Management and Organisational Behaviour in an Ethical Context

We work with leading authors to develop the strongest educational materials bringing cutting-edge thinking and best learning practice to a global market.

Under a range of well-known imprints, including Financial Times/Prentice Hall, Addison Wesley and Longman, we craft high quality print and electronic publications which help readers to understand and apply their content, whether studying or at work.

Pearson Custom Publishing enables our customers to access a wide and expanding range of market-leading content from world-renowned authors and develop their own tailor-made book. You choose the content that meets your needs and Pearson Custom Publishing produces a high-quality printed book.

To find out more about custom publishing, visit www.pearsoncustom.co.uk

A Pearson Custom Publication

Management and Organisational Behaviour in an Ethical Context

Compiled from:

Business Ethics and Values: Individual, Corporate and International Perspectives
Second Edition
Colin Fisher and Alan Lovell

Management and Organisational Behaviour
Eighth Edition
Laurie J. Mullins

Pearson Education Limited
Edinburgh Gate
Harlow
Essex CM20 2JE

And associated companies throughout the world

Visit us on the World Wide Web at:
www.pearsoned.co.uk

First published 2008

Compiled From:

Business Ethics and Values: Individual, Corporate and International Perspectives
Second Edition
Colin Fisher and Alan Lovell
ISBN 978 0 273 69478 6

Management and Organisational Behaviour
Eighth Edition
Laurie J. Mullins
ISBN 978 0 273 70888 9

ISBN 978 1 84658 940 9

Printed and bound in Great Britain by Henry Ling Limited at the Dorset Press, Dorchester, DT1 1HD.

Contents

The Organisational Setting 1

Selected Chapters from
Management and Organisational Behaviour
Eighth Edition
Laurie J. Mullins

Chapter 1 'The Nature of Organisational Behaviour' 2

Chapter 2 'Approaches to Organisation and Management' 39

Chapter 3 'The Nature and Context of Organisations' 74

The Individual 117

Selected Chapters from
Management and Organisational Behaviour
Eighth Edition
Laurie J. Mullins

Chapter 7 'Work Motivation and Job Satisfaction' 119

Groups, Teams and Leadership 163

Selected Chapters from
Management and Organisational Behaviour
Eighth Edition
Laurie J. Mullins

Chapter 8 'The Nature of Work Groups and Teams' 164

Chapter 9 'Working in Groups and Teams' 196

Chapter 10 'The Nature of Leadership' 228

The Nature of Management 271

Selected Chapters from
Management and Organisational Behaviour
Eighth Edition
Laurie J. Mullins

Chapter 11 'The Role of the Manager' 272

Chapter 12 'Managerial Behaviour and Effectiveness' 304

Structures of Organisation 341

Selected Chapters from
Management and Organisational Behaviour
Eighth Edition
Laurie J. Mullins

Chapter 14 'Corporate Strategy and Responsibilities' 342

Chapter 15 'Organisation Structures and Design' 377

Chapter 16 'Patterns of Structure and Work Organisation' 415

Business, Ethics and Values 449

Selected Chapters from
Business Ethics and Values: Individual, Corporate and International Perspectives
Second Edition
Colin Fisher and Alan Lovell

Chapter 1 'Perspectives on Business Ethics and Values' 451

Chapter 7 'Whistleblower or Witness?' 486

Chapter 8 'Corporate Responsibility, Corporate Governance and Corporate Citizenship' 519

Chapter 9 'Sustainability and the Responsible Corporation' 562

Chapter 10 'Ethical Conformance: Codes, Standards, Culture, Leadership and Citizen Power' 601

Chapter 12 'Globalisation and International Business' 641

Organisation Management 683

Selected Chapters from
Management and Organisational Behaviour
Eighth Edition
Laurie J. Mullins

Chapter 19 'Organisation Development, Culture and Change' 684

The Organisational Setting

THE NATURE OF ORGANISATIONAL BEHAVIOUR

When people are engaged and committed they are more likely to behave in the interests of the company and they have less need to be controlled and measured. In essence, engaged people can be trusted to behave in the interests of the company, in part because they perceived their interests to be the same as, or aligned with, the interests of the company.

Lynda Gratton – global authority on the people implications of strategy

The Democratic Enterprise, Financial Times Prentice Hall (2004), p. 208

The scope for the examination of behaviour in organisations is very wide. There is a multiplicity of interrelated factors that influence the behaviour and performance of people as members of a work organisation. It is important to recognise the role of management as an integrating activity and the increasingly global business environment. People and organisations need each other. The manager needs to understand the main influences on behaviour in work organisations and the nature of the people–organisation relationship.

Learning outcomes

After completing this chapter you should be able to:

- explain the meaning and nature of organisational behaviour;
- detail main interrelated influences on behaviour in work organisations;
- outline contrasting perspectives of organisations and different orientations to work;
- explain the importance of management as an integrating activity;
- assess the nature and importance of the new psychological contract;
- recognise the need for a global context to management and organisational behaviour;
- review the changing nature of work organisations.

Critical reflection

Although a commonly used term, organisational behaviour is a misnomer: rarely do all members act collectively in such a way as to represent the behaviour of the organisation as a whole. In practice, we are talking about the attitudes and actions of individuals or small group within the organisation.

Do you agree? What term would you suggest best explains this subject area?

THE MEANING OF ORGANISATIONAL BEHAVIOUR

We live in an organisational world. Organisations of one form or another are a necessary part of our society and serve many important needs. The decisions and actions of management in organisations have an increasing impact on individuals, other organisations and the community. It is important, therefore, to understand how organisations function and the pervasive influences which they exercise over the behaviour of people.[1]

Organisational behaviour is concerned with the study of the behaviour of people within an organisational setting. It involves the understanding, prediction and control of human behaviour.[2] Common definitions of organisational behaviour (OB) are generally along the lines of: **the study and understanding of individual and group behaviour and patterns of structure in order to help improve organisational performance and effectiveness.**[3]

However much of a cliché it may sound, it is still an inescapable fact that people are the main resource of any organisation. Without its members, an organisation is nothing; an organisation is only as good as the people who work within it. In today's increasingly global and competitive environment the effective management of people is even more important for organisational survival and success.

There is a close relationship between organisational behaviour and management theory and practice. Some writers seem to suggest that organisational behaviour and management are synonymous, but this is something of an over-simplification because there are many broader facets to management. Organisational behaviour does not encompass the whole of management; it is more accurately described in the narrower interpretation of providing a behavioural approach to management.

THE STUDY OF ORGANISATIONAL BEHAVIOUR

The use of separate topic areas is a recognised academic means of aiding study and explanation of the subject. In practice, however, the activities of an organisation and the job of management cannot be isolated neatly into discrete categories. The majority of actions are likely to involve a number of simultaneous functions that relate to the total processes within an organisation.[4]

Consider, for example, a manager briefing departmental staff on an unexpected, important and urgent task that has to be undertaken quickly. Such a briefing is likely to include consideration of goals and objectives, organisation structure, management system, process of delegation and empowerment, systems of communication, leadership style, motivation and control systems. The behaviour of the staff will be influenced by a combination of individual, group, organisational and environmental factors.

Topic studies in organisational behaviour should not be regarded, therefore, as entirely free-standing. Any study inevitably covers several aspects and is used to a greater or lesser extent to confirm generalisations made about particular topic areas. The use of the same studies to illustrate different aspects of management and organisational behaviour serves as useful revision and reinforcement and helps to bring about a greater awareness and understanding of the subject.

The relevance of theory

In the study of management and organisational behaviour you will come across many theories. However, you should not be put off by the use of the word 'theory'. Most rational decisions are based on some form of theory. Theory contains a message on how managers might behave. This will influence attitudes towards management practice and lead to changes in actual patterns of behaviour. **Theory helps in building generalised models applicable to a range of organisations or situations. It further provides a conceptual framework and gives a perspective for the practical study of the subject**. Thus theory and practice are inseparable. Together they lead to a better understanding of factors influencing patterns of behaviour in work organisations and applications of the process of management.[5]

However, to be of any help to the practising manager, theory has to be appropriate. For example, *Lee* refers to:

> *... the danger of adopting theories because they are teachable, rather than because they are effective ... [however] without appropriate theory, there would be very little communication of the insights of scientific theory to practising managers.*[6]

Although it is not always easy to establish their exact origins, ideas do percolate through to best practice.[7]

Patching suggests that all managers who think about what they do are practical students of organisational theory.

> *Theory is not something unique to academics, but something we all work with in arriving at our attitudes, beliefs and decisions as managers. It seems obvious to most of us that some theories are better than others. Many managerial discussions which we undertake in meetings focus upon trying to agree upon which theory will be best for a particular decision.*[8]

Alternative approaches

There is a number of alternative approaches to the study of organisational behaviour. For example, in addition to a managerialist approach, *Drummond* refers to two other intellectual standpoints, interpretative and critical.

The interpretative standpoint views ambiguity, paradox and contradictions as part of the natural experiences of organisations, with an emphasis upon understanding the subtleties and dynamics of organisational life. The critical standpoint believes that reality is very real and people have only a marginal amount of freedom, and regards management science as bogus, a means of legitimising economic exploitation.[9]

While acknowledging the existence and potential contributions of both these standpoints, **the main thrust of this book is to present a managerial approach to organisational behaviour**. It is concerned with interactions among the structure and operation of organisations, the process of management and the behaviour of people at work. The underlying theme of the book is the need for organisational effectiveness and the importance of the role of management as an integrating activity.

A FRAMEWORK OF STUDY

The behaviour of people, however, cannot be studied in isolation. It is necessary to understand interrelationships with other variables that together comprise the total organisation. This involves consideration of interactions among the formal structure, the tasks to be undertaken, the technology employed and methods of carrying out work, the process of management and the external environment.

The study of organisational behaviour embraces therefore an understanding of:

- the behaviour of people;
- the process of management;
- the organisational context in which the process of management takes place;
- organisational processes and the execution of work; and
- interactions with the external environment of which the organisation is part.

This provides us with a basic, but convenient, framework of analysis (*see* Figure 1.1).

> *Organisational Behaviour is one of the most complex and perhaps least understood academic elements of modern general management, but since it concerns the behaviour of people within organisations it is also one of the most central ... its concern with individual and group patterns of behaviour makes it an essential element in dealing with the complex behavioural issues thrown up in the modern business world.*
>
> Financial Times Mastering Management Series[10]

Wilson, however, suggests that the meaning of the term organisational behaviour is far from clear. She challenges what constitutes organisational behaviour and questions whether we should be interested only in behaviour that happens within organisations. There is a reciprocal relationship in what happens within and outside organisations. Wilson suggests that we also look outside of what are normally thought of as organisations and how we usually think of work. We can also gain insight into organisational life and behaviour by looking at what happens in rest and play; considering emotion and feeling; considering the context in which work is defined as men's or women's work; and looking at less organised work, for example work on the fiddle and the meaning of work for the unemployed.[11] These suggestions arguably add an extra dimension to the meaning and understanding of organisational behaviour.

Figure 1.1 Organisational behaviour: a convenient framework of analysis

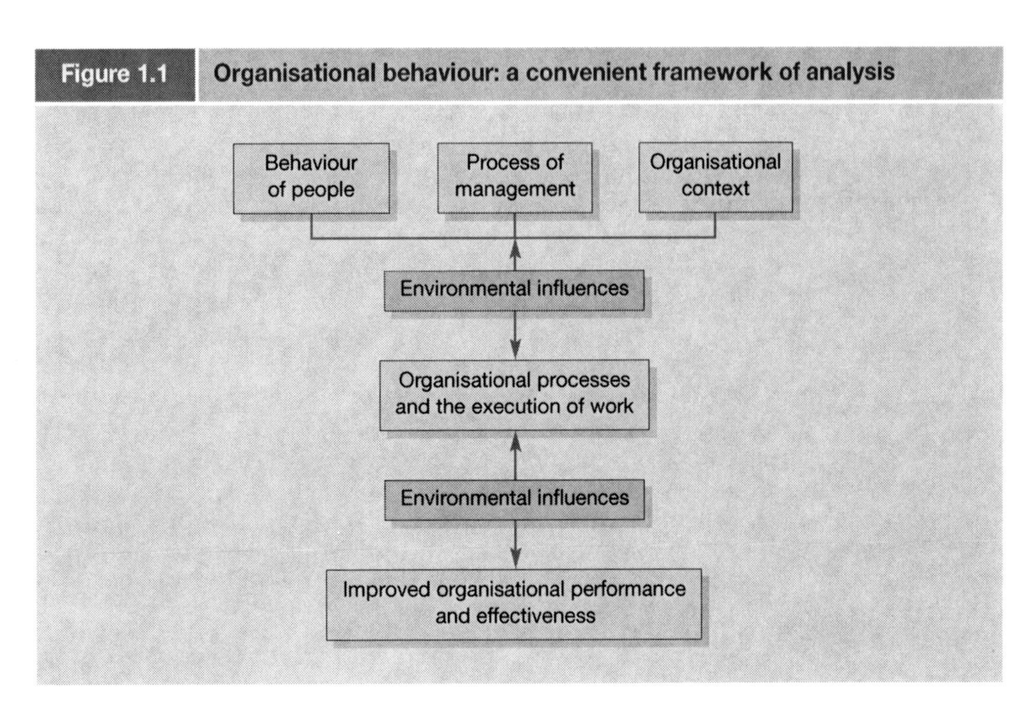

INFLUENCES ON BEHAVIOUR

The variables outlined above provide parameters within which a number of interrelated dimensions can be identified – the individual, the group, the organisation and the environment – which collectively influence behaviour in work organisations.

The individual Organisations are made up of their individual members. The individual is a central feature of organisational behaviour, whether acting in isolation or as part of a group, in response to expectations of the organisation, or as a result of the influences of the external environment. Where the needs of the individual and the demands of the organisation are incompatible, this can result in frustration and conflict. It is the task of management to integrate the individual and the organisation and to provide a working environment that permits the satisfaction of individual needs as well as the attainment of organisational goals.

The group Groups exist in all organisations and are essential to their working and performance. The organisation comprises groups of people and almost everyone in an organisation will be a member of one or more groups. Informal groups arise from the social needs of people within the organisation. People in groups influence each other in many ways and groups may develop their own hierarchies and leaders. Group pressures can have a major influence over the behaviour and performance of individual members. An understanding of group structure and behaviour complements a knowledge of individual behaviour and adds a further dimension to organisational behaviour.

The organisation Individuals and groups interact within the structure of the formal organisation. Structure is created by management to establish relationships between individuals and groups, to provide order and systems and to direct the efforts of the organisation into goal-seeking activities. It is through the formal structure that people carry out their organisational activities in order to achieve aims and objectives. Behaviour is affected by patterns of organisation structure, technology, styles of leadership and systems of management through which organisational processes are planned, directed and controlled. The focus of attention, therefore, is on the impact of organisation structure and design, and patterns of management, on the behaviour of people within the organisation. *McPhee* refers to the growth in the nature and importance of organisational structures and their essence, and for greater emphasis on business-to-business (B2B) depth or group interviewing as part of an insight into business and organisational behaviour.[12]

The environment The organisation functions as part of the broader external environment of which it is a part. The environment affects the organisation through, for example, technological and scientific development, economic activity, social and cultural influences and governmental actions. The effects of the operation of the organisation within its environment are reflected in terms of the management of opportunities and risks and the successful achievement of its aims and objectives. The increasing rate of change in environmental factors has highlighted the need to study the total organisation and the processes by which the organisation attempts to adapt to the external demands placed upon it.

Increasing globalisation means that organisations must respond to different market demands and local requirements. 'In globalization, strategy and organisation are inextricably twined.'[13] Globalisation impacts on organisational behaviour and has placed greater emphasis on processes within organisations rather than functions of the organisation.

Contrasting but related approaches

These different dimensions provide contrasting but related approaches to the understanding of human behaviour in organisations. They present a number of alternative pathways for the study of the subject and level of analysis. It is possible, for example, to adopt a **psychological** approach with the main emphasis on the individuals of which the organisation is comprised. Psychological aspects are important but by themselves provide too narrow an approach for the understanding of management and organisational behaviour. Our main concern is not with the complex detail of individual differences and attributes *per se* but with the behaviour and management of people within an organisational setting.

It is also possible to adopt a **sociological** approach concerned with a broader emphasis on human behaviour in society. Sociological aspects can be important. A number of sociology writers seem set on the purpose of criticising traditional views of organisation and management. Many of the criticisms and limitations to which such writers refer are justified and help promote healthy academic debate. Unfortunately, however, much of the argument tends to be presented in the abstract and is lacking in constructive ideas on how, in practical terms, action can be taken to improve organisational performance.

A MULTIDISCIPLINARY APPROACH

Whatever the approach, the study of organisational behaviour cannot be undertaken entirely in terms of a single discipline. It is necessary to provide a multidisciplinary, behavioural science perspective (*see* Figure 1.2). Although there are areas of overlap among the various social sciences, their sub-divisions and related disciplines such as economics and political science, the study of behaviour can be viewed in terms of three main disciplines – **psychology, sociology** and **anthropology**. All three disciplines have made an important contribution to the field of organisational behaviour.

- **Psychologists** are concerned, broadly speaking, with the study of human behaviour, with traits of the individual and membership of small social groups. The main focus of attention is on the individual as a whole person, or what can be termed the 'personality system', including, for example, perception, attitudes and motives.

Figure 1.2 Organisational behaviour – a multidisciplinary approach

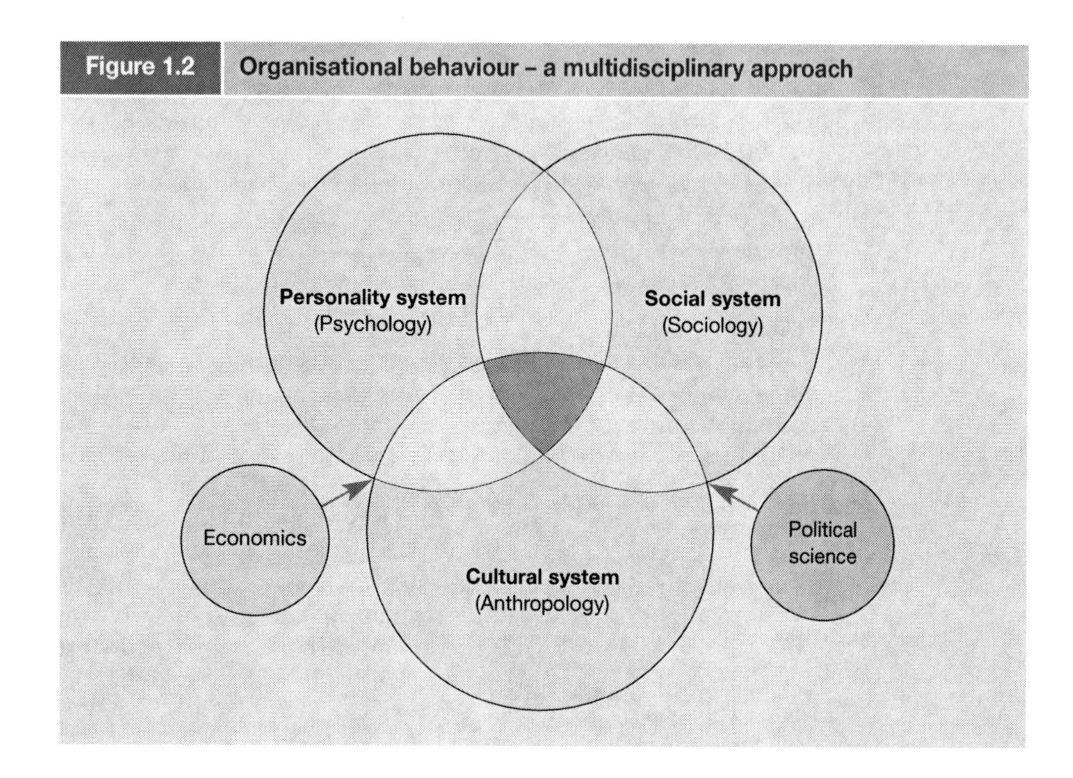

- **Sociologists** are more concerned with the study of social behaviour, relationships among social groups and societies, and the maintenance of order. The main focus of attention is on the analysis of social structures and positions in those structures – for example, the relationship between the behaviour of leaders and followers.
- **Anthropologists** are more concerned with the science of mankind and the study of human behaviour as a whole. As far as organisational behaviour is concerned the main focus of attention is on the cultural system, the beliefs, customs, ideas and values within a group or society, and the comparison of behaviour among different cultures – for example, the importance to Muslim women of wearing trousers to work. People learn to depend on their culture to give them security and stability and they can suffer adverse reactions to unfamiliar environments.

The contribution of relevant aspects of psychology, sociology and anthropology underpins the field of organisational behaviour. Behavioural science attempts to structure organisations in order to secure the optimum working environment. It is concerned with reconciling the needs of the organisation for the contribution of maximum productivity, with the needs of individuals and the realisation of their potential. In terms of the applications of behavioural science to the management of people, we need also to consider the relevance and applications of philosophy, ethics and the law.

Critical reflection

A significant feature of organisational behaviour is the invariable difficulty in identifying a single solution to a particular situation. To what extent do you find that the absence of one, 'right answer' not only makes study of the subject complex and frustrating but also brings into question the value of studying the subject at all?

ORGANISATIONAL METAPHORS

Organisations are complex social systems that can be defined and studied in a number of ways. A significant approach to this broad perspective on the nature of organisations and organisational behaviour is provided by *Morgan*. Through the use of metaphors, Morgan identifies eight different ways of viewing organisations – as machines, organisms, brains, cultures, political systems, psychic prisons, flux and transformation, and instruments of domination. According to Morgan, these contrasting metaphors aid the understanding of the complex nature of organisational life and the critical evaluation of organisational phenomena.[14]

- **Machines**. This suggests that organisations can be designed as if they are machines, with orderly relations between clearly defined parts. Viewing organisations as machines can provide the basis for efficient operation in a routine, reliable and predictable way. This form of bureaucratic structure offers form, continuity and security. However, it may have adverse consequences and limit the development of human capacities. Organisations viewed as machines function better in a stable and protected environment.
- **Organisms**. The organisation is seen as behaving like a living system. In the same way that biological mechanisms adapt to changes in their environment, so organisations, as open systems, adapt to the changing external environment. Organisations operating within a turbulent and dynamic environment require an adaptable type of structure.
- **Brains**. Viewing organisations as brains involves thinking about the organisation as inventive and rational and in a manner that provides for flexibility and creative action. The challenge is to create new forms of organisation capable of intelligent change and that can disperse brain-like capacities.

- **Cultures**. This sees organisations as complex systems made up of their own characteristic sets of ideology, values, rituals and systems of belief and practice. Attention to specific aspects of social development helps to account for variations among organisations.
- **Political systems**. In the sense that ways must be found to create order and direct people, organisations are intrinsically political. They are about authority, power, superior–subordinate relationships and conflicting interests. Viewing organisations as political systems helps in an understanding of day-to-day organisational life, the wheeling and dealing, and pursuit of special interests.
- **Psychic prisons**. This views organisations as psychic phenomena created and sustained by conscious and unconscious processes. Organisations and their members are constrained by their shadows or 'psychic prisons' and become trapped by constructions of reality. Their inherited or created mythical past places affect the representation of the organisation to the outside world. Viewing organisations as psychic prisons provides an understanding of the reality and illusions of organisational behaviour.
- **Flux and transformation**. The universe is in a constant state of flux, embodying characteristics of both permanence and change. Organisations can be seen as in a state of flux and transformation. In order to understand the nature and social life of organisations, it is necessary to understand the sources and logic of transformation and change.
- **Instruments of domination**. In this view organisations are associated with processes of social domination, and individuals and groups imposing their will on others. A feature of organisations is asymmetrical power relations that result in the pursuit of the goals of the few through the efforts of the many. Organisations are best understood in terms of variations in the mode of social domination and control of their members.

A broader view of organisational behaviour

Although the main concern of this book is with a managerial approach to organisational behaviour, these contrasting metaphors offer an interesting perspective on how to view organisations. They provide a broader view of the dynamics of organisational behaviour and how to manage and design organisations. However, Morgan points out that these metaphors are not fixed categories and are not mutually exclusive. An organisation can be a mix of each and predominantly a combination of two or three metaphors. Furthermore, these combinations may change over a period of time.

A number of writers use metaphors to help describe organisations. For example, in discussing the role and logic of viewing the organisation in terms of metaphors, *Drummond* raises questions such as what an organisation is like and the power of metaphors in shaping our thinking, but also points out that all metaphors are partial and no metaphor can explain fully a particular phenomenon.[15]

ORIENTATIONS TO WORK AND THE WORK ETHIC

People differ in the manner and extent of their involvement with, and concern for, work. From information collected about the work situation, organisational participation and involvement with work colleagues, and life outside the organisation, *Goldthorpe et al.* identified three main types of orientation to work: instrumental, bureaucratic and solidaristic.[16]

- Individuals with an instrumental orientation define work not as a central life issue but in terms of a means to an end. There is a calculative or economic involvement with work and a clear distinction between work-related and non-work-related activities.
- Individuals with a bureaucratic orientation define work as a central life issue. There is a sense of obligation to the work of the organisation and a positive involvement in terms of a career structure. There is a close link between work-related and non-work-related activities.

- Individuals with a **solidaristic orientation** define the work situation in terms of group activities. There is an ego involvement with work groups rather than with the organisation itself. Work is more than just a means to an end. Non-work activities are linked to work relationships.

Different work situations

Some people may well have a set motivation to work, whatever the nature of the work environment. However, different work situations may also influence the individual's orientation to work. For example, the lack of opportunities for team work and the satisfaction of social expectations may result in an instrumental orientation to work and a primary concern for economic interests such as pay and security. In other situations where there are greater opportunities to satisfy social needs, membership of work groups may be very important and individuals may have a more solidaristic orientation to work.

According to *Herman*, the work ethic has been deeply challenged by two trends – the division of labour and the destruction of continuity in employment. Work has been fractured in task and sub-divided into specialised sub-tasks or branches, creating new kinds of work altogether. The division of labour has generated tens of thousands of discrete functions in the workplace. A more recent trend is the destruction of continuity in employment, with many employees likely to re-enter the job market multiple times. This discourages the development of bonds of loyalty or employees investing themselves in their work with the hope of long-term employment.[17]

Knights and Willmott contend that most management textbooks do not make the connection between managing and everyday life. By drawing on a number of contemporary novels they attempt to 'bring to life' what they see as the reality of managing and organising, and dimensions of human experience at work and elsewhere. They explore, in an interesting way, the changing meaning of work and orientations to it, and how different kinds of work are meaningful to some people and not to others.[18]

International and cultural influences

National culture is also a significant influence on orientations to work. For example, *Reeves* comments on the importance of conversation for effective organisational relationships but how this is resisted in the British work culture.

> *The Protestant version of the work ethic prevails, implying heads-down work, focused agendas, punctuality, efficiency. In French and Spanish offices, it takes the first hour to kiss everyone, the second to discuss local gossip and the third to pop out for a coffee and croissant. In Britain, these activities would count as sexual harassment, time-wasting and absenteeism. Many firms have built cafés or break out areas and then discovered people are too scared to use them for fear of looking work-shy.*[19]

As another example, the author experienced for himself how in parts of Australia work-related activities could often be undertaken comfortably in local coffee houses without concern about 'presenteeism' or being seen as being away from the place of work.

Cartwright comments on the psychological process of culture that has the power and authority not only to determine lifestyle but also to form individual personality traits, behaviours and attitudes.

> *It is the cultural environment that motivates people to do their best and to give of their best, often irrespective of or even in spite of their working or living environment. In this respect we make a clear distinction between social conditions and the cultural environment. In the same way that a first-class system does not guarantee first-class results, good living and working conditions do not, in themselves, guarantee high morale and motivation. People in the best working and living conditions can still have low morale and motivation without the benefit of a supportive culture.*[20]

Work/life balance Popular newspaper articles often suggest that work is still a large component of what gives meaning to people's lives and give examples of lottery or pools winners staying in work and often in their same old job. Other surveys and reports suggest that the workplace is no longer a central feature of social activity. For a majority of people the main reason for work remains the need for money to fulfil the necessities of life. However, much still appears to depend on the extent of an individual's social contacts and activities outside of the work situation.

From a survey conducted among subscribers to *Management Today*, the majority of Britain's managers are engaged in a perpetual juggling act with the work/life balance and in meeting both personal and work commitments. For many of those surveyed, however, work remains a huge source of satisfaction.[21] The work/life balance is discussed more fully in Chapter 3.

MANAGEMENT AS AN INTEGRATING ACTIVITY

Whatever the individual's orientations to work or cultural influences, it is through the process of management that the efforts of members of the organisation are co-ordinated, directed and guided towards the achievement of organisational goals. Management is the cornerstone of organisational effectiveness (*see* Figure 1.3).

Patterns of human behaviour It is the responsibility of management to manage. But organisations can achieve their aims and objectives only through the co-ordinated efforts of their members. This involves the effective management of human resources. However, it is important always to remember that it is people who are being managed and people should be considered in human terms.

Figure 1.3 Management as the cornerstone of organisational effectiveness

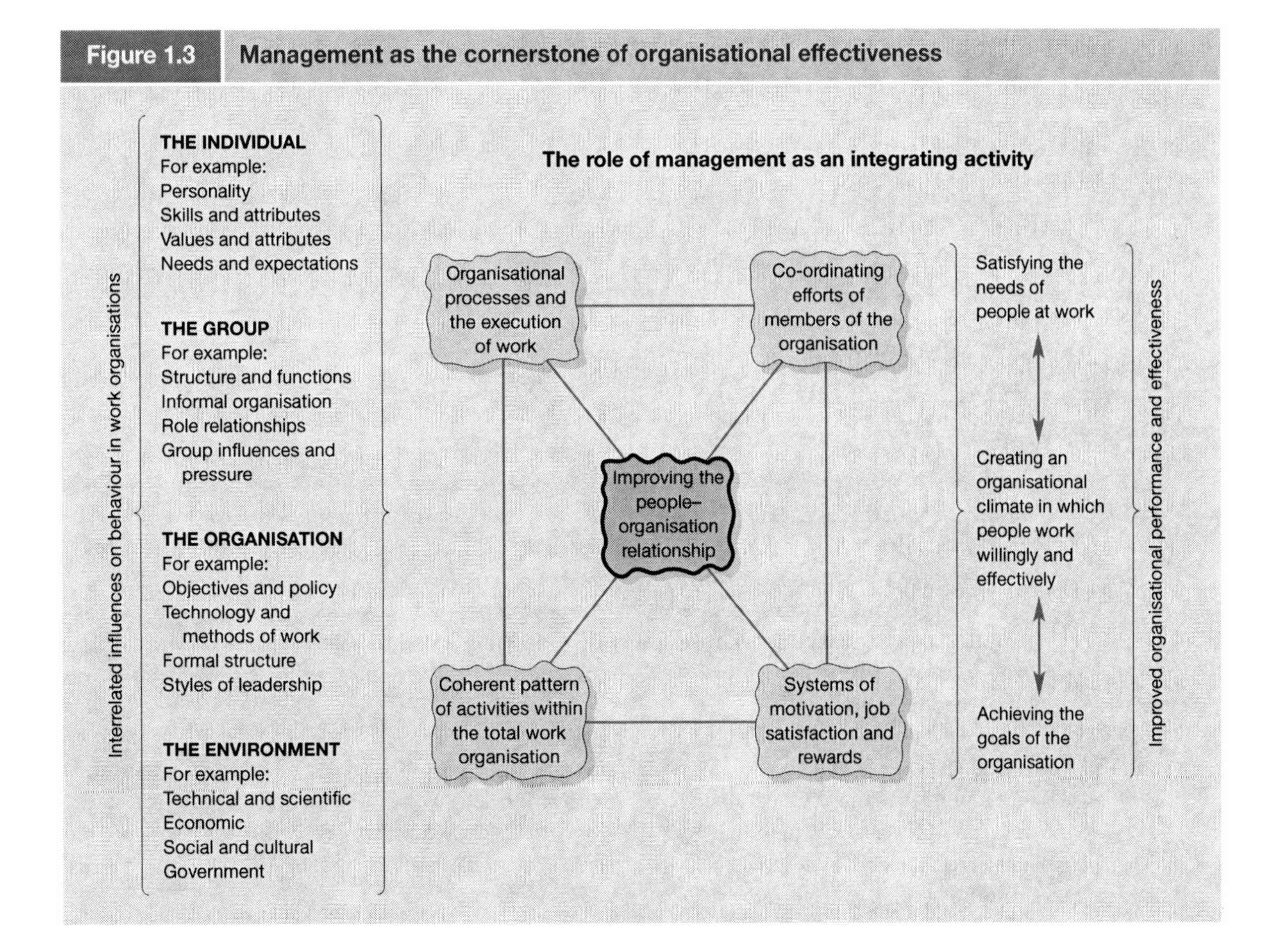

Unlike physical resources, people are not owned by the organisation. People bring their own perceptions, feelings and attitudes towards the organisation, systems and styles of management, their duties and responsibilities, and the conditions under which they are working. At the heart of successful management is the problem of integrating the individual and the organisation, and this requires an understanding of both human personality and work organisations.[22]

For example, *Egan* refers to the importance of the shadow side of the organisation: that is, those things not found on organisation charts or in company manuals – the covert, and often undiscussed, activities of people which affect both the productivity and quality of the working life of an organisation.[23]

Human behaviour is capricious and scientific methods or principles of behaviour cannot be applied with reliability. For example, in his study of job satisfaction, Bassett comments that:

> *There seem to be no universal generalizations about worker dissatisfaction that permit easy management policy solutions to absenteeism and turnover problems ... There are almost never any exact conditions of cause and effect in the realm of human behaviour.*[24]

It is also widely observed that you cannot study the behaviour of people without changing it.

Critical reflection

The performance of people at work is influenced by a complex combination of social and cultural factors, and the idiosyncratic behaviour of individuals. Do you agree therefore that effective management is all about the human aspects of the organisation? Do you think that tensions, conflicts and politics are almost inevitable, as are informal structures of organisation and unofficial working methods?

The people–organisation relationship

It could be argued that the majority of people come to work with the **original** attitude of being eager to do a good job and desirous of performing well and to the best of their abilities. **People generally respond in the manner in which they are treated**. Where actual performance fails to match the ideal this is largely a result of how staff perceive they are treated by management.

Many problems in the people–organisation relationship arise not so much from what management does but from **the manner in which it is done**. Often, it is **not so much the intent but the manner of implementation** that is the root cause of staff unrest and dissatisfaction. For example, staff may agree on the need to introduce new technology to retain the competitive efficiency of the organisation, but feel resentment about the lack of pre-planning, consultation, retraining programmes, participation in agreeing new working practices and wage rates, and similar considerations arising from the manner of its introduction.

Therefore, a heavy responsibility is placed on managers and the activity of management – on the processes, systems and styles of management. Attention must be given to the work environment and appropriate systems of motivation, job satisfaction and rewards. It is important to remember that improvement in organisational performance will come about only through people.[25]

Providing the right balance

Management should, therefore, endeavour to create the right balance between the interrelated elements that make up the total organisation and to weld these into coherent patterns of activity best suited to the external environment in which the organisation is operating. Consideration must be given to developing an organisational climate in which people work willingly and effectively.

People and organisations need each other. **Attention should be focused, therefore, on improving the people–organisation relationship.** Management is an integral part of this relationship. It should serve to reconcile the needs of people at work with the requirements of the organisation. Management is essentially an integrating activity that permeates every facet of the organisation's operations. The style of management adopted can be seen as a function of the manager's attitudes towards people and assumptions about human nature and behaviour (discussed in Chapter 12).

The general movement towards flatter organisation structures, flexible working and greater employee involvement has placed increasing emphasis on an integrating rather than a hierarchical/controlling style of management.

Refresh your understanding
Activity 1B
www.pearsoned.co.uk/mullins

Management processes in the new millennium will be much more behavioural in nature, focusing on the key human resource-driven issues: learning, team-based visions, driving human resource processes, incentives to enhance growth, holistic budgeting, and proactive controls.[26]

Organisational environment and culture

It is important to bear in mind that the activity of management takes place within the broader context of the organisational setting and subject to the organisational environment and culture. There are also variations in systems and styles of management and in the choice of managerial behaviour. The simple, five-stage framework (Figure 1.4) provides a basic framework of study.

THE PSYCHOLOGICAL CONTRACT

One significant aspect of organisational behaviour and the relationship between the individual and the process of management is the concept of the **psychological contract**. This is not a written document but implies a series of mutual expectations and satisfaction of needs arising from the people–organisation relationship. It involves a process of giving and receiving by the individual and by the organisation. The psychological contract covers a range of expectations of rights and privileges, duties and obligations, which do not form part of a formal agreement but still have an important influence on people's behaviour.[27]

The nature and extent of individuals' expectations vary widely, as do the ability and willingness of the organisation to meet them. It is difficult to list the range of implicit expectations that individuals have and they change over time. These expectations are notwithstanding any statutory requirements placed upon the organisation; instead they relate more to the idea of a social responsibility of management, discussed in Chapter 14. The organisation will also have implicit expectations of its members. The organisational side of the psychological contract places emphasis on expectations, requirements and constraints that may differ from, and may conflict with, an individual's expectations. Some possible examples of the individual's and the organisation's expectations are given in Figure 1.5.

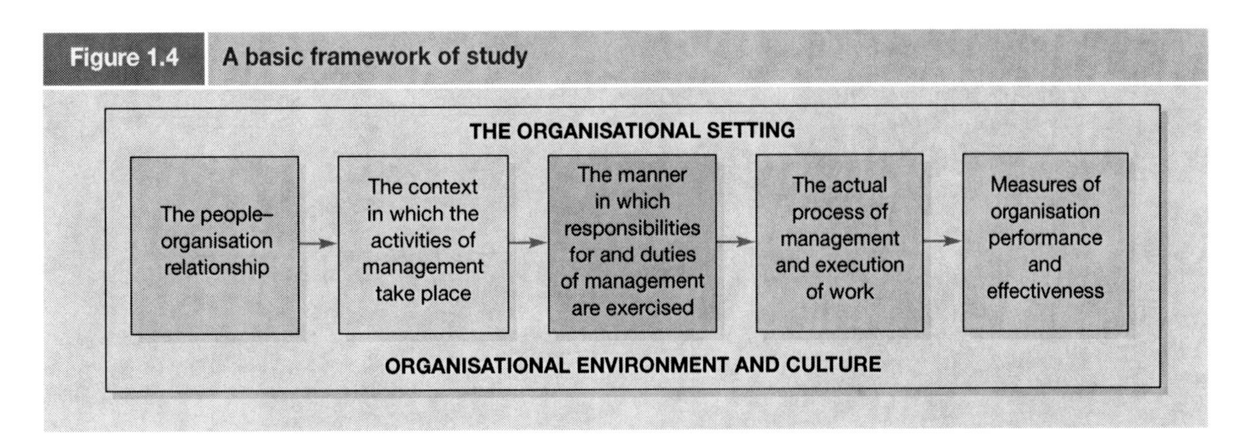

Figure 1.4 A basic framework of study

Figure 1.5 The psychological contract: possible examples of individual and organisational expectations

INDIVIDUALS' EXPECTATIONS OF THE ORGANISATION

- Provide safe and hygienic working conditions.
- Make every reasonable effort to provide job security.
- Attempt to provide challenging and satisfying jobs, and reduce alienating aspects of work.
- Adopt equitable human resource management policies and procedures.
- Respect the role of trade union officials and staff representives.
- Consult fully with staff and allow genuine participation in decisions which affect them.
- Implement best practice in equal opportunity policies and procedures.
- Reward all staff fairly according to their contribution and performance.
- Provide reasonable opportunities for personal development and career progression.
- Treat members of staff with respect.
- Demonstrate an understanding and considerate attitude towards personal problems of staff.

ORGANISATIONAL EXPECTATIONS OF THE INDIVIDUAL

- Uphold the ideology of the organisation and the corporate image.
- Work diligently in pursuit of organisational objectives.
- Adhere to the rules, policies and procedures of the organisation.
- Respect the reasonable authority of senior members of staff.
- Not take advantage of goodwill shown by management.
- Be responsive to leadership influence.
- Demonstrate loyalty and not betray positions of trust.
- Maintain harmonious relationships with work colleagues.
- Not abuse organisational facilities such as email or Internet access.
- Observe reasonable and acceptable standards of dress and appearance.
- Show respect and consolidation to customers and suppliers.

Implications for organisational strategy

The Chartered Institute of Personnel and Development (CIPD) suggests that the psychological contract may have implications for organisational strategy in a number of areas, for example:

- **process fairness** – people want to know their interests will be taken into account, treated with respect and consulted about change;
- **communications** – an effective two-way dialogue between employer and employee;
- **management style** – adopting a more 'bottom-up' style and drawing on the strategic knowledge of employees;
- **managing expectations** – making clear what new recruits can expect and distinguishing rhetoric from reality;

- **measuring employees' attitudes** – regular monitoring of employee attitudes and acting on the results.[28]

Process of balancing

It is unlikely that all expectations of the individual or of the organisation will be met fully. There is a continual process of balancing, and explicit and implicit bargaining. The nature of these expectations is not defined formally and although the individual member and the organisation may not be consciously aware of them, they still affect relationships between them and have an influence on behaviour.

The psychological contract is a useful concept in examining the socialisation of new members of staff to the organisation. According to *Kotter*, early experiences have a major effect on an individual's subsequent career in an organisation and influence job satisfaction, attitude and level of productivity. The extent of the matches between individual and organisational expectations also influences the willingness of people to stay with the organisation and of the organisation to continue to employ them.[29]

Stalker suggests that successful companies are those that have the ability to balance the unwritten needs of their employees with the needs of the company. Such companies use a simple formula of Caring, Communicating, Listening, Knowing and Rewarding:

- **Caring** – demonstrating genuine concern for individuals working in the organisation.
- **Communicating** – really talking about what the company is hoping to achieve.
- **Listening** – hearing not only the words but also what lies behind the words.
- **Knowing** – the individuals who work for you, their families, personal wishes, desires and ambitions.
- **Rewarding** – money is not always necessary; a genuine thank-you or public recognition can raise morale.[30]

The significance of the psychological contract depends on the extent to which it is perceived as fair by both the individual and the organisation, and will be respected by both sides. *Cartwright*, refers to mutuality as the basic principle of the psychological contract:

> *A psychological contract is not only measured in monetary value or in the exchange of goods or services, it is in essence the exchange or sharing of beliefs and values, expectations and satisfactions. Mutuality is the basic principle of the psychological contract and consensus or mutual understanding is the basis of mutuality. Ideally therefore self-interest should be balanced with common interest in a 'win–win' arrangement.*[31]

The nature of the employer–employee relationship is clearly a central feature of the psychological contract. *Emmott* points out that good people-management practices are the basis for a positive psychological contract and this means managers having to deal with the 'soft stuff'. Properly managed, the psychological contract delivers hard, bottom-line results and improved business performance.

> *Managers at all levels can have an influence on employees' perceptions of the psychological contract. It is, however, the* ***relationship between individual employees and their line manager*** *that is likely to have most influence in framing and managing employees' expectations.*[32]

News that Barclay would be off-shoring 1,800 jobs subjected the bank to intense scrutiny from government, trade unions, shareholders, customers and, of course, employees. The bank recognised it needed to do something to strengthen the 'psychological contract' it had with its employees if it was to redeploy them elsewhere within the organisation.

Management Today[33]

CHANGING NATURE OF THE PSYCHOLOGICAL CONTRACT

The changing nature of organisations has placed increasing emphasis on the importance of effective human resource management, including the importance of the psychological contract within the employment relationship. From a review of research, *McBain* maintains that human resource management plays a key role in ensuring the promotion of business success and managing change. This involves paying attention to the psychological contract and the establishment of expectations and obligations with all groups of employees within the organisation.[34] The Institute of Administrative Management has introduced a new module on 'The Individual and the Organisation in Context' that has come about because of the need to keep abreast of changes affecting the individual at work.

> *There is a need for managers to be aware of the new psychological contracts the individual members of their teams are bringing to work. Managers will have to consider alternative management styles to meet this new need and to use new skills to motivate and train their staff. People no longer come to work to be 'told what to do', but are aspiring to be part of the whole, with a real role as stakeholders in the success of 'their' organisation. Wise managers will harness this commitment for the benefit of everyone concerned.*[35]

Hiltrop suggests that the increasing pressure for organisations to change has prompted growing disillusionment with the traditional psychological contract based on lifetime employment and steady promotion from within. Companies must develop new ways to increase the loyalty and commitment of employees. This includes attention to reward strategies based on recognition of contribution rather than status or position; systematic training and development including the skills for working in cross-functional teams; and the training of managers in counselling, coaching and leadership skills.[36]

According to CIPD, changes currently affecting the workplace have persuaded people to take the psychological contract seriously. These changes include more employees on part-time and temporary contracts and more jobs outsourced; delayering and 'leanness' of organisations; more demanding customers and improved quality and service standards; the increasing importance of human capital as a source of competitive advantage; and more fluid organisation structures. The effect of these changes is that employees are increasingly recognised as the key business drivers. The psychological contract offers a framework for monitoring employee attitudes and priorities.[37]

Performance management

Stiles et al. also draw attention to how new competitive conditions and dynamic environments have brought performance management to centre stage as a major element in the changing nature of the psychological contract. From an examination of three large UK organisations, the authors explore 'how performance management processes are being used to support moves from the traditional contract of job security and clear career paths, while attempting to maintain commitment and morale'. The authors conclude that there are two main areas of difficulty in changing the psychological contract so that it focuses on performance management. The presence of mixed messages from employers is undermining the employment relationship and changes are being driven in a top-down manner with a lack of consultation. There is also disenchantment and concern about the accuracy and fairness of performance management processes, with employees expressing scepticism towards managerial attempts to implement change.[38]

A new moral contract

The changing nature of organisations and individuals at work has placed increasing pressures on the awareness and importance of new psychological contracts. *Ghosal et al.* suggest that in a changing social context the law of masters and servants that underlies the old psychological contract is no longer acceptable to many people. Forces of global competition and turbulent change make employment guarantees unfeasible and also enhance the need for levels of trust and teamwork. The new management philosophy needs to be grounded in a very different moral contract with people. Rather than seeing people as a corporate asset from which value can be appropriated, people are seen as a responsibility and a resource to be added to. The new moral contract also demands much from employees, who need to abandon the stability of lifetime employment and embrace the concept of continuous learning and personal development.[39]

However, *Furnham and Taylor* assert that despite the importance of the psychological contract, as many as two-thirds of employees believe their employers 'patently violated' this understanding.[40]

ORGANISATIONAL PRACTICES

It is convenient, here, to consider two sets of observations on the nature of human behaviour and what may actually happen, in practice, in organisations: the Peter Principle and Parkinson's Law. Although these observations are presented in a satirical manner, they nevertheless make a serious and significant point about the management and functioning of organisations and the actual nature and practice of organisational behaviour.

THE PETER PRINCIPLE

This is concerned with the study of occupational incompetence and the study of hierarchies. The analysis of hundreds of cases of occupational incompetence led to the formulation of the '**Peter Principle**', which is:

In a hierarchy every employee tends to rise to their level of incompetence.[41]

Employees competent in their position are promoted and competence in each new position qualifies for promotion to the next highest position until a position of incompetence is reached. The principle is based on perceived incompetence at all levels of every hierarchy – political, legal, educational and industrial – and ways in which employees move upwards through a hierarchy and what happens to them after promotion.

Among the many examples quoted by Peter are those from the teaching occupation. *A* is a competent and conforming college student who becomes a teacher following the textbook, curriculum guide and timetable schedule, and who works well except when there is no rule or precedent available. *A* never breaks a rule or disobeys an order but will not gain promotion because, although competent as a student, *A* has reached a level of incompetence as a classroom teacher.

B, a competent student and inspiring teacher, although not good with paperwork, is promoted to head of the science department because of success as a teacher. The head of science is responsible for ordering all science supplies and keeping extensive records and *B*'s incompetence becomes evident.

C, a competent student, teacher and head of department, is promoted to assistant principal and being intellectually competent is further promoted to principal. *C* is now required to work directly with higher officials. By working so hard at running the school, however, *C* misses important meetings with superiors and has no energy to become involved with community organisations. *C* thus becomes regarded as an incompetent principal.

Means of promotion

Peter suggests two main means by which a person can affect their promotion rate, 'Pull' and 'Push'.

- Pull is an employee's relationship – by blood, marriage or acquaintance – with a person above the employee in the hierarchy.

- Push is sometimes manifested by an abnormal interest in study, vocational training and self-improvement.

In small hierarchies, Push may have a marginal effect in accelerating promotion; in larger hierarchies the effect is minimal. Pull is, therefore, likely to be more effective than Push.

Never stand when you can sit; never walk when you can ride; never Push when you can Pull.[42]

PARKINSON'S LAW

A major feature of Parkinson's Law is that of the 'rising pyramid', that is, 'Work expands so as to fill the time available for its completion'.[43] General recognition of this is illustrated in the proverb, 'It is the busiest person who has time to spare.' There is little, if any, relationship between the quantity of work to be done and the number of staff doing it. Underlying this general tendency are two almost axiomatic statements:

- An official wants to multiply subordinates, not rivals.
- Officials make work for each other.

Parkinson goes on to give the following example. If a civil servant, *A*, believes he is overworked, there are three possible remedies: (i) resignation; (ii) ask to halve the work by having it shared with a colleague, *B*; or (iii) seek the assistance of two subordinates, *C* and *D*. The first two options are unlikely. Resignation would involve loss of pension rights, while sharing work with a colleague on the same level would only bring in a rival for promotion. So *A* would prefer the appointment of two junior members of staff, *C* and *D*. This would increase *A*'s status. There must be at least two subordinates, so that by dividing work between *C* and *D*, A will be the only person to understand the work of them both. Furthermore, each subordinate is kept in order by fear of the other's promotion.

When, in turn, *C* complains of overwork, *A*, with the agreement of *C*, will advise the appointment of two assistants, *E* and *F*. However, as *D*'s position is much the same and to avoid internal friction, two assistants, *G* and *H*, will also be recommended to help *D*. There are now seven people, *A, C, D, E, F, G, H*, doing what one person did before, and *A*'s promotion is almost certain.

People making work for each other

With the seven people now employed, the second stage comes into operation. The seven people make so much work for each other that they are all fully occupied and *A* is actually working harder than ever. For example, an incoming document comes before each of them in turn. *E* decides it is *F*'s concern; *F* places a draft reply for *C*, who makes drastic amendments before consulting with *D*, who asks *G* to action it. But then *G* goes on leave and hands the file to *H*, who drafts a minute signed by *D* and returned to *C*, who revises the first draft and puts the new version before *A*. What does *A* do? *A* could find many excuses for signing *C*'s draft unread. However, being a conscientious person, and although beset with problems created by subordinates both for *A* and for themselves, *A* reads through the draft carefully, deletes the fussy paragraphs added by *C* and *H* and restores it to the format presented in the first instance by *F*.

Among other features of organisational practice that Parkinson discusses are principles of personnel selection; the nature of committees; personality screen; high finance – and the 'Law of Triviality', which means in a committee that the time spent on any agenda item will be in inverse proportion to the sum involved; layout of the organisation's administration block; and 'injelitis' – the disease of induced inferiority.

Relevance of observations

Despite the light vein of Parkinson's writing, the relevance of his observations can be gauged from comments in the Introduction by HRH The Duke of Edinburgh.

The most important point about this book for serious students of management and administration is that it illustrates the gulf that exists between the rational/intellectual approach to human organisation and the frequent irrational facts of human nature ... The law should be compulsory reading at all business schools and for all management consultants. Management structures solve nothing if they do not take the facts of human nature into proper consideration, and one of the most important facts is that no one really likes having to make decisions. Consequently structures may generate a lot of activity but little or no useful work.[44]

I first read Parkinson's Law when studying for Economics A-level. Many of the laws are just as relevant today as they were then. They include: how to 'manage' a meeting, and how time spent in meetings is inversely proportional to the importance of each issue – his example is a short discussion on a £10 million power plant followed by a lengthy debate over a £350 bicycle shed. Ever been there? ... Parkinson's most famous law is that 'work expands to fill the time available – as we all make work for one another'. This is still true today.

Iain Herbertson, Managing Director of Manpower[45]

THE CHANGING NATURE OF WORK ORGANISATION

The effective management of people takes place in the context of the wider environmental setting, including the changing patterns of organisations and attitudes to work. It is frequently documented that a global economy, increased business competitiveness, the move towards more customer-driven markets, and advances in scientific knowledge, especially telecommunications and office automation, have led to a period of constant change and the need for greater organisational flexibility.

The power and influence of private and public organisations, the rapid spread of new technology and the impact of various socio-economic and political factors have attracted increasing attention to the concept of corporate social responsibilities and business ethics. Increasing attention is also being focused on the ethical behaviour that underlies the decisions and actions of managers and staff; many responsible organisations and professional bodies now choose to publish a Code of Ethics.

The changing nature of organisations and individuals at work has placed growing pressure on the awareness and importance of new psychological contracts. Forces of global competition and turbulent change make employment guarantees unfeasible and demand a new management philosophy based on trust and teamwork. People are seen as a responsibility and a resource to be added to. Employees need to abandon the stability of lifetime employment and embrace the concept of continuous learning and personal development.[46]

According to an Economic and Social Research Council (ESRC) publication, in any analysis of the transformation of Britain's employment relations we cannot neglect the changing nature of work. The influence of technological innovation, work restructuring and job redesign are all helping to reshape shopfloor attitudes among managers, unions and workers.[47]

In their discussion of the 21st-century organisation, *Bouchikhi and Kimberly* refer to the customised workplace that represents a radical departure from commonly accepted management principles and techniques. They summarise the main differences between 19th-, 20th- and 21st-century management – *see* Table 1.1.[48]

New approaches to management and organisational behaviour

In discussing new approaches to management practices for the next decade, *Muzyka* suggests that: 'Organisational behavior has moved from an emphasis on the structural aspects of functional and cross-functional organisations to more flexible models, including enhanced consideration of short-term, high performance teams.'

Table 1.1 Contrasting the paradigms

	19th century	20th century	21st century
Theory of personhood	Interchangeable muscle and energy	A subordinate with a hierarchy of needs	Autonomous and reflexive individual
Information and knowledge	The province of management alone	Management-dominated and shared on a limited basis	Widely diffused
The purpose of work	Survival	Accumulation of wealth and social status	Part of a strategic life plan
Identification	With the firm and/ or with the working class	With a social group and/or the firm	The disenfranchised self
Conflict	Disruptive and to be avoided	Disruptive but tolerated and can be settled through collective bargaining	A normal part of life
Division of labour	Managers decide, employees execute	Managers decide, employees execute thoughtfully	Employees and managers decide and execute
Power	Concentrated at the top	Limited, functional sharing/empowerment	Diffused and shared

Source: Bouchikhi, H. and Kimberly, J. R., 'The customized workplace', in Chowdhury, S. (ed.) *Management 21C*, Financial Times Prentice Hall (2000), p. 215. Reproduced with permission from Pearson Education Ltd.

New ideas of how to motivate and deploy people have developed. A new contract is evolving that involves the exchange of value. Individuals need to be encouraged and permitted to achieve: to perform to their highest potential, for their benefit and that of the employer. Organisations are encouraging staff to craft more flexible, value-laden, and specific rules governing their relationships.[49]

Cloke and Goldsmith refer to the age of traditional management coming to an end and the decline of hierarchical, bureaucratic, autocratic management. They contend that management is an idea whose time is up and organisations that do not recognise the need to share power and responsibility with all their workers will lose them.[50]

GLOBALISATION AND THE INTERNATIONAL CONTEXT

One major challenge facing managers in the early 21st century arises from what many commentators have identified as an increasingly international or **global** business environment. The following factors are frequently cited as potential explanatory factors underlying this trend:

- improvements in international communication facilities leading to an increased consciousness of differences in workplace attitudes and behaviour in other societies;
- international competitive pressure – for example, the emergence of newly industrialised and/or free-market nations (the Far East region and former communist bloc countries are often viewed as examples of this phenomenon);
- the spread of production methods and other business processes *across* nations and regions;

- international business activity, for example: overseas franchising or licensing agreements; outsourcing of business units to other countries (call centres provide a topical example); direct foreign investment and the activities of multinational corporations which, by definition, operate outside national boundaries.

In broad terms, **globalisation** refers to organisations integrating, operating and competing in a worldwide economy. The organisations' activities are more independent across the world rather than confined nationally. Globalisation will also impact on the nature of business ethics and international corporate social responsibilities, discussed in Chapter 14. With globalisation, strategy and structure are inextricably linked. As organisations, and especially large business organisations, adopt a more global perspective this will have a significant effect on the broader context of management and organisational behaviour.

For example, *Francesco and Gold* refer to the globalisation of the economy that has created new types of structures such as the 'boundaryless organisation' which breaks the traditional demarcations of authority and task specialisation associated with bureaucracies and other structures. 'Features of a boundaryless organization include a widespread use of project teams, interfunctional teams, networks, and similar structural mechanisms, thus reducing boundaries that typically separate organizational functions and hierarchical levels.' A key management challenge is the socialisation and training of members of the organisation away from the effects of the bureaucratic mentality. Although there is still some form of authority structure, and task and political boundaries, such boundaries are flexible and unlike the rigid horizontal and vertical dimensions of traditional organisations.[51]

However, according to *McLean*, globalisation has ultimately and importantly altered the terms of reference and resulted in a paradigm shift for the way organisations are managed.

> *It has altered the way we work, via, for example, sophisticated systems and procedures aimed at streamlining and 'internationalising' business activities and practices. It has brought companies closer together through opening up new markets and through technological innovations, such as e-business and e-commerce via the World Wide Web. It has increased competition, the speed of innovation, the ubiquity of change and environmental complexity and uncertainty.*[52]

However, although national action may be informed by global thinking, an underlying guideline for multinational organisations is to 'think globally; act locally'. Consider the area of strategic human resource management (HRM). To what extent do differences in, for example, legislation, social security provisions, the philosophy of employment relations, arrangements for collective bargaining, management practices, regulation of the employment contract, the informal organisation, as well as communications over long distances and different time zones, demand attention to HRM at primarily a national level?

The future of globalisation

Globalisation has been subjected to much criticism in part at least due to lack of clarity as to its exact meaning and to the confusion about organisations that are very large-scale (such as Walmart in the USA) but have only a small proportion of their operations on a global basis. Globalisation has also become the source of demonstrations and has been blamed for escalating inequalities in the developing world and endangering regional cultures. There appears to be a return to strong nationalistic tendencies in countries such as America and France. *Rugman* refers to the illusion of the global company and maintains that there is no trend towards globalisation but strong evidence of a hardening of triad blocs and regional groups of the EU, USA and Japan.[53] *Saul* dates the rise of globalisation from 1971 but contends that its heyday was in the mid-1990s and it is now in retreat.[54]

According to *Child*, globalisation is a complex phenomenon and the term is used in so many different ways it is in danger of losing any useful purpose. Globalisation is a trend rather than a condition that necessarily already exists, it is not spreading evenly across the world and many unsubstantiated and sweeping claims have been made. 'The trend towards globalisation is a strong one, but it remains to be seen how far and how fast it will spread. It has powerful opponents.'[55]

Meanwhile, *McLean* maintains that globalisation is here to stay – it won't go away and if anything will get worse. 'We must face the realism that the world, and indeed organisations and the way they are managed, will never be the same. We must encompass these changes and harness the opportunities they present.'[56]

Whatever the extent of globalisation, there are clear implications for organisational behaviour in accommodating international dimensions of management and cultural differences.

Cultural environment

The importance of people in business understanding cultural differences is illustrated by IBM which publishes for members of staff a comprehensive guide to main dimensions of culture and business, and an introduction to concepts, tips, resources and tools for building cross-cultural competencies across national, organisational, team and interpersonal barriers.

Within the global civilisation there are of course many differences in cultural values and attitudes. According to *Dana*, it is essential for people in business to understand cultural differences, but this is not just a matter of noting different ways but rather rooting out the reasons behind these differences. 'Complex cultural environments require fluency not only in words, but more importantly in understanding what is not said – and this takes time, patience and dedication.' For example, the Japanese believe in sharing and the concept of harmony (*wa*) and will often ponder and think through responses as part of a conciliatory relationship and to avoid conflict. Other cultures may find the periodic silence awkward and a sign of mistrust.[57]

In America, there is a strong commitment to the organisation (the corporation) and work and career are taken very seriously (as the author has experienced for himself). Hard work is accepted as part of the American way of life and good timekeeping is important. It is a long-hours culture and generally there is little concern for the work/life balance. There is a strong emphasis on political correctness and little banter or humour at work (again as the author found out to his cost), especially not in formal meetings. Americans do not like self-deprecation and find it strange that the British are prepared to laugh at themselves.[58]

In China there is an enormous bureaucracy and the hierarchy is an important indication of authority. In the business world you may need to deal with several ascending levels of management before reaching the senior manager. There can be an apparent lack of courtesy – and rather than given, respect and trust have to be earned. There is a strong superior–subordinate relationship, with staff often undertaking menial tasks for their boss.[59]

In Japan and Korea, where society tends to be male dominated, in the business world men are more likely to be taking the main role in setting agendas, communications and decision-making.

Cross-cultural approach to management

One rationale for taking a cross-cultural approach to management lies in the potential benefits to be gained in performance terms. *Schneider and Barsoux*, in advocating cultural awareness of one's own society, note:

> *Each country has its unique institutional and cultural characteristics, which can provide sources of competitive advantage at one point, only to become liabilities when the environment changes. Managers therefore need to evaluate the extent to which national culture can interfere with their company's efforts to respond to strategic requirements, now and in the future.*'[60]

In addition to practically based benefits in considering our own 'home' culture, there has been a long tradition of looking to other cultures for examples of 'successful' practice which could be transplanted into work organisations in different societies. Different models may be dominant at different times. *Thompson and McHugh* note: 'In the post-war period the giant US corporations transferred work organisation and managerial techniques across capitalist countries.'[61] However, in subsequent eras Scandinavian autonomous work group arrangements and Japanese management techniques were examined by and, to some extent, implemented in, organisations across the world. Such a search for good practice in other countries is, of course, ongoing and an awareness of how other cultures organise work and manage people is likely to be of continuing benefit in the future.

It is not only businesses that choose to operate in more than one country or import foreign business and management techniques that are affected by cross-cultural concerns. *Tayeb* reported United States Department of Labor statistics indicating that in the period from 1985 to 2000, only 15 per cent of new entrants to the workforce in the USA were white males.[62] This highlights the importance of managing diversity in workforces *within* national boundaries. The management of diversity is discussed in Chapter 4.

Managing people from different cultures

Another advantage of adopting a cross-cultural approach to the study of organisational behaviour, and to the management of people more generally, lies in the recognition of variations in workplace attitudes and behaviour between individuals and groups in different cultural contexts. *Brooks* notes: 'Differences in national culture may have a bearing on how organisations deal with each other and also on behaviour within organisations which comprise a mix of nationalities.'[63] If we accept this fundamental point then it follows that key topics within the subject area of organisational behaviour may be influenced by national culture and that we should therefore re-evaluate models and concepts when applying them to other societies.

One leading writer in the field of cross-cultural studies, *Trompenaars*, commenting on his own work, suggests: 'It helped managers to structure their experiences and provided new insights for them and their organisations into the real source of problems faced when managing across cultures or dealing with diversity.'[64] In examining the centrally important topic of motivation, *Francesco and Gold* inform their readers: 'Managers must develop organisational systems that are flexible enough to take into account the meaning of work and the relative value of rewards within the range of cultures where they operate.'[65] A practical example of the impact of cultural diversity in the organisational behaviour area is provided in the recollections of an international human resource manager cited in *Schneider and Barsoux*: 'Indonesians manage their culture by a group process, and everyone is linked together as a team. Distributing money differently among the team did not go over all that well; so we've come to the conclusion that pay for performance is not suitable for Indonesia.'[66] It may be extremely useful therefore to examine academic frameworks and research findings within the field of organisational behaviour to indicate the extent to which they are applicable worldwide or, alternatively, subject to meaningful variation in different cultural contexts.

Critical reflection

To what extent do you support the suggestion that national culture is not only an explanation of human beliefs, values and actions but arguably the most significant feature in the study of organisational behaviour? What examples can you give in support of your view?

IS ORGANISATIONAL BEHAVIOUR CULTURE-BOUND?

While it can be valuable to apply organisational behaviour concepts to diverse cultural settings, it should also be borne in mind that some **universal** theories and models may, in reality, contain important culturally derived assumptions. When examining classical frameworks for understanding organisation structure (discussed in Chapter 2), *Schneider and Barsoux* point out: 'Theories about how best to organise – Max Weber's (German) bureaucracy, Henri Fayol's (French) administrative model, and Frederick Taylor's (American) scientific management – all reflect societal concerns of the times as well as the cultural background of the individuals.'[67] That writers on work organisations may themselves be influenced by their own cultural backgrounds when compiling their work is unsurprising: however, equally it should not be ignored.

More significant still is the possibility that whole topics within organisational behaviour, *per se*, may be underpinned by a particular culturally derived frame of reference. *Francesco and Gold*, addressing the issue of leadership, claim: 'One difficulty is that not all cultures have the term leader.'[68] This raises the possibility that meanings we may assume to be taken for granted could be interpreted differently or **not even perceived at all** in different parts of the world.

Culture as understanding

'For our most basic common link is that we all inhabit this small planet, we all breathe the same air, we all cherish our children's future, and we are all mortal' (John. F. Kennedy, 10 June 1963). There are a number of very good reasons why we could usefully understand cultural difference (and similarity) at work, based on new awareness contributing to our own effectiveness and moreover to the accomplishment of organisational goals. It could also be true to say that an appreciation of culture and its effects may be of intrinsic value. There could therefore be advantages of cross-cultural awareness which include:

- increased self-awareness;
- sensitivity to difference;
- questioning our own assumptions and knowledge;
- lessening ignorance, prejudice and hatred.

However, it would be wrong to think that increased cross-cultural awareness or activity will automatically bring about any of these outcomes.

Adler listed the following inbuilt dangers when multicultural teams operate in a business setting;

- mistrust – including stereotyping;
- miscommunication with potential for reduced accuracy and resultant stress;
- process difficulties, that is failure to agree when agreement is needed or even what constitutes agreement when arriving at decisions.

Adler goes on to examine research on the success of multicultural work teams and concludes that the evidence suggests that they either perform *much better or much worse* than teams composed of one cultural group.[69] There are clearly risks as well as benefits in working across cultures. It is hoped that an appreciation of cross-cultural aspects of organisational behaviour can help in this regard.

Brooks is one of several commentators who draw our attention to the interlinked nature of culture. Figure 1.6 illustrates the interplay between relevant factors affecting any one national culture.[70] You may wish to consider how these factors have combined to shape your own 'home' culture and that of one other country with which you are familiar.

FIVE DIMENSIONS OF CULTURE: THE CONTRIBUTION OF HOFSTEDE

Geert Hofstede is one of the most significant contributors to the body of knowledge on culture and workplace difference. His work has largely resulted from a large-scale research programme involving employees from the IBM Corporation, initially in 40 countries. In

Figure 1.6 Factors affecting national culture

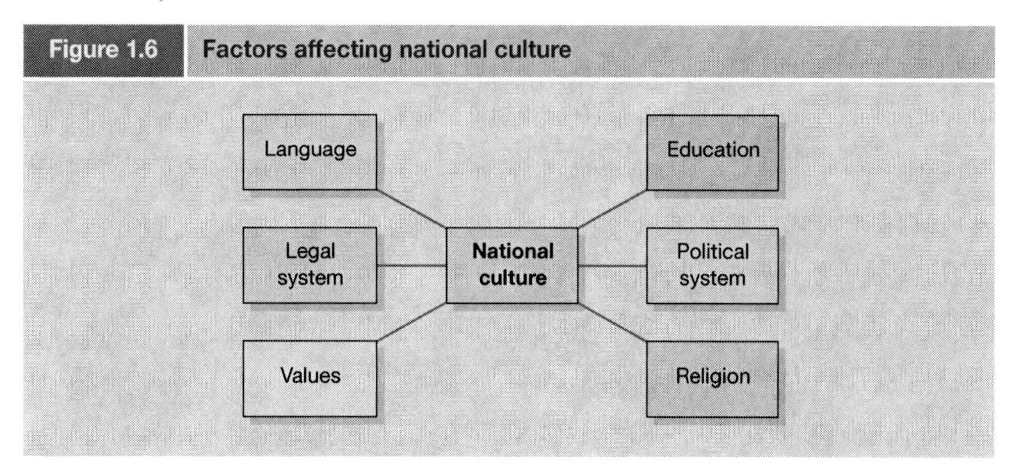

Source: From Brooks, I., *Organisational Behaviour: Individuals, Groups and Organisation*, Third Edition, Financial Times Prentice Hall (2006), p. 272, with permission from Pearson Education Ltd.

focusing on one organisation Hofstede felt that the results could be more clearly linked to national cultural difference. Arguing that culture is, in a memorable phrase, **collective programming** or **software of the mind**, Hofstede initially identified four dimensions of culture: power distance, uncertainty avoidance, individualism and masculinity.[71]

- **Power distance** is essentially used to categorise levels of inequality in organisations, which Hofstede claims will depend upon management style, willingness of subordinates to disagree with superiors, and the educational level and status accruing to particular roles. Countries which displayed a high level of power distance included France, Spain, Hong Kong and Iran. Countries as diverse as Germany, Italy, Australia and the USA were characterised as low power distance societies. Britain also emerged as a low power distance society according to Hofstede's work.
- **Uncertainty avoidance** refers to the extent to which members of a society feel threatened by unusual situations. High uncertainty avoidance is said to be characteristic in France, Spain, Germany and many of the Latin American societies. Low to medium uncertainty avoidance was displayed in the Netherlands, the Scandinavian countries and Ireland. In this case Britain is said to be 'low to medium' together with the USA, Canada and Australia.
- **Individualism** describes the relatively individualistic or collectivist ethic evident in that particular society. Thus, the USA, France and Spain display high individualism. This contrasts with Portugal, Hong Kong, India and Greece which are low individualism societies. Britain here is depicted as a high individualism society.
- **Masculinity** is the final category suggested by Hofstede. This refers to a continuum between 'masculine' characteristics, such as assertiveness and competitiveness, and 'feminine' traits, such as caring, a stress upon the quality of life and concern with the environment. High masculinity societies included the USA, Italy, Germany and Japan. More feminine (low masculinity) societies included the Netherlands and the Scandinavian countries. In this case Britain was located within the high masculinity group.

A fifth dimension of culture, long-term/short-term orientation, was originally labelled **Confucian work dynamism**. This dimension developed from the work of *Bond* in an attempt to locate Chinese cultural values as they impacted on the workplace.[72] Countries which scored highly on Confucian work dynamism or long-term orientation exhibited a strong concern with time along a continuum and were therefore both past- and future-oriented, with a preoccupation with tradition but also a concern with the effect of actions and policies on future generations.

Evaluation of Hofstede's work

Extremely influential, the seminal work of Hofstede has been criticised from certain quarters. In common with other writers in this area there is a focus on the national rather than the regional level. The variations within certain countries, for example Spain, can be more or less significant. Again in common with other contributors Hofstede's classifications include medium categories which may be difficult to operationalise, accurate though they may be. Some may also find the masculinity/femininity dimension unconvincing and itself stereotypical. Other writers have questioned whether Hofstede's findings remain current. *Holden* summarises this view: 'How many people have ever thought that many of Hofstede's informants of three decades ago are now dead? Do their children and grandchildren really have the same values?'[73]

Ultimately, readers can assess the value of his work in the light of their own experiences and interpretations of the business world. Hofstede in his extensive research has attempted to locate the essence of work-related differences across the world and to relate these to preferred management styles.

CULTURAL DIVERSITY: THE CONTRIBUTION OF TROMPENAARS

Another significant contributor to this area of study is *Fons Trompenaars* whose later work is co-authored with *Charles Hampden-Turner*.[74] Trompenaars's original research spanned 15 years, resulting in a database of 50,000 participants from 50 countries. It was supported by cases and anecdotes from 900 cross-cultural training programmes. A questionnaire method comprised a significant part of the study which involved requiring participants to consider their underlying norms, values and attitudes. The resultant framework identifies seven areas in which cultural differences may affect aspects of organisational behaviour.

- Relationships and rules. Here societies may be more or less **universal**, in which case there is relative rigidity in respect of rule-based behaviour, or **particular**, in which case the importance of relationships may lead to flexibility in the interpretation of situations.
- Societies may be more oriented to the **individual** or **collective**. The collective may take different forms: the corporation in Japan, the family in Italy or the Catholic Church in the Republic of Ireland. There may be implications here for such matters as individual responsibility or payment systems.
- It may also be true that societies differ to the extent it is thought appropriate for members to show emotion in public. **Neutral** societies favour the 'stiff upper lip', while overt displays of feeling are more likely in **emotional** societies. Trompenaars cites a survey in which 80 employees in each of various societies were asked whether they would think it wrong to express upset openly at work. The numbers who thought it wrong were 80 in Japan, 75 in Germany, 71 in the UK, 55 in Hong Kong, 40 in the USA and 29 in Italy.
- In **diffuse** cultures, the whole person would be involved in a business relationship and it would take time to build such relationships. In a **specific** culture, such as the USA, the basic relationship would be limited to the contractual. This distinction clearly has implications for those seeking to develop new international links.
- **Achievement**-based societies value recent success or an overall record of accomplishment. In contrast, in societies relying more on **ascription**, status could be bestowed on you through such factors as age, gender or educational record.
- Trompenaars suggests that societies view **time** in different ways which may in turn influence business activities. The American dream is the French nightmare. Americans generally start from zero and what matters is their present performance and their plan to 'make it' in the future. This is 'nouveau riche' for the French, who prefer the 'ancien pauvre'; they have an enormous sense of the past.

- Finally it is suggested that there are differences with regard to attitudes to the **environment**. In Western societies, individuals are typically masters of their fate. In other parts of the world, however, the world is more powerful than individuals.

Trompenaars' work is based on lengthy academic and field research. It is potentially useful in linking the dimensions of culture to aspects of organisational behaviour which are of direct relevance, particularly to people approaching a new culture for the first time.

The high- and low-context cultures framework

This framework for understanding cultural difference has been formulated by Ed Hall; his work is in part co-authored with Mildred Reed Hall.[75] *Hall* conceptualises culture as comprising a series of 'languages', in particular:

- language of time;
- language of space;
- language of things;
- language of friendships;
- language of agreements.

In this model of culture Hall suggests that these 'languages', which resemble shared attitudes to the issues in question, are communicated in very different ways according to whether a society is classified as 'high' or 'low' context.

The features of 'high' context societies, which incorporate Asian, African and Latin American countries, include:

- a high proportion of information is 'uncoded' and internalised by the individual;
- indirect communication styles ... words are less important;
- shared group understandings;
- importance attached to the past and tradition;
- 'diffuse' culture stressing importance of trust and personal relationships in business.

'Low' context societies, which include the USA, Australia, Britain and the Scandinavian countries, exhibit contrasting features including:

- a high proportion of communication is 'coded' and expressed;
- direct communication styles ... words are paramount;
- past context is less important;
- 'specific' culture stressing importance of rules and contracts.

Other countries, for example France, Spain, Greece and several Middle Eastern societies, are classified as 'medium' context.

To take one example as an illustration: American managers visiting China may find that a business transaction in that country will take more time than at home. They may find it difficult to interpret the true feelings of their Chinese host and may need to decode non-verbal communication and other signals. They may seek to negotiate a rules-based contract whereas their Chinese counterpart may lay greater stress upon building a mutually beneficial reciprocal relationship. There is scope for potential miscommunication between the two cultures and interesting differences in interpersonal perception. In so far as much of the management literature canon originates from the Anglo-American context, there is again considerable merit in adopting a cross-cultural perspective.

A concept map of some issues for discussion on cross-cultural organisational differences is set out in Figure 1.7.

Figure 1.7 Concept map of cross-cultural organisational differences

CROSS-CULTURAL ORGANISATIONAL DIFFERENCES
(– some issues for discussion)

- FEATURES OF CULTURES
- 4 DIMENSIONAL SPECTRA OF NATIONAL CULTURES

CULTURE is a collective mental programming of the people of/in a particular environment – encompassing a number of people conditioned by the same education and life experiences
GEERT HOFSTEDE 1980

FEATURES
- They are difficult to change. Any change is usually very slow (years) and is resisted.
- Cultures may be identified in diverse groupings e.g. family; organisations; nations; etc.

- MASCULINITY v FEMININITY
  – Identified in the dominant values of the society

MASCULINITY
concerned with:
– Assertiveness
– Acquisition of wealth and things
– Live to work
– Clear sex roles, leading to male dominance

FEMININITY
concerned with:
– Quality of life
– Working to live
– Fluid sex roles, leading to equality

- UNCERTAINTY AVOIDANCE
  – Low U.A. suggests a culture of risk takers; a concern with performance and doing something to satisfy needs as suggested by Maslow

– Having a powerful superior whom one can blame (and praise) satisfies the need to avoid uncertainty
– Cultures with strong uncertainty avoidance trends don't take risks and don't conform to Maslow's perception of a hierarchy of human needs (Western)

- USA/UK e.g. place Esteem > Social Needs > Security
- Other value systems Security > Social Needs > Esteem and achievement (belonging)

- POWER DISTANCE
  dimension relates to people as subordinates and their attitude to superiors. Large power distance mean superiors are held in awe as inaccessible (probably autocratic) persons/leaders

– Leadership complements subordinateship/followership
– Small power distances relate to more participative leadership styles
– What is feasible depends on the cultural conditioning of subordinates
– Western leadership theories advocate participation in decision making by subordinates
– Medium power distances (USA/UK) initiatives taken by the manager
– Larger power distances initiatives taken by the leader

– Initiatives taken by subordinates

- COLLECTIVIST ENVIRONMENT
  local employees need ties with the organisation for mutual loyalty and emotional dependence. Emphasises 'belonging' (prefers non-capitalist order)

– Capitalism more associated with 'individualist' cultures e.g. US and UK
– Individualism is characterised by a society where people care for themselves and immediate family. Any involvement with the organisation is calculative, we seek autonomy and financial security

COMPANY POLICY IMPLICATIONS
- If differences in environmental cultures are obvious, Western management theories are constrained
- If culture matters, policies are less effective in different cultural environments
- Identical personnel policies may have differing effects in different countries
- Also perceptions of absenteeism; financial incentives; performance; quality costs; grievance procedures; labour turnover, etc.

IMPLICATIONS FOR TRAINING MANAGERS (INTL)
If destined to work abroad, they need a thorough familiarisation with the new culture using:–
- Specialised cross-cultural training institutes, or
- Host country personnel to advise them

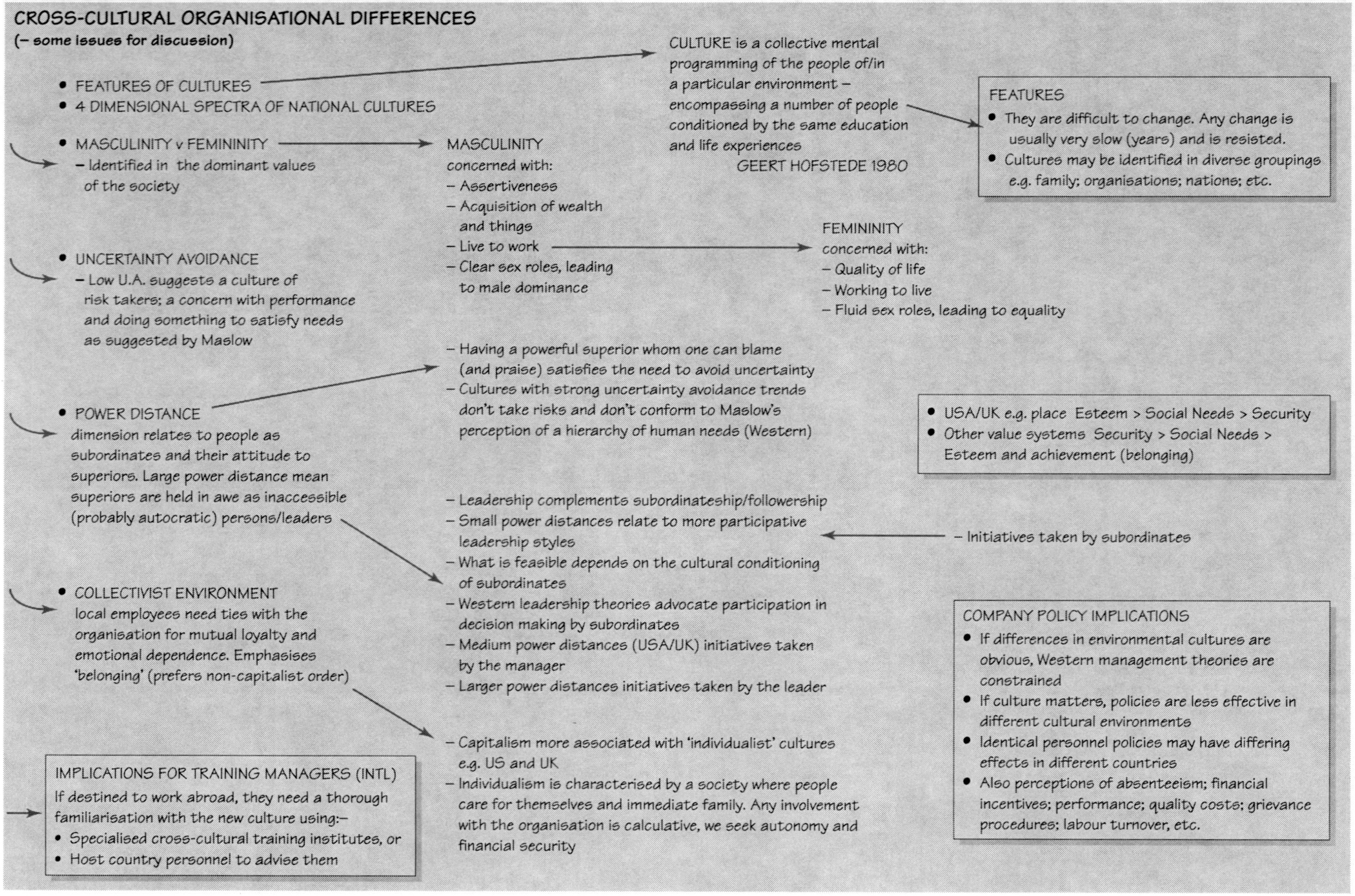

Source: Training Learning Consultancy Ltd, Bristol, England. Reproduced with permission.

CONVERGENCE OR CULTURE-SPECIFIC ORGANISATIONAL BEHAVIOUR

There is evidence of a narrowing or even increasing elimination of cultural differences in business. *Grint* sees both positive and negative consequences of aspects of globalisation. While noting that 'at last we are approaching an era when what is common between people transcends that which is different; where we can choose our identity rather than have it thrust upon us by accident of birth', the same author goes on to suggest: 'We are heading for global convergence where national, ethnic and local cultures and identities are swamped by the McDonaldization ... and/or Microsoftization of the world.'[76]

There is an undoubted narrowing of cultural differences in work organisations and such narrowing may apply to individual and group behaviour at work. *Thompson and McHugh* note, 'Russia is now experiencing rampant individualism and uncertainty following the collapse of the old solidaristic norms', thus implying convergence of work values.[77] For the most part, however, it is argued here that growing similarity and harmonisation relate more often to production, IT and quality systems which are more likely to converge due to best-practice comparisons and universal computer standards. Human resource management is, contrastingly, less likely to converge due to national institutional frameworks and culturally derived preferences. Recent significantly different responses to the need for greater workplace 'flexibility' in Britain and France illustrate this point. Above all, those aspects of organisational behaviour which focus on individual differences, groups and managing people are the most clearly affected by culture and it is argued strongly here that it is and is likely to remain essential to take a cross-cultural approach to the subject.

THE IMPORTANCE OF PEOPLE AND ORGANISATIONAL BEHAVIOUR

However one looks at the nature or disciplines of organisational behaviour it is important to remember, as *Morgan* reminds us, that 'the reality of organisational life usually comprises numerous different realities!'[78]

Hellriegel, Slocum and Woodman suggest:

> *... One way to recognise why people behave as they do at work is to view an organisation as an iceberg. What sinks ships isn't always what sailors can see, but what they can't see.*[79]

The overt, formal aspects focus only on the tip of the iceberg (organisation). It is just as important to focus on what you can't see – the covert, behavioural aspects (*see* Figure 1.8).

As part of the *Financial Times Mastering Management* series, *Wood*, in his discussion of the nature of organisational behaviour, suggests that in its concern for the way people behave in an organisational context, organisational behaviour can be regarded as the key to the whole area of management.

> *Is the study of behaviour in organisations important? I think it is vital. What the social sciences, humanities and the arts are to university education, OB is to business school education. The more technical a manager's training, the more important organisational behaviour becomes. It is arguably the one area that can carry the burden of bringing the collective wisdom of human history into the decision-making calculus of developing managers. And this is no trivial task.*[80]

In the foreword to Cloke and Goldsmith's thought-provoking book *The End of Management*, *Bennis* claims that a distinct and dramatic change is taking place in the philosophy underlying organisational behaviour, calling forth a new concept of humanity.

Figure 1.8 The organisational iceberg

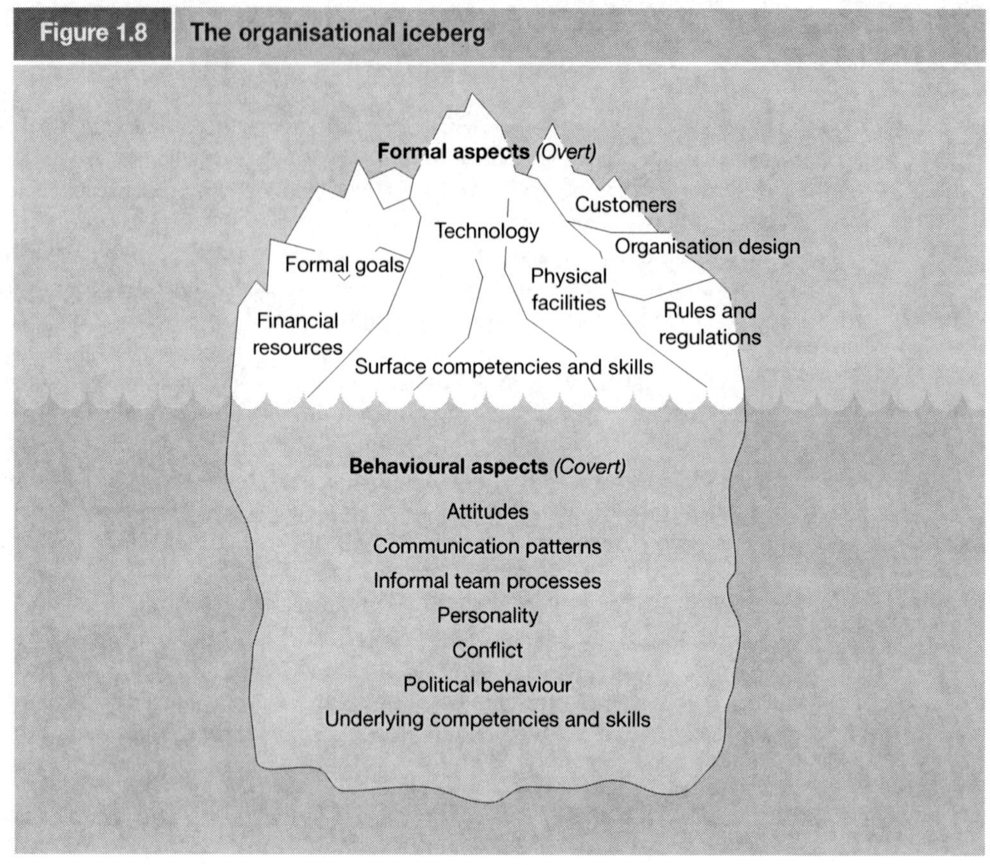

Source: Hellriegel, D., Jackson, S.E. and Slocum, J. W., Jr., *Management*, Eighth Edition, South-Western Publishing (1998), p. 6. Reprinted with the permission of South-Western, a division of Thomson Learning (www.thomsonrights.com / Fax: 800-730-2215).

This new concept is based on expanded knowledge of our complex and shifting needs, replacing an oversimplified, innocent, push-button idea of humanity. This philosophical shift calls for a new concept of organisational depersonalized, mechanistic value system of bureaucracy. With it comes a new concept of power, based on collaboration and reason, replacing a model based on coercion and threat ... The real push for these changes stems from the need not only to humanize organisations, but to use them as crucibles for personal growth and self-realization.[81]

Refresh your understanding
Activity 1E
www.pearsoned.co.uk/mullins

Critical reflection

'The study of organisational behaviour is really an art that pretends it is a science and produces some spurious research findings in a vain attempt to try to prove the point.' How far do you agree with this statement? Do you think the study of organisational behaviour is too subjective ever to be a science?

MANAGEMENT IN THE NEWS

Organisations, strategy and culture

How global strategy can get lost in translation

Stefan Stern

Business leaders pull levers, issue uplifting statements, announce eye-catching initiatives ... and then what? Not even the most hyperactive executive team can be everywhere at all times to monitor what is going on in the furthest reaches of the organisation. The actions of managers and staff on the ground will determine whether quarterly targets are hit and whether grand strategies are realised. Knowing this does not make it any less frustrating when carefully thought-out plans fail to deliver or seem to be simply ignored out in the field. An imposing corporate headquarters may impress visitors, but managers in distant time zones are unlikely to be so easily intimidated. As the old Chinese proverb has it: 'The mountains are high and the emperor is far away.'

Irritation at the persistent failure of managers lower down the corporate ladder to perform partly explains the huge popularity of the hottest management buzzword of the early 21st century – execution. 'There is nothing wrong with our strategy,' senior management teams can console themselves. 'What we lack is the ability to execute it.' It is not only CEOs who suffer while trying to change vast organisations. As Philip Stephens reported in the *Financial Times* last week, Tony Blair, the British prime minister, is exasperated at his lack of success in reforming the UK's public sector. For almost a decade now the prime minister has been giving roughly the same speech, every three to six months, on the need for painful and radical reform. Every time the speech is delivered, front-line public sector managers look up wearily from their desks with a mixture of incomprehension and despair.

When strategy and culture are at odds, it is said, culture always wins. Large organisations are complex. A great deal can get lost in translation between the brilliant PowerPoint presentation to the board and the daily hand-to-hand combat of the marketplace. We use the misleadingly simple term 'globalisation' to describe how the largest corporations do business internationally, as though there is only one way of behaving. But trading across borders inevitably means running up against cultural differences. As the consultant and guru Fons Trompenaars has pointed out, culture can be a very slippery customer. So, understand the vagaries of the different cultures you are dealing with and all will be well with your global corporate strategy, right? Sadly, no. Indeed, blaming 'cultural differences' has become an easy excuse for business leaders who have failed either to devise the right strategy in the first place or to appreciate how to put it into effect.

Andrew Kakabadse, a professor at Cranfield University's school of management in the UK, argues that cultural issues are often a red herring when international businesses are struggling to perform.

> *In the best-run companies the culture of individual countries makes no difference to the performance of the business. The company creates its own powerful culture which supersedes the country culture.*

Business leaders need to mind the gap between head office and the rest of the company. Communicating strategy effectively will take longer, much longer, than you imagine. And 'communication' should mean a frank and unhurried two-way exchange of views, not simply a lavish print run of gleaming corporate brochures.

'What about the workers?' was the traditional cry of organised labour in the last century. Before launching your next big strategic move, spare a moment to ask: what about the managers?

Source: Stern, S., 'How global strategy can get lost in translation', *Financial Times*, 31 July 2006.

Discussion questions

1. **Analyse the content of this article using the framework for organisational behaviour given in Figure 1.1. What can we learn from it about the nature of organisational behaviour?**
2. **Discuss and explain why Trompenaars and Kakabadse might seem to have different views about the relative importance of cultural factors and communication systems in the achievement of organisational goals. Can these views be reconciled?**

SYNOPSIS

- Organisations play a major and continuing role in the lives of us all, especially with the growth of large-scale business organisations. It is important, therefore, to understand how organisations function and the pervasive influences they exercise over the behaviour of people. Organisational behaviour is broadly concerned with the study of the behaviour of people within an organisational setting. It is also necessary to understand interrelationships with other variables that together comprise the total organisation.

- The behaviour of people in work organisations can be viewed in terms of multirelated dimensions concerning the individual, the group, the organisation and the environment. The study of organisational behaviour cannot be understood fully in terms of a single discipline. It is necessary to provide a behavioural science approach drawing on selected aspects of the three main disciplines of psychology, sociology and anthropology together with related disciplines and influences.

- Organisations are complex social systems that can be defined and studied in a number of ways. One approach is to view organisations in terms of contrasting metaphors. Gauging the effectiveness or success of an organisation is not an easy task, however, although one central element is the importance of achieving productivity through the effective management of people. People differ in the manner and extent of their involvement with, and concern for, work. Different situations influence the individual's orientation to work and work ethic. A major concern for people today is balancing work and personal commitments.

- It is through the process of management that efforts of members of the organisation are co-ordinated, directed and guided towards the achievement of organisational objectives. It is essentially an integrating activity and concerned with arrangements for the carrying out of organisational processes and the execution of work. How managers exercise the responsibility for, and duties of, management is important. Attention should be focused on improving the people–organisation relationship.

- One particular aspect of the relationship between the individual and the organisation is the concept of the psychological contract. This is not a formal, written document but implies a series of mutual expectations and satisfaction of needs arising from the people–organisation relationship. There is a continual process of explicit and implicit bargaining. The nature of expectations has an important influence on the employment relationship and behaviour in work organisations. The changing nature of organisations and individuals at work has placed increasing focus on the awareness and importance of a different moral contract with people.

- A major challenge facing managers today arises from an increasingly international or global business environment. This highlights the need for a cross-cultural approach to the study of organisational behaviour and the management of people. In an increasingly global context, managers need to recognise and understand the impact of national culture. However, culture is a multifaceted concept and notoriously difficult to pin down. But it has important repercussions for the effective management of people and the study and understanding of workplace behaviour.

Refresh your understanding, assess your progress and begin your research with online resources at www.pearsoned.co.uk/mullins

REVIEW AND DISCUSSION QUESTIONS

1. Discuss critically what you believe are the main factors to bear in mind with, and particular difficulties presented by, the study of organisational behaviour.
2. Suggest main headings under which interrelated factors that influence behaviour in work organisations can best be identified. Where possible, give practical examples based on your experience.
3. Discuss how organisations may be viewed in terms of contrasting metaphors. Explain how you would apply these metaphors to an understanding of your own organisation.
4. Discuss the role of management as an integrating activity. Give your views on the responsibility of management and the manner in which you believe this responsibility should be exercised.

5 Explain the nature of the people–organisation relationship. Why is it important to distinguish between the 'intent' and the 'implementation' of management decisions and actions?

6 Discuss with supporting examples the changing nature of the psychological contract. List (i) the personal expectations you have of your own organisation and (ii) what you believe to be the expectations of the organisation.

7 Why is it increasingly important for managers to adopt an international approach? Discuss critically the likely longer-term impact of Britain's membership of the European Union.

8 Debate fully the importance of national culture to the study of management and organisational behaviour. Where possible, give your own actual examples.

ASSIGNMENT 1

Five figures are shown below.

(a) (c) (e)

(b) (d)

You are required to:

1 Select the one that is different from all the others.

2 Discuss in small groups reasons for the individual selections and be prepared to justify your own decision.

3 See whether you can reach a consensus on a single group answer.

Discussion

- To what extent did members of the group understand the thought processes of others?
- If you were persuaded to change your mind, on what basis was this decision made?
- What conclusions do you draw from this exercise?

ASSIGNMENT 2

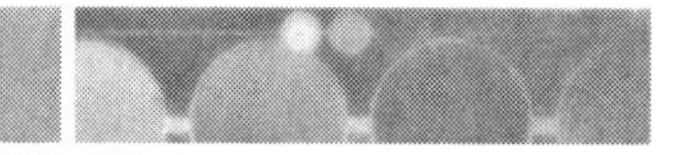

Provide for classroom discussion short descriptions (suitably disguised if necessary) to illustrate the practical application of:

1 The Peter Principle.

2 Parkinson's Law.

Include in your descriptions what you believe to be the relevance of each of these sets of observations and the effects on other members of staff.

Objectives

Completing this exercise should help you to enhance the following skills:

- Obtain a clearer picture of your own and other people's work ethic.
- Explore the importance of work to you and your fixed attitudes about work.
- Recognise the significance of individuals' orientations to work within an organisation.

Exercise

You are required to start by asking yourself this question: is it a good thing to be a worker? Then think carefully about your responses to the following questions.

How do you feel ...

- when you hear the word 'work'?
- as you get ready for work?
- when you know the day is over?
- about the work you've accomplished?
- about someone who chooses not to work?
- about taking time off?
- when you hear the word 'management'?
- about taking control of your career?

Compare your responses with those of your colleagues. What conclusions do you draw about the work ethic?

Source: 'So what's your work ethic?' *Professional Manager*, May 2003, p. 38. Reproduced with permission from the Chartered Management Institute; and Walmsley, C.J., *Your Future Looks Bright*, Preston Beach (2002), p. 98.

Discussion

- What do you see as the character traits of a person with a healthy work ethic?
- To what extent do you agree with the contention that 'we are employed for our skills but valued for our attitude'?
- What effect might different orientations to work have within an organisation and how might they all be accommodated?

CASE STUDY

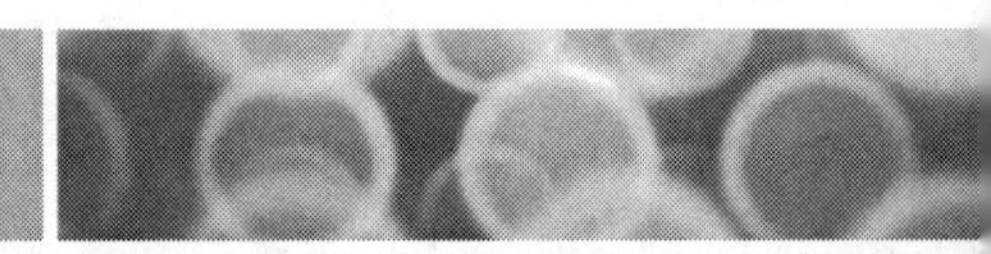

Virgin Atlantic and Ryanair

This case examines two organisations that have many similarities as well as a number of significant differences. The essential technology and systems behind each organisation may be very similar, but the nature and style of management and its consequent impact on the way people working in these organisations think, feel and behave have created very different organisational cultures. So what are the similarities and what are the differences?

The most obvious similarity is that both Virgin Atlantic and Ryanair operate in the UK passenger air transport industry. Both are relatively recent creations and might be seen as new entrants to the sector: Virgin's air transport business was founded by Richard Branson in 1984[82] and Michael O'Leary took over as Chief Executive at Ryanair, a small Irish airline which had been founded as Guinness Peat Aviation in 1985.[83] Both started life in competition with major national flag-

Source: Empics/Associated Press

Source: Empics Sports Photo Agency

Michael O'Leary (left) and Richard Branson (right) have both created very successful airline companies, but their organisational cultures and values are very different from each other.

carrier airlines (British Airways and Aer Lingus respectively) and grew to be major challengers to these established companies. As they grew, their scale of operations brought them into competition with a much larger number and range of airlines operating from the UK: Branson's Virgin Atlantic competes with some major US and other intercontinental companies such as American Airlines and United Airlines; O'Leary competes with the likes of Flybe and EasyJet in the short-haul market. Both Branson, who was born in 1950, and O'Leary, who is ten years younger, are individuals with strong and distinctive personalities, who have a relentless appetite for media presence and who make extensive use of themselves in their frequent marketing communications. They engage in advertising stunts, readily appear on the news media in relation to stories about the industry, and their faces and personalities are easily associated with their companies.

Charting different courses

There are, however, some major differences. First, they differ in their choice of markets. Virgin's air transport business originated in the long-haul, mainly transatlantic market which might be highly profitable but is also extremely competitive. As the business grew, offshoots were founded as independent companies; for instance, Virgin Blue in Australia and Virgin Express which has its hub in Brussels and serves European destinations outside the UK and does not compete directly with Ryanair. Ryanair started as a short-haul carrier and has remained so, focusing on European destinations from a small number of airports in the UK and Eire. The two companies' competitive positioning is also very different. Ryanair is well known as 'The Low Cost Airline'; the first thing that hits you in its publicity material is the price[84] and this is very clearly the core of its business strategy. The 'no frills' approach means just that: even the in-flight food is limited to sandwiches and costs extra. Virgin, by contrast, attracts passengers by offering a superior experience and is firmly positioned at the quality end of the market. Publicity material emphasises style and comfort, and there is a range of in-flight extras which, even at the economy end of the price range, includes in-flight food and drinks and packs of 'amenities' such as flight socks, eye shades and lip balm.

As was noted, both men love publicity stunts and often use humour in their public communications. Branson is usually smiling and in poses which indicate fun and a desire to show close links with his staff and popularity with employees, customers and the public in general. O'Leary is much more likely to be acerbic, critical and uses what might euphemistically be called 'colourful' language in his public statements. He seems to care little about public opinion of him as an individual and has been in trouble with the advertising standards authorities in the UK and Eire on more than one occasion for 'offensive' adverts that have upset people from British Airways (who were accused of being 'Expensive ba****ds' in an *Evening Standard* advert in 1999) and the Catholic Church (the 'Fourth Secret of Fatima' advert of 2000 featured the Pope).[85]

The brand values are also very different. Virgin as a collection of businesses does everything from running trains to manufacturing contraceptives via cosmetics and financial services. All these enterprises are linked by the single powerful central image of the founder and the characteristic red livery. Ryanair does one thing and one thing only, but in doing so sets an almost buccaneering tone, readily taking on authorities such as the European Union over competition policy and the British Airports Authorities over charging practices. Branson has certainly had his conflicts with British Airways, notably over the 'dirty tricks' affair of the early 1990s, but is not likely to challenge governments.

Virgin tries hard to build customer loyalty and gain repeat business through brand-related service values; Ryanair's repeat business (and for some customers the Ryanair experience is one which inspires the thought 'never again') is on price, not loyalty to the brand. These differences have a significant effect on the nature of employment relations and the psychological contract between the two companies and their employees.

Working for Richard and Michael

Each company's brand image and treatment of customers have a bearing on the nature of organisational relationship with staff, and vice versa. Aspects of organisational behaviour therefore show through in a variety of interconnected ways to create consistent and very different cultures.

At Virgin Atlantic, cabin crew are there to be helpful and welcoming; they are important projectors of the brand image and their job is partly to encourage the all-important customer loyalty which generates continuing profit. The importance of staff as carriers of company values is clearly reflected in the recruitment material and other statements about the nature of work at Virgin Atlantic.

> *Virgin Atlantic brings together all manner of people in all manner of roles, all playing a crucial role in the smooth running of a very complex operation. But whoever you are and wherever you join us, you'll never stop thinking of our customers and what we can do for them. From frontline cabin crew to IT analysts, everyone here plays a role in delivering the Virgin brand. That means using initiative, taking responsibility for your actions and being ready to support those around you at all times. Similarly, you'll play your part in maintaining the friendly, unconventional professionalism that makes Virgin Atlantic such a unique place of work.*[86]

The recruitment process is lengthy and includes a group interview which acts as a filter for further tests before job offers are made. Training programmes for cabin crew and other staff are run from a dedicated training centre, and there is a wide range of benefits for full-time staff including seven free flights a year, private pensions and medical schemes and discounted goods and services across the Virgin group.

At Ryanair, the cabin crew work for a supplier organisation called Crewlink. You can discover whether you qualify to apply for a job by answering a series of 11 online questions. Successful applicants for cabin crew posts are trained at one of Crewlink's centres and are expected to pay an up-front charge of €1,200 for the five-week course (or with a €400 deposit it can be offset against initial year's salary at a total cost of €1,300). Students are not paid to attend the course; successful graduates get a three-year contract with Crewlink to work on Ryanair flights on a shift-work basis. Ryanair crew are not expected to make overnight stops at its destinations. Post-tax starting salary is listed as being £1,100 per month (£13,200 pa); Crewlink suggests that after the initial three years, and subject to satisfactory performance, a permanent job with Ryanair itself might be available at a salary of up to £25,000 pa. Staff must be flexible in terms of their work location across the 15 European centres and Crewlink does not guarantee work if individuals specify a preferred work location.[87]

By comparison with long haul, a short-haul operation involves very tight turnaround times and Ryanair aims for 20 minutes. This creates a very different pace and set of pressures on the workforce compared with those at Virgin, which is likely to have higher staffing levels and to give crew longer rest breaks in the destination locations between flights. The nature of customer relations, by contrast, might be more demanding at Virgin than at Ryanair – staff and customers are together for longer and the brand image must be maintained.

Complaints and horror stories can be found about work at both organisations; however, Ryanair is subject to a more systematic and organised campaign of criticism for its employment practices by trade union organisations. In particular, the International Transport Workers' Federation[88] has run a major campaign on its website since 2004 called 'Ryan-be-fair', the purpose of which is to pressurise the management at Ryanair into accepting the role of trade unions in representing the workforce. It collects comments from disgruntled crew and former workers which give a flavour of the operational stresses and organisational culture.

Both organisations have been successful – Ryanair has turned in significant profits for several years in a sector which is prone to disruption and financial loss and which has seen a number of brands disappear[89] (Buzz, Go and Debonair). Virgin also continues to go from strength to strength commercially.[90] But the cultures and values which get them off the ground could hardly be more different.

Your tasks

1. Using the organisational metaphors of Morgan given on (p. 8) identify two which you think might be applied appropriately to Virgin Atlantic and two to Ryanair. How would you justify your choices?
2. Critically evaluate both organisations in terms of one or more of the descriptions of the psychological contract given in the chapter (for instance that of Stalker, Cartwright or Emmott) (p. 15).
3. Identify the different demands which might be made of managers to achieve organisational effectiveness in each business (you could use Figure 1.3 as a framework). What are the implications for the role and development of managers in each case?

Notes and references

1 A summary of some merits in understanding organisational behaviour theory and the role of management is given in Mullins, L. J. 'The Organisation and the Individual', *Administrator*, vol. 7, no. 4, April 1987, pp. 11–14.
2 See, for example: Luthans, F. *Organisational Behaviour*, Seventh Edition, McGraw-Hill (1995).
3 See, for example: Robbins, S. P. and Judge, T. A. *Organisational Behavior*, Twelfth edition, Pearson Prentice Hall (2007).
4 A similar view is taken by Watson, T. J. *Organising and Managing Work: organisational, managerial and strategic behaviour in theory and practice*, Financial Times Prentice Hall (2002).
5 See, for example: Billsberry, J. (ed.) 'There's Nothing So Practical as a Good Theory: how can theory help managers become more effective?', in *The Effective Manager: perspectives and illustrations*, Sage Publications (1996), pp. 1–27; and Naylor, J. *Management*, Financial Times Pitman Publishing (1999), pp. 18–20.
6 Lee, R. A. 'There Is Nothing so Useful as an Appropriate Theory', in Wilson, D. C. and Rosenfeld, R. H. *Managing Organisations: text, readings and cases*, McGraw-Hill (1990), p. 31.
7 Crainer, S. 'The Rise of Guru Scepticism', *Management Today*, March 1996, pp. 48–52.
8 Patching, K. *Management and Organisation Development*, Macmillan Business (1999), p. 11.
9 Drummond, H. *Introduction to Organisational Behaviour*, Oxford University Press (2000).
10 'Introduction to Module 6, Organisational Behaviour', *Financial Times Mastering Management*, FT Pitman Publishing (1997), p. 216.
11 Wilson, F. M. *Organisational Behaviour and Work: a critical introduction*, Second edition, Oxford University Press (2004), pp. 1–2.
12 McPhee, N. 'Gaining Insight on Business and Organisational Behaviour: the Qualitative Dimension', *International Journal of Market Research*, vol. 44, Winter 2002, pp. 53–72.
13 Yip, G. S. 'Global Strategy in the Twenty-first Century', in Crainer, S. and Dearlove, D. (eds) *Financial Times Handbook of Management*, Second edition, Financial Times Prentice Hall (2001), p. 151.
14 Morgan, G. *Creative Organisation Theory*, Sage Publications (1989), p. 26.
15 Drummond, H. *Introduction to Organisational Behaviour*, Oxford University Press (2000).
16 Goldthorpe, J. H., Lockwood, D., Bechofer, F. and Platt, J. *The Affluent Worker*, Cambridge University Press (1968).
17 Herman, S. W. 'How Work Gains Meaning in Contractual Time: a narrative model for reconstructing the work ethic', *Journal of Business Ethics*, vol. 38, no. 1–2, June 2002, pp. 65–79.
18 Knights, D. and Willmott, H. *Management Lives: power and identity in work organisations*, Sage Publications (1999).
19 Reeves, R. 'Reality Bites', *Management Today*, March 2003, p. 35.
20 Cartwright, J. *Cultural Transformation*, Financial Times Prentice Hall (1999), p. 27.
21 Oliver, J. 'Losing Control', *Management Today*, June 1998, pp. 32–8.
22 See, for example: Argyris, C. *Integrating the Individual and the Organisation*, John Wiley & Sons (1964).
23 Egan, G. 'The Shadow Side', *Management Today*, September 1993, pp. 33–8.
24 Bassett, G. 'The Case Against Job Satisfaction', *Business Horizons*, vol. 37, no. 3, May–June 1994, pp. 62, 63.
25 See, for example: Robinson, G. 'Improving Performance Through People', *The British Journal of Administrative Management*, September/October 1999, pp. 4–5.
26 Chowdhury, S. *Management 21C*, Financial Times Prentice Hall (2000), p. 119.
27 See, for example: Schein, E. H. *Organisational Psychology*, Third Edition, Prentice Hall (1988).
28 CIPD, *Managing the Psychological Contract*, Chartered Institute of Personnel and Development, December 2004.
29 Kotter, J. P. 'The Psychological Contract: managing the joining-up process', *California Management Review*, vol. 15, no. 3, 1973, pp. 91–9.
30 Stalker, K. 'The Individual, the Organisation and the Psychological Contract', *The Institute of Administrative Management*, July/August 2000, pp. 28, 34.
31 Cartwright, J. *Cultural Transformation*, Financial Times Prentice Hall (1999), p. 39.
32 Emmott, M. 'The Psychological Contract: Managers Do Make a Difference', *Manager, The British Journal of Administrative Management*, September/October 2001, p. 15.
33 M.C.A. Awards, *Management Today*, April 2005, p. xix.
34 McBain, R. 'The Role of Human Resource Management and the Psychological Contract', *Manager Update*, vol. 8, no. 4, Summer 1997, pp. 22–31.
35 Stalker, K. 'The Individual and the Organisation', *Student Adviser*, no. 51, The Institute of Administrative Management, Spring 2003.
36 Hiltrop, J. M. 'Managing the Changing Psychological Contract', *Employee Relations*, vol. 18, no. 1, 1996, pp. 36–49.
37 CIPD, *Managing the Psychological Contract*, Chartered Institute of Personnel and Development, December 2004.
38 Stiles, P., Gratton, L., Truss, C., Hope-Hailey, V. and McGovern, P. 'Performance Management and the Psychological Contract', *Human Resource Management Journal*, vol. 7, no. 1, 1997, pp. 57–66.
39 Ghoshal, S., Bartlett, C. A. and Moran, P. 'Value Creation: the new millennium management manifesto', in Chowdhury, S. *Management 21C*, Financial Times Prentice Hall (2000), pp. 121–40.
40 Furnham, A. and Taylor, J. *The Dark Side of Behaviour at Work*, Palgrave Macmillan (2004).
41 Peter, L. J. and Hull, R. *The Peter Principle*, Pan Books (1970), p. 22.
42 Ibid., p. 56.
43 Parkinson, C. N. *Parkinson's Law*, Penguin Modern Classics (2002), p. 14.
44 HRH The Duke of Edinburgh, 'Introduction' to Parkinson, C. N. *Parkinson's Law*, Penguin Modern Classics (2002), pp. 9–10.
45 Herbertson, I. 'Books', *Management Today*, May 2000, p. 4.
46 Ghoshal, S., Bartlett, C. A. and Moran, P. 'Value Creation: the new millennium management manifesto', in Chowdhury, S. *Management 21C*, Financial Times Prentice Hall (2000), pp. 121–40.

47 Taylor, R. 'The Future of Employment Relations', Economic and Social Research Council, September 2001, pp. 7–8.
48 Bouchikhi, H. and Kimberly, J. R. 'The Customized Workplace', in Chowdhury, S. *Management 21C*, Financial Times Prentice Hall (2000), pp. 207–19.
49 Muzyka, D. 'Thriving on the Chaos of the Future', in Pickford, J. (ed.) *Financial Times Mastering Management 2.0*, Financial Times Prentice Hall (2001), p. 8.
50 Cloke, K. and Goldsmith, J. *The End of Management and the Rise of Organisational Democracy*, Jossey-Bass (2002).
51 Francesco, A. M. and Gold, B. A. *International Organisational Behavior*, Second Edition, Pearson Prentice Hall (2005), p. 246.
52 McLean, J. 'Globalisation is here to stay', *Manager, The British Journal of Administrative Management*, June/July 2006, p. 16.
53 Rugman, A. 'The Illusion of the Global Company' in Pickford, J. (ed.) *Mastering Management 2.0*, Financial Times Prentice Hall (2001), pp. 129–33.
54 Saul, J. R. *The Collapse of Globalism*, Atlantic Books (2005).
55 Child, J. *Organisation: contemporary principles and practice*, Blackwell Publishing (2005), p. 30.
56 McLean, J. 'Globalisation is Here to Stay', *Manager, The British Journal of Administrative Management*, June/July 2006, p. 16.
57 Dana, L. 'Culture is of the Essence in Asia', in Pickford, J. (ed.) *Mastering Management 2.0*, Financial Times Prentice Hall (2001), pp. 139–43.
58 See, for example: Fletcher, W. 'The American Way', *Management Today*, August 2005, pp. 46–9.
59 See, for example: Slater, D. 'When in China ...', *Management Today*, May 2006, pp. 46–50.
60 Schneider, S. C. and Barsoux, J. *Managing Across Cultures*, Second Edition, Financial Times Prentice Hall (2003), p. 9.
61 Thompson, P. and McHugh, D. *Work Organisations: A Critical Introduction*, Third edition, Palgrave (2002), p. 81.
62 Tayeb, M. *The Management of a Multicultural Workforce*, John Wiley & Sons (1996).
63 Brooks, I. *Organisational Behaviour: Individuals, Groups and Organisation*, Third edition, Financial Times Prentice Hall (2006), p. 270.
64 Trompenaars, F. 'Trans-Cultural Competence', *People Management*, 22 April 1999, p. 31.
65 Francesco, A. M. and Gold, B. A. *International Organisational Behavior*, Second Edition, Pearson Prentice Hall (2005), p. 140.
66 Schneider, S. C. and Barsoux, J. *Managing Across Cultures*, Second Edition, Financial Times Prentice Hall (2003), p. 167.
67 Ibid., p. 86.
68 Francesco, A. M. and Gold, B. A. *International Organisational Behavior*, Second edition, Pearson Prentice Hall (2005), p. 213.
69 Adler, N. J. *International Dimensions of Organisational Behaviour*, Fourth edition, South Western College Publishing (2002).
70 Brooks, I. *Organisational Behaviour: Individuals, Groups and Organisation*, Third edition, Financial Times Prentice Hall (2006), p. 272.
71 Hofstede, G. *Culture's Consequences: International Differences in Work-related Values*, Sage Publications (1980).
72 Hofstede, G. and Bond, M. H. 'The Confucius Connection: From Cultural Roots to Economic Growth', *Organisational Dynamics*, Spring 1988, pp. 4–21.
73 Holden, N. J. *Cross-Cultural Management: A Knowledge Management Perspective*, Financial Times Prentice Hall (2002), p. 51.
74 Trompenaars, F. and Hampden-Turner, C. *Riding the Waves of Culture*, Second edition, Nicholas Brearley (1999).
75 Hall, E. T. and Hall, M. R. *Understanding Cultural Differences*, Intercultural Press (1990).
76 Grint, K. *The Sociology of Work*, Second edition, Polity Press (1998), p. 298.
77 Thompson, P. and McHugh, D. *Work Organisations: A Critical Introduction*, Third edition, Palgrave (2002), p. 74.
78 Morgan, G. *Creative Organisation Theory*, Sage Publications (1989), p. 26.
79 Hellriegel, D., Slocum, J. W. and Woodman, R. W. *Organisational Behavior*, Eighth edition, South-Western Publishing (1998), p. 5.
80 Wood, J. 'Deep Roots and Far From a "Soft" Option', *Financial Times Mastering Management*, FT Pitman Publishing (1997), p. 217.
81 Bennis, W. 'Foreword', in Cloke, K. and Goldsmith, J. *The End of Management and the Rise of Organisational Democracy*, Jossey-Bass (2002), p. ix.
82 Virgin Atlantic website *All About Us* avaliable at http://www.virginatlantic.com/en/us/allaboutus/ourstory/history.jsp.
83 Creaton, S. *Ryanair – How a Small Irish Airline Conquered Europe*, Aurum (2004).
84 See the Ryanair website at *www.ryanair.com*.
85 Creaton, op.cit. Chapter 15.
86 Virgin Atlantic website, *Working for Us*, http://www.virginatlantic.com/en/gb/careers/workingforus/index.jsp.
87 Crewlink website www.crewline.ie.
88 International Transport Workers' Federation website, www.iftglobal.org.
89 BBC news website, *Ryanair Profits Jump on Hot Spots*, news.bbd.co.uk (1 August 2006).
90 BBC news website, *Profits Jumps at Virgin Atlantic*, news.bbc.co.uk (27 May 2005).

APPROACHES TO ORGANISATION AND MANAGEMENT

If there were such a thing as Management Science, presumably there would be scientific laws and rules. I was to be grievously disappointed. I read endless hypotheses that tried to explain why people and organisations behaved the way they did but no proof … Managing a business, or any organisation, I came to see was more practical art than applied science.

Charles Handy – management writer and broadcaster

Myself and Other More Important Matters, William Heinemann (2006), p. 61

Organisational behaviour is a discursive subject and much has been written about it. The study of organisations and management theory has, therefore, to proceed on a broad front. It is the comparative study of the different approaches that will yield benefits to the manager. The study of organisations, their structure and management is important for the manager. Identification of major trends in management and organisational behaviour, and the work of leading writers, provide a perspective on concepts and ideas discussed in more detail in other chapters.[1]

Learning outcomes

After completing this chapter you should be able to:

- identify major trends in the development of organisational behaviour and management thinking;
- contrast main features of different approaches to organisation and management;
- evaluate the relevance of these different approaches to the present-day management of organisations;
- explain the relationships between management theory and practice;
- assess the value of the study of different approaches to organisation and management;
- recognise the relationship between the development of theory, behaviour in organisations and management practice;
- establish a basis for consideration of aspects of organisational behaviour discussed in subsequent chapters.

Critical reflection

It is often claimed that what leading writers say is an important part of the study of management and organisational behaviour. Others say that all these different ideas are little more than short-term fads and have little practical value. What do you think? What role does management theory have in helping us solve problems we face in our organisational lives today?

MANAGEMENT THEORY

Writing on organisation and management, in some form or another, can be traced back thousands of years.[2] However, the systematic development of management thinking is viewed, generally, as dating from the end of the nineteenth century with the emergence of large industrial organisations and the ensuing problems associated with their structure and management.[3 4]

A central part of the study of organisation and management is the development of management thinking and what might be termed management theory. The application of theory brings about change in actual behaviour. Managers reading the work of leading writers on the subject might see in their ideas and conclusions a message about how they should behave. This will influence their attitudes towards management practice. As *McGregor* puts it:

> *Every managerial act rests on assumptions, generalizations, and hypotheses – that is to say, on theory. Our assumptions are frequently implicit, sometimes quite unconscious, often conflicting; nevertheless, they determine our predictions that if we do a, b will occur. Theory and practice are inseparable.*[5]

Importance of management theory

The study of management theory is important, therefore, for the following reasons:

- It helps to view the interrelationships between the development of theory, behaviour in organisations and management practice.
- An understanding of the development of management thinking helps in understanding principles underlying the process of management.
- Knowledge of the history helps in understanding the nature of management and organisational behaviour and reasons for the attention given to main topic areas.
- Many of the earlier ideas are of continuing importance to the manager and later ideas on management tend to incorporate earlier ideas and conclusions.
- Management theories are interpretive and evolve in line with changes in the organisational environment.

> *There is much truth in the saying that every living practitioner is prisoner to the ideas of a dead theorist. Immunized by their daily confrontation with the 'real world' corporate managers typically exhibit a healthy distrust of theory that has, in general, served them well.*[6]

DEVELOPMENTS IN MANAGEMENT AND ORGANISATIONAL BEHAVIOUR

It is helpful, therefore, to trace major developments in management and organisational behaviour and what has led to the concentration of attention on such topics as structure, motivation, groups, leadership and organisation development.

Miner makes the point that the more that is known about organisations and their methods of operation, the better the chances of dealing effectively with them. Understanding may be more advanced than prediction, but both provide the opportunity to influence or to manage the future. Theory provides a sound basis for action.[7] However, if action is to be effective, the theory must be adequate and appropriate to the task and to improved organisational performance. It must be a 'good' theory.

In order to help identify main trends in the development of organisational behaviour and management theory, it is usual to categorise the work of writers into various 'approaches', based on their views of organisations, their structure and management. Although a rather simplistic process, it does provide a framework in which to help direct study and focus attention on the progression of ideas concerned with improving organisational performance.

A framework of analysis

There are, however, many ways of categorising these various approaches. For example, *Skipton* attempts a classification of 11 main schools of management theory.[8] Whatever form of categorisation is adopted, it is possible to identify a number of other approaches, or at least sub-divisions of approaches, and cross-grouping among the various approaches. The choice of a particular categorisation is therefore largely at the discretion of the observer.

The following analysis will revolve around a framework based on four main approaches:

- classical – including scientific management and bureaucracy;
- human relations – including neo-human relations;
- systems;
- contingency (*see* Figure 2.1).

However, attention is also drawn to other 'approaches' or ideas, including:

- decision-making;
- social action;
- postmodernism (*see* Figure 2.3, p. 60).

Figure 2.1 Main approaches to organisation, structure and management

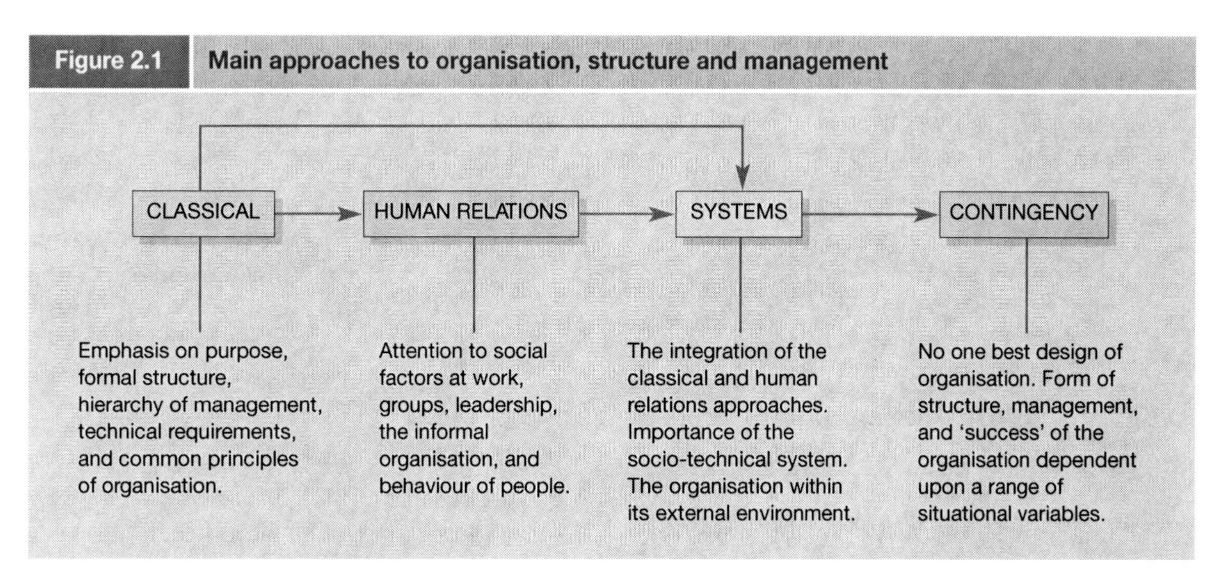

THE CLASSICAL APPROACH

The classical writers thought of the organisation in terms of its purpose and formal structure. They placed emphasis on the planning of work, the technical requirements of the organisation, principles of management, and the assumption of rational and logical behaviour. The analysis of organisation in this manner is associated with work carried out initially in the early part of the last century, by such writers as *Taylor*, *Fayol*, *Urwick*, *Mooney and Reiley*, and *Brech*. Such writers were laying the foundation for a comprehensive theory of management.

A clear understanding of the purpose of an organisation is seen as essential to understanding how the organisation works and how its methods of working can be improved. Identification of general objectives would lead to the clarification of purposes and responsibilities at all levels of the organisation and to the most effective structure. Attention is given to the division of work, the clear definition of duties and responsibilities, and maintaining specialisation and co-ordination. Emphasis is on a hierarchy of management and formal organisational relationships.

Sets of principles

The classical writers (also variously known as the formal or scientific management writers – although scientific management is really only a part of the classical approach) were concerned with improving the organisation structure as a means of increasing efficiency. They emphasised the importance of principles for the design of a logical structure of organisation. Their writings were in a normative style and they saw these principles as a set of 'rules' offering general solutions to common problems of organisation and management.

Most classical writers had their own set of principles but among the most publicised are those of *Fayol* and *Urwick*. Fayol recognised there was no limit to the principles of management but in his writing advocated 14.[9] Urwick originally specified eight principles, but these were revised to ten in his later writing.[10] (*See* Chapters 11 and 15.)

Mooney and Reiley set out a number of common principles which relate to all types of organisations. They place particular attention on:

- **the principle of co-ordination** – the need for people to act together with unity of action, the exercise of authority and the need for discipline;
- **the scalar principle** – the hierarchy of organisation, the grading of duties and the process of delegation; and
- **the functional principle** – specialisation and the distinction between different kinds of duties.[11]

Brech attempts to provide a practical approach to organisation structure based on tried general principles as opposed to the concentration on specific cases or complex generalisations of little value to the practising manager. He sets out the various functions in the organisation and the definition of formal organisational relationships.[12] Although clearly a strong supporter of the formal approach in some of his views such as, for example, on the principle of span of control, Brech is less definite than other classical writers and recognises a degree of flexibility according to the particular situation.

Brech does place great emphasis, however, on the need for written definition of responsibilities and the value of job descriptions as an aid to effective organisation and delegation. This work builds on the ideas of earlier writers, such as Urwick, and therefore provides a comprehensive view of the classical approach to organisation and management.

Evaluation of the classical approach

The classical writers have been criticised generally for not taking sufficient account of personality factors and for creating an organisation structure in which people can exercise only limited control over their work environment. The idea of sets of principles to guide managerial action has also been subject to much criticism. For example, *Simon* writes:

Organisational design is not unlike architectural design. It involves creating large, complex systems having multiple goals. It is illusory to suppose that good designs can be created by using the so-called principles of classical organisation theory.[13]

Research studies have also expressed doubt about the effectiveness of these principles when applied in practice.[14] However, the classical approach prompted the start of a more scientific view of management and attempted to provide some common principles applicable to all organisations. These principles are still of relevance in that they offer a useful starting point in attempting to analyse the effectiveness of the design of organisation structure. The application of these principles must take full account of:

- the particular situational variables of each individual organisation; and
- the psychological and social factors relating to members of the organisation.

Major sub-groupings

Two major 'sub-groupings' of the classical approach are:

1 scientific management, and
2 bureaucracy.

SCIENTIFIC MANAGEMENT

Many of the classical writers were concerned with the improvement of management as a means of increasing productivity. At this time emphasis was on the problem of obtaining increased productivity from individual workers through the technical structuring of the work organisation and the provision of monetary incentives as the motivator for higher levels of output. A major contributor to this approach was *F.W. Taylor* (1856–1917), the 'father' of scientific management.[15] Taylor believed that in the same way that there is a best machine for each job, so there is a best working method by which people should undertake their jobs. He considered that all work processes could be analysed into discrete tasks and that by scientific method it was possible to find the 'one best way' to perform each task. Each job was broken down into component parts, each part timed and the parts rearranged into the most efficient method of working.

Principles to guide management

Taylor was a believer in the rational–economic needs concept of motivation. He believed that if management acted on his ideas, work would become more satisfying and profitable for all concerned. Workers would be motivated by obtaining the highest possible wages through working in the most efficient and productive way. Taylor was concerned with finding more efficient methods and procedures for co-ordination and control of work. He set out a number of principles to guide management. These principles are usually summarised as:

- the development of a true science for each person's work;
- the scientific selection, training and development of the workers;
- co-operation with the workers to ensure work is carried out in the prescribed way;
- the division of work and responsibility between management and the workers.

In his famous studies at the Bethlehem Steel Corporation, Taylor, who was appointed as a management consultant, applied his ideas on scientific management to the handling of pig iron. A group of 75 men were loading an average of $12\frac{1}{2}$ tons per man per day. Taylor selected a Dutch labourer, called Schmidt, whom he reported to be a 'high-priced' man with a reputation for placing a high value on money, and a man of limited mental ability. By following detailed instructions on when to pick up the pig iron and walk, and when to sit and rest, and with no back talk, Schmidt increased his output to $47\frac{1}{2}$ tons per day. He maintained this level of output throughout the three years of the study. In return Schmidt received a 60 per cent increase in wages compared with that paid to the other men.

One by one other men were selected and trained to handle pig iron at the rate of $47\frac{1}{2}$ tons per day and in return they received 60 per cent more wages. Taylor drew attention to the need for the scientific selection of the workers. When the other labourers in the group were trained in the same method, only one in eight was physically capable of the effort of loading $47\frac{1}{2}$ tons per day, although there was a noticeable increase in their level of output.

Reactions against scientific management

There were strong criticisms of, and reaction against, scientific management methods from the workers who found the work boring and requiring little skill. Despite these criticisms Taylor attempted to expand the implementation of his ideas in the Bethlehem Steel Corporation. However, fears of mass redundancies persuaded the management to request Taylor to moderate his activities. Yet Taylor's belief in his methods was so strong that he would not accept management's interference and eventually they dispensed with his services.

Scientific management was applied for a time in other countries with similar criticisms and hostile reactions. The ideas of scientific management were also adopted in the American Watertown Arsenal despite the lingering doubts of the controller. He was not convinced about the benefits of paying bonuses based on methods which reduced time taken to complete a job; also the workers reacted unfavourably to time and motion studies and he was fearful of a strike. The controller eventually gave way, however, and the scientific management approach was adopted – to be followed almost immediately by a strike of moulding workers. The strike at Watertown Arsenal led to an investigation of Taylor's methods by a House of Representatives Committee which reported in 1912.

The conclusion of the committee was that scientific management did provide some useful techniques and offered valuable organisational suggestions, but gave production managers a dangerously high level of uncontrolled power. The studies at Watertown Arsenal were resumed but the unions retained an underlying hostility towards scientific management. A subsequent attitude survey among the workers revealed a broad level of resentment and hostility, by both union and non-union members, to scientific management methods. As a result of this report the Senate banned Taylor's methods of time study in defence establishments.

Taylorism as management control

There has also been considerable interest in 'Taylorism' as representing a system of management control over workers. Taylor placed emphasis on the content of a 'fair day's work' and on optimising the level of workers' productivity. A major obstacle to this objective was 'systematic soldiering' and what Taylor saw as the deliberate attempt by workers to promote their best interests and to keep employers ignorant of how fast work, especially piece-rate work, could be carried out.

According to *Braverman*, scientific management starts from the capitalist point of view and method of production, and the adaptation of labour to the needs of capital. Taylor's work was more concerned with the organisation of labour than with the development of technology. A distinctive feature of Taylor's thought was the concept of management control.[16] Braverman suggests Taylor's conclusion was that workers should be controlled not only by the giving of orders and maintenance of discipline but also by removing from them any decisions about the manner in which their work was to be carried out. By division of labour, and by dictating precise stages and methods for every aspect of work performance, management could gain control of the actual process of work. The rationalisation of production processes and division of labour tends to result in the de-skilling of work and this may be a main strategy of the employer.[17]

Cloke and Goldsmith also suggest that Taylor was the leading promoter of the idea that managers should design and control the work process scientifically in order to guarantee maximum efficiency. He believed in multiple layers of management to supervise the work process and in rigid, detailed control of the workforce.

> *Taylor's theories justified managerial control over the production process and removed decision making from employees and from owners as well. The increasingly authoritative operational role of management diminished the direct involvement of owners in day-to-day decision making. Managers saw this as an opportunity to solidify their power and adopted Taylor's ideas wholesale. In the process, they affirmed efficiency over collaboration, quantity over quality, and cost controls over customer service.*[18]

Critical reflection

The work of the classical writers drew attention to the importance of general guidelines for technical and structural efficiency, and design of the work organisation. But do you think the work of these writers stands the test of time or has it been rendered redundant for the new challenges of modern organisations?

RELEVANCE OF SCIENTIFIC MANAGEMENT

While Taylor's work is often criticised today it should be remembered that he was writing at a time of industrial reorganisation and the emergence of large, complex organisations with new forms of technology. Taylor's main concern was with the efficiency of both workers and management. He believed his methods of scientific management would lead to improved management–labour relations and contribute to improved industrial efficiency and prosperity.

Taylor adopted an instrumental view of human behaviour together with the application of standard procedures of work. Workers were regarded as rational, economic beings motivated directly by monetary incentives linked to the level of work output. Workers were viewed as isolated individuals and more as units of production to be handled almost in the same way as machines. Hence, scientific management is often referred to as a machine theory model.

Taylor's work continues to evoke much comment and extreme points of view. For example, *Rose* suggests:

> *It is difficult to discuss the 'contribution' of F. W. Taylor to the systematic study of industrial behaviour in an even-tempered way. The sheer silliness from a modern perspective of many of his ideas, and barbarities they led to when applied in industry, encourage ridicule and denunciation.*[19]

The theme of inefficiency

Rose argues that Taylor's diagnosis of the industrial situation was based on the simple theme of inefficiency. Among his criticisms are that Taylor selected the best workers for his experiments and assumed that workers who were not good at one particular task would be best at some other task. There is, however, no certainty of this in practice. Taylor regarded workers from an engineering viewpoint and as machines, but the one best way of performing a task is not always the best method for every worker.

The reduction of physical movement to find the one best way is not always beneficial and some 'wasteful' movements are essential to the overall rhythm of work. Rose also argues that the concept of a fair day's pay for a fair day's work is not purely a technical matter. It is also a notion of social equity and not in keeping with a scientific approach.

Drucker, however, claims:

> *Frederick Winslow Taylor may prove a more useful prophet for our times than we yet recognize ... Taylor's greatest impact may still be ahead ... the under-developed and developing countries are now reaching the stage where they need Taylor and 'scientific management' ... But the need to study Taylor anew and apply him may be the greatest in the developed countries.*[20]

According to Drucker, the central theme of Taylor's work was not inefficiency but the need to substitute industrial warfare by industrial harmony. Taylor sought to do this through:

- higher wages from increased output;
- the removal of physical strain from doing work the wrong way;
- development of the workers and the opportunity for them to undertake tasks they were capable of doing; and
- elimination of the 'boss' and the duty of management to help workers.

Drucker also suggests that Taylor's idea of functional foremen can be related to what is now known as matrix organisation (matrix organisation is discussed in Chapter 15). Support for Drucker's views appears to come from *Locke* who asserts that much of the criticism of Taylor is based on a misunderstanding of the precepts and that many of his ideas are accepted by present-day managers.[21]

Impetus to management thinking

Whatever the opinions on scientific management, Taylor and his disciples have left to modern management the legacy of such practices as work study, organisation and methods, payment by results, management by exception and production control. The development of mass assembly line work, invented by Henry Ford in 1913 ('Fordism') and which dominated production methods in Western economies, can be seen to have many common links with the ideas of scientific management.[22]

The principles of Taylor's scientific approach to management appear still to have relevance today. We can see examples of Taylorism alive and well, and management practices based on the philosophy of his ideas. As an example, Figure 2.2 shows a 'Hanger Insertion Programme' for a large American department store. Large hotel organisations often make use of standard recipes and performance standard manuals and it is common for housekeeping staff to have a prescribed layout for each room, with training based on detailed procedures and the one best way. Staff may be expected to clean a given number of rooms per shift with financial incentives for additional rooms.

Whatever else Taylor did, at least he gave a major impetus to the development of management thinking and the later development of organisational behaviour. For example, *Crainer and Dearlove* suggest that although Taylor's theories are now largely outdated, they still had a profound impact throughout the world and his mark can be seen on much of the subsequent management literature.[23] And *Stern* goes a stage further:

> *The 'scientific management' of Frederick Taylor ... shaped the first coherent school of thought with application to the industrialised world. He was our first professional guru and Taylorism – with its twin goals of productivity and efficiency – still influences management thinking 100 years on.*[24]

It is difficult to argue against the general line of Taylor's principles but they are subject to misuse. What is important is the context and manner in which such principles are put into effect. There is arguably one best way *technically* to perform a job, particularly, for example, with factory assembly line production. However, account needs to be taken of human behaviour. People tend to have their preferred way of working and the need for variety and more interesting or challenging tasks. Provided work is carried out safely and to a satisfactory standard and completed on time, to what extent should management *insist* on the 'one best way'?

It seems that Taylor did not so much ignore (as is often suggested) but was more unaware of the complexity of human behaviour in organisations and the importance of the individual's feelings and sentiments, group working, managerial behaviour and the work environment. However, we now have greater knowledge about social effects within the work organisation and about the value of money, incentives, motivation, and job satisfaction and performance.

Figure 2.2 Hanger Insertion Programme: an example of scientific management

KEY IDEAS

Hanger Insertion

- The new programme involving the process of hanging merchandise on hangers efficiently and effectively.

The purposes of this new programme:

- To assist the stores in better customer service – by having the merchandise ready to go on the floor, saving space in the stockroom, and creating customer goodwill.
- To increase the units per hour produced.
- To perform the job duties as efficiently and effectively as possible.

TECHNIQUES

- Keep the necessary items needed in your range. All supplies should be within arm's reach. For example, place the trash bin next to you, have your hanger supply near you. You should not need to take any steps.
- For ANY prepack, Unpack merchandise in the prepack or unpack enough of the prepack in the amount to be placed on the trolley, tearing the plastic off of the entire group.
  Lay the merchandise out on the unpack table, and if applies, unfold each piece, removing tissue, etc.
  Insert the hangers and hang the *entire group* of merchandise at once.
- When removing hangers from the merchandise, have the merchandise in a group on the unpack table; remove these hangers working from the front to the back.
- When inserting hangers, as a group, insert working from the back to the front of the group on the unpack table. Hang pieces as a group.
- If merchandise is bulky, Leave merchandise folded, **remove all of the plastic at once**, insert hangers for merchandise unpacked, hang all pieces on the trolley, then remove at the same time all excess plastic, clips, etc.
- When possible, it is more efficient to remove all the plastic at once after the merchandise is hung.
- When hanging pants, skirts, etc., slip the hanger over both sides of the piece of merchandise and push metal clips down at the same time. This will alleviate additional steps.
- When pants are in plastic and hangers have to be removed, hang them first, take pants off hangers, lay on table, throw away plastic, insert hangers.
- When having to button pants, skirts, etc., take the top of the button through the hole first. This makes the process flow easier and more efficient.
- Put your supply of hangers in the cover of a tote and place on the table next to you.

BUREAUCRACY

A form of structure to be found in many large-scale organisations is bureaucracy. Its importance in the development of organisation theory means that it is often regarded as a sub-division under the classical heading and studied as a separate approach to management and the organisation of work. The ideas and principles of the classical writers were derived mainly from practical experience. Writers on bureaucracy, however, tend to take a more theoretical view.

Weber, a German sociologist, showed particular concern for what he called 'bureaucratic structures', although his work in this area came almost as a side issue to his main study on power and authority.[25] He suggested that 'the decisive reason for the advance of bureaucratic organisation has always been its purely technical superiority over any other form of organisation'. Weber pointed out that the definition of tasks and responsibilities within the structure of management gave rise to a permanent administration and standardisation of work procedures notwithstanding changes in the actual holders of office.

The term 'bureaucracy' has common connotations with criticism of red tape and rigidity, though in the study of organisations and management it is important that the term is seen not necessarily in a deprecative sense but as applying to certain structural features of formal organisations. Weber analysed bureaucracies not empirically but as an 'ideal type' derived from the most characteristic bureaucratic features of all known organisations. He saw the development of bureaucracies as a means of introducing order and rationality into social life.

Main characteristics of bureaucracies

Weber did not actually define bureaucracy but did attempt to identify the main characteristics of this type of organisation. He emphasised the importance of administration based on expertise (rules of experts) and administration based on discipline (rules of officials).

- The tasks of the organisation are allocated as official duties among the various positions.
- There is an implied clear-cut division of labour and a high level of specialisation.
- A hierarchical authority applies to the organisation of offices and positions.
- Uniformity of decisions and actions is achieved through formally established systems of rules and regulations. Together with a structure of authority, this enables the co-ordination of various activities within the organisation.
- An impersonal orientation is expected from officials in their dealings with clients and other officials. This is designed to result in rational judgements by officials in the performance of their duties.
- Employment by the organisation is based on technical qualifications and constitutes a lifelong career for the officials.[26]

The four main features of bureaucracy are summarised by *Stewart* as specialisation, hierarchy of authority, system of rules and impersonality.

- **Specialisation** applies more to the job than to the person undertaking the job. This makes for continuity because the job usually continues if the present jobholder leaves.
- **Hierarchy of authority** makes for a sharp distinction between administrators and the administered or between management and workers. Within the management ranks there are clearly defined levels of authority. This detailed and precise stratification is particularly marked in the armed forces and in the civil service.
- **System of rules** aims to provide for an efficient and impersonal operation. The system of rules is generally stable, although some rules may be changed or modified with time. Knowledge of the rules is a requisite of holding a job in a bureaucracy.
- **Impersonality** means that allocation of privileges and the exercise of authority should not be arbitrary, but in accordance with the laid-down system of rules. In more highly developed bureaucracies there tend to be carefully defined procedures for appealing against certain types of decisions. Stewart sees the characteristic of impersonality as the feature of bureaucracy which most distinguishes it from other types of organisations. A bureaucracy should not only be impersonal but be seen to be impersonal.[27]

CRITICISMS OF BUREAUCRACY

Weber's concept of bureaucracy has a number of disadvantages and has been subject to severe criticism.

- The over-emphasis on rules and procedures, record keeping and paperwork may become more important in its own right than as a means to an end.

- Officials may develop a dependence upon bureaucratic status, symbols and rules.
- Initiative may be stifled and when a situation is not covered by a complete set of rules or procedures there may be a lack of flexibility or adaptation to changing circumstances.
- Position and responsibilities in the organisation can lead to officious bureaucratic behaviour. There may also be a tendency to conceal administrative procedures from outsiders.
- Impersonal relations can lead to stereotyped behaviour and a lack of responsiveness to individual incidents or problems.

Restriction of psychological growth

One of the strongest critics of bureaucratic organisation, and the demands it makes on the worker, is *Argyris*.[28] He claims that bureaucracies restrict the psychological growth of the individual and cause feelings of failure, frustration and conflict. Argyris suggests that the organisational environment should provide a significant degree of individual responsibility and self-control; commitment to the goals of the organisation; productiveness and work; and an opportunity for individuals to apply their full abilities.

When these ideas are related to the main features of bureaucracy discussed above, such as specialisation, hierarchy of authority, system of rules and impersonality, it is perhaps easy to see the basis of Argyris' criticism.

A similar criticism is made by *Caulkin* who refers to the impersonal structure of bureaucracy as constructed round the post rather than the person and the ease with which it can be swung behind unsocial or even pathological ends.

> *The overemphasis on process rather than purpose, fragmented responsibilities and hierarchical control means that it's all too easy for individuals to neglect the larger purposes to which their small effort is being put.*[29]

EVALUATION OF BUREAUCRACY

The growth of bureaucracy has come about through the increasing size and complexity of organisations and the associated demand for effective administration. The work of the classical writers has given emphasis to the careful design and planning of organisation structure and the definition of individual duties and responsibilities. Effective organisation is based on structure and delegation through different layers of the hierarchy. Greater specialisation and the application of expertise and technical knowledge have highlighted the need for laid-down procedures.

Bureaucracy is founded on a formal, clearly defined and hierarchical structure. However, with rapid changes in the external environment, de-layering of organisations, empowerment and greater attention to meeting the needs of customers, there is an increasing need to organise for flexibility. *Peters and Waterman* found that excellent American companies achieved quick action just because their organisations were fluid and had intensive networks of informal and open communications.[30] By contrast, the crisis IBM experienced in the 1980s/1990s over the market for personal computers is explained at least in part by its top-heavy corporate structure, cumbersome organisation and dinosaur-like bureaucracy.[31]

According to *Cloke and Goldsmith*, management and bureaucracy can be thought of as flip sides of the same coin. The elements of bureaucracy generate organisational hierarchy and management, while managers generate a need for bureaucracy.

> *Bureaucracies provide a safe haven where managers can hide from responsibility and avoid being held accountable for errors of judgement or problems they created or failed to solve. In return, managers are able to use bureaucratic rules to stifle self-management and compel employees to follow their direction ... Yet bureaucratic systems can be broken down and transformed into human-scale interactions. We have seen countless managers recreate themselves as leaders and facilitators, employees reinvent themselves as responsible self-managing team members, and bureaucracies transform into responsive, human-scale organisations. Alternatives to organisational hierarchy are both practical and possible.*[32]

Organisational solutions

As organisations face increasing global competitiveness and complex demands of the information and technological age, the need arises for alternative forms of corporate structure and systems. For example, *Ridderstrale* points out that in the past century the hallmark of a large company was hierarchy, which rests on principles at odds with the new strategic requirements. 'Bureaucracies allowed people with knowledge to control ignorant workers. Now, new structures are needed as knowledge spreads.' Ridderstrale suggests four specific ways in which high-performing organisations have responded to increasingly complex knowledge systems by developing organisational solutions which depart from the traditional bureaucratic model:

- more decentralised and flatter structures in order that quick decisions can be taken near to where the critical knowledge resides. Flatter structures can be achieved by increasing the span of control and reducing layers from the top or removing layers of middle management;
- the use of more than a single structure in order that knowledge may be assembled across the boundaries of a traditional organisation chart. If people have less permanent places in the hierarchy they are more readily able to move across functional and geographical borders;
- converting companies into learning organisations and giving every employee the same level of familiarity with personnel and capabilities. Successful companies develop a detailed inventory of core competencies. In order to fully exploit current knowledge, managers need to know what the company knows;
- the broader sharing of expertise and knowledge, which may be located in the periphery where little formal authority resides. Managers need to share principles to ensure co-ordination, encourage 'lowest common denominators' and the development of 'tribal' qualities through shared ownership and rewards, common norms, culture and values.[33]

Public sector organisations

In the case of public sector organisations, in particular, there is a demand for uniformity of treatment, regularity of procedures and accountability for their operations. This leads to adherence to specified rules and procedures which limit the degree of discretion exercised by management, and to the keeping of detailed records. For example, *Green* argues that, although bureaucracies are becoming less and less the first-choice format for organisational shape, there is still a place for bureaucracy in parts of most organisations and especially public sector organisations such as local authorities and universities. The use and implementation of tried and tested rules and procedures help to ensure essential values and ethics, and that necessary functions are run on a consistent and fair basis.[34]

New forms of information technology such as electronic transactions processed from home or public access terminals are likely to change processes of government service delivery, administrative workloads and the nature of bureaucracy.[35]

Relevance today

By their very nature, bureaucracies are likely to attract criticism. For example, there appears to be a particular dilemma for management in personal service industries. The underlying characteristics of bureaucracy would seem to restrict personal service delivery which requires a flexible approach, responsiveness to individual requirements and the need for initiative and inventiveness.[36] Much of this criticism is valid, but much also appears unfair comment.

Stewart suggests that more organisations today contain mainly or a considerable number of professionals. Such organisations will still have bureaucratic features although there is more reliance on professional discretion and self-regulation than on control through rules and regulations.[37] However, despite new forms of organisation which have emerged, many writers suggest that bureaucracy is still as relevant today as a major form of organisation structure.[38]

Critical reflection

Whatever the validity of the criticism or demands for alternative forms of structure, it is difficult to envisage how large-scale organisations could function effectively without exhibiting at least some of the features of a bureaucracy. For example, in their dealings with public sector organisations people often call for what amounts to increased bureaucracy, even though they may not use that term. How would you defend the benefits of bureaucratic structures?

STRUCTURALISM

Sometimes Weber's work is associated with the ideas of writers such as Karl Marx under the sub-heading of the **structuralism** approach, which is a synthesis of the classical (or formal) school and the human relations (or informal) school.[39] A major line of thought was that the earlier approaches were incomplete and lacked adequate theoretical assumptions and background. The structuralism approach provides a radical perspective of social and organisational behaviour.[40] Greater attention should be given to the relationship between the formal and informal aspects of the organisation, and the study of conflict between the needs of the individual and the organisation, and between workers and management. (*See also* the discussion on conflict in Chapter 19.) Structuralism is sometimes associated as part of a broader human relations approach, which is discussed below.

THE HUMAN RELATIONS APPROACH

The main emphasis of the classical writers was on structure and the formal organisation, but during the 1920s, the years of the Great Depression, greater attention began to be paid to the social factors at work and to the behaviour of employees within an organisation – that is, to **human relations**.

The Hawthorne experiments

The turning point in the development of the human relations movement ('behavioural' and 'informal' are alternative headings sometimes given to this approach) came with the famous Hawthorne experiments at the Western Electric Company in America (1924–32) and the subsequent publication of the research findings.[41] Among the people who wrote about the Hawthorne experiments was *Elton Mayo* (1880–1949), who is often quoted as having been a leader of the researchers. However, there appears to be some doubt as to the extent to which Mayo was actually involved in conducting the experiments and his exact contribution to the human relations movement.[42]

There were four main phases to the Hawthorne experiments:

- the illumination experiments;
- the relay assembly test room;
- the interviewing programme;
- the bank wiring observation room.

The illumination experiments The original investigation was conducted on the lines of the classical approach and was concerned, in typical scientific management style, with the effects of the intensity of lighting upon the workers' productivity. The workers were divided into two groups, an experimental group and a control group. The results of these tests were inconclusive as production in the experimental group varied with no apparent relationship to the level of lighting, but actually increased when conditions were made much worse. Production also increased in the control group although the lighting remained unchanged. The level of production was influenced, clearly, by factors other than changes in physical conditions of work. This prompted a series of other experiments investigating factors of worker productivity.

The relay assembly test room

In the relay assembly test room the work was boring and repetitive. It involved assembling telephone relays by putting together a number of small parts. Six women workers were transferred from their normal departments to a separate area. The researchers selected two assemblers who were friends with each other. They then chose three other assemblers and a layout operator. The experiment was divided into 13 periods during which the workers were subjected to a series of planned and controlled changes to their conditions of work, such as hours of work, rest pauses and provision of refreshments. The general environmental conditions of the test room were similar to those of the normal assembly line.

During the experiment the observer adopted a friendly manner, consulting the workers, listening to their complaints and keeping them informed of the experiment. Following all but one of the changes (when operators complained too many breaks made them lose their work rhythm) there was a continuous increase in the level of production. The researchers formed the conclusion that the extra attention given to the workers, and the apparent interest in them shown by management, were the main reasons for the higher productivity.

The interviewing programme

Another significant phase of the experiments was the interviewing programme. The lighting experiment and the relay assembly test room drew attention to the form of supervision as a contributory factor to the workers' level of production. In an attempt to find out more about the workers' feelings towards their supervisors and their general conditions of work, a large interviewing programme was introduced. More than 20,000 interviews were conducted before the work was ended because of the depression.

Initially, the interviewers approached their task with a set of prepared questions, relating mainly to how the workers felt about their jobs. However, this method produced only limited information. The workers regarded a number of the questions as irrelevant; also they wanted to talk about issues other than just supervision and immediate working conditions. As a result, the style of interviewing was changed to become more non-directive and open-ended. There was no set list of questions and the workers were free to talk about any aspect of their work.

The interviewers set out to be friendly and sympathetic. They adopted an impartial, non-judgemental approach and concentrated on listening.

Using this approach, the interviewers found out far more about the workers' true feelings and attitudes. They gained information not just about supervision and working conditions but also about the company itself, management, work group relations and matters outside of work such as family life and views on society in general. Many workers appeared to welcome the opportunity to have someone to talk to about their feelings and problems and to be able to 'let off steam' in a friendly atmosphere. The interviewing programme was significant in giving an impetus to present-day personnel management and the use of counselling interviews, and highlighting the need for management to listen to workers' feelings and problems.

Being a good listener is arguably even more important for managers in today's work organisations and it is a skill which needs to be encouraged and developed.[43]

The bank wiring observation room

Another experiment involved the observation of a group of 14 men working in the bank wiring room. It was noted that the men formed their own informal organisation with sub-groups or cliques, and with natural leaders emerging with the consent of the members. The group developed its own pattern of informal social relations and 'norms' of what constituted 'proper' behaviour. Despite a financial incentive scheme where the workers could receive more money the more work produced, the group decided on a level of output well below the level they were capable of producing.

Group pressures on individual workers were stronger than financial incentives offered by management. The group believed that if they increased their output, management would raise the standard level of piece rates. The importance of group 'norms' and informal social relations are discussed in Chapter 8.

EVALUATION OF THE HUMAN RELATIONS APPROACH

The human relations approach has been subjected to severe criticism. The Hawthorne experiments have been criticised, for example, on methodology and on failure of the investigators to take sufficient account of environmental factors – although much of this criticism is with the value of hindsight. The human relations writers have been criticised generally for the adoption of a management perspective, their 'unitary frame of reference' and their over-simplified theories.[44]

Other criticisms of the human relations approach are that it is insufficiently scientific and that it takes too narrow a view. It ignores the role of the organisation itself in how society operates.

Sex power differential

There are a number of interpretations of the results of the Hawthorne experiments, including the possible implications of the 'sex power differential' between the two groups. In the relay assembly room where output increased, the group was all female, while in the bank wiring room where output was restricted, the group was all male. The workers in the relay assembly test room were all young unmarried women. All except one were living at home with traditional families of immigrant background. In the work environment of the factory the women had been subjected to frequent contact with male supervisors and therefore 'the sex power hierarchies in the home and in the factory were congruent'. It is suggested, therefore, that it was only to be expected that the women agreed readily to participate with management in the relay assembly test room experiment.[45]

Importance of the Hawthorne experiments

Whatever the interpretation of the results of the Hawthorne experiments, they did generate new ideas concerning the importance of work groups and leadership, communications, output restrictions, motivation and job design. They placed emphasis on the importance of personnel management and gave impetus to the work of the human relations writers. The Hawthorne experiments undoubtedly marked a significant step forward in providing further insight into human behaviour at work and the development of management thinking. The Hawthorne experiments are regarded as one of the most important of all social science investigations and are recognised as probably the single most important foundation of the human relations approach to management and the development of organisational behaviour.

In a review of humane approaches to management, *Crainer* asserts: 'The Hawthorne Studies were important because they showed that views of how managers behaved were a vital aspect of motivation and improved performance. Also, the research revealed the importance of informal work groups.'[46]

Humanisation of the work organisation

Whereas supporters of the classical approach sought to increase production by rationalisation of the work organisation, the human relations movement has led to ideas on increasing production by humanising the work organisation. The classical approach adopted more of a managerial perspective, while the human relations approach strove for a greater understanding of people's psychological and social needs at work as well as improving the process of management. It is usually regarded as the first major approach to organisation and management to show concern for industrial sociology.

The human relations approach recognised the importance of the informal organisation which will always be present within the formal structure. This informal organisation will influence the motivation of employees who will view the organisation for which they work through the values and attitudes of their colleagues. Their view of the organisation determines their approach to work and the extent of their motivation to work well or otherwise.

Human relations writers demonstrated that people go to work to satisfy a complexity of needs and not simply for monetary reward. They emphasised the importance of the wider social needs of individuals and gave recognition to the work organisation as a social organisation and the importance of the group, and group values and norms, in influencing individual behaviour at work. It has been commented that the classical school was concerned about 'organisations without people' and the human relations school about 'people without organisations'.

NEO-HUMAN RELATIONS

Certainly there were shortcomings in the human relations approach and assumptions which evolved from such studies as the Hawthorne experiments were not necessarily supported by empirical evidence.

For example, the contention that a satisfied worker is a productive worker was not always found to be valid. However, the results of the Hawthorne experiments and the subsequent attention given to the social organisation and to theories of individual motivation gave rise to the work of those writers in the 1950s and 1960s who adopted a more psychological orientation. New ideas on management theory arose and a major focus of concern was the personal adjustment of the individual within the work organisation and the effects of group relationships and leadership styles. This group of writers is often (and more correctly) categorised separately under the heading of '**neo-human relations**'. The works of these writers are examined in more detail in subsequent chapters but are summarised broadly here.

The work of Maslow

A major impetus for the neo-human relations approach was the work of *Maslow* who, in 1943, put forward a theoretical framework of individual personality development and motivation based on a hierarchy of human needs.[47] The hierarchy ranges through five levels from, at the lowest level, physiological needs, through safety needs, love needs, esteem needs, to the need for self-actualisation at the highest level. Individuals advance up the hierarchy only as each lower-level need is satisfied. Although Maslow did not originally intend this need hierarchy to be applied necessarily to the work situation it has, nevertheless, had a significant impact on management approaches to motivation and the design of work organisation to meet individual needs. The work of Maslow provides a link with the earlier human relations approach.

Some leading contributors

Among the best-known contributors to the neo-human relations approach are *Herzberg* and *McGregor*. Herzberg isolated two different sets of factors affecting motivation and satisfaction at work. One set of factors comprises those which, if absent, cause dissatisfaction. These are 'hygiene' or 'maintenance' factors which are concerned basically with job environment. However, to motivate workers to give of their best, proper attention must be given to a different set of factors, the 'motivators' or 'growth' factors. These are concerned with job content.[48]

McGregor argued that the style of management adopted is a function of the manager's attitudes towards human nature and behaviour at work. He put forward two suppositions called Theory X and Theory Y which are based on popular assumptions about work and people.[49]

Other major contributors to the neo-human relations approach are *Likert*, whose work includes research into different systems of management;[50] *McClelland*, with ideas on achievement motivation;[51] and *Argyris*, who considered the effects of the formal organisation on the individual and psychological growth in the process of self-actualisation.[52] Argyris' major contributions include his work on organisational learning and on effective leadership.[53]

The neo-human relations approach has generated a prolific amount of writing and research not only from original propounders but also from others seeking to establish the validity, or otherwise, of their ideas. This has led to continuing attention being given to such matters as organisation structuring, group dynamics, job satisfaction, communication and participation, leadership styles and motivation. It has also led to greater attention to the importance of interpersonal interactions, the causes of conflict and recognition of 'industrial relations' problems.

THE SYSTEMS APPROACH

More recently, attention has been focused on the analysis of organisations as 'systems' with a number of interrelated sub-systems.

The classical approach emphasised the technical requirements of the organisation and its needs – 'organisations without people'; the human relations approaches emphasised the psychological and social aspects, and the consideration of human needs – 'people without organisations'.

The **systems approach** attempts to reconcile these two earlier approaches and the work of the formal and the informal writers. Attention is focused on the total work organisation and the interrelationships of structure and behaviour, and the range of variables within the organisation. This approach can be contrasted with a view of the organisation as separate parts. The systems approach encourages managers to view the organisation both as a whole and as part of a larger environment. The idea is that any part of an organisation's activities affects all other parts.

Systems theory

Systems theory is not new and has been used in the natural and physical sciences for a number of years. One of the founders of this approach was the biologist *Ludwig von Bertalanffy* who used the term 'systems theory' in an article published in 1951 and who is generally credited with having developed the outline of General Systems Theory.[54] The systems approach to organisation has arisen, at least in part, therefore, from the work of biologists, and *Miller and Rice* have likened the commercial and industrial organisation to the biological organism.[55]

Using a General Systems Theory (GST) approach, *Boulding* classified nine levels of systems of increasing complexity according to the state of development and knowledge about each level.[56] Organisations are complex social systems and are more open to change than lower-level simple dynamic or cybernetic systems. Boulding felt there were large gaps in both theoretical and empirical knowledge of the human level and the social organisations level of systems, although some progress has now been made with recent theories of organisational behaviour.

The business organisation as an open system

The business organisation is an open system. There is continual interaction with the broader external environment of which it is part. The systems approach views the organisation within its total environment and emphasises the importance of multiple channels of interaction. Criticisms of earlier approaches to organisation are based in part on the attempt to study the activities and problems of the organisation solely in terms of the internal environment. The view of the organisation as an open system is examined in Chapter 3.

The systems approach views the organisation as a whole and involves the study of the organisation in terms of the relationship between technical and social variables within the system. Changes in one part, technical or social, will affect other parts and thus the whole system.

Longwall coal-mining study

The idea of socio-technical systems arose from the work of *Trist* and others, of the Tavistock Institute of Human Relations, in their study of the effects of changing technology in the coal-mining industry in the 1940s.[57] The increasing use of mechanisation and the introduction of coal-cutters and mechanical conveyors enabled coal to be extracted on a 'longwall' method.

Shift working was introduced, with each shift specialising in one stage of the operation – preparation, cutting or loading. However, the new method meant a change in the previous system of working where a small, self-selecting group of miners worked together, as an independent team, on one part of the coalface – the 'single place' or 'shortwall' method.

Technological change had brought about changes in the social groupings of the miners. It disrupted the integration of small groups and the psychological and sociological properties of the old method of working. There was a lack of co-operation between different shifts and within each shift, an increase in absenteeism, scapegoating and signs of greater social stress. The 'longwall' method was socially disruptive and did not prove as economically efficient as it could have been with the new technology.

The researchers saw the need for a socio-technical approach in which an appropriate social system could be developed in keeping with the new technical system. The result was the 'composite longwall' method with more responsibility to the team as a whole and shifts carrying out composite tasks, the reintroduction of multiskilled roles and a reduction in specialisation. The composite method was psychologically and socially more rewarding and economically more efficient than the 'longwall' method.

The socio-technical system

The concept of the organisation as a 'socio-technical' system directs attention to the transformation or conversion process itself, to the series of activities through which the organisation attempts to achieve its objectives. The **socio-technical system** is concerned with the interactions between the psychological and social factors and the needs and demands of the human part of the organisation, and its structural and technological requirements.

Recognition of the socio-technical approach is of particular importance today. People must be considered as at least an equal priority along with investment in technology. For example, *Lane et al.* point out that major technological change has brought about dramatic changes in worker behaviour and requirements. It is people who unlock the benefits and opportunities of information communication technology.[58]

Technology determinism

The concept of socio-technical systems provides a link between the systems approach and a sub-division, sometimes adopted – the **technology approach**. Writers under the technology heading attempt to restrict generalisations about organisations and management and emphasise the effects of varying technologies on organisation structure, work groups and individual performance and job satisfaction. This is in contrast with the socio-technical approach which did not regard technology, *per se*, as a determinant of behaviour.

Under the heading of the technology approach could be included the work of such writers as *Walker and Guest* (effects of the assembly-line production method on employee behaviour);[59] *Sayles* (relationship between technology and the nature of work groups);[60] and *Blauner* (problems of 'alienation' in relation to different work technologies).[61] Technological determinism is discussed more fully in Chapter 17.

THE CONTINGENCY APPROACH

The classical approach suggested one best form of structure and placed emphasis on general sets of principles while the human relations approach gave little attention at all to structure. In contrast the **contingency approach** showed renewed concern with the importance of structure as a significant influence on organisational performance. The contingency approach, which can be seen as an extension of the systems approach, highlights possible means of differentiating among alternative forms of organisation structures and systems of management. There is no one optimum state. For example, the structure of the organisation and its 'success' are dependent, that is contingent upon, the nature of tasks with which it is designed to deal and the nature of environmental influences.

Refresh your understanding
Activity 2C
www.pearsoned.co.uk/mullins

The most appropriate structure and system of management is therefore dependent upon the contingencies of the situation for each particular organisation. The contingency approach implies that organisation theory should not seek to suggest one best way to structure or manage organisations but should provide insights into the situational and contextual factors which influence management decisions. Contingency models of organisation and management are discussed in Chapter 16.

OTHER APPROACHES TO THE STUDY OF ORGANISATIONS

The four-fold framework of classical, human relations, systems and contingency approaches provides a helpful, although rather simplistic, categorisation. The study of organisations, their structure and management is a broad field of inquiry. Depending on the views and preferences of the writer, other possible main approaches include decision-making and social action.

THE DECISION-MAKING APPROACH

The systems approach involves the isolation of those functions most directly concerned with the achievement of objectives and the identification of main decision areas or sub-systems. Viewing the organisation as a system emphasises the need for good information and channels of communication in order to assist effective decision-making in the organisation. Recognition of the need for decision-making and the attainment of goals draws attention to a sub-division of the systems approach, or a separate category, that of the **decision-making (or decision theory) approach**. Here the focus of attention is on managerial decision-making and how organisations process and use information in making decisions.

Successful management lies in responding to internal and external change. This involves the clarification of objectives, the specification of problems and the search for and implementation of solutions. The organisation is seen as an information processing network with numerous decision points. An understanding of how decisions are made helps in understanding behaviour in the organisation. Decision-making writers seek to explain the mechanisms by which conflict is resolved and choices are made.

Some leading writers

Leading writers of the decision-making approach include *Barnard*, *Simon* and *Cyert and March*. The scope of the decision-making approach, however, is wide and it is possible to identify contributions from engineers, mathematicians and operational research specialists in addition to the work of economists, psychologists and writers on management and organisation.

Barnard stressed the need for co-operative action in organisations. He believed that people's ability to communicate, and their commitment and contribution to the achievement of a common purpose, were necessary for the existence of a co-operative system.[62]

These ideas were developed further by Simon. He sees management as meaning decision-making and his concern is with how decisions are made and how decision-making can be improved. Simon is critical of the implication of man as completely rational and proposes a model of 'administrative man' who, unlike 'economic man', 'satisfices' rather than maximises. Administrative decision-making is the achievement of satisfactory rather than optimal results in solving problems.[63]

Economic models of decision-making, based on the assumption of rational behaviour in choosing from known alternatives in order to maximise objectives, can be contrasted with behavioural models based not so much on maximisation of objectives as on short-term expediency where a choice is made to avoid conflict and to stay within limiting constraints. Managers are more concerned with avoiding uncertainties than with the prediction of uncertainties.[64]

SOCIAL ACTION

Social action represents a contribution from sociologists to the study of organisations. Social action writers attempt to view the organisation from the standpoint of individual members (actors) who will each have their own goals and interpretation of their work situation in terms of the satisfaction sought and the meaning that work has for them. The goals of the individual, and the means selected and actions taken to achieve these goals, are affected by the individual's perception of the situation. Social action looks to the individual's own definition of the situation as a basis for explaining behaviour. Conflict of interests is seen as normal behaviour and part of organisational life. According to *Silverman*:

> *The action approach ... does not, in itself, provide a theory of organisations. It is instead best understood as a method of analysing social relations within organisations.*[65]

Criticisms of earlier approaches

A main thrust of social action is the criticism of earlier approaches to organisation and management and of what is claimed to be their failure to provide a satisfactory basis for the explanation or prediction of individual behaviour. For example, criticism is directed at approaches which focused on the goals and needs of the organisation rather than on considerations of the effectiveness of an organisation in meeting the needs of its individual members.

The human relations approaches have been criticised because of their focus on generalised theories of good management, group psychology and the suggestion of needs common to all individuals at work. The technology approach has been criticised for attributing feelings of alienation to the nature of technology and the status of work groups rather than an analysis which focused on concern for the individual's expectations of, and reactions to, work. The systems approach has been criticised for failure to examine the orientation of individual members to the organisation, the different expectations people have of their work or ways in which the environment influences expectations of work.

Unitary or pluralistic view

Important contributors to a social action approach include *Goldthorpe* (industrial attitudes and behaviour patterns of manual workers)[66] and *Fox*. In a research paper written for the Royal Commission on Trade Unions and Employers' Associations (the Donovan Report), Fox suggests two major ways of perceiving an industrial organisation – a 'unitary' approach and a 'pluralistic' approach.[67]

With the unitary approach the organisation is viewed as a team with a common source of loyalty, one focus of effort and one accepted leader. The pluralistic approach views the organisation as made up of competing sub-groups with their own loyalties, goals and leaders. These competing sub-groups are almost certain to come into conflict.

The unitary and pluralistic perspectives of the organisation are discussed in Chapter 13.

Action theory

A theory of human behaviour from an 'action approach' is presented by *Bowey*.[68] She suggests that action theory, systems theory and contingency theory are not necessarily incompatible approaches to the understanding of behaviour in organisations. It would be possible to take the best parts of the different approaches and combine them into a theory that would model empirical behaviour and also facilitate the analysis of large numbers of people in organisations. Bowey goes on to present such a theory as a particular form of an action theory approach. According to Bowey, action theory is not capable of dealing with the analysis of the behaviour of a large number of people in organisations. Her theory is based, therefore, on three essential principles of action theory, augmented by four additional concepts taken from systems theory.

The three essential principles of action theory can be summarised as below:

- Sociology is concerned not just with behaviour but with 'meaningful action'.
- Particular meanings persist through reaffirmation in actions.
- Actions can also lead to changes in meanings.

Additional concepts

Bowey suggests that these three principles apply mainly to explanations of individual, or small-scale, behaviour. She gives four additional concepts, taken from systems theory, on which analysis of large-scale behaviour can be based. These concepts are redefined in accordance with an action approach.

- **Role**. This is needed for the analysis of behaviour in organisations. It explains the similar action of different people in similar situations within the organisation and the expectations held by other people.
- **Relationships**. This is needed to explain the patterns of interaction among people and the behaviours displayed towards one another.
- **Structure**. The relationships among members of an organisation give rise to patterns of action which can be identified as a 'transitory social structure'. The social factors, and non-social factors such as payment systems, methods of production and physical layout, together form the behavioural structure.
- **Process**. Human behaviour can be analysed in terms of processes, defined as 'continuous interdependent sequences of actions'. The concept of process is necessary to account for the manner in which organisations exhibit changes in structure.

The three principles of action theory, together with the four additional concepts from systems theory, provide an action approach to the analysis of behaviour in organisations. Bowey goes on to illustrate her theory with case studies of five different types of organisations, all in the restaurant industry.

A NUMBER OF APPROACHES

We can now see that within the broad four-fold classification of classical, human relations, systems and contingency approaches it is possible to identify a number of other approaches or at least sub-divisions of approaches, although there is no consensus on the categorisation of these different approaches or on the identification of the various contributors to one particular approach. So far we have established a possible nine-fold classification: classical (including scientific management); bureaucracy; human relations; neo-human relations; systems; technology; contingency; decision-making; and social action – and if structuralism is included, we have a ten-fold classification. This classification could be extended still further. For example, another more recent categorisation sometimes identified as a separate approach is management science – with emphasis on quantitative analysis, mathematical models, operational research and computer technology (*see* Figure 2.3.).

Figure 2.3 An outline of developments of approaches to organisation and management

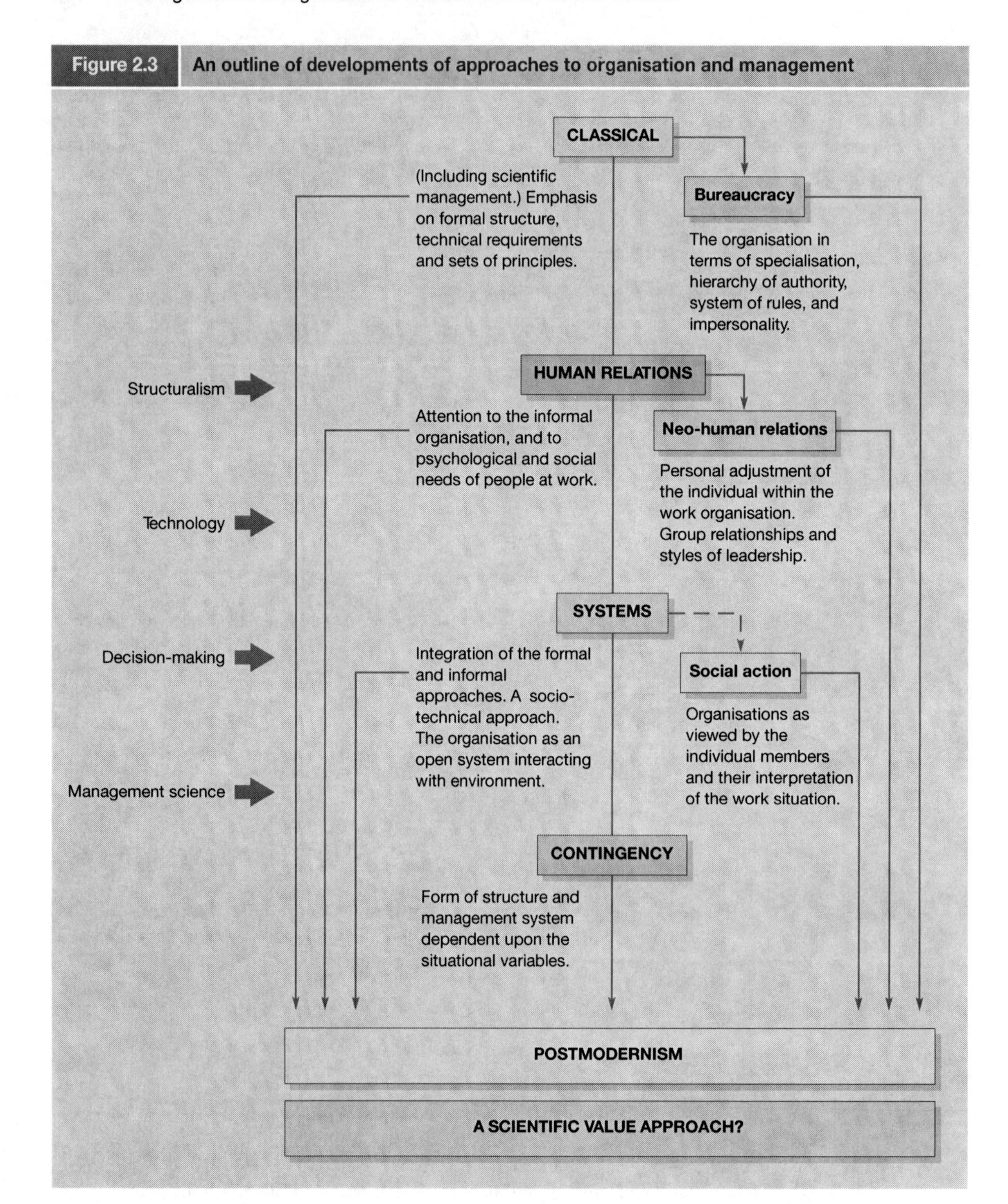

POSTMODERNISM

The work of contemporary writers discussed above together with the achievements of practitioners such as Alfred P. Sloan Jr (1875–1966, Chief Executive and Honorary Chairman of General Motors) gave rise to the so-called 'modern organisation'.[69] With the development of the information and technological age a more recent view of organisations and management is the idea of **postmodernism**. In the 1990s, writers such as *Clegg* described the postmodern organisation in terms of the influence of technological determinism, structural flexibility, premised on niches, multiskilled jobs marked by a lack of demarcation, and more complex employment relationships including subcontracting and networking.[70]

Postmodernism rejects a rational systems approach to our understanding of organisations and management and to accepted explanations of society and behaviour. Highly flexible, free-flowing and fluid structures with the ability to change quickly to meet present demands form the basis of the new organisation. For example, *Watson* suggests that the modernism inherent in the systems-control approach to understanding work organisations and their management is naïve and unrealistic. The possibility of any kind of complete and coherent body of management knowledge has increasingly been brought into question.

> *To enable us to move toward a more realistic or pragmatically reasonable way of 'framing' work organisation and its management, a shift has first to be made in our deeper assumptions about the social world. These are the modernist assumptions which inevitably underpin the whole edifice of work organisation and management thinking.*[71]

By contrast, postmodernism places greater attention on the use of language and attempts to portray a particular set of assumptions or versions of the 'truth'. Watson defines postmodernism as:

> *A way of looking at the world that rejects attempts to build systematic (or 'foundationalist') explanations of history and society and which, instead, concentrates on the ways in which human beings 'invent' their words, especially through the use of language or 'discourse'.*[72]

The idea of postmodernism is, however, not easy to explain fully in clear and simple terms. It is arguably more of a generalised sociological concept rather than a specific approach to organisation and management. There is even some discussion of two connotations, and theories or philosophies of the concept depending on whether the term is hyphenated or not.[73] Perhaps understandably therefore the concept of postmodernism appears to have little interest or appeal to the practical manager.

Indeed Watson, for example, questions the value of labelling more flexible forms of bureaucratic structure and culture as postmodern or post-bureaucratic and differentiating these from the modernist bureaucratic organisation.

> *There is no postmodern or post-bureaucratic organisational form available to us that is essentially different from the modernist bureaucratic organisation. We are indeed seeing different mixes of direct and indirect management control attempts as the world changes. But the world was always changing. Probably from the very beginning of industrialisation there has been a mixing of direct and indirect controls with emphases in one direction and then the other being made at different times.*[74]

Nevertheless, postmodernist organisation can arguably be seen as a healthy challenge to more traditional approaches. It puts forward alternative interpretations of rationality, credibility and ambiguity; a thoughtful critical perspective on disorders in work organisations; and reminds us of the complexities in our understanding of management and organisational behaviour.

Critical reflection

The majority of research and writing on approaches to organisations and management has originated from North America or Western Europe. Do you think that this results in a culturally biased view of organisational behaviour and managerial theory that has only limited value or relevance anywhere else?

RELEVANCE TO MANAGEMENT AND ORGANISATIONAL BEHAVIOUR

The different possible categorisations are not necessarily a bad thing; they illustrate the discursive and complex nature of management. The possible sub-divisions and cross-groupings help illustrate the many factors relevant to the study and practice of management and organisational behaviour. Discussion on the various categorisations of approaches and the identification of individual writers within a particular approach can provide a useful insight into the subject.

Positive advantages

Whatever form of categorisation is adopted, the division of writers on organisation and management into various approaches offers a number of positive advantages.

- It is helpful to students in the arrangement and study of their material.
- It provides a setting in which to view the field of management and to consider the contribution of individual writers.
- It traces the major lines of argument developed by writers seeking to advise practising managers on how they might improve performance.
- It provides a framework in which the principles enunciated can be set and against which comparisons with management practice can be made.
- It helps in organisational analysis and in the identification of problem areas. For example, is the problem one of structure, of human relations or of the socio-technical process?
- It enables the manager to take from the different approaches those ideas which best suit the particular requirements of the job. For example, in dealing with a problem of structure, the ideas of the classical writers or of contingency theory might be adopted. When there is a problem relating to personnel management, ideas from the human relations movement might be of most value. If the problem is one of environmental influence, insights from the systems approach might prove most helpful. For problems of a more quantitative nature, ideas from the decision-making approach or from management science might be applicable.

Caveats to be noted

There are, however, a number of important caveats that should be noted.

- The various approaches represent a progression of ideas, each building on from the other and adding to it. Together they provide a pattern of complementary studies into the development of management thinking. The different approaches are not in competition with each other and no one approach should be viewed as if it were the only approach, replacing or superseding earlier contributions. Many ideas of earlier writers are still of relevance today and of continuing importance in modern management practice.
- Any categorisation of individual writers into specific approaches is inevitably somewhat arbitrary and not all writers can be neatly arranged in this manner. This is only to be expected. Such writers are expounding their current thoughts and ideas in keeping with the continual development of management theory and changes in management practice. The comment made about some management writers that they are saying different things at different times might therefore be taken more as a compliment than as a criticism.

- Even when there is agreement on the nature of the contribution from different writers, the actual division into varying approaches may take a number of forms. In other words, while there might be acceptance of the need for a framework, there is no agreement on its shape. Different authors have adopted different formats in which to set out the developments in management thinking.
- Some of the literature categorises management thinkers into divisions called 'schools'. The use of this term suggests a clarity of distinction between each division and a uniformity of beliefs within each division. This is perhaps an exaggeration. The distinction between these so-called schools is not clear-cut and there is not necessarily a consistency of thinking among the various contributors in each division. The term 'approaches' to management is more indicative of the obscure lines between the different categorisations and, paradoxically, it is the suggestion of vagueness that, arguably, makes it a more appropriate term to use.

> *Of course, management theories have often been the subject of discourse and criticism. Some critics see organisational philosophies as management fads that will be replaced by new ones as other theories are proposed. That may well be the case, but it is good for management theories to evolve, because organisations change, the environment changes, and as a result, management practices and techniques change ... Theories provide us with valuable insights into how we can be more understanding, influential and ultimately more successful in managing organisations and the turbulent dynamic environments in which they operate ... you of course, may have a different view!*
>
> Jacqueline McLean [75]

The importance of cultural contexts

A major criticism of the attempt to define generalised models of management theory is the assumption of national culture. *Schneider and Barsoux* draw attention to how the different theories on how to organise all reflect societal concerns of the times as well as the cultural backgrounds of the individuals. Different approaches reflect different cultural assumptions regarding, for example, human nature and the importance of task and relationships.[76]

Cheng, Sculli and Chan also question the universality of theories of management and organisational behaviour on the ground that they have not adequately addressed the factor of culture. 'Traditionally, the greatest aspiration of researchers is to discover objective, universalistic principles of behaviour. The tacit assumption behind this is that these principles may be discovered without reference to cultural contexts.' They conclude that while there may be some universality to organisation structures, for example the need for some form of hierarchy whatever its shape may be, different national cultures frequently give those structures different meanings.[77]

In a review of management theory and practice, *Heller* contrasts British and American thinking with methods employed by the Japanese. In the 1960s, Western managements showed a total lack of curiosity about competition from Japan; British and European managers were still obsessed by the American example. The Japanese built hugely on what they had borrowed from the USA. However, the Japanese also practised and perfected what management scientists often only preached.[78]

Although British management has failed to live up to Japanese standards, professional standards among managers in Britain have improved greatly over the past 25 years. The potential of a widening Europe and the Japanese penchant for locating more plants in Britain provide the best reasons for brighter prospects.

TOWARDS A SCIENTIFIC VALUE APPROACH?

It might be that the study of organisations, their structure and management is moving towards a more scientific approach. Management science can assist managers in the analysis of complex problems that are subject to quantitative constraints and in the optimisation of decisions in such problems. It may also assist in the establishment of broad theory. However, many operational problems in organisations relate to the nature of human behaviour and the people–organisation relationship and do not lend themselves to the application of a scientific answer.

There are no definitive or final solutions to the problems of organisations. The nature of work organisations and the environment in which they operate is becoming increasingly complex and subject to continual change. However, at least we do understand more about the dynamics of management and organisational behaviour as a basis for the analysis of human behaviour in organisations.[79]

> *It is obvious from even a cursory glance at the history of management science that science and technology are considered to be key instruments in solving workplace problems and in controlling workplaces ... While Taylorist scientific management may have its academic critics, management science is thriving. It is itself a large business, providing employment for management consultants whose sole concern is solving workplace problems of other corporations.*[80]

Balance between philosophy and science

Miner, however, suggests that although the degree of commitment to the scientific value system is increasing, as yet there is insufficient research to move the field entirely into science, completely divorced from philosophy. At present management theory is clearly in the 'schools' phase. As discussed earlier, it is possible to argue over the use of the term 'schools'. However, whatever terminology is used, and whatever the state of our knowledge, the message from Miner is clear:

> *... schools of management thought are very much a reality, and the management student who approaches the field without at least a minimal understanding of them does so at some risk.*[81]

According to *Crainer*, management is active, not theoretical. But management is nothing without ideas.

> *Ideas drive management as surely as the immediate problems which land on managers' desks or which arrive via their email. Decisions have to be based on ideas, as well as instinct. Without ideas managers flit desperately from crisis to crisis. They cannot know where they are going, why they are doing something or what they will achieve, without the fuel of ideas.*[82]

BENEFITS TO THE MANAGER

Whatever the balance between philosophy and science, a knowledge and understanding of management theory will help with the complexities of management in modern work organisations. No single approach to organisation and management provides all the answers. It is the comparative study of different approaches which will yield benefits to the manager.[83] There is, of course, no shortage of new ideas on organisational behaviour and management thinking. To what extent, however, do these ideas lead to improved organisational performance?

There is undoubtedly much scepticism about and criticism of management gurus. For example, according to *Crainer*, the past 30 years have seen management thinking in a state of perpetual flux with a relentless quest for new ideas, such as corporate strategy, the nature of management, culture, quality and the Japanese approach, excellence, the re-emergence of leadership, competitive advantage, empowerment and re-engineering. Crainer believes that this is what managers have been doing all along, but how well they have succeeded is a matter of debate.

> *Comparing past and present is diverting, but provides more questions than answers. What can be said is that managers remain open to new lights and that over 30 years the sheer profusion of ideas has, at times, been overwhelming.*[84]

Crainer also suggests that as one idea after another fails to translate into sustainable practice, there is a growing disillusionment with the pedlars of managerial wisdom.

> *Yet, the desire for instant solutions which tackle all managerial problems in one fell swoop remains strong ... Amid the hard sell, the quick fixes and organisational placebos, it is true to say that there is little that's original. But, without gurus, managers would lose a rich source of inspiration, information and controversy.*[85]

Reporting on a 12-year study of the knowledge and use of management concepts in technical organisations, *Flores and Utley* suggest that a look back at the theories and principles that have been taught in the past could give an indication of the success of any new approach and help prepare today's and tomorrow's managers for the future.[86] And *Stern* has this to say: 'Management thinkers still have a lot to tell us. You don't have to believe everything they say, but they may at least offer stimulation; they might provoke senior managers into abandoning complacency and trying to see problems in a new light.'[87]

There are, then, many aspects to management. There are no simple solutions, no one best way to manage. However, the study of organisations, their structure and management is still important for the manager and remains an indispensable part of the job.

Activity 2E
www.pearsoned.co.uk/mullins

Critical reflection

'The study of different approaches to organisation and management and the development of organisation theory have no practical relevance for today's managers. It is really no more than a luxury for students and the time could be spent better on more important topic areas.' How would you present a *counter* argument?

MANAGEMENT IN THE NEWS

Professionalism

FT

Problem with performance-managing professionals

Stefan Stern

When our first child was born last spring my wife and I indulged in that traditional speculation practised by many new parents: what did we want the dear girl to do when she grew up? I instinctively veered towards the conventional. She would, of course, pursue a brilliant professional career, achieving both financial security and social respectability. Put your trust in the professions and you can't go wrong. My wife, less hidebound than me, was more pragmatic. 'I bet she'd make a good plumber,' she said.

At only 15 months, my daughter has not yet had to face the literacy and numeracy tests that will soon be coming her way from the UK's Department for Education and Skills. It is therefore too early to say in which direction she is headed – although, to judge by her talent for destroying order, plumbing may indeed turn out to be a favoured option.

But Mrs Stern's scepticism does provoke other, more immediate, questions. What does it mean to be a professional today? Where in the past the term covered

Management in the news – continued

What does it mean to be a professional today? Is dedication to your craft being undermined by a need to meet targets?

the established disciplines of law, medicine or accountancy, today it is used to cover even the work done by security guards or contract cleaners. Has the term 'professional' been devalued through its ever wider application to ever more lines of work? And what implications does the changing nature of professionalism have for both employees and their organisations?

One afternoon last month, Demos, a London-based think-tank, gathered together a selection of professional people and gave them a few minutes to describe the challenges they face doing their jobs. The effect was remarkable. In both the public and private sectors, managers are agonising over similar things. In this age of targets, monitoring and performance management, professional people wonder how much autonomy they retain over how they go about their work. They had originally entered a profession because of a vocation, a calling. Now they found themselves pursuing a managerial agenda set remotely by bosses who often did not share the same personal commitment to the work in hand that they do. Richard Sennett, a professor at the London School of Economics, argues that many professional people have lost 'a sense of craft' in their day-to-day work. They are being judged according to their position in an occupational hierarchy, not by what it is about their work that makes them feel professional: their dedication to their craft.

> *We have misunderstood the idea of quality, and how people go about doing quality work. A most important motivator for professionals is being able to do a good job for its own sake, rather than just to meet a target. If you take that ability away from professionals they get very unhappy.*

Sometimes, of course, professionalism is in the eye of the beholder. This is a theme film-maker Quentin Tarantino explores in his 1992 crime thriller, *Reservoir Dogs*. Professionalism is the film's leitmotif. A gang of armed robbers collapses into violent disarray as a planned heist goes wrong. Appalled by a colleague's displays of brutality, Mr White, played by Harvey Keitel, issues the most damning criticism imaginable.

> *What you're supposed to do is act like a f****** professional. A psychopath is not a professional. You can't work with a psychopath, 'cause ya don't know what those sick assholes are gonna do next.*

I have wandered a little from this column's usual territory. How unprofessional. But that is my point. The early 21st-century version of professionalism risks becoming narrow and impoverished. The under-40s coming up through the ranks seek variety and autonomy in their work, as well as financial rewards. They do not want their true professionalism to be performance-managed out of them.

Source: Stern, S., 'Problem with performance-managing professionals', *Financial Times*, 10 July 2006.

Discussion questions

1. **Identify and review the arguments for and against regarding management as another 'profession' like law and medicine. How far can the different approaches be seen as a conflict between the 'classical' and 'human relations' approaches to organisation and management?**
2. **The author of the article suggests that people today seek autonomy and variety in their work. Using the concept of social action theory, discuss the implications for the way in which organisations might be structured and managed in the 21st century.**

SYNOPSIS

- The study of organisational behaviour has to proceed on a broad front. A central part of this study is the development of management thinking and what might be termed management theory. In order to help identify main trends in the development of organisational behaviour, it is usual to categorise the work of leading writers into various 'approaches' based on their views of organisations, their structure and management. This provides a simplistic framework on which to direct study and focus attention.

- The classical writers placed emphasis on purpose and structure, on the technical requirements of the organisation, and on the assumption of rational and logical behaviour. The human relations writers emphasised the importance of the informal organisation and the psychological and social needs of people at work. The systems approach focuses attention on the interactions between technical and social variables. The organisation is seen in continual interaction with the external environment. Contingency theory highlights possible means of differentiating between alternative forms of structures and systems of management.

- This four-fold categorisation provides a useful starting point for the identification of main trends in the development of management thinking. Within this framework, however, it is possible to identify a number of other approaches or sub-divisions of approaches. The decision-making approach emphasises the need for good information and channels of communication. Social action writers attempt to view the organisation from the position of individual members who will each have their own interpretation of the work situation in terms of the satisfaction sought and the meaning that work has for them.

- With the development of the information and technological age the need arises for alternative forms of corporate structure and systems. A more recent view is the idea of postmodernism. This rejects a rational systems approach to our understanding of organisations and management, and to accepted explanations of society and behaviour. Postmodernism is arguably more of a generalised sociological concept rather than a specific approach to organisation and management. Nevertheless, postmodernist organisation can arguably be seen as a healthy challenge to more traditional approaches and reminds us of the complexities in our understanding of management and organisational behaviour.

- Whatever form of categorisation is adopted, the division of writers on organisation and management into various approaches offers a number of advantages. It helps in organisational analysis and the identification of problem areas. It enables the manager to take from the different approaches those ideas that suit best the particular requirements of the job. There are, however, a number of caveats that should also be noted, including the significance of cultural contexts. In more recent years attention has been given to potential applications of Japanese management.

- It might be that the study of organisations is moving towards a more scientific value approach. However, whatever the balance between philosophy and science, a knowledge of management theory will help with the complexities of management in modern work organisations. There is much scepticism and criticism of management gurus but the study of organisation theory is an indispensable part of the job. Ideas are as important to management decisions as is instinct. It is necessary to view the interrelationships among the development of theory, behaviour in organisations and management practice.

Refresh your understanding, assess your progress and begin your research with online resources at www.pearsoned.co.uk/mullins

REVIEW AND DISCUSSION QUESTIONS

1. Assess critically the relevance of scientific management to present-day organisations. Illustrate your answer with reference to your own organisation.
2. To what extent is there anything positive to be said for bureaucratic structures? Select a large-scale organisation of your choice and suggest ways in which it displays characteristics of a bureaucracy.
3. What are the main conclusions that can be drawn from the Hawthorne experiments? Discuss critically the relevance of these experiments for management and organisational behaviour today.

→

Review and discussion questions – continued

4 Summarise the main features of the neo-human relations approach to organisation and management. How does it differ from other approaches?

5 Evaluate the application of the systems approach to the analysis of work organisations. Suggest an example of a work situation in which the systems approach might be appropriate.

6 Contrast approaches to improving organisational performance based on attention to technical and structural requirements with those based on concern for psychological and social factors.

7 Explain what is meant by a social action approach. Assess critically the practical relevance of 'action theory'.

8 Identify, and outline briefly, major trends in management theory since the beginning of this century. Debate critically the extent to which the ideas of management gurus have any practical relevance or benefits for managers.

ASSIGNMENT

a Answer each question 'mostly agree' or 'mostly disagree'. Assume that you are trying to learn something about yourself. Do not assume that your answer will be shown to a prospective employer.

		Mostly agree	*Mostly disagree*
1	I value stability in my job.	☐	☐
2	I like a predictable organisation.	☐	☐
3	The best job for me would be one in which the future is uncertain.	☐	☐
4	The army would be a nice place to work.	☐	☐
5	Rules, policies and procedures tend to frustrate me.	☐	☐
6	I would enjoy working for a company that employed 85,000 people worldwide.	☐	☐
7	Being self-employed would involve more risk than I'm willing to take.	☐	☐
8	Before accepting a job, I would like to see an exact job description.	☐	☐
9	I would prefer a job as a freelance house painter to one as a clerk for the Department of Motor Vehicles.	☐	☐
10	Seniority should be as important as performance in determining pay increases and promotion.	☐	☐
11	It would give me a feeling of pride to work for the largest and most successful company in its field.	☐	☐
12	Given a choice, I would prefer to make £30,000 per year as a vice-president in a small company to £40,000 as a staff specialist in a large company.	☐	☐
13	I would regard wearing an employee badge with a number on it as a degrading experience.	☐	☐
14	Parking spaces in a company lot should be assigned on the basis of job level.	☐	☐
15	If an accountant works for a large organisation, he or she cannot be a true professional.	☐	☐
16	Before accepting a job (given a choice), I would want to make sure that the company had a very fine programme of employee benefits.	☐	☐
17	A company will probably not be successful unless it establishes a clear set of rules and procedures.	☐	☐
18	Regular working hours and holidays are more important to me than finding thrills on the job.	☐	☐
19	You should respect people according to their rank.	☐	☐
20	Rules are meant to be broken.	☐	☐

Source: DuBrin, A. J., *Human Relations: A Job-Oriented Approach*, Reston Publishing/Prentice Hall/Pearson Education (1978), pp. 296–7. Reproduced with permission.

b You should then consider and discuss the further information supplied by your tutor.

PERSONAL AWARENESS AND SKILLS EXERCISE

Objectives

Completing this exercise should help you to enhance the following skills:

- Demonstrate your knowledge and understanding of scientific management techniques.
- Write an objective set of instructions for undertaking a simple piece of work.

Exercise

Using the example from Figure 2.2 on p. 47 as a model, **you are required** to develop a *detailed* programme using scientific management techniques for any **two** of the following simple domestic tasks:

- booking an airline ticket;
- cooking a simple meal (for example spaghetti bolognese);
- bathing a small child;
- rearranging 100 CDs in some form of order, 10 to each shelf;
- washing up after a small dinner party;
- renewing your passport.

Discussion

- What are the potential up- and downsides of removing operator discretion in this way?
- Explain with supporting reasons those tasks or activities that you believe are particularly suited to a scientific management approach.
- How do you feel about carrying out routine tasks on an ongoing basis over which you are given little personal discretion?

CASE STUDY

Dell Computers: the world at your fingertips

Breaking the mould

The growth of the home personal computer (pc) market is one of the most remarkable success stories of the last quarter century. If you own a home pc or an electronic notebook and you live in the United States, then there is a one in three possibility that it arrived on your doorstep packed in boxes labelled 'Dell'. Whilst Dell has a smaller proportion of the pc market outside the USA (approximately 17 per cent worldwide, and locked in close competition with its nearest rival, Hewlett-Packard), there remains a strong possibility that your new pc was assembled in Limerick, Penang or Xiamen. Any of these is a very long way from the bedroom of a campus dormitory at the University of Texas at Austin, which is where Michael Dell began to build and sell computers directly to customers in 1984 before dropping out of college to run his business full-time.

In 1984, building a pc from components was still a specialised activity, and while some people were able to assemble their own equipment in order to save money and get precisely what they wanted, the majority of domestic customers bought ready-made products from retailers. The distribution channel for the industry usually contained five components: supplier (of components, chips, software, etc.), manufacturer, distributor, retailer and customer. Michael Dell's idea was to sell direct and at the same time allow customers to have a pc partly tailored to their personal requirements by choosing options from a list of components and specifications which he would then assemble to order. This move eliminated two of the five elements of the distribution channel (the distributors and the retailers), leaving only three players: the suppliers, Dell and the customer.[88] The opportunity to

Source: Rex Features

Michael Dell transformed a business run from his bedroom at university to one of the leading companies in the IT market.

develop this new approach into a successful business was made possible by the coalescence of three trends: increased levels of consumer confidence and knowledge about the product itself; better and faster software which enabled first the phone-based and then the internet-based ordering system to run effectively; and finally technological and manufacturing advances which enabled Dell to lower the price of a pc to a level where it clearly became good value for money.

Whilst Dell supplied both business and individual customers, it was in the home pc market that the approach had particular success. Each computer was assembled to order, with components purchased from suppliers as they were required, so Dell was able to identify and respond to customer preferences and industry trends very quickly and without a significant amount of capital being tied up in inventory or stock (the value of which would be declining rapidly as new and better products emerged). The system had the added advantage that customers pre-paid for the goods, thus placing Dell on a firm financial footing from the outset.

While this approach to the manufacture of consumer goods is by no means unique (the 'lean manufacturing' approach is widely used in the car industry, for example) and other players in the IT market adopted it, Dell was able to make it work more successfully than its competitors. The basic business model transferred readily to the Internet, where the process of 'mass customisation' can be managed even more effectively online.[89] Dell's growth at the turn of the century took it worldwide and it was placed first in a ranking of the 'Most Admired Companies' by *Fortune* magazine in February 2005.[90] Dell has also won accolades for ethical standards of corporate behaviour.

Not all plain sailing

The brand image which helped put Dell at the top of *Fortune's* list in 2005 depended very heavily on its ability to pull together both its own efforts and those of other organisations (i.e. component manufacturers, transport and logistics organisations, delivery companies, etc.), often in far-flung regions of the world, to put together a package which offered both reliability and value for money for its customers. As we have seen, its original strength was in its ability to cut out the 'middle man' and deliver that package quickly and cheaply. But the IT business is both highly competitive and a dizzyingly fast-moving environment and in the early years of the 21st century Dell had to rebalance the content of its package.

The area where the Dell operation proved most vulnerable was that of customer service and technical support. In the more traditional world of retail outlets, customers were able to discuss purchases and return faulty equipment or seek support at a store. Such a network of customer support was absent from the Dell model. Initially Dell outsourced customer support (along with delivery), but as expectations about after-sales service rose, its call centre support lagged behind these expectations, resulting in some very public criticism[91] not least of which was in the form of a long-running critical blog by dissatisfied customer and journalist Jeff Jarvis.[92] Dell brought its technical support centres back in-house; two were based in Canada, but mostly they were 'off-shored' (but not 'outsourced') to the Philippines and India, where Dell expects to employ 15,000 workers by 2008.[93] It also launched its own blog[94] as a means of capturing and responding to customer complaints. In July 2006, Dell's share price dropped substantially after a profit warning was issued following the decision to make a major investment in customer support systems.[95] The task then facing Dell's management was to persuade investors that the proposed plan would result in a long-term improvement in the company's ability to stay ahead of the game and ultimately deliver a good return on investment.

Why was this move necessary? To a large extent, the very success of Dell at the cheaper end of the market meant that similar low-cost operators ceased to be a major competitive threat by the end of the 1990s. However, as home computers became big business for more up-market companies and those which had previously focused on business customers, Dell found itself competing directly with the very companies it had side-stepped in the 1990s: Hewlett-Packard, Lenovo (the Chinese company which bought the IBM computer manufacturing arm in 2005) and even Sony. These organisations were not only able to provide high-quality, reliable products but also had much stronger customer service support. This revealed a strategic weakness in Dell's operation and forced it to raise its game not only in terms of the computing power it delivers but also in terms of its after-sales service.

The Soul of Dell

Dell is keen to balance business performance with responsible operations – the overall general philosophy is described by the company as 'The Soul of Dell'[96] and the Code of Conduct reflects its ambitions to:

> *... conduct business the Dell Way – the right way, which is 'Winning with Integrity.' Simply put, we want all members of our team, along with our shareholders, customers, suppliers and other stakeholders, to understand that they can believe what we say and trust what we do.*[97]

Feedback from the workforce as well as customers is clearly critical to Dell's success, and the workforce is encouraged to get involved in the process through its 'Tell Dell' system.

> *There is change happening all across Dell, creating a revolution in how we interact and drive for business results. Processes are changing, attitudes are shifting, objectives are being aligned, careers are being enhanced and people are listening. Closely. At the core of it is Tell Dell.*
>
> *The Tell Dell survey program has been continually refined over the past several years from being a good informational instrument to its current use as a critical analytic and diagnostic tool for making Dell a better place to work and a stronger company. Part of the Winning Culture philosophy is to engage directly with our employees, the way we do with our customers. As managers at Dell, it is critical that we support our Winning Culture by working to deliver an unbeatable employee experience each and every day.*
>
> Ro Parra and Joe Marengi,
> Senior Vice Presidents of Americas.[98]

Talking to Hyderabad

This case study is being written on a Dell computer. It was ordered from the front room of a terraced house in the south of England at about 10pm one March evening. Within minutes, I had an email from Sunita at the Hyderabad Customer Experience Centre to say she would be tracking my order to completion and giving me updates on its progress. I could look at the progress it was making by following events on the website, which told me that the components were on their way to Limerick, then that the pc had been assembled, then that it had been dispatched to the distribution hub where it was joined by the chosen accessories. I could see when it crossed from Ireland to the UK, when it had reached the local distribution centre and finally Sunita phoned me to announce the delivery day and time about one week after the order was placed.

She rang again to ensure that it had arrived and was operating to my satisfaction. When I mentioned that the cooling fan seemed rather noisy, she logged a call to the technical support team (also in India) and I found myself, phone in one hand, screwdriver in the other, involved in what can only be described as the postmodern experience of running a diagnostic test on my pc, with Sunita's colleague talking me through the process of opening the operating unit, dismantling the fan and checking the nature of the fault. As a result, a local engineer was dispatched with a replacement component. Within ten days the whole operation was complete to both my and Sunita's satisfaction and we said our farewells.

Your tasks

1. Analyse the organisational choices that Dell has made using two of the four main analytical models presented in Figure 2.1. Which approach do you think is more appropriate and why?
2. What are the main organisational challenges which Dell faces in order to 'conduct business the Dell Way'? What are the implications for line managers and supervisors of creating a corporate culture based on the Dell Way?
3. Dell is using technologically sophisticated methods to collect 'soft' data about its performance from both customers (one2one) and staff (Tell Dell). Evaluate these initiatives and discuss the value of such information in relation to 'hard' data (such as sales figures, share price, etc.) as a management tool.
4. Critically review the concept of postmodernism as a means of understanding the nature of highly diverse (in terms of geography, technology, organisation, technical specialisation and culture) organisations such as Dell.

Notes and references

1. This chapter is based in parts on a development of the author's articles: Mullins, L. J. 'Approaches to Management', *Management Accounting*, vol. 57, no. 4, April 1979, pp. 15–18, and Mullins, L. J. 'Some Further Approaches to Management Theory', *Management Accounting*, vol. 58, no. 3, March 1980, pp. 30–3.
2. See, for example: George, C. S. *The History of Management Thought*, Second edition, Prentice Hall (1972).
3. For a review of management thinking see, for example: Sheldrake, J. *Management Theory: From Taylorism to Japanization*, International Thomson Business Press (1996).
4. See also: Flores, G. N. and Utley, D. R. 'Management Concepts in Use – a 12-year Perspective', *Engineering Management Journal*, vol. 12, no. 3, September 2000, pp. 11–17.
5. McGregor, D. *The Human Side of Enterprise*, Penguin (1987), p. 6.
6. Ghoshal, S., Barlett, C. A. and Moran, P. 'Value Creation: The new millennium management manifesto', in Chowdhury, S. *Management 21C*, Financial Times Prentice Hall (2000), p. 122.
7. Miner, J. B. *Theories of Organizational Behaviour*, Dryden Press (1980).
8. Skipton, M. D. 'Management and the Organisation', *Management Research News*, vol. 5, no. 3, 1983, pp. 9–15.
9. Fayol, H. *General and Industrial Management*, Pitman (1949). See also: Gray, I. *Henri Fayol's General and Industrial Management*, Pitman (1988).
10. Urwick, L. *Notes on the Theory of Organization*, American Management Association (1952).
11. Mooney, J. D. and Reiley, A. C. *The Principles of Organization*, Harper and Bros (1939); revised by Mooney, J. D., Harper & Row (1947).
12. Brech, E. F. L. *Organisation: The Framework of Management*, Second edition, Longman (1965).
13. Simon, H. A. *Administrative Behaviour*, Third edition, Free Press (1976), p. xxii.
14. Woodward, J. *Industrial Organization: Theory and Practice*, Second edition, Oxford University Press (1980).
15. Taylor, F. W. Scientific Management, Harper & Row (1947). Comprises 'Shop Management' (1903), 'Principles of Scientific Management' (1911) and Taylor's testimony to the House of Representatives' Special Committee (1912).
16. Braverman, H. *Labor and Monopoly Capital*, Monthly Review Press (1974).
17. For a study of employers' labour relations policies, including comments on the work of Braverman, see: Gospel, H. F. and Littler, C. R. (eds) *Managerial Strategies and Industrial Relations*, Heinemann Educational Books (1983).
18. Cloke, K. and Goldsmith, J. *The End of Management and the Rise of Organizational Democracy*, Jossey-Bass (2002), p. 27.
19. Rose, M. *Industrial Behaviour*, Penguin (1978), p. 31. See also: Rose, M. *Industrial Behaviour*, Second edition, Penguin (1988), Chapter 2.
20. Drucker, P. F. 'The Coming Rediscovery of Scientific Management', *The Conference Board Record*, vol. 13, June 1976, pp. 23–7. Reprinted in Drucker, P. F. *Towards the Next Economics and Other Essays*, Heinemann (1981).
21. Locke, E. A. 'The Ideas of Frederick W. Taylor: An Evaluation', *Academy of Management Review*, vol. 7, no. 1, January 1982, pp. 14–24.
22. For a discussion on 'Fordism', see, for example: Fincham, R. and Rhodes, P. S. *The Individual, Work and Organization*, Second edition, Weidenfeld and Nicolson (1992).
23. Crainer, S. and Dearlove, D. *Financial Times Handbook of Management*, Second edition, Financial Times Prentice Hall (2001).
24. Stern, S. 'Guru Guide', *Management Today*, October 2001, pp. 83–4.
25. Weber, M. *The Theory of Social and Economic Organization*, Collier Macmillan (1964).
26. Blau, P. M. and Scott, W. R. *Formal Organizations*, Routledge and Kegan Paul (1966).
27. Stewart, R. *The Reality of Management*, Third edition, Butterworth-Heinemann (1999).
28. Argyris, C. *Integrating the Individual and the Organization*, John Wiley & Sons (1964).
29. Caulkin, S. 'Faceless Corridors of Power', *Management Today*, January 1988, p. 65.
30. Peters, T. J. and Waterman, R. H. *In Search of Excellence*, Harper & Row (1982).
31. Tibballs, G. *Business Blunders*, Robinson Publishing (1999).
32. Cloke, K. and Goldsmith. J. *The End of Management and the Rise of Organizational Democracy*, Jossey-Bass (2002), pp. 92–4.
33. Ridderstrale, J. 'Business Moves Beyond Bureaucracy', in Pickford, J. (ed.) *Financial Times Mastering Management 2.0*, Financial Times Prentice Hall (2001), pp. 217–20.
34. Green, J. 'Is Bureaucracy Dead? Don't Be So Sure', *Chartered Secretary*, January 1997, pp. 18–19.
35. See, for example: Waller, P. 'Bureaucracy takes new form', *Professional Manager*, May 1998, p. 6.
36. See, for example: Mullins, L. J. *Hospitality Management and Organisational Behaviour*, Fourth edition, Longman (2001).
37. Stewart, R. *The Reality of Management*, Third edition, Butterworth-Heinemann (1999).
38. See, for example: Wilson, F. A. *Organizational Behaviour: A Critical Introduction*, Oxford University Press (1999).
39. For example, see: Etzioni, A. *Modern Organizations*, Prentice-Hall (1964), p. 41.
40. See, for example: Aktouf, O. 'Management and Theories of Organizations in the 1990s: Towards a Critical Radical Humanism?', *Academy of Management Review*, vol. 17, no. 3, 1992, pp. 407–31.
41. There are many versions of the Hawthorne experiments. Among the most thorough accounts is Roethlisberger, F. J. and Dickson, W. J. *Management and the Worker*, Harvard University Press (1939). See also: Landsberger, H. A. *Hawthorne Revisited*, Cornell University Press, Ithaca (1958).
42. See, for example: Rose, M. *Industrial Behaviour*, Second edition, Penguin (1988).
43. See, for example: Buggy, C. 'Are you really listening?', *Professional Manager*, July 2000, pp. 20–2.
44. Silverman, D. *The Theory of Organisations*, Heinemann (1970).
45. Stead, B. A. *Women in Management*, Prentice-Hall (1978), p. 190.
46. Crainer, S. *Key Management Ideas: The thinkers who changed the management world*, Third edition, Financial Times Prentice Hall (1998), p. 111.
47. Maslow, A. H. 'A Theory of Human Motivation', *Psychological Review*, vol. 50, no. 4, July 1943, pp. 370–96.
48. Herzberg, F. W., Mausner, B. and Snyderman, B. B. *The Motivation to Work*, Second edition, Chapman and Hall (1959).

49 McGregor, D. *The Human Side of Enterprise*, Penguin (1987).
50 Likert, R. *New Patterns of Management*, McGraw-Hill (1961). See also: Likert, R. *The Human Organization*, McGraw-Hill (1967), Likert, R. and Likert, J. G. *New Ways of Managing Conflict*, McGraw-Hill (1976).
51 McClelland, D. C. *Human Motivation*, Cambridge University Press (1988).
52 Argyris, C. *Understanding Organizational Behavior*, Tavistock Publications (1960) and *Integrating the Individual and the Organization*, Wiley (1964).
53 See, for example: Caulkin, S. 'Chris Argyris', *Management Today*, October 1997, pp. 58–9.
54 Bertalanffy, L. von 'Problems of General Systems Theory: A new approach to the unity of science', *Human Biology*, vol. 23, no. 4, December 1951, pp. 302–12.
55 Miller, E. J. and Rice, A. K. *Systems of Organization*, Tavistock Publications (1967).
56 Boulding, K. 'General Systems Theory – The Skeleton of Science', *Management Science*, vol. 2, no. 3, April 1956, pp. 197–208.
57 Trist, E. L, Higgin, G. W., Murray, H. and Pollock, A. B. *Organizational Choice*, Tavistock Publications (1963).
58 Lane, T., Snow, D. and Labrow, P. 'Learning to succeed with ICT', *The British Journal of Administrative Management*, May/June 2000, pp. 14–15.
59 Walker, C. R. and Guest, R. H. *The Man on the Assembly Line*, Harvard University Press (1952). See also: Walker, C. R., Guest, R. H. and Turner, A. N. *The Foreman on the Assembly Line*, Harvard University Press (1956).
60 Sayles, L. R. *Behaviour of Industrial Work Groups*, Wiley (1958).
61 Blauner, R. *Alienation and Freedom*, University of Chicago Press (1964).
62 Barnard, C. *The Functions of the Executive*, Oxford University Press (1938).
63 Simon, H. A. *The New Science of Management Decision*, Revised edition, Prentice-Hall (1977).
64 Cyert, R. M. and March, J. G. *A Behavioural Theory of the Firm*, Second edition, Blackwell (1992).
65 Silverman, D. *The Theory of Organisations*, Heinemann (1970), p. 147.
66 Goldthorpe, J. H., Lockwood, D., Bechhofer, F. and Platt, J. *The Affluent Worker*, Cambridge University Press (1968).
67 Fox, A. *Industrial Sociology and Industrial Relations*, HMSO (1966).
68 Bowey, A. M. *The Sociology of Organisations*, Hodder & Stoughton (1976).
69 For further information see Crainer, S. *Key Management Ideas: The thinkers who changed the management world*, Third edition, Financial Times Prentice Hall (1998).
70 Clegg, S. R. *Modern Organizations: Organization Studies in the Postmodern World*, Sage (1990).
71 Watson, T. J. *Organising and Managing Work*, Financial Times Prentice Hall (2002), p. 51.
72 Ibid., p. 50.
73 See, for example: Legge, K. *Human Resource Management: Rhetorics and Realities*, Macmillan Business (1995).
74 Watson, T. J. *Organising and Managing Work*, Financial Times Prentice Hall (2002), p. 254.
75 McLean, J. 'Management techniques and theories', *Manager, The British Journal of Administrative Management*, August/September 2005, p. 17.
76 Schneider, S. C. and Barsoux, J. *Managing Across Cultures*, Second edition, Financial Times Prentice Hall (2003).
77 Cheng, T., Sculli, D. and Chan, F. 'Relationship Dominance – Rethinking Management Theories from the Perspective of Methodological Relationalism', *Journal of Managerial Psychology*, vol. 16, no. 2, 2001, pp. 97–105.
78 Heller, R. 'The Change Managers', *Management Today: 25th Anniversary Issue*, 1991, pp. 12–16.
79 See, for example: Klein, S. M. and Ritti, R. R. *Understanding Organizational Behavior*, Second edition, Kent Publishing (1984), Chapter 1.
80 Bradley, H., Erickson, M., Stephenson, C. and Williams, S. *Myths at Work*, Polity Press (2000), pp. 96–7.
81 Miner, J. B. *Management Theory*, Macmillan (1971), p. 145. See also: Miner, J. B. *Theories of Organizational Behaviour*, Holt, Rinehart and Winston (1980), Chapter 1.
82 Crainer, S. *Key Management Ideas: The thinkers who changed the management world*, Third edition, Financial Times Prentice Hall (1998), p. xi.
83 For a critical account on competing views about organisation theory and its applications, see: Perrow, C. *Complex Organizations*, Second edition, Scott, Foresman (1979). For a discussion of British and American ideas on conceiving and selling management theory, see: Foster, G. 'Management's Missing Ideas', *Management Today*, March 1980, pp. 72–5, 152–6.
84 Crainer, S. 'That Was The Idea That Was', *Management Today*, May 1997, pp. 18–19.
85 Crainer, S. 'The Rise of Guru Scepticism', *Management Today*, March 1997, pp. 48–52.
86 Flores, G. N. and Utley, D. R. 'Management Concepts in Use – a 12-year Perspective', *Engineering Management Journal*, vol. 12, no. 3, September 2000, pp. 11–17.
87 Stern, S. 'Guru Guide', *Management Today*, October 2001, p. 87.
88 Kraemer, K. Dedrick, J. and Yamashiro, S. 'Refining and Extending the Business Model with Information Technology: Dell Computer Corporation', in *The Information Society*, 2000, vol. 16, pp. 5–21.
89 Visit any of the Dell direct-order websites to see how this operates; in the UK the address is www.dell.co.uk. The corporate address with wider company information is at www.dell.com.
90 *Fortune*, 22 February 2005.
91 Lee, L. 'Dell: Facing up to Past Mistakes' Business Week On-line, 19 June 2006, www.businessweek.com [accessed July 2006].
92 Jeff Jarvis' blog is at www.buzzmachine.com.
93 BBC News website 'Dell to Employ 50% More in India', 30 January 2006, news.bbc.co.uk [accessed July 2006].
94 www.dellone2one.com.
95 Allison, K. and Nuttall, C. 'Dell shares tumble after warning over sales', FT online, 21 July 2006.
96 'The Soul of Dell' can be found at the Dell website [accessed 23 July 2006].
97 Dell's 'Code of Conduct' also at the Dell website [accessed 23 July 2006].
98 'Tell Dell' is described in the recruitment pages of the Dell website [accessed 23 July 2006].

THE NATURE AND CONTEXT OF ORGANISATIONS

> **In the final resort, it is vital that we understand what organization is, what it does, and the grounds on which it can be justified because it is not just a means to achieving better economic performance but also exerts a profound influence on the societies in which we live ...The form of organization we employ transports values back into society and carries a message about how to treat other people.**
>
> **John Child** – chair of Commerce University of Birmingham),
> *Organization: Contemporary principles and practices*, Blackwell Publishing (2005), p. 399

Applications of organisational behaviour and the process of management take place not in a vacuum but within the context of a particular organisational setting and environment. The organisation is a complex social system and is the sum of many interrelated variables. It is important to understand the main features which affect the structure, management and functioning of the work organisation. The manager also needs to recognise the role of the organisation within the broader social context and in influencing the lives of its members.

Learning outcomes

After completing this chapter you should be able to:

- explain the perspectives of the organisation, and basic components of an organisation;
- distinguish alternative types and classifications of organisations, and relate different organisations to these classifications;
- examine the organisation in terms of an open systems model;
- explain the nature and importance of the informal organisation;
- review the sources and impact of organisational conflict;
- explore the role of organisations in terms of the work/life balance;
- assess the nature and impact of stress at work.

Critical reflection

The activities of management take place within an organisational setting. No two organisations are the same and managers are concerned only with what takes place in their own unique organisational environment. Do you believe generalised models or theories of organisations serve any useful purpose?

PERSPECTIVES OF THE ORGANISATION

Organisations in one form or another have always been an integral feature of human civilisation. Although the origins of modern organisations can be traced back thousands of years, they evolve continually and the organisations of today are clearly very different. The beginning of the 20th century with the emergence of large corporate entities, and the work of writers such as Frederick Taylor on scientific management and Max Weber on bureaucracy, drew attention to the importance of the work organisation.[1]

All **organisations** have some function to perform. They exist in order to achieve objectives and to provide satisfaction for their members. Organisations enable objectives to be achieved that could not be achieved by the efforts of individuals on their own. It must be remembered that organisations are structures of people. Through co-operative action, members of an organisation can provide a synergistic effect. Organisations are an integral part of society involving both public and private sectors. For example, in their discussion of the new public services, Farnham and Horton define organisations as:

> *... social constructs created by groups in society to achieve specific purposes by means of planned and co-ordinated activities. These activities involve using human resources to act in association with other inanimate resources in order to achieve the aims of the organisation.*[2]

Common factors in organisations

There are, then, many different types of organisations which are set up to serve a number of purposes and to meet a variety of needs. Organisations come in all forms, shapes and sizes. Not only are there many different types of organisations, there is some suggestion that cultural differences in countries can reflect different conceptions of what actually is an organisation.[3] However, despite the differences, there are at least three common factors in any organisation:

- people
- objectives
- structure.

It is the interaction of **people** in order to achieve **objectives** which forms the basis of an organisation. Some form of **structure** is needed by which people's interactions and efforts are channelled and co-ordinated. To which we can add a fourth factor:

- management.

Some process of **management** is required by which the activities of the organisation, and the efforts of its members, are directed and controlled towards the pursuit of objectives. The actual effectiveness of the organisation will be dependent upon the quality of its people, its objectives and structure, and the resources available to it. The interrelationship of people, objectives and structure, together with the efficient use of available non-human and human resources, will determine the success or failure of the organisation and the extent of its effectiveness (*see* Figure 3.1).

Figure 3.1 Common factors in organisations

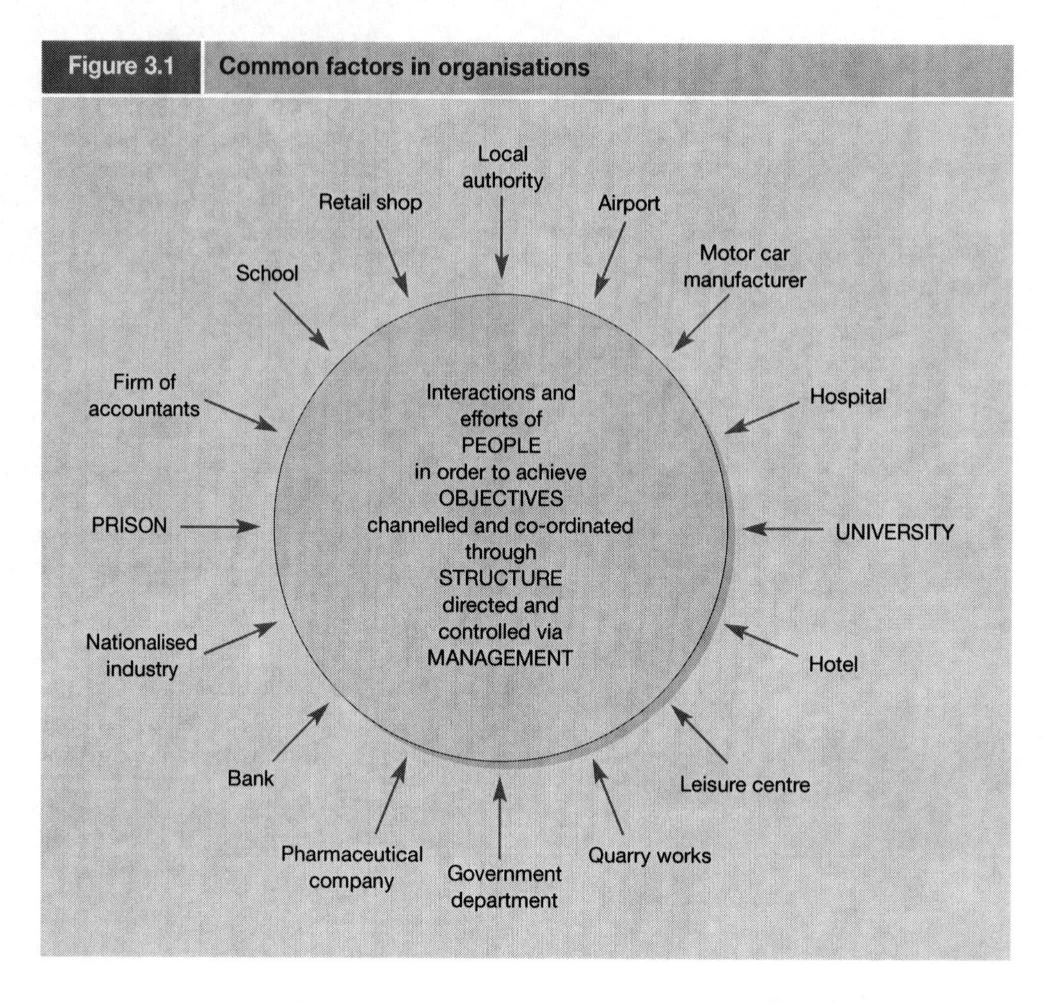

Among the variety of approaches to organisation theory, *Watson* refers to one which stresses three common aspects of organisational life:

- the importance of the creative, critical and situation-defining characteristics of the individuals who make up the organisation;
- the varieties of interests and goals among individuals and groups in the organisation, and the emphasis on conflict and political behaviour; and
- the interactions between the organisation and the general environment, and recognition that organisations make their environment as much as it makes them.[4]

Differences in applications

Despite these common factors, the structure, management and functioning of these organisations will all vary because of differences in the nature and type of the organisation, their respective goals and objectives, and the behaviour of the people who work in them. Let us now consider just two types of organisations towards the opposite ends of a possible continuum – say a maximum security prison and a university largely concerned with research – as a framework on which to focus attention. We can appreciate readily that although both types of organisation will be concerned with the basic activities of organisation and management, their goals and objectives, actual procedures and methods of operation, structure, systems and style of management, and orientation and behaviour of members will differ considerably (*see* Figure 3.2).

Figure 3.2 The nature of organisations

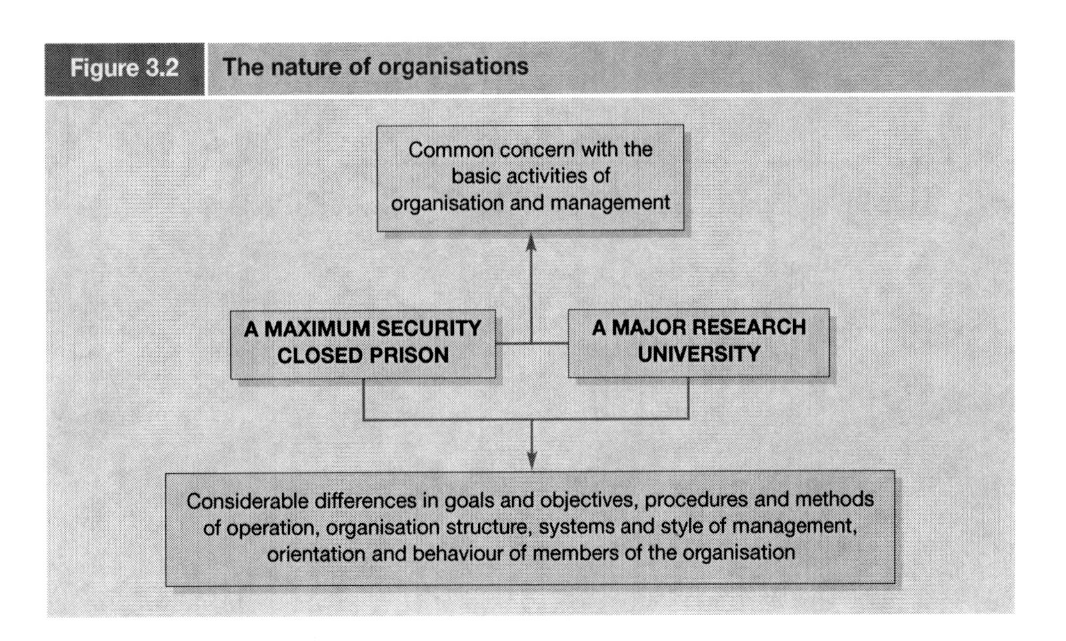

THE FORMAL ORGANISATION

The formal organisation can be distinguished from the informal organisation (which is discussed later in this chapter) – the difference between them is a feature of the degree to which they are structured.

A **formal organisation** has been defined by *Schein* as:

> *the planned co-ordination of the activities of a number of people for the achievement of some common, explicit purpose or goal, through division of labor and function, and through a hierarchy of authority and responsibility.*[5]

An organisation is a pattern of roles and a blueprint for their co-ordination. The object of co-ordination is activities, not people. The formal organisation can exist independently of the membership of particular individuals.

The formal organisation is:

- deliberately planned and created;
- concerned with the co-ordination of activities;
- hierarchically structured with stated objectives; and
- based on certain principles such as the specification of tasks, and defined relationships of authority and responsibility.

An organisation chart, for example, gives a representation of the formal structure. Other examples of the formal organisation are rules and regulations, policy manuals, standing orders and job descriptions (*see* Figure 3.9 on p. 91).

The organisation as a coalition

The formal organisation can be seen as a coalition of individuals with a number of sub-coalitions.[6] Membership of the coalition will be dependent upon the type of organisation but could include, for example, managers, administrators, workers, elected representatives, appointed officials, volunteers, shareholders, suppliers, trade union officials, leaders of interest groups, customers, clients, patrons, donors, specialists, consultants and representatives of external agencies.

It is difficult to define specific, permanent boundaries for an organisational coalition. However, by focusing on participants over a given period, or participants concerned with particular decision-making processes, it is possible to identify the main members of a coalition. Strategies adopted by particular sectional interests or sub-coalitions will sometimes be part of the formal organisation structure – for instance, in the pursuit of manifest managerial goals – and will sometimes be related to the informal structure – for example, heads of department vying with each other for limited resources, or workers indulging in restrictive practices.

BASIC COMPONENTS OF AN ORGANISATION

Any organisation can be described, broadly, in terms of an operating component and an administrative component.[7]

- The **operating component** comprises the people who actually undertake the work of producing the products or providing the services.
- The **administrative component** comprises managers and analysts and is concerned with supervision and co-ordination.

Developing this description, we can analyse the work organisation in terms of five basic components: the operational core, operational support, organisational support, top management and middle management (*see* Figure 3.3.).

- The **operational core** is concerned with direct performance of the technical or productive operations and the carrying out of actual task activities of the organisation – for example, people putting together parts on an assembly line, teaching in a classroom, treating a patient, cooking meals in a hotel, serving in a bank, repairing a hole in the road.
- **Operational support** is concerned indirectly with the technical or productive process but closely related to the actual flow of operational work – for example, people working in quality control, work study, progress planning, storekeeping, works maintenance, technical services.
- **Organisational support** is concerned with provision of services for the whole organisation, including the operational core, but which are usually outside the actual flow of operational work – for example, people working in personnel, medical services, canteen, management accounting, office services.

Figure 3.3 Five basic components of an organisation

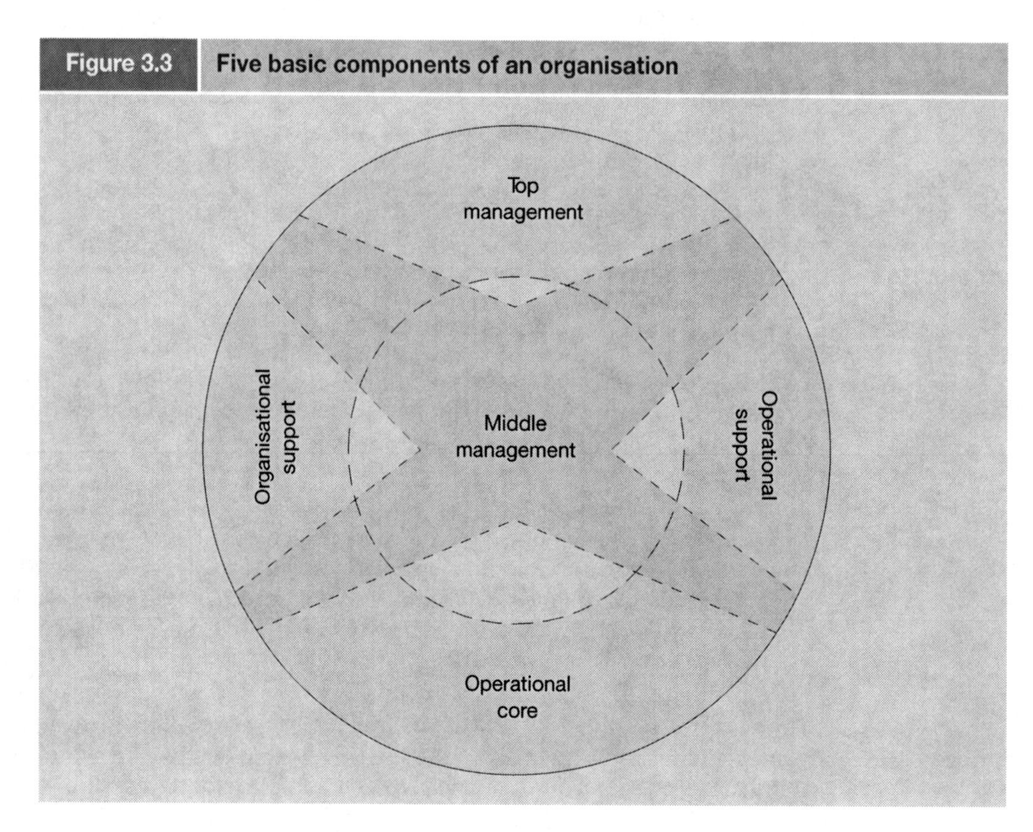

- **Top management** is concerned with broad objectives and policy, strategic decisions, the work of the organisation as a whole and interactions with the external environment – for example, managing director, governors, management team, chief executive, board of directors, council members.
- **Middle management** is concerned with co-ordination and integration of activities and providing links with operational support staff and organisational support staff, and between the operational core and top management.

PRIVATE AND PUBLIC SECTOR ORGANISATIONS

Organisations can, traditionally, be distinguished in terms of two generic groups:

- private enterprise organisations; and
- public sector organisations.

The distinction can be made on the basis of ownership and finance, and the profit motive. **Private enterprise organisations** are owned and financed by individuals, partners or shareholders in a joint stock company and are accountable to their owners or members. They vary widely in nature and size, and the type and scope of goods and services provided. The main aim is of a *commercial* nature such as profit, return on capital employed, market standing or sales level.

Public sector organisations are created by government and include, for example, municipal undertakings and central government departments, which do not have profit as their goal. Municipal undertakings such as local authorities are 'owned' by the council tax payers and ratepayers and financed by council taxes, rates, government grants, loans and charges for certain services. Central government departments are 'state owned' and financed by funds granted by parliament. Public sector organisations have political purposes and do not distribute profits. Any surplus of revenue over expenditure may be reallocated through improved services or reduced charges. The main aim is a *service* to and the *well-being of the community*.

> *How well our public services are operating, how effectively they are meeting the needs of those they serve, and how they are delivering those services are all questions that we need to ask. We all need to be confident that public money, our money, is being well spent and is achieving the results that we, the public, require.*
>
> Robert Coffey, 'The Service Principle'[8]

Privatisation

The extent of the state ownership of public sector operations, or of their '**privatisation**', and the balance between commercial and social interests is determined by the government of the day. In recent years there has been a vigorous policy of creating freedom from state control and the transfer of business undertakings to private hands (privatisation).

There are other public sector organisations whose aims involve both a commercial interest and a service interest. Nationalised industries such as the postal service at present run as public corporations with autonomy on day-to-day management, a degree of commercial freedom but with ultimate government control in the national interest. These public corporations are required to make efficient use of their resources by ensuring a given minimum rate of return on their investments and to charge prices based on the actual cost of supplying goods or services to certain groups of consumers. However, provision may also be made for certain activities to be undertaken on social grounds as a service to the community even though these activities might be run at a financial loss.

There have been increasing moves to encourage contracting-out of certain local authority services and putting them to compulsory competitive tender (CCT) and a greater degree of competition has also been introduced. The exposure to competition and demands for economical and high-quality service have prompted local authorities to replace administration with business management.[9] (Management in private and public sector organisations is discussed in Chapter 11.)

Not-for-profit organisations

The increasing scale of privatisation and the blurring of commercial interests and social interests have led to an alternative classification of organisations:

- **profit**; and those clearly
- **not-for-profit**.

Not-for-profit organisations include on the one hand charities, private societies and most religious organisations, and on the other hand National Health Service hospitals, universities, prisons, and most government and local authority departments. However, even in not-for-profit, public sector organisations there has been increased government pressure to ensure cost-effectiveness, investment by private sector involvement, and efficiency and economy in their operations.

The same blurring of distinctions can also be seen in the case of charities. For example, *Arnott* points out that there is very little about the 21st-century charity which is straightforward and they exist in a highly complex context.

> *The old distinctions between private, public and not-for-profit sectors have been blurred as charities have taken on an ever-increasing role in the delivery of public services. Tough competition for funds and growing public scrutiny have led many charities to adopt practices once more commonly associated with the commercial sector.*[10]

The private–public interface

Smith points out that although the private–public sector divide is part of the British economic and political landscape, the divisions are being broken down and moves between the two sectors – in both directions – are becoming more frequent. Business people are being introduced to the public sector in an unprecedented way and bringing their expertise to bear on efficiency across Whitehall.[11]

Rose and Lawton also suggest that the extent of privatisation, the introduction of so-called business styles of management and the development of an intense competitive performance culture have all served to challenge the traditional concept of a public sector. 'Privatisation and quasi-privatisation, in the form of contracting out and agency provision, have meant an increasing interface with non-public-sector organisations. Part of the rationale for this development is that these organisations have expertise and competencies which are not as well developed in the public sector. This has facilitated the transfer of technologies such as business process re-engineering and the business excellence model.'[12]

However, in spite of the fashion for applying private sector techniques in government, Sir David Wright refers to the difficult issues which remain about the way government performs and delivers its services. The challenge of management change has shifted to the public sector with the call for improved delivery of public services. In the private sector there is the bottom line of follow the money or achieve the sale or deal. But in government the link between inputs and outcomes remains hard to establish and the challenge is aggravated by the inability to focus activity on a small number of immediately realisable targets. As a function of the democratic process, government departments are responsible for a large number of activities and are subject to political initiatives, both of which can leach valuable resources and affect any assessment of how private sector techniques can be applied.[13]

PRODUCTION AND SERVICE ORGANISATIONS

Another major distinction is arguably between production and service organisations. Compared with 'production' industries, services tend to display a number of characteristic features, including the following.

- The consumer is a participant in the service process. This requires particular attention to the surroundings and characteristics of the service operations.
- Services cannot be stored, they are time perishable and if they are not used they are likely to be wasted. For example, the income lost from a hotel room unsold on one day is lost for ever.
- Unlike physical products, services are less tangible and more difficult to explain or communicate. Benefits derived from services tend to be associated with feelings and emotions.
- In service operations work activities are people-oriented and the characteristics of the workforce are particularly important in determining organisational effectiveness.
- Measurement of output is difficult and there is unlikely to be a single, important criterion by which to measure effective performance.[14]

Different from other industries

To what extent, then, are service industries any different from other industries? According to *Levitt*, it is only in a matter of degree:

> *Purveyors of service, for their part, think that they and their problems are fundamentally different from other businesses and their problems. They feel that service is people-intensive, while the rest of the economy is capital-intensive. But these distinctions are largely spurious. There are no such things as service industries. There are only industries whose service components are greater or less than those of other industries. Everybody is in service.*[15]

Other writers such as *Macdonald*, however, maintain that service organisations are different. 'Product quality and service quality are the same inasmuch as they apply to the results of different activities. There are, however, some fundamental differences in the organisation of an operation to provide products and services. There are also intrinsic differences between products and services.'[16](*See* Table 3.1.)[17]

Table 3.1 Differences between products and services

Product	Service
The customer receives a tangible product in the form of goods which can be seen and touched	The customer receives an intangible service which may or may not satisfy
The goods remain with the customer	Services are consumed at the moment of delivery
The production and delivery of goods are usually separated	Production, delivery and consumption of services are often at the same time
Few producers deal with customers	Most producers deal with customers
The customer is rarely involved with production	The customer is often closely involved with production
Goods can be serviced	Services have already been consumed and cannot be serviced
Goods are subject to liability but the producer has more opportunity to ameliorate the effect on the customer and thus the financial penalty	Services which do not meet the requirements are difficult to replace – the financial impact is usually total
Goods can be purchased to store in inventory to satisfy the customer's needs	Services cannot be stored but must still be available on customer demand
Goods can be transported to the point of sale	Some services are transportable (e.g. information through communication lines) but most require the transportation of the service provider
The quality of goods is relatively easy for customers to evaluate	The quality of services is more dependent on subjective perception and expectation
Goods are often technically complex – the customer therefore feels more reliant on the producer	Services appear less complex – the customer therefore feels qualified to hassle the producer

Source: Macdonald, J., 'Service is different', *The TQM Magazine*, vol. 6, no. 1, 1994, p. 6. Reproduced with permission from Emerald Publishing Group Limited.

Critical reflection

The basic components of organisations are the same and all organisations are concerned with the effective management of people in order to achieve their goals and objectives. To what extent therefore is there any meaningful difference between private enterprise and public sector organisations or between production and service organisations?

TYPES OF AUTHORITY AND ORGANISATIONS

In one of the earliest studies of formal organisations, *Weber* distinguished three types of authority: **traditional**, **charismatic** and **legal–rational**.[18] These types of authority are based on the form of control regarded as legitimate by subordinates and their acceptance of the power of superiors. The three types of authority relate to different types of organisations.

- In **traditional organisations**, authority is legitimised by custom and a longstanding belief in the natural right to rule, or is possessed by traditional ('proper') procedure. Examples would be the authority of the Pope, kings or queens or a paternalistic employer.
- In **charismatic organisations**, authority is legitimised by belief in the personal qualities of the leader; authority is based on the leader's strength of personality and inspiration. Winston Churchill might be quoted as an example. The practical need for some routine, for procedures and systems and for economic support means that if the movement is to continue it must become organised. On the impending demise of the charismatic leader the movement might collapse unless a 'legitimate' heir is found. This process tends to transform a charismatic organisation into either a traditional organisation or a bureaucratic organisation.
- In **bureaucratic organisations**, authority is based on the acceptance of the law of formal rules and procedures, and on impersonal principles. There is a legal–rational authority which stems from hierarchical position in the organisation and not from personality. Examples are the armed forces and the authority of government ministers or a college principal.

The concept of legal–rational authority is of most interest to us because most business organisations, particularly large-scale ones, tend to be of the bureaucratic type of structure, although there are variations in degree. Bureaucracy, as applying to certain structural features of organisation, is the most dominant type of formal organisation.

THE CLASSIFICATION OF ORGANISATIONS

In order to relate the study of management and organisational behaviour to one particular type of organisation as distinct from another, it is necessary to group similar types of organisations together. This enables generalisations to be made on the basis of certain characteristic features of organisations within a particular grouping. Organisations can be distinguished by, for example, their nature and type, goods or services provided, size, aims and objectives, and the people who are employed by or who work in them. Organisations can, therefore, be classified in a number of ways and different writers have emphasised particular features of organisations.

Classification by major purpose

A common classification of organisations is by their major purpose. This leads to a distinction between, for example:

- business firms (**economic organisations**);
- armies, trade unions and police forces (**protective organisations**);
- clubs and societies (**associative organisations**);

- local authorities and hospitals (**public service organisations**); and
- churches (**religious organisations**).

Further distinctions could be made, for example, into political organisations, educational organisations, military organisations and voluntary organisations.

Such a distinction tends to lack refinement and not all organisations fit simply into one classification. Many universities combine research with teaching. Some hospitals are concerned as much with training and/or research as with treatment of patients. One could debate the main purpose of a prison: is it, for example, corrective, protective, penal or educational? The main purpose of a trade union is seen, presumably, as protection of the interests of its members through their wages and working conditions, but many trade unions also have strong social, educational and political interests.

Many organisations serve more than one goal, but although they are multi-purpose organisations it is usually possible to identify one predominant goal (or purpose) by which the organisation can be classified, however crude this classification may be. It is of interest, however, to note the comment by *Etzioni* that:

> *To the extent that such things can be measured, it appears that many multi-purpose organisations tend to serve each of their goals separately and all of them together more effectively and efficiently than single-purpose organisations of the same category.*[19]

PRIME BENEFICIARY OF THE ORGANISATION

Blau and Scott propose a classification on the basis of the prime beneficiary.[20] Four groups of people involved in a relationship with any organisation are categorised into:

- the members, or rank-and-file participants;
- the owner or managers of the organisation;
- the clients or, more generally, the 'public-in-contact' who are technically 'outside' the organisation yet have regular direct contact with it;
- the public at large – that is, the members of the society in which the organisation operates.

Organisations are then classified on the basis of who benefits – that is, which of the four categories is the prime beneficiary of its operations. Four types of organisation are identified on this basis:

- **mutual-benefit associations**, where the prime beneficiary is the membership, such as political parties, trade unions and professional associations;
- **business concerns**, where the owners are the prime beneficiaries, such as industrial and other firms privately owned and operated for profit;
- **service organisations**, where the client group is the main beneficiary, such as hospitals, schools and welfare agencies;
- **commonweal organisations**, where the prime beneficiary is the public at large, such as central government departments, the armed services and the police.

Problems associated with each type of organisation

It is emphasised that the prime beneficiary is not necessarily the only beneficiary. Each of the various groups which make a contribution to an organisation do so only in return for certain benefits received.

Blau and Scott suggest that special problems are associated with each type of organisation.

- In **mutual-benefit organisations** the main problem is that of providing for participation and control by the membership and of maintaining internal democracy.
- In **business concerns** the central problem is that of maximising operational efficiency in a competitive environment.
- In **service organisations** the problem is reconciling conflict between professional service to clients and administrative procedures.
- In **commonweal organisations** the important problem is ensuring democratic procedures by which they are held accountable to the public for their actions.

PRIMARY ACTIVITY OF THE ORGANISATION

It is not easy to find a comprehensive classification into which all organisations can be simply and satisfactorily categorised; a degree of generalisation, assumption and qualification is required. An alternative form of classification is provided by *Katz and Khan*. Their classification is based on 'genotypic (first-order) factors' and on 'second-order factors'.[21] In terms of the genotypic function, which is the primary activity of the organisation as a sub-system within the larger society, there are four broad types of organisations:

- **productive or economic** – concerned with the creation of wealth, the manufacture of goods, and the provision of services for the public;
- **maintenance** – for example, schools and churches, concerned with the socialisation of people to fulfil roles in other organisations and in society;
- **adaptive** – for example, research establishments, concerned with the pursuit of knowledge and the development and testing of theory;
- **managerial or political** – for example, government departments, trade unions and pressure groups. These are concerned with adjudication, co-ordination and control of physical and human resources and other sub-systems.

Object-moulding or people-moulding

Organisations can, then, be described in terms of second-order factors. Among other things these factors relate to structure; the system of intrinsic or extrinsic rewards to attract and retain members and to achieve satisfactory performance from them; and the nature of the throughput – the transformation or processing of objects or the moulding of people as the end product of the organisation. A distinction can be made between

- object-moulding organisations, and
- people-moulding organisations.

Object-moulding organisations are concerned with physical or material objects as the nature of work being carried out – for example, a manufacturing plant, a car plant or an oil company. **People-moulding organisations** are concerned with human beings as the basis of the nature of work being carried out – for example, a school or a leisure centre. In people-moulding organisations a further distinction can be made between

- people-processing organisations – for example, an employment agency or a social security benefit office, and
- people-changing organisations – for example, a mental hospital or an open prison.

THE ORGANISATION AS AN OPEN SYSTEM

We have seen that organisations differ in many important respects, but they also share common features. By adopting the systems view of organisations, we can identify principles and prescriptions of organisation and management that apply to business organisations in general. Differences in the application and operation of these principles and prescriptions as between one business organisation and another is largely a matter only of degree and emphasis. Organisations can be viewed as open systems which take inputs from the environment (outputs from other systems) and through a series of activities transform or convert these inputs into outputs (inputs to other systems) to achieve some objective (*see* Figure 3.4).

In terms of this **open systems model** the business organisation, for example, takes in resources such as people, finance, raw materials and information from its environment, transforms or converts these and returns them to the environment in various forms of outputs such as goods produced, services provided, completed processes or procedures in order to achieve certain goals such as profit, market standing, level of sales or consumer satisfaction.

Figure 3.4 The open systems model of organisations

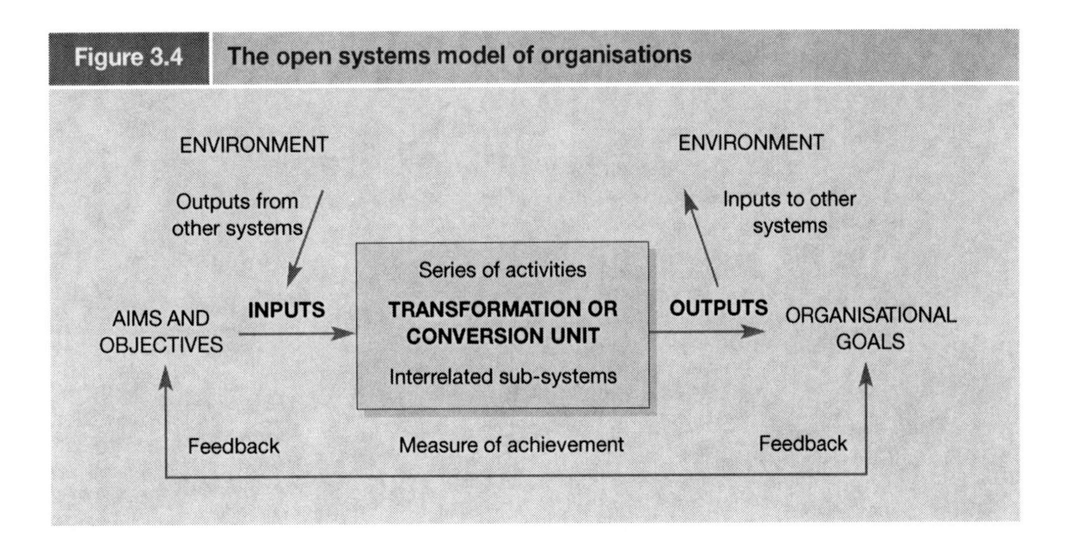

A common point of reference

There are, of course, differences in the activities and methods of operation of the various forms of business organisations. There will also be differences between business organisations of the same type – for example, in relation to their size and scale of activities. Using this systems model, the same form of analysis can be applied to all types of organisations. This provides a common point of reference and enables us to take a general approach to the study of organisations, to analyse them and to derive general principles and prescriptions.[22]

An example of the open systems model applied to the environment systems division of a major heating and ventilation company is given in Figure 3.5.

INTERACTIONS WITH THE ENVIRONMENT

The structure, management and functioning of an organisation are not only determined by internal considerations and choices but are also influenced strongly by a range of volatile, **external, environmental factors**. In order to be effective and maintain survival and growth, the organisation must respond to the opportunities and challenges, and the risks and limitations, presented by the external environment of which it is part. Changes in the environment will affect inputs, and changes in inputs will affect the transformation or conversion process and hence the outputs. The open systems approach views the organisation within its total environment and emphasises the importance of multiple channels of interaction.

The increasing rate of change in major environmental factors (technical, economic, social and governmental) has highlighted the need to study the total organisation and to adopt a systems approach. In addition to these major environmental factors, there is a multiplicity of constantly changing environmental influences that affect the operation of an organisation (*see* Figure 3.6). In order to understand the operations of organisations, and to improve organisational performance, it is necessary to consider how they achieve an internal and external balance and how they are able to adapt to changes in their environment and the demands placed upon them.[23]

Consider, for example, how the management and operation of a large comprehensive school might be affected by such external influences as government proposals for reform of education, changing demographic trends, the general economic climate, advances in information technology, changing views of the role of education in society, greater diversity of people in the catchment area, reports from Her Majesty's Inspectors, increased health and safety concerns, representations from employers' associations and trade unions, parent groups and equality campaigners.

Figure 3.5 An example of the open systems model

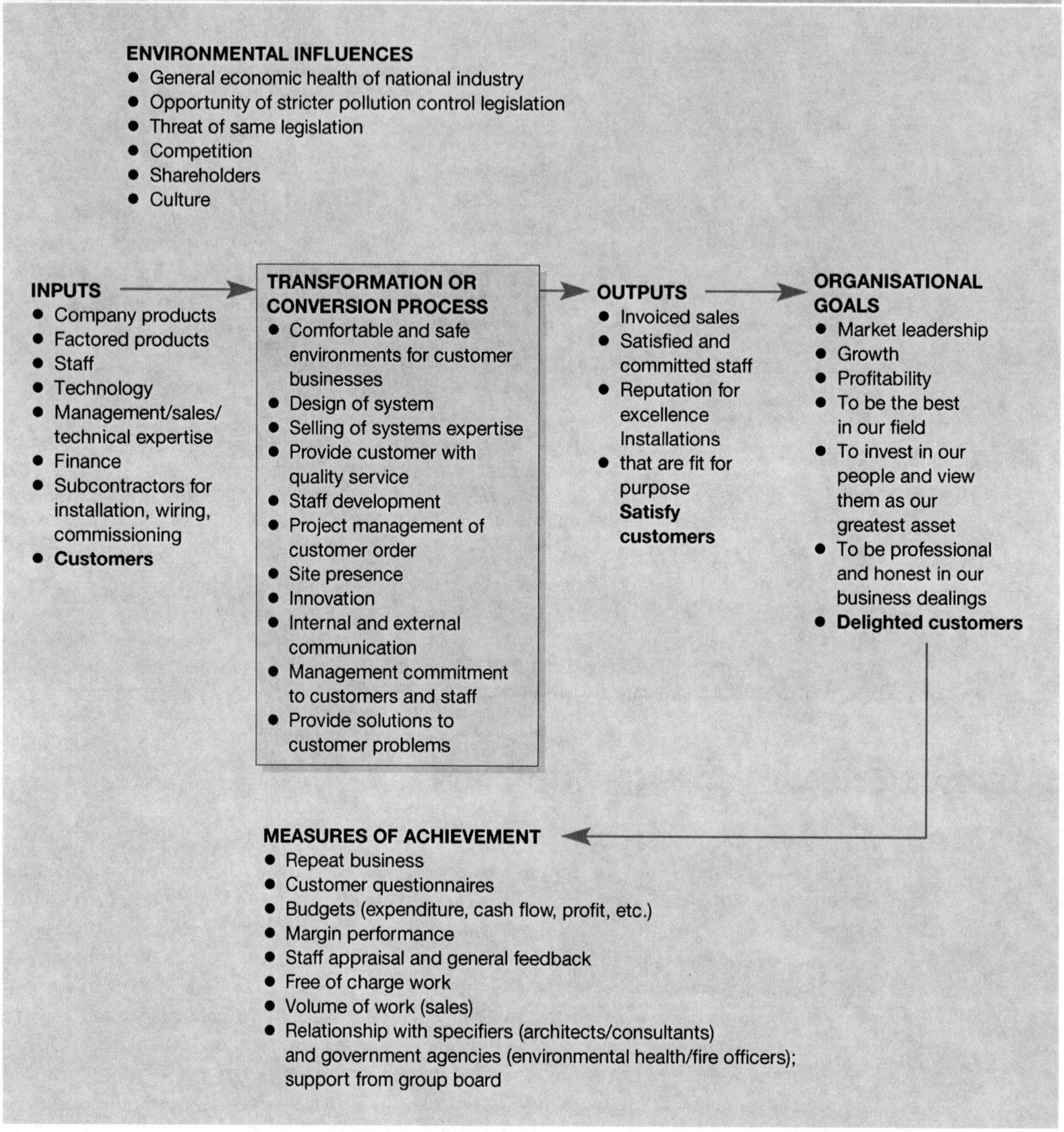

ENVIRONMENTAL INFLUENCES
- General economic health of national industry
- Opportunity of stricter pollution control legislation
- Threat of same legislation
- Competition
- Shareholders
- Culture

INPUTS →
- Company products
- Factored products
- Staff
- Technology
- Management/sales/ technical expertise
- Finance
- Subcontractors for installation, wiring, commissioning
- **Customers**

TRANSFORMATION OR CONVERSION PROCESS →
- Comfortable and safe environments for customer businesses
- Design of system
- Selling of systems expertise
- Provide customer with quality service
- Staff development
- Project management of customer order
- Site presence
- Innovation
- Internal and external communication
- Management commitment to customers and staff
- Provide solutions to customer problems

OUTPUTS →
- Invoiced sales
- Satisfied and committed staff
- Reputation for excellence Installations
- that are fit for purpose **Satisfy customers**

ORGANISATIONAL GOALS
- Market leadership
- Growth
- Profitability
- To be the best in our field
- To invest in our people and view them as our greatest asset
- To be professional and honest in our business dealings
- **Delighted customers**

MEASURES OF ACHIEVEMENT
- Repeat business
- Customer questionnaires
- Budgets (expenditure, cash flow, profit, etc.)
- Margin performance
- Staff appraisal and general feedback
- Free of charge work
- Volume of work (sales)
- Relationship with specifiers (architects/consultants) and government agencies (environmental health/fire officers); support from group board

PESTEL analysis Organisational performance and effectiveness will be dependent upon the successful management of the opportunities, challenges and risks presented by changes in the external environment. One popular technique for analysing the general environment is a **PESTEL analysis** – that is, Political, Economic, Socio-cultural, Technological, Environmental and Legal influences. As an example, *Lynch* presents the main issues that might be considered when undertaking a PESTEL analysis (*see* Figure 3.7).[24]

Figure 3.6 Environmental influences on the organisation

External influences are almost infinite in number and variety and no study could hope to consider them all. For students of business and for managers alike, the requirement is to recognise the complexity of the external environment and to pay greater attention to those influences which appear the most pertinent and pressing for the organisation in question, rather than to attempt to consider all possible contingencies.

I. Worthington and C. Britton, *The Business Environment*[25]

THE COMPARATIVE STUDY OF ORGANISATIONS

All organisations need clear aims and objectives that will determine the nature of inputs, the series of activities to achieve outputs and the realisation of organisational goals. Feedback about the performance of the system, and the effects of its operation on the environment, are measured in terms of achieving the aims and objectives.

Basic principles of organisation and management apply in any series of activities in any organisation. For example:

- attention must be given to the design of a suitable structure;
- the common elements of management – clarification of objectives, planning, organising, directing and control – apply to a greater or lesser extent in all cases;
- essential financial, legal, personnel and administrative functions must be carried out in all types of organisation.

These common features make possible the application of general principles of management and organisational behaviour (including, for example, in both a prison or a university) and the meaningful study of organisation theory.

While general principles and prescriptions apply to all organisations, differences in their aims and objectives, organisational goals and environmental influences will result in differences in the input–conversion–output process and in the series of activities involved in this process. The nature of inputs, the throughputs and the form of the outputs will emphasise

Figure 3.7 Checklist for a PESTEL analysis

Political future

- Political parties and alignments at local, national and European or regional trading-bloc level
- Legislation, e.g. on taxation and employment law
- Relations between government and the organisation (possibly influencing the preceding items in a major way and forming a part of future corporate strategy)
- Government ownership of industry and attitude to monopolies and competition

Socio-cultural future

- Shifts in values and culture
- Change in lifestyle
- Attitudes to work and leisure
- 'Green' environmental issues
- Education and health
- Demographic changes
- Distribution of income

Economic future

- Total GDP and GDP per head
- Inflation
- Consumer expenditure and disposable income
- Interest rates
- Currency fluctuations and exchange rates
- Investment, by the state, private enterprise and foreign companies
- Cyclicality
- Unemployment
- Energy costs, transport costs, communications costs, raw materials costs

Technological future

- Government and EU investment policy
- Identified new research initiatives
- New patents and products
- Speed of change and adoption of new technology
- Level of expenditure on R&D by organisation's rivals
- Developments in nominally unrelated industries that might be applicable

Environmental future

- 'Green' issues that affect the environment
- Level and type of energy consumed – renewable energy?
- Rubbish, waste and its disposal

Legal future

- Competition law and government policy
- Employment and safety law
- Product safety issues

Source: Lynch, R., *Corporate Strategy*, Fourth Edition, Financial Times Prentice Hall (2006), p. 84. Reprinted with permission of Pearson Education Ltd.

characteristic features of a particular organisation. These features highlight alternative forms of structure, management, methods of operation and behaviour of people employed by or working in different types of organisations.

THE ANALYSIS OF WORK ORGANISATIONS

Whatever the type or classification of organisations, the transformation or conversion of inputs into outputs is a common feature. Within the organisation (system) as a whole, each of the different transformation or conversion activities may themselves be viewed as separate **organisational sub-systems** with their own input–conversion–output process interrelated to, and interacting with, the other sub-systems.

The interrelationship and interdependence of the different parts of the system raise the question of the identification of these sub-systems. What are the boundaries that distinguish one sub-system from other sub-systems and from the system as a whole? In practice the boundaries are drawn at the discretion of the observer and sub-systems are identified according to the area under study. These sub-systems may be identified, therefore, in a number of ways, although there is a degree of similarity among the alternative models.

However these sub-systems are identified, it is the task of management to co-ordinate the sub-systems and to ensure that the activities of the organisation as a whole are directed towards the accomplishment of its goals and objectives. We can suggest, therefore, five main interrelated sub-systems as a basis for the analysis of work organisations (*see* Figure 3.8).

- **Task** – the goals and objectives of the organisation. The nature of inputs and outputs, and the work activities to be carried out in the transformation or conversion process.
- **Technology** – the manner in which the tasks of the organisation are carried out and the nature of work performance. The materials, systems and procedures, and equipment used in the transformation or conversion process.

Figure 3.8 Organisational sub-systems

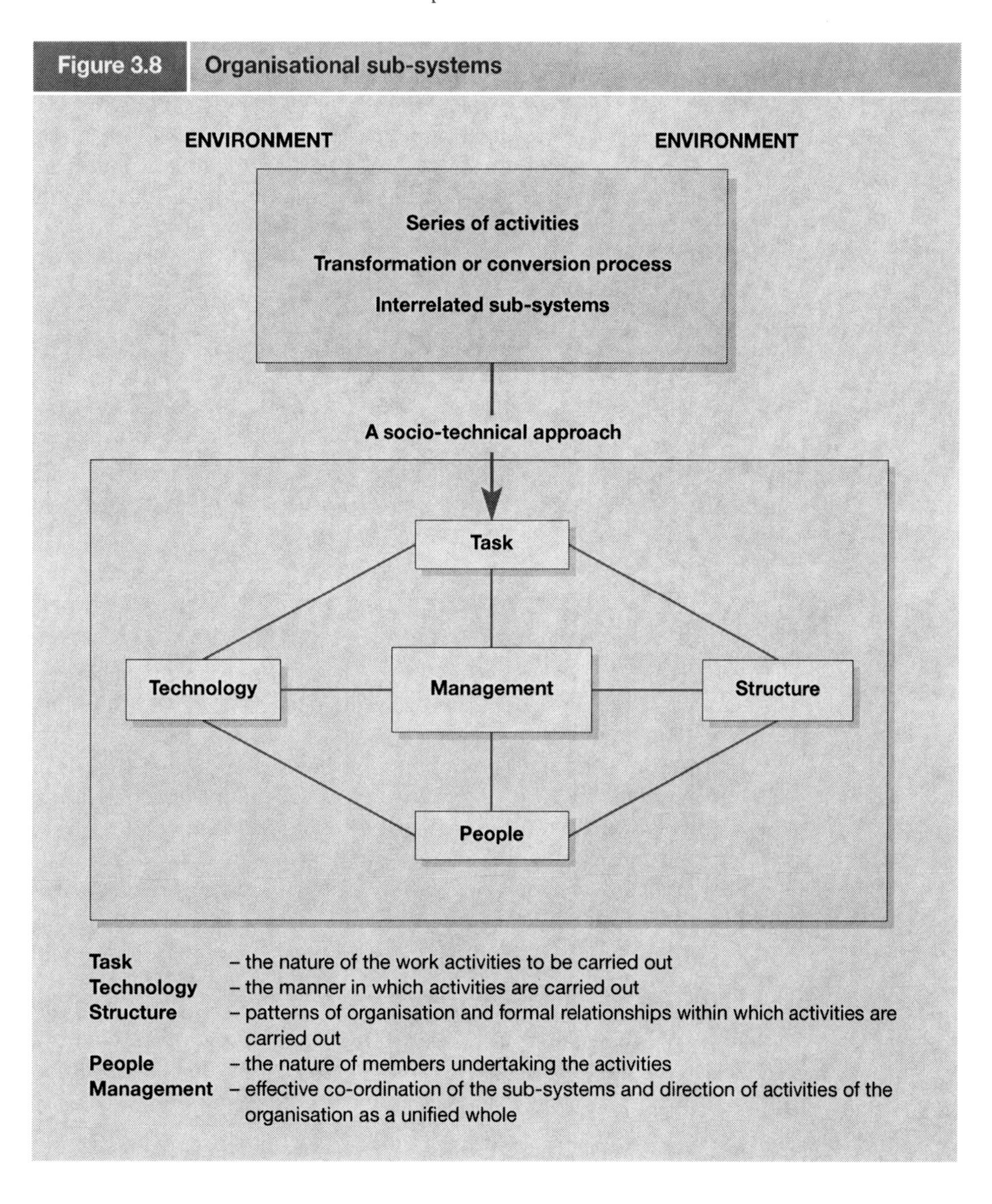

- **Structure** – patterns of organisation, lines of authority, formal relationships and channels of communication among members. The division of work and co-ordination of tasks by which the series of activities is carried out.
- **People** – the nature of the members undertaking the series of activities. For example, their attitudes, skills and attributes; needs and expectations; interpersonal relations and patterns of behaviour; group functioning and behaviour; informal organisation and styles of leadership.
- **Management** – co-ordination of task, technology, structure and people, and policies and procedures for the execution of work. Corporate strategy, direction of the activities of the organisation as a whole and its interactions with the external environment.

A broader view of the organisation's activities

The study of organisations as open systems serves to indicate both the common features and the main distinguishing features between different types of organisations. It provides a useful framework for the comparative study of organisations. The systems view of organisations enables managers to view their own organisation in perspective and to compare it in meaningful terms with other types of organisations. Managers cannot afford to take a narrow, blinkered view; they need to adopt a broader view and recognise the interrelationships between various activities and the effects that their actions and decisions have on other activities. The above framework of five main interrelated sub-systems – task, technology, structure, people and management – provides a useful basis for the analysis of organisational performance and effectiveness. Attention should be focused on the total work organisation and on the interrelationships between the range of variables which affect organisational performance.

Critical reflection

The traditional analysis of an organisation is usually based upon the departmental structure and whether individual departments are operating efficiently. Do you think this form of analysis is still relevant or does it lead only to blinkered sectional interests rather than to the interrelationships and co-ordination of sub-systems of the organisation as an integrated whole?

CONTINGENCY MODELS OF ORGANISATION

The analysis of organisational effectiveness requires an understanding of relationships within the organisation's structure, the interrelated sub-systems and the nature of its external environment.

Irrespective of the identification of sub-systems, the nature and scale of the series of activities involved in converting inputs to outputs will differ from one organisation to another in terms of the interrelationships between technology, structure, methods of operation and the nature of environmental influences. 'Contingency' models of organisation highlight these interrelationships and provide a further possible means of differentiation between alternative forms of organisation and management.

The contingency approach takes the view that there is no one best, universal form of organisation. There is a large number of variables, or situational factors, that influence organisational performance. Contingency models can be seen as an '*if–then*' form of relationship. *If* certain situational factors exist, *then* certain organisational and managerial variables are most appropriate. Managers can utilise these models to compare the structure and functioning of their own organisation. Contingency models are examined in Chapter 16.

THE INFORMAL ORGANISATION

Whatever the type or nature of an organisation or its formal structure, an **informal organisation** will always be present (*see* Figure 3.9). The informal organisation arises from the interaction of people working in the organisation, their psychological and social needs, and the development of groups with their own relationships and norms of behaviour, irrespective of those defined within the formal structure.

- The informal organisation is flexible and loosely structured.
- Relationships may be left undefined.
- Membership is spontaneous and with varying degrees of involvement.

Group relationships and norms of behaviour exist outside the official structure and the informal organisation may, therefore, be in conflict with the aims of the formal organisation. A summary of differences between the formal and the informal organisation is given in Table 3.2.

Functions of the informal organisation

The informal organisation can serve a number of important functions.

- It provides satisfaction of members' social needs and a sense of personal identity and belonging.
- It provides for additional channels of communication – for example, through the 'grapevine', information of importance to particular members is communicated quickly.

Figure 3.9 Formal and informal organisation

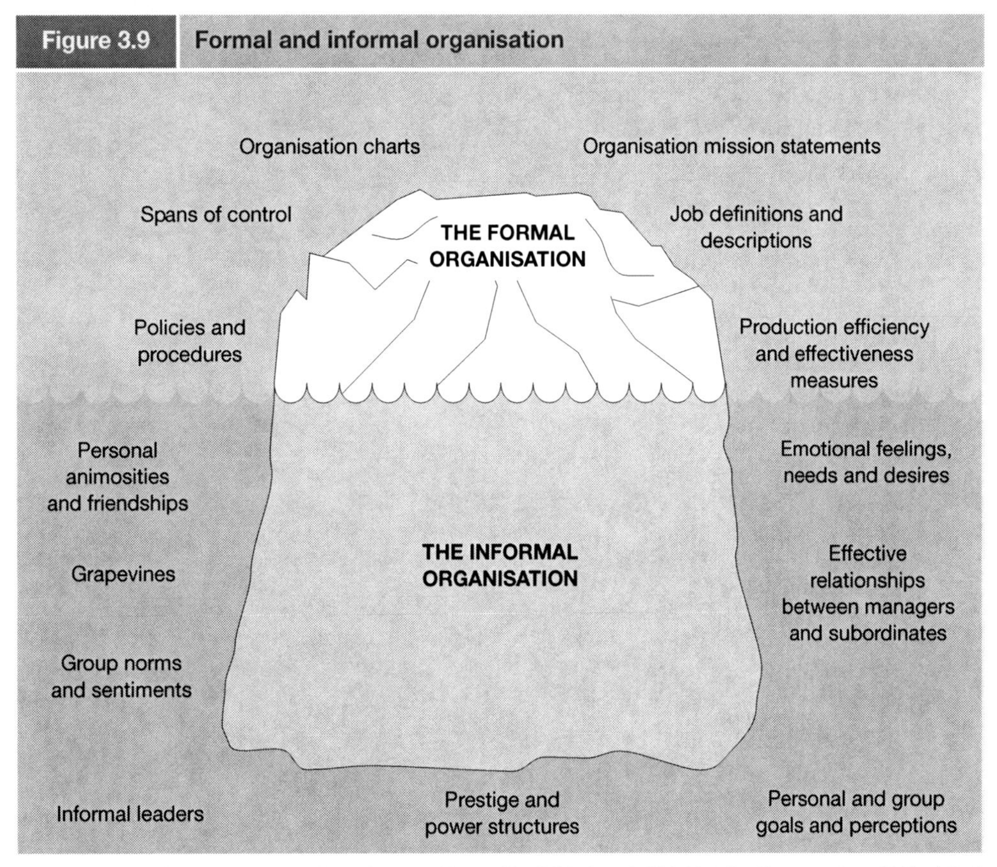

Source: Lysons, K., 'Organisational analysis', supplement to *Manager, The British Journal of Administrative Management*, no. 18, March/April (1997). Reproduced with permission of The Institute of Administrative Management.

- It provides a means of motivation – for example, through status, social interaction, variety in routine or tedious jobs, and informal methods of work.
- It provides a feeling of stability and security, and through informal 'norms' of behaviour can exercise a form of control over members.
- It provides a means of highlighting deficiencies or weaknesses in the formal organisation – for example, areas of duties or responsibilities not covered in job descriptions or outdated systems and procedures. The informal organisation may also be used when formal methods would take too long, or not be appropriate, to deal with an unusual or unforeseen situation.

Buying a coffee machine and water cooler could be the most important investments a company ever makes in its future. For it's at these social hubs of office life that the real business often gets done, as part of a casual chat or chance meeting.

Sue Law, 'Beyond the Water Cooler'[26]

Table 3.2 Comparison of the formal and the informal organisation

Characteristic	Formal organisation	Informal organisation
1 Structure		
A Origin	Planned	Spontaneous
B Rationale	Rational	Emotional
C Characteristics	Stable	Dynamic
2 Position terminology	Job	Role
3 Goals	Profitability or service to society	Member satisfaction
4 Influence		
A Base	Position	Personality
B Type	Authority	Power
C Flow	Top–down	Bottom–up
5 Control mechanisms	Threat of firing, demotion	Physical or social sanctions (norms)
6 Communication		
A Channels	Formal channels	Grapevine
B Networks	Well-defined, follow formal lines	Poorly defined, cut across regular channels
C Speed	Slow	Fast
D Accuracy	High	Low
7 Charting the organisation	Organisation chart	Sociogram
8 Miscellaneous		
A Individuals included	All individuals in work group	Only those 'acceptable'
B Interpersonal relations	Prescribed by job description	Arise spontaneously
C Leadership role	Assigned by organisation	Result of membership agreement
D Basis for interaction	Functional duties or position	Personal characteristics, ethnic background, status
E Basis for attachment	Loyalty	Cohesiveness

Source: Adapted from Gray, J. L. and Starke F. A., *Organizational Behavior: Concepts and Applications*, Fourth Edition, Merrill Publishing Company (1988), p. 432. Reproduced with permission from Pearson Education Inc.

Relationship between people and organisation

The overall effectiveness of the organisation will be affected both by sound structural design and by the individuals filling the various positions within the structure. Management will need to acknowledge the existence of the informal organisation that arises from the interactions of people working in the organisation. The operation of the organisation and actual working arrangements will be influenced by the style of management, the personalities of members and the informal organisation. These factors may lead to differences between the formal structure of the organisation and what happens in practice. *Stewart* found the relationship between people and organisation to be reciprocal.

> *People modify the working of the formal organization, but their behaviour is also influenced by it. It may make demands on them which they find an undue strain, so that they seek ways of modifying these pressures. The method of work organization can determine how people relate to one another, which may affect both their productivity and their morale. Managers, therefore, need to be conscious of the ways in which methods of work organization may influence people's attitudes and actions. Before behaviour is put down to individual or group cussedness, managers should look for its possible organizational causes.*[27]

Building an organisation involves more than concern for structure, methods of work and technical efficiency. The hallmark of many successful business organisations is the attention given to the human element; to the development of a culture which helps to create a feeling of belonging, commitment and satisfaction.[28] Structure must be designed, therefore, so as to maintain the balance of the socio-technical system and the effectiveness of the organisation as a whole. Attention must be given to the interactions between both the structural and technological requirements of the organisation, and social factors and the needs and demands of the human part of the organisation.

The informal organisation, therefore, has an important influence on the morale, motivation, job satisfaction and performance of staff. It can provide members with greater opportunity to use their initiative and creativity in both personal and organisational development. Covert and informal activities may also have economic consequences for the organisation in terms of added values and/or costs that escape ordinary accounting procedures.[29] The importance and nature of groups, and reasons why people form into groups, both formal and informal, are discussed in Chapter 8.

ORGANISATIONAL CONFLICT

It might be expected that a healthy organisational climate would be reflected by complete harmony in working relationships and loyalty and common commitment to the goals and objectives of the organisation. This view of work organisations as 'happy families' is perhaps a worthwhile and creditable ideal and as such appears to be implied by a number of management writers.

Drucker makes the following point:

> *Any business enterprise must build a true team and weld individual efforts into a common effort. Each member of the enterprise contributes something different, but they must all contribute towards a common goal. Their efforts must all pull in the same direction, and their contributions must fit together to produce a whole – without gaps, without friction, without unnecessary duplication of effort ... The manager must know and understand what the business goals demand of him in terms of performance, and his superior must know what contribution to demand and expect of him – and must judge him accordingly. If these requirements are not met, managers are misdirected. Their efforts are wasted. Instead of teamwork, there is friction, frustration and conflict.*[30]

Such traditional views appear to imply a **unitary perspective** of the organisation. The organisation is viewed as an integrated and harmonious whole. Conflict is seen as a dysfunctional outcome and can be explained, for example, by poor communications, personality clashes or the work of agitators. But if one accepts the views of, for example, the social action writers and the idea of a **pluralistic approach** to work organisations, then conflict among competing sub-groups will be seen as inevitable. Conflict is seen as an inherent feature of organisations and induced, in part, by the very structure of the organisation. The pluralistic manager is more likely to accept that conflict in organisations requires careful handling and attempt to reconcile rival interests.

The radical perspective

The radical perspective is associated with the ideas of writers such as *Karl Marx* and the structuralist approach to organisations and management discussed in Chapter 2.[31] It challenges the traditional view of conflict and sees organisations in terms of the disparity in power and control. Conflict is a feature of the unequal nature of organisational life and a means of bringing about change.[32] Collective bargaining is not seen as particularly helpful in a system stacked against the workers. Conflict is a natural part of the class struggle. The design of organisation structure, management systems and the choice of technology all form part of the struggle for power and control within the work organisation.

According to the radical approach, the design of organisation structure, management systems and the choice and use of technology all form part of the struggle for power and control within the work organisation. Greater attention should be given to relationships between the formal and informal aspects of the organisation and the study of conflict between the needs of the individual and those of the organisation, and between workers and management.

CONTRASTING VIEWS OF CONFLICT

Most of us will understand what is commonly meant by organisational conflict and will be aware of its existence and effects. Conflict can be related to power and politics. Yet conflict is a term that can be defined and interpreted in a number of ways. For our purpose we can see conflict as behaviour intended to obstruct the achievement of some other person's goals. Conflict is based on the incompatibility of goals and arises from opposing behaviours. It can be viewed at the individual, group or organisation level. *Ackroyd and Thompson* use the term 'organizational misbehaviour' to refer to 'anything you do at work which you are not supposed to'. Management establish boundaries that distinguish acceptable and non-acceptable behaviour from employees. The actions of employees are then judged as falling one side or the other of these boundaries.[33]

Common definitions of conflict tend to be associated with negative features and situations which give rise to inefficiency, ineffectiveness or dysfunctional consequences. The traditional view of conflict is that it is bad for organisations. Conflict is perceived as disruptive and unnatural and represents a form of deviant behaviour that should be controlled and changed. Clearly, extreme cases of conflict in organisations can have very upsetting, or even tragic, consequences for some people and have adverse effects on organisational performance. Conflict situations can give rise to excessive emotional or physical stress.

Positive and negative outcomes

Conflict is not *necessarily* a bad thing, however. It can be seen as a 'constructive' force and in certain circumstances it can be welcomed or even encouraged. For example, it can be seen as an aid to incremental improvement in organisation design and functioning, and to the decision-making process. Conflict can be an agent for evolution, and for internal and external change. Properly identified and handled, it can help to minimise the destructive influences of the win–lose situation.

From a survey of practising managers, who reported that they spend approximately 20 per cent of their time dealing with conflict situations, *Schmidt* records a number of both positive and negative outcomes of conflict.[34] Positive outcomes include:

*situations could be changed if we could also view it as positive and manageable! What if we think of these situations as raising **questions of difference**? What if we were to make a shift away from blaming individuals and their personalities, recognizing instead that it is through normal human interaction that outward expressions of difference are produced?*[37]

THE SOURCES OF CONFLICT

Much has been written about the implications of conflict as a social process. Whilst recognising the importance of this debate, it is not the intention here to enter into a detailed discussion of the ideologies of conflict. The important point is not so much whether competing sub-groups and conflict are seen as inevitable consequences of organisation structure, but how conflict, when found to exist, is handled and managed.

There are many potential sources of organisational conflict, including the main ones summarised below.

- **Differences in perception**. We all see things in different ways. We all have our own, unique picture or image of how we see the 'real' world. Differences in perception result in different people attaching different meanings to the same stimuli. As perceptions become a person's reality, value judgements can be a potential major source of conflict. (The importance of perception is discussed in Chapter 6.)
- **Limited resources**. Most organisational resources are limited and individuals and groups have to fight for their share; for example, at the time of the allocation of the next year's budget or when cutbacks have to be made. The greater the limitation of resources, then usually the greater the potential for conflict. In an organisation with reducing profits or revenues, the potential for conflict is likely to be intensified.
- **Departmentalisation and specialisation**. Most work organisations are divided into departments with specialised functions. Because of familiarity with the manner in which they undertake their activities, managers tend to turn inwards and to concentrate on the achievement of their own particular goals. When departments need to co-operate, this is a frequent source of conflict. Differing goals and internal environments of departments are also a potential source of conflict. In *Woodward's* study of management organisation of firms in this country she comments on the bad relationships between accountants and other managers. One reason for this hostility was the bringing together of two quite separate financial functions.

  People concerned with works accounting tended to assume responsibility for end results that was not properly theirs; they saw their role as a controlling and sanctioning one rather than as a servicing and supportive one. Line managers resented this attitude and retaliated by becoming aggressive and obstructive.[38]

- **The nature of work activities**. Where the task of one person is dependent upon the work of others there is potential for conflict; for example, if a worker is expected to complete the assembly of a given number of components in a week but the person forwarding the part-assembled components does not supply a sufficient number on time. If reward and punishment systems are perceived to be based on keeping up with performance levels, then the potential for conflict is even greater. If the work of a department is dependent upon the output of another department, a similar situation could arise, especially if this situation is coupled with limited resources; for example, where the activities of a department, whose budget has been reduced below what is believed necessary to run the department efficiently, are interdependent with those of another department, which appears to have received a more generous budget allocation.
- **Role conflict**. A role is the expected pattern of behaviours associated with members occupying a particular position within the structure of the organisation. In practice, the manner in which people actually behave may not be consistent with their expected

- better ideas produced;
- people forced to search for new approaches;
- long-standing problems brought to the surface and resolved;
- clarification of individual views;
- stimulation of interest and creativity;
- a chance for people to test their capacities.

Negative outcomes include:

- some people felt defeated and demeaned;
- the distance between people increased;
- a climate of mistrust and suspicion developed;
- individuals and groups concentrated on their own narrow interests;
- resistance developed rather than teamwork;
- an increase in employee turnover.

Broad interpretation of conflict

The current view appears to recognise that conflict can be interpreted more broadly than in the traditional view. *Townsend* sees conflict as a sign of a healthy organisation – up to a point.

> *A good manager doesn't try to eliminate conflict; he tries to keep it from wasting the energies of his people ... If you're the boss and your people fight you openly when they think you're wrong – that's healthy. If your people fight each other openly in your presence for what they believe in – that's healthy. But keep all the conflict eyeball to eyeball.*[35]

A more recent view of conflict is the **interactionist perspective**, which believes that conflict is a positive force and necessary for effective performance. This approach encourages a minimum level of conflict within the group in order to encourage self-criticism, change and innovation, and to help prevent apathy or too great a tolerance for harmony and the status quo.[36]

Conflict, *per se*, is not necessarily good or bad but an inevitable feature of organisational life and should be judged in terms of its effects on performance. Even if organisations have taken great care to try to avoid conflict, it will still occur. Conflict will continue to emerge despite management attempts to suppress it.

Critical reflection

'Conflict should be accepted as a reality of management and organisational behaviour, and properly managed can be an energising and vitalising force within groups and the organisation.' Do you believe that managers should therefore be encouraged to invoke constructive conflict? Or do you think the negative aspects of conflict arguably outweigh the potential benefits?

Conflict and 'difficult people'

The idea of conflict as inevitable is discussed by *Irvine* who suggests that if you ask a group of managers about the nature and level they experience, the majority will tell you honestly that apart from the odd minor tiff, there is not much conflict about. There are, however, 'difficult people'.

> *Perhaps our reluctance to identify, and then directly address, conflict within organisations is based upon the widely held belief that conflict is inevitable, negative and unmanageable. There is a tendency to see conflict as a result of one person's personality. Conflict may be inevitable, but how dramatically*

pattern of behaviour. Problems of role incompatibility and role ambiguity arise from inadequate or inappropriate role definition and can be a significant source of conflict. (Role conflict is discussed in Chapter 8.)

- **Inequitable treatment**. A person's perception of unjust treatment, such as in the operation of personnel policies and practices, or in reward and punishment systems can lead to tension and conflict. For example, according to the equity theory of motivation (discussed in Chapter 7), the perception of inequity will motivate a person to take action to restore equity, including changes to inputs or outputs, or through acting on others.
- **Violation of territory**. People tend to become attached to their own 'territory' within work organisations; for example, to their own area of work, or kinds of clients to be dealt with, or to their own room, chair or parking space. Jealousy may arise over other people's territory – for example, size of room, company car, allocation of an assistant or other perks – through access to information or through membership of groups.[39] A stranger walking into a place of work can create an immediate feeling of suspicion or even resentment because people do not usually like 'their' territory entered by someone they do not know and whose motives are probably unclear to them.

  Ownership of territory may be **conferred formally**, for example by organisation charts, job descriptions or management decisions. It may be **established through procedures**, for example circulation lists or membership of committees. Or it may **arise informally**, for example through group norms, tradition or perceived status symbols. The place where people choose to meet can have a possible, significant symbolic value. For example, if a subordinate is summoned to a meeting in a manager's office this might be taken that the manager is signalling higher status. If the manager chooses to meet at the subordinate's place of work, or on neutral territory, this may be a signal that the manager wishes to meet the subordinate as an equal. If a person's territory is violated this can lead to the possibility of retaliation and conflict.
- **Environmental change**. Changes in an organisation's external environment, such as shifts in demand, increased competition, government intervention, new technology or changing social values, can cause major areas of conflict. For example, a fall in demand for, or government financial restrictions on, enrolments for a certain discipline in higher education can result in conflict for the allocation of resources. If the department concerned is a large and important one and led by a powerful head, there could be even greater potential for conflict.

  There are many other potential sources of organisational conflict, including:
  - **individual** – such as attitudes, personality characteristics or particular personal needs, illness or stress;
  - **group** – such as group skills, the informal organisation and group norms;
  - **organisation** – such as communications, authority structure, leadership style, managerial behaviour;
  - **the age gap** – *Hart* discusses how relationships between older employees and younger managers, where experience is on one side and power on the other, can lead to conflict.

  > *The problem for the inexperienced manager in conflict with an older employee is that it is all too easy to label someone 'difficult' rather than intelligently trying to explore the reasons behind their behaviour. If steps are not taken to improve the relationship both manager and employee can end up feeling threatened and undermined.*[40]

STRATEGIES FOR MANAGING CONFLICT

Although a certain amount of organisational conflict may be seen as inevitable, there are a number of ways in which management can attempt to avoid the harmful effects of conflict. Many of these ideas will be discussed in later chapters. The strategies adopted will vary according to the nature and sources of conflict outlined above.

- **Clarification of goals and objectives**. The clarification and continual refinement of goals and objectives, role definitions and performance standards will help to avoid misunderstandings and conflict. Focusing attention on superordinate goals, that are shared by the parties in conflict, may help to defuse hostility and lead to more co-operative behaviour.
- **Resource distribution**. Although it may not always be possible for managers to increase their allocated share of resources, they may be able to use imagination and initiative to help overcome conflict situations – for example, making a special case to higher management; greater flexibility to transfer funds between budget headings; delaying staff appointments in one area to provide more money for another area.
- **Human resource management policies and procedures**. Careful and detailed attention to just and equitable HRM policies and procedures may help to reduce areas of conflict. Examples are job analysis, recruitment and selection; systems of reward and punishment; appeals, grievance and disciplinary procedures; arbitration and mediation; recognition of trade unions and their officials.
- **Non-monetary rewards**. Where financial resources are limited, it may be possible to pay greater attention to non-monetary rewards. Examples are job design; more interesting, challenging or responsible work; increased delegation or empowerment; improved equipment; flexible working hours; attendance at courses or conferences; unofficial perks or more relaxed working conditions.
- **Development of interpersonal/group process skills**. This may help to encourage a better understanding of one's own behaviour, the other person's point of view, communication processes and problem-solving. It may also encourage people to work through conflict situations in a constructive manner.
- **Group activities**. Attention to the composition of groups and to factors which affect group cohesiveness may reduce dysfunctional conflict. Overlapping group membership with a 'linking-pin' process, and the careful selection of project teams or task forces for problems affecting more than one group, may also be beneficial.
- **Leadership and management**. A more participative and supportive style of leadership and managerial behaviour is likely to assist in conflict management – for example, showing an attitude of respect and trust; encouraging personal self-development; creating a work environment in which staff can work co-operatively. A participative approach to leadership and management may also help to create greater employee commitment.
- **Organisational processes**. Conflict situations may be reduced by attention to such features as the nature of the authority structure; work organisation; patterns of communication and sharing of information; democratic functioning of the organisation; unnecessary adherence to bureaucratic procedures, and official rules and regulations.
- **Socio-technical approach**. Viewing the organisation as a socio-technical system, in which psychological and social factors are developed in keeping with structural and technical requirements, will help in reducing dysfunctional conflict.

A summary of conflict management is given in the concept map in Figure 3.10.

THE ORGANISATION OF THE FUTURE

We have looked at the nature and type of organisations and their components. It is, however, important to remember that organisations are living organisms and evolving constantly. The changing nature of work organisations and the social context has led to a climate of constant change and the need for greater organisational flexibility. Managers need to be aware of new psychological contracts and to adopt alternative styles of management.

As *Chowdhury* points out: 'The organization of the 21st century will be characterized by unprecedented complexity and will require a different breed of leader.'[41] *Ulrich* also suggests that with the changing and dynamic contextual factors:

Figure 3.10 Concept map of conflict management

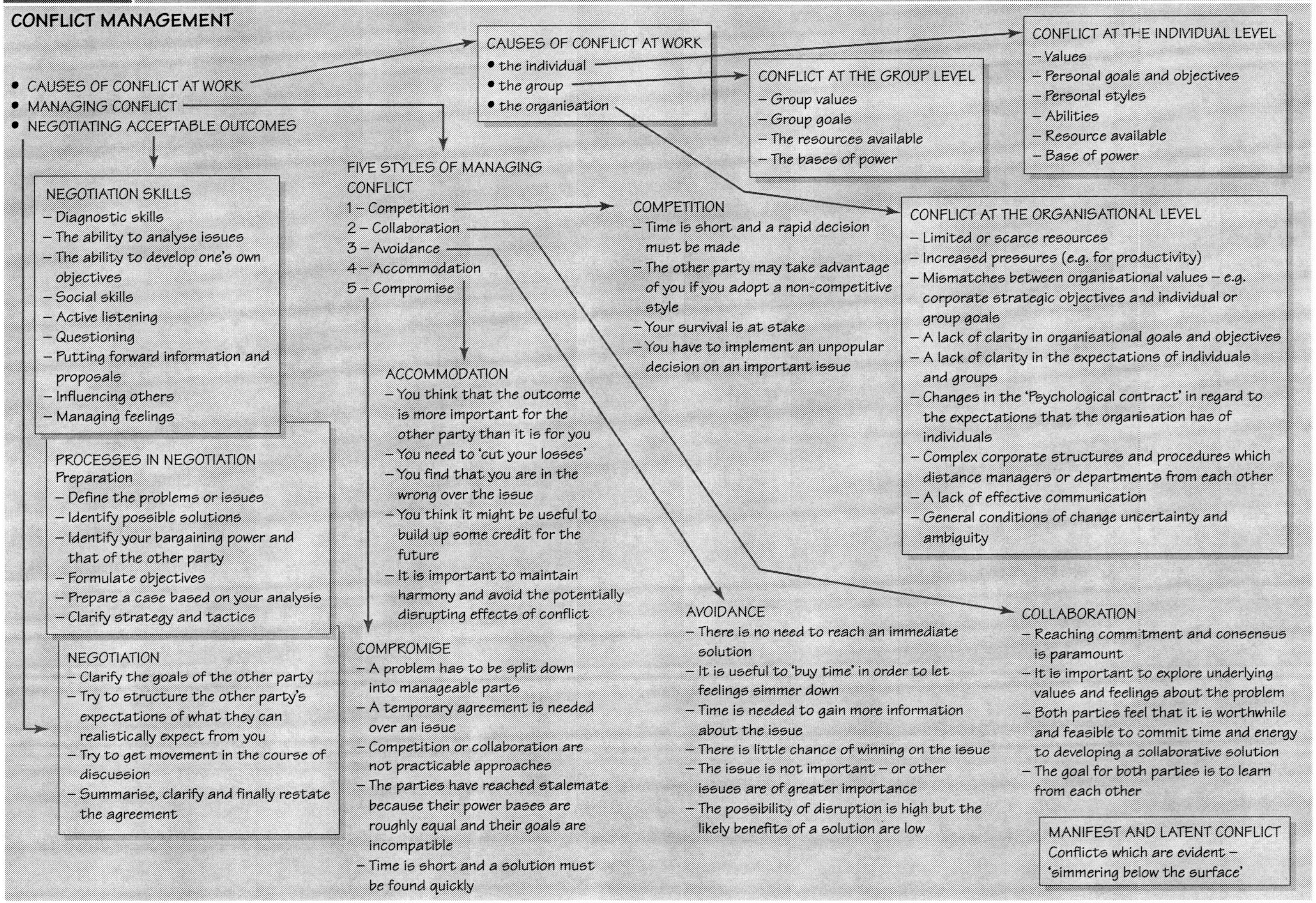

CONFLICT MANAGEMENT

- CAUSES OF CONFLICT AT WORK
- MANAGING CONFLICT
- NEGOTIATING ACCEPTABLE OUTCOMES

CAUSES OF CONFLICT AT WORK
- the individual
- the group
- the organisation

CONFLICT AT THE INDIVIDUAL LEVEL
– Values
– Personal goals and objectives
– Personal styles
– Abilities
– Resource available
– Base of power

CONFLICT AT THE GROUP LEVEL
– Group values
– Group goals
– The resources available
– The bases of power

CONFLICT AT THE ORGANISATIONAL LEVEL
– Limited or scarce resources
– Increased pressures (e.g. for productivity)
– Mismatches between organisational values – e.g. corporate strategic objectives and individual or group goals
– A lack of clarity in organisational goals and objectives
– A lack of clarity in the expectations of individuals and groups
– Changes in the 'Psychological contract' in regard to the expectations that the organisation has of individuals
– Complex corporate structures and procedures which distance managers or departments from each other
– A lack of effective communication
– General conditions of change uncertainty and ambiguity

FIVE STYLES OF MANAGING CONFLICT
1 – Competition
2 – Collaboration
3 – Avoidance
4 – Accommodation
5 – Compromise

COMPETITION
– Time is short and a rapid decision must be made
– The other party may take advantage of you if you adopt a non-competitive style
– Your survival is at stake
– You have to implement an unpopular decision on an important issue

ACCOMMODATION
– You think that the outcome is more important for the other party than it is for you
– You need to 'cut your losses'
– You find that you are in the wrong over the issue
– You think it might be useful to build up some credit for the future
– It is important to maintain harmony and avoid the potentially disrupting effects of conflict

COMPROMISE
– A problem has to be split down into manageable parts
– A temporary agreement is needed over an issue
– Competition or collaboration are not practicable approaches
– The parties have reached stalemate because their power bases are roughly equal and their goals are incompatible
– Time is short and a solution must be found quickly

AVOIDANCE
– There is no need to reach an immediate solution
– It is useful to 'buy time' in order to let feelings simmer down
– Time is needed to gain more information about the issue
– There is little chance of winning on the issue
– The issue is not important – or other issues are of greater importance
– The possibility of disruption is high but the likely benefits of a solution are low

COLLABORATION
– Reaching commitment and consensus is paramount
– It is important to explore underlying values and feelings about the problem
– Both parties feel that it is worthwhile and feasible to commit time and energy to developing a collaborative solution
– The goal for both parties is to learn from each other

MANIFEST AND LATENT CONFLICT
Conflicts which are evident – 'simmering below the surface'

NEGOTIATION SKILLS
– Diagnostic skills
– The ability to analyse issues
– The ability to develop one's own objectives
– Social skills
– Active listening
– Questioning
– Putting forward information and proposals
– Influencing others
– Managing feelings

PROCESSES IN NEGOTIATION
Preparation
– Define the problems or issues
– Identify possible solutions
– Identify your bargaining power and that of the other party
– Formulate objectives
– Prepare a case based on your analysis
– Clarify strategy and tactics

NEGOTIATION
– Clarify the goals of the other party
– Try to structure the other party's expectations of what they can realistically expect from you
– Try to get movement in the course of discussion
– Summarise, clarify and finally restate the agreement

Source: Training Learning Consultancy Ltd, Bristol, England. Reproduced with permission.

> *The essence of organizations has shifted and will continue to shift from focusing on structure to capability. Capability represents what the organization is able to do and how it does it rather than the more visible picture of who reports to whom and which rules govern work ... Organizations will operate in the future to identify and nurture a handful of critical capabilities.*[42]

The importance of people in the organisation

Lynda Gratton emphasises the importance of putting people at the heart of corporate purpose. We are part of organisations stamped by technology that has created the patents, ideas and innovations that brought success. However, while this past has been essential to our success, it will not bring sustainable competitive advantage for the future unless we build the potential of people and human capital in our organisations. This requires a new agenda, a new set of challenges for leaders and a redefined set of managerial capabilities that includes an understanding of the reality of the organisation. Gratton suggests that you should build a model for your organisation around what causes high levels of trust and inspiration and to consider the organisation against these key influences:

- Do people understand the context in which they operate and the competitive threats and challenges the business faces?
- Are employees confident about the ability of the organisation to adapt?
- Are they involved in decisions about themselves and the organisation?

It is also important to understand the complexity of the organisation and the changes necessary to move from the present to the future.[43]

Cloke and Goldsmith refer to the rise of organisational democracy. There is a demand for alternative organisational practices and a far-reaching transformation has already begun, based on the idea that management as a system fails to open the heart or free the spirit. The age of management is coming to an end and the real push for the future is for more authentic human relationships and the humanisation of organisations as crucibles for personal growth and development.[44]

THE WORK/LIFE BALANCE

We have looked at the nature and importance of organisations as an integral feature of human civilisation. But what role do, or should, organisations play in the lives of their staff or with broader concerns for the work/life balance? And how much also depends upon the individual's orientations to work (discussed in Chapter 1)?

Attitude to work

An interesting point of view is put forward by *Reeves* who contends that our attitude to work needs a radical overhaul and that it is nonsense that 'wicked work' gets the blame for most of our ills. Work is our community, how we identify ourselves, and it is becoming more central to our lives. It is a provider of friends, gossip, networks, fun, creativity, purpose, comfort, belonging, identity – and even love. Work is where life is. People doing work they enjoy are happy – not only at work but generally in the other areas of their lives too. Happiness lies in meaningful work for us all. The line between 'work' and 'life' is rapidly being rubbed out. Few people want to put their work in a box labelled 'nine to five'.[45]

In contrast, however, *Armitage* maintains that the image presented by the media is one where work is made so attractive to the extent it surpasses the Protestant ethic of being good for the soul and becomes something we must all do for the good of our well-being. Armitage questions whether it is time to re-assess what we do and whether we get satisfaction from it. Although we may not have unlimited control over what we do, we have to make a greater effort to balance the amount of time and effort we put into our work and our personal lives. 'Once work begins to take over one's life to the exclusion of all other interests, that is the time to call a halt. If not, then we run the very real risk of not only becoming a workaholic, but also of endangering personal relationships and friendships and maybe even suffering the longer-term effects of ill health.'[46]

Work–life balance is an issue of growing concern within the UK. The declining influence of trade unions in regulating the employment relationship, job insecurity, the extension of operating and opening hours, and the impact of new forms of information and communications technology on work are just some of the factors that have made it increasingly difficult for workers to balance their work and their personal lives.

European Industrial Relations Review[47]

MEANING TO PEOPLE'S LIVES

Popular press articles often suggest that work is still a large component of what gives meaning to people's lives and give examples of big lottery or pools winners staying in work and often in their same, even apparently routine, jobs. Other surveys and reports continue to suggest that the workplace is no longer a central feature of social activity. For a majority of people the main reason for work remains the need for money to fulfil the necessities of life. However, much still appears to depend on the extent of an individual's social contacts and activities outside of the work situation.

A survey from Roffey Park Management Research and Training Institute found that the vast majority of managers are looking for a greater sense of meaning in their working lives.[48]

A recent study from the Department of Trade and Industry (DTI) draws attention to the fact that the workplace has altered dramatically over the last decade and old methods are no longer appropriate as employers accept that their most valuable asset is their workforce.

> *Employers worldwide are recognising of their own accord that it makes good business sense to provide opportunities for their workforce to achieve a better work–life balance – with a pay back of increased morale, better effectiveness and productivity, and the ability to embrace change.*[49]

The results also show there is no one standard work/life balance policy that will suit every business. Arguably there is no such thing as work/life balance but different work/life balances with different parts of the jigsaw taking on greater importance at different times in our working lives.[50] *Summers and Nowicki* suggest that the more secure the organisation and the less competitive the environment, the more latitude the manager has to encourage employees to lead balanced lives.[51]

Ethical considerations

It is not easy to determine the extent to which attention to the quality of working life and the work/life balance is based on the exercise of a genuine social responsibility and a moral or ethical motivation (discussed in Chapter 14) or based primarily on the pursuit of economic efficiency and motivated through good business practice and enlightened self-interest.

But to what extent should the work/life balance form part of the ethical concern or underlying values of an organisation? Opinions appear to be divided. For example, *Sternberg*, whilst recognising the importance of treating employees ethically, does not support the belief that a business should be run for the benefit of its employees or should by action or by omission encourage employees to have inappropriate expectations of the business.

Despite widespread notions to the contrary, it is not the role of business to give meaning to the lives of its employees or to provide social welfare or full employment; business is not a substitute for family or community, the church or the state.[52]

Meanwhile, *Browning* suggests that a meaningful work community is one that concentrates on the overlap between individual values and aspirations, the organisation's values, and the wider concerns and expectations of modern society. Employees are looking for more meaning at work. Bringing them closer into the organisation and giving them responsibility for its vision and values is the key.

We are increasingly looking forward for the workplace to provide us with the meaning that we once expected from the more traditional sources in our lives, such as community, religion and family. For companies this means balancing commercial goals with the aims of employees, and it is not simply about culture.[53]

The Advisory, Conciliation and Arbitration Service (ACAS) draws attention to the reinforcing nature of its mission to improve both organisations and working life. These objectives are not mutually exclusive.

Unless improving working life is taken into account, employers will not get the motivation, commitment and loyalty that are increasingly needed for success. Unless there is an improvement in performance, employers will not have the wherewithal to bring about a sustained improvement in working lives – improving performance is the most practical way of improving working life.[54]

ORGANISATIONAL STRESS

In addition to organisational conflict, a major and related influence on the work/life balance is the extent to which employees suffer from organisational stress. There appears little doubt that stress at work is one of the biggest problems in European companies and one of the major adverse influences on the quality of working life and work performance. **Stress** is a complex and dynamic concept. It is a source of tension and frustration, and can arise through a number of interrelated influences on behaviour, including the individual, group, organisational and environmental factors discussed in Chapter 1.

The Health and Safety Executive (HSE) defines stress as: 'The adverse reaction people have to excess pressure. It isn't a disease. But if stress is intense and goes on for some time, it can lead to a mental and physical ill health (e.g. depression, nervous breakdown, heart disease).'[55]

However, *York* contends that despite all the business-speak, people get seriously vague when it comes to definitions and raises the question: What is stress? Is it a new name for an old-fashioned condition such as unhappiness or overwork, or is it peculiar to our uniquely pressured times? York suggests there is something in the idea that stress isn't just about hard work or unhappiness, but about conflict, confusion and frustration. It's about the anxiety generated by multi-tasking and balancing priorities, meeting contradictory demands, about knowing where to start and papering over the cracks when you want to do too much.[56]

Levels of stress

An increasing number of surveys report, perceived or actual, increases in levels of stress. There have also been a number of highly publicised reports of successful legal claims based on the effects of stress. Understandably, however, there is also a level of scepticism about the amount of emphasis placed on stress, and a number of press and other articles feature the 'myth' of work stress.

An interesting report from the Institute for Social and Economic Research suggests that claims of workplace pressure may be misplaced. Levels of job satisfaction and mental distress vary systematically according to the day of the week on which respondents are interviewed. Stress appears to disappear on Friday and Saturday. When genuine dissatisfaction was found, it tended to be because employees were working too few or too many hours. However, the main cause of stress was money difficulties, caused by unemployment or debt. The research casts a question mark over the generous compensation regularly handed out by the courts to employees claiming they suffer from stress.[57] *Randall* also makes the point that: 'Whichever lawyer first hit on the idea of promoting stress as either a reason for not going to work or a way to make others cough up could hardly have done more damage to Britain's work ethic than if he or she had arranged a quintupling of dole payments.'[58]

IS STRESS NECESSARILY TO BE AVOIDED?

Stress, however, is a very personal experience, as is the response of each individual to it and their beliefs about how best to cope with the causes and effects. *Orpen* questions the prevalent view among managers in Britain which seems to be that stress at work is something to be avoided at all costs. Just as there are circumstances when individuals may have too much stress, there are also circumstances when individuals may have too little stress for effective performance.[59] This view also appears to be supported by *Guyther*, who points out that although stress appears to have become public health enemy number one and is viewed as the culprit of myriad complaints, the term is bandied about far too readily and there is a need to stand back and attempt to get things into some sort of perspective. A measure of stress is natural. A degree of stress at work is no unhealthy thing and without it nothing would ever get done.[60] However, it is important to bear in mind that stress can potentially be very harmful.

A certain amount of stress may **arguably** not necessarily be seen as a bad thing and may even help promote a higher level of performance. But what is the distinction between pressure and stress? 'Pressure' can be seen as a positive factor that may be harnessed to help people respond to a challenge and function more effectively. 'Stress' may be regarded as a continuous negative response arising from extreme pressure or other demands and the individual's inability to cope.

> *Personal performance may improve with pressure, up to a certain point. Beyond that point, continuous pressure leads to a fall in performance as the person is no longer able to cope. Signs of this are fatigue, poor judgement and bad decision making. In turn, this can lead to serious business problems.*[61]

Research by organisations such as the Health and Safety Executive have identified stress, anxiety and depression as among the most commonly reported illnesses, and wider research has also indicated that stress, brought about through work intensification and conflicts between home and work, is related to the risks of disease and ill-health.[62]

A study by *van ZylKobus Lazenby* found that South African managers in affirmative action positions are functioning in a stressful environment that can give rise to unethical acts. Results indicated that high stress correlates substantially with claiming credit for a subordinate's work, failing to report a co-worker's violation of company policy, offering potential clients fully paid holidays and purchasing shares upon hearing privileged company information.[63]

> *The results of unrelieved stress on the individual and on business are worrying. The result may be higher accident rates, sickness absence, inefficiency, damaged relationships with clients and colleagues, high staff turnover, early retirement on medical grounds, and even premature death ... The cost of stress is huge. It is devastating to the individual and damaging to the business at a time when the need to control business costs and ensure an effective and healthy workforce is greater than ever. It is in everyone's interest to tackle the taboo on talking about emotional problems because it is this which inhibits individuals from seeking help.*
>
> Simon Armson, Chief Executive, The Samaritans[64]

CAUSES OF STRESS

Stress is part of everyday working life and occurs for a variety of reasons, including individual differences and types of personality; occupation and actual nature of the job, and whether working in the private or public sector; and both conflict and the work/life balance discussed above. Others sources of stress at work include the following:

- Demands for improved business competitiveness and lower operating costs have frequently led to restructuring of organisations and reductions in staffing levels. This has placed greater pressures on remaining staff and resulted in a growing number of work-related health problems, work stress and a less efficient workforce.[65]
- The long-hours culture, increased workloads and work intensification, together with unreasonable deadlines.
- Excessive rules and regulations, and greater bureaucratic burdens especially among professional groups.
- Developments in information and communications technology (ICT) that mean staff are far more constantly and easily contactable and expected to deliver everything faster. This can lead to greater pressure on individuals, a reluctance to switch off and a blurring between work and home life.
- Organisational changes such as redundancies and the loss of key members of staff that place extra demands on managers.
- Interpersonal relationships at work, especially with immediate superiors, poor communications and office politics.
- Lack of delegation and autonomy over control of work. Research into managers in various types of organisation in Western Australia showed that delegation of responsibility to middle managers required great skill, which was too seldom present. Replies from 532 managers in 36 organisations indicated a clear correlation between lack of autonomy and stress at work. Stress was often caused by the hierarchical structure of the organisation not permitting sufficient autonomy. As a result, projects were frequently delayed and also managers' authority within their departments was undermined.[66]
- Organisation structure and role relationships. Lack of clarity about expected patterns of behaviour or role conflict is a potential source of role stress (discussed in Chapter 8). In the case of customer service, *Jamison* suggests that if there is a conflict between the requirements of a customer and the requirements of the organisation, this will induce unhelpful behaviour as a result of stress.[67]

COPING WITH STRESS

There are a number of measures by which individuals and organisations can attempt to reduce the causes and effects of stress. There are also many suggested techniques to help individuals bring stress under control – for example, changing your viewpoint, identifying causes of distress, laughing and telling jokes, working on stress reduction and appreciating that some stress can be useful.[68] However, there are not always easy remedies for stress and much depends upon the personality of the individual. Techniques such as relaxation therapy may help some people, although not others, but still tend to address the symptoms rather than the cause. As *Vine and Williamson* point out, stress-inducing hazards are hard to pin down, much less eliminate. It is important to know how people feel about the things that cause them stress as well as which 'stressors' are most common in a particular industry and occupation. Human resource policy should include several stress management building blocks within the organisation structure including management education, employee education, counselling and support, critical incident briefing, and good sound management.[69]

Organisations also need to give greater attention to training, support and counselling and to the work organisation and job design.

Effective communications and conversation

Effective communications at all levels of the organisation are clearly important in helping to reduce or overcome the level of stress. However, in addition to good communications, *Reeves* refers to the importance of conversation for maintaining relationships and suggests a case for a conversation culture. The ability to hold good-quality conversations is becoming a core organisational and individual skill. Unlike communication, conversations are intrinsically creative and roam freely across personal issues, corporate gossip and work projects. 'Conversations are a defence against stress and other mental health problems. People with good social relationships at work are much less likely to be stressed or anxious.'[70]

A growing number of organisations are introducing an email-free day to encourage staff to use the telephone or walk across the corridor to talk more with one another.

Checklist of strategies

The Engineering Employers' Federation set out a checklist of strategies relating to building corporate awareness and managerial understanding, and avoiding and minimising stress by attention to:

- job design;
- structure of the organisation and resources;
- management style; and
- helping the individual to cope.

Effective management of stress can reduce absence, increase work quality and performance, reduce resistance to change, improve relationships with customers, colleagues and suppliers, and reduce staff turnover.[71]

HSE's stress management standards

As part of its Fit for Work Fit for Life Fit for Tomorrow Strategic Programme, the HSE is working with businesses on health issues, including work-related stress, to enable them to be managed more effectively in the workplace. With input from a range of businesses, professional bodies and trade unions, the HSE has developed a new approach to tackle this problem. The Stress Management Standards encourage employers and employees to work in partnership to adopt agreed standards of good management practice to prevent stress at an organisational level.

The adoption of the Management Standards is a key element in bringing about the reductions in worker ill-health absence outlined above. The Standards provide a framework that allows an assessment to be made about the degree of exposure to seven key workplace stressors – culture, control, relationships, change, demands of the job, role, and support and the individual – and promotes better working conditions by identifying where action can be taken by management (*see* Figure 3.11).

The HSE has also negotiated a written protocol with ACAS to enable the HSE Stress Partners to call on the expertise of a team of ACAS advisers as required. In return, the participating organisations are expected to provide data to help the HSE further refine the Standards and encourage wider implementation of the Standards.[72]

Critical reflection

'Management models are a crude representation of our organisational existence that only serve to dull our awareness of the richness of our environment and prevent us from finding new ways of looking at the world of organisations and work.' How would you argue *against* this statement?

Figure 3.11 Work-related stressors

CULTURE

Problems that can lead to stress
- lack of communication and consultation
- a culture of blame when things go wrong, denial of potential problems
- an expectation that people will regularly work excessively long hours or take work home with them

What management can do
- provide opportunities for staff to contribute ideas, especially in planning and organising their own jobs
- introduce clear business objectives, good communication, and close employee involvement, particularly during periods of change
- be honest with yourself, set a good example, and listen to and respect others
- be approachable – create an atmosphere where people feet it is OK to talk to you about any problems they are having
- avoid encouraging people to work excessively long hours

CONTROL

Problems that can lead to stress
- lack of control over work activities

What management can do
- give more control to staff by enabling them to plan their own work, make decisions about how that work should be completed and how problems should be tackled

RELATIONSHIPS

Problems that can lead to stress
- poor relationships with others
- bullying, racial or sexual harassment

What management can do
- provide training in interpersonal skills
- set up effective systems to prevent bullying and harassment (i.e. a policy, agreed grievance procedure and proper investigation of complaints)

CHANGE

Problems that can lead to stress
- uncertainty about what is happening
- fears about job security

What management can do
- ensure good communication with staff
- provide effective support for staff throughout the process

DEMANDS OF THE JOB

Problems that can lead to stress
- too much to do, too little time
- too little/too much training for the job
- boring or repetitive work, or too little to do
- the working environment

What management can do
- prioritise tasks, cut out unnecessary work, try to give warning of urgent or important jobs
- make sure individuals are matched to jobs, provide training for those who need more, increase the scope of jobs for those who are over-trained
- change the way jobs are done by moving people between jobs, giving individuals more responsibility, increasing the scope of the job, increasing the variety of tasks, giving a group of workers greater responsibility for effective performance of the group
- make sure other workplace hazards, such as noise, harmful substances and the threat of violence, are properly controlled

ROLE

Problems that can lead to stress
- staff feeling that the job requires them to behave in conflicting ways at the same time
- confusion about how everyone fits in

What management can do
- talk to people regularly to make sure that everyone is clear about what their job requires them to do
- make sure that everyone has clearly defined objectives and responsibilities linked to business objectives, and training on how everyone fits in

SUPPORT AND THE INDIVIDUAL

Problems that can lead to stress
- lack of support from managers and co-workers
- not being able to balance the demands of work and life outside work

What management can do
- support and encourage staff, even when things go wrong
- encourage a healthy work–life balance
- see if there is scope for flexible work schedules (e.g. flexible working hours, working from home)
- take into account that everyone is different, and try to allocate work so that everyone is working in the way that helps them work best

Source: Health and Safety Executive, *Work-related Stress: A Short Guide*, (INDG281Rev1) (2003). © Crown Copyright 2003. Crown copyright material is reproduced with permission of the Controller of Her Majesty's Stationery Office (HMSO).

MANAGEMENT IN THE NEWS

Crossing continents

A spun-out tale of two corporate cultures

Geoff Dyer

Liu Zhengrong's job is emblematic of the times – to bring some Chinese dynamism to corporate Germany and to introduce some German rigour to management in China. Aged 37, Mr Liu is probably the highest-placed executive from mainland China in corporate Europe. The Shanghai-born manager was appointed in 2004 as head of human resources at Lanxess, the chemicals group spun off from German conglomerate Bayer in January last year.

Anyone thinking the HR title sounds a little lightweight should remember that in Germany the human resources executive represents the company in important negotiations with trade unions, giving him or her a central role in corporate life. For Mr Liu, the position meant an unenviable first task at the newly spun-out Lanxess. Bayer had kept its healthcare and agrochemicals operations, leaving Lanxess with a collection of low-margin and low-growth chemicals businesses that Bayer no longer wanted. Mr Liu had to persuade the unions to accept the loss of 1,000 jobs as the company desperately tried to cut €100m ($128m) of costs. To add to the political sensitivity of job losses in corporate Germany, the company also wanted to shift some production to China.

Putting forward a Chinese executive to negotiate such a drastic package caused much scepticism among union officials. 'They were asking, what does he really want to do?' says the wiry-framed Mr Liu. 'But in Germany everyone gets a fair chance.' The talks took four months and often lasted well into the night. In the end, two arguments won over the unions, he says. They had witnessed Bayer stagnate in the 1990s when a number of difficult strategic decisions were avoided. And they knew the competitive threat from regions such as China was rapidly approaching.

Dealing with the unions has been a 'rich experience', he says, but the system has its flaws. 'There is lots of bureaucracy and ritual, all of which cost speed and efficiency and affect the bottom line,' he says. 'I have tried to get across to people that we need to change things a bit.' Yet there are also strengths in the German system that China could learn from: 'German companies have more respect for their employees and make a huge effort at having transparency in decision-making. That is not usually the case in China.'

The difference in attitudes to the workplace between Asia and Europe was most apparent to Mr Liu when he introduced a new profit-sharing scheme. In the past, a complicated mathematical formula was used to determine how much each person got. Instead, Mr Liu gave line managers discretion over a large part of the bonus pool. 'They are much clearer than anyone else about who are the pillars in the company,' he says. The plan was also a way of giving employees more honest feedback. 'We need managers who dare to tell employees who are not good that they do not have a place in my team,' he says. 'In the past, managers would give someone a 75 per cent evaluation, when the team average was 85 per cent, and hope that they got the message.'

In Europe, the proposal caused considerable disquiet. Many German staff feared bonuses would depend on 'the nose factor', whether an employee is liked or not, rather than ability. Yet in China, the idea that anyone would get any form of bonus after a mediocre performance – as happened under the old system – was considered to be like the old 'iron rice bowl', when the state guaranteed living conditions.

Source: Dyer, G., 'A spun-out tale of two corporate cultures', *Financial Times*, 22 May 2006.

Discussion questions

1 **Summarise and critically review what this article reveals about the main strengths and weaknesses of both Chinese and German corporate management styles.**

2 **Discuss and explain the extent to which the business environment, rather than management style, influences the way in which managers need to behave and act.**

SYNOPSIS

- The application of organisational behaviour and process of management take place not in a vacuum but within the context of an organisational setting. There are many different types of organisations set up to serve different purposes and needs, and they come in all forms, shapes and sizes. However, there are at least three common factors in any organisation: people, objectives and structure. To which can be added a fourth factor – management. The qualities of these factors determine organisational effectiveness.

- Organisations can, traditionally, be distinguished in terms of two generic groups: private enterprise and public sector. The increasing rate of privatisation has led, however, to a blurring of commercial interests and service to the community. Another major distinction is arguably between production and service organisations. In order to relate the study of management and organisational behaviour to one particular type of organisation as distinct from another, it is necessary to group similar types of organisations together.

- Organisations differ in many important respects but they also share common features. Business organisations can be viewed as open systems in continual interaction with the external environment of which they are part. Within the organisation as a whole there are a number of sub-systems interrelating and interacting with each other. Contingency models of organisation draw attention to interrelationships among technology, structure, methods of operation and environmental influences.

- Whatever the type or nature of an organisation or its formal structure, an informal organisation will always be present and arises from the interactions of people and their psychological and social needs. It serves a number of important functions and has an influence on the morale, motivation, job satisfaction and performance of staff. Organisations of the future will be characterised by technology and complexity. It is important to emphasise the importance of people and the need for authentic human relationships, and the humanisation of organisations.

- It might be expected that a healthy organisational climate would be reflected by complete harmony in working relationships, but conflict is a reality of management and organisational behaviour. There are contrasting views of conflict and it can be seen to have both positive and negative outcomes. The important point is how conflict is handled and managed. Managers need to adopt appropriate strategies for dealing with the harmful effects of conflict. The organisation of the future will be characterised by complexity and the essence will continue to shift from structure to capability.

- Increasing attention is focused on the role organisations play in the lives of staff and with broader concerns for the work/life balance and meaning to people's lives. It is not easy to determine the extent to which concerns for the quality of working life are based on a genuine social responsibility or motivated by economic efficiency. There appears little doubt that stress at work is a major concern and a potential source of mental and physical ill-health. However, a certain amount of pressure may, *arguably*, help promote a higher level of performance.

Refresh your understanding, assess your progress and begin your research with online resources at www.pearsoned.co.uk/mullins

REVIEW AND DISCUSSION QUESTIONS

1. What is an organisation and why do organisations exist? What are the common factors in any organisation?
2. Contrast various organisations, including your own, in terms of classifications based on: (i) prime beneficiary, and (ii) primary activity.
3. Discuss critically the extent to which differences among various organisations limit the value of the study of management and organisational behaviour.
4. Assess critically the practical value to both the student and the manager of adopting an open systems view of organisational analysis.
5. Distinguish between the formal and the informal organisation and explain their main characteristics. What functions are served by the informal organisation?

6 To what extent do you accept the view that conflict is an inevitable feature of management and organisational behaviour?

7 Why do you think increasing attention is being given to the work/life debate? As a senior manager, what steps would you take to help improve the quality of working life for staff?

8 Give your own critical views on how *you* see the organisation of the future and the humanisation of organisations.

ASSIGNMENT 1

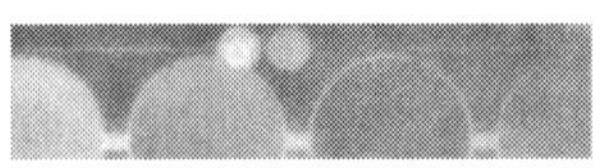

Overview

Undoubtedly you have had recent experiences with numerous organisations. Ten to fifteen minutes of reflective thinking should result in a fairly large list of organisations. Don't be misled by thinking that only large organisations, such as your college or General Motors, are relevant for consideration. How about the clinic with the doctor(s), nurse(s) and secretary/bookkeeper? Or the corner garage or service station? The local tavern, McDonald's and the neighbourhood theatre are all organisations. You should not have any difficulty in listing a number of organisations with which you have had recent contact.

The second part of the exercise, however, gets tougher. You are asked to describe several of the key characteristics of the organisations that you have listed. One of the major issues in studying and describing organisations is deciding what characteristics or factors are important. Some of the more common characteristics considered in the analysis of organisations are:

1 size (small to very large);
2 degree of formality (informal to highly structured);
3 degree of complexity (simple to complex);
4 nature of goals (what the organisation is trying to accomplish);
5 major activities (what tasks are performed);
6 types of people involved (age, skills, educational background, etc.);
7 location of activities (number of units and their geographic location).

You should be able to develop a list of characteristics that you think is relevant for each of your organisations.

Now to the third, final and most difficult task. Think about what is involved in the *management* of these organisations. For example, what kinds of functions do their managers perform? How does one learn the skills necessary to be an effective manager? Would you want to be a manager in any of these organisations?

In effect, in this exercise you are asked to think specifically about organisations you have been associated with recently, develop your own conceptual model for looking at their characteristics, and think more specifically about the managerial functions in each of them. You probably already know a great deal more about organisations and their management than you think. This exercise should be useful in getting your thoughts together.

Procedure

Step 1

Prior to class, list up to ten organisations (e.g. work, living group, club) in which you have been involved or with which you have had recent contact.

Step 2

Enter five organisations from your list on the form 'Profile of Organisations' (below).

a List the organisations.

b Briefly outline the characteristics that you consider most significant.

c Describe the managerial functions in each of these organisations.

Assignment 1 – continued

Step 3

During the class period, meet in groups of five or six to discuss your list of organisations, the characteristics you consider important and your descriptions of their management. Look for significant similarities and differences across organisations.

Step 4

Basing your selections on this group discussion, develop a list entitled 'What We Would Like to Know about Organisations and Their Management'. Be prepared to write this list on the board and to share your list with other groups in the class.

PROFILE OF ORGANISATIONS

Organisation	Key characteristics	Managerial functions
1 ________	________	________
2 ________	________	________
3 ________	________	________
4 ________	________	________
5 ________	________	________

Source: Kast, F. E. and Rosenzweig. J. E., 'Our organizational society: your association with organizations', in *Experimental Exercises and Cases in Management*, McGraw-Hill (1976), pp. 13–15, Reproduced with permission from the McGraw-Hill Companies.

ASSIGNMENT 2

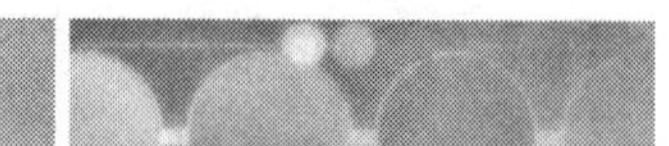

Think of any organisation with which you are familiar and be prepared to give a descriptive account to your colleagues on:

- the unusual, strange, interesting or 'quirky' features of, and people in, the organisation; and
- how things actually happen and work in practice.

PERSONAL AWARENESS AND SKILLS EXERCISE

Objectives

Completing this exercise should help you to enhance the following skills:

- Demonstrate your ability to analyse an organisation in terms of an open systems model.
- Identify and analyse the transformation or conversion process in terms of main interrelated sub-systems.

Exercise

You are required to:

1 With the aid of a diagram, depict your own or some other organisation well known to you in terms of its:
   - main aims and objectives;
   - inputs;
   - nature of the transformation or conversion process;
   - outputs;
   - measurement of effectiveness in achieving organisational goals.
2 Provide specific examples of ways in which the structure, management and functioning of the organisation are affected by external environmental influences.

Discussion

- How effective are the interactions and interrelationships among the sub-systems? Give practical examples to support your view.
- Comment critically on the effectiveness of management in co-ordinating the sub-systems and directing the activities of the organisation as a unified whole towards the accomplishment of its goals and objectives.

CASE STUDY

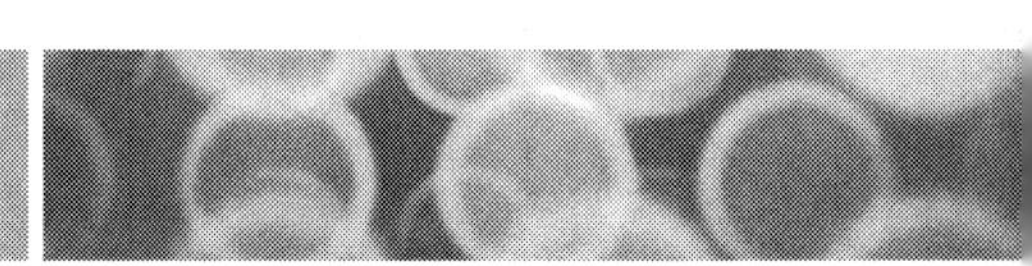

Grameen Bank: a case of applied business ethics

The issue of third world poverty is one which is rarely far from Western headlines, sometimes as the result of a particular humanitarian crisis or natural disaster, but often in association with debates about the effects of globalisation and in particular the impact of global business activities on individuals and communities in poor countries. It is an issue which inspires heated argument, as well as demands for money or action, or both. A comparison between the agendas of Live Aid and Live 8, for example, show a shift from demands for charity (in Sir Bob Geldof's famously exasperated plea to 'Give us your f***ing money!' at Live Aid) to concern about the trading position of third world countries in a global context; hence the lobbying of the G8 leaders at the 2005 summit. Discussion of the topic often tends to focus on the behaviour of specific business organisations and the 'ethical' status of their activities in poorer parts of the world. Some participants in the debate question whether business can ever truly be 'ethical' because its very existence depends upon acts of exploitation. So can business ever really help improve the condition of poor people in developing countries?

When considering such issues, it is important to remember that poverty is not the same thing as helplessness. The development of the Grameen Bank, a Bangladeshi banking business, illustrates one way in which ingenuity coupled with enterprise can present an alternative to charity and government aid as a route out of poverty.

Why banks are important to the poor

The development of any successful enterprise relies not only on the ingenuity, creativity and hard work of the entrepreneur but also on a number of social and economic preconditions, including such things as property rights and the ability to amass or borrow capital for investment in equipment and materials.[73] Borrowing power among the poor is very limited, as they are unlikely to be able to provide adequate security for loans from a commercial lending institution such as a bank. Without the ability to purchase the tools of their trade or raw materials, many individual workers remain dependent upon friends, family, moneylenders or employers to loan them what they need, often at extortionate rates and at the risk of physical violence if repayments are not made on time. Poor workers are therefore generally unable to amass sufficient funds to become independent economic operators. This situation of dependency upon an employer or other intermediary for both paid work and the means to do the work is often described as 'debt bondage' or 'debt peonage'. The effect of such structures is often to ensure that the poorest in society remain unable, by their own efforts, to break free from a form of servitude which stifles more general economic growth.

Mohammed Yunus and the Grameen Bank

Traditional banks developed from places where rich people were able to deposit their money safely, into

Mohammed Yunus and the Grameen Bank he founded won the 2006 Nobel Peace Prize.

commercial institutions where customers' money is used to make loans to other customers. In the earlier stages of their development they competed for the business of large customers such as companies and wealthy individuals since these were low-risk borrowers and provided high growth prospects. Until the standardisation and automation of many banking operations, most working-class people in developed economies did not have ready access to banking services. For poor people in developing countries, access to commercial banking services, including loans, remains a remote prospect indeed.

Mohammed Yunus is a Bangladeshi economist who, after studying and working in the United States, returned home to become an economics professor at the University of Chittagong. He became familiar with the problems of poor local people, mainly women, in his lunchtime strolls around the city of Dhaka and realised that many of the people he met would be greatly helped by the injections of very small amounts of capital, as little as US$1–2. He developed the idea of a specific type of what is usually termed 'microcredit' and in 1976, using $26 of his own money, began to make very small loans to poor local women so that they could invest in animals or other materials which would enable them to make money. Such tiny loans were out of the question for standard commercial banks because of the high administrative costs relative to the investment, the lack of loan security and the impossibility of proper credit referencing. Thus Yunus invented a new type of organisation: a low-cost, local operation which runs from the homes and community centres of the village (*grameen* literally means village). The loans are unsecured, so rely on local knowledge and trust, and need to be very precisely targeted. Both the investors and the creditors of grameen banks know each other and members meet regularly to monitor the progress of business, including loan repayments. Social capital is the mainstay of the banks and borrowers are highly involved in loan decisions and the general operation of the banks. This social nexus leads to a very unusual feature of the banks, which is their policy of making loans only to the very poor and, in the vast majority of cases, to women, who are generally more trustworthy in their handling of money than men. Yunus believes that this type of credit can lead to significant change in the status of poor individuals and can help provide a route out of extreme poverty without reliance on external sources of money.

> *Grameencredit is based on the premise that the poor have skills which remain unutilised or under-utilised. It is definitely not the lack of skills which make poor people poor. Grameen believes that the poverty is not created by the poor, it is created by the institutions and policies which surround them. In order to eliminate poverty all we need to do is to make appropriate changes in the institutions and policies, and/or create new ones. Grameen believes that charity is not an answer to poverty. It only helps poverty to continue. It creates dependency and takes away individual's initiative to break through the wall of poverty. Unleashing of energy and creativity in each human being is the answer to poverty.*[74]

The system proved highly successful; the 2004 annual report recorded over 4 million members and 3.7 million active borrowers with just under 96% of these being women.[75]

Iqbal Quadir and Grameen Phone

The Grameen business model, small-scale, local and trust-based with a focus on helping the poorest members of a community, was also behind the development of a number of offshoot enterprises, which now make up the Grameen family. One significant one, the Grameen Phone, involves local village women setting themselves up as 'telephone ladies' by enabling them to purchase a mobile phone with a Grameen bank loan and then renting it out for local use. Iqbal Quadir's idea for this communication business was directly inspired by the principles behind the grameen bank, and indeed the bank network also provides part of the infrastructure, as the local bank offices often provide the base for the GSM towers needed to make the network operate. From its inception in 1997, this initiative has brought communication technology to rural areas which are otherwise largely isolated; villagers can now make contact with friends and relatives, but also with hospitals and other services. It can also improve the market position of Grameen Phone customers who are engaged in other sorts of work.

An example is described by Roland Buerk, in a BBC report on one of the Grameen 'telephone ladies', Roshinara Begum in the Bangladeshi village of Kalimajani. One of her customers is local fish farmer Mohammed Abul Hashem, who uses the phone service to order food and supplies from the capital. He is quoted as explaining:

If the phone wasn't here then I'd have to travel to Dhaka. It's a very long and unpleasant journey. Now I can use the phone I am saving time and it makes my business more competitive.[76]

Similarly, farmers are able to compare seed prices rather than relying on a single company representative who happens to be in their area, thus giving them some economic muscle in the market.

Grameen Phone is far from being a charitable activity relying on benevolence; its spread has been possible only because it entered into a profitable partnership with the Norwegian telecoms company Telenor, which owns 62 per cent of the business and provides both the technical knowledge and the equipment to run the network successfully. In 2004 Grameen Phone numbered 95,000 phone ladies operating in 50,000 villages, each making, on average, $700 a year, with the Bangladeshi government benefiting to the tune of $200 million in taxes. As Quadir has observed:

Governments don't always need to support the poor. The poor can support the government. Poor people aren't a recipient – they're a resource. It's not too expensive to provide services to the poor – the involvement of the poor reduces the cost of services. Poor people are eager learners because they don't have the luxury of not learning.[77]

The Grameen Bank and associated Grameen Trust continue to develop their range of business support activities to suit local circumstances, with activities as diverse as fish farming programmes, and Internet access centres across rural Bangladesh. Finally, Yunus and Grameen are also achieving recognition on a world scale; their contribution to the alleviation of poverty through an approach that translates 'visions into practical action for the benefit of millions' won the bank and Yunus the 2006 Nobel Peace Prize.

Your tasks

1. How would you classify an organisation such as the Grameen Bank? Which of the approaches (classification by purpose, by prime beneficiary, by primary activity) do you think provides the most accurate description of the Bank and why?
2. How far can the concepts of the 'formal' and the 'informal' organisation apply to this case?
3. Two of the significant features of the Grameen Bank are its focus on helping individuals to achieve independence and its strong preference for loans to women. What problems might this cause and what risks does it take in the communities and societies (mainly Islamic) where it operates? Can its continued operation be ethically justified if it creates serious social disruption?
4. Find out what you can about 'debt bondage' or 'debt peonage'. Contrast this system of work organisation with the way in which a Western multinational organisation (such as a manufacturing organisation or a traditional bank) operates in a developing country. Critically evaluate each system of work organisation in ethical terms.

Main sources

Banker to the Poor, biography of Mohammed Yunus.

The Economist, which ran a special issue about Third World debt on 3 November 2005

Grameen Bank homepage – www.grameen-info.org – which has information about the Grameen Bank and many of its related activities, including Grameen Phone and other specific programmes supported by the Trust. There are articles by and about Mohammed Yunus, and a number of case studies; also news items about the activities of the Trust.

Notes and references

1 For an account of developments in organisations see: Peters, G. 'Creating the Modern Organization', in Crainer, S. and Dearlove, D. (eds) *Financial Times Handbook of Management*, Second edition, Financial Times Prentice Hall (2001), pp. 24–45.

2 Farnham, D. and Horton, S. (eds) *Managing the New Public Services*, Second edition, Macmillan (1996), p. 26.

3 Schneider, S. C. and Barsoux, J. *Managing Across Cultures*, Second edition, Financial Times Prentice Hall (2003).

4 Watson, T. J. *Management Organisation and Employment Strategy*, Routledge and Kegan Paul (1986).

5 Schein, E. H. *Organizational Psychology*, Third edition, Prentice-Hall (1988), p. 15.

6 Cyert, R. M. and March, J. G. *A Behavioral Theory of the Firm*, Second edition, Blackwell (1992).

7 Mintzberg, H. *The Structuring of Organizations*, Prentice-Hall (1979).

8 Coffey, R. 'The Service Principle', *Chartered Secretary*, March 2005, p. 26.

9 See, for example: Dodds, O. 'Implications of Change for Local Government Managers', *Professional Manager*, November 1995, pp. 15–17.

10 Arnott, J. 'Cause and Ethics', *Chartered Secretary*, December 2002, pp. 22–4.

11 Smith, D. 'Crossing the Private–Public Divide', *Management Today*, August 1998, pp. 26–30.

12 Rose, A. and Lawton, A. *Public Services Management*, Financial Times Prentice Hall (1999), p. 74.

13 Wright, Sir David 'In My Opinion', *Management Today*, March 2003, p. 14.

14 Fitzsimmons, J. A. and Sullivan, R. S. *Service Operations Management*, McGraw-Hill (1982).

15 Levitt, T. 'Production-Line Approach to Service', *Harvard Business Review*, September–October 1972, p. 41.

16 Macdonald, J. 'Service is Different', *The TQM Magazine*, vol. 6, no. 1, 1994, p. 5.

17 For a discussion on the nature of service industries, see, for example: Mullins, L. J. *Hospitality Management and Organisational Behaviour*, Fourth edition, Longman (2001).

18 Weber, M. *The Theory of Social and Economic Organization*, Collier Macmillan (1964).

19 Etzioni, A. *Modern Organizations*, Prentice-Hall (1964), p. 14.

20 Blau, P. M. and Scott, W. R. *Formal Organizations*, Routledge and Kegan Paul (1966).

21 Katz, D. and Khan, R. L. *The Social Psychology of Organizations*, Second edition, Wiley (1978).

22 See, for example: Mullins, L. J. 'The Hotel and the Open Systems Model of Organisational Analysis', *The Services Industry Journal*, vol. 13, no. 1, January 1993, pp. 1–16.

23 For a more detailed discussion of environmental influences, see, for example: Worthington, I. and Britton, C. *The Business Environment*, Fifth edition, Financial Times Prentice Hall (2006).

24 Lynch, R. *Corporate Strategy*, Fourth edition, Financial Times Prentice Hall (2006).

25 Worthington, I and Britton, C. *The Business Environment*, Fifth edition, Financial Times Prentice Hall (2006), p. 13.

26 Law, S. 'Beyond the Water Cooler', *Professional Manager*, January 2005, p. 26.

27 Stewart, R. *The Reality of Management*, Third edition, Butterworth-Heinemann (1999), p. 125.

28 For a fuller discussion, see: Sadler, P. *Designing Organisations: The Foundation for Excellence*, Mercury (1991).

29 Egan, G. 'The Shadow Side', *Management Today*, September 1993, pp. 33–8.

30 Drucker, P. F. *The Practice of Management*, Heinemann Professional (1989), p. 119.

31 For an account of the Marxist critique, see, for example: Johnston, R. 'Hidden Capital', in Barry, J., Chandler, J., Clark, H., Johnston, R. and Needle, D. (eds), *Organization and Management: A Critical Text*, International Thomson Business Press (2000), pp. 16–35.

32 Salaman, G. *Class and Corporation*, Fontana (1981).

33 Ackroyd, S. and Thompson, P. *Organizational Misbehaviour*, Sage Publications (1999).

34 Schmidt, W. H. 'Conflict: A Powerful Process for (Good or Bad) Change', *Management Review*, Issue 63, December 1974, pp. 4–10.

35 Townsend, R. *Further Up the Organisation*, Coronet Books (1985), p. 39.

36 See, for example: Robbins, S. P. *Organizational Behavior: Concepts, Controversies, Applications*, Eighth edition, Prentice-Hall (1998).

37 Irvine, L. 'Conflicts of Interest', *The British Journal of Administrative Management*, March/April 1998, pp. 8–10.

38 Woodward, J. *Industrial Organization: Theory and Practice*, Second edition, Oxford University Press (1980), p. 113.

39 See, for example: James, J. *Body Talk at Work*, Judy Piatkus Limited (2001).

40 Hart, J. 'Mind the Gap', *Professional Manager*, November 2002, pp. 22–3.

41 Chowdhury, S. *Management 21C*, Financial Times Prentice Hall (2000), p. 205.

42 Ulrich, D. 'Context, Capability amd Response', in Chowdhury, S. *Management 21C*, Financial Times Prentice Hall (2000), p. 240.

43 Gratton, L. *Living Strategy: Putting People at the Heart of Corporate Purpose*, Financial Times Prentice Hall (2000).

44 Cloke, K. and Goldsmith, J. *The End of Management and the Rise of Organizational Democracy*, Jossey-Bass (2002).

45 Reeves, R. 'The Joy of Work', *Management Today*, May 2001, pp. 60–3.

46 Armitage, K. 'Can We Really Achieve a Life/Work Balance?' *The British Journal of Administrative Management*, July/August 2001, pp. 14–15.

47 'Work-life Balance: evidence from across the UK', *European Industrial Relations Review*, Issue 380, September 2005, p. 27.

48 Hoar, R. 'Work with Meaning', *Management Today*, May 2004, pp. 45–53.

49 'Work-Life Balance: The Business Case', Department of Trade and Industry, September 2001, p. 3.

50 Rice, M. 'Balancing Acts', *Management Today*, September 2002, pp. 52–9.

51 Summers, J. and Nowicki, M. 'Achievement and Balance: What do Managers Really Want?', *Healthcare Financial Management*, vol. 56, no. 3, March 2003, pp. 80–4.

52 Sternberg, E. *Just Business: Business Ethics in Action*, Second edition, Oxford University Press (2000), pp. 124–5.

53 Browning, G. 'The Search for Meaning', *People Management*, 29 December 2005.

54 'Improving the World of Work', ACAS, August 2005, p. 16.

55 'Work-related stress: A short guide', Health and Safety Executive, November 2001. See also: 'Organisational Interventions for Work Stress: A risk management approach', Health and Safety Executive, 2000.
56 York, P. 'Getting a Grip on Stress', *Management Today*, October 2001, p. 105.
57 Taylor, M. 'Tell Me Why I Don't Like Mondays', Working Paper of the Institute for Social and Economic Research, October 2002.
58 Randall, J. 'Home Truths', *Management Today*, June 2001, p. 31.
59 Orpen, C. 'Want The Best? Get Stressed!' *Chartered Secretary*, August 1996, pp. 18–20.
60 Gwyther, M. 'Stressed for Success', *Management Today*, January 1999, pp. 22–6.
61 'Managing Stress at Work', Engineering Employers' Federation, 2001.
62 'Work-life Balance: evidence from across the UK', *European Industrial Relations Review*, Issue 380, September 2005.
63 Van ZylKobus Lazenby, E. 'The Relation Between Ethical Behaviour and Work Stress amongst a Group of Managers Working in Affirmative Action Positions', *Journal of Business Ethics*, vol. 40, no. 2, October 2002, pp. 111–19.
64 Armson, S. 'Putting Stress on the Bottom Line', *Management Today*, September 1997, p. 5.
65 See, for example: Ridd, J. 'Hidden Costs of Work Stress', *The British Journal of Administrative Management*, October/November 1994, pp. 14–15.
66 Hall, K. and Savery, L. K. 'Stress Management', *Management Decision*, vol. 25, no. 6, 1987, pp. 29–35.
67 Jamison, C. 'Top 10 Myths of Customer Service', *The British Journal of Administrative Management*, July/August 1999, pp. 19–21.
68 Black, O. 'Making Stress Work for You', *Management Today*, December 2001, p. 19.
69 Vine, P. and Williamson, J. 'Run Down, Stressed Out', *The British Journal of Administrative Management*, January/February 1998, pp. 14–17.
70 Reeves, R. 'Reality Bites', *Management Today*, March 2003, p. 35.
71 'Managing Stress at Work', Engineering Employers' Federation, 2001.
72 Information kindly provided by HSE Press Office, January 2006.
73 DeSoto, H. *The Mystery of Capital*, Black Swan (2001).
74 Yunus, M. 'What is Microcredit?' www.grameen-info.org/bank [accessed 8 May 2006].
75 Grameen Bank, Performance Indicators and Ratio Analysis, www.grameen.com/bank [accessed 30 May 2006].
76 Buerk, R. 2005 '"Telephone Ladies" Connect Bangladesh' BBC News website, 26 November 2005, http://news.bbc.co.uk [accessed 28 May 2006].
77 Iqbal Quadir at PUSH conference 2005, 'People United to Serve Humanity' reported at http://www.ethanzuckerman.com/blog/?m=200506&paged=2.

The Individual

> **If your staff do something good, tell them. And then tell them again. And again. Keep it up. Put it in writing. Send them a memo – something they can keep. Put in the company newsletter. Add a note to their file. Whatever, but make it widely known they did good. This is a quick and cheap method of praising and motivating your team and it lets everyone know you are monitoring, praising, motivating.**
>
> **Richard Templar** – bestselling author of the popular rules books
>
> *The Rules of Management*, Pearson Prentice Hall (2005), p. 66

WORK MOTIVATION AND JOB SATISFACTION

The relationship between the organisation and its members is influenced by what motivates them to work and the rewards and fulfilment they derive from it. The work organisation, and the design and content of jobs, can have a significant effect on the satisfaction of staff and their levels of performance. The manager needs to know how best to elicit the co-operation of staff and direct their efforts to achieving the goals and objectives of the organisation.

Learning outcomes

After completing this chapter you should be able to:

- explain the meaning and underlying concept of motivation;
- detail main types of needs and expectations of people at work;
- explain frustration-induced behaviour and possible reactions to frustration at work;
- examine main theories of motivation and evaluate their relevance to particular work situations;
- assess the meaning, nature and dimensions of job satisfaction;
- review broader approaches to job design;
- evaluate the relationship between motivation, job satisfaction and work performance.

Critical reflection

'The most important motivating influences for people at work are to identify with the values of the organisation, and genuine recognition and praise. These are more important than high wages or good working conditions.' Do you agree? In your own words, what motivates you most?

THE MEANING OF MOTIVATION

The study of **motivation** is concerned, basically, with why people behave in a certain way. The basic underlying question is, 'Why do people do what they do?'[1] In general terms, motivation can be described as the direction and persistence of action. It is concerned with why people choose a particular course of action in preference to others, and why they continue with a chosen action, often over a long period and in the face of difficulties and problems.[2]

From a review of motivation theory, *Mitchell* identifies four common characteristics which underlie the definition of motivation:[3]

- **Motivation is typified as an individual phenomenon.** Every person is unique and all the major theories of motivation allow for this uniqueness to be demonstrated in one way or another.
- **Motivation is described, usually, as intentional.** Motivation is assumed to be under the worker's control, and behaviours that are influenced by motivation, such as effort expended, are seen as choices of action.
- **Motivation is multifaceted.** The two factors of greatest importance are: (i) what gets people activated (arousal) and (ii) the force of an individual to engage in desired behaviour (direction or choice of behaviour).
- **The purpose of motivational theories is to predict behaviour.** Motivation is not the behaviour itself and it is not performance. Motivation concerns action and the internal and external forces which influence a person's choice of action.

On the basis of these characteristics, Mitchell defines motivation as 'the degree to which an individual wants and chooses to engage in certain specified behaviours'.

Underlying concept of motivation

The underlying concept of motivation is some driving force within individuals by which they attempt to achieve some goal in order to fulfil some need or expectation. This concept gives rise to the basic motivational model, which is illustrated in Figure 7.1.

People's behaviour is determined by what motivates them. Their performance is a product of both ability level and motivation.

$$\text{Performance} = \text{function}\ (\text{ability} \rightarrow \text{motivation})$$

Kreitner et al. suggest that although motivation is a necessary contributor for job performance, it is not the only one. Along with ability, motivation is also a combination of level of skill, knowledge about how to complete the task, feelings and emotions, and facilitating and inhibiting conditions not under the individual's control.[4] However, what is clearly evident is that if the manager is to improve the work of the organisation, attention must be given to the level of motivation of its members. The manager must also encourage staff to direct their efforts (their driving force) towards the successful attainment of the goals and objectives of the organisation.

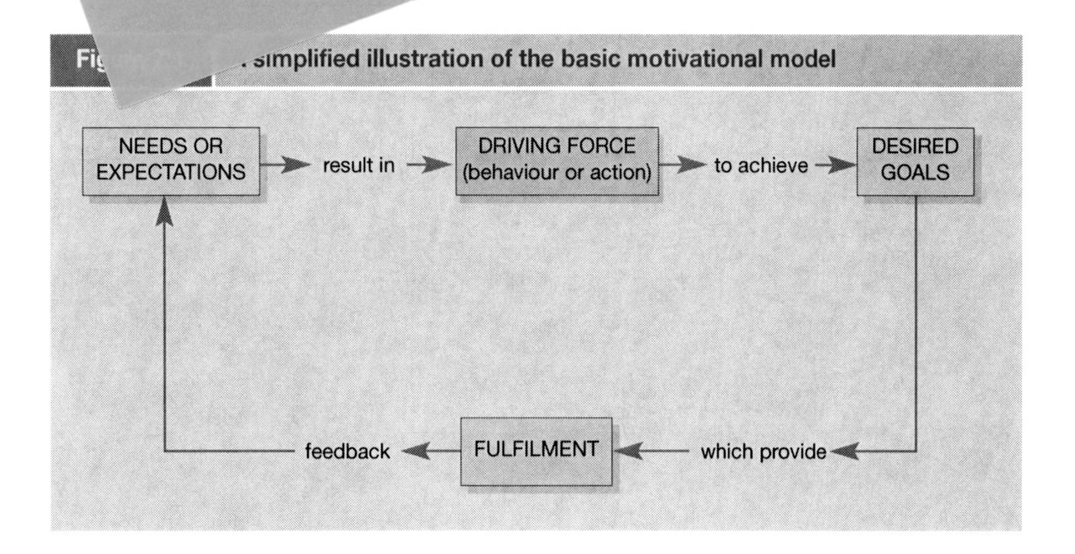

Fi… simplified illustration of the basic motivational model

NEEDS AND EXPECTATIONS AT WORK

But what is this driving force? What are people's needs and expectations and how do they influence behaviour and performance at work? Motivation is a complex subject, it is a very personal thing, and it is influenced by many variables. *Farren* reminds us of the 12 human needs that have been around since the beginning of recorded history: family, health and well-being, work/career, economic, learning, home/shelter, social relationships, spirituality, community, leisure, mobility, and environment/safety. 'Work and private life in the new millennium will continue to revolve around the 12 human needs.'[5]

The various needs and expectations at work can be categorised in a number of ways – for example the simple divisions into physiological and social motives or into intrinsic and extrinsic motivation.

Extrinsic motivation is related to 'tangible' rewards such as salary and fringe benefits, security, promotion, contract of service, the work environment and conditions of work. Such tangible rewards are often determined at the organisational level and may be largely outside the control of individual managers.

Intrinsic motivation is related to 'psychological' rewards such as the opportunity to use one's ability, a sense of challenge and achievement, receiving appreciation, positive recognition and being treated in a caring and considerate manner. The psychological rewards are those that can usually be determined by the actions and behaviour of individual managers.[6]

Higher set of motivational needs

According to *Kets de Vries*, the best-performing companies possess a set of values that creates the right conditions for high performance; he questions whether in such best companies there is something more going on that touches upon a deeper layer of human functioning, causing people to make an extra effort. The emphasis is on widening choice that enables people to choose more freely, instead of being led by forces of which they are unaware; and it is a motivational needs system on which such choice is based. Kets de Vries suggests that in addition to the motivation needs system for physiological needs, sensual and enjoyment needs, and the need to respond to threatening situations, companies that get the best out of their people are characterised by a higher set of motivational needs system:

- **attachment/affiliation** – concerning the need for engagement and sharing, a feeling of community and a sense of belonging to the company; and

- **exploration/assertion** – concerning th[illegible]ork, a sense of fun and enjoyment, the need for self-assertion an[illegible]hoose.[7]

Broad classification for motivation to work

Given the complex and variable nature of needs and expectations, the following is a simplistic but useful, broad three-fold classification as a starting point for reviewing the motivation to work (*see* Figure 7.2):

- **Economic rewards** – such as pay, fringe benefits, pension rights, material goods and security. This is an **instrumental** orientation to work and concerned with 'other things'.
- **Intrinsic satisfaction** – derived from the nature of the work itself, interest in the job, and personal growth and development. This is a **personal** orientation to work and concerned with 'oneself'.
- **Social relationships** – such as friendships, group working and the desire for affiliation, status and dependency. This is a **relational** orientation to work and concerned with 'other people'.

A person's motivation, job satisfaction and work performance will be determined by the comparative strength of these sets of needs and expectations and the extent to which they are fulfilled. For example, some people may make a deliberate choice to forgo intrinsic satisfaction and social relationships (particularly in the short term or in the earlier years of their working life) in return for high economic rewards. Other people are happy to accept comparatively lower economic rewards in favour of a job that has high intrinsic satisfaction and/or social relationships. Social relationships would appear to be an important feature for many people, especially, for example, for those working in the hospitality industry where interactions with other people and the importance of supportive working relationships and good teamwork can be strong motivators at work.[8]

Broader concerns

Popular press reports appear to indicate that many people are increasingly motivated by broader concerns such as their work/life balance, opportunities for flexible working, career advancement and personal development and growth, and a feeling of identification with the values of the organisation. The motivation to work is also influenced by the changing nature of the work environment and the concept of the 'psychological contract', which was discussed in Chapter 1.

Figure 7.2 Needs and expectations of people at work

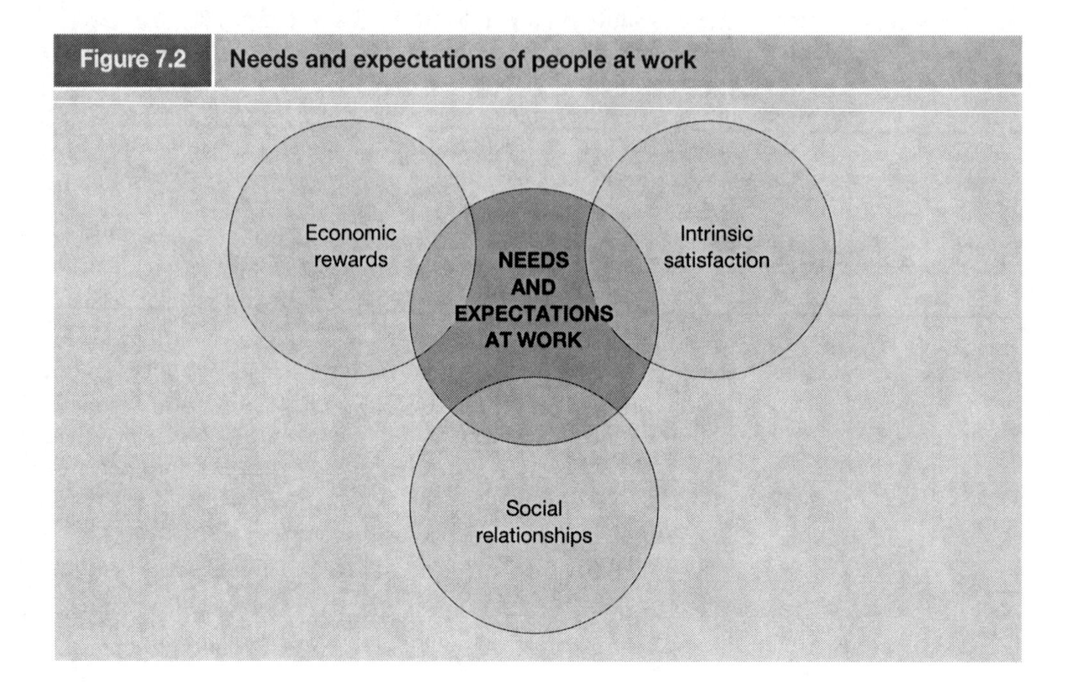

> *Today's managers are clearly more motivated by the intrinsic rewards of work such as challenge and a sense of purpose rather than with jobs that simply provide an income. Whilst they are driven by key organisational values such as customer focus and professionalism, they are most personally motivated by environments that foster innovation and staff development and a climate of trust.*
>
> Chartered Management Institute, 'Motivation Matters'[9]

FRUSTRATION-INDUCED BEHAVIOUR

What happens if a person's motivational driving force is blocked and they are unable to satisfy their needs and expectations, and what is the likely effect on their work performance? There are two possible sets of outcomes: constructive behaviour or frustration (*see* Figure 7.3).

Constructive behaviour

Constructive behaviour is a positive reaction to the blockage of a desired goal and can take two main forms: problem-solving or restructuring.

- **Problem-solving** is the removal of the barrier – for example repairing a damaged machine or bypassing an unco-operative superior.
- **Restructuring**, or compromise, is the substitution of an alternative goal, although such a goal may be of a lower order – for example taking an additional part-time job because of failure to be promoted to a higher grade.

Figure 7.3 A basic model of frustration

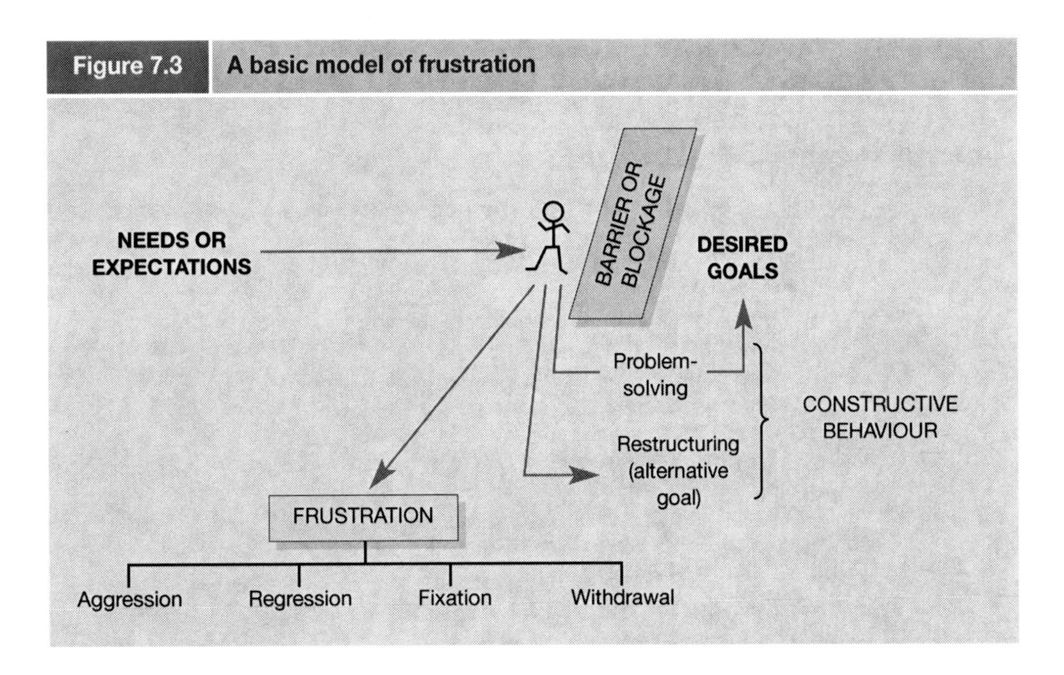

Note: Even if a person engages in constructive behaviour in response to a barrier or blockage, it could be said that the person was 'frustrated', if only mildly or in the short term, in an attempt to satisfy a desired goal. However, the term 'frustration' is usually interpreted as applying to **negative responses** to a barrier or blockage which prevents satisfaction of a desired goal.

Frustration (negative responses)

Frustration is a negative response to the blockage of a desired goal and results in a defensive form of behaviour. There are many possible reactions to frustration caused by the failure to achieve a desired goal. These can be summarised under four broad headings: aggression, regression, fixation, and withdrawal.[10] However, these categories are not mutually exclusive. Most forms of frustration-induced behaviour at work are a combination of aggression, regression and fixation.

Aggression is a physical or verbal attack on some person or object, for example striking a supervisor, rage or abusive language, destruction of equipment or documents, malicious gossip about a superior. This form of behaviour may be directed against the person or object that is perceived as the source of frustration, that is the actual barrier or blocking agent. However, where such a direct attack cannot be made, because, for example, the source of frustration is not clear or not specific, or where the source is feared, such as a powerful superior, aggression may be displaced towards some other person or object.

With **displaced aggression** the person may find an easier, safer person or object as a scapegoat for the outlet of frustration – for example picking arguments with colleagues, being short-tempered with subordinates, shouting at the cleaners or kicking the waste-paper bin. A more constructive form of displaced aggression is working off frustrated feelings through demanding physical work or sport, or perhaps by shouting/cursing when alone or in the company of an understanding colleague.

Regression is reverting to a childish or more primitive form of behaviour – for example sulking, crying, tantrums or kicking a broken machine or piece of equipment.

Fixation is persisting in a form of behaviour which has no adaptive value and continuing to repeat actions which have no positive results – for example the inability to accept change or new ideas, repeatedly trying a machine which clearly will not work, insisting on applying for promotion even though not qualified for the job.

Withdrawal is apathy, giving up or resignation – for example arriving at work late and leaving early, sickness and absenteeism, refusal to accept responsibility, avoiding decision-making, passing work over to colleagues or leaving the job altogether.

Factors influencing frustration

Among the factors which determine an individual's reaction to frustration are the:

- level and potency of need (*see*, for example, Maslow's theory of motivation, discussed below);
- degree of attachment to the desired goal;
- strength of motivation;
- perceived nature of the barrier or blocking agent; and
- personality characteristics of the individual.

It is important that managers attempt to reduce potential frustration, for example, through:

- effective recruitment, selection and socialisation;
- training and development;
- job design and work organisation;
- equitable personnel policies;
- recognition and rewards;
- effective communications;
- participative styles of management;
- attempting to understand the individual's perception of the situation.

Proper attention to motivation and to the needs and expectations of people at work will help overcome boredom and frustration-induced behaviour.

MONEY AS A MOTIVATOR

Earlier writers, such as F. W. Taylor, believed in economic needs motivation. Workers would be motivated by obtaining the highest possible wages through working in the most efficient and productive way. Performance was limited by physiological fatigue. For Taylor, motivation was a comparatively simple issue – what the workers wanted from their employers more than anything else was high wages. This approach is the **rational–economic concept of motivation**. The ideas of F. W. Taylor and his 'rational–economic needs' concept of motivation (discussed in Chapter 2) and subsequent approaches to motivation at work have fuelled the continuing debate about financial rewards as a motivator and their influence on productivity.

Where there is little pleasure in the work itself or the job offers little opportunity for career advancement, personal challenge or growth, many people may appear to be motivated primarily, if not exclusively, by money. Weaver suggests that for many hourly workers in the hospitality industry, such as dishwashers, waiting or housekeeping staff, the work does not change much among different companies and there is little attachment to a particular company. For such staff, Weaver proposes a 'Theory M' programme of motivation based on direct cash rewards for above-average performance. A percentage base is calculated from the average performance of workers on the staff.[11]

Yet we frequently see pronouncements from prominent business figures that motivation is about much more than money.

> *Work is about letting people know they are important, their hard work and efforts matter, and they're doing a good job. And this kind of recognition, in fact, can sometimes be more important than money.*
>
> Gary Kusin, CEO, FedEx Kinko's[12]

The short answer appears to be that for the vast majority of people, money is clearly important and a motivator at work **but** to what extent and **how** important depends upon their personal circumstances and the other satisfactions they derive from work. The bottom line is surely the extent to which money motivates people to work **well** and to the best of their abilities. Although pay may still make people tick, there are now a number of other important influences on motivation. For many people, the feeling of being recognised and valued appears more important than money in motivating them to stay in a particular job. (*See* Herzberg's two-factor theory of motivation, discussed below.)

Motivation other than by money

As *Grayson and Hodges* point out, historically loyalty was bought and employers offered gradual progression up the hierarchy, a decent salary and job security in return for a hard day's work. 'Increasingly, motivation is based on values rather than purely on financial reward.'[13] A similar point is made by *Saunders*:

> *If the 1980s were all about money, and people were only as good as their last bonus, in more recent years time has become the new money, and quality-of-life issues have come to the fore. Benefits that replenish the psychological contract are becoming the most valuable. So holiday arrangements, career breaks and potential for flexible hours and homeworking are now on the agenda.*[14]

A recent study from the Economic & Social Research Council analysed the influences on employee behaviour and productivity and raises the question: What if employees are guided not only by monetary incentives but also by social norms? Social norms interact with economic incentives and may have a large effect upon organisational performance.[15]

Critical reflection

'Whatever people may say or would like us to believe, in the real world money is the most potent need and strongest motivator.' Do you agree?

'All the ideas and theories that abound around motivation at work are redundant when it comes to basic issues.' Do you believe that you can motivate employees to do anything as long as they feel their job is under threat?

THEORIES OF MOTIVATION

There are many competing theories that attempt to explain the nature of motivation. These theories may all be at least partially true and help to explain the behaviour of certain people at certain times. It is often most acute for younger people starting on their career, for people at mid-career positions or for those who find limited opportunities for promotion or further advancement. For employers there may be difficulties in motivating staff both in the longer term as well as in the short run. It is because of the complexity of motivation and the fact that there is no ready-made solution or single answer to what motivates people to work well that the different theories are important to the manager. They show there are many motives that influence people's behaviour and performance. Collectively, the different theories provide a framework within which to direct attention to the problem of how best to motivate staff to work willingly and effectively.

Criticisms and reservations

It is important to emphasise, however, that these various theories are not conclusive. They all have their critics (this is particularly true of the content theories of motivation) or have been subject to alternative findings that purport to contradict original ideas. Many of these theories were not intended, initially to have the significance that some writers have subsequently placed upon them. It is always easy to quote an example that appears to contradict any generalised observation on what motivates people to work. Despite these reservations the different theories provide a basis for study and discussion, and for review of the most effective motivational style (*see* Figure 7.4).

> *You don't motivate individuals. You provide them with an environment to be self-motivated. It is a personal decision, but it's management's job to provide the right environment.*
>
> Kathy Schofield, Director of Human Resources, HFC Bank[16]

The manager, therefore, must judge the relevance of these different theories, how best to draw upon them, and how they might effectively be applied in particular work situations. The manager should be aware of at least the main theories of motivation.

Content theories and process theories

The usual approach to the study of motivation is through an understanding of internal cognitive processes – that is, what people feel and how they think. This understanding should help the manager to predict likely behaviour of staff in given situations. These different cognitive theories of motivation are usually divided into two contrasting approaches: content theories and process theories.

- **Content theories** attempt to explain those specific things that actually motivate the individual at work. These theories are concerned with identifying people's needs and their relative strengths, and the goals they pursue in order to satisfy these needs. Content theories place emphasis on the nature of needs and **what motivates**.

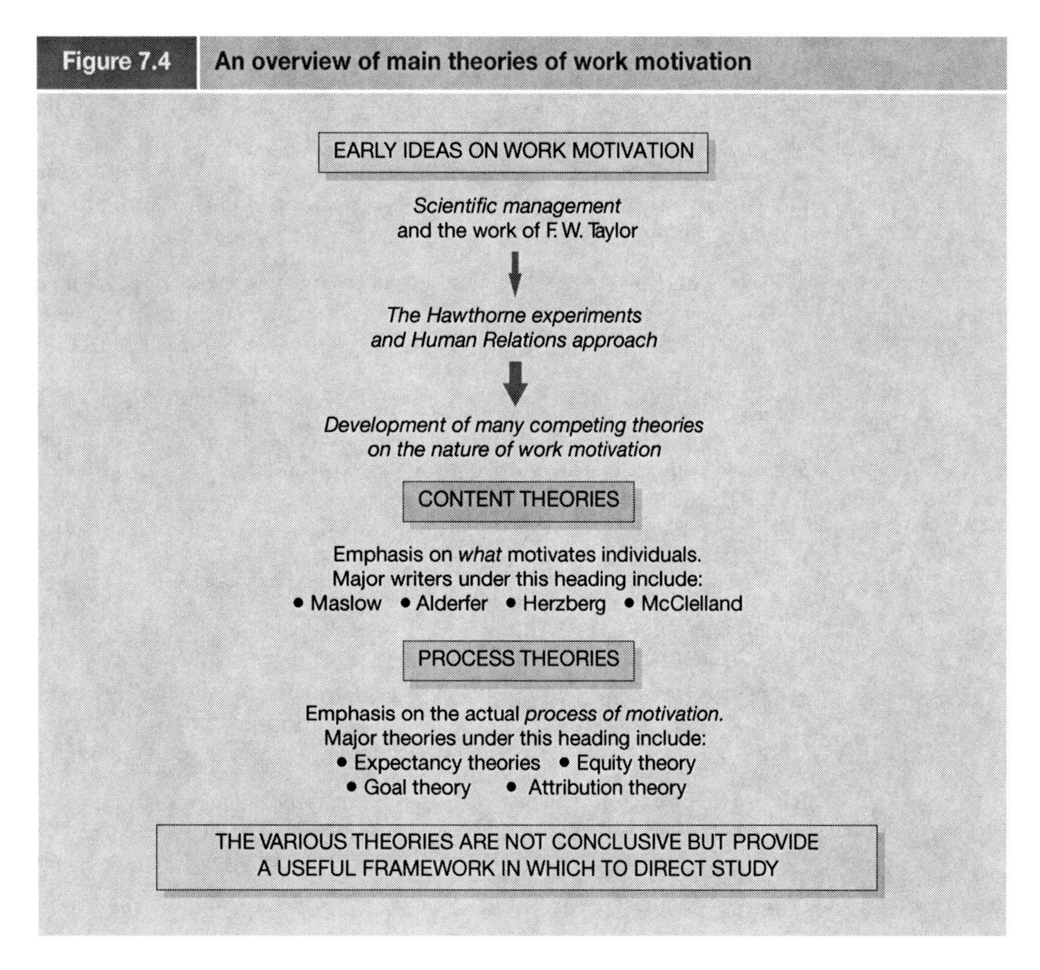

- **Process theories** attempt to identify the relationship among the dynamic variables that make up motivation. These theories are concerned more with how behaviour is initiated, directed and sustained. Process theories place emphasis on the **actual process of motivation**. These theories are discussed later in this chapter.

CONTENT THEORIES OF MOTIVATION

Major content theories of motivation include:

- *Maslow's* hierarchy of needs model;
- *Alderfer's* modified need hierarchy model;
- *Herzberg's* two-factor theory;
- *McClelland's* achievement motivation theory.

MASLOW'S HIERARCHY OF NEEDS THEORY

A useful starting point is the work of *Maslow* and his theory of individual development and motivation, published originally in 1943.[17] Maslow's basic proposition is that people are wanting beings, they always want more, and what they want depends on what they already have. He suggests that human needs are arranged in a series of levels, a hierarchy of importance.

Maslow identified eight innate needs, including the need to know and understand, aesthetic needs and the need for transcendence. However, the hierarchy is usually shown as ranging through five main levels, from, at the lowest level, physiological needs, through safety needs, love needs and esteem needs, to the need for self-actualisation at the highest level. The **hierarchy of needs** may be shown as a series of steps but is usually displayed in the form of a pyramid (Figure 7.5). This is an appropriate form of illustration as it implies a thinning out of needs as people progress up the hierarchy.

- **Physiological needs**. These include homeostasis (the body's automatic efforts to retain normal functioning) such as satisfaction of hunger and thirst, the need for oxygen and to maintain temperature regulation. Also sleep, sensory pleasures, activity, maternal behaviour and, arguably, sexual desire.
- **Safety needs**. These include safety and security, freedom from pain or threat of physical attack, protection from danger or deprivation, the need for predictability and orderliness.
- **Love needs** (often referred to as social needs). These include affection, sense of belonging, social activities, friendships, and both the giving and receiving of love.
- **Esteem needs** (sometimes referred to as ego needs). These include both self-respect and the esteem of others. Self-respect involves the desire for confidence, strength, independence and freedom, and achievement. Esteem of others involves reputation or prestige, status, recognition, attention and appreciation.
- **Self-actualisation needs**. This is the development and realisation of one's full potential. Maslow sees this as 'What humans can be, they must be' or 'becoming everything that one is capable of becoming'. Self-actualisation needs are not necessarily a creative urge and may take many forms which vary widely from one individual to another.

Once a lower need has been satisfied, it no longer acts as a strong motivator. The needs of the next higher level in the hierarchy demand satisfaction and become the motivating influence. Only unsatisfied needs motivate a person. Thus Maslow asserts that *'a satisfied need is no longer a motivator'*.

Not necessarily a fixed order

Although Maslow suggests that most people have these basic needs in about the order indicated, he also makes it clear that **the hierarchy is not necessarily a fixed order**. There will be a number of exceptions to the order indicated. For some people there will be a reversal of the hierarchy, for example:

- Self-esteem may seem to be more important than love to some people. This is the most common reversal of the hierarchy. It is often based on the belief that the person most

Figure 7.5 Maslow's hierarchy of needs model

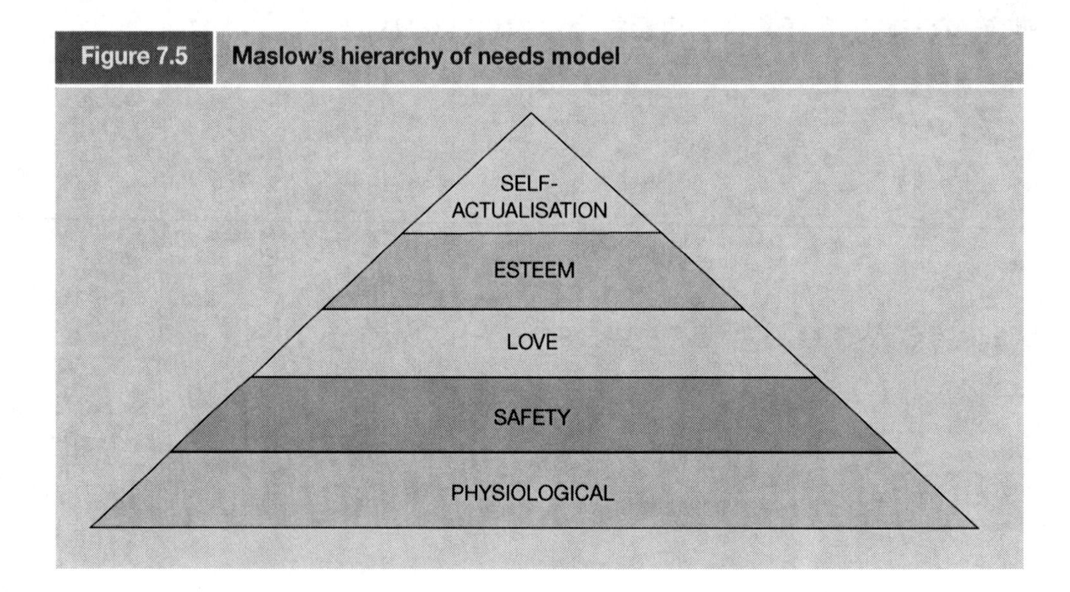

loved is strong, confident or inspires respect. People seeking love try to put on a show of aggressive, confident behaviour. They are not really seeking self-esteem as an end in itself but for the sake of love needs.

- For some innately creative people the drive for creativity and self-actualisation may arise despite lack of satisfaction of more basic needs.
- Higher-level needs may be lost in some people who will continue to be satisfied at lower levels only: for example, a person who has experienced chronic unemployment.
- Some people who have been deprived of love in early childhood may experience the permanent loss of love needs.
- A need which has continued to be satisfied over a long period of time may be undervalued. For example, people who have never suffered from chronic hunger may tend to underestimate its effects, and regard food as rather an unimportant thing. Where people are dominated by a higher-level need this may assume greater importance than more basic needs.
- People with high ideals or values may become martyrs and give up everything else for the sake of their beliefs.

Maslow claims that the hierarchy is relatively universal among different cultures, but he recognises that there are differences in an individual's motivational content in a particular culture.

Degrees of satisfaction

Maslow points out that a false impression may be given that a need must be satisfied fully before a subsequent need arises. **He suggests that a more realistic description is in terms of decreasing percentages of satisfaction along levels of the hierarchy**. For example, arbitrary figures for the average person may be: satisfied 85 per cent in physiological needs; 70 per cent in safety needs; 50 per cent in love needs; 40 per cent in esteem needs; and 10 per cent in self-actualisation needs. There is a gradual emergence of a higher-level need as lower-level needs become more satisfied. The relative importance of these needs changes during the psychological development of the individual. Maslow subsequently modified his views by noting that satisfaction of self-actualisation needs by growth-motivated individuals can actually enhance these needs rather than reduce them. Furthermore, he accepted that some higher-level needs may still emerge after long deprivation of lower-level needs rather than only after their satisfaction.

Evaluation of Maslow's theory

Based on Maslow's theory, once lower-level needs have been satisfied (say at the physiological and safety levels), giving more of the same does not provide motivation. Individuals advance up the hierarchy as each lower-level need becomes satisfied. Therefore, to provide motivation for a change in behaviour, the manager must direct attention to the next higher level of needs (in this case, love or social needs) that seek satisfaction.

Applications to the work situation

There are a number of problems in relating Maslow's theory to the work situation. These include the following:

- People do not necessarily satisfy their needs, especially higher-level needs, just through the work situation; they satisfy them through other areas of their life as well. Therefore the manager would need to have a complete understanding of people's private and social lives, not just their behaviour at work.
- There is doubt about the time that elapses between the satisfaction of a lower-level need and the emergence of a higher-level need.
- Individual differences mean that people place different values on the same need. For example, some people prefer what they might see as the comparative safety of working in a bureaucratic organisation to a more highly paid and higher status position, but with less job security, in a different organisation.

- Some rewards or outcomes at work satisfy more than one need. Higher salary or promotion, for example, can be applied to all levels of the hierarchy.
- Even for people within the same level of the hierarchy, the motivating factors will not be the same. There are many different ways in which people may seek satisfaction of, for example, their esteem needs.
- Maslow viewed satisfaction as the main motivational outcome of behaviour. But job satisfaction does not necessarily lead to improved work performance.

A useful basis for evaluation

Although Maslow did not originally intend that the need hierarchy should necessarily be applied to the work situation, it remains popular as a theory of motivation at work. Despite criticisms and doubts about its limitations, the theory has had a significant impact on management approaches to motivation and the design of organisations to meet individual needs. It is a convenient framework for viewing the different needs and expectations that people have, where they are in the hierarchy, and the different motivators that might be applied to people at different levels.

The work of Maslow has drawn attention to a number of motivators and stimulated study and research. The need hierarchy model provides a useful base for the evaluation of motivation at work. For example, *Steers and Porter* suggest a list of general rewards and organisational factors used to satisfy different needs (*see* Table 7.1).[18]

Saunders contends that despite the time that has elapsed, Maslow's theory remains watertight.

> *When prehistoric man first took shelter in a cave and lit a fire, he was satisfying his lowest – physiological and safety needs. When a Buddhist achieves a state of nirvana, she is satisfying the fifth and highest – self-actualisation ... The cave these days might be a three-bedroom semi with garden and off-street parking, but the fact remains that once we've got enough to feed, clothe and house our families money is a low-level motivator for most people. The dash for cash is soon replaced by the desire for recognition, status and ultimately (although Maslow reckoned that a lot of us never get this far) the need to express yourself through your work.*[19]

Table 7.1 Applying Maslow's need hierarchy

Needs levels	General rewards	Organisational factors
1 Physiological	Food, water, sex, sleep	a Pay b Pleasant working conditions c Cafeteria
2 Safety	Safety, security, stability, protection	a Safe working conditions b Company benefits c Job security
3 Social	Love, affection, belongingness	a Cohesive work group b Friendly supervision c Professional associations
4 Esteem	Self-esteem, self-respect, prestige, status	a Social recognition b Job title c High-status job d Feedback from the job itself
5 Self-actualisation	Growth, advancement, creativity	a Challenging job b Opportunities for creativity c Achievement in work d Advancement in the organisation

Source: Steers, R. M. and Porter, L. W., *Motivation and Work Behaviour*, Fifth Edition, McGraw-Hill (1991), p. 35.

ALDERFER'S MODIFIED NEED HIERARCHY MODEL

A modified need hierarchy model has been presented by *Alderfer*.[20] This model condenses Maslow's five levels of need into only three levels based on the core needs of existence, relatedness and growth (ERG theory) (*see* Table 7.2. p. 263).

- **Existence needs** are concerned with sustaining human existence and survival and cover physiological and safety needs of a material nature.
- **Relatedness needs** are concerned with relationships to the social environment and cover love or belonging, affiliation and meaningful interpersonal relationships of a safety or esteem nature.
- **Growth needs** are concerned with the development of potential and cover self-esteem and self-actualisation.

A continuum of needs

Like Maslow, Alderfer suggests that individuals progress through the hierarchy from existence needs to relatedness needs to growth needs as the lower-level needs become satisfied. However, Alderfer suggests these needs are more a continuum than hierarchical levels. More than one need may be activated at the same time. Individuals may also progress down the hierarchy. There is a frustration–regression process. For example, if an individual is continually frustrated in attempting to satisfy growth needs, relatedness needs may reassume most importance. The lower-level needs become the main focus of the individual's efforts.

Alderfer proposed a number of basic propositions relating to the three need relationships. Some of these propositions followed Maslow's theory, some were the reverse of the theory. A number of studies were undertaken to test these propositions across different samples of people in different types of organisations. Results from the studies were mixed. For example, the proposition that the less existence needs are satisfied the more they will be desired received constant support from all six samples. However, the proposition that satisfaction of existence needs activates desire for relatedness needs was not supported in any of the six samples.

Satisfaction of needs

Unlike Maslow's theory, the results of Alderfer's work suggest that lower-level needs do not have to be satisfied before a higher-level need emerges as a motivating influence. The results, however, do support the idea that lower-level needs decrease in strength as they become satisfied. ERG theory states that an individual is motivated to satisfy one or more basic sets of needs. Therefore if a person's needs at a particular level are blocked, attention should be focused on the satisfaction of needs at the other levels. For example, if a subordinate's growth needs are blocked because the job does not allow sufficient opportunity for personal development, the manager should attempt to provide greater opportunities for the subordinate to satisfy existence and relatedness needs.

HERZBERG'S TWO-FACTOR THEORY

Herzberg's original study consisted of interviews with 203 accountants and engineers, chosen because of their growing importance in the business world, from different industries in the Pittsburgh area of America.[21] He used the critical incident method. Subjects were asked to relate times when they felt exceptionally good or exceptionally bad about their present job or any previous job. They were asked to give reasons and a description of the sequence of events giving rise to that feeling. Responses to the interviews were generally consistent and revealed that there were two different sets of factors affecting motivation and work. **This led to the two-factor theory of motivation and job satisfaction.**

Hygiene and motivating factors

One set of factors are those which, if absent, cause dissatisfaction. These factors are related to job context, they are concerned with job environment and extrinsic to the job itself. These factors are the **'hygiene' or 'maintenance' factors** ('hygiene' being used as analogous to the medical term meaning preventive and environmental). They serve to prevent dissatisfaction. The other set of factors are those that, if present, serve to motivate the individual to superior effort and performance. These factors are related to job content of the work itself. They are the **'motivators' or growth factors**. The strength of these factors will affect feelings of satisfaction or no satisfaction, but not dissatisfaction. **The opposite of dissatisfaction is not satisfaction but, simply, no dissatisfaction** (*see* Figure 7.6).

The hygiene factors can be related roughly to Maslow's lower-level needs and the motivators to Maslow's higher-level needs (*see* Table 7.2, p. 263). To motivate workers to give of their best, the manager must give proper attention to the motivators or growth factors. Herzberg emphasises that hygiene factors are not a 'second-class citizen system'. They are as important as the motivators, but for different reasons. Hygiene factors are necessary to avoid unpleasantness at work and to deny unfair treatment. 'Management should never deny

Figure 7.6 Representation of Herzberg's two-factor theory

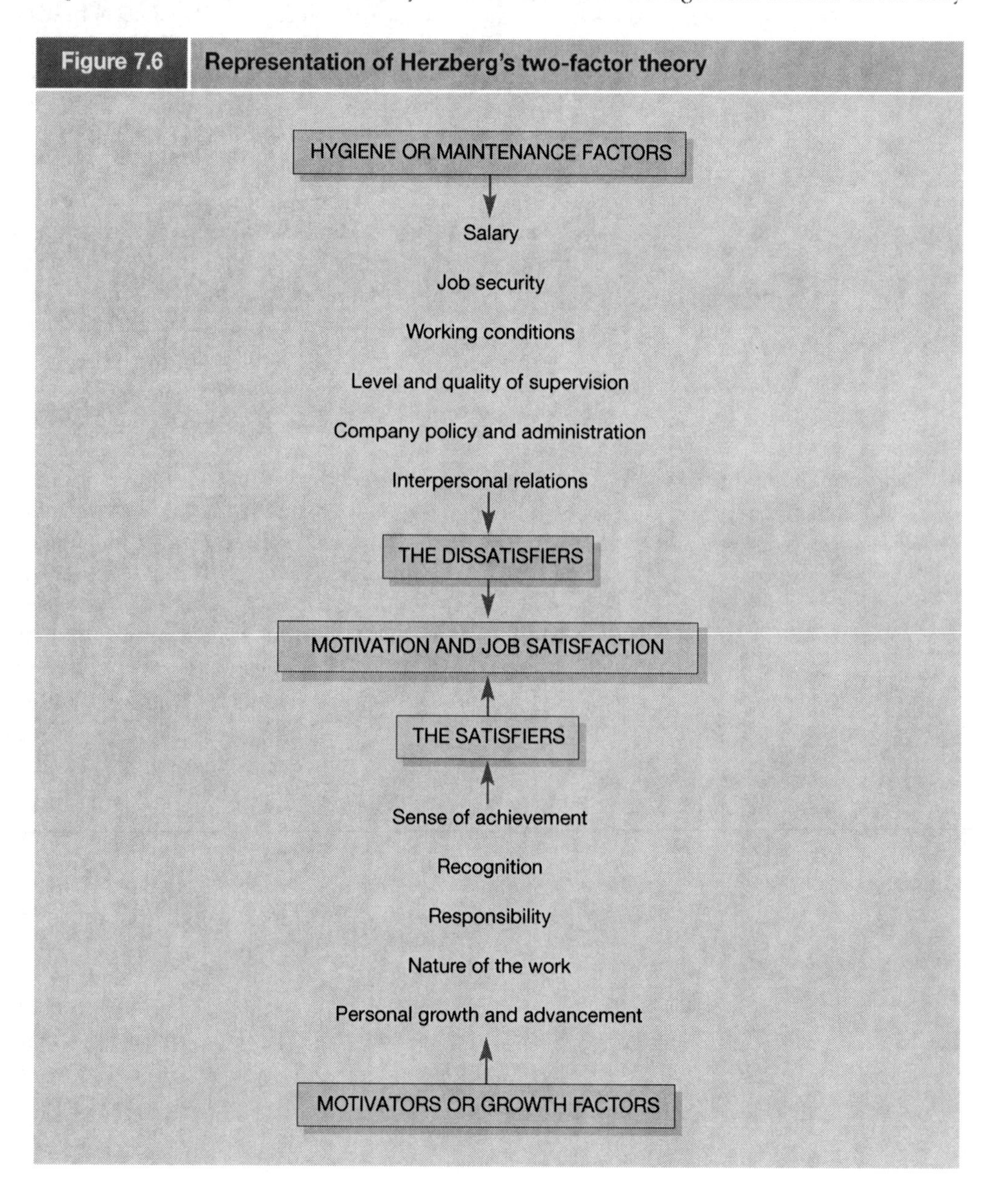

people proper treatment at work.' The motivators relate to what people are allowed to do and the quality of human experience at work. They are the variables which actually motivate people. The work of Herzberg indicates that it is more likely good performance leads to job satisfaction rather than the reverse.

Evaluation of Herzberg's work

Herzberg's theory is, however, a source of frequent debate. There have been many other studies to test the theory. The conclusions have been mixed. Some studies provide support for the theory. However, it has also been attacked by a number of writers. There are two common general criticisms of Herzberg's theory. One is that the theory has only limited application to 'manual' workers. The other is that the theory is 'methodologically bound'.

It is often claimed that the theory applies least to people with largely unskilled jobs or whose work is uninteresting, repetitive and monotonous, and limited in scope. Yet these are the people who often present management with the biggest problem of motivation. Some workers do not seem greatly interested in the job content of their work or with the motivators or growth factors.

A second, general criticism concerns methodology. It is claimed that the critical incident method, and the description of events giving rise to good or bad feelings, influences the results. People are more likely to attribute satisfying incidents at work, that is the motivators, as a favourable reflection on their own performance. The dissatisfying incidents that is the hygiene factors, are more likely to be attributed to external influences and the efforts of other people. Descriptions from the respondents had to be interpreted by the interviewers. This gives rise to the difficulty of distinguishing clearly between the different dimensions and to the risk of possible interviewer bias.

Despite such criticisms, there is still evidence of support for the continuing relevance of the theory. According to *Crainer and Dearlove*:

> *Herzberg's work has had a considerable effect on the rewards and remuneration packages offered by corporations. Increasingly, there is a trend towards 'cafeteria' benefits in which people can choose from a range of options. In effect, they can select the elements they recognise as providing their own motivation to work. Similarly, the current emphasis on self-development, career management and self-managed learning can be seen as having evolved from Herzberg's insights.*[22]

Whatever the validity of the two-factor theory, much of the criticism is with the benefit of hindsight, and *Herzberg* did at least attempt an empirical approach to the study of motivation at work and job satisfaction. Furthermore, his work has drawn attention to the importance of job design in the 'quality of work life'.

Table 7.2 Linking Maslow's, Alderfer's and Herzberg's theories of motivation

Maslow's hierarchy of needs	Alderfer's ERG theory	Herzberg's two-factor theory
PHYSIOLOGICAL	EXISTENCE	HYGIENE FACTORS
SAFETY		
LOVE	RELATEDNESS	
ESTEEM		MOTIVATORS
SELF-ACTUALISATION	GROWTH	

McCLELLAND'S ACHIEVEMENT MOTIVATION THEORY

McClelland's work originated from investigations into the relationship between hunger needs and the extent to which imagery of food dominated thought processes. From subsequent research McClelland identified four main arousal-based, and socially developed, motives:

- the Achievement motive;
- the Power motive;
- the Affiliative motive;
- the Avoidance motive.[23]

The first three motives correspond, roughly, to Maslow's self-actualisation, esteem and love needs. The relative intensity of these motives varies between individuals. It also tends to vary between different occupations. Managers appear to be higher in achievement motivation than in affiliation motivation. McClelland saw the achievement need (n-Ach) as the most critical for the country's economic growth and success. The need to achieve is linked to entrepreneurial spirit and the development of available resources.

Use of projective tests

Research studies by McClelland use a series of projective 'tests' – Thematic Apperception Test (TAT) – to gauge an individual's motivation. For example, individuals are shown a number of pictures in which some activity is depicted. Respondents are asked to look briefly (10–15 seconds) at the pictures and then to describe what they think is happening, what the people in the picture are thinking and what events have led to the situation depicted.[24] An example of a picture used in a projective test is given in Assignment 1 at the end of this chapter. The descriptions are used as a basis for analysing the strength of the individual's motives.

People with high achievement needs

Despite the apparent subjective nature of the judgements, research studies tend to support the validity of TAT as an indicator of the need for achievement.[25] McClelland has, over years of empirical research, identified four characteristics of people with a strong achievement need (n-Ach): a preference for moderate task difficulty, personal responsibility for performance, the need for feedback, and innovativeness.

- They prefer **moderate task difficulty** and goals as an achievement incentive. This provides the best opportunity of proving they can do better. If the task is too difficult or too risky, it would reduce the chances of success and of gaining need satisfaction. If the course of action is too easy or too safe, there is little challenge in accomplishing the task and little satisfaction from success.
- They prefer **personal responsibility for performance**. They like to attain success through the focus of their own abilities and efforts rather than by teamwork or chance factors outside their control. Personal satisfaction is derived from the accomplishment of the task and recognition need not come from other people.
- They have the need for **clear and unambiguous feedback** on how well they are performing. A knowledge of results within a reasonable time is necessary for self-evaluation. Feedback enables them to determine success or failure in the accomplishment of their goals and to derive satisfaction from their activities.
- They are **more innovative**. As they always seek moderately challenging tasks they tend always to be moving on to something a little more challenging. In seeking short cuts they are more likely to cheat. There is a constant search for variety and for information to find new ways of doing things. They are more restless and avoid routine and also tend to travel more.

Characteristics of achievement motivation

The extent of achievement motivation varies between individuals. Some people rate very highly in achievement motivation. They are challenged by opportunities and work hard to achieve a goal. Money is not an incentive but may serve as a means of giving feedback on performance. High achievers seem unlikely to remain long with an organisation that does not pay them well for good performance. Money may seem to be important to high achievers, but they value it more as symbolising successful task performance and goal achievement.

McClelland's research has attempted to understand the characteristics of high achievers. He suggests that n-Ach is not hereditary but results from environmental influences and he has investigated the possibility of training people to develop a greater motivation to achieve.[26] McClelland suggests four steps in attempting to develop achievement drive:

- Striving to attain feedback on performance. Reinforcement of success serves to strengthen the desire to attain higher performance.
- Developing models of achievement by seeking to emulate people who have performed well.
- Attempting to modify their self-image and to see themselves as needing challenges and success.
- Controlling day-dreaming and thinking about themselves in more positive terms.

McClelland was concerned with economic growth in underdeveloped countries. He has designed training programmes intended to increase the achievement motivation and entrepreneurial activity of managers.

McClelland has also suggested that as effective managers need to be successful leaders and to influence other people, they should possess a high need for power.[27] However, the effective manager also scores high on inhibition. Power is directed more towards the organisation and concern for group goals and is exercised on behalf of other people. This is 'socialised' power. It is distinguished from 'personalised' power that is characterised by satisfaction from exercising dominance over other people, and personal aggrandisement.

PROCESS THEORIES OF MOTIVATION

Process theories, or extrinsic theories, attempt to identify the relationships among the dynamic variables that make up motivation and the actions required to influence behaviour and actions. They provide a further contribution to our understanding of the complex nature of work motivation. Many of the process theories cannot be linked to a single writer, but major approaches and leading writers under this heading include:

- expectancy-based models – *Vroom*, and *Porter and Lawler*;
- equity theory – *Adams*;
- goal theory – *Locke*;
- attribution theory – *Heider* and *Kelley* (this was discussed in Chapter 6).

Expectancy theories of motivation

The underlying basis of **expectancy theory** is that people are influenced by the expected results of their actions. Motivation is a function of the relationship between:

1 effort expended and perceived level of performance; and
2 the expectation that rewards (desired outcomes) will be related to performance.

There must also be:

3 the expectation that rewards (desired outcomes) are available.

These relationships determine the strength of the 'motivational link' (*see* Figure 7.7).

Figure 7.7 Expectancy theory: the motivational link

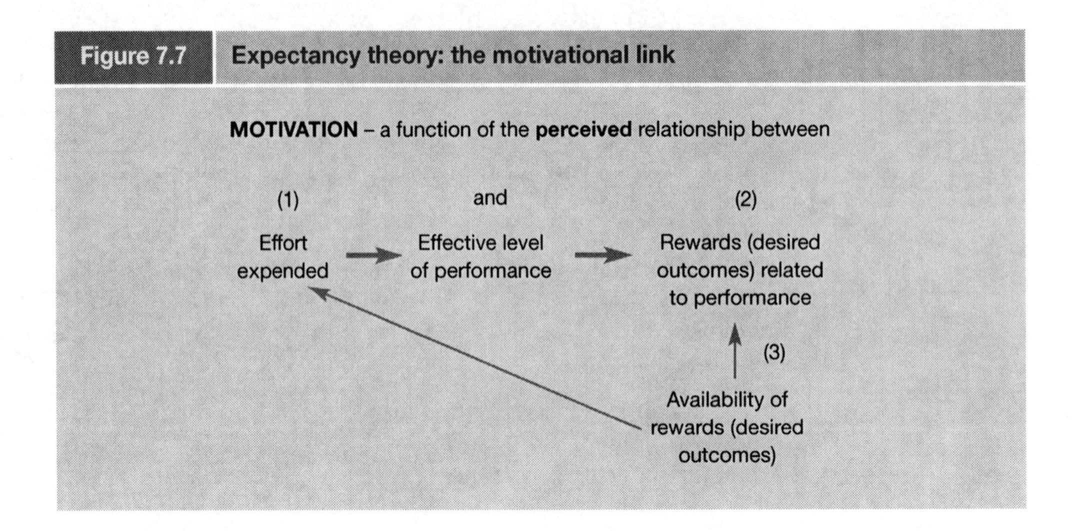

Performance therefore depends upon the perceived expectation regarding effort expended and achieving the desired outcome. For example, the desire for promotion will result in high performance only if the person believes there is a strong expectation that this will lead to promotion. If, however, the person believes promotion to be based solely on age and length of service, there is no motivation to achieve high performance. A person's behaviour reflects a conscious choice between the comparative evaluation of alternative behaviours. **The choice of behaviour is based on the expectancy of the most favourable consequences.**

Expectancy theory is a generic theory of motivation and cannot be linked to a single individual writer. There are a number of versions and some of the models are rather complex. More recent approaches to expectancy theory have been associated with the work of *Vroom* and of *Porter and Lawler*.

VROOM'S EXPECTANCY THEORY

Vroom was the first person to propose an expectancy theory aimed specifically at work motivation.[28] His model is based on three key variables: **valence**, **instrumentality** and **expectancy** (VIE theory or expectancy/valence theory). The theory is founded on the idea that people prefer certain outcomes from their behaviour over others. They anticipate feelings of satisfaction should the preferred outcome be achieved.

Valence The feeling about specific outcomes is termed **valence**. **This is the attractiveness of, or preference for, a particular outcome to the individual.** *Vroom* distinguishes valence from value. A person may desire an object but then gain little satisfaction from obtaining it. Alternatively, a person may strive to avoid an object but find, subsequently, that it provides satisfaction. **Valence is the anticipated satisfaction from an outcome.** This may differ substantially from value, which is the actual satisfaction provided by an outcome.

The valence of certain outcomes may be derived in their own right, but more usually they are derived from the other outcomes to which they are expected to lead. An obvious example is money. Some people may see money as having an intrinsic worth and derive satisfaction from the actual accumulation of wealth. Most people, however, see money in terms of the many satisfying outcomes to which it can lead.

Instrumentality The valence of outcomes derives, therefore, from their instrumentality. This leads to a distinction between first-level outcomes and second-level outcomes.

- **The first-level outcomes are performance-related.** They refer to the quantity of output or to the comparative level of performance. Some people may seek to perform well 'for its own sake' and without thought to expected consequences of their actions. Usually, however, performance outcomes acquire valence because of the expectation that they will lead to other outcomes as an anticipated source of satisfaction – second-level outcomes.
- **The second-level outcomes are need-related.** They are derived through achievement of first-level outcomes – that is, through achieving high performance. Many need-related outcomes are dependent upon actual performance rather than effort expended. People generally receive rewards for what they have achieved rather than for effort alone or through trying hard.

On the basis of *Vroom's* expectancy theory it is possible to depict a general model of behaviour (*see* Figure 7.8).

Expectancy

When a person chooses between alternative behaviours which have uncertain outcomes, the choice is affected not only by the preference for a particular outcome but also by the probability that such an outcome will be achieved. People develop a **perception** of the degree of probability that the choice of a particular action will actually lead to the desired outcome. This is **expectancy**. It is the relationship between a chosen course of action and its predicted outcome. Expectancy relates effort expended to the achievement of first-level outcomes. Its value ranges between 0, indicating zero probability that an action will be followed by the outcome, and 1, indicating certainty that an action will result in the outcome.

Motivational force

The combination of valence and expectancy determines the person's motivation for a given form of behaviour. This is the **motivational force**. The force of an action is unaffected by outcomes which have no valence or by outcomes that are regarded as unlikely to result from a course of action. Expressed as an equation, motivation (M) is the sum of the products of the valences of all outcomes (V), times the strength of expectancies that action will result in

Figure 7.8 Basic model of expectancy theory

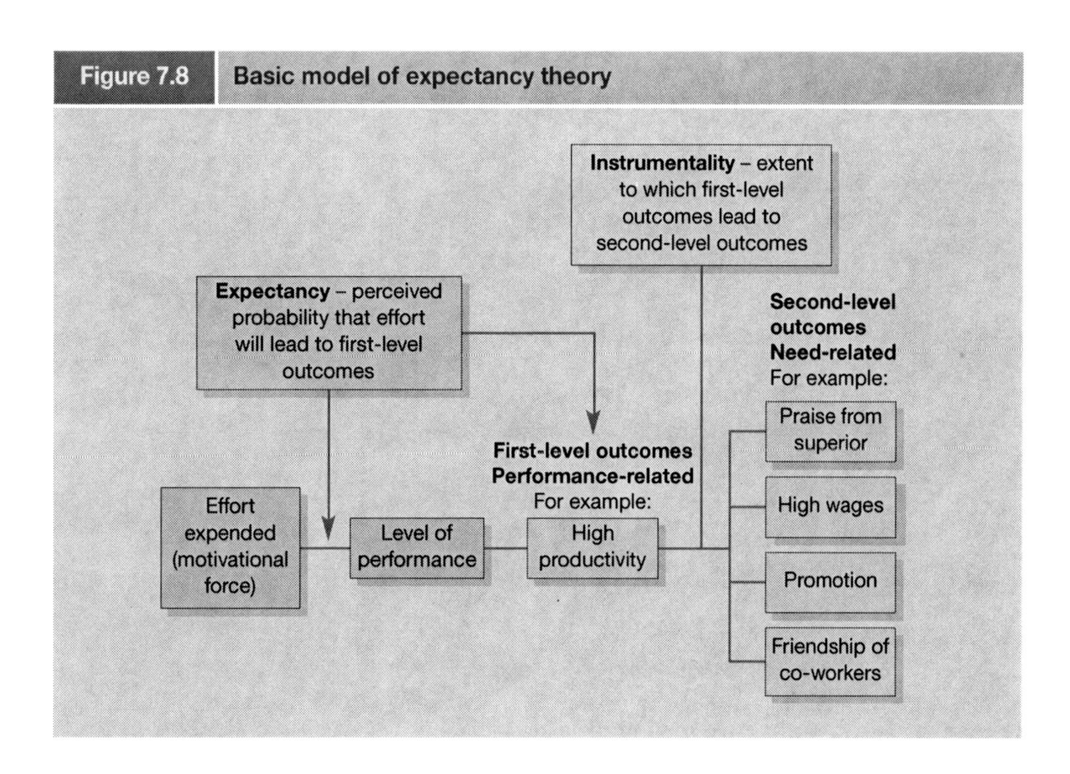

achieving these outcomes (E). Therefore, if either, or both, valence or expectancy is zero, then motivation is zero. The choice between alternative behaviours is indicated by the highest attractiveness score.

$$M = \sum^{n} E \cdot V$$

There are likely to be a number of outcomes expected for a given action. Therefore, the measure of $E \cdot V$ is summed across the total number of possible outcomes to arrive at a single figure indicating the attractiveness for the contemplated choice of behaviour.

THE PORTER AND LAWLER EXPECTANCY MODEL

Vroom's expectancy/valence theory has been developed by *Porter* and *Lawler*.[29] Their model goes beyond motivational force and considers performance as a whole. They point out that effort expended (motivational force) does not lead directly to performance. It is mediated by individual abilities and traits, and by the person's role perceptions. They also introduce rewards as an intervening variable. Porter and Lawler see motivation, satisfaction and performance as separate variables and attempt to explain the complex relationships among them. Their model recognises that job satisfaction is more dependent upon performance, than performance is upon satisfaction.

Explanation of relationships

These relationships are expressed diagrammatically (Figure 7.9) rather than mathematically. In contrast to the human relations approach which tended to assume that job satisfaction leads to improved performance, Porter and Lawler suggest that satisfaction is an effect rather than a cause of performance. It is performance that leads to job satisfaction.

- **Value of reward** (Box 1) is similar to valence in Vroom's model. People desire various outcomes (rewards) which they hope to achieve from work. The value placed on a reward depends on the strength of its desirability.

Figure 7.9 The Porter and Lawler motivation model

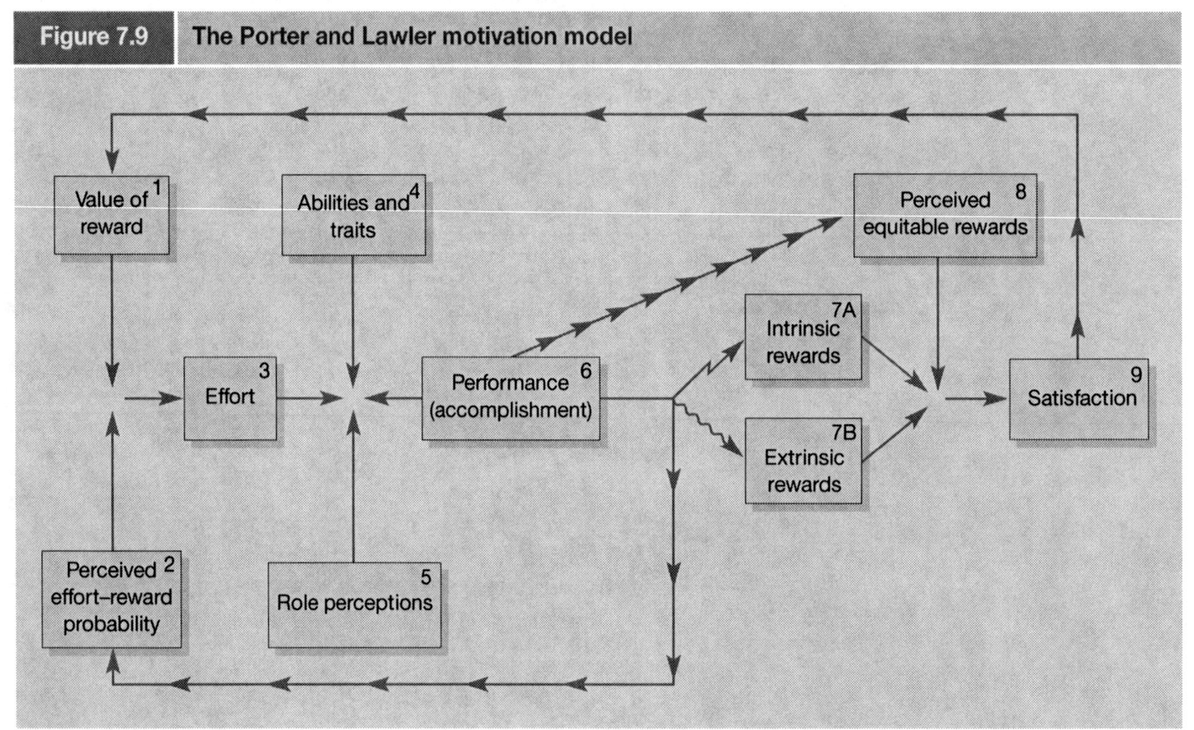

Source: From Porter, I. W. and Lawler, E. E., *Managerial Attitudes and Performance*. Copyright © Richard D. Irwin Inc. (1968) p. 165.

- **Perceived effort–reward probability** (Box 2) is similar to expectancy. It refers to a person's expectation that certain outcomes (rewards) are dependent upon a given amount of effort.
- **Effort** (Box 3) is how hard the person tries, the amount of energy a person exerts on a given activity. It does not relate to how successful a person is in carrying out an activity. The amount of energy exerted is dependent upon the interaction of the input variables of value of reward and perception of the effort–reward relationship.
- **Abilities and traits** (Box 4). Porter and Lawler suggest that effort does not lead directly to performance but is influenced by individual characteristics. Factors such as intelligence, skills, knowledge, training and personality affect the ability to perform a given activity.
- **Role perceptions** (Box 5) refer to the way in which individuals view their work and the role they should adopt. This influences the type of effort exerted. Role perceptions will influence the direction and level of action which is believed to be necessary for effective performance.
- **Performance** (Box 6) depends not only on the amount of effort exerted but also on the intervening influences of the person's abilities and traits, and their role perceptions. If the person lacks the right ability or personality, or has an inaccurate role perception of what is required, then the exertion of a large amount of energy may still result in a low level of performance or task accomplishment.
- **Rewards** (Boxes 7A and 7B) are desirable outcomes. Intrinsic rewards derive from the individuals themselves and include a sense of achievement, a feeling of responsibility and recognition (for example Herzberg's motivators). Extrinsic rewards derive from the organisation and the actions of others and include salary, working conditions and supervision (for example Herzberg's hygiene factors). The relationship between performance and intrinsic rewards is shown as a jagged line. This is because the extent of the relationship depends upon the nature of the job. If the design of the job permits variety and challenge, so that people feel able to reward themselves for good performance, there is a direct relationship. Where job design does not involve variety and challenge, there is no direct relationship between good performance and intrinsic rewards. The wavy line between performance and extrinsic rewards indicates that such rewards do not often provide a direct link to performance.
- **Perceived equitable rewards** (Box 8). This is the level of rewards people feel they should fairly receive for a given standard of performance. Most people have an implicit perception about the level of rewards they should receive commensurate with the requirements and demands of the job, and the contribution expected of them. Self-rating of performance links directly with the perceived equitable reward variable. Higher levels of self-rated performance are associated with higher levels of expected equitable rewards. The heavily arrowed line indicates a relationship from the self-rated part of performance to perceived equitable rewards.
- **Satisfaction** (Box 9). This is not the same as motivation. It is an attitude, an individual's internal state. Satisfaction is determined by both actual rewards received and perceived level of rewards from the organisation for a given standard of performance. If perceived equitable rewards are greater than actual rewards received, the person experiences dissatisfaction. The experience of satisfaction derives from actual rewards that meet or exceed the perceived equitable rewards.

LAWLER'S REVISED EXPECTANCY MODEL

Following the original Porter and Lawler model, further work was undertaken by *Lawler* (*see* Figure 7.10).[30] He suggests that in deciding on the attractiveness of alternative behaviours, there are two types of expectancies to be considered: effort–performance expectancies (E → P) and performance–outcome expectancies (P → O).

The first expectancy (E → P) is the person's perception of the probability that a given amount of effort will result in achieving an intended level of performance. It is measured on a scale between 0 and 1. The closer the perceived relationship between effort and performance, the higher the E → P expectancy score.

The second expectancy (P → O) is the person's perception of the probability that a given level of performance will actually lead to particular need-related outcomes. This is measured also on a scale between 0 and 1. The closer the perceived relationship between performance and outcome, the higher the P → O expectancy score.

Motivational force to perform

The multiplicative combination of the two types of expectancies, E → P and the sum of the products P → O, determines expectancy. The motivational force to perform (effort expended) is determined by multiplying E → P and P → O by the strength of outcome valence (V).

$$E(\text{Effort}) = (E \rightarrow P) \times \Sigma\,[(P \rightarrow O) \quad V]$$

The distinction between the two types of expectancies arises because they are determined by different conditions. E → P expectancy is determined in part by the person's ability and self-confidence, past experience and the difficulty of the task. P → O expectancy is determined by the attractiveness of the outcomes and the belief about who controls the outcomes, the person him/herself or other people.

Figure 7.10 An illustration of the Lawler expectancy model

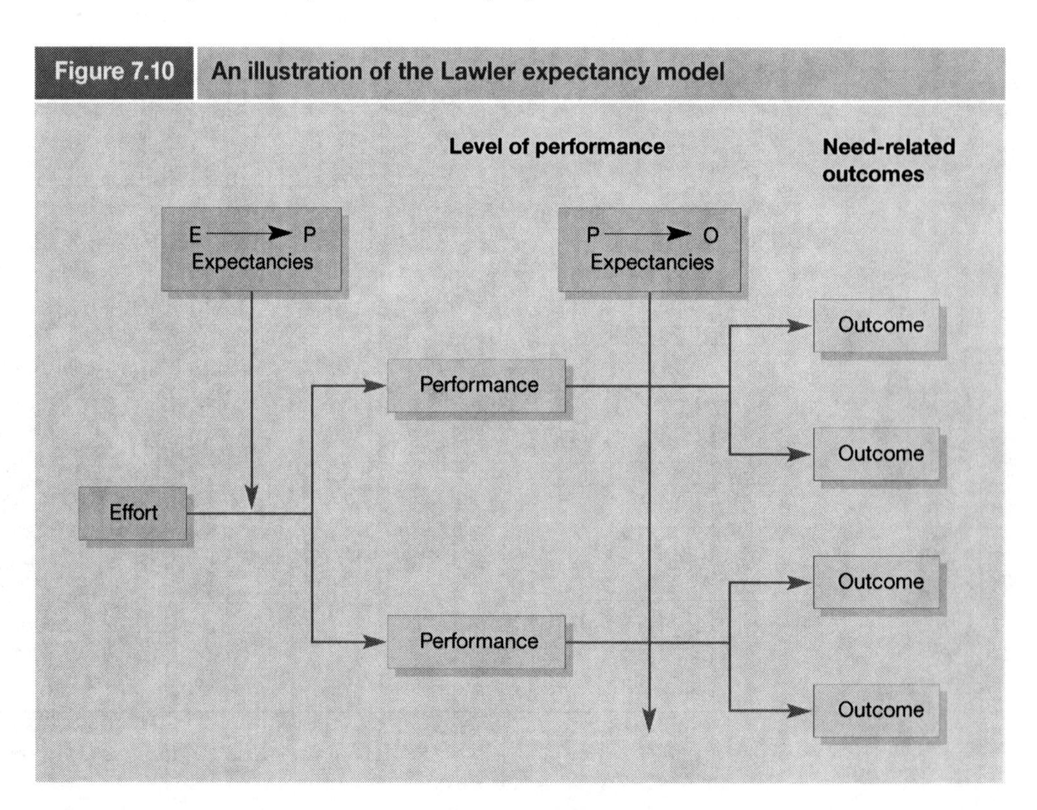

IMPLICATIONS FOR MANAGERS OF EXPECTANCY THEORIES

There are a number of versions of expectancy theory. The main elements tend to be very similar, however, and this suggests the development of a generally accepted approach. Expectancy models are not always easy to understand, or to apply. There are many variables which affect behaviour at work. A problem can arise in attempting to include a large number of variables or in identifying those variables which are most appropriate in particular situations.

Expectancy theory does, however, draw attention to the complexities of work motivation. It provides further information in helping to explain the nature of behaviour and motivation in the work situation, and helps to identify problems in performance. Expectancy theory indicates that managers should give attention to a number of factors, including the following:

- Use rewards appropriate in terms of individual performance. Outcomes with high valence should be used as an incentive for improved performance.
- Attempt to establish clear relationships between effort–performance and rewards, as perceived by the individual.
- Establish clear procedures for the evaluation of individual levels of performance.
- Pay attention to intervening variables such as abilities and traits, role perceptions, organisational procedures and support facilities, which, although not necessarily direct motivational factors, may still affect performance.
- Minimise undesirable outcomes which may be perceived to result from a high level of performance, such as industrial accidents or sanctions from co-workers, or to result despite a high level of performance, such as short-time working or layoffs.

Porter and Lawler also emphasise that the expectancy model is just a model and that expectancy theory applies only to behaviours which are under the voluntary control of the individual. The two general types of choices over which individuals have voluntary control of work performance in organisations are:

1 the amount of effort and energy expended; and
2 the manner in which they go about performing their work.

There is always a choice about the way you do your work, even if there is not a choice about the work itself. You always have a choice about the attitude you bring to the job.

World famous Pike Place Fish Market, Seattle[31]

Critical reflection

'Expectancy theories of motivation appear to make sense in the classroom and form the basis of an interesting academic debate, but it is unlikely the practising manager will be impressed or take much notice.' What do you think? How would you explain the potential benefits of expectancy theory to a sceptical manager?

EQUITY THEORY OF MOTIVATION

One of the major variables of satisfaction in the Porter and Lawler expectancy model is perceived equitable rewards. This leads to consideration of another process theory of motivation – **equity theory**. Applied to the work situation, equity theory is usually associated with the work of *Adams*.[32]

Equity theory focuses on people's feelings of how fairly they have been treated in comparison with the treatment received by others. It is based on exchange theory. Social relationships involve an exchange process. For example, a person may expect promotion as an outcome of a high level of contribution (input) in helping to achieve an important organisational objective. People also compare their own position with that of others. They determine the perceived equity of their own position. Their feelings about the equity of the exchange are affected by the treatment they receive when compared with what happens to other people. Most exchanges involve a number of inputs and outcomes. According to equity theory, people place a weighting on these various inputs and outcomes according to how they perceive their importance. When there is an unequal comparison of ratios the person experiences a sense of **inequity**.

Behaviour as a consequence of inequity

A feeling of inequity causes tension, which is an unpleasant experience. The presence of inequity therefore motivates the person to remove or to reduce the level of tension and the perceived inequity. The magnitude of perceived inequity determines the level of tension. The level of tension created determines the strength of motivation. Adams identifies six broad types of possible behaviour as consequences of inequity (*see* Figure 7.11):

- **Changes to inputs**. A person may increase or decrease the level of their inputs, for example through the amount or quality of work, absenteeism, or working additional hours without pay.
- **Changes to outcomes**. A person may attempt to change outcomes such as pay, working conditions, status and recognition, without changes to inputs.
- **Cognitive distortion of inputs and outcomes**. In contrast to actual changes, people may distort, cognitively, their inputs or outcomes to achieve the same results. Adams suggests that although it is difficult for people to distort facts about themselves, it is possible, within limits, to distort the utility of those facts: for example, the belief about how hard they are really working, the relevance of a particular qualification, or what they can or cannot obtain with a given level of pay.

Figure 7.11 An illustration of Adams's equity theory of motivation

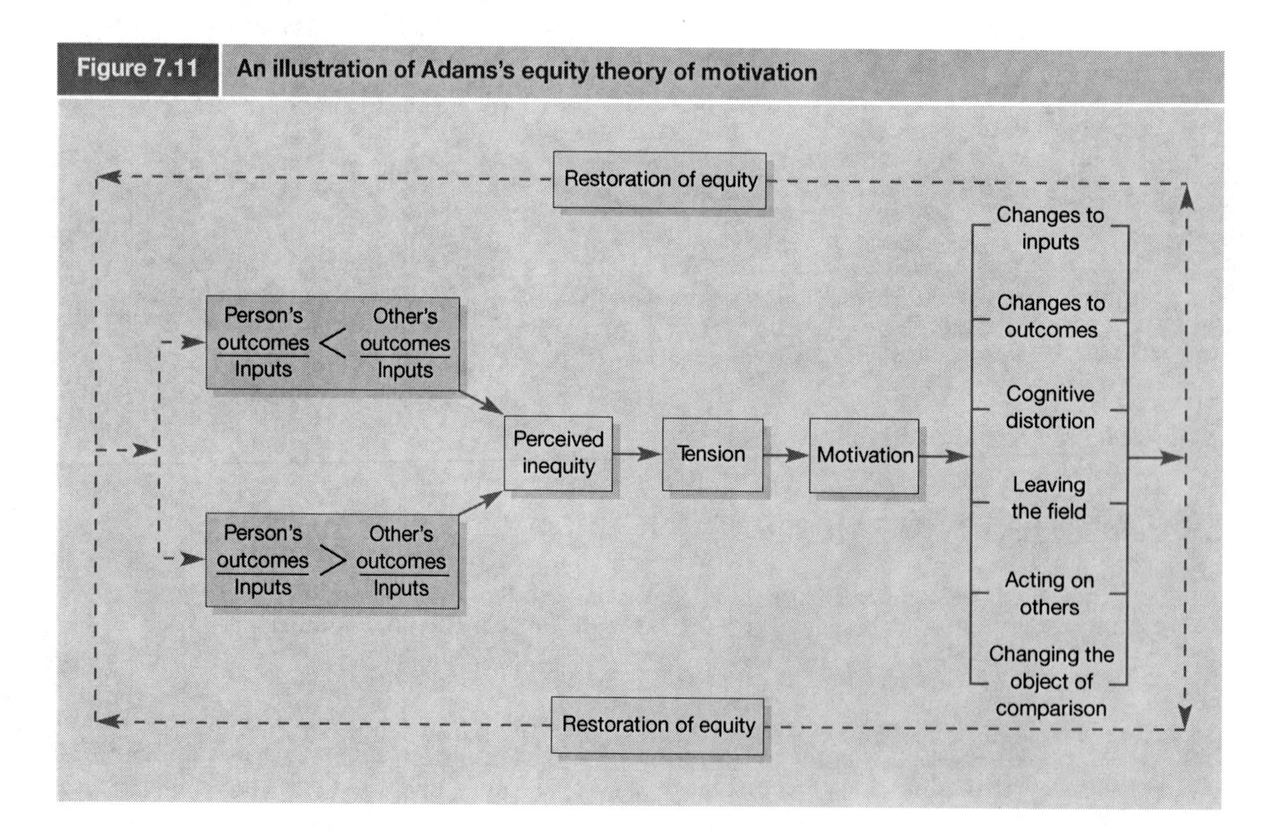

- **Leaving the field.** A person may try to find a new situation with a more favourable balance, for example by absenteeism, request for a transfer, resigning from a job or from the organisation altogether.
- **Acting on others.** A person may attempt to bring about changes in others, for example to lower their inputs or accept greater outcomes. Or the person may cognitively distort the inputs and outcomes of others. Alternatively, a person may try to force others to leave the field.
- **Changing the object of comparison.** This involves changing the reference group with whom comparison is made. For example, where another person with a previously similar outcome–input ratio receives greater outcomes without any apparent increase in contribution, that other person may be perceived as now belonging to a different level in the organisation structure. The comparison need not necessarily be made with people who have the same inputs and outcomes. The important thing is a similar ratio of outcomes to inputs.

Under the control of the manager

The manager may seek to remove or reduce tension and perceived inequity among staff by influencing these types of behaviour – for example by attempting to change a person's inputs or encouraging a different object of comparison. However, there are likely to be only two courses of action under the direct control of the manager. Outcomes can be changed by, for example, increased pay, additional perks or improved working conditions, or by instigating a person leaving the field through transfer, resignation or, as an extreme measure, dismissal.

GOAL THEORY

Another theory usually considered under the heading of motivation to work is **goal theory**, or the theory of goal-setting (*see* Figure 7.12). This theory is based mainly on the work of *Locke*.[33] The basic premise of goal theory is that people's goals or intentions play an important part in determining behaviour. Locke accepts the importance of perceived value, as indicated in expectancy theories of motivation, and suggests that these values give rise to the experience of emotions and desires. People strive to achieve goals in order to satisfy their emotions and desires. Goals guide people's responses and actions. Goals direct work behaviour and performance and lead to certain consequences or feedback. Locke subsequently pointed out that 'goal-setting is more appropriately viewed as a motivational technique rather than as a formal theory of motivation.'[34]

Figure 7.12 An illustration of Locke's theory of goal-setting

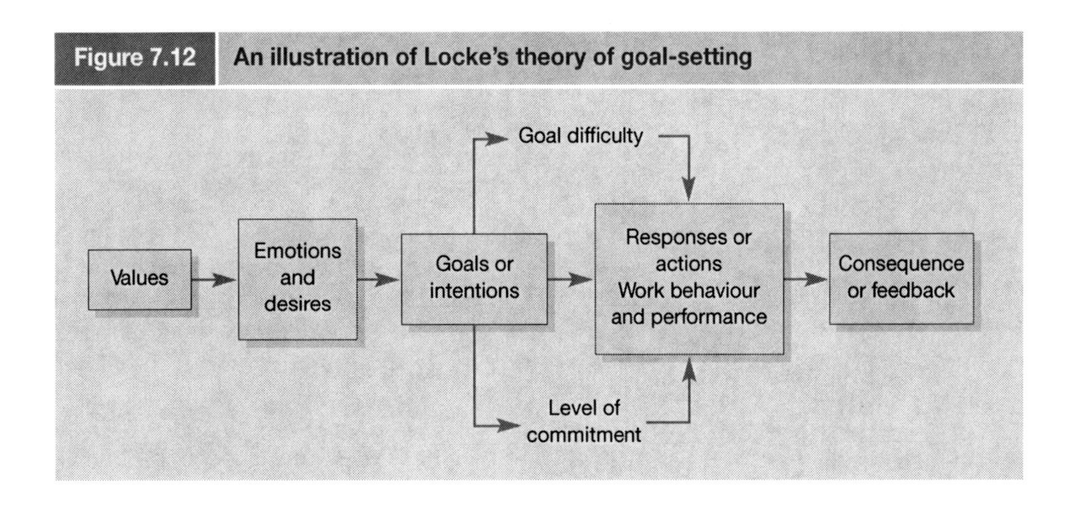

Goal-setting and performance

The combination of goal difficulty and the extent of the person's commitment to achieving the goal regulates the level of effort expended. People with specific quantitative goals, such as a defined level of performance or a given deadline for completion of a task, will perform better than people with no set goal or only a vague goal such as 'do the best you can'. People who have difficult goals will perform better than people with easier goals.

Gratton refers to 'stretch goals' which are ambitious, highly targeted opportunities for breakthrough improvements in performance. These goals should stem from critical success indicators and come from deep discussions within the company, and from collaboration within and across task forces, and lead to development of activities and tactics to achieve the goals.[35] People lacking positive motivation at work may also help gain improved results and a better sense of achievement by setting themselves specific goals and identifying tasks directly related to their work and measurable targets of time and performance.

Practical implications for the manager

Goal theory has a number of practical implications for the manager:

- Specific performance goals should systematically be identified and set in order to direct behaviour and maintain motivation.
- Goals should be set at a challenging but realistic level. Difficult goals lead to higher performance. However, if goals are set at too high a level or are regarded as impossible to achieve, performance will suffer, especially over a longer period.
- Complete, accurate and timely feedback and knowledge of results is usually associated with high performance. Feedback provides a means of checking progress on goal attainment and forms the basis for any revision of goals.
- Goals can be determined either by a superior or by individuals themselves. Goals set by other people are more likely to be accepted when there is participation. Employee participation in the setting of goals may lead to higher performance.

Much of the theory of goal-setting can be related to the system of management by objectives (discussed in Chapter 12). MBO is often viewed as an application of goal-setting, although it was devised originally before the development of goal-setting theory. However it is viewed, the theory of goal-setting provides a useful approach to work motivation and performance. And *Hannagan* goes so far as to suggest: 'At present goal-setting is one of the most influential theories of work motivation applicable to all cultures'.[36]

ATTRIBUTION THEORY

A more recent approach to the study of motivation is attribution theory. Attribution is the process by which people interpret the perceived causes of behaviour. This is discussed in Chapter 6.

RELEVANCE OF THEORIES OF MOTIVATION

Given that most major theories of motivation date back many years it is inevitable that questions will be raised about their relevance today. *Reis and Pena* question whether motivating people to work in the 21st century with theories conceived during the past 100 years is likely to be feasible. They conclude that the core message is that managers should reconsider the outdated motivational patterns utilised to maintain role performance in organisations and adopt a fresh motivation formula for the 21st century based on friendship, work and respect.[37]

However, we have seen from the discussions above that there still appears to be general support for the theories – and, perhaps ironically, particularly for the early theories of

Maslow and Herzberg and McClelland. A Chartered Management Institute checklist maintains that these theories are still valid today. 'A basic understanding of their main principles will be invaluable for building a climate of honesty, openness and trust.'[38] From a 12-year study of the use of management concepts in technical organisations, *Flores and Utley* found the work of Maslow and McGregor the most popular motivational theories and also refer to the relationship between Maslow and Herzberg and the successful implementation of quality systems.[39]

THE MOTIVATION OF KNOWLEDGE WORKERS

Recent advantages in telecommunications and in scientific and technological knowledge have led to greater emphasis on the knowledge and expertise of staff and the importance of creativity. *Tampoe* suggests that at the core of the new industrial trend are the 'knowledge workers' – those employees who apply their theoretical and practical understanding of a specific area of knowledge to produce outcomes of a commercial, social or personal value. The performance of knowledge workers should be judged on both the cleverness of ideas and the utility and commercial value of their applied knowledge. Creativity is necessary and needs to be encouraged but should be bounded by commercial realism. This presents management with a new challenge of how to motivate the knowledge workers.[40]

Tampoe suggests that the personal motivation of knowledge workers is based on the value they place on the rewards they expect to earn at work. In addition to the individual's own motivation, the performance of knowledge workers is dependent upon four key characteristics (*see* Figure 7.13):

- task competence;
- peer and management support;
- task and role clarity; and
- corporate awareness.

The challenge to management is to ensure the effectiveness of the four key variables and to recognise the need for staff to supervise and manage themselves and the wider rewards expected by knowledge workers.

Figure 7.13 Motivating knowledge workers

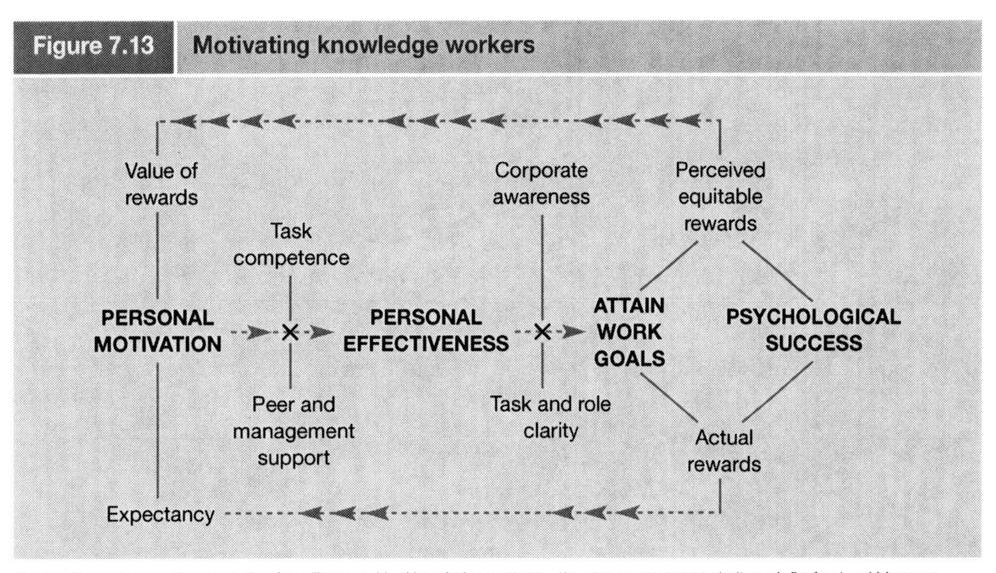

Source: Reproduced with permission from Tampoe, M., 'Knowledge workers – the new management challenge', *Professional Manager*, Institute of Management, November 1994, p. 13.

A climate of creativity

Lucas draws attention to skills shortages as one of the biggest challenges facing employers in the new millennium. In order to attract and keep talented individuals, the so-called knowledge workers, organisations cannot rely simply on a pay rise or cash bonus but have to be more creative about the way they structure remuneration packages. Individual performance-related pay is still the most widely used reward strategy, but attention is also given to employee share ownership, competence-related pay and team reward – and also to non-cash incentives such as gift vouchers. However, Lucas points out that employees, especially high flyers, rank challenging and interesting work and freedom higher on their motivational list than money and performance-related pay. 'Research suggests that most organisations haven't recognised the need to identify and tap into their employees' personal motivators.'[41]

A report from the *Chartered Institute of Personnel and Development* draws attention to the management of knowledge workers, highlighting the importance of autonomy, challenging work and sharing in the creation of organisational values. With the development of new technology it is important to motivate employees to capture, share and transfer knowledge.[42]

Whitmore suggests that in order to create a climate for creativity among employees, recognition must be given to the importance of two human needs that rise above all others and exist independent of race, creed and culture – the need for self-belief and the development of emotional intelligence; and the ever-present need that every human being has for a sense of meaning and purpose in their lives. 'Self-belief and meaningful work are the fundamental bedrocks that underlie business performance. Of course, pay and conditions are important too, but we know that. It is these two others that are barely recognised ... but business leaders ignore them at their peril.'[43]

CROSS-CULTURAL DIMENSIONS OF MOTIVATION

Whatever the popularity of different theories of motivation, doubts are raised about their universality on the ground that they have not adequately addressed the factor of culture.[44] Are theories of motivation universally applicable or are there meaningful differences in motivation at work, or in life more generally, in different societies? Many readers may feel able to recognise perceived variations in extrinsic, intrinsic and relational aspects of motivation as a result of experience of foreign cultures. Do similarities in workplace attitudes and behaviour outweigh differences? A number of writers have questioned whether motivational theories and models originating in one culture are amenable to transference to other parts of the world. *Francesco and Gold* devote a substantial proportion of a discussion of motivation to examining the extent to which American motivation theories are applicable outside the United States.

When discussing Maslow's contribution to this topic and, in particular, the concept of a hierarchy of needs, Francesco and Gold suggest: 'In an international context the circumstances and values of a particular culture can influence the ordering and importance of needs. The values of individualism and collectivism can make the hierarchy more or less relevant.'[45] In evaluating McClelland's work, Francesco and Gold question whether the meaning of an underlying concept, in this case achievement, can even be understood worldwide in the sense it was intended: 'Another concern with Learning Needs Theory is that the concept of achievement is difficult, if not impossible, to translate into languages other than English.'[46]

It has already been suggested that one criticism of content theories of motivation centres on its relative applicability in different circumstances and the suggestion that there may be variations across cultures falls within this line of reasoning. However, perhaps less obviously, process theories of motivation have also been criticised for being culture-bound. As they focus on process rather than content, such theories may appear to be more applicable in diverse cultural contexts. Nonetheless it has been suggested that process theories of motivation contain certain inbuilt assumptions that are themselves culturally derived.

Adler reminds us that expectancy models of motivation assume that individuals believe that they can, to some extent, control their environment and influence their fate. If, as in the cases of more fatalistic cultures such as China, people do not have the same sense of internal attribution, the expectancy model may have less force and therefore applicability. When Adams's equity theory is applied across the world, differences in interpretation have been recorded.[47] *Chen* suggests that while individualistic cultures place a high regard on equity, collectivist cultures value equality more than equity. Again we see here the possibility that while a theory of motivation may be essentially valid in principle, it is legitimate to think about the ways in which national culture can intervene in terms of its interpretation in different societies.[48]

THE MEANING AND NATURE OF JOB SATISFACTION

Attempting to understand the nature of job satisfaction and its effects on work performance is not easy. Job satisfaction is a complex and multifaceted concept, which can mean different things to different people. It is usually linked with motivation, but the nature of this relationship is not clear. Satisfaction is not the same as motivation. **Job satisfaction** is more of an attitude, an internal state. It could, for example, be associated with a personal feeling of achievement, either quantitative or qualitative.

It is often suggested that job satisfaction is necessary in order to achieve a high level of motivation and performance. However, although the level of job satisfaction may well affect strength of motivation, this is not always the case. The relationship between job satisfaction and performance is an issue of continuing debate and controversy. One view, associated with the early human relations approach, is that satisfaction leads to performance. An alternative view is that performance leads to satisfaction. *Reeves* draws attention to the relationship between accomplishment at work and the need to 'work harder'.

> *All this busy-ness and stress is creating more heat than light. It is a sign not of work being too hard but too shallow. Human nature is driven by a desire to accomplish things, and so the fewer opportunities for accomplishment a job contains, the more likely we are to fill the void by tearing around in a frenzy in an effort to persuade ourselves and others that our work has a purpose, that it is important.*[49]

DIMENSIONS OF JOB SATISFACTION

There is some doubt whether job satisfaction consists of a single dimension or a number of separate dimensions. Some workers may be satisfied with certain aspects of their work and dissatisfied with other aspects. Job satisfaction is itself a complex concept and difficult to measure objectively. The level of job satisfaction is affected by a wide range of variables relating to individual, social, cultural, organisational and environmental factors.

- **Individual factors** include personality, education and qualifications, intelligence and abilities, age, marital status, orientation to work.
- **Social factors** include relationships with co-workers, group working and norms, opportunities for interaction, informal organisation.
- **Cultural factors** include underlying attitudes, beliefs and values.
- **Organisational factors** include nature and size, formal structure, HR policies and procedures, employee relations, nature of the work, technology and work organisation, supervision and styles of leadership, management systems, working conditions.
- **Environmental factors** include economic, social, technical and governmental influences.

These different factors all affect the job satisfaction of certain individuals in a given set of circumstances but not necessarily in others.

Five contractual areas

Mumford examines job satisfaction in two ways:

1 in terms of the fit between what the organisation requires and what the employee is seeking; and
2 in terms of the fit between what the employee is seeking and what they are actually receiving.

On the basis of various schools of thought on job satisfaction, Mumford identifies five contractual areas by which this organisational/employee relationship can be examined: the knowledge contract, the psychological contract, the efficiency/reward contract, the ethical contract and the task structure contract (*see* Table 7.3).[50]

The work environment

An increasingly important issue affecting job satisfaction and efficiency is the nature of the work environment and workplace facilities. *Handy* argues that an inspired workplace will result in inspired workers and draws attention to the importance for work performance of the atmosphere, quality and style of buildings and offices.[51]

A 2003 study by the Chartered Management Institute reports on UK managers' attitudes to and experiences of their physical working environment. The study was undertaken among a random sample of 4,000 managers across all levels and sectors and size of organisation. Topics addressed included hours worked, commuting and travel, flexible working, the existing and preferred layout of offices and the use of new technologies. Concerns were expressed about the need for more quiet areas, under-equipped meeting rooms, lack of adequate meeting space, and their offices not making a good impression on clients and visitors. Nearly half of those surveyed would relinquish one week's annual leave for a better office and sizeable numbers would forgo £1,000 in salary or private medical insurance for a significantly upgraded workspace. And even if the role, salary and benefits were no better, 45 per cent would contemplate changing companies in return for an improved work environment.[52, 53]

Table 7.3 Five contractual areas relating to job satisfaction

	The firm	The employee
The knowledge contract	Needs a certain level of skill and knowledge in its employees if it is to function efficiently	Wishes the skills and knowledge they bring with them to be used and developed
The psychological contract	Needs employees who are motivated to look after its interests	Seeks to further interests private to self, e.g. to secure: achievement, recognition, responsibility, status
The efficiency/rewards contract	Needs to implement generalised output, quality standards and reward systems	Seeks a personal, equitable effort–reward bargain and controls, including supervisory ones, which are perceived as acceptable
The ethical (social value) contract	Needs employees who will accept the firm's ethos and values	Seeks to work for an employer whose values do not contravene their own
The task structure contract	Needs employees who will accept technical and other constraints which produce task specificity or task differentiation	Seeks a set of tasks which meets their requirements for task differentiation, e.g. which incorporate variety, interests, targets, feedback, task identity and autonomy

Source: Mumford, E., 'Job satisfaction: a method of analysis', *Personnel Review*, vol. 20, no. 3, 1991, p. 14. Reproduced with permission from Emerald Group Publishing Limited.

> *More than any other element, fun is the secret of Virgin's success. I am aware that the idea of business being fun and creative goes right against the grain of convention, and it's certainly not how they teach it at some of those business schools, where business means hard grind and lots of 'discounted cash flows' and 'net present values' ... For us, our employees matter most. It just seems common sense to me that, if you start off with a happy, well motivated workforce, you're much more likely to have happy customers. And in due course the resulting profits will make your shareholders happy.*
>
> Richard Branson, *Losing My Virginity*[54]

Alienation at work

One main approach to job satisfaction is in terms of frustration and **alienation** at work. Job satisfaction can be seen as the obverse of frustration at work (discussed above). Alienation refers to the detachment of the person from their work role. The concept of alienation at work is associated originally with the views of **Marx**.[55] He saw the division of labour in pursuit of profit, and exploitation by employers, as a denial of the workers' need for self-expression. Workers become estranged from the product of their work. Work no longer provided a satisfying experience in itself, but represented a means of satisfying other external demands. The concept of alienation has been extended by *Blauner*.[56] He describes alienation in terms of four dimensions: powerlessness, meaninglessness, isolation and self-estrangement.

- **Powerlessness** denotes the workers' lack of control over management policy, immediate work processes, or conditions of employment.
- **Meaninglessness** stems from standardisation and division of labour. It denotes the inability to see the purpose of work done or to identify with the total production process or finished product.
- **Isolation** is not belonging to an integrated work group or to the social work organisation and not being guided by group norms of behaviour.
- **Self-estrangement** is the failure to see work as an end in itself or as a central life issue. Workers experience a depersonalised detachment and work is seen solely as a means to an end.

In recent years attention to job satisfaction has also become more closely associated with broader approaches to improved job design and work organisation, and the quality of working life movement, and with stress and the work/life balance (discussed in Chapter 3).

Critical reflection

Job satisfaction is very subjective. It is affected by many variables including unknown domestic situations and personal relationships outside of work. Management models of job satisfaction appear to be a complete waste of time. Do you agree? What do you think are the most powerful influences on job satisfaction?

BROADER APPROACHES TO JOB SATISFACTION

Broader approaches to job satisfaction aim to give the person improved empowerment and job enrichment through greater autonomy and authority over the planning, execution and control of their work. It focuses attention on intrinsic satisfaction. Job enrichment increases the complexity of the work. It should provide the person with a more meaningful and challenging job and offer greater opportunities for psychological growth.

The main methods of achieving job enrichment include the following:

- permitting workers greater freedom and control over the scheduling and pacing of their work as opposed to machine pacing;
- allowing workers to undertake a full task cycle, build or assemble a complete product or component, or deliver a complete service;
- providing workers with tasks or jobs which challenge their abilities and make fuller use of their training, expertise and skills;
- giving workers greater freedom to work in self-managing teams with greater responsibility for monitoring their own performance and the minimum of direct supervision; and
- providing workers with the opportunity to have greater direct contact with clients, consumers or users of the product or service.

In an organisation, empowerment means that each staff member is responsible for creating that organisation's culture. There aren't many motivating forces more potent than giving your staff an opportunity to exercise and express their idealism.

Anita Roddick, *Business As Unusual*[57]

A COMPREHENSIVE MODEL OF JOB ENRICHMENT

Attempts to improve intrinsic motivation must not only include considerations of job characteristics but also take account of individual differences and attributes, and people's orientation to work. A popular and comprehensive model of job enrichment has been developed by *Hackman and Oldham* (*see* Figure 7.14).[58] The model views job enrichment in terms of increasing five core job dimensions: skill variety, task identity, task significance, autonomy and feedback. These core job characteristics create three psychological states:

- experienced meaningfulness of the work;
- experienced responsibility for the outcomes of the work; and
- knowledge of the actual results of the work activities.

Figure 7.14 A job characteristics model of work motivation

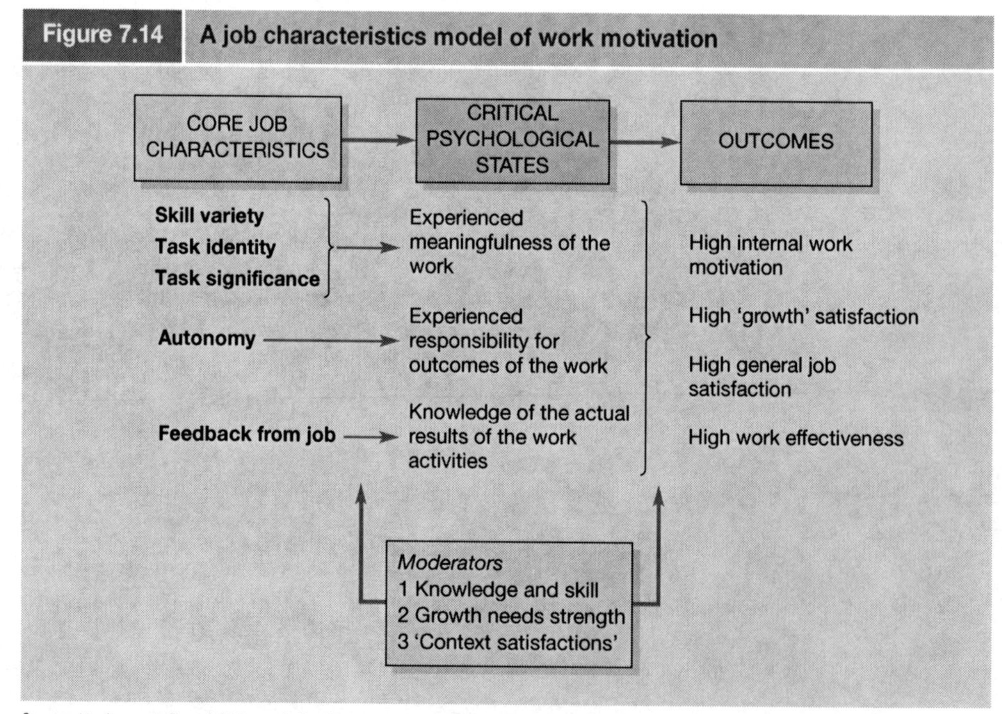

Source: Hackman, J. R. and Oldham, G. R., *Work Redesign*, Addison-Wesley Publishing Company, Inc. (1980), Figure 4.6, p. 90. Reproduced with permission from Pearson Education, Inc.

Five core dimensions

The five core job dimensions can be summarised as follows:

- **skill variety** – the extent to which a job entails different activities and involves a range of skills and talents;
- **task identity** – the extent to which a job involves completion of a whole piece of work with a visible outcome;
- **task significance** – the extent to which a job has a meaningful impact on other people, either inside or outside the organisation;
- **autonomy** – the extent to which a job provides freedom, independence and discretion in planning the work and determining how to undertake it;
- **feedback** – the extent to which work activities result in direct and clear information on the effectiveness of job performance.

An example of a job with little enrichment could be that of a production assembly line worker or a kitchen porter, where all five core characteristics are likely to score low. An example of an enriched job could be that of a parish priest who draws upon a wide range of social skills and talents, who can usually identify with the whole task and whose job has clear and important meaning and significance. There is a very high level of autonomy and likely to be direct and clear feedback.

Motivating potential score

From these five core job dimensions, Hackman and Oldham have developed an equation which gives a single index of a person's job profile. By answering a questionnaire – the Job Diagnostic Survey (JDS) – and by giving a score (between 1 and 7) to each job dimension, the person can calculate an overall measure of job enrichment, called the motivating potential score (MPS).

Examples of questions from the JDS are:

- How much variety is there in your job?
- To what extent does your job involve doing a whole and identifiable piece of work?
- In general, how significant or important is your job?
- How much autonomy is there in your job?
- To what extent does doing the job itself provide you with information about your work performance?

$$\text{MPS} = \frac{\{\text{skill variety} + \text{Task variety} + \text{Task significance}\}}{3} \times \text{Autonomy} \times \text{Feedback}$$

The first three job dimensions of skill variety, task identity and task significance are averaged, since it is the combination of these dimensions which contributes to experienced meaningfulness of work. The remaining two job dimensions, autonomy and feedback, stand on their own. Since scores for skill variety, task identity and task significance are additive, this means that the absence of one dimension can be partially offset by the presence of the other dimensions. However, if either autonomy or feedback is absent then, because of the multiplicative relationship, the MPS would be zero. The job would offer no potential to motivate the person.

Empirical support for the model

Empirical support for the model is mixed. From their studies, Hackman and Oldham claim that people with enriched jobs and high score levels on the Job Diagnostic Survey experienced more satisfaction and internal motivation. The core job dimensions of skill variety, task identity and task significance combined to predict the level of experienced meaningfulness of the work. The core dimensions of autonomy and feedback did not relate so clearly to experienced responsibility and knowledge of results. Some of the other dimensions were as good, or better, in predicting these psychological conditions. In general, however, the results of their studies showed that jobs that scored high on the core dimensions were associated with high levels of personal and work outcomes.

In a study of a sample of six hotels (with between 35 and 65 bedrooms) in Great Yarmouth, *Lee-Ross* undertook an examination of the reliability of the JDS among seasonal workers. From an analysis of 163 questionnaires, Lee-Ross concludes that in general, reliability scores were compatible with those of Hackman and Oldham. The JDS appears to hold just as well for hotel workers as for workers in other industries.[59]

Based on integrating Hackman and Oldham's job characteristics model with Maslow's hierarchy of needs, *Roe et al.* propose a general model of work motivation, tested with Bulgarian, Hungarian and Dutch workers. The model indicates that situational characteristics lead to critical psychological factors, inducing two main motivational factors – **job involvement** and **organisational commitment** – which in turn lead to two proximal outcomes of work motivation – **effort** and **job satisfaction** – which affect **performance, stress** and **tendency to leave the organisation**. Although there were some differences that draw attention to cultural variables, there was also a large degree of similarity in results across the three countries.[60]

FLEXIBLE WORKING ARRANGEMENTS

An increasingly significant aspect of motivation and job satisfaction is flexible working. According to CIPD: 'This relates to an organisation's working arrangements in terms of working time, working location and the pattern of working.'[61] Moves towards greater flexibility may afford opportunities for employees to have more freedom and control over their working arrangements and have noticeable effects on their job satisfaction and performance. Flexible working arrangements are discussed in Chapter 16.

CONTEXTUAL FACTORS IN JOB DESIGN

The different methods of job design are not necessarily separate approaches. They are interrelated and there is some overlapping among them. For example, goal-setting is sometimes viewed as another approach to job design. Goal-setting involves building goals, feedback and incentives into the structure of the job. In addition, there are many other associated (contextual) factors which affect job design, including, for example: organisational culture, structure, systems of management and style of leadership, trade unions, HR policies and procedures, communications, group norms, ergonomics, the management of change, and the working environment.

Management style and culture

The potential benefits of improved job design are unlikely to be realised if attention is focused on the content of jobs alone. Of equal, if not more, importance is the process by which redesign is carried out. This has led to recognition of the importance of management style and, increasingly, of organisation culture.[62] Central to improving the quality of working life is a participative, open style of management involving employees in decisions that affect them, including the design or choice of technology. Management should attempt to develop a relationship of trust among all members and sections of the organisation and a meaningful partnership approach with trade unions.

Job satisfaction and HRM

Theories of work motivation and job satisfaction have influenced management systems and styles of leadership, and developments in HR policies and procedures. The human resource management function is centred on people's needs while working in an organisation and ways in which their work promotes or frustrates the fulfilment of these needs.[63] The practice of modern human resource management is directed towards providing conditions under which people work willingly and effectively, and contribute to the success of the organisation. This involves concern for employee motivation and job satisfaction.

Refresh your understanding
Activity 7E
www.pearsoned.co.uk/mullins

A concept map of job satisfaction is set out in Figure 7.15.

Figure 7.15 Concept map of job satisfaction

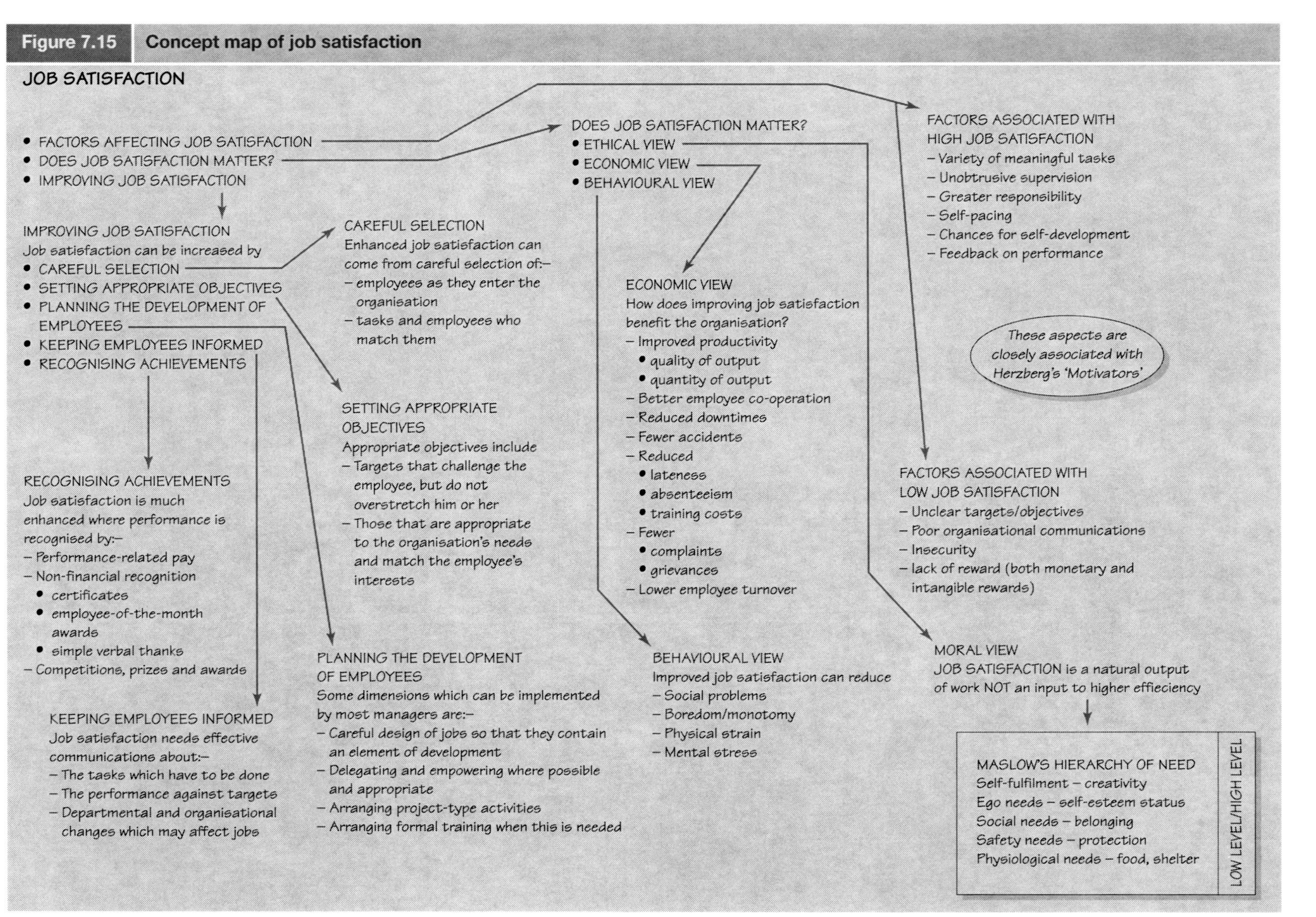

Source: Training Learning Consultancy Ltd, Bristol, England. Reproduced with permission.

Critical reflection

Motivation varies over time and according to circumstances. Individuals have a variety of changing, and often conflicting, needs and expectations which they attempt to satisfy in a number of ways. How do you think your motivation will change in five years' time? Do you agree that the search for a generalised theory of motivation at work is a vain quest and all these competing theories are just a waste of time?

MANAGEMENT IN THE NEWS

Towels and talent

FT

Microsoft plans perks to retain staff

Richard Waters

Microsoft said it would supply free towels in company showers, better food in staff canteens and on-site laundry service in an effort to boost employee morale as it battles for talent with Google and other recent start-ups. The outbreak of the internet 'perks war' is the latest sign of Microsoft's attempt to keep some of the trappings of a fast-growing Silicon Valley start-up as it takes on more of the characteristics of other large, slower-growing blue chip companies.

Google has become the most visible exponent of Silicon Valley's entitlement culture, using the free food in its highly rated cafeteria, along with the availability at its campus of services ranging from massages to automobile oil changes, to help attract and retain workers. The tech companies defend the on-site perks as a way to reward employees who often work long hours and who would otherwise have to leave the premises, making them less efficient.

Microsoft's decision to offer new employee perks, initially only at its headquarters campus near Seattle but eventually also in other sites around the world, marks a reversal of an earlier, unpopular cost-cutting policy. A decision to scrap the free towel service two years ago became a lightening rod for employee dissatisfaction. Under Ken DiPietro, who was hired as head of human resources from Dell, a technology company renowned for its low-cost ways, Microsoft abandoned a number of perks, echoing a wider attempt at the time to bring a new and more stringent financial discipline to the software company.

Mr DiPietro was replaced a year ago by Lisa Brummel, an internal appointment that signalled the company's desire to repair some of the damage to morale. In an internal email to staff earlier this week, Ms Brummel unveiled a number of changes to Microsoft's compensation system and other management systems. They include adding 15 per cent to the amount of restricted stock that Microsoft sets aside each year to reward employees. Its decision recently to abandon stock options, a form of compensation that had famously created thousands of 'Microsoft Millionaires', has left it at a disadvantage to Google and other fast-growing companies, which use the incentives liberally to attract talent.

Ms Brummel also said Microsoft would scrap a system that had forced managers to rate a certain number of workers as sub-standard each year, and that it would adjust its compensation system to keep 'top talent' at the company. The new perks, which include a grocery delivery service and 'dinners to go from Wolfgang Puck', a celebrity chef who runs a catering service, 'are designed to ease the burden given the hectic pace of life', Ms Brummel wrote.

Source: Waters, R., 'Microsoft plans perks to retain staff', *Financial Times*, 20 May 2006.

Discussion questions

1. **With reference to Figure 7.2, assess the extent to which you think Microsoft meets the needs and expectations of its employees.**
2. **Discuss the extent to which you think that organisational success is the *cause* or the *effect* of meeting employee needs and expectations.**
3. **What does the experience of Microsoft reveal about the 'psychological contract' between the company and its employees?**

SYNOPSIS

- The study of motivation is concerned, basically, with why people behave in a certain way. The underlying concept of motivation is some driving force within individuals by which they attempt to achieve some goal in order to fulfil some need or expectation. Individuals have a variety of changing, and often competing, needs and expectations which they attempt to satisfy in a number of ways. If a person's motivational driving force is blocked and they are unable to satisfy their needs and expectations, this may result either in constructive, problem-solving behaviour or in frustration-induced behaviour.

- There are many competing theories that attempt to explain motivation at work. The different theories may be divided into two contrasting groups: content theories and process theories. Content theories place emphasis on what motivates and are concerned with identifying people's needs and their relative strengths, and the goals they pursue in order to satisfy these needs. Main content theories include Maslow's hierarchy of needs model, Alderfer's modified need hierarchy model, Herzberg's two-factor theory and McClelland's achievement motivation theory.

- Process theories place emphasis on the actual process of motivation. These theories are concerned with the relationships among the dynamic variables that make up motivation, and with how behaviour is initiated, directed and sustained. Many of the process theories cannot be linked to a single writer, but major approaches under this heading include expectancy-based models, equity theory, goal theory and attribution theory.

- These different theories are not conclusive. However, it is because of the complexity of motivation that these different theories are important to the manager and many writers still expound their relevance today. They help demonstrate the many motives that influence people's behaviour at work. They provide a framework within which to direct attention for how best to motivate and reward staff to work willingly and effectively. One major doubt concerning the different theories of motivation is about their universality, on the grounds that they do not adequately address the factor of culture.

- Attempting to understand the nature of job satisfaction and links with work performance is not easy. Although the level of job satisfaction may well affect the strength of motivation, this is not always the case. Job satisfaction is more of an internal state and could be associated, for example, with a feeling of personal achievement. Job satisfaction is a complex concept and difficult to measure objectively. The level of job satisfaction is affected by a wide range of individual, social, organisational and cultural variables.

- Broader approaches to satisfaction aim to give the person improved empowerment and job enrichment through greater autonomy and control over their work. Attention has also been given to a comprehensive model of job enrichment and five core dimensions. Moves towards greater flexibility may have noticeable effects on job satisfaction and performance of staff. Despite many theories and studies there are still doubts as to how best to manage an organisation so that staff have both high job satisfaction and productivity. Account must also be taken of contextual factors, including management style and culture, and developments in human resource management.

Refresh your understanding, assess your progress and begin your research with online resources at **www.pearsoned.co.uk/mullins**

REVIEW AND DISCUSSION QUESTIONS

1. Explain what you understand by the underlying concept of motivation. Summarise the main needs and expectations to be taken into account in considering the motivation of people at work.
2. What do you understand by frustration-induced behaviour? Give a practical example, preferably from your work experience, of each of the main forms of this behaviour.
3. Critically assess the practical value of Maslow's hierarchy of needs model to improving the motivation of people at work. Give examples of the extent to which the theory could meaningfully be applied to staff in your own organisation.

Review and discussion questions – continued

4 Discuss critically the validity of the contention that the motivation for staff to work well depends on more than a high salary and good working conditions.

5 Explain your understanding of expectancy-based theories of motivation. Use a simple diagram to help explain an expectancy theory of your choice. What implications do expectancy theories of motivation have for the manager?

6 Give practical examples of situations in which each of the following theories of motivation might be appropriate: (i) achievement motivation; (ii) equity theory; (iii) goal theory.

7 What exactly do you understand by job satisfaction? What are the main dimensions of job satisfaction? Give specific examples of causes of job dissatisfaction that you have experienced.

8 Evaluate critically the relationship between motivation, job satisfaction and effective work performance. Give reasons in support of your views.

ASSIGNMENT 1

a List, as far as possible in rank order, the specific needs and expectations that are most important **to you as an individual**. (Do *not* include basic physiological needs such as to satisfy thirst or hunger, or a *minimal* standard of accommodation.)

b Explain, briefly, to what extent these needs and expectations are met currently by your present work situation and/or to what extent you anticipate they will be met by your future career ambitions.

c Think of any work experience that you have had – even a short-term, vacation or part-time job. Briefly describe those aspects of the job and/or experiences that:

(i) motivated you to work well and to the best of your ability; and

(ii) had a demotivating influence on your behaviour and performance.

Be prepared to share your feelings and comments as part of a class discussion.

ASSIGNMENT 2

a Write a brief description of what you think is happening to the people in the picture and what you think will happen to them in the future.

b After you have written your description, compare your response with those of your colleagues.

PERSONAL AWARENESS AND SKILLS EXERCISE

Objectives

Completing this exercise should help you to enhance the following skills:

- Analyse and review what determines your motivation to work.
- Reflect upon your perceptions about the motives of other people.
- Take account of individual needs and expectations at work.

Exercise

1 Put in writing as openly and precisely as possible, and in rank order, those factors that have the strongest influence on your own motivation and job satisfaction. *Exchange accounts with a partner before proceeding further.*

2 Now assume you are the newly appointed general manager of a 50-room hotel with restaurant. You have been brought in as a trouble shooter and at interview you were informed there is serious concern about the generally poor level of work performance, that morale is low and there is a disturbing high level of staff turnover.
   - Detail fully the likely actions you would take to help overcome the present situation.
   - Indicate clearly the priorities you would have in mind.
   - Make clear any necessary, reasonable assumptions.
   - Explain how you might draw upon those theories/studies you consider relevant.

3 Write, fully and honestly, the extent to which there is disparity between your own motives and, based on the above, motivating other people. How would you explain and rationalise differences?

4 Compare and discuss critically accounts with your partner, and be prepared to explain and justify your views.

Discussion

- How far did you avoid generalisations about what motivates other people?
- What assumptions did you make about the work ethic of staff at the hotel?
- To what extent where you able to distance your own motivations?
- What conclusions do you draw from this exercise?

CASE STUDY

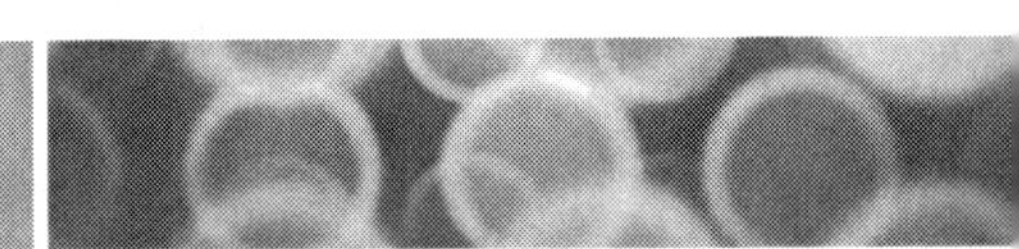

Don't get mad, get online!

In 2005 the word 'blog', meaning an on-line journal or web log which is regularly updated by the author, entered the *Oxford English Dictionary* for the first time. Figures collected by academic researchers and other internet monitoring organisations suggest that by the time the word made it into the dictionary there were about 30 million blogs in existence, and the numbers were increasing at the rate of about 70,000 per day.[64] Not all blogs are about work, but the fact that life in the office or workplace is a significant part of many people's lives means that many blogs include references to work, bosses, colleagues and customers alongside other normal daily experiences, opinions about news events and so on. A number of blogs are specifically about work and these are the ones which tend to hit the headlines, usually when an employee gets into trouble for airing their opinions about the organisation they work for in the blogosphere.

Why do individuals blog about work? At one level, blogging is no different from gossip. Many bloggers expect to have small audiences, possibly of like-minded people who have similar experiences to discuss; the content of blogs may be much like the discussions with colleagues that are routinely held in the round the water cooler or coffee machine; or with friends in a pub or bar after work. Most blogs include opportunities for email and on-line discussion and so become a lively mix of intimate diary items and chat-room style comments. For some authors the aim is to give an insight into their working life, perhaps discussing the type of job which many people know about but few really understand. In the UK, at least one chief police constable and a number of ambulance service workers are known to blog primarily about their work.[65] However, many see it is a way of letting off steam about aspects of their work which enrage them, be it the organisation, their individual managers, their annoying colleagues and often the absurd behaviour of members of the general public and customers in particular.[66] This can make blogging a particularly risky activity, at least if the blogger wishes to keep their job.

Careless blogging can get you dooced

In 2004 Ellen Simonetti hit the headlines[67] when she was sacked by her employer, the American Delta Airlines, essentially for identifying it as the company about which she was blogging on her 'Queen of the Sky' website.[68] The offence which got her sacked was not the blog itself but the fact that by posting photographs of herself draped across the seats of an aircraft in her uniform (pictures which were described by the company as 'inappropriate'), she identified the organisation itself and therefore was considered to have brought it into disrepute. In January 2005, in a similar British case, Joe Gordon, an employee of 11 years' standing at Waterstones book shop in Edinburgh, was dismissed for gross misconduct[69] after 'bringing the company into disrepute' by complaining about his 'evil boss' at the fictionalised but nevertheless sufficiently recognisable bookstore 'Bastardones' in his blog 'The Wolamaloo Gazette.'[70]

The term 'doocing' has since been used to describe the phenomenon of being sacked for blogging, a fate which also befell Catherine Sanderson or 'La Petite Anglaise', who was dismissed from the Parisian branch of British accounting firm Dixon Wilson in July 2006 for committing the 'real and serious' offence of blogging mischievously but anonymously about her boss and colleagues.[71] As with Simonetti, it was when she posted photographs of herself on the site that the company decided that she, and therefore it, could be identified and that it had to act against its employee.

Learning to love bloggers

Not every organisation has reacted with hostility to bloggers. The Chief Constable and the ambulance workers mentioned above are at least tolerated and at best supported by their employers (the Chief Constable's blog is hosted by the North Wales Police website). The same was also true for Robert Scoble, at Microsoft, whose blog (Scobleizer) not only turned him into a cyber-celebrity but also acted to help humanise the previously monolithic corporate face of the company.[72]

Source: www.petiteanglaise.com/Catherine Sanderson

Is it acceptable to blog about your company? Catherine Sanderson, "La Petite Anglaise" was sacked for her light-hearted (but anonymous) online account of events in her workplace.

Other organisations have actively embraced blog culture and sought to use it to their advantage. In the UK, Cadbury Schweppes decided to use blogging as a tool in its graduate recruitment programme and in 2005 enabled new graduates to blog their work experiences as a way of communicating to potential applicants about working life with the company.[73] Dell, the US computer giant, has also created its own blog (one2one) as a means of engaging with customer criticism. Yet other businesses have developed on the back of the blogging bandwagon. Market Sentinel offers an internet monitoring service (much like that of a press agency) to companies which want to know what is being blogged about them and be alerted to potential threats posed to their brand image in the blogosphere.

However, the blogging community is not entirely comfortable with attempts by 'corporates' to colonise this corner of cyberspace. Some companies, for example Wal-Mart, which used its public relations agency Edelman to 'feed' positive stories to well-known bloggers, have come in for criticism.[74] Other organisations have recognised the impossibility of controlling employees' private blogs, but have offered guidance and codes of practice for their workforce as a means of establishing out company policy and thereby establishing boundaries of acceptable behaviour. IBM, for example, has developed a set of 11 guidelines for its staff, some of which are summarised below:[75]

- Know and follow IBM's Business Conduct Guidelines.
- IBMers are personally responsible for their posts.
- You must make it clear that you are speaking for yourself and not on behalf of IBM.
- Respect copyright, fair use and financial disclosure laws.
- Don't provide IBM's or another's confidential or other proprietary information.
- Don't use ethnic slurs, personal insults, obscenity, etc. and show proper consideration for others' privacy and topics that may be considered objectionable or inflammatory, such as politics and religion.
- Don't pick fights, be the first to correct your own mistakes and don't alter previous posts without indicating that you have done so.
- Try to add value. Provide worthwhile information and perspective.

Organisational consequences: possibilities and challenges

IBM's approach, the development of guidelines for employees, is increasingly being seen as the way forward for organisations which are concerned about blogging. It prevents them from appearing heavyhanded, avoids the adverse publicity that can sometimes be stirred up by a sacking, and might also preclude legal challenges, for instance on the grounds of unfair dismissal or as an attempt to curtail freedom of speech. Simonetti, Gordon and Sanderson all challenged their dismissals using employment tribunals or their equivalents, opening the question of the validity of dismissal for blogging. The existence of company guidelines which have clearly been breached by a blogger is likely to support an employer's case for dismissal.

The UK Chartered Institute of Personnel and Development considers that there are occasions when blogging might be easily identifiable as a disciplinary offence but would not necessarily support a dismissal; for instance, the abuse of company equipment and time by workers 'blogging on the job' might not be deemed to warrant dismissal by an employment tribunal unless the blog additionally caused harm to the organisation's reputation and interests.[76] Yet disclosure of confidential information might well breach company data protection policies, and dismissal for libellous or defamatory comments might stand up to the test of a tribunal. Similarly, it seems possible that if employees are using blogs to air their work grievances rather than using the more normal (and in the UK statutorily required) grievance procedures, they might well be risking fair dismissal. However, it is also worth considering how far disgruntled employees' blogs indicate that organisational grievance procedures or other employee feedback mechanisms (such as attitude surveys) are not operating very successfully and that important information about employee morale and job dissatisfaction is being overlooked.

Finally, it might also be necessary to consider how far blogs are acceptable as a form of whistleblowing and whether employees who use blogs in this way would be protected by relevant legislation such as the Public Interest Disclosure Act (PIDA) of 1998 in the UK. The PIDA extends protection to whistleblowers, but normally on the basis that they have already exhausted internal organisational methods of raising their concerns before going public. Here again, blogs might be of enormous value to senior managers within an organisation whose ability to monitor the reality of working life in relation to aims regarding (for example) employee morale or issues of corporate social responsibility is limited.

The last word should perhaps go to an anonymous blogger who reported to *Personnel Today* magazine:

> *Blogging, with its potential audience of millions, is an easy way to exercise my creativity and make my views heard. I'm dissatisfied with my job and unhappy with the way recent restructuring and management decisions have led to low morale, although I do not have an 'evil boss' like the Waterstone's employee. Most of my work-related moans on my blog are minor, everyday niggles about annoying colleagues or the dull nature of my employment, but I am not afraid to occasionally pull out the big guns over issues I feel passionately about.*[77]

Your tasks

1 Using a basic model of expectancy theory such as that in Figure 7.8 or of goal setting theory such as Locke's (Figure 7.12), assess the various motivational forces which might be operating when employees blog about their employer.

2 It seems that for some people, blogging about work can be viewed as a form of frustration-induced behaviour. Critically review the process of blogging as a method of expressing job dissatisfaction. How do you think managers should respond to cases of work-related blogging by frustrated employees?

3 Organisational responses to employee blogs outlined in the case study might be categorised as either hostile (sack and sue), accepting (control and monitor) or creative (encourage and use). For each of these approaches, identify some basic guidelines for handling cases such as those of Simonetti, Gordon and Sanderson, bearing in mind the motivational effects that your proposals might have on both bloggers and other employees.

Notes and references

1 See, for example: Pate, L. E. 'Understanding Human Behaviour', *Management Decisions*, vol. 26, no. 1, 1998, pp. 58–64.
2 Krech, D., Crutchfield, R. S. and Ballachey, E. L. *Individual in Society*, McGraw-Hill (1962).
3 Mitchell, T. R. 'Motivation: New Directions for Theory, Research, and Practice', *Academy of Management Review*, vol. 7, no. 1, January 1982, pp. 80–8.
4 Kreitner, R., Kinicki, A. and Buelens, M. *Organizational Behaviour*, First European edition, McGraw-Hill (1999).
5 Farren, C. 'Mastery: The Critical Advantage' in Chowdhury, S. *Management 21C*, Financial Times Prentice Hall (2000), p. 95.
6 See, for example: Rudolph, P. A. and Kleiner, B. H. 'The Art of Motivating Employees', *Journal of Managerial Psychology*, vol. 4, no. 5, 1989, pp. i–iv.
7 Kets de Vries, M. 'Beyond Sloan: trust is at the core of corporate values' in Pickford, J. (ed.) *Financial Times Mastering Management 2.0*, Financial Times Prentice Hall (2001), pp. 267–70.
8 For a fuller discussion, see: Mullins, L. J. *Hospitality Management and Organisational Behaviour*, Fourth edition, Longman (2001).
9 Cook, P. and Jackson, N. 'Motivation Matters', Chartered Management Institute, October 2005, p. 11.
10 See, for example: Brown, J. A. C. *The Social Psychology of Industry*, Penguin (1954 and 1986).
11 Weaver, T. 'Theory M: Motivating with Money', *Cornell HRA Quarterly*, vol. 29, no. 3, November 1988, pp. 40–5.
12 Kusin, G. 'A 360-Degree Spin', *Hemisphere United*, October 2005, p. 76
13 Grayson, D. and Hodges, A. *Everybody's Business: Managing risks and opportunities in today's global society*, Financial Times (2001), p. 76.
14 Saunders, A. 'Keep Staff Sweet', *Management Today*, June 2003, p. 73.
15 Huck, S., Kubler, D. and Weibull, J. 'Social Norms and Economic Incentives in Firms', Economic & Social Research Council, 5 March 2003.
16 Cited in Crainer, S. 'Re-engineering the Carrot', *Management Today*, December 1995, p. 66.
17 Maslow, A. H. 'A Theory of Human Motivation', *Psychological Review*, 50, July 1943, pp. 370–96 and Maslow, A. H. *Motivation and Personality*, Third edition, Harper and Row (1987).
18 Steers, R. M. and Porter, L. W. *Motivation and Work Behaviour*, Fifth edition, McGraw-Hill (1991).
19 Saunders A, 'Keep Staff Sweet', *Management Today*, June 2003, p. 75.
20 Alderfer, C. P. *Existence, Relatedness and Growth*, Collier Macmillan (1972).
21 Herzberg, F., Mausner, B. and Snyderman, B. B. *The Motivation to Work*, Second edition, Chapman and Hall (1959).
22 Crainer, S and Dearlove, D. (eds) *Financial Times Handbook of Management*, Second edition, Financial Times Prentice Hall (2001), p. 361.
23 McClelland, D. C. *Human Motivation*, Cambridge University Press (1988).
24 For examples of pictures, see: Osland, J. S., Kolb, D. A. and Rubin, I. M. *Organizational Behaviour: An experimental approach*, Seventh edition, Prentice Hall (2001).
25 See, for example: Spangler, W. D. 'Validity of Questionnaire and TAT Measures of Need for Achievement Two Meta-Analyses', *Psychological Bulletin*, July 1992, pp. 140–54.
26 McClelland, D. C. 'Business Drive and National Achievement' *Harvard Business Review*, vol. 40, July–August 1962, pp. 99–112.
27 McClelland, D. C. and Burnham, D. H. 'Power is the Great Motivation', *Harvard Business Review*, vol. 54, March–April 1976, pp. 100–10.
28 Vroom, V.H. *Work and Motivation*, Wiley (1964) Also published by Krieger (1982).
29 Porter, L. W. and Lawler, E. E. *Managerial Attitudes and Performance*, Irwin (1968).
30 Lawler, E. E. *Motivation in Work Organizations*, Brooks/Cole (1973).
31 Lundin, S, Paul, H and Christensen, *Fish: A Remarkable Way to Boost Morale and Improve Results*, Hyperion Press (2001), p. 37.

32 Adams, J. S. 'Injustice in Social Exchange', in Berkowitz, L. (ed) *Advances in Experimental and Social Psychology*, Academic Press (1965). Abridged in Steers, R. M. and Porter, L. W. *Motivation and Work Behavior*, Second edition, McGraw-Hill (1979), pp. 107–24.
33 Locke, E. A. 'Towards a Theory of Task Motivation and Incentives', *Organizational Behavior and Human Performance*, vol. 3, 1968, pp. 157–89.
34 Locke, E. A. 'Personal Attitudes and Motivation', *Annual Review of Psychology*, vol. 26, 1975, pp. 457–80.
35 Gratton, L. *Living Strategy: Putting people at the heart of corporate purpose*, Financial Times Prentice Hall (2000), p. 193.
36 Hannagan, T. *Management*, Fourth edition, Financial Times Prentice Hall (2005), p. 363.
37 Reis, D. and Pena, L. 'Reengineering the Motivation to Work', *Management Decision*, vol. 39, no. 8, (2001), pp. 666–75.
38 'Motivating Your Staff in a Time of Change', *Management Checklist 068*, Chartered Management Institute, 2001.
39 Flores, G. N. and Utley, R. 'Management Concepts in Use – a 12-year perspective', *Engineering Management Journal*, vol. 12, no. 3, September 2000, pp. 11–17.
40 Tampoe, M. 'Knowledge Workers – The New Management Challenge', *Professional Manager*, November 1994, pp. 12–13.
41 Lucas, E. 'Turning on the Knowledge Workers', *Professional Manager*, May 1999, pp. 10–12.
42 'Managing Knowledge Workers: the HR dimension', Chartered Institute of Personnel and Development, January 2002.
43 Whitmore, Sir John 'Breaking Down the Barriers to Management Creativity', *Manager, The British Journal of Administrative Management*, May/June 2002, pp. 24–6.
44 See, for example: Cheng, T., Sculli, D. and Chan, F. S. 'Relationship Dominance – Rethinking management theories from the perspective of methodological relationalism', *Journal of Managerial Psychology*, vol. 16, no. 2, 2001, pp. 97–105.
45 Francesco, A. M. and Gold, B. A. *International Organizational Behavior*, Second edition, Pearson Prentice Hall (2005), p. 126.
46 Ibid., p. 129.
47 Adler, N. J. *International Aspects of Organizational Behaviour*, Third edition, South Western College Publishing (1997).
48 Chen, C. C. 'New Trends in Reward Allocation Preferences: A Sino-US Comparison', *The Academy of Management Journal*, vol. 38, no. 2, 1995, pp. 402–28.
49 Reeves, R. 'Reality Bites', *Management Today*, May 2003, p. 37.
50 Mumford, E. 'Job Satisfaction: A Method of Analysis', *Personal Review*, vol. 20, no. 3, 1991, pp. 11–19.
51 Handy, C. 'Boring Workplace, Boring Worker', *Management Today*, November 1997, p. 29.
52 'The Workplace Survey', Chartered Management Institute, March 2003.
53 Myerson, J. 'Workspace Heaven?', *Management Today*, June 2003, pp. 53–61.
54 Branson, R. *Losing My Virginity*, Virgin Publishing (1998), pp. 431, 444.
55 Marx, K. 'The Notion of Alienation', in Coser, L. A. and Rosenburg, B. *Sociological Theory*, Collier Macmillan (1969), pp. 505–10.
56 Blauner, R. *Alienation and Freedom*, University of Chicago Press (1964).
57 Roddick, A. *Business As Unusual*, Thorsons (2000), p. 70.
58 Hackman, J. R. and Oldham, G. R. *Work Redesign*, Addison-Wesley (1980).
59 Lee-Ross, D. 'The Reliability and Rationale of Hackman and Oldham's Job Diagnostic Survey and Job Characteristics Model among Seasonal Hotel Workers', *International Journal of Hospitality Management*, 17, 1998, pp. 391–406.
60 Roe, R. A., Zinovieva, I. L., Dienes, E. and Ten Horn, L. A., 'A Comparison of Work Motivation in Bulgaria, Hungary and the Netherlands: Test of a model', *Applied Psychology: An International Review*, vol. 49, 2000, pp. 658–87.
61 'Flexible Working: The Implementation Challenge', CIPD, October 2005, p.6.
62 See, for example: Cartwright, J. *Cultural Transformation*, Financial Times Prentice Hall (1999).
63 See, for example: Torrington, D., Hall, L. and Taylor, S. *Human Resource Management*, Sixth edition, Financial Times Prentice Hall (2005).
64 Personnel Today 2006 'Blogging: Waste of time or corporate tool?' published 21 March 2006 and available at www.personneltoday.com [accessed 26 July 2006].
65 Richard Brunstrom, Chief Constable of North Wales at http://www.north-wales.police.uk/nwp/public/en/blogs/; and two blogs by members of the London Ambulance service Random Acts of Reality (www.randomreality.blogware.com) and Nee Naw (www.neenaw.co.uk).
66 E.g. waiterrant.net, youareworthmore.org (Wal-Mart employees).
67 BBC News website 2004 'US Blogger fired by her airline' at http://news.bbc.co.uk dated 3 November 2004 [accessed 26 July 2006].
68 Queen of the Sky; Journal of a (fired) Flight Attendant http://queenofsky.journalspace.com.
69 Personnel Today 2005 'Don't blog your way into trouble published 17 January 2005 available at www.personneltoday.com [accessed 26 July 2006].
70 The Wolamaloo Gazette, www.wolamaloo.org.uk.
71 Smith-Spark, L. 2006 'How to Blog and keep your job' BBC news website http://news.bbc.co.uk published 20 July 2006 [accessed 26 July 2006].
72 Watkins, D. 2006 'How big business barged in on the bloggers' *The Guardian* 20 March 2006.
73 Paton, N. 2006 'This is what I did at work today...' *Daily Mail*, 29 January 2006.
74 Watkins, D. 2006 'How big business barged in on the bloggers' *The Guardian*, 20 March 2006.
75 For the full guidelines and discussion about how they should be managed, visit the IBM website http://www-128.ibm.com/developerworks/blogs/dw_blog_comments.jspa?blog=351&entry=81328.
76 Spencer, S. 2005 'Illegal blogging', *People Management*, 27 January 2005.
77 Personnel Today 2005 'Don't blog your way into trouble' 17 January 2005 available at www.personneltoday.com [accessed 26 July 2006].

Groups, Teams and Leadership

THE NATURE OF WORK GROUPS AND TEAMS

"To build good teams you need a wide pool of staff with different talents to draw upon … Good managers should delight in the diversity and excellence of their staff and know that one of their main jobs is to manage the problems that come with any diverse group of talented people. In any group of talented people you will naturally get interpersonal tensions. It is important that you show you respect all the different skills and personalities in your team."

Nic Peeling – frontline manager with QinetiQ

Brilliant Manager: What the Best Managers Know, Do and Say, Pearson Prentice Hall (2005), pp. 129–30

Groups and teams are a major feature of organisational life. The work organisation and its sub-units are made up of groups of people. Most activities of the organisation require at least some degree of co-ordination through the operation of groups and teamwork. An understanding of the nature of groups is vital if the manager is to influence the behaviour of people in the work situation. The manager must be aware of the impact of groups and teams and their effects on organisational performance.

Learning outcomes

After completing this chapter you should be able to:

- explain the meaning and importance of work groups and teams;
- distinguish between groups and teams, and between formal and informal groups;
- explain the main reasons for the formation of groups and teams;
- examine factors which influence group cohesiveness and performance;
- review the characteristics of an effective work group;
- analyse the nature of role relationships and role conflict;
- evaluate the importance of groups and teams for effective organisational performance.

Critical reflection

'Groups are an essential part of the structure of an organisation but "teamworking" is no more than a fashionable term used by management to give workers an exaggerated feeling of importance and empowerment. In reality, however, an emphasis on teamworking is only likely to lead to more work, less freedom and even closer control from other team members.' How far do you agree with this comment? What is your experience of teamworking?

THE MEANING AND IMPORTANCE OF GROUPS AND TEAMS

Groups are an essential feature of any organisation. Individuals seldom work in isolation from others. Work is a group-based activity and if the organisation is to function effectively it requires collaboration and co-operation among its members Although there is no single accepted definition, most people will readily understand what constitutes a group. The essential feature is that its members regard themselves as belonging to the group. A popular definition defines the group in psychological terms as:

> *any number of people who (1) interact with one another; (2) are psychologically aware of one another; and (3) perceive themselves to be a group.*[1]

Another useful way of defining a work group is a collection of people who share most, if not all, of the following characteristics:

- a definable membership
- group consciousness
- a sense of shared purpose
- interdependence
- interaction
- ability to act in a unitary manner.[2]

Essential features of work organisations

Groups are a characteristic of all social situations and almost everyone in an organisation will be a member of one or more groups. The working of groups and the influence they exert over their membership is an essential feature of human behaviour and of organisational performance. Members of a group must co-operate in order for work to be carried out, and managers themselves will work within these groups. People in groups influence each other in many ways and groups may develop their own hierarchies and leaders. Group pressures can have a major influence over the behaviour of individual members and their work performance.

DIFFERENCES BETWEEN GROUPS AND TEAMS

In common usage and literature, including to some extent in this book, there is a tendency for the terms 'groups' and 'teams' to be used interchangeably. It is not easy to distinguish clearly between a group and a team. *Guzzo and Dickson*, for example, go so far as to suggest that it is probably pointless and in any case more or less impossible to distinguish groups from teams.[3]

According to *Holpp*, while many people are still paying homage to teams, teamwork, empowerment and self-management, others have become disillusioned. Holpp poses the question: What are teams? 'It's a simple enough question, but one that's seldom asked. We all think we know intuitively what teams are. Guess again. Here are some questions to help define team configurations.'

- Are teams going to be natural work groups, or project-and-task oriented?
- Will they be self-managed or directed?
- How many people will be on the teams; who's in charge?
- How will the teams fit into the organisation's structure if it shows only boxes and not circles or other new organisational forms?

Holpp also poses the question: Why do you want teams? If teams are just a convenient way to group under one manager a lot of people who used to work for several downsized supervisors, don't bother. But if teams can truly take ownership of work areas and provide the kind of up-close knowledge that's unavailable elsewhere, then full speed ahead.[4]

Teamwork a fashionable term

The use of the word 'teams' has become increasingly fashionable in recent years. *Crainer* refers to the use of 'teamworking' as a side effect of increasing concentration on working across functional divides and fits neatly with the trend towards empowerment. However, despite the extensive literature about teams and teamworking, the basic dynamics of teamworking often remain clouded and uncertain.

Teams occur when a number of people have a common goal and recognise that their personal success is dependent on the success of others. They are all interdependent. In practice, this means that in most teams people will contribute individual skills many of which will be different. It also means that the full tensions and counter-balance of human behaviour will need to be demonstrated in the team.[5]

Cane suggests that organisations are sometimes unsure whether they have teams or simply groups of people working together.

It is certainly true to say that any group of people who do not know they are a team cannot be one. To become a team, a group of individuals needs to have a strong common purpose and to work towards that purpose rather than individually. They need also to believe that they will achieve more by co-operation than working individually.[6]

Whereas all teams are, by definition, groups, it does not necessarily follow that all groups are teams.

Belbin points out that to the extent that teamwork was becoming a fashionable term, it began to replace the more usual reference to groups and every activity was now being described as 'teamwork'. He questions whether it matters whether one is talking about groups or teams and maintains that the confusion in vocabulary should be addressed if the principles of good teamwork are to be retained. Belbin suggests there are several factors that characterise the difference between groups and teams (*see* Figure 8.1). The best differentiator is size: groups can comprise any number of people but teams are smaller with a membership between (ideally) four and six. The quintessential feature of a small, well-balanced team is that leadership is shared or rotates whereas large groups typically throw up solo leaders.[7]

While acknowledging the work of Belbin it appears that the term 'group' is often used in a more general sense and 'team' in a more specific context. We continue to refer to 'group' or 'team' according to the particular focus of attention and the vocabulary of the quoted authors.

Figure 8.1 Differences between a team and a group

	Team	Group
Size	Limited	Medium or Large
Selection	Crucial	Immaterial
Leadership	Shared or rotating	Solo
Perception	Mutual knowledge understanding	Focus on leader
Style	Role spread co-ordination	Convergence conformism
Spirit	Dynamic interaction	Togetherness persecution of opponents

Source: Belbin, R. M., *Beyond the Team*, Butterworth-Heinemann, (2000). Copyright © 2000, reproduced with permission from Elsevier Ltd.

Another possible distinction is based on the development and maturity of the 'group'. For example, in terms of Tuckman's model (discussed on p. 310), not until a group proceeds beyond the stages of forming, norming and storming and successfully reaches the performing stage does it become a team.

GROUP VALUES AND NORMS

The classical approach to organisation and management tended to ignore the importance of groups and the social factors at work. The ideas of people such as F. W. Taylor popularised the concept of the 'rabble hypothesis' and the assumption that people carried out their work, and could be motivated, as solitary individuals unaffected by others. The human relations approach, however (discussed in Chapter 2), gave recognition to the work organisation as a social organisation and to the importance of the group, and group values and norms, in influencing behaviour at work.

One experiment involved the observation of a group of 14 men working in the bank wiring room. The men formed their own sub-groups or cliques, with natural leaders emerging with the consent of the members. Despite a financial incentive scheme where workers could receive more money the more work they did, the group decided on 6,000 units a day as a fair level of output. This was well below the level they were capable of producing. Group pressures on individual workers were stronger than financial incentives offered by management.

Informal social relations

The group developed its own pattern of informal social relations and codes and practices ('norms') of what constituted proper group behaviour.

- **Not to be a 'rate buster'** – not to produce at too high a rate of output compared with other members or to exceed the production restriction of the group.

Figure 8.2 Concept map of group norms

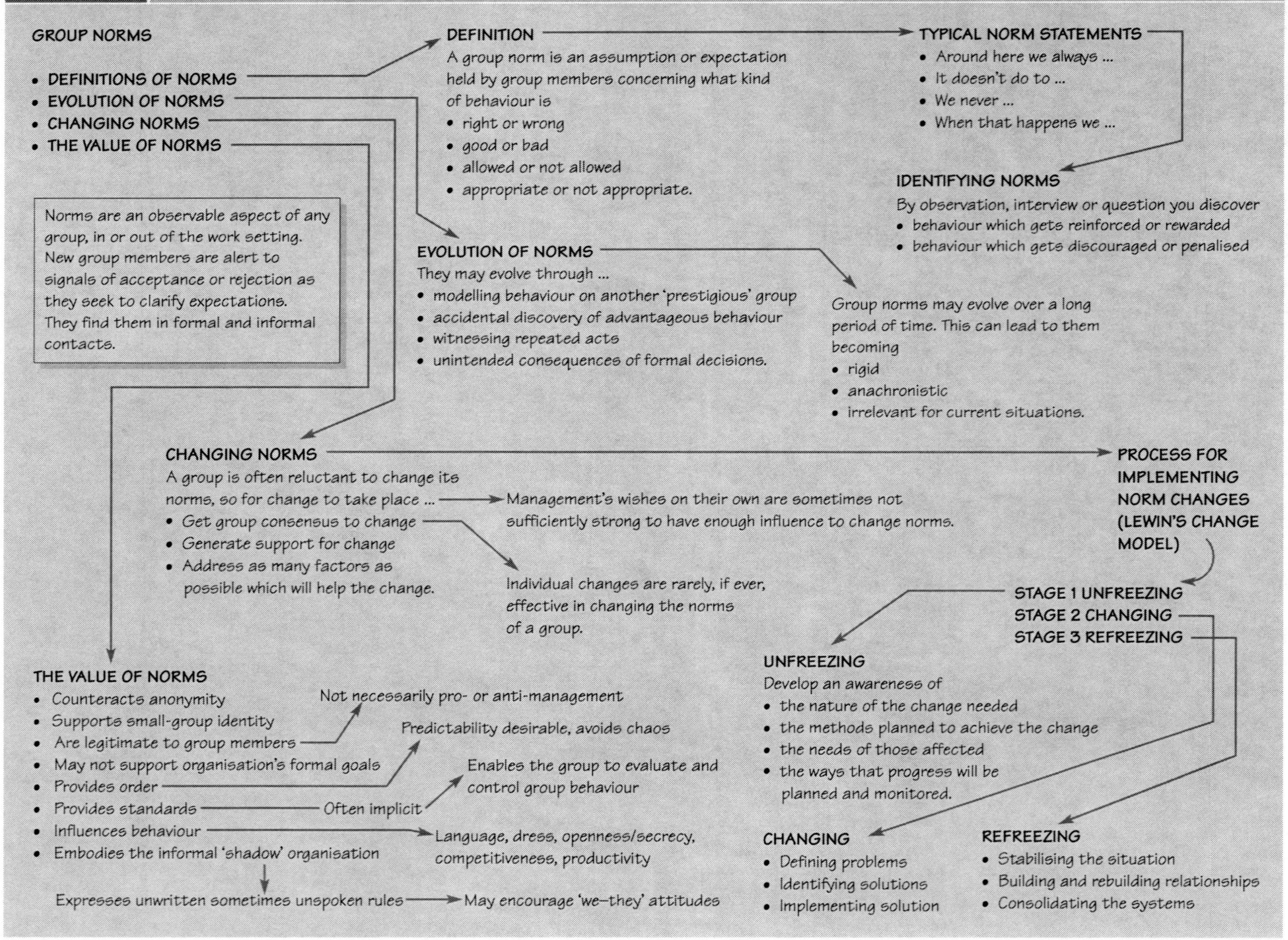

GROUP NORMS

- DEFINITIONS OF NORMS
- EVOLUTION OF NORMS
- CHANGING NORMS
- THE VALUE OF NORMS

Norms are an observable aspect of any group, in or out of the work setting. New group members are alert to signals of acceptance or rejection as they seek to clarify expectations. They find them in formal and informal contacts.

DEFINITION

A group norm is an assumption or expectation held by group members concerning what kind of behaviour is

- right or wrong
- good or bad
- allowed or not allowed
- appropriate or not appropriate.

TYPICAL NORM STATEMENTS

- Around here we always ...
- It doesn't do to ...
- We never ...
- When that happens we ...

IDENTIFYING NORMS

By observation, interview or question you discover

- behaviour which gets reinforced or rewarded
- behaviour which gets discouraged or penalised

EVOLUTION OF NORMS

They may evolve through ...

- modelling behaviour on another 'prestigious' group
- accidental discovery of advantageous behaviour
- witnessing repeated acts
- unintended consequences of formal decisions.

Group norms may evolve over a long period of time. This can lead to them becoming

- rigid
- anachronistic
- irrelevant for current situations.

CHANGING NORMS

A group is often reluctant to change its norms, so for change to take place ... → Management's wishes on their own are sometimes not sufficiently strong to have enough influence to change norms.

- Get group consensus to change → Individual changes are rarely, if ever, effective in changing the norms of a group.
- Generate support for change
- Address as many factors as possible which will help the change.

PROCESS FOR IMPLEMENTING NORM CHANGES (LEWIN'S CHANGE MODEL)

STAGE 1 UNFREEZING
STAGE 2 CHANGING
STAGE 3 REFREEZING

UNFREEZING

Develop an awareness of

- the nature of the change needed
- the methods planned to achieve the change
- the needs of those affected
- the ways that progress will be planned and monitored.

CHANGING

- Defining problems
- Identifying solutions
- Implementing solution

REFREEZING

- Stabilising the situation
- Building and rebuilding relationships
- Consolidating the systems

THE VALUE OF NORMS

- Counteracts anonymity
- Supports small-group identity
- Are legitimate to group members → Not necessarily pro- or anti-management
- May not support organisation's formal goals
- Provides order → Predictability desirable, avoids chaos
- Provides standards — Often implicit → Enables the group to evaluate and control group behaviour
- Influences behaviour → Language, dress, openness/secrecy, competitiveness, productivity
- Embodies the informal 'shadow' organisation

Expresses unwritten sometimes unspoken rules → May encourage 'we–they' attitudes

Source: Training Learning Consultancy Ltd, Bristol, England. Reproduced with permission.

- **Not to be a 'chiseller'** – not to shirk production or to produce at too low a rate of output compared with other members of the group.
- **Not to be a 'squealer'** – not to say anything to the supervisor or management which might be harmful to other members of the group.
- **Not to be 'officious'** – people with authority over members of the group, for example inspectors, should not take advantage of their seniority or maintain a social distance from the group.

The group had their own system of sanctions including sarcasm, damaging completed work, hiding tools, playing tricks on the inspectors and ostracising those members who did not conform with the **group norms**. Threats of physical violence were also made and the group developed a system of punishing offenders by 'binging' that involved striking someone a fairly hard blow on the upper part of the arm. This process of binging also became a recognised method of controlling conflict within the group.

Team performance

According to *Riches*, one way to improve team performance is to establish agreed norms or rules for how the team is to operate and rigorously stick to them. Norms could address the obligations of individual members to the team, how it will assess its performance, how it will work together, what motivation systems will be used, how it will relate to customers, and the mechanisms to facilitate an honest exchange about the team norms and behaviour.[8]

A 2003 study by the *Economic & Social Research Council* draws attention to the importance of social norms among employees and questions whether employees are guided not only by monetary incentives but also by peer pressure towards social efficiency for the workers as a group. 'Intuitively, social norms among workers must be important if they work in teams where bonuses are dependent on group rather than individual effort.'[9] (You may see some similarity here with the bank wiring room experiment, discussed above.)

A concept map of group norms is set out in Figure 8.2.

FORMAL AND INFORMAL GROUPS

Groups are deliberately planned and created by management as part of the formal organisation structure. However, groups will also arise from social processes and the informal organisation that was discussed in Chapter 3. The informal organisation arises from the interaction of people working within the organisation and the development of groups with their own relationships and norms of behaviour, irrespective of those defined within the formal structure. This leads to a major distinction between formal and informal groups.

Formal groups

Groups are formed as a consequence of the pattern of organisation structure and arrangements for the division of work, for example the grouping together of common activities into sections. Groups may result from the nature of technology employed and the way in which work is carried out, for example the bringing together of a number of people to carry out a sequence of operations on an assembly line. Groups may also develop when a number of people of the same level or status within the organisation see themselves as a group, for example departmental heads of an industrial organisation or chief officers of a local authority. **Formal groups** are created to achieve specific organisational objectives and are concerned with the **co-ordination of work activities**. People are brought together on the basis of defined roles within the structure of the organisation. The nature of the tasks to be undertaken is a predominant feature of the formal group. Goals are identified by management, and certain rules, relationships and norms of behaviour established.

Formal groups tend to be relatively permanent, although there may be changes in actual membership. However, temporary formal groups may also be created by management, for example the use of project teams in a matrix organisation. Formal work groups can be differentiated in a number of ways, for example on the basis of membership, the task to be performed, the nature of technology, or position within the organisation structure.

Virtuoso teams *Boynton and Fischer* draw attention to '**virtuoso teams**' that are formed specifically for big change in organisations. They are comprised of individual superstars or virtuosos with a single clear, ambitious mandate and not to remain together over multiple initiatives or projects. Virtuoso teams require a special kind of leadership and to be managed in a manner that unleashes the maximum contribution from each individual superstar. Although most organisations rarely form such teams, they are required for radical change opportunities that represent a significant departure from prior practice and/or how an organisation conducts its business. Examples of big changes that represented a virtuoso team are the Manhattan Project, Thomas Edison's inventory factory and Roald Amundsen's polar expedition.[10]

Informal groups

The formal structure of the organisation, and system of role relationships, rules and procedures, will always be augmented by interpretation and development at the informal level. **Informal groups** are based more on personal relationships and agreement of group members than on defined role relationships. They serve to satisfy psychological and social needs not related necessarily to the tasks to be undertaken. Groups may devise ways of attempting to satisfy members' affiliation and other social motivations lacking in the work situation. Membership of informal groups can cut across the formal structure. They may comprise individuals from different parts of the organisation and/or from different levels of the organisation, both vertically and diagonally, as well as from the same horizontal level. An informal group could also be the same as the formal group, or it might comprise a part only of the formal group (*see* Figure 8.3).

Members of an informal group may appoint their own leader who exercises authority by the consent of the members themselves. The informal leader may be chosen as the person who reflects the attitudes and values of the members, helps to resolve conflict, leads the group in satisfying its goals, or liaises with management or other people outside the group. The informal leader may often change according to the particular situation facing the group.

Figure 8.3 **Examples of informal groups within the formal structure of an organisation**

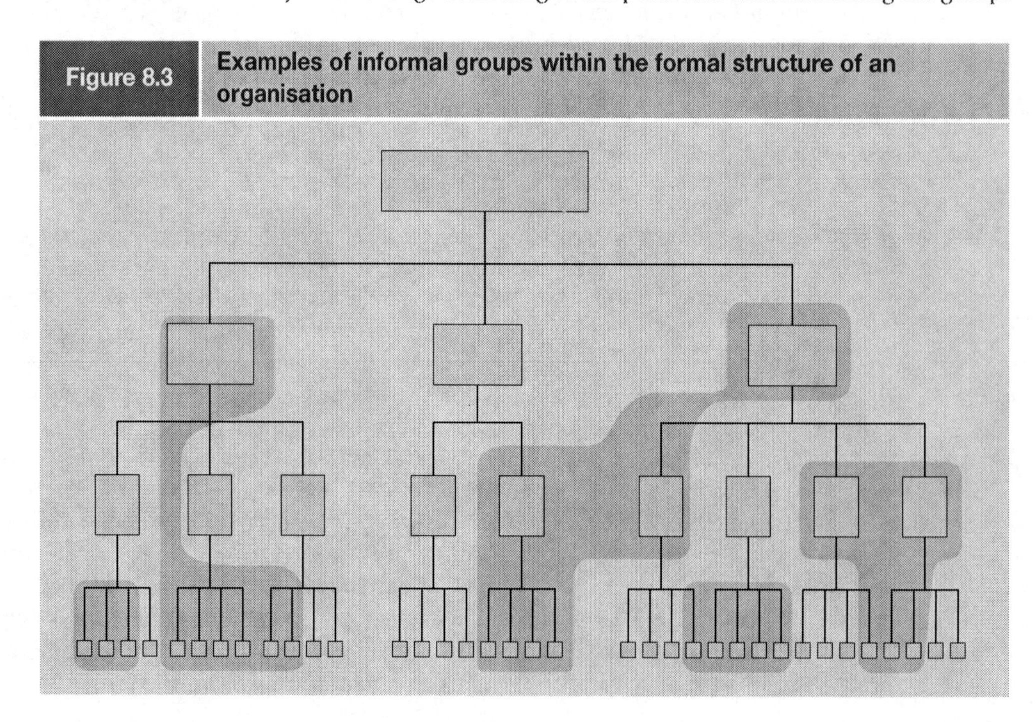

Although not usually the case, it is possible for the informal leader to be the same person as the formal leader appointed officially by management.

Major functions of informal groups

Lysons suggests four main reasons for informal groups.

- **The perpetuation of the informal group 'culture'**. Culture in this context means a set of values, norms and beliefs which form a guide to group acceptance and group behaviour. Unless you broadly subscribe to the group culture, you will not belong and will be an 'outsider' or 'isolate'.
- **The maintenance of a communication system**. Groups want all the information that affects their welfare, either negatively or positively. If groups are not apprised of policies and motives behind actions, they will seek to tap into formal communication channels and spread information among group members.
- **The implementation of social control**. Conformity to group culture is enforced by such techniques as ridicule, ostracism and violence. This is illustrated, for example, by the enforcement of group norms in the bank wiring room discussed above.
- **The provision of interest and fun in work life**. Many jobs are monotonous and fail to hold workers' attention. Work may also offer few prospects. Workers may try to compensate by interpersonal relations provided by the group and in such activities as time wasting by talking, gambling, practical joking and drinking.[11]

> *We humans are a gregarious lot. We like to gather together and establish our own social networks, which are often the real key to creativity and innovation in organisations ... But many managers are unaware that seemingly pointless social networking does in fact play a crucial part in the way people interact with each other and get work done.*
>
> Sue Law, 'Beyond the Water Cooler'[12]

An example of informal groups

A lack of direction and clear information flow within the formal structure can give rise to uncertainty and suspicion. In the absence of specific knowledge, the grapevine takes on an important role, rumours start and the informal part of the organisation is highlighted, often with negative results. A typical example concerned an industrial organisation in a highly competitive market and experiencing a drop in sales. Two top managers had suddenly lost their jobs without any apparent explanation and there were board meetings seemingly every other day. Although there was no specific information or statements from top management, the general feeling among the staff was that whatever was about to happen was most unlikely to be good news.

At lunchtime three junior members of staff, one female and two male, each from different departments, were having a chat. With a half smile the female member said to the others that she could well be seeing a lot more of both or at least one of them before long. She said that she had heard, unofficially, from her manager that the department was about to be awarded a very profitable order. She surmised that other departments, which she had also heard had lost their parts of the same contracts and not had many orders recently, would have to integrate into the successful department with the possible loss of certain jobs. The other two members both believed this and talked about it within their own departments as if it were a fact. The result? Even more uncertainty throughout the organisation, increased gloom and distraction from the task. In fact, no such integration did take place, only a minor restructuring of the organisation with no direct loss of jobs other than through voluntary early retirement. However, it proved very difficult for top management to effectively quash the rumour and restore trust and morale.

Critical reflection

Given the obvious importance of social networks for both the morale and job satisfaction of staff and their levels of work performance, do you think that the main focus in the study of organisational behaviour should be on the operations and effective management of the informal organisation?

REASONS FOR FORMATION OF GROUPS OR TEAMS

Individuals will form into groups or teams, both formal and informal, for a number of reasons.

- **Certain tasks can be performed only through the combined efforts of a number of individuals working together.** The variety of experience and expertise among members provides a synergetic effect that can be applied to the increasingly complex problems of modern organisations.
- **Collusion between members** in order to modify formal working arrangements more to their liking – for example, by sharing or rotating unpopular tasks. Membership therefore provides the individual with opportunities for initiative and creativity.
- **Companionship and a source of mutual understanding and support from colleagues.** This can help in solving work problems and also to militate against stressful or demanding working conditions.
- **Membership provides the individual with a sense of belonging.** It provides a feeling of identity and the chance to acquire role recognition and status within the group or team.
- **Guidelines on generally acceptable behaviour.** It helps to clarify ambiguous situations such as the extent to which official rules and regulations are expected to be adhered to in practice, the rules of the game and what is seen as the correct actual behaviour. The informal organisation may put pressure on members to resist demands from management on such matters as higher output or changes in working methods. Allegiance to the group or team can serve as a means of control over individual behaviour and individuals who contravene the norms are disciplined – for example, the process of 'binging' in the bank wiring room, mentioned above.
- **Protection for its membership.** Group or team members collaborate to protect their interests from outside pressures or threats.

Expectations of group membership

Individuals have varying expectations of the benefits from group membership, relating to both work performance and social processes. However, working in groups may mean that members spend too much time talking among themselves rather than doing. Groups may also compete against each other in a non-productive manner. It is a question of balance. It is important, therefore, that the manager understands the reasons for the formation of groups and is able to recognise likely advantageous or adverse consequences for the organisation.

GROUP COHESIVENESS AND PERFORMANCE

Social interaction is a natural feature of human behaviour but ensuring harmonious working relationships and effective teamwork is not an easy task. The manager's main concern is that members of a work group co-operate in order to achieve the results expected of them. Co-operation among members is likely to be greater in a united, cohesive group. Membership of a cohesive group can be a rewarding experience for the individual, can contribute to the promotion of morale and aid the release of creativity and energy. Members of a high-morale group are more likely to think of themselves as a group and work together effectively. Strong and cohesive work groups can, therefore, have beneficial effects for the organisation. There are many factors which affect group cohesiveness and performance that can be summarised under four broad headings, as shown in Figure 8.4.

Figure 8.4 Factors contributing to group cohesiveness and performance

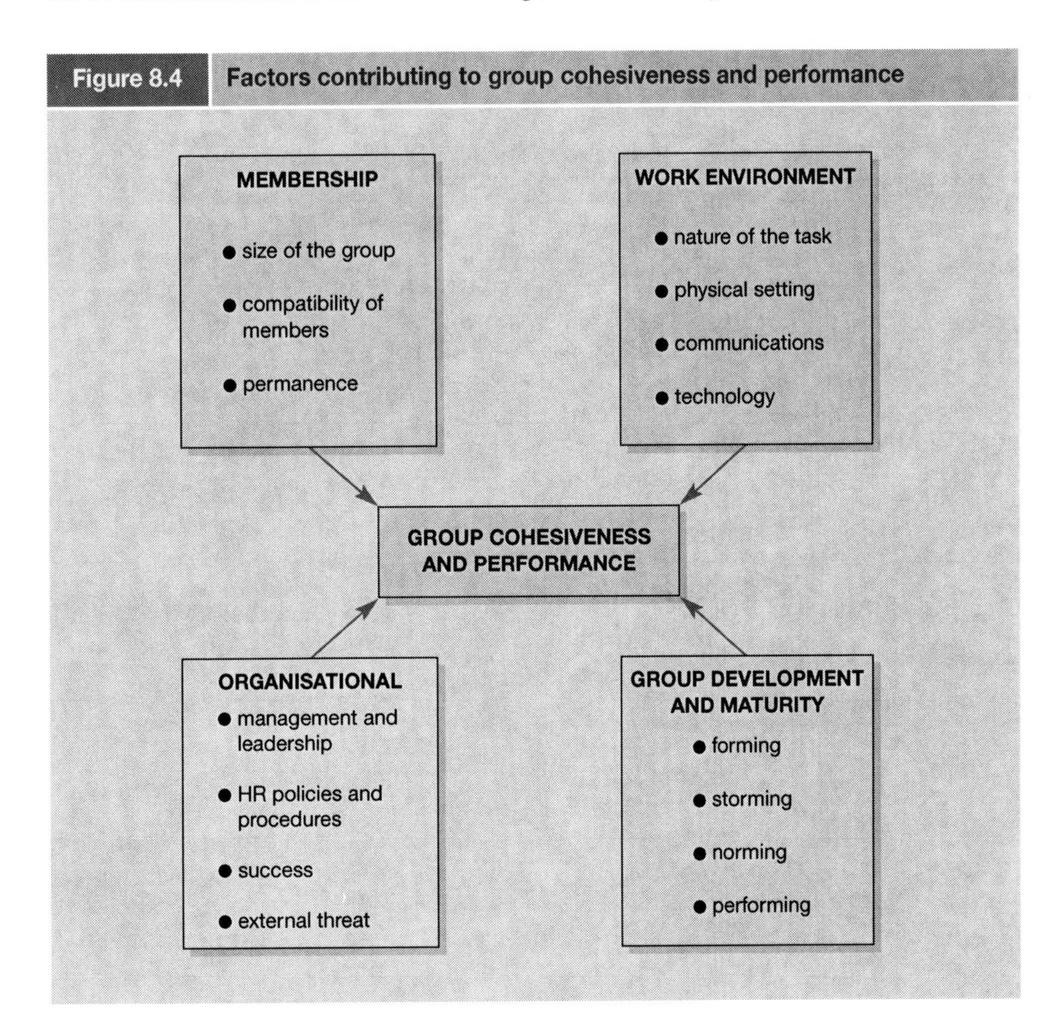

MEMBERSHIP

Size of the group As a group increases in size, problems arise with communications and co-ordination. Large groups are more difficult to handle and require a higher level of supervision. Absenteeism also tends to be higher in larger groups. When a group becomes too large it may split into smaller units and friction may develop between the sub-groups.

It is difficult to put a precise figure on the ideal size of a work group and there are many conflicting studies and reports. Much will depend upon other variables, but it seems to be generally accepted that cohesiveness becomes more difficult to achieve when a group exceeds 10–12 members.[13] Beyond this size the group tends to split into sub-groups. A figure of between five and seven is often quoted as an apparent optimum size for full participation within the group. Many readers will be familiar with the classic 1957 movie *Twelve Angry Men* in which one juror persuades the other 11 to change their minds over a murder verdict. This drew attention to a range of intra-group conflicts and the difficulty in groups of more than ten people attempting to reach consensus.

Cane asks the question: how many people should be in a team?

The answers from different organisations as to what is the perfect number vary from between four and fifteen depending on a whole range of variables. Fifteen is about the maximum number of people anyone can communicate with without having to raise their voice significantly and any less than four has a restriction in the amount of creativity and variety that can be produced. It is interesting to note that these figures range between the maximum and minimum numbers of sports teams – perhaps less of a coincidence than it seems.[14]

Compatibility of the members The more homogeneous the group in terms of such features as shared backgrounds, intests, attitudes and values of its members, the easier it is usually to promote cohesiveness. Variations in other individual differences, such as the personality or skills of members, may serve to complement each other and help make for a cohesive group. However, such differences may be the cause of disruption and conflict. Conflict can also arise in a homogeneous group where members are in competition with each other. Individual incentive payment schemes, for example, may be a source of conflict.

Permanence of group members Group spirit and relationships take time to develop. Cohesiveness is more likely when members of a group are together for a reasonable length of time and changes occur only slowly. A frequent turnover of members is likely to have an adverse effect on morale and on the cohesiveness of the group.

WORK ENVIRONMENT

The nature of the task Where workers are involved in similar work, share a common task or face the same problems, this may assist cohesiveness. The nature of the task may serve to bring people together when it is necessary for them to communicate and interact regularly with each other in the performance of their duties – for example, members of a research and development team. Even if members of a group normally work at different locations they may still experience a feeling of cohesiveness if the nature of the task requires frequent communication and interaction – for example, security guards patrolling separate areas who need to check with each other on a regular basis. However, where the task demands a series of relatively separate operations or discrete activities – for example, on a machine-paced assembly line – it is more difficult to develop cohesiveness. Individuals may have interactions with colleagues on either side of them but little opportunity to develop a common group feeling.

Physical setting Where members of a group work in the same location or in close physical proximity to each other this will generally help cohesiveness. However, this is not always the case. For example, in large open-plan offices staff often tend to segregate themselves from colleagues and create barriers through the strategic siting of such items as filing cabinets, bookcases or indoor plants. The size of the office and the number of staff in it are, of course, important considerations in this case. Isolation from other groups of workers will also tend to build cohesiveness. This often applies to a smaller number of workers on a night shift.

Communications The more easily members can communicate freely with each other, the greater the likelihood of group cohesiveness. Communications are affected by the work environment, by the nature of the task and by technology. For example, difficulties in communication can arise with production systems where workers are stationed continuously at a particular point with limited freedom of movement. Even when opportunities exist for interaction with colleagues, physical conditions may limit effective communication. For example, the technological layout and high level of noise with some assembly line work can limit contact between workers. Restrictions on opportunities for social interaction can hamper internal group unity.

Technology We can see that the nature of technology and the manner in which work is carried out have an important effect on cohesiveness and relate closely to the nature of the task, physical setting and communications. Where the nature of the work process involves a craft or skill-based 'technology' there is a higher likelihood of group cohesiveness. However, with machine-paced assembly line work it is more difficult to develop cohesiveness. Technology also has wider implications for the operation and behaviour of groups and therefore is considered in a separate section later.

ORGANISATIONAL FACTORS

Management and leadership The form of management and style of leadership adopted will influence the relationship between the group and the organisation and are major determinants of group cohesiveness. In general terms, cohesiveness will be affected by such things as the manner in which the manager gives guidance and encouragement to the group, offers help and support, provides opportunities for participation, attempts to resolve conflicts and gives attention to both employee relations and task problems. *McKenna and Maister* draw attention to the importance of the group leader establishing a level of trust among the group by helping them understand the behaviours that build trust. 'The job of the group leader is to encourage people to earn the trust of others in their group and then show them how it can translate into greater commitment, greater creativity, greater professional satisfaction, and better performance.'[15]

HR policies and procedures Harmony and cohesiveness within the group are more likely to be achieved if HR policies and procedures are well developed and perceived to be equitable, with fair treatment for all members. Attention should be given to the effects that appraisal systems, discipline, promotion and rewards, and opportunities for personal development have on members of the group.

Success The more successful the group, the more cohesive it is likely to be, and cohesive groups are more likely to be successful. Success is usually a strong motivational influence on the level of work performance. Success or reward as a positive motivator can be perceived by group members in a number of ways, for example the satisfactory completion of a task through co-operative action, praise from management, a feeling of high status, achievement in competition with other groups, benefits gained, such as high wage payments from a group bonus incentive scheme.

External threat Cohesiveness may be enhanced by members co-operating with one another when faced with a common external threat, such as changes in their method of work or the appointment of a new manager. Even if the threat is subsequently removed, the group may continue to have a greater degree of cohesiveness than before the threat arose. Conflict between groups will also tend to increase the cohesiveness of each group and the boundaries of the group become drawn more clearly.

GROUP DEVELOPMENT AND MATURITY

The degree of cohesiveness is affected also by the manner in which groups progress through the various stages of development and maturity before getting down to the real tasks in hand. This process can take time and is often traumatic for the members. *Bass and Ryterband* identify four distinct stages in group development:

- mutual acceptance and membership;
- communication and decision-making;
- motivation and productivity; and
- control and organisation.[16]

An alternative, and more popular, model by *Tuckman* identifies five main successive stages of group development and relationships: **forming, storming, norming, performing** and **adjourning**.[17]

- **Stage 1** – forming. The initial formation of the group and the bringing together of a number of individuals who identify, tentatively, the purpose of the group, its composition and terms of reference. At this stage consideration is given to hierarchical structure of the group, pattern of leadership, individual roles and responsibilities, and codes of conduct. There is likely to be considerable anxiety as members attempt to create an impression, to test each other and to establish their personal identity within the group.
- **Stage 2** – storming. As members of the group get to know each other better they will put forward their views more openly and forcefully. Disagreements will be expressed and challenges offered on the nature of the task and arrangements made in the earlier stage of development. This may lead to conflict and hostility. The storming stage is important because, if successful, there will be discussions on reforming arrangements for the working and operation of the group, and agreement on more meaningful structures and procedures.
- **Stage 3** – norming. As conflict and hostility start to be controlled, members of the group will establish guidelines and standards and develop their own norms of acceptable behaviour. The norming stage is important in establishing the need for members to co-operate in order to plan, agree standards of performance and fulfil the purpose of the group.
- **Stage 4** – performing. When the group has progressed successfully through the three earlier stages of development it will have created structure and cohesiveness to work effectively as a team. At this stage the group can concentrate on the attainment of its purpose and performance of the common task is likely to be at its most effective.
- **Stage 5** – adjourning. This refers to the adjourning or disbanding of the group because of, for example, completion of the task, members leaving the organisation or moving on to other tasks. Some members may feel a compelling sense of loss at the end of a major or lengthy group project and their return to independence is characterised by sadness and anxiety. Managers may need to prepare for future group tasks and engendering team effort.

Another writer suggests that new groups go through the following stages:

- the polite stage;
- the why are we here, what are we doing stage;
- the power stage, which dominant will emerge;
- the constructive stage when sharing begins; and
- the unity stage – this often takes weeks, eating together, talking together.[18]

POTENTIAL DISADVANTAGES OF STRONG, COHESIVE GROUPS

Although there are potential disadvantages of cohesive groups (discussed below) they may result in greater interaction between members, mutual help and social satisfaction, lower turnover and absenteeism, and often higher production.[19]

If the manager is to develop effective work groups, attention should be given to those factors that influence the creation of group identity and cohesiveness. However, strong and cohesive groups also present potential disadvantages for management. Cohesive groups do not necessarily produce a higher level of output. Performance varies with the extent to which the group accepts or rejects the goals of the organisation. Furthermore, with a very high level of cohesiveness and attention to social activities, there may even be a fall in output. The level of production is likely to conform to a standard acceptable as a norm by the group. It may be remembered that in the bank wiring room experiment of the Hawthorne studies, group norms imposed a restriction on the workers' level of output.

Once a group has become fully developed and created cohesiveness, it is more difficult for the manager successfully to change the attitudes and behaviour of the group. It is important that the manager should attempt to influence the group during the norming stage when members are establishing guidelines and standards and their own norms of acceptable behaviour. When a group has become fully developed and established its own culture it is more difficult to change the attitudes and behaviour of its members.

Inter-group conflict

Strong, cohesive groups may develop a critical or even hostile attitude towards people outside the group or members of other groups. This can be the case, for example, when group cohesiveness is based on common status, qualifications, technical expertise or professional standing. Group cohesiveness may result in lack of co-operation with, or opposition to, non-members. As a result, resentment and intergroup conflict may arise to the detriment of the organisation as a whole. In order to help prevent, or overcome, unconstructive intergroup conflict, the manager should attempt to stimulate a high level of communication and interaction between the groups and to maintain harmony. Rotation of members among different groups should be encouraged.

Yet, intergroup rivalry may be deliberately encouraged as a means of building stronger within-group cohesiveness. The idea is that a competitive element may help to promote unity within a group. However, intergroup rivalry and competition need to be handled carefully. The manager should attempt to avoid the development of 'win–lose' situations. Emphasis should be placed on overall objectives of the organisation and on superordinate goals. These are goals over and above the issues at conflict and which, if they are to be achieved, require the co-operation of the competing groups.

CHARACTERISTICS OF AN EFFECTIVE WORK GROUP

The characteristics of an effective work group are not always easy to isolate clearly. The underlying feature is a spirit of co-operation in which members work well together as a united team and with harmonious and supportive relationships. This may be evidenced when members of a group exhibit:

- a belief in shared aims and objectives;
- a sense of commitment to the group;
- acceptance of group values and norms;
- a feeling of mutual trust and dependency;
- full participation by all members and decision-making by consensus;
- a free flow of information and communications;
- the open expression of feelings and disagreements;
- the resolution of conflict by the members themselves;
- a lower level of staff turnover, absenteeism, accidents, errors and complaints.

However, as *Brooks* points out, as teams operate at the higher order of group dynamics this list is arguably more reflective of 'effective **work teams** rather than work groups and this is how it should be – these are teams not groups'.[20]

The effects of technology

Technology is clearly a major influence on the pattern of group operation and behaviour. The work organisation may limit the opportunities for social interaction and the extent to which individuals are able to identify themselves as members of a cohesive work group.

This in turn can have possible adverse effects on attitudes to work and the level of job satisfaction. In many assembly line production systems, for example, relationships between individual workers are determined by the nature of the task, the extent to which individual jobs are specified and the time cycle of operations.

ACAS draws attention to technological advances and how new technology enables production to be tailored quickly to customer requirements, often on an individual basis.

> *Mass production techniques, where jobs are broken down into simple tasks, are not suitable for the new customer focused manufacturing nor the expectations of an educated workforce. Organisations need workers to be more flexible, to co-operate with other workers, supervisors and managers throughout the organisation, to operate sophisticated technology and to be more adaptable. In addition, the sheer complexity of operations in industry, commerce and the services places them beyond the expertise and control of any one individual. In these circumstances some form of teamwork becomes not just desirable but essential.*[21]

Impact of information technology

The impact of information technology demands new patterns of work organisation and affects the formation and structure of groups. It will influence where and how people interact. Movement away from large-scale centralised organisation to smaller working units can help create an environment in which workers may relate more easily to each other. Improvements in telecommunications mean, on one hand, that support staff need no longer be located within the main production unit. On the other hand, modern methods of communication mean that individuals may work more on their own, from their homes, shared offices or hotels, or work more with machines than with other people.[22]

VIRTUAL TEAMS

The combination of increasing globalisation and widespread developments in information communications and technology has given greater emphasis to the opportunities for, and need of, **virtual teams**. Instead of face-to-face proximity, virtual teams are a collection of people who are geographically separated but still work together closely. The primary interaction among members is by some electronic information and communication process.[23] This enables organisations to function away from traditional working hours and the physical availability of staff. Computer-based information systems and increased wireless connectivity further the opportunities for virtual working. By their very nature, virtual teams are likely to be largely self-managed.

According to *Hall*, the virtual team is a potential future compromise between fully fledged teams and well-managed groups.

> *I am watching the rise of this idea with interest but am sceptical that it will actually create a 'third way'. Real teams can only be forged in the crucible of personal interaction: videoconferences and Net communications are still poor substitutes for this. Of course, once a team has formed it can use these media, as members will know each other well, but that's not the important bit. It's the forming, norming and storming that make a team.*[24]

Communication and leadership skills

However, *Parker* highlights that remote working may also have an impact on the social aspects of organisational working with an increasing feeling of isolation. 'Remote teamworking is not simply a matter of ensuring staff have access to a laptop and telephone line, and assuming that they will be able to continue with their work. The management and communication skills that this new working culture requires are also key to success.'[25]

A similar point is made by *Norval* who maintains that many remote workers can feel isolated and that the organisation is ignoring them, and this can affect their motivation. Without the visual sense and informal communications within the office, managers need to make a more conscious effort to build rapport and to rethink their management style.[26]

Symons considers one advantage of virtual teamworking using asynchronous media is the clarity and richness of contributions when respondents are removed from the urgency of immediate interaction and this can be particularly relevant in cross-cultural groups. However, as the leader cannot influence by their physical presence, and as hierarchies fade online, managing dispersed teams requires a range of subtly different leadership skills. It is important to develop mutual trust, a democratic approach of shared control and decision-making, and to adopt the role and style of a coach. 'The leader has to establish and maintain "credit" with the group, as "position power" has little or no currency in virtual working.'[27]

Cultural diversity

One reason for the growth in virtual teams is because of increasing globalisation and team members working and living in different countries. This gives rise to potential difficulties of cultural diversity. As *Francesco and Gold* point out: 'The more culturally diverse the members, the more difficult it is to manage a virtual team. Cultural diversity, which will be increasingly common, adds to the complexity of managing virtual teams because different values, customs, and traditions require more leadership under conditions that reduce the ability to use direct leadership.'[28] And according to *Murray*, although virtual working presents some unexpected benefits, if managing diversity in the workplace is a tough task for business leaders, the challenges of keeping executives from different backgrounds working together in various parts of the world is even more difficult. Virtual working does not eradicate the sort of cultural misunderstandings that can arise in a face-to-face situation. 'Cultural or behavioural differences that can manifest themselves in face-to-face working situations can be exacerbated in virtual teamworking, particularly when the group has members from different backgrounds.'[29]

Critical reflection

Self-interest and opportunism are natural features of human behaviour and will always take preference over the demands and best interests of the group or teamwork.' How would you present a *counter* point of view? How far are you prepared to put the interests of a work group before your own interests?

Remote teamworking at the Prudential[30]

Remote teamworking is not simply a matter of ensuring staff have access to a laptop and a telephone line and assuming that they will be able to continue with their work. The management and communications skills that this new working culture requires are also key to success. When one of Britain's leading financial services providers, Prudential, *decided to introduce extensive remote working as part of its drive to build stronger customer relationships they called on the experience and expertise of* Chameleon Training & Consulting. *The Prudential were keen to ensure that their employees not only had the technology but also the skills to maximise the individual and business benefits offered by this new way of working. Chris Parker, Chameleon's Marketing Manager, explains how technology is only the starting point to developing an effective remote team.*

Technology has been a constant driver for change in British business over the last decade. The myth has been that the technological changes alone have single-handedly propelled workplace culture from the age of telephone and typewriters into the broadband world of high speed networks, email and mobile communication, mobile phones and laptops. The reality is a need to adapt management techniques, working culture and employee skill levels. Working in the training and HR industry we know that these requirements cannot be ignored. In addition, many companies have attempted to introduce technology for the sake of it, or brought in 'new' gadgets without looking

Remote teamworking at the Prudential – continued

at the impact on the organisation, or individual workers, and have spent even less time looking at the role training can play in integrating the new technology into the processes and working culture of an organisation.

The pace of change

Prudential is one of the largest and most prestigious financial services organisations, with more than 150 years' experience building long and successful relationships with shareholders, customers and policyholders alike. The financial services industry has changed and continues to change at a faster pace than almost any other, and for this reason, technology, and the delivery of the skills required to integrate new ways of working into employees' daily processes and functions, is more important than in any other area of business.

Practice Head of Prudential's B2B division, and responsible for the development of the team, Martin Boniface says that this changing marketplace was one of the core reasons Prudential decided to change their working culture, embracing technology, and ensuring that their employees have the skills to work effectively in this new environment. 'We realised that technology, and the effective utilisation of it through training, offered us a flexible, customer facing approach to our business, offering benefits for the company, its customers and Prudential employees.'

How to achieve this was going to be another matter entirely, and one which would prove to be far more wide-ranging than originally thought.

A question of image

According to Boniface, 'We wanted to develop a culture where we were able to be proactive, rather than reactive to the needs of our customers. One of the challenges that Prudential faced in this changeable market was to move away from the traditional view of the "man from the Pru" that policyholders know, towards a more modern image in keeping with the changing market's requirements, and this needed to be replicated throughout the business. Representatives were spending hours travelling to visit corporate customers, while still spending time at a centralised office. We realised that in order to offer a more customer focused approach to our corporate clients, we would have to fundamentally change our working culture.' Remote working was positively encouraged for staff in the B2B division at Prudential, with employees using laptops and mobile phones to allow the team to function effectively, but initially this was the exception rather than the rule.

Focus on the customer

'In the B2B division, we made some fairly radical changes,' says Boniface. 'We realised that remote working was the way forward for us, and reorganised our business to focus on our customers, rather than their geographical location – as had been the way in the past. This meant that remote working now became the rule, with the exception of members of our support team who still had a centrally based office location. The ability of our employees to work remotely allowed us to spend more time concentrating on the individual requirements of our corporate customers, and offered financial and efficiency benefits for both the company and our employees. We weren't asking our staff to travel from their homes to an office, and spend hours travelling out to customers' premises, back to the office, before heading home in the evening. This energised and invigorated the team instantly.'

Managing culture change

Having implemented this new way of working for a couple of months, it became obvious that while much of the culture change was beneficial, there were also areas which could be improved, and some that emerged which had not been expected. 'It was at this point that Prudential looked for expert help in remote team management, in order to refine and improve the new remote teamworking practices, and develop solutions designed to enable staff to manage their new working environment and the change of culture,' says Philippa Muress, Chameleon's Head of Consultancy Services. 'Having trialled remote working, Prudential carried out a number of focus groups to identify areas which needed refining. As a result, we were presented with a number of management challenges and objectives.'

Whilst the remote teamworking had been generally successful, with Prudential ensuring that staff had been supported in terms of hardware, with budgets provided for selecting computer technology, installing high speed communications access, and addressing Health and Safety issues, an overwhelming need for emotional support and remote, or virtual, team building had been identified.

The significant difference between central office-based working and remote working is that it is difficult to develop a team spirit, a sense of camaraderie, working remotely through new electronic and telecommunications methods. Morale and motivation had also been identified as areas with which Prudential's new virtual team required some assistance.

'Communication and trust are key elements of developing strong remote teamworking,' says Philippa Muress. 'There is a difference between managing a team in a traditional office environment, and managing a remote team of workers which requires new skills and new management techniques. Some of these skills can be adapted from traditional management methodology, but there are also specific techniques and skills, which are critical in the development of an effective remote team. These are exactly the areas which we help organisations to develop through our Managing Remote Teams programmes.'

'You can't control the volume of email,' adds Boniface. 'You have no way of knowing the emotional state of the recipient of an email, or how they perceive the content of the message, which means that trust has to be central to the team, and clarity is essential to avoid misunderstandings.' The ability for open discussion where things are unclear forms a central part of ensuring that the team is both effective and efficient. 'The last thing you want is for conflicts to grow from small misunderstandings because someone has not picked up the phone to say, "Do I understand this correctly?"'

The delivery of the course has taken a number of different forms, with Chameleon using a blend of input sessions, assessment tools and role-play techniques during the implementation of the first phase of Prudential's Remote Teams training. Issues of management techniques, motivation and empowerment, and developing a team spirit from remote locations have all been central in the work, ensuring that staff have received a totally bespoke solution tailored to the specific needs of the organisation. Philippa Muress says, 'One of the most important parts of developing a training programme is ensuring that the development and implementation addresses the aims and objectives of both the team and the wider organisation. When developing an effective remote team it is important that you don't isolate the remote members from the rest of the organisation.'

The programme has highlighted the development needs, not only of the managers and remote workers, but also of those who provide support back in the office, and one-day workshops have been arranged for the whole team. 'We recognise the need for a strategic and co-ordinated programme of change in order to develop long-standing effective and successful remote teams,' says Boniface. 'There is a very important coaching element to the remote teams programme which Chameleon has developed for us, which offers vital support and reassurance. Working remotely can be a lonely experience if the necessary skill training is not a place, and we're delighted with the way that Chameleon has been there at every step. Our single point of contact has been one of their Remote Team experts, who understands our business, our aims and our specific business focus.'

Enjoying the benefits of managed change

The benefits of this new virtual team are already being experienced at 'the Pru'. Their vision of creating a more customer-faced commercial approach is generating more business with less cost (which has occurred, in part, as a result of the reduced requirement for desk space), and has raised customer satisfaction levels in the process.

In a market which has experienced considerable change, this has generated substantial competitive advantage for the company, and boosted morale within the CRM team. Chameleon's Philippa Muress says that the benefits experienced by the Prudential are all classic traits of effective Remote Teams training. 'Technology is only the beginning of developing a remote team environment – without the necessary tools to manage the new working practices, the new approach to managing and being managed, and the new communication and emotional skills, remote teamworking will not bring the efficiencies and financial rewards which can be achieved with a co-ordinated, structured and expertly delivered programme.'

Source: 'Remote team working at Prudential', *Manager, the British Journal of Administrative Management*, March/April 2002, pp. 30–1 and with the permission of Murray Blair.

ROLE RELATIONSHIPS

In order that the organisation can achieve its goals and objectives, the work of individual members must be linked into coherent patterns of activities and relationships. This is achieved through the 'role structure' of the organisation.

A 'role' is the expected pattern of behaviours associated with members occupying a particular position within the structure of the organisation. It also describes how a person perceives their own situation. The concept of 'role' is important to the functioning of groups and for an understanding of group processes and behaviour. It is through role differentiation that the structure of the work group and relationships among its members are established. Some form of structure is necessary for teamwork and co-operation. The concept of roles helps to clarify the structure and to define the pattern of complex relationships within the group.

The formal organisational relationships (line, functional, staff or lateral) – discussed later in Chapter 15 – can be seen as forms of role relationships. These individual authority relationships determine the pattern of interaction with other roles.

The role, or roles, that the individual plays within the group is influenced by a combination of:

- **situational factors**, such as the requirements of the task, the style of leadership, position in the communication network; and
- **personal factors** such as values, attitudes, motivation, ability and personality.

The role that a person plays in one work group may be quite different from the role that person plays in other work groups. However, everyone within a group is expected to behave in a particular manner and to fulfil certain role expectations.

A person's role-set

In addition to the role relationships with members of their own group – peers, superiors, subordinates – the individual will have a number of role-related relationships with outsiders – for example, members of other work groups, trade union officials, suppliers, consumers. This is a person's 'role-set'. The role-set comprises the range of associations or contacts with whom the individual has meaningful interactions in connection with the performance of their role (*see* Figure 8.5).

Role incongruence

An important feature of role relationship is the concept of 'role incongruence'. This arises when a member of staff is perceived as having a high and responsible position in one respect but a low standing in another respect. Difficulties with role incongruence can arise from the nature of groupings and formal relationships within the structure of the organisation. There are a number of work-related relationships such as doctor and nurse, chef and waiter, senior manager and personal assistant which can give rise to a potential imbalance of authority and responsibility.

Difficulties with role incongruence can also arise in line-staff relationships: for instance, a relatively junior member of the HR department informing a senior departmental manager that a certain proposed action is contrary to the policies of the organisation. Another example with staff relationships is where a person establishes themselves in the role of 'gatekeeper' to the boss[31] – for instance, where a comparatively junior personal assistant passes on the manager's instructions to one of the manager's more senior subordinates or where the personal assistant attempts to block a more senior member of staff having access to the manager.

Role expectations

Many role expectations are prescribed formally and indicate what the person is expected to do and their duties and obligations. Formal role prescriptions provide guidelines for expected behaviours and may be more prevalent in a 'mechanistic' organisation. Examples are written contracts of employment, rules and regulations, standing orders, policy deci-

Figure 8.5 Representation of a possible role-set in the work situation

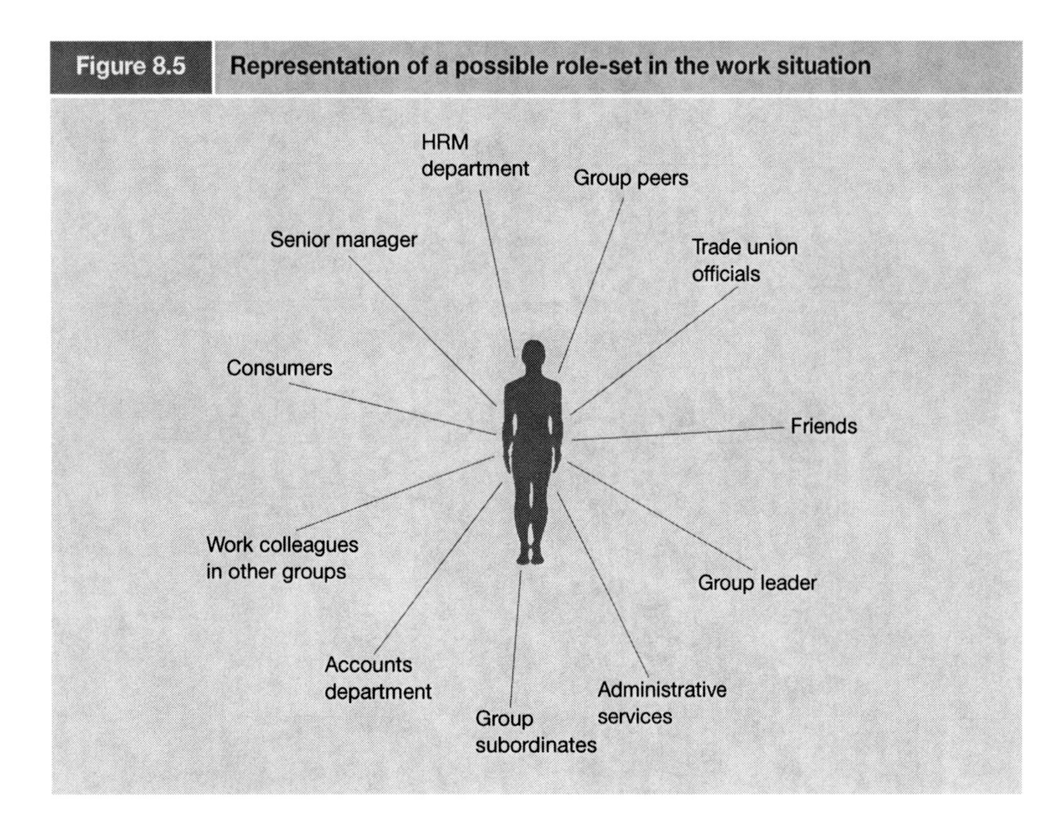

sions, job descriptions, or directives from superiors. Formal role expectations may also be derived clearly from the nature of the task. They may, in part at least, be defined legally, for example under the Health and Safety at Work Act, or as with the obligations of a company secretary under the Companies Acts, or the responsibilities of a district auditor under the Local Government Acts.

Not all role expectations are prescribed formally, however. There will be certain patterns of behaviour that although not specified formally will nonetheless be expected of members. These informal role expectations may be imposed by the group itself or at least communicated to a person by other members of the group. Examples include general conduct, mutual support to co-members, attitudes towards superiors, means of communicating, dress and appearance. Members may not always be consciously aware of these informal expectations yet they still serve as important determinants of behaviour. Under this heading could be included the concept of a psychological contract which was discussed in Chapter 1.

Some members may have the opportunity to determine their own role expectations, where, for example, formal expectations are specified loosely or only in very general terms. Opportunities for **self-established** roles are more likely in senior positions, but also occur within certain professional, technical or scientific groups, for example senior research staff, or where there is a demand for creativity or artistic flair, for example head chefs. Such opportunities may be greater within an 'organic' organisation and will also be influenced by the style of leadership adopted – for example, where a *laissez-faire* approach is adopted.

ROLE CONFLICT

Patterns of behaviour result from both the role and the personality. The concept of role focuses attention on aspects of behaviour existing independently of an individual's personality. **Role conflict** arises from inadequate or inappropriate role definition and needs to be distinguished from personality clashes. These arise from incompatibility between two or more people as individuals even though their roles may be defined clearly and understood fully. In practice, the manner in which a person actually behaves may not be consistent with their expected pattern of behaviours. This inconsistency may be a result of role conflict. Role conflict as a generic term can include:

- role incompatibility
- role ambiguity
- role overload
- role underload.

These are all problem areas associated with the creation of role expectations (*see* Figure 8.6).

Figure 8.6 Role relationships and conflicts

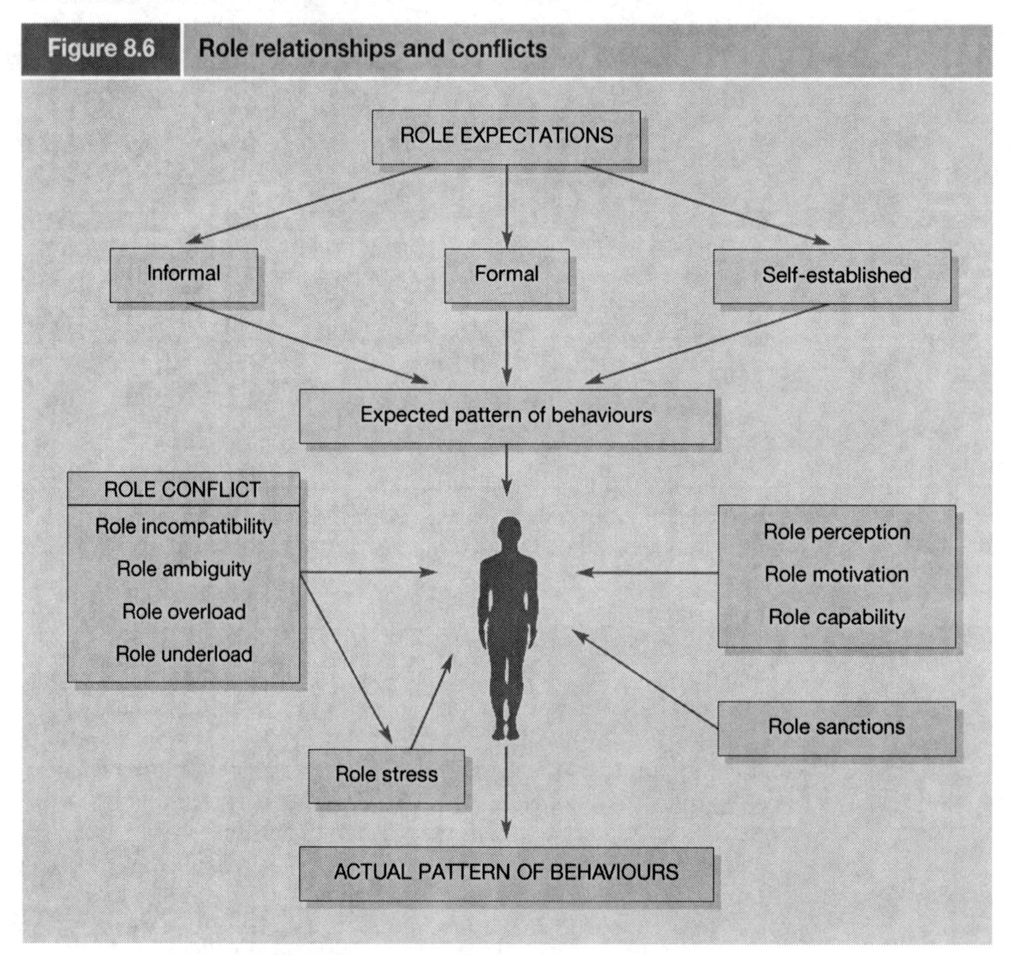

Source: Adapted from Miner, J. B., *Management Theory*, Macmillan (1971) p. 47.

- **Role incompatibility** arises when a person faces a situation in which simultaneous different or contradictory expectations create inconsistency. Compliance with one set of expectations makes it difficult or impossible to comply with other expectations. The two role expectations are in conflict. A typical example concerns the person 'in the middle', such as the supervisor or section head, who faces opposing expectations from workers and from management. Another example might be the situation of a manager who believes in a relaxed, participative style of behaviour more in keeping with a Theory Y approach, but whose superior believes in a Theory X approach and expects the manager to adopt a more formal and directive style of behaviour.

- **Role ambiguity** occurs when there is lack of clarity as to the precise requirements of the role and the person is unsure what to do. The person's perception of their role may differ from the expectations of others. This implies that insufficient information is available for the adequate performance of the role. Role ambiguity may result from a lack of formally prescribed expectations. It is likely to arise in large, diverse groups or at times of constant change. Uncertainty often relates to such matters as the method of performing tasks, the extent of the person's authority and responsibility, standards of work, and the evaluation and appraisal of performance.
- **Role overload** is when a person faces too many separate roles or too great a variety of expectations. The person is unable to meet satisfactorily all expectations and some must be neglected in order to satisfy others. This leads to a conflict of priority. Some writers distinguish between role overload and work overload. Role overload is seen in terms of the total role-set and implies that the person has too many separate roles to handle. Where there are too many expectations of a single role – that is, a problem of quantity – this is work overload.
- **Role underload** can arise when the prescribed role expectations fall short of the person's perception of their role. The person may feel their role is not demanding enough and that they have the capacity to undertake a larger or more varied role, or an increased number of roles. Role underload may arise, for example, when a new member of staff is first appointed or from the initial effects of empowerment.

Role conflict and matrix organisation

Problems of role conflict can often arise from the matrix form of organisation (which is discussed in Chapter 15) and, for example, from the use of flexible project teams. Where staff are assigned temporarily, and perhaps on a part-time basis, from other groups this creates a two-way flow of authority and responsibility.

Unless role differentiations are defined clearly this can result in conflicting expectations from the manager of the person's own functional grouping and from the manager of the project team (role incompatibility). It can also lead to uncertainty about the exact requirements of the part the person is expected to play as a member of the project team (role ambiguity). The combinations of expectations from both managers may also result in role overload.

Role stress

Role conflict can result in role stress. As discussed in Chapter 3, although a certain amount of stress may **arguably** be seen as a good thing, and especially at managerial level helps to bring out a high level of performance, it is also potentially very harmful. Stress is a source of tension, frustration and dissatisfaction. It can lead to difficulties in communication and interpersonal relationships and can affect morale, effectiveness at work and health. There are a number of ways in which management might attempt to avoid or reduce role conflict and the possibilities of role stress.

- Increase specification and clarity of prescribed role expectations, for example through written statements on objectives and policy, use of manuals and set procedures, introduction of appropriate rules, and detailed job descriptions. However, such measures may be resented by staff. They may restrict the opportunity for independent action and personal development, giving rise to even more role conflict.
- Improved recruitment and selection and the careful matching of abilities, motivation, interests and personalities to the demands of a particular role.
- Attention to induction and socialisation programmes, job training and retraining, staff development and career progression plans.
- Medical examinations and health screening to give early indications of potential stress-related problems.

- The creation of new roles or assimilation of existing roles. The reallocation or restructuring of tasks and responsibilities. The clarification of priorities, and the elimination or downgrading of minor roles.
- Giving advance notice and explanation of what is likely to happen, for example of an expected, additional heavy workload which must be completed urgently. Where possible and appropriate provide an opportunity for practice or experience.
- Attention to factors which may help improve group structure and group cohesiveness, and help overcome intergroup conflict.
- Review of organisation structure, information flow and communication networks, for example members of staff being answerable to more than one superior.

Other influences on behaviour

Even if there is an absence of role conflict and role stress, a person's actual behaviour may still be inconsistent with their expected pattern of behaviours. *Miner* gives three reasons that may account for this disparity.[32]

- The person does not perceive their job in the way the role prescriptions specify. This is a form of role ambiguity but may arise not because the role prescriptions themselves are unclear but because the person misunderstands or distorts them.
- Motivation is lacking and the person does not want to behave in the way prescribed.
- The person does not have the capabilities – knowledge, mental ability or physical skills – required to behave in the way the role prescriptions specify.

Application of sanctions

Organisations apply a number of both positive and negative sanctions as inducements for members to contribute and behave in accordance with their prescribed roles. Typical examples are: an increase in salary or wages; promotion; a sideways or downwards move in the organisation structure; the threat of dismissal.

There are also a number of less direct sanctions that may be adopted. These include the size of office or work area, the allocation of unpopular tasks, giving opportunities for paid overtime work, level of supervision or empowerment, the amount of information given or the extent of consultation, granting or withholding privileges.

Role sanctions may also be applied through the operation of the informal organisation. Members of the group may impose their own sanctions and discipline individuals who contravene the norms of the group or expected standards of behaviour.

THE IMPORTANCE OF TEAMWORK

How people behave and perform as members of a group is as important as their behaviour or performance as individuals. Harmonious working relationships and good teamwork help make for a high level of staff morale and work performance. Effective teamwork is an essential element of modern management practices such as empowerment, quality circles and total quality management, and how groups manage change. Teamwork is important in any organisation but may be especially significant in service industries, such as hospitality organisations where there is a direct effect on customer satisfaction.[33]

According to ACAS, teams have been around for as long as anyone can remember and there can be few organisations that have not used the term in one sense or another. In a general sense, people talk of teamwork when they want to emphasise the virtues of co-operation and the need to make use of the various strengths of employees. Using the term more specifically, teamworking involves a reorganisation of the way work is carried out. Teamwork can increase competitiveness by:

- improving productivity;
- improving quality and encouraging innovation;
- taking advantage of the opportunities provided by technological advances;
- improving employee motivation and commitment.[34]

The general movement towards flatter structures of organisation, wider spans of control and reducing layers of middle management, together with increasing empowerment of employees, all involve greater emphasis on the importance of teamworking. 'There's no doubt that effective teamwork is crucial to an organisation's efforts to perform better, faster and more profitably than their competitors.'[35]

Skills of effective teamworking

From a recent study of Europe's top companies, *Heller* refers to the need for new managers and new methods, and includes as a key strategy for a new breed of managers in a dramatically changed environment: 'making team-working work – the new, indispensable skill'. Heller refers to the happy teams at Heineken. Part of the cultural strength of Heineken is a realisation that 'the best culture for an organisation is a team culture' and that 'any large organisation is a team of teams – and people who have to work together as a team must also think together as a team'.[36] Heller also lists Heineken's manifesto for 'professional team-thinking' and maintains that 'arguing with any of these eleven points is absurd'.

1. The aim is to reach the best decision, not just a hasty conclusion or an easy consensus. The team leader always has the ultimate responsibility for the quality of the decision taken – and, therefore, for the quality of the team-thinking effort that has led up to the decision.
2. To produce the best professional team-thinking, the team leader must ensure that ego-trips, petty office politics and not-invented-here rigidity are explicitly avoided. There should be competition between ideas – not between individual members of the team.
3. The team-thinking effort must first ensure that the best question to be answered is clearly and completely formulated.
4. The team-thinking process is iterative – not linear. Therefore, the question may have to be altered later and the process repeated.
5. The team leader is responsible for seeing that sufficient alternatives and their predicted consequences have been developed for evaluation by the team.
6. The team leader will thus ask, 'What are our alternatives?' – and not just, 'What is the answer?'
7. The team leader also recognizes that it is wiser to seek and listen to the ideas of the team before expressing his or her own ideas and preferences.
8. In any professional team-thinking effort, more ideas will have to be created than used. But any idea that is rejected will be rejected with courtesy and with a clear explanation as to why it is being rejected. To behave in this way is not naive, it is just decent and smart.
9. A risk/reward equation and a probability of success calculation will be made explicitly before any important decision is taken.
10. Once a decision is made professionally, the team must implement it professionally.
11. When you think, think. When you act, act.

Source: From Robert Heller, *In Search of European Excellence*, Profile Books (1997), p. 231. Reproduced with permission.

According to *Guirdham*, the growth of teamwork has led to the increased interest in interface skills at work.

> *More and more tasks of contemporary organisations, particularly those in high technology and service businesses, require teamwork. Taskforces, project teams and committees are key elements in the modern workplace. Teamwork depends not just on technical competence of the individuals composing the team, but on their ability to 'gel'. To work well together, the team members must have more than just team spirit. They also need collaborative skills – they must be able to support one another and to handle conflict in such a way that it becomes constructive rather than destructive.*[37]

A similar point is made by *Ashmos and Nathan*: 'The use of teams has expanded dramatically in response to competitive challenges. In fact, one of the most common skills required by new work practices is the ability to work as a team.'[38]

The nature and importance of teamwork is discussed further in Chapter 9.

Activity 8D
www.pearsoned.co.uk/mullins

Critical reflection

Groups and teamworking are an essential and integral part of the work organisation, but people value their individuality and own identity and enjoy the right of self-expression. The real skill of management should therefore be to make full use of people's individuality for the mutual benefit of the group as a whole. Do you agree? How do you think managers might best be trained to enhance the contribution and performance of groups?

MANAGEMENT IN THE NEWS

The Pink Ladies mean business

No men please, we're cabbies

Robert Watts

While government reports and official statistics seem to suggest that women are still lagging behind men in terms of pay and status, and many commentators focus on making existing organisations more female friendly, there may also be other solutions. The story of the Pink Ladies Cabs service is one example of an organisation which shows how women can take successful business initiatives and run their own show.

'Pink Ladies Cabs' was founded by Tina Dutton and Andrea Winders in Warrington, Cheshire, in June 2005. The idea was simple and had been lurking in Tina's mind for some time when a family conversation triggered her to take action. Leanna, Tina's daughter, mentioned that she was anxious about being the last person in a taxi after a night out with friends. There were many taxi companies to choose from, but not all were operating legally and there were a number of reported attacks on women by taxi drivers, especially in London. Here was a small but significant market niche. Together Tina and Andrea did some market research and came up with a distinctive package to fit the gap.

Is it 'a man's world?' The successful Pink Ladies Cab service run for women by women suggests that it doesn't have to be.

The basic idea is to provide safe transport for women. The drivers are all women and Pink Ladies makes sure they are trained in self-defence and first aid. All their cabs (conspicuously bright pink Renault Kangoos) are fitted with satellite navigation and tracking devices, and have extra safety features such as gel-filled tyres to minimise the risk of the cab being stranded with a puncture. Bookings are made for specific times and customers receive text or telephone messages when the cabs are two minutes away, so that they don't have to wait around outside to be picked up. When a client is dropped off, the Pink Ladies driver will wait until they can see that she is safely inside her destination before driving away. Further security measures include a no-cash policy which means that the cabs never have money on board; instead clients have a pre-payment card which can be recharged over the internet or by phone.

But is it legal? At first glance a business which serves and employs only women (for the most part; they do have a male mechanic) might seem to be in contravention of the Sex Discrimination Act. However, Tina and Andrea know that by operating as a club, not a taxi company, they are able to run this women-only service. If you want to use a Pink Cab you pay a small membership fee to have access to the service and your membership card is also the pre-pay card you use to book and pay for the ride. As for employment, the EOC agreed with their interpretation of one part of the law on sex discrimination which allows a 'women only' policy if the holder of the job provides individuals with personal services promoting their welfare.

And it's not just Warrington; they have developed an operation in London, and their service is already featuring in foreign tourist guides for visitors to London. They are planning further expansion through franchise operations. Pink Ladies are certainly going places!

Source: Watts, R., 'No men please, we're cabbies', *Daily Telegraph*, 5 January 2006.

Discussion questions

1 **'Pink Ladies' have created a women's organisation rather than seeking to feminise an existing one. Critically evaluate the ways in which this factor might affect the group values and norms of the company.**

2 **How does modern technology (such as satellite navigation) affect the roles that individuals can play within this organisation? Does the organisation challenge or reinforce stereotypes of women's roles?**

SYNOPSIS

- Work is a group-based activity, and groups and teams are a major feature of human behaviour and work organisation. Members must co-operate for work to be carried out. Harmonious working relationships and good teamwork help make for a high level of staff morale and organisational performance. There is a tendency for the terms 'groups' and teams' to be used interchangeably. Whereas all teams are groups, it does not necessarily follow that all groups are teams. Groups develop their own pattern of values and norms of behaviour.

- Groups are formed as a consequence of the pattern of organisation structure and arrangements for the division of work. There are two main types of groups at work, formal and informal. Formal groups are deliberately planned and created by management as part of the organisation structure and to achieve specific organisational objectives. Informal groups are based on personal relationships and develop irrespective of the formal structure. Informal groups serve to satisfy members' psychological and social needs. Groups are formed, therefore, for a number of reasons relating to both work performance and social processes.

- Individuals will form into groups or teams, both formal and informal, for a number of reasons relating to both work performance and social processes. The manager's main concern is that members co-operate. Factors that affect group cohesiveness can be considered under the broad headings of membership, work environment, organisational and group development and maturity. Membership of strong and cohesive groups can be a rewarding experience for the individual and have beneficial effects for the organisation.

- There are, however, potential disadvantages of strong, cohesive groups and the manager should attempt to prevent unconstructive intergroup conflict. However, intergroup rivalry may be deliberately encouraged as a means of building stronger within-group cohesiveness. Individuals make a contribution to the work of the organisation in different ways. The effective management of work groups requires an understanding of the psychological and social influences on behaviour within organisations.

- The characteristics of an effective work group are not always easy to isolate. The underlying feature is a spirit of co-operation in which members work well together as a united team, and with harmonious and supportive relationships. The combination of increasing globalisation and widespread developments in information communications and technology has given greater emphasis to the opportunities for, and need of, virtual teams. Members are geographically separated but still work together closely.

- The concept of 'role' is important to the functioning of groups and for an understanding of group processes and behaviour. It is through role differentiation that the structure of work groups and relationships among members is established. Role expectations may be established formally, they may be informal or they may be self-established. Inadequate or inappropriate role definition can result in role conflict, including role incompatibility, role ambiguity, role overload and role underload. It is important that the manager makes every effort to minimise role conflict and the causes of role stress.

Refresh your understanding, assess your progress and begin your research with online resources at **www.pearsoned.co.uk/mullins**

REVIEW AND DISCUSSION QUESTIONS

1. What is a group? Explain the importance and influence of group values and norms and give practical examples from within your own organisation.
2. How would you distinguish between a 'group' and a 'team'? To what extent do you believe the distinction has practical significance for managers?
3. Distinguish between formal and informal groups and provide your own supporting examples. What functions do groups serve in an organisation?
4. Identify different stages in group development and maturity. What other factors influence the cohesiveness of work groups? Give examples by reference to a work group to which you belong.
5. Discuss critically the advantages and disadvantages of virtual teams and how you believe they are likely to develop in the future.
6. What is meant by the role structure of an organisation? Construct a diagram that shows your own role-set within a work situation. Give examples of informal role expectations to which you are, or have been, a party.
7. Explain different forms of role conflict that can result in role stress. Give an account of a work situation in which you have experienced role conflict/role stress. As a manager, what action would you have taken in an attempt to rectify the situation?
8. Detail fully what you believe are the essential characteristics of a successful work group or team. As a manager, explain how you would attempt to develop effective group/team relationships and performance.

ASSIGNMENT 1

Recall your experience of a work group or team with which you are familiar and comment critically on:

1. the extent to which members were clear about the goals of the group, what they were expected to achieve, and how their performance would be evaluated;
2. the diversity of group membership, and significances of diversity for the operations and success of the group;

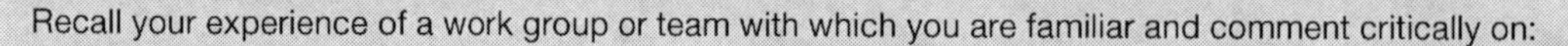

3. and what *exactly* made the group effective or fall apart?

ASSIGNMENT 2

Obtain, or prepare, a chart depicting the formal groupings within your organisation or a large department of the organisation.

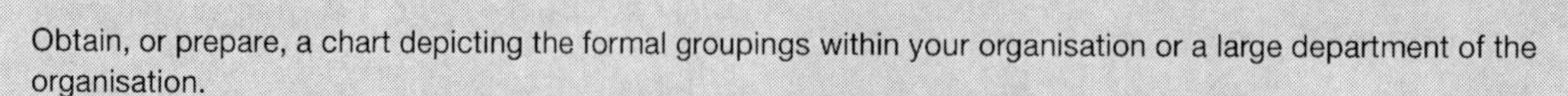

1. Using this chart, identify clearly the informal groups that exist within the formal structure.

2 Discuss ways in which these informal groups aid, and/or conflict with, the work of the organisation/department.
3 Explain the extent to which management recognises the influence of the informal groups.
4 What conclusions do you draw from this assignment?

PERSONAL AWARENESS AND SKILLS EXERCISE

Objectives

Completing this exercise should help you to enhance the following skills:

- Observe and record the development and maturity of a small work group.
- Analyse the behaviour of individual members of the group.
- Identify those factors that most influence the cohesiveness of the group.

Exercise

You are required to observe a small group or project team at work; *alternatively*, recall the working of any small group of which you have recently been a member.

1 Complete the following grid by giving a tick in the appropriate box to denote each contribution by individual members.

	Names of group members (or reference numbers)				
Forming					
Storming					
Norming					
Performing					
Adjourning (if appropriate)					

2 Give specific examples of the group values or norms that constituted 'proper' behaviour of group members.
3 Detail sanctions applied to those members who did not conform to the group norms and the apparent effectiveness of these sanctions.
4 Comment critically on the effectiveness of the group as a whole.

Discussion

- To what extent do you believe groups develop clearly through the five main successive stages of forming, storming, norming, performing and adjourning?
- Which in your opinion is the most crucial stage?
- Give your views, with supporting reasons, on the apparent satisfaction derived by individuals from membership of the group.

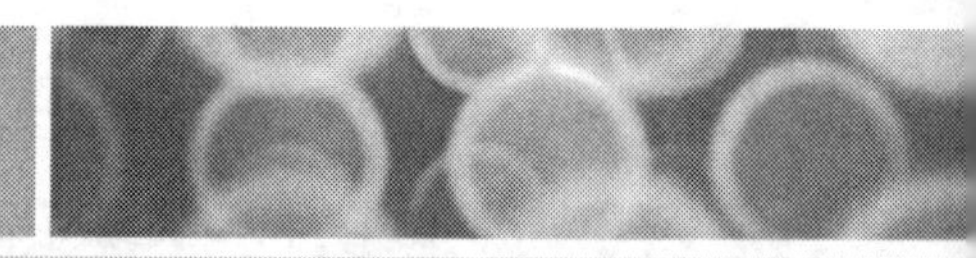

CASE STUDY

Mumbai's Dabbawalahs a world-class quality service

Those studying organisational behaviour often find themselves reading about the issues faced by global businesses, whose managerial excellence is supported by cutting-edge technology and major financial investment. The organisation in this case study has neither cutting-edge technology nor major investment and never has had. However, it has become famous in recent years, as the world's business schools have beaten a path to its door to study the extraordinary organisation of Mumbai's dabbawalahs.

Dabbawalahs (or 'tiffinwalahs') run a service in Mumbai whose purpose is easy enough to describe: each working day, they arrange the collection and delivery from Bombay's suburbs of about 175,000 lunches in the traditional tiffin boxes. These meals are prepared by wives or mothers (or sometimes local restaurants) for individual workers in central Mumbai: obviously, the contents of each box are unique, which is the central appeal of the service. A little later in the day, the dabbawalahs collect the empties and return them to the workers' homes.

In some ways, the design of the system resembles that of a modern international courier service. It is based on local collection of the tiffin boxes, which are then loaded on to local trains for bulk transportation into the centre of Mumbai (special compartments are reserved for the boxes). At each of the central stations, other members of the team unload the boxes for destinations near the station and sort them for hand delivery to the offices and workshops where the individual recipients work. They also load any boxes for delivery further down the line. The train stops for about 20 seconds at these stations, resulting in a turnaround time that would make many of Europe's low-cost airlines look up in surprise. Delivery to the hungry workers is achieved by 12.45 sharp, following which the process is reversed to return the boxes to the homes.[39] The service costs Rs300–350 per month ($US6–7) and the dabbawalahs earn about Rs5,000 (about $US115) a month. Customers pay one month's bonus to the organisation for the Diwali festival. This intricate, precisely co-ordinated operation takes place in a city famous for its bustle, traffic delays and occasional chaos – the dabbawalahs negotiate the traffic on foot and by bicycle at a cracking pace, whatever the weather: the tiffin must get through. The error rate is said to be vanishingly small: one box may go astray every two months.

Source: Nick Hanna/Alamy

The amazing dabbawallahs deliver 175,000 lunchtime tiffin boxes a day in Bombay in a well co-ordinated and highly effective team operation.

A team to beat the best

There is no IT support for this daily miracle – no track and trace, no computers, no bar codes, just a handwritten code on each box that allows the dabbawalah to recognise which station the box has to be sent to and unloaded, its ultimate destination and its return address. Many of the dabbawalahs have low levels of literacy, but their ability to decode and correctly route the 40 or so boxes that they each carry through the crowded streets is key to the whole system. The very high levels of effectiveness and efficiency achieved in this service have attracted the attention of business schools from many countries. As the dabbawalahs proudly proclaim, the reliability of the system is at Six Sigma levels (one error in 1 million), a performance that is comparable to that of the world's leading corporations.[40] Business strategy expert C.K. Prahalad was struck by the performance level of this system as well as by its very low levels of capital-intensiveness:

> *That's a good thing by itself because you can dramatically reduce the capital intensity of a business. A lot of the float there is between points of production and consumption can be reduced dramatically around the world.*[41]

However, the interest in this case is not so much in the technical details of the logistics but in the team that makes the service happen. The dabbawalah service is said to have originated in 1890,[42] and to have been invented by Indian entrepreneur Mahadeo Havaji Bacchex.[43] At the same time, a then much smaller Mumbai was starting to experience a strong growth of daily commuting into the centre. From the outset, the design of the service was much the same as today – the local trains were hauled by steam engines and the traffic jams on the streets were animal rather than automotive, but the challenge was essentially the same. There has always been strong cultural preference for home cooking among workers in India: in Mumbai, which has always drawn its working population from all over India, 'home cooking' means a kaleidoscope of different regional styles and traditions. Clearly, a service that can bring this diverse range of home-prepared meals reliably to the individual in the workplace is going to be in demand. The service grew to its present levels by the 1950s.

There are about 5,000 dabbawalahs in Mumbai today, organised into teams of 20–25 under an experienced group leader. Ragunath Medge is President of Nutan Mumbai Tiffin Box Suppliers Charity Trust (and a regular guest speaker these days at business school conferences). As he explains, those who work for the organisation are mostly shareholders, rather than employees:

> *If you have employees, then you have unions and strikes. We are all shareholders in the Trust and thus we share in the earnings.*

He explains that the dabbawalahs mainly come from the same region, the Pune district and that most are related to each other:

> *We all come from the region east of the Sahyadri (Western Ghats), and everyone who joins us, is known to us. If an outsider does join in, we initially employ him on a fixed salary, and if in a couple of years he wins our trust, we may make him a shareholder.*[44]

These sentiments are echoed in the comments of one of the dabbawalahs in an article published in *The Guardian* in 2002:

> *It's a very sociable job,' Sapan Mare, a tiffin-wallah since 1970 explained, as we rattled into central Bombay* [Mumbai].*'I like the fact that I meet so many people every day. Between 100 to 110 members of my family are in the tiffin business. I come from a family where four generations have been tiffin-wallahs,' he added proudly.*[45]

Mr Medge explains that the job for Trust shareholders lasts for as long as the member is strong enough to do the work. Notes on a blogspot (weblog) of a talk given by Mr Medge provide further detail of the discipline that characterises the dabbawalah team: members are mainly vegetarians and most don't drink alcohol.[46] Drinking at work is against the rules: the first and second offence will result in a fine and the third will result in removal from the service. There is also a dress code for team members, presumably to show pride and confidence in the high standards of the service and also perhaps to secure public co-operation with the smooth daily running of the operation. The organisation sets great store by the integrity and trustworthiness of its members: dabbawalahs just do not have police records.

The future of the service

As any services marketing textbook will confirm, customers often take part in the production of services. In this case, the expertise and hard work of the dabbawalahs will come to nothing if the meals are not ready for collection on time: those who prepare the meals in homes and local restaurants can also be seen as part of the team. Sometimes, it is suggested that customers also use the network as an informal communications medium, sending each other little notes in the tiffin boxes.

The city of Mumbai is at the forefront of the huge economic and social changes that are sweeping through India. The dabbawalah system is still a mainstay of the working day in the city, but is starting to experience and respond to change. The growth of fast food is a global phenomenon that has been relatively slow to penetrate the Indian market but is now starting to make its mark. Mr Medge's operation is still resolutely uncomputerised (what good would gigabytes and parallel processors be in the traffic in Mumbai?), but it does have a website and is now able to accept orders via the site or by SMS. Its website also seeks to re-assert the traditional core values of the organisation in the face of the tide of global fast food.[47] Among the 'top ten reasons for using the Dabbawalahs' services' are the following appeals to the good sense of Mumbai workers:

1. *Home made food is best for health … Outside junk foods may take your life and makes you sick…*
2. *Home made food is cheaper … It's simple maths.*
3. *Do you not love your mother or wife and like to eat food made by her?*

The dabbawalahs have fed thousands of people for more than a century. Their astonishingly effective logistics continue to deliver reliable, low-priced service every working day. As can be seen on their website, they have admirers all around the world – Prince Charles (who invited the two dabbahwalahs quoted in this case to his wedding to Camilla), Richard Branson (of course) and – perhaps paradoxically – the Slow Food movement. For generations, the cohesion, dedication and discipline of this team have been the main guarantees of their legendary service and it seems likely to retain a place in the hearts of Mumbai residents as modernisation proceeds.

Your tasks

1. If a team can be defined as a group of people working towards a common goal, discuss the advantages and disadvantages of the dabbawalah practice of making team members shareholders rather than employees. Would the same arguments apply to other logistically similar operations?
2. Use the framework in Figure 8.4 to analyse the cohesiveness and performance of the dabbawalah team. To what extent does the dabbawalah service display the characteristics of an effective work group?
3. Why has technology played such a small part in the development of the dabbawalah service so far? Is this likely to change in future? Identify ways in which this might affect the team spirit of the organisation.

Notes and references

1 Schein, E. H. *Organizational Psychology*, Third edition, Prentice-Hall (1988), p. 145.
2 Adair, J. *Effective Teambuilding*, Gower (1986).
3 Guzzo, R. A. and Dickson, M. W. 'Teams in Organizations: recent research on performance and effectiveness', *Annual Review of Psychology*, vol. 47, (1996), pp. 307–38.
4 Holpp, L. 'Teams: It's All in the Planning', *Training & Development*, vol. 51, no. 4, April 1997, pp. 44–7.
5 Crainer, S. *Key Management Ideas: Thinkers that changed the management world*, Third edition, Financial Times Prentice Hall (1998), p. 237.
6 Cane, S. *Kaizen Strategies for Winning Through People*, Pitman Publishing (1996), p. 116.
7 Belbin, R. M. *Beyond the Team*, Butterworth-Heinemann (2000).
8 Riches, A. 'Emotionally Intelligent Teams', Organisational Change & Leadership Development, www.anneriches.com.au, accessed 11 March 2003.
9 Huck, S., Kubler, D. and Weibull, J. 'Social Norms and Economic Incentives in Firms', *Economic & Social Research Council*, 5 March 2003.
10 Boynton, A. and Fischer B. *Virtuoso Teams: Lessons from teams that changed their worlds*, Financial Times Prentice Hall (2005).
11 Lysons, K. 'Organisational Analysis', *Supplement to The British Journal of Administrative Management*, no. 18, March/April 1997.
12 Law, S. 'Beyond the Water Cooler', *Professional Manager*, January 2005, pp. 26–8.
13 See, for example: Jay, A. *Corporation Man*, Penguin (1975). In an amusing historical account of the development of different forms of groups, Jay suggests that ten is the basic size of human grouping.
14 Cane, S. *Kaizen Strategies for Winning Through People*, Pitman Publishing (1996), p. 131.
15 McKenna, P. J. and Maister, D. H. 'Building Team Trust', *Consulting to Management*, vol. 13, no. 4, December 2002, pp. 51–3.
16 Bass, B. M. and Ryterband, E. C. *Organizational Psychology*, Second edition, Allyn and Bacon (1979).
17 Tuckman, B. W. 'Development Sequence in Small Groups', *Psychological Bulletin*, vol. 63, 1965, pp. 384–99; and Tuckman, B. W. and Jensen, M. C. 'Stages of Small Group Development Revised', *Group and Organizational Studies*, vol. 2, no. 3, 1977, pp. 419–27.
18 Cited in Green, J. 'Are your teams and groups at work successful?', *Administrator*, December 1993, p. 12.
19 Argyle, M. *The Social Psychology of Work*, Second edition, Penguin (1989).
20 Brooks, I. *Organisational Behaviour: Individuals, Groups and Organisation*, Third edition, Financial Times Prentice Hall (2006) p. 99.
21 Teamwork: Success Through People', Advisory Booklet, ACAS, April 2003, p. 9.
22 See, for example: Kinsman, F. 'The Virtual Office and The Flexible Organisation', *Administrator*, April 1994, pp. 31–2; and Chowdhury, S. *Management 21C*. Financial Times Prentice Hall (2000).
23 See, for example: Johnson, P., Heimann, V. and O'Neill, K. 'The "Wonderland" of Virtual Teams', *The Journal of Workplace Learning*, vol. 13, no. 1, 2001, pp. 24–30.
24 Hall, P. 'Team Solutions Need Not Be the Organisational Norm', *Professional Manager*, July 2001, p. 45.
25 Parker, C. 'Remote Control – a Case Study', *Manager, The British Journal of Administrative Management*, March/April 2002, p. 30.
26 Norval, D. in conversation with Law, S. 'Beyond the Water Cooler', *Professional Manager*, January 2005, pp. 26–8.
27 Symons, J. 'Taking Virtual Team Control', *Professional Manager*, vol. 12, no. 2, March 2003, p. 37.
28 Francesco, A. M. and Gold, B. A. *International Organizational Behavior*, Second edition, Pearson Prentice Hall (2005), p. 118.
29 Murray, S. 'Virtual teams: Global harmony is their dream', *Financial Times*, May 11, 2005.
30 Reproduced with permission from *Manager, The British Journal of Administrative Management*, March/April 2002, pp. 30–31 and with the permission of Murray Blair, Chameleon Training and Consulting, Surrey.
31 See, for example: Lerner, P. M. 'Beware the Gatekeeper', *Amtrak Express*, July/August 1994, pp. 14–17.
32 Miner, J. B. *Management Theory*, Macmillan (1971).
33 See, for example: Mullins, L. J. *Hospitality Management and Organisational Behaviour*, Fourth edition, Longman (2001).
34 *Teamwork: Success Through People*, Advisory Booklet, ACAS, April 2003.

35 Lucas, E. 'And the Winner is Everyone', *Professional Manager*, January 2001, p. 10.
36 Heller, R. *In Search of European Excellence*, HarperCollins Business (1997), p. 229.
37 Guirdham, M. *Interactive Behaviour at Work*, Third edition, Financial Times Prentice Hall (2002), p. 12.
38 Ashmos, D. P. and Nathan, M. L. 'Team Sense-Making: A mental model for navigating uncharted territories', *Journal of Managerial Issues*, vol. 14, no. 2, Summer 2002, p. 198.
39 Harding, L. 'A Bombay Lunchbox', *The Guardian* on-line 24 June 2002.
40 The Dabbawalah website http://www.mydabbawala.com/ [accessed 4 August 2006].
41 Anderson, B. Fast food delivers lunchtime lesson 17 August 2004 CNN.com website http://www.cnn.com/2004/ BUSINESS/ 08/16/ mumbai.dabbawallahs/index.html [accessed 4 August 2006].
42 The Dabbawalah website http://www.mydabbawala.com/ [accessed 4 August 2006].
43 Harding, L. *A Bombay Lunchbox*, The Guardian on-line, 24 June 2002 http://www.guardian.co.uk/elsewhere/ journalist/story/0,7792,743042,00.html [accessed 4 August 2006].
44 The Dabbawalah website http://www.mydabbawala.com/ [accessed 4 August 2006].
45 Harding, L. 'A Bombay Lunchbox', *The Guardian* on-line 24 June 2002. http://www.guardian.co.uk/ elsewhere/journalist/ story/0,7792,743042,00.html [accessed 4 August 2006].
46 Nomad(i) Blogspot of an unknown Indian http:// nomad-i.blogspot.com.
47 The Dabbawalah website http://www.mydabbawala.com/ [accessed 4 August 2006].

WORKING IN GROUPS AND TEAMS

> **We know everyone is different. When selecting people for your team, the most important thing to look for is ones who are decent, honest, bright and capable. You will find that good people will naturally work together as a team, will interrelate well and will want each other to succeed. And while I'm on the subject of teams, don't send people off on those terrible outward-bound weekends. Have a party instead.**
>
> **(Sir) Gerry Robinson** – one of the UK's most powerful businessmen
>
> *I'll Show Them Who's Boss*, BBC Books (2004), p. 183

If the manager is to make the most effective use of staff, it is important to have an understanding of working in groups and teams. It is necessary to recognise the nature of human relationships and the functions, roles and factors that influence team performance and effectiveness. Attention should be given to the analysis of behaviour of individuals in group situations and to their effective performance. The manager needs to be aware of the interactions and operation of work groups and teams.

Learning outcomes

After completing this chapter you should be able to:

- explain interactions among members of a group and membership of successful teams;
- detail main types of contributions or team roles;
- contrast patterns of communication networks within small work groups;
- examine methods of analysing the behaviour of individual members;
- distinguish different group functions and member roles, and explain the use of frameworks of behavioural analysis;
- evaluate the nature of individual or group or team performance;
- review the importance of, and influences on, successful teamworking.

Critical reflection

Much is written and talked about the nature of groups and teams, but how well do you think all this theory works in practice? Despite all the hype and myths, is it simply a question of ensuring the right mix of skills and that all the members of the group co-operate with each other? Or is this an over-simplification?

INTERACTIONS AMONG MEMBERS

In the previous chapter we mentioned that how people behave and perform as members of a group is as important as their behaviour or performance as individuals, and drew attention to the importance of effective teamwork. The main focus of attention in this chapter is the actual roles, behaviours and performance of people working in groups or teams. Once again, however, we should be aware of the tendency for the terms 'groups' and 'teams' to be used interchangeably. If groups are to be successful and perform effectively, there must be a spirit of unity and co-operation. Members of a group must work well together as a team. As *Crainer* reminds us, in most teams people will contribute individual skills, many of which will be different. However, referring to the work of *Obeng*,[1] Crainer points out that it is not enough to have a rag-bag collection of individual skills.

> *The various behaviors of the team members must mesh together in order to achieve objectives. For people to work successfully in teams, you need people to behave in certain ways. You need some people to concentrate on the task at hand (doers). You need some people to provide specialist knowledge (knowers) and some to solve problems as they arise (solvers). You need some people to make sure that it is going as well as it can and that the whole team is contributing fully (checkers). And you need some people to make sure that the team is operating as a cohesive social unit (carers).*[2]

As ACAS points out: 'To remain competitive organisations need to make optimum use of equipment and people if they are to thrive or even survive ... In a general sense people talk of teamwork when they want to emphasise the virtues of co-operation and the need to make use of the various strengths of employees.'[3]

In order to understand the functions and processes of a group, it is necessary to understand what happens when people meet; the actions and behaviour of individual members; the parts people play; the patterns of interactions and forces within the group; and influences on individual and group performance. According to *Guirdham*, for example:

> *Many of the concepts that have helped us understand interactive behaviour in work relationships are also needed for understanding it in groups, including role behaviour, norms and co-operation, competition, conflict and conflict resolution. Most of what there is to understand about group work applies equally to both decision-making groups and teams but there are some further issues particular to the two different kinds of groups. There is, however, no suggestion that teams do not have to solve problems!*[4]

BELBIN'S TEAM-ROLES

One of the most popular and widely used analyses of individual roles within a work group or team is that developed by *Meredith Belbin*. Following years of research and empirical study, Belbin concludes that groups composed entirely of clever people, or of people with similar personalities, display a number of negative results and lack creativity. The most consistently successful groups comprise a range of roles undertaken by various members. The constitution of the group itself is an important variable in its success.[5] Initially, Belbin identified eight useful types of contribution – or team-roles.

A **team-role** is described as a pattern of behaviour, characteristic of the way in which one team member interacts with another whose performance serves to facilitate the progress of the team as a whole. In a follow-up publication, Belbin discusses the continual evolution of team-roles, which differ in a few respects from those originally identified and adds a ninth role.[6] Strength of contribution in any one role is commonly associated with particular weaknesses. These are called allowable weaknesses. Members are seldom strong in all nine team-roles. A description of the evolved nine team-roles is given in Table 9.1.

The types of people identified are useful team members and form a comprehensive list. These are the key team-roles and the primary characters for successful teams. Creative teams require a balance of all these roles and comprise members who have characteristics complementary to each other. 'No one's perfect, but a team can be.' Belbin claims that good examples of each type would prove adequate for any challenge, although not all types are necessarily needed. Other members may be welcome for their personal qualities, for example a sense of humour, but experience suggests there is no other team-role that it would be useful to add.

Table 9.1 Belbin's evolved nine team-roles

Roles and descriptions – team-role contribution		Allowable weaknesses
Plant	Creative, imaginative, unorthodox. Solves difficult problems.	Ignores details. Too preoccupied to communicate effectively.
Resource investigator	Extrovert, enthusiastic, communicative. Explores opportunities. Develops contacts.	Over-optimistic. Loses interest once initial enthusiasm has passed.
Co-ordinator	Mature, confident, a good chairperson. Clarifies goals, promotes decision-making. Delegates well.	Can be seen as manipulative. Offloads personal work.
Shaper	Challenging, dynamic, thrives on pressure. Has the drive and courage to overcome obstacles.	Can provoke others. Hurts people's feelings.
Monitor-Evaluator	Sober, strategic and discerning. Sees all options. Judges accurately.	Lacks drive and ability to inspire others.
Teamworker	Co-operative, mild, perceptive and diplomatic. Listens, builds, averts friction.	Indecisive in crunch situations.
Implementer	Disciplined, reliable, conservative and efficient. Turns ideas into practical actions.	Somewhat inflexible. Slow to respond to new possibilities.
Completer	Painstaking, conscientious, anxious. Searches out errors and omissions. Delivers on time.	Inclined to worry unduly. Reluctant to delegate.
Specialist	Single-minded, self-sharing, dedicated. Provides knowledge and skills in rare supply.	Contributes on only a narrow front. Dwells on technicalities.

Source: Belbin, R. M., *Team Roles at Work*, Butterworth-Heinemann (a division of Reed Elsevier UK Ltd) and Belbin Associates (1993) p. 23. Reproduced with permission.

Back-up team-roles and functional roles

The most consistently successful teams were 'mixed' with a balance of team-roles. The role that a person undertakes in a group is not fixed and may change according to circumstances. Individuals may have a 'back-up team-role' with which they have some affinity other than their primary team-role. If certain roles were missing members would call upon their back-up roles. Team-roles differ from what Belbin calls 'functional-roles'. These are the roles that members of a team perform in terms of the specifically technical demands placed upon them. Team members are typically chosen for functional roles on the basis of experience and not personal characteristics or aptitudes.

Belbin has developed a Self-Perception Inventory designed to provide members of a group with a simple means of assessing their best team-roles.

The value of Belbin's team-roles inventory

Despite possible doubts about the value of Belbin's Self-Perception Inventory, it remains a popular means of examining and comparing team-roles. For example, in order to explore whether local government managers were distinctively different from the model of private sector management, *Arroba and Wedgwood-Oppenheim* compared samples of the two groups of managers and Belbin's key team-roles. There were noticeable similarities between the two groups, with the noticeable exception of the marked difference between private sector managers and local government officers in the score for teamworkers and the team-roles they preferred to adopt. The individual characteristics of managers in the two sectors differed. The data implied that local government officers were committed to organisational objectives and dedicated to task achievement, but the low score for teamworkers suggested the high commitment to organisational tasks was not supplemented by a concern for interpersonal processes. In local government, the drive and enthusiasm and emphasis on task were exaggerated, while attention to idea generation and productive interpersonal relationships was less marked.[7]

Distribution of team roles among UK managers

Using Belbin's model, *Fisher et al.* undertook a study of the distribution of team roles among managers. Over the past 15 years many layers of management have been removed and the gap in people to lead and motivate has increasingly been filled by the creation of multitudes of teams. The participants of the study were 1441 male and 355 female managers, all with some management experience. All had completed a personality questionnaire and were candidates short-listed for a range of management positions in both the private and public sectors. The study analysed data supplied by ASE/NFER Publishing Company and results were then compared with the Belbin model. The data broadly agreed with the Belbin model. The authors conclude that as much is still unknown about teams, it is reassuring that further support has been found for the popular Belbin team-role model. There are several unresolved problems with teamworking but these might lie more with practices in staff recruitment than in team theory.[8]

PATTERNS OF COMMUNICATION

The level of interaction among members of a group or team is influenced by the structuring of channels of communication. Laboratory research by *Bavelas*[9] and subsequent studies by other researchers such as *Leavitt*[10] have resulted in the design of a series of communication networks. These networks were based on groups of five members engaged in a number of problem-solving tasks. Members were permitted to communicate with each other by written notes only and not everyone was always free to communicate with everyone else.

There are five main types of communication networks – wheel, circle, all-channel, Y and chains (*see* Figure 9.1).

Figure 9.1 Communication networks

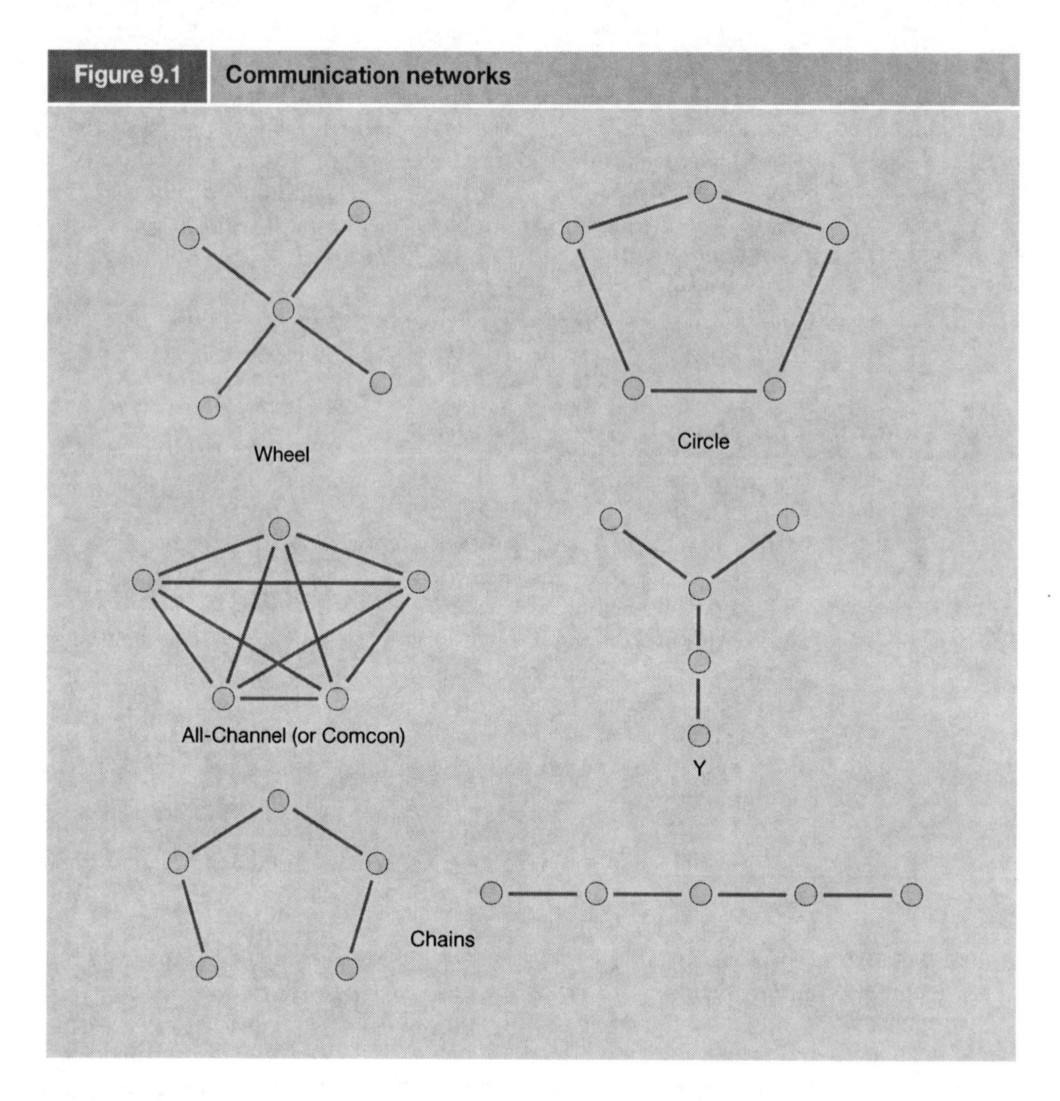

- **The wheel**, also sometimes known as the star, is the most **centralised network**. This network is most efficient for simple tasks. Problems are solved more quickly with fewer mistakes and with fewer information flows. However, as the problems become more complex and demands on the link person increase, effectiveness suffers. The link person is at the centre of the network and acts as the focus of activities and information flows and the co-ordinator of group tasks. The central person is perceived as leader of the group and experiences a high level of satisfaction. However, for members on the periphery, the wheel is the least satisfying network.
- **The circle** is a more **decentralised network**. Overall it is less efficient. The group is unorganised, with low leadership predictability. Performance tends to be slow and erratic. However, the circle is quicker than the wheel in solving complex problems and also copes more efficiently with change or new tasks. The circle network is most satisfying for all the members. Decision-making is likely to involve some degree of participation.
- **The all-channel (or comcon) network** is a decentralised network that involves full discussion and participation. This network appears to work best where a high level of interaction is required among all the members in order to solve complex problems. Leadership predictability is very low. There is a fairly high level of satisfaction for members. The all-channel network may not stand up well under pressure, in which case it will either disintegrate or reform into a wheel network.

- **A 'Y' or chain network** might be appropriate for more simple problem-solving tasks, requiring little interaction among members. These networks are more centralised, with information flows along a predetermined channel. Leadership predictability is high to moderate. There is a low to moderate level of satisfaction for members.

The relationship between centralised and decentralised networks and performance of the group is outlined in Figure 9.2.

Figure 9.2 Communication networks and task complexity

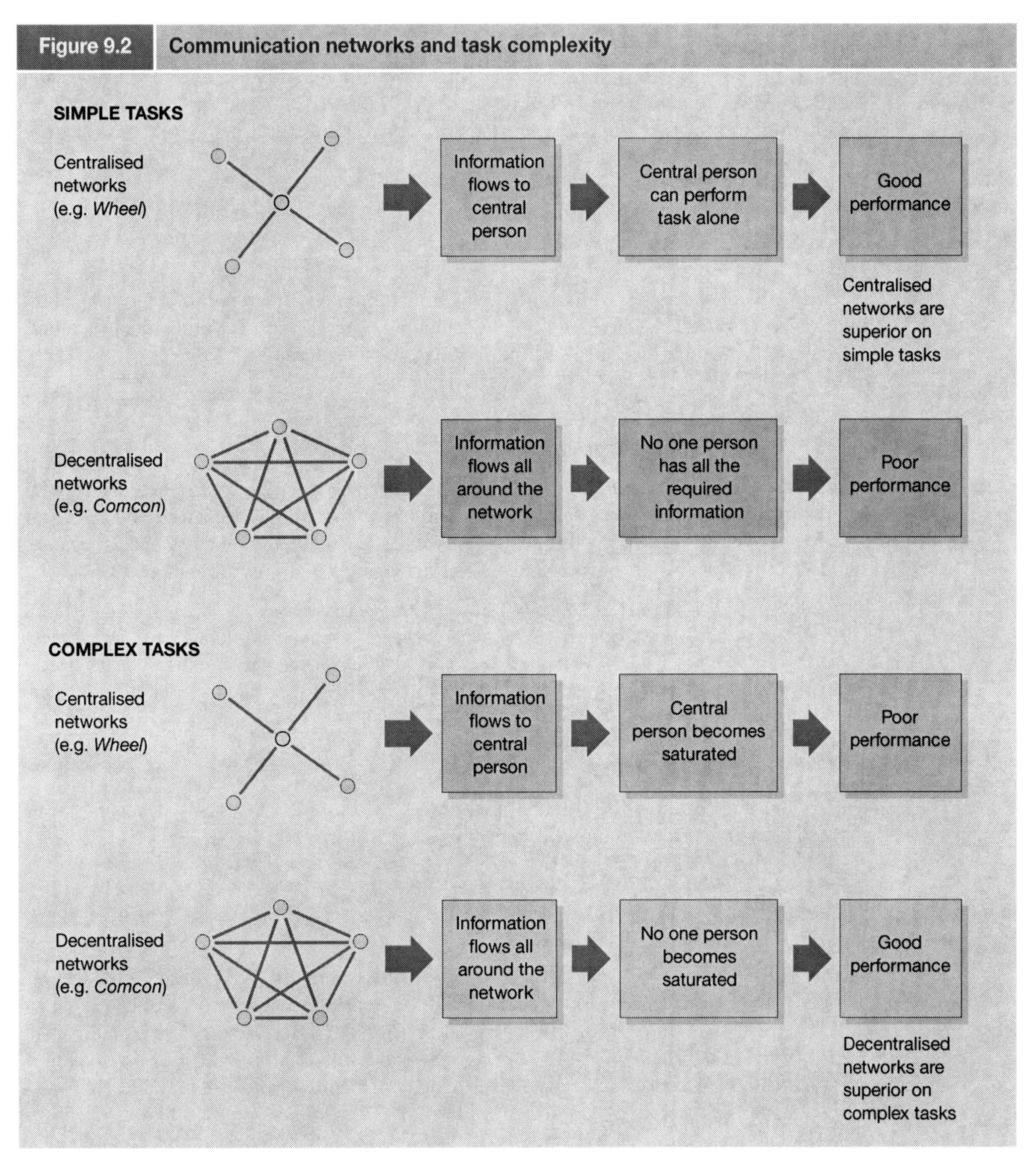

Source: Greenberg, J. and Baron, R. A., *Behavior in Organizations*, Sixth Edition, Prentice-Hall Inc. (1995), p. 306. Reproduced with permission from Pearson Education, Inc.

Implications for the manager

Despite the obvious artificiality and limitations of these communication network studies, they do have certain implications for the manager. Knowledge of the findings may be applied to influence the patterns of communication in meetings and committees. They also provide a reasonable representation of the situations that might apply in large organisations. It will be interesting for the manager to observe the patterns of communication adopted by different groups in different situations. The manager can also note how communication networks change over time and how they relate to the performance of the group.

No one network is likely to be effective for a range of given problems. The studies draw attention to the part of the manager's job that is to ensure the most appropriate communication network for the performance of a given task. Problems which require a high level of interaction among members of the group may not be handled efficiently if there are inadequate channels of communication or sharing of information. The choice of a particular communication network may involve trade-offs between the performance of the work group and the satisfaction of its members.

ANALYSIS OF INDIVIDUAL BEHAVIOUR

In order to understand and to influence the functioning and operation of a group or team, it is necessary to study patterns of interaction and the parts played by individual members. For example, in a more recent publication *Belbin* acknowledges:

> *Teamwork does not, of course, guarantee in itself good results. As in sport, there can be good teams and poor teams. And as in sport, it all depends on how the players play together.*[11]

It is necessary to balance the requirement for effective performance of the team with respect for the individuality of its members and to achieve the right mix. Not all skilled and capable individuals are necessarily good team players and it may sometimes be an advantage to have someone who will have a more sceptical attitude and be more open to change. For example, *Stanley* refers to the challenge of managing a high-performance team.

> *When assembling a high-performance team, you are gathering together energy-packed employees, who are a lot like thoroughbreds. Keep in mind, they have an innate drive to excel. Their thoughts run outside the mundane and familiar. With a flare for the unique, they are extraordinary and can generate new ideas that will keep the organisation ahead of the competition … Along with assigning each member appropriate tasks, the manager must monitor individual performance. By encouraging members to maximise their individual effort, the team will greatly increase the probability of success.*[12]

Two of the main methods of analysing the behaviour of individuals in group situations are **sociometry** and **interaction process analysis**.

SOCIOMETRY

Originally developed by *Moreno* in 1953, **sociometry** is a method of indicating the feelings of acceptance or rejection among members of a group.[13] A sociogram is a diagrammatical illustration of the pattern of interpersonal relationships derived from sociometry. The sociogram depicts the choices, preferences, likes or dislikes and interactions between individual members. It can also be used to display the structure of the group and to record the observed frequency and/or duration of contacts among members.

The basis of sociometry, however, is usually 'buddy rating' or 'peer rating'. Each member is asked to nominate or to rate, privately, other members in terms of some given context or characteristic – for example, with whom they communicate, or how influential or how likeable they are. Questions may relate to either work or social activities. For example:

- Who would you most prefer or least prefer as a workmate?
- Who would make a good leader?
- With whom would you choose and not choose to go on holiday?

Positive and negative choices may be recorded for each person, although sometimes positive choices only are required. The choices may be limited to a given number or they may be unlimited. Sometimes individuals may be asked to rank their choices.

Sociograms

Members' choices could be shown in tabular form. For example, Table 9.2 shows first and second choices for a group of final-year degree students. Members were asked to indicate, in confidence, those whom they would most prefer to talk to about: (i) a major work-related problem, and (ii) a difficult personal problem. Positive choices only were requested.

An advantage of the diagrammatical illustration, however, is that the sociogram provides a visual description of the sociometric structure of a group. It can indicate cliques and sub-groups, compatibility, and members who are popular, isolated or who act as links. Figure 9.3 gives a simple illustration of an actual sociogram for a group of 15 members with single, positive choices only.

1. G and M are popular (the stars) and most often chosen by members.
2. M is the link between two overlapping cliques, KML and MNO.
3. H and P are unpopular (isolated) and chosen least by members.
4. JKMO is a chain.
5. ABCD is a sub-group and separated from the rest of the members.

It should be noted, however, that there are several methods of compiling and drawing sociograms, and a number of potential criticisms and limitations. Problems also arise over *how* to draw the sociogram and how to interpret the roles of individual members. In the experience of the author, less concern should be given to the concept of sociometry itself. It

Table 9.2 Example of a 'tabulated' sociogram (positive choices only)

Work-related problem			Personal problem	
Second choice	**First choice**		**First choice**	**Second choice**
		A		///
		B	/	//
///	/	C	//	/
/		D	//	
		E	/	
		F	/	//
	/	G	//	
/////	//	H	//	
		J	/	/
	//	K		
////	///////	L		//
	/	M	/	/
		N		//
/		O	/	
14	14		14	14

Figure 9.3 A simple illustration of a sociogram

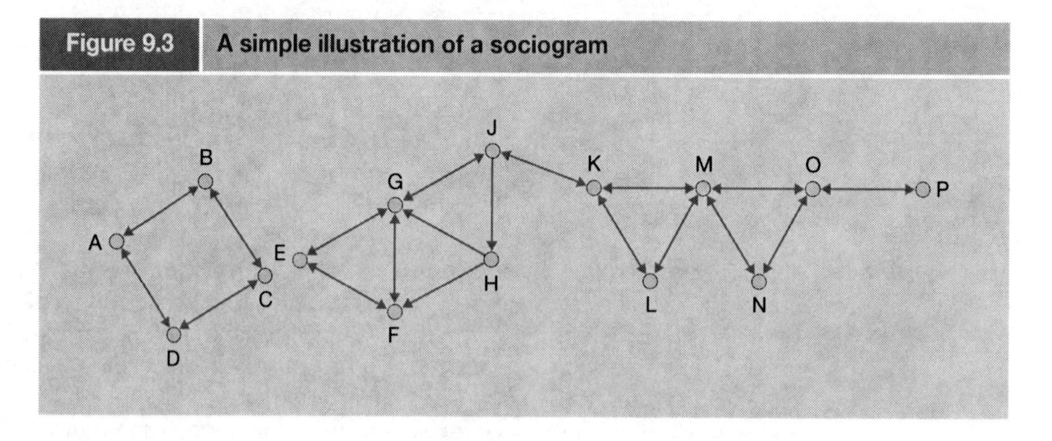

is better seen as a useful vehicle that, if handled sensitively, can serve to encourage meaningful discussions on patterns of social interactions, group behaviour and the perceptions of individual members towards each other.

Critical reflection

How would you argue that all first-year students should be encouraged to participate in a sociometry exercise with members of their class? What possible difficulties or opposition would you foresee?

INTERACTION ANALYSIS

The basic assumption behind **interaction analysis** is that behaviour in groups may be analysed from the viewpoint of its function. This approach has developed largely from the work of *Bales* on methods for the study of small groups. This aim is to provide ways of describing group process and indications of factors influencing the process.[14] In Bales' 'Interaction Process Analysis' every act of behaviour is categorised, as it occurs, under twelve headings. These differentiate between 'task' functions and 'socio-emotional' functions. The categories apply to both verbal interaction and non-verbal interaction.

A **Socio-emotional: positive reactions**
- 1 **Shows solidarity**, raises others' status, gives help, reward.
- 2 **Shows tension release**, jokes, laughs, shows satisfaction.
- 3 **Agrees**, shows passive acceptance, understands, concurs, complies.

B **Task: attempted answers**
- 4 **Gives suggestion**, direction, implying autonomy for others.
- 5 **Gives opinion**, evaluation, analysis, expresses feeling, wish.
- 6 **Gives orientation**, information, repeats, clarifies, confirms.

C **Task: questions**
- 7 **Asks for orientation**, information, repetition, confirmation.
- 8 **Asks for opinion**, evaluation, analysis, expression of feeling.
- 9 **Asks for suggestion**, direction, possible ways of action.

D **Socio-emotional: negative reactions**
- 10 **Disagrees**, shows passive rejection, formality, withholds help.
- 11 **Shows tension**, asks for help, withdraws out of field.
- 12 **Shows antagonism**, deflates others' status, defends or asserts self.

Task and maintenance functions

If the group is to be effective, then, whatever its structure or the pattern of interrelationships among members, there are two main sets of functions or processes that must be undertaken – **task functions** and **maintenance functions**.

- **Task functions** are directed towards problem-solving, the accomplishment of the tasks of the group and the achievement of its goals. Most of the task-oriented behaviour will be concerned with 'production' activities or the exchange and evaluation of ideas and information.
- **Maintenance functions** are concerned with the emotional life of the group and directed towards building and maintaining the group as an effective working unit. Most of the maintenance-oriented behaviour will be concerned with relationships among members, giving encouragement and support, maintaining cohesiveness and the resolution of conflict.

Task and maintenance functions may be performed either by the group leader or by members. Ultimately it is the leader's responsibility to ensure that both sets of functions are carried out and the right balance is achieved between them. The appropriate combination of task-oriented behaviour and maintenance-oriented behaviour is essential to the success and continuity of the group.

In addition to these two types of behaviour, members of a group may say or do something in attempting to satisfy some personal need or goal. The display of behaviour in this way is termed **self-oriented behaviour**. This gives a classification of three main types of functional behaviour that can be exhibited by individual members of a group: **task-oriented, maintenance-oriented** and **self-oriented**.

Classification of member roles

A popular system for the classification of member roles in the study of group behaviour is that devised originally by *Benne and Sheats*.[15] The description of member roles performed in well-functioning groups is classified into three broad headings: **group task roles, group building and maintenance roles** and **individual roles**.

- **Group task roles**. These assume that the task of the group is to select, define and solve common problems. For example, initiator-contributor, opinion seeker, co-ordinator, evaluator, recorder. Any of the roles may be performed by the various members or the group leader.
- **Group building and maintenance roles**. The analysis of member functions is oriented towards activities which build group-centred attitudes or maintain group-centred behaviour. For example, encourager, gatekeeper, standard setter, group commentator. Contributions may involve a number of roles and members or the leader may perform each of these.
- **Individual roles**. These are directed towards the satisfaction of personal needs. Their purpose is not related either to group task or to the group functioning. For example, aggressor, blocker, dominator, help-seeker.

FRAMEWORKS OF BEHAVIOURAL ANALYSIS

Several frameworks have been designed for observers to categorise patterns of verbal and non-verbal behaviour of group or team members. Observers chart members' behaviour on specially designed forms. These forms may be used to focus on single individuals or to record the total interaction with no indication of individual behaviour. The system of categorisation may distinguish between different behaviours in terms of the functions they are performing. The completed observation forms can be used as a basis for discussion of individual or group performance in terms of the strengths/weaknesses of different functional behaviour.

Use of different frameworks

Different frameworks use a different number of categories for studying behaviour in groups. The interaction analysis method can become complex, especially if non-verbal behaviour is included. Many of the categories in different frameworks may at first sight appear to be very similar. It is important, therefore, to keep the framework simple and easy to understand and complete. The observer's personality, values and attitudes can influence the categorisation of behaviour. For these reasons it is preferable to use trained observers, and wherever possible and appropriate to use more than one observer for each group. The observers can then compare the level of consistency between their categorisations. Observation sheets can be designed to suit the particular requirements of the group situation and the nature of the activity involved. An example of a reasonably simple, ten-point observation sheet used by the author is given in Figure 9.4.

Completing the observation sheet

Where appropriate, it may be helpful to note the initial seating, or standing, arrangements of the group. This will help in the identification of group members. Depending on the nature of the activity involved, it might also be possible to indicate main channels of interaction among individuals – for example, to whom eye contact, hand movements or ideas and questions are most frequently directed. A note could also be made of changes in arrangements during, and at the end of, the activity. Headings on the observation sheet are not necessarily exclusive. For example, leadership could be included under Taking Initiative, or under Performing Group Roles. Similarly, the role of humorist could be included under Performing Group Roles, but might also appropriately be included under the heading of Harmonising.

Observers will tend to use their own methods for completing the sheet: for example, a simple stroke or tick for each contribution and perhaps a thick stroke for a particularly significant contribution. Some observers might use some other distinguishing mark to indicate non-verbal behaviour such as body movements, smiles or eye contact. The most important point, however, is that the charting should not become too complex. The observer should feel happy with the framework and be capable of explaining the entries in a meaningful way. Where more than one observer is present there should be some degree of consistency between them.

BALANCE BETWEEN THE TEAM AND THE INDIVIDUAL

Groups and teams are an essential feature in the life of work organisations. Individuals on teams interact extensively with each other and with other teams in the organisation. Team-based management is used to improve communication, co-ordination and co-operation within the organisation.[16] For example, as *Green* maintains:

> *The generally perceived advantages of working in teams are the release of creativity and energy, much more interaction between people satisfying the need to belong ... teamworking can improve efficiency by people planning activities together with cooperation and communication. Team members together should be able to identify many ways to improve work organisation; how information, ideas and outputs flow and how team-working can reduce costs and improve productivity.*[17]

We mentioned previously the need to balance effective team performance with respect for the individual members. Although everyone operates fundamentally as a loner at work, *James* draws attention to the need in most jobs for the eponymous teamworking. 'Effective teams need equilibrium, no matter how uneasy. The perfect team will have balance, with each member aware of their role and happy to add that value to the task. The natural leaders for any given job will be in charge and their leadership will be cherished by mutual consent.

Figure 9.4 **Observation sheet for behaviour in groups**

Nature of group

Nature of activity

Date *Name of observer(s)*

Initial arrangement of group

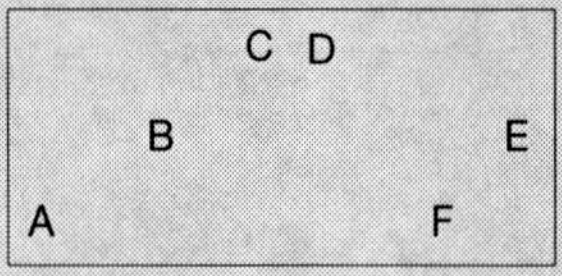

C D
B E
A F

Name of group members (or reference letters)

	A	B	C	D	E	F
Taking initiative – e.g. attempted leadership, seeking suggestions, offering directions						
Brainstorming – e.g. offering ideas or suggestions, however valid						
Offering positive ideas – e.g. making helpful suggestions, attempting to problem-solve						
Drawing in others – e.g. encouraging contributions, seeking ideas and opinions						
Being responsive to others – e.g. giving encouragement and support, building on ideas						
Harmonising – e.g. acting as peacemaker, calming things down, compromising						
Challenging – e.g. seeking justification, showing disagreement in constructive way						
Being obstructive – e.g. criticising, putting others down, blocking contributions						
Clarifying/summarising – e.g. linking ideas, checking progress, clarifying objectives/proposals						
Performing group roles – e.g. spokesperson, recorder, time keeper, humorist						

Other comments

Being a perfect team member means commitment to the task and overrides personal ambition and glory. Unfortunately this is rarely achieved in the workplace.'[18]

Successful organisations are good at building teams and exploiting teamwork. People need to be able to work in teams; they need to subordinate their own agenda to the wellbeing of the group. Further, organisations need to foster diversity, which entails respect for the individual and makes group decision making more creative.

M. Kets de Vries, 'Beyond Sloan: Trust is at the Core of Corporate Values'.[19]

In order to help improve the performance of the organisation it is necessary to understand the nature of human relationships and what goes on when groups of people meet. Working in a group is likely to be both a psychologically rewarding, and a potentially demanding experience for the individual. Group performance and the satisfaction derived by individuals are influenced by the interactions among members of the group. As an example of this, Figure 9.5 gives an unsolicited commentary from five final-year business studies degree students after completing a group-based assignment.

Figure 9.5 Unsolicited commentary from students after completing a group-based assignment

WHAT WE FEEL WE HAVE LEARNED FROM WORKING IN A GROUP

1. 'We learned that we had to listen to everybody's points of view and take these into consideration.'
2. 'We found that we had to be prepared to make certain sacrifices and adopted a democratic decision process. However, if an individual felt very strongly about a specific point and persisted with a valid argument then this had to be included.'
3. 'We often felt frustrated.'
4. 'It was time-consuming and difficult to schedule meetings due to differences in timetables and preferences in working hours.'
5. 'We learned that it is good to pool resources because this increased the overall standard of the piece of work. We feel this was only because we all set high personal standards and expected these from our fellow group members. We learned that it is possible to work in other less productive groups where individual levels of achievement may decrease.'
6. 'We learned that it is better to work in a smaller and not a larger group, as there is a tendency for individual ideas to be diluted.'
7. 'Groups formed on the basis of friendship alone are not as effective as groups formed with work as the major influence. The former tend to be unproductive.'
8. 'We found that it was good to get positive response, encouragement and feedback from team members. Likewise, it was demotivating to receive a negative response.'
9. 'We learned a lot about our individual personalities.'
10. 'We benefited from sharing personal experiences from our industrial placements.'
11. 'It is important to separate work and personal relationships.'

Critical reflection

'The nature of the hierarchical structure and the inevitable role conflicts, power struggles, politics and personality clashes means that individuals will usually complete a task more quickly and effectively than a group or team.' To what extent do you think this is fair comment? What has been your experience?

INDIVIDUAL COMPARED WITH GROUP OR TEAM PERFORMANCE

It is, however, difficult to draw any firm conclusions from a comparison between individual and group or team performance. An example of this can be seen from a consideration of decision-making. Certain groups, such as committees, may be concerned more specifically with decision-making, but all groups must make some decisions. Group decision-making can be costly and time-consuming.

One particular feature of group versus individual performance is the concept of social loafing and the 'Ringelmann effect', which is the tendency for individuals to expend less effort when working as a member of a group than as an individual. A German psychologist, *Ringelmann*, compared the results of individual and group performance on a rope-pulling task. Workers were asked to pull as hard as they could on a rope, performing the task first individually and then with others in groups of varying size. A meter measured the strength of each pull. Although the total amount of force did increase with the size of the work group, the effort expended by each individual member decreased with the result that the total group effort was less than the expected sum of the individual contributions.[20] Replications of the Ringelmann effect have generally been supportive of the original findings.[21]

According to *Hall*, there is a danger of elevating teams into a 'silver bullet' – a magic solution to all business problems. 'It is not that I don't think teams work. They clearly do and it would be difficult to run an organisation of any size if you couldn't create and manage a team ... The truth is that teams are not always the right answer to a problem. Often a well-briefed and well-managed group of individuals will do a task fine ... A further point is that some very skilled individuals are not good team players.'[22]

However, the general feeling appears to be that the collective power of a group outshines individual performance.[23] 'Even though individuals working on their own are capable of phenomenal ingenuity, working together as a team can produce astounding results and a better decision.'[24] *Guirdham* believes that: 'Compared with individuals, groups can make objectively better decisions to which people feel more commitment, while teams can perform functions and carry out projects better and more efficiently. This can only happen, however, if the people have the special skills and abilities needed.'[25]

One might expect, therefore, a higher standard of decision-making to result from group discussion. However, on the one hand, there is the danger of compromise and decisions being made in line with the 'highest common view' and, on the other hand, there is the phenomenon of the so-called risky-shift.

The risky-shift phenomenon

This suggests that instead of the group taking fewer risks and making safer or more conservative decisions, the reverse is often the case. Pressures for conformity means there is a tendency for groups to make more risky decisions than would individual members of the group on their own. Studies suggest that people working in groups generally advocate more risky alternatives than if they were making an individual decision on the same problem.[26]

Presumably, this is because members do not feel the same sense of responsibility for group decisions or their outcomes. 'A decision which is everyone's is the responsibility of no one.' Other explanations offered for the **risky-shift** phenomenon include:

1 People inclined to take risks are more influential in group discussions than more conservative people.
2 Risk-taking is regarded as a desirable cultural characteristic that is more likely to be expressed in a social situation such as group working.[27]

However, groups do appear to work well in the evaluation of ideas and to be more effective than individuals for problem-solving tasks requiring a range of knowledge and expertise. From a review of the research *Shaw* suggests that evidence supports the view that groups produce more solutions and better solutions to problems than do individuals.[28]

'Groupthink'

The effectiveness of group behaviour and performance can be adversely affected by the idea of **'groupthink'**. From an examination of some well-known government policy-making groups, *Janis* concluded that decisions can be characterised by groupthink which he defines as 'a deterioration of mental efficiency, reality testing, and moral judgment that results from in-group pressures'.[29] Groupthink results in the propensity for the group to just drift along. It is a generalised feature and can be apparent in any organisational situation where groups are relied upon to make important decisions.

Janis identifies a number of specific symptoms of groupthink:

1. There is an illusion of invulnerability with excessive optimism and risk-taking.
2. The discounting or discrediting of negative feedback that contradicts group consensus results in rationalisation in order to explain away any disagreeable information.
3. An unquestioned belief in the inherent morality of the group which leads members to be convinced of the logical correctness of what it is doing and to ignore ethical or moral consequences of decisions.
4. The group's desire to maintain consensus can lead to negative stereotyping of opponents or people outside the group, or to the acceptance of change.
5. There is pressure on individual members to conform and reach consensus so that minority or unpopular ideas may be suppressed.
6. Each member of the group may impose self-censorship in order to suppress their own objectives, or personal doubts or disagreements.
7. As a result of self-censorship, there is an illusion of unanimity with a lack of expressed dissent and a false sense of unity.
8. In the unlikely event of dissent or contrary information, this will give rise to the emergence of 'mind guards' who act as filters, guarding group leaders, deflecting opposition and applying pressure on deviants.

According to *Hambrick*: 'Groupthink tends to occur when group members have very similar experiences and frame of references, particularly when they have relatively long tenures in the group. A company head who dislikes conflict or who punishes dissenters also creates the conditions for groupthink.'[30]

Three central criteria

Drawing on the work of Vroom and Yetton, discussed in Chapter 7, *Misselhorn* puts forward a framework for determining when to make a decision on your own and when to involve a group. Three central overall criteria are taken into account:

- the **competence** of the people to make the decision – this would include knowledge, experience, skill, access to information and their practical experience to make it work in practice;
- the **context** in which they are working – which would include the relationships among those involved as well as the physical conditions and culture of the organisation; and
- the **commitment** to the decision through the way it affects those involved, and the rewards and punishments they will experience.

The framework provides a set of criteria to help the leader/manager to make a systematic and rational choice. It also draws attention to low ratings where the leader/manager may need to take precautions when deciding whether to involve a group or leave it to an appropriate individual.[31]

BRAINSTORMING

A **brainstorming** approach (sometimes now referred to as 'thought showers') involves the group adopting a 'freewheeling' attitude and generating as many ideas as possible, the more wild or apparently far-fetched the better.[32] As an illustrative exercise a group may be asked to generate as many and varied possible uses as they can for, for example, a house brick or a car fan belt.

There are a number of basic procedures for brainstorming:

- It is based on maximum freedom of expression with a totally informal approach.
- The initial emphasis is on the quantity of ideas generated, not the quality of ideas.
- No individual ideas are criticised or rejected at this stage, however wild or fanciful they may appear.
- Members are encouraged to elaborate or build on ideas expressed by others and to bounce suggestions off one another.
- There is no comment on or evaluation of any particular idea until all ideas have been generated.

Brainstorming is based on encouraging members to suspend judgement, the assumption that creative thinking is achieved best by encouraging the natural inclinations of group members, and the rapid production and free association of ideas. The quantity of ideas will lead to quality of ideas.

An interesting and popular exercise to help illustrate the suspension of initial perceived barriers and the encouragement of creative thinking is given in Figure 9.6. This exercise may also be used to compare individual and group/team-based performance. Your tutor will provide the (or least one) answer. There may be others that the author is unaware of!

Figure 9.6 An example of creative thinking

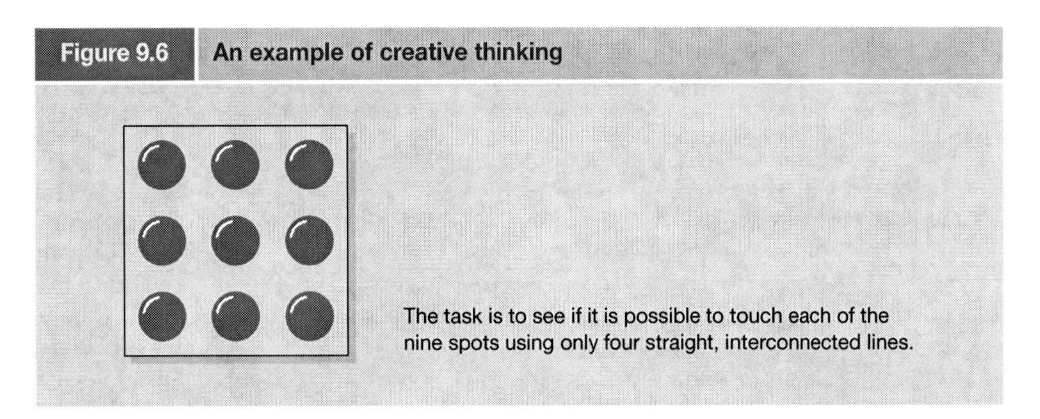

Effectiveness of brainstorming groups

One might reasonably expect that members of a brainstorming group would produce more creative problem-solving ideas than if the same members worked alone as individuals. Availability of time is an important factor. Over a longer period of time the group may produce more ideas through brainstorming than individuals could. Perhaps surprisingly, however, there appears to be doubt about the effectiveness of brainstorming groups over an individual working under the same conditions. Nevertheless, brainstorming still appears to have many advocates and is a popular activity for staff development programmes[33] (*see* Figure 9.7). Despite the rather negative view of nominal group brainstorming, we should recognise the importance of innovation for successful organisational performance.[34]

Figure 9.7 Advantages of brainstorming

BRAINSTORMING

Brainstorming is a problem-solving/solution-finding technique which can be used by individuals, groups or teams. Its full benefit is gained by sharing ideas and possibilities with others.

The first step is to define the problem or situation to which the group or team wants solutions or ideas. Ideally one person should act as scribe and write up ideas on a flipchart. He or she can contribute, but should not comment on others' suggestions. Every idea should be written up, however far-fetched or silly it might seem, without challenge from others.

Everyone should be encouraged to participate.

When all possibilities have been exhausted, suggestions can be examined, clarified, amended, accepted or rejected.

It may be that several options are accepted as possible ways forward. Reverse brainstorming looks at the possibilities and then brainstorms all the *problems* associated with the ideas. This helps give an objective view of ideas or solutions.

If performed correctly, brainstorming is an excellent, non-threatening way to include all members of a team in the problem-solving/decision-making process. It has the added benefit of producing many and various ideas, some of which will be of no value but others which may be of immediate or future benefit. Creativity is contagious and one idea will spark off another. Often, it is one of the most apparently silly ideas that points the way to a solution.

Brainstorming:

- involves everyone;
- focuses the mind;
- encourages creativity;
- meets individual needs for team inclusion;
- encourages communication – listening, information sharing;
- maximises ideas/possible solutions to problems;
- minimises risk of overlooking elements of the problem or issue under question.

Source: Bishop, S. and Taylor, D., *Developing Your Staff*, Pitman Publishing/Longman Training (1994). Reproduced with permission from Pearson Education Ltd.

Aid to creativity Any procedure which aids the process of creativity should be welcomed and there are a number of potential positive achievements in terms of related structural techniques for stimulating innovation. These include the Delphi technique and quality circles.

The **Delphi technique** is based on multiple, anonymous inputs from individual members of the group. Ideas and suggestions are recorded by a central manager and then recirculated to other members for their feedback. The central manager collates the responses and continues the circulation process again until consensus is reached. Although a time-consuming process, the Delphi technique helps to overcome the limitations of face-to-face brainstorming and symptoms of groupthink.

QUALITY CIRCLES

A **quality circle** is a group of people within an organisation who meet on a regular basis to identify, analyse and solve problems relating to quality, productivity or other aspects of day-to-day working arrangements using problem-solving techniques. Although quality circles actually originated in America they were exported to Japan and are more usually associated with their wide applications (since 1962) in Japanese manufacturing industries, as well as in some white-collar operations. Since the refinement of the quality circle process in Japan there has been increasing interest in their use in America and Britain as well as in many other countries. In America, quality circles appear to have been first implemented in 1974.[35]

The essential features of a quality circle group include the following:

- membership is voluntary;
- the group usually numbers between five and ten members;
- membership is normally drawn from people undertaking similar work or from the same work station;
- the group selects the problems to be tackled and the methods of operation;
- a leader can be chosen from within the group but is usually the immediate supervisor;
- the group members receive training in communication and problem-solving skills, quality control techniques and group processes;
- the group recommends solutions to management and, where possible, has authority to implement agreed solutions.

Potential limitations

There are a number of potential limitations on the effectiveness of quality circles:

- Any attempt at solving organisational problems cannot be considered as a single dimension. The promotion of quality circles needs to be approached in terms of possible effects on related sub-systems of the organisation, for example human resource management and industrial relations procedures.
- Quality circles can rely too heavily on intrinsic motivation and the assumption that involvement and recognition are sufficient rewards in themselves. This reflects a major difference between the operation of quality circles in the West and in Japan. Workers in Japan appear, for example, to accept that financial gains will go to the organisation.
- The greater involvement of members in problem-solving and decision-making may be resented by some groups, for example quality control departments, or by managers or trade union officials who may be suspicious of possible challenges to their traditional authority.

The application of quality circles does appear simple and straightforward, but early experience must be viewed in the context of Japanese culture and management systems. However, quality circles offer a number of potential benefits. They provide problem-solving at a more local level and the participation of employees in work-related decisions which concern them. Quality circles do work and have been used successfully by a number of British organisations. There are some doubts, however, as to the extent to which the hopes for, or potential benefits of, quality circles are realised fully in organisations.[36]

GROUP DYNAMICS

Interest in the study of group process and behaviour has led to the development of group dynamics and a range of group training methods aimed at increasing group effectiveness through improving social interaction skills. A central feature of group dynamics is **sensitivity training**, in which members of a group direct attention to the understanding of their own behaviour and to perceiving themselves as others see them. The objectives are usually stated as:

- to increase sensitivity (the ability to perceive accurately how others react to oneself);
- diagnostic ability (the skill of assessing behavioural relationships between others and reasons for such behaviour); and
- behavioural flexibility or action skill (the ability to relate one's behaviour to the requirements of the situation).

T-groups

A usual method of sensitivity training (which is increasingly used as a generic term) is the T-group (training group), sometimes called laboratory training. A **T-group** has been defined as:

an approach to human relations training which, broadly speaking, provides participants with an opportunity to learn more about themselves and their impact on others, and in particular to learn how to function more effectively in face-to-face situations.[37]

The original form of a T-group is a small, leaderless, unstructured, face-to-face grouping. The group normally numbers between eight and twelve members who may be strangers to each other or who may come from the same organisation (a family group). A deliberate attempt is made to minimise any status differentials among members. There is no agenda or planned activities. Trainers are present to help guide the group, but do not usually take an active role or act as formal leader. The agenda becomes the group's own behaviour in attempting to cope with the lack of structure or planned activities. Training is intended to concentrate on process rather than content, that is on the feeling level of communication rather than the informational value of communication.

Faced with confusion and lack of direction, individuals will act in characteristic ways. With the guidance of the trainers these patterns of behaviour become the focus of attention for the group. Participants are encouraged to examine their self-concepts and to be more receptive to the feelings and behaviours of others. Feedback received by individuals from other members of the group is the main mechanism for learning. This feedback creates a feeling of anxiety and tension, and the individual's self-examination leads to consideration of new values, attitudes and behaviour. Typically, the group meets for a 1–2 hour session each day for up to a fortnight. The sessions are supported by related lectures, study groups, case studies and other exercises.

The Johari window

A simple framework for looking at self-insight, which is used frequently to help individuals in the T-group process, is the 'Johari window' (*see* Figure 9.8). This classifies behaviour in matrix form between what is known–unknown to self and what is known–unknown to others.[38] A central feature of the T-group is reduction of the individual's 'hidden' behaviour through self-disclosure and reduction of the 'blind' behaviour through feedback from others.

- **Hidden behaviour** is that which the individual wishes to conceal from, or not to communicate to, other group members. It is part of the private self. An important role of the group is to establish whether members conceal too much, or too little, about themselves from other members.
- **The blind area** (that is behaviour known to others but unknown to self) includes mannerisms, gestures and tone of voice and represents behaviour of the impact of which on others the individual is unaware. This is sometimes referred to as the 'bad breath' area.

Members must establish an atmosphere of openness and trust in order that hidden and blind behaviours are reduced and the public behaviour enhanced.

Figure 9.8 The Johari window

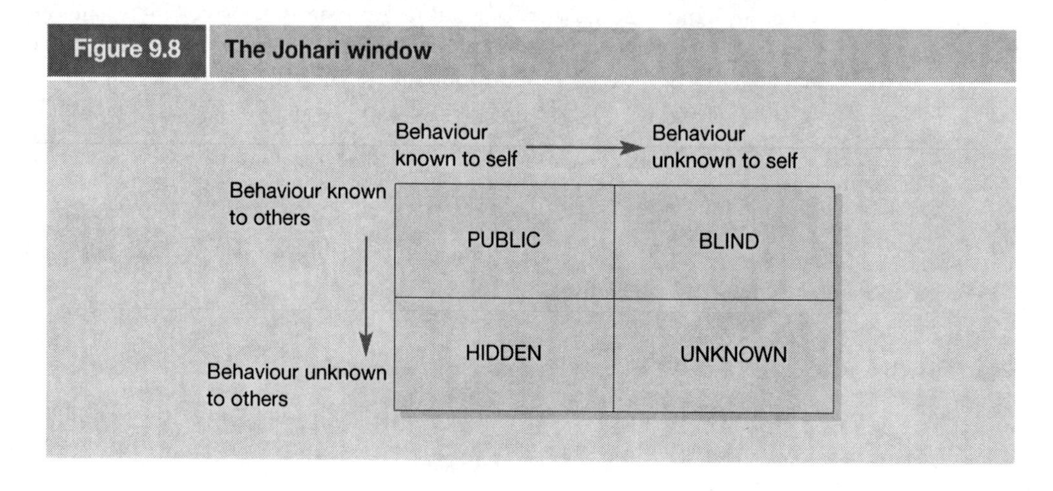

Value and effectiveness of T-groups

Reactions to the value and effectiveness of T-group training are very mixed. The experience can be disturbing and unpleasant, at least for some members. T-group training is difficult to evaluate objectively and there is still a main problem of the extent to which training is transferred 'back home' to practical work situations. However, a number of studies do suggest that participation as a member of a T-group does increase interpersonal skills, induce change and lead to open communications and more flexible behaviour. T-groups probably do result in a change of behaviour but it is not always clear whether such change is positive or related to improved organisational performance.[39]

T-groups now take a number of forms. Some place emphasis on the understanding of group processes, others place more emphasis on the development of the individual's self-awareness and feelings towards the behaviour of other people. They are now used frequently as a means of attempting to improve managerial development and organisational performance. The *Blake and Mouton* managerial grid seminars, discussed in Chapter 12, can be seen as an applied, and refined, form of T-group. A number of training packages have been designed, often under the broad heading of interpersonal skills, which are less confrontational and less disturbing for participants.

Critical reflection

'Sensitivity training programmes are an unnecessary activity that have no practical value as a means of increasing the long-term standard of group performance, and for many people they are an embarrassing and demeaning experience.' Do you think this is fair comment or under what circumstances can such programmes be justified? How do you feel about participating in such a programme?

SELF-MANAGED WORK GROUPS

An important development in work redesign and job enrichment is a form of work organisation based on self-managed work groups (or autonomous work groups). This involves a socio-technical approach with technological processes, production methods and the way in which work is carried out integrated with the social system of the organisation, including the informal group structure. Members of the group assume greater autonomy and responsibility for the effective performance of the work. With greater empowerment the belief is that members will feel more committed to the objectives and operations of the group. Key features of the self-managed work group include the following:

- specific goals are set for the group but members decide the best means by which these goals are to be achieved;
- group members have greater freedom and choice and wider discretion over the planning, execution and control of their work;
- collectively members of the group have the necessary variety of expertise and skills to successfully undertake the tasks of the group;
- the level of external supervision is reduced and the role of supervisor becomes more one of giving advice and support to the group;
- feedback and evaluation are related to the performance of the group as a whole.

There is, however, a potential danger that a self-managed group is more likely to establish its own values and norms (discussed in Chapter 8) that may be at variance with those of the organisation.

Popularity and applications

Wilson points out that self-directed teams feature high in the list of most popular management tools in a study by the Institute of Management with Bain & Company. 'Once people are fully committed to teamworking and enthusiastic about getting on with it, training can be a rewarding experience for everyone involved and also great fun.'[40] However, despite the apparent potential advantages, to date self-managed teams appear to have only limited applications. For example, *Torrington, Hall and Taylor* suggest that teamwork has evolved from autonomous working groups and although it is still used as a means of empowering employees and facilitating their development, there is of late a more critical perspective. 'There remain many strong supporters of teamwork and many organisations are committed to this approach, although it is also criticised as management control by another means and has often failed to improve performance.'[41]

Autonomy and control

A strong supporter of the idea of the autonomous work group is *Waterman*. In order to build spirit, morale and commitment in any organisation Waterman believes that people should be in control of at least some part of their lives and that they should be given some influence over things that affect them. The quintessence of this belief is the self-managing team – groups of three to ten people who work without any direct supervision. Employees should be organised into teams that cut across old boundaries, trained and placed in jobs that challenge their abilities, given the information they need, informed of what they need to accomplish and then turned loose.[42]

ACAS also strongly supports autonomous work groups for both increased competitiveness and for the quality of working life.

> *The concept of autonomous teams may be misleading as teams will always be answerable to management and rely on the provision of resources and other support. Nevertheless, one of the best ways to ensure that teams continue to develop is to move towards self-regulation – an important way of monitoring the progress of teams is to assess the level of dependence on management. It is for management to encourage progress by helping the teams develop greater independence.*
>
> *Reorganising the workforce into teams is not easy but when successfully developed, teamworking has been shown to be a way of improving competitiveness and at the same time enhancing the quality of working life for employees.*[43]

BUILDING SUCCESSFUL TEAMS

Whatever the debate about a comparison between individual and group or team performance, or self-managed groups, effective teamworking is of increasing importance in modern organisations. This demands that the manager must be aware of, and pay attention to, a number of interrelated factors, including:

- clarification of objectives and available resources;
- organisational processes and the clarification of roles;
- empowerment, decision-making and channels of communication;
- patterns of interaction, and attention to both task and maintenance functions;
- social processes and the informal organisation;
- management systems and style of leadership;
- training and development.

The effectiveness of the team will also be influenced by the tasks to be undertaken, the nature of technology and the organisational environment. Ultimately, however, the performance of the team will be determined very largely by the characteristics of its members. The nature of group personality means that what works well for one team may not work well for an apparently similar team in the organisation.

As *Wilson* points out, for example, although teamworking, like most management ideas, is very simple, nevertheless this simplicity conceals a great challenge.

> *The principles of teamworking may be easily understood, but the task of installing it can be quite daunting. Introducing teamworking is not a straightforward grafting job, the simple matter of adding a new idea to those already in place. It is about making a fundamental change in the way people work. Every teamworking application is different. Each organisation, department and individual group is faced with unique problems and in some situations it is more about getting rid of old ways of doing things than injecting new ones.*
>
> J. Wilson, 'Building Teams – with Attitude'[44]

A concept map of effective work groups is set out in Figure 9.9.

Skills for successful teamwork

The increasing need for collaboration and teamwork together with recognition for the individual has highlighted the need for attention to social skills and effectively relationships among people. If people are not working together they are essentially a collection of individuals. *Douglas* refers to the importance of helping people to master the so-called 'soft' skills:

> *Organisations in most sectors – and especially in ones that are particularly demanding from a scientific or technical point of view – are operating in environments where collaboration, teamwork, and an awareness of the commercial consequences and implications of technical research are as important as scientific and technical skills themselves. Personnel with scientific and technical skills significantly disproportionate to their 'people' skills – by which I primarily mean people management capabilities and the knowledge of how to work with maximum effectiveness as part of a team – are increasingly unlikely to be as much of an asset to their organisation as they ought to be.*[45]

However, Douglas points out that as we all interact with people to a greater or lesser extent in our everyday lives, there is a tendency to assume that people management skills are merely an extension of our natural abilities. In fact, people management skills are the more difficult and rare type of skill but to a large extent they can be learned.

Cloke and Goldsmith refer to the special skills required for successful teamwork and list ten skills team members can develop in order to build innovative self-managing teams. All of these skills are interrelated, mutually reinforcing and dependent upon each of the others.[46]

- **Skill of self-management** – overcoming obstacles together and in the process building a sense of ownership, responsibility, commitment and efficiency within each team member.
- **Skill of communication** – collaboratively developing their skills in becoming better listeners, commiserating with others, reframing communications so they can be heard, and communicating honestly about things that really matter.
- **Skill of leadership** – creating opportunities for each member to serve as leader. Employees need to be skilled in linking, organising, co-ordinating, collaborating, planning, facilitating, coaching and mentoring.
- **Skill of responsibility** – everyone is personally responsible not only for their own work but for the work of every other member of the team. Team members have to exercise responsibility in order to become self-managing.
- **Skill of supportive diversity** – collaborative experiences allow team members to overcome prejudices and biases and not create winners and losers, reject outsiders or mistrust people who are different.
- **Skills of feedback and evaluation** – essential to improving learning, team communication and the quality of products, processes and relationships. In a true team environment, self-critical perspectives are expected, welcomed, acknowledged and rewarded.

Figure 9.9 Concept map of effective work groups

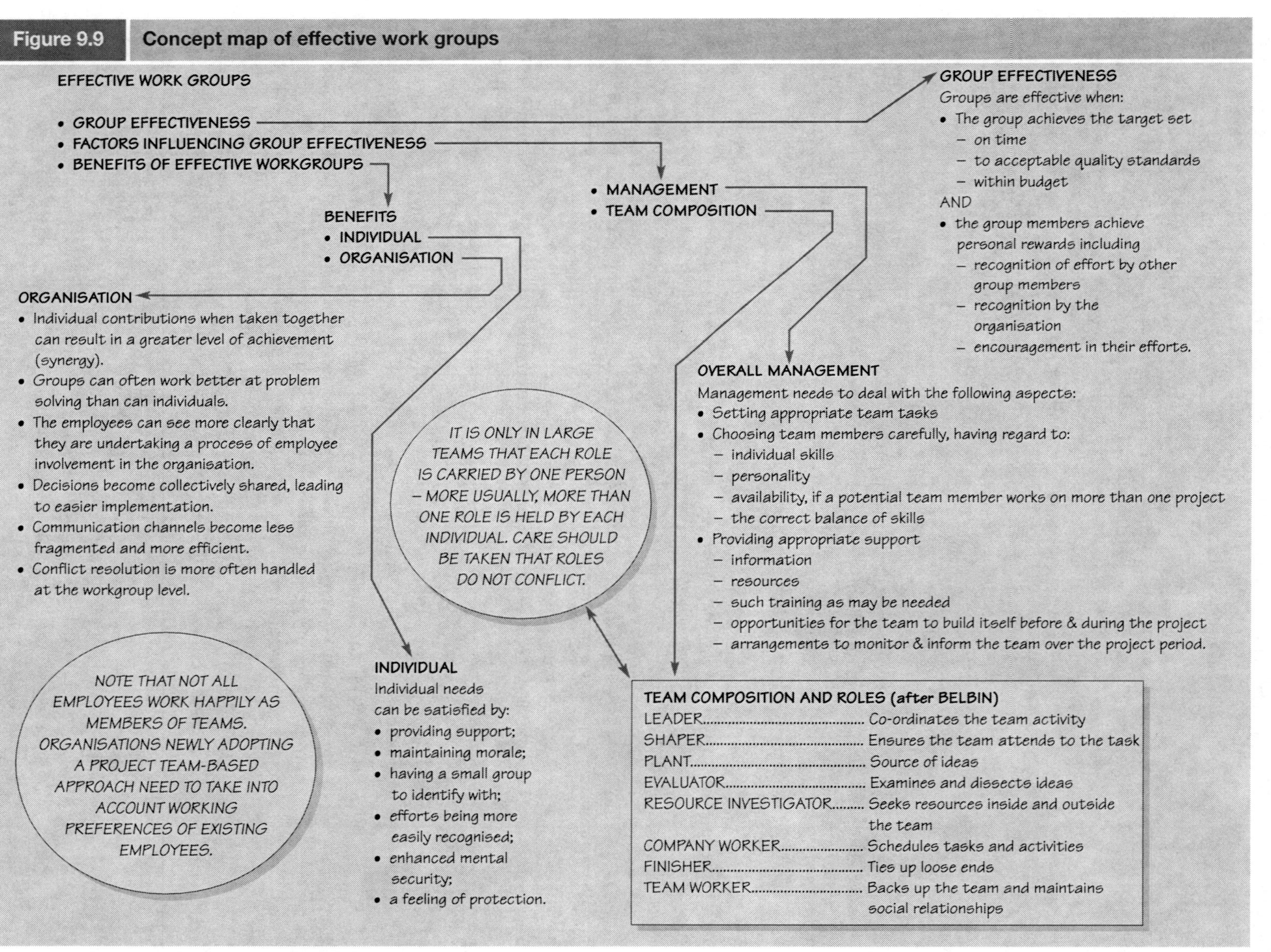

Source: Training Learning Consultancy Ltd, Bristol, England. Reproduced with permission.

- **Skill of strategic planning** – to identify challenges and opportunities collaboratively and influence the environment in which problems emerge. Strategic planning encourages employees to think long term, be proactive and preventative and focus on solutions rather than problems.
- **Skill of shaping successful meetings** – team meetings can be streamlined and made shorter, more satisfying and more productive, and result in expanded consensus.
- **Skill of resolving conflicts** – encouraging team members to improve skills in problem solving, collaborative negotiation, responding to difficult behaviour and conflict resolution.
- **Skill of enjoyment** – most team members enjoy working together to accomplish difficult tasks. Their pleasure derives from meeting high-performance challenges and producing results that benefits themselves and their teams, organisations and communities.

The role of team leader

Building successful teams also requires effective leadership with an emphasis on trust, clear communications, full participation and self-management. 'The influence and usefulness of team leaders comes, not from their delivery of traditional supervisory and control methods, but from their ability to lead from the front and in training, coaching and counselling their team members to high standards of performance.'[47]

In her discussion of the 'democratic enterprise' (organisations which can flourish economically and can also be places of excitement and stimulation, fulfilment and tranquillity), *Gratton* maintains that it is the leaders of the teams across the organisation who make the company vision a reality on a day-to-day basis. The team leaders are the creator of space in which choice and freedom can be exercised; they delineate the obligations and accountabilities contained within the business goals; they become a role model for how members should behave; and they bring the philosophy of autonomy and personal development to realisation by the manner in which they act as mentor and coach.[48]

Continuous process of improvement and innovation

The requirement for continual development and improvement is a necessary part of effective teamwork. However, as *Riches* points out: 'Understandably, teams are pre-occupied with getting the job done. Few teams regularly take time out to reflect on how the team itself is working and what it needs to do to improve the way its modus operandi ... Even fewer set measurable objectives for team functioning and/or get feedback from internal and external customers about the team's effectiveness.'[49]

The ACAS advisory booklet concludes that although self-regulation is necessary if the potential of teamworking is to be realised, teams will always need some degree of management direction. The task of management is to oversee the development of teams and provide the necessary support and training. Even when in place, teams will need constant monitoring and development. Teamworking is not a finite project but a process of continuous improvement and innovation.

> *The introduction of teamworking is a major step for an organisation to take. It is important that management, trade unions and employees ensure they know how teamworking will contribute to their business strategy and that it is likely to involve a long-term transformation ... The early challenge and excitement of establishing teams may fade and it is easy for organisations to accept a level of performance which is short of optimum ... In order to achieve high performance, teams require regular changes and challenges. These may include: changes to team personnel; new tasks; re-examining the contribution the team makes to the overall business aims; and ensuring that the team has regular dealings with other teams.*[50]

Critical reflection

All this discussion about group membership and building successful teams is very interesting and sounds fine in the classroom. But how far do you think it works in practice, for example with managing groups of workers in a restaurant kitchen, on a production assembly line, in a gay pub, or with professionals such as lecturers, doctors or lawyers?

MANAGEMENT IN THE NEWS

Winning teams

FT

Football's example can help companies score

John Kay

Like many lecturers, I have a library of presentation slides. The most frequently used is 15 years old and relates the performance of English soccer league clubs to their expenditure on players. Both wages and transfer fees over a 25-year period are included. The message is that you get what you pay for. There is a strong relationship between cash spent and average league position. There were some outliers, but the outstanding story was Liverpool. Liverpool and Manchester United had invested more than others. But while the performance of Manchester United was exactly what our equations predicted, Liverpool had done much better. Manchester United had assembled a group of outstanding players. Liverpool had assembled an outstanding team.

The story of the 2006 World Cup is that outstanding teams defeated groups of outstanding players. All players in top sides are very good. The reason the countries in the final four were not the ones pundits expected was that their predictions were based on the quality of individual players. But the trophy goes not to the best players but to the best team.

My slide is popular because references to football bring back to life audiences battered into somnolence by harangues on transformational change. The serious purpose is to illustrate that business success is not simply a matter of acquiring the best people, technology or resources. Businesses create value by establishing a difference between the cost of their input and the effectiveness of their output. The Italian team was more than the sum of its parts, the Brazilian team was not.

The difference between output and value added is relevant to every type of business, but especially important for the professional services company – whether it is a football team or an investment. Goldman Sachs and McKinsey do not simply attract exceptional people – so did Manchester United and

Source: Neil Tingle/actionplus

Is a team more than the sum of its parts? Would another group of equally talented players have had Liverpool's successes?

Brazil. Like Liverpool and Italy, these businesses achieve more than would be predicted from the quality of the people alone. That makes these companies very profitable. By sharing that excess profitability with their talented employees they keep them in post and maintain their leadership position.

But what are the characteristics that distinguish a great team from a group of great players? Organisational knowledge belongs to the business rather than the individuals who make up the business. My group was impressed by the systematic way in which Liverpool assembled through post-match debriefing and disseminated through pre-match briefing extensive information about other players, clubs and pitches. But their main explanation of Liverpool's relative success came from a simple economic model of the game of football. A player can kick for goal or pass the ball to a better situated player. His choice will depend on the degree to which his incentives relate to the performance of the team rather than his performance as an individual and on his expectations about whether the next player will shoot or pass in turn. Because an individual's behaviour depends on expectations of the behaviour of others, teams will become locked into particular states. Individuals joining a team will find it best to conform to the local style, so these equilibria are stable.

That is why transformational change cannot be achieved by talking about it and my audiences were right to be more interested in the footballing metaphor than in the guff that had gone before.

Source: Kay, J., 'Football's example can help companies score', *Financial Times*, 10 July 2006. Copyright © 2006 The Financial Times Limited, reproduced with permission.

Discussion questions

1 Analyse the commentary on teamwork in this article using the concept map outline of effective work groups given in Figure 9.9. Which features of the model appear to be present and which are missing?

2 Critically evaluate the comments about Liverpool football club in terms of communication patterns. What skills and activities might help managers to achieve effective communication between the members of their team?

SYNOPSIS

● Organisational performance and the satisfaction derived by individuals are influenced by the interactions among members of the group. Members must work well together as a team and there must be a spirit of unity and co-operation. One of the most popular analyses of individual roles is that developed by *Belbin*, who suggests nine key contributions or team-roles for successful groups. The level of interaction is influenced by the channels of communication. There are five main types of communication networks – wheel, circle, all-channel, Y and chains.

● In order to understand and influence the functioning and operation of a group, it is necessary to study the behaviour of individual members. Two main methods are: (i) sociometry, and (ii) interaction analysis. Sociometry is usually based on 'buddy rating' or 'peer rating'. It is a method of indicating feelings of acceptance and/or rejection among members of a group. A sociogram gives a diagrammatical illustration of the pattern of interpersonal relationships derived from sociometry.

● Interaction analysis is based on the assumption that the behaviour of individuals may be analysed from the viewpoint of its function or process. Two essential functions necessary for the success and continuity of a group are: (i) task-oriented behaviour, and (ii) maintenance-oriented behaviour. In addition, members may display self-oriented behaviour. Several frameworks have been designed for observers to categorise patterns of verbal and non-verbal behaviour of members. It is important, however, that the frameworks do not become too complex.

● Groups and teams are an essential feature in the life of the organisation but there must be a balance with respect for the individual members. Working in a group is likely to be a rewarding but also potentially demanding experience for the individual. In order to help improve the performance of the organisation it is necessary to understand the nature of human relationships and what goes on when groups of people meet. It is difficult to draw any firm comparison with individual performance. Group decision-making would appear to offer a number of advantages but can be adversely affected by the 'risky-shift' phenomenon and by 'groupthink'.

● Brainstorming (or thought showers) is an attempt to help a group produce more creative problem-solving ideas. However, there appears to be some doubt about the effectiveness of brainstorming over an individual working under the same conditions. Interest in the study of groups and teams has led to the development of training methods aimed at improving social interaction skills and self-insight. Attention is also given to self-managed (or autonomous) work groups. Quality circles are another potential aid to group problem-solving, innovation and creativity.

● Building successful teams is of increasing importance in modern organisations. It is necessary to take into account a variety of interrelated factors, including the characteristics and behaviour of their members, social skills and relationships among people and effective leadership with an emphasis on trust and clear communications. The task of management is to oversee the development of teams and provide the necessary support and training. Although self-regulation is necessary if the potential of team-working is to be realised, teams will always need some degree of management direction. The requirement for continual development and improvement is a necessary part of effective teamwork.

Refresh your understanding, assess your progress and begin your research with online resources at **www.pearsoned.co.uk/mullins**

REVIEW AND DISCUSSION QUESTIONS

1. Discuss critically and with supporting practical examples the likely advantages and disadvantages of working in a small work group.
2. Contrast different types of communication networks. Give examples of a situation in which each type of network is likely to be most appropriate.
3. Assess the practical value to the manager of the analysis of individual behaviour. Explain how you would go about constructing a sociogram.
4. Distinguish between (a) group task roles, (b) group building and maintenance roles, and (c) individual roles. Give your own examples of each of these types of group member roles.
5. Suggest a framework for the analysis and categorisation of patterns of individual behaviour in group situations. What considerations need to be kept in mind when using such frameworks?
6. Explain what is meant by (a) 'groupthink', (b) the risky-shift phenomenon, and (c) brainstorming (or thought showers). Assess critically the likely standard of individual compared with group or team performance.
7. Explain the meaning and purpose of sensitivity training. Give your views on the relevance and practical value of group dynamics.
8. Detail fully the main factors to be considered in a review of effective teamworking.

ASSIGNMENT 1

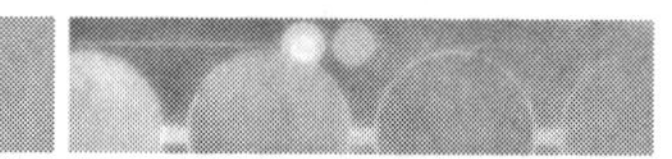

Attempt, *preferably*, to observe a small group or project team at work; *alternatively*, next time you are involved in a small group discussion, observe the members of your group.

- Explain the nature of the content of the group's discussion, and contrast this with the process of the discussion.
- Complete the grid below by giving a tick in the appropriate box to denote the behaviour of individual members in terms of:
  - group task roles;
  - group building and maintenance roles;
  - individual roles.
- What conclusions do you draw concerning the conduct and apparent effectiveness of the group?

	Names of group members (or reference numbers)						
							Totals
Group task roles							
Group building/maintenance roles							
Individual roles							
Totals							

ASSIGNMENT 2

Working within a small group and as directed by your tutor, adopt a brainstorming approach to providing as many uses as possible for:

- a 1970 edition of an American 900-page textbook on management;
- a man or woman's leather belt.

Elect a member to record **all** of your responses. At the end of the allotted time, delete any **obvious** duplication, total the numbers of ideas for each separate exercise and then be prepared to share and compare ideas and total scores from other groups.

What conclusions do you draw from this assignment?

PERSONAL AWARENESS AND SKILLS EXERCISE

Objectives

Completing this exercise should help you to enhance the following skills:

- Evaluate the role(s) you play within the team and the contribution you make.
- Explore your relationships with other members of the team.
- Receive and give honest feedback about strengths and personal weaknesses.

Exercise

In order to work well with other people you need to know and understand yourself and be prepared to receive honest feedback from your colleagues. The effectiveness of a team can be enhanced by a genuine openness among its members.

You are required to work in pairs with another team member – preferably one you do not know very well and if possible from a different ethnicity, culture, gender or age group – and to ask the following questions of each other.

You should both agree to honour confidentiality and to conduct the exercise as a means of providing constructive feedback.

1 For what role do you think I am most suited – and why?
2 In what ways can I contribute more to the work of the team?
3 Which member of the team do you believe I am most close to and which member most distant from?
4 What do you see as my major strengths and personal weaknesses as a member of the team?
5 What is it about me that you find most annoying?
6 In what ways could we help each other in our work?
7 How can I be a better all-round member of the team?

After you have both completed these questions consider carefully and honestly:

8 What have you learned about yourself from this activity and what response from your colleague surprised you the most? Put this in writing as an aid to discipline and for your personal reflection.

CASE STUDY

When does a team become a crowd? Innocent Drinks

In July 2006 Innocent Drinks won the 'company of the year' award in a ceremony organised by the UK entrepreneurship magazine, *Business XL*. The judges commented that despite its growth to over £37 million worth of revenue and 100 employees, it had managed to retain the culture and enthusiasm of a small enterprise.[51] Although the company had not yet reached its tenth birthday (it was formed in August 1998 and sold its first batch of smoothies the following May), this award was not the first it had notched up in its short life.[52] Many are accolades for the products themselves – it won Best UK Soft Drink at the Quality Food and Drink Awards or so-called 'foodie oscars' for four successive years from 2002–2005 – and others are awards for entrepreneurship and business success. But one, the Guardian Employer of the Year Award in 2005, was made for the company's approach to managing people, an approach which clearly has a strong focus on the development and maintenance of a strong team culture.

As with many small businesses, the ethos of the founder or founders is critical to the values and behaviours which are adopted by other members of the organisation; the challenge for any enterprise is to retain that ethos when it becomes a big business. So how did Innocent manage to turn a team of three into a team of 100?

Innocent was probably a team before it was a company. The three co-founders, Richard Reed, Jon Wright and Adam Balon, were university friends who, while they had gone their separate ways after graduating, continued to share a dream of setting up their own business. The story of their search for a good business idea (e.g. the Amazing Electric Bath)[53] and the inspiration which gave them their winning one, i.e. developing an easy way for busy people to get some healthy nutrition into their diet, is well documented (they famously did their first piece of market research with the aid of two dustbins).[54] It seems that fun and friendship became keystones for the success of the business, and its most significant values.

Shared values

Reed has stated that the original friendship which founded the business set the tone for all their business relationships; that the organisation views itself as a network of friends, of people with differing skills (Wright is in charge of production, Balon deals with the commercial aspects such as trade contacts, Reed handles product development and marketing) but with shared

Source: Innocent Drinks

As this van's unusual corporate livery shows, there has always been a strong element of fun in the way that Innocent's team works together.

values and ambitions. The importance of shared values became evident in the initial stages when the trio were attempting to find a juice-manufacturing company which would produce their recipes at a commercial level. Most fruit juice suppliers in the UK used concentrates as the basis for their products and could not believe that the smoothies could be made without using the industry-standard processes of reconstitution and the addition of preservatives. But the unique selling point for Innocent is that the product is *nothing but* fresh fruit; as the innocent promise on the packs explains:

> *No concentrates, no stabilisers, no flavourings, no GM stuff, no preservatives, no added sugar, no E numbers, no funny business. And if we do you can tell our mums.*

It took them nine months to find not only a juicing company which shared their vision but a like-minded 'business angel' who would put up enough starting capital to enable their concept to be brought to market.

The phenomenal growth of the business is partly accounted for by the fact that it was based on an idea which squarely hit the zeitgeist of the new millennium, in terms of both its appeal to an increasingly health-conscious generation of busy urban workers and concerns about the ethics of food production. This growth necessitated a very rapid increase in personnel; the days of experimenting with new recipes in home kitchens were soon over and the trio had to get help on board quickly. One of their earliest recruits and first employee was Dan Germain, another university friend, who initially helped with deliveries as a summer job. As the company grew, Germain not only stayed on but became their Head of Creative, designing much of their communication material (such as packaging), copywriting publicity, creating the company website and writing imaginative and quirky recipe books.[55]

In all its communications, from the childishly scribbled logo and information on packaging to the delivery vans made to look like meadows or cows, Innocent creates a strong sense of its brand: youthful, irreverent, full of self-deprecating humour, but above all dedicated to its founding ideals (and seriously cool). A brief tour around the website gives an insight into life at 'Fruit Towers', the idiosyncratically restyled office building on a Shepherds Bush industrial estate with its famous carpet of green astroturf. News events recorded on the website reflect the concerns and happenings in the Innocent 'family' (the search for a cat one of the employees was cat-sitting and who had gone missing; a request for birthday present ideas for another employee's granny), as well as incidents in the life of the company itself (new packaging, a favourable write-up in the French newspaper *Le Monde*, burglaries at the Amsterdam office). Joining Innocent as an employee is clearly joining a very close-knit group.

Induction, innocent-style

In his October 2005 contribution to *The Guardian* column 'Diary of an Entrepreneur', Reed describes the way in which Innocent welcomes new employees on board (the company had then reached 83; it celebrated taking on its 100th member of staff with a lunch party in June 2006).

> *As a business, we are saying hello to plenty of new people ... How do we make sure every single one of them understands what we are about? As we sell more drinks in more places to more people, how do we keep everything feeling, well, innocent? Our business is growing at a phenomenal rate. In the past three months alone, we've welcomed 18 new people to our HQ, Fruit Towers. We now total 83 Innocent people across Europe. And we want each of these people to have an amazing time from the day they start their jobs. We want person number 83 (he's called Ben) to feel as passionate about things as person number 1.*
>
> *So, when it comes to people, we start at the beginning. We treat people the way we'd like to be treated ourselves, and we keep things personal. If you get a job at Innocent, your offer arrives with a case of drinks. Once the legal bit is over, we send you a little handbook that tells you all about life at Fruit Towers. And we make sure we give you a ring in the month before you join, just to say 'hi' and make sure everything is OK. We've found it's the little things that are appreciated best. Things like having flowers on your desk when you arrive, and a nice little timetable that maps out your first two weeks. We also give people a pack of photos of the people they'll be working with and a map of the office, so they can recognise and find their new mates.*
>
> *But the bit that Innocent people remember about their first few days is the 'lunchmate'. In your first two weeks, you are scheduled a series of lunch dates with all sorts of people. So, as well as doing all the boring work stuff, you get to find out the office gossip and make a bunch of new friends. No more sitting in the local park on your own nibbling at a sandwich on a bench because you don't know anyone yet'.*[56]

This description illustrates an important aspect of the way in which Innocent manages its people. In keeping with the informal culture of the business, Reed avoids the more 'technical' terms like induction or orientation; and the first two weeks' activities are clearly designed to create the sense of belonging to a team. The company offers many traditional benefits such as share options and a healthcare plan, but also scholarships, clubs and numerous celebratory events (its annual free music festival 'Fruitstock' started as a way of thanking staff, suppliers and customers for a good year). Reed explains:

> *Being an entrepreneur means many things. First and foremost, it's about organising and operating your own business and assuming the risk for that venture. When you first start out, the desire is very much to create something of your own.*
>
> *But very soon you learn that, even though you might have a great idea and a solid business plan, the whole thing is going to take a lot more work and effort than you ever thought. And you won't be able to do it all yourself. In short, you'll need a dedicated, clever and beautiful bunch of people to accompany you as you grow your venture.*
>
> *Two out of three new businesses fail within the first three years, and I'm convinced that this happens because they don't recruit the right people. Even if you do recruit wisely, you still need to have the right environment and support in place, so that people feel happy, respected and motivated along the way. Last but not least, people love to be rewarded and recognised for a job well done, and our business is no different.'*[57]

Beyond that, it has created the Innocent Foundation to help plough some of the profits back into the communities which supply its fruit in less developed countries, a move which further supports the ideal of natural products which are good for people – growers as well as consumers – and considers them part of the Innocent 'family'. In 2006 it was the UK's biggest smoothie brand with sales expected to gross £50 million; the Innocent team was clearly flying high. But the problem with flying high is that you have a long way to fall. Now, if they don't find that cat ...

Your tasks

1 Critically review Reed's account of Innocent's approach to its staff in relation to the difference between 'task' functions and 'maintenance' functions as described on p. 339.

2 Do you think Innocent is vulnerable to 'groupthink'? What measures could the management team put in place to avoid such a risk?

3 Discuss way in which the Belbin model of team roles might be applied to the recruitment and selection of new team members in growing organisations like Innocent. Consider and outline both its strengths and its limitations.

NOTES AND REFERENCES

1 Obeng, E. *All Change*, Pitman Publishing (1994).
2 Crainer, S. *Key Management Ideas: Thinkers that changed the management world*, Third edition, Financial Times Prentice Hall (1998), p. 238.
3 'Teamwork: Success Through People', Advisory Booklet, ACAS, April 2003, pp. 6–7.
4 Guirdham, M. *Interactive Behaviour at Work*, Third edition, Financial Times Prentice Hall (2002), p. 463.
5 Belbin, R. M. *Management Teams: Why They Succeed or Fail*, Butterworth-Heinemann (1981).
6 Belbin, R. M. *Team Roles at Work*, Butterworth-Heinemann (1993).
7 Arroba, T. and Wedgwood-Oppenheim, F. 'Do Senior Managers Differ in The Public and Private Sector? An Examination of Team-Role Preferences', *Journal of Managerial Psychology*, vol. 9, no.1, 1994, pp. 13–16.
8 Fisher, S. G., Hunter, T. A. and Macrosson, W. D. K. 'The Distribution of Belbin Team Roles among UK Managers', *Personnel Review*, vol. 29, no. 2, 2000, pp. 124–40.
9 Bavelas, A. 'A Mathematical Model for Group Structures', *Applied Anthropology*, vol. 7, 1948, pp. 19–30, and Bavelas, A. 'Communication Patterns in Task-Oriented Groups', in Lasswell, H. N. and Lerner, D. (eds) *The Policy Sciences*, Stanford University Press (1951).
10 Leavitt, H. J. 'Some Effects of Certain Communication Patterns on Group Performance', *Journal of Abnormal and Social Psychology*, vol. 46, 1951, pp. 38–50. See also: Leavitt, H. J. *Managerial Psychology*, Fourth edition, University of Chicago Press (1978).
11 Belbin, R. M. *Changing The Way We Work*, Butterworth-Heinemann (1997), p. 13.
12 Stanley. T. J. 'The Challenge of Managing a High-Performance Team', *SuperVision*, vol. 63, no. 7, July 2002, pp. 10–12.
13 Moreno, J. L. *Who Shall Survive?* Beacon House (1953). See also: Moreno, J. L. and Jennings, H. H. *The Sociometry Reader*, Free Press of Glencoe (1960).
14 Bales, R. F. 'A Set of Categories for the Analysis of Small Group Interaction', *American Sociological Review*, vol. 15, April 1950, pp. 257–63.
15 Benne, K. D. and Sheats, P. 'Functional Roles of Group Members', *Journal of Social Issues*, vol. 4, 1948, pp. 41–9.
16 Whitfield, J. M., Anthony, W. P. and Kacmar, K. M. 'Evaluation of Team-Based Management: A Case Study', *Journal of Organizational Change Management*, vol. 8, no. 2, 1995, pp. 17–28.
17 Green, J. R. 'Team Building in Practice', *Chartered Secretary*, November 1997, pp. 34–5.
18 James, J. *Body Talk at Work*, Judy Piatkus (2001), p. 212.
19 Kets de Vries, M. 'Beyond Sloan: Trust is at the Core of Corporate Values', in Pickford, J. (ed.), *Financial Times Mastering Management 2.0*, Financial Times Prentice Hall (2001), p. 268.
20 Kravitz, D. A. and Martin, B. 'Ringelmann Rediscovered: The Original Article', *Journal of Personality and Social Psychology*, May 1986, pp. 936–41.
21 See, for example: Karau, S. J. and Williams, K. D. 'Social Loafing: A Meta-Analysis Review and Theoretical Integration', *Journal of Personality and Social Psychology*, October 1993, pp. 681–706.
22 Hall, P. 'Team Solutions Need Not Be the Organisational Norm', *Professional Manager*, July 2001, p. 45.
23 See, for example: Blanchard, K. and Bowles, S. *High Five: None of Us Is As Smart As All of Us*, HarperCollins Business (2001).
24 Stanley, T. J. 'The Challenge of Managing a High-Performance Team', *SuperVision*, vol. 63, no. 7, July 2002, pp. 10–12.
25 Guirdham, M. *Interactive Behaviour at Work*, Third edition, Financial Times Prentice Hall (2002), p. 498.
26 Kogan, N. and Wallach, M. A. 'Risk-Taking as a Function of the Situation, the Person and the Group', in Newcomb, T. M. (ed.) *New Directions in Psychology III*, Holt, Rinehart and Winston (1967).
27 For a comprehensive review of the 'risky-shift' phenomenon, see, for example: Clarke, R. D. 'Group Induced Shift Towards Risk: A Critical Appraisal', *Psychological Bulletin*, vol. 76, 1971, pp. 251–70. See also: Vecchio, R. P. *Organizational Behavior*, Third edition, Harcourt Brace and Company (1995).
28 Shaw, M. E. *Group Dynamics*, McGraw-Hill (1976).
29 Janis, J. L. *Victims of Groupthink*, Houghton Mifflin (1972) and Janis, J. L. Groupthink, Second edition, Houghton Mifflin (1982).
30 Hambrick, D. 'Putting the Team into Top Management', in Pickford, J. (ed.), *Financial Times Mastering Management 2.0*, Financial Times Prentice Hall (2001), p. 289.
31 Misselhorn, H, *Understanding and Managing Your Organization*, Third edition M.O.D. Consulting (2001).

32 Osborn, A.F. *Applied Imagination: Principles and Procedures of Creative Thinking*, Scribner's (1963).
33 See, for example: Bishop, S. and Taylor, D. *Developing Your Staff*, Pitman Publishing/Longman Training, (1994).
34 See, for example: Waterman, R. *The Frontiers of Excellence*, Nicholas Brearley (1994).
35 Meyer, G. W. and Scott, R. G. 'Quality Circles: Panacea or Pandora's Box', *Organizational Dynamics*, Spring 1985, pp. 34–50.
36 See, for example: Hill, S. 'Why Quality Circles Failed But Total Quality Management Might Succeed', *British Journal of Industrial Relations*, vol. 29, no. 4, 1991, pp. 541–68.
37 Cooper, C. L. and Mangham, I. L. (eds) *T-Groups: A Survey of Research*, Wiley (1971), p. v.
38 Luft, J. *Group Processes: An Introduction to Group Dynamics*, Second edition, National Press (1970). (The term 'Johari Window' was derived from a combination of the first names of the original authors, Joseph Luft and Harry Ingham.)
39 See, for example: McKenna, E. Business *Psychology and Organisational Behaviour*, Lawrence Erlbaum (1994).
40 Wilson, J. 'Building Teams – with Attitude', *Professional Manager*, September 1998, pp. 12–13.
41 Torrington, D., Hall, L. and Taylor, S. *Human Resource Management*, Sixth edition, Financial Times Prentice Hall, (2005), p. 280.
42 Waterman, R. *The Frontiers of Excellence*, Nicholas Brearley (1994).
43 *Teamwork: Success Through People*, Advisory Booklet, ACAS, April 2003, p. 34.
44 Wilson, J. 'Building Teams – with Attitude', *Professional Manager*, September 1998, p. 13.
45 Douglas, M. 'Why Soft Skills Are an Essential Part of the Hard World of Business', *Manager, The British Journal of Administrative Management*, New Year 2003, pp. 34–5.
46 Cloke, K. and Goldsmith, J. *The End of Management and the Rise of Organizational Democracy*, Jossey-Bass (2002).
47 *'Teamwork: Success Through People'*, Advisory Booklet, ACAS, April 2003, p. 31.
48 Gratton, L. *The Democratic Enterprise*, Financial Times Prentice Hall (2004).
49 Riches, A. 'Emotionally Intelligent Teams', Organisational Change & Leadership Development, www.anneriches.com.au [accessed 28 January 2006].
50 *Teamwork: Success Through People*. Advisory Booklet, ACAS, April 2003, p. 34.
51 *The Independent*, 'Innocent Drinks wins "company of the year" award', 4 July 2006.
52 A list of its awards under various categories can be located on the company website, www.innocentdrinks.co.uk
53 Richard Reed, 4 February 2005. Speech to the Advancing Enterprise 2005 Conference, available at HM Treasury website: www.hm-treasury.gov.uk
54 Not only at Innocent's own website, but also by in a major article by Rowan Gibson at www.rethinkinggroup.com.
55 Girton Newsletter Spring 2006; Alumni Interview with Dan Germain, pp. 22–3.
56 Richard Reed 'Diary of an Entrepreneur', *The Guardian*, 15 October 2005.
57 Richard Reed 'Diary of an Entrepreneur', *The Guardian*, 17 November 2005.

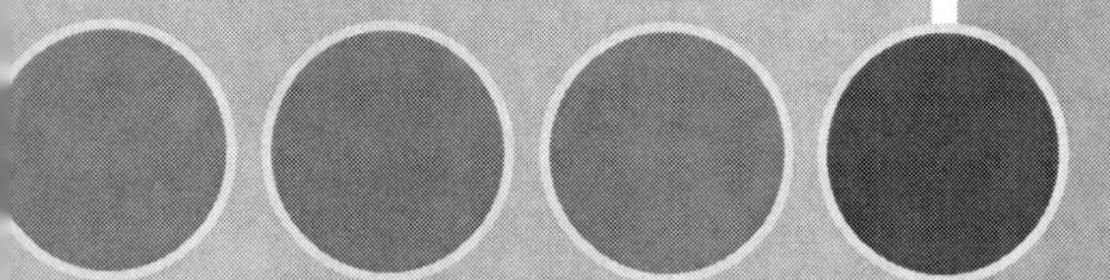

THE NATURE OF LEADERSHIP

"Leadership is not about the leader, it is about how he or she builds the confidence of everyone else. Leaders are responsible for both the big structures that serve as the cornerstone of confidence, and for the human touches that shape a positive emotional climate to inspire and motivate people … Leaders deliver confidence by espousing high standards in their messages, exemplifying these standards in the conduct they model and establishing formal mechanisms to provide a structure for acting on those standards."

Rosabeth Moss Kanter – prominent business thought leader and award-winning author

Confidence: Leadership and the Psychology of Turnarounds, Random House (2004), pp. 325–6

An essential part of management is co-ordinating the activities of people and guiding their efforts towards the goals and objectives of the organisation. This involves the process of leadership and the choice of an appropriate form of action and behaviour. Leadership is a central feature of organisational performance. The manager needs to understand the nature of leadership influence, factors that determine relationships with other people and the effectiveness of the leadership relationship.

Learning outcomes

After completing this chapter you should be able to:

- explain the meaning and importance of leadership in work organisations;
- contrast main approaches to, and studies of, leadership;
- examine leadership as an aspect of behaviour, and different styles of leadership;
- explore contingency theories of leadership;
- evaluate the nature and main components of transformational leadership and inspirational leadership;
- explain the leadership relationship and the exercise of leadership power and influence;
- review the variables which determine effective leadership and development.

Critical reflection

Leadership is all about determination, personality and innate ability at the right time for a particular competitive situation. Many business leaders have no formal academic qualifications and each has their own individual leadership style. Does this suggest that great leaders are born to be so? Or do you think it is possible to train a person to be an effective leader?

THE MEANING OF LEADERSHIP

There are many ways of looking at **leadership** and many interpretations of its meaning. Leadership might be interpreted in simple terms, such as 'getting others to follow' or 'getting people to do things willingly', or interpreted more specifically, for example as 'the use of authority in decision-making'. It may be exercised as an attribute of position or because of personal knowledge or wisdom. Leadership might be based on a function of personality or it can be seen as a behavioural category. It may also be viewed in terms of the role of the leaders and their ability to achieve effective performance from others. According to *Crainer* there are over 400 definitions of leadership and 'it is a veritable minefield of misunderstanding and difference through which theorists and practitioners must tread warily'.[1]

It is difficult, therefore, to generalise about leadership, but essentially it is a **relationship through which one person influences the behaviour or actions of other people**. This means that the process of leadership cannot be separated from the activities of groups and effective teambuilding.

According to *Useem*, leadership is a matter of making a difference. It entails changing an organisation and making active choices among plausible alternatives, and depends on the development of others and mobilising them to get the job done.

> *Leadership is at its best when the vision is strategic, the voice persuasive and the results tangible. In the study of leadership, an exact definition is not essential but guiding concepts are needed. The concepts should be general enough to apply to many situations, but specific enough to have tangible implications for what we do.*[2]

However, Useem suggests vision and strategy have been joined by new critical capabilities – leading out and leading up. With the increasing use of outsourcing, managers need the skill to lead out: not just to send work downwards to subordinates but also to have a talent for lateral leadership in arranging work with colleagues. And as organisations decentralise authority, managers must be able to lead their own bosses, to have the capacity to lead up and muster support from above as well as below.

Inspiring and influencing other people

Today, leadership is increasingly associated not with command and control but with the concept of inspiration, of getting along with other people and creating a vision with which others can identify. According to a recent CBI report: 'Effective leaders, who can inspire their people to realise their personal and collective potential, are often the deciding factor between a company being good at what it does and achieving greatness.'[3]

> *The vision is absolutely key to getting your troops together. It has to be qualitative, daring and grab the imagination. The test of it should be how quickly people will latch on to where you are going; you can entrust them with the how. You only get a company going where you want it to go by leadership by example and by honest and endless communication. Everyone in the business has to buy into your vision.*
>
> Sir John Harvey-Jones [4]

According to *Levine*, leaders need to focus on moving people and organisations forward by increasing the competency of staff and the co-operation of teams in order to improve the organisation. A leader's job is to constantly challenge the bureaucracy that smothers individual enthusiasm and the desire to contribute to an organisation. Leaders in the new millennium will create an environment that encourages the development of skills, learning and openness so that those on their team can participate in the deployment of financial and human resources.[5]

Inspirational leadership is discussed more fully later in this chapter.

The importance of leadership

The changing nature of work organisations, including flatter structures and recognition of the efficient use of human resources, coupled with advances in social democracy, have combined to place growing importance on leadership. The nature of management is moving away from an emphasis on getting results by the close control of the workforce and towards an environment of coaching, support and empowerment.

Leadership is related to motivation, interpersonal behaviour and the process of communication. According to *Sir Paul Judge*: 'Thirty years ago it was very much about what you knew, the technicalities of things. Managers now are leaders of their groups, their departments. Although they may well need some specialist knowledge, the human relations part of the management job is more important than ever. People have more flexibility and more choice in their careers, which are themselves more fluid, so keeping people motivated is very important.'[6]

Good leadership involves the effective process of delegation and empowerment. The leadership relationship is not limited to leader behaviour resulting in subordinate behaviour. Leadership is a dynamic process. The leader–follower relationship is reciprocal and effective leadership is a two-way process that influences both individual and organisational performance. A major report from the Advanced Institute of Management Research refers to the dual role of leadership. 'Leaders both motivate employees and design effective organisations. There are two broad conceptions of what leaders do – they motivate their followers and they design organisational contexts to enable their followers to function effectively.'[7]

Fullan discusses leadership in a culture of change and points out that leadership is key to large-scale improvement. It is essential for leaders to understand the change process and moral purpose without change will lead to moral martyrdom. Leaders must be able to operate under complex, uncertain circumstances.[8]

Leadership development in the public sector

A research report by the Chartered Management Institute highlights the attitudes and opinions of managers working in the public sector on the key issues of leadership and performance. The report indicates a strong positive relationship between the organisational priority given to leadership development and the level of employee motivation and satisfaction.[9]

LEADERSHIP AND MANAGEMENT

What is the relationship between leadership and management? Although the two terms are often used interchangeably, management is more usually viewed as getting things done through other people in order to achieve stated organisational objectives. The manager may react to specific situations and be more concerned with solving short-term problems. Management is regarded as relating to people working within a structured organisation and with prescribed roles. To people outside the organisation the manager might not necessarily be seen in a leadership role. The emphasis of leadership is on interpersonal behaviour in a broader context. It is often associated with the willing and enthusiastic behaviour of followers. **Leadership does not necessarily take place within the hierarchical structure of the organisation.** Many people operate as leaders without their role ever being clearly established or defined. *Belbin* suggests that:

> *there is a clear implication that leadership is not part of the job but a quality that can be brought to a job ... The work that leadership encompasses in the context clearly is not assigned but comes about spontaneously.*[10]

The 7-S organisational framework

The differences between leadership and management have been applied by Watson to the 7-S organisational framework. Watson suggests that whereas managers tend towards reliance on strategy, structure and systems, leaders have an inherent inclination for utilisation of the 'soft' Ss of style, staff, skills and superordinate (or shared) goals. Watson also suggests, although cautiously, that 7-S management could be seen as the province of leaders. Managers will not ordinarily be capable of achieving sufficient mastery of all seven factors to attain a consistently high level of organisational performance.[11]

Differences in attitudes and relations with others

There are other differences between leadership and management. *Zaleznik* explores difference in attitudes towards goals, conceptions of work, relations with others, self-perception and development.

- Managers tend to adopt impersonal or passive attitudes towards goals. Leaders adopt a more personal and active attitude towards goals.
- In order to get people to accept solutions, the manager needs continually to co-ordinate and balance in order to compromise conflicting values. The leader creates excitement in work and develops choices that give substance to images that excite people.
- In their relationships with other people, managers maintain a low level of emotional involvement. Leaders have empathy with other people and give attention to what events and actions mean.
- Managers see themselves more as conservators and regulators of the existing order of affairs with which they identify and from which they gain rewards. Leaders work in, but do not belong to, the organisation. Their sense of identity does not depend upon membership or work roles and they search out opportunities for change.[12]

Close relationship between management and leadership

Despite a continuing debate on differences between management and leadership, there is a close relationship between them and it is not easy to separate them as distinct activities. Today, there appears an increasing tendency to emphasise the interrelationship between management and leadership and to see them more as synonymous.

> *I have never been fond of distinguishing between leadership and management: they overlap and you need both qualities.*[13]

> *Increasingly, management and leadership are being seen as inextricably linked. It is one thing for a leader to propound a grand vision, but this is redundant unless the vision is managed so it becomes real achievement.*[14]

Many methods of management training can also be used as a means of measuring leadership style. For example, the Leadership Grid (discussed in Chapter 12) was until recently known as the Managerial Grid. Note also that the new framework of effective leadership introduced by Investors in People is called the 'Leadership and Management Model'.[15]

Figure 10.1 A framework for the study of managerial leadership

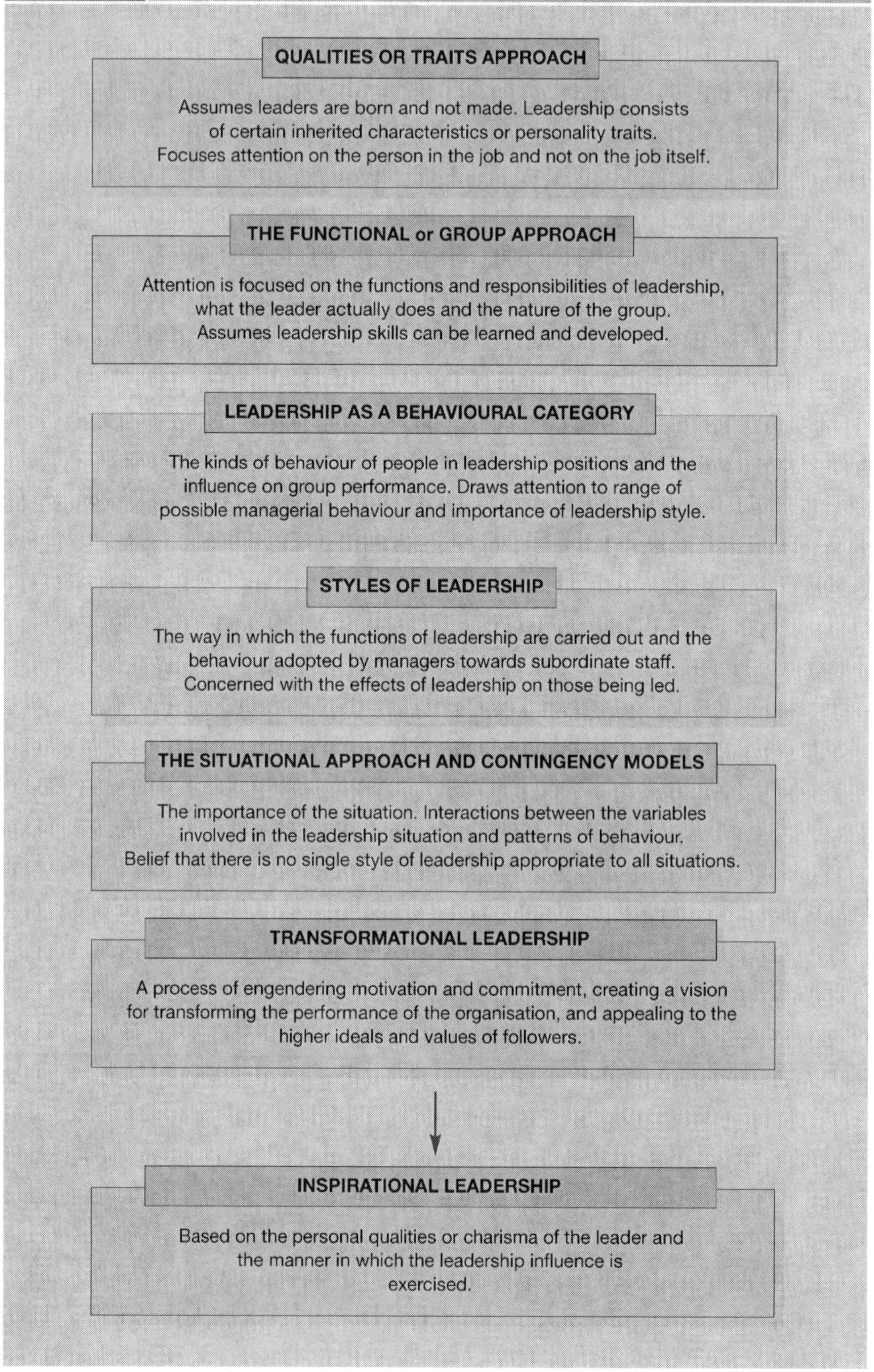

QUALITIES OR TRAITS APPROACH

Assumes leaders are born and not made. Leadership consists of certain inherited characteristics or personality traits. Focuses attention on the person in the job and not on the job itself.

THE FUNCTIONAL or GROUP APPROACH

Attention is focused on the functions and responsibilities of leadership, what the leader actually does and the nature of the group. Assumes leadership skills can be learned and developed.

LEADERSHIP AS A BEHAVIOURAL CATEGORY

The kinds of behaviour of people in leadership positions and the influence on group performance. Draws attention to range of possible managerial behaviour and importance of leadership style.

STYLES OF LEADERSHIP

The way in which the functions of leadership are carried out and the behaviour adopted by managers towards subordinate staff. Concerned with the effects of leadership on those being led.

THE SITUATIONAL APPROACH AND CONTINGENCY MODELS

The importance of the situation. Interactions between the variables involved in the leadership situation and patterns of behaviour. Belief that there is no single style of leadership appropriate to all situations.

TRANSFORMATIONAL LEADERSHIP

A process of engendering motivation and commitment, creating a vision for transforming the performance of the organisation, and appealing to the higher ideals and values of followers.

↓

INSPIRATIONAL LEADERSHIP

Based on the personal qualities or charisma of the leader and the manner in which the leadership influence is exercised.

The debate between Leadership and Management is well rehearsed, and usually produces shades of two perspectives, presented here as extremes: A hierarchical relationship with Leadership at the top; Leadership and Management equal in status, but at opposite ends of a continuum. Frankly, there is little evidence to support one view over the other. But there is overwhelming evidence that people like the idea of being a 'leader'. Indeed this may be the reason why the debate still rages, as it fulfils a need for differentiation.

Ray Moorcroft, 'To lead or to manage? That is the question'[16]

Critical reflection

In universities, many lecturers inspire students and are viewed as leaders but not usually as managers. In sport, we frequently hear talk about great leaders who are not managers of the team. There appears to be a clear and accepted distinction between leadership and management. Why do you think this distinction does not appear to apply in the same way within business organisations?

APPROACHES TO LEADERSHIP

Due to its complex and variable nature there are many alternative ways of analysing leadership. It is helpful, therefore, to have some framework in which to consider different approaches to study of the subject.

One way is to examine managerial leadership in terms of:

- the qualities or traits approach;
- the functional or group approach, including action-centred leadership;
- leadership as a behavioural category;
- styles of leadership;
- contingency theories;
- transitional or transformational leadership; and
- inspirational or visionary leadership.

(*See* Figure 10.1.)

THE QUALITIES OR TRAITS APPROACH

The first approach assumes that leaders are born and not made. Leadership consists of certain inherited characteristics, or personality traits, which distinguish leaders from their followers: the so-called Great Person theory of leadership. The **qualities approach** focuses attention on the man or woman in the job and not on the job itself. It suggests that attention is given to the selection of leaders rather than to training for leadership.

Drucker (writing originally in 1955) makes the point that:

> *Leadership is of utmost importance. Indeed there is no substitute for it. But leadership cannot be created or promoted. It cannot be taught or learned.*[17]

There have been many research studies into the common traits of leadership. However, attempts at identifying common personality, or physical and mental, characteristics of different 'good' or 'successful' leaders have met with little success.[18] Investigations have identified lists of traits that tend to be overlapping, contradictory or with little correlation for most features. It is noticeable that 'individuality' or 'originality' usually features in the list. This itself suggests that there is little in common between specific personality traits of different leaders. It is perhaps possible therefore to identify general characteristics of leadership ability, such as self-confidence, initiative, intelligence and belief in one's actions, but research into this area has revealed little more than this.

Limitations of the traits approach

There are three further limitations with this approach.

- First, there is bound to be some subjective judgement in determining who is regarded as a 'good' or 'successful' leader.
- Second, the lists of possible traits tend to be very long and there is not always agreement on the most important.
- Third, it ignores the situational factors.

Even if it were possible to identify an agreed list of more specific qualities, this would provide little explanation of the nature of leadership. It would do little to help in the development and training of future leaders. Although there is still limited interest in the qualities, or traits, approach, attention has been directed more to other approaches to leadership. The qualities or traits approach gives rise to the questions of whether leaders are born or made and whether leadership is an art or a science, The important point, however, is that **these are not mutually exclusive alternatives**. Even if there are certain inborn qualities that make for a good leader, these natural talents need encouragement and development. Even if leadership is something of an art, it still requires the application of special skills and techniques.

THE FUNCTIONAL (OR GROUP) APPROACH

This approach to leadership focuses attention not on the personality of the leader, nor on the man or woman in the job, *per se*, but on the **functions of leadership**. Leadership is always present in any group engaged in a task. The functional approach views leadership in terms of how the leader's behaviour affects, and is affected by, the group of followers. This approach concentrates on the nature of the group, the followers or subordinates. It focuses on the content of leadership. Greater attention can be given to the successful training of leaders and to the means of improving the leaders' performance by concentrating on the functions which will lead to effective performance by the work group.

The functional approach believes that the skills of leadership can be learned, developed and perfected. In contrast to the view of Drucker (referred to above), *Kotter* makes the point that successful companies do not wait for leaders to come along. 'They actively seek out people with leadership potential and expose them to career experiences designed to develop that potential. Indeed, with careful selection, nurturing and encouragement, dozens of people can play important leadership roles in a business organisation.'[19] A similar point is made by *Whitehead*: 'There has been a dramatic change in how management thinkers regard leadership today. Leaders are not born, they say, but made. And the good news is everyone can do it. You don't have to be promoted to a management position. You can be a leader whatever job you do. You don't have to be the boss to be a leader.'[20]

Action-centred leadership

A general theory on the functional approach is associated with the work of *John Adair* and his ideas on **action-centred leadership** which focuses on what leaders actually *do*.[21] The effectiveness of the leader is dependent upon meeting three areas of need within the work group: the need to achieve the common **task**, the need for **team maintenance**, and the **individual needs** of group members. Adair symbolises these needs by three overlapping circles (*see* Figure 10.2).

Figure 10.2 Interaction of needs within the group

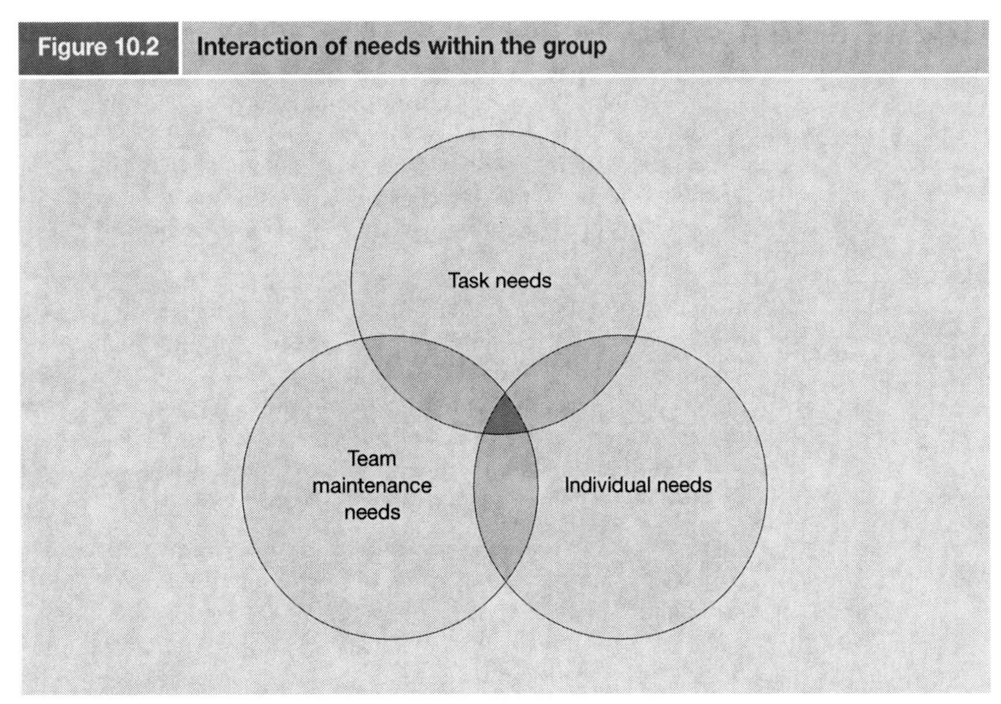

Source: Adair, J., *Action-Centred Leadership*, Gower Press (1979), p. 10. Reproduced with permission from Gower Publishing Ltd.

Task functions involve:

- achieving the objectives of the work group;
- defining group tasks;
- planning the work;
- allocation of resources;
- organisation of duties and responsibilities;
- controlling quality and checking performance;
- reviewing progress.

Team functions involve:

- maintaining morale and building team spirit;
- the cohesiveness of the group as a working unit;
- setting standards and maintaining discipline;
- systems of communication within the group;
- training the group;
- appointment of sub-leaders.

Individual functions involve:

- meeting the needs of the individual members of the group;
- attending to personal problems;
- giving praise and status;
- reconciling conflicts between group needs and needs of the individual;
- training the individual.

The action by the leader in any one area of need will affect one or both of the other areas of need. The ideal position is where complete integration of the three areas of need is achieved. The three-circle approach used by Adair also serves to illustrate the close relationship between leadership and management. Building the team and satisfying individual needs would include leadership. Achieving the common task clearly involves the process of management.

LEADERSHIP AS A BEHAVIOURAL CATEGORY

This approach draws attention to the kinds of behaviour of people in leadership situations. One of the most extensive research studies on behavioural categories of leadership was the Ohio State Leadership Studies undertaken by the Bureau of Business Research at Ohio State University. The focus was on the effects of leadership styles on group performance. Results indicated two major dimensions of leadership behaviour, labelled 'consideration' and 'initiating structure'.[22]

- **Consideration** reflects the extent to which the leader establishes trust, mutual respect and rapport with the group and shows concern, warmth, support and consideration for subordinates. This dimension is associated with two-way communication, participation and the human relations approach to leadership.
- **Structure** reflects the extent to which the leader defines and structures group interactions towards attainment of formal goals and organises group activities. This dimension is associated with efforts to achieve organisational goals.

Consideration and initiating structure can be seen as the same as maintenance function (building and maintaining the group as a working unit and relationships among group members) and task function (accomplishment of specific tasks of the groups and achievement of goals) that were discussed in Chapter 9. Consideration and initiating structure were found to be uncorrelated and independent dimensions. Leadership behaviour could, therefore, be shown on two separate axes. A high-consideration, high-structure style appears to be generally more effective in terms of subordinate satisfaction and group performance, but the evidence is not conclusive and much seems to depend upon situational factors. However, later findings suggest that the best leadership style entails high levels of both people-centred and task-centred dimensions.[23]

Employee-centred and production-centred supervisors

Another major research study was carried out at the University of Michigan Institute for Social Research at the same time as the Ohio State studies. Effective supervisors (measured along dimensions of group morale, productivity and cost reduction) appeared to display four common characteristics:

- delegation of authority and avoidance of close supervision;
- an interest and concern in their subordinates as individuals;
- participative problem-solving; and
- high standards of performance.

Likert, who has summarised the findings of the University of Michigan studies, used the terms **employee-centred** and **production-centred** supervisors.[24] These terms are similar to the dimensions of consideration and structure. The first three of these supervisory characteristics are examples of consideration. The fourth characteristic exemplifies structure. Like consideration and structure, employee-centred and production-centred supervision need to be balanced. Likert concluded that employee-centred supervisors who get best results tend to recognise that one of their main responsibilities is production. Both the Ohio State and the University of Michigan studies appear to support the idea that there is no single behavioural category of leadership that is superior. There are many types of leadership behaviour and their effectiveness depends upon the variables in any given situation.

Major dimensions of managerial leadership

Despite the many types of actual leadership behaviour, we have seen that there appears to be general agreement on two major dimensions of managerial leadership. This can be extended to include the works of McGregor and of Blake and McCanse, discussed as part of managerial behaviour in Chapter 12 (*see* Figure 10.3).

Figure 10.3 Two major dimensions of managerial leadership

Group interaction analysis	*Task functions*	*Maintenance functions*
Ohio State leadership study	Initiating structure	Consideration
University of Michigan study	Production-centred supervision	Employee-centred supervision
McGregor, assumptions about people and work	Theory X	Theory Y
Blake and McCanse, Leadership Grid	Concern for production	Concern for people

STYLES OF LEADERSHIP

Attention to leadership as a behavioural category has drawn attention to the importance of leadership style. In the work situation it has become increasingly clear that managers can no longer rely solely on the use of their position in the hierarchical structure as a means of exercising the functions of leadership. In order to get the best results from subordinates the manager must also have regard for the need to encourage high morale, a spirit of involvement and co-operation, and a willingness to work. This gives rise to consideration of the style of leadership and provides another heading under which to analyse leadership behaviour.

Leadership style is the way in which the functions of leadership are carried out, the way in which the manager typically behaves towards members of the group.

The attention given to leadership style is based on the assumption that subordinates are more likely to work effectively for managers who adopt a certain style of leadership than they will for managers who adopt alternative styles.

Broad classification of leadership style

There are many dimensions to leadership and many possible ways of describing leadership style, such as dictatorial, unitary, bureaucratic, benevolent, charismatic, consultative, participative and abdicatorial. The style of managerial leadership towards subordinate staff and the focus of power can, however, be classified, broadly, within a simplified three-fold heading.

- The **authoritarian (or autocratic) style** is where the focus of power is with the manager and all interactions within the group move towards the manager. The manager alone exercises decision-making and authority for determining policy, procedures for achieving goals, work tasks and relationships, control of rewards or punishments.
- The **democratic style** is where the focus of power is more with the group as a whole and there is greater interaction within the group. The leadership functions are shared with members of the group and the manager is more part of a team. The group members have a greater say in decision-making, determination of policy, implementation of systems and procedures.
- A ***laissez-faire* (genuine) style** is where the manager observes that members of the group are working well on their own. The manager consciously makes a decision to pass the focus of power to members, to allow them freedom of action 'to do as they think best', and not to interfere; but is readily available if help is needed. There is often confusion over this style of leadership behaviour. The word 'genuine' is emphasised because this is

to be contrasted with the manager who could not care, who deliberately keeps away from the trouble spots and does not want to get involved. The manager just lets members of the group get on with the work in hand. Members are left to face decisions that rightly belong with the manager. This is more a non-style of leadership or it could perhaps be labelled as abdication.

Attention to style of leadership

Attention to the manager's style of leadership has come about because of a greater understanding of the needs and expectations of people at work. It has also been influenced by such factors as:

- increasing business competitiveness and recognition of efficient use of human resources;
- changes in the value system of society;
- broader standards of education and training;
- advances in scientific and technical knowledge;
- changes in the nature of work organisation;
- pressure for a greater social responsibility towards employees, for example through schemes of participation in decision-making and work/life balance; and
- government legislation, for example in the areas of employment protection, and the influence of the European Union.

All of these factors have combined to create resistance against purely autocratic styles of leadership.

CONTINUUM OF LEADERSHIP BEHAVIOUR

One of the best-known works on leadership style is that by *Tannenbaum and Schmidt* (Figure 10.4).[25] Originally written in 1958 and updated in 1973, their work suggests a continuum of possible leadership behaviour available to a manager and along which various styles of leadership may be placed. The continuum presents a range of action related to the degree of authority used by the manager and to the area of freedom available to non-managers in arriving at decisions. The Tannenbaum and Schmidt continuum can be related to McGregor's supposition of Theory X and Theory Y. Boss-centred leadership is towards Theory X and subordinate-centred leadership is towards Theory Y.

Four main styles of leadership

Moving along the continuum, the manager may be characterised according to the degree of control that is maintained. Neither extreme of the continuum is absolute as there is always some limitation on authority and on freedom. This approach can be seen as identifying four main styles of leadership by the manager: tells, sells, consults, joins.

- **Tells.** The manager identifies a problem, makes a decision and announces this to subordinates, expecting them to implement it without an opportunity for participation.
- **Sells.** The manager still makes a decision but recognises the possibility of some resistance from those faced with the decision and attempts to persuade subordinates to accept it.
- **Consults.** The manager identifies the problem but does not make a decision until the problem is presented to the group, and the manager has listened to the advice and solutions suggested by subordinates.
- **Joins.** The manager defines the problem and the limits within which the decision must be made and then passes to the group, with the manager as a member, the right to make decisions.

Figure 10.4 Continuum of manager–non-manager behaviour

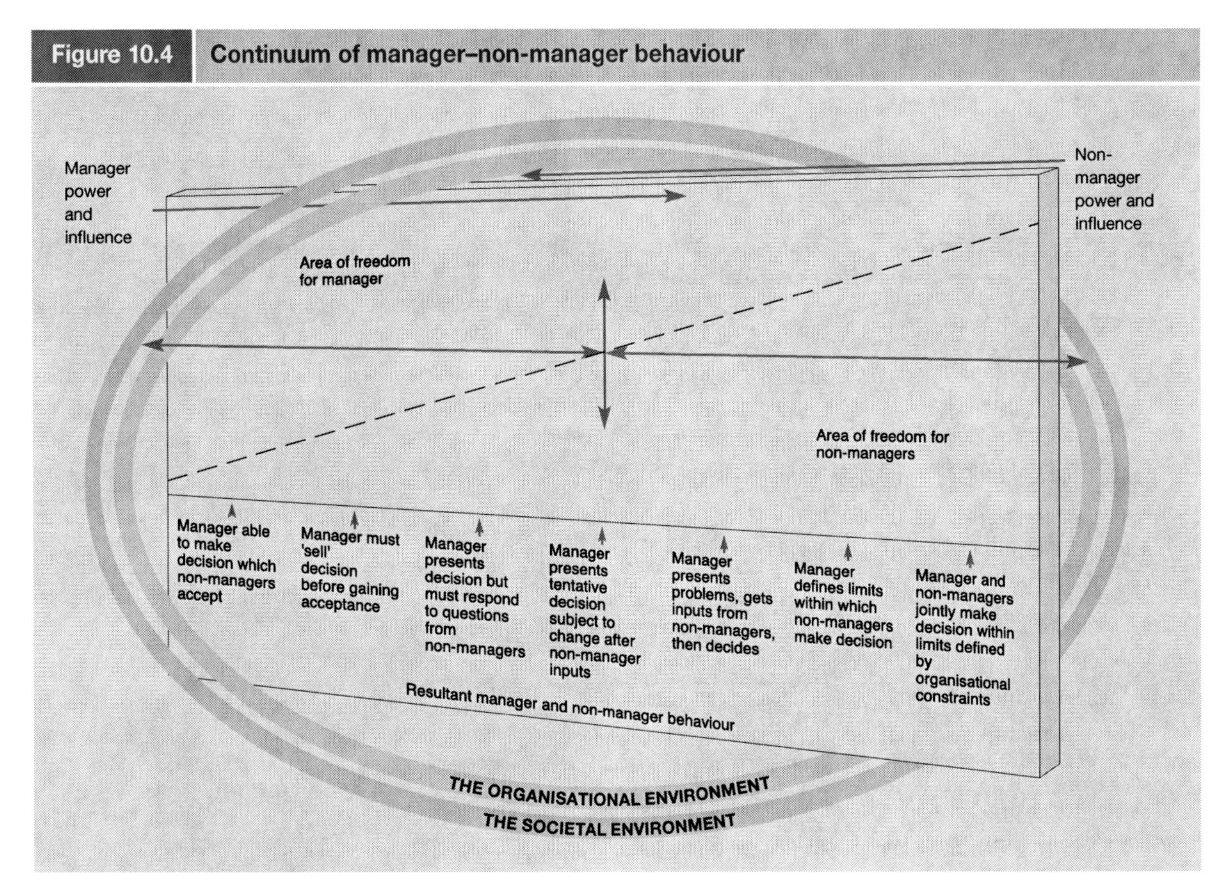

Source: Tannenbaum, R. and Schmidt, W. H., 'How to choose a leadership pattern', *Harvard Business Review*, May/June 1973, p. 167.

Main forces in deciding type of leadership

Tannenbaum and Schmidt suggest that there are three factors, or forces, of particular importance in deciding what types of leadership are practicable and desirable. These are: forces in the manager, forces in the subordinate and forces in the situation.

1 **Forces in the manager.** The manager's behaviour will be influenced by their personality, background, knowledge and experiences. These internal forces will include:
   - value systems;
   - confidence in subordinates;
   - leadership inclinations; and
   - feelings of security in an uncertain situation.

2 **Forces in the subordinate.** Subordinates are influenced by many personality variables and their individual set of expectations about their relationship with the manager. Characteristics of the subordinate are:
   - the strength of the need for independence;
   - the readiness to assume responsibility for decision-making;
   - the degree of tolerance for ambiguity;
   - interest in the problem and feelings as to its importance;
   - understanding and identification with the goals of the organisation;
   - necessary knowledge and experience to deal with the problem; and
   - the extent of learning to expect to share in decision-making.

   The greater the positive response to these characteristics, the greater freedom of action can be allowed by the manager.

3 **Forces in the situation.** The manager's behaviour will be influenced by the general situation and environmental pressures. Characteristics in the situation include:
- type of organisation;
- group effectiveness;
- nature of the problem; and
- pressure of time.

Tannenbaum and Schmidt conclude that successful leaders are keenly aware of those forces which are most relevant to their behaviour at a particular time. They are able to behave appropriately in terms of their understanding of themselves, the individuals and the group, the organisation, and environmental influences. Successful managers are both perceptive and flexible. Forces lying outside the organisation are also included. Recognition is given to the possibility of the manager and/or subordinates taking initiatives to change the boundaries of the rectangle through interaction with external forces. Recognition is also given to the power available to all parties in the organisation (for example individual workers and trade unions) and to the factors which underlie decisions on the use of power by the manager. Tannenbaum and Schmidt suggest a new continuum of patterns of leadership behaviour in which the total area of freedom shared between managers and non-managers is redefined constantly by interactions between them and the forces in the environment.

CONTINGENCY THEORIES OF LEADERSHIP

The continuum of leadership behaviour draws attention to forces in the situation as one of the main forces influencing the nature of managerial behaviour. The **situational approach** emphasises the situation as the dominant feature in considering the characteristics of effective leadership. There are, however, limitations to the situational approach. There are people who possess the appropriate knowledge and skills and appear to be the most suitable leaders in a given situation, but who do not emerge as effective leaders. Another limitation is that it does not explain fully the interpersonal behaviour or the different styles of leadership and their effect on members of the group. Finally, in the work organisation, it is not usually practicable to allow the situation continually to determine who should act as the leader.

Despite the limitations of the situational approach, situational factors are important in considering the characteristics of leadership. More recent studies focus on the interactions between the variables involved in a leadership situation and patterns of leadership behaviour, and provide another general approach to the study of leadership – contingency theory. Contingency theories are based on the belief that there is no single style of leadership appropriate to all situations. Major contingency models of leadership include:

- **Favourability of leadership situation** – *Fiedler*
- **Quality and acceptance of leader's decision** – *Vroom and Yetton* and *Vroom and Jago*
- **Path–goal theory** – *House*, and *House and Dessler*
- **Readiness level of followers** – *Hersey and Blanchard*.

FIEDLER'S CONTINGENCY MODEL

One of the first leader–situation models was developed by *Fiedler* in his contingency theory of leadership effectiveness.[26] Fiedler's contingency model was based on studies of a wide range of group situations and concentrated on the relationship between leadership and organisational performance. In order to measure the attitudes of the leader, Fiedler developed a 'least preferred co-worker' (LPC) scale. This measures the rating given by leaders about the person with whom they could work least well. The questionnaire contains up to 20 items. Examples of items in the LPC scale are pleasant/unpleasant, friendly/unfriendly, helpful/frustrating, distant/close, co-operative/unco-operative, boring/interesting, self-assured/hesitant, open/guarded.

Each item is given a single ranking of between one and eight points, with eight points indicating the most favourable rating. For example:

Pleasant	:	:	:	:	:	:	:	:	Unpleasant
	8	7	6	5	4	3	2	1	

The LPC score is the sum of the numerical ratings on all the items for the 'least preferred co-worker'. The original interpretation of the LPC scale was that the leader with a high LPC score derived most satisfaction from interpersonal relationships and, when relationships with subordinates need to be improved, is motivated to act in a supportive, considerate manner. The leader with a low LPC score derived most satisfaction from performance of the task and achieving objectives. Establishing good relationships with subordinates is a secondary motivation. It was thought that high LPC scores would be associated with effective performance by the group. However, the interpretation of LPC has changed a number of times and there is still uncertainty about its actual meaning.

Favourability of leadership situation

Fiedler suggests that leadership behaviour is dependent upon the favourability of the leadership situation. There are three major variables which determine the favourability of the situation and which affect the leader's role and influence:

- **Leader–member relations** – the degree to which the leader is trusted and liked by group members, and their willingness to follow the leader's guidance.
- **The task structure** – the degree to which the task is clearly defined for the group and the extent to which it can be carried out by detailed instructions or standard procedures.
- **Position power** – the power of the leader by virtue of position in the organisation, and the degree to which the leader can exercise authority to influence (for example) rewards and punishments, or promotions and demotions.

From these three variables, Fiedler constructed eight combinations of group–task situations through which to relate leadership style (*see* Figure 10.5).

When the situation is

- **very favourable** (good leader–member relations, structured task, strong position power), or
- **very unfavourable** (poor leader–member relations, unstructured task, weak position power),
- then a **task-oriented leader** (low LPC score) with a directive, controlling style will be more effective.

When the situation is

- **moderately favourable** and the variables are mixed, then the leader with an interpersonal relationship orientation (high LPC score) and a **participative approach** will be more effective.

Fiedler is suggesting, therefore, that leadership style will vary as the favourability of the leadership situation varies.

Organisational variables

Fiedler's work has been subject to much debate and criticism but it does provide a further dimension to the study of leadership.[27] It brings into consideration the organisational variables that affect leadership effectiveness and suggests that in given situations a task-oriented, or structured, style of leadership is most appropriate. The 'best' styles of leadership will be dependent upon the variable factors in the leadership situation.

Figure 10.5 Correlations between leader's LPC scores and group effectiveness

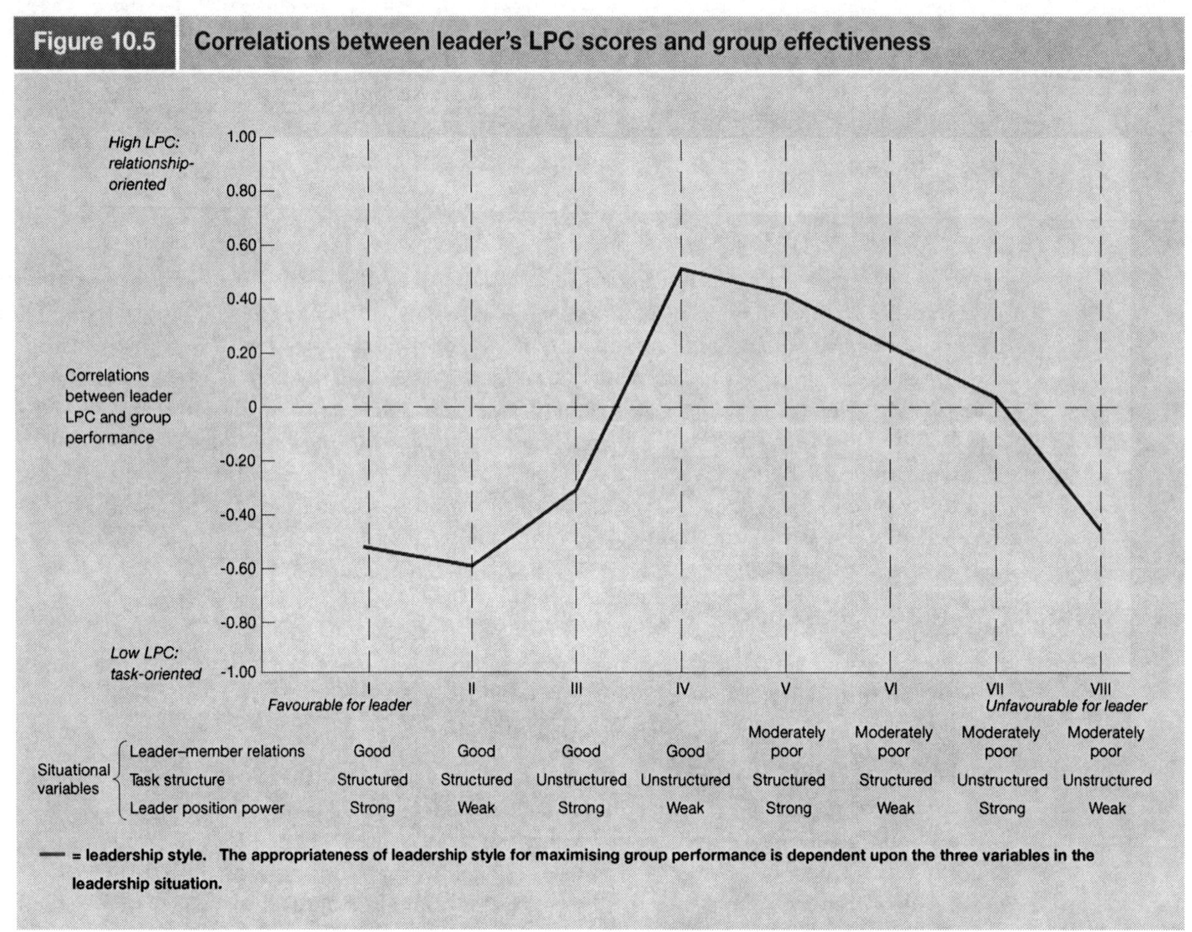

Source: Adapted from Fielder, F .E., *A Theory of Leadership Effectiveness*. McGraw-Hill (1967), p. 146. Reproduced with permission from The McGraw-Hill Companies, Inc.

Fiedler argues that leadership effectiveness may be improved by changing the leadership situation. Position power, task structure and leader–member relations can be changed to make the situation more compatible with the characteristics of the leader. Leaders with a low LPC score could be placed in a leadership situation that is very favourable or very unfavourable. Leaders with a high LPC score could be placed in a leadership situation that is of moderate favourability.

VROOM AND YETTON CONTINGENCY MODEL

Another contingency model of leadership is provided by *Vroom and Yetton*.[28] They base their analysis on two main aspects of a leader's decision: its quality and its acceptance.

- **Decision quality**, or rationality, is the effect that the decision has on group performance.
- **Decision acceptance** refers to the motivation and commitment of group members in implementing the decision.

A third consideration is

- the amount of **time required** to make the decision.

The Vroom and Yetton model suggests five main management decision styles:

- Autocratic
  A.I: Leader solves the problem or makes the decision alone using information available at the time.
  A.II: Leader obtains information from subordinates but then decides on solution alone.
- Consultative
  C.I: The problem is shared with relevant subordinates, individually. The leader then makes the decision that may or may not reflect the influence of subordinates.
  C.II: The problem is shared with subordinates as a group. The leader then makes the decision that may or may not reflect the influence of subordinates.
- Group
  G.II: The problem is shared with subordinates as a group. The leader acts as chairperson rather than an advocate. Together the leader and subordinates generate and evaluate alternatives and attempt to reach group consensus on a solution.

Decision rules Vroom and Yetton suggest seven decision rules to help the manager discover the most appropriate leadership style in a given situation. The first three rules protect the **quality of decisions.**

1 Is there a quality requirement such that one solution is likely to be more rational than another?
2 Is there sufficient information to make a high-quality decision?
3 Is the problem structured? The last four rules protect the **acceptance of decisions**.
4 Is acceptance of the decision by subordinates critical to effective implementation?
5 If you were to make the decision yourself, is it reasonably certain that it would be accepted by subordinates?
6 Do subordinates share the organisational goals to be obtained in solving the problem?
7 Is conflict among subordinates likely in preferred solutions?

These rules indicate decision styles that the manager should **avoid** in a given situation and indicate the use of others. Decision tree charts can be produced to help in the application of the rules and to relate the situation to the appropriate leadership style.

THE VROOM AND JAGO REVISED DECISION MODEL

In a revised version of the original model, *Vroom and Jago* retain the five main decision-making styles but incorporate a larger number – 12 – of contingency variables.[29] The new model specifies that any of the five decision styles may be effective in given situations. The contingency variables relate to:

- quality requirement;
- commitment requirement;
- leader information;
- problem structure;
- commitment probability;
- goal congruence;
- subordinate conflict;
- subordinate information;
- time constraint;
- geographical dispersion;
- motivation time; and
- motivation development.

Unlike the Vroom and Yetton model that requires a definite yes/no answer, ten of these situational variables are answered on a five-point scale. For example, to the question 'How important is subordinate commitment to the decision?', the manager selects one of the following responses: no importance; low importance; average importance; high importance; critical importance.

Use of decision trees

Vroom and Jago developed four decision trees relating to a generic type of managerial problem:

- an individual-level problem with time constraints;
- an individual-level problem in which the manager wishes to develop an employee's decision-making ability;
- a group-level problem in which the manager wishes to develop employees' decision-making abilities; and
- a time-driven group problem.

The manager selects one of the trees and moves along the branches by answering the questions at each decision point. This leads to one of the five described decision-making styles.

PATH–GOAL THEORY

A third contingency model of leadership is the path–goal theory, the main work on which has been undertaken by *House*,[30] and by *House and Dessler*.[31] The model is based on the belief that the individual's motivation is dependent upon expectations that increased effort to achieve an improved level of performance will be successful, and expectations that improved performance will be instrumental in obtaining positive rewards and avoiding negative outcomes. This is the 'expectancy' theory of motivation, which is discussed in Chapter 7.

Four main types of leadership behaviour

The path–goal theory of leadership suggests that the performance of subordinates is affected by the extent to which the manager satisfies their expectations. Path–goal theory holds that subordinates will see leadership behaviour as a motivating influence to the extent that it means:

- satisfaction of their needs is dependent upon effective performance; and
- the necessary direction, guidance, training and support, which would otherwise be lacking, is provided.

House identifies four main types of leadership behaviour:

- **Directive leadership** involves letting subordinates know exactly what is expected of them and giving specific directions. Subordinates are expected to follow rules and regulations. This type of behaviour is similar to 'initiating structure' in the Ohio State Leadership Studies.
- **Supportive leadership** involves a friendly and approachable manner and displaying concern for the needs and welfare of subordinates. This type of behaviour is similar to 'consideration' in the Ohio State Leadership Studies.
- **Participative leadership** involves consulting with subordinates and the evaluation of their opinions and suggestions before the manager makes the decision.
- **Achievement-oriented leadership** involves setting challenging goals for subordinates, seeking improvement in their performance and showing confidence in subordinates' ability to perform well.

Path–goal theory suggests that the different types of behaviour can be practised by the same person at different times in varying situations. By using one of the four styles of leadership behaviour the manager attempts to influence subordinates' perceptions and motivation, and smooth the path to their goals (*see* Figure 10.6).

Figure 10.6 Representation of the path–goal theory of leadership

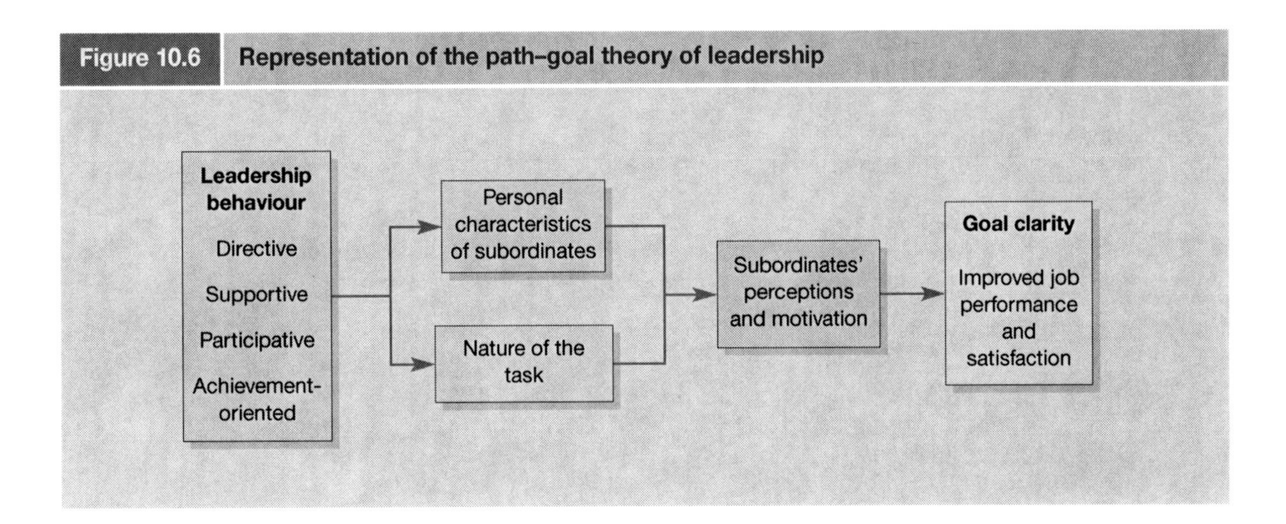

Two main situational factors

Leadership behaviour is determined by two main situational factors: the personal characteristics of subordinates and the nature of the task.

- **The personal characteristics of subordinates** determine how they will react to the manager's behaviour and the extent to which they see such behaviour as an immediate or potential source of need satisfaction.
- **The nature of the task** relates to the extent that it is routine and structured or non-routine and unstructured.

For example, when a task is highly structured, the goals readily apparent and subordinates are confident, then attempts to further explain the job or to give directions are likely to be viewed as unacceptable behaviour. However, when a task is highly unstructured, the nature of the goals is not clear and subordinates lack experience, then a more directive style of leadership behaviour is likely to be welcomed by subordinates. Effective leadership behaviour is based, therefore, on both the willingness of the manager to help subordinates and the needs of subordinates for help. Leadership behaviour will be motivational to the extent that it provides necessary direction, guidance and support, helps clarify path–goal relationships and removes any obstacles which hinder attainment of goals.

READINESS OF THE FOLLOWERS OR GROUP

A major variable in the style of leadership adopted by the manager is the nature of subordinate staff. This view is developed by *Hersey and Blanchard* who present a form of situational leadership based on the 'readiness' level of the people the leader is attempting to influence. Readiness is the extent to which followers have the ability and willingness to accomplish a specific task. It is not a personal characteristic of the individual but how ready the individual is to perform a particular task.[32]

Readiness (R) is divided into a continuum of four levels: R1 (low), R2 and R3 (moderate) and R4 (high).

- **R1 – low follower readiness** – refers to followers who are both *unable and unwilling* and who lack commitment and motivation; or who are *unable and insecure*.
- **R2 – low to moderate follower readiness** – refers to followers who are *unable but willing* and who lack ability but are motivated to make an effort; or who are *unable but confident*.
- **R3 – moderate to high follower readiness** – refers to followers who are *able but unwilling*, and who have the ability to perform but are unwilling to apply their ability; or who are *able but insecure*.

- **R4 – high follower readiness** – refers to followers who are both *able and willing* and who have the ability and commitment to perform; or who are *able and confident*.

Task behaviour and relationship behaviour

For each of the four levels of maturity, the appropriate style of leadership is a combination of task behaviour and relationship behaviour.

- **Task behaviour** is the extent to which the leader provides directions for the actions of followers, sets goals for them and defines their roles and how to undertake them.
- **Relationship behaviour** is the extent to which the leader engages in two-way communication with followers, listens to them and provides support and encouragement.

From the combination of task behaviour and relationship behaviour derive four leadership styles (S): telling (S1), selling (S2), participating (S3) and delegating (S4). The appropriate leadership style corresponds with the readiness of the followers (*see* Figure 10.7).

Figure 10.7 Situational Leadership® model

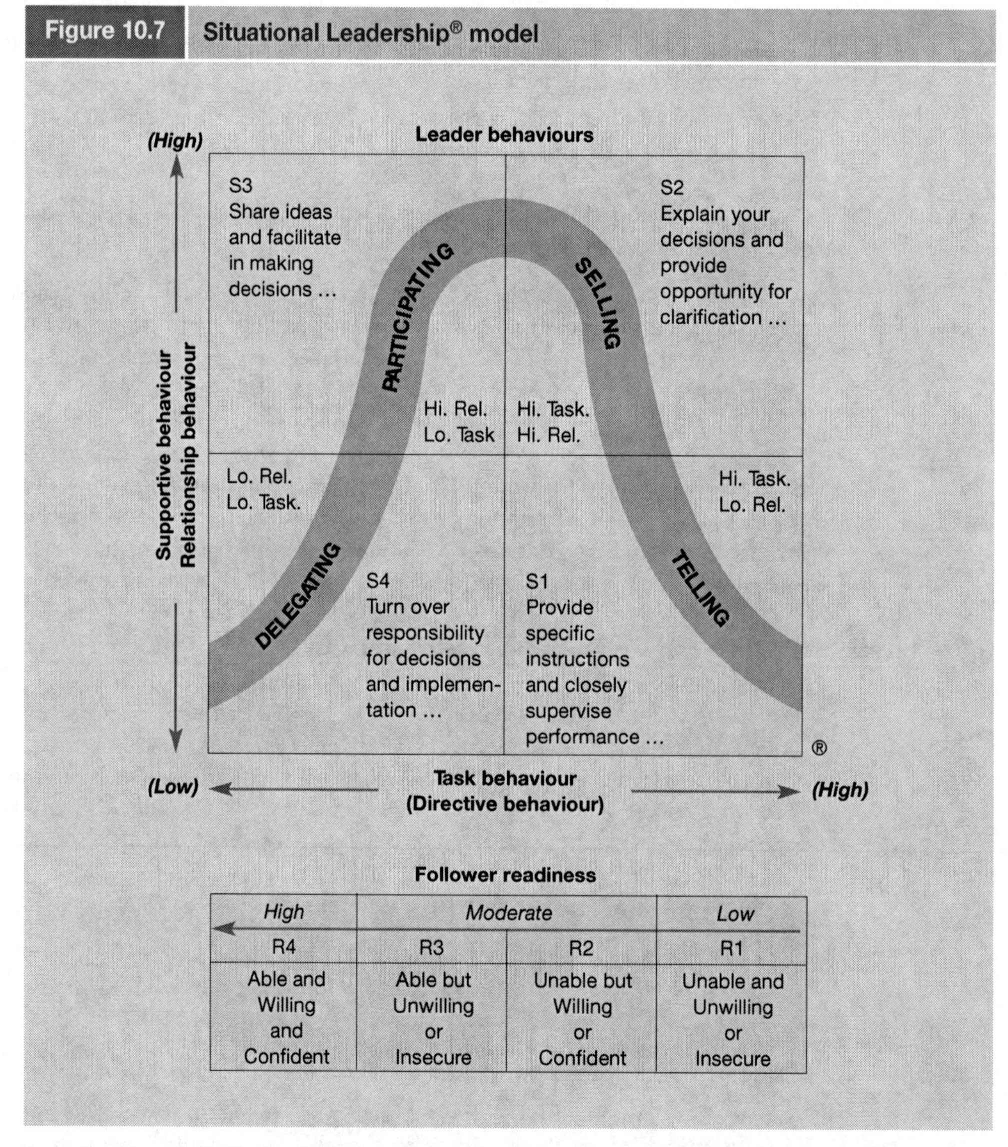

High	*Moderate*		*Low*
R4	R3	R2	R1
Able and Willing and Confident	Able but Unwilling or Insecure	Unable but Willing or Confident	Unable and Unwilling or Insecure

Source: From Hersey, P., *The Situational Leader*, Center for Leadership Studies (1984) p. 63.

- S1 – **telling** – emphasises high amounts of guidance (task behaviour) but limited supportive (relationship) behaviour. This style is most appropriate for *low follower readiness* (R1).
- S2 – **selling** – emphasises high amounts of both directive (task) and relationship behaviours. This style is most appropriate for *low to moderate follower readiness* (R2).
- S3 – **participating** – emphasises a high amount of two-way communication and supportive (relationship) behaviour but low amounts of guidance (task behaviour). This style is most appropriate for *moderate to high follower readiness* (R3).
- S4 – **delegating** – emphasises little direction or support with low levels of both task and relationship behaviours. This style is most appropriate for *high follower readiness* (R4).

Development of subordinates

Hersey and Blanchard suggest that the key to using situational leadership is that any leader behaviour may be more or less effective according to the readiness of the person the leader is attempting to influence. The model draws attention to the importance of developing the ability, confidence and commitment of subordinates. The manager should help subordinates to develop in readiness to the extent that they are able and willing to go. This development should take place by adjusting leadership behaviour through the four styles of telling, selling, participating and delegating.

Critical reflection

The situational approach rejects the idea of one generalised model of leadership and draws attention to the importance of prevailing variables. However, most workers like to know exactly where they stand with their boss and become confused and unsettled with constant changes in leadership style. Do you accept therefore that contingency theories of leadership have little real value or relevance to modern organisations?

TRANSFORMATIONAL LEADERSHIP

In recent years increasing business competitiveness and the need for the most effective use of human resources has resulted in writers on management focusing attention on how leaders revitalise or transform organisations. Based on the work of writers such as *Burns* this has given rise to a distinction between two fundamental forms of leadership: transactional or transformational.[33]

- Transactional leadership is based on legitimate authority within the bureaucratic structure of the organisation. The emphasis is on the clarification of goals and objectives, work task and outcomes, and organisational rewards and punishments. Transactional leadership appeals to the self-interest of followers. It is based on a relationship of mutual dependence and an exchange process of 'I will give you this, if you do that.'
- Transformational leadership, by contrast, is a process of engendering higher levels of motivation and commitment among followers. The emphasis is on generating a vision for the organisation and the leader's ability to appeal to higher ideals and values of followers, and creating a feeling of justice, loyalty and trust. In the organisational sense, transformational leadership is about transforming the performance or fortunes of a business.

Components of transformational leadership

According to *Bass*, the transformational leader motivates followers to do more than originally expected and the extent of transformation is measured in terms of the leader's effects on followers. Applying the ideas of Burns to organisational management, Bass proposed a theory of transformational leadership that argues that the leader transforms and motivates followers by:

1 generating greater awareness of the importance of the purpose of the organisation and task outcomes;
2 inducing them to transcend their own self-interests for the sake of the organisation or team; and
3 activating their higher-level needs.[34]

Transformational leadership is comprised of four basic components:

- **idealised influence** – the charisma of the leader, and the respect and admiration of the followers;
- **inspirational motivation** – the behaviour of the leader which provides meaning and challenge to the work of the followers;
- **intellectual stimulation** – leaders who solicit new and novel approaches for the performance of work and creative problem solutions from followers; and
- **individualised consideration** – leaders who listen and give special concern to the growth and developmental needs of the followers.[35]

Yukl provides a set of guidelines for transformational leadership:

- **Articulate a clear and appealing vision** of what the organisation could accomplish or become to help people understand the purpose, objectives and priorities of the organisation, and to help guide the actions and decisions of members.
- **Explain how the vision can be attained** and establish a clear link between the vision and a credible conventional yet straightforward strategy for attaining it.
- **Act confident and optimistic** about likely success, demonstrate self-confidence and conviction, and emphasise positive aspects of the vision rather than the obstacles and dangers.
- **Express confidence in followers** and their ability to carry out the strategy for accomplishing the vision, especially when the task is difficult or dangerous, or when members lack confidence in themselves.
- **Use dramatic, symbolic actions to emphasise key values** and demonstrate leadership behaviour through dramatic, highly visible actions including risking personal loss, self-sacrifice or acting unconventionally.
- **Lead by example** by recognising actions speak louder than words, through exemplary behaviour in day-to-day interactions with subordinates and by demonstrating consistency in daily behaviour.[36]

INSPIRATIONAL OR VISIONARY LEADERSHIP

Many writers see transformational leadership as the same thing as charismatic, visionary or inspirational leadership. *Kreitner et al.* refer to charismatic leadership as transforming employees to pursue organisational goals over self-interests: 'Charismatic leaders transform followers by creating changes in their goals, values, needs, beliefs, and aspirations. They accomplish this transformation by appealing to followers' self-concepts – namely, their values and personal identity.'[37] Writers such as *Burns* and *Bass* identified leaders by their actions and the impact those actions have on other people.

Successful transformational leaders are usually identified in terms of providing a strong vision and sense of mission, arousing strong emotions in followers and a sense of identification with the leader. As mentioned at the start of this chapter, leadership today is increasingly associated with the concept of creating a vision with which others can identify, getting along with other people and the concept of inspiration. This might be considered as part of transformational leadership or arguably it has given rise to a new approach to leadership – that of **inspirational or visionary leadership**. Inspirational leadership is not concerned so much with the theory of leadership but more with the skills of motivating and inspiring people.

Personal qualities or charisma

Leadership may be based on the personal qualities, or charisma, of the leader and the manner in which influence is exercised. The importance of charisma for effective leadership is emphasised by *Conger*, who also believes that many of the traits that make a successful leader can be taught, including charisma.

> *Now the big question is whether you are born with charisma or whether you can develop it. I believe you can develop elements of it. For example, you can take courses to improve your speaking skills. You can learn to stage events that send powerful messages. You can learn to think more critically about the status quo and its shortcomings. You can do more on a daily basis to motivate your team. What you simply cannot learn is how to be passionate about what you do. You have to discover that for yourself, and passion is a big part of what drives a charismatic leader. It is also what motivates and inspires those who work for the charismatic leader.*[38]

Is charisma enough?

However, the extent to which charismatic or inspirational leadership helps bring about improvement in organisational performance is open to much debate. Conger also draws attention to the danger that the leader's vision, dynamism and inspirational nature are highly attractive to followers, which leads to a natural dependence. Staff see this extraordinary figure as a model to be emulated and the leader's abilities become the yardstick by which they measure their own performance. This is a potential source of leadership derailment. Dependence makes the followers more susceptible to deception.[39]

Dearlove draws attention to the increasing focus on leaders as real people managing in a consensus-seeking manner. 'While traditional views of leadership tend eventually to concentrate on vision and charisma, the message now seems to be that charisma is no longer enough to carry leaders through.'[40] *Bloomfield* also refers to the cult of the individual, supposedly charismatic leader and the danger that this leads businesses into deep water far more often than the application of rational leadership. Too often the charismatic leader, aided and abetted by the language of current management fashion, attempts to 'inspire', to delight with their vision and to produce a mission statement of where the business might be – at the expense of real substance.[41]

Adair argues that to be a truly inspirational leader one must understand the spirit within. All people have the potential for greatness. The inspirational leader connects with the led, appreciates the capabilities of others and through trust will unlock the powers in others. Adair refers to 'the inspired moment' – a recognition and seizure of a brief window of opportunity that can act as a powerful catalyst that inspires both the leader and the led.[42]

The importance of vision

Effective transformational leaders are those who inspire people and create a vision for the organisation and its future direction. According to *Whitehead*:

> *The big word now associated with leadership is vision. The ability to see the bigger picture. To take the long-term view. What the ultimate objectives of the organisation are and how people can work together to achieve them ... Perhaps the most important attribute is that a good leader inspires people by creating a climate where it is OK for people to make mistakes and learn from them, rather than what happened in the past which was to blame and punish them. Leading from this position, they gain a higher level of commitment from their people than mere compliance.*[43]

Kahan sees visionary leadership as transformative. It involves greatness, penetrating the ordinary, and requires total involvement. Among the qualities visionary leaders cultivate are imagination, engagement, tangible results and penetrating self-reflection. They engage society with its competitive, divergent viewpoints. Visionary leadership is ultimately about increasing performance but also with the rewards of tangible results to your membership and deep personal satisfaction.[44]

Need for visionary leadership

In her discussion of the creation of the democratic enterprise (organisations that can flourish economically and can also be places of excitement and stimulation, fulfilment and tranquillity), *Gratton* maintains that it is the creation of a shared purpose and the role of the leadership team that are most vital. The role of the leader as visionary is fundamental to creating the broad philosophical context of democracy and as the architect of shared purpose.[45]

Referring to the work of Goffee and Jones, *Witzel* suggests: 'Leadership is one of the most vital and yet elusive ingredients in modern business. Leaders provide vision, direction, inspiration, give the business a sense of purpose and at the same time act as a moral compass.'[46] *Goffee and Jones* point out that the need for visionary leadership is becoming increasingly important. Traditional business hierarchies gave managers and workers a sense of their own position and what was expected of them. Now, as these hierarchies break down, it is leaders themselves who must fill the void, helping subordinates to understand their place and purpose. Personal leadership is beginning to replace organisational structure.[47]

> *What sets great leaders apart is their ability to engage those around them in a shared vision of the future. By making the right decisions, they demonstrate their commitment to turning that vision into reality; and by doing so successfully, they instil in others the confidence to trust in their leadership.*
>
> Sir Bryan Nicholson[48]

The inspirational gap

According to a survey by the Chartered Management Institute, the power to inspire is rated highest among desirable leadership qualities. A detailed survey of almost 1500 practising managers in a broad cross-section of organisations found that the key characteristic that leaders should ideally possess, inspiration, was identified by 55 per cent of managers. However, most leaders appeared to lack this characteristic, with only 11 per cent of respondents saying they experienced this in reality.[49]

The survey from the Chartered Management Institute highlighted a significant 'inspirational gap' in leadership across UK organisations. The Department of Trade and Industry undertook a research project to explore how to start closing this critical leadership inspiration gap.[50] 'It is now accepted that for the UK to maintain its competitiveness there is a growing need for companies to adopt strategies that will enable a greater level of innovation and the provision of higher value and services.' The report is based on a study of 568 followers at different management levels working in a wide variety of organisations. It confirms that today's workforce is more diverse, informed and sophisticated than ever before. Ultimately people are still looking for something different and better in organisational leadership.

Key conclusions of the report include:

- For the past 30 years there have been increasing amounts of data to suggest that leadership has a lot more to do with inspiration and vision than with straightforward technical competence. Leadership is now recognised as a transferable skill, it can be developed by continued learning and development throughout a person's career.
- Managers demand visionary leaders who win not only results but also the trust and respect of their teams. It is the relationship between people that results in action.

Figure 10.8 Concept map of leadership and management

LEADERSHIP AND MANAGEMENT

- MANAGEMENT → Leadership by function
- LEADERSHIP → Leadership by personality

Managers have to ensure their subordinates collectively or separately reach their goals → MANAGERS have the authority to direct work and behaviour

LEADERS have influence through example, persuading, motivating, teaching → Leadership may be situationally governed – arising due to a set of circumstances Some managers are more suitable to operate in one set of situations than others

LEADERSHIP
– the ability to ensure subordinates perform their tasks and duties up to the standards required, by inspiration or inducement

Leaders cannot achieve the goals by themselves
Subordinates require direction to obtain the goals

Therefore co-operation or coercion required → Charisma ↔ Technocrat
– Leaders are those individuals who are perceived most frequently to perform those roles and functions which initiate or control behaviour of others towards the achievement of group goals or sub goals (Gibb)

No single trait or group of characteristics has been isolated which sets off the leader from members of groups (Jenkins)

FOUR VARIABLES
1 Characteristics/traits of the leader
2 Attitudes of the folllowers
3 Organisation purpose, technology, ethos, values, structure
4 Social economic and political milieu (McGregor) between countries between cultures

- Group tasks usually complex
- Organisations require stability not continuous change in leader
- Situational Theory Leadership is specific to the situation under investigation, i.e. a leader emerges in response to the problem or challenge
- Personnel with highly technical skills possessing wide sapiential (knowledge) gives authority/ leadership

LEADERSHIP TRAITS
- Intelligence
- Self Confidence
- Initiative talking
- Empathy
- Self-awareness
- Objectivity (human relationships)

THE ESSENTIALS OF LEADERSHIP
– Social skills
– Ability to communicate
– Flexibility/judgement as to which management style to adopt

ACTION-CENTRED LEADERSHIP (ADAIR)

INDIVIDUAL NEEDS
– Concern for the individual
- fairness and consistency in disciplinary matters
- help with training, career prospects with ... preparation for retirement recognition of performance
- good or adequate with ...
- commendation or helpful criticism

– Job enrichment
– Giving status

Group Needs / Individual Needs / Task Needs

GROUP NEEDS
Defence of the group needs
– laterally and vertically
Building up teamwork, recognising informal groups
Protection of interests which may lead to disruption e.g. relocation to another site; uneven work loads; accomodation; pay differentials

TASK NEEDS
Task definition
Planning
Allocating work and resources
Controlling quality, pace of work
Monitoring
Amending the plans
Co-ordinating with other groups
Obtaining resources required

Use of authority by manager / Area of freedom by subordinate

tell	sell	consult	share	delegate	abdicate	
1	2	3	4	5	6	7

1 Tell them
2 Tell them and sell it to them
3 Tell them and talk about it
4 Tentative decision and talk
5 Problem – talk and manager decides
6 Manager gives limits; all discuss, group decides
7 Manager gives limits; group discusses and decides

- Organisational leadership
- Personal leadership ... contribution by the individual in the post showing – charisma/energy/vision

Authoritarian ↔ Democratic

KINDS OF LEADERSHIP
Formal
– appointed in the hierarchy by the management
Informal
– exercises influence but is not in formal position; can initiate or block actions; can be in conflict with the formal leader; can set the group norms

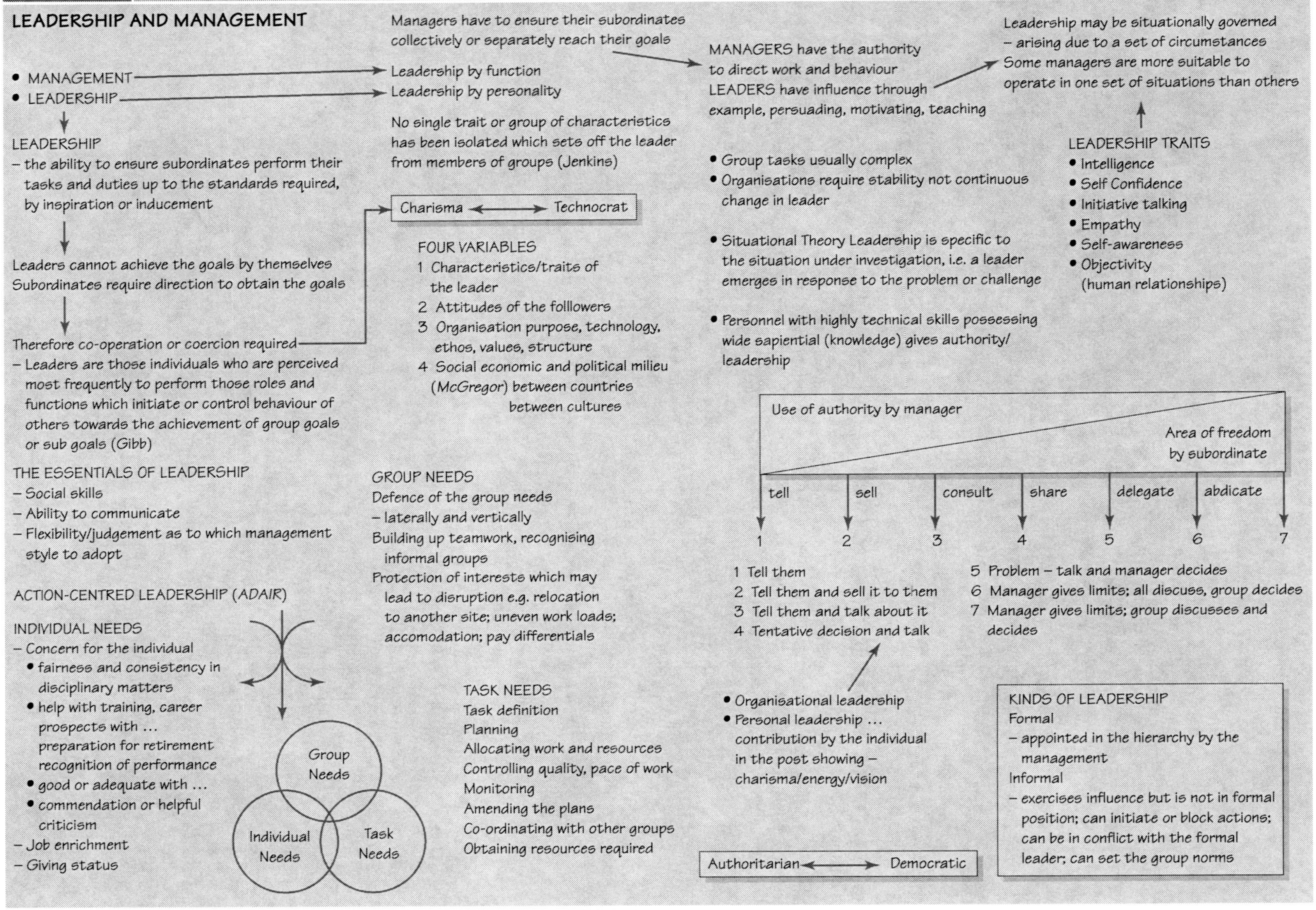

Source: Training Learning Consultancy Ltd., Bristol, England. Reproduced with permission.

- In order to keep followers motivated and committed in an era of unrelenting change, leaders must be able to create organisation cultures that foster not only performance but also a sense of pride and fun.

Critical reflection

There is a great deal of support today for the idea that effective leaders need to demonstrate the qualities of commitment and vision, and to inspire loyal followers to higher levels of performance. However, it is also clear that identifying the profile of such leaders, and defining their distinctive characteristics and skills, is still subject to uncertainty and debate. So do you think we are any further forward in establishing what makes a good leader?

A summary of leadership and management is set out in the concept map in Figure 10.8.

LEADERSHIP AND INNOVATION

A 2005 report by the Advanced Institute of Management Research in co-operation with the Chartered Management Institute draws attention to the impact of leadership on innovation.[51] The report refers to the dual role of leaders, first as motivators, inspiring people to transcend the ordinary, and second as architects, designing an organisational environment that enables employees to be innovative. 'The impact of leadership on innovation goes well beyond the motivating effect of the inspirational or charismatic leader. Leaders also affect innovation through organisational design and must create appropriate organisational environments to suit the different innovation processes.' The primary challenges for organisational leaders in promoting innovation are to:

- recognise and develop appropriate leadership for the different stages of the innovation process; and
- create organisational contexts that support complete innovation processes of different degrees of novelty.

Conceptual framework

The report distinguishes between leaders who primarily motivate through transformational actions – a 'motivational' perspective – and those take a more transactional approach and emphasise the co-ordination of organisational tasks – a 'structuralist' perspective. In order to address the question of how leadership affects innovation within organisations, the report proposes a conceptual framework that reflects the complex interaction among leadership, the organisational context and innovation (Figure 10. 9).

There is, however, a need for being mindful that leadership:

- can manifest itself at all levels in the organisation, not just the top;
- need not be concentrated in the person of a single leader but may act through distributed leadership systems; and
- sets the organisational context for followers' activities both through motivation and the administrative co-ordination of systems that support innovation.

Figure 10.9 The 'leadership for innovation' conceptual framework

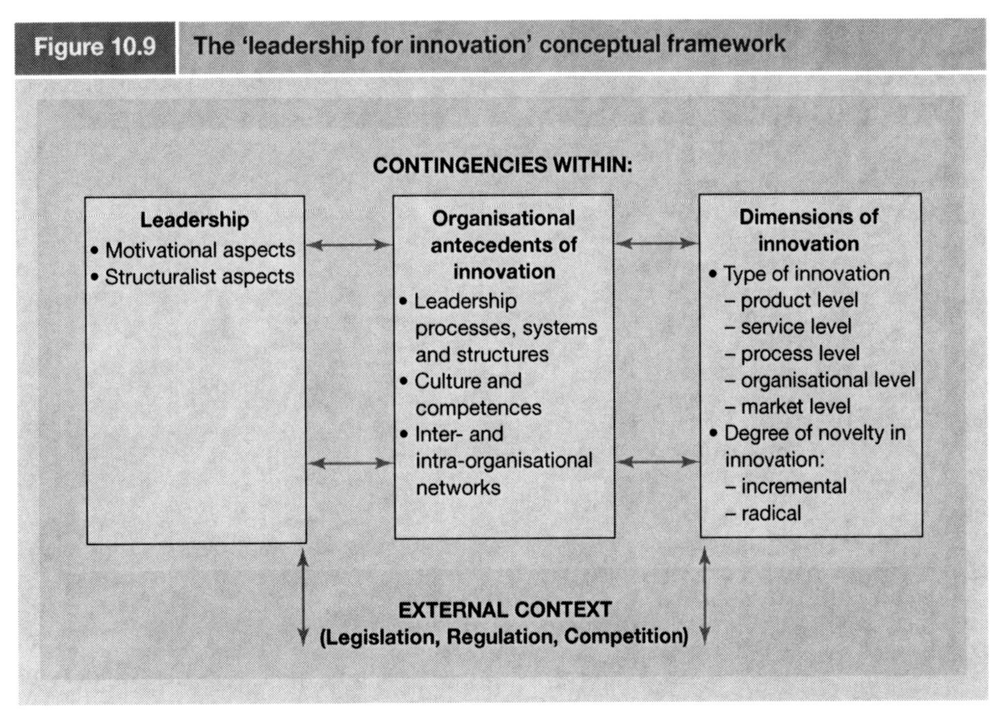

Source: From Munshi, N. *et al.*, *Leadership for Innovation: The Impact of Leadership on Innovation*, Advanced Institute of Management Research (AIM) (2005), Figure 5, p.18. Reproduced with permission from the Advanced Institute of Management Research.

THE LEADERSHIP RELATIONSHIP

Whatever the perceived approach to leadership, the most important point is the nature of the leadership relationship and the manner in which the leader influences the behaviour and actions of other people.

Leadership is a dynamic form of behaviour and there are a number of variables that affect the leadership relationship. Four major variables are identified by *McGregor* as:

- the characteristics of the leader;
- the attitude, needs and other personal characteristics of the followers;
- the nature of the organisation, such as its purpose, its structure, the tasks to be performed; and
- the social, economic and political environment.

McGregor concludes that 'leadership is not a property of the individual, but a complex relationship among these variables'.[52]

According to *Kouzes and Posner*, 'credibility is the foundation of leadership'. From extensive research in over 30 countries and response to the question of what people 'look for and admire in a leader, in a person whose direction they would willingly follow', people have consistently replied that they want:

> *leaders who exemplify four qualities: they want them to be honest, forward-looking, inspiring and competent. In our research our respondents strongly agree that they want leaders with integrity and trustworthiness, with vision and a sense of direction, with enthusiasm and passion, and with expertise and a track record for getting things done.*[53]

Fullan refers to the importance of relationship building as a basic component of the change process and effective leadership: 'Leaders must be consummate relationship builders with diverse people and groups – especially with people different from themselves. Effective leaders constantly foster purposeful interaction and problem solving, and are wary of easy consensus.'[54]

Power and leadership influence

Within an organisation, leadership influence will be dependent upon the type of power that the leader can exercise over the followers. The exercise of power is a social process which helps to explain how different people can influence the behaviour/actions of others. Five main sources of power upon which the influence of the leader is based have been identified by *French and Raven* as reward power, coercive power, legitimate power, referent power and expert power.[55] We shall consider these in terms of the manager (as a leader) and subordinate relationship.

- **Reward power** is based on the subordinate's *perception* that the leader has the ability and resources to obtain rewards for those who comply with directives; for example, pay, promotion, praise, recognition, increased responsibilities, allocation and arrangement of work, granting of privileges.
- **Coercive power** is based on fear and the subordinate's *perception* that the leader has the ability to punish or to bring about undesirable outcomes for those who do not comply with directives; for example, withholding pay rises, promotion or privileges; allocation of undesirable duties or responsibilities; withdrawal of friendship or support; formal reprimands or possibly dismissal. This is in effect the opposite of reward power.
- **Legitimate power** is based on the subordinate's *perception* that the leader has a right to exercise influence because of the leader's role or position in the organisation. Legitimate power is based on authority, for example that of managers and supervisors within the hierarchical structure of an organisation. Legitimate power is therefore 'position' power because it is based on the role of the leader in the organisation, and not on the nature of the personal relationship with others.
- **Referent power** is based on the subordinate's *identification* with the leader. The leader exercises influence because of perceived attractiveness, personal characteristics, reputation or what is called 'charisma'. For example, a particular manager may not be in a position to reward or punish certain subordinates, but may still exercise power over the subordinates because the manager commands their respect or esteem.
- **Expert power** is based on the subordinate's *perception* of the leader as someone who is competent and who has some special knowledge or expertise in a given area. Expert power is based on credibility and clear evidence of knowledge or expertise; for example, the expert knowledge of 'functional' specialists such as the personnel manager, management accountant or systems analyst. The expert power is usually limited to narrow, well-defined areas or specialisms.

Finlay suggests that in addition to the five sources of power identified by French and Raven can be added:

- personal power, supported and trusted by their colleagues and subordinates; and
- connection power, which results from personal and professional access to key people and information.[56]

Subordinates' perception of influence

It is important to note that these sources of power are based on the subordinate's *perception* of the influence of the leader, whether it is real or not. For example, if a leader has the ability to control rewards and punishments but subordinates *do not believe this*, then in effect the leader has no reward or coercive power. Similarly, if subordinates in a line department *believe* a manager in a (different) staff department has executive authority over them then even if, *de facto*, that manager has no such authority there is still a *perceived* legitimate power.

French and Raven point out that the five sources of power are interrelated and the use of one type of power (for example, coercive) may affect the ability to use another type of power (for example, referent). Furthermore, the same person may exercise different types of power, in particular circumstances and at different times.

> *You have to look at leadership through the eyes of the followers and you have to live the message. What I have learned is that people become motivated when you guide them to the source of their own power and when you make heroes out of employees who personify what you want to see in the organisation.*
>
> Anita Roddick[57]

NO ONE BEST FORM OF LEADERSHIP

We have seen that there are many alternative forms and styles of managerial leadership. Within an organisation different individuals may fulfil the functions of leadership and there are many different styles of leadership. A potential danger with the contingency approach is that the manager may appear to lack consistency in leadership style. However, although subordinates may reasonably expect some degree of consistency from the manager in approaching the same type of problem with the same style, this is not to say that different types of problems should be approached in the same manner. Subordinates would ordinarily expect a different style of managerial leadership according to the contingencies of the situation.

The right leader for the right situation

As *Rajan* also points out: 'Of course, different leadership styles are needed to cope with different situations: for example, the autocratic style makes sense when an organisation is in deep trouble and needs to achieve a rapid turn-around. That style would be counter-productive when the organisation is in a growth situation.'[58] And *Stern* maintains that although in more carefree times business gurus exalted leaders who admitted to frailty, not any more. The task of sustaining growth in a sluggish market calls for driven, leather-skinned bosses. Instead of touchy-feely management the quality of 'mental toughness' is needed to help elite performers to prevail.[59]

Different styles at different stages of a business

Different types of leadership may also be most appropriate at different stages in the development of a business organisation. Leadership can also vary between public and private sectors and depend upon the size of the organisation. According to the DTI, a primary challenge for organisational leaders in promoting innovation is:

> *Recognise and develop appropriate leadership for the different stages of the innovation process. How leaders are selected, supported, evaluated, motivated and developed is likely to differ depending upon the stage of the innovation process they are responsible for. For instance, transformational leadership skills may be more useful in early-stage innovation activity, such as R & D and product development, but transactional leadership skills are also essential to the smooth functioning of commercialisation.*[60]

National cultural dimensions

Another major variable influencing choice of leadership style may be national culture. *McGregor* concluded that the social, economic and political environment affected the leadership relationship, together with the attitudes and needs of 'followers'.[61] *Tannenbaum and Schmidt* identify leaders' own value systems as factors that influence their chosen style. They also highlight subordinates' – or non-managers' – needs for independence and tolerance of ambiguity as relevant variables in the choice of style.[62] These factors vary according to the cultural context in which the leadership relationship takes place. One should be wary of stereotyping the behaviour of leaders or subordinates, and many myths appear to have grown around notions of 'orderly' German, 'undisciplined' Italian and even 'obstructive' British workers. However, there are reasons to suggest that there may indeed be national cultural differences that are relevant to an understanding of leadership.

Refresh your understanding
Activity 10D
www.pearsoned.co.uk/mullins

Culture as a contingent factor in leadership?

The contribution of contingency approaches to understanding leadership suggest that contrasting types and styles of leadership may be more or less appropriate in different situations. *Tayeb* draws attention to cross-cultural leadership and points out that in a global business landscape, national culture affects leadership styles and behaviours. It is clear that people living in different parts of the world have different expectations from those in a leadership position. The way in which employees perceive their leaders, as employee-oriented or task-oriented, appears to vary from culture to culture.[63]

LEADERSHIP EFFECTIVENESS

Research undertaken by the consulting firm Hay/McBer, as reported by Goleman, has studied which precise leadership behaviours yield positive results. The research drew on a sample of 3871 executives worldwide and identified six, well-known different styles of leadership, each springing from different components of emotional intelligence:

- coercive leaders – who demand immediate compliance;
- authoritative leaders – who mobilise people towards a vision;
- affiliative leaders – who create emotional bonds and harmony;
- democratic leaders – who build consensus through participation;
- pacesetting leaders – who expect excellence and self-direction;
- coaching leaders – who develop people for the future.

However, only four of these leadership styles had a positive effect. The coercive style demanded immediate compliance, lacked flexibility and motivation, and was the least effective style. The pacesetting style set high standards of performance but led to a drop in morale and had a largely negative impact.

Reliance on more than one style

Goleman reports that the most effective executives use a collection of distinct leadership styles, each in the right measure, at just the right time. Although the authoritative style of leadership can be occasionally overbearing, it was found to be most effective and can motivate and inspire commitment to the goals of the organisation. The affiliative style has potential to create harmony within teams and can be used in conjunction with the authoritative style. The democratic approach was seen as positive, and encourages input from staff and helps build consensus through participation. The coaching style, although the least frequently used, can help staff identify their strengths and encourage long-term development goals. The study concludes that the most effective leaders rely on more than one leadership style, and were able to master a mixture of authoritative, democratic, affiliative and coaching styles. Leaders with the best results use most of the styles in a given week – seamlessly and in different measure – depending on the business situation.[64]

Variables affecting leadership effectiveness

Clearly, there is no one 'best' form of leadership that will result in the maintenance of morale among group members and high work performance. Three main aspects to be considered in determining the most appropriate style of leadership are: the manager, the group and the work environment.

However, there are many variables that underlie the effectiveness of leadership in work organisations. More specifically, these include the following:

- the characteristics of the manager, personality, attitudes, abilities, value system, and the personal credibility of the manager;
- the type of power of the manager and the basis of the leadership relationship;

- the characteristics of the followers: diversity, their needs and expectations, attitudes, knowledge, confidence and experience, and their motivation and commitment;
- the relationship between the manager and the group, and among members of the group;
- the type and nature of the organisation, organisation culture, and different stages in innovation and development;
- the nature of the tasks to be achieved, the extent to which structured or routine;
- the technology, systems of communication and methods of work organisation;
- organisation structure and systems of management;
- the type of problem and the nature of the manager's decisions;
- the nature and influence of the external environment;
- the social structure and informal organisation, and the psychological contract;
- the influence of national culture.

The shadow of leadership

McCabe suggests that leaders who want to transform their performance and the effectiveness of the team should look at how their own shadow could be getting in the way. Leaders focus on what they see as important and they are typically quite unconscious of the unintended but massive impact they are having on their colleagues, teams and clients. All leaders cast a shadow and whatever a particular leadership style, the shadow will affect others and can compromise people's engagement at work and business effectiveness. Leaders need to be fully aware of the shadow they cast and the impact they have on others.

> *To be successful, leaders today have to find ways to engage people's ideas, energy and inspiration and this means they will have to build much stronger relationships – and what will prevent such relationships from occurring is their shadow.*[65]

Leadership attributes

Valenti suggests that by whatever means a person attains a leadership position, there are five essential qualities that he or she must possess to be a successful leader over time. A leader must have:

- **courage** – to do what is right and to overcome obstacles;
- **confidence** – the unshakeable belief in yourself to make happen what you want to happen;
- **concentration** – persistence and the unwillingness to quit, and focus to stay on track;
- **passion** – for what they do and what they believe in with enthusiasm and commitment;
- **values** – a strong sense of enduring standards of behaviour.[66]

The DTI found that the three most frequently identified leadership attributes are vision (79 per cent), trust (77 per cent), and respect (73 per cent). However, less than four in ten followers see these behaviours demonstrated within their own company.[67]

LEADERSHIP DEVELOPMENT

Education and training in management needs to emphasise not only interpersonal skills but also a flexibility of approach, diagnostic ability and the realisation that the most effective form of leadership behaviour is a product of the total leadership situation.

According to Investors in People, leadership development is not just a corporate issue: 'The ability to create and communicate a clear vision, and motivate people to deliver it, is as important to the small entrepreneur as to the leader of 1000 people. All organisations should be identifying the managers they will need in a few years' time and developing them. All top managers should be planning their succession and supporting the people who will step into their shoes when it's time to move on.'[68] (The Investors in People 'Leadership and Management Model' is discussed in Chapter 20.)

Leadership development in the public sector

Extensive research undertaken by the Chartered Management Institute reveals that consistently poor ratings accorded to public sector leaders is a key cause for concern during a period of major reform. The survey of 1900 public sector managers, mostly at middle and junior level, reveals that only 33 per cent of managers rate the leadership demonstrated by their most senior management team as high quality. Although a wide and varied range of training activities is taking place, the majority of managers perceive a low priority placed on leadership development. Only a quarter of respondents claimed their organisational budget for developing leaders is adequate and organisations are still tending to rely on traditional and formalised methods of developing their leaders.[69]

Seven principles for developing leaders

Referring to his action-centred leadership model (discussed earlier in this chapter), *Adair* identifies seven key principles of leadership development that can be applied successfully in different kinds of organisations in both the public and private sectors.

1 **Development of a strategy for leadership development** for each of the three levels of leadership – operational, strategic and team.
2 **Selection** of those with high potential for becoming effective leaders.
3 **Training for leadership** that implies instruction with a specific end in view. Identify your business training needs in the leadership context and assign them priorities.
4 **Career development** through giving a person the right job at the right time. People grow as leaders through the actual practice of leading.
5 **Line managers as leadership developers** by developing the individual's potential and sharing their knowledge of leadership.
6 **Corporate culture** that is valued at all levels and should encourage a climate of self-development in leadership.
7 **The chief executive** who should be leading from the front and who owns the problem of growing leaders.

The seven principles are complementary and are likely to have a synergetic effect if applied as a whole. Although a simple framework, Adair maintains the seven principles form the first coherent and effective approach for growing leaders.[70]

The leadership jigsaw

The DTI report referred to previously found that around a third of employees surveyed had never worked for, or been motivated by, an exceptional leader. In order that aspiring leaders can find out if they have the necessary skills, *Cutler* has designed a 'jigsaw' of best practice. There are six interlinking pieces: vision, example, relationships, motivation, empowerment and communications as a guide to the measurement and development of leadership skills. Cutler believes that leadership is not such a difficult role if condensed to these essential elements and has devised a set of questions to help aspiring leaders to find out if they have all the necessary pieces of the jigsaw (*see* Figure 10.10).[71]

LEADERS OF THE FUTURE

Gratton points out that while we are part of organisations shaped by technology that created the patents, ideas and innovations that brought success, the past will not bring sustainable competitive advantage for the future. To do this we have to build the potential of people in our organisations, the knowledge they bring and their commitment and enthusiasm.

Figure 10.10 The leadership 'jigsaw'

VISION – Do you:
1 Work hard at communicating your vision for the organisation to all staff at all levels?
2 Understand that your vision must appeal to your staff at both an emotional and practical level if they are to join you on your journey?
3 Understand the culture and values of your organisation and their impact on its future development?
4 Recognise blind alleys!

MOTIVATION – Do you:
1 Understand that every member has a different set of motivational stimuli?
2 Explain your decisions in terms of their benefit to the organisation and its members?
3 Celebrate and reward individual and team achievements?
4 Prefer to offer carrots, rather than weird sticks!

EXAMPLE – Do you:
1 Match your words with your actions?
2 Take full responsibility for organisational problems, even if you were not directly responsible?
3 Occasionally muck in when your staff are under pressure at work?
4 Regularly consider what you see in the bathroom mirror!

EMPOWERMENT – Do you:
1 Believe that people generally respond well when given greater responsibility for their own performance?
2 Allocate sufficient resources to training and development?
3 Get a buzz when staff set and achieve their own goals?
4 Realise that the organisation would still function if you were not there!

RELATIONSHIPS – Do you:
1 Work hard at countering a them and u s' culture within your organisation?
2 Set clear codes of acceptable conduct and take action against breaches of them?
3 Stress that everyone contributes to the success of the team(s) they belong to?
4 Admit when you make a mistake!

COMMUNICATIONS – Do you:
1 Use your influence to encourage two-way communications at all levels in your organisation?
2 Encourage personal contact rather than written, mechanical or technological alternatives?
3 Encourage a diversity of opinion and constructive criticism?
4 Walk the talk!

Source: Adapted from Cutler, A., 'A good fit is essential', *Professional Manager*, vol. 15, no. 3, May 2005, p. 38. Reproduced with permission from Chartered Management Institute and the author.

Building human potential demands a new agenda, a new set of challenges for leaders and a redefined set of managerial capabilities. This new agenda creates a set of expectations of the leaders. Gratton sets out four expectations as the message for leaders.

- **Expectation 1: dream collectively** – create a time and a process for you and your colleagues to dream about the future; create enthusiasm and excitement and a vision for the future; view the present as a pathway to the future; allow people to work independently but within the frame of the general direction; and work to identify and co-ordinate the major themes for action.
- **Expectation 2: balance the short term with the longer term** – think in the past, the present and the future; be aware of the human scale of change and create plans of action that reflect human time scales and a capacity in human potential; build a vision for the future that engages people and allows them to understand their future role.
- **Expectation 3: build an organisation that values people** – treat people with respect and have their ideas taken seriously and allow them to believe they can make a difference; be aware of the need to create communication channels with employees; demonstrate a commitment to people; treat people with politeness, respect and dignity and create a strong role model for others to follow.

- **Expectation 4: understand the reality of the organisation** – create a deep, shared understanding of the current state of the business, and examine the metaphor of the organisation; put the building of a highly committed workforce at the centre of strategy; build a model of your organisation around high levels of trust, commitment and inspiration; develop an understanding of process fairness and justice, and understand employees' perceptions of integrity, consistency and pride.[72]

Leaders as architects of collectives

According to *Hill*, world-class companies in the 21st century will be ever-evolving collectives of talented, passionate and diverse individuals. Leaders will be the architects of these collectives. With more companies having access to the same technology, markets, production method and channels of distribution, the competitive element has fundamentally changed. The strategic management of talent has become the key to competitive advantage. Leadership is about providing the moral and strategic vision that defines the collective's identity and binds the individuals together. A significant portion of leaders' time will be spent on locating, assessing, attracting and, when necessary, developing the needed talent. Once leaders have clarified the vision and collected the talent, they have to execute the vision. This entails shaping the collective, the culture, processes and the structure.[73]

New skills and competencies

Bennis hails the arrival of new leadership and suggests that 'the leaders of the future will have to cast off the heavy burden of command and control, hierarchically based leadership'. Leaders will have to learn an entirely new set of skills and that four competencies will determine the success of new leadership.

1 **The new leader understands and practises the power of appreciation** – as a generalisation most organisations are woefully neglectful of bestowing acknowledgement or appreciation, yet it is one of the most powerful motivators, especially for knowledge workers.
2 **The new leader keeps reminding people of what is important** – organisations drift into entropy and bureaucratisation of imagination when they forget what's important. Reminding people of what is important can give meaning and value to work, and collective focused energy.
3 **The new leader generates and sustains trust** – the terms of the new social contract of work have changed and no one can depend on lifelong loyalty or commitment to any organisation. Trust has powerful connotations and the ingredients are a combination of competencies, constancy, caring, fairness, candour and, most of all, authenticity.
4 **The new leader and the led are intimate allies** – new leadership is all about great leaders being made by great groups and by organisations that create the social architecture of respect and dignity, and great leadership brings that about. Without each other, the leader and the led are culturally impoverished.

The post-bureaucratic organization requires a new kind of alliance between leaders and the led. Today's organizations are evolving into federations, networks, clusters, cross-functional teams, temporary systems, ad hoc task forces, lattices, modules, matrices – almost anything but pyramids with their obsolete top–down leadership. The new leader will encourage healthy dissent and value those followers courageous enough to say no. It will go to the leader who exults in cultural differences and knows that diversity is the best hope for long-term survival and success. This does not mark the end of leadership. Rather the need for a new, far more subtle and indirect form of influence for leaders to be effective.[74]

Refresh your understanding
Activity 10E
www.pearsoned.co.uk/mullins

Critical reflection

Despite the vast amount of writing on the subject by both academics and practising managers, it is extremely difficult to give a precise and agreed definition of leadership. Do you find this confusing and a hindrance to your studies? Nor is there agreement on one best model or style of leadership, or how leadership potential can best be developed. What do you believe are the essential characteristics that make for an effective leader?

MANAGEMENT IN THE NEWS

Learning to lead

Leadership: ways to instil those elusive qualities

Richard Donkin

Leadership studies have become a multi-million-pound earner for business schools and consultants on both sides of the Atlantic, as companies clamour to imbue their executives with the qualities needed to create, transform and sustain successful businesses. Underpinning this 'market' are scores of leadership books, all adding a particular view or facet to the genre. Leadership is the number one topic in the *Harvard Business Review* and few large companies have neglected to develop their own leadership or talent management programmes.

Like art, leadership tends to defy attempts at framing precise definitions. Warren Bennis, the world's leading exponent of leadership theory, has described it as 'the capacity to create a compelling vision and translate it into action and sustain it'. But, also like art, leadership is subject to competing influences and popular movements that are constantly changing the way it is perceived.

Harvard-based Ronald Heifetz, one of the most influential of the modern generation of theorists, says leadership is about 'mobilising people to make progress on the hardest of problems'. Debate still rages on the extent to which leadership must be a quality not only of a recognised leader but of managers and other employees throughout a business. The vast majority of leadership programmes, however, are designed to prepare people for senior positions at the head of organisations, divisions or departments in roles that have become invested with authority.

One of the biggest challenges facing companies is preparing people for leadership positions who may have excelled in their specialist role but have little experience of managing or leading. Here, some of the latest thinking is directed not at creating leadership positions but towards investing specialists with influencing and interventionist behaviours that equip them to lead without designated authority.

'New research we have undertaken among clients points to an identified need for more of the so-called soft skills of leadership such as emotional intelligence, rather than concerns with position and function,' says Kim Lafferty, country director, UK and Ireland, at the Center for Creative Leadership (Europe). 'Interdependent decision-making is coming to be valued more than independent decision making and companies are becoming far more interested in collaboration than used to be the case,' she says.

While some leadership issues may be universal, there is also a growing recognition among business schools that companies may have specific leadership issues. Some companies, including IBM in a recent exercise, seek to identify leadership competencies based on traits, behaviours and skills identified in high performers. Future leaders are then selected or developed against the competency base.

According to Prof Heifetz, most students of leadership turn up to class with a list of what he calls 'technical problems' that have ready solutions. His task, he believes, is to confront his classes less with issues of power, persuasion and personality – what might be classed as traditional concerns of leadership – and more with their capacity to deal with competing values, changing attitudes and new learning.

'We used to talk about the 'knowing–doing' gap. Now we are talking about the 'knowing–being' gap,' says Ms Lafferty. 'It's a subtle difference but it makes

Management in the news – continued

leadership something more inclusive than exclusive and that's important.'

Discussion questions

1. What different skills do you think might be necessary for organisational leaders who hold positions of authority, and those who do not? How far do the requirements overlap?
2. Review and discuss the implications of this trend away from leadership on the basis of designated authority for both the design and structure of organisations, and the selection and training of managers.

SYNOPSIS

- There are many ways of looking at leadership and many interpretations of its meaning, but essentially it is a relationship through which one person influences the behaviour or actions of other people. The leader–follower relationship is reciprocal and effective leadership is a two-way process. Leadership is related to motivation, the process of communication, the activities of groups and the process of empowerment. The changing nature of business organisations has placed increasing importance on leadership.

- There is a close relationship between leadership and management, especially in work organisations, and an increasing tendency to see them as synonymous. However, arguably there are differences between the two and it does not follow that every leader is a manager. Leadership may be viewed in more general terms, with emphasis on interpersonal behaviour in a broader context.

- Due to its complex nature there are many alternative ways of analysing leadership. Leadership may be examined in terms of the qualities or traits approach, in terms of the functional or group approach, as a behavioural category, in terms of styles of leadership, through the situational approach and contingency models, and in terms of the distinction between transactional or transformational leadership.

- Contingency theories draw attention to the interactions between the variables involved in a leadership situation and patterns of leadership behaviour. The most appropriate form of leadership is dependent upon the variables in a particular leadership situation. Different contingency theories have concentrated on different situational variables. These include favourability of the leadership situation, decision acceptance and decision quality, path–goal theory, and the 'readiness' of followers.

- The attention given to transformational leadership and the importance of charisma has given rise to an increasing focus on the concept of leaders creating a vision with which others can identify and inspiring followers to improve organisational performance. There is, however, doubt about the extent to which leaders possess these personal qualities. Attention is also given to the impact of leadership on innovation and to the dual role of leaders as both motivators and organisational architects.

- Leadership is a dynamic form of behaviour and the leader's influence is dependent upon the type of power exercised over other people. However, there is no one best form or style of leadership. There are many variables that underlie the effectiveness of leadership, including dimensions of national culture. The most successful form of leadership behaviour is a product of the total leadership situation. Attention needs to be given to leadership development. Leaders of the future will face new expectations and will need to learn new sets of skills.

Refresh your understanding, assess your progress and begin your research with online resources at **www.pearsoned.co.uk/mullins**

REVIEW AND DISCUSSION QUESTIONS

1 Explain clearly what you understand by the meaning of leadership. How would you distinguish leadership from management?

2 Distinguish between different approaches to the study of leadership and discuss critically what you see as the relevance today of each of these approaches.

3 Using the Tannenbaum and Schmidt continuum, identify, with reasons, your preferred style of leadership. Give an example of a situation in which you might need to adopt an alternative style of leadership.

4 What do you understand by leader–situation models of leadership? Assess the practical value to the manager of: (i) Fiedler's contingency model of leadership effectiveness, and (ii) Hersey and Blanchard's model of situational leadership.

5 Discuss the main sources of power and leadership influence. Give a practical example of each of these main sources of power and influence within your own organisation.

6 Explain clearly the nature and main features of transformational leadership. Give your own examples of people you would regard as transformational leaders. Discuss critically the relevance of personal qualities or charisma for effective leadership.

7 Discuss the main situational variables that are likely to influence the most appropriate form of managerial leadership behaviour. Detail three work situations in which a different style of leadership is likely to be most effective.

8 If you were a consultant on leadership, what areas of needs would you include in designing a leadership development programme for managers in a large work organisation? Justify your ideas.

ASSIGNMENT 1

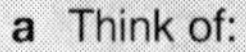

a Think of:
  (i) one of the 'best' leaders, *and*
  (ii) one of the 'worst' leaders that you have experienced, preferably in a work situation.

b Identify and list those specific qualities, or lack of them, which were characteristic of *each* leader. Where possible, draw up your list under three broad headings of:
  (i) personal attributes – for example, intelligence, appearance;
  (ii) social relationships – for example, approachability, interests;
  (iii) task performance – for example, delegation, discipline.

c Give a brief description of an actual situation that illustrates the behaviour/actions of *each* leader and the results of such behaviour/action. Keep your answer balanced. Try to be as objective as possible and avoid personal bias.

d Draw up your *own* list, with brief supporting descriptions, of the main characteristics you would expect to be exhibited by a successful leader. Be prepared to justify your lists and descriptions in class discussion.

ASSIGNMENT 2

Your leadership style

For each of the following ten pairs of statements, divide five points between the two according to your beliefs, perceptions of yourself, or according to which of the two statements characterises you better. The five points may be divided between the A and B statements in any way you wish with the constraint that only whole positive

Assignment – continued

integers may be used (i.e. you may not split 2.5 points equally between the two). Weigh your choices between the two according to the one that better characterises you or your beliefs.

1 A As leader I have a primary mission of maintaining stability. ______
B As leader I have a primary mission of change. ______

2 A As leader I must cause events. ______
B As leader I must facilitate events. ______

3 A I am concerned that my followers are rewarded equitably for their work. ______
B I am concerned about what my followers want in life. ______

4 A My preference is to think long range: What might be. ______
B My preference is to think short range: What is realistic. ______

5 A As a leader I spend considerable energy in managing separate but related goals. ______
B As a leader I spend considerable energy in arousing hopes, expectations, and aspiration among my followers. ______

6 A While not in a formal classroom sense, I believe that a significant part of my leadership is that of a teacher. ______
B I believe that a significant part of my leadership is that of a facilitator. ______

7 A As leader I must engage with followers at an equal level of morality. ______
B As leader I must represent a higher morality. ______

8 A I enjoy stimulating followers to want to do more. ______
B I enjoy rewarding followers for a job well done. ______

9 A Leadership should be practical. ______
B Leadership should be inspirational. ______

10 A What power I have to influence others comes primarily from my ability to get people to identify with me and my ideas. ______
B What power I have to influence others comes primarily from my status and position. ______

Details of scoring and interpretation will be provided by your tutor.

Source: From Schermerhorn, J. R., Jr., *et al. Managing Organizational Behaviour*, Fourth Edition, John Wiley & Sons (1991), p. 484. Reproduced with permission from John Wiley & Sons Inc.

PERSONAL AWARENESS AND SKILLS EXERCISE

Evaluate your skills

Self-knowledge is crucial for evaluating achievements and potential. Below is a list of attributes associated with leadership. Read through these statements and evaluate the leadership skills demonstrated by your team and those that you display. Score yourself from one to ten for each attribute or put ticks or crosses in the boxes. Use this information to consider areas where you or your team could develop.

1 Demonstrating initiative, delivering operational excellence, implementing decisions and delivering results.

I reinforce people's determination to do the right thing. ☐

I have a strong work ethic. ☐

I do things right for the first time. ☐
I stay focused on priorities and recognise when to delegate tasks. ☐
I stretch myself to meet the values of others and myself simultaneously. ☐
I demonstrate values by tangible and visible actions. ☐
I choose service over self-interest. ☐
I act with integrity. ☐

2 Drawing groups together, enjoying team management and placing importance on the development of others.

I reward and recognise team members daily. ☐
I use analogy to simplify conceptual ideas. ☐
I connect and integrate values into the working operation of the organisation. ☐
I clarify future direction in terms that make sense. ☐
I reduce strategic plans to simple ideas which can be easily communicated. ☐
I communicate effectively with internal and external stakeholders. ☐
I target communication to the needs of the audience in pace, level and method of delivery. ☐
I break complex targets down into digestible pieces. ☐

3 Offering support, demonstrating active listening and encouraging others to achieve objectives.

I demonstrate trust in others to perform effectively. ☐
I recognise that leadership is a process of upward as well as downward influence. ☐
I inspire excitement with my communication style. ☐
I encourage hard-hitting debate and dialogue. ☐
I display stature and presence to gain commitment and loyalty. ☐
I put aside personal ambition for the sake of the whole. ☐
I take time to connect with each team member. ☐
I set clear goals and success criteria, allowing people to use their initiative. ☐

4 Demonstrating decisiveness, offering inspiration and eliciting respect by touching hearts, not just minds.

I take pride in winning as a team, not just individually. ☐
I foster the development of a common vision. ☐
I appear consistently enthusiastic and inspirational about the vision. ☐
I build the capacity of the next generation of leaders by investing in the team ☐
I hold myself accountable, without blaming others. ☐
I hold myself accountable with the clear understanding that ethical standards must never be comprised. ☐
I manage the ambiguity of leadership and power. ☐
I find a sense of continuity through others. ☐

Source: *The Path to Leadership: Developing a Sustainable Model within Organisations*, CBI (in association with Harvey Nash), September 2005. Reproduced with permission from CBI.

CASE STUDY

Being Apple: Steve Jobs

Steve Jobs is CEO of Apple and one of the world's best-known business leaders.

The many biographies of Jobs on the Internet agree on the basic details.[75] He was born in 1955 in California. In 1976, he and Steve Wozniak founded the Apple Computer Company. The next year saw the launch of the company's second computer – the Apple II – whose success established Apple as one of the main brands in the fledgling personal computer (PC) industry. Apple went public in 1980 and by 1983 Jobs was looking for an experienced corporate manager to oversee the company's continuing expansion – he hired John Sculley from Pepsi Cola. In 1984, Apple launched the Macintosh, whose innovative design was surely one of the key steps forward in the development of today's user-friendly PCs.[76]

In 1985, Jobs fell out with the Apple board and with Sculley and resigned from the company. He went on to found the computer company NeXT, whose workstation products were seen as innovative and influential, but which were too expensive for mass market success. By the early 1990s, NeXT was concentrating on software rather than hardware and Apple was experiencing significant financial problems as the PC market started to mature. In 1996, Apple bought NeXT and installed Jobs as interim CEO in 1997. Jobs was back and set about some radical surgery to improve Apple's profitability. The technology that arrived with the NeXT purchase allowed a new operating system to be developed and Jobs was closely associated with the development and launch of the brightly coloured and inspirational iMac in 1998.

The 'i' prefix was adopted by Apple for a series of further innovations as its renaissance under Jobs continued, including the launch in 2001 of the spectacularly successful iPod music player and the iTunes service to support it. This success has provided the company with a whole new set of strategic options in music and entertainment. Steve Jobs, however, is not someone to concentrate his efforts on a single industry. In 1986, he bought a computer graphics operation from Lucasfilm and renamed it Pixar, which became one of the leading players in computer animation. In partnership with Disney it produced a stream of immensely successful animation movies from *Toy Story* (1995) to *The Incredibles* (2004). In 2006, Disney and Pixar merged, leaving Jobs as a significant shareholder in Disney and a member of the Disney board.

Source: Empics/Associated Press

Where would they be without him? Apple's way of doing business has been strongly influenced by its charismatic founder Steve Jobs.

Cool entrepreneurship

At one level, Steve Jobs can be seen as one of the group of successful young men who made the information revolution happen over the last three decades. These new entrepreneurs did not fit the traditional model of the buttoned-down businessman – they were not always academically successful (like Michael Dell, Jobs dropped out of college), they dressed casually and thought unconventionally. While they may differ greatly in leadership style and manner, they share a dedicated, driven, even obsessive approach to work, coupled with a strong vision of the change they want to create. There has always, however, been something distinctive about the Apple way of doing things, resulting in the fierce loyalty that often inspires Apple users. As one commentator put it:

> *Lodged in the DNA of Silicon Valley, there is a rebel gene known as Apple Computer. Most of the other ingredients are the generally uniform, inoffensive elements you would expect to find in the soul of an engineer ... The Apple gene comes from an altogether different place. Its essence is one part design flair, two parts marketing hype. It carries elements of risk-taking and inventiveness. It is closely intertwined with the technical drive that pervades Silicon Valley and is the source of occasional startling originality, yet the technology is always subservient to something else. If Apple's genetic make-up stands apart, it owes much to Steve Jobs.*[77]

Evidence that Apple is centred on the personality of its leader is plentiful. Jobs supplies the inspiration and vision and is the company's face. When there is a key new product to launch, it is usually the CEO who reveals it to the world, having been personally involved in whatever it took to bring the product into being. As a recent report observed, his keynote speeches at Apple conferences are 'more like rock concerts than corporate events', with Jobs centre stage.[78]

What is it about Steve Jobs' leadership that commands such attention? He values pure creativity very highly, but in the thousands of words written about him on the Internet, adjectives such as 'tolerant' or 'easy going' do not feature very often. The words 'passionate, charming, inspirational, abrasive' are much more representative, with many expressing much stronger views.[79] Jobs seems to be someone who sets himself very high standards and then demands the same of everyone around him. This can lead to disappointment, frustration, anger and – on occasion – harsh treatment of those who are seen as having let him and the company down. Jobs provided an insight into this mentality in an interview in 1995 with the Smithsonian Institution:[80]

> *I always considered part of my job was to keep the quality level of people in the organisations I work with very high. That's what I consider one of the few things I actually can contribute individually … to instil in the organisation the goal of only having 'A' players … the difference between the worst taxi cab driver and the best taxi cab driver to get you crosstown Manhattan might be two to one. The best one will get you there in fifteen minutes, the worst one will get you there in a half an hour … In the field that I'm in the difference between the best person and the worst person is about a hundred to one or more. The difference between a good software person and a great software person is fifty to one ... Therefore, I have found, not just in software, but in everything I've done it really pays to go after the best people in the world. It's painful when you have some people who are not the best people in the world and you have to get rid of them; but I found that my job has sometimes exactly been that: to get rid of some people who didn't measure up and I've always tried to do it in a humane way. But nonetheless it has to be done and it is never fun.*

Although Jobs became and remained wealthy over most of his career, his motivation seems not to centre on money. His annual salary as Apple's CEO is famously set at $1. What drives him is innovation: he is famously the man who wants 'to put a ding in the universe'.[81] This means not purely technical innovation but the ability to imagine products that are revolutionary in their impact on everyday life. Design and marketing have been integral to the Apple appeal, resulting in some truly transformative (and very successful) products such as the Macintosh and the iPod, but also many that did not really connect commercially. This demanding agenda has had its costs, both for the company and for Jobs personally. Business strategy commentators sometimes observe that the real money is to be made by changing the way a business works, not by pure innovation.

> *Technical innovation will earn you lots of adoring fans (think Apple). Business-model innovation will earn you lots of money (think Dell)… If your cool new thing doesn't generate enough money to cover costs and make a profit, it isn't innovation. It's art.*[82]

If wealth is the scorecard, then Steve Jobs' position at 140 in the 2006 *Forbes* list of the world's richest people doesn't come close to Bill Gates at number one or Michael Dell at 15.[83] The overall impression, though, is that this is not the point for Jobs; changing the world is more important than building the biggest pile of money.

The succession problem

The comparison with Bill Gates leads to another issue that often crops up for organisations that are dominated by a strong and charismatic leader: that of succession. A business news article in 2005 pointed out that Microsoft had gone to some lengths to plan for Bill Gates' gradual retirement from the company.[84] Gates' role had been split into two, with a successor lined up within the company for each part. The pre-announced two-year transition was intended to reassure the markets about the future for a post-Gates Microsoft. At Apple, things weren't so clear. In August 2004, Jobs underwent surgery for a rare form of pancreatic cancer. He survived and was back at work after just one month, but his brush with mortality caused many to wonder about Apple's prospects without Jobs. This remains an important question for the company. A quote from venture capitalist Michael Moritz sums up Jobs' importance to Apple:

> *Steve is an utterly remarkable man – one of the most interesting, original and creative businessmen of the last 50 years. His achievements at both Apple and Pixar over the last ten years put paid to the doubters who say that no individual can change the course of a company or industry – let alone two companies or industries.*[85]

Apple has never done things in a conventional way and it may be that asking about succession planning is missing the point about the way the organisation is run. As a leader, Steve Jobs' charismatic and demanding presence has pervaded Apple and made it what it is today. Its products have had a significant impact on everyday life, even for those who have never chosen Apple, and the company seems to be set to deliver more surprises in the world of digital media.

Your tasks

1. How and to what extent does Steve Jobs' career illuminate the difference between management and leadership?
2. How can Steve Jobs' leadership style be analysed? To what extent does the evidence so far conform to the Burns model of transformational leadership?
3. Jobs' career has been in two industries that are characterised by rapid market change, fast technological development and considerable turbulence. Critically examine the extent to which these situational factors bear upon the leadership style that Jobs has shown over the years.

Notes and references

1. Crainer, S. 'Have the Corporate Superheroes had their Day?', *Professional Manager*, March 1995, pp. 8–12.
2. Useem, M. 'How to Groom Leaders of the Future', in Pickford, J. (ed.) *Financial Times Mastering Management 2.0*, Financial Times Prentice Hall (2001), p. 297.
3. CBI, 'The Path to Leadership: Developing a sustainable model within organisations', Caspian Publishing, September 2005, p. 4.
4. Havey-Jones, J. (Sir) in Mann, S. 'Top Guru', *Professional Manager*, September 2002, p. 17.
5. Levine, S. R. 'The Value-Based Edu-Leader', in Chowdhury, S. *Management 21C*, Financial Times Prentice Hall (2000), p. 90.
6. Judge, P. (Sir), 'Standard-bearer', *Professional Manager*, vol. 12, no. 1, January 2003, p. 19.
7. 'Leadership for Innovation', Advanced Institute of Management Research, 2005.
8. Fullan, M. *Leading in a Culture of Change*, Jossey-Bass (2001).
9. Charlesworth, K. Cook, P. and Crozier, G. *Leading Change in the Public Sector: Making the Difference*, Chartered Management Institute, May 2003.
10. Belbin, R.M. *Changing the Way We Work*, Butterworth-Heinemann (1997), p. 98.
11. Watson, C. M. 'Leadership, Management and the Seven Keys', *Business Horizons*, March–April 1983, pp. 8–13.
12. Zaleznik, A. 'Managers and Leaders: Are They Different?' *Harvard Business Review*, May–June 1977, pp. 67–78.
13. Fullan, M. *Leading in a Culture of Change*, Jossey-Bass (2001), p. 2.
14. Dearlove, D. 'Reinventing Leadership', in Crainer, S. and Dearlove, D. (eds) *Financial Times Handbook of Management*, Second edition, Financial Times Prentice Hall (2001), p. 538.
15. '*The Leadership and Management Model*', Investors in People UK, 2003.
16. Moorcroft, R. 'To lead or to manage? That is the question'. *Manager, The British Journal of Administrative Management*, November 2005, p. 4.
17. Drucker, P. F. *The Practice of Management*, Heinemann Professional (1989), p. 156.
18. See for example Bryman, A. 'Leadership in Organisations' in Clegg, S. Hardy, C. and Nord, W. (eds), *Managing Organsations: Current Issues*, Sage (1999), pp. 26–62.
19. Kotter, J. P. 'What Leaders Really Do', *Harvard Business Review*, May–June 1990, p. 103.
20. Whitehead, M. 'Everyone's a Leader Now', *Supply Management*, 25 April 2002, pp. 22–4.
21. Adair, J. *Action-Centred Leadership*, Gower (1979). See also: Adair, J. *The Skills of Leadership*, Gower (1984).
22. Fleishman, E. A. 'Leadership Climate, Human Relations Training and Supervisory Behavior', in Fleishman, E. A. and Bass, A. R. *Studies in Personnel and Industrial Psychology*, Third edition, Dorsey (1974).
23. Bryman, A. 'Leadership in Organisations', in Clegg, S. Hardy, C. and Nord, W. (eds), *Managing Organsations: Current Issues*, Sage (1999), pp. 26–62.
24. Likert, R. *New Patterns of Management*, McGraw-Hill (1961).
25. Tannenbaum, R. and Schmidt, W. H. 'How to Choose a Leadership Pattern', *Harvard Business Review*, May–June 1973, pp. 162–75, 178–80.
26. Fiedler, F.E. *A Theory of Leadership Effectiveness*, McGraw-Hill (1967).
27. See, for example: Yukl, G. *Leadership in Organizations*, Fifth edition, Prentice Hall (2002).
28. Vroom, V. H. and Yetton, P. W. *Leadership and Decision-Making*, University of Pittsburgh Press (1973).
29. Vroom, V. H. and Jago, A. G. *The New Leadership: Managing Participation in Organizations*, Prentice-Hall (1988).
30. House, R. J. 'A Path–Goal Theory of Leadership Effectiveness', *Administrative Science Quarterly*, vol. 16, September 1971, pp. 321–38.
31. House, R. J. and Dessler, G. 'The Path–Goal Theory of Leadership', in Hunt, J. G. and Larson, L. L. (eds) *Contingency Approaches to Leadership*, Southern Illinois University Press (1974).
32. Hersey, P. and Blanchard, K. H. *Management of Organizational Behavior: Utilizing Human Resources*, Sixth edition, Prentice-Hall (1993).
33. Burns, J. M. *Leadership*, Harper & Row (1978).
34. Bass, B. M. *Leadership and Performance Beyond Expectations*, Free Press (1985).
35. Bass, B. M. and Avolio, B. J. *Improving Organizational Performance Through Transformational Leadership*, Sage Publications (1994).
36. Yukl, G. *Leadership in Organizations*, Sixth edition, Pearson Prentice-Hall (2006).
37. Kreitner, R., Kinicki, A. and Buelens, M. *Organizational Behaviour*, First European edition, McGraw-Hill (1999), p. 487.

38 Conger, J. 'Charisma and How to Grow It', *Management Today*, December 1999, pp. 78–81.
39 Conger, J. 'Danger of Delusion. The qualities that make leaders great can also cause their downfall. Success and self-confidence often breed narcissism and a sense of infallibility', *Financial Times*, 29 November 2002.
40 Dearlove, D. 'Reinventing Leadership', in Crainer, S. and Dearlove, D. (eds) *Financial Times Handbook of Management*, Second edition, Financial Times Prentice Hall (2001), p. 538.
41 Bloomfield, S. 'Charismatic Leaders are Passe', *Professional Manager*, vol. 12, no. 1, January 2003, p. 37.
42 Adair, J. *The Inspirational Leader: How to Motivate, Encourage and Achieve Success*, Kogan Page (2003).
43 Whitehead, M. 'Everyone's a Leader Now', *Supply Management*, 25, April 2002, pp. 22–4.
44 Kahan, S. 'Visionary Leadership' *The Great Washington Society of Association Executives*, www.leader-values.com [accessed 28 January 2006].
45 Gratton, L. *The Democratic Enterprise*, Financial Times Prentice Hall (2004).
46 Witzel, M. 'Book review: A rewarding read if you want to lead' www.ft.com [accessed 31 January 2006].
47 Goffee, R. and Jones, G. *Why Should Anyone Be Led By You?* Harvard Business School Press (2006).
48 Nicholson, Bryan (Sir), 'In my opinion', *Management Today*, January 2006, p. 10.
49 Horne, M. and Jones, D. S. *Leadership: the Challenge for All?*, Chartered Management Institute, December 2001.
50 'Inspired Leadership: Insights into people who inspire exceptional performance', Department of Trade and Industry, August 2004.
51 'Leadership for Innovation', Advanced Institute of Management Research, March 2005.
52 McGregor, D. *The Human Side of Enterprise*, Penguin (1987), p. 182.
53 Kouzes, J. M. and Posner, B. Z. 'The Janusian Leader', in Chowdhury, S. *Management 21C*, Financial Times Prentice Hall (2000), p. 18.
54 Fullan, M. *Leading in a Culture of Change*, Jossey-Bass (2001), p. 5.
55 French, J. R. P. and Raven, B. 'The Bases of Social Power', in Cartwright, D. and Zander, A. F. (eds) *Group Dynamics: Research and Theory*, Third edition, Harper and Row (1968).
56 Finlay, P. *Strategic Management: An Introduction to Business and Corporate Strategy*, Financial Times Prentice Hall (2000), p. 103.
57 Roddick, A. *Body and Soul*, Ebury Press (1991), p. 214.
58 Rajan, A. 'Meaning of Leadership in 2002', *Professional Manager*, March 2002, p. 33.
59 Stern, S. 'If You Think You're Hard Enough', *Management Today*, March 2003, pp. 46–51.
60 'Leadership for Innovation', Advanced Institute of Management Research, March 2005.
61 McGregor, D, *The Human Side of Enterprise*, Penguin (1987).
62 Tannenbaum, R. and Schmidt, W. H. 'How to Choose a Leadership Pattern', *Harvard Business Review*, May–June 1973, pp. 162–75, 178–80.
63 Tayeb, M. 'Cross-cultural leadership' in CBI, *The Path to Leadership: Developing a sustainable model within organisations*, Caspian Publishing, September 2005, pp. 14–20.
64 Goleman, D. 'Leadership That Gets Results', *Harvard Business Review*, vol. 78, no. 2, March–April 2000, pp. 78–90.
65 McCabe, B. 'The disabling shadow of leadership', *Manager, British Journal of Administrative Management*, April/May 2005, pp. 16–17.
66 Valenti, A. 'Five Essential Qualities of Leadership' www.leader-values.com [accessed 28 January 2006].
67 'Inspired Leadership: Insights into people who inspire exceptional performance', Department of Trade and Industry, August 2004.
68 *The Leadership and Management Model*, Investors in People UK, 2003, p. 3.
69 Charlesworth, K., Cook, P. and Crozier, G. *Leading Change in the Public Sector: Making the Difference*, Chartered Management Institute, May 2003.
70 Adair, J. *How to Grow Leaders*, Kogan Page (2005).
71 Cutler, A. 'A good fit is essential', *Professional Manager*, vol.14, no. 3 May 2005, p. 38.
72 Gratton, L. *Living Strategy: Putting People at the Heart of Corporate Purpose*, Financial Times Prentice Hall (2000).
73 Hill, L. 'Leadership as Collective Genius', in Chowdhury, S. *Management 21C*, Financial Times Prentice Hall (2000), pp. 45–65.
74 Bennis, W. 'The New Leadership', in Crainer, S. and Dearlove, D. (eds) *Financial Times Handbook of Management*, Second edition, Financial Times Prentice Hall (2001), pp. 546–50.
75 See, for example, the selection at http://www.answers.com/topic/steve-jobs.
76 Those around in that year may recall the iconic Orwellian '1984' television advert which cost $1.5m, was directed by Ridley Scott, aired only once in the USA during the 1984 Superbowl, and made advertising history with its implied critique of IBM. If you missed it, then you can view it at www.apple-history.com.
77 Waters, R (2005), 'Apple Bites Back', *Financial Times*, 10 June 2005.
78 Naughton, J and Mathiason, N (2005), Will Jobs' departure cut Apple to the core?' Observer Business and Media, 30 July 2006.
79 Waters, R (2005), 'Apple Bites Back', *Financial Times*, 10 June 2005.
80 http://americanhistory.si.edu/collections/comphist/sj1.html 'Oral and Video Histories: Steve Jobs', interview dated 20 April 1995.
81 http://www.quotationsbook.com/quotes/215/view and many others.
82 Hawn, C. (2004), 'If he's so smart ... Steve Jobs, Apple and the Limits to Innovation', *Fast Company Magazine*, January 2004, at http://www.fastcompany.com/magazine/78/jobs.html.
83 http://www.forbes.com/lists/2006/10/Rank_1.html.
84 Naughton, J and Mathiason, N (2005), Will Jobs' departure cut Apple to the core?' *Observer Business and Media*, 30 July 2006.
85 Quoted in: Waters, R (2005), 'Apple Bites Back', *Financial Times*, 10 June 2005.

The Nature of Management

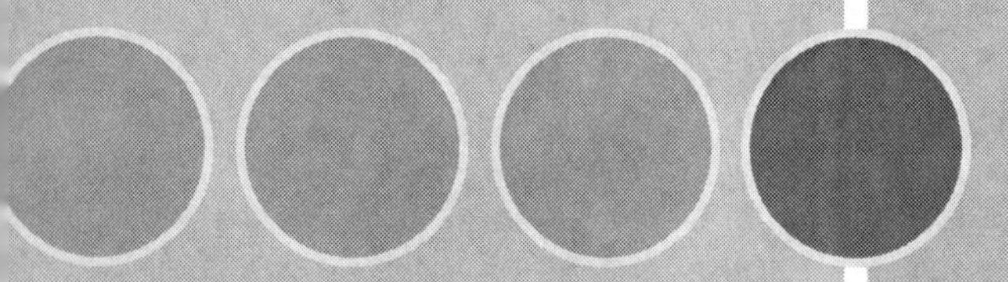

THE ROLE OF THE MANAGER

> **Management is about human beings. Its task is to make people capable of joint performance, to make their strengths effective and their weaknesses irrelevant. This is what organization is all about, and it is the reason that management is the critical, determining factor … We depend on management for our livelihoods and our ability to contribute and achieve.**

Peter F. Drucker – internationally renowned author and consultant

Classic Drucker, Harvard Business School (2006), p. 194

Organisations can achieve their goals and objectives only through the co-ordinated efforts of their members and it is the task of management to get work done through other people. Management is fundamental to the effective operation of work organisations. It is by the process of management and execution of work that the activities of the organisation are carried out. Management is an integral part of the people–organisation relationship. It is essentially an integrating activity that permeates every facet of the operations of an organisation.

Learning outcomes

After completing this chapter you should be able to:

- explain the meaning of management and main activities, or functions, of management;
- analyse the essential nature of managerial work;
- contrast management in private enterprise and public sector organisations;
- outline empirical studies on the nature of managerial work and behaviour;
- debate the attributes and qualities of a successful manager;
- review the nature of management and the changing role of managers;
- evaluate the importance of management for effective organisational performance.

Critical reflection

'Despite all the rhetoric, surely management is simply about taking charge of people in order to get the job done – and you cannot learn this from any textbook or classroom.' How far do you agree with this contention? What relevance do theories of organisational behaviour have for effective management practice in modern organisations?

THE MEANING OF MANAGEMENT

Management is a generic term and subject to many interpretations. A number of different ideas are attributed to the meaning of management and to the work of a manager.[1] In certain respects everyone can be regarded as a manager, at least to some extent. We all manage our own time and everyone has some choice whether or not to do something, and some control, however slight, over the planning and organisation of their work. *Knights and Willmott* refer to managing as an everyday activity that involves interactions between people that are not unrelated or entirely dissimilar to other spheres of life, except perhaps in the rhetoric and hype that surround management. They contend that most established textbooks about management and organisation provide little that enables practising managers to make sense of their particular problem or dilemma, and in order to appreciate the living of management draw on a number of contemporary novels.[2]

However, we are concerned with management as involving people looking beyond themselves and exercising formal authority over the activities and performance of other people. For our purposes, therefore, we can regard management as:

- taking place within a structured organisational setting with prescribed roles;
- directed towards the attainment of aims and objectives;
- achieved through the efforts of other people; and
- using systems and procedures.

At its most basic, management may be viewed as 'making things happen'.

Management is active, not theoretical. It is about changing behaviour and making things happen. It is about developing people, working with them, reaching objectives and achieving results. Indeed, all the research into how managers spend their time reveals that they are creatures of the moment, perpetually immersed in the nitty-gritty of making things happen.[3]

Significance of cultural influences

Schneider and Barsoux contend that trying to define the meaning of management shows up differences in beliefs and values. Cultural influences are a significant feature of management. Managers in some countries might have more concern for the 'spiritual' aspects of management, while in others there would be greater concern for the business sense. Developing people through work could be seen as an intrusion of privacy, and others may perceive empowerment as another name for manipulation.[4] According to *Francesco and Gold,* if international managers are to perform successfully in the global economy they need to understand the affects of different cultures on organisational behaviour. Reliance on theories developed in one culture is not sufficient.[5]

The emergence of management *Peter Drucker*, who is widely regarded as the guru of management gurus, has written about the significance in social history of the emergence of management:

> *The emergence of management as an essential, a distinct and a leading institution is a pivotal event in social history. Rarely, if ever, has a new basic institution, a new leading group, emerged as fast as has management since the turn of this [20th] century. Rarely in human history has a new institution proven indispensable so quickly; and even less often has a new institution arrived with so little opposition, so little disturbance, so little controversy.*[6]

Drucker sees management as denoting a function as well as the people who discharge it, a social position and authority, and also a discipline and field of study. 'Management is tasks. Management is a discipline. But management is also people. Every achievement of management is the achievement of a manager. Every failure is a failure of a manager.'[7] Other writers, however, take the view that management is not a separate discipline. The problem is identifying a single discipline that encompasses the work of a manager, or agreeing the disciplines that a manager needs in order effectively to carry out this work. Note, however, the discussion on 'The Changing Role of Managers' at the end of this chapter.

Manager as a job title Even within a work organisation you cannot identify a manager necessarily by what a person is called or by their job title. In some organisations there is a liberal use of the title 'manager' in an apparent attempt to enhance the status and morale of staff. As a result there are a number of people whose job title includes the term manager but who, in reality, are not performing the full activities of a manager. Yet there are many people whose job title does not include the term manager (for example, group accountant, head chef, chief inspector, captain, headteacher, production controller, district nursing officer, company secretary) but who, in terms of the activities they undertake and the authority and responsibility they exercise, may be very much a manager.

Managers born or made? Management an art or science? There is frequent debate about whether managers are born or made or whether management is an art or a science. Briefly, the important point is that neither of these is a mutually exclusive alternative. The answer to either question is surely a combination of both. Even if there are certain innate qualities that make for a potentially good manager, these natural talents must be encouraged and developed through proper guidance, education and training, and planned experience.

Clearly, management must always be something of an art, especially in so far as it involves practice, personal judgement and dealing with people. However, it still requires knowledge of the fundamentals of management, and competence in the application of specific skills and techniques – as illustrated, for example, with developments in information technology.

> *The trouble is that, for all the techniques at their disposal, managers generally act at a very intuitive level. Managers may have absorbed the latest thinking on core competencies, but are more likely to base a decision on prejudice or personal opinion rather than a neat theory.*[8]

The discussion of management as an art or a science is developed by *Watson* who suggests that in order to make sense of the complex and highly ambiguous situations in which managers find themselves, management can be viewed as both art and science but also magic and politics (*see* Figure 11.1).[9]

Management and administration

There is often confusion over different interpretations of the two terms '**management**' and '**administration**'. One of the main reasons for this confusion would seem to result from the translation of *Fayol's* book *Administration industrielle et générale* from the French into English. In the original (1929) English edition there was a direct translation of 'administration', but in the wider republication of the book in 1949 the term 'management' replaced 'administra-

Figure 11.1 Management as art, science, magic and politics

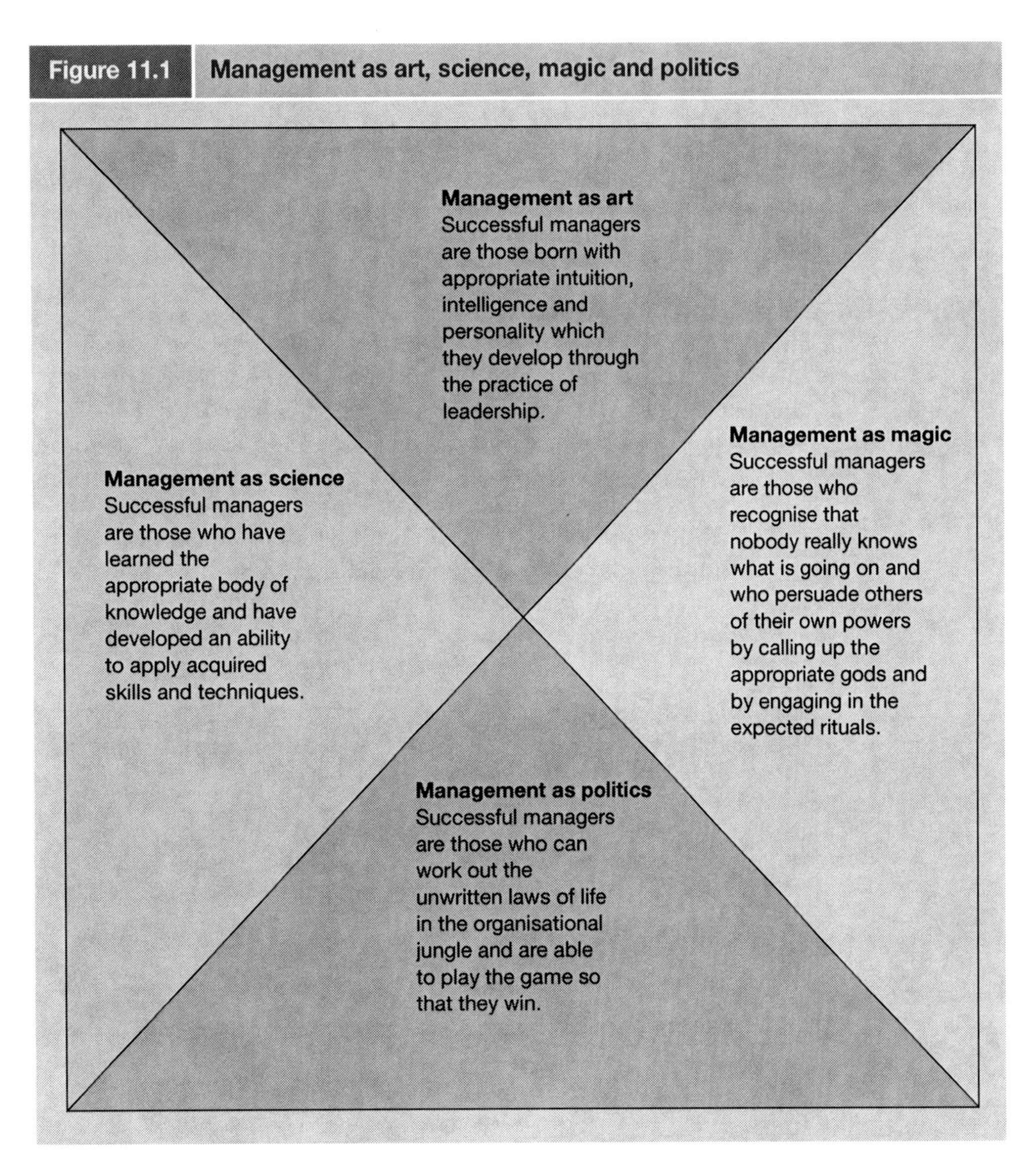

Source: From Watson, T. J., *Management, Organisation and Employment Strategy*, Routledge & Kegan Paul (1986), p. 29. Reproduced by permission of the publisher, Routledge, a division of Taylor & Francis, Ltd.

tion' in the title. In the introduction to the revised edition, Urwick indicates regret at this change and also expresses concern at the possible division between management being seen to apply only to business organisations, and (public) administration as applying to the same functions in public service organisations.[10]

Dictionary definitions tend to see the two words as synonymous. Management is sometimes referred to as 'administration of business concerns' and administration as 'management of public affairs'. However, the term 'management' is now used far more widely within the public sector. There is clearly an overlap between the two terms and they tend to be used, therefore, in accordance with the convenience of individual writers. This confirms the feeling that although most people perceive a difference between the two terms, this difference is not easy to describe. (A comparison of management in private enterprise and public sector organisations is to be found later in this chapter.)

Administration part of management

There appears, therefore, to be growing acceptance of the term management as the general descriptive label and **administration** as relating to the more specific function of the implementation of systems and procedures instigated by management. Administration can be seen as taking place in accordance with some form of rules or procedures, whereas management implies a greater degree of discretion. For our purposes, management is viewed as applying to both private and public sector organisations; and administration is interpreted as part of the management process, and concerned with the design and implementation of systems and procedures to help meet stated objectives. Systems of communication and procedures relating to information technology are particularly important today.

THE PROCESS OF MANAGEMENT

The nature of management is variable. Management relates to all activities of the organisation and is undertaken at all levels of the organisation. Management is not a separate, discrete function. It cannot be departmentalised or centralised. An organisation cannot have a department of management in the same way as it can have a department for other functions, such as production, marketing, accounting, or human resources. Management is seen best, therefore, as a process common to all other functions carried out within the organisation. **Management is essentially an integrating activity**. (*See* Figure 11.2.)

But what does the process of management actually involve and what activities does it encompass? Management is a complex and discursive subject. Despite the widespread use of

Figure 11.2 The central focus of management

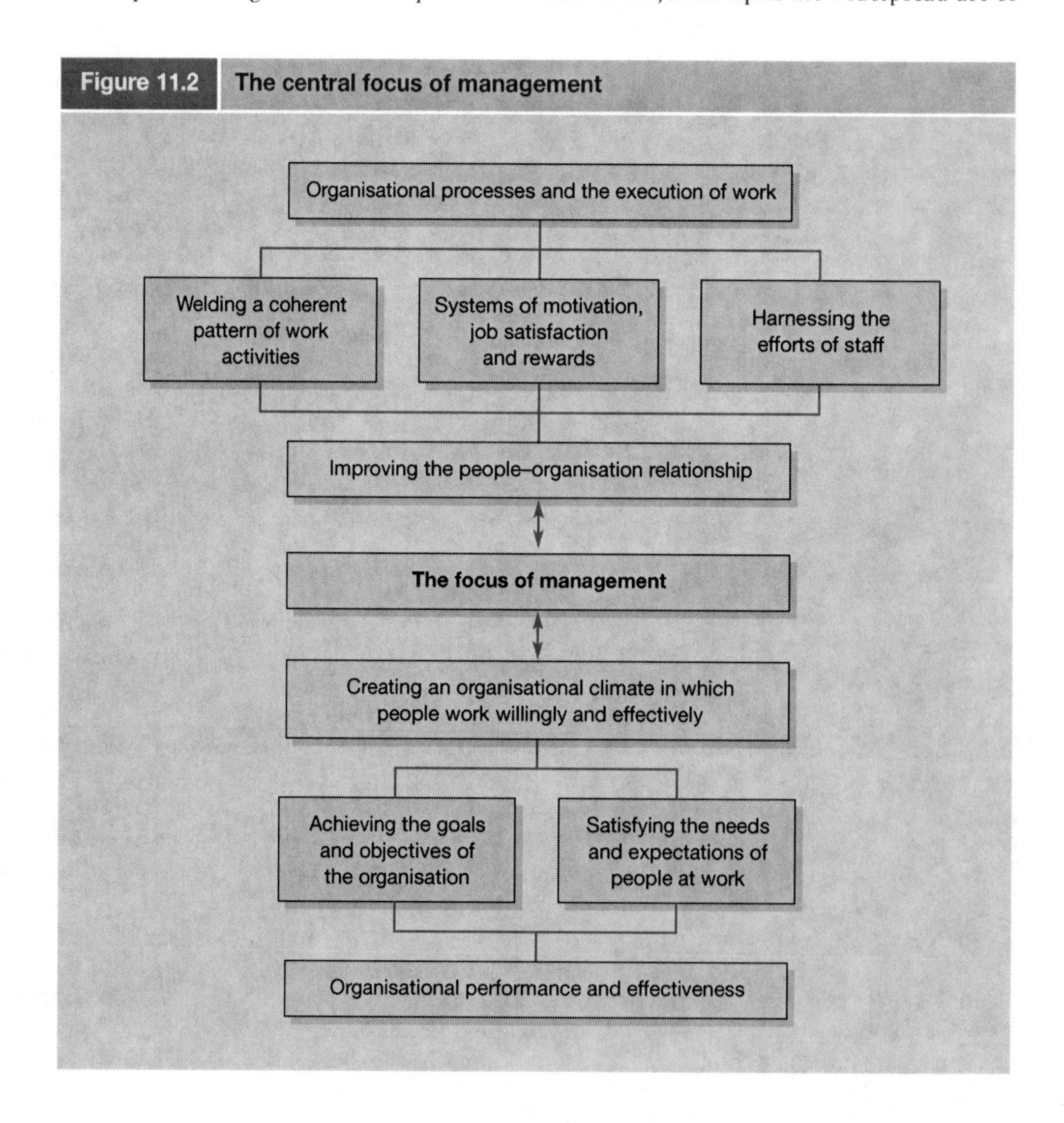

the term and the large amount written about the subject, it is not easy to find agreement on a simple yet comprehensive definition of management or of a manager. Moreover, **'management' is not homogeneous. It takes place in different ways and at different levels of the organisation**. One approach, especially favoured by classical writers, is to analyse the nature of management and to search for common activities (or functions, or elements) applicable to managers in all organisations.

Common activities of management

One of the first, and most widely quoted, analyses is that given by *Henri Fayol*, who analysed the activities of industrial undertakings into six groups:

- technical (production, manufacture and adaptation);
- commercial (buying, selling, exchange and market information);
- financial (obtaining capital and making optimum use of available funds);
- security (safeguarding property and persons);
- accounting (information on the economic position, stocktaking, balance sheet, costs, statistics); and
- managerial. (The term 'management' is a translation of the French term 'administration'.)[11]

The managerial activity is divided into five elements of management, which are defined as: 'to forecast and plan, to organise, to command, to co-ordinate and to control'. Fayol describes these elements as:

- **Planning** (translated from the French *prevoyer* = to foresee, and taken to include forecasting) – examining the future, deciding what needs to be achieved and developing a plan of action.
- **Organising** – providing the material and human resources and building the structure to carry out the activities of the organisation.
- **Command** – maintaining activity among personnel, getting the optimum return from all employees in the interests of the whole organisation.
- **Co-ordination** – unifying and harmonising all activities and effort of the organisation to facilitate its working and success.
- **Control** – verifying that everything occurs in accordance with plans, instructions, established principles and expressed command.

PRINCIPLES OF MANAGEMENT

Fayol also suggests that a set of well-established principles would help concentrate general discussion on management theory. He emphasises, however, that these principles must be flexible and adaptable to changing circumstances. Fayol recognised that there was no limit to the principles of management but in his writing advocated 14 of them.

1. **Division of work**. The object is to produce more and better work from the same effort, and the advantages of specialisation. However, there are limits to division of work which experience and a sense of proportion tell us should not be exceeded.
2. **Authority and responsibility.** Responsibility is the corollary of authority. Wherever authority is exercised responsibility arises. The application of sanctions is essential to good management, and is needed to encourage useful actions and to discourage their opposite. The best safeguard against abuse of authority is the personal integrity of the manager.
3. **Discipline** is essential for the efficient operation of the organisation. Discipline is in essence the outward mark of respect for agreements between the organisation and its members. The manager must decide on the most appropriate form of sanction in cases of offences against discipline.
4. **Unity of command**. In any action an employee should receive orders from one superior only; if not, authority is undermined and discipline, order and stability threatened. Dual command is a perpetual source of conflicts.

5 **Unity of direction.** In order to provide for unity of action, co-ordination and focusing of effort, there should be one head and one plan for any group of activities with the same objective.
6 **Subordination of individual interest to general interest.** The interest of the organisation should dominate individual or group interests.
7 **Remuneration of personnel.** Remuneration should as far as possible satisfy both employee and employer. Methods of payment can influence organisational performance and the method should be fair and should encourage keenness by rewarding well-directed effort, but not lead to overpayment.
8 **Centralisation** is always present to some extent in any organisation. The degree of centralisation is a question of proportion and will vary in particular organisations.
9 **Scalar chain.** The chain of superiors from the ultimate authority to the lowest ranks. Respect for line authority must be reconciled with activities which require urgent action, and with the need to provide for some measure of initiative at all levels of authority.
10 **Order.** This includes material order and social order. The object of material order is avoidance of loss. There should be an appointed place for each thing, and each thing in its appointed place. Social order involves an appointed place for each employee, and each employee in his or her appointed place. Social order requires good organisation and good selection.
11 **Equity.** The desire for equity and for equality of treatment are aspirations to be taken into account in dealing with employees throughout all levels of the scalar chain.
12 **Stability of tenure of personnel.** Generally, prosperous organisations have a stable managerial personnel, but changes of personnel are inevitable and stability of tenure is a question of proportion.
13 **Initiative.** This represents a source of strength for the organisation and should be encouraged and developed. Tact and integrity are required to promote initiative and to retain respect for authority and discipline.
14 **Esprit de corps** should be fostered, as harmony and unity among members of the organisation is a great strength in the organisation. The principle of unity of command should be observed. It is necessary to avoid the dangers of divide and rule of one's own team, and the abuse of written communication. Wherever possible verbal contacts should be used.

Figure 11.3 Ten new principles for effective administrative management

1	Manage information through people.
2	Change is a constant, and must be managed.
3	Technology is the future.
4	Relationships matter.
5	Investment in training and development is important.
6	Measure only against the best.
7	The market is global.
8	Unity of direction is important.
9	Equity is expected.
10	Initiative is important.

Source: From Moorcroft, R., 'Managing in the 21st century', *Manager, The British Journal of Administrative Management*, January/February 2000, p. 10. Reproduced with permission from The Institute of Administrative Management.

A number of these principles relate directly to, or are influenced by, the organisation structure in which the process of management takes place. Fayol's set of principles can be compared therefore with those given by Urwick and discussed in Chapter 15.

Relevance for the 21st century

In an article bringing together the thinking of senior members of the Institute of Administrative Management, *Moorcroft* suggests that Fayol's five elements of management are still recognised as relevant and appropriate for the managers of today and tomorrow. However, although some of the principles of management remain fresh and relevant, at the start of a new millennium a new set of principles is needed to guide a manager's everyday actions. These 'principles' are not offered as an exclusive or authoritative list but are proposed as a thought-provoking starting point to address the management problems awaiting us in the new millennium (*see* Figure 11.3, page 416).[12]

MANAGEMENT AS A SOCIAL PROCESS

Another well-known analysis is given by *Brech* who defines management as:

> *A social process entailing responsibility for the effective and economical planning and regulation of the operations of an enterprise, in fulfilment of given purposes or tasks, such responsibility involving:*
> *(a) judgement and decision in determining plans and in using data to control performance and progress against plans;*
> *(b) the guidance, integration, motivation and supervision of the personnel composing the enterprise and carrying out its operations.*[13]

Brech identifies four main elements of management:

- **Planning** – determining the broad lines for carrying out operations, preparing methods by which they are carried out and setting standards of performance.
- **Control** – checking actual performance against standards to ensure satisfactory progress and performance, and recording as a guide to possible future operations.
- **Co-ordination** – balancing and maintaining the team by ensuring a suitable division of work and seeing that tasks are performed in harmony.
- **Motivation** – or inspiring morale. Getting members of the team to work effectively, to give loyalty to the group and to the task, to carry out their tasks properly, and to play an effective part in the activities of the organisation. This general inspiration is accompanied by a process of supervision or leadership to ensure the teams are carrying out their activities properly.

Other analyses Many other writers have provided an analysis of the elements of management. At first sight these analyses may appear to differ in certain aspects, but on closer study they show a basic similarity. Debate on the inclusion or exclusion of a particular element of management tends to revolve round the use and interpretation of different terms, and the emphasis which is placed upon them.

For example, what *Fayol* calls **command** – maintaining activity among personnel and getting optimum return from employees – might be taken to mean what *Brech* refers to as **motivation** – getting members of the team to work effectively and to carry out properly the activities allocated to them. Brech does not use the term **organising** but this appears to be covered under the headings of **planning** and **co-ordination**.

Critical reflection

'It is difficult to think of any aspect of the functioning of the organisation, or behaviour of people, which does not concern, or relate back to, management in some way. For example, personality clashes could be traced back to management procedures for recruitment and selection, socialisation and training, delegation or the level and style of supervision. And personality clashes are likely to affect the attitudes and work performance of the members concerned, and also affect the morale of other staff.' Can you give an example which contradicts this assertion?

THE TASKS AND CONTRIBUTION OF A MANAGER

Yet another approach to describing management is given by *Drucker* who identifies three tasks, equally important but essentially different, that have to be performed:

1 fulfilling the specific purpose and mission of the institution, whether business enterprise, hospital, or university;
2 making work productive and the worker achieving;
3 managing social impacts and social responsibilities.[14]

Drucker then goes on to identify five basic operations in the work of the manager:

- **Sets objectives** – determines objectives and the goals for each area of objectives, and describes what needs to be done to achieve these objectives.
- **Organises** – analyses the activities, decisions and relations required, classifies and divides work, creates organisation structure and selects staff.
- **Motivates and communicates** – creates a team out of people responsible for various jobs.
- **Measures** – establishes targets and measurements of performance which focus on both the individual and the organisation as a whole.
- **Develops people** – directs, encourages and trains. How well subordinates develop themselves depends on the way a manager manages.

These categories require a combination of analytical ability, synthesising ability, integrity, human perception and insight and social skill.

Responsibility for the work of other people

Drucker argues that the traditional definition of management based on the responsibility for the work of other people is unsatisfactory and too narrow, and emphasises a secondary rather than a primary characteristic. There are people, often in responsible positions, who are clearly 'management' but who do not have responsibility for the work of other people.

A person's function and contribution may be unaffected by the number of subordinate staff. A 'manager' is someone who performs the tasks of management whether or not they have power over others.

> *Who is a manager can be defined only by that person's function and by the contribution he or she is expected to make. And the function that distinguishes the manager above all others is the function no one but the manager can perform. The one contribution a manager is uniquely expected to make is to give others vision and ability to perform. It is vision and moral responsibility that, in the last analysis, define the manager.*[15]

ESSENTIAL NATURE OF MANAGERIAL WORK

Despite the view expressed by Drucker on the tasks and contribution of a manager, one of the most popular ways of defining management is that it involves getting work done second-hand, that is through the efforts of other people. Managers are judged not just on their own performance but on the results achieved by subordinate staff. If we look at how people at work actually spend their time, we should be able to distinguish between those whose main occupation is the carrying out of discrete tasks and the actual doing of work themselves, and those who spend proportionally more of their time in determining the nature of work to be undertaken by other people, the planning and organising of their work, issuing them with instructions and giving advice, and checking on their performance.

'Managing' and 'doing'

By distinguishing 'managing' from 'doing' in this way we can see management as clarifying objectives and the planning of work, organising the distribution of activities and tasks to other people, direction of subordinate staff and controlling the performance of other people's work. **This provides us with a convenient description and summary of managerial work as clarification of objectives, planning, organising, directing and controlling** (*see* Figure 11.4).

Figure 11.4 Summary of essential nature of managerial work

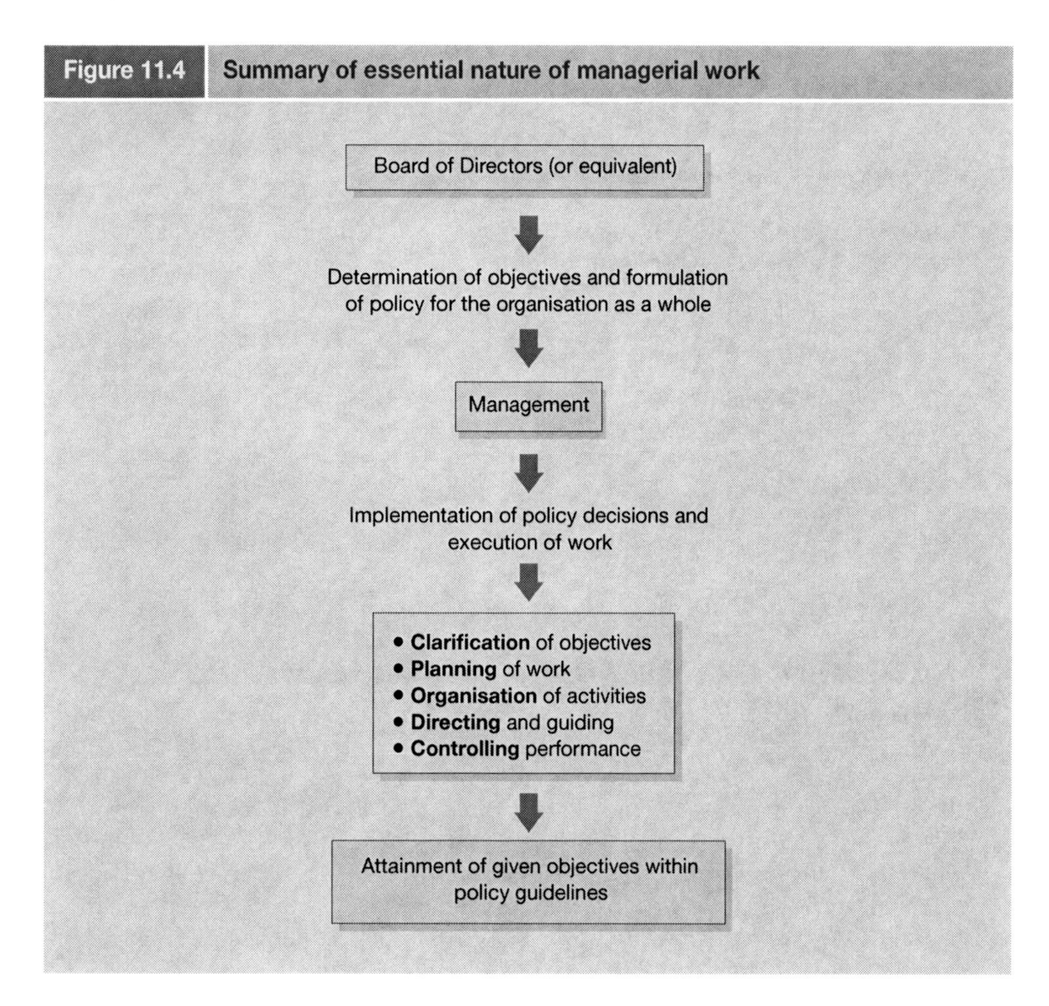

The degree of emphasis given to these different activities may vary widely, however, from one manager to another. Some managers are likely to spend more time on certain activities than other managers. The application of these activities reflects a wide range of management practice and managerial style.

Direction, motivation and control

Having already identified direction, of the organisation as a whole, as a responsibility of the board of directors (or equivalent body), it is tempting to use the term 'motivating' instead of 'directing' in our definition of the activities of management. This would avoid possible confusion over terminology: and motivation is perhaps a less emotive word. But is motivating an adequate description? It is certainly part of the manager's job to motivate staff but it involves more than this. Subordinate staff also need development and guidance. They need to be motivated **to perform well in the right areas**. The manager has a responsibility to see that subordinate staff are effective as well as efficient. Their efforts must be **directed** towards the achievement of given objectives in accordance with stated policy. This involves the process of control. It is acknowledged that control is another emotive word and some writers prefer alternatives such as monitoring, inspecting or checking – although whatever the wording the functions that it embraces are usually very similar. The real importance is not the particular term itself but what it is intended to achieve and the manner in which 'control' is exercised (*see* Chapter 18).

Management is all about control. Success gives you control and control gives you longevity as a manager. In football very few managers achieve a position of complete control over their teams.

Sir Alex Ferguson[16]

The efforts of other people

Stewart attempts to integrate the various definitions of management and summarises the manager's job, broadly defined as:

> *deciding what should be done and then getting other people to do it. A longer definition would be concerned with how these tasks are to be accomplished. The first task comprises setting objectives, planning (including decision-making), and setting up formal organization. The second consists of motivation, communication, control (including measurement), and the development of people. The two tasks are separated for convenient analysis, but in practice they may often overlap.*[17]

The definition of management as 'getting work done through the efforts of other people' may not perhaps meet all criteria or satisfy everyone's perception of the nature of managerial work. It does, however, have the advantage of simplicity and focuses on what in reality is at the heart of effective management.

MANAGEMENT IN PRIVATE ENTERPRISE AND PUBLIC SECTOR ORGANISATIONS

The increasing scale of privatisation and the general movement of major organisations away from local authority jurisdiction and towards greater responsibility for managing their own affairs have led to blurring of the traditional distinction between private and public sector management. Divisions between the two sectors are increasingly being broken down. There are, however, still perceived differences between management in the private and public sectors. These differences arise from particular features of public sector organisations. For example:

- aims concerned with providing a service for, and for the well-being of, the community rather than just of a commercial nature;

- the scale, variety and complexity of their operations;
- the tendency for them to be subject more to press reports on their activities;
- the political environment in which they operate, and in the case of local government, for example, the relationship between elected members and permanent officers;
- high levels of statutory controls, legislation and ministerial guidance;
- the generally high level of trade union involvement;
- the difficulties in measuring standards of performance of services provided compared with profitability;
- the demand for uniformity of treatment and public accountability for their operations; and
- the tendency towards more rigid HR policies, for example specific limitations on levels of authority and responsibility, fixed salary gradings based on general pay scales, long-term career structures and set promotion procedures.

A number of these features frequently combine to result in increased bureaucracy within public sector organisations.

The same general problems of management

Both private enterprise and public sector organisations, however, face the same general problems of management. Both are concerned with, for example:

- the efficiency and effectiveness of their operations;
- the clarification of aims and objectives;
- the design of a suitable structure; and
- carrying out essential administrative functions.

Basic principles of management apply in any series of activities in any organisation. Although actual methods and procedures will of necessity differ, the common activities and concerns of management apply to a greater or lesser extent in both private enterprise and public sector organisations. As *Robinson* points out:

> *Innovation in industry and commerce is a given. In local government organisations some may find it a more curious concept. But this simplistic, stereotypical view of management is wrong. Managers must manage professionally in whatever sector they function – or leave themselves vulnerable to the threats in an increasingly global and competitive environment. This applies to managers of public sector organisations as well as to private sector managers – and survival for many will be dependent upon the effective management of change and innovation.*[18]

Common challenges for all management

Fenlon suggests that 'public and private leadership are fundamentally alike and different in important respects'. Although public sector executives also confront unique challenges in every aspect of their leadership, the essentials of leadership and management in the public sector are the same as those in the private sector. In both sectors classical managerial activities are required such as designing organisational structures and processes that support strategies, building systems for staffing, budgeting and planning, and measuring results. While public sector executives must also develop strategies that create benefits, as opposed to profits, at an acceptable rate of return on political capital employed, the skills of leading and managing are fundamentally alike.[19]

Hannagan refers to the need to continuously improve productivity faster than the competition as the challenge for all management in both the private and public sectors. Management theories apply to all managers and both sectors face a central factor of the management of change.

> *In the public sector the challenge may be measured in different ways to those used in the private sector. Profit may not play a part, but measurement of activity against costs may replace monitoring of the*

return on capital invested. Income is now often linked to output and outcomes, while expenditure is firmly controlled and audited. Public sector managers are increasingly being asked to manage their organisations in a more commercial and effective way, exposed to competition without any guarantee of survival. In many areas, public sector management is little different from that in the private sector, with the same urgencies and pressures. This is exemplified by the increasing frequency of movement between the two sectors.[20]

The importance of task and context

However, according to Stewart, the belief that one should manage the public sector in the same way as the private sector is an illusion of our times. Within all categories of work there are critical differences in the nature of management depending on the tasks to be undertaken and their context. The good manager will be one who recognises the need to relate their management style and approach to context and task, and this is as important in the public sector as in the private sector. The management of difference can be seen at work in local government, where the sheer diversity of services means that different services are managed in different ways. Stewart maintains that many of the dominant management approaches advocated for local government assume a uniformity of approach which promises to ignore difference. The belief in a generic type of management for all situations can be misleading in that it conceals the need for the hard analysis of the nature of task and context.[21]

Management in service industries

In Chapter 3 we discussed the distinction between production and service organisations. In order to operate effectively, service industries need management like any other industry. Both require attention to the same general problems of management in the same way as management in public and private sector organisations. The open systems model applies in exactly the same way to service organisations as to any other business organisation. Increasing attention is being given to the applications of general management theory within the service industry and to the links between management in service and other industries.[22]

THE WORK OF A MANAGER

Despite similarities in the general activities of management, the jobs of individual managers will differ widely. The work of the manager is varied and fragmented. In practice, it will be influenced by such factors as:

- the nature of the organisation, its philosophy, objectives and size;
- the type of structure;
- activities and tasks involved;
- technology and methods of performing work;
- the nature of people employed; and
- the level in the organisation at which the manager is working.

These differences do not just exist between organisations in the private and public sectors; they are often more a matter of degree. For example, many large business organisations may have more in common in their management and operations with public sector organisations than with small private firms.

The environmental setting

A major determinant of the work of the manager is the nature of the environment, both internal and external, in which the manager is working. Managers have to perform their jobs in the situation in which they find themselves (*see* Figure 11.5).

The **internal environment** relates to the culture and climate of the organisation – 'how things are done around here' – and to the prevailing atmosphere surrounding the organisation.

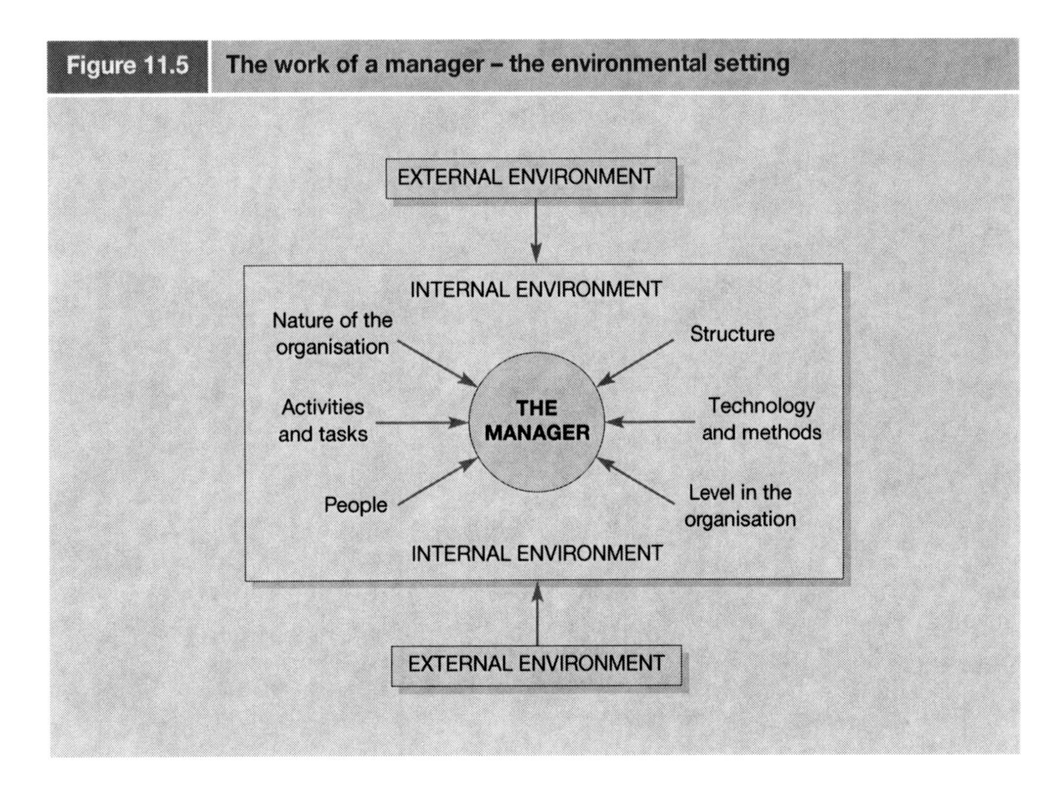

Figure 11.5 The work of a manager – the environmental setting

Organisational culture and climate are discussed in Chapter 19. The **external environment** relates to the organisation as an open system, as discussed in Chapter 3. Managers must be responsive to the changing opportunities and challenges, and risks and limitations facing the organisation. External environmental factors are largely outside the control of management.

The diversity of management

More recent studies on the nature of management have been based on wider observation and research, and have concentrated on the diversity of management and differences in the jobs of managers. Among the best-known empirical studies on the nature of managers' jobs, and how managers actually spend their time, are those by *Mintzberg*, *Kotter*, *Luthans* and *Stewart*.[23]

Critical reflection

There are many ways of looking at the meaning of management. The essential nature of managerial work is not easy to describe as aspects that are common in many applications escape us in others. How do you view the role of the manager? All managers have their individual way of working. The basic criteria must therefore be no more than a compromise between the ideas of some of the more lucid writers on the subject. Do you agree therefore that the study of management is of only limited value?

MANAGERIAL ROLES

Based on the study of the work of five chief executives of medium-sized to large organisations, *Mintzberg* classifies the activities which constitute the essential functions of a top manager's job.[24] What managers do cannot be related to the classical view of the activities of management. The manager's job can be described more meaningfully in terms of various 'roles' or organised sets of behaviour associated with a position.[25] Mintzberg recognises that people who 'manage' have formal authority over the unit they command and this leads to a special position of status in the organisation.

As a result of this formal authority and status, managerial activities can be seen as a set of ten **managerial roles** which may be divided into three groups: (i) interpersonal roles, (ii) informational roles and (iii) decisional roles (*see* Figure 11.6).

Figure 11.6 The manager's roles

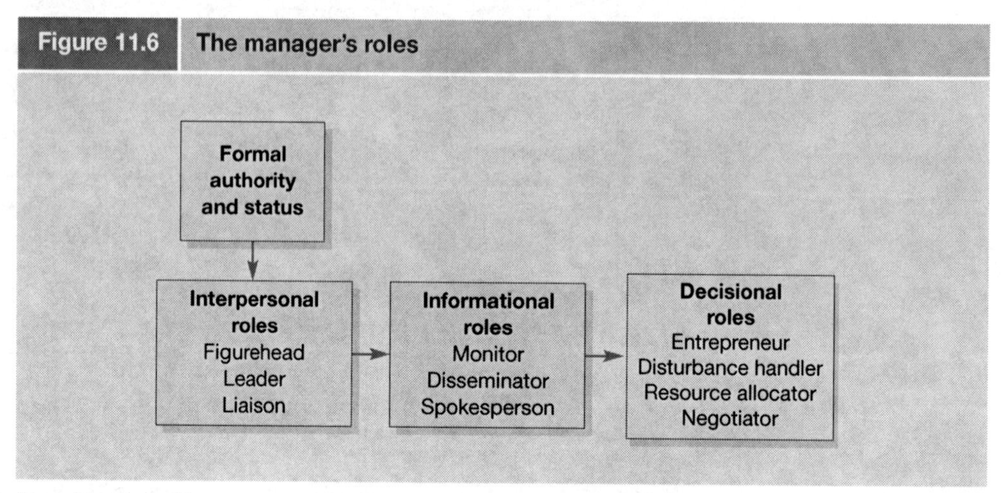

Source: Mintzberg, H., 'The manager's job: folklore and fact', *Harvard Business Review Classic*, March–April 1990, p. 168.

Interpersonal roles

The **interpersonal roles** are relations with other people arising from the manager's status and authority.

1 **Figurehead role** is the most basic and simple of managerial roles. The manager is a symbol and represents the organisation in matters of formality. The manager is involved in matters of a ceremonial nature, such as the signing of documents, participation as a social necessity, and being available for people who insist on access to the 'top'.
2 **Leader role** is among the most significant of roles and it permeates all activities of a manager. By virtue of the authority vested in the manager there is a responsibility for staffing, and for the motivation and guidance of subordinates.
3 **Liaison role** involves the manager in horizontal relationships with individuals and groups outside their own unit, or outside the organisation. An important part of the manager's job is the linking between the organisation and the environment.

Informational roles

The informational roles relate to the sources and communication of information arising from the manager's interpersonal roles.

4 **Monitor role** identifies the manager in seeking and receiving information. This information enables the manager to develop an understanding of the working of the organisation and its environment. Information may be received from internal or external sources, and may be formal or informal.
5 **Disseminator role** involves the manager in transmitting external information through the liaison role into the organisation, and internal information through leader role between the subordinates. The information may be largely factual or may contain value judgements. The manager is the nerve centre of information. If the manager feels unable, or chooses not, to pass on information this can present difficulties for delegation.
6 **Spokesperson role** involves the manager as formal authority in transmitting information to people outside the unit, such as the board of directors or other superiors, and the general public such as suppliers, customers, government departments and the press.

Decisional roles The decisional roles involve the making of strategic organisational decisions on the basis of the manager's status and authority, and access to information.

7 **Entrepreneurial role** is the manager's function to initiate and plan controlled (that is, voluntary) change through exploiting opportunities or solving problems, and taking action to improve the existing situation. The manager may play a major part, personally, in seeking improvement, or may delegate responsibility to subordinates.
8 **Disturbance handler role** involves the manager in reacting to involuntary situations and unpredictable events. When an unexpected disturbance occurs the manager must take action to correct the situation.
9 **Resource allocator role** involves the manager in using formal authority to decide where effort will be expended, and making choices on the allocation of resources such as money, time, materials and staff. The manager decides the programming of work and maintains control by authorising important decisions before implementation.
10 **Negotiator role** is participation in negotiation activity with other individuals or organisations, for example a new agreement with a trade union. Because of the manager's authority, credibility, access to information, and responsibility for resource allocation, negotiation is an important part of the job.

Mintzberg emphasises that this set of ten roles is a somewhat arbitrary division of the manager's activities. It presents one of many possible ways of categorising the view of managerial roles. The ten roles are not easily isolated in practice but form an integrated whole. If any role is removed, this affects the effectiveness of the manager's overall performance.

Why organisations need managers As a result of describing the nature of managerial work in terms of a set of ten roles, *Mintzberg* suggests six basic purposes of the manager, or reasons why organisations need managers:

- to ensure the organisation serves its basic purpose – the efficient production of goods or services;
- to design and maintain the stability of the operations of the organisation;
- to take charge of strategy-making and adapt the organisation in a controlled way to changes in its environment;
- to ensure the organisation serves the ends of those people who control it;
- to serve as the key informational link between the organisation and the environment; and
- as formal authority to operate the organisation's status system.

BEHAVIOUR PATTERN OF GENERAL MANAGERS

From a detailed study of 15 successful American general managers involved in a broad range of industries, *Kotter* found that although their jobs differed and the managers undertook their jobs in a different manner, they all had two significant activities in common: **agenda-setting** and **network-building**.[26]

- **Agenda-setting** is a constant activity of managers. This is a set of items, or series of agendas involving aims and objectives, plans, strategies, ideas, decisions to be made and priorities of action in order to bring about desired end-results. This requires individual managers responsible for achieving targets to have a continual and changing series of agendas to help bring intentions into reality.
- **Network-building** involves the managers interacting with other people and establishing a network of co-operative relations. These networks are outside the formal structure. They have often included a very large number of people, many of whom were in addition to their boss or direct subordinates, and also included individuals and groups outside the organisation. Meetings provided exchanges of information over a wide range of topics in

a short period of time. A major feature of network-building was to establish and maintain contacts that could assist in the successful achievement of agenda items.

Typical pattern of behaviour

On the basis of interviews, observations, questionnaires and relevant documents, *Kotter* found the following features of a typical pattern of daily behaviour for a general manager (GM).[27]

1. They spent most of their time with others.
2. The people they spent time with included many in addition to their superior and direct subordinates.
3. The breadth of topics covered in discussions was very wide.
4. In these conversations GMs typically asked a lot of questions.
5. During these conversations GMs rarely seemed to make 'big' decisions.
6. Discussions usually contained a considerable amount of joking, kidding and non-work-related issues.
7. In not a small number of these encounters, the substantive issue discussed was relatively unimportant to the business or organisation.
8. In such encounters, the GMs rarely gave 'orders' in a traditional sense.
9. Nevertheless, GMs frequently attempted to influence others.
10. In allocation of time with other people, GMs often reacted to the initiatives of others.
11. Most of their time with others was spent in short, disjointed conversations.
12. They worked long hours. (The average GM studied worked just under 60 hours per week. Although some work was done at home and while commuting or travelling, they spent most of their time at work.)

DETERMINING WHAT REAL MANAGERS DO

Developing the work of Mintzberg and Kotter, *Luthans* and associates undertook a major investigation into the true nature of managerial work through the observation of 44 'real' managers.[28] A detailed record was maintained of the behaviours and actions of managers from all levels and many types of organisations, mostly in the service sector and a few manufacturing companies. The data collected were reduced into 12 descriptive behavioural categories under four managerial activities of real managers:

- **communication** – exchanging information, paperwork;
- **traditional management** – planning, decision-making, controlling;
- **networking** – interacting with outsiders, socialising/politicking;
- **human resource management** – motivating/reinforcing, disciplining/punishing, managing conflict, staffing, training/developing.

Frequency of activities

Following determination of the nature of managerial activity, Luthans then went on to study a further, different set of 248 real managers in order to document the relative frequency of the four main activities. Trained observers completed a checklist at random times once every hour over a two-week period. The time and effort spent on the four activities varied among different managers. The 'average' manager, however, spent 32 per cent of time and effort on traditional management activities, 29 per cent on communication activities, 20 per cent on human resource management activities and 19 per cent on networking activities.

PATTERNS OF MANAGERIAL WORK AND BEHAVIOUR

Based on earlier studies of managerial jobs,[29] *Stewart* has developed a model for understanding managerial work and behaviour.[30] The model directs attention to the generalisations that can be made about managerial work, and differences that exist among managerial jobs. It acknowledges the wide variety, found from previous studies, among different managers in similar jobs in terms of how they view their jobs and the work they do.

Demands, constraints and choices

The three main categories of the model are **demands, constraints** and **choices**. These identify the flexibility in a managerial job.

- **Demands** are what anyone in the job has to do. They are not what the manager ought to do, but only what must be done: for example, meeting minimum criteria of performance, work which requires personal involvement, complying with bureaucratic procedures which cannot be avoided, meetings that must be attended.
- **Constraints** are internal or external factors which limit what the manager can do: for example, resource limitations, legal or trade union constraints, the nature of technology, physical location, organisational constraints, attitudes of other people.
- **Choices** are the activities that the manager is free to do, but does not have to do. They are opportunities for one job-holder to undertake different work from another, or to do the work in a different way: for example, what work is done within a defined area, to change the area of work, the sharing of work, participation in organisational or public activities.

The flexibility of managerial jobs

Stewart suggests that the model provides a framework for thinking about the nature of managerial jobs, and about the manner in which managers undertake them. To understand what managerial jobs are really like it is necessary to understand the nature of their flexibility. Account should be taken of variations in behaviour and differences in jobs before attempting to generalise about managerial work. Study of managers in similar jobs indicates that their focus of attention differs. Opportunities for individual managers to do what they believe to be most important exist to a greater or lesser extent in all managerial jobs. Stewart also concludes that the model has implications for organisational design, job design, management effectiveness, selection, education and training, and career decisions.

How managers really behave

From a review of research into managerial behaviour, Stewart concludes that the picture built up gives a very different impression from the traditional description of a manager as one who plans, organises, co-ordinates, motivates, and controls in a logical, ordered process. Management is very much a human activity.

> *The picture that emerges from studies of what managers do is of someone who lives in a whirl of activity, in which attention must be switched every few minutes from one subject, problem, and person to another; of an uncertain world where relevant information includes gossip and speculation about how other people are thinking and what they are likely to do; and where it is necessary, particularly in senior posts, to develop a network of people who can fill one in on what is going on and what is likely to happen. It is a picture, too, not of a manager who sits quietly controlling but who is dependent upon many people, other than subordinates, with whom reciprocating relationships should be created; who needs to learn how to trade, bargain, and compromise; and a picture of managers who, increasingly as they ascend the management ladder, live in a political world where they must learn how to influence people other than sub-ordinates, how to manoeuvre, and how to enlist support for what they want to do. In short, it is a much more human activity than that commonly suggested in management textbooks.*[31]

Critical reflection

'Someone with poor social skills or lacking political astuteness can never become an effective manager ... you can't make a silk purse out of a sow's ear. And in any case, management is all about relevant job experience.' To what extent do you agree that training makes very little difference?

WHAT GREAT MANAGERS DO

According to *Buckingham*, an average manager sees employees as workers who fill roles; an exceptional manager sees them as individuals to build roles around. Great managers perform their magic by discovering developing and celebrating what is different about each person who works for them. 'While there are as many styles of management as there are managers, there is one quality that sets truly great managers apart from the rest: They discover what is unique about each person and then capitalize on it ... Great managers know and value the unique abilities and even the eccentricities of their employees, and learn how best to integrate them into a coordinated plan of attack.'

Identifying and capitalising on each person's uniqueness is a powerful tool because it saves time in the allocation of roles; makes each person more accountable; builds a stronger sense of team through creating interdependency; and introduces a healthy degree of disruption by shuffling existing hierarchies and existing assumptions about who is allowed to do what. Managers need to know to collate what they know about each person and put their idiosyncrasies to use. In order to manage people well, this demands that the manager knows:

- their strengths;
- the triggers that activate those strengths; and
- how they learn.

Great managers do not try to change a person's style. The majority of differences in traits and talents are enduring and resistant to change.

> *A manager's most precious resource is time, and great managers know that the most effective way to invest their time is to identify exactly how each employee is different and then to figure out how best to incorporate those enduring idiosyncrasies into the overall plan.*[32]

THE ATTRIBUTES AND QUALITIES OF A MANAGER

The 'Quality of Management' is one of nine ingredients of success by which *Management Today* rates performance in its annual survey of Britain's Most Admired Companies. In 2003 The Investors in People introduced a 'Leadership and Management Model' that focuses on the development of organisational leadership and management capability. The model is discussed in Chapter 20. Whatever the role of the manager or whether in the private or public sector, in order to carry out the process of management and the execution of work, the manager requires a combination of technical competence, social and human skills, and conceptual ability.[33]

As the manager advances through the organisational hierarchy, greater emphasis is likely to be placed on conceptual ability, and proportionately less on technical competence (*see* Figure 11.7). (*See also* the discussion on levels of organisation in Chapter 15.)

- **Technical competence** relates to the application of specific knowledge, methods and skills to discrete tasks. Technical competence is likely to be required more at the supervisory level and for the training of subordinate staff, and with day-to-day operations concerned in the actual production of goods or services.

Figure 11.7 The combination of attributes of a manager

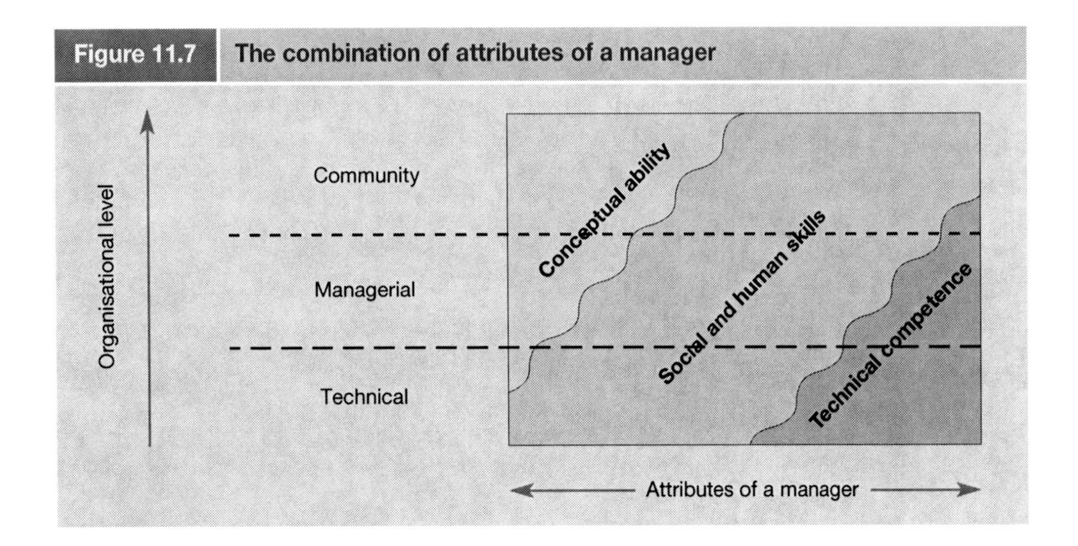

- **Social and human skills** refer to interpersonal relationships in working with and through other people, and the exercise of judgement. A distinctive feature of management is the ability to secure the effective use of the human resources of the organisation. This involves effective teamwork and the direction and leadership of staff to achieve co-ordinated effort. Under this heading can be included sensitivity to particular situations, and flexibility in adopting the most appropriate style of management.
- **Conceptual ability** is required in order to view the complexities of the operations of the organisation as a whole, including environmental influences. It also involves decision-making skills. The manager's personal contribution should be related to the overall objectives of the organisation and to its strategic planning.

Although a simplistic approach, this framework provides a useful basis from which to examine the combination and balance of the attributes of an effective manager. For example the extent of technical competence or conceptual ability will vary according to the level of the organisation at which the manager is working. However, major technological change means that managers at all levels of the organisation increasingly require technical competence in the skills of information communications technology.

Balance of 'hard' and 'soft' skills

Management has become more about managing people than managing operations, however, and social and human skills which reflect the ability to get along with other people are increasingly important attributes at all levels of management. *Green* suggests that most managers will spend most time operating between the spectrum of 'hard' skills such as conducting disciplinary matters or fighting one's corner in a debate about allocation of budgets; and 'soft' skills such as counselling, or giving support and advice to a member of staff. The most successful managers are those able to adjust their approach and response to an appropriate part of the spectrum.[34]

And as *Douglas* also reminds us, although there is a clear need for mastery of technical expertise, 'soft skills' are also an essential part of the world of business.

> *Living as we do in a society that is technologically and scientifically extremely advanced, most kinds of professional advancement are close to impossible without the mastery of one or more specialised branches of systematic technical knowledge ... What is the downside? Organisations in most sectors – and especially in ones that are particularly demanding from a scientific or technical point of view – are operating in environments where collaboration, teamwork, and an awareness of the commercial implications of technical research are as important as scientific and technical skills themselves. Personnel with scientific and technical skills significantly disproportionate to their 'people' skills – by which I primarily mean people management capabilities and knowledge of how to work with maximum effectiveness as part of a team – are increasingly unlikely to be as much of an asset to their organisation as they ought to be.*[35]

Importance of job experience

A recent report from the Chartered Management Institute found changing perceptions of what makes a good manager. For the first time since the question was asked in 1986, the belief that 'leaders are born not made' has been eclipsed by the view that relevant job experience makes good managers (*see* Figure 11.8). The report also points out that a clear trend emerges in those skills that employers will be developing in the future: the ability to manage change and manage risk will be the key for managers in the coming years. The ability to facilitate organisational learning and to lead through ethical/value-based behaviour are identified as priority areas.[36]

Figure 11.8 Changing perceptions of what makes a good manager

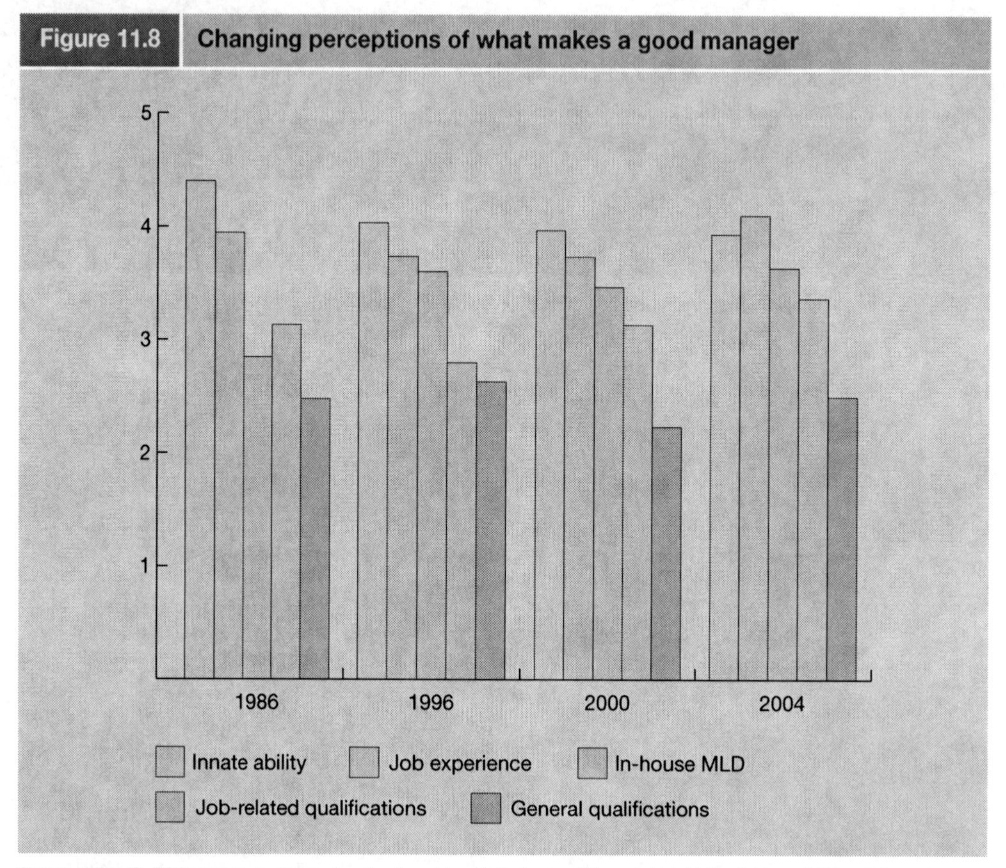

Source: Mabey, C., 'Management development works: the evidence', *Professional Manager*, Vol. 14, No. 2, March 2005, p. 4. Reproduced with permission from Chartered Management Institute.

Situational management

According to *Misslehorn*, the challenge for managers is to sharpen their ability to **perceive** more accurately, **process** the information more wisely, **respond** more appropriately and examine the **feedback** from the actions taken in order to learn and keep things on track. Managers need to **think** through situations, bringing their rational and creative brainpower to bear on them. They also need to involve others through appropriate **interaction** and communication. The way managers think about the situation and interact with others has a direct bearing on their **perceptions** of the situation – helping to curb some of the distortions from their past experience, values, bias, fears, feelings and prejudices. And the way managers think about a situation and interact with others also has a direct bearing on their **responses** and the results produced and outcomes of their actions. This interplay between thinking and interacting takes place in complex strategic organisational situations. This process of **situational management** is illustrated in Figure 11.9.[37]

Figure 11.9 Situational management

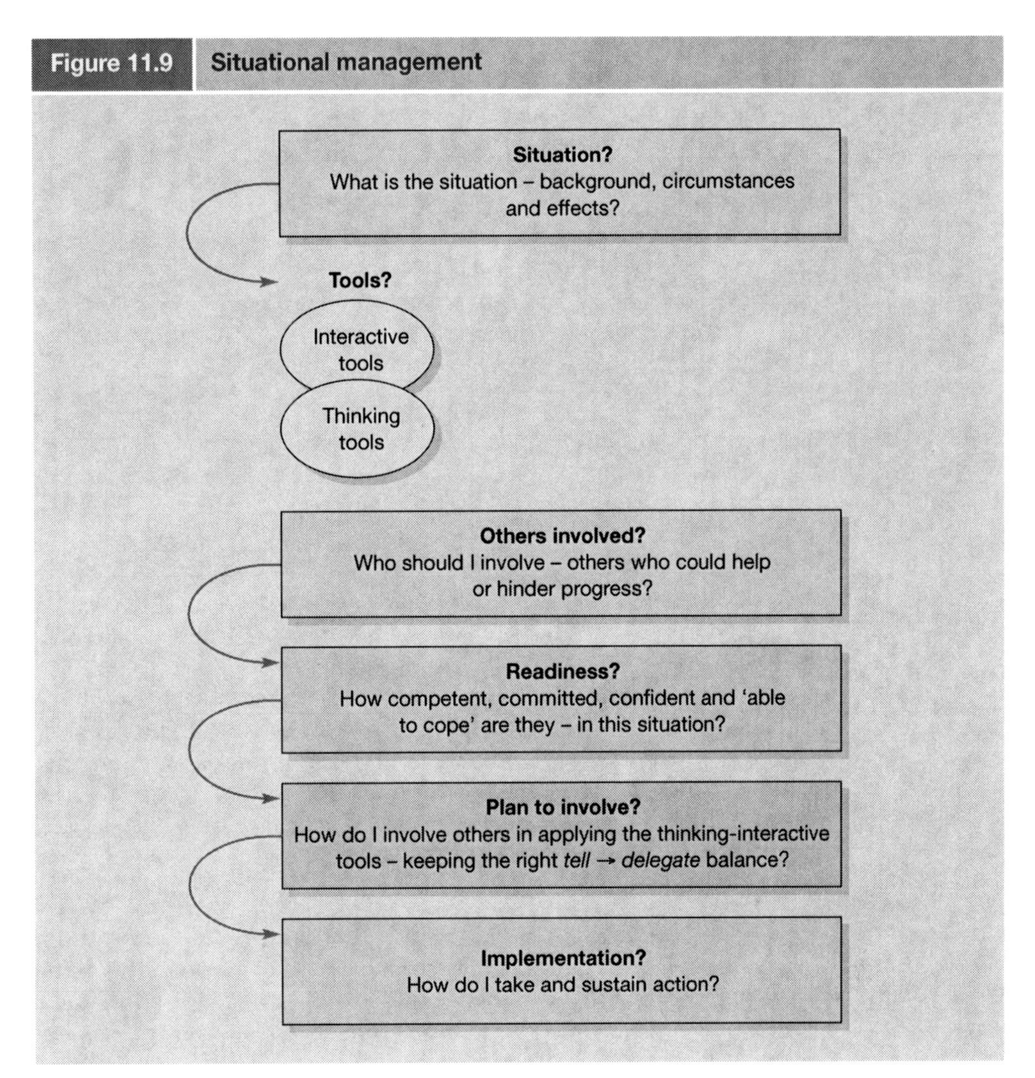

Source: Adapted from Misselhorn, H., *The Head and Heart of Management*, Management and Organization Development Consultants (2003), p. 13.

> *The fact is that management ultimately depends on an understanding of human nature. I suggest it goes much further than that. In the first place, good management depends on the acceptance of certain basic values. It cannot be achieved without honesty and integrity, or without consideration for the interests of others. Secondly, it is the understanding of human foibles that we all share, such as jealousy, envy, status, prejudice, perception, temperament, motivation and talent, which provides the greatest challenge to managers.*
>
> HRH The Duke of Edinburgh[38]

THE CHANGING ROLE OF MANAGERS

Billsberry points out that the number of people who are managers has been growing rapidly and also that the scope and variety of what managers are required to do has been continually expanding.[39] By contrast, *Belbin* contends that many of the quintessential managerial activities that fell within the everyday domain of the manager, such as communicating, motivating and organising, have now become shared with an assortment of well-educated executives such as technical experts, advisers and specialists, including human resource professionals, industrial relations officers and consulting firms. Responsibility for direction of effort and setting objectives is taken over by directors. Managers in the traditional sense of 'a person who assigns tasks and responsibilities to others' have become a dwindling minority. This has had cultural consequences. 'The flattening of hierarchy in opening up opportunities to non-managerial executives has helped to create resistance to the authority and status of the manager–boss.'[40]

Ten key strategies

Whatever the debate, we should note the comments of *Heller* who from his study of Europe's top companies refers to the need for new managers and new methods to obey the imperatives of a dramatically changed environment.

> *Today, managements whose minds and deeds are stuck in the status quo are obsolescent, weak and failing. In the next few years, they will be obsolete – and failed. Renewal and nimbleness have become paramount necessities for the large and established. For the younger business, staying new and agile is equally imperative.*[41]

Heller goes on to identify ten key strategies for Europe's new breed of managers:

1. **Developing leadership** – without losing control or direction.
2. **Driving radical change** – in the entire corporate system, not just in its parts.
3. **Reshaping culture** – to achieve long-term success.
4. **Dividing to rule** – winning the rewards of smallness while staying or growing large.
5. **Exploiting the 'organisation'** – by new approaches to central direction.
6. **Keeping the competitive edge** – in a world where the old ways of winning no longer work.
7. **Achieving constant renewal** – stopping success from sowing the seeds of decay.
8. **Managing the motivators** – so that people can motivate themselves.
9. **Making team-working work** – the new, indispensable skill.
10. **Achieving total management quality** – by managing everything much better.

Six critical elements

We have referred previously to the changing nature of work organisations and *Prahalad*, for example, suggests that the change in the work of managing is obvious. Issues of formal structure and hierarchy, authority and power, industry experience and seniority, and control and co-ordination are all open to challenge. The changing role of managing requires that special attention should be given to the role of senior managers. Prahalad suggests the need to concentrate on six critical elements:

1. The importance of a **shared competitive agenda**.
2. Creating a clear charter of **values and behaviours**.
3. Focusing on **influence without ownership**.
4. **Competing for talent** and building the skill mix of the organisation.
5. **Speed of reaction** in the organisation.
6. **Leveraging corporate resources** to address emerging opportunities.

Prahalad concludes: 'The emerging dimensions of managerial work are clear. The soft issues such as values and behaviors, often dismissed as unimportant, are critical.'[42]

According to a report from the Chartered Management Institute, British managers are now placing concern for consumers, themselves as managers and other employee groups above their traditional concern for owners and shareholders of their organisation. Looking to the future, managers believe the most important issues facing their organisation over the next decade will be managing change, customer satisfaction, use of the Internet, motivation of core staff, managing diversity and the development of human resources.[43]

The end of management?

Note, however, that according to *Cloke and Goldsmith*: 'Managers are the dinosaurs of our modern organisational ecology. The Age of Management is finally coming to a close.' Cloke and Goldsmith suggest that the ever-extending reach of globalisation, continuously rising productivity, growing complexity of information, expanded sensitivity of the environment and swelling pace of technological innovation are all increasing the demand for alternative organisational practices. They contend that management is an idea whose time is up. Organisations that do not recognise the need to share power and responsibility with all their workers will lose them. The most significant trends in the theory and history of management are the decline of hierarchical, bureaucratic, autocratic management and the expansion of collaborative self-management and organisational democracy.[44]

But what is actually 'new'?

There is much written today about changes in the workforce and new approaches to management. It is interesting to note, however, the ideas on the nature of managerial behaviour put forward over 60 years ago by Mary Parker Follett. Her thinking was based on concern for social, evolutionary progress, and the organisation and management of people for effective performance and a fuller life. Follett envisioned the successful operation of groups, and management responsibility diffused through the organisation and not just concentrated at the top of the hierarchy. One of her most notable contributions was emphasis on the situational approach as one of the main forces in influencing the manager–subordinate relationship through the depersonalising of orders and obeying 'the law of the situation'.[45]

Parker suggests that Follett's ideas on human relations in the workforce foreshadowed the state of things to come and continue to offer managers in the new century fresh food for thought. Her proposals for best management practice have not only reflected much of what is portrayed as new today but offer managers fresh insight into the task of leadership and management.[46]

While the nature of managerial work changes constantly, the fundamental truth remains unchanged: management continues to represent a huge challenge to those who put it into practice every day throughout the world.[47]

Critical reflection

According to Peter Drucker, management is a practice rather than a science or a profession so there are no precise solutions, and the ultimate test of management is achievement and business performance. To what extent can you argue, therefore, that in the effective management of business organisations, the ends justify the means?

MANAGEMENT IN THE NEWS

Too close for comfort

Managers who want to get up close and personal

Lucy Kellaway

Are you a success as a person? If this is too large a question, let me ask something less open-ended: Are you a success as a parent? I have just put both questions to myself and am at a loss. Being a person is a mixed bag and so is being a parent. There are good bits and bad bits about each, but the concept of success does not really apply to either. What would the criteria be? Even if I could assess my success as a

Management in the news – continued

person, it would surely be a personal matter. Yet last week I found that two large organisations were boldly placing their employees' personal and parental success at the heart of company policy.

The first is Goldman Sachs, which has set up a Wellness Exchange for all its busy workers. The very name gives a hint that all is not well. Wellness is an annoying new word that is spreading across the corporate world like some lethal virus. Gyms are now called wellness centres and even respectable companies such as Nestlé have a wellness division. But what does it mean? I cannot find it in my dictionary, and the online definition goes like this: 'Wellness as defined by the National Wellness Association is an active process of becoming aware of and making choices toward a more successful existence.' Which does not leave you any the wiser. The idea of a wellness *exchange* is positively sinister. Goldman gives wellness to its employees but, in return, what do they give back? Their working lives, with their souls thrown in, one fears.

'The driving force behind the Wellness Exchange is to recognise Goldman Sachs employees in all aspects of their lives, personally and professionally,' it says on the company website. So there are wellness fairs you can go to, seminars and lectures on personal growth and, more prosaically (and usefully), gyms and doctors. The bank offers everything you need to combat the non-wellness of working so hard. It even gives adoption assistance, infertility treatment and manages 'fitness activities' that 'allow for interaction outside the work environment'. One of the offerings at the Wellness Exchange is one-on-one counselling for employees, 'empowering them with the tools to make positive lifestyle choices'. Quite a few Goldman employees do seem to have made a positive lifestyle choice recently: they have left the bank.

The other policy I studied last week was from Ernst & Young and is all about helping 'parents manage their personal and professional goals' (in other words, stopping mothers from quitting). The policy is called My JournEY, which raises the question: journey to where? To and from work via the daycare centre, one assumes. This policy is about 'new moms' and 'veteran moms' networking and sharing best practice. There is a lot of reaching out and talk of 'connectivity' but there is something more practical on offer, too: a new lactation programme, which includes a 'hospital-grade pump'.

The only thing that one might be able to borrow from My JournEY is the clever way that the Ernst & Young brand is reflected in the name. There are surely possibilities for the Financial Times here and I have just spent an enjoyable and creative hour or so brainstorming and have come up with this: aFTer childbirth you oFTen go soFT and daFT. That might be true but it is not really a good name for a policy for new moms.

Source: Kellaway, L. 'Managers who want to get up close and personal', *Financial Times*, 25 June 2006.

Discussion questions

1 Outline and evaluate the reasons why organisations might set up programmes like these to support the personal lives of their employees.

2 What role conflicts might this concern with people's domestic and personal lives cause for individual managers and members of their staff? Can such conflicts be successfully reconciled?

SYNOPSIS

- 'Management' is a generic term and subject to many interpretations. Our concern is with management within a structured organisational setting and involving the exercise of formal authority over the work of other people. The nature of management is variable. It relates to all activities of the organisation and is undertaken at all levels. Management is essentially an integrating activity that permeates all other aspects of the organisation.

- It is not easy to find agreement on the definition of management, or of a manager. Management is not homogeneous but takes place in different ways. One approach is to analyse the nature of management and to identify common activities and principles. By distinguishing 'managing' from 'doing' we can summarise the nature of managerial work as clarification of objectives, planning, organising, directing and controlling. The degree of emphasis given to these different activities may vary widely from one manager to another. There are, however, many other approaches to the analysis of management.

- There are important differences between management in private enterprise and public sector organisations. However, all organisations face the same general problems of management. Although there are perceived differences between management in the private and public sectors, increasing attention is being given to applications of general management theory and the adoption of business practices in the public sector. There are common challenges for all managers. Management theories apply to all managers and the skills of managing are fundamentally alike.

- Despite similarities in the general activities of management, the jobs of individual managers differ widely. Empirical studies have concentrated on the diversity of management and differences in the nature of managerial work. These studies have drawn attention to such features as managerial roles, agenda-setting and network-building, what real managers do, and demands, constraints and choices in a managerial job.

- In order to carry out the process of management and execution of work, the manager requires a combination of technical competence, social and human skills, and conceptual ability. Growing attention is attached to managerial competencies including skills in information communication technology. Despite the increasing emphasis on technical expertise, it is important that managers have a balance of both 'hard' and 'soft' skills, including people skills.

- While the importance and responsibility of management is still widely recognised there is a need for a changed role for managers. Europe's new breed of managers need to focus attention on key strategies including the importance of values and behaviours. Important issues for the future include managing change, leadership and motivation of staff, managing diversity, the development of human resources, and demands for alternative organisational practices. One can, however, question what is really new about managerial behaviour.

Refresh your understanding, assess your progress and begin your research with online resources at **www.pearsoned.co.uk/mullins**

REVIEW AND DISCUSSION QUESTIONS

1. How would you summarise the essential nature of managerial work? In what ways does the job of a manager differ from any other job in a work organisation?
2. Explain fully and with supporting reasons what you see as the most important attribute(s) or quality(ies) required of a successful manager.
3. To what extent is it possible to establish rules or principles of good management? Assess critically the practical applications of these rules or principles.
4. Contrast critically the nature of management in (i) service and production industries, and (ii) private enterprise and public sector organisations.
5. Why do organisations need managers? Suggest how the flexibility in managerial jobs might be identified and compare and contrast any two different managerial jobs.
6. Suggest which *one* writer has in your opinion made the greatest contribution to our understanding of the nature of management. Justify your answer.
7. Discuss critically the suggestion that management is a much more human activity than is commonly suggested in management textbooks. Support your discussion with practical examples.
8. Explain fully how you see the nature of managerial activities and the likely role of the manager in ten years' time.

ASSIGNMENT 1

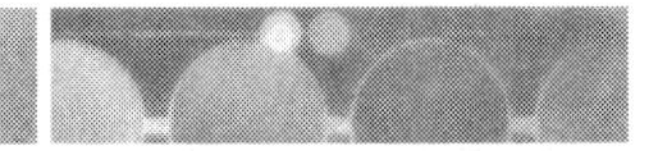

Select a particular managerial job and observe the manager in action, preferably over an extended period of time.

a Make notes, with supporting examples, of the proportion of the manager's work and time which is spent on:

1 the carrying out of discrete tasks and the actual 'doing' of work personally, and

2 deciding what work is to be done and planning, organising, directing or controlling the work of other people.

Assignment – continued

- **b** Analyse particular ways in which features of the internal and external environment influence the work of the manager.
- **c** Suggest, with supporting reasons, the **particular** attributes or qualities that appear to be necessary for successful performance of the manager's job.
- **d** Analyse the job in terms of the activities of: (i) agenda-setting, and (ii) network-building.
- **e** Identify clearly those factors that determine the demands, constraints and choices of the job. Comment critically on how these factors determine the flexibility in the manager's job.
- **f** State clearly the conclusions you draw from your observations and compare with those of your colleagues.

ASSIGNMENT 2

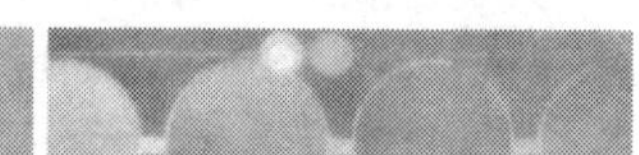

Examine the nature of managerial activity within your own university/college.

- **a** Explain clearly those factors that distinguish the general nature of management from that in other (private sector) business organisations and identify clearly the main internal and environmental influences.
- **b** Using a framework of your choice, examine the specific functions of one particular management position (such as, for example, a head of department).
- **c** Contrast the specific attributes and abilities required of that manager with those required by managers at different levels of the university/college.
- **d** Explain fully whether you believe your lecturer can reasonably be regarded as a manager.
- **e** State clearly the conclusions you draw and compare with those of your colleagues.

PERSONAL AWARENESS AND SKILLS EXERCISE

Objectives

Completing this exercise should help you to enhance the following skills:

- Act in the role of the manager to handle a number of real-life situations.
- Conduct management–staff interviews and discussions.
- Review critically your ability to deal with emotionally difficult situations.

Exercise

Given below are a number of real-life situations. You are required to:

1. Think through each one and explain how you as the manager might best handle the discussion with your member of staff.
2. Record how you would approach each discussion/interview and the type of questions you might be likely to ask.

Example 1

One of your employees continually arrives late for work. This is the sixth time this has happened. Their excuse is that they have to take their child to nursery because they are getting divorced and their spouse refuses to do this task.

Example 2

You receive a complaint from one of your female employees that another one of your employees has pornographic data on his PC that she finds offensive.

Example 3

One of your permanent employees has been accused of assaulting another member of staff who works for the same organisation but is an independent contractor.

Example 4

You overhear a member of your department comment of you that 'he/she has no idea of the technical complexity of my work ... I don't know how he/she can manage a department like this!'

Example 5

A key client calls you to complain about sarcastic and impatient comments made by one of your more experienced technicians. Comments like 'Your people must be really thick if they think that's how it works ...' have proved less than helpful. You know this person has been working long hours, achieving excellent results and is clearly committed to their job and the department. In fact, you have just promoted the technician for these very reasons.

Example 6

In a recent management meeting, a relatively new colleague repeatedly contradicted you and appeared to be 'scoring points' at your expense. Although the colleague had made some valid, even perceptive comments, it isn't exactly helping your relationship get off to an encouraging start. Furthermore, this has happened on a previous occasion.

Discussion

- How would you summarise the essential nature of the manager–subordinate relationship?
- Using your own examples, explain the importance of using appropriate approaches when dealing with potentially difficult situations.
- What do you learn about the nature of the manager–subordinate relationship?

CASE STUDY

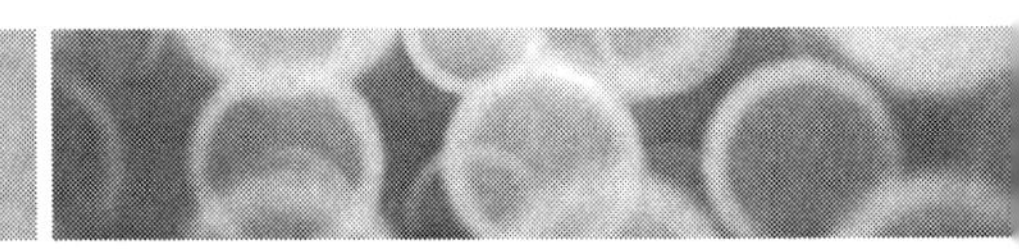

Stuck in the middle?

In August 2005, two studies of organisational life made unhappy reading for many of Britain's managers. An Investors in People survey discovered that 80 per cent of staff believed that some of their colleagues were lazy and often not up to their jobs, and half of them blamed managers for allowing the situation to continue.[48] On the same day, a major Sirota Survey Intelligence report which had questioned 3.5 million staff over three years found that most workers believed that their bosses were overly bureaucratic, made inconsistent decisions and generally hampered their staff rather than helping them to do their jobs.[49] Taken together with the trend for delayering (removing layers of management from organisations to streamline business activity and achieve cost savings), and some further warnings that managers who fail to adapt to the changing nature of the workplace are likely to face 'mass lay-offs',[50] one might forgive the average middle manager for feeling somewhat unloved. However, some more recent research by *Management Today* magazine suggests that perhaps all is not doom and gloom at the centre of organisational life.[51]

Middle Managers: telling it like it is

The *Management Today* survey was conducted during early 2006 and reported in the March 2006 edition of the magazine. Part of its purpose was to match a similar survey of top business leaders which had taken place six months earlier and to discover more about the role and

Source: Paul Risdale/PhotoFusion

Are middle managers stressed out by bureaucracy and organisational politics, or inspired by their role and prospects?

nature of mid-ranking managers, many of whom might not have the ambition to become chief executives or captains of industry, but upon whom most organisations depend for the regular delivery of core activities. Over 1000 managers took part in the survey, representing both public and private sector organisations, and a good 40 per cent of respondents were women. Some of the headline figures demonstrated a strong sense of job satisfaction, and in answer to a question about whether, if they had their time again, they would choose to become a manager, 92 per cent respondents answered that they had not regretted their choice. A small majority, 54 per cent, were not actively seeking promotion and a significant majority, almost 69 per cent, did not want to step into their boss's job. Clearly the picture here is one of broad satisfaction with the work and the nature of their managerial role. However, perhaps unsurprisingly given the findings of the other surveys mentioned, 43 per cent felt that they were not valued.

The survey seemed to highlight a number of common reasons why managers enjoyed their work. Chief among these were:

- influence and achievement: the ability to see themselves making positive contributions to the organisation and the way it worked. A significant 88 per cent of those surveyed said that this was one of the strongest motivating factors for them;
- autonomy: 79 per cent considered that a relative degree of autonomy was also a source of satisfaction. The managers who were happiest in their work were those whose bosses were able to allow them a relatively free rein;
- developing people: again, almost 80 per cent of the managers considered that their role in developing others, helping people to achieve better levels of performance and encouraging newer or younger workers to be a major source of work-related pleasure.

Things which managers reported as being demotivating and which frustrated them in their jobs were:

- bureaucracy: 48 per cent cited excessive and bureaucratic systems as being what they disliked most about their work;
- pressure to do more with less: this was often what stressed managers most. As customers and clients become more demanding, the lack of resources, coupled with increasing spans of control, was clearly putting managers under significant strain. Indeed, middle managers were also reported as being more likely to take time off sick than any other employee group;[52]
- politics: 45 per cent of the survey respondents believed that office politics was damaging to their organisations.

There were some marked differences of opinion about how the question of organisational politics should be approached – one manager who was interviewed in detail for the *Management Today* report considered it was something which had to be understood and handled, but others were very critical of the sort of behaviour which caused different units or departments of (mostly larger) organisations to become close-knit and focused on protecting their own interests, often at the expense of overall organisational success.

Leading isn't easy

Becoming a manager means, for many, a significant change in role and perspective, and the transition causes a number of common problems for those who find themselves in 'the middle'. One aspect of their managerial work which many reported as problematic was the need to learn effective delegation, and to become a leader rather than a 'doer'. One respondent from Hewlett-Packard illustrated this point:

> *When I first became a manager, I tried to do everything myself, my old job plus my new responsibilities, but I soon realised this was a mistake.*

She also noted that being judged on the success of her team, rather than on her individual performance, was difficult to get used to. This unwillingness or inability to delegate was also reported in a 2003 survey of UK middle managers by the HR consultancy DDI.[53] Not only did many (over 60 per cent) of the managers questioned believe that the best way to get a job done was to do it themselves, but over half felt that they were unable to delegate, either because their staff did not have adequate skills or because they could not be trusted to deliver on time. And yet, as one of the directors of DDI observed:

> *If you've not made the transition from doing to leading in your first management promotion, you'll become badly unstuck when you move up another level.*[54]

The problems surrounding delegation might also be related to the first headline reported above; the difficulty of identifying and dealing with under-performing staff. While workers might believe their colleagues to be lazy, they also clearly felt that managers were not doing enough to tackle matters of poor performance.

As Ruth Spellman, Chief Executive of IIP, observed in her commentary on the findings:

> *It is clear from the findings that UK managers are aware that dead wood is a problem that can damage their organisation – but are failing to do anything about it. However, left unchecked … (it).. can breed resentment amongst colleagues and cripple an organisation's productivity.*[55]

Yet if this is set against the complaints of micro-management which many employees voiced, it becomes clear that the delicate balance between effective monitoring and interference is a difficult one to achieve.

Another common theme running through the *Management Today* and the DDI surveys was that of middle manager stress. This arises partly from the causes highlighted above, but also from the ambiguity which often surrounds the role. Middle managers might be pivotal to the actual running of the day-to-day activities of the organisation, but while they are accountable to senior people who are often the strategic decision-makers, they are also embroiled in the minutiae of daily work. This results in two very different sets of demands from two different directions, as the HR director at Centrica summarised:

> *It's difficult to report to the top team and order the paper clips as well.*[56]

In some cases, managers felt that the additional stresses of taking on a managerial workload not only removed them from the work they enjoyed as specialists, but that the additional pay was scarcely adequate to compensate for the added pressure. One respondent noted that:

> *There's only £2k difference in a managerial role pay and an analyst below, but the workload increases by 45 per cent.*[57]

Similarly, while middle managers are the key players in organisational change and development, they report that they often find themselves driving through initiatives which have been developed and determined by those above them in the organisation, who are sometimes those who lack recent knowledge of the realities of life at the front line. One of the *Management Today* respondents who works at British Petroleum noted that the company has initiated a system which is designed to overcome this type of horizontal segmentation. All senior managers have to spend four days a year working in the company's forecourt stores and a further four hours each quarter answering the phones in its call centres.

Finally, what are the prospects for middle managers? The *Management Today* survey reported that fewer than half of those surveyed were actively looking for promotion (46 per cent) compared with 54 per cent who were not. This matches closely with the figure of 47 per cent who saw themselves as very ambitious. Few in the survey wanted their boss's job, and only 27 per cent believed that, in five years' time, they would be holding a more senior role in their current organisations. This might indicate relatively strong sense of job satisfaction, but it might equally be a realistic assessment of the impact of structural delayering and the consequently reduced career opportunities open via traditional forms of promotion. For some, career development might take place through sideways moves or opportunities to be mentors and coaches to less experienced managers. For others, however, despite the stresses and frustrations, being stuck in the middle is quite a comfortable place to be.

Your tasks

1. Analyse the survey results using one or more of the models from the text about the nature of management (for example that of Fayol, p. 415, Drucker, p. 418 or Mintzberg, p. 423). Which of the models do you find offers the best analysis of the work of middle managers and why?
2. What training and development needs are suggested by the material from the surveys? Suggest appropriate content and methods of an effective development programme for a newly appointed middle manager. How will your choice be affected by your overall view of the nature of management as suggested by Watson and outlined in Figure 11.1?
3. Is it harder or easier to be a senior manager than a middle manager? Explain the reasons for your answer.

Notes and References

1 See, for example: Margretta, J. *What Management Is: How it Works and Why it's Everyone's Business*, HarperCollins (2002).
2 Knights, D. and Willmott, H. *Management Lives: Power and Identity in Work Organizations*, Sage Publications (1999), p. iix.
3 Crainer, S. *Key Management Ideas: Thinkers that Changed the Management World*, Third edition, Financial Times Prentice Hall (1998), p. xi.
4 Schneider, S. C. and Barsoux, J. *Managing Across Cultures*, Second edition, Financial Times Prentice Hall (2003).
5 Francesco, A. M. and Gold, B. A. *International Organizational Behavior*, Second edition, Prentice Hall (2005).
6 Drucker, P. F. *The Practice of Management*, Heinemann Professional (1989), p. 3.
7 Drucker, P. F. *Management*, Pan Books (1979), p. 14.
8 Crainer, S. 'The Rise of Guru Scepticism', *Management Today*, March 1996, p. 51.
9 Watson, T. J. *Management, Organisation and Employment Strategy*, Routledge & Kegan Paul (1986).
10 Fayol, H. *General and Industrial Management*, Pitman (1949). See also: Gray, I. *Henri Fayol's General and Industrial Management*, Pitman Publishing (1988).
11 Fayol, H. *General and Industrial Management*, Pitman (1949).
12 Moorcroft, R. 'Managing in the 21st Century', *The British Journal of Administrative Management*, January/ February 2000, pp. 8–10.
13 Brech, E. F. L. *Principles and Practice of Management*, Third edition, Longman (1975), p. 19.
14 Drucker, P. F. *People and Performance*, Heinemann (1977), p. 28.
15 Ibid., p. 59.
16 Ferguson, A. (Sir) in Gwyther M. and Saunders, A. 'United they stand?' *Management Today*, April 2005, p. 41.
17 Stewart, R. *The Reality of Management*, Third edition, Butterworth Heinemann (1999), p. 6.
18 Robinson, G. 'Improving Performance through People', *The British Journal of Administrative Management*, September/ October 1999, p. 4.
19 Fenlon, M. 'The Public Spirit', Mastering Leadership, *Financial Times*, 22 November 2002, pp. 4–5.
20 Hannagan, T. *Management: Concepts and Practices*, Fourth edition, Financial Times Prentice Hall (2005), p. 32.
21 Stewart, J. 'Managing Difference', *Chartered Secretary*, October 2003, p. 31.
22 See, for example: Mullins, L. J. *Hospitality Management and Organisational Behaviour* Fourth edition, Longman (2001).
23 For a useful summary of the work of the manager, see for example: Birchall, D. W. 'What Managers Do', in Crainer, S. and Dearlove, D. (eds) *Financial Times Handbook of Management*, Second edition, Financial Times Prentice Hall (2001), pp. 110–31.
24 Mintzberg, H. *The Nature of Managerial Work*, Harper and Row (1973).
25 Mintzberg, H. 'The Manager's Job: Folklore and Fact', *Harvard Business Review Classic*, March–April 1990, pp. 163–76.
26 Kotter, J. P. *The General Managers*, The Free Press (1982).
27 Kotter, J. P. 'What Effective General Managers Really Do', *Harvard Business Review*, vol. 60, no. 6, November–December 1982, pp. 156–67.
28 Luthans, F. 'Successful vs. Effective Real Managers', *The Academy of Management Executive*, vol. 11, no. 2, May 1988, pp. 127–32.
29 Stewart, R. *Contrasts in Management*, McGraw-Hill (1976).
30 Stewart, R. *Choices for the Manager*, McGraw-Hill (1982). See also, Stewart, R. *Managing Today and Tomorrow*, Macmillan (1991).
31 Stewart, R. 'Managerial Behaviour: How Research has Changed the Traditional Picture', in Earl, M. J. (ed.) *Perspectives on Management: A Multidisciplinary Analysis*, Oxford University Press (1983), pp. 96–7.
32 Buckingham, M. 'What Great Managers Do', *Harvard Business Review*, vol. 83, no. 3, March 2005, pp. 70–9.
33 Katz, R. L. 'Skills of an Effective Administrator', *Harvard Business Review*, September–October 1974, pp. 90–102.
34 Green, J. 'When Was Your Management Style Last Applauded?', *Chartered Secretary*, December 1998, pp. 28–9.
35 Douglas, M. 'Why "Soft Skills" Are an Essential Part of the Hard World of Business', *Manager, The British Journal of Administrative Management*, No. 34, Christmas 2002/New Year 2003, p. 34.
36 Mabey, C. 'Management Development Works: The Evidence' Chartered Management Institute, January 2005.
37 Misselhorn, H. *The Head and Heart of Management*, Management and Organization Development Consultants, South Africa (2003), pp. 12–13.
38 'In Celebration of the Feel-good Factor', *Professional Manager*, March 1998, p. 6.
39 Billsberry, J. (ed.) *The Effective Manager: Perspectives and Illustrations*, Sage Publications (1996).
40 Belbin, R. M. *Changing the Way we Work*, Butterworth-Heinemann (1997), p. 95.
41 Heller, R. *In Search of European Excellence*, HarperCollins Business (1997), p. xvi.
42 Prahalad, C. K. 'Emerging Work of Managers', in Chowdhury, S. *Management 21C*, Financial Times Prentice Hall (2000) pp. 141–50.
43 Poole, M. and Mansfield, R. *Two Decades of Management*, Chartered Management Institute, June 2001.
44 Cloke, K. and Goldsmith, J. *The End of Management; and the Rise of Organizational Democracy*, Jossey-Bass (2002).
45 Metcalfe, H. and Urwick, L (eds), *Dynamic Administration – The Collected Papers of Mary Parker Follett*, Harper (1941).
46 Parker, L. E. 'Shock of the New a Century on', *Professional Manager*, vol. 14, no. 6, November 2005, pp. 34–5.
47 Crainer, S. *Key Management Ideas*, Third edition, Financial Times Prentice Hall (1998), p. xvi.
48 BBC news website, 'Staff brand colleagues as "lazy"' 12 August 2006 [accessed 12 August 2006].
49 BBC news website, 'Workers want bosses to "get lost"' 12 August 2006 [accessed 12 August 2006].
50 Thomas, D. 'Middle managers face mass lay-offs' *Personnel Today* available from www.personneltoday.com 2 June 2005 [accessed 12 August 2006].
51 Kennett, M. 'View from the Middle' *Management Today* March 2006 pp. 35–42.
52 Rigby, R. 2006 Employee Absence; Sick Notes, *HR Magazine* 1 January 2006 available at www.hrmagazine.co.uk [accessed 12 August 2006].
53 DDI 2003 'Leading on the Fault Line' Research report published by DDI and available from www.ddiworld.com [accessed 12 August 2006].

54 *Personnel Today* 2006 'How to Lead from the Middle' 9 May 2006 and available from www.personneltoday.com [accessed 12 August 2006].
55 IIP Press Release 19.08.05 available at www.investorsinpeople.co.uk [accessed 12 August 2006].
56 Rigby, R. 2006 'The best bit is in the middle', *HR Magazine* 6 July 2006 available at www.hrmagazine.co.uk [accessed 12 August 2006].
57 Kennett, M. 'View from the Middle', *Management Today* March 2006 pp. 35–42.

MANAGERIAL BEHAVIOUR AND EFFECTIVENESS

Very often, your resources are greater than you might think. I don't like it when people underestimate me, and I try not to underestimate anyone else, either. People are multifaceted, and its important to let them function in a way that will allow them to shine. Most people would rather succeed than fail, but sometimes the leader has to be the catalyst for putting 'success' into their personal vocabulary.

Donald J. Trump – Head of the Trump Organisation

How to Get Rich, BBC Books (2004), p. 27

It is the responsibility of managers to achieve results through the utilisation of human resources and the efforts of other people. The way in which managers exercise their responsibilities and duties is important. The behaviour of managers and their style of management will influence the effort expended and level of performance achieved by subordinate staff. Attention must be given to the skills of management and to influences on managerial effectiveness.

Learning outcomes

After completing this chapter you should be able to:

- contrast different attitudes and assumptions of managers about human nature and behaviour at work;
- examine managerial styles in terms of concern for production and concern for people;
- assess different systems of management;
- debate suggested philosophies for the successful management of people;
- analyse criteria for evaluating the effectiveness of managers;
- explain the importance of the management of time and distinguish activity from effectiveness;
- recognise the importance of adopting an appropriate style of managerial behaviour.

Critical reflection

People respond according to the manner in which they are treated. 'The majority of people come to work eager to do a good job and to perform to the best of their abilities. Therefore if individual performance fails to match the ideal, this is a result of poor management.' What is your response to this view? What is your experience of the workplace?

MANAGERIAL STYLE AND BEHAVIOUR

The changing nature of the work environment and the association between organisations and individuals draws attention to the traditional boss–subordinate relationship. There appears to be a growing recognition that managers can no longer rely solely on their perceived formal authority as a result of a hierarchical position in the structure of the organisation. For example, according to *ACAS*, much of the emphasis in employee relations today has to be on the individual and their position in the workplace.[1] This changing relationship suggests that more than ever an essential ingredient of any successful manager is the ability to handle people successfully. There is therefore a heavy responsibility on managers and on the styles and systems of management adopted.

It is, however, interesting to note the views of *Watson* who, while acknowledging that to create the goods, services and quality of life that people look for in the modern world, rather complex patterns of co-operative behaviour have to be orchestrated and 'managed', identifies three major problems in thinking about organising and managing work in terms of 'managing people'. First, in a modern democratic society, is it realistic even to contemplate the possibility of managing people and that there are people willing to be managed? Second, can it be argued that a manager has no moral right to direct, manage or boss any individual? Third, does the focus on people management tend to blur the part played by structures, systems, cultures, processes and the rest?[2]

Nevertheless, whatever the veracity of these problems or the importance attached to the management of systems, the organising and management of work depends ultimately on the people who make up the organisation. Without people, systems and procedures and indeed organisations themselves are meaningless. And people need to be managed. What, of course, are of increasing importance are the style of managerial behaviour and its effectiveness for *both* organisational performance and the satisfaction of its members. As *Austin* points out, good people management produces financial success. Companies which look after their staff on average out-perform the stock market by two or three times and there is no moral dilemma in either choosing to make money or look after people. If employees feel valued, they give more of themselves and are more productive.[3]

With the general movement towards flatter organisation structures, flexible working and greater employee empowerment, there is more emphasis on an integrating rather than a traditional controlling style of management. Management style and behaviour can be as important as management competence. As *Greenhalgh* points out, it is clear that managers today face a new era for business and need to face up to the new opportunities and constraints. Successful management involves adapting to the new order.

> *Gone is the notion of the corporate leader as the person who supplied the vision, decided on the appropriate strategy and tactics to achieve that vision, then assigned tasks of implementation to a hierarchy of subordinates. Also gone is the notion of worker-as-robot, someone who didn't think but merely performed as instructed ... The new generation of knowledge workers don't think of themselves as 'subordinates': they consider themselves independent professionals who can be given a general goal and be left to accomplish it without 'micromanagement'. They look to managers to facilitate their achievement rather than to direct and control their work.*[4]

Human capital management (HCM)

Increasingly, attention is drawn to the concept of human capital management (discussed in Chapter 13) as a key indicator of a company's success and to good people management. *Lloyd* raises the question of the similarities and differences between a good people manager and human capital management. It could be argued that HCM is frequently identified with a more formalised, technical and manipulative approach, although despite the language of words such as 'capital' and 'assets' it is not inherently incompatible with a good people manager. However: 'In the end, management is not about more manipulation – people quickly see through this and hence the high levels of cynicism in many organisations. It is about helping people really to believe in what they are doing (pure McGregor Theory Y?).'[5] McGregor's Theory X and Theory Y are discussed below.

MANAGERS' ATTITUDES TOWARDS PEOPLE

The way in which managers approach the performance of their jobs and the behaviour they display towards subordinate staff is likely to be conditioned by predispositions about people, and human nature and work. Drawing on Maslow's hierarchy of needs model (which is discussed in Chapter 7), *McGregor*, in 1960, put forward two suppositions about human nature and behaviour at work. He argued that the style of management adopted is a function of the manager's attitudes towards people and assumptions about human nature and behaviour. The two suppositions are called Theory X and Theory Y and are based on polar assumptions about people and work.[6]

Theory X assumptions about human nature

Theory X represents the carrot-and-stick assumptions on which traditional organisations are based. Its assumptions are that:

- the average person is lazy and has an inherent dislike of work;
- most people must be coerced, controlled, directed and threatened with punishment if the organisation is to achieve its objectives;
- the average person avoids responsibility, prefers to be directed, lacks ambition and values security most of all; and
- motivation occurs only at the physiological and security levels.

The central principle of Theory X is direction and control through a centralised system of organisation and the exercise of authority. McGregor questioned whether the Theory X approach to human nature is correct and the relevance of management practices which are based upon it. Assumptions based on a Theory X approach, and the traditional use of rewards and sanctions exercised by the nature of the manager's position and authority, are likely to result in an exploitative or authoritarian style of management.

Theory Y assumptions about human nature

At the other extreme to Theory X is Theory Y which represents the assumptions consistent with current research knowledge. **The central principle of Theory Y is the integration of individual and organisational goals**. Its assumptions are:

- for most people work is as natural as play or rest;
- people will exercise self-direction and self-control in the service of objectives to which they are committed;
- commitment to objectives is a function of rewards associated with their achievement;
- given the right conditions, the average worker can learn to accept and to seek responsibility;
- the capacity for creativity in solving organisational problems is distributed widely in the population;
- the intellectual potential of the average person is only partially utilised; and
- motivation occurs at the affiliation, esteem and self-actualisation levels as well as at the physiological and security levels.

McGregor implies that a Theory Y approach is the best way to elicit co-operation from members of an organisation. It is the task of management to create the conditions in which individuals may satisfy their motivational needs and in which they achieve their own goals through meeting the goals of the organisation. McGregor develops an analysis of the implications of accepting Theory Y in regard to performance appraisal, administration of salaries and promotions, participation, staff–line relationships, leadership, management development and the managerial team.

Managerial strategies

Although Theory X and Theory Y are based on polar extremes and are an over-simplification, they do represent identifiable philosophies that influence managerial behaviour and strategies. Most people have the potential to be self-motivating. They can best achieve their personal goals through self-direction of their efforts towards meeting the goals of the organisation. Broadening educational standards and changing social values mean that people today have wider expectations of the quality of working life, including opportunities for consultation and participation in decisions that affect them. Managers should develop practices based more on an accurate understanding of human behaviour and motivation.

The Theory Y approach, however, is not a 'soft' option. In practice it is often difficult to achieve successfully. It can be frustrating and time-consuming, and mistakes will occur.

> *Since 1952 I've been stumbling around buildings and running primitive Theory Y departments, divisions, and finally one whole Theory Y company: Avis. In 1962, after thirteen years, Avis had never made a profit (except one year when they jiggled their depreciation rates). Three years later the company had grown internationally (not by acquisitions) from $30 million in sales to $75 million in sales, and had made successive annual profits of $1 million, $3 million, and $5 million. If I had anything to do with this, I ascribe it all to my application of Theory Y. And a faltering, stumbling, groping, mistake-ridden application it was.*
>
> Robert Townsend, *Further Up the Organisation* [7]

Demands of the situation

The two views of Theory X and Theory Y tend to represent extremes of the natural inclination of managers towards a particular style of behaviour. In practice, however, the actual style of management behaviour adopted will be influenced by the demands of the situation.[8] Where the job offers a high degree of intrinsic satisfaction or involves a variety of tasks, an element of problem-solving and the exercise of initiative, or where output is difficult to measure in quantitative terms, an informal, participative approach would seem to be more effective. It is more likely to lead to a higher level of staff morale. In many cases this would apply to work of a scientific, technical or professional nature. Where commitment to the goals of the organisation is almost a prerequisite of membership, such as in certain voluntary or charity organisations, for example, then a Theory Y approach would clearly seem to be most appropriate.

Use of a Theory X approach

However, even if a manager has a basic belief in Theory Y assumptions, there may be occasions when it is necessary, or more appropriate, to adopt a Theory X approach. When the nature of the job itself offers little intrinsic reward or limited opportunities to satisfy higher-level needs, a more dictatorial style of management might work best. Some jobs are designed narrowly, with highly predictable tasks and output measured precisely. This is the case, for example, with many complex production processes in manufacturing firms. With these types of jobs a Theory X approach may be needed if an adequate level of performance is to be maintained.

A Theory X approach may also be indicated in emergency situations, or where shortage of time or other overriding factors demand the use of authority in directing actions to the tasks in hand. For example, in the hustle, heat and noise of a busy hotel kitchen preparing fresh meals for a large banquet, with many tasks to be co-ordinated over very short time scales, it seems to be recognised that a Theory X style of management is most appropriate. In such circumstances this style of management appears to be accepted by the kitchen staff.

If subordinates match the Theory Y assumptions of the manager, then this style of management may well be effective. However, there are many staff who, whatever the nature of their job, do not wish to accept responsibility at work. They seem to prefer, and respond better to, a more directed and controlled style of management. There are times, therefore, when the manager may be justified in adopting Theory X assumptions about staff.

JAPANESE 'THEORY Z' ENVIRONMENT

Developing the work of *McGregor*, a comparison of management style and practice in different cultural settings is provided by *Ouchi* (1981). In contrast to the traditional, more bureaucratic American organisational environment, Ouchi recommends a Japanese-style **'Theory Z'** environment.

> *The problem of productivity in the United States will not be solved with monetary policy nor through more investment in research and development. It will only be remedied when we learn how to manage people in such a way that they can work together more effectively. Theory Z offers several such ways.*[9]

The characteristics of a Theory Z organisation are described by Ouchi as:

- long-term employment, often for a lifetime;
- relatively slow process of evaluation and promotion;
- development of company-specific skills, and moderately specialised career path;
- implicit, informal control mechanisms supported by explicit, formal measures;
- participative decision-making by consensus;
- collective decision-making but individual ultimate responsibility;
- broad concern for the welfare of subordinates and co-workers as a natural part of a working relationship, and informal relationships among people.

Japanese industry and management

According to Ouchi, type Z organisations would be more effective as a result of an emphasis on trust, which goes hand in hand with productivity; a less hierarchical and bureaucratic structure; and higher levels of worker involvement – all of which would create a distinctive company style and culture. His ideas generated considerable debate about the nature of Japanese industry and Japanese managers that to some extent continues today.

Note also that while many British and US organisations once attempted to emulate Japanese methods and styles of management, with mixed results, there is now evidence of a reversal of this trend, with Japanese corporations moving away from a Theory Z environment and restructuring along the lines of Western organisations.[10]

> *The cynic might describe efforts to turn Theory Y into practice as doing with difficulty what comes naturally to the Japanese. There, excellent managers apply principles of behaviour which translate perfectly into western language – and which have long been echoed in the progressive areas of the west. Yet you still encounter the old ostrich attitudes that caused western companies so much damage in the past: for instance, the argument that to emulate Japan is impossible because of its peculiar culture. But the famous national enthusiasm for good business and effective management isn't simply a product of Japan's culture. After all, sloppy western habits, like investing too little in productive capacity, new products, training, quality and marketing are hardly cultural – not unless bad business economics are built into the western mentality.*
>
> Robert Heller, *In Search of European Excellence*[11]

Critical reflection

A first step in the effective management of other people is confidence in your own ability and awareness of your own strengths and weaknesses. It might follow that acknowledgement of '*mea culpa*' and responsibility for failings should be part of the philosophy and language of successful managers. Why, then, do you think that many managers find it difficult to admit, or apologise publicly for, their mistakes?

THE MANAGERIAL/LEADERSHIP GRID®

One means of describing and evaluating different styles of management is the *Blake and Mouton* Managerial Grid® (*see* Figure 12.1). First published as the **Managerial Grid** in 1964, restated in 1978 and 1985[12] and republished in 1991 as the **Leadership Grid**,[13] the Grid provides a basis for comparison of managerial styles in terms of two principal dimensions:

- concern for production; and
- concern for people.

Concern for production is the amount of emphasis that the manager places on accomplishing the tasks in hand, achieving a high level of production and getting results or profits. This is represented along the horizontal axis of the Grid.

Concern for people is the amount of emphasis that the manager gives to subordinates and colleagues as individuals and to their needs and expectations. This is represented along the vertical axis of the Grid.

Five basic combinations

'Concern for' is not how much concern, but indicates the character and strength of assumptions which underlie the manager's basic attitudes and style of management. The significant point is 'how' the manager expresses concern about production or about people. The four corners and the centre of the Grid provide five basic combinations of degree of concern for production coupled with degree of concern for people (*see* Figure12.1(a)):

- **the impoverished manager** (1,1 rating), low concern for production and low concern for people;
- **the authority–compliance manager** (9,1 rating), high concern for production and low concern for people;
- **the country club manager** (1,9 rating), low concern for production and high concern for people;
- **the middle-of-the-road manager** (5,5 rating), moderate concern for production and moderate concern for people; and
- **the team manager** (9,9 rating), high concern for production and high concern for people.

Managers with a 1,1 rating tend to be remote from their subordinates and believe in the minimum movement from their present position. They do as little as they can with production or with people. Too much attention to production will cause difficulties with staff and too much attention to the needs of staff will cause problems with production.

Managers with a 9,1 rating are autocratic. They tend to rely on a centralised system and the use of authority. Staff are regarded as a means of production and motivation is based on competition between people in order to get work done. If staff challenge an instruction or standard procedure they are likely to be viewed as unco-operative.

Figure 12.1 The Leadership Grid®

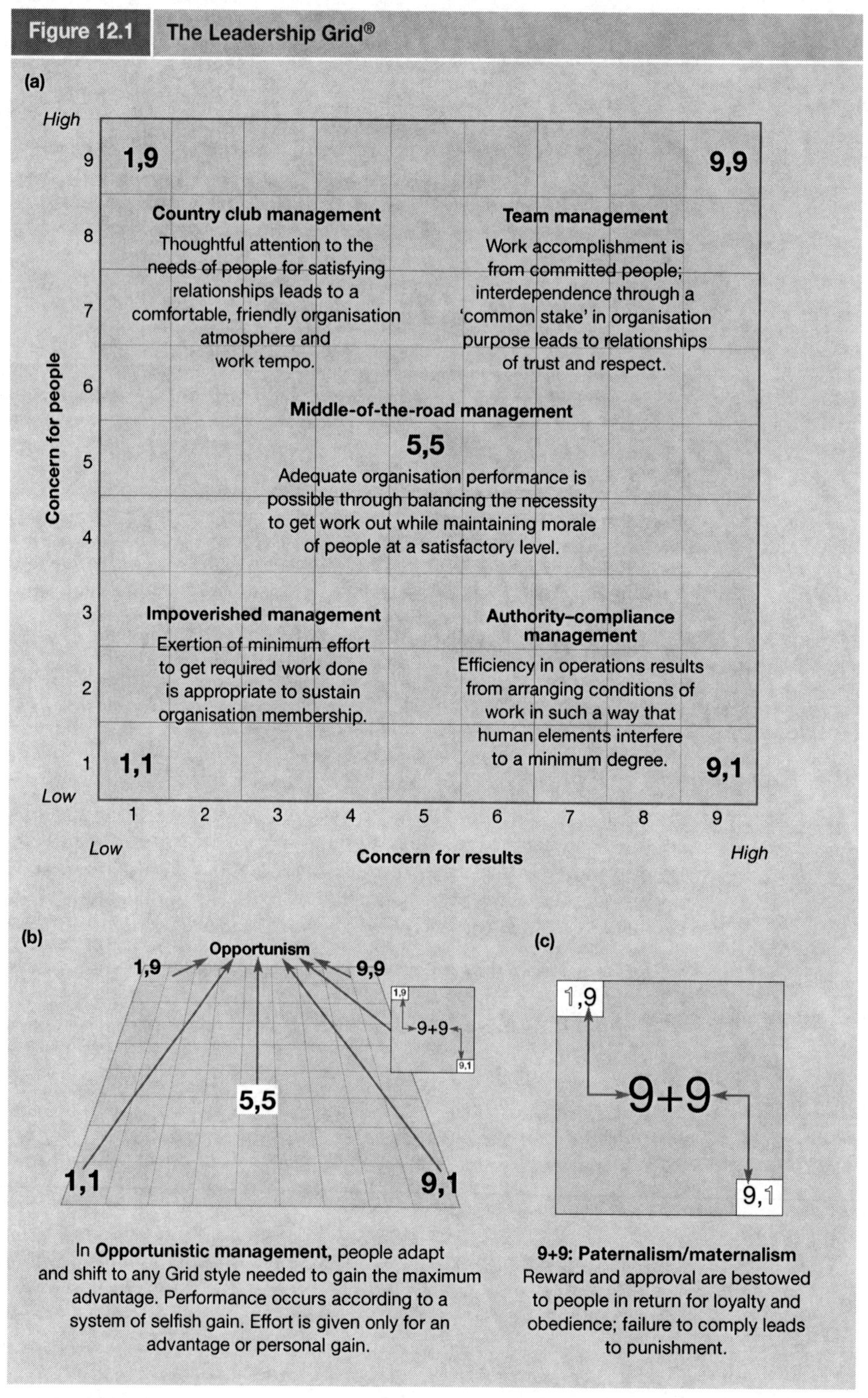

In **Opportunistic management,** people adapt and shift to any Grid style needed to gain the maximum advantage. Performance occurs according to a system of selfish gain. Effort is given only for an advantage or personal gain.

9+9: Paternalism/maternalism
Reward and approval are bestowed to people in return for loyalty and obedience; failure to comply leads to punishment.

Source: Blake, R. R. and McCanse, A. A., *Leadership Dilemmas – Grid Solutions*, Gulf Publishing Co. (1991), Grid Figure, p. 29, Paternalism Figure, p. 30, Opportunism Figure, p. 31. Reproduced by permission of Grid International, Inc., Houston, Texas.

The 1,9 rating managers believe that a contented staff will undertake what is required of them and achieve a reasonable level of output. Production is secondary to the avoidance of conflict and maintenance of harmony among the staff. Managers will seek to find compromises between staff and solutions acceptable to everyone. Although innovation may be encouraged, they tend to reject good ideas if likely to cause difficulties among the staff.

The 5,5 rating is the middle-of-the-road management with the approach of 'live and let live' and a tendency to avoid the real issues. This style of management is the 'dampened pendulum' with managers swinging between concern for production and concern for people. Under pressure, this style of management tends to become task management (9,1). Where this strains relations and causes resentment from staff, however, pressure is eased and managers adopt a compromise approach. If there is a swing too much the other way (towards 1,9), managers are likely to take a tighter and more hardened approach.

Managers with a 9,9 rating believe in the integrating of the task needs and concern for people. They believe in creating a situation whereby people can satisfy their own needs by commitment to the objectives of the organisation. Managers will discuss problems with the staff, seek their ideas and give them freedom of action. Difficulties in working relationships will be handled by confronting staff directly and attempting to work out solutions with them.

These five styles of management represent the extremes of the Grid. With a nine-point scale on each axis there is a total of 81 different 'mixtures' of concern for production and concern for people. Most people would come up with a score somewhere in an intermediary position on the Grid.

Two additional grid styles

The 1991 edition of the Grid covers two additional styles: opportunism and 9+9 paternalism/maternalism, which take account of the reaction of subordinates.

- In **opportunistic management**, organisational performance occurs according to a system of exchanges, whereby effort is given only for an equivalent measure of the same. People adapt to the situation to gain maximum advantage of it (*see* Figure 12.1(b)).
- In **9+9 paternalistic/maternalistic management**, reward and approval are granted to people in return for loyalty and obedience; and punishment is threatened for failure to comply (*see* Figure 12.1(c)).

A summary of the seven basic combinations of the Grid is given in Table 12.1.

Framework for patterns of behaviour

The Managerial Grid provides a framework in which managers can identify, study and review their patterns of behaviour. Instead of viewing management styles as a dichotomy of 'either/or', Blake and Mouton claim that the Managerial Grid illustrates that the manager can gain the benefits of maximising, simultaneously, methods which are both production-oriented and people-oriented. The 9,9 position, although an ideal, is worth working for. Based on their experience of using the original Grid, Blake and Mouton give three reasons why it is important to consider which style of management is used to achieve production through people:

- the 9,9 style of management correlates positively with bottom line productivity;
- 9,9 oriented managers enjoy maximum career success;
- there is now greater knowledge about the correlation between extreme grid styles of management and mental and physical health.

Dominant style of management

From their research, Blake and Mouton emphasise that managers may switch from one style to another or combine elements of different styles. However, they also found that managers tend to have one dominant style of management that they use more often than any other. In

Table 12.1 Leadership Grid® style definitions

9,1 Authority–compliance management	Managers in this position have great concern for production and little concern for people. People are seen as 'tools' for production. They demand tight, unilateral control in order to complete tasks efficiently. They consider creativity and human relations to be unnecessary.
1,9 Country club management	Managers in this position have great concern for people and little concern for production. They try to avoid conflicts and concentrate on being liked, even at the expense of production. To them the task is less important than good interpersonal relations. Their goal is to keep people happy. (This is a soft Theory X and not a sound human relations approach.)
1,1 Impoverished management	This style is often referred to as *laissez-faire*. Leaders in this position have little concern for people or productivity. They avoid taking sides and stay out of conflicts. They do just enough to maintain group membership.
5,5 Middle-of-the-road management	Leaders in this position have medium concern for both people and production. They rely on tried and true techniques and avoid taking untested risks. They attempt to balance their concern for both people and production, but are not committed strongly to either. Conflict is dealt with by avoiding extremes and seeking compromise rather than sound resolution.
9+9 Paternalistic 'father knows best' management	This leader takes the high 9 level of concern from 9,1 and 1,9 to create a combined style of controlling paternalism. The paternalist strives for high results (high 9 from 9,1) and uses reward and punishment to gain compliance (high 9 from 1,9). The paternalist uses a high level of concern for people to reward for compliance or punish for rejection.
Opportunistic 'what's in it for me' management	The opportunist uses whatever Grid style is needed to obtain selfish interest and self promotion. They adapt to situations to gain the maximum advantage. They may use 9,1 to push their own goals with one person, and 1,9 to gain trust and confidence with another. Performance occurs according to a system of exchanges. Effort is given only for an equivalent measure of the same.
9,9 Team management	These managers demonstrate high concern for both people and production. They work to motivate employees to reach their highest levels of accomplishment. They explore alternatives openly and aggressively. They are flexible and responsive to change. This style is considered ideal.

Source: Blake, R. R. and McCanse, A. A., *Leadership Dilemmas – Grid Solutions*, Gulf Publishing Company (1991), p. 29. Reproduced with permission from Grid International, Inc., Houston, Texas.

addition, they found that many managers have a 'back-up' style that they adopt if their dominant style does not work in a particular situation.

The dominant style of management is influenced in any particular situation by any of four conditions:

- **organisation** – the nature of the organisation in which the manager is employed, and the extent to which there are rigid rules and regulations;
- **values** – the personal values, beliefs or ideals that the manager holds concerning how to treat people or to manage results;
- **personal history** – the deep-rooted personal history of the manager may be an important factor and may lead to a preference for a particular approach because that style may have been experienced frequently in the past;

- **chance** – the manager may not have been confronted with, or had personal experience of, alternative sets of assumptions about how to manage. 'Chance' has not provided the manager with an opportunity to learn.

Relevance today From a review of the Managerial Grid programme, *Lester* believes it undoubtedly lends itself supremely well to training programmes. Although its relevance to real-life issues is less sure, in presenting a sophisticated learning package the Grid provides many potential applications for those who wish to study organisation development.[14]

According to *Newborough*, 'an organisation's structure, plan and concept are crucial to its effectiveness. Yet beyond these, the most significant single factor is the behaviour of the management team. Its members must act as leaders. They must accomplish their objectives through their ability to guide, motivate and integrate the efforts of others'. The ultimate purpose of studies of managerial style is to aid in the training and development of those who wish to become better leaders. Grid organisation development identifies and applies relevant aspects of behavioural science, and Newborough maintains that the Managerial/Leadership Grid is as relevant today as when it was first launched.[15] And according to *Crainer and Dearlove*: 'Crude at it is, the Grid helps people who are not conversant with psychology to see themselves and those they work with more clearly, to understand their interactions, and identify the sources of resistance and conflicts.'[16]

MANAGEMENT SYSTEMS

Work by McGregor, and by Blake and Mouton, suggests that an organisation is more likely to harness its staffing resources effectively if there is a participative style of management. This view is supported by the work of *Likert*, writing in the 1960s and 1970s. On the basis of a questionnaire to managers in over 200 organisations and research into the performance characteristics of different types of organisations, Likert identifies a four-fold model of management systems.[17] These systems are designated by number:

System 1	Exploitive authoritative
System 2	Benevolent authoritative
System 3	Consultative
System 4	Participative

- **System 1 – Exploitive authoritative.** Decisions are imposed on subordinates, motivation is based on threats, there is very little teamwork or communication; responsibility is centred at the top of the organisational hierarchy.
- **System 2 – Benevolent authoritative.** There is a condescending form of leadership, motivation is based on a system of rewards, there is only limited teamwork or communication; there is responsibility at managerial levels but not at lower levels of the organisational hierarchy.
- **System 3 – Consultative.** Leadership involves some trust in subordinates, motivation is based on rewards but also some involvement, there is a fair degree of teamwork, and communication takes place vertically and horizontally; responsibility for achieving the goals of the organisation is spread more widely throughout the hierarchy.
- **System 4 – Participative.** Leadership involves trust and confidence in subordinates, motivation is based on rewards for achievement of agreed goals, there is participation and a high degree of teamwork and communication; responsibility for achieving the goals of the organisation is widespread throughout all levels of the hierarchy.

Profile of organisational characteristics Likert has also established a 'profile of organisational characteristics' describing the nature of the four different management systems. The profile compares the four systems in terms of a table of organisational variables under the headings of:

1 leadership processes;
2 motivational forces;
3 communication process;
4 interaction–influence process;
5 decision-making process;
6 goal-setting or ordering; and
7 control processes.

Using this table, Likert undertook a survey of several hundred managers comprising different groups from a wide range of experience, and in both line and staff positions. His studies confirmed that least productive departments or units tended to employ management practices within Systems 1 and 2, and the most productive departments or units employed management practices within Systems 3 and 4.[18]

Supportive relationships

The nearer the behavioural characteristics of an organisation approach System 4, the more likely this will lead to long-term improvement in staff turnover and high productivity, low scrap, low costs and high earnings. Likert sets out three fundamental concepts of System 4 management. These are the use of:

- the principle of supportive relationships among members of the organisation and in particular between superior and subordinate;
- group decision-making and group methods of organisation and supervision; and
- high performance aspirations for all members of the organisation.

Supportive relationships are intended to enhance self-esteem and ego-building, contribute to subordinates' sense of personal worth and importance, and maintain their sense of significance and dignity. The superior's behaviour is regarded as supportive when this entails:

- mutual confidence and trust;
- helping to maintain a good income;
- understanding of work problems and help in doing the job;
- genuine interest in personal problems;
- help with training to assist promotion;
- sharing of information;
- seeking opinions about work problems;
- being friendly and approachable; and
- giving credit and recognition where due.

Group decision-making Group decision-making and supervision use an overlapping form of structure. Individuals known as 'linking-pins' are members not only of their own group but also of the next superior group and, where appropriate, of peer groups. This enables each work group to be linked to the rest of the organisation. In System 4 management interaction and decision-making rely heavily on group processes, and discussions focus on the decisions to be made. Likert emphasises that group methods of decision-making should not be confused with the use of committees. With the group method of decision-making the superior is held responsible for the quality and implementation of decisions. The superior is responsible for developing subordinates into an effective group.

In considering high performance aspirations, Likert refers to studies that suggest that employees generally want stable employment and job security, opportunities for promotion and satisfactory compensation. They want, also, to feel proud of their organisation and its performance and accomplishments. In System 4 management, superiors should therefore have high performance aspirations, but so also should every member of the organisation. To be effective, these high performance goals should not be imposed but set by a participative mechanism involving group decision-making and a multiple overlapping group structure. The mechanism should enable employees to be involved in setting high performance goals that help to satisfy their needs.

Causal, intervening and end-result variables

Likert also refers to three broad classes of variables relating to the firm's human organisation and its operations: (i) causal, (ii) intervening, and (iii) end-result.

- **Causal variables** are independent variables that can be amended by the organisation and its management, for example management policies, the structure of an organisation, and leadership strategies. Causal variables determine development of an organisation and the results it achieves.
- **Intervening variables** indicate the internal health of the organisation, for example the loyalties, attitudes, motivations and performance of members and their collective capacity for interaction, communication and decision-making.
- **End-result variables** indicate the final outcome and reflect the influences of intervening variables. The end-result variables reflect the achievement of the organisation, for example productivity, costs, scrap, earnings.

Attempts to improve the intervening variables are likely to be more successful through changing the causal variables, rather than changing directly the intervening variables. End-result variables are most likely to be improved by changing the causal variables, rather than the intervening variables.

In Figure 12.2 Likert gives a simplified example of the interrelationships between causal, intervening and end-result variables in the System 1 or 2 and System 4 management. The arrows indicate the pattern of relationships between the three classes of variables.

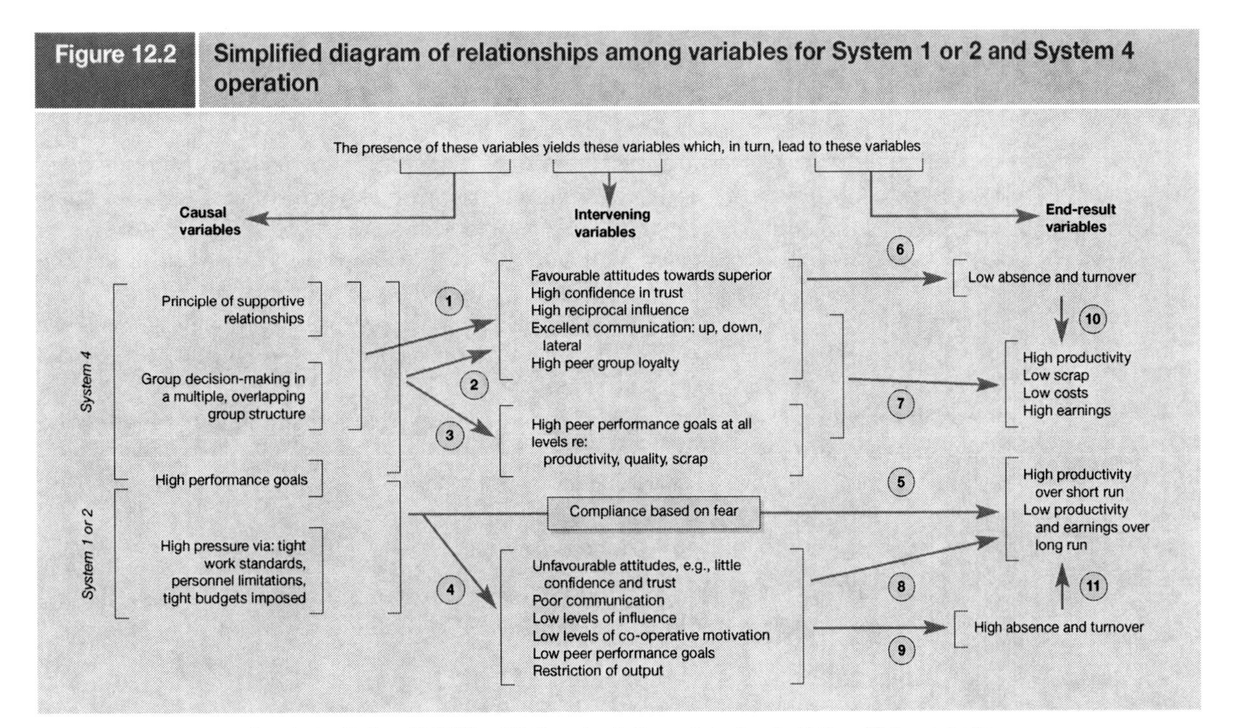

Figure 12.2 Simplified diagram of relationships among variables for System 1 or 2 and System 4 operation

Source: Likert, R., *The Human Organization*, McGraw-Hill (1967) p. 137. Reproduced with permission from the McGraw-Hill Companies, Inc.

Critical reflection

There is an organisational cliché that says 'managing people is like trying to herd cats'. This being the case, then, believing that people can be effectively managed through a behavioural approach might be a lost cause and perhaps the scientific management concept of rational-economic motivation is still the best way to improve performance and satisfy members of staff. To what extent do you support this view?

MANAGEMENT BY OBJECTIVES (MBO)

One particular participative approach to the activities involved in planning, organisation, direction and control, and to the execution of work, is **management by objectives (MBO)**. MBO is a phrase used to describe a style or system of management that attempts to relate organisational goals to individual performance and development through the involvement of all levels of management. The underlying basis of a system of MBO is:

- the setting of objectives and targets;
- participation by individual managers in agreeing unit objectives and criteria of performance; and
- the continual review and appraisal of results.

The phrase 'management by objectives' appears to have been introduced by *Drucker* in 1954.[19] The approach was taken up by McGregor who advocated its use as a preferred means of goal-setting, appraisal of managerial performance and self-assessment. The system of MBO has been adopted in a wide range of organisational settings, in the public as well as the private sector.

The cycle of MBO activities

MBO involves a continuous cycle of interrelated activities (*see* Figure 12.3):

- the clarification of organisational goals and objectives. These should be communicated clearly to, and understood fully by, all members of staff;
- review of organisational structure. The need is for a flexible structure and systems of management that make for effective communications, quick decision-making and timely feedback information;
- participation with subordinates in order to gain their willing acceptance of objectives and targets, key result areas and standards and measurements of performance;
- agreement on performance improvement plans that will enable subordinates to make the optimum contribution to: (i) meeting their own objectives and targets, and (ii) improved organisational performance;
- establishment of an effective monitoring and review system for appraisal of progress and performance, including self-checking and evaluation;
- undertaking any necessary revisions to, or restatement of, subordinates' objectives and targets;
- review of organisational performance against stated goals and objectives.

To be fully effective, MBO also needs to be linked with a meaningful system of rewards and career progression that recognises the subordinate's level of contribution and performance.

Figure 12.3 The cycle of MBO activities

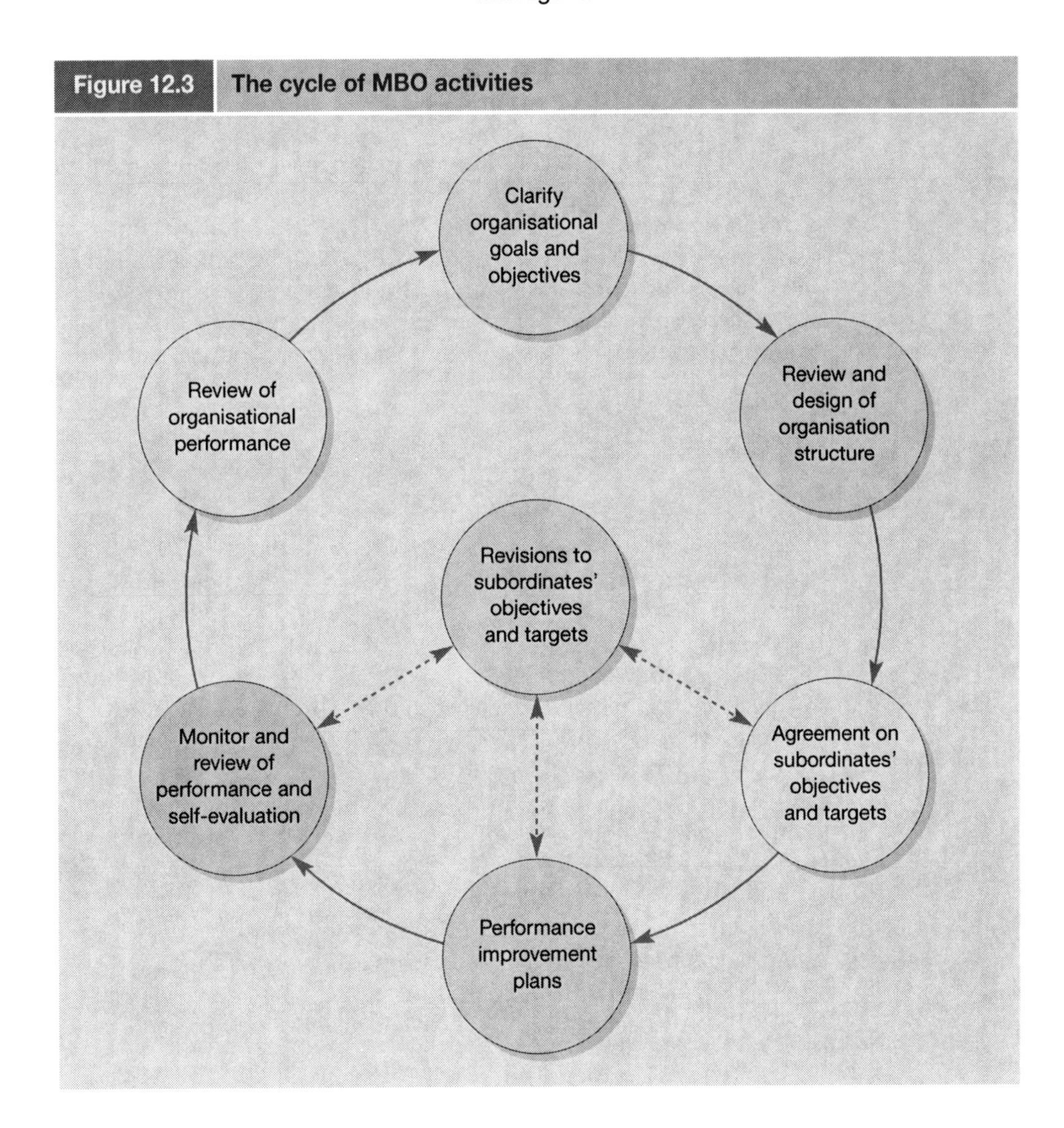

Relevance today

MBO is potentially an attractive system. It provides an opportunity for staff to accept greater responsibility and to make a higher level of personal contribution. There is much to recommend it to both the organisation and individual managers. MBO, however, is not a panacea and it is subject to a number of criticisms and potential limitations. It is not always easy to set specific targets or figures for certain more senior jobs or where the work involves a high degree of self-established role prescriptions (discussed in Chapter 8). The same might apply to jobs that require a high level of interpersonal relationships, especially where this involves confidential matters, such as counselling. There is a potential danger that where objectives and targets are more difficult to specify and measure in precise terms, these are neglected and greater emphasis is placed on objectives that are more easily monitored.

MBO appears to have suffered a decline in popularity. However, there are still differences in opinion. *Heller* paints a far less optimistic picture. He suggests:

> *MBO had only one defect: it didn't work. No matter how much care had been taken in formulating the objectives, drawing up the plans and involving all the managers, the corporate targets were invariably missed. So the technique passed away as one of the more fashionable management theories, defeated by the refusal of reality to conform to the plan.*[20]

By contrast, however, *Gratton* refers to a quote from David Packard (founder of Hewlett-Packard) that 'no operating policy has contributed more to Hewlett-Packard's success than the policy of management by objective'.[21]

Arguably, a major reason for the apparent demise of MBO is that the basic idea and fundamental features are now incorporated into modern systems of staff appraisal and performance management systems. Greater attention to the setting of clear objectives and levels of expected performance, flexible organisation structures and self-managed teams, and empowerment and self-regulating feedback can be related to the essential elements of MBO. *Hannagan* suggests: 'Although it [MBO] has fallen out of fashion as a system, many present day methods are very similar to MBO in their approach and results.'[22]

MANAGING PEOPLE

We have stated previously that, although there are many aspects to management, the one essential ingredient of any successful manager is the ability to handle people effectively. Recall the discussion in Chapter 1 on people and organisational behaviour. An increasing number of organisations take apparent delight in expounding (in their mission statements, corporate objectives, annual reports and the such) that their employees are their greatest assets. It is, however, arguable how much an understanding, people-centred approach to management is exercised in practice and the extent to which there still appears to be an emphasis on the use of rules, systems, procedures and paperwork rather than **with and through people**. And as *Gratton*, for example, points out on the basis of six years of study in conjunction with the London Business School, there has been no uniform progress in people management and 'yet for many people the reality of life in an organisation is that they do not feel they are treated as the most important asset, or that their knowledge is understood or used'.[23]

It is important that managers have a highly developed sense of **people perception** and understand the feelings of staff, and their needs and expectations. It is people who are being managed and people should be considered in human terms. A genuine concern for people and for their welfare goes a long way in encouraging them to perform well.

Basic managerial philosophies

A positive policy of investment in people and an interpersonal relationship approach to management is, in the longer term, worth the effort. For example, the UK government-sponsored initiative Investors in People is based on a commitment to the benefits organisations can gain through their people and on the vital role of managers. (Investors in People is discussed in Chapter 13.)

It is possible to put forward a number of underlying philosophies that *arguably* are likely to make for the successful management of people, and lead to both improved work performance and more contented staff (*see* Figure 12.4). **These philosophies are not intended to be prescriptive but to encourage discussion on the extent to which you agree with the points of view.**

Consideration, respect and trust

People generally respond according to the way they are treated. If you give a little, you will invariably get a lot back. Make people feel important and give them a sense of personal worth. The majority of staff will respond constructively if treated with consideration and respect, and as responsible individuals who wish to serve the organisation well. *Gratton* makes the point: 'Treat people with politeness, respect and dignity and in doing so create a strong role model for others to follow. Building a reputation of fairness gives you a buffer against the times when the policy is wrong, or you behave badly.'[24] A similar point is made by *Lloyd*:

Figure 12.4 The effective management of people

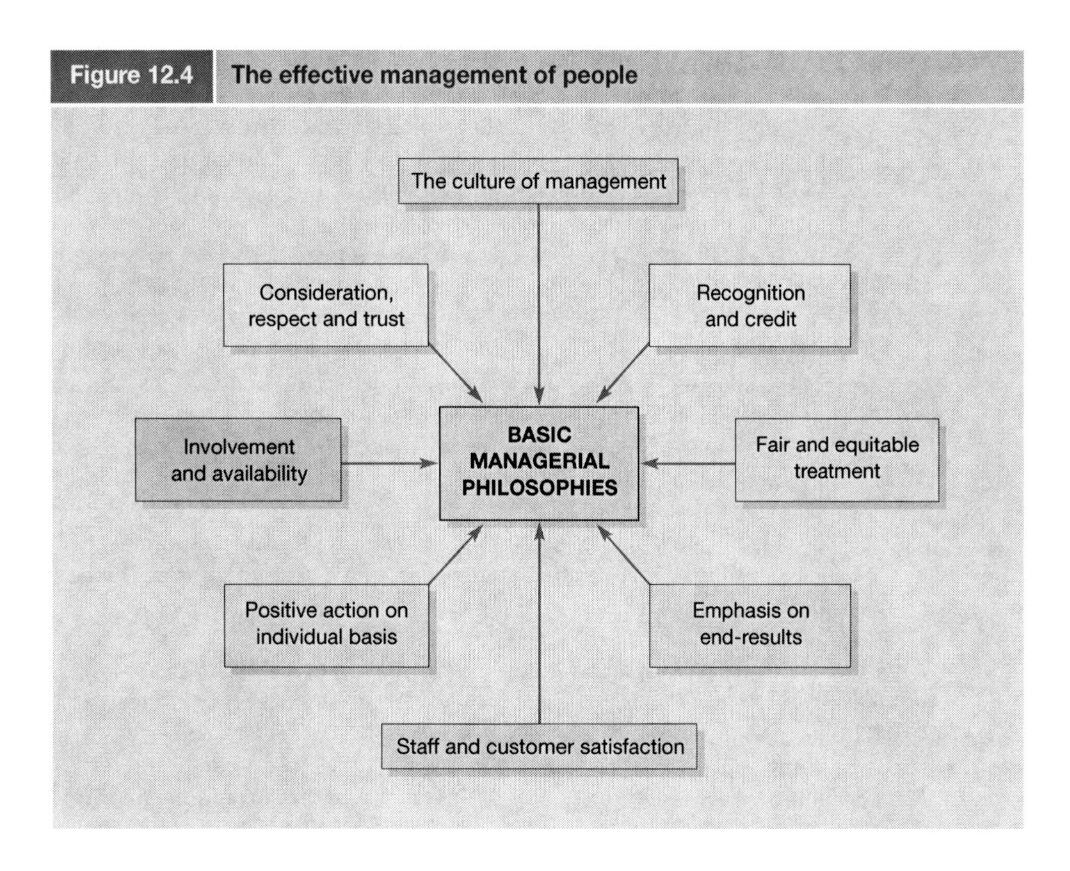

A good people manager believes in the value of people, treats them fairly and with respect: hence that vital element of trust is established and grown. But how often does this happen in practice? Management, of course, involves a combination of what you do and the way that it is done.[25]

However, how can members of staff show that they can be trusted unless trust is first placed in them? **The initiative must come from management**. 'Lack of trust is probably one of the greatest time and resource wasters in the workplace. Managers who do not trust their employees are probably wasting hours every week checking up on them at every turn and failing to utilise the resources at their disposal.'[26]

Recognition and credit

People can be praised to success. Give full recognition and credit when it is due and let people know you appreciate them. Too often managers are unresponsive to good performance, which may occur the vast majority of the time, and appear to take this for granted, but are quick to criticise on the few occasions when performance falls below expectations. **However, it should not be assumed that staff would necessarily take a lack of response as a sign of positive recognition rather than just the absence of criticism.** So often you hear the comment: 'Well nobody has complained so I suppose everything is all right.' What a poor indictment of management style! Positive feedback on good performance is a strong motivator *and* staff are then more likely to accept and respond to constructive criticism. If staff are to take a pride in their work they need to know when they are performing well and to receive appropriate recognition for their efforts.

A sincere word of thanks from the right person at the right time can mean more to an employee than a formal award ... What is important is that someone takes the time to notice an achievement, seeks out the employee responsible and personally gives praise in a timely way.

Federico Castellanos, Vice President, Human Resources, IBM (EMEA)[27]

Involvement and availability

Involve yourself with the work of the staff and make sure you fully understand the difficulties and distastes of their duties and responsibilities. Ensure an open flow of communications and encourage participation and feedback. Take an active interest in the work of staff but without excessive supervision or inhibiting their freedom of action. Wherever possible be available to staff as a priority, rather than to administration. Remember the importance of giving time to listen genuinely to the feelings and problems of staff. This means giving staff your full attention including adopting appropriate body language. Even if you disagree with their point of view it is important to show that you understand, and are sensitive to, what they are saying. It is, however, also important to note that being a good listener is a skill which needs to be developed and as *Fletcher* reminds us: 'Hearing is not listening. Listening is not a passive activity. It is hard work. It demands attention and concentration.'[28]

The approach of Management By Walking About (MBWA), together with informal communication processes, is often heralded as a positive management practice – and indeed it may well be so. However, there is the danger of arousing mistrust among staff, the suspicion of management snooping and doubts about 'what are you doing here?'. MBWA is unlikely to be effective unless perceived by staff as part of a broader, genuine belief by management in the continuing importance of giving time to listen to, and understand, the feelings and problems of staff.

Fair and equitable treatment

Treat people fairly but according to merit. Ensure justice in treatment, equitable systems of motivation and rewards, clear human resource management policies and procedures, avoidance of discrimination, and full observance of all laws and codes of conduct relating to employment. People expect certain outcomes in exchange for certain contributions or inputs. A feeling of inequality causes tension and motivates the person to indulge in certain forms of behaviour in order to remove or to reduce the perceived inequity.[29] Recall also the discussion on the psychological contract in Chapter 1.

Positive action on an individual basis

Treat members of staff as individuals. Deal with individual situations on an individual basis and avoid the 'blanket' approach. For example, it has come to the manager's attention that a couple of members of staff have failed to provide some urgently requested information on time. The manager's reaction is to send a circular to *all* members of the department reminding them of the need for, and importance of, meeting deadlines. This may appear to be an easy way out to the manager. But what are likely to be the reactions of staff?

The two members concerned might shield behind the generality of the circular and persuade themselves that it doesn't apply particularly to them. They might even choose to believe that the manager must be referring to other members of staff, perhaps in a different section, and take little notice of the circular. In contrast, the majority of staff in the department who do have a good record of providing requested information on time may well be annoyed or upset by the circular.

There could be some staff who despite pressing personal difficulties have taken great pride in their work and made a special effort to maintain an excellent record of co-operation – quite possibly without any previous positive recognition from management. **It would be understandable if the reaction of these staff was one of resentment and disillusionment, and with a possible adverse effect on their future attitude to work.** The manager has more to lose than to gain from adopting a 'blanket' approach to a particular problem and by the failure to take selective, positive action on an individual basis.

Emphasis on end-results

Place emphasis on end-results and levels of actual performance and achievement rather than on compliance with detailed instructions, rules or regulations. For example, where set attendance times are *clearly* seen as a necessary requirement of the job, it is right that managers should ensure that time-keeping is adhered to and enforced as appropriate. But in many cases rigid times of attendance are not an essential requirement for effective performance.

Who makes the greatest contribution to the work of the organisation? Person A who is always on time, keeps to the exact lunch break and never leaves early (or late), but spends much of the day in idle conversation and gossip, shuffling papers and looking at the work, and achieves only adequate performance? Or Person B who may 'not be seen about the place so much', but always gives maximum effort, makes full use of time and is never idle, is flexible, delivers whatever is expected on time and achieves a consistently high level of performance?

Good time-keeping can be an important part of the job. However, if 'always being there' is not a requirement, *per se*, for effective performance, what is to be gained by insisting on rigid times of attendance? Such a requirement is likely to be perceived by Person B-type staff as an unwarranted bureaucratic style of management. Furthermore, it could turn a Person B into a Person A – with an adverse effect on the level of effective performance. The increasing movement to flexible working patterns and teleworking coupled with demands to boost productivity are placing growing emphasis on what staff actually achieve rather than the time spent at work. The important criteria are the level and quality of performance.

Staff and customer satisfaction

The starting point for customer, or consumer, satisfaction is good manager–subordinate relationships. Supportive and harmonious working relationships are more likely to create a working environment that results in high levels of both staff *and* consumer satisfaction. Managers need to adopt a positive attitude towards staff and to develop a spirit of mutual co-operation. Staff should feel that they are working *with* the manager rather than *for* the manager.

Make all staff part of the management team

- *Virgin pays some of the lowest salaries in the industry yet its staff are very talented and loyal – paradox?*
- *The company's success in this field is down to Sir Richard's (Branson) management philosophy where all staff feel valued and Branson is just as interested in a flight stewardess's opinion as he is in his marketing director's.*
- *Successful people management is about inclusion and Branson works on making all his staff like a team where each is valued not only for fulfilling their job remit but for contributing to the development of the business as a whole.*

The Virgin Factor[30]

Critical reflection

In your interactions with people at work, as in life more generally, there will always be some people you just cannot seem to please. Give them a bag of gold and they will complain that the bag is the wrong colour, or it is too heavy to carry, or why could you not give them a cheque instead! How would you behave towards a 'bag of gold' person?

CHOICE OF MANAGERIAL STYLE

Some might well consider that these philosophies are too idealistic and that given the harsh realities of the working environment managers need to adopt a more dominant stance. However, it is not suggested that managers should in any way give up the right to manage: it is a question of *how* they manage and how they use their authority – for example, a 'Theory X' style with emphasis on direction and control, and the use of rewards and sanctions exercised by nature of the manager's position and authority; or a 'Theory Y' style in which individuals may satisfy their motivational needs through integration with meeting the goals of the organisation.

Management may also be based on 'organisational power' derived from status or position within the hierarchical structure, and the use of formal authority; or 'personal power' derived from competence and expertise, identification with subordinates, commanding respect, and urging and encouraging people in the performance of their tasks.[31] *Green* contends that most successful managers are able to adjust their approach and response between a continuum of hard skills and soft skills, and react appropriately to different situations.[32]

The nature of people at work

Galunic and Weeks refer to the changing nature of the employment relationship and that developing people, not just managing them, has become a necessary yet tricky task. Fortunately, however, some things have not changed.

> *Human nature remains remarkably stable. People want to feel competent and secure, they are consistent in reciprocating good or bad deeds; and they are influenced by, and often imitate, behaviours that surround them. Nothing changes from the sandpit to the boardroom, so managers should revisit these truths as they think about investing in people.*[33]

Golden rule management

One example of an interesting and enlightened people approach is put forward by *Mary Kay Ash*, founder of the huge, multi-million-dollar company Mary Kay Cosmetics in the USA.[34] Ash writes about the intentional development of a management concept that allows fairness to flourish in business, the belief that people will shine if given a chance, and methods that are applicable to any organisation. Her concept of the management of people is based on the Golden Rule 'Do unto others as you would have them do unto you', with emphasis on being a 'people company'. (Again, this is a philosophy very much in line with the views of the author.)

> *People come first at Mary Kay Cosmetics – our beauty consultants, sales directors and employees, our customers, and our suppliers. We pride ourselves as a 'company known for the people it keeps'. Our belief in caring for people, however, does not conflict with our need as a corporation to generate a profit.*[35]

The philosophy of 'Golden Rule Management' is applied in such ways as, for example:

- **Treat people fairly but according to merit.** In order to balance responsibilities to the company, the employee, and all other employees, every manager must be able to say 'no'. But employees should be encouraged to turn a 'no' into the motivation to accomplish more.
- However busy you are, **make the other person feel important** and let people know you appreciate them.
- **Motivate people through giving praise.** A good manager must understand the value of praising people to success.
- **Encourage feedback** and don't undervalue the ability to listen.
- **Sandwich every bit of criticism between two layers of heavy praise.**
- **An open-door philosophy.**
- **Help other people get what they want** – and you will get what you want. Good managers' success is reflected in the success of their people.
- **Never hide behind policy or pomposity.**

MANAGERIAL EFFECTIVENESS

The importance of managerial performance and effectiveness has long been recognised by major writers such as *Drucker* who, originally in 1955, propounded that:

> *The manager is the dynamic, life-giving element in every business. Without their leadership 'the resources of production' remain resources and never become production. In a competitive economy,*

above all, the quality and performance of the managers determine the success of a business; indeed they determine its survival. For the quality and performance of its managers is the only effective advantage an enterprise in a competitive economy can have.[36]

The importance of management performance has also been more recently emphasised by *Foppen*:

Management is of pivotal importance for modern society. It is for this reason that, no matter what, thinking about management, certainly at university level, is of great relevance to management practice. So apart from the question of whether management's claim that it is indispensable is really valid or not, the fact that practically everyone believes it is, is what counts.[37]

The overall responsibility of management can be seen as the attainment of the given objectives of the organisation. Upon the attainment of its aims and objectives will rest the success and ultimate survival of the organisation. There is therefore a clear and important need for effective management. And this need is just as strong in public sector organisations as in private enterprise organisations. Indeed, it could be argued that in local government, for example, the accountability of public servants to elected members for their actions means that professional standards of management of the highest order are even more essential. Whether in private or public sector organisations, however, managerial effectiveness is a difficult concept both to define and to measure.

Efficiency and effectiveness

Managerial efficiency can be distinguished from managerial effectiveness. **Efficiency** is concerned with 'doing things right' and relates to inputs and what the manager does. **Effectiveness** is concerned with 'doing the right things' and relates to outputs of the job and what the manager actually achieves.

To be efficient the manager must attend therefore to the **input requirements of the job** – to clarification of objectives, planning, organisation, direction and control. But in order to be effective, the manager must give attention to **outputs of the job** – to performance in terms of such factors as obtaining best possible results in the important areas of the organisation, optimising use of resources, increasing profitability, and attainment of the aims and objectives of the organisation.

Effectiveness must be related to the achievement of some purpose, objective or task – to the performance of the process of management and the execution of work. Criteria for assessing the effectiveness of a manager should be considered in terms of measuring the results that the manager is intended to achieve. But **what is also important is the manner in which the manager achieves results and the effects on other people**. This may well influence effectiveness in the longer term. Managerial effectiveness results from a combination of personal attributes and dimensions of the manager's job in meeting the demands of the situation, and satisfying the requirements of the organisation.

Stewart suggests that effectiveness is more important than efficiency.

> *Managers who want to improve should review both their effectiveness and their efficiency. Effectiveness is doing the right things. Efficiency is making the most economic use of the resources. Effectiveness is more important than efficiency because one must be doing the right kind of work. Only then does it matter whether the work is done efficiently.*[38]

Effective and successful managers

From a study of what real managers do (discussed in Chapter 10), *Luthans* attempted to distinguish between effective and successful managers.

- **Effective managers** are defined in terms of the quantity and quality of standards of performance, and the satisfaction and commitment of subordinates.
- **Successful managers** are defined operationally in terms of the speed of their promotion within an organisation.

Effective managers had a different emphasis from successful managers and do almost the opposite activities, and Luthans found few real managers who were both effective and successful. The biggest contribution to **effectiveness** came from first, communicating and second, human resource management; with the least relative contribution from the networking activity. By contrast, for a significant number of managers by far the strongest key to success came from the networking activity, with the weakest contribution from the human resource management activity.[39]

MEASURES OF EFFECTIVENESS

Management involves getting work done through the co-ordinated efforts of other people. **Managers are most likely to be judged not just on their own performance but also on the results achieved by other staff.** The manager's effectiveness may be assessed *in part*, therefore, by such factors as:

- the strength of motivation and morale of staff;
- the success of their training and development; and
- the creation of an organisational environment in which staff work willingly and effectively.

The difficulty is determining objective measurement of such factors. Some possible indication might be given by, for example:

- the level of staff turnover;
- the incidence of sickness;
- absenteeism;
- poor time-keeping; and
- accidents at work.

However, such figures are likely to be influenced also by broader organisational or environmental considerations, for example poor job security due to the economic climate, which are outside the direct control of the individual manager. In any case, there is the general question of the extent to which such figures bear a direct relationship to the actual performance of subordinate staff.

Other criteria of effectiveness

Other criteria that may give some indication of managerial effectiveness include the efficiency of systems and procedures, and the standard of services afforded to other departments. Again, however, there is the question of how to determine objective measurement of such criteria.

For some management jobs it might be possible to identify more quantitative factors which *may* give an indication of managerial effectiveness, including:

- meeting important deadlines;
- accuracy of work carried out by the department, perhaps measured by the number of recorded errors;
- level of complaints received from superiors, other departments, customers or clients, suppliers, the public;
- adherence to quality standards, for example, the amount of scrap or waste material;
- keeping within agreed cost or budgetary control limits; and
- levels of output and productivity (*see* Figure 12.5).

Another broad, qualitative criterion of increasing significance today is in terms of perceived social accountability, and the ethical behaviour of individual managers and the organisation as a whole (discussed in Chapter 14).

Figure 12.5 Possible indicators of managerial effectiveness

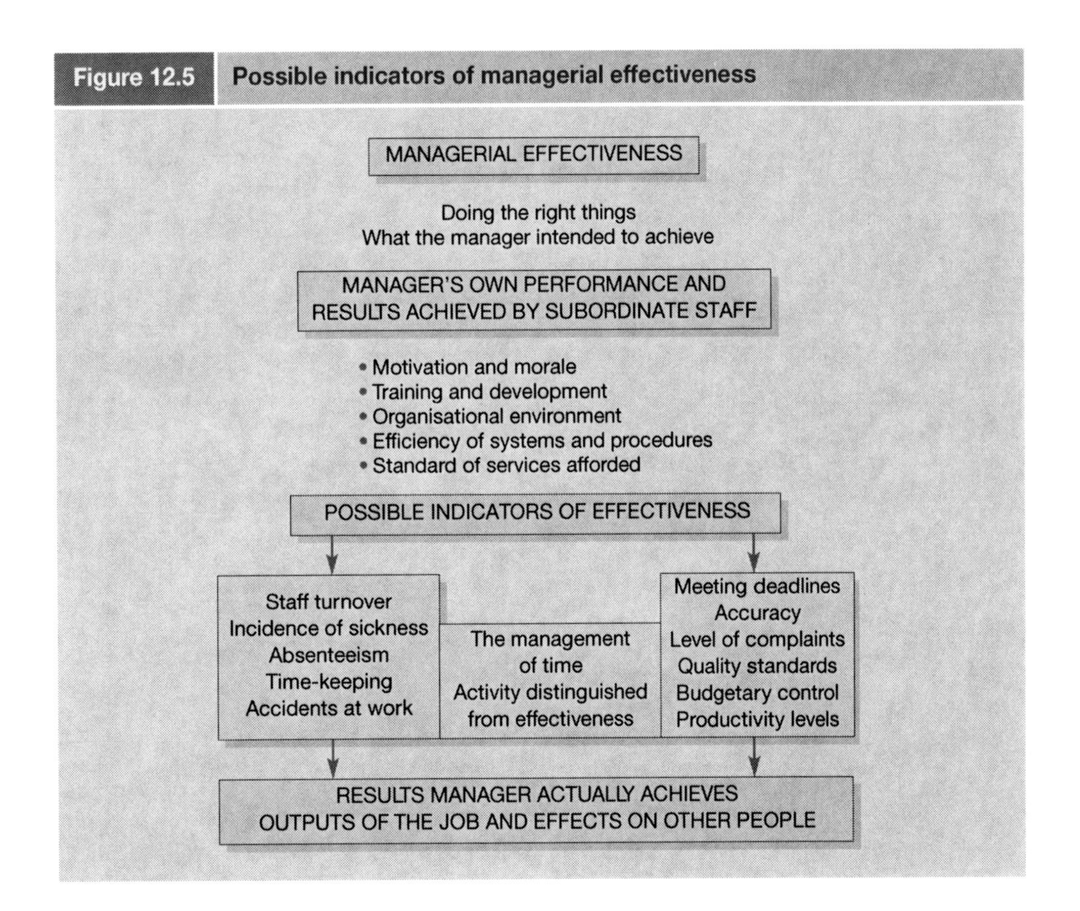

MANAGEMENT STANDARDS CENTRE

The Management Standards Centre (MSC) is the government-recognised standards-setting body for the management and leadership areas. Upgrading the skills of managers is fundamental to the government's aim to raise UK productivity and competitiveness. The MSC was responsible for developing a new set of National Occupational Standards (NOS) for management and leadership in May 2004. They describe the level of performance expected in employment for a range of management and leadership functions/activities.

As an employer-led organisation which champions management and leadership, the MSC is working with the Skills for Business Network to identify and address the skills gaps and shortages on a sector-by-sector basis, thereby contributing to the profitability of the UK.

> **Our vision** – *To create a UK partnership of employers and other key stakeholders to lead the professional development of all those working in the field of management and leadership.*
>
> **Our mission** – *To fulfil the needs of employers by developing a skilled management workforce through promoting our nationally recognised set of standards and qualifications which have full employer relevance and 'ownership'.*[40]

Components of the Management and Leadership Standards

The MSC undertook a review of World Class National Occupational Standards for Management and Leadership during 2004 with the aim of producing a new set of standards which:

- identify the full range of management and leadership functions/activities typically undertaken in organisations; and
- describe what individuals need to know, understand and be able to do in undertaking the identified functions/activities to the level or 'standard' expected in employment.

The new Management and Leadership Standards were approved in May as benchmarks to help managers – and the organisations in which they work – improve their performance. The underlying principle is **individual development, corporate gain**. The standards are arranged in a logical sequence to cover every aspect of management at every level in an organisation. There are six key roles or functional groupings divided into a total of 47 units (Table 12.2).

Table 12.2 New Management Standards 2004

A	**Managing self and personal skills**
A1	Manage your own resources
A2	Manage your own resources and professional development
A3	Develop your personal networks
B	**Providing direction**
B1	Develop and implement operational plans for your area of responsibility
B2	Map the environment in which your organisation operates
B3	Develop a strategic business plan for your organisation
B4	Put the strategic business plan into action
B5	Provide leadership for your team
B6	Provide leadership in your area of responsibility
B7	Provide leadership for your organisation
B8	Ensure compliance with legal, regulatory, ethical and social requirements
B9	Develop the culture of your organisation
B10	Manage risk
B11	Promote equality of opportunity and diversity in your area of responsibility
B12	Promote equality of opportunity and diversity in your organisation
C	**Facilitating change**
C1	Encourage innovation in your team
C2	Encourage innovation in your area of responsibility
C3	Encourage innovation in your organisation
C4	Lead change
C5	Plan change
C6	Implement change
D	**Working with people**
D1	Develop productive working relationships with colleagues
D2	Develop productive working relationships with colleagues and stakeholders
D3	Recruit, select and keep colleagues
D4	Plan the workforce
D5	Allocate and check work in your team
D6	Allocate and monitor the progress and quality of work in your area of responsibility
D7	Provide learning opportunities for colleagues
E	**Using resources**
E1	Manage a budget
E2	Manage finance for your area of responsibility
E3	Obtain additional finance for the organisation
E4	Promote the use of technology within your organisation
E5	Ensure your own actions reduce risks to health and safety
E6	Ensure health and safety requirements are met in your area of responsibility
E7	Ensure an effective organisational approach to health and safety

Table 12.2 Continued

F	**Achieving results**
F1	Manage a project
F2	Manage programme of complimentary projects
F3	Manage business processes
F4	Develop and review a framework for marketing
F5	Resolve customer service problems
F6	Monitor and solve customer service problems
F7	Support customer service improvements
F8	Work with others to improve customer service
F9	Build your organisation's understanding of its market and customers
F10	Develop a customer focused organisation
F11	Manage the achievement of customer satisfaction
F12	Improve organisational performance

Source: From the Management Standards Centre (www.management-standards.org). I am grateful to Dr Kion Ahadi, Policy and Projects Manager, Management Standards Centre for providing this information.

3-D MODEL OF MANAGERIAL BEHAVIOUR

However effectiveness is measured, managers are likely to be effective only if they adopt the most appropriate style of behaviour.

A development of the Blake and Mouton Managerial Grid, discussed earlier, is the three-dimensional (3-D) model of managerial behaviour suggested by *Reddin*.[41] By adding a third dimension of managerial effectiveness to task orientation and relationship orientation, the 3-D model identifies eight possible styles of managerial behaviour.

- **Task orientation (TO)** is the extent to which the manager directs both personal and subordinates' efforts through planning, organisation and control.
- **Relationship orientation (RO)** is dependent upon the manager's personal job relationships. This is characterised by consideration for subordinates' feelings, mutual trust and encouragement.

The combination of TO and RO determines the manager's basic style of behaviour. The four possible basic styles (*see* Figure 12.6) are similar to those identified by Blake and Mouton in the Managerial Grid.

Figure 12.6 The four basic styles of managerial behaviour

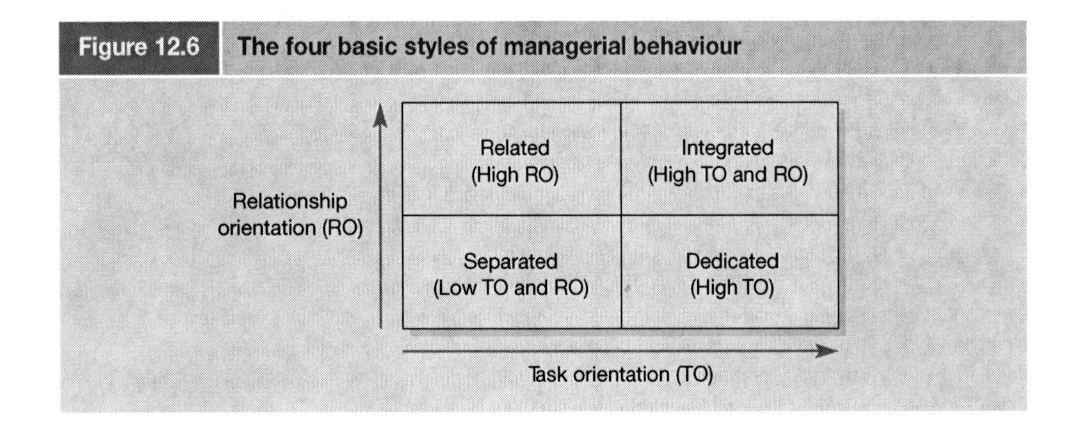

Apparent effectiveness and personal effectiveness

Each of these four basic styles of management can be effective or ineffective depending on the situation in which they are applied. Effectiveness is defined by Reddin as:

> *the extent to which a manager achieves the output requirements of his position ... Managerial effectiveness has to be defined in terms of output rather than input, by what a manager achieves rather than by what he does.*

Reddin distinguishes managerial effectiveness from (i) apparent effectiveness, and (ii) personal effectiveness.

- **Apparent effectiveness** is the extent to which the behaviour of the manager – for example punctuality, giving prompt answers, tidiness, making quick decisions and good public relations – gives the appearance of effectiveness. Such qualities may or may not be relevant to effectiveness.
- **Personal effectiveness** is the extent to which the manager achieves personal objectives – for example power and prestige – rather than the objectives of the organisation.

Eight styles of managerial behaviour

Applying the third dimension of managerial effectiveness provides eight styles of managerial behaviour – four effective styles, which achieve output requirements, and four ineffective styles (*see* Figure 12.7). For each of the basic styles – separated, dedicated, related or integrated – there is a more effective or less effective version. Effectiveness results from the appropriateness of a particular style of management to the demands of the situation in which it is applied. When one of the basic styles (for example 'separated') is adopted in an appropriate situation, a more effective style ('bureaucrat') results. When the basic style is adopted in an inappropriate situation, the result is a less effective style ('deserter').

Figure 12.7 The 3-D model of managerial effectiveness

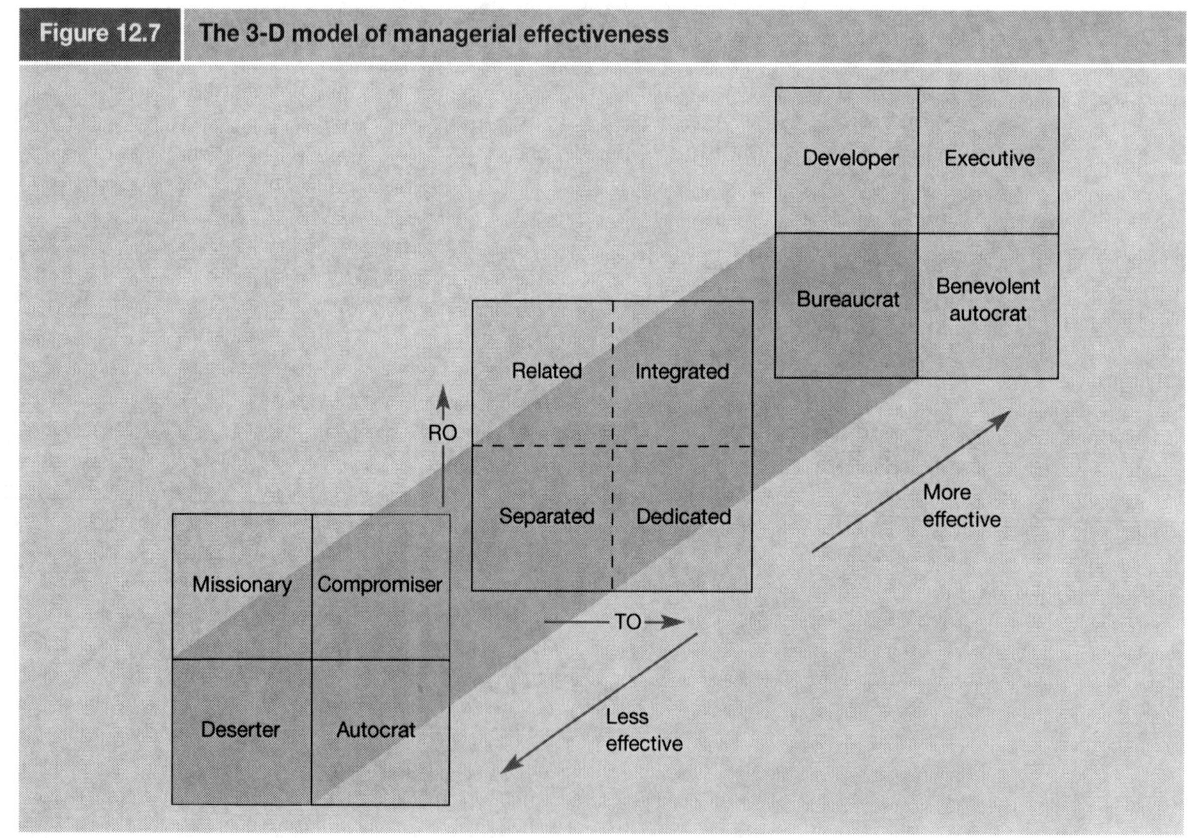

Source: Reddin, W.J., *Managerial Effectiveness*, McGraw-Hill (1970), p. 206.

The eight styles of management may be described briefly as follows.

More effective styles

1 **Bureaucrat** – a low concern for both task and relationships. The manager adopting this style is seen as being interested mainly in rules and procedures to control the situation, and as conscientious.
2 **Benevolent autocrat** – a high concern for task and a low concern for relationships. Managers adopting this style know what they want and how to achieve it without causing resentment.
3 **Developer** – a high concern for relationships and a low concern for task. The manager adopting this style is seen as having implicit trust in people and concerned mainly with developing them as individuals.
4 **Executive** – a high concern for both task and relationships. The manager adopting this style is seen as a good motivator, sets high standards, treats people as individuals, and favours team management.

Less effective styles

5 **Deserter** – low concern for both task and relationships in a situation where such behaviour is inappropriate. The manager lacks involvement and is passive or negative.
6 **Autocrat** – a high concern for task and a low concern for relationships in a situation where such behaviour is not appropriate. The manager is seen as lacking confidence in others, unpleasant and interested only in the task in hand.
7 **Missionary** – a high concern for relationships and a low concern for task where such behaviour is inappropriate. The manager is seen as interested mainly in preserving harmony.
8 **Compromiser** – a high concern for both task and relationships in a situation requiring high concern for neither, or for only one orientation. The manager is seen as a poor decision-maker, too easily influenced by the pressures of the situation, and as avoiding immediate pressures and problems at the expense of maximising long-term output.

Appropriate style of behaviour

According to Reddin's 3-D theory, managerial effectiveness cannot be measured simply in terms of achieving production or relationships with other people. The manager must also be adaptable in adopting the appropriate style of behaviour that will determine effectiveness in achieving the output requirements of the job. Reddin has developed a 'management-style-diagnosis' test to identify styles of management and of organisations. The test comprises 64 paired statements which compare one style of management with another. From each pair of statements is selected the one statement which describes best the manager's behaviour in their present job. Analysis of the answers can help the manager to evaluate their own perceived style of management.

THE MANAGEMENT OF TIME

Whatever the attributes or qualities of a successful manager, one essential underlying criterion is the effective use of time. With many managers who complain that they do not have sufficient time it may be more a case that they have failed to organise themselves or their work properly. The most important members of staff to be managed are themselves. Although it is currently a popular topic of attention, the importance of time management has long been recognised as an inherent feature of management. *Drucker*, writing in 1988, refers to time as the limiting factor for effective executives. Time is a unique resource – you cannot rent, hire, buy or otherwise obtain more time. The supply of time is totally inelastic; time is totally irreplaceable and everything requires time.[42]

There are a number of suggested procedures and techniques for managing time but the essential requirements of good time management include:

- clear objectives;
- careful forward planning;
- the definition of priorities and action;
- the ability to delegate successfully; and
- flexible working.

A 'concept map' of the management of time is presented in Figure 12.8.

Effectiveness and activity

For many managers, appearing always to be busy, a cluttered desk and a continual flurry of activity are outward signs of their effectiveness. The trouble is that such managers may be too busy 'doing' rather than **thinking about what they, and their staff, should be doing and how they should be doing it**. Activity may be a substitute for actual achievement. It is important therefore to distinguish effectiveness from activity. *Rees and Porter* suggest that:

> *Activity-centred behaviour is in any case much more likely to spring from incompetence and/or insecurity rather than adroit political behaviour. Activity-centred behaviour is likely to aggravate the position of the manager in the long run rather than ameliorate it.*[43]

Beware the busy manager

A recent study by *Bruch and Ghoshal* suggesting that we should beware of the busy manager raises the question: 'Are the least effective executives the ones who look like they are doing the most?' They refer to unproductive busyness and what they call 'active non-action'. After ten years of studying the behaviour of busy managers in nearly a dozen large companies, Bruch and Ghoshal claim that fully 90 per cent of managers squander their time in all sorts of ineffective activities.

> *No doubt, executives are under incredible pressure to perform, and have far too much to do, even when they work 12-hour days. But the fact is, very few managers use their time as effectively as they could. They think they're attending to pressing matters, but they're really just spinning their wheels ... A mere 10 per cent of managers are purposeful – that is, both highly energetic and highly focused. They use their time effectively by carefully choosing goals and then taking deliberate actions to reach them. Managers that fall into the other groups, by contrast, are usually just spinning their wheels; some procrastinate, others feel no emotional connection to their work, and still others are easily distracted from the task at hand. Although they look busy, they lack either the focus or the energy required for making any sort of meaningful change.*[44]

Manager's checklist

Stewart suggests that it is often salutary for managers to compare what they think they do against what happens in practice. Answers to the following questions will help managers decide what, if anything, they should check, and to review their effective management of time.[45]

1. Am I giving adequate attention to current activities, to reviewing the past and to planning for the future? In particular, am I giving enough thought to the future?
2. Am I dividing my time correctly between different aspects of my job? Is there, perhaps, one part of my job on which I spend too much of my time?
3. Have I changed what I am trying to do, and how I work to allow for the effects of changes in my work?
4. Am I certain that I am not doing any work that I ought to have delegated?
5. Who are the people that I ought to be seeing? Am I spending too much or too little time with any of them?

Figure 12.8 Concept map of the management of time

THE MANAGEMENT OF TIME

- WHY MUST MANAGERS MANAGE THEIR OWN TIME?
- THEIR STAFF'S TIME

MANAGING YOUR TIME
- Importance of time management
- Where does time go?
- Conserving time
- Time management tools

WHY IS IT IMPORTANT?
- Managers usually face more jobs than there is time to do them
- Jobs have different priorities
- Some jobs have to be done and some delegated – which?

WHERE DOES PRODUCTIVE TIME GO?
- Routine jobs (minor jobs but important)
- Regular duties
- Maintenance role as part of the organisation
  e.g. – meetings
  – selection/recruitment
  – seeing visitors
- Special assignments (unpredictable)
- Creative work (requires time)

?

PARKINSON'S LAW
– Work expands in such a way as to fill the time available

MANAGING DEPARTMENTAL TIME
Requires:
- Responding to external time pressures
- Maximising the time capacity available
- Analysing the components of total job time
- Using time planning techniques
- Recording time spent

IMPROVING DEADLINE TIMES PRODUCTION COMPLETION DELIVERY DEADLINES
– Changing working practices
– Using better equipment
– Training staff
– Collecting more/better information

Careful network planning will assist the manager to reorganise and reduce time pressures, eliminate wasted time and maximise time usage

PARETO PRINCIPLE
In any series of events which you do
e.g. your job: 80% of the ouput arises from 20% of your input
(the %s may vary but the principle remains)
e.g. 20% of the customer base leads to 80% of the income

RECORDING TIME
- for future reference – record and keep times for specific jobs
- for estimating and quoting
- for buying in replacement labour – sub-contracting/out-sourcing

TIME MANAGEMENT
A systematic step approach to using time effectively
1 – Analysis of time usage in the past
2 – The time budget in the future
3 – Allocate time to specific tasks
- Plan and adhere to a weekly time schedule
- Record activities

4 – Classify activities

COSTING TIME
- What is your total cost?
- How much productive time do you achieve?
- What utilisation do you obtain?
- How much would a consultant/teleworker /subcontractor charge?

WHERE DOES THE REMAINDER GO?
Wasted and lost time due to:–
- Lack of focus on task
  (Poor directions/lack of understanding)
- Failure to delegate
  (Assumes there is someone to delegate to)
- Interruptions
  (Should you have an 'open door'?)
- Fatigue – losing concentration
  (Take the breaks especially lunch)
- Failure to communicate
  – instructions not clear
  – failure to listen
- Failure to anticipate
  ('I never thought')

- Advance planning can
  – avoid problems later
  – anticipate trouble in different situations
  – allow an overview of the task

METHODS/TECHNIQUES FOR TIME PLANNING
- Network planning for long jobs (and Critical Path Analysis)
  – explore benefits of project management computer software
- GANTT charts
- Plan priority sequences
- Ordered sequences
- Short-term scheduling
  – consider value/costs of setting up specific 'jobbing' capacity for quick repeat order, or

– Fill-in jobs for waiting time between longer or larger jobs

MANAGING TIME USAGE
- Work sampling and time study techniques may be applicable
- Set time standards for jobs with realistic (+/–) allowances
- Use standard data catalogues for estimating job durations

– Give time allowances for an end-of-day activity to prepare for tomorrow

CONSERVING TIME
- Learn to communicate effectively
- Train subordinates to listen by Question & Answer techniques
- Organise meetings effectively – don't just hold them
- Reduce paperwork (form filling is slow, is it all necessary?)
- Control interruptions
- Set time objectives for tasks

COMPONENTS OF TOTAL JOB TIME
- Inherent time – sum of labour time, machine time and handling time
- Set-up time – time to prepare or tear-down after work; % time wastage reduced by scheduling longer runs
- Lost time – personal time for breaks, toilet, sickness, holidays, etc.
- Technical time – machinery failure or component shortage
- Learning time – familiarisation with the job. Can only be estimated and is often inaccurate

FOR EFFECTIVE TIME MANAGEMENT YOU SHOULD:–
- Establish the KEY TASKS (the six most important tasks you do)
- Set your OBJECTIVES (the achievements you are trying to attain in the key post)
- Identify PERFORMANCE STANDARDS (the quantifiable measure of the objectives)
- Identify CONSTRAINTS (things standing in the way of your objectives)
- Decide on ACTION PLANS (ways of removing the constraints)

Source: Training Learning Consultancy Ltd, Bristol, England. Reproduced with permission.

6 Do I organise my working day and week, as far as possible, according to priorities, or do I tend to deal with each problem as it turns up, or even as I think of it, without stopping to think whether there is something more important that I should be working on?
7 Am I able to complete a task, or am I constantly interrupted? If the latter, are all these interruptions an essential part of my work?

There are three questions that managers should ask of each of their activities:

- Should it be done at all?
- If so, when should it be done?
- Should it be delegated?

The Chartered Management Institute has published a checklist which explains that:

Good time management has always been an important skill, but it is now essential. Factors such as widespread corporate restructuring, accelerating change, information overload and the need to balance private and working lives have put the squeeze on managers to get more from their working day.[46]

Presenteeism and output

Despite growing interest in time management, it should not be viewed in isolation from related activities of management such as leadership and delegation. For example, a key aspect of managerial leadership (discussed in Chapter 10) is visibility. Time management needs to be balanced against potential benefits from maintaining an open-door policy or the MBWA approach. When making a conscious effort to find more time for themselves, managers need to take account of their availability for consultation with subordinates, superiors or colleagues and for ensuring effective processes of communication.

Clegg suggests that working more flexibly can be managed in a variety of ways but essentially it is about using our time, and the time of other people, more intelligently.

Traditionally we managed input. The time that an individual spent at his or her desk (or wherever) was a measure of their contribution. But there is a snag with this approach because there is no linkage between presenteeism and value to the company. Some staff could sit at their desk from 7am to 9pm keeping intensely busy all the time and never do anything to improve the bottom line. Others could, in minutes, boost revenue or slash costs by thousands or even millions of pounds. To cope with this paradox we need to change the focus to outputs – measuring what an individual produces, particularly the value of that output.[47]

Critical reflection

'Many of the 'newer' pronouncements on managerial behaviour are no more than the repetition of well-established concepts in a more contemporary context. In fact, management thinking has advanced little since the work of original authors such as Peter Drucker in 1955 or Douglas McGregor in 1960. How much truth do you think there is in this statement?

MANAGEMENT IN THE NEWS

Bad Manners and Bad Managers

Bosses with 'no time to be nice'

Alison Maitland

Lucy quit her job in university administration after finding herself routinely ignored and undermined by a manager. On one occasion, the female boss returned from leave and sent everyone in the department except Lucy an email thanking them for their work during her absence. On another, she told some of Lucy's peers that she could not be trusted. Lucy, whose name has been changed, says things rapidly went downhill. 'I found it exceptionally rude,' she says. 'It made me extremely negative towards her. It shut me down. I felt she was someone I didn't really want to get to know or work with. Communication became very poor, which made the job difficult.'

Her experience is echoed in a survey of workplace behaviour in the UK which shows that people in positions of power are often the worst perpetrators of incivility. Respondents accuse their bosses of dressing down employees in front of colleagues or customers, delivering unpleasant messages by email, ignoring the contribution of more junior staff and even tearing up someone's work in public.

'I have been shouted at in front of 20 people by the MD who said that the work I had done was 'crap' and I was to do it again,' says an employee in her 30s. In a similar vein, a 30-year-old female employee of an accountancy firm recalls 'one of the partners clicking his fingers at a senior manager to get his attention and calling him down the office, as though he were a puppy'. In a case of eye-popping discourtesy, a 29-year-old employee reports that 'a director who has since left asked me to go out in the pouring rain for his sandwich when I was eight months pregnant'.

'The lesson in manners must be taught from the top,' says Colette Hill, chief executive of CHA, the consultancy that commissioned the survey, Business Behaving Badly. 'In an organisation whose leaders are selectively courteous, fail to attend scheduled meetings, are cavalier about deadlines or casually bully their direct reports, others will inevitably follow the unspoken rules of engagement.'

While some of the 1,100 respondents to the online survey say that the only rude people they encounter at work are customers and that their colleagues are scrupulously polite, others report endemic incivility. email abuse is a particular bugbear, especially when people use it to avoid face-to-face contact. A respondent in his 40s says: 'One so-called member of the local management team regularly makes snide comments by email and presses the 'send' button as he puts on his coat and heads for home, knowing he won't see the people he's targeting for several days because of their shift pattern.'

The erosion of hierarchy and authority, and the growing pluralism of society, has left people less clear about how to behave at work, says Nigel Nicholson, professor of organisational behaviour at London Business School. 'We used to know where we stood a bit better. Now everybody has different standards, so there is much more room to perceive these [uncivil] things as happening.'

Despite persisting cases of rudeness and bullying by managers, Prof Nicholson sees some cause for optimism. Employees are speaking out more, he says. 'Bosses have always indulged themselves. In the old days, people used to knuckle under. Now they won't accept it.'

Source: Maitland, A., 'Bosses with "no time to be nice"', *Financial Times*, 11 May 2006.

Discussion Questions

1 **Critically review what this article reveals about the changing nature of managerial authority.**

2 **Discuss the extent to which 'good manners' are simply a matter of individual perception and personal standards, and the implications this might have for managerial behaviour.**

SYNOPSIS

- It is the responsibility of managers to achieve results through the efforts of other people. This involves the effective management of human resources. The way in which managers exercise their authority and carry out their responsibilities is important. The changing nature of the work environment is reflected in changes in the traditional boss–subordinate relationship. The style of management adopted, and the behaviour displayed towards subordinate staff, is likely to be conditioned by predispositions about people, human nature and work.

- One means of describing different styles of management is the Managerial Grid, now republished as the Leadership Grid®, and the combination of concern for production and concern for people. There are five basic combinations with a total of 81 different 'mixtures' of concern for production and concern for people. Managers tend to have one dominant style of management but may switch from one style to another. The Grid provides a framework in which managers can identify, study and review their patterns of behaviour, and aid training and development.

- An organisation is arguably more likely to harness its staffing resources effectively if there is a participative style of management. Likert identifies a four-fold model of management systems that can be related to a profile of organisational characteristics. System 4 is based on the principle of supportive relationships and group processes. One particular style or system of management is management by objectives (MBO). There are, however, a number of limitations and criticisms and, arguably, MBO has now been incorporated into modern systems of staff appraisal and performance management.

- There are many aspects to management but one essential ingredient of any successful manager is the ability to handle people effectively. It is important that managers have a highly developed sense of 'people perception' and understand the feelings of staff, and their needs and expectations. It is people who are being managed, and people should be considered in human terms. There are a number of views on what is likely to make for the successful management of people and lead to improved work performance.

- There is a clear and important need for managerial effectiveness, which can be distinguished from managerial efficiency and from activity. Effectiveness is concerned with doing the right things and relates to outputs of the job and to what the manager actually achieves. Managers are likely to be judged not just on their own performance but also on results achieved by other staff. The concept of managerial effectiveness is, however, difficult both to define and to measure. The Management Standards Centre provides a list of standards as benchmarks to help managers and their organisations improve performance.

- The combination of task orientation and relationship orientation results in four basic styles of managerial behaviour. Each of these styles can be effective or ineffective depending on the situation in which it is applied. One essential underlying criterion is the management of time. With the changing nature of the work organisation, good time management is arguably more essential than ever. However, studies suggest that activity may be a substitute for actual achievement and that busy managers are not necessarily effective managers.

Refresh your understanding, assess your progress and begin your research with online resources at www.pearsoned.co.uk/mullins

REVIEW AND DISCUSSION QUESTIONS

1 Distinguish between different sets of attitudes and assumptions about people at work that managers might hold. Suggest how these different attitudes and assumptions might influence actual managerial behaviour.

2 Critically assess the value and relevance today of management by objectives (MBO) as a means of improving organisational performance.

3 From your experience, explain fully a situation that you believe demonstrates a successful way of dealing with subordinate staff. To what extent can you relate this situation to the application of theories or principles of management?

4 Discuss what you see as the most important considerations in adopting a people-centred approach to management.
5 How would you, as a senior manager, attempt to manage your staff effectively as knowledge workers rather than subordinates?
6 How would you attempt to distinguish between an effective and an ineffective manager? Give specific examples of the criteria you would apply to assess the effectiveness of a particular managerial job of your choice.
7 Explain Reddin's 3-D model of managerial behaviour. Give a practical example of situations that demonstrate (i) a more effective style, and (ii) a less effective style.
8 Debate critically what you believe are the essential features relating to the effective management of time.

ASSIGNMENT

Complete the 'Your Management Style' questionnaire. Move quickly and do not think too deeply about each question but give your first immediate response.

Your Management Style Questionnaire

There are ten pairs of statements. Assign a weight from 0 to 10 to each statement to show the relative strength of your belief in the statements in each pair. The points assigned for each pair must total 10 in each case. Be as honest with yourself as you can and resist the natural tendency to respond as you would 'like to think things are'. This instrument is not a test. There are no right or wrong answers. It is designed to be a stimulus for personal reflection and discussion.

1 It's only human nature for people to do as little work as they can get away with. ______ (A)
When people avoid work, it's usually because their work has been deprived of its meaning. ______ (B)
10

2 If employees have access to any information they want, they tend to have better attitudes and behave more responsibly. ______ (C)
If employees have access to more information than they need to do their immediate tasks, they will usually misuse it. ______ (D)
10

3 One problem in asking for employees' ideas is that their perspective is too limited for their suggestions to be of much value. ______ (E)
Asking employees for their ideas broadens their perspective and results in the development of useful suggestions. ______ (F)
10

4 If people don't use much imagination and ingenuity on the job, it's probably because relatively few people have much of either. ______ (G)
Most people are imaginative and creative but may not show it because of limitations imposed by supervision and the job. ______ (H)
10

5 People tend to raise their stakes if they are accountable for their own behaviour and for correcting their own mistakes. ______ (I)
People tend to lower their stakes if they are not punished for their misbehaviour and mistakes. ______ (J)
10

Assignment – continued

6 It's better to give people both good and bad news because most employees want the whole story, no matter how painful. ______ (K)

It's better to withhold unfavourable news about business because most employees really want to hear only the good news. ______ (L)

10

7 Because a supervisor is entitled to more respect than those below him or her in the organisation, it weakens the supervisor's prestige to admit that a subordinate was right and he or she was wrong. ______ (M)

Because people at all levels are entitled to equal respect, a supervisor's prestige is increased when he or she supports this principle by admitting that a subordinate was right and he or she was wrong. ______ (N)

10

8 If you give people enough money, they are less likely to be concerned with such intangibles as responsibility and recognition. ______ (O)

If you give people interesting and challenging work, they are less likely to complain about such things as pay and supplemental benefits. ______ (P)

10

9 If people are to set their own goals and standards of performance, they tend to set them higher than the boss would. ______ (Q)

If people are allowed to set their own goals and standards of performance, they tend to set them lower than the boss would. ______ (R)

10

10 The more knowledge and freedom people have regarding their jobs, the more controls are needed to keep them in line. ______ (S)

The more knowledge and freedom people have regarding their jobs, the fewer controls are needed to ensure satisfactory job performance. ______ (T)

10

Source: Adapted from Myers, M. S., *Every Employee a Manager*, McGraw-Hill (1970). Reproduced with permission from the McGraw-Hill Companies, Inc.

PERSONAL AWARENESS AND SKILLS EXERCISE

Objectives

Completing this exercise should help you to enhance the following skills:

- Discover the level of trust that people have in you.
- Gain a deep appreciation of factors influencing interpersonal relationships.
- Examine and review those factors that influence your management style.

Exercise

You are required to ask yourself the following 11 questions:

1 Do people tend to open up to you and tell you things about themselves that they don't tell many others?

2 Are you generally accepting and non-judgemental of others?

3 Do people freely offer you help and support?

4 Do people come and seek your advice?

5 Do people feel comfortable being vulnerable around you?
6 Do you readily admit when you are wrong or have made a mistake?
7 Do you tend to use sarcasm and make putdown comments about people?
8 Do you gossip about others more than just occasionally?
9 Do you tell lies if it will benefit you to do so?
10 Do you like to make yourself look good even if it is at the expense of others?
11 Do you take credit for things that others have done?

Source: From Bibb, S. and Kourdi, J., 'Do people trust you?' *Professional Manager*, vol. 14, July 2004, p. 32. A Chartered Management Institute publication, reproduced with permission.

Discussion

- How important is trust to the success of an organisation?
- What do you believe are the characteristics of a trusted leader?
- How can managers develop and retain trust?

CASE STUDY

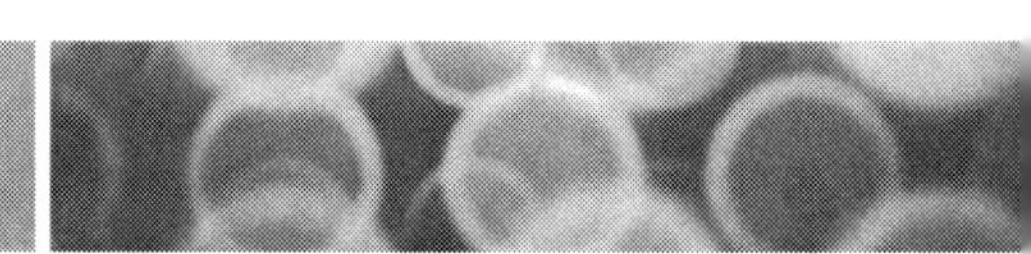

Effective management: a question of context?

As this chapter has illustrated, the nature of management effectiveness is to some degree dependent upon context. There may be a number of skills, personal qualities and behaviours which are central to effective management in any context, but the need for a contingency approach based upon the nature and environment of an organisation is highlighted by many of the authors whose work is discussed here.

Talented people with successful careers can sometimes fail to fulfil expectations in new roles or changed circumstances; for instance, the problems surrounding the Morrison's supermarket company illustrates the way in which a major organisational change (the acquisition of Safeway) resulted in the under-performance of a previously very successful company chairman, Sir Ken Morrison. At many levels of organisational life, management training and development programmes can help to smooth out individual transitions, for example as the result of promotion, but experience and performance remain key to the assessment of managerial effectiveness. An increasing amount of academic research is revealing that the *perceived* effectiveness of managers may also be of significance in relation to both the evaluation of an individual's success in a managerial role and with regard to decisions about their future promotion. This mix of fact and perception can sometimes have a damaging effect on the careers of both specific individuals and others in the group to which they might be seen to belong. In particular, we might consider the long-running debate about the effectiveness of women as managers.

Part of this debate has centred on the difficulty which some women have experienced in performing effectively in organisations and sectors of the economy which have traditionally been a male preserve. The evolutionary result of traditional work patterns is often seen in organisational structures and cultures which can be viewed as highly male-oriented, both in their overt features – aggressive language, open, personal competitiveness between colleagues, and loud banter in the workplace – and in their systems and practices – long working hours, the assumption of 24/7 availability and performance measures which seem to lock individuals into long working hours as a means to success. This naturally has an impact in defining and institutionalising behaviours which are both *regarded* as effective and which are likely to *be* effective (the term patriarchal is often used to describe such institutionalised 'maleness'). As more and more women gain professional expertise through improved opportunities and access to education, their expectations of having a working life and a career outside the family are likely to become the norm. This naturally raises questions about how women might react to the experience of using their talent in a masculine organisation and how they can both become and be recognised as effective managers. The issue of gender in relation to managerial effectiveness is likely to remain firmly on the agenda. In this case, we will examine some of the reactions.

If you can't join them, beat them

The Chartered Institute of Personnel and Development (CIPD) published a study in 2004 of the attitudes of a small sample of women in their 30s and 40s who had achieved significant management positions in commercial organisations. This study was set against a background of figures that showed both increasing female participation at managerial level and a 20 per cent rise in the number of women appointed to director level on the boards of FTSE 100 companies. It suggested that women in senior organisational roles could be classified into three groups depending upon their attitude towards careers in the upper layers of business organisations, and they describe the categories as:

- **corporate high-flyers** – those who have stayed within corporate life and have achieved senior roles;
- **soloists and pioneers** – those who have struck out alone, either working on their own or setting up businesses on their own terms;
- **submarines** – talented women who have chosen not to work towards traditional career advancement, but have put their energy into other areas.'[48]

In fact, the first two categories are closely linked, as this and many other cases show.[49] It comes from the world of investment banking, a classic zone of macho culture, and one which has frequently been under the media spotlight about its treatment of senior women.

From High Flyer to Pioneer

Nicola Horlick first hit the headlines in 1997 when, after a very successful career as a fund manager with Morgan Grenfell, she was suspended from her job because senior managers of the parent company, Deutsche Bank, believed she was about to leave and take a number of her team with her into a new venture. Refusing to take it quietly, she denied the story and flew to Germany with a posse of reporters trailing in her wake to demand her job back. She stayed sacked, but gained the tabloid title of 'Superwoman' when journalists realised she had five children. The following year she was in the news again when her oldest daughter died of leukaemia, and she wrote a book which seemed to give a positive answer to its title question, 'Can You Have it All?' Her next career move was to set up the UK branch of Société Générale Asset Management. Then she was very close to moving to Australia in 2004 to take up a job with AMP, but pulled out essentially because of the disruptive effect such a move would have had on her children's schooling.

Nicola Horlick denies that she is a 'superwoman' and sees effective delegation and strong teamwork as the cornerstones of good management

Her most recent venture is Bramdean Asset Management, a small investment company which she founded and launched in 2005 shortly after divorcing. With Bramdean, she moved from a corporate high flyer to become a soloist and pioneer in the CIPD survey terms. Her business is designed to fit around her, in the sense that she lives close to the office, can walk to work and ensures she is able to combine work and family commitments (her youngest child was three and the oldest sixteen when Bramdean was founded). It is highly collaborative in style, unlike many similar businesses, and in that sense she is pioneering a different style of asset management that involves a diverse team monitoring investments rather than focusing control in the hands of individual fund managers. This reduces the risk for investors who benefit from a variety of styles and a diverse portfolio. She describes her personal style as being essentially nurturing; she claims that this is essential for the development of talent in organisations and considers that she uses her parenting skills in the workplace just as much as in her home life.

> *One of the things I notice about really successful people is that they are not afraid to be surrounded by people as good as, if not better than, them. That's what I try and do: I employ successful people and try to make their life as interesting and as fun as possible.*[50]

She emphasises the importance of building a team and how this affects the way in which people need to be rewarded:

If you're going to have a team-based approach you cannot reward people on their individual performance alone. You have to have a big element that is related to the performance of the team as a whole, and you have to keep ramming home that message. As long as you keep doing that, people will then try very hard to make sure that they do contribute.[51]

She also emphasises the importance of delegation, which she sees as a particularly important skill and one which would enable her (with six maternity breaks in her career by the time she was 40) to achieve a better balance between work and family life.

I never knew when I wasn't going to be in the office. I had to teach everyone what to do when I was out. It honed my delegation skills.[52]

Furthermore, she has a clear view of the purpose of work and the importance of focusing on the job. She dislikes office politics; in her view work is not a holiday camp or a social occasion and bickering and in-fighting should be squashed so that the team is focused on the job rather than jockeying for position in a hierarchy. She does not, however, complain about sexism in the workplace. She sees advantages in being female in a male world and often claims that being the only woman pitching for business to investors makes the bid more memorable. She also admits that women and men work differently and that using the 'softer' side of the female psyche to lead teams and nurture staff is more effective for her than attempting to emulate male aggression. In this she strikes a very different tone from some of the high-profile women (such as Stephanie Villalba) who have used sex discrimination legislation as a means of fighting against the macho culture of investment banks (perhaps the CIPD should include a further category of 'Litigators' in future revisions of its typology). As for the 'superwoman' tag, she dismisses this view by observing that it is easier to do what she does when there is money to provide support systems:

If you're a single mother living on a council estate with three children, having to work with no assistance whatsoever, no man in sight, THAT person is a superwoman. I have lots of help.[53]

Your tasks

1. It has been argued that some effective managerial behaviours are universal and others contextually determined. Using the chapter and the case as a starting point, identify what you believe to be examples of each. Discuss and justify your choice.
2. Critically review the suggestion in this case that some parenting skills can be used by managers in an organisational setting. What sorts of parenting skills might be effective and under what organisational circumstances?
3. The case illustrates the way in which a successful and talented individual has designed an organisation to suit her specific abilities and requirements. What might managers in larger and more traditional organisations learn from her experience and how could they apply it in practice?

Notes and references

1 'Improving the World of Work', ACAS, August 2005.
2 Watson, T. *Organising and Managing Work*, Second edition, Financial Times Prentice Hall, (2006).
3 Austin, J., in Law, S. 'Good employees reap rewards', *Professional Manager*, vol. 13, no. 2, March 2004, pp. 34–5.
4 Greenhalgh, L. 'Managers Face Up to the New Era', in Pickford, J. (ed.) *Financial Times Mastering Management 2.0*, Financial Times Prentice Hall (2001), p. 17.
5 Lloyd, B. 'Words, meaning and managementspeak' *Professional Manager*, vol. 13, no. 5, September 2004, p. 37.
6 McGregor, D. *The Human Side of Enterprise*, Penguin (1987).
7 Townsend, R. *Further Up the Organisation*, Coronet Books (1985), pp. 168–9.
8 See, for example: Mullins, L. J. ' Management and Managerial Behaviour', *International Journal of Hospitality Management*, vol. 4, no. 1, 1985, pp. 39–41.
9 Ouchi, W. G. *Theory Z: How American Business Can Meet the Japanese Challenge*, Addison-Wesley (1981), p. 4.
10 For a detailed discussion on Japanese management practices see: Hannagan, T. *Management: Concepts and Practices*, Fourth edition, Financial Times Prentice Hall (2005).
11 Heller, R. *In Search of European Excellence*, HarperCollins Business (1997), p. 138.
12 Blake, R. R. and Mouton, J. S. *The Managerial Grid III*, Gulf Publishing Company (1985).

13 Blake, R. R. and McCanse, A. A. *Leadership Dilemmas – Grid Solutions*, Gulf Publishing Company (1991).
14 Lester, T. 'Taking Guard on the Grid', *Management Today*, March 1991, pp. 93–6.
15 Newborough, G. 'People vs Production', *The British Journal of Administrative Management*, May/June 1999, pp. 13–14.
16 Crainer, S. and Dearlove, D. (eds) *Financial Times Handbook of Management*, Second edition, Financial Times Prentice Hall (2001), p. 364.
17 Likert, R. *New Patterns of Management*, McGraw-Hill (1961).
18 Likert, R. and Likert, J. G. *New Ways of Managing Conflict*, McGraw-Hill (1976).
19 Drucker, P. F. *The Practice of Management*, Heinemann Professional (1989).
20 Heller, R. *In Search of European Excellence*, HarperCollins Business (1997), p. 252.
21 Gratton, L. *The Democratic Enterprise*, Financial Times Prentice Hall (2004), p. 180.
22 Hannagan, T. *Management: Concepts and Practices*, Fourth edition, Financial Times Prentice Hall (2005), p. 181.
23 Gratton, L. *Living Strategy: Putting People at the Heart of Corporate Purpose*, Financial Times Prentice Hall (2000), p. xiii.
24 Gratton, L. *Living Strategy: Putting People at the Heart of Corporate Purpose*, Financial Times Prentice Hall (2000), p. 206.
25 Lloyd, B. 'Words, meaning and managementspeak' *Professional Manager*, vol. 13, no. 5, September 2004, p. 37.
26 Mann, S. 'Give a little gain a lot', *Professional Manager*, March 1999, p. 32.
27 Castellanos, F. 'Getting the rewards', *Read.Me*, IBM team publication for the UK and Ireland, May/June 1998, no. 11, p. 32.
28 Fletcher, W. 'Good Listener, Better Manager', *Management Today*, January 2000, p. 30.
29 Adams, J. S. 'Injustice in Social Exchange', abridged in Steers, R. M. and Porter, L. W. *Motivation and Work Behavior*, Second edition, McGraw-Hill (1979), pp. 107–24.
30 'Management Insights, 'The Virgin Factor', *Management Today*, May 2000.
31 See, for example: Beggs, A. 'The Real Meaning of Empowerment', *Financial Times Mastering Management Review*, September 1997, pp. 14–15.
32 Green, J. 'When Was Your Management style Last Applauded?', *Chartered Secretary*, December 1998, pp. 28–9.
33 Galunic, G. and Weeks, J. 'Survey – Mastering People Management', *Financial Times*, 12 November 2001.
34 Ash, M. K. *On People Management*, Macdonald & Co. (1985).
35 Ibid., p. xix.
36 Drucker, P. *The Practice of Management*, Heinemann Professional (1989), p. 3.
37 Foppen, J. W. 'Knowledge leadership', in Chowdhury, S. *Management 21C*, Financial Times Prentice Hall (2000), pp. 160–1.
38 Stewart, R. *The Reality of Management*, Third edition, Butterworth Heinemann (1999), p. 179.
39 Luthans, F. 'Successful vs. Effective Real Managers', *The Academy of Management Executive*, vol. 11, no. 2, 1988, pp. 127–32.
40 Ahadi, K. Management Standards Centre, 2006.
41 Reddin, W. J. *Managerial Effectiveness*, McGraw-Hill (1970).
42 Drucker, P. F. *The Effective Executive*, Heinemann Professional (1988).
43 Rees, W. D. and Porter, C. *Skills of Management*, Fifth edition, Thomson Learning (2001), p. 22.
44 Bruch, H. and Ghoshal, S. 'Beware the Busy Manager', *Harvard Business Review*, February 2002, pp. 62–9.
45 Stewart, R. *Managers and Their Jobs*, Second edition, Macmillan (1988), p. 123.
46 'Managing Your Time Effectively', *Management Checklist 016*, Chartered Management Institute, June 2005.
47 Clegg, B. 'Making the most of time', *Professional Manager*, vol. 13, no. 1, January 2004, pp. 20–1.
48 CIPD 2004 'Women in the Boardroom; a bird's eye view', London, CIPD.
49 See, for instance, the creation of Sapphire Partners, a new style of business founded by two former corporate high fliers, Kate Grussing and Shirley Soskin, which offers a mix of consultancy and executive search services to match senior professionals who want flexible jobs with companies that need their skills; or Charlton House catering company, founded by Robyn Jones, one of the women interviewed for the CIPD study. Both examples show women using their expertise to create a 'girl-shaped' organisation in which they can be successful and effective rather than attempting to fit into standard 'boy-shaped' ones at the expense of both family and sanity.
50 Butcher, S. 2005 'Nicola Horlick delivers career tips' eFinancialCareers website www.efinancialcareers.co.uk 4 November 2005 [accessed 27 June 2006].
51 Horlick, N. 2005 'Fifty lessons: teamwork takes all kinds' Telegraph.co.uk 30 June 2005 [accessed 27 June 2006].
52 Horlick, N. 2005 'Fifty lessons: teamwork takes all kinds' Telegraph.co.uk 30 June 2005 [accessed 27 June 2006].
53 Walters, S. 2005 'Superwoman Nicola still battling for "the girls"'. *Manchester Evening News* (on line version) www.Manchesteronline.co.uk 14 February 2005 [accessed 27 June 2006].

Structures of Organisation

ORGANISATIONAL STRATEGY, ETHICS AND RESPONSIBILITIES

> **"The traditional perspective is that managers in business organizations are agents who represent the interests of the owners in achieving economic success for the organization. From this perspective, ethical leadership is satisfied by maximizing economic outcomes that benefit owners while not doing anything strictly prohibited by laws and moral standards."**
>
> **Gary Yukl** – State University of New York
>
> *Leadership in Organizations*, Sixth Edition, Pearson Prentice Hall (2006), p. 423

The overall function and direction of a work organisation is determined by the nature of its corporate strategy. Strategy provides goals, objectives and guidelines for the structure and operations of the organisation. Organisations play a major and increasingly important role in the lives of us all. The power and influence of a business organisation must also be tempered by decisions relating to its broader social obligations and ethical responsibilities. Corporate strategy and responsibilities are important features in the study of management and organisational behaviour.

Learning outcomes

After completing this chapter you should be able to"

- explain the nature of, and functions served by, corporate strategy;
- assess the importance of organisational ideologies and principles;
- examine the need for objectives and policy, and the importance of the profit objective;
- assess the concept of corporate social responsibilities and organisational stakeholders;
- explore approaches to the consideration of values and ethics in organisations;
- evaluate the nature and scope of business ethics and codes of conduct;
- review the importance of corporate strategy and responsibilities for the effective management of a work organisation.

Critical reflection

'The idea of corporate strategy may serve as a management control system but has little value to the day-to-day activities undertaken within the organisation or as a guideline for human behaviour or actions.' Do you agree? What benefits do you see from the corporate strategy in your college/university?

THE IMPORTANCE OF STRATEGY

In Chapter 3 we saw that the context of the organisational setting is central to the application of organisational behaviour and the process of management. It is the interaction of people in order to achieve objectives that forms the basis of the particular organisation. If you do not know where you are going, you cannot tell whether you have arrived! Underlying the effective management of people, therefore, is the requirement for a clear understanding of the nature of the business that the organisation is in and how best to provide customer or consumer satisfaction.[1] In order to study organisational behaviour you need to understand the nature of corporate strategy for the formal organisation as a whole.

Johnson et al. define strategy as

The direction and scope of an organisation over the long term, which achieves advantage in a changing environment through its configuration of resources and competences with the aim of fulfilling stakeholders expectations.[2]

An alternative definition, cited in Lynch, is given by *Andrews*:

Corporate strategy is the pattern of major objectives, purposes or goals and essential policies or plans for achieving those goals, stated in such a way as to define what business the company is in or is to be in and the kind of company it is or is to be.[3]

Together, these definitions highlight the importance of the overall direction of the organisation, its goals and objectives and the expectations of stakeholders. Some writers distinguish different terms and various levels of 'strategy' but corporate strategy is seen here as a generic term embracing a link among organisation structure, the process of management and applications of organisational behaviour. All organisations have some function to perform, some contribution to make to the environment of which they are part. The function of the business organisation may be seen, for example, as the creation and/or supply of goods and services. This involves bringing together the factors of production and their successful mix and direction, to provide products or services in order to create value added. Others might see the function of business organisations as, for example, providing a source of employment and of income.

Explicit statement of strategy

Objectives and policy are formalised within the framework of a **corporate strategy**, which serves to describe an organisation's sense of purpose, and plans and actions for its implementation. *Tilles* has suggested that without an explicit statement of strategy it becomes more difficult for expanding organisations to reconcile co-ordinated action with entrepreneurial effort.[4] An explicit strategy for the business organisation is necessary for the following reasons. First, there is the need for people to co-operate together in order to achieve the benefits of mutual reinforcement. Second, there are the effects of changing environmental conditions.

The absence of an explicit concept of strategy may result in members of the organisation working at cross-purposes. The intentions of top management may not be communicated clearly to those at lower levels in the hierarchy who are expected to implement these intentions. Obsolete patterns of behaviour become very difficult to modify. Change comes about from either subjective or intuitive assessment, which become increasingly unreliable as the rate of change increases. Developing a statement of strategy demands a creative effort. If strategic planning is to be successful, it requires different methods of behaviour and often fundamental change in the nature of interactions among managers.

People and strategy

Johnson et al. draw attention to the importance of the relationship between people and successful strategies. This goes beyond the traditional HR agenda and is concerned with behaviours as well as competences. The people dimension of strategy is concerned with three related issues:

- people as a resource – personal and organisational competences, and performance management;
- people and behaviour – personal behaviours and collective behaviour;
- organising people – HR function, line managers, structures and processes.

> *The ability to change behaviours may be the key ingredient for success. Creating a climate where people strive to achieve success and the motivation of individuals are crucial roles of any manager and are a central part of their involvement in their organisation's strategy.*[5]

Allen and Helms suggest that different types of reward practices may more closely complement different generic strategies and are significantly related to higher levels of perceived organisational performance.[6]

Managers' skills and competencies

Increased business competitiveness and the dynamic external environment have placed important emphasis on corporate strategy and the competencies of managers. For example, *Richardson and Thompson* argue that if organisations are to be effective in strategic terms they must be able to deal with the pressures and demands of change. Managers should be strategically aware and appreciate the origins and nature of change. They should possess a comprehensive set of skills and competencies and be able to deal effectively with the forces which represent opportunities and threats to the organisation. Effective strategic management creates a productive alliance between the nature and the demands of the environment, the organisation's culture and values, and the resources that the organisation has at its disposal.[7]

> *Strategy is about first asking questions, then improving the quality of those questions through listening to the answers and acting on the new knowledge. Any effective strategy requires the successful integration of thoughts about tomorrow's new business opportunities with both past experience and the pattern of today's behaviours.*[8]

Corporate approach in the public sector

Some form of corporate strategy or planning is necessary for all organisations, particularly large organisations and including service organisations and those in the public sector. In a discussion on strategy developments, *Lynch* suggests that many of the same considerations apply to both public and private organisations. The major difference has been the lack of the objective to deliver a profit in government-owned institutions. The trend in most parts of the world is now towards privatising large public companies in the utilities and telecommunications sectors. The principal impact of privatisation on strategy will depend on the form that privatisation takes. Some companies may remain monopolies even though in the private sector. Lynch sets out the following key strategic principles for public and non-profit organisations:

- Public organisations are unlikely to have a profit objective. Strategy is therefore governed by broader public policy issues such as politics, monopoly supply, bureaucracy and the battle for resources from the government to fund the activities of the organisation.
- Strategy in non-profit organisations needs to reflect the values held by the institutions concerned. Decision-making may be slower and more complex.
- Within the constraints outlined above, the basic strategic principles can then be applied.[9]

In the public sector, the establishment of objectives and policy requires clarification of the respective roles of both elected members and permanent officials. This dual nature of management requires harmonious relationships between the two parties and emphasises the need for a corporate approach.

The concept of synergy

An important aspect of corporate strategy and the growth and development of organisations is the **concept of synergy** that was developed in management applications by *Ansoff*.[10] **Synergy** results when the whole is greater than the sum of its component parts. It can be expressed, simply, in terms of the 2 + 2 = 5 effect. An example could be an organisation integrating its retail and online operations.

Synergy is often experienced in situations of expansion or where one organisation merges with another, such as an organisation responsible for the development and production of a product merging with an organisation that markets the product. The new organisation could benefit from the combined strengths and opportunities, skills and expertise, shared fixed overheads and technology, and from the streamlining and economy of its operations. An example could be the merger of a computer firm with expertise in the design and marketing of hardware, with a firm expert in software manufacture and systems design. In the search for synergy and increased productivity, a number of organisations are creating a more streamlined structure and concentrating on its key activities with the outsourcing of non-core activities. (The ethical issues that arise from outsourcing are discussed later in this chapter.)

It is possible, however, to experience negative synergy or the 2 + 2 = 3 situation. Such a situation might arise when a merger occurs between organisations operating in different fields, with different markets or with different methods, or where the new organisation becomes unwieldy or loses its cost-effectiveness. Another example could be customer and/or union resistance to the outsourcing of call centres to other countries.

ORGANISATIONAL GOALS

In addition to performing some function, all organisations have some incentive for their existence and for their operations. The goals of an organisation are the reason for its existence. The activities of the organisation are directed to the attainment of its goals. A goal is a future expectation, some desired future state. It is something the organisation is striving to accomplish. The meaning of a goal is, however, subject to a number of interpretations. It can be used in a very broad sense to refer to the overall purpose of an organisation – for example, to produce television sets. A goal may also be used to refer to more specific desired accomplishments – for example, to produce and sell a given number of a range of television sets within a given period of time.

Organisational goals are more specific than that of the function of an organisation. The goals of an organisation will determine the nature of its inputs and outputs, the series of activities through which the outputs are achieved, and interactions with its external environment. The extent to which an organisation is successful in attaining its goals is a basis for the evaluation of organisational performance and effectiveness.

Goals are therefore an important feature of work organisations. To be effective, goals should be emphasised, stated clearly and communicated to all members of the organisation. The movement towards greater delegation and empowerment down through the hierarchy means that staff at all levels must be aware of their key tasks and actions, and exactly what is expected of them and their department/section. For example, goal-setting theory is widely recognised as a successful means of increasing work motivation and performance.[11]

> *In today's environment, old-style command and control structures no longer work. People want freedom, but it must be freedom within a framework. Organisations, like individuals, need goals. Ensuring that appropriate goals are set is every manager's responsibility. Although currently it is popular to encourage commitment by letting the organisation set its own goals, this approach frequently yields only modest results. More challenging goals, created top-down, can have far more dramatic effects on business performance ... Setting ambitious goals forces the organisation to dig deeper for creative solutions and to rethink how the business should be run.*
>
> Sir Brian Pitman, Chairman of Lloyds TSB[12]

Balance of empowerment and control

To be effective, organisational goals should encourage the use of empowerment but still incorporate an element of traditional management measurement and control.

Mills and Friesen suggest that to be effective, goals must exhibit several characteristics:

- **be understandable** – otherwise those who are given them seek further input before acting. If they cannot act on their own it follows they have not been empowered;
- **contain a time element** – in order that those being empowered will know when their progress will be measured. This helps them to accept empowerment and stop looking for direction;
- **be carefully drawn** – broad enough to support independent action but not so broad that confounding factors prevent their achievement. For example, asking a team to keep company stock price above target is too broad as factors influencing share prices are beyond the control of any one team;
- **be subject to alignment** – with other goals across the organisation in order to facilitate co-ordination among teams and to 'roll up' into collective company goals.[13]

The goal-setting process is of importance to all types of organisations and facilitates the attainment of objectives. In the public sector, for example, organisations such as hospitals, local authorities and universities have complex, diverse and competing goals. The clarification of goals and objectives is the basis for corporate planning, and a planning, programming, budgeting systems (PPBS) approach to decision-making.

An ambiguous concept

However, the concept of organisational goals is ambiguous. Goals may be expressed very simply: in the case of business organisations, for example, to make a profit, or to increase productivity. Such broadly based goals might be taken for granted and they tell us little about the emphasis placed on the various activities of the organisation in meeting its goals. In any case, profit might more correctly be interpreted as a reward to the shareholders or providers of capital, and a means of ensuring the continued existence of the organisation and maintaining its growth and development. *Watson* questions whether it is necessary to have the notion of organisational goals as giving focus or direction to the idea of an organisation when such a purpose could readily and more simply be achieved using the notions of 'tasks'.[14]

INTEGRATION OF GOALS

Strictly, organisations have no goals; only people do. Organisational goals are established by people, either individually or, more usually, by a number of individuals co-operating. For example, a group of senior managers may collectively agree on a particular desired course of action that may then come to be referred to as an organisational goal. However, this is still the goal of those managers who initially determined it.

Success of the organisation is measured by the progress of people towards goals set by people. This gives rise to the questions:

- To what extent has the organisation one common set of goals, or is there diversity among the various goals of different departments or divisions of the organisation?
- How far are the goals of management compatible with the goals of the organisation?
- To what extent do individual members obtain satisfaction of their own goals through the attainment of organisational goals?

Informal goals

Members of the organisation have different, and often conflicting, goals. As a result, the goals which the organisation actually pursues (**informal goals**) may be distinguished from the officially stated goals (**formal goals**) that are set out in broad terms as the reasons for the purpose of the organisation. Informal goals may be inferred from the actual decisions made and actions taken within the organisation. Managers, and other members of the organisation, will have:

- their own perception of the goals of the organisation – for example, to produce high-quality television sets which satisfy requirements of the customers; and
- their personal goals – for example to earn high wages, to achieve promotion, to gain social satisfaction, to achieve status – which they expect to fulfil by participating in the activities of the organisation (*see* Figure 14.1).

Figure 14.1 Compatibility of goals within an organisation

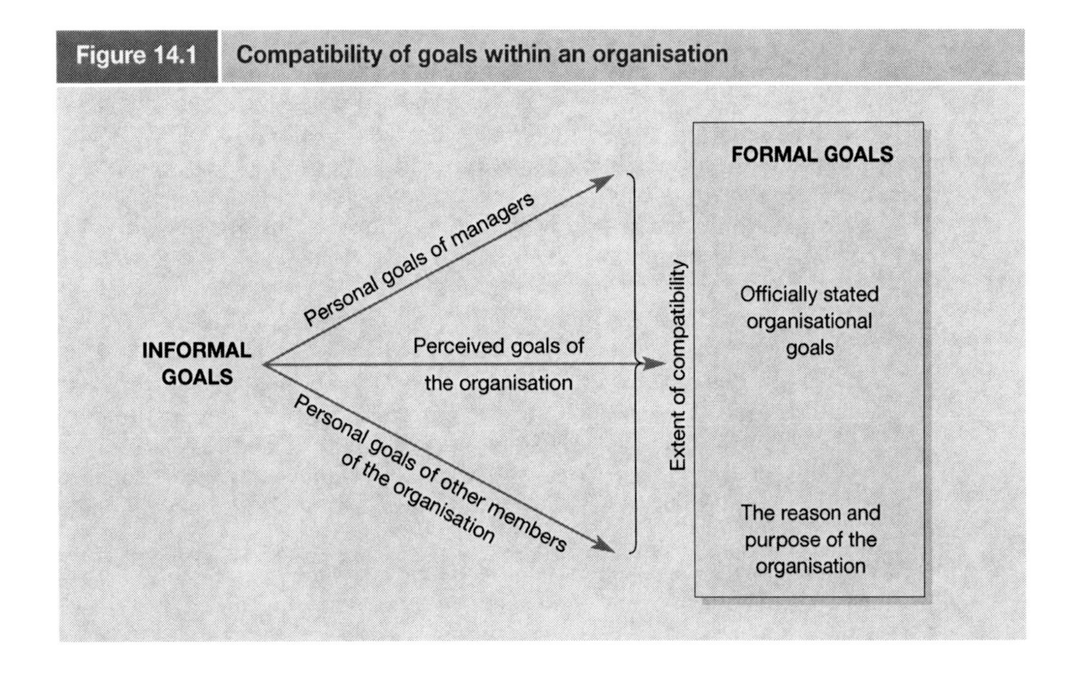

Compatibility of personal goals and organisational goals

If organisational goals and personal goals are pulling in different directions, conflict will arise and performance is likely to suffer. An organisation will be more effective when personal goals are compatible with organisational goals. Organisational performance will depend ultimately on the extent to which individuals are provided with the opportunity to satisfy their own goals by contributing to the goals of the organisation.

Management has a responsibility to clarify organisational goals and to attempt to integrate personal goals (including their own) with the overall objectives of the organisation. Only when organisational goals are shared by all members of the organisation will complete integration be achieved. In practice, this is unlikely. As McGregor points out:

> *Perfect integration of organizational requirements and individual goals and needs is, of course, not a realistic objective. In adopting this principle, we seek that degree of integration in which the individual can achieve his goals best by directing his efforts towards the success of the organisation.*[15]

Management should endeavour, therefore, to structure the organisation so that people may realise their own (personal) goals by helping the organisation to satisfy its goals. One attempt at integrating organisational goals with the needs of the individual members of the organisation is provided by the approach of Management by Objectives. This is discussed in Chapter 12.

Critical reflection

In large-scale organisations, the goals and objectives of the organisation, management and the workforce are never likely to be fully compatible. Do you think attempts at harmonisation are worth the effort? Or should one just accept the inevitability of organisational conflict?

ORGANISATIONAL IDEOLOGIES AND PRINCIPLES

The goals of the organisation may be pursued in accordance with an underlying ideology, or philosophy, based on beliefs, values and attitudes. This **organisational ideology** determines the 'culture' of the organisation and provides a set of principles that govern the overall conduct of the organisation's operations, codes of behaviour, the management of people and its dealings with other organisations.[16] These sets of principles may be recognised and implemented informally as 'accepted conventions' of the organisation or they may be stated formally in writing.

Certain aspects of an organisation's philosophy may be so dominant that they become the 'hallmark' of that organisation and place constraints on other areas or forms of activities. An example is the high quality standard of Marks & Spencer's merchandise and the company's explicit policy of buying primarily from United Kingdom sources. In the case of the Walt Disney Company, quality service is embedded deeply within its corporate culture. The overriding byword of The Body Shop is honesty and this underlies its policy of: 'We WILL be the most honest cosmetic company.' As another example, the highest-quality hallmark of Rolls-Royce cars would presumably prevent entry into the cheaper mass-production market.

Organisational values and beliefs

More than 30 years ago, *Brech* wrote about the ideology of an organisation related to the idea of both an ethical foundation and an organisational or operational foundation.

- **Ethical foundation** embodies the basic principles which govern the external and internal relations of the organisation. External relations concern standards of fair trading and relations with, for example, customers, suppliers and the general public. Internal relations are concerned with fair standards of employment and relations with members of the organisation, including authorised union representatives.

- **Organisational or operational foundation** is concerned with the structure, operation, and conduct of the activities of the organisation. External aspects relate to, for example, methods of trading and channels of distribution. Internal aspects include methods of production, use of equipment and managerial practices relating to organisational performance, productivity and profitability.[17]

In more recent years organisations have given growing attention to a set of stated corporate values displayed prominently for all to see. *Lucas* questions whether such grand statements of corporate principles really mean anything and concludes that they actually have a point and values can be used with success. 'A set of values is obviously a nice thing for an organisation to have; something to pin on the notice board. But for those organisations that have learned to walk the talk, deeply embedded values can attract the right people, underpin the business in times of crisis and provide direction for the future.'[18]

Dainty and Anderson point out that values are the guidelines a person uses to make choices and within organisations, basic beliefs affect what decisions are made, how people interact, and the kind of work practices that are pursued and developed. They form the glue that binds an organisation's culture. 'Building an understanding of values that are shared within an organisation will be as important in the 21st century as it is today. In fact, many feel that organisations and people should be returning to more fundamental values, rather than moving away from them. Increasingly, organisations are spending time working out and agreeing the values by which they want their organisation to be managed.'[19]

Cloke and Goldsmith contend that organisations can increase their integrity, coherence, and integration and improve their performance by reaching consensus on shared values. They can bolster value-based relationships by recognising and encouraging behaviours that uphold their values; communicate and publicise their values, and encourage individual and team responsibility for implementing them; and develop methods for monitoring compliance with values, providing feedback and identifying potential conflicts of interest. Most importantly consensus on shared values means organisations can accomplish these goals without moralising, preaching, excusing or imposing their values on others.[20]

MISSION STATEMENTS

In recent years it has become increasing popular for an organisation to produce a **mission statement** and/or its 'vision' that sets out the purpose and general direction for the organisation. There is sometimes an apparent uncertainty of the distinction between the terms 'mission' and 'vision'. It seems to be generally accepted that the vision provides the overall frame of reference within which mission statements are written and goals selected. 'If vision is ill formed, mission statements will be vague and goal achievement hard to measure.'[21]

Mission statements vary in length, the extent of specific or general content, and according to the type of organisation. For example, the mission and vision of the Chartered Management Institute as set out in its Royal Charter is to: **'promote the art and science of management'**. Its vision is to be the **'authoritative and influential champion for professional management'**.

In fulfilling its mission, the Institute will:

- encourage and support the lifelong development of managers;
- raise the level of competence and qualification of management;
- initiate, develop, evaluate and disseminate management thinking, tools, techniques and practices;
- influence employers, policy makers and opinion formers on management.[22]

Value of mission statements

The desire to identify with as many stakeholders as possible means that many mission statements are all embracing with bland and abstract wording. The value of a mission statement is dependent, however, upon the extent to which it is understood and accepted throughout the organisation, and translated in meaningful terms to all members of staff including those at the operational level. *Perrin and Tavakoli* raise doubts over managers who have a naïve notion that the production and dissemination of a well-crafted statement will create a sense of mission:

> *The picture will remain gloomy while managers and consultants believe that creating a mission statement is synonymous with creating a sense of mission. You only create the latter if your mission statement is understood, believed and acted upon by a majority of organisation members.*[23]

A mission statement is only likely to be of any value if the organisation actually practices what it preaches. *Reeves* maintains that the problem with vision statements is that they are just that – statements, and typically they are disconnected from those they are meant to inspire. However, when values, mission and values are aligned to behaviour, this has an enormous impact on the productivity of organisations.[24]

A similar point is made by *Gratton*:

> *How often do corporate plans and mission statements remain simply that: senior executive rhetoric with little meaning to those people whose job it is to deliver customer satisfaction or bring complex products rapidly to the marketplace? Employees may hear corporate mission statements extolling the virtues of customer satisfaction or product innovation, but when the communication fanfare is over, the customer-focus workshops completed, and the lights dim on the business video, what is left? A group of employees trying to make sense and create meaning from the many messages and cues they have received.*[25]

OBJECTIVES AND POLICY

In accordance with its ideology or philosophy, the goals of the organisation are translated into objectives and policy. Terminology and use of the two terms varies but objectives are seen here as the 'what' and policy as the 'how', 'where' and 'when' – the means that follow the objectives.

- **Objectives** set out more specifically the goals of the organisation, the aims to be achieved and the desired end-results.
- **Policy** is developed within the framework of objectives. It provides the basis for decision-making and the course of action to follow in order to achieve objectives.

The establishment of objectives and policy is therefore an integral part of the process of management, and a necessary function in every organisation. In terms of a systems approach, the objectives of an organisation are related to the input–conversion–output cycle. In order to achieve its objectives and satisfy its goals the organisation takes inputs from the environment, through a series of activities transforms or converts these inputs into outputs and returns them to the environment as inputs to other systems. The organisation operates within a dynamic setting and success in achieving its goals will be influenced by a multiplicity of interactions with the environment (*see* Figure 14.2).

Objectives Clearly defined and agreed objectives are the first stage in the design of organisation structure and help facilitate systems of communication between different parts of the organisation. The choice of objectives is an essential part of corporate strategy and the

Figure 14.2 A systems view of organisational goals and objectives

decision-making process involving future courses of action. Objectives may be set out either in general terms or in more specific terms. General objectives are determined by top management. Specific objectives are formulated within the scope of general objectives and usually have more defined areas of application and time limits.

Objectives may be just implicit but the formal, explicit definition of objectives will assist communications and reduce misunderstandings, and provide more meaningful criteria for evaluating organisational performance. However, objectives should not be stated in such a way that they detract from the recognition of possible new opportunities, potential danger areas, the initiative of staff or the need for innovation or change.

Policy A policy is a guideline for organisational action and the implementation of goals and objectives. Policy is translated into rules, plans and procedures; it relates to all activities of the organisation and to all levels of the organisation. Clearly stated policy can help reinforce the main functions of the organisation, make for consistency and reduce dependency on the actions of individual managers. Policy clarifies the roles and responsibilities of managers and other members of staff and provides guidelines for managerial behaviour. Some policy decisions are directly influenced by external factors – for example government legislation on equal opportunities and diversity.

Corporate guidelines

Whatever the type of organisation, there is a need for lines of direction through the establishment of objectives and determination of policy. Objectives and policy together provide corporate guidelines for the operations and management of the organisation. The activities of the organisation derive their significance from the contribution they make to achieving objectives in the manner directed. The formulation of objectives and policy, and the allocation of resources, provide the basis for strategic planning which is the first stage in the planning and control processes of business organisations. Clearly stated, good objectives help provide unity of direction and the basis for employee commitment and motivation. Recall, for example, the discussion on management by objectives in Chapter 12. A commonly used mnemonic is that objectives should be 'SMART':

Specific Measurable Achievable Realistic Timebound

THE PROFIT OBJECTIVE

In order to be successful, the primary objectives of the business organisation may be seen as:

- to continue in existence – that is, to **survive**;
- to maintain **growth and development**; and
- to make a **profit**.

All three objectives are inextricably linked and it is a matter of debate whether the organisation survives and develops in order to provide a profit, or makes a profit by which it can survive and develop.

Summers and Nowicki suggest that using a Maslow-like hierarchy of needs (discussed in Chapter 7), the first concern for organisations is survival. After organisational survival is ensured, managers then have considerable latitude in what they want the organisation to be and do.[26]

If we accept survival as the ultimate objective of the business organisation, this involves the need for a steady and continuous profit. Organisations must be prepared to accept the possibility of a reduction in short-term profitability in order to provide for future investments. The profit goal is achieved through the process of management and the combined efforts of members of the organisation. In times of economic recession the survival objective takes on particular importance, especially for small businesses.

> *Managers today have a problem. They know their companies must grow. But growth is hard, especially given today's economic environment where investment capital is difficult to come by and firms are reluctant to take risks. Managers know innovation is the ticket to successful growth. But they just can't seem to get innovation right.*[27]

Not a sufficient criterion

Although the objective of profit maximisation is undoubtedly of great importance, it is not, by itself, a sufficient criterion for the effective management of a business organisation. In practice, there are many other considerations and motivations which affect the desire for the greatest profit or maximum economic efficiency and the accompanying assumptions which underlie the economic theory of the firm.

The meaning of 'profit maximisation' is not, by itself, very clear. Consideration has to be given to the range and quality of an organisation's products or services, to the costs of its operations and to environmental influences. Reducing attention to longer-term 'investments' such as quality and after-sales service, research and development, sales promotion, management development, satisfaction of staff and their employment conditions may increase profitability in the short term, but is likely to jeopardise future growth and development, and possibly even the ultimate survival of the organisation.

A business organisation has to provide some commodity or service by which it contributes to the economic and/or social needs of the community. It also has broader social responsibilities to society. (Social responsibilities are discussed later in this chapter.) Profit can be seen as the incentive for an organisation to carry out its activities effectively. Profit does at least provide some broad measure of effectiveness and highlights the difficulty in evaluating the effectiveness of not-for-profit organisations, such as National Health Service hospitals, prisons or universities.

Furthermore, as discussed earlier, members of the organisation will have their own personal goals and their own perception of the goals of the organisation.

Fallacy of the single objective

The reality is that managers are usually faced with the challenge of several, often competing and/or conflicting objectives. *Drucker* has referred to the fallacy of the single objective of a business. The search for the one, right objective is not only unlikely to be productive, but is certain to harm and misdirect the business enterprise.

To emphasize only profit, for instance, misdirects managers to the point where they may endanger the survival of the business. To obtain profit today they tend to undermine the future ... To manage a business is to balance a variety of needs and goals ... the very nature of business enterprise requires multiple objectives which are needed in every area where performance and results directly and vitally affect the survival and prosperity of the business.[28]

Drucker goes on to suggest eight key areas in which objectives should be set in terms of performance and results:

1 **Market standing** – for example: share of market standing; range of products and markets; distribution; pricing; customer loyalty and satisfaction.
2 **Innovation** – for example: innovations to reach marketing goals; developments arising from technological advancements; new processes and improvements in all major areas of organisational activity.
3 **Productivity** – for example: optimum use of resources; use of techniques such as operational research to help decide alternative courses of action; the ratio of 'contributed value' to total revenue.
4 **Physical and financial resources** – for example: physical facilities such as plant, machines, offices and replacement of facilities; supply of capital and budgeting; planning for the money needed; provision of supplies.
5 **Profitability** – for example: profitability forecasts and anticipated timescales; capital investment policy; yardsticks for measurement of profitability.
6 **Manager performance and development** – for example: the direction of managers and setting up their jobs; the structure of management; the development of future managers.
7 **Worker performance and attitude** – for example: union relations; the organisation of work; employee relations.
8 **Public responsibility** – for example: demands made upon the organisation, such as by law or public opinion; responsibilities to society and the public interest.

The balanced scorecard

The **balanced scorecard (BS)** is an attempt to combine a range of both qualitative and quantitative indicators of performance which recognise the expectations of various stakeholders and relates performance to a choice of strategy as a basis for evaluating organisational effectiveness. Citing the work of *Kaplan and Norton* in a year-long study of a dozen US companies,[29] Anita van de Vliet refers to the approach of a 'balanced scorecard' and the belief that

... relying primarily on financial accounting measures was leading to short-term decision-making, over-investment in easily valued assets (through mergers and acquisitions) with readily measurable returns, and under-investment in intangible assets, such as product and process innovation, employee skills or customer satisfaction, whose short-term returns are more difficult to measure.

van de Vliet suggests that in the information era, there is a growing consensus that financial indicators on their own are not an adequate measure of company competitiveness or performance and there is a need to promote a broader view.

The balanced scorecard does still include the hard financial indicators, but it balances these with other, so-called soft measures, such as customer acquisition, retention, profitability and satisfaction; product development cycle times; employee satisfaction; intellectual assets and organisational learning.[30]

The balanced scorecard can also be used in the public sector where there is an increasing need for organisations to improve their performance and to be seen as more businesslike in the delivery of services (including an employee perspective).

Given that the public sector has the difficult task of fulfilling a wide range of very different objectives, the BS could help in formal recognition and measurement of these objectives.[31]

Critical reflection

'The single most important objective for the business organisation is profit maximisation; and for the workers high monetary rewards. These are the only realistic criteria by which organisational effectiveness can reasonably be judged.' To what extent do you think this is a realistic view or is it an oversimplification?

STRATEGY, OPPORTUNITIES AND RISKS

Every business needs to have a strategy and this strategy must be related to changing environmental conditions. In order to survive and maintain growth and expansion top management must protect the business from potentially harmful influences, and be ready to take maximum advantage of the challenges and opportunities presented. While top management must always accept the need for innovation, there is still the decision as to which opportunities it wishes to develop in relation to its resources and those it chooses not to pursue. An effective business strategy depends upon the successful management of opportunities and risks.

Drucker suggests that strategy should be based on the priority of maximising opportunities, and that risks should be viewed not as grounds of action but as limitations on action. He points out that while it is not possible to ensure that the right opportunities are chosen, it is certain that the right opportunities will not be selected unless:

- the focus is on maximising opportunities rather than on minimising risks;
- major opportunities are scrutinised collectively and in respect of their characteristics rather than singly and in isolation;
- opportunities and risks are understood in terms of the appropriateness of their fit to a particular business; and
- a balance is struck between immediate and easy opportunities for improvement, and more difficult, long-range opportunities for innovation and changing the character of the business.[32]

If the business is to be successful then its organisation structure must be related to its objectives and to its strategy. The structure must be designed so as to be appropriate to environmental influences, the continued development of the business, and the management of opportunities and risks. According to *Stern*, with the fast-changing world and competitive environment it becomes harder for leaders to distinguish between threats and opportunities, and between risks and rewards.[33]

E-business strategies

Advances in information technology and the Internet mean that organisations have to embrace successful e-commerce and **e-business** strategies. According to *Earl*:

> *Quite simply, IT affects business strategy. It is an input to business strategy as well as an output. The Internet, mobile communications, and future media present both threats and opportunities. So business strategy that ignores how technology is changing markets, competition, and processes is a process for the old economy, not the new economy. That is what 'e-everything' is about.*[34]

Kermally points out that in order to operate within the new macro-economic environment, organisations have to seriously consider the arrival of the new economy and strategies. They have to embrace e-business in order to deal with the complexity of the new business environment. Apart from scenario planning, e-businesses also have to focus special attention on recruiting and retaining staff. It is important to keep up with competitors and not to become complacent about adopting e-business. Kermally maintains that the e-business model is important because it:

- makes it possible for information to be shared more quickly and easily;
- facilitates human interaction;
- enables organisational resources and capabilities to be stretch strategically;
- provides global reach in marketing;
- allows consumers to shop 24 hours a day from any location; and
- promotes economic growth.[35]

SWOT ANALYSIS

In order to evaluate the nature of the business environment and its strategic capability, an organisation may undertake a **SWOT analysis** (sometimes also known as 'WOTS up'), which focuses on the Strengths, Weaknesses, Opportunities and Threats facing the organisation. The SWOT analysis provides convenient headings under which to study an organisation in its environmental setting and may provide a basis for decision-making and problem-solving. You may therefore find the analysis helpful in tackling case studies.

- **Strengths** are those positive aspects or distinctive attributes or competencies which provide a significant market advantage or upon which the organisation can build – for example, through the pursuit of diversification. These are characteristics of the organisation such as present market position, size, structure, managerial expertise, physical or financial resources, staffing, image or reputation. By searching out opportunities that match its strengths the organisation can optimise the effects of synergy.
- **Weaknesses** are those negative aspects or deficiencies in the present competencies or resources of the organisation, or its image or reputation, which limit its effectiveness and which need to be corrected or need action taken to minimise their effect. Examples of weaknesses could be operating within a particular narrow market, limited accommodation or outdated technology, a high proportion of fixed costs, a bureaucratic structure, a high level of customer complaints or a shortage of key managerial staff.
- **Opportunities** are favourable conditions and usually arise from the nature of changes in the external environment. The organisation needs to be sensitive to the problems of business strategy and responsive to changes in, for example, new markets, technology advances, improved economic factors, or failure of competitors. Opportunities provide the potential for the organisation to offer new, or to develop existing, products, facilities or services.
- **Threats** are the converse of opportunities and refer to unfavourable situations that arise from external developments likely to endanger the operations and effectiveness of the organisation. Examples could include changes in legislation, the introduction of a radically new product by competitors, political or economic unrest, changing social conditions and the actions of pressure groups. Organisations need to be responsive to changes that have already occurred and to plan for anticipated significant changes in the environment and to be prepared to meet them.

Although SWOT can offer a number of potential advantages for helping to evaluate corporate performance, care must be taken that the process does not lead to an over-simplified and misleading analysis. There are many ways of evaluating organisational performance and effectiveness, and varying criteria for success. *Levine* suggests that the new criteria for assessing the strength of an organisation will be in the area of quality results achieved through people.[36]

CORPORATE SOCIAL RESPONSIBILITIES

Organisations play a major and increasingly important role in the lives of us all, especially with the growth of large-scale business and expanding globalisation. The decisions and actions of management in organisations have an increasing impact on individuals, other organisations and the community. The power and influence that many business organisations now exercise should be tempered, therefore, by an attitude of responsibility by management.

In striving to satisfy its goals and achieve its objectives, the organisation cannot operate in isolation from the environment of which it is part. The organisation requires the use of factors of production and other facilities of society. The economic efficiency of organisations is affected by governmental, social, technical and cultural variables. In return, society is in need of the goods and services created and supplied by organisations, including the creation and distribution of wealth. Organisations make a contribution to the quality of life and to the well-being of the community.

Organisational survival is dependent upon a series of exchanges between the organisation and its environment. These exchanges and the continual interaction with the environment give rise to a number of broader responsibilities to society in general. These broader responsibilities, which are both internal and external to the organisation, are usually referred to as **corporate social responsibilities** (CSR). These social responsibilities arise from the interdependence of organisations, society and the environment.

According to the All Party Parliamentary Group on Management, there are varying definitions of what CSR stands for, but in general terms, it refers to:

> *The comprehensive approach organisations take to meet or exceed the expectations of stakeholders beyond such measures as revenue, profit and legal obligations. It covers community investment, human rights and employee relations, environmental practices and ethical conduct.*[37]

The recognition of the importance of social responsibilities can be gauged in part by the extent of government action and legislation on such matters as employment protection, equal opportunities and diversity, companies acts, consumer law, product liability and safeguarding the environment. This has formalised certain areas of social responsibilities into a legal requirement. It is doubtful, however, whether legislation alone is sufficient to make management, or other members of an organisation, behave in what might be regarded as a 'proper' manner.

Growing attention to social responsibilities

There has been growing attention given to the subject of CSR and an increasing amount of literature on the subject and on a new work ethic. The importance of CSR can also be gauged by the extent of coverage included in the annual report of most major companies. Many businesses, both in the UK and in other parts of Europe, are attempting to provide a more open and transparent view of their operations.[38] The European Commission is encouraging firms to assess their performance not on profit margins alone but also on the welfare of their workforce and care for the environment.[39]

Ann Chant, Director General, HM Revenue & Customs, suggests that rather than worrying about exactly what it is, CSR might simply be one of those things where it is best to get on and try it. Chant argues that CSR should be a two-way partnership.

> *I believe the key to understanding CSR in the community is to recognise that when done properly, it is a partnership. Both parties – the organisation and the section of the community or group of individuals that the organisation is linking with – should have something to give and something to gain.*[40]

Global responsibilities Today there is also greater concern for business communities to accept their global responsibilities. This is recognised, for example, in the foreword to a book by Grayson and Hodges, by HRH The Prince of Wales.

> *For the business community of the twenty-first century, 'out of sight' is no longer 'out of mind'. Global communications and media operations can present every aspect of a company's operations directly to customers in stark, unflattering and immediate terms. Those customers increasingly believe that the role of large companies in our society must encompass more than the traditional functions of obeying the law, paying taxes and making a profit. Survey after survey reveals that they also want to see major corporations helping 'to make the world a better place'. That may be in some respects a naïve ambition, but it is, nevertheless, a clear expectation, and one that companies ignore at their peril ... It is immensely encouraging to find that there are business leaders who recognise the challenge of running their companies in ways that make a positive and sustainable contribution to the societies in which they operate. It is a huge task, not least in finding ways of reaching out to the thousands of managers at the 'sharp end' of the business who, every day, take the decisions that have real impact on employees, on whole communities and on the environment.*
>
> HRH The Prince of Wales[41]

ORGANISATIONAL STAKEHOLDERS

We have seen that social responsibilities are often viewed in terms of **organisational stakeholders** – that is, those individuals or groups who have an interest in and/or are affected by the goals, operations or activities of the organisation or the behaviour of its members.[42] Managers, for example, are likely to have a particular interest in, and concern for, the size and growth of the organisation and its profitability, job security, status, power and prestige. Stakeholders, meanwhile, include a wide variety of interests and may be considered, for example, under six main headings of:

- employees;
- providers of finance;
- consumers;
- community and environment;
- government; and
- other organisations or groups.

Employees People and organisations need each other. Responsibilities to employees extend beyond terms and conditions of the formal contract of employment and give recognition to the worker as a human being. People today have wider expectations of the quality of working life, including justice in treatment, democratic functioning of the organisation and opportunities for consultation and participation, training in new skills and technologies, effective HRM policies and practices, and provision of social and leisure facilities. Responsibilities to employees involve considerations of the new psychological contracts discussed in Chapter 1.

Providers of finance Joint stock companies are in need of the collective investments of shareholders in order to finance their operations. Shareholders are drawn from a wide range of the population. The conversion of a number of building societies and insurance companies from mutual societies to public companies extended significantly the range of share ownership and stakeholding among private individuals. Many people also subscribe indirectly as shareholders through pension funds and insurance companies. Shareholders expect a fair financial return as payment for risk bearing and the use of their capital. In addition, social responsibilities of management extend to include the safeguarding of investments, and the opportunity for shareholders to exercise their responsibility as owners of the company, to participate in policy decisions and to question top management on the affairs of the company. In the case of public sector organisations, finance may be provided by government grants/subsidies – which are funded 'compulsorily' by the public through taxation and rates – as well as loans, and charges for services provided. There is, therefore, a similar range of responsibilities to the public as subscribers of capital.

Consumers To many people, responsibilities to consumers may be seen as no more than a natural outcome of good business. There are, however, broader social responsibilities including:

- providing good value for money;
- the safety and durability of products/services;
- standard of after-sales service;
- prompt and courteous attention to queries and complaints;
- long-term satisfaction – for example, serviceability, adequate supply of products/services, and spare and replacement parts;
- fair standards of advertising and trading;
- full and unambiguous information to potential consumers.

Increasing concern for social responsibilities to consumers can be seen by the activities of such bodies as the Consumers' Association, and the number of television and radio programmes devoted to this subject. In the case of public corporations there are Users' National Councils or consumers' regulatory bodies which are independent and look after the interests of customers. In the case of local government there is a system of Commissioners for Local Administration (popularly referred to as 'Ombudsmen'), designed to provide an independent investigation of citizens' complaints over alleged maladministration.

Community and environment It is in the area of concern for the community at large that social responsibilities can be seen most clearly. Organisations have a responsibility not to misuse the scarce factors of production upon which the wealth of the country depends. Organisations have a responsibility to society, to respect environmental considerations and take care of amenities. Some examples under this heading include:

- the effects and potential dangers of pollution, noise, disposal of waste;
- the siting and appearance of new buildings;
- transportation policies, such as the routing of heavy vehicles through narrow village roads; and
- avoidance of excessive packaging and more use of biodegradable materials.

Government Another important area of social responsibility could arguably be to the government. Organisations should, of course, respect and obey the law even where they regard it as not in their best interests. What is debatable, however, is the extent to which organisations should co-operate voluntarily with actions requested by the government. Some examples are restraint from trading with certain overseas countries, and the acceptance of controls over imports or exports, actions designed to combat inflation, such as limits on the level of wage settlements, assisting in the control of potential social problems – for example, the sale of tobacco or alcohol and the display of health warnings.

Other organisations or groups The potential range of social responsibilities is substantial. Other organisations or groups to whom organisations might be regarded as having a social responsibility, or obligation, are **suppliers, trade unions, business associates** and even **competitors**. Examples of social responsibilities might include fair standards of trading, honouring terms and conditions of purchase or sale, and settlement dates (for example, payment of accounts), assistance to smaller organisations, engagement only in fair competition, respect for copyright and patents. Some organisations extend the range of social responsibilities even further – for example, by giving recognition to the needs of developing countries; limiting the extent of political involvement or campaigning; donations to, or sponsorship of, the arts, educational or research institutions, sporting organisations or charities.

A blurred distinction

It should be recognised, however, that the distinction is blurred between the exercise of a genuine social responsibility, on the one hand, and actions taken in pursuit of good business practice and the search for organisational efficiency on the other. One approach is that attention to social responsibilities arises out of a moral or ethical motivation and the dictates of conscience – that is, out of genuine philanthropic objectives. An alternative approach is that the motivation is through no more than enlightened self-interest and the belief that, in the long term, attention to social responsibilities is simply good business sense. In practice, it is a matter of degree and balance, of combining sound economic management with an appropriate concern for broader responsibilities to society.

Whatever the view of corporate social responsibility, management has as its priority the need to ensure the survival and effective performance of the organisation. As *Drucker* puts it:

> *The first responsibility to society is to operate at a profit, and only slightly less important is the necessity for growth. The business is the wealth-creating and wealth-producing organ of our society. Management must maintain its wealth-producing resources intact by making adequate profits to offset the risk of economic activity. And it must besides increase the wealth-creating and wealth-producing capacity of these resources and with them the wealth of society.*[43]

The attention given to social responsibilities must involve weighing the costs of meeting these responsibilities against the benefits derived. Provided the cost/benefit analysis is not detrimental to economic and/or competitive performance, management must then determine the extent to which, and the manner in which, the organisation will attempt to satisfy its social responsibilities. The recognition of social responsibilities should form an integral part of strategy and the establishment of objectives and policies of the organisation.

> *It is inevitable that sometimes there will be a tension between a business' obligation to be ethical and its desire to be financially successful: the question is how these conflicts are dealt with ... In order for business leaders to win back the trust they have lost, ethics must be more than a quick bolt-on or a new-fangled job title. It has to go to the heart of the way in which they create wealth.*
>
> R. Reeves, 'Do the right thing'[44]

Critical reflection

A National Health Service trust chairperson was heavily criticised for maintaining that the primary loyalty of doctors was owed to their employers and that their duty to patients came third, after themselves. When demands upon the health service are limitless and resources finite, do you believe the idea of owing first loyalty to the organisation for which you work is such a bad thing?

VALUES AND ETHICS

In the last few years, there have been more and more reports of UK and US service sector jobs being transferred to lower-cost Anglophone locations elsewhere in the world (India, Sri Lanka and others). Financial services organisations have provided notable examples of this 'offshoring', as have IT helpdesk services and many other customer service offices. It is now commonplace for customers in the UK to find themselves talking to someone thousands of miles away: stories circulate about how some call centre employees are briefed on UK weather conditions in order to appear more 'local'.

The availability of much cheaper, high-capacity international telecommunications is obviously a prime driver of this prominent feature of globalisation, as is the availability of educated English-speakers to perform these services. Like so many other aspects of globalisation, however, the development of offshoring also raises a range of *ethical* issues. For those who may be made redundant as jobs in the UK are moved offshore, for example, the news – at least in the short term – is mainly bad. For UK customers, the effects of lower costs in the new locations may be favourable, but there are some reports of customer dissatisfaction in some cases, with some companies choosing to bring this type of work back to the UK.[45] There have also been reports of security lapses in some financial services offshore operations[46] and of possibly serious errors in the transcription of medical notes carried out in offshore locations for UK NHS Trusts.[47]

In Indian cities, by contrast, the arrival of this type of work has had a mainly positive effect: for all that the pay rates may appear to be low by UK standards, many of these opportunities are very attractive in the local labour market, to the extent that concerns have been expressed about qualified professionals abandoning their work to seek call centre work. Shareholders in the offshoring companies will expect to benefit if the same quality of service can be delivered at lower cost, while there will also be indirect effects in both countries due to changes in things like demand for local services, tax revenues and social security payments.

Ethics is to do with good and bad (or right and wrong): it seeks to understand what makes good things good, for example, in ways that can be generalised to other similar cases. The example of offshoring shows how complex these questions can be – goodness or badness appears to depend on where you stand. But ethical questions are important because of their effect on people in organisations, as well as people outside organisations who are affected by the choices made by the people in organisations. Ethical complexity is probably the rule in real life, but the ethical aspects of organisational behaviour are too important to ignore. In this section, we outline the influence of ethical considerations in terms of the actions taken by the organisation in pursuit of its strategic objectives, together with the ethical implications of interpersonal interaction, both inside the organisation and between individuals across organisational boundaries.

Ethics and business

Ethics is concerned with the study of morality: practices and activities that are considered to be importantly right or wrong, together with the rules that govern those activities and the values to which those activities relate.[48] Business ethics can be seen as an example of applied ethics – just as medical ethics is about the application of general ethics to the human activity called medicine, business ethics seeks to explore the implications of general ethics for the conduct of business. This apparently obvious point is important: by taking this stance, one rejects the view that moral principles have no bearing on business, or that 'the business of business is business', as the common saying has it.

This is not to say that it is easy, or uncontroversial, to apply ethics to business: on the contrary, this fast-growing subject is characterised by a range of sharply contrasting views. Some of this controversy is inherent in ethics itself – as will be discussed below, there is no single clear view of how to judge good and bad, and this must impact on any application such as business ethics. This particular application of ethics, however, is also complicated by the fact that ethics mainly deals with good or bad conduct on the part of individuals, resulting in possible difficulties in applying these ideas to impersonal corporate entities like companies. Is it appropriate to regard companies as if they were individual people and if not, what allowances should be made? Or, can the subject be satisfactorily seen as relating to the conduct of individuals as employees of businesses? Clearly, for very small businesses, the two views merge into one, but for larger, corporate entities, the position is more complex.

A discussion of ethics in business organisations has to take account of the purpose of the organisation, as well as its strategy (what it is trying to achieve, usually in competition with other similar businesses). These two factors are important because of their influence on what the organisation chooses to do and thus on the consequences for people inside and outside the organisation. A decision by an airline, for example, to pursue a low-cost strategy will have significant impacts on what is required of its staff and how well that business fares in the market. A successful implementation of such a strategy may mean fast growth, with attractive career development opportunities for some staff, but also more negative consequences for others. Yet, the failure of a strategy can lead to the end of the organisation as an independent entity, with more widespread adverse consequences for the organisation's people.

ETHICS AND CORPORATE SOCIAL RESPONSIBILITY

One illustration of the complexity of issues in business ethics is the diversity of opinion on the issue of corporate social responsibility (discussed above). On one side of the debate are those who would share *Milton Friedman's* view that the social responsibility of business is to make as much money as possible for the shareholders, within the rules of the game (fair competition, no deception or fraud, and so on).[49] This shareholder-centred view sees the directors of a company as agents of the owners, who are duty bound to act so as to maximise the interests of those owners, this being taken as the reason for owners having made the investment in the first place.

A more recent development of this general approach is that of *Sternberg* who proposes a teleological view of business ethics, based upon the pursuit of the business purpose – that of maximising long-term owner wealth by selling products and services.[50] Actions by a firm that are consistent with this aim and which satisfy the additional tests of common decency (for example refraining from stealing, cheating, coercion, and so on) and distributive justice (that is ensuring that rewards are proportional to contributions made) are ethical. Actions that fail any one of these three tests are, in this model, unethical.

At the other end of the spectrum are some forms of **stakeholder theory**, which emphasise a much broader set of social responsibilities for business. *Cannon* suggests that:

> *There exists an implicit or explicit contract between business and the community in which it operates. Business is expected to create wealth; supply markets; generate employment; innovate and produce a sufficient surplus to sustain its activities and improve its competitiveness while contributing to the maintenance of the community in which it operates. Society is expected to provide an environment in which business can develop and prosper, allowing investors to earn returns while ensuring that the stakeholders and their dependants can enjoy the benefits of their involvement without fear of arbitrary or unjust action. The interdependence between society and business cannot be overstated.*[51]

Differing assumptions about a business

The two perspectives provide very different views of how a business should act, because of their differing assumptions concerning what a business is *for*. In the shareholder-centred view, a business is principally for the shareholders and its actions should mainly be judged on the criterion of maximising their interests. In the stakeholder view quoted above, a business is for its stakeholders (who are potentially a very large and diverse group) and its actions should be designed to balance stakeholder interests. From the point of view of business ethics – the study of good and bad conduct in business – this distinction is very important. The use of company resources to support a local community project, for example, might be seen as admirable in the stakeholder view but unethical in the shareholder-centred view, in that it would be a misapplication of funds that belong to the owners (unless, of course, such an investment could be shown to be consistent with the shareholders' best interests).

Each of the two approaches adopts a different yardstick for judging the 'goodness' of a proposed action by a company. In the shareholder-centred view, the action has to be shown to be consistent with the duty of maximising owner wealth, which is conceptually relatively simple, but which necessarily involves assumptions concerning the likely effect of the proposed action. In the stakeholder view (or, at least in those versions of the stakeholder view that emphasise an accountability to stakeholders), the task of management is to balance stakeholder interests. However, managers seeking to do this – often in the face of loud opposing claims from the various interests – will very quickly encounter the practical problem of how that 'balance' should be defined and recognised.

Although difficult to reconcile in practice, the two approaches are not completely incompatible: to a stakeholder theorist, shareholders count as one type of stakeholder, but not the only type to which duties are owed by the firm. Likewise, *Sternberg* acknowledges the importance of understanding and remaining aware of the various stakeholder groups and of actively managing relationships between the company and these groups, because doing so is likely to be consistent with maximising owner wealth. As she points out, however, 'taking account' of something is importantly different from 'being accountable' to it.[52]

Intelligent self-interest

It is also worth emphasising that a company seeking to maximise its owners' long-term wealth may well do very good things for its 'stakeholders', not necessarily through any direct intent but in pursuit of its main duty. Providing customers with excellent products and services is the central example, of course, but this form of intelligent self-interest may also – for example – drive a firm to build strong, trusting relationships with its suppliers and distributors (because it will be better off as a result), or an attractive working environment for its employees (because it wishes to recruit and keep the best, in order to be able to compete more effectively).

Even beyond its immediate commercial relationships, an intelligently self-interested company may deliberately set out to build strong relationships with other stakeholders, or to take a principled stance on an issue such as the use of child labour, because to do so is to maximise owner value. The 'value' in question is not just next year's dividends, but refers to the value of the investment as a whole and thus obliges the management to think long term as well as short term and to consider the impact of company actions as broadly as possible.

Offshoring example

In the 'offshoring' example at the beginning of this section, the shareholder-centred view would place emphasis on the unit cost savings to be achieved by moving the operation to a lower-cost area, provided that the required quality of service can be maintained. Other things being equal, lower unit costs obviously allow higher margins and improved rewards to shareholders. However, the assessment would also take into account the possibility of additional risks to be managed, such as security and quality control issues mentioned at the beginning of this section. Furthermore, this view would also consider the competitive implications of the decision: if other suppliers all outsource and reduce their prices to customers, a decision not to do the same could damage the company. Yet, being different could be a viable competitive stance for one or more competitors, particularly if some customers are concerned about reduced quality of service from offshoring: NatWest in the UK seemed to take this stance in its advertising.

A stakeholder-centred company would place more emphasis on the impacts of the decision on the various stakeholder groups, notable including UK employees in this case. Although the decision to offshore might still be seen as competitively necessary by such a company, it might feel impelled to make more generous arrangements for those whose jobs are to be replaced, both out of a sense of long-term obligation and also to preserve its image in the UK labour market. The question as to whether the group defined as 'those that the company has not yet recruited in the offshore location' should also be considered to be a stakeholder group with a legitimate claim for attention is one of the numerous judgements to be made in this approach.

Refresh your understanding
Activity 14C
www.pearsoned.co.uk/mullins

In the UK, the report of the RSA inquiry 'Tomorrow's Company' referred to the concept of an imaginary 'operating licence' granted to a company by the public, which can be effectively suspended or withdrawn if a company appears to be behaving badly.[53] Doing business effectively and well relies upon hundreds, sometimes thousands of transactions every day of the year. If some of these transactions become more difficult because trust has been squandered and co-operation has been withdrawn, then the firm will start to lose out to its better-behaved competitors and its owners' wealth will start to suffer.

BUSINESS ETHICS

The large-scale issues of corporate social responsibility are to do with how a company should conduct itself within society: these questions certainly have an ethical aspect, as has been discussed, but they are not the whole of business ethics. Day-to-day decisions made by individual managers are not usually made on the basis of some detailed calculation of the consequences for shareholder value (however theoretically desirable that might be) and more general ethical considerations must play a part in resolving the dilemmas that sometimes arise in practice.

The scope of **business ethics** is very broad, because anything done by a company or its employees can be done ethically or unethically. The following list is not intended to be exhaustive, but rather to illustrate the all-pervasive nature of ethical questions in business:

- behaviour towards customers, suppliers, distributors and competitors: for example, marketing and selling, fair competition, intelligence gathering, inducements and incentives;
- treatment of employees: for example, recruitment, rewards, training, promotion, dismissal, employee and employer rights and duties;
- treatment of other stakeholder groups: for example, local communities, governments, interest groups;
- effect on the natural environment: for example, pollution, recycling, sustainability;
- conduct in international operations: for example, use of power, respect for human rights, respect for local cultural values, offshoring, and so on.

No single view of right or wrong

These questions can be complex, since there is no single view in general ethics of what makes something right or wrong. One school of thought emphasises **duties**, things that must be done (or refrained from) irrespective of the consequences. This deontological point of view holds that goodness or badness is evident only in the action itself: that, for example, lying is bad because it is bad in itself. By contrast, a **consequentialist** view of ethics holds that the goodness or badness of a proposed action is evident only in the consequences of that action: whether a lie is good or bad depends upon the consequences of that particular lie at the time. Utilitarianism, for example, is a consequentialist theory, in that it seeks to maximise the net happiness for everyone affected by a particular action ('the greatest good for the greatest number', as it is sometimes expressed). Both of the perspectives on corporate social responsibility discussed above are also to some extent consequentialist, in that they are mainly concerned with an assessment of the effects of a firm's actions.

Both duties and consequences (or 'means' and 'ends' in the familiar Machiavellian saying about the latter justifying the former) are plainly important in the way we deal with ethical issues in everyday life. Unfortunately, however, they are very different ways of reasoning, which can lead to contradictory outcomes in some cases. An exclusively duty-based view of ethics, for example, must sooner or later run into problems such as absolutism, or the difficulty of deciding which duty should take precedence over others in a particular situation. If, for example, both lying and killing are held to be inherently wrong, is it acceptable to lie in order to avoid a killing? And whatever answer is given, how do we know?

Nonetheless, duties and principles clearly do inform our views of how people should treat each other at work. An exclusively consequentialist view of ethics also entails methodological problems of forecasting reliably what the consequences of an action may be and of deciding how to measure those consequences. Some forms of utilitarianism can be very unjust to small minorities, by allowing their unhappiness (i.e. as a result of some proposed action) to be offset by the increased happiness of a much larger number. Again, however, we can hardly deny that our assessment of the likely consequences of different actions plays a part in our view of acceptable and unacceptable behaviour in an organisation.

By way of illustration, a deontological approach to the ethics of offshoring would focus on aspects of the proposal that might be in breach of clear principles and duties. While no business can reasonably accept a general duty to keep existing employees on the payroll for ever (or not ever to relocate operations), a contemplation of duties might cause a company to do as much as possible to soften the impact of the job losses, including the possibility of internal transfer, retraining, outplacement and more-than-minimum redundancy packages. A utilitarian analysis would seek to identify all who would be affected – anywhere in the world – by the proposed offshoring decision and then assess the impact (positive or negative) on each person (or, more realistically, groups).

This would allow a sort of 'trial balance' of the consequences to be drawn up and an evaluation of the net impact on aggregate happiness. Necessarily in this method, the reduction in happiness for others, such as those who are made involuntarily redundant is offset by the extra happiness created for some – those who get the offshore jobs, for example. Obviously, this is of little comfort to the former group, which illustrates one of the important criticisms of the utilitarian approach.

Further approaches

Nor is the choice restricted to means and ends in ethics: several further approaches can be distinguished in Western thought, including the following:

- **Virtue** ethics, based upon an analysis of desirable human qualities that lie between undesirable extremes (the virtue of 'courage', for example, lies between the undesirable extremes of 'cowardice', at one end and 'foolhardiness' at the other). We might want to explore, for example, what virtues are found in good chief executives, and whether different virtues apply to good entrepreneurs.
- **Ethical relativism**, which holds that goodness and badness are largely or entirely determined by the prevailing values of the time in question and may thus change from one period to another, or one culture to another. Although it is clearly true that values and standards have changed over time (in the attitude towards child labour, for example), pure relativism is an uncomfortable stance for most people, who have intuitive conscience-based convictions that some things are just plain wrong.
- **Emotivism**, which suggests that statements about ethics are essentially statements about the speaker's attitudes, and that it is therefore futile to search for any ethical 'truths'. The statement 'lying is bad' is, from this point of view, saying little more than 'I don't like lying'.

Ethical decision-making at work

How, then, are ethical choices to be made by people working for organisations? No simple and universal answer is available – ethical awareness is something that can be cultivated and the different perspectives will often help to shed light on a particular dilemma. Some perspectives may appear to be better suited to particular situations: whereas, for example, it is difficult to avoid some sort of consequentialist component in thinking about how a company should act, it is also clear that duty-based arguments must also weigh heavily in thinking about the ethical treatment of people such as employees. The German philosopher Kant's view that we should always treat other people as ends in themselves and never simply as means is surely an important principle for decent human resource management and one that would often be seen as more important than the prospect of short-term gain.[54]

Personal integrity and individual values are important elements in ethical decision-making at work, but the increasingly common company, professional or industry codes of conduct may also provide support and guidance. This is not to say that these ethical 'resources' will always provide clear and comfortable guidance – sometimes, people in organisations will experience tension between the conflicting demands of, say, their own personal values and the demands placed on them by their organisation. If these conflicts become intolerable and cannot be resolved through normal means, then an individual may decide to become a 'whistleblower' in the public interest, by taking the high-risk approach of placing the problem in the public domain for resolution. Codes of conduct can help to reduce the risk of painful situations like this by providing a published set of values to which the individual can appeal, rather than taking the risk wholly personally.

(I am grateful to my colleague, Richard Christy, Department of Human Resource and Marketing Management, University of Portsmouth for providing the above information on Values and Ethics.)

A concept map outlining some issues of ethics at work is given in Figure 14.3.

CODES OF ETHICS

In American and Canadian organisations, codes of conducts are very common and in many cases members of the organisation are required to sign to indicate formally their acceptance. Codes may be updated on a regular basis and in some cases such as investment companies this may be at least once a year. In the UK an increasing number of organisations, of all types, are also now publishing a code of ethics (or code of conduct). For example, according to The Chartered Management Institute:

> *There is a growing belief that organisations can succeed only if they are seen to observe high ethical standards. As a result, more are choosing to make a public commitment to ethical business by formulating and publishing a code of operating principles. The key difficulty they face in doing so is translating high sounding principles into practical guidelines, and thence into actual practice.*

The Institute provide a checklist for codes of ethics that provides initial guidelines that apply equally to public, private and voluntary sectors.[55]

IBM publishes a document of business conduct relating to the ethical practices and values of the company. The document includes a comprehensive set of guidelines on:

- You and Your Job in IBM;
- Conducting IBM's Business; and
- On Your Own Time.

Figure 14.3 Concept map of ethics at work

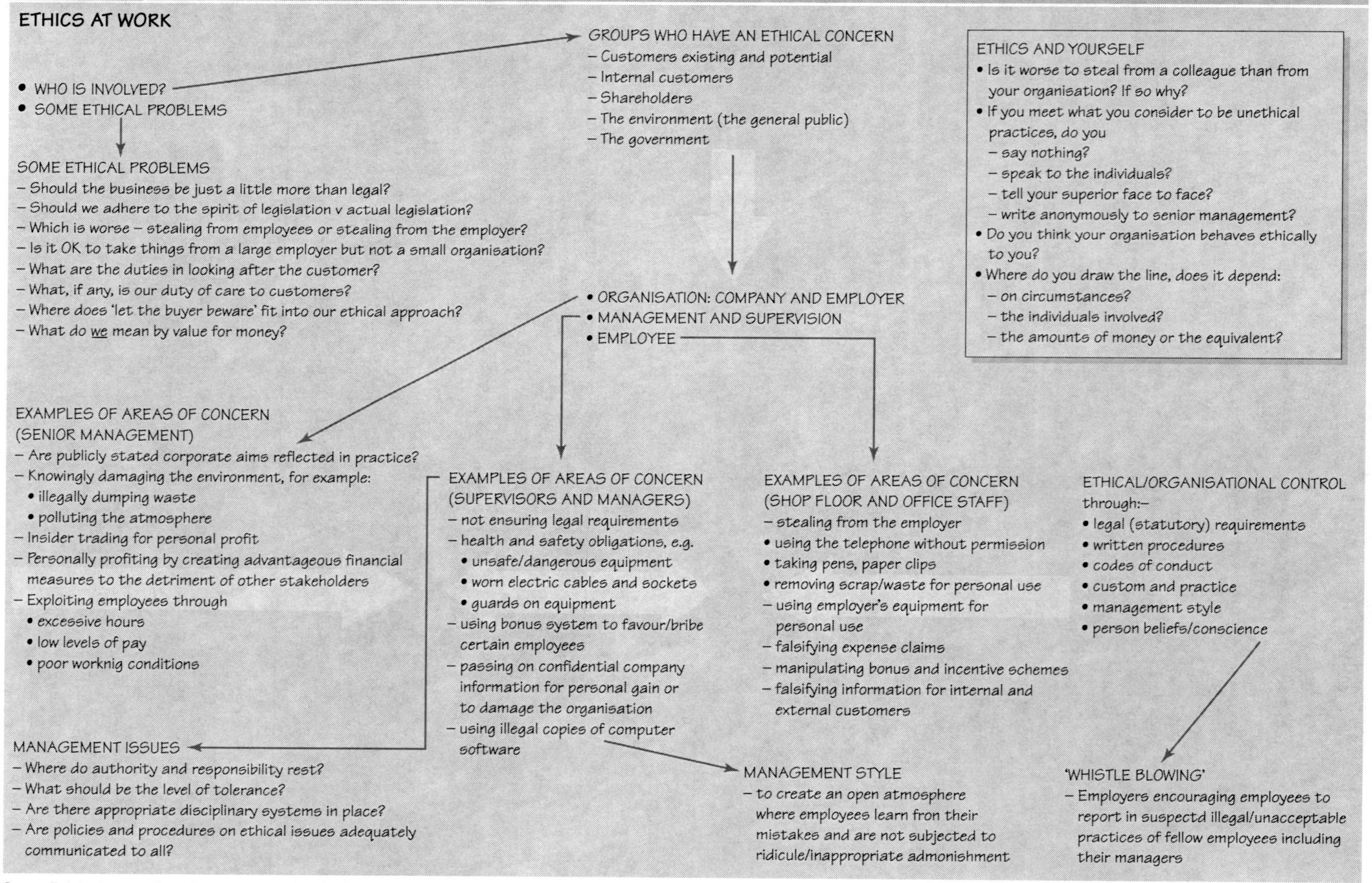

ETHICS AT WORK

- WHO IS INVOLVED?
- SOME ETHICAL PROBLEMS

GROUPS WHO HAVE AN ETHICAL CONCERN
- Customers existing and potential
- Internal customers
- Shareholders
- The environment (the general public)
- The government

ETHICS AND YOURSELF
- Is it worse to steal from a colleague than from your organisation? If so why?
- If you meet what you consider to be unethical practices, do you
  - say nothing?
  - speak to the individuals?
  - tell your superior face to face?
  - write anonymously to senior management?
- Do you think your organisation behaves ethically to you?
- Where do you draw the line, does it depend:
  - on circumstances?
  - the individuals involved?
  - the amounts of money or the equivalent?

SOME ETHICAL PROBLEMS
- Should the business be just a little more than legal?
- Should we adhere to the spirit of legislation v actual legislation?
- Which is worse – stealing from employees or stealing from the employer?
- Is it OK to take things from a large employer but not a small organisation?
- What are the duties in looking after the customer?
- What, if any, is our duty of care to customers?
- Where does 'let the buyer beware' fit into our ethical approach?
- What do we mean by value for money?

- ORGANISATION: COMPANY AND EMPLOYER
- MANAGEMENT AND SUPERVISION
- EMPLOYEE

EXAMPLES OF AREAS OF CONCERN (SENIOR MANAGEMENT)
- Are publicly stated corporate aims reflected in practice?
- Knowingly damaging the environment, for example:
  - illegally dumping waste
  - polluting the atmosphere
- Insider trading for personal profit
- Personally profiting by creating advantageous financial measures to the detriment of other stakeholders
- Exploiting employees through
  - excessive hours
  - low levels of pay
  - poor worknig conditions

EXAMPLES OF AREAS OF CONCERN (SUPERVISORS AND MANAGERS)
- not ensuring legal requirements
- health and safety obligations, e.g.
  - unsafe/dangerous equipment
  - worn electric cables and sockets
  - guards on equipment
- using bonus system to favour/bribe certain employees
- passing on confidential company information for personal gain or to damage the organisation
- using illegal copies of computer software

EXAMPLES OF AREAS OF CONCERN (SHOP FLOOR AND OFFICE STAFF)
- stealing from the employer
  - using the telephone without permission
  - taking pens, paper clips
  - removing scrap/waste for personal use
- using employer's equipment for personal use
- falsifying expense claims
- manipulating bonus and incentive schemes
- falsifying information for internal and external customers

ETHICAL/ORGANISATIONAL CONTROL through:–
- legal (statutory) requirements
- written procedures
- codes of conduct
- custom and practice
- management style
- person beliefs/conscience

MANAGEMENT ISSUES
- Where do authority and responsibility rest?
- What should be the level of tolerance?
- Are there appropriate disciplinary systems in place?
- Are policies and procedures on ethical issues adequately communicated to all?

MANAGEMENT STYLE
- to create an open atmosphere where employees learn from their mistakes and are not subjected to ridicule/inappropriate admonishment

'WHISTLE BLOWING'
- Employers encouraging employees to report in suspectd illegal/unacceptable practices of fellow employees including their managers

Source: Training Learning Consultancy Ltd, Bristol, England. Reproduced with permission.

At one level, the IBM Business Conduct Guidelines are a document of conduct we establish for ourselves to help us comply with laws and good ethical practices. We regularly review and update it as business and the world at large become more complex, and as the need for such guidelines becomes greater. But this is not just about compliance with the law and general standard of ethics. By establishing these guidelines and giving them the weight of a governing document, we are acknowledging that our choices and actions help define IBM for others. We are ensuring that our relationships – with clients, investors, colleagues and the communities in which we live and work – are built on trust. In other words, the Business Conduct Guidelines are a tangible example of our values and an expression of IBMer's personal responsibility to uphold them.[56]

In the public sector, the Local Government Act 2000 specifies the following principles to govern the conduct of members of relevant English authorities and Welsh police authorities: selflessness, honesty and integrity, objectivity, accountability, openness, personal judgement, respect for others, duty to uphold the law, stewardship and leadership. These principles are intended to underpin the mandatory provisions of the model codes of conduct for English local authorities.[57]

A matter of degree and balance

Allen, however, questions whether the emphasis on the caring sharing company of the new millennium and social responsibility is all going a bit far. There is scarcely a company without a loftily worded mission statement and high-minded references to shareholders. There are now numerous codes and standards and any company wishing to keep up to date with latest developments in social responsibility needs to look in many directions at once, and companies are talking of 'codemania'. While many codes offer voluntary guidelines, companies that fail to meet these can see themselves receiving a bad press or disinvestments. Nevertheless, the burden of social responsibilities can be seen as part of the response to ever-changing social conditions.[58] And, according to *Cook*, although it is easy to be cynical following the fall of big companies there are many organisations which are 'putting something back'. There is evidence about reversing the decline in public trusts and that in response to stakeholder and customer attitudes, corporate values are changing.[59]

According to *Philippa Foster Back*, OBE (Director, Institute of Business Ethics), the globalisation of business has raised questions of applying ethical values to the different cultures and societies in which organisations operate. The challenge for everyone concerned with ethics now is to ensure that values are embedded throughout an organisation. A code of ethics needs to be translated into reality through training and enforcement and driven from the top.[60]

Related legislation

As part of the growing attention to the concept of corporate social responsibilities there are a number of pieces of recent legislation that arguably relate to the concept of business ethics and organisational accountability. Although it is not in the scope of this book to provide detailed aspects of legal provisions, we should recognise the existence of such legislation, including the Human Rights Act 1998, the Public Interest Disclosure Act 1998, the Local Government Act 2000 and the Freedom of Information Act 2000.

The **Human Rights Act 1998** came into force on 2 October 2000 and incorporates into English law rights and liberties enshrined in the European Convention on Human Rights. The provisions apply to the acts of 'public authorities' and make it unlawful for them to act in a way incompatible with a right under the Convention. The Act is designed to provide greater protection for individuals, and to protect them from unlawful and unnecessary interference. Everyone has the right to respect for their private and family life, their home and their correspondence. The Act has a significant effect on people both as citizens and at work.

The **Public Interest Disclosure Act 1998**, which has become known widely as the 'Whistleblower's Act', is designed to protect people who expose wrongdoing at their workplace, to provide reassurance that there is a safe alternative to silence and to provide a safeguard against retaliation. Employers need to establish clear internal procedures by which members of staff can raise any matters of personal concern.

The **Local Government Act 2000**, the so-called 'New Ethical Framework', requires all local authorities to provide codes of conduct to promote high standards of behaviour. The government has distinguished between general principles of conduct in public service and the code of conduct containing specific actions and prohibitions that demonstrate the principles are being observed.

The **Freedom of Information Act 2000** gives the public one simple right to access information held by public authorities. Under the Act, the public have a 'right to know'.

An integrated approach

McEwan summarises the separate histories of corporate social responsibility, business ethics and corporate governance, and suggests a method of enquiry that attempts to integrate these different perspectives on business through three broad levels of enquiry:

- a **descriptive** approach that draws attention to the values and beliefs of people from different cultures and societies that influence their attitudes towards the various activities of business in their home countries and abroad;
- a **normative** approach that identifies sets of values and beliefs as a basis for making ethical decisions at the individual, group, or senior management level in an organisation;
- an **analytical** approach that attempts to explore the relationship between these normative values and beliefs and other value-systems or ideologies such as political or religious beliefs and culture or other social customs.[61]

Critical reflection

'Without EU intervention, government legislation and the threat of adverse press or television reports, the majority of business organisations would give little regard to their social responsibilities or to business ethics.' To what extent do you support this contention? What do you think is the single most important social responsibility of organisations?

MANAGEMENT IN THE NEWS

Power to the people

The cost of not caring for your customers

Tom Lester

If you have a complaint with the ferry service between Stranraer in Scotland and Belfast, employees are allowed to spend up to £1,000 to solve the problem for you – without having to obtain management approval. Stena Line, the Swedish operator, credits the 'satisfaction strategy' developed on the crossing with boosting its market share, and it has now been extended to all other Stena routes.

Such cases illustrate the growing commitment of companies to pay closer attention to their customers and help resolve complaints. Most consumers have personal horror stories of bank letters demanding payment of a non-existing account, helplines that can't or won't help and managers who cower behind expensive automated systems. Moreover, the problem is getting worse, surveys show. Research by

Source: Neil Setchfield

Good customer relations can boost market share. Stena Line employees are empowerd to spend up to £1,000 solving a customer's compaint.

Accenture, the management consultancy, found that when telephoning to complain, customers spent an average of six minutes on hold, and spoke to more than two service representatives. Researchers at Birmingham's Aston University found that the majority of chief executives regard complaining customers as a nuisance and too demanding. Yet most chief executives would swear their companies are 'customer-oriented'.

Research by Frederick Reichheld, director emeritus at Bain & Company, the strategy consultancy, provides a reality check. He has shown that over the past decade the only reliable guide to customer loyalty (and future purchases) is the answer to the question 'Would you recommend [company X] to a friend or colleague?'

Mere satisfaction is not enough to bring customers back, while those who come away vaguely dissatisfied won't complain, but next time simply vote with their credit cards – and quite probably, tell their friends. Chief executives must remember even when profits are tight that repeat purchases are several times cheaper than new business. Once the volume of complaints is reduced, the handling staff can concentrate on creating value for customers and company.

Alan Gordon, Stena Line's route director who came up with the scheme for ferry staff, says that he has never had to pay out the £1,000. Where five years ago they expected to receive four complaints for every compliment, now they find they get three compliments for every complaint. In what he believes is a direct consequence, 'We carry 60 per cent of foot passengers to Northern Ireland, and 56 per cent of cars.'

Whereas many companies are content merely to cut the rate of complaints, careful monitoring of the handling process reveals where products or services can be improved, and how they are best sold to customers. Charles Reed, customer services director at Nationwide, says that 40 per cent of complainants have been found to go on to consider other products. 'They're your best advocates,' he adds. For that reason, he strongly opposes any move to outsource the building society's four call centres. 'It is a core part of our business to talk to customers. Our directors regularly meet 100 or more customers in evening sessions, and we record and analyse their comments.' There will always be some mistakes, so ensure that staff nearest the customers are empowered to remedy them.

Source: Lester, T., 'The cost of not caring for your customers', *Financial Times*, 29 January 2006. Copyright © Tom Lester, reproduced with permission.

Discussion questions

1. **Identify and discuss the implications for managers and supervisors of giving this type of decision-making power to front-line employees.**
2. **Analyse and explain how the implications of empowering front-line staff might differ if the organisation is a public sector one (for instance, a benefits agency or a hospital) rather than a business.**

SYNOPSIS

- Underlying the study of organisational behaviour is the nature of corporate strategy for the organisation as a whole. The effective management of people requires a clear understanding of the business that the organisation is in. Corporate strategy highlights the importance of the overall direction of the organisation, its goals and objectives and the expectations of shareholders. All organisations have some function to perform and some incentive for their existence and for their operations. The goals of an organisation determine the nature of its outputs and the series of activities through which the outputs are achieved.

- The goals of the organisation may be pursued in accordance with an underlying ideology or philosophy that determines the culture of the organisation and governs the overall conduct of its operations. The concept of organisational goals serves a number of important functions, but there are potential disadvantages and limitations with this approach. Strictly, organisations have no goals, only people do.

Members of an organisation have different and often conflicting goals. Management has a responsibility to clarify organisational goals and to attempt to integrate personal goals with the overall objectives of the organisation.

- Organisational survival is dependent upon a series of exchanges between the organisation and its environment. In recent years it has become increasingly popular for organisations to produce a mission statement and/or vision of their purpose and general direction. However, such a statement is likely to be of value only if the organisation actually practises what it preaches. The goals of an organisation are translated into objectives and policy that provide corporate guidelines for the operation and management of the organisation.

- The choice of objectives is an essential part of the decision-making process involving future courses of action. Policy is developed within the framework of objectives. It provides the basis for decision-making and the course of action to follow in order to achieve objectives. Although the objective of profit maximisation is undoubtedly important, it is not by itself a sufficient criterion for the effective management of a business organisation. In practice, there are many other considerations and motivations which affect the desire for the greatest profit or maximum economic efficiency.

- In striving to satisfy its goals and achieve its objectives, the organisation cannot operate in isolation from the environment of which it is part. The power and influence of business organisations should be tempered with its broad corporate social responsibilities (CSR). These responsibilities are often viewed in terms of organisational stakeholders. There is growing attention to the subject of CSR, including concerns for global responsibilities. There is, however, a blurred distinction between the exercise of genuine social responsibilities and actions taken in pursuit of organisational efficiency.

- The importance of CSR and how a company should conduct itself within society draws attention to values and ethics. There are differing assumptions about how a business should act, such as shareholder-centred or a stakeholder view. An example is the debate over the increasing number of organisations 'offshoring' activities to locations elsewhere in the world. The scope of business ethics is very broad and gives rise to a number of questions with no single view of what is right or wrong. An increasing number of organisations now publish a code of ethics (or code of conduct) but this needs to be embedded throughout the organisation and translated into reality.

Refresh your understanding, assess your progress and begin your research with online resources at **www.pearsoned.co.uk/mullins**

REVIEW AND DISCUSSION QUESTIONS

1. Discuss critically the purpose, nature and practical value of corporate strategy.
2. What do you see as the importance of organisational ideology or philosophy? Explain the extent to which there is a clear ideology or set of principles that govern the overall conduct of your organisation.
3. Distinguish between objectives and policy. Identify examples of objectives and policy in your organisation, and comment on how effectively you believe they have been implemented.
4. To what extent do you believe that profit maximisation is a sufficient criterion for the effective management of a business organisation? What other indicators might be applied in terms of organisational performance and results?
5. Assess the practical relevance of (i) the balanced scorecard and (ii) a SWOT analysis.
6. Discuss critically the extent to which you accept the concept of corporate social responsibilities.
7. How would you attempt to explain the meaning and significance of organisational values and business ethics?
8. Comment critically on the code of ethics (or code of conduct) for your organisation; or if one does not exist, draw up your own suggested code.

ASSIGNMENT 1

Obtain the mission/vision statements for three different organisations (including your university, college or work organisation).

Critically evaluate the extent to which each of these statements:

- gives a clear indication of the main purpose and general direction of the organisation;
- is written in clear, specific, substantial and meaningful language; and
- appears likely to inspire members of the organisation.

In the case of your own organisation, comment critically with supporting examples on the perceived value of the mission statement and the extent to which the wording is put into practice at the operational level. Explain what changes, if any, you would make to the mission statement.

What conclusions do you draw from this assignment?

ASSIGNMENT 2

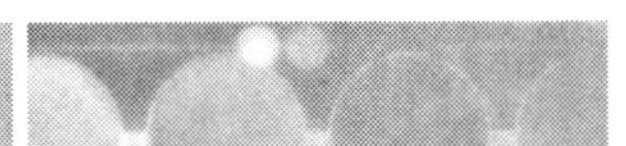

a Detail fully what you believe are the social responsibilities or obligations of your own, or some other work organisation of your choice, and identify the major stakeholders.

b Give specific examples of the ways in which the organisation has attempted to satisfy, and/or has failed to satisfy, responsibilities or obligations to these stakeholders.

c Specify the extent to which attention has been given to values in the organisation, and to the principles, standards and expected practices or judgements of 'good' (ethical) behaviour.

d Compare your observations with those of your colleagues and summarise what conclusions you draw.

PERSONAL AWARENESS AND SKILLS EXERCISE

Objectives

Completing this exercise should help you to enhance the following skills:

- Clarify the work values and beliefs that are important to you.
- Examine your sensitivity to, and dealings with, other people.
- Debate and justify with colleagues the nature of your values and beliefs.

Exercise

You are required to:

a rate the following items: 5 (extremely important for me); 4 (very important for me); 3 (average importance for me); 2 (not important for me); 1 (I would oppose this). What is required are your genuine beliefs and feelings about each item, not what others think or believe, but what you personally and honestly believe and feel about each item.

1 There should be clear allocation of objectives and accountability for them ____

2 We should be open and honest in all our dealings with each other ____

3 People's talents should be recognised, developed and correctly utilised ____

Personal awareness and skills exercise – continued

4 One should give acknowledgement and praise to those in authority ____
5 There are clear rules about what we should and should not do in getting the job done ____
6 Conflicts should be surfaced and resolved rather than allowed to simmer ____
7 The causes of problems should be directed away from oneself ____
8 Encouragement and support should be placed above criticism ____
9 Problems should be tackled and resolved in co-operation with others ____
10 What is right should be placed above who is right ____
11 Clear standard procedures should be in place for all important jobs ____
12 One should become visible and build up one's personal image ____
13 Equity and fairness should be applied to all regardless of status or standing ____
14 Excellence should be our aim in all that we do professionally and administratively ____
15 We give close attention to codes of conduct since this is what builds character ____
16 We should keep each other informed and practise open and friendly communication ____
17 We know who should be making the decisions and refer decisions to the right person ____
18 Everyone and their contribution should be treated with respect and dignity ____
19 We should meet all our commitments to one another – we do what we say we will do ____
20 One should form networks of support among those with influence ____
21 There are clear reporting relationships – who reports to whom – and we stick to them ____
22 People should take responsibility for their own decisions and actions ____
23 Everyone should be committed to personal growth and life-long learning ____
24 Situations or events should be created so as to justify the advancement of one's goals ____
25 Performance should be assessed against objectives and standards declared up-front ____
26 Policies should be clear and not changed until there is proof that they need changing ____
27 Everyone's needs should be given equal standing regardless of their position or status ____
28 We should be committed to the service of others rather than ourselves ____
29 Positive relationships should be established with those who have influence ____
30 Warmth and affection should be demonstrated in our work relationships ____
31 Individual productivity and performance should be encouraged and actively promoted ____
32 We all know what our jobs are and we stick to our defined responsibilities ____
33 Those from disadvantaged backgrounds should be helped to catch up with others ____
34 One should expect to get support from those to whom we have given past support ____
35 Goals should be challenging and stretch people to higher levels of achievement ____

b In small groups, compare and discuss, frankly and openly, your ratings with those of your colleagues. Be prepared to justify your ratings but also listen with an open mind to the views of your colleagues.

Further information will be provided by your tutor.

Source: Misselhorn, A., *The Head and Heart of Management*, Organization Develeopment Consultants (SA) (2003), p. 36. Reproduced with permission from Organization Development Consultants.

Discussion

- How difficult was it for you to complete your ratings?
- How much agreement was there among members of your group? Did this surprise you?
- To what extent were you influenced to rethink your values or beliefs?

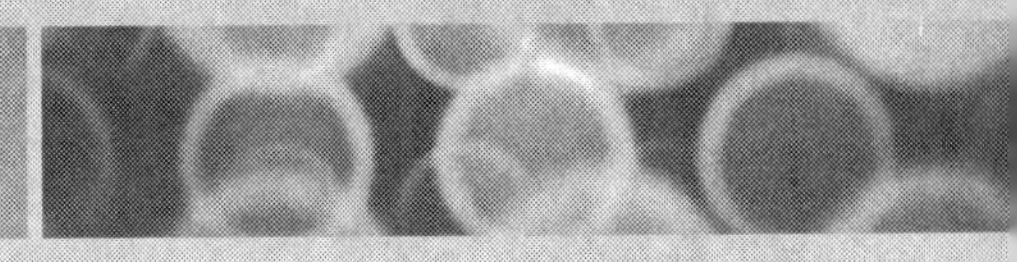

CASE STUDY

318 Mondays To Go ... The London Olympics

> *There's no complacency here, because we will need every one of those 318 Mondays there are between now and the opening ceremony.*[62]

All organisations have objectives, which may be expressed more or less formally. Sometimes, such objectives provide a very clear and very public statement of the whole purpose of the organisation, as well as a stark binary test of its effectiveness. The organisation established to make the London 2012 Olympics happen is one such case – as its website (with its real-time countdown graphic) explains, the games will run from Friday 27 July 2012, by which time everything has to be ready.[63] And being ready in 2012 will be the result of successfully co-ordinating the efforts of dozens of other independent organisations – 'only slightly late' is just not an option.

Recent experience of major UK sports facility development has often been mixed, with a number of very public delays to the redevelopment of the Wembley football ground for example, so it is unsurprising that media reports about the 2012 Olympics often focus on the potential for failure. At a different level, this critical time-dependence will be familiar to many organisations; specialist events management firms, for example, make a business from the effective co-ordination of a range of inputs towards a fixed target date. At a personal level we might even consider the organisation of a graduation ceremony, birthday party or wedding in the same way.

The quote at the top of this case is from a BBC radio interview with Lord Coe, Chairman of the London Organising Committee for the Olympic Games and Paralympic Games (LOCOG) on the first anniversary of the award of the 2012 games to London. In the preamble to the interview, the reporter recounted the apocryphal story of the International Olympic Committee official who visited Athens in early 2004 to check on the progress towards the summer Olympics in that year. 'All going well?' he asked the head building contractor. 'Sure, yes, we're making good progress', replied the contractor. 'So, it's all going to be ready for the Opening Ceremony, then?' enquired the official, a little tensely. 'Oh yes, that'll be OK ... What date's that again?' said the contractor with practised assurance. 'Friday 13 August', said the official, expectantly. There was a pause' 'Err ... would that be morning or afternoon?'

The London Organising Committee for the Olympic Games may have a clear objective, but that doesn't make the task easy for Chairman Sebastian Coe.

Organising, publicising and staging London 2012 is the responsibility of Lord Coe's LOCOG organisation, which will report to the International Olympic Committee. In the early stages, LOCOG will be a relatively small organisation, co-ordinating the efforts of many other bodies, but it is envisaged that around 100 000 people will be working on the games by 2012: 3 000 directly employed staff, 70 000 volunteers and a large number of contractors. Carrying out LOCOG's development programme will be the responsibility of a separate organisation – the Olympic Delivery Authority (ODA), which is co-located with LOCOG in Canary Wharf, East London.

The end product of London 2012 is diverse and complex – the Olympics will include 26 sports and the Paralympics 19. These events will require a total of 25 venues in five groups of centres, with the all-new Olympic Park in East London as the prime location. Operationally, 500 000 spectators are expected on each of the days of the games, with train facilities to be developed to the capacity to deliver 240 000 visitors per hour at peak. Stage-managing and co-ordinating these events efficiently and safely will be a task of immense complexity in itself, but perhaps less challenging than the co-ordination task in the preceding six years.

A marathon project

Funding London 2012 is also complex: a public sector funding of more than £2 billion for the infrastructure development has been agreed, comprising contributions from the National Lottery, London council tax (local tax paid by London residents) and the London

Development Agency (responsible for assisting economic development in the London area). The UK government is also funding a substantial programme of transport and other infrastructural improvement in East London. Running the Games themselves is expected to cost about £2 billion, which is expected to come from the private sector. In addition, LOCOG will receive a share of the International Olympic Committee's broadcasting revenues and the benefits of its own marketing programme.

Before 2012 the project led by the ODA must ensure the preparation of the Olympic Park infrastructure and surrounding site; this entails building new permanent venues, Olympic transport projects, the Olympic Village and a number of temporary facilities. Developing the facilities for this worldwide event was challenging from the outset. The land designated for the Olympic Park, for example, was already in use in one way or another when the Games were awarded to London, raising questions of ownership, compensation and regulation. The ODA has been equipped with statutory powers to enable it to deal with these issues before the substantial tendering process can begin. Some of the facilities to be provided will be temporary in nature, but the project as a whole also aims to provide a lasting legacy to the area and to London and the UK as a whole. Throughout the development, the theme of environmental sustainability must also be emphasised. ODA Chief Executive David Higgins commented in a recent interview[64] that long-term legacy development planning was likely to take the most time in developing the main planning application. The ODA identifies a number of key partners in this project, including Transport for London, the London Development Agency, the London Thames Gateway Development Corporation, as well as a number of other local government organisations. Working with this range of independent partners will require considerable skills of communication and co-ordination, and skill in balancing the range of interests that is likely to arise. ODA also needs to ensure that development contracts are awarded to the very best providers that can be attracted. Towards that end, ODA has been associated with the London 2012 Roadshow around the UK in 2006, the aim of which is to ensure that maximum awareness, interest and participation can be achieved and to make the Olympics a national, not just a London, event.

As mentioned above, London residents will be making a substantial contribution to the funding of the infrastructure development from their local tax payments. Not surprisingly, the Mayor of London's website goes to some lengths to explain the benefits to London of the 2012 Olympics.[65] For the Mayor, the benefits to London are in terms of economic development and regeneration, employment, infrastructure improvement, culture and sustainability.

Learning from experience

One year after the initial announcement, the International Olympic Committee reported itself to be pleased with progress in London. At the same time, Olympics Minister Tessa Jowell expressed confidence about budgetary management'

> *We are carrying out a review of all the costs, and that will be a continuing discipline,' she said. 'We expect some costs to rise, but others will come down. We are right on top of that process.*[66]

LOCOG is also taking the opportunity to learn from its counterparts in Italy, where the Winter Olympics took place in 2006, and China which hosts the Beijing 2008 Olympics. Its chief executive Paul Deighton commented that the Beijing experience had highlighted the importance of getting the long-term use of the facilities decided as early as possible, in order that construction could proceed continuously.[67]

After just one year, change and development could be seen on all fronts: the key appointments had been made and a strong team assembled. Eighty-six per cent of the land needed had been acquired, although some local resistance to the compulsory purchase orders remained. Fifty electricity pylons and transmission cables had been buried as a key preparatory task to redevelopment and work was under way on developments to the transport infrastructure. Problems such as contaminated land are likely to arise in some places, which will test the resilience of the plans. In commercial terms, already 60 per cent of the major sponsorship of the Games had been signed up and a new parliamentary bill passed to provide safeguards against ticket touts and 'ambush marketing' (the intrusion of unauthorised publicity).[68]

As the Mayor of London commented in a newspaper article in 2003, while the bid was being prepared

> *The lessons of the Dome, Wembley and Picketts Lock will serve as cautionary tales for whoever heads the team for the Olympic bid, but they cannot be used as an excuse for avoiding ambitious projects. Our competitor cities too will have learned from previous failed sporting bids and less than successful projects. The expected battle between New York, London, Paris and Moscow will be a clash of the titans. Hosting the 2012 Olympics is one of the most ambitious projects we will have seen in Britain for many years, but as any sportsperson will tell you, you don't get anywhere without ambition.*[69]

The organisation created to achieve that ambition has been careful to assign clear responsibilities for the many tasks involved. Some of the tasks will be carried out by direct employees of the LOCOG/ODA organisation, but the bulk of the work will be done by contractors to the ODA and by the co-ordinated efforts of independent partner organisations. The unique combination of scale, complexity, prominence and complete inflexibility of the opening date make this an extraordinary organisational challenge. When asked whether the Olympic Park will be built in time, David Higgins, whose experience is based on the successful Sydney 2000 Olympics, replied simply:

Of course it will. Every Olympic city always builds it; they eventually finish it, some with more heartaches than others.[70]

Your tasks

1 The London 2012 project has a single overriding goal. How could the ideas of the goal model approach be applied to understand how that overriding goal might be achieved?

2 Make a list of stakeholders of the London 2012 project. Analyse the interest of each group in the project and identify the main issues that the London 2012 project will have to manage in balancing stakeholder interests.

3 Outline a SWOT analysis for the London 2012 project. What are the key organisational resources and skills that will need to be deployed in managing these opportunities and risks?

4 Identify ways in which the experience of managing a major project with a single goal differ from that of managing a regular process which does not have such a simple 'binary test' of success or failure. Suggest what different demands might be made of a manager in each of the two types of circumstance and what different skills might be required.

Notes and references

1 See, for example: Morley, M. 'What Business Are You In?', *Professional Manager*, March 1997, pp. 12–13.

2 Johnson, G., Scholes, K. and Whittington, R. *Exploring Corporate Strategy*, Seventh edition, Financial Times Prentice Hall (2005), p. 9.

3 Andrews, K. *The Concept of Corporate Strategy*, Irwin (1971), in Lynch, R. *Corporate Strategy*, Fourth edition, Financial Times Prentice Hall (2006), p. 6.

4 Tilles, S. 'Making Strategy Explicit', in Ansoff, H. I. (ed.) *Business Strategy*, Penguin (1969).

5 Johnson, G., Scholes, K. and Whittington, R. *Exploring Corporate Strategy*, Seventh edition, Financial Times Prentice Hall (2005), p. 448.

6 Allen, R. S. and Helms, M. M. 'Employee Perceptions of the Relationship Between Strategy, Rewards and Organizational Performance', *Journal of Business Strategies*, vol. 19, no. 2, Fall 2002, pp. 115–39.

7 Richardson, B. and Thompson, J. 'Strategic Competency in the 1990s', *Administrator*, July 1994, pp. 2–6.

8 Lloyd, B. 'In my Opinion', *Management Today*, August 2001, p. 8.

9 Lynch, R. *Corporate Strategy*, Fourth edition, Financial Times Prentice Hall (2006), p. 22.

10 Ansoff, H. I. (ed.) *Business Strategy*, Penguin (1969).

11 See, for example: Hannagan, T. *Management: Concepts & Practices*, Fourth edition, Financial Times Prentice Hall (2005), p. 363.

12 Pitman, B. (Sir) 'In my Opinion', *Management Today*, June 2000, p.14.

13 Mills, D. Q. and Friesen, G. B. 'Empowerment', in Crainer, S. and Dearlove, D. *Financial Times Handbook of Management*, Second edition, Financial Times Prentice Hall (2001), p. 335.

14 Watson, T. *Organising and Managing Work*, Second edition, Financial Times Prentice Hall (2006)

15 McGregor, D. *The Human Side of Enterprise*, Penguin (1987), p. 55.

16 See, for example: Brown, A. 'Organizational Culture: The Key to Effective Leadership and Organizational Development', *Leadership and Organization Development Journal*, vol. 13, no. 2, 1992, pp. 3–6.

17 Brech, E. F. L. (ed.) *The Principles and Practice of Management*, Third edition, Longman (1975).

18 Lucas, E. 'Believe It or Not, Values Can Make a Difference', *Professional Manager*, November 1999, pp. 10–12

19 Dainty, P. and Anderson, M. 'Mindsets For Managers', in Chowdhury, S. *Management 21C*, Financial Times Prentice Hall (2000), p. 110.

20 Cloke, K. and Goldsmith, J. The End of Management and the Rise of Organizational Democracy, Jossey-Bass (2002).

21 Mills, D. Q. and Friesen, G. B. 'Empowerment', in Crainer, S. and Dearlove, D. *Financial Times Handbook of Management*, Second edition, Financial Times Prentice Hall (2001), p. 334.

22 www.managers.org.uk (accessed 26 June 2006).

23 Perrin, L. and Tavakoli, I. 'Mission Impossible Without Commitment', *Professional Manager*, July 1997, pp. 14–15.

24 Reeves, C. 'Making vision statements meaningful', *Manager, British Journal of Administrative Management*, April/May 2006.
25 Gratton, L. *Living Strategy: Putting People at the Heart of Corporate Purpose*, Financial Times Prentice Hall (2000), p. 55.
26 Summers, J. and Nowicki, M. 'Achievement and Balance: What Do Managers Really Want?', *Healthcare Financial Management*, vol. 56, no. 3, March 2002, pp. 80–4.
27 Christensen, C. M., Raynor, M. E. and Anthony, S. D. 'Six Keys to Creating New-Growth Businesses', *Harvard Management Update*, 2003, p. 3.
28 Drucker, P. F. *The Practice of Management*, Heinemann Professional (1989), p. 59.
29 Kaplan, R. S. and Norton, D. P. *The Balanced Scorecard: Translating Strategy into Action*, Harvard Business School Press (1996).
30 van de Vliet, A. 'The New Balancing Act', *Management Today*, July 1997, pp. 78–80.
31 Tonge, R. and Callaghan, C. 'Using the Balanced Scorecard in the Public Sector', *Chartered Secretary*, October 1997, pp. 18–19.
32 Drucker, P. F. *Managing for Results*, Heinemann Professional (1989). See also: Drucker, P. F. *Managing in Turbulent Times*, Heinemann (1980).
33 Stern, S. 'Leading Lights', *Management Today*, June 2004, pp. 72–3.
34 Earl, M. 'IT Strategy in The New Economy', in Pickford, J. (ed), *Financial Times Mastering Management 2.0*, Financial Times Prentice Hall (2001), p. 109.
35 Kermally, S. 'E-strategy is Key to Future Success', *Professional Manager*, July 2001, pp. 28–9.
36 Levine, S. R. 'The Value-Based Edu-Leader', in Chowdhury, S. *Management 21C*, Financial Times Prentice Hall (2000), p. 90.
37 Cable, Vincent (MP) 'Hard-nosed case for CSR' *Professional Manager*, vol. 14, no. 3, May 2005, p. 11.
38 See, for example: Piggott, G. 'Open Relationships', *Holland Herald*, January 2003, pp. 54–64.
39 Harris, J. 'EU Acts to Promote More Socially Responsible Companies', *Social Agenda*, October 2002, pp. 3–4.
40 Chant, Ann 'In my opinion', *Management Today*, May 2005, p. 12.
41 HRH The Prince of Wales, Foreword to Grayson, D. and Hodges, A. *Everybody's Business: Managing Global Risks and Opportunities in Today's Global Society*, Financial Times (2001), pp. 8–9.
42 See, for example: Worthington, I. and Britton, C. *The Business Environment*, Fifth edition, Financial Times Prentice Hall (2006).
43 Drucker, P. F. *The Practice of Management*, Heinemann Professional (1989), p. 380.
44 Reeves, R. 'Do the right thing', *Management Today*, July 2005, pp. 549.
45 BBC News, 'Powergen shuts India call centres', 15 June 2006.
46 BBC News, 'Man held in HSBC India scam probe', 28 June 2006.
47 *The Guardian*, 'Overseas Transcription errors "putting patients' lives at risk"', 21 June 2006.
48 De George, R. T. *Business Ethics*, Fifth edition, Prentice Hall (1999).
49 Friedman, M. 'The Social Responsibility of Business is to Increase Its Profits', *New York Times Magazine*, 13 September 1970, pp. 32, 122–6.
50 Sternberg, E. *Just Business*, Little Brown (1994).
51 Cannon, T. *Corporate Responsibility*, Pitman (1994), pp. 32–3.
52 Sternberg, E. *Just Business*, Little Brown (1994).
53 RSA, *Tomorrow's Company – The Role of Business in a Changing World*, Royal Society for Arts, Manufactures and Commerce (1995).
54 For a discussion, see: De George, R. T. *Business Ethics*, Fifth edition, Prentice Hall (1999).
55 Chartered Management Institute, 'Codes of Ethics' Checklist 028, August 2005.
56 Palmisano, S. 'IBM Business Conduct Guidelines' IBM, December 2005. (With thanks to Lynn Thomson, First Line Manager, IBM (UK) Ltd.)
57 Dobson, N. 'Prejudicial Interests?', *Chartered Secretary*, May 2003, pp. 22–4.
58 Allen, A. 'Up the Moral Mountain', *Chartered Secretary*, May 2001, pp. 21–2.
59 Cook, S. 'Who Cares Wins', *Management Today*, January 2003, pp. 40–7.
60 Back, P. F. 'Taking a proactive approach to ethics' *Professional Manager*, vol. 15, no. 3, May 2006, p. 37.
61 McEwan, T. *Managing Values and Beliefs in Organisations*, Financial Times Prentice Hall (2001).
62 BBC Radio interview with Lord Coe, Radio 4 'The Today Programme', 2 July 2006.
63 The London 2012 website is at www.london2012.com.
64 *Daily Telegraph*, 20 July 2006.
65 Greater London Authority 'Mayor applauds procurement principles to create truly sustainable Games' press release 8 September 2005 www.london.gov.uk/mayor/olympics [accessed 22 July 2006].
66 BBC Sport website 2006 'IOC Pleased with London progress' 21 April 2006 http://news.bbc.co.uk/sport1 [accessed 22 July 2006].
67 London 2012 11 April 2006 'Masterclass in Olympic Planning' The London 2012 Website http://www.london2012.com [accessed 22 July 2006].
68 BBC news website 6 July 2006 'Preparing for 2012' accessed 22 July 2006 http://news.bbc.co.uk/sport1.
69 Livingstone, K. 2003 'We must go for gold with London's Olympic bid' *The Observer* 12 January 2003. http://observer.guardian.co.uk [accessed 24 July 2006].
70 *Daily Telegraph*, 20 July 2006.

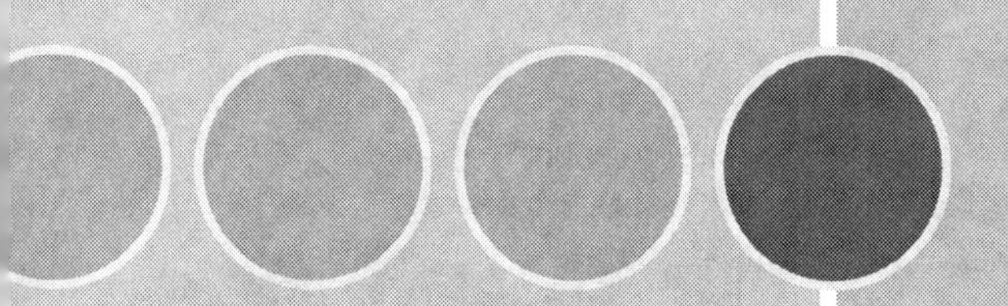

ORGANISATION STRUCTURE AND DESIGN

> **The quality of the relationship between line and functional managers lies at the heart of achieving both compliance to rules and an ability to work with the principles behind them. If the relationship is good, and trust and respect high, then both sides understand the importance of each other's role … Line management knows they will always be pressing to drive harder on performance, but understand the functional roles are there to help create, and strengthen, the boundaries they must not cross.**
>
> **Carolyn Taylor** – partner in the Mettle Group
> *Walking the Talk: building a culture for success*, Random House (2005), p. 290

In order to achieve its goals and objectives, the work of an organisation has to be divided among its members. Some structure is necessary to make possible the effective performance of key activities and to support the efforts of staff. Structure provides the framework of an organisation and its pattern of management. It is by means of structure that the purpose and work of the organisation are carried out. The manager needs to understand the importance and effects of organisation structure and design.

Learning outcomes

After completing this chapter you should be able to:

- explain the meaning and nature of organisation structure;
- identify levels of organisation and debate the importance of the hierarchy;
- explore the main factors to be considered in the design of organisation structure and different methods for the division of work;
- debate the relevance and applications of principles of organisation and organisational relationships;
- explain the importance of good structure and the consequences of a deficient structure;
- assess the importance of structure for organisational performance;
- review the relationship between the structure of an organisation and the people who work within it.

Critical reflection

The trend is towards more horizontal structures, teamwork, empowerment, flexible working arrangements and informal relationships. Do you believe this has reduced significantly the need for, and importance of, formal organisation structures? What do you see as the likely effects of developments in information communications technology for structural design?

THE MEANING AND NATURE OF ORGANISATION STRUCTURE

The purpose of structure is the division of work among members of the organisation, and the co-ordination of their activities so they are directed towards the goals and objectives of the organisation. Structure is the pattern of relationships among positions in the organisation and among members of the organisation. Structure makes possible the application of the process of management and creates a framework of order and command through which the activities of the organisation can be planned, organised, directed and controlled. The structure defines tasks and responsibilities, work roles and relationships, and channels of communication.

Structure is clearly important for any organisation, whatever its size. However, in the smaller organisations there are likely to be fewer problems of structure. The distribution of tasks, the definition of authority and responsibility, and the relationship between members of the organisation can be established on a more personal and informal basis. With increasing size, however, there is greater need for a carefully designed and purposeful form of organisation. There is need for a formal **organisational structure**. There is also need for a continual review of structure to ensure that it is the most appropriate form for the particular organisation, and in keeping with its growth and development. This is likely to be of particular importance for the very large companies.

Birkinshaw discusses the structures behind global companies and the problem for international companies of balancing bureaucracy with the benefits of size.

> *There are many ways of addressing this balancing act. One way is to work on culture, to get people to think entrepreneurially. Another way is through systems – reward systems, career management and so on. A third way is through structure – the basic lines of reporting and accountability that are typically drawn on an organisation chart. The structure is never the whole story, it is just a way of dividing responsibilities among executives. It is meaningless unless supported by appropriate systems and a consistent culture. However, structure is still surprisingly informative about strategic priorities and the work going on, so it is as good a place to start as any.*[1]

Objectives of structure

The objectives of structure may be summarised as to provide for:

- the economic and efficient performance of the organisation and the level of resource utilisation;
- monitoring the activities of the organisation;
- accountability for areas of work undertaken by groups and individual members of the organisation;
- co-ordination of different parts of the organisation and different areas of work;
- flexibility in order to respond to future demands and developments, and to adapt to changing environmental influences; and
- the social satisfaction of members working in the organisation.[2]

These objectives provide the criteria for structural effectiveness. Structure, though, is not an end in itself but a means of improving organisational performance. For example, as *Heller* points out:

> *No amount of reorganising and reshuffling will increase the long-term capability of a business unless you suit the organisation to the people and to a genuinely shared purpose.*[3]

Organisation structure and culture

In previous chapters we have made the point that the organisation does not exist independently but is open to, and in continual interaction with, the broader external environment of which it is part. A major determinant of an organisation's structure is its culture. The pervasive nature of culture in terms of both external influences and 'how things are done around here' and common values, beliefs and attitudes will have a significant effect on organisational processes including the design of structure. *Watson* suggests that we must be careful not to treat structures or cultures as if they were solid 'things' that exist separately from the processes and relationships that the two concepts are intended to help us make sense of. The structure of work organisations also involves the wider context of societal structures and cultures. 'Societal structures both contribute to and result from organisational structures.' *Watson* also refers to the closeness and overlap of structure and culture. 'Many of the processes and practices we observe in an organisation could as readily be said to be part of the structure of the organisation as part of its culture.'[4] (Culture as a contingency factor of structure is discussed in Chapter 16.)

THE IMPORTANCE OF GOOD STRUCTURE

According to *Drucker*, it is the correct design of structure that is of most significance in determining organisational performance.

> *Good organisation structure does not by itself produce good performance. But a poor organisation structure makes good performance impossible, no matter how good the individual managers may be. To improve organisation structure ... will therefore always improve performance.*[5]

The importance of good structure is also emphasised by *Child*:

> *A basic structure distributes responsibilities among the members of a company. Its purpose is to contribute to the successful implementation of objectives by allocating people and resources to necessary tasks and designing responsibility and authority for their control and coordination.*[6]

The structure of an organisation affects not only productivity and economic efficiency but also the morale and job satisfaction of the workforce. Getting the structure right is the first step in organisational change.[7] Structure should be designed, therefore, so as to encourage the willing participation of members of the organisation and effective organisational performance. There is also a close relationship between organisation structure and corporate strategy although the nature of this relationship, and whether structure follows strategy or strategy follows structure, is the subject of debate.[8]

The human element

The functions of the formal structure, and the activities and defined relationships within it, exist independently of the members of the organisation who carry out the work. However, personalities are an important part of the working of the organisation. In practice, the actual operation of the organisation and success in meeting its objectives will depend upon the behaviour of people who work within the structure and who give shape and personality to the framework. *Lord Forte*, for example, has drawn attention to the importance of the human element in organisation structure:

> *The human aspect in a business is vital: you can keep drawing squares and lines, but within these squares you must have people and they must be deeply involved with the business. If this does not happen, then the lines and squares and the diagrams mean nothing.*[9]

In an IMD survey, the commitment and involvement of employees ranked second only to top management as a key success factor for restructuring. Yet the survey also showed that almost 40 per cent of restructuring obstacles related to the failure to achieve employee commitment.[10] According to *Hannagan*, softer corporate values are being emphasised now compared to the harder values by concentrating more on staff training, developing skills and ensuring that all employees understand the organisation's values. There is a shift from the harder values of strategy, structure and systems to the softer ones of staff, skills and style.[11]

The human relations writers are critical of the emphasis on the formal organisation. They favour a structure in which there is increased participation from people at all levels of the organisation, greater freedom for the individual, and more meaningful work organisation and relationships. One of the strongest critics of the formal organisation is *Argyris*.[12] He claims that the formal, bureaucratic organisation restricts individual growth and self-fulfilment and, in the psychologically healthy person, causes a feeling of failure, frustration and conflict. Argyris argues that the organisation should provide a more 'authentic' relationship for its members.

The view of the human relations writers represents more of an attitude towards organisation than specific proposals, but it reminds us of the importance of the human element in the design of structure. Managers need to consider how structural design and methods of work organisation influence the behaviour and performance of members of the organisation.

LEVELS OF ORGANISATION

Organisations are layered. The determination of policy and decision-making, the execution of work, and the exercise of authority and responsibility are carried out by different people at varying levels of seniority throughout the organisation structure. In small organisations, these activities tend to be less distinct but in the larger organisations it is possible to look at organisations in terms of three broad interrelated levels in the hierarchical structure: **the technical level, the managerial level** and **the community level**.[13] These last two levels are often referred to as middle management and senior management.

The **technical level** is concerned with specific operations and discrete tasks, with the actual job or tasks to be done, and with performance of the technical function. Examples are the physical production of goods in a manufacturing firm, administrative processes giving direct service to the public in government departments, and the actual process of teaching in an educational establishment.

The technical level interrelates with the **managerial level**, or organisational level, which is concerned with the co-ordination and integration of work at the technical level. Decisions at the managerial level relate to the resources necessary for performance of the technical function, and to the beneficiaries of the products or services provided. Decisions will be concerned with (i) mediating between the organisation and its external environment, such as the users of the organisation's products or services, and the procurement of resources, and (ii) the 'administration' of the internal affairs of the organisation including the control of the operations of the technical function.

In turn, the managerial level interrelates with the **community level** or institutional level, concerned with broad objectives and the work of the organisation as a whole. Decisions at the community level will be concerned with the selection of operations, and the development of the organisation in relation to external agencies and the wider social environment. Examples of the community level within organisations are the board of directors of joint stock companies, governing bodies of educational establishments which include external representatives, and trustees of non-profit organisations. Such bodies provide a mediating link between the managerial organisation and co-ordination of work of the technical organisation, and the wider community interests.

Interrelationship of levels

In practice, there is not a clear division between determination of policy and decision-making, co-ordination of activities and the actual execution of work (see Figure 15.1). Most decisions are taken with reference to the execution of wider decisions, and most execution of work involves decision. Decisions taken at the institutional level determine objectives for the managerial level, and decisions at the managerial level set objectives for the technical level. Therefore, if the organisation as a whole is to perform effectively there must be clear objectives, a soundly designed structure and good communications, both upwards and downwards, among the different levels of the organisation.

The managerial level, for example, would be unable to plan and supervise the execution of work of the technical function without the knowledge, expertise, practical know-how and enthusiasm of people who are closest to the actual tasks to be undertaken. People operating at the technical level should, therefore, make known to higher levels the practical difficulties and operational problems concerning their work. It is the duty of the managerial level to take appropriate action on this information, and to consult with people at the community or institutional level.

Not all activities concerned with the management of an organisation can be considered, necessarily, in terms of these three levels of work. There will be certain activities that are analysed more meaningfully in terms of a greater, or possibly a smaller, number of levels. In many cases movements towards more democratic organisations, empowerment, an increase in knowledge workers and technological advances have contributed to a blurring of a clear differentiation between policy, management and the execution of work. However, the three broad levels provide a basis for a critical analysis of the interrelated activities of the organisation.

Figure 15.1 Interrelated levels of organisation

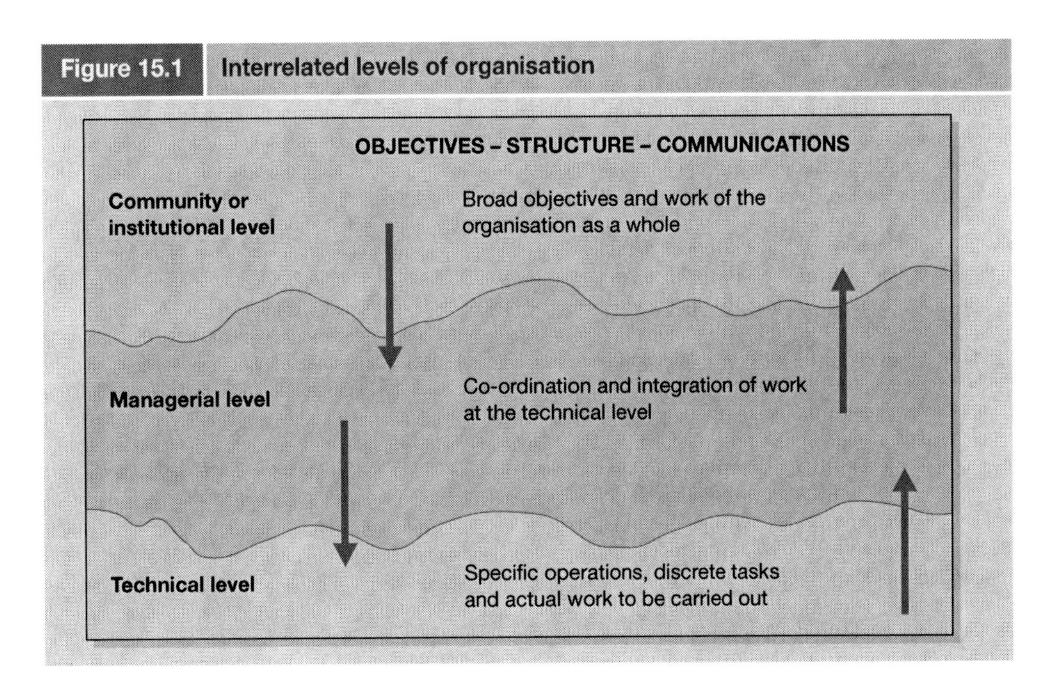

The management process in local government

An example of the interrelationship between the different levels of an organisation can be seen from the comments in the Bains Report on management in local government. The report recognises that elected members remain responsible for ultimate direction and control of the authority, key decisions on objectives and plans to attain them, and reviewing progress and performance of services. However, the report also refers to the dual nature of management and to the changing relationship between permanent officers and elected members at the different stages of the management process.

The report concludes:

> *We doubt whether it is possible to divide the total management process into two separate halves, one for members and the other for officers ... That process itself can be seen as a scale, with the setting of objectives and allocation of major resources at one end, moving through the designing of programmes and plans, to the execution of those plans at the other end. As one moves through that management scale, the balance between the two elements changes from member control with officer advice at the 'objective' end to officer control with member advice at the 'execution' end.*[14]

More recently, The Audit Commission has referred to the harmful gaps caused in local government and the National Health Service by the de-layering and the stripping out of middle managers which have been carried out without a full understanding of the impact on the council's management structures as a whole.[15]

Divide between senior and middle management

Rawson draws attention to the increasing absence of mutuality between senior and middle managers in both the public and private sector.

> *Traditionally, senior managers have been concerned with setting the strategic direction and objectives for the organisation; middle managers with making it happen – resourcing and managing the changes. The corollary is that senior managers are concerned with results and middle managers with how these are achieved. The divide appears as middle levels complain that their seniors are solely concerned with short-term financial results and as seniors reply that the middle strata devote more effort to voicing problems than to finding solutions. In both sectors the delayering of organisations has dramatically reduced the resources available to middle managers. The divide deepens as each accuses the other of pursuing their own personal rather than organisational ends. Middle accuse senior of being concerned with their own career advancement: senior accuse middle of directing their efforts to protecting their positions.*[16]

THE IMPORTANCE OF THE HIERARCHY

We have referred previously to the significance of the changing nature of the work organisation. Early writers on management, for example Weber (discussed in Chapter 2), drew attention to the importance of the hierarchy of authority. However, the increasing use of group or team approaches, the growth of flexible employment, increasing use of subcontracting, an emphasis on participation and empowerment, and many workers involved in decision-making have all led to changes in the traditional boss–subordinate relationship. This has lead to a discussion on the role of the hierarchy in modern organisations and the extent to which managers can rely solely on their perceived formal authority within the structure of the organisation.

Stewart maintains that: 'Authority is, and is likely to continue to be, less acceptable than in the past. This reflects a major change in society: what has been termed the end of the grateful society. Better educated and more independent people expect to be consulted rather than to be told what to do.'[17] However, according to *Jebb*: 'The hierarchy is not dead. It has merely changed its form. The trappings of power in the modern workplace may have been toned down but the boss is still the boss.' Jebb refers to Hampden Turner who maintains that to confuse informality with the end of the organisational pecking order is a mistake.

There is a lot of muddled thinking about hierarchies and the whole issue of how equally we treat people within companies. But treating someone as an equal does not mean they are equal. Any smart person wanting the best out of a person treats them as an equal. However informal the environment, you can't escape from a functional hierarchy although the more skilled the company's work, the fewer tiers of management and the fewer individual managers should be required.[18]

The importance of the hierarchy is also strongly emphasised by *Drucker* who asserts that: 'One hears a great deal today about "the end of the hierarchy". This is blatant nonsense. In any institution there has to be a final authority, that is, a "boss"– someone who can make the final decisions and who can expect them to be obeyed.'[19]

Is the hierarchy obsolete?

However, contrary to the views of writers such as Jebb and Drucker, *Butcher* maintains that hierarchy is in principle obsolete in the knowledge economy:

Intellectual capital possessed by knowledge workers implies management based on fragile coalition rather than control. The arguments for de-emphasizing hierarchical control are now well rehearsed. Hierarchical assignment of tasks worked well when central planning worked well, but those days are gone. Local autonomy and accountability are essential for creating organisational ability.[20]

A similar point is made by Cloke and Goldsmith who question whether we are accustomed to and have accepted that hierarchy, rules and managers are an essential part of organisational life. Have managers been seduced by the apparent power over others that a hierarchical organisation offers and by the disproportionate rewards it can provide to those at the top? If so, this is depriving individuals of the chance to develop themselves to their full potential and cluttering organisations with wasteful and counter-productive processes.[21]

According to *Gratton*, more than at any other point in time, there is now a chance to create the democratic enterprise.

Over the last decade it has become increasingly clear that through the forces of globalization, competition and more demanding customers, the structure of many companies has become flatter, less hierarchical, more fluid and virtual. The breakdown of hierarchies provides us with fertile ground on which to create a more democratic way of working.[22]

Critical reflection

'Organisations are a form of social stratification. Advancement through the hierarchy can reasonably be seen as an indication of merit and achievement, and a reward for hard work.' Do you think this statement has any relevance for modern work organisations? Is the idea of hierarchy still important as an indication of promotion and career progression?

THE DESIGN OF ORGANISATION STRUCTURE

It is important to bear in mind that there are many variables that influence the most appropriate organisation structure and system of management, including situational factors and the contingency approach. Changing patterns of work organisation, the demand for greater flexibility and the multi-skilling challenge, and managerial processes such as delegation and empowerment also have a major interrelationship with structure and influence decisions on structural design, as discussed in Chapter 16.

Basic principles and considerations

While recognising that there is clearly no one right organisation, there is nevertheless, in the final analysis, an underlying need to establish a framework of order and system of command by which the work to be undertaken is accomplished successfully. This demands that attention be given to certain basic principles and considerations in the design of organisation structure, or in reviewing the effectiveness of an existing structure (*see* Figure 15.2).

These principles and considerations may perhaps appear prescriptive for the study of organisational behaviour, but they still present management with a series of important decision points.

> *Organisations are collections of people brought together for a purpose. To achieve this purpose successfully, people need to be organised within the best possible structure. Decisions on structure are primary strategic decisions. Structure can make or break an organisation.*[23]

Structure provides the framework for the activities of the organisation and must harmonise with its goals and objectives. The first step, therefore, is to examine the objectives of the organisation. Only when objectives have been clearly defined, can alternative forms of structure be analysed and compared.[24]

Figure 15.2 Basic considerations in the design of organisation structure

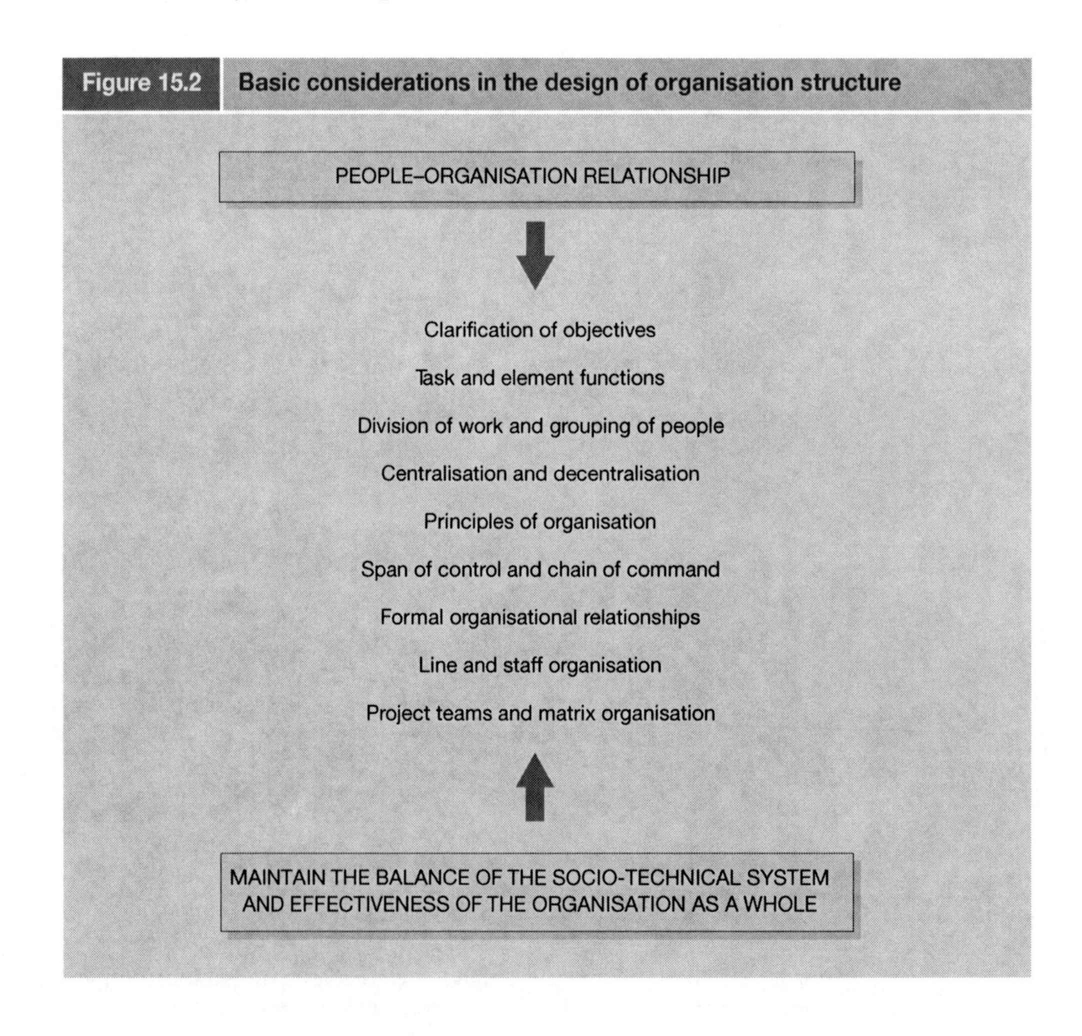

CLARIFICATION OF OBJECTIVES

A clear definition of objectives is necessary in order to provide a basis for the division of work and grouping of duties into sub-units. The objectives for these sub-units must be related to the objectives of the organisation as a whole in order that an appropriate pattern of structure can be established. Clearly stated and agreed objectives (discussed in Chapter 14) will provide a framework for the design of structure, and a suitable pattern of organisation to achieve those objectives. The nature of the organisation and its strategy will indicate the most appropriate organisational levels for different functions and activities, and the formal relationships between them. Clearly defined objectives will help facilitate systems of communication between different parts of the organisation and the extent of decentralisation and delegation. The formal structure should help make possible the attainment of objectives. It should assist in the performance of the essential functions of the organisation and the major activities that it needs to undertake.

TASK AND ELEMENT FUNCTIONS

In order to produce some good, or provide some service, there are four essential functions that the organisation must perform.

1 The good or service must be developed.
2 Something of value must be created. In the case of the business organisation this might be the production or manufacture of a product; in the case of the public sector organisation the provision of a service.
3 The product or services must be marketed. They must be distributed or made available to those who are to use them.
4 Finance is needed in order to make available the resources used in the development, creation and distribution of the products or services provided.

These essential functions of developing the good or service, manufacturing the good or providing the service, marketing them, and financing the organisation, are what *Woodward* refers to as the **'task' functions**. These are the basic activities of the organisation that are related to the actual completion of the productive process and directed towards specific and definable end-results. To ensure the efficient achievement of overall objectives of the organisation, the results of the task functions must be co-ordinated.[25]

Other activities of the organisation are not directed towards specific and definable ends but are supportive of the task functions and an intrinsic part of the management process. These are referred to as **'element' functions** and include, for example, human resources, planning, management services, public relations, quality control and maintenance. In other organisations, noticeably in service industries involving direct customer contact, human resource management can be seen as closely associated with a task function.[26] In the majority of organisations, however, the personnel function does not normally have any direct accountability for the performance of a specific end-task.

Implications for organisation structure

The two kinds of functions, task and element, differ in a number of ways and these differences have important implications for organisation. Failure to distinguish between the two types of functions can lead to confusion in the planning of structure and in the relationship between members of the organisation. For example, in her study of the management organisation of firms in this country, *Woodward* comments on the bad relationships between accountants and other managers referred to during the study. One reason for this hostility was the bringing together of two quite separate financial functions essential to the efficient operation of a business.

> *People concerned with works accounting tended to assume responsibility for end results that was not properly theirs; they saw their role as a controlling and sanctioning one rather than as a servicing and supportive one. Line managers resented this attitude and retaliated by becoming aggressive and obstructive.*[27]

According to Woodward, activities concerned with raising funds for the business, keeping accounts and determination of financial policy are task functions. Management accounting, however, concerned with prediction and control of production administration, is an element function, and is primarily a servicing and supportive one. Relationships between the accountants and other managers seemed better when the two functions were organisationally separate. This was noticeable especially in divisionalised organisation when each product division had its own accounting staff providing line managers with the necessary information to control their own departments. In these cases the task function of finance was completely divorced from the element function of management accounting in which the servicing and supportive role is of most importance.

THE DIVISION OF WORK

Within the formal structure of an organisation work has to be divided among its members and different jobs related to each other. The division of work and the grouping together of people should, wherever possible, be organised by reference to some common characteristic which forms a logical link between the activities involved. It is necessary to maintain a balance between an emphasis on subject matter or function at higher levels of the organisation, and specialisation and concern for staff at the operational level.

Work can be divided, and activities linked together, in a variety of ways.

Major purpose or function

The most commonly used basis for grouping activities is according to specialisation, the use of the same set of resources, or the shared expertise of members of staff. It is a matter for decision in each organisation as to which activities are important enough to be organised into separate functions, departments or sections. Work may be departmentalised and based, for example, on differentiation between task and element functions, discussed above (*see* Figure 15.3).

Product or service

In division by product or service, the contributions of different specialists are integrated into separate, semi-autonomous units with collective responsibility for a major part of the business process or for a complete cycle of work. This form of grouping is more common in the

Figure 15.3 Division of work by major purpose or function

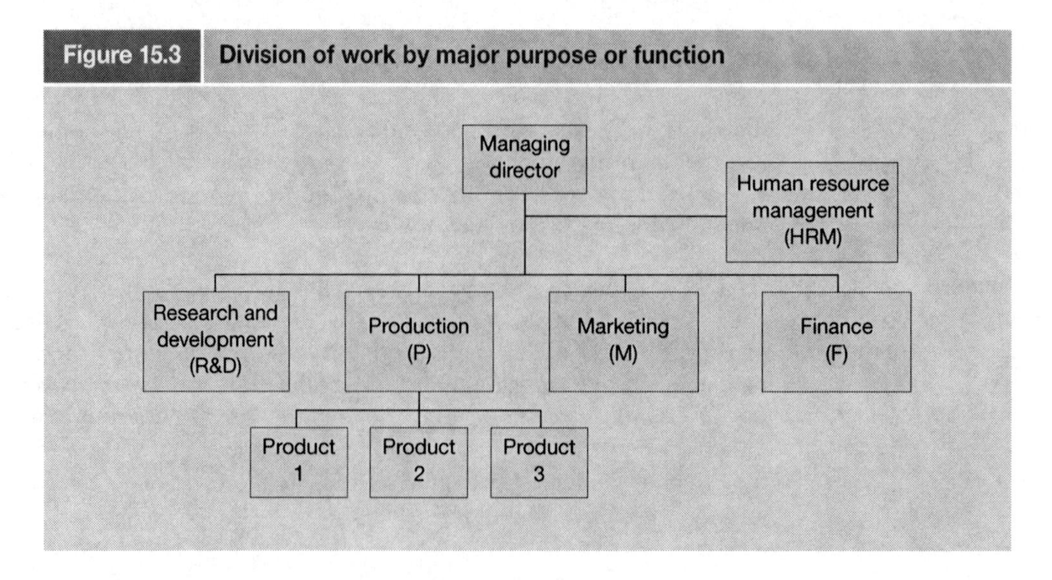

larger diversified organisations and may be used as a means of sub-dividing departments into sections. An example is the bringing together of all activities concerned with a particular production line, product or service (*see* Figure 15.4). Another example is a hospital where medical and support staff are grouped together in different units dealing with particular treatments such as accidents and emergency, medical or surgery. With grouping by product or service there is a danger that the divisions may attempt to become too autonomous, presenting management with a problem of co-ordination and control.

Location In division by location, different services are provided by area or geographical boundaries according to particular needs or demands, the convenience of consumers, or for ease of administration (*see* Figure 15.5). Examples are the provision of local authority services for people living in a particular locality, the siting of hospitals or post offices, the provision of technical or agricultural further education in industrial or rural areas, sales territories for business firms or the grouping of a number of retail shops under an area manager. Another example is provided by organisations with multi-site working and the grouping of a range of similar activities or functions located together on one site. The improvement in communications, particularly telecommunications, tends, however, to reduce the importance of location. For example, administrative staff may no longer need to be located within the main production unit.

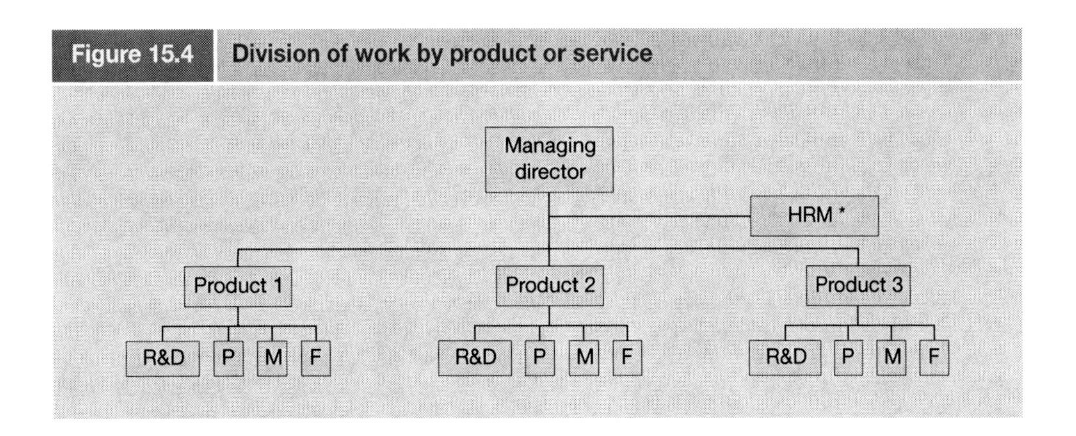

Figure 15.4 Division of work by product or service

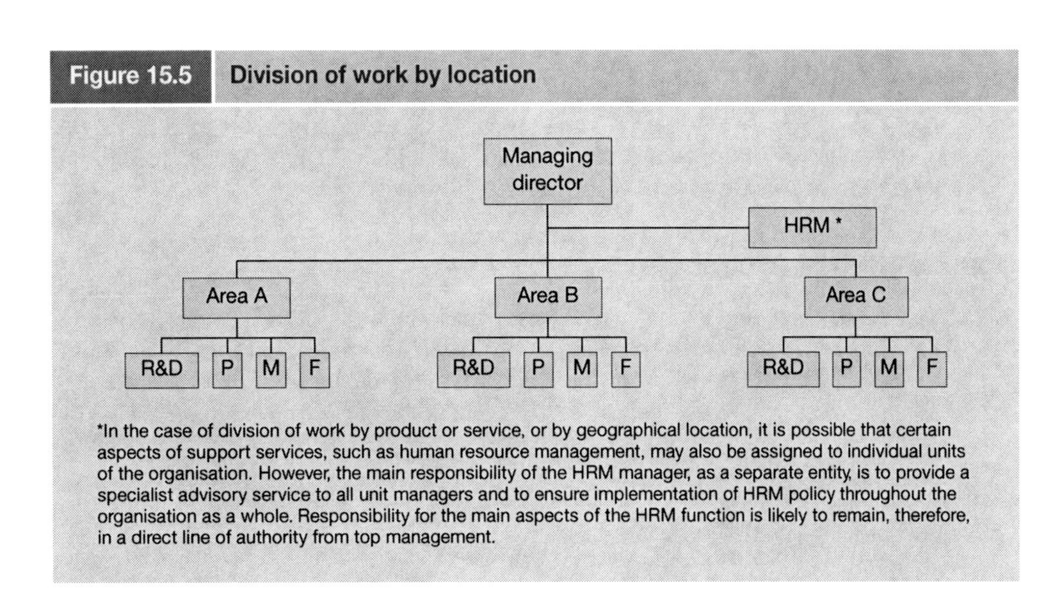

Figure 15.5 Division of work by location

*In the case of division of work by product or service, or by geographical location, it is possible that certain aspects of support services, such as human resource management, may also be assigned to individual units of the organisation. However, the main responsibility of the HRM manager, as a separate entity, is to provide a specialist advisory service to all unit managers and to ensure implementation of HRM policy throughout the organisation as a whole. Responsibility for the main aspects of the HRM function is likely to remain, therefore, in a direct line of authority from top management.

Nature of the work performed Division may be according to the nature of the work performed where there is some special common feature of the work such as the need for speedy decisions, accuracy, confidentiality/security, or where local conditions require first-hand knowledge not immediately available elsewhere. Another example may be the grouping of equipment or machinery which is noisy or which produces dust, fumes or unpleasant odours. When common processes are used in a range of different activities, this may also be used as the basis of division. This method of grouping includes, for example, the decision as to whether to establish a centralised resource centre for all departments of the organisation or to allow each department to have its own service. With manufacturing industries, a range of products may pass through a common production facility or configuration of machines that may be grouped together in a single unit – for example, a batch production engineering firm having departments based on like skills or methods of operation.

Common time scales Division may be according to time scales, for example shift working and the extent to which different tasks should be undertaken by different shifts. In a further education college there may be separate departments or groupings to deal with the different needs of full-time day students and part-time evening students. Another example of activities grouped according to time is in a hotel. Activities in the kitchen tend to be short term, especially when guests in the restaurant are waiting to be served, and a range of different tasks have to be co-ordinated very quickly. Other activities, for example market research and forecasting future room occupancy, are longer-term decisions and subject to different organisational requirements.

Staff employed The allocation of duties and responsibilities may be according to experience or where a particular technical skill or special qualification is required – for example, the division of work between surgeons, doctors and nurses, or between barristers, solicitors and legal executives. Another example is the sharing of routine work processes among members of a supervised group. In smaller organisations the allocation of work may be on an *ad hoc*, personal basis according to the knowledge and skills contributed by individuals. Work may also be planned deliberately to give a variety of tasks and responsibilities to provide improved job satisfaction or to assist in the training of staff.

Customer or people to be served Separate groups may be established to deal with different consumer requirements – for example, the division between trade or retail customers or between home or export sales. In hospitals there are different groupings dealing with, for example, patients in the gynaecology, geriatric and children's wards. In large clothes shops there may be separate departments for men's, women's and children's clothing. Government departments are often grouped by this method and work is divided according to for whom the services are provided – for example, the unemployed, low-pay families, students, young people or senior citizens. A further example is the provision of canteen services which may be grouped by customer demand according to price, range or standard of meals available, speed of service, or type of customer; this gives rise to separate facilities such as the directors' dining room, or for staff and students in educational establishments.

Combination of groupings

These different ways of dividing work can be combined in various forms and most organisations will contain examples of alternative combinations for grouping activities. Some activities might be grouped according to one method and other activities according to a different method. Decisions on the methods of grouping will include considerations of:

- the need for co-ordination;
- the identification of clearly defined divisions of work;
- economy;
- the process of managing the activities;

- avoiding conflict; and
- the design of work organisation which takes account of the nature of staff employed, their interests and job satisfaction.

Management must decide upon the most significant factors that will determine the methods for division of work and linking of activities appropriate to the changing circumstances within the particular organisation.

CENTRALISATION AND DECENTRALISATION

A critical decision point that arises from division of work and grouping of activities is the extent of centralisation or **decentralisation**. Most organisations necessarily involve a degree of decentralisation arising from such features as an increase in size, the geographical separation of different parts of the organisation, or the need to extend activities or services to remote areas. Our main concern is with decentralisation or devolution in terms of specific delegation or empowerment to sub-units or groups within the organisation such that they enjoy a measure of autonomy or independence.

The advantages often claimed for centralisation tend to relate to economic and administrative considerations. However, such advantages frequently are not realised fully, and do not lead to an actual improvement in service. There are a number of contrary arguments against centralisation, including the criticism that it creates a more mechanistic structure and may result in lengthening the chain of command. There are also positive arguments, which tend to relate more to behavioural considerations, in favour of decentralisation (*see* Figure 15.6).

Extent of decentralisation

The balance between centralisation and decentralisation is one of the major debates in organisation structure. The advisability of decentralisation must be considered in terms of the nature

Figure 15.6 Advantages of centralisation or decentralisation

Advantages of centralisation

- the easier implementation of a common policy for the organisation as a whole;
- providing a consistent strategy across the organisation;
- preventing sub-units becoming too independent;
- making for easier co-ordination and management control;
- improved economies of scale and a reduction in overhead costs;
- greater use of specialisation, including better facilities and equipment;
- improved decision-making which might otherwise be slower and a result of compromise because of diffused authority.

Advantage of decentralisation

- enables decisions to be made closer to the operational level of work;
- increased responsiveness to local circumstances;
- improved level of personal customer service;
- more in keeping with developments in flatter and more flexible structures;
- support services, such as adminstration, are more likely to be effective if provided as close as possible to the activities they are intended to serve;
- provides opportunities for training and development in management;
- usually, it has an encouraging effect on the motivation and morale of staff.

of the product or service provided, policy-making, the day-to-day management of the organisation and the need for standardisation of procedures, or conditions or terms of employment of staff. Decentralisation generally tends to be easier to implement in private sector organisations than in the public sector organisations where there is a greater demand for the accountability of their operations, regularity of procedures and uniformity of treatment.

However, it is not always easy to gauge the true extent of decentralisation. With flatter organisation structures, managements may claim a greater degree of decentralisation but in reality this may not always be the case. The extent and nature of decentralisation will vary from organisation to organisation and also over time. The balance between centralisation and decentralisation will be affected by such factors as the importance of decision-making, the urgency of the situation and time scales and also by technological developments, changes in structure, the prevailing organisational climate and the nature of staff employed.

The growing emphasis on participation and empowerment suggests a focus of attention on the principles of decentralisation, yet senior management still needs to maintain effective co-ordination and overall control of the activities of the organisation as a whole. Ideally, business organisations should attempt to blend the benefits of decentralisation for customer orientation and increased responsiveness, with the advantages of size, common resources and economies of scale. In the case of the big company, *Barnevik*, for example, believes in both the vital importance of decentralisation for local entrepreneurship, and exploiting the advantages of a big company: 'We want to be global and local, big and small, radically decentralised with central reporting and control. If we can resolve those contradictions we can create real organisational advantage.'[28]

Critical reflection

'The trend towards flatter structures, de-layering and virtual working leads to confusion and uncertainty, and can promote a climate of mistrust and low morale.' Do you think there is any truth in this statement? 'The reality is that most people would prefer to have a clearly established formal relationship with management and with their fellow workers.' To what extent do you agree with this contention?

PRINCIPLES OF ORGANISATION

The classical writers placed emphasis on the definition of structure in terms of division of work, chain of command, span of control and reporting relationships. Attention was focused on the requirements of the formal organisation and the search for a common set of principles applicable to all circumstances. Probably the leading authority in the UK was *Lyndall Urwick*, who originally specified eight principles of organisation, but revised these to ten in his later writing.[29]

1 **The principle of the objective**
'Every organisation and every part of the organisation must be an expression of the purpose of the undertaking concerned, or it is meaningless and therefore redundant.'
2 **The principle of specialisation**
'The activities of every member of any organised group should be confined, as far as possible, to the performance of a single function.'
3 **The principle of co-ordination**
'The purpose of organising *per se*, as distinguished from the purpose of the undertaking, is to facilitate co-ordination: unity of effort.'

4 **The principle of authority**
'In every organised group the supreme authority must rest somewhere. There should be a clear line of authority to every individual in the group.'
5 **The principle of responsibility**
'The responsibility of the superior for the acts of the subordinate is absolute.'
6 **The principle of definition**
'The content of each position, both the duties involved, the authority and responsibility contemplated and the relationships with other positions should be clearly defined in writing and published to all concerned.'
7 **The principle of correspondence**
'In every position, the responsibility and the authority should correspond.'
8 **The principle of span of control**
'No person should supervise more than five, or at the most, six direct subordinates whose work interlocks.'
9 **The principle of balance**
'It is essential that the various units of an organisation should be kept in balance.'
10 **The principle of continuity**
'Re-organisation is a continuous process: in every undertaking specific provision should be made for it.'

Relevance of principles

As mentioned in Chapter 2, the idea of common sets of principles on organisation and management has been subject to much criticism. Many of the principles are bland statements expressed in non-operation terms and give little basis for specific managerial action; they tend to view people as a given rather than as a variable in the system. However, despite such limitations, the principles do provide general guidance on the structuring of organisations and, as such, it is difficult to argue against them. It is also interesting to note that much of the more recent writing on the subject appears to be based on the ideas of the original statements.[30] The basic concept can be of value to the practical manager, **if modified to suit the demands of the particular situation**, including the nature of staffing in the organisation. The proper application of these principles is likely to help improve organisational performance.

Two of the more specific principles of general interest in the structuring of organisations are, (i) the span of control, and (ii) the chain of command.

SPAN OF CONTROL

The span of control arises in line authority and refers to the **number of subordinates who report directly** to a given manager or supervisor. It does not refer to the total of subordinate operating staff, that is those staff who report first to another person. Hence the term 'span of responsibility' or 'span of supervision' is sometimes considered to be more appropriate.

V. A. Graicunas developed a mathematical formula for the span of control.[31] The limitation of the number of subordinates who can effectively be supervised is based on the total of direct and cross relationships,

$$R = n\left(\frac{2n}{n} + n - 1\right)$$

where n is the number of subordinates, and R is the number of interrelationships.

For example, with five subordinates the total number of interrelationships requiring the attention of the manager is 100; with six subordinates the number of interrelationships is 222. Urwick supports the idea of Graicunas and, as we have seen from his list of principles, states that the span of control should not exceed five or at the most six direct subordinates whose work interlocks. At lower levels of the organisation, however, where there is less interlocking, or where responsibility is concerned more with the performance of specific tasks, the span of control may be larger.

Factors influencing span of control

Practical studies of span of control, however, show that it varies widely in different organisations and that the average span is larger than suggested by Graicunas and Urwick. For example, in *Woodward*'s study of 100 manufacturing firms in south-east Essex (discussed in Chapter 16) she found that the size of span of control varied directly with technology and type of production system.[32]

In addition to the type of technology or production system there are a number of other factors that will influence the limit of span of control. These include:

- the nature of the organisation, the complexity of the work and the similarity of functions, and the range of responsibilities;
- the ability and personal qualities of the manager including the capacity to cope with interruptions;
- the amount of time the manager has available from other activities to spend with subordinates;
- the ability and training of subordinate staff, the strength of their motivation and commitment, and the extent of direction and guidance needed;
- the effectiveness of co-ordination and the nature of communication and control systems;
- the physical location or geographical spread of subordinates;
- the length of the scalar chain, discussed in the following section.

Importance of span of control

If the span of control is **too wide**, it becomes difficult to supervise subordinates effectively and this places more stress on the manager. With larger groupings, informal leaders and sub-groups or cliques are more likely to develop and these may operate contrary to the policy of management. There may be lack of time to carry out all activities properly. Planning and development, training, inspection and control may suffer in particular, leading to poor job performance. A wide span of control may limit opportunities for promotion. Too wide a span of control may also result in a slowness to adapt to change or to the introduction of new methods or procedures.

If the span of control is **too narrow**, this may present a problem of co-ordination and consistency in decision-making and hinder effective communications across the organisation structure. Morale and initiative of subordinates may suffer as a result of too close a level of supervision. Narrow spans of control increase administrative costs and can prevent the best use being made of the limited resource of managerial talent. They can lead to additional levels of authority in the organisation creating an unnecessarily long chain of command.

THE CHAIN OF COMMAND

This refers to the number of different levels in the structure of the organisation, the chain, or lines, of hierarchical command sometimes known as the 'scalar chain'. The **chain of command** establishes the vertical graduation of authority and responsibility, and the framework for superior–subordinate relationships in an unbroken line down from the top of the organisation (*see* Figure 15.7). Every person must know their position within the structure of the organisation. Most organisation charts demonstrate that this principle is used widely as a basis for organisational design. A clear line of authority and responsibility is necessary for the effective operation of the organisation.

It seems to be generally accepted, however, that for reasons of morale and to help decision-making and communications there should be as few levels as possible in the chain of command. There is the danger of adding to the structure in such a way that it results in increased hierarchical authority and control, leads to the risk of empire building and the creation of unnecessary work in justification of the new position. If efforts are made to reduce the number of levels, however, this may bring about an increase in the span of control with the resulting difficulties already discussed. The design of structure necessitates, therefore, maintaining an appropriate balance between span of control and chain of command.

Need for a balanced structure

The combination of span of control and chain of command determines the overall pyramid shape of the organisation and whether the hierarchical structure is 'flat' or 'tall' (*see* Figure 15.7). The pyramid represents the structure of authority. Broader spans of control and few levels of authority result in a **flat hierarchical structure** as tends to be found, for example, in universities. Narrower spans of control and more levels of authority result in a **tall hierarchical structure** as tends to be found, for example, in the civil service or the armed forces. There is no one, ideal combination of span of control and scalar chain, which depends upon the particular situation for each organisation, but it is important to provide an appropriate, balanced structure.

Figure 15.7 How the span of control affects organisational structure

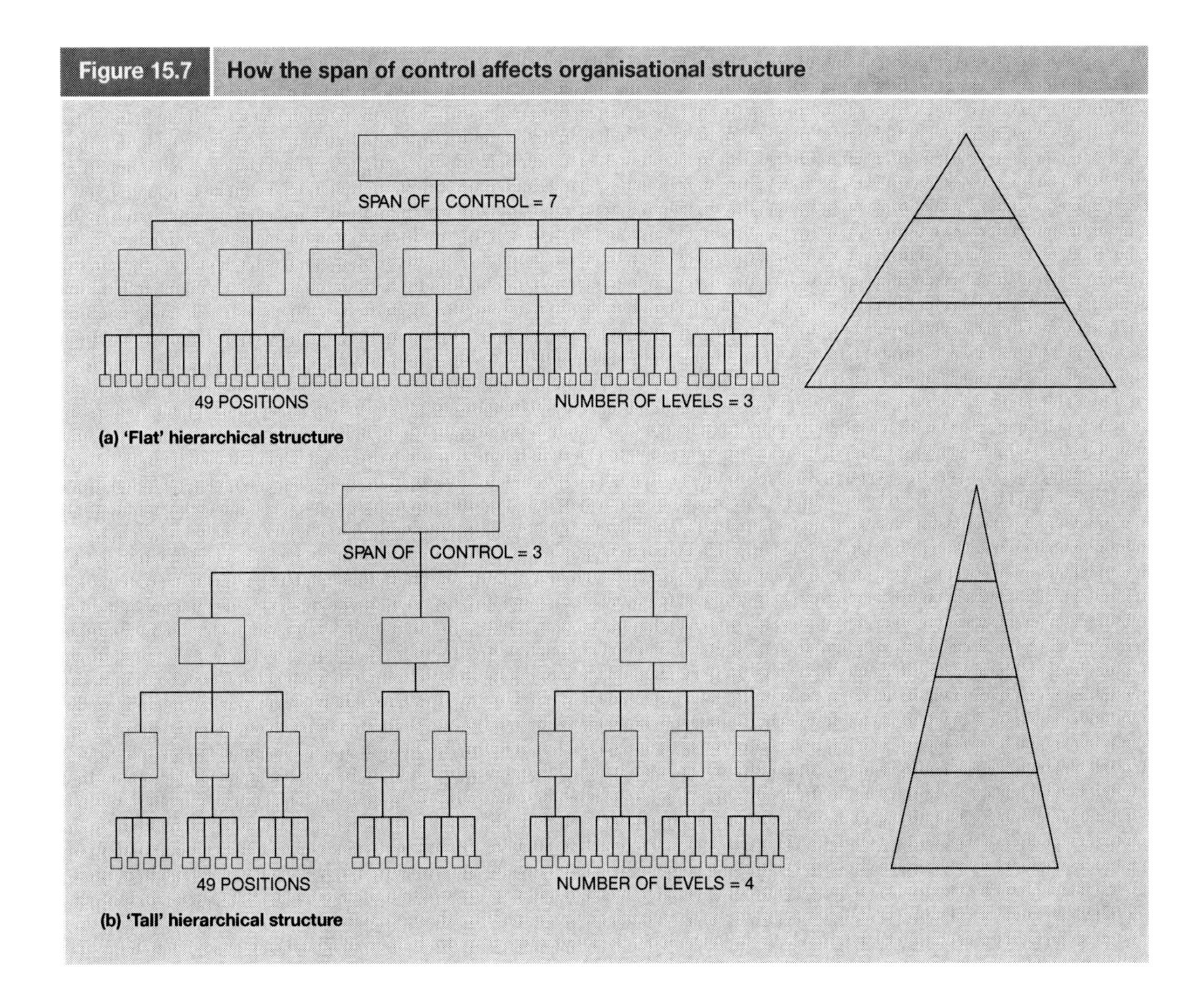

Information technology

An additional dimension of structural design is **information technology**. The impact of information technology will have significant effects on the structure, management and functioning of most organisations. It demands new patterns of work organisation and affects individual jobs, the formation and structure of groups, the nature of supervision and managerial roles. Information technology results in changes to lines of command and authority, and influences the need for restructuring the organisation and attention to job design. Computer-based information and decision-support systems influence choices in design of production or service activities, hierarchical structures and organisation of support staffs. Information technology may influence the centralisation/decentralisation of decision-making and control systems.

New technology has typically resulted in a 'flatter' organisational pyramid with fewer levels of management required. In the case of new office technology it allows the potential for staff at clerical/operator level to carry out a wider range of functions and to check their own work. The result is a change in the traditional supervisory function and a demand for fewer supervisors.

FORMAL ORGANISATIONAL RELATIONSHIPS

In any organisation structure certain formal relationships between individual positions will arise from the defined pattern of responsibilities. There is often confusion over the meaning of different terms and their implications for organisational structure, but these **individual authority relationships** may be identified as:

- line
- functional
- staff or
- lateral (*see* Figure 15.8).

The design of organisation structure in terms of the principle of line, functional, staff or lateral, determines the pattern of role relationships and interactions with other roles, discussed in Chapter 8.

Line relationships

In **line relationships**, authority flows vertically down through the structure – the chain of command – for example, from the managing director to managers, section leaders, supervisors and other staff. There is a direct relationship between superior and subordinate, with each subordinate responsible to only one person. Line relationships are associated with functional or departmental division of work and organisational control. Line managers have authority and responsibility for all matters and activities within their own department.

Functional relationships

Functional relationships apply to the relationship between people in specialist or advisory positions, and line managers and their subordinates. The specialist offers a common service throughout all departments of the organisation, but has no direct authority over those who make use of the service. For example, the human resources manager has no authority over staff in other departments – this is the responsibility of the line manager. However, as the position and role of the HR manager would have been sanctioned by top management, other staff might be expected to accept the advice which is given. The HR manager, however, could be assigned some direct, executive authority for certain specified responsibilities such as health and safety matters throughout the whole organisation. Note, however, that specialists in a functional relationship with other managers still have a line relationship with both their own superior and their own departmental subordinate staff.

Figure 15.8 Illustration of formal organisational relationships

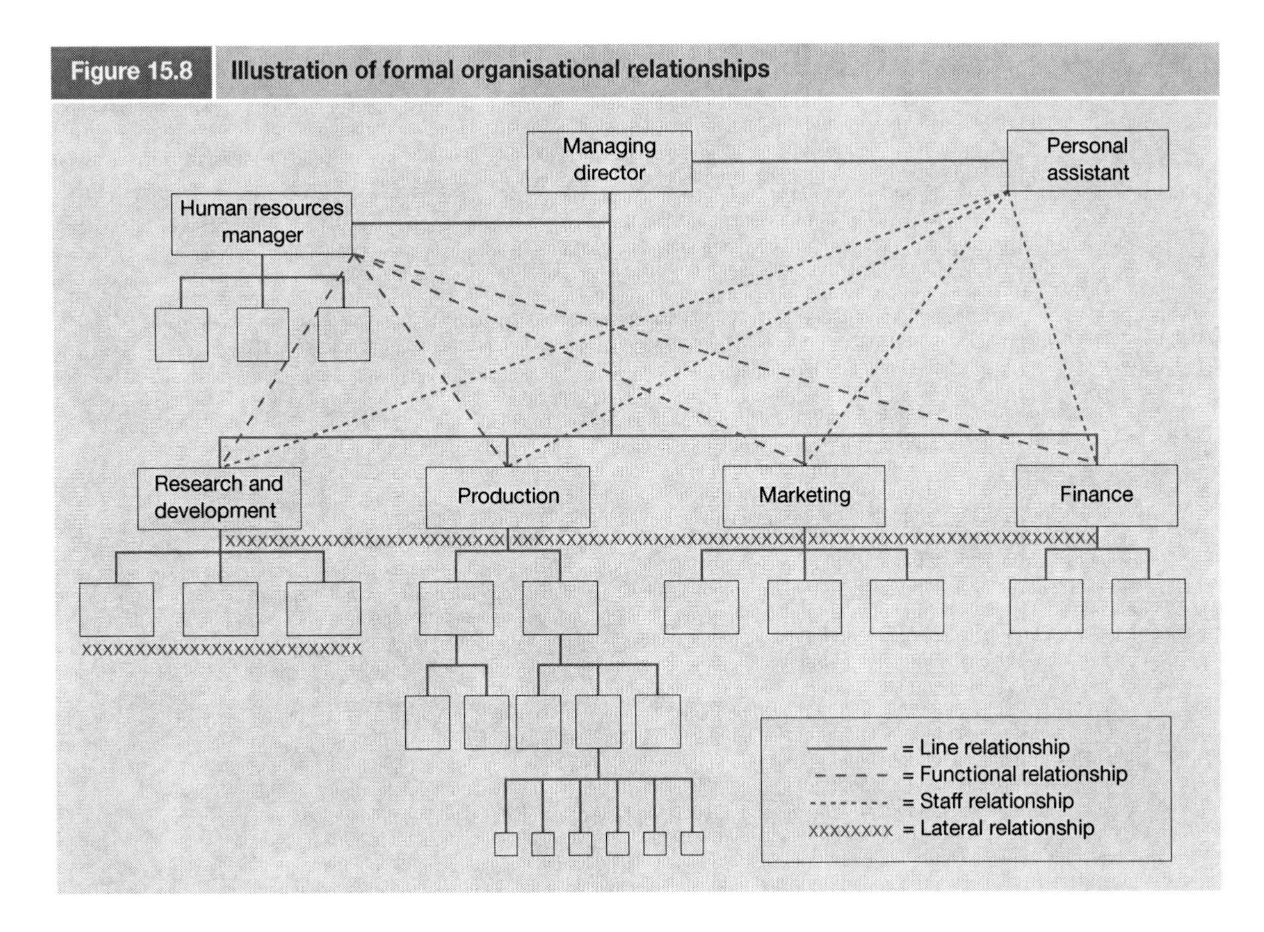

Staff relationships

Staff relationships arise from the appointment of personal assistants to senior members of staff. Persons in a staff position normally have little or no direct authority in their own right but act as an extension of their superior and exercise only 'representative' authority. They often act in a 'gatekeeper' role. There is no formal relationship between the personal assistant and other staff except where delegated authority and responsibility have been given for some specific activity. In practice, however, personal assistants often do have some influence over other staff, especially those in the same department or grouping. This may be partially because of the close relationship between the personal assistant and the superior, and partially dependent upon the knowledge and experience of the assistant, and the strength of the assistant's personality.

> *In business and governmental agencies, from doctors' offices to licensing and regulatory boards, one may come face to face with people who have established themselves as gatekeeper to the boss. Gatekeepers aspire to and are rewarded with various titles, like administrative assistant, office manager or special assistant to such-and-such. But the essential role is usually that of secretary to the boss ... Aspiring gatekeepers typically evoke polarised reactions among the office staff ... Peers, unlike the boss, quickly recognise the individual's lack of integrity and willingness to step on all toes en route to the position of guardian and the gate.*[33]

Lateral relationships

Lateral relationships exist between individuals in different departments or sections, especially individuals on the same level. These lateral relationships are based on contact and consultation and are necessary to maintain co-ordination and effective organisational performance. Lateral relationships may be specified formally but in practice they depend upon the co-operation of staff and in effect are a type of informal relationship.

LINE AND STAFF ORGANISATION

As organisations develop in size and work becomes more complex, the range of activities and functions undertaken increases. People with specialist knowledge have to be integrated into the managerial structure. Line and staff organisation is concerned with different functions that are to be undertaken. It provides a means of making full use of specialists while maintaining the concept of line authority. It creates a type of informal matrix structure (*see* Figure 15.9).

Line organisation relates to those functions concerned with specific responsibility for achieving the objectives of the organisation and to those people in the direct chain of command. **Staff organisation** relates to the provision of specialist and support functions for the line organisation and creates an advisory relationship. This is in keeping with the idea of

Figure 15.9 Representation of line and staff organisation

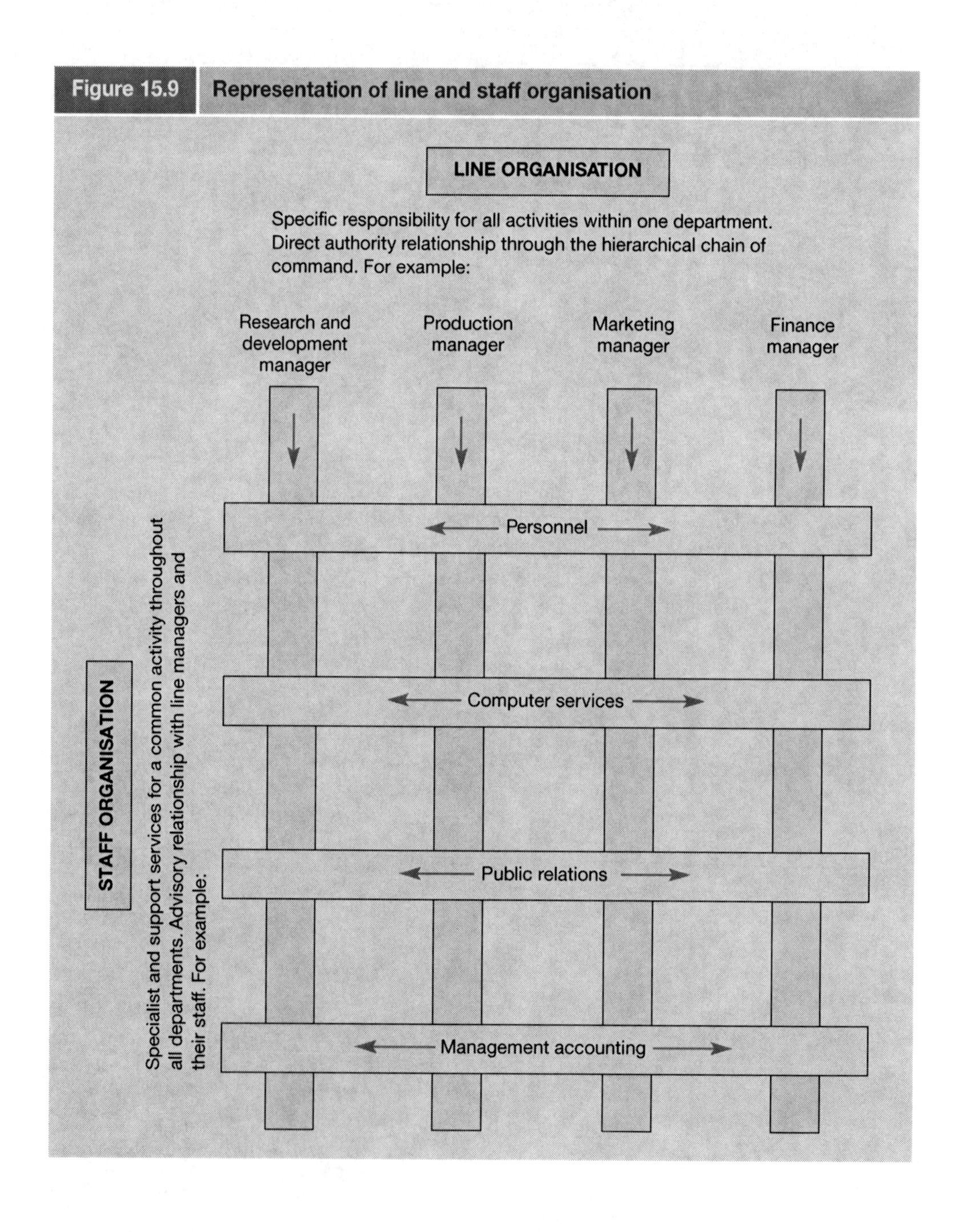

task and element functions discussed earlier. Again, confusion can arise from conflicting definitions of terminology. In the line and staff form of organisation, the individual authority relationship defined previously as 'functional' now becomes part of the actual structure under the heading of staff relationships.

Difficulties with line and staff relations

The concept of line and staff relations presents a number of difficulties. With the increasing complexity of organisations and the rise of specialist services it becomes harder to distinguish clearly between what is directly essential to the operation of the organisation, and what might be regarded only as an auxiliary function. The distinction between a line manager and a staff manager is not absolute. There may be a fine division between offering professional advice and the giving of instructions. Friction inevitably seems to occur between line and staff managers. Neither side may fully understand or appreciate the purpose and role of the other. Staff managers are often criticised for unnecessary interference in the work of the line manager and for being out of touch with practical realities. Line managers may feel that the staff managers have an easier and less demanding job because they have no direct responsibility for producing a product or providing a service for the customer, and are free from day-to-day operational problems.

Staff managers may feel that their difficulties and work problems are not appreciated fully by the line manager. Staff managers often complain about resistance to their attempts to provide assistance and co-ordination, and the unnecessary demands for departmental independence by line managers. A major source of difficulty is to persuade line managers to accept, and act upon, the advice and recommendations which are offered. The line and staff relationship can also give rise to problems of 'role incongruence', discussed in Chapter 8.

Internal marketing of staff departments

Clutterbuck suggests that a common feature of commercial life is staff departments, such as human resources and information technology, that have poor reputations with line managers. Even where line managers are clear what they want staff departments to do, they are rarely credited with initiative or much relevance to business objectives. In order to raise their profile, their perceived value and their contribution to the organisation there are a number of critical activities in the internal marketing of staff departments:

- understanding and responding effectively to the needs of internal customers;
- linking all the department's activities closely with the strategic objectives of the business;
- developing excellent communications and relationships with internal customers;
- ensuring internal customers' expectations are realistic; and
- continuously improving professionalism and capability in line with internal customers' needs.[34]

THE INVERTED ORGANISATION

Greater awareness of the importance of service delivery, total quality management and the continual search for competitive advantage has resulted in the concept of an inversion of the traditional hierarchical structure with customers at the summit and top management at the base. This will be accompanied by the devolution of power and delegation to the empowered, self-managing workers near the top of the inverted pyramid.[35]

> *In inverted organizations the line hierarchy becomes a support structure. The function of line managers becomes bottleneck breaking, culture development, consulting on request, expediting resource movements and providing service economies of scale. Generally, what was line management now performs essentially staff activities. The inverted organization poses certain unique challenges. The apparent loss of formal authority can be very traumatic for former line managers.*[36]

PROJECT TEAMS AND MATRIX ORGANISATION

The division of work and methods of grouping described earlier tend to be relatively permanent forms of structure. With the growth in newer, complex and technologically advanced systems it has become necessary for organisations to adapt traditional structures in order to provide greater integration of a wide range of functional activities. Although bureaucratic structures and hierarchies still exist in many organisations, increasing attention has been given to the creation of groupings based on project teams and matrix organisation. Members of staff from different departments or sections are assigned to the team for the duration of a particular project.

Project teams A project team may be set up as a separate unit on a temporary basis for the attainment of a particular task. When this task is completed the project team is disbanded or members of the unit are reassigned to a new task. Project teams may be used for people working together on a common task or to co-ordinate work on a specific project such as the design and development, production and testing of a new product; or the design and implementation of a new system or procedure. For example, project teams have been used in many military systems, aeronautics and space programmes. A project team is more likely to be effective when it has a clear objective, a well-defined task and a definite end-result to be achieved, and the composition of the team is chosen with care.

According to *Mann*, project-based working is as old as the pyramids but for increasing numbers of organisations it is very much the new way to do things. 'In today's leaner and meaner organisational set-up it seems that everything is a project and everyone a project worker.' Mann suggests two main drivers bringing about this change in the way work is managed. First, organisations have been stripped down to the core and resources are limited. Second, every area of the business has to contribute and be accountable as a cost centre. To be effective, projects require clarity at the outset, skills development, a supportive culture, managing communications and maintaining good working relationships.[37]

The matrix organisation

The matrix organisation is a combination of:

1 functional departments which provide a stable base for specialised activities and a permanent location for members of staff; and
2 units that integrate various activities of different functional departments on a project team, product, programme, geographical or systems basis. As an example, ICI is organised on matrix lines, by territory, function and business.

A **matrix structure** might be adopted in a university or college, for example, with grouping both by common subject specialism, and by association with particular courses or programmes of study. The matrix organisation therefore establishes a grid, or matrix, with a two-way flow of authority and responsibility (see Figure 15.10). Within the functional departments authority and responsibility flow vertically down the line, but the authority and responsibility of the 'project' manager (or course programme manager) flow horizontally across the organisation structure.

A matrix design might be adopted in the following circumstances:

1 **More than one critical orientation to the operations of the organisation**. For example, an insurance company has to respond simultaneously to both functional differentiation (such as life, fire, marine, motor) and to different geographical areas.
2 **A need to process simultaneously large amounts of information**. For example, a local authority social services department seeking help for an individual will need to know where to go for help from outside agencies (such as police, priest, community relations officer) and at the same time whom to contact from internal resources within the organisation (such as the appropriate social worker, health visitor or housing officer).

Figure 15.10 Outline of a matrix structure in a university

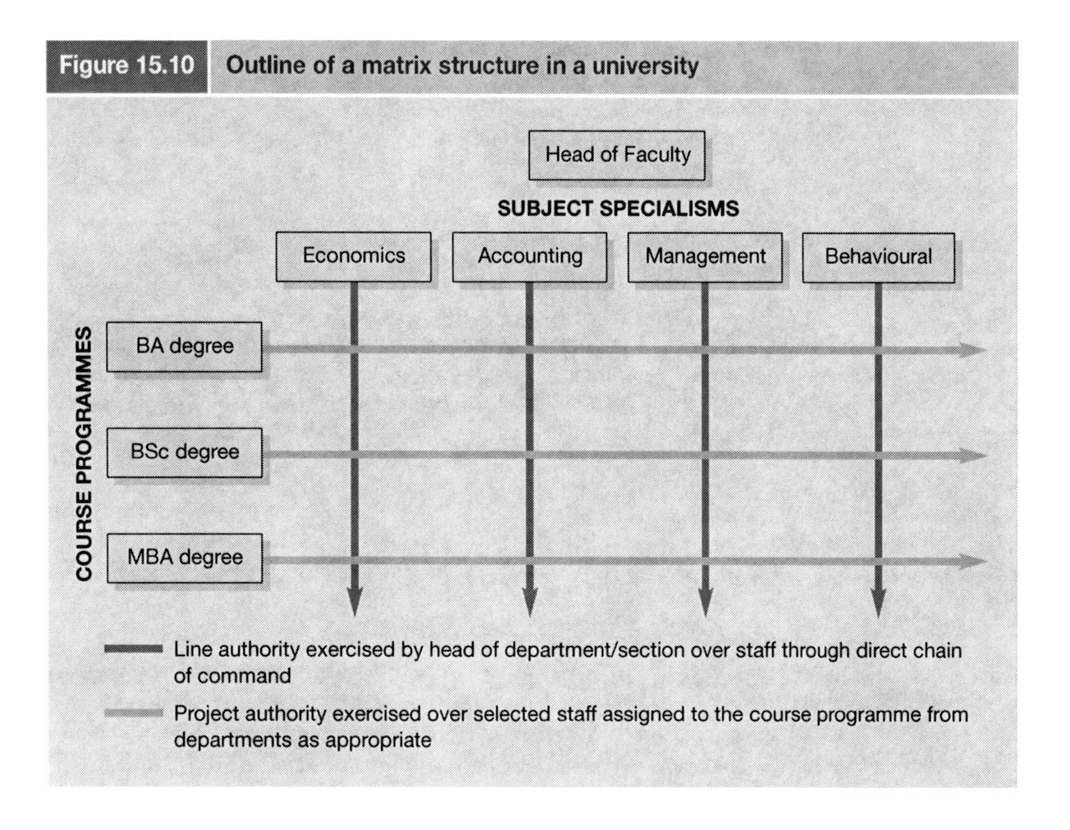

3 **The need for sharing of resources.** This could be justified only on a total organisational basis such as the occasional or part-time use by individual departments of specialist staff or services.

Developing an effective matrix organisation, however, takes time and a willingness to learn new roles and behaviour; this means that matrix structures are often difficult for management to implement effectively.[38]

Difficulties with matrix structures

Matrix organisation offers the advantages of flexibility, greater security and control of project information, and opportunities for staff development. There are, however, a number of potential difficulties and problem areas:

- There may be a limited number of staff reporting directly to the project manager with extra staff assigned as required by departmental managers. This may result in a feeling of ambiguity. Staff may be reluctant to accept constant change and prefer the organisational stability from membership of their own functional grouping.
- Matrix organisation can result in a more complex structure. By using two methods of grouping it sacrifices the unity of command and can cause problems of co-ordination.
- There may be a problem in defining the extent of the project manager's authority over staff from other departments and in gaining the support of other functional managers.
- Functional groups may tend to neglect their normal duties and responsibilities.

An underlying difficulty with matrix structures is that of divided loyalties and role conflict with individuals reporting simultaneously to two managers; this highlights the importance of effective teamwork. According to *Bartlett and Ghoshal,* matrix structures have proved all but unmanageable. Dual reporting leads to conflict and confusion; the proliferation of channels of communication creates informational log-jams; and overlapping responsibilities result in a loss of accountability.[39] And *Senior* makes the point that:

Matrix structures rely heavily on teamwork for their success, with managers needing high-level behavioural and people management skills. The focus is on solving problems through team action ... This type of organisational arrangement, therefore, requires a culture of co-operation, with supportive training programmes to help staff develop their teamworking and conflict-resolution skills.[40]

Critical reflection

'The idea of a matrix structure may appeal to those critical of a so-called prescriptive approach to organisational structure. But in reality a matrix structure is an unnecessary complication and creates more potential problems than it answers.' What do you think? What role do you believe the matrix structure serves?

EFFECTS OF A DEFICIENT ORGANISATION STRUCTURE

It is not easy to describe, in a positive manner, what constitutes a 'good' or effective organisation structure although, clearly, attention should be given to the design principles discussed above. However, the negative effects of a poorly designed structure can be identified more easily. In his discussion on the principles of organisation and co-ordination, *Urwick* suggests that 'lack of design is Illogical, Cruel, Wasteful and Inefficient'.

- It is **illogical** because in good social practice, as in good engineering practice, design should come first. No member of the organisation should be appointed to a senior position without identification of the responsibilities and relationships attached to that position and its role within the social pattern of the organisation.
- It is **cruel** because it is the individual members of the organisation who suffer most from lack of design. If members are appointed to the organisation without a clear definition of their duties or the qualifications required to perform those duties, it is these members who are likely to be blamed for poor results that do not match the vague ideas of what was expected of them.
- It is **wasteful** because if jobs are not put together along the lines of functional specialisation then new members of the organisation cannot be trained effectively to take over these jobs. If jobs have to be fitted to members of the organisation, rather than members of the organisation fitted to jobs, then every new member has to be trained in such a way as to aim to replace the special, personal experience of the previous job incumbent. Where both the requirements of the job and the member of the organisation are unknown quantities, this is likely to lead to indecision and much time wasted in ineffective discussion.
- It is **inefficient** because if the organisation is not founded on principles, managers are forced to fall back on personalities. Unless there are clearly established principles, which are understood by everyone in the organisation, managers will start 'playing politics' in matters of promotion and similar issues.

Urwick lays emphasis on the technical planning of the organisation and the importance of determining and laying out structure before giving any thought to the individual members of the organisation. Although Urwick acknowledges that the personal touch is important and part of the obvious duty of the manager, it is not a substitute for the need for definite planning of the structure.

In short, a very large proportion of the friction and confusion in current society, with its manifest consequences in human suffering, may be traced back directly to faulty organisation in the structural sense.[41]

Consequences of badly designed structure

Urwick's emphasis on the logical design of organisation structure rather than the development around the personalities of its members is typical of the classical approach to organisation and management. Despite this rather narrow view, more recent writers have drawn similar conclusions as to the consequences of badly designed structure.

Child points out that:

> *Certain problems arise time and time again in struggling companies. Even at the best of times they can point to incipient dangers that have to be dealt with. Deficiencies in organisation can play a part in exacerbating each of these problems. High on the list are (1) low motivation and morale, (2) late and inappropriate decisions, (3) conflict and lack of co-ordination,(4) a generally poor response to new opportunities and external change, and (5) rising costs.*[42]

Child then goes on to explain the consequences of structural deficiencies.

- **Low motivation and morale** may result from: apparently inconsistent and arbitrary decisions; insufficient delegation of decision-making; lack of clarity in job definition and assessment of performance; competing pressures from different parts of the organisation; and managers and supervisors overloaded through inadequate support systems.
- **Late and inappropriate decisions** may result from: lack of relevant, timely information to the right people; poor co-ordination of decision-makers in different units; overloading of decision-makers due to insufficient delegation; and inadequate procedures for re-evaluation of past decisions.
- **Conflict and lack of co-ordination** may result from: conflicting goals and people working at cross-purposes because of lack of clarity on objectives and activities; failure to bring people together into teams or through lack of liaison; and lack of effective systems for communicating the modification of tasks.
- **Poor response to new opportunities and external change** may result from: failure to establish specialist jobs concerned with forecasting environmental change; failure to give adequate attention to innovation and planning of change as main management activities; inadequate use of teamwork and attention to relevant aspects of new projects.
- **Rising costs** may result from: a long hierarchy of authority with a high proportion of senior positions; an excess of rules, procedures and administrative work at the expense of productive work; and the presence of some, or all, of the other organisational problems.

Shortcomings in structure may also provide greater opportunities for the illicit activities of staff. For example, the collapse of Britain's oldest merchant bank, Barings, and the activities of 'rogue trader' Nick Leeson were made more straightforward by the major reorganisation and expanded structure of the Barings empire.[43]

ORGANISATION CHARTS

The structure of an organisation is usually depicted in the form of an organisation chart. This will show, at a given moment in time, how work is divided and the grouping together of activities, the levels of authority and formal organisational relationships. The organisation chart provides a pictorial representation of the overall shape and structural framework of an organisation. Some charts are very sketchy and give only a minimum amount of information. Other charts give varying amounts of additional detail such as an indication of the broad nature of duties and responsibilities of the various units.

Charts are usually displayed in a traditional, vertical form such as those already depicted in Figures 15.7 and 15.8 above. They can, however, be displayed either horizontally with the information reading from left to right, or concentrically with top management at the centre. The main advantage of both the horizontal and the concentric organisation charts is that they tend to reduce the indication of superior or subordinate status. They also offer the practical advantage of more space on the outer margin. In addition, the concentric chart may help to depict the organisation more as a unified whole. Organisation charts are useful in explaining the outline structure of an organisation. They may be used as a basis for the analysis and review of structure, for training and management succession, and for formulating changes. The chart may indicate **apparent weaknesses** in structure such as, for example:

- too wide a span of control;
- overlapping areas of authority;
- lack of unity of command;
- too long a chain of command;
- unclear reporting relationships and/or lines of communication;
- unstaffed functions.

Probably the most immediate and accessible way to describe any formal organisation is to outline its structure. For the student of organisations, knowledge of its structure is indispensable as a first step to understanding the processes which occur within it. When asked to describe their organisation, managers will frequently sketch an organisation chart to show how their organisation 'works'.[44]

Limitations of organisation charts

There are, however, a number of limitations with traditional organisation charts. They depict only a static view of the organisation, and show how it looks and what the structure should be. Charts do not show the comparative authority and responsibility of positions on the same level, or lateral contacts and informal relations. Neither do charts show the extent of personal delegation from superior to subordinates, or the precise relationships between line and staff positions. Organisation charts can become out of date quickly and are often slow to be amended to reflect changes in the actual structure.

Despite these limitations, the organisation chart can be a valuable and convenient way of illustrating the framework of structure – **provided the chart is drawn up in a comprehensible form**. There is always the question of what the chart does not show and what the observer interprets from it. There are a number of conventions in drawing up organisation charts. It is not the purpose here to go into specific details, but it is important to remember that the chart should always give:

- the date when it was drawn up;
- the name of the organisation, branch or department (as appropriate) to which it refers;
- whether it is an existing or proposed structure;
- the extent of coverage, for example if it refers to the management structure only, or if it excludes servicing departments;
- a reference to identify the person who drew up the chart.

While acknowledging that organisation charts have some uses, Townsend likens them to 'rigor mortis' and advises that they should be drawn in pencil.

Never formalize, print and circulate them. Good organisations are living bodies that grow new muscles to meet challenges. A chart demoralizes people. Nobody thinks of himself as below other people. And in a good company he isn't. Yet on paper there it is ... In the best organizations people see themselves working in a circle as if around one table.[45]

A summary of formal organisations and organisation charts is set out in the concept map in Figure 15.11.

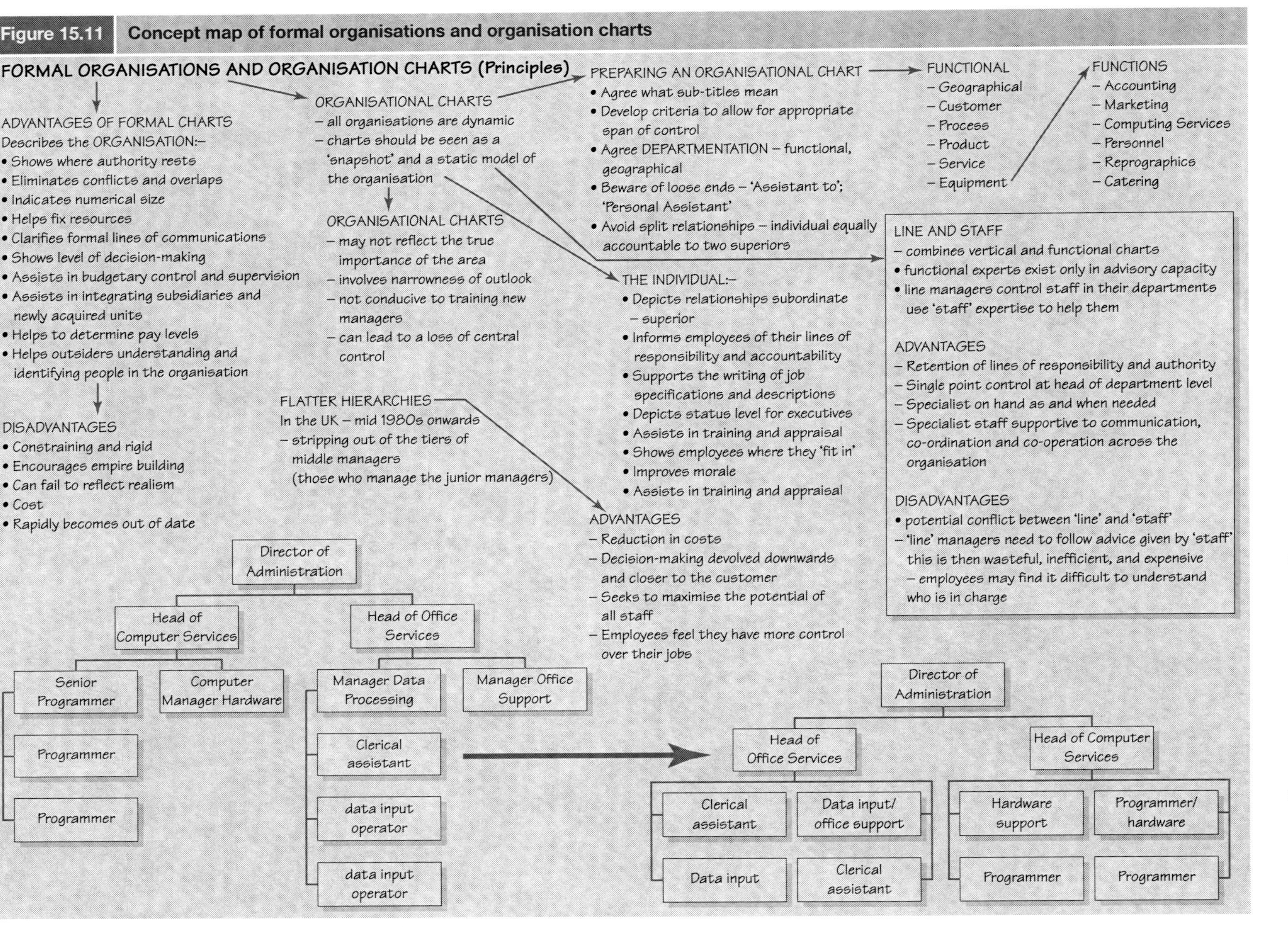

Figure 15.11 Concept map of formal organisations and organisation charts

Source: Training Learning Consultancy Ltd, Bristol, England. Reproduced with permission.

STRUCTURE AND ORGANISATIONAL BEHAVIOUR

It is clear, then, that it is essential to give full attention to the structure and design of an organisation. However, this is not always an easy task.

> *Designing structures which achieve a balance between co-operation and competition, which combine team behaviours and individual motivation, is one of the hardest parts of building organisations – or designing economic systems.*[46]

Structuring an organisation involves balancing a series of trade-offs.[47] In analysing the effectiveness of structure, consideration should be given to both the formal and technological requirements and principles of design and to social factors and the needs and demands of the human part of the organisation. Structure should be designed so as to maintain the balance of the socio-technical system and to encourage the willing participation of members and effective organisational performance.

> *An organisation can be separated into two parts or structures which can then be examined. One section is a definable structure that will be present in every company, the other is the structure caused by human intervention. The latter provides the company with its distinctive appearance, and may be regarded as the manager's particular response to the design requirements of organised behaviour. Essentially the effectiveness of an organisation depends on how accurately human design matches the structure of organised behaviour.*[48]

'Realities' of organisational behaviour

The structure or charts do not describe what really happens in work organisations. For example, as *Watson* points out, a systems-control framing of organisations tends to take for granted that managerially designed structures and cultures more or less make organisations what they are. Account must be taken of both official and unofficial aspects of structure and culture.

> *An important element of the struggle for management control is one of the coming to terms with the fact that the formal or official arrangements that managers make when they 'design' organisations do not work out as expected, in practice.*[49]

To conclude our discussion we need to remind ourselves of the 'realities' of organisational behaviour and of points made in previous chapters. Rarely do all members of an organisation behave collectively in such a way as to represent the behaviour of the organisation as a whole. In practice, we are referring to the behaviour of individuals, or sections or groups of people, within the organisation. Human behaviour is capricious and prescriptive methods or principles cannot be applied with reliability. Individuals differ and people bring their own perceptions, feelings and attitudes towards the organisation, styles of management and their duties and responsibilities. The behaviour of people cannot be studied in isolation and we need to understand interrelationships with other variables that comprise the total organisation, including the social context of the work organisation and the importance of the informal organisation. The behaviour and actions of people at work will also be influenced by a complexity of motivations, needs and expectations.

Gray and Starke provide a humorous but perhaps realistic illustration of how an organisation actually works (*see* Figure 15.12).[50]

Heller also refers to:

> *the gap between the aims of big company organisations and what actually happens. Organisational form and organisational behaviour are not one and the same thing.*[51]

The changing world of organisations and management

Birchall refers to the changing world of organisations and its impact on management. As a consequence of factors such as global competition, the convergence of information and communications technology, the emergence of the digital economy, recession in most Western economies, the emergence of customer power and changing political philosophy, much of the work undertaken by middle management no longer requires the considerable layers of management. Tasks that used to take up a great deal of management time in hierarchical structures are now possible with minimal supervision or intervention. Much of the organisation's work is carried out in projects. Many managers will find themselves managing people who spend much of their time outside the office. There is a strong move towards the use of consultants. Managers will need to be familiar with electronic networks, the operation of dispersed teams and virtual organisations.[52]

Birchall draws attention to management as no longer the sole prerogative of an elite group called managers. The functions of management are being much more widely shared within an enterprise and possibly the greatest potential in managing complex organisations lies in releasing the organisation's creative capabilities. A similar point is made by *Cloke and Goldsmith* who maintain that management is an idea whose time is up and the days of military command structures are over.

> *Rather than building fixed structures with layers of middle management, many innovative organisations function as matrixed webs of association, networks, and fast-forming high-performance teams ... The most significant trends we see in the theory and history of management are the decline of the hierarchical, bureaucratic, autocratic management and the expansion of collaborative self-management and organisational democracy.*[53]

Figure 15.12 How the organisation should be compared with how it actually works

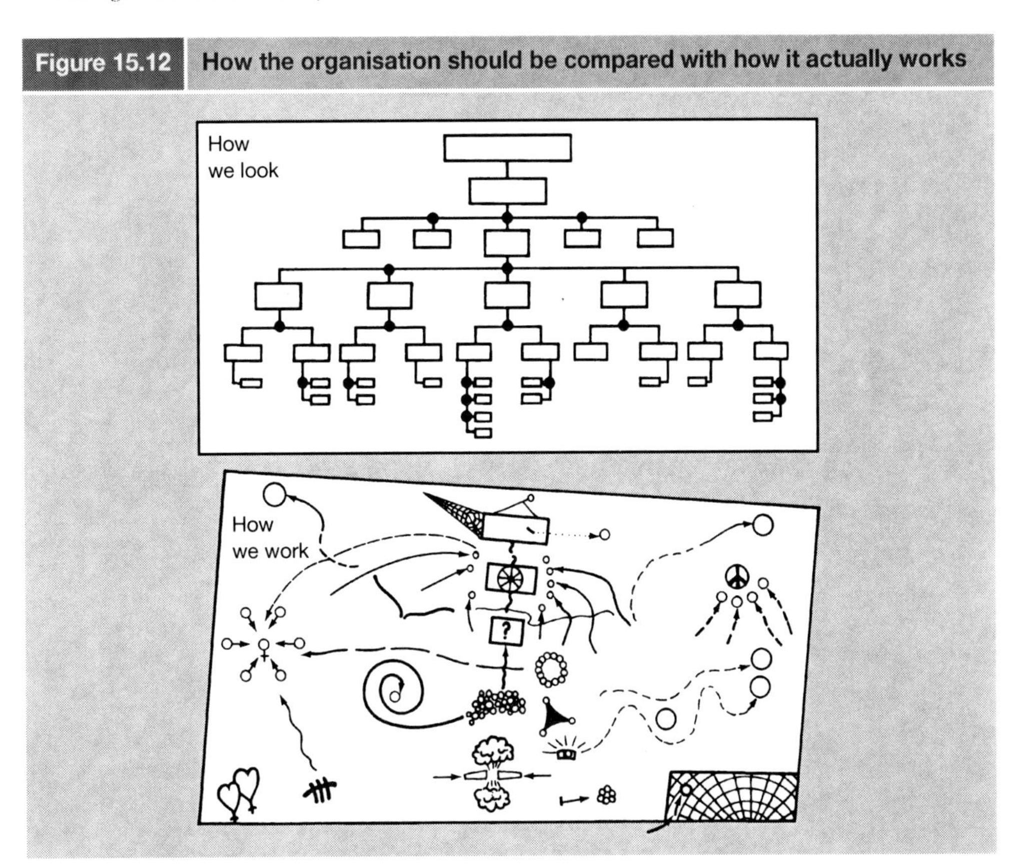

Source: Gray, J. L. and Starke, F. A., *Organisational Behaviour: Concepts and Applications*, Fourth Edition, Merrill Publishing Company (1988), p. 431. Reproduced with permission from Pearson Education, Inc.

Refresh your understanding
Activity 15D
www.pearsoned.co.uk/mullins

Critical reflection

'Given the changing nature of organisations, the formal structure is unimportant. The only thing that really matters is whether individuals know what is expected of them, work well with other people and perform their tasks successfully.' Do you agree? What do you see as the purpose and importance of structural design for modern work organisations?

MANAGEMENT IN THE NEWS

Freewheeling at Google

Can Google's random genius last?

Simon London

Googlemania has been in full swing for more than a year. Unless you devote your life to the subject, you have probably struggled to keep pace with the adventures of Sergey, Larry and their hoard of gifted geeks. You might even be asking yourself: do I really care? There are two important reasons why you should. The first has to do with Google's business model, the second with how the world's most written about company is run.

What does the original search engine have in common with Gmail, Google News, Google Earth and the myriad other services to have poured forth from Mountain View, California? They are all piped to your computer via the Internet and they are all free, in the sense of being funded by targeted advertising. Thus Google has found a way to turn almost anything you look at on your computer screen into advertising-supported media.

For traditional media companies, including the Financial Times, this is worrisome. Advertisers suddenly have a nifty new way to spend their money. For software companies – notably, but not only, Microsoft – the implications are super-scary: why should consumers pay for software if Google and its imitators can provide the basics (word processing, email, calendars, spreadsheets) for free? Perhaps even more significant than the business model, however, is the way Google is run. The company is reluctant to let management journalists roam freely around the Googleplex, but it seems to be engaged in nothing less than a giant experiment in 'emergence'.

Management gurus have for years been telling companies to abandon the traditional top–down, process-driven approach to strategy. Harness the imagination of employees, they exhort. Do not be afraid to experiment. Create an internal market for ideas. Place bets. Build a 'portfolio' of initiatives from which a winning strategy can emerge.

Yet old habits die hard. The strategic planning process remains an annual ritual. Chief executives talk about the need to experiment, then mete out punishment when experiments go wrong, or fail to champion unconventional projects when it matters most. Now compare that with Google, where software engineers can spend up to 20 per cent of their time on projects of their own choosing ... since when did big companies allow such latitude? Imagine what delights might result if General Motors followed suit.

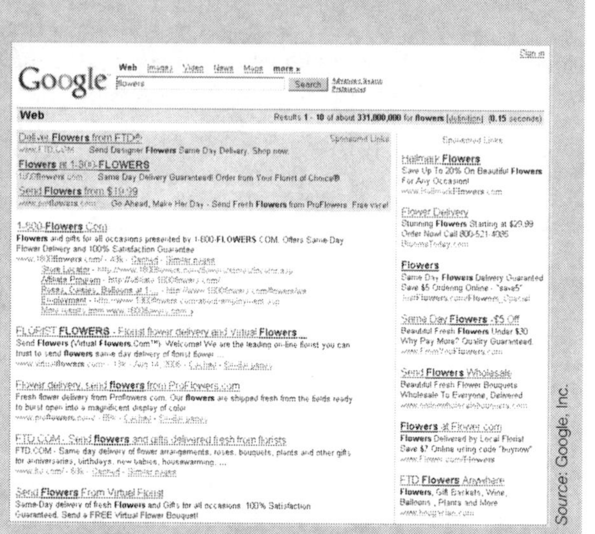

Source: Google, Inc.

Giving employees freedom to choose their own projects has expanded Google from a search engine to a provider of countless services across the globe.

Command-and-control managers will respond that such practices are a recipe for slacking and wasted resources. A more enlightened interpretation is that Google is trying to harness the collective wisdom of employees about how resources should be allocated. Interesting projects attract talent, irrespective of whether they have been sanctioned by top management. While some initiatives at Google seem to be driven from the top, the company remains open to the possibility that internal market forces will come up with better decisions than committees.

None of this implies that Google is free from the normal headaches of project management. Froogle, its online shopping search service, has been in beta for so long that it is a standing Silicon Valley joke. Nor does its riotous run imply that the emergent approach will continue to deliver results. What works for a few dozen or even a few hundred programmers may not produce results in an international company of several thousand employees. The business model may have almost limitless potential, but will the organisation scale? This, as of the time of writing, is a $126bn (£71bn) question.

Source: London, S., 'Can Google's random genius last?', *Financial Times*, 31 January 2006.

Discussion questions

1 Critically examine the extent to which Google's approach supports the idea that 'management is an idea whose time is up' as outlined in the final quote of the chapter.

2 Outline the implications for managers of adopting a 'freewheeling' approach that allows organisational strategy to emerge from the workforce rather than being a choice made by organisational chiefs. Identify the benefits and problems that would occur in transferring such an approach to other types of organisation, for instance those in the public sector.

SYNOPSIS

- Structure provides the framework of an organisation and makes possible the application of the process of management. The structure of an organisation affects not only productivity and economic efficiency but also the morale and job satisfaction of its members. The overall effectiveness of the organisation will be influenced both by sound structural design, and by the behaviour of people who work within the structure. Attention must be given to integrating the structural and technological requirements of the organisation, and the needs and demands of the human part of the organisation.

- Some structure is necessary to make possible the effective performance of key activities and to support the efforts of staff. Organisations are layered and within the hierarchical structure there are three broad, interrelated levels: technical, managerial and community. The changing nature of the work organisation has led to discussion on the role of the hierarchy, the traditional boss–subordinate relationship and the extent to which managers can rely solely on their perceived formal authority within the structure of the organisation. However, although the hierarchy has changed its form, arguably it is not dead.

- There are many variables and situational factors which influence the most appropriate structure. However, there is an underlying need to establish a framework of order and system of command through which the activities of the organisation can be planned, organised, directed and controlled. This demands attention to certain basic considerations in the design of organisation structure. Although this may appear a prescriptive approach, it still presents management with a series of important decision points.

- The essence of structure is the division of work among members of the organisation, the co-ordination of activities and different jobs related to each other. Work can be divided and activities linked in a number of ways. Most organisations will contain examples of alternative combinations for grouping activities and relating different jobs to each other. A critical decision point arising from division of work and grouping of activities is the extent of centralisation and decentralisation.

- A particular form of relationship that can cause difficulty is the line and staff organisation, and the integration of people with specialist knowledge into the managerial structure. With the need to provide integration of a wide range of functional activities, greater attention has been given to more flexible forms of structure, such as project teams and matrix organisation. There are, however, a number of potential difficulties with matrix structures.

- A badly designed structure can have a number of negative effects and is likely to give rise to inefficiency, low motivation and morale, late and inappropriate decisions, conflict, rising costs and lack of development. The structure of an organisation is depicted usually in the form of a chart although there are a number of limitations with traditional organisation charts. It is important to remember relationships between structure and the realities of organisational behaviour. Some writers draw attention to the changing world of management and organisational democracy.

Refresh your understanding, assess your progress and begin your research with online resources at **www.pearsoned.co.uk/mullins**

REVIEW AND DISCUSSION QUESTIONS

1 What are the objectives of organising? To what extent do you think there are different levels in the hierarchical structure of an organisation?

2 What is the importance of good structure? How does structure relate to the overall effectiveness of an organisation? Discuss critically the continuing importance of the hierarchy.

3 Explain the main factors to be considered in the design of organisation structure. Debate critically the value of 'principles' of organisation.

4 Distinguish clearly between 'span of control' and 'chain of command'. Discuss the practical implications for the structure and effective operation of a large organisation.

5 Prepare your own diagrams to help explain: (i) line and staff organisation, and (ii) a matrix form of organisation structure. What are the reasons for adopting each of these forms of structure and what problem areas might arise?

6 To what extent would you agree with the contention that a logical structure for organisation is better for efficiency and morale than a structure allowed to develop around personalities? What are the likely consequences of a poorly designed structure?

7 Debate critically how the 'realities' of organisational behaviour influence organisation structure and design. Give your own examples.

8 What are *your* views on the idea of 'the end of management and the rise of organisational democracy'?

ASSIGNMENT 1

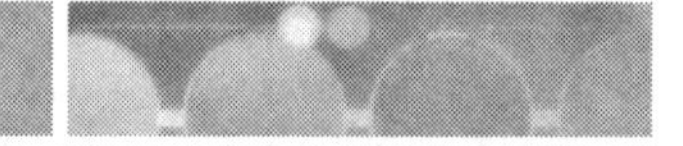

Examine closely arrangements for the division of work and linking together of activities in your own or some other organisation of your choice.

a Investigate and make notes on the variety of ways in which work is divided and combinations for grouping of activities within the organisation.

b Comment critically on the apparent effectiveness of different methods adopted for the division of work among members of the organisation.

c Give reasons, together with practical examples, in support of your comments.

d Explain fully changes you would recommend in order to help improve organisational performance. Where appropriate, prepare a revised, or a new, organisation chart.

ASSIGNMENT 2

Checklist for symtoms of organisational deficiencies

Read through the questionnaire and tick the questions (if any) for which you answer 'yes' for (1) your organisation as a whole and (2) your team or unit within it.

Symptoms	*Your organisation*	*Your team or unit*
Do morale and motivation seem noticeably low?	☐	☐
Do decisions seem inconsistent and arbitrary, without reference to rules or criteria?	☐	☐
Are people unclear about what is expected of them and how their contribution might be assessed?	☐	☐
Do people perceive they have too little responsibility and opportunity for achievement?	☐	☐
Are individuals subject to competing pressures from different parts of the organisation?	☐	☐
Are people overloaded?	☐	☐
Is decision-making delayed and lacking in quality?	☐	☐
Does vital information fail to reach decision-makers in time?	☐	☐
Are decision-makers segregated in separate units with insufficient co-ordination of their activities?	☐	☐
Are decision-makers overloaded because they have failed to delegate sufficiently?	☐	☐
Are there inadequate procedures for evaluating the results of similar decisions made in the past?	☐	☐
Is there noticeable conflict and lack of co-ordination?	☐	☐
Do individuals or groups have conflicting goals that are not in line with overall organisational objectives and priorities?	☐	☐
Have opportunities been missed for co-ordinating people's activities by forming teams or other ways of ensuring liaison between them?	☐	☐
Are systems lacking for ensuring that information on operational changes is communicated adequately to other parts of the company?	☐	☐
Does the organisation fail to respond innovatively to changing circumstances?	☐	☐
Is it no one's special responsibility to monitor change that is going on outside the organisation?	☐	☐
Do innovation and the planning of change get inadequate support from the top?	☐	☐
Is there inadequate co-ordination between the people who can identify new opportunites and those who might be able to develop ways of satisfying them (for example, between sales and R&D)?	☐	☐
Are costs rising (over and above inflation), especially in the administrative areas?	☐	☐
Does the organisation have too many managers and too few people carrying out the work?	☐	☐
Is there too much procedure and paperwork, distracting people from productive work and requiring additional administrative staff?	☐	☐

Source: From Child, J., *Organization: Contemporary Principles and Practice*, Blackwell Publishing (2005), p. 22. Reproduced with permission from Blackwell Publishing, Ltd.

a After completing the checklist compare your responses with colleagues.

b What conclusions did you draw from this exercise?

PERSONAL AWARENESS AND SKILLS EXERCISE

Objectives

Completing this exercise should help you to enhance the following skills:

- Depict how organisations are represented formally by charts.
- Explore the complex patterns of interrelationships that exist below the surface.
- Distinguish between how organisations look and how they actually work.

Exercise

Using the pictorial example in Figure 15.12 and working in small self-selecting groups, you are required to:

1. Refer to an organisation with which you are familiar (or a department of a large organisation) and obtain or draw a formal 'How we look' organisation chart.
2. Identify key people in the organisation and interview them informally. From your discussions and own observations draw an alternative 'How we work' organisation chart.
3. Detail the significant variables that impact upon the alternative chart and give an honest evaluation of how realistic you believe your chart to be.
4. Using you 'How we work' chart as a visual aid be prepared to give a short presentation to the class describing clearly how the organisation ACTUALLY works.

Discussion

- How difficult was it for you to find out what is 'really going on' in the organisation?
- How would you explain the differences between the two charts? What actual or potential difficulties do you foresee?
- Is there ever such a thing as a 'real' and 'factual' view of organisations?

CASE STUDY

Zara: a dedicated follower of fashion

The retail fashion industry is probably one of the most fast-moving and fickle businesses that can be imagined. The whole process of predicting next season's colours, fabrics, styles and hemlines is partly determined by the creativity of the major fashion designers, and the reports from the catwalk shows of Paris, Milan or London are expected to set a trend six months or so ahead. The reality of what most people buy, however, is usually more mundane than the fantastic, occasionally shocking, items that parade before the assembled press and celebrities at the spring or autumn shows. On the high street, sales of a genuinely trendy item can be hit dramatically by such uncontrollable factors as the weather, and demand is easily influenced by the whims of celebrities, or even politicians (in 2002 Teresa May, chairman of the UK opposition Tory party, became an unlikely trendsetter when the press noticed her wearing a pair of leopard-print kitten-heeled shoes).[54]

The business, therefore, of selling the image and the clothing of the moment is a complex one. The organisational structures which support the retail fashion industry are heavily focused on two main tasks: making reliable predictions about design trends and then achieving cost reduction in the production process. To achieve these cost reductions, most fashion businesses source both raw materials and finished products globally. The production of cotton cloth, for instance, is now firmly situated in lower-cost economies such as Turkey, India and China. To spread the risk and achieve further cost savings, fashion chains generally outsource many aspects of their business, particularly the garment manufacturing and distribution operations, to separate supply companies. Often other more creative aspects, such as the design of clothing ranges, are

Zara's unusual organisational structure keeps it well ahead of the latest trends in high street fashion.

contracted to individual designers or fashion houses. Designer George Davies, who founded the fashion chain Next, has created successful clothing ranges for both Asda and Marks & Spencer, and Stella McCartney was commissioned to design a range for H&M in 2005.

The industry standard time to get a newly designed and approved range of clothing into high street stores is somewhere between six and nine months.[55] The whole process therefore involves a high degree of risk; misinterpretation of this highly ephemeral market can lead to serious under- or over-stocking of a particular design or product, and the company will suffer substantial loss of revenue either through loss of custom, or by having to sell off failed lines cheaply or through discount or 'outlet' stores. Occasionally the whole business can be de-railed by politics, as happened during the so-called 'bra wars' incident in the summer of 2005. Between 70 and 80 million items of Chinese-made clothing were subject to quotas and a European Union trade embargo after the EU and China had failed to negotiate a replacement for the Multi-Fibre Agreement which had ended in January 2005. Retailers became increasingly anxious as their autumn ranges spent several weeks stockpiled in European ports and warehouses instead of making their way to the shops. One company which has designed itself to minimise risks such as these is the Spanish textile and clothing company Inditex, whose most well-known outlet is Zara.

The Galician way

Amancio Ortega founded the textile company which was to become Inditex in the 1960s in the city of La Coruña in the Galicia region of northern Spain. He opened his first fashion retail store in the same city in 1975 and by the turn of the millennium it had grown to become a worldwide enterprise with a turnover of €1615 million and over 30000 employees.[56] In addition to Zara, the Inditex group comprises other brands such as Pull & Bear (young men's fashion), Massimo Dutti and Often (which pitch at the quality end of the market), Oysho (lingerie), Tempe (shoes) and Bershka and Kiddy's Class for teenagers and young children. The Zara arm of the business has outlets across the world from Austria to Venezuela, and in March 2006 reported a 26 per cent rise in profits for the previous year (four times that of its Swedish rival H&M) as well as plans to open well over 400 new outlets during 2006, thus continuing to expand at roughly the same speed as it had during 2005. By any measure, this has been a fast-growing and profitable business in a market characterised by high risk and where there are already many well-established, dominant global brands.

There are many reasons for the extraordinary effectiveness of Zara in the capricious and frenetic world of high street fashion. Analysts have suggested that some of its key attributes are geographically specific.[57] Galicia had a limited textile industry prior to the 1970s and when the regional and national governments in Spain decided to boost domestic textile production in the area, the developments took the Galician industry in a different direction to that followed in other more traditional Spanish textile-producing areas. The main difference was a tendency to integrate design, production, logistics and sales within companies rather than, as is common elsewhere, to separate and outsource these different business elements. Ortega's creation was typical of the region and this very commitment to the principle of vertical integration (keeping control of all major operations) is what has underpinned Zara's success.

But control, in this case, does not mean rigidity. In order to achieve its business aim of adapting constantly to the demands of the market, the company deliberately rejected rigid organisational structures in favour of a more flexible approach. As has been noted already, and unlike many of its rivals, it has not attempted to achieve this by extensive use of subcontracting. Instead, its flexibility comes from the use of a highly integrated, fast and efficient form of communication between its global network of outlets and the central hub of operations in Spain, combined with possibly one of the most sophisticated just-in-time (JIT) operations in the world. As mentioned above, the industry average time for bringing a design into the shops is somewhere between six and nine months. Zara routinely achieves this task in 3–4 weeks. In his 2004 book, James Surowiecki describes the Zara operation in New York as follows:

Every Tuesday and Saturday in SoHo, a big truck pulls to the curb on the east side of Broadway to have its cargo unloaded. From out of the truck emerge ... stacks of dress shirts in soft colors, slim-cut black skirts, and elegant women's jackets that look – from a distance – like they just came off a Milan runway. All the pieces of clothing have two things in common. They come from a million-square-foot warehouse owned by a company called Zara, in the town of La Coruña ... And, in all likelihood, three weeks before they were unloaded, they weren't even a glint in their designers' eyes.[58]

Managing a fashion laboratory

Unlike other companies which design and order their clothing ranges many months in advance, then stock up distribution centres with about three months' supply ahead of expected sales, Zara makes only what is selling at the moment. Its design team is based in La Coruña (other Inditex brand designers are based in Barcelona and Alicante) and with its hi-tech and highly integrated manufacturing centres close by, individual designers can see their creations turned into small batches of finished products within days and shipped out to stores within a few weeks. If the design sells well, more is produced and shipped out; if it flops, the company has lost very little as the volume of remaindered items is small and the design is scrapped. This small batch production process can enhance sales, as customers snap up eye-catching items quickly in case they aren't there tomorrow. As the recruitment page for fashion designers on the company website explains:

At Inditex collections are launched to enrich every week with new designs and proposals that improve our product offer. We re-invent trends because we adapt them to what our customers want, and win the battle of the very latest style.[59]

The close integration of design, production and logistics is only part of the story. The other crucial element in the company's design is the role of the stores, and in particular the store managers. Inditex describes its stores as 'fashion laboratories'.

They are where customers tell us what they want to wear. We listen to their opinions and tastes, and the store team passes it on to us. With this valuable information our fashion industry swings into action to offer our customers new items every week. Thanks to our store teams we have changed the rules of the fashion game ... [they are] *... teams of entrepreneurs with initiative, who take fashion into the streets every day.*

Store assistants and managers constantly collect information about what is selling and how quickly it leaves the racks, meaning that local managers have a strong influence on the success of their stores and thus the company overall. If customers are asking for items in a different colour, or want certain styles that they can't find, their comments are recorded on hand-held computers, and a digest of both sales and customer feedback is transmitted daily to Zara HQ to alert the designers to trends. This degree of flexibility also allows Zara's store and regional product managers to adapt collections to local preferences – if Mexican customers want their strappy summer dresses in vivid reds and yellows but the Swiss prefer them in pastel pinks and blues, Zara can deliver.

With its flexible and integrated organisational structure, Inditex, and Zara in particular, has clearly rewritten many of the rules of the industry. The structure affects the nature of both the work (the work of a designer, for instance, becomes a blend of both long-range forecasting based on trends unveiled at catwalk shows and constant innovation based on day-by-day sales data) and the relationships within a global company which put individual store managers in direct and regular contact with design and production. It may have become a trendsetter in more ways than one.

Your tasks

1. Analyse Zara's structure in relation to the 'Interrelated levels of organisation' diagram at Figure 15.1. How does it match and how does it differ from the model?
2. Critically assess Zara's structure against each of Urwick's principles of organisation as outlined on pp. 576–7.
3. Organisations could be said to sit somewhere along a continuum between complete vertical integration, i.e. in-house control of all aspects of the operation, and complete outsourcing, i.e. externalisation of all operational aspects, with the core acting as a co-ordinating agent. What are the advantages and disadvantages of each structure in terms of responsiveness, resilience and efficiency?
4. How transferable is the Zara model to non-business sectors? Discuss this in relation to either a public sector operation (such as an NHS hospital) or a not-for-profit one.

Notes and references

1 Birkinshaw, J. 'The Structure behind Global Companies', in Pickford, J. (ed.), *Financial Times Mastering Management 2.0*, Financial Times Prentice Hall (2001), p. 75.

2 Adapted from Knight, K. (ed.) *Matrix Management: A Cross-functional Approach to GOrganization*, Gower (1977), pp. 114–15.

3 Heller, R. 'Resist That Urge to Reorganise', *Management Today*, January 1996, p. 21.

4 Watson, T. *Organising and Managing Work*, Second edition, Financial Times Prentice Hall (2006) pp. 254–62.

5 Drucker, P. F. *The Practice of Management*, Heinemann Professional (1989), p. 223.

6 Child, J. *Organization: Contemporary Principles and Practice*, Blackwell Publishing (2005), p. 6.

7 See, for example: Heller, R. *In Search of European Excellence*, HarperCollins Business (1997), p. 34.

8 See, for example: Lynch, R. *Corporate Strategy*, Fourth edition, Financial Times Prentice Hall (2003), Chapter 16.

9 Forte, C. (Lord Forte) *Forte: The Autobiography of Charles Forte*, Sidgwick and Jackson (1986), p. 122.

10 Vollmann, T. 'Restructuring: How to Improve your Success Ratio', *FT Mastering Management*, The Reader 2, Financial Times, June 1997.

11 Hannagan, T. *Management: Concepts and Practices*, Third edition, Financial Times Prentice Hall (2002).

12 Argyris, C. *Integrating the Individual and the Organization*, Wiley (1964).

13 Parsons, T. 'Some Ingredients of a General Theory of Formal Organization', in Litterer, J. A. *Organizations: Structure and Behaviour*, Third edition, Wiley (1980).

14 Department of the Environment, *The New Local Authorities: Management and Structure* (The Bains Report), HMSO (1972) pp. 10–11.

15 Audit Commission *Form Follows Function*, HMSO (1996).

16 Rawson, M. 'Whose Side Are You On?', *Professional Manager*, November 1997, p. 3.

17 Stewart, R. *The Reality of Management*, Third edition, Butterworth-Heinemann (1999), p. 190.

18 Jebb, F. 'Don't Call Me Sir (Everyone Knows I'm the Boss)', *Management Today*, August 1998, pp. 44–7.

19 Drucker, P. F. *Management Challenges for the 21st Century*, Butterworth-Heinemann (1999), p. 11.

20 Butcher, D. 'Breaking out of Organizational Mindsets', in Crainer, S. and Dearlove, D. (eds), *Financial Times Handbook of Management*, Second edition, Financial Times Prentice Hall (2001), p. 91.

21 Cloke, K. and Goldsmith, J. *The End of Management and the Rise of Organizational Democracy*, Jossey-Bass (2002).

22 Gratton, L. *The Democratic Enterprise*, Financial Times Prentice Hall (2004), pp. xii–xiv.

23 Lundy, O. and Cowling, A. *Strategic Human Resource Management* (1996), p. 141.

24 For a fuller discussion on strategy and structure see: Lynch, R. *Corporate Strategy*, Fourth edition, Financial Times Prentice Hall (2006), Chapter 16.

25 Woodward, J. *Industrial Organization: Theory and Practice*, Second edition, Oxford University Press (1980).

26 See, for example: Mullins, L. J. *Hospitality Management and Organisational Behaviour*, Fourth edition, Longman (2001).

27 Woodward, J. *Industrial Organization: Theory and Practice*, Second edition, Oxford University Press (1980), p. 113.

28 Barnevik, P. cited in Evans, P. A. L. 'The Dualistic Leader: Thriving On Paradox', in Chowdhury, S. *Management 21C*, Financial Times Prentice Hall (2000), p. 71.

29 Urwick, L. *Notes on the Theory of Organization*, American Management Association (1952).

30 See, for example: Moorcroft, R. 'Managing in the 21st Century', *The British Journal of Administrative Management*, January/February 2000, pp. 8–10.

31 Graicunas, V. A. 'Relationship in Organization', in *Papers on the Science of Administration*, University of Columbia (1937).

32 Woodward, J. *Industrial Organization: Theory and Practice*, Second edition, Oxford University Press (1980).

33 Learner, P. M. 'Beware the Gatekeeper', *Amtrak Express*, July/August 1994, pp. 14–17.

34 Clutterbuck, D. 'Marketing the Staff Departments', *Professional Manager*, January 1994, pp. 7–9.

35 Heller, R. 'The Manager's Dilemma', *Management Today*, January 1994, pp. 42–7.

36 Quinn, J. B., Anderson, P. and Finkelstein, S. 'Leveraging Intellect', in Crainer, S. and Dearlove, D. (eds), *Financial Times Handbook of Management*, Second edition, Financial Times Prentice Hall (2001), p. 592.

37 Mann, S. 'Working around Projects', *Professional Manager*, November 2002, pp. 29–32.

38 Adapted from Kolondy, H. F. 'Managing in a Matrix', *Business Horizons*, March/April 1981, pp. 17–24.

39 Bartlett, A. and Ghoshal, S. 'Matrix Management: Not a Structure, a Frame of Mind', *Harvard Business Review*, July–August 1990, pp. 138–45.

40 Senior, B. *Organisational Change*, Second edition, Financial Times Prentice Hall (2002), p. 87.

41 Urwick, L. *The Elements of Administration*, Second edition, Pitman (1947), pp. 38–9.

42 Child, J. *Organization: Contemporary Principles and Practice*, Blackwell Publishing (2005), p. 17.

43 Tibballs, G. *Business Blunders*, Robinson Publishers (1999), Chapter 2.

44 Rosenfeld, R. H. and Wilson, D. C., *Managing Organizations: Text, Readings & Cases*, Second edition, McGraw-Hill (1999), p. 255.

45 Townsend, R. *Further Up the Organisation*, Coronet Books (1985), p. 159.

46 Kay, J. *Financial Times*, 17 January 1997.

47 See for example, Galbraith, J. R. *Designing Organizations*, Jossey-Bass (1995).

48 Dunderdale, P. 'Analysing Effective Organisations', *Professional Manager*, September 1994, pp. 23–4.

49 Watson, T. *Organising and Managing Work*, Second edition, Financial Times Prentice Hall (2006), p. 259.

50 Gray, J. L. and Starke, F. A. *Organizational Behavior: Concepts and Applications*, Fourth edition, Merrill Publishing Company, an imprint of Macmillan Publishing (1988).

51 Heller, R. *In Search of European Excellence*, HarperCollins Business (1997), p. 4.

52 Birchall, D. W. 'What Managers Do', in Crainer, S. and Dearlove, D. (eds), *Financial Times Handbook of Management*, Second edition, Financial Times Prentice Hall (2001), pp. 110–31.
53 Cloke, K. and Goldsmith, J. *The End of Management and the Rise of Organizational Democracy*, Jossey-Bass (2002), p. 41.
54 D'Argy Smith, M. BBC News Website 'The Seaside Fashion Shows' 11 October 2002.
55 Elliott, B. 'What's really new in supply chains?' FT.com, 28 June 2006 [assessed 3 August 2006].
56 Revilla Bonnin, A. 'The Fashion Industry in Galicia: Understanding the "Zara" Phenomenon', *European Planning Studies*, vol. 10, no. 4, pp. 519–27.
57 Ibid.
58 Surowiecki, J. 'The Wisdom of Crowds', Abacus (2004), p. 192.
59 Inditex website; www.InditexJobs.com [accessed 3 August 2006].

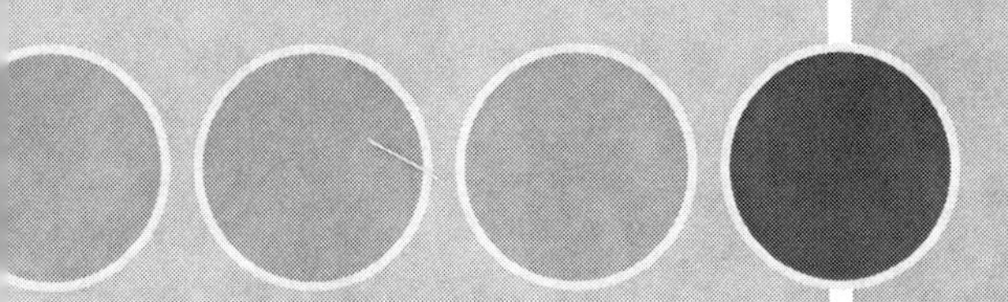

PATTERNS OF STRUCTURE AND WORK ORGANISATION

> There are no formal management structures in my companies – much to the disapproval of many. I know what is going on partly because I have told people what to do, and ensured the team is in place to deliver, and partly because I ask what's going on. It's not always easy to implement, but in theory it really is that simple.

(Sir) Alan Sugar – CEO and Chairman of Amstrad

The Apprentice, BBC Books (2005), p. 90

There are many variables that influence the most appropriate organisation structure and system of management. It is necessary to analyse structure in terms of the relationships among its components. Attention needs to be given to pressures for greater flexibility in patterns of organisation and the workforce, and the nature of the manager–subordinate relationship. The 'fit' between structure, systems of management and the behaviour of people will depend upon situational variables for each particular organisation.

Learning outcomes

After completing this chapter you should be able to:

- explain the meaning and nature of the contingency approach to organisation structure;
- examine main contingency models and assess their implication for management;
- assess the importance of changing external environments for the management and structure of organisations;
- evaluate the relevance and value of the contingency approach, and the importance of culture;
- recognise the changing face of the workplace and the demand for flexibility;
- explain the significance of the flexible firm, outsourcing and the shamrock organisation;
- review the importance of situational variables for patterns of structure and work organisation.

Critical reflection

'We trained very hard, but it seemed every time we were beginning to form up into teams we would be reorganised. I was to learn later in life that we tend to meet any new situation by reorganising and a wonderful method it can be for creating the illusion of progress while producing confusion, inefficiency and demoralisation' (Gaius Petronius, AD 66). To what extent do you think this is still true for modern work organisations?

VARIABLES INFLUENCING ORGANISATION STRUCTURE

In the previous chapter we looked at structure as providing the framework of management and at a number of basic principles and considerations that underlie the design of organisation structure. These principles and considerations suggest a prescriptive stance towards structure. There are, however, a number of variables and other factors which affect the most appropriate organisation structure and systems of management, the manner in which the work of the organisation is carried out and how people actually behave within the formal structure and system of the organisation.

Earlier approaches to organisation and management

Earlier approaches to organisation and management believed in one best form of structure and tended to concentrate on limited aspects of organisation. They also tended to study the organisation in isolation from its environment.

- The **classical approach** focused attention on the formal structure, technical requirements of the organisation and general sets of principles. There was an assumption of rational and logical behaviour. The identification of general objectives and the clarification of purposes and responsibilities at all levels of the organisation would lead to the most effective structure. Bureaucracy, as a sub-group of the classical approach, views the structure of the organisation in terms of specialisation, hierarchy of authority, system of rules and impersonality.
- The **human relations approach** focused attention on the informal organisation, and on the psychological and social needs of people at work. The neo-human relations writers concentrated on the personal adjustment of individuals within the structure of the organisation. Members were assumed to be committed to achieving the goals of the organisation. Attention was given to design of a structure that removed alienating aspects of work and restrictions on effective performance.
- The **systems view** of organisation and management placed emphasis on the socio-technical approach, the interrelationships of sub-systems and multiple channels of interaction, and recognised the importance of the external environment.

Given the speed of technological change, an increasing rate of innovation, and growing demands by a more highly educated work force, many scholars suggest that the classical view of organizations will become outdated. In response to the resulting frustration, bureaucracies will begin to fade away and will be replaced by more creative forms of organization.

R. P. Vecchio, *Organizational Behavior, Core Concepts*[1]

According to *Bouchikhi and Kimberly*, a feature that differentiates the 19th-, 20th- and 21st-century management paradigms is that as customers and shareholders have been more proactive, market-driven strategies and flexible organisations have developed as a consequence.[2] The changing nature of the work environment, the increasing demands for flexibility and concerns with the contextual factors influencing structure have drawn attention to the contingency approach to organisational design.

THE CONTINGENCY APPROACH

The **contingency approach** can be seen as a development of the systems approach; it goes a stage further in relating the environment, and other variables, to specific structures of organisation. The contingency approach takes the view that there is no one best, universal structure. There are a large number of variables, or situational factors, which influence organisational design and performance. **The contingency approach emphasises the need for flexibility.**

As *Vecchio* puts it: 'The goal of the contingency view is to explain how differences in the contextual and structural dimensions are related. As the term *contingency* implies, this approach does not seek universal principles that can be used for every situation, but instead seeks to explain how one attribute or characteristic depends upon another.'[3]

The most appropriate structure is dependent, therefore, upon the contingencies of the situation for each individual organisation. These situational factors account for variations in the structure of different organisations.

Lynch points out: 'Every organisation is unique in size, products or services, people, leadership and culture' and provides helpful examples of some of the possible implications for organisation design (*see* Figure 16.1).[4]

Figure 16.1 Examples of the connection between purpose and organisation design

Purpose	Implications for organisation design
• 'Ideas factory' such as an advertising or promotions agency	• Loose, fluid structure with limited formalised relationships. As it grows in size, however, more formal structures are usually inevitable
• Multinational company in branded goods	• Major linkage and resource issues that need carefully co-ordinated structures, e.g. on common suppliers or common supermarket customers for separate product ranges
• Government civil service	• Strict controls on procedures and authorisations. Strong formal structures to handle major policy directions and legal issues
• Non-profit-making charity with a strong sense of mission	• Reliance on voluntary members and their voluntary contributions may require a flexible organisation with responsibility devolved to individuals
• Major service company such as a retail bank or electricity generating company	• Formal structures but supported by some flexibility so that variations in demand can be met quickly
• Small business attempting to survive and grow	• Informal, willingness to undertake several business functions such as selling or production, depending on the short-term circumstances
• Health service with strong professional service ethics, standards and quality	• Formalised structure that reflects the seniority and professional status of those involved while delivering the crucial complex service provisions
• Holding company with subsidiaries involved in diverse markets	• Small centralised headquarters acting largely as a banker, with the main strategic management being undertaken in individual companies

Source: Adapted from Lynch, R., *Corporate Strategy*, Fourth Edition, Financial Times Prentice Hall (2006), p. 582. Reprinted by permission of Pearson Education Ltd.

An 'if–then' relationship

The contingency approach can be seen as a form of 'if–then' matrix relationship.[5] If certain situational factors exist, then certain variables in organisation structure and systems of management are most appropriate. A simplified illustration of contingency relationships is given in Figure 16.2.

Situational factors may be identified in a number of ways. The more obvious bases for comparison include the type of organisation and its purpose (discussed in Chapter 3), power and control, history, and the characteristics of the members of the organisation such as their abilities, skills and experience and their needs and motivations. The choice of structure can also be influenced by the preferences of top management.[6] Another significant contingent factor is the culture of the organisation, which is discussed below and also in Chapter 19. Other important variables are size, technology and environment. A number of studies have been carried out into the extent to which these contingency factors influence organisational design and effectiveness. Among the most significant contingency influences are those shown in Figure 16.3.

Figure 16.2 The 'If–then' contingency relationship

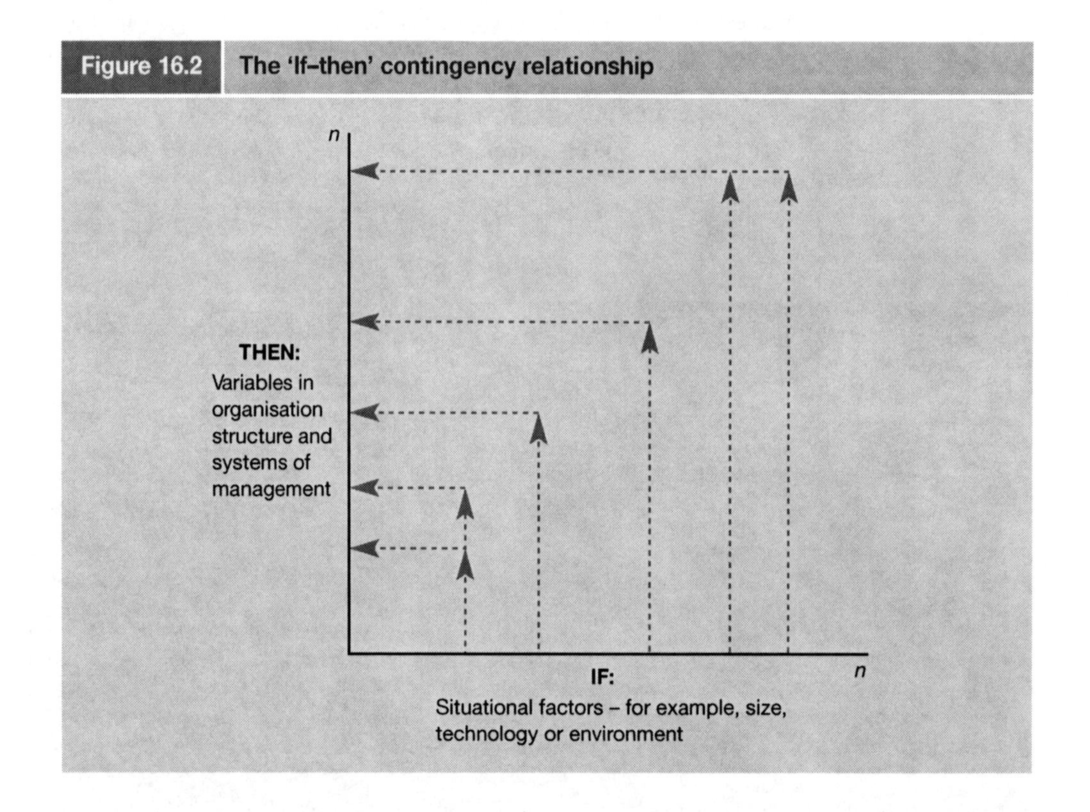

Critical reflection

According to the contingency approach, different situational factors may have some relevance for certain types of organisations at some time given a particular set of circumstances, and these situational factors may influence patterns of organisation structure. Do you think this is a sensible view of modern work organisations? Or is this approach too vague and with too many variables to have any practical value for managers?

Figure 16.3 Main influences on the contingency approach

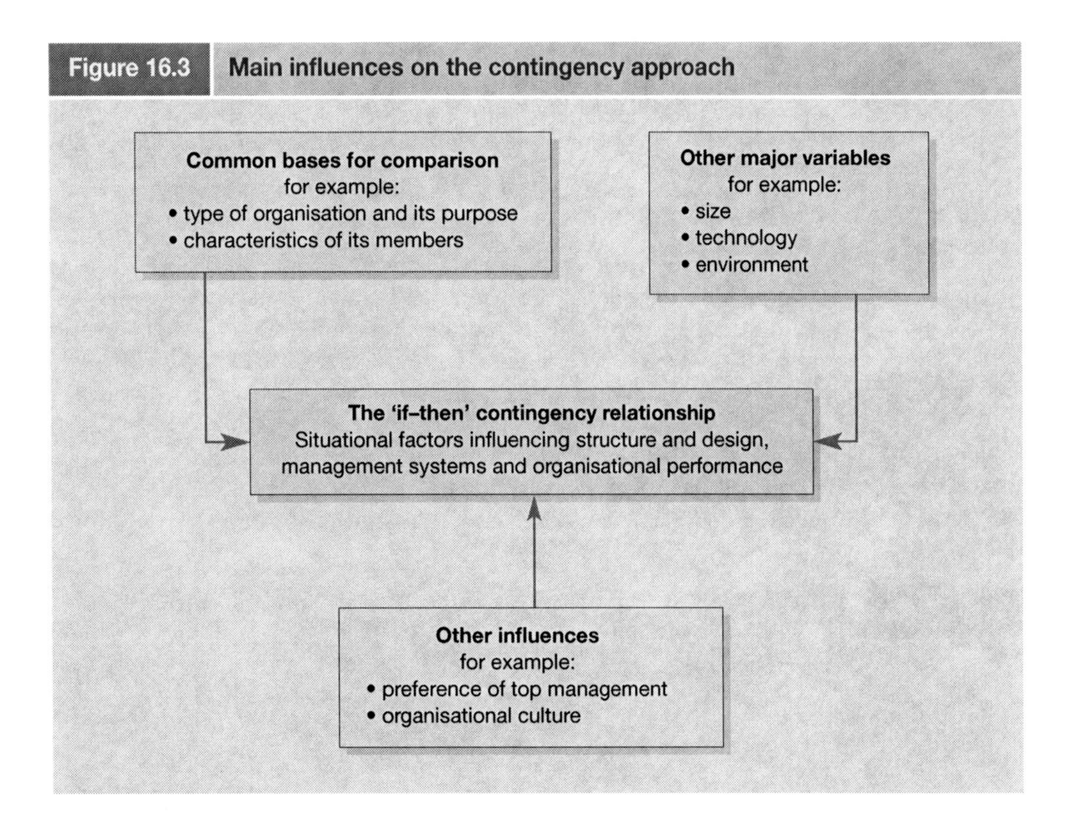

SIZE OF ORGANISATION

The size of an organisation has obvious implications for the design of its structure. In the very small organisations there is little need for a formal structure. With increasing size, however, and the associated problems of the execution of work and management of staff, there are likely to be more formalised relationships and greater use of rules and standardised procedures. Size explains best many of the characteristics of organisation structure, for example the importance of standardisation through rules and procedures as a mechanism for co-ordination in larger organisations.

Size, however, is not a simple variable. It can be defined and measured in different ways, although the most common indication of size is the number of persons employed by the organisation. There is the problem of distinguishing the effects of size from other organisational variables. Furthermore, there is conflicting evidence on the relationship of size to the structure and operation of the organisation.

Size and economic performance

In a study of the effects of size on the rate of growth and economic performance, *Child* acknowledges the tendency for increased size to be associated with increased bureaucracy. He argues that the more bureaucratised, larger organisations perform better than the less bureaucratised, larger organisations. Child found that:

> *Much as critics may decry bureaucracy ... the more profitable and faster growing companies, in the larger size category of 2000 employees and above, were those that had developed this type of organisation. The larger the company, the greater the association between more bureaucracy and superior performance. At the other end of the scale, among small firms of only a hundred or so employees, the better performers generally managed with very little formal organization.*[7]

There is a continuing debate about the comparative advantages of large and small organisations, or whether 'bigger is best' or 'small is beautiful'. The conclusion appears to be that managers should attempt to follow a middle line in terms of the size of the organisations and that complexity rather than size may be a more influential variable.[8]

Structures of global companies

Refresh your understanding
Activity 16A
www.pearsoned.co.uk/mullins

Birkinshaw draws attention to size as a particular feature of the structures of global companies. 'The reality is that global companies end up being perceived as complex, slow-moving and bureaucratic. The challenge for top managers lies in minimizing these liabilities, while retaining the benefits of size.' The pure matrix (discussed in Chapter 15) with equal stress on two lines of accountability does not work. Attention must be given to strong but informal horizontal relationships and country managers in developing markets. The organisation of a global company depends on a host of factors including number of businesses and countries in which it operates, the type of industry, location of major customers, and its own heritage. Birkinshaw identifies four (simplified) models for the structure of a global company (*see* Figure 16.4).[9]

Figure 16.4 Four models for global company structure

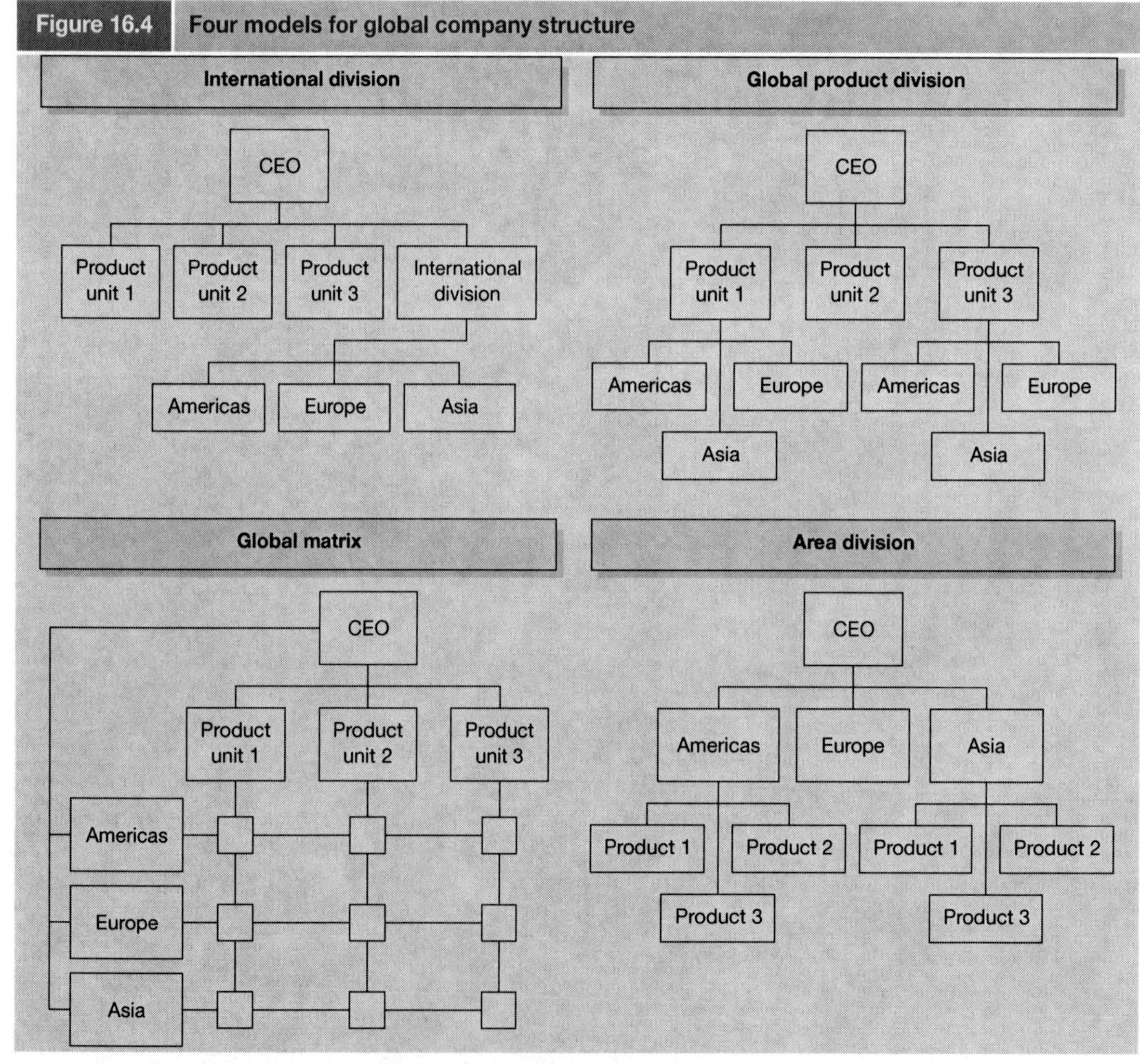

Source: From Birkinshaw, J., 'The structures behind global companies', in Pickford, J. (ed.) *Mastering Management 2.0*, Financial Times Prentice Hall (2001), p. 76. Reproduced with permission from Pearson Education Ltd.

TECHNOLOGY

Two major studies concerning technology are:

- Woodward – patterns of organisation, production technology and business success; and
- Perrow – main dimensions of technology and organisation structure.

THE WOODWARD STUDY

A major study of the effects of technology on organisation structure was carried out by *Joan Woodward*.[10] Her pioneering work presents the results of empirical study of 100 manufacturing firms in south-east Essex and the relationships between the application of principles of organisation and business success. The main thesis was:

> *that industrial organisations which design their formal organisational structures to fit the type of production technology they employ are likely to be commercially successful.*[11]

Information was obtained from each of the firms under the four headings of:

1. history, background and objectives;
2. manufacturing processes and methods;
3. forms and routines used in the organisation and operation of the firm;
4. information relating to an assessment of commercial success.

The firms were divided into nine different types of production systems, from least to most technological complexity, with three main groupings of:

- unit and small batch production;
- large batch and mass production;
- process production.

The research showed that the firms varied considerably in their organisation structure and that many of the variations appeared to be linked closely with differences in manufacturing techniques.

Principles of organisation and business success

There appeared to be no direct link between principles of organisation and business success. As far as organisation was concerned, the 20 outstandingly successful firms had little in common. The classical approach appeared to fail in providing a direct and simple basis for relating organisational structure and business success. **There was, however, a stronger relationship between organisation structure and success within each of the three main groupings of production systems.**

Organisational patterns were found to be related more to similarity of objectives and production techniques than to size, type of industry or the business success of the firm. Among the organisational characteristics showing a direct relationship to technology were span of control and levels of management, percentage of total turnover allocated to wages and salaries, ratio of managers to total personnel, and ratio of clerical and administrative staff to manual workers. The more advanced the technology, the longer the length of the line.

Patterns of organisation and technology

Woodward acknowledges that technology is not the only variable that affects organisation but is one that could be isolated more easily for study. She does, however, draw attention to the importance of technology, organisation and business success.

> *The figures relating to the span of control of the chief executive, the number of levels in the line of command, labour costs, and the various labour ratios showed a similar trend. The fact that*

organizational characteristics, technology and success were linked together in this way suggested that not only was the system of production an important variable in the determination of organizational structure, but also that one particular form of organization was most appropriate to each system of production. In unit production, for example, not only did short and relatively broad based pyramids predominate, but they also appeared to ensure success. Process production, on the other hand, would seem to require the taller and more narrowly based pyramid.[12]

Relationship between development, production and marketing

Another important finding of Woodward's study was the nature of the actual cycle of manufacturing and the relationship between three key 'task' functions of development, production and marketing. The most critical of these functions varied according to the type of production system (*see* Table 16.1).

- **Unit and small batch**. Production was based on firm orders only, with marketing the first activity. Greater stress was laid on technical expertise, and the quality and efficiency of the product. Research and development were the second, and most critical, activities. The need for flexibility, close integration of functions and frequent personal contacts meant that an organic structure was required.
- **Large batch and mass**. Production schedules were not dependent directly on firm orders. The first phase of manufacturing was product development, followed by production that was the most important function and third, marketing. The three functions were more independent and did not rely so much on close operational relationships among people responsible for development, production and sales.
- **Process**. The importance of securing a market meant that marketing was the central and critical activity. Products were either impossible or difficult to store, or capacity for storage was very limited. The flow of production was directly determined, therefore, by the market situation. The emphasis of technical knowledge was more on how products could be used than on how they could be made.

Table 16.1 Characteristics of production sytems

Production systems	Manufacturing cycle			Relationship between task functions
Unit and small batch	Marketing	Development (Most critical function)	Production	Day-to-day operational relationship
Large batch and mass	Development	Production (Most critical function)	Marketing	Normally exchange of information only
Process	Development	Marketing (Most critical function)	Production	Normally exchange of information only

Source: Woodward, J., *Industrial Organization: Theory and Practice*, Second Edition, Oxford University Press (1980), p. 128. Reproduced with permission from Oxford University Press.

Subsequent studies A subsequent study by *Zwerman* supported, very largely, the findings of Woodward. Zwerman's study involved a slightly different sample of organisations and was carried out in Minneapolis in the USA.[13] In other respects, however, the study attempted to replicate Woodward's work. Zwerman reached a similar conclusion, that the type of production technology was related closely to variations in organisation structure. Another study in Japan also supported Woodward's findings and the relationship between technology and structure.[14]

However, a further study by *Collins and Hull* of 95 American manufacturing firms questioned the extent to which span of control is a by-product of main types of production technology. Variations in the span of control of production operations were attributed to the underlying effects of size, task complexity and automation. Collins and Hull suggest that the technology versus size debate has moved beyond an 'either–or' proposition to a 'both–and' proposition.[15]

MAJOR DIMENSIONS OF TECHNOLOGY: THE WORK OF PERROW

The work by Woodward was extended by *Perrow*, who drew attention to two major dimensions of technology:

- the extent to which the work task is predictable or variable; and
- the extent to which technology can be analysed.[16]

Variability refers to the number of exceptional or unpredictable cases and the extent to which problems are familiar. For example, a mass production factory is likely to have only a few exceptions but the manufacture of a designer range of clothing would have many exceptional and unpredictable cases. The **analysis of technology** refers to the extent to which the task functions are broken down and highly specified, and the extent to which problems can be solved in recognised ways or by the use of routine procedures.

Combining the two dimensions provides a continuum of technology from Routine → Non-routine. With non-routine technology there are a large number of exceptional cases involving difficult and varied problem-solving. The two dimensions of variability and the analysis of problems can also be represented as a matrix (*see* Figure 16.5).

Technology and structure The classification of each type of technology relates to a particular organisation structure. *Perrow* suggests that by classifying organisations according to their technology and predictability of work tasks, we should be able to predict the most effective form of structure. Variables such as the discretion and power of sub-groups, the basis of co-ordination and the interdependence of groups result from the use of different technologies.

Figure 16.5 Matrix of technology variables

	FEW EXCEPTIONS	MANY EXCEPTIONS
PROBLEMS CANNOT BE ANALYSED	*Craft technology* Making a whole product probably in the same way each time, e.g. fine glassware	*Non-routine technology* e.g. psychiatric care in a mental hospital; manufacture of nuclear fuel systems
PROBLEMS CAN BE ANALYSED	*Routine technology* Manufacture of standard products; highly mechanised mass production	*Engineering technology* e.g. made-to-order machines such as electrical components; research consultancy

Source: Adapted from Perrow, C., *Organisational Analysis: A Sociological View*, Tavistock Publications (1970) p. 78; and Mitchell, T. R. *People in Organisations*, Second Edition. McGraw-Hill (1982) p. 32. Reproduced with permission from the McGraw-Hill Companies Inc.

In the **routine type of organisation** there is minimum discretion at both the technical and supervisory levels, but the power of the middle management level is high, co-ordination is based on planning and there is likely to be low interdependence between the two groups. This arrangement approaches a bureaucratic structure.

In the **non-routine type of organisation** there is a high level of discretion and power at both the technical and supervisory levels, co-ordination is through feedback and there is high group interdependence. This model resembles an organic structure.

ENVIRONMENT

Two important studies that focused not just on technology but also on the effects of uncertainty and a changing external environment on the organisation, and its management and structure, are those by:

- Burns and Stalker – divergent systems of management practice, 'mechanistic' and 'organic'; and
- Lawrence and Lorsch – the organisation of specific departments, and the extent of 'differentiation' and 'integration'.

THE BURNS AND STALKER STUDY

The study by Burns and Stalker was an analysis of 20 industrial firms in the UK and the effects of the external environment on their pattern of management and economic performance.[17] The firms were drawn from a number of industries: a rayon manufacturer, a large engineering company, Scottish firms attempting to enter the electronics field and English firms operating in varying sectors of the electronics industry.

Mechanistic and organic systems

From an examination of the settings in which the firms operated, Burns and Stalker distinguished five different kinds of environments ranging from 'stable' to 'least predictable'. They also identified two divergent systems of management practice and structure – the **'mechanistic' system** and the **'organic' system**. These represented the polar extremes of the form that such systems could take when adapted to technical and commercial change. Burns and Stalker suggested that both types of system represented a 'rational' form of organisation which could be created and maintained explicitly and deliberately to make full use of the human resources in the most efficient manner according to the circumstances of the organisation.

The **mechanistic system** is a more rigid structure and more appropriate to stable conditions. The characteristics of a mechanistic management system are similar to those of bureaucracy.

The **organic system** is a more fluid structure appropriate to changing conditions. It appears to be required when new problems and unforeseen circumstances arise constantly and require actions outside defined roles in the hierarchical structure.

A summary of the characteristics of mechanistic and organic organisations is provided by *Litterer* (*see* Table 16.2).[18] The mechanistic organisation is unable to deal adequately with rapid change; it is therefore more appropriate for stable environmental conditions. An example might be a traditional high-class and expensive hotel operating along classical lines with an established reputation and type of customer. However, major fast-food chains that tend to operate along the lines of scientific management (discussed in Chapter 3) also require a mechanistic structure. By contrast, a holiday or tourist hotel with an unpredictable demand, offering a range of functions and with many different types of customers, requires an organic structure.

Location of authority Although the organic system is not hierarchical in the same sense as the mechanistic system, Burns and Stalker emphasise that it is still stratified, with positions differentiated according to seniority and greater expertise. The location of authority, however, is by consensus and the lead is taken by the 'best authority', that is the person who is seen to be most informed and capable. Commitment to the goals of the organisation is greater in the organic system, and it becomes more difficult to distinguish the formal and informal organisation. The development of shared beliefs in the values and goals of the organisation in the organic system runs counter to the co-operation and monitoring of performance achieved through the chain of hierarchical command in the mechanistic system.

A study of 42 voluntary church organisations in the USA found that as the organisations became more mechanistic, the intrinsic motivation, sense of freedom and self-determination of their members decreased.[19]

Burns and Stalker point out that there are intermediate stages between the two extreme systems that represent not a dichotomy but a polarity. The relationship between the mechanistic and organic systems is not rigid. An organisation moving between a relatively stable and a relatively changing environment may also move between the two systems.

Organic cultures for high-technology organisations According to *Reigle*, knowledge workers in today's high-technology organisations require environments with organic characteristics. As technology continues to expand throughout the world, an organic organisational culture will become increasingly important. In order to retain highly skilled knowledge workers, managers should undertake investigations using an organisational culture assessment (OCA) to measure whether their organisations exhibit mechanistic or organic cultures. The OCA is based on five cultural elements of language, tangible artefacts and symbols, patterns of behaviour, rites and rituals, espoused values and beliefs and underlying assumptions.[20]

Table 16.2 Characteristics of mechanistic and organic organisations

Mechanistic		Organic
High, many and sharp differentiations	SPECIALISATION	Low, no hard boundaries, relatively few different jobs
High, methods spelled out	STANDARDISATION	Low, individuals decide own methods
Means	ORIENTATION OF MEMBERS	Goals
By superior	CONFLICT RESOLUTION	Interaction
Hierarchical, based on implied contractual relation	PATTERN OF AUTHORITY CONTROL AND COMMUNICATION	Wide net based upon common commitment
At top of organisation	LOCUS OF SUPERIOR COMPETENCE	Wherever there is skill and competence
Vertical	INTERACTION	Lateral
Directions, orders	COMMUNICATION CONTENT	Advice, information
To organisation	LOYALTY	To project and group
From organisational position	PRESTIGE	From personal contribution

Source: Litterer, J. A., *The Analysis of Organisations*, Second Edition, John Wiley & Sons (1973), p. 339. Reproduced with permission from the estate of Joseph A. Litterer.

'MIXED' FORMS OF ORGANISATION STRUCTURE

Organisations *tend* towards mechanistic or organic, and many will be hybrid – that is, a mix of both mechanistic and organic structures – and often this is an uneasy mix that can lead to tension and conflict. For example, a group of people engaged on a set of broad functional activities might prefer, and perform best in, an organic structure, while another group tends to prefer a mechanistic structure and to work within established rules, systems and procedures. The different perceptions of appropriate organisational styles and working methods present a particular challenge to management. There is need for a senior member of staff, in an appropriate position in the hierarchy and who has the respect of both groups, to act in a bridging role and to help establish harmony between them.[21]

A typical example of a hybrid organisation could be a university with differences in perception between the academic staff and the non-teaching staff. The non-teaching staff have an important function in helping to keep the organisation operational and working effectively, and may fail to understand why academics appear to find it difficult, or resent, working within prescribed administrative systems and procedures. The academic staff may well feel that they can work effectively only within an organic structure, and tend to see non-teaching staff as bureaucratic and resistant to novel or different ideas. Universities may also tend to be more mechanistic at top management level, with an apparent proliferation of committees and sub-committees, because of their dealings with, for example, government bodies and other external agencies.

The distinction between mechanistic and organic structures is often most pronounced between 'production' and 'service' functions of an organisation. An example of a hybrid organisation from the private sector could be a large hotel. Here the work tasks and operations of the kitchen (the production element) suggest that a more mechanistic structure might be appropriate. Other departments, more concerned with a service element, such as front-office reception, may work better with a more organic structure.[22]

Matching structures, systems and styles of management

The design of an organisation is an exercise in matching structures, systems and style of management, and the people employed, to the various activities of the organisation. If there is a mismatch, problems can arise. *Parris* gives an example from the television programme *M*A*S*H* (Mobile Army Surgical Hospital):

> *Activities that are concerned with keeping things going but work in unstable conditions is an area where mismatching can occur as they contain elements of work that could be made systematic and simplified but as a consequence of their need to react quickly to changes to systematisation could make them less flexible. However, since they are often dealing with complex problems a degree of systematisation is necessary. An example of this would be the 4077th MASH, where to meet the demands of treating emergencies in battle they need to react quickly. But to treat complex injuries with complex technology and maintain records, etc. for the future treatment and other associated administration, a certain level of routine is necessary. Similarly when the unit is overloaded and necessary medical supplies are not available, considerable 'negotiation' and 'dealing' with other units, etc. is undertaken. The organisation that has evolved is a sort of Task Culture where everyone works as a team to process the work with easy working relationships, etc., but it does have role elements in the efficiency with which paperwork is processed. It has power culture elements for ...* [the Company Clerk] *to negotiate and bargain with other units and the unit commander has to use personal intervention to keep the unit going and protect it from the rest of the organisation in which it exists.*
>
> *The problems of imposing an inappropriate organisational design exists in the shape of* [those who] *represent the dominant role organisation in which the unit exists. Their attempts to impose military rules and procedures and impose the formal rank in the unit are seen as highly inappropriate, often farcical.*[23]

Critical reflection

Many organisational behaviour students express a preference for working within an organic organisation. Why do you think this is? Is it true for you? Do you agree that hierarchical, mechanistic structures are still necessary for effective management and the execution of work?

THE LAWRENCE AND LORSCH STUDY

Lawrence and Lorsch undertook a study of six firms in the plastics industry followed by a further study of two firms in the container industry and two firms in the consumer food industry.[24] They attempted to extend the work of Burns and Stalker and examined not only the overall structure but also the way in which specific departments were organised to meet different aspects of the firm's external environment.

Lawrence and Lorsch sought to answer the following questions:

1 What are the differences in the environmental demands facing various organisations, and how do these demands relate to the internal functioning of effective organisations?
2 Do organisations operating in a stable environment make greater use of the formal hierarchy to achieve integration, and if so, why? Is it because less integration is required, or because decisions can be made more effectively at higher levels of the organisation or by fewer people?
3 Is the same degree of differentiation in orientation and departmental structure found in organisations in different industrial environments?
4 If greater integration is required among functional departments in different industries, does this influence problems of integrating different parts of the organisation and the methods of achieving integration?

Differentiation and integration

The internal structures of the firms were analysed in terms of 'differentiation' and 'integration'.

Differentiation describes 'the difference in cognitive and emotional orientation among managers in different functional departments' with respect to:

- the goal orientation of managers – for example, the extent to which attention was focused on particular goals of the department;
- the time orientation of managers in relation to aspects of the environment with which they are concerned – for example, longer-term horizons or short-term horizons and problems requiring immediate solutions;
- the interpersonal relations of managers to other members – for example, a managerial style based on concern for the task, or on concern for people relationships; and
- the formality of structure – for example, the extent of mechanistic or organic design.

Integration describes 'the quality of the state of collaboration that exists among departments that are required to achieve unity of effort by the demands of the environment'. It is the degree of co-ordination and co-operation between different departments with interdependent tasks. Lawrence and Lorsch's view of integration was not the minimising of differences between departments and the provision of a common outlook. It was the recognition that different departments could have their own distinctive form of structure according to the nature of their task, and the use of mediating devices to co-ordinate the different outlooks of departments.

Different structures for individual departments

Given the possibility that different demands of the environment are characterised by different levels of uncertainty, it follows that individual departments may develop different structures. The study of the firms in the plastics industry supported this hypothesis and Lawrence and Lorsch found a clear differentiation between the major departments of research, production and sales.

- **Research** was more concerned with the long-run view and was confronted with pressures for new ideas and product innovation. The department operated in a dynamic, scientific environment and had the least bureaucratic structure.
- **Production** was more concerned with the here and now, short-term problems such as quality control and meeting delivery dates. The department operated in a fairly stable, technical environment and had the most bureaucratic structure.
- **Sales** was in the middle between research and production. The department was concerned with chasing production and had a moderately stable market environment.

The two most successful firms were those with the highest degree of integration and were also among the most highly differentiated.

Organisation structure and different environments

This view of differentiation and integration was confirmed in the subsequent study of firms in the container and consumer food industries. In this part of the study a comparison was made of both high- and low-performance firms operating in different environments. The aim was to discover what forms of organisation structure were required for different environments. It was concluded that the extent of differentiation and integration in effective organisations will vary according to the demands of the particular environment.

- The more diverse and dynamic the environment, the more the effective organisation will be differentiated and highly integrated.
- In more stable environments, less differentiation will be required but a high degree of integration is still required. Differences in the environment will require different methods of achieving integration.

Integrating mechanisms

The mechanisms used to achieve integration depend on the amount of integration required and the difficulty in achieving it.

- In mechanistic structures, integration may be attempted through the use of policies, rules and procedures.
- In organic structures, integration may be attempted through teamwork and mutual co-operation.
- As the requirements for the amount of integration increase, additional means may be adopted, such as formal lateral relations, committees and project teams.
- When there is a high degree of differentiation, the use of assigned 'integrators' or possibly a separate unit with a number of integrators were suggested. Because they are not dominated by any particular perspective, these integrators can help resolve problems of co-ordination and work programming between different departments.

Refresh your understanding
Activity 16B
www.pearsoned.co.uk/mullins

It is important, however, to achieve the right balance of integration. Too high a level of integration may involve costs that are likely to exceed possible benefits. Too low a level of integration is likely to result in departments 'doing their own thing', poorer quality decisions and failure to make the best use of resources.[25]

Patterns of organisation and management

Lawrence and Lorsch do not see the classical and human relations approaches as being out of date but as part of a continuum of patterns of organisation and management related to the environment in which they operate. The work of Lawrence and Lorsch is an extension of this continuum and their case for 'a contingency theory of organisations' has provided a further insight into the relationship between organisation structure and the demands of the environment.

EVALUATION OF THE CONTINGENCY APPROACH

The contingency approach draws attention to the situational factors that account for variations in the structure of organisations. It is more concerned with differences among organisations than with similarities. It rejects a number of assumptions of the classical and human relations approaches, and the idea of one best form of structure. For its part, however, the contingency approach tends to assume that organisational performance is dependent upon the degree to which the structure of the organisation matches the prevailing contingencies.

Hunt explains the concept of contingency as follows:

> *The concept of contingency also implies that there is no one, absolute 'best' design; rather, there is a multitude of possibilities and the best or preferred choice will be contingent on the situation being analysed. Universal models designed to suit all situations are therefore rejected. This is consistent with the fact that most organizations are networks of a variety of bits of design rather than conforming, as one entity, to a particular model. So we might find units of bureaucracy, units of matrix structures, units with project teams, units with extremely loose, almost ad hoc structures – and all these within, say, the same oil company. In this sense, the contingency theorists merely reflected the findings of hundreds of researchers. There are common elements in the hierarchies of different organisations but there are also very many differences peculiar to the local situation.*[26]

Criticisms/limitations

As with other approaches to organisation and management, contingency theory has been subject to a number of criticisms or doubts about its practical value to management. Among the writers who have assessed the contribution and relevance of the contingency approach are *Child*,[27] *Dawson*[28] and *Mintzberg*.[29]

The criticisms, difficulties and limitations of the contingency approach usually revolve around seven main issues.

1 **Causal relationship**. The nature of the causal relationship between organisation and performance is open to question. Most contingency models imply a causal relationship between structure, as an intervening variable, and performance as a dependent variable. It is probable, however, that certain factors such as the personal characteristics of management and staff, and changes in product markets and market conditions, influence performance independently of structure. It is also possible that organisational performance is an influence on structural design. Managers may be stimulated to make changes to structure as a result of feedback of information on performance.
2 **Organisational performance**. Implicit in contingency theory is the notion that the fit among components of the organisation and situation variables is related to maximising organisational performance. However, organisational performance is multifaceted and the measurement of performance applied in many of the contingency studies has not been precise. It is impossible to derive a single criterion for the appropriateness of the fit among various features of organisation and improved performance.
3 **Independent variables**. The supposed status of the independent 'contingent' variables as the 'given' and beyond the control of members of the organisation is open to question. Large organisations may be in a position to exercise control over certain aspects of their environment. For example, an organisation may be in a monopoly position or have its own protected niche in the environment. Organisations may also be able to influence their environment through, for example, advertising or political pressure groups. Some organisations, therefore, may be less dependent upon their environment and in a more secure position compared with other organisations. Any mismatch in contingency factors is likely to have less severe consequences for survival and level of performance.

4 **Multiple contingencies**. Different patterns of contingency factors have distinctive implications for organisational design. Organisations face multiple contingencies and there is potential for multi-way relationships among the range of organisational variables. Different contingencies may result in the need for different patterns of structure (as with a hybrid form of organisation discussed above) – for example, a department operating within a dynamic environment and demanding a more organic structure, within an organisation where other departments function within a more bureaucratic structure.
5 **Planned change**. Contingency models of organisation fail to give sufficient emphasis to unanticipated consequences of planned change – for example, the effects of the introduction of new technology on the internal working of the organisation or on the social interactions among groups of people engaged in certain activities.
6 **Power factors**. Organisation structure is not necessarily determined only by impersonal contingency conditions, but also by what are referred to as 'power' factors. The pressure of external control – such as government control of public sector organisations; the political context; the power needs of various members and managerial preferences; the culture of the organisation and the power of social norms – also enters into the design of structure.
7 **Timing of organisational change**. Most organisations operate under conditions of constant change, and this raises the question of the frequency and timing of organisational change. Developing organisations cannot, without difficulty, change their formal structure at too frequent an interval. There must be a significant change in contingency factors before an organisation will respond. Changes in structure tend to lag behind situational change. There is, therefore, a degree of luck about whether at any moment in time there is a good fit between structure and prevailing contingency factors.

> *Organization structure, like so many other aspects of business, is hostage to fads and fashions ... In looking at contemporary trends, we should note that many 'new' ideas have in fact been around in some form for decades.*
>
> J. Birkinshaw, *Mastering Management 2.0*[30]

CONTRIBUTION OF CONTINGENCY THEORY

Despite the criticisms and limitations of contingency theory, it has provided a further insight into our understanding of relationships among factors influencing the structure, management and operations of work organisations. An appropriate form of organisation will help prevent problems caused by unsuitable structures. The contingency approach has relevance in terms of, for example, division of work and co-ordination of activities, hierarchy and definition of responsibilities, methods of work, motivation and commitment of staff, and style and systems of management.

The basic concepts of the contingency approach help managers to develop a more thorough understanding of complex situations and to take appropriate action.[31] It also draws attention to the difficulties with mixed forms of organisation, and to the importance of different structures for different activities and situations – as illustrated in the example of *M*A*S*H* given earlier in the chapter.

Not every situation is unique

According to *Robey*, modern contingency theory provides an increasing amount of empirical research, it defines variables ignored in earlier work, and it directs the attention of the manager to the contingencies to be considered in the design of organisation structure. However, the contingency approach runs the risk of concluding that 'it all depends on everything', and the greatest danger is the over-emphasis on differences between organisations and the exclusion of similarities. If the contingency approach is to be useful in guiding organisation design it should not treat every situation as being unique. 'Rather it must strike a balance between universal prescriptions and the statement that all situations are different (which is really no theory at all). Thus, modern theory uses a limited number of contingencies to help explain structural differences between organizations.'[32]

Vecchio also refers to the contingency approach as 'it depends'. However, this is not meaning to be evasive but assuming that there are a number of important dependencies, and acknowledges:

> *the difficulty of offering simple general principles to explain or predict behavior in organizational settings ... If you ask a contingency researcher for a simple answer to a seemingly simple question, you should expect to be given a fairly complex and highly qualified answer. Because human behavior is itself complex, a statement of behavioral principles must also be complex.*[33]

CULTURE AS A CONTINGENT FACTOR

Several writers have sought to examine whether the principles of contingency theory hold true in different national contexts. For example, in Chapter 1 we drew attention to national culture as a feature of management and organisational behaviour including the contribution of *Hofstede*[34] and of *Trompenaars*.[35] *Hickson et al.* investigated 70 manufacturing units in Britain, the USA and Canada. They discovered that while there were differences in organisational arrangements, these could not be attributed to cultural effects. The relationship between variables, such as size, and the degree of specialisation and formality was found to be constant in all three countries, and the researchers suggested this would 'hold for work organisations in all societies'.[36]

Maurice, Sorge and Warner, however, concluded that 'matched' organisations in different societies grow in contrasting ways, which may be the result of distinctive patterns in the wider society. For example, their research showed that British organisations appeared to grow laterally – that is, to develop large numbers of specialised managers. This may be a reflection of the comparatively specialised nature of British education and the influential role played by the professions. In contrast, the smaller number of categories of workers found in the German organisations studied may be traced back to the notion of the company apprenticeship prevalent in that country. In this way culture can itself be seen as a contingent factor.[37]

Whatever the perspective, it is important for future managers to understand the effect of national culture on behaviour. This is of increasing significance with the growth of multicultural workforces and the effects of the European Union on organisational design.

Historical and societal context

Schneider and Barsoux suggest that while managers are ready to accept national culture as an influence on the way people relate to each other, they are less convinced of its real effect on the structure, systems and process of the organisation. However, the emerging approaches to management reflect different cultural assumptions and models of management have diffused across countries at different rates in different ways. Historical and societal context needs to be considered to understand the adoption of and diffusion of different forms of organisation across countries. Schneider and Barsoux discuss the multidimensional impact of culture on organisations and management and maintain that it would be a mistake to base a prediction regarding structure or process on a single cultural dimension.

> *Managers need to recognise that the relationship between cultural dimensions and structure (or processes) are not simple cause–effect links, but instead, are multidetermined. Similar approaches may exist for the same reason. Thus formalized rules and procedures or participative management approaches may have a different raison d'être on different sides of the national border.*
>
> S. C. Schneider and J. Barsoux, *Managing Across Cultures*[38]

An interesting set of caricatures for organisation charts of different countries is given in Figure 16.6.

Cultural variations and organisation structure

Francesco and Gold draw attention to cultural variations in the governance of business that affect organisational structure. For example, two forms of corporate governance substantially different from the West are the Japanese *keiretsu* and the Korean *chaebol*. The Japanese *keiretsu* are complex interfirm networks that combine market exchange and non-economic social relations. The group is usually in a large number of industries and often includes a bank at the core and a general trading company. Control and co-ordination is facilitated through each member firm of the *keiretsu* owning a small part, up to 20 per cent, of the

Figure 16.6 Caricatures of organisation charts for different countries

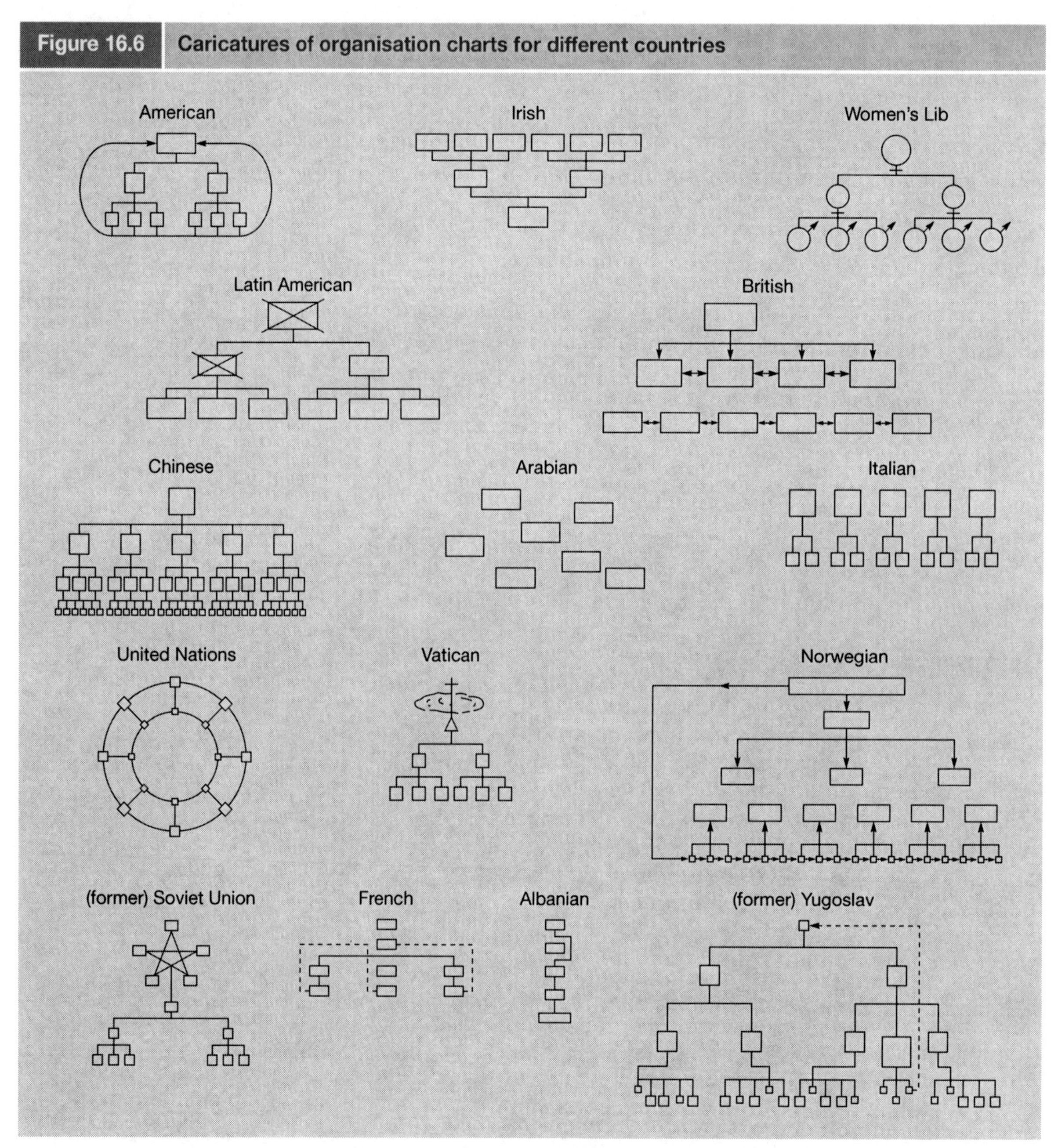

Source: Copyright © Reed Business Information Ltd, reprinted with permission.

stock of other firms in the group. *Chaebols* are large conglomerates or financial cliques that dominate the South Korean economy. The business group is owned and managed by family members or relatives. The founders are active in the operations of the *chaebols* and influence their business philosophy and management style. Most financial investment comes from government-controlled banks and in return the *chaebols* make political contributions for favourable treatment.[39]

THE CHANGING FACE OF THE WORKPLACE

The effects of increased economic pressures and demands for greater competitiveness have drawn attention to the importance of structural variables. The movement towards tighter and leaner organisations has emphasised the importance of alternative forms of structure and of the demand for flexibility. *Morgan* argues that we are leaving the age of organised structures and moving into an era where self-organisation will become a key competence. Looser organisations and different forms of control will entail a close examination of such issues as growth and size, teamwork, decentralisation, franchising and subcontracting.[40] And *Eden* maintains that:

> *It is important to design at least parts of the organisation so that it can recognise early on the direction in which uncertain situations will unfold, and so respond to change and uncertainty in an opportunistic, flexible and effective manner.*[41]

Seven habits of new organisations

Crainer suggests that the organisation is changing and the world of work is moving into a new age and lists 'seven habits of the new organisation':

1 flexible and free-flowing;
2 non-hierarchical;
3 based on participation;
4 creative and entrepreneurial;
5 based round networks;
6 driven by corporate goals;
7 utilising technology as a key resource.[42]

Relationship between the organisation and individuals

Management Consultancies Association (MCA) and *Management Today* carried out a survey of 1200 managers, from all types of organisations, in order to understand their attitudes to their employers and how these are likely to change in the future. The survey draws attention to the changing relationship between organisations and individuals and that ties to the workplace will increasingly cease to be a hindrance.

There are four interconnected forces that have brought about this changing relationship:

- changes in the shape of organisations themselves with outsourcing leading to a range of previously in-house processes and functions fulfilled elsewhere;
- changing pattern of people's working days with constant reference to flexibility. More than two-thirds of respondents spent a significant amount of time working outside the organisation;
- the pattern of people's working lives taking a very different shape with the ending of jobs for life and the active pursuit of career changes. Individuals increasingly choose employment that allows them to work from home or provides the latest technology;
- the impact of new technology enabling greater workforce mobility. However, although technology is usually an enabler, it can also be disabling. For example, email is the most important activity in helping people get their job done but it is also a burden.

It follows that as people are expected to operate more autonomously, so their responsibilities grow. Greater personal autonomy suggests greater fluidity in the workforce as a whole.

If there is one current that underlies the responses from a wide range of individuals about their expectations for the future of organisations and perceptions of management failings, it is that power in the workplace is shifting inexorably away from the organisation and towards employees.[43]

Outsourcing

In order to free management to concentrate on core activities, businesses are making increasing use of outsourcing and having a wider range of non-core services provided to them by specialist service providers.[44] The MCA/MT survey refers to the significant increase in outsourcing with some of the highest growth in business process outsourcing (BPO) where entire functions are moved outside the organisation. Although BPO applies mostly to larger companies, it is becoming more attractive to small and medium-sized organisations (SMEs). Delivery via cheap online technology puts a growing range of business processes within reach of SMEs which are also being targeted by service providers attempting to benefit from economies of scale. However, one of the consequences of increased outsourcing is that the boundaries of the organisation are becoming blurred. *Vernon* suggests that the debate on what can be successfully outsourced will continue. Despite the anxieties the outsourcing trend will continue with organisations becoming more transparent or 'virtual'. 'But how far outsourcing can go (as opposed to what can be outsourced) is also being debated now: at what point does a company outsource so much that it no longer has the critical mass to function?'[45]

Critical reflection

We are in an era of the end of jobs for life, the active pursuit of career changes and greater freedom and autonomy for the individual. How do you feel about this? Do you think that it might have an adverse effect on the desire to succeed, and commitment and loyalty to the organisation?

THE DEMAND FOR FLEXIBILITY

The nature of work is being redefined and this has created strong pressures for greater flexibility in patterns of work organisation and in the workforce. *Bouchikhi and Kimberly* suggest that the major challenge to organisations by external world trends is one of openness to individuals' needs and democratisation. Organisations must change into 'customised workplaces'. The challenge for management in the 21st century is to fully internalise the diverse and changing needs of individuals, and to investigate employee-driven flexibility.[46]

As ACAS points out, the UK workforce is now more diverse than ever, reflecting changes in society and the make-up of the population. Women comprise almost half the workforce and this figure is rising, while the workforce is also ageing. The demand for part-time and other flexible working patterns is increasing. Many employers are acknowledging that it makes good business sense to introduce flexible working arrangements to enable their employees to achieve a better work–life balance. They recognise that as well as providing a better quality of life for their employees they can increase the competitiveness and profitability of the business.[47]

The business case for flexibility is clear. In common with many other businesses, Lloyds TSB operates in an extremely competitive environment. Customers increasingly wish to access their finances whenever convenient for them and it is therefore no longer possible to be a 9 to 5 organisation. Flexibility is the key to staying competitive and we have to consider when, where and how to deliver services to ensure that we can provide a high quality customer service ... Implementing flexible management that really works, however, is not for the faint-hearted. We had to radically rethink our approach, which had become associated with arrangements for women and children, with most of the uptake at junior clerical level. This has involved looking at the way work is organised and at organisational culture.

Sir Brian Pitman, Chairman of Lloyds TSB Group plc[48]

The flexible firm A significant approach was *Atkinson's* idea of the flexible firm.[49] He suggests that firms are really looking for three kinds of flexibility:

- **functional flexibility** in order to permit the rapid redeployment of employees among different activities and tasks (perhaps involving the practice of multi-skilling);
- **numerical flexibility** in order to restructure so as to adjust the number of employees to match the level of demand for labour;
- **financial flexibility** in order that pay and other employment costs reflect the supply and demand of labour and in order to shift to new pay and remuneration systems.

As a result, Atkinson suggests that flexible firms have attempted to develop an organisation structure based on a central, stable 'core' group of full-time permanent career employees who undertake the organisation's key, firm-specific activities and with emphasis on functional flexibility, supported by peripheral and numerically flexible groups of workers including agency temporaries, subcontracting, self-employed and part-time staff, whose numbers, in theory, can expand or contract according to market conditions.

Flexible working arrangements

Flexible working arrangements are a range of options designed to help employees balance work and home life. There is a wide range of flexible working practices, which in many instances can be used in a wide variety of workplaces:

- part-time working;
- flexitime;
- shift swapping;
- annual hours;
- work at or from home;
- term-time working;
- staggered hours;
- self-rostering;
- career breaks from work;
- mobile working/teleworking;
- compressed working hours;
- time off in lieu;
- job sharing;

The DTI provides illustrations of how innovative companies have used policies to reduce absenteeism, boost productivity and reduce long hours.[50] Case study examples of flexible working practices are also provided by the Equal Opportunities Commission[51] and the CIPD.[52]

A survey from the Chartered Management Institute found a significant relationship between levels of motivation and business performance. A high proportion of managers are motivated in their work and looking to be stretched. However, although a long hours culture is a reality, most managers want more freedom and personal choice in managing their long hours through flexible working to help ensure the right balance between work and home life. While part-time working and the use of temporary staff are now relatively common, options to work flexibly through options such as a compressed working week, annualised hours and sabbaticals are much less common.[53]

The European Commission has drawn attention to the rapid expansion of temporary work in the European Union in recent years. 'The trend towards temporary work is likely to continue, because it suits both individuals and business by encouraging job creation and flexibility. It enables companies to cope with workload fluctuations, and to use agencies when they need employees with specific skills.'[54]

However, despite the apparent popularity of flexible working, *Lucas* suggests that it is still causing organisations much anxiety.

> *It seems that for every organisation proactively embracing the many and varied forms of flexible working practices, there are those that are still tending to be reactive. Legislation and worries about the logistics appear to be putting some organisations and their management team on the back foot. They appear to view flexible working as just another problem or issue rather than an option which can be a motivational, performance enhancing and overhead cost-saving opportunity.*[55]

Telecommuting Recent advances in computerisation and telecommunications have had a further significant effect on the opportunities for flexible working. People can work from almost any geographic location: from head office, a satellite office, a shared access telecentre; or from their home, hotel room or car. An increasingly popular means of teleworking is **telecommuting** where staff work from home with a computer network telephone and fax.

From a discussion of the opportunities and challenges of telecommuters, *Manochehri and Pinkerton* conclude that telecommuting has come of age. The technological developments have made it possible, and economic and social factors have made it necessary. Managers have no choice but to learn how to take advantage of this new approach.

> *The advantages of telecommuting are already clear and distinct. Several trends such as further growth in information technology, the expanding role of the service sector, the emergence of virtual corporations and the diverse needs of the employees will guarantee a higher reliance on telecommuting as a viable alternative ... Managers have to appreciate the telecommuting management challenges and determine how to overcome them. If implemented and managed properly, telecommuting can be a valuable asset to an organization and to the people it employs.*[56]

A challenge for managers

The use of information communications technology and moves towards an increasingly flexible workforce call for attention to appropriate structures of organisation and systems of management. *Lucas* maintains that the big challenge for managers in the new millennium is: 'How do you create trust, communicate effectively, and foster teamwork with a group of people who could be working anywhere from their dining room table to an airport lounge?' Lucas suggests that this requires a sound performance management system, the effective management of virtual teams and managing communication. Flexible working calls for flexible managers who can cope with uncertainty, ambiguity and constant change, management development programmes, and a fundamental review of the role of a manager in the new world of work.[57]

Rigby suggests that for the first time, it is reasonable to say that the technological and financial barriers to some sort of mass home working have finally come down. 'The technology and communications infrastructure is now robust and fast enough – no, really – for a wide range of employees to do their job effectively without going past their front door.' There is, however, a downside. Home working flexibility blurs the boundaries between home and office. There are questions of measurement and the managerial fear that home workers do not actually work, and for whom this technology is most appropriate.[58]

Also, working from home does not appeal to everyone and it needs to be managed well, especially for full-time home workers. An increasing number of home workers report a feeling of detachment from the work situation and that they miss the interaction with colleagues.

Home Alone Stir Crazy

Unless managed well, the dream of working from home can turn into a nightmare, says former full-time home worker Rosemary Eatherden.

It's one o'clock, I've been at my laptop for five hours and I'm ready for a break. I need conversation. Across the office, I catch the eye of my only colleague. I walk over, fondly press his hand – well, paw actually – and he delivers my favourite conversational opener: 'Got any jelly babies?'

Even if you don't have a life-size talking Basil Brush to keep you company, if you work from home you'll know where I'm coming from. There are times for home workers when the exam-like intensity of your day leaves you desperate for human contact. Fox contact, even.

But surely home working is every weary commuter's dream? Well, no. Regular week-long home working can easily become a nightmare. I'm glad to have left it behind. On paper, I was the perfect home worker: disciplined, self-motivated and conscientious. But you also need to be happy working in isolation, able to survive without a daily fix of office chat.

I thought that was for me. After three years working at home, I knew it was not. It wasn't so much the gossip I missed, it was the interacting. I found I'd lost the knack. When you spend ten hours a day bonding with a laptop in a room on your own, you don't have a rich fund of stories with which to entertain your friends.

But why should all that matter to your employers? You're probably 25 per cent more productive, they're saving several grand a year on your desk space, and few of us are ever too sick to crawl across the hall to get to work.

I've heard the CIO of a big blue-chip company describe his utopia: a world where we can get information any time, any place, and where the office is redundant. We've pretty near got the technology cracked. So that leaves us with the hard bit: searching for a way to survive and thrive with almost zero interaction. Because if employers want creative, problem-solving team players, maybe solitary confinement, although it might boost the balance sheet, isn't the best answer.

You can have creative thoughts and solve problems on your own, but batting ideas around with colleagues in the same room is often so much better. Pressures that drag you down when you're on your own lighten or disappear when you laugh about them with others. Feeling part of a team helps you get through the day.

Occasional forays into the office don't give you the fix you need. You either hog the floor, delirious at the chance to speak, or wonder what everyone is talking about because you were sitting at home when the topic under discussion had an airing.

And many organisations find they have managers who are ill-equipped to cope with home workers. Trust is the hurdle, not technology. Yet trust is not the biggest challenge firms face. If home working is to be a success, they need to be smarter at understanding the long-term effects on people's health and well-being.

Working on your own, all day, every day, will wear down even the most resilient and spirited individual. Many full-time home workers say they feel forgotten and undervalued as a result of their isolation. Or could that be paranoia? That's another home-working hazard.

Rosemary Eatherden is a communications consultant[59]

Source: Eatherden, R., 'Home alone stir crazy', *Management Today,* March 2005, p. 75.

THE SHAMROCK ORGANISATION

One particular approach to flexible structural design and the core and complementary model of employment is *Handy's* concept of the 'shamrock' organisation.[60] The three leaves to each stem of the shamrock are symbolic of the organisation which is seen as made up of three distinct groups of people who are managed, organised and paid differently, and with different expectations: the professional core; the contractual fringe; and the flexible labour force (*see* Figure 16.7).

Figure 16.7 Representation of Handy's shamrock organisation

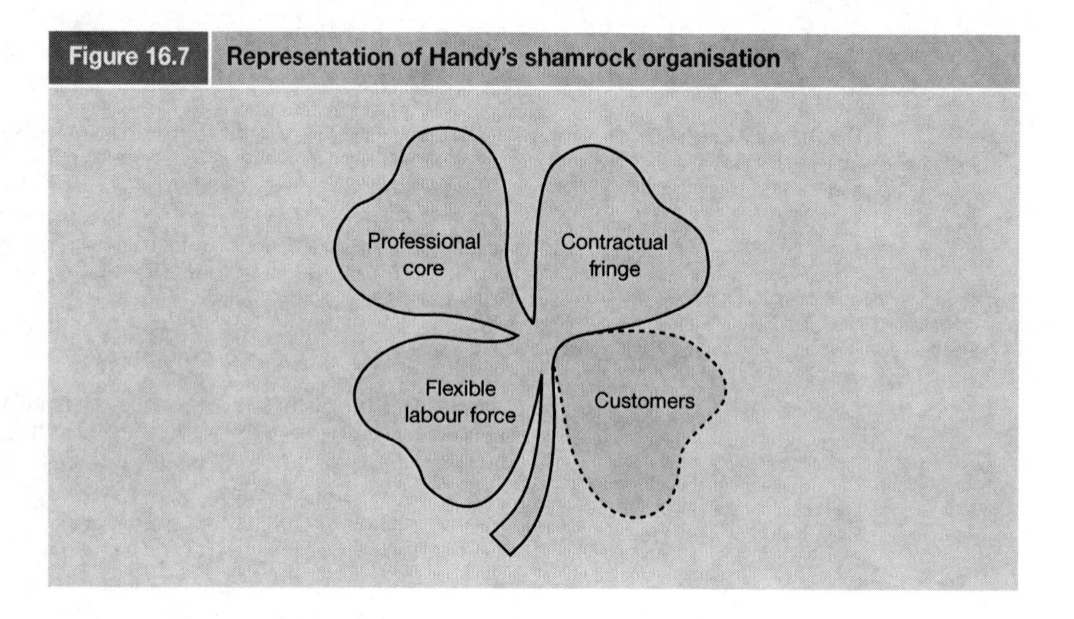

- **The professional core** comprises qualified professionals, technicians and managers essential to the existence and effective performance of the organisation. Collectively, these people own the knowledge that distinguishes the organisation. They get most of their identity and purpose from their work and are likely to be committed to it and dependent on it. The professional core are expensive and the tendency has been for organisations to restructure in order to reduce their numbers.
- **The contractual fringe** comprises those people, or other organisations, outside the organisation who provide specialist services and undertake all non-essential work which can be done by somebody else, and in theory are able to do it better for less. The organisational principle is that the contractual fringe are paid for results not for time, in fees and not wages. It is wise for the shamrock organisation to put boring and repetitive work out to contract, specifying the results expected and paying the fee.
- **The flexible labour force** represents all those part-time and temporary workers who make up the fastest growing group in the pattern of employment. It provides for flexibility in human resourcing. People are brought in as occasional extra part-time labour or temporary staff as changing work situations demand. Their commitment will be to a job and work group rather than to a career or organisation. Part-time or temporary work may be a matter of choice, not just a necessity.

Three significant workforces

According to Handy, organisations now have three significant workforces, each with a different kind of commitment to the organisation and a different set of expectations, and each workforce needs to be managed in different ways. The concept of the shamrock organisation can encourage managers to question the operations of their organisations. It gives rise to important decisions concerning what activities, and which people, should belong to the core, and concerning the management and control of subcontracting and of the flexible workforce. Managers could use the concept of the shamrock organisation and how this might best be adapted and utilised in a review of structure to suit the particular circumstances of the nature and operations of their organisation.

The increase in the flexible labour force is particularly noticeable with the growth of service industries. Services are created and consumed simultaneously. Unlike manufacturing, services are time-perishable and cannot be stored. The flexible labour force has increasingly been used as a cheaper and more convenient means of dealing with the peaks and troughs of demands, and as a means of adjusting the level of service to match changing customer requirements. Although casual and part-time staff are unlikely to have the same degree of commitment or ambition as the core it is important that they are taken seriously and regarded as a valuable part of the organisation. If treated as casual labour such people respond casually. The flexible workforce should be treated with respect, given fair and equitable treatment, adequate training and status, and decent pay and conditions. If casual and part-time staff are to respond in a positive way and provide a high standard of service, they have to be managed in a considerate and effective manner.

Customers as the fourth leaf?

Handy also refers to the growing practice of saving labour in the core by introducing another, informal and unpaid form of subcontracting – that of getting customers to do some of the work of the organisation. Examples include the collection rather than the delivery of goods, self-assembly furniture, automated banking facilities and self-serve petrol. In the hospitality industry, there are many examples of this 'serve yourself' philosophy. Examples include the provision of shoe-cleaning equipment or machines, hotel guests making their own tea and coffee in their rooms, restaurant self-service breakfast and buffet meals, and the provision of vending machines for snacks and beverages.

Challenges of the shamrock

Handy suggests that although on the face of it the shamrock is logical, these are not easy organisations to run. Each leaf of the shamrock has to be managed differently, yet as part of the whole. The core is the critical hub of the organisational network and this raises important questions as to what activities belong in the core; and which people belong in the core, and for how long. Fixed-term contracts will be an increasing feature. Employing fewer people brings with it the need for better people, and pressure for alertness and quality will place greater demands on the core people.

EMPOWERMENT AND CONTROL

Whatever its structural design, the various operations of the organisation have to be distributed among its members. It is necessary to plan, organise, direct and control their activities. The demand for flexibility and greater freedom and autonomy for individuals raises questions about the location of decision-making within the organisation, the extent and nature of delegation and empowerment, the manager–subordinate relationship, and the maintenance of management control within the formal structure of the organisation. This is discussed more fully in Chapter 18.

Refresh your understanding
Activity 16D
www.pearsoned.co.uk/mullins

Critical reflection

'The potential problem with alternative patterns of structure and the changing nature of the work environment is the risk of undermining line of authority and clearly established management–subordinate relationships.' Do you believe there is a threat to the underlying basis of effective organisational control and performance? Or do you think the new patterns of structure benefit individuals and the organisation?

MANAGEMENT IN THE NEWS

Dead end or turning point?

Another side of a 'McJob'

Mc Job; colloq. derog., An unstimulating, low-paid job with few prospects, esp. one created by the expansion of the service sector.

Both the Oxford English and the Merriam-Webster Dictionaries ran into a regular 'McFlurry of trouble with US fast-food giant McDonald's when they included the word 'McJob'. McDonald's then Chief Executive, Jim Cantalupo, took exception to the Merriam-Webster definition of 'a low-paying job that requires little skill and provides little opportunity for advancement'[62] and argued, in an open letter of 2003, that

more than 1,000 of the men and women who own and operate McDonald's restaurants today got their start by serving customers behind the counter.[63]

In recent years, McDonald's has been working hard to overturn the image which affects the fast-food industry in particular. A number of initiatives, some very imaginative, have been launched in the UK by David Fairhurst, appointed vice-president of McDonald's UK in 2005 from Tesco.[64] Some key statistics about employment at McDonald's include the facts that for over a third of its UK staff it is their first job, and that the 90 day turnover for hourly-paid staff is on a steady course downwards. A high proportion (60 per cent) of staff (crew) is aged 16–21 years, and five of its board members together with 80 per cent of managers (average length of service a respectable 10 years) started out as crew.[65]

Source: Empics/Associated Press

Fancy a career at McDonald? Far from being a low-paid, dead-end 'McJob', working at McDonalds can prove the gateway to a long-term, sucessful career for many young people.

The 'unskilled young worker' factor was perhaps behind one initiative, unveiled in September 2006, to help employees gain qualifications by both studying and taking exams at their place of work. A website, called 'Our Lounge', is available to all 67,000 staff, giving access to an online tutor who can help them towards NVQ or GCSE-equivalent qualifications in basic literacy and numeracy. Exams are taken at work using staff areas or training rooms, and Fairhurst expects that 1,000 employees would be taking up the initiative in its first year. He observed:

we recruit on qualities, not qualifications, but we want to ensure that no one is held back by not having the basics of numeracy and literacy.[66]

More unusually, McDonald's has launched an experimental form of shared contract to encourage flexibility by giving workers more personal control over their hours and shifts. The 'family contract' enables two people from the same family who work in the same restaurant to cover each other's shifts without having to notify the manager in advance. Fairhurst believes that pairings like this will help employees to manage their shift and family commitments more easily, thus increasing their job satisfaction and motivation.[67]

The company has also attempted to turn round its public image through a recruitment poster campaign 'Not Bad for a McJob' which draws on research carried out by Professor Adrian Furnham of University College London. Furnham's report suggests that a job at McDonald's can have a positive impact on workers' lives, especially younger low-skilled workers, who experience increased self-esteem, confidence and motivation. Amongst workers questioned, 90 per cent showed high levels of engagement, 85 per cent said the job was better than they'd expected, 83 per cent had seen positive change in themselves since starting work and 74 per cent saw a long-term career at McDonald's.

The youngsters we spoke to started work viewing a McJob like most other people. But there is an amazing change in perception once they start. They are happy, motivated and the work gives them confidence and self-esteem. The evidence indicates that these types of jobs are positive for young people.[68]

Furnham's report quotes Jason Hersey who left school at age 16 without any qualifications and little confidence. Nine years after getting a job at McDonald's he manages a store with an annual turnover of £1.7m.

Management in the news – continued

'I went into the job so I could get a bit of money to have a laugh with my mates,' he says. 'My perception was the same as most other people – it was a means to an end and was not going to take me anywhere. My mum was just happy I'd got a job but me working for McDonald's wasn't something she was going to sing about to her mates. Now you can't shut her up. While other business wouldn't have given me a chance, I showed I was willing to work and they rewarded that. They realise it's not in their interest to hold someone back who wants to do well.'[69]

Discussion questions

1 What are generally considered to be the main characteristics of a McJob? How, and how far, do the initiatives described in the case, and the research by Adrian Furnham, challenge these assumptions?

2 Review the way in which the structure and technology of this type of organization determine the nature of the work itself. What are the implications for the management of people in such organizations?

SYNOPSIS

- There are a number of variables and other factors that affect organisation structures and systems of management. Earlier approaches to organisation and management believed in one best form of structure and tended to concentrate on limited aspects of organisation. The contingency approach, however, emphasises the need for flexibility and takes the view that there is no one best structure or system of management. If certain situational factors exist, **then** certain variables in organisation structure and systems of management are most appropriate.

- Situational factors may be identified in a number of ways and various studies have been carried out into the extent to which these contingency factors influence organisational design and effectiveness. Among the most important contingency factors are size of organisation, technology and environment. A particular concern for global companies is the need to balance the benefits of size with the liabilities of a complex, slow-moving and bureaucratic structure.

- Important studies concerning technology include those by Woodward, who draws attention to patterns of organisation and production systems, and business success, and Perrow on the variability and analysis of technology. Two important studies on the effects of the environment on the management and structure of organisations include work by Burns and Stalker, who have drawn attention to the significance of the distinction between the characteristics of mechanistic and organic structures, and Lawrence and Lorsch on the differentiation and integration of internal structures.

- As with other approaches to organisation and management, the contingency approach has been subject to a number of criticisms or doubts about its practical value to management. However, despite the criticisms and limitations it has provided a further insight into our understanding of relationships among factors influencing the structure, management and operations of organisations. The contingency approach also draws attention to the importance of different structures for different activities of the organisation.

- The effects of increased economic pressures and demands for greater competitiveness have drawn attention to the importance of structural variables. The movement towards tighter and leaner organisations has emphasised the importance of alternative forms of structure, of the demand for flexibility and greater freedom for the individual. There is a wide range of flexible working practices, which in many instances can be used in a variety of workplaces. In order to free management to concentrate on core activities, businesses are making increasing use of outsourcing and having a wider range of non-core services provided to them by specialist service providers.

- One particular approach to flexible structural design, and the core and complementary model of employment is Handy's concept of the 'shamrock' organisation which is seen as made up of three distinct groups of people who are managed, organised and paid differently, and with different expectations: the professional core, the contractual fringe and the flexible labour force. The demand for flexibility raises questions about the location of decision-making within the organisation, the extent and nature of delegation and empowerment, and the manager–subordinate relationship.

Refresh your understanding, assess your progress and begin your research with online resources at **www.pearsoned.co.uk/mullins**

REVIEW AND DISCUSSION QUESTIONS

1. Explain what is meant by the contingency approach to organisation. How does the contingency approach differ from other approaches to organisation and management?
2. Contrast 'mechanistic' and 'organic' systems of management practice and structure. What is the significance of this distinction?
3. Explain what is meant by 'differentiation' and 'integration' of the internal structure of an organisation. What are the implications of differentiation and integration, and what mechanisms might be adopted to achieve integration?
4. Assess critically the value and contribution of contingency theory to the structure, management and operation of work organisations. Give your own examples of situational factors that are likely to account for variations in the structure and management of different organisations.
5. Discuss the demand for increased flexibility in patterns of work organisation and structural design, and give examples of flexible working arrangements in an organisation of your choice.
6. To what extent have you seen evidence of the 'shamrock organisation' in relation to the structure of your own or some other chosen organisation?
7. What are *your* views on the influence of recent advances in computerisation and telecommunications for patterns of structure and work organisation?
8. Discuss critically the questions that are raised by the increased demand for flexibility and greater freedom for individuals.

ASSIGNMENT 1

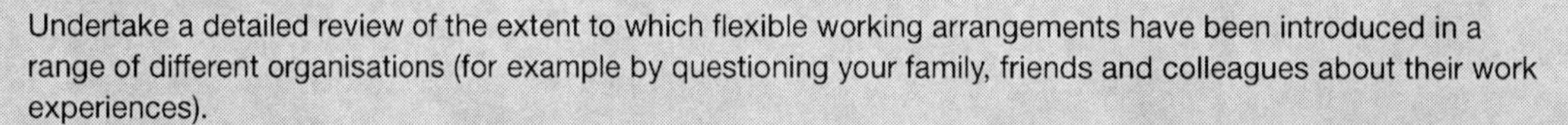

Undertake a detailed review of the extent to which flexible working arrangements have been introduced in a range of different organisations (for example by questioning your family, friends and colleagues about their work experiences).

a Detail critically the apparent effectiveness of these arrangements and their influence on job satisfaction and perceived work performance.

b Explain fully why, despite the many apparent potential advantages, working from home has not proved as popular to the extent that might have been expected.

ASSIGNMENT 2

Given the speed of technological change, an increasing rate of innovation, and growing demands by a more highly educated work force, many scholars suggest that the classical view of organisations will become outdated. In response to the resulting frustration, bureaucracies will begin to fade away and will be replaced by more creative forms of organisation.

Vecchio, R. P. *Organisational Behavior*, Core Concepts, Fourth Edition, Dryden Press (2000), p. 320.

a Detail fully how would you design a more creative form for your own (or some other chosen) organisation.

b Where appropriate prepare a revised organisation chart.

c Be prepared to lead a class discussion, including a question and answer session, to discuss your findings.

PERSONAL AWARENESS AND SKILLS EXERCISE

Objectives

Completing this exercise should help you to enhance the following skills:

- Identify and contrast actual features of different structures within organisations.
- Evaluate the significance today of this distinction.
- Recognise the effect of different structures on people within organisations.
- Act the role of a senior manager.

Exercise

Drawing on the information given in Table 16.2, you are required to:

1 Prepare a detailed comparison and analysis of ways in which your own organisation (or some other organisation well known to you) tends to displays characteristic features of mechanistic and organic structures.

2 Prepare detailed notes on:
- the effectiveness of structure in relation to systems and styles of management, the various activities of the organisation and the people employed; and
- different perceptions of both mechanistic and organic features, and examples of tension and conflict which arise from a mix of both structures.

3 As a senior manager, explain fully what actions you would recommend in order to help overcome these tensions and conflicts.

Discussion

- What is the real strategic value of organisational structure and who should be involved in the design of structure?
- What is the impact of technology and technological change on the significance of mechanistic or organic structures?
- Given a forced choice, explain, with supporting reasons, which form of structure you would most prefer to work within.

CASE STUDY

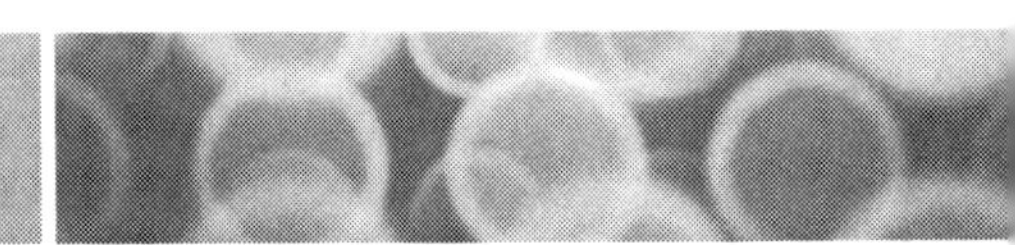

John Lewis, Waitrose and Ocado: distinctively successful

The Business and the Partnership

The John Lewis Partnership is one of the UK's top ten retail businesses with 27 John Lewis department stores and 179 Waitrose supermarkets. It is also the country's largest example of worker co-ownership. All 64,000 permanent staff are Partners in the business. We believe that the commitment of Partners to the business is a unique source of competitive advantage which has fuelled 75 years of profitable growth and a reputation amongst customers and suppliers unparalleled in the UK retail industry[70]

John Lewis opened his Oxford Street department store for business in 1864. In its early days it was a traditional family-owned business, and his two sons followed him into the firm. John Spedan Lewis, later to found the John Lewis Partnership, became Director of a second store (Peter Jones in Sloane Square) in 1905. Possibly influenced by the egalitarian social and political movements of the early 20th century, he wanted to change the way in which the business was managed and to involve its employees more centrally in its running. In 1920 he launched an employee profit-sharing scheme at the Peter Jones store. His views were not accepted by his father and initially caused a rift in the running of the business, but father and son were reconciled before the former's death in 1928, when Spedan inherited the whole enterprise. The following year Spedan Lewis drew up the First Trust Settlement which left him in control of the business but gave employees shares in its profits. Shortly before the Second World War the business acquired the Waite, Rose and Taylor grocery stores, and in 1940 bought the Selfridge Provincial Stores Group. In 1950 the Second Trust Settlement created the John Lewis Partnership (JLP) as it is today, owned and run entirely by its employees. John Spedan Lewis died in 1963.

As a business, the John Lewis Partnership is therefore organisationally very different to its major competitors in the UK. It operates in a variety of highly competitive business environments: the UK food retail business is dominated by Tesco, Sainsbury's and Walmart (Asda), and John Lewis department stores compete not only with other department stores but also with specialist high-street retailers of clothing, electrical goods, furniture and furnishings. Success in these markets requires very high standards of efficiency and effectiveness, and it is interesting to consider the extent to which JLP's distinctive organisation and culture explain its success.

How successful is it and how is it successful?

> *The supreme purpose of the John Lewis Partnership is simply the happiness of its members.*[71]

John Spedan Lewis' words, quoted in the JLP corporate brochure, set an unusual objective for a business organisation. While many commercial organisations consider the happiness of the workforce as one among several key aims, few hold it to be an overriding one. JLP's structure is an example of representative democracy: all partners elect representatives to the governing Partnership Council; elected representatives account for 80 per cent of Council members, with the remaining 20 per cent appointed by the Chairman. The Chairman and senior directors are required to give an annual account of their stewardship at a full council meeting. Further means of communication and decision-making include branch forums and divisional councils which reflect the various operating units including warehouses and factories as well as stores. Partners can therefore influence decisions and affect the company's activities, and there is a direct pay-off in the shape of an annual bonus based on the company's profits. The Chairman and other directors must ensure the continuing solvency of the business as well as keeping funds available for growth, but beyond whatever is necessary for these purposes, the annual profits are redistributed to members. All partners receive

Source: Roger Bamber/Alamy

The John Lewis Partnership, including Waitrose, has a unique organisational structure which has contributed to its business success.

bonuses which are calculated as a percentage of their base pay; in the financial year 2005/06 this resulted in £120 million of profit being redistributed at a rate of 15 per cent of salary.[72] In some years this has gone as high as 22 per cent, although a range of 9–15 per cent appears to be more usual. This direct form of 'industrial democracy' and high level of worker participation means that the management of JLP does not recognise or negotiate with trade unions.

A further aspect of the objective of 'partner happiness' is the extensive range of benefits and services which JLP provides to its workforce. There is a non-contributory final-salary pension scheme and many direct forms of assistance including a loans scheme. Holiday entitlements are generous, as are discounts on purchases, and the partnership owns social and sporting amenities as well as several estates which provide leisure activities and accommodation for partners and their families.

Its commercial success, as we have noted, depends on performance in some very tough markets. How has JLP maintained and grown its business?

Keeping the customer satisfied

> *The Partnership was ahead of its time in recognising that commercial success depended on showing the highest level of good citizenship in its behaviour within the community. Today we are best known for the fact that our business is owned for the benefit of our employees, but we know that to cut our way through tough competitive conditions, we have to continue to prize sound relationships with our customers and suppliers, and sustain a keen sense of civic responsibility.*[73]

In January 2006 the John Lewis Partnership and Waitrose came first and second in a regular Verdict survey of customer satisfaction with retail stores.[74] It also 'trumped' its arch rival Marks and Spencer by posting higher growth in like-for-like sales during the first quarter of 2006 at a time when M&S was recovering strongly from a period of low growth and was publicly discussing plans to start selling electrical goods in competition with John Lewis.[75] Clearly the partnership's growth and the high levels of customer satisfaction are very closely linked. Unlike a number of its rivals, JLP does not use loyalty cards, although it does offer both store cards and a credit card with relatively modest rewards. What it does claim to do is to focus on quality and to offer value for money (John Spedan Lewis introduced the 'never knowingly undersold' principle in 1925).

Taking Waitrose as the main example, this has meant a defining principle of 'Quality food, honestly priced'. The effect can be seen in a number of ways, including a relatively early decision to integrate local products into its range (many major food retailers have preferred to stock only products which can be made available at all their stores nationally), thus anticipating a growing interest in localism and the environmental problems associated with long-distance haulage (food miles). In 2001 its television advertising campaign announced that it was selling only free range eggs and it has gone on to establish links with farmers whose meat and poultry are produced according to high standards of animal welfare. In 2005 it was named the first winner of 'Food Retailer of the Year' by the RSPCA in its 'Conscientious Consumer' campaign.[76] Once again, this fitted well with a trend towards concern amongst UK consumers about the ethical production of food and questions about food safety and traceability (knowing the precise source of food products enables a retailer to react very quickly to environmental health alerts such as that surrounding 'bird flu' at the start of 2006). In 2005, the year of Live8, the partnership launched the Waitrose Foundation, which runs parallel to its commitment to fair trade and seeks to do more for local citrus fruit producers in southern Africa than simply guarantee a fair price for their products. The Trust sponsors social, educational and health care initiatives among these farming communities, viewing it as a means of encouraging sustainable and long-term development in the country.

These initiatives have been supported by superior advertising since 1997 and the award-winning television campaigns from 2001 gave a distinctive and stylish edge to its marketing which has been copied by rival Marks and Spencer. The advertisements generally focus on the provenance of the products and the lives and work of individual producers and suppliers. Indeed, the company name appears only at the end of the advertisements, in a way which emphasises the relationship between producer and consumer and positions the company as a discreet intermediary between the two rather than a dominant brand.

Of course, no food retailer can afford to ignore the value of Internet shopping, but Waitrose adopted an unusual model for its home delivery service. It decided, in 2001, to enter into partnership with the newly formed venture Ocado rather than to create an own-brand delivery service as did most of its rivals. This distinctive approach has enabled the company both to spread the risk of such a venture and to deliver a better standard of service than many other comparable operations. All goods are picked from the central warehouse in Hertfordshire, placed into 'pods' which are then distributed by truck to car parks around the region; then the pods are reloaded onto small delivery vans which carry eight pods to their destination. This contrasts with the model adopted by Tesco and others where goods are picked from the shelves at local stores, which tends to mean a higher risk of stock shortages and the inclusion of alternative or replacement items.[77] The Waitrose website also won an RNIB award for accessibility in 2005.

And so?

Any company can start spending money on corporate social responsibility ventures; all the main supermarkets do and many publicly announce a specific percentage of profits for the purpose. What appears to make Waitrose different is the coherence and integration of a number of features, including:

- structure, systems and culture (the partnership, its consultative councils);
- segmentation and positioning (its market is clearly identified as middle-class educated professionals in metropolitan and suburban areas);
- product strategy and upstream relationships (high-quality, locally sourced, Fairtrade, and its civilised, non-bullying approach and indeed lionisation of producers in TV adverts);
- customer service (universally appreciated in surveys and delivered by people who have every reason to care about the difference between adequate and very good);
- specific CSR initiatives (the Waitrose Foundation, its 'model' estate farm at Leckford in Hampshire);
- marketing communications (innovative, engaging, memorable, perfectly targeted, and understated).

Ten years ago, Waitrose was admirable but not very exciting. Today, the Waitrose brand is cool, with a seemingly effortless stylishness that makes some of the others look flatfooted, loud and desperate. It has formed a strong bond with a very profitable niche market of customers who love being treated that way. And it works only because the offering as a whole fits together and is utterly credible.

Your tasks

1. Using the Burns and Stalker model (Table 16.2) and the Handy model (Figure 16.7) as the basis for analysis, identify the degree to which the John Lewis Partnership, Waitrose and Ocado reflect mechanistic, organic and 'shamrock' structures of organisation.
2. Critically review the governing structure of the John Lewis partnership. What are the strengths and weaknesses of such a structure in a fast-moving competitive environment?
3. Discuss and evaluate the possible impact of this democratic style of organisation on the role and behaviour of managers. How is it likely to differ from the role and behaviour of managers in a more traditional, shareholder-owned company?

Notes and references

1. Vecchio, R. P. *Organizational Behavior, Core Concepts*, Fourth edition, Dryden Press (2000), p. 320.
2. Bouchikhi, H and Kimberly, J. R. 'The Customized Workplace', in Chowdhury, S. *Management 21C*, Financial Times Prentice Hall (2000), pp. 207–19.
3. Vecchio, R. P. *Organizational Behavior: Core Concepts*, Fourth edition, Dryden Press (2000), p. 338.
4. Lynch, R. *Corporate Strategy*, Fourth edition, Financial Times Prentice Hall (2006), p. 582.
5. See, for example: Luthans, F. *Organisational Behaviour*, Fourth edition, McGraw-Hill (1985).
6. See, for example: Miller, D. and Droge, C. 'Psychological and Traditional Determinants of Structure', *Administrative Science Quarterly*, 31 December 1986, pp. 539–60.
7. Child, J. *Organization: A Guide to Problems and Practice*, Second edition, Paul Chapman (1988), p. 221.
8. See, for example: McKinley, W. 'Decreasing Organisational Size: To Untangle or Not to Untangle?', *Academy of Management Review*, January 1992, pp. 112–23; and Shapiro, E. 'Power, Not Size Counts', *Management Review*, September 1996.
9. Birkinshaw, J. 'The Structures behind Global Companies', in Pickford, J. (ed.), *Financial Times Mastering Management 2.0*, Financial Times Prentice Hall (2001), pp. 75–80.
10. Woodward, J. *Industrial Organization: Theory and Practice*, Second edition, Oxford University Press (1980).
11. Dawson, S. and Wedderburn, D. 'Introduction' to Woodward, J. *Industrial Organisation: Theory and Practice*, Second edition, Oxford University Press (1980), p. xiii.
12. Woodward, J. *Industrial Organisation: Theory and Practice*, Second edition, Oxford University Press (1980), pp. 69, 71.
13. Zwerman, W. L. *New Perspectives on Organisation Theory*, Greenwood (1970).
14. Marsh, R. M. and Mannari, H. 'Technology and Size as Determinants of the Organisational Structure of Japanese Factories', *Administrative Science Quarterly*, 26, 1981, pp. 35–56.
15. Collins, P. D. and Hull, F. 'Technology and Span of Control: Woodward Revisited', *Journal of Management Studies*, vol. 23, no. 2, March 1986, pp. 143–64.
16. Perrow, C. *Organisational Analysis: A Sociological View*, Tavistock Publications (1970).
17. Burns, T. and Stalker, G. M. *The Management of Innovation*, Tavistock Publications (1966).
18. Litterer, J. A. *The Analysis of Organizations*, Second edition, Wiley (1973).
19. Sherman, J. D. and Smith, H. L. 'The Influence of Organisational Structure on Intrinsic Versus Extrinsic Motivation', *Academy of Management Journal*, December 1984, p. 883.
20. Reigle, R. F. 'Measuring Organic and Mechanistic Cultures', *Engineering Management Journal*, vol. 13, no. 4, December 2001, pp. 3–8.
21. Wilkins, R. 'The Management Challenge of Hybrid Organisations', *Administrator*, vol. 7, no. 8, September 1987, p. 3.
22. Mullins, L. J. *Hospitality Management and Organisational Behaviour*, Fourth edition, Longman (2001).
23. Parris, J. 'Designing your Organisation', *Management Services*, vol. 23, no. 10, October 1979, p. 14.
24. Lawrence, P. R. and Lorsch, J. W. *Organisation and Environment*, Irwin (1969).
25. Boschken, H. L. 'Strategy and Structure: Reconceiving the Relationship', *Journal of Management*, vol. 16, no. 1, March 1990, pp. 135–50.
26. Hunt, J. W. *Managing People at Work: A Manager's Guide to Behaviour in Organisations*, Third edition, McGraw-Hill (1992), p. 170.
27. Child, J. *Organisation: A Guide to Problems and Practice*, Second edition, Paul Chapman (1988).
28. Dawson, S. 'Organisational Analysis and the Study of Policy Formulation and Implementation', *Public Administration Bulletin*, 31, December 1979, pp. 52–68.
29. Mintzberg, H. *The Structuring of Organisations*, Prentice Hall (1979).
30. Birkinshaw, J, *Mastering Management 2.0*, Financial Times Prentice Hall (2001), p. 78.
31. See, for example: Fincham, R. and Rhodes, P. S. *The Individual, Work and Organisation*, Second edition, Weidenfeld and Nicolson (1992).

32 Robey, D. *Designing Organisations*, Irwin (1982), p. 59.
33 Vecchio, R. P., *Organisational Behavior: Core Concepts*, Fourth edition, Dryden Press (2000), pp. 11–12.
34 Hofstede, G. *Culture's Consequences: International Differences in Work-related Values'*, Sage Publications (1980).
35 Trompenaars, F. and Hampden-Turner, C. *Riding the Waves of Culture*, Second edition, Nicholas Brearley (1999).
36 Hickson, D., Hinings, C., McMillan, C. and Schwitter, J. 'The Culture Free Context of Organisation Structures: A Tri National Comparison', *Sociology*, vol. 8, 1974, pp. 59–80.
37 Maurice, M., Sorge, A. and Warner, M. 'Societal Differences in Organising Manufacturing Units: A Comparison of France, West Germany and Britain', *Organisational Studies*, vol. 1, no. 1, 1980, pp. 59–86.
38 Schneider, S. C. and Barsoux, J. *Managing Across Cultures*, Second edition, Financial Times Prentice Hall (2003), p. 101.
39 Francesco, A. M. and Gold, B. A. *International Organisational Behavior*, Second edition, Pearson Prentice Hall (2005).
40 Morgan, G. *Imaginisation: The Art of Creative Management*, Sage Publications (1993).
41 Eden, C. 'Coping with strategic risk', in Crainer, S. and Dearlove, D. (eds) *Handbook of Management*, Financial Times Prentice Hall (2001).
42 Crainer, S., *Key Management Ideas: Thinkers that Changed the Management World*, Third edition, Financial Times Prentice Hall (1998), p. 47.
43 Czerniawska, F. 'From bottlenecks to blackberries: How the relationship between organisations and individuals is changing', Management Consultancies Association, Executive Report, September 2005; and Vernon, M. 'The Changing Face of the Workplace' *Management Today*, September 2005, pp. 62–7.
44 See, for example: Hains, G. 'BPO: The Next Generation of Outsourcing', *Institute of Business Ideas and Solutions'*, December 2002, pp. 12–13.
45 Vernon, M. 'The Changing Face of the Workplace' *Management Today*, September 2005, pp. 62–7. See also Czerniawska, F. 'From bottlenecks to blackberries: How the relationship between organisations and individuals is changing', Management Consultancies Association, Executive Report, September 2005.
46 Bouchikhi, H. and Kimberly, J. R., 'The Customized Workplace', in Chowdhury, S., *Management 21C*, Financial Times Prentice Hall (2000), pp. 207–19.
47 'Advice Leaflet – Flexible Working' ACAS, November 2005. www.acas.org.uk [accessed 24 April 2006].
48 Pitman, B. (Sir) 'Flexibility is the Key to Competitiveness', *Professional Manager*, March 2000, p. 6.
49 Atkinson, J. 'Manpower Strategies for Flexible Organisations', *Personnel Management*, vol. 16, no. 8, August 1984, pp. 28–31.
50 'Work–Life Balance: The Business Case' Department of Trade and Industry, September 2001.
51 'Flexible Working – Case studies', Equal Opportunities Commission, www.eoc.org.uk, 24 June 2003.
52 'Flexible Working: The Implementation Challenge', CIPD, October 2005.
53 Cook, P. and Jackson, N. 'Motivation Matters', Chartered Management Institute, October 2005.
54 'Commission Proposal Supports Temporary Agency Work', *Social Agenda*, European Commission Employment and Social Affairs, Issue No. 2, July 2002.
55 Lucas, E. 'Riding the flexible working wave', *Professional Manager*, January 2006, pp. 22–4.
56 Manochehri, G. and Pinkerton, T. 'Managing Telecommuters: Opportunities and Challenges', *American Business Review*, vol. 21, no. 1, January 2003, pp. 9–16.
57 Lucas, E., 'Keep it Formal for Maximum Flexibility', *Professional Manager*, March 2000, pp. 10–12.
58 Rigby, R. 'Homing In', *Management Today*, March 2005, pp. 72–4.
59 Eatherden, R. 'Home Alone Stir Crazy' *Management Today*, March 2005, p. 75.
60 Handy, C. B. *The Age of Unreason*, Business Books (1989).
61 Oxford English Dictionary Online version
62 Merriam-Webster Dictionary, Online version
63 *McDonald's anger over McJob entry*, BBC online news, news.bbc.co.uk, 11 September 2003 [accessed 19 January 2006].
64 Thomas, D. 'HR challenges ... I'm lovin' it' *Personnel Today*, 6 September 2005, www.personneltoday.com [accessed 19 January 2006].
65 Ibid.
66 People Management, *Large on Learning*, www.peoplemanagement.co.uk [accessed 19 January 2006].
67 Thomas, D. 'McDonald's agrees shift swapping contract' *Personnel Today*, 25 January 2006, www.personneltoday.com [accessed 19 January 2006].
68 Winterman, D. 'The flip side of a McJob' BBC online news, news.bbc.co.uk, 6 August 2006 [accessed 19 January 2006].
69 Ibid
70 John Lewis Partnership website http://www.johnlewispartnership.co.uk/
71 John Spedan Lewis, quoted in the JLP corporate brochure.
72 John Lewis Partnership Annual Report and Accounts 2005–6.
73 Sir Stuart Hampson, Chairman of JLP.
74 Verdict, 2006 Consumer Satisfaction Index.
75 Wallop, H. 2006 'John Lewis Trumps M&S', *Daily Telegraph* 30 May 2006.
76 RSPCA Website www.rspca.org.uk [accessed 26 June 2006].
77 Day, P. 2005 'Right up Your Street'. BBC online news.bbc.co.uk, 9 August 2005 [accessed 26 June 2006].

Business, Ethics and Values

Perspectives on business ethics and values

Learning outcomes

Having read this chapter and completed its associated activities, readers should be able to:

- Identify the good, tragic, comic, satirical and farcical elements in the way in which people and organisations deal with matters of ethics and morality.
- Explain the basic features of stakeholder theory.
- Evaluate the business case for business ethics and the validity of its claims.
- Give an account of the various arguments about the moral status of business, organisations and management.

Stories and business ethics

The study of business ethics begins with stories. Families and societies have always used stories to illustrate and reinforce their sense of values, justice and fairness. And so it is in business and organisations. There are the stories often found in organisational glossy newsletters of good deeds done by staff volunteering to work among disadvantaged groups and the benefits that the organisation has brought to the communities it works within. Then there are the more gossipy stories that are told, and half told, as episodes are interrupted by work or authority figures, that tell of jealousies and spites, corruption and abuse, lying and distortion.

Czarniawska (2004: 21) pointed out that there are four types of dramatic story in the European classical tradition – romances, tragedies, comedies and satires, each of which has its characteristic figure of speech. Each of them can represent different kinds of business ethics issues.

Figures of speech

DEFINITIONS

Metaphor

Makes comparisons by referring to one thing as a different thing. So calling all the employees in an organisation 'assets' is a metaphor. If you said of a chief executive officer 'she is a Branson among business leaders', this would be a use of metaphor and a means of making a hero of her. It could also be a kind of paralipsis in which attention is drawn to something – that the CEO is a woman and Branson a man – while pretending to pass over it. As a form of irony this paralipsis could be taken as a criticism of the CEO.

Metonymy

Uses an attribute of something to represent the thing itself. Chairpersons sit in a chair when they hold a board meeting. The chair is their attribute, so they become known as chairs. In tragedy a single attribute can undermine a person's integrity; a good person is often brought low because of a part of their behaviour or character.

Synecdoche

Uses a part of something to represent the whole. Business people wear suits and so that particular aspect of them comes to represent them and their role. Others refer to them as suits, as in 'are the suits arriving today to check us out?'. Suits are also a means by which business people present a good image of themselves. In comedy synecdoche points out the comic pretensions between ambition and reality. The smartness of the clothes can emphasise the vacuity of the wearer.

Irony

Speaking or writing in such a way as to imply the opposite of what is being said. Often used to imply mockery or jest. It is therefore the basis of much satire.

Romances are based on the quest of a single individual to achieve some noble goal that is only achievable because human beings have an innate, if sometimes well disguised, goodness. The Quaker heroes of the past such as Joseph Rowntree who built model factories and villages for model workers, or more modern heroes such as Anita Roddick who sought, against the odds, to make selling beauty products a beautiful process, are good examples. Such heroes become metaphors for their particular brand of ethical management.

Tragedies tell of people who try to behave well but who, by challenging fate, come to personal grief. The stories of whistleblowers who reveal corporate wrong-doing but in so doing lose their families, their homes and their livelihoods are a good example. Tragedy is based on metonymy, as in the film *The China Syndrome* (Bridges, 1979) in which Jack Lemmon plays an engineer in a malfunctioning nuclear power station who is the only person to be troubled by a vibration felt as a test procedure was conducted. The vibration is a metonym for the potential cataclysm that is waiting to happen.

Comedies are stories about how human imperfections and weaknesses make the achievement of a happy ending difficult. The ways in which companies that are foreign to a new country they have begun to operate in often get their attempts to integrate wrong are a strong source of comedy. The western businessmen, for it is mostly men who would do this, who ignorantly offend their Arab business partners by putting their feet up on their desk after concluding a deal in an attempt to show that the formal business is over and everyone can relax, and so revealing the soles of their shoes, have a degree of comic potential. The dirty soles of the shoes act as a synecdoche, a part of the businessman, which stands for the unwholesomeness of the whole man.

Satires work ironically. By contrasting people's behaviour with their words, or by defining the context in which the words are said, it is made clear that people meant the opposite of what they said. When corporations are accused of not taking care of

- customers, by not closing the doors on the *Herald of Free Enterprise* (*see* p. 328), or
- employees, as in the Bhopal incident in which 20,000 people were killed or harmed by a chemical leak from an American owned chemical works in the city (*see* p. 469) (the leak could have been prevented if procedures, management and maintenance had been rigorous), or
- the environment when the oil companies are accused of despoiling the Niger Delta (*see* p. 475),

organisations often reply by saying that the objects and subjects they have damaged are in fact their top priority. They thereby make themselves the object of satire. People then take such claims as ironies. In the film *Super Size Me*, Morgan Spurlock (2004) tested McDonald's claim that its food is not intrinsically unhealthy by living for a month on its products. Of course such a diet made him an unhealthier person (that is irony).

Connexion point

The ethical issues raised by the film *Super Size Me* are discussed in Case study 2.23 (pp. 91–2).

There is, in business ethics as in life generally, a narrow point of balance

- between romance and satire
- and between tragedy and comedy.

These tensions are the narrative dynamic behind business ethics issues. The heroes of romances can easily become the subject of satirists' scorn. In the struggles between heroes and villains the heroes can overreach themselves and believe they really do have magical powers, in some cases literally. In 1999 in the oil producing delta region of Nigeria members of a cult known as the *Egbesu* began a violent campaign against, as they saw it, the despoliation of their homeland by the oil companies (Ibeanu, 2000: 28). It was believed that the charms they wore made them impervious to bullets. The heroes may then become ridiculous and the villains begin to look more benign. Tragedy can, uncomfortably, have comic elements. As Marx (1963: 1) pointed out, history repeats itself, 'first time as tragedy, second time as farce'. Just as commonly comedy can descend into tragedy. The difference between an organisational comedy of incompetence and a tragedy may be no more than the operation of chance. If luck remains with the organisation then we can all laugh at its bumbling, but if luck runs out the story can become tragic, for some. In December 2004 (Harding, 2004) a Delhi schoolboy from one of the elite schools, doubtless anxious to show off his new mobile phone with built-in camera, used it to take a video clip of his girlfriend providing him with oral sex. Unfortunately for him within a few days the video clip was on sale on Bazee.com, the Indian version of eBay, and indeed owned by eBay. The company took the item off the website as soon as they became aware of it but nevertheless an uproar ensued in India and a mildly, if in poor taste, comic event turned serious. The boy was taken to juvenile court and expelled from school. Avnish Bajaj, the CEO of Bazee.com and a US citizen, was arrested and thrown into the notoriously overcrowded Tihar gaol. For three people at least tragedy was a tale of prosperity, for a time, that ended in wretchedness. The matter was debated in the Indian parliament and the BJP party denounced the incident as the result of American 'interference'. The American government in its turn was taking a serious interest in Mr Bajaj's imprisonment. Condoleeza Rice, the soon to be American Secretary of State, was reported to be furious at the humiliating treatment meted out to an American citizen. The Indian software industry association called for Bajaj's immediate release.

It would appear that the issues and problems that form the subject of business ethics can appear in different forms, sometimes as romances, sometimes as tragedies, sometimes as comedies and sometimes as satires. It follows that stories are a good mechanism through which business issues can be studied and understood. If we can understand how the plots of these stories can lead to either good or bad outcomes we can develop an intuitive knowledge of how to encourage more happy endings than bad ones. Or at least the stories might palliate, or help us come to terms with, the dilemmas we face (Kirk, 1974: 83).

Case study 1.1

The *Hindustan Times*, Monday 29 November 2004

I am writing this part of the chapter in a hotel room in New Delhi, India. A copy of the newspaper has been slid under the door to my room. A number of its stories show the range of business ethics issues. The lead story is a *romance*: a hero entrepreneur and philanthropist, in this case Sir Richard Branson, is reported to have attended a party in New Delhi at which 4.5 crore (a crore is ten million) rupees had been raised for a children's educational charity. 'The creation of wealth is fine. But businesses need to pay back to the society in a number of ways', said Branson. The next day it was also reported that the Government of India might allow Branson to buy a personal stakeholding in a domestic airline, even though the rules on foreign direct investment would not allow Virgin Atlantic, his own airline, to buy such a stake.

Tragedy was represented by a story that a former High Court judge was likely to be charged with receiving bribes and manipulating judgments to favour the person who had paid the bribes. It is a tragedy because a judge appointed to uphold the law, and who no doubt originally intended to do so, allowed himself to give way to external pressures and so destroyed his reputation.

A story that *satirises* itself is that twenty years after the Bhopal incident American scientists are proposing to recreate the gas leak under controlled experimental conditions. In particular they want to discover whether deadly chemicals such as carbon monoxide and hydrogen cyanide were released as well as other chemicals in the original leak. The irony is that it seems that, when only Indian citizens had been harmed and killed by such a leak, the Americans had been content to ignore the possibility that these two gases were involved. But, by 2004, when it was possible that American citizens might be subject to such a chemical attack by terrorists, then it was suddenly important to know the truth. The *Hindustan Times* reported that Indian scientists already know the truth, from their clinical studies of the victims, that these gases had been released. The report was also *ironic* (in the technically incorrect meaning of its being an unhappy coincidence) in that on the same day *BBC World* reported that an Amnesty International report had condemned both Union Carbide and the Government of India for not ensuring that past and continuing victims of the incident were properly compensated.

Comedy was represented by a report on how fog was, as in the past, causing airline passengers at Delhi's airport to become unhappy because it delayed their flights. This should not have been the case, but the proposed anti-fog landing system had not been implemented as planned. The *Hindustan Times* poked gentle fun at the airport's management who had proposed to avert passengers' displeasure by providing a gallery of pictures of Delhi's ancient monuments to entertain and inform them. This apparent dedication to customer service when their solution was comically inadequate ('but what if, after viewing all the sketches, the foreign tourist still has time to kill before he could catch his flight?') indicates a bureaucratic disdain for customers. (When I arrived at the airport the sketches were found to be few in number, unexceptionable and unviewed by anyone but me.)

There is one other story in the paper that suggests a fifth dramaturgical genre is needed – *farce*. The characteristic figure of speech of farce is hyperbole or excessive exaggeration to the point of silliness. Laloo Prasad Yadav is a notorious figure in Indian politics (Dalrymple, 1999: 10–25). When he was imprisoned for corruption, while Chief Minister of the State of Bihar, he was replaced in the post by his wife. When the new national government was formed in 2004, Laloo was made Minister for Railways. The paper reported he was in a bitter spat with a ministerial colleague, Ram Vilas Paswan, who had been railway minister in the 1990s. Both wanted the railway job: allegedly it is a rich source of kickbacks. In a speech to a political rally in Patna, the capital of Bihar, Laloo said 'Lots of money was made in that time [when Paswan had the portfolio]. I will make all those files that show corruption public. He is now in deep trouble.' The farcical elements are that the pot is calling the kettle black; that a government department has had files proving alleged corruption for ten years but has not taken any action; and that a politician has claimed the moral high ground by the unethical practice of revealing confidential official papers in an attempt to gain a political advantage over a rival.

Activity 1.1

Choose a daily newspaper or weekly magazine and identify as many stories in it as you can that deal with an aspect of business ethics. Read each story in turn and decide whether it has elements of romance, tragedy, comedy, satire or farce within it.

One of the long running business ethics stories concerns a moral decision that faces profit seeking organisations. It is a conflict between public duty and self-interest. Should they only exercise their social and environmental duty if it coincides with the financial interests of their owners? In this case they will be heroes in the stories of the owners but villains in the tales of everyone else. Or should they prevent the organisation harming society and the environment, beyond the demands of the law if necessary, even if it will hurt the owners' immediate interests? In this case their ascription to the roles of hero and villain in the stories will be reversed.

Following the Asian tsunami in 2004 many Australian companies made donations to the appeal fund. Stephen Matthews, a spokesman for the Australian Shareholders' Association, criticised the companies, saying that they had no approval for their philanthropy. He implied that companies should not make such donations without expecting something in return.

> Boards of directors don't have a mandate from their shareholders to spend money in this way. [ ] There is a role for business to make a contribution in relation to the tsunami, particularly those businesses who have activities up in South Asia. [ ] Where their businesses are dependent on those sorts of markets there could possibly be a benefit for shareholders in them making donations to relief.
>
> (ABC News Online, 2005a)

Later the Association's chief executive tried to limit the damage of the ensuing public disdain by clarifying the statement. The ASA was not opposed to companies making donations because 'it is in everyone's interests that the affected communities and economies recover as soon as possible'. Companies should however disclose to the shareholders the extent of their giving (ABC News Online, 2005b). Some commentators thought, uncharitably, that the rapid donations of cash and goods to the affected regions by some large companies was an attempt to have their brands associated with humanitarian good works (Simpson, 2005).

The story illustrates the question of whether a business case should be proven for acting in a socially and environmentally responsible way before it is necessary for an organisation to adopt the role. This is dealt with in the next section.

The business case for business ethics

Should private, profit seeking organisations behave in a socially responsible and moral way, beyond the requirement of the law, because it is the right thing to do or because it pays them to do so? This might be seen as a moral dilemma; indeed in many ways it is the central issue in business ethics. If it is true that corporations that behave in a responsible and ethical manner do in fact make better returns for their owners than do those organisations that cut corners or behave badly, then the philosophical question of whether organisations ought to behave well is redundant. Do the well-behaved hero companies actually achieve their reward and despite their tribulations win through and enter into a successful long-term relationship with their investors and reach the top of the corporate financial performance league tables, or, in folk story terms, marry the princess and ascend the throne (Czarniawska, 2004: 78)? Several people have sought to answer this question.

There are sensible arguments that can be used to suggest that corporate bad behaviour can be bad for business. It would be logical to assume that a business that was seen to behave badly would lose the esteem and respect of its customers and so lose sales and profitability. A poor image would counteract the large sums that companies spend on developing their brands. Conversely if a company is associated with good behaviour, using renewable resources, not employing child labour in its factories in developing countries and providing good training and development opportunities for its staff, it should be good for sales. This is one of the motivations behind the fair trade movement.

The fair trade labels

The fair trade (or alternative trade) movement began in the late 1960s as an attempt to give small and independent farmers and artisans in the third world a better return on their efforts. As such, small-scale producers did not have access to first world markets and as they were many and the purchasers were relatively few they received only a small percentage of the price that their products eventually sold for in the developed countries. This situation was made worse because much of the processing and packaging of the basic products, which adds much of the value to a product, was done in the developed countries and not in the countries of origin. At this stage large NGOs such as Oxfam started selling third world products in their shops at terms that were beneficial to the producers. They also encouraged the setting up of cooperatives and credit unions and local processing plants that all added value to the producers.

In the 1980s a Dutch priest who worked, with the support of a church-based NGO, alongside small-scale Mexican coffee producers realised that there could be a marketing advantage in selling the coffee under a 'fair trade' label. The development of such labels meant that fair trade products were not just available in charity and ethnic shops but in mainstream supermarkets and retailers (IRC, 1998). Some research conducted in Belgium (de Pelsmacker *et al.*, 2003) distinguished four groups of coffee buyers:

- Fair trade lovers – 10% of sample who are willing to, and sometimes do, pay the premium price for fair trade coffee.
- Fair trade likers – 40% of the sample who were well disposed to fair trade products and could be encouraged to buy them by effective marketing.
- The flavour lovers (24%) and the brand lovers (25%) were not influenced at all by the fair trade label.

As the range of fair trade label goods increased to include tea, honey, chocolate and clothes, the researchers concluded a large potential and profitable market would open up for such products.

In 2002, the Co-op in the UK announced that it would make all its own brand chocolate products fair trade. This was seen as a major change that would enable it to charge a premium for its products and achieve a good level of sales. Cadbury Schweppes (2004) take a different view and point out that only 0.1 per cent of worldwide cocoa sales goes through the fair trade system which pays the producers a social premium on top of the going market price. One reason why this is so is that fair trade works best through producer cooperatives and there are still very few of these in the producing countries. They also argue that if most producers were paid a social premium this would result in a cocoa glut that would eventually lead to a collapse in cocoa prices. Their approach is to work directly with producers and provide programmes that can improve the farmers' efficiency and the value they can add to their crops.

However, these benefits of good behaviour are not guaranteed. A brand untarnished by a poor reputation is most likely to affect the buying decisions of consumers, but less likely to influence business purchasers, who will rate a good deal before a sense of social responsibility. Bad corporate behaviour will only diminish reputation, and good behaviour boost it, if it becomes known. Many companies of course have public relations departments and corporate communications departments that are designed to prevent harm being done to their brands and reputation. Making bad behaviour known requires that wrongdoing is seen and made public and that there are ways of measuring good behaviour so that credit can be given to those corporations that score well on some kind of ethics scale. There are measures of social, ethical and environmental performance, but these are mostly designed to meet the needs of the ethical investment community rather than consumers and purchasers.

Measures of corporate social, ethical and environmental performance

DEFINITIONS

There are a number of standard measures, or more properly indices, that are available for assessing the social and environmental performance of corporations.

FTSE4Good: This index is calculated from a number of factors that cover the three areas of:

- working towards environmental sustainability
- developing positive relationships with stakeholders
- upholding and supporting Universal Human Rights.

The factors are sometimes but not always measurable things. Judgements about whether a company is complying with international ethical standards are also included. A panel of experts meets to decide whether companies' performance entitles them to be included in the index.

- **Dow Jones Sustainability Indices**
  The DJSI tracks the financial performance of companies that have committed to long-term sustainability. It is a guide for those who wish to invest in companies that are ethical or that profess a philosophy of sustainability.
- **SERM rating:** This stands for Socio-Ethical Risk Management. It is designed to assess the degree to which companies are actively managing the risk they would be subject to in areas such as abuse of human rights, engagement in bribery and corruption, degradation of the physical environment, negative impacts of new technology, and many other factors.
- **Ethical Investment Research Service (EIRIS)**
  EIRIS carries out research on companies worldwide and provides information to those who wish to invest ethically. It is a charity set up in 1983 by churches and charities who did not wish to invest any of their money in ethically dubious organisations.

The indices are all professionally designed and include checks and tests to ensure that the judgements they contain are valid; this however makes starker the fact that they are judgements rather than measures of social and environmental outcomes.

Webley and More (2003) have sought an empirical answer to the question whether business ethics pays. They faced the technical problem that there is no single and definitive measure of ethical performance. They happily admit that they have had to choose proxy or surrogate measures that are indicative of whether a company is behaving in an ethical and environmentally protective way but not conclusive proof that they are. (Commentators have taken a satirical delight in the fact that Enron was often commended for its ethics policies.) Webley and More chose the following measures:

- Whether a company has a published code of ethics that has been revised within the past five years.
- Companies' SERM rating.
- Companies' ratings on *Management Today*'s 'Britain's Most Admired Companies' survey that is carried out by Michael Brown of Nottingham Business School.

Their analysis showed that companies that had a code of ethics had better ratings on both SERM and the 'Most Admired Company' league tables than those that did not. Therefore, to keep things simple all they needed to check was whether companies with a code performed better financially than those that did not.

It might have been anticipated that when Webley and More (2003) came to consider how to measure the financial performance of companies the task would be easier, but there is a wide range of possible measures. They chose:

- Market value added (MVA) – This is the difference between what investors have put into a company over a number of years and what they would get from it if they sold it at current prices.
- Economic value added (EVA) – This is the amount by which investors' current income from the company is greater or less than the return they would get if they had invested the money in something else of equal risk. In other words it is the opportunity cost of placing money in a particular company.
- Price earnings ratio (P/E ratio) – This is the market value of a share in a company divided by the shareholders' earnings.
- Return on capital employed (ROCE) – This is a measure of the return that the capital invested in a company makes for its owners.

The results of their research into the relationship between a company's ethical standing and its financial performance is shown graphically in Figures 1.1, 1.2, 1.3 and 1.4.

Two cohorts, each a little short of 50, of large companies were chosen from the FTSE 350 for the study. The results indicate, *prima facie*, that companies within the sample that have a code of ethics (and hence score better on the SERM ratings and the 'Most Admired Company' tables than those who do not) also achieved a better MVA and EVA over the four-year period 1997–2000. Between 1997 and 2000 companies without a code had a greater ROCE than those that did, but by 2001 the position had reversed and those with a code performed better. The P/E ratio was more stable over the period of the study for companies with codes than it was for companies without. There is a strong indication that having a code, managing the non-financial risks of a company (as measured by SERM), and being rated by one's peers as a reputable company are associated with higher and more stable financial returns.

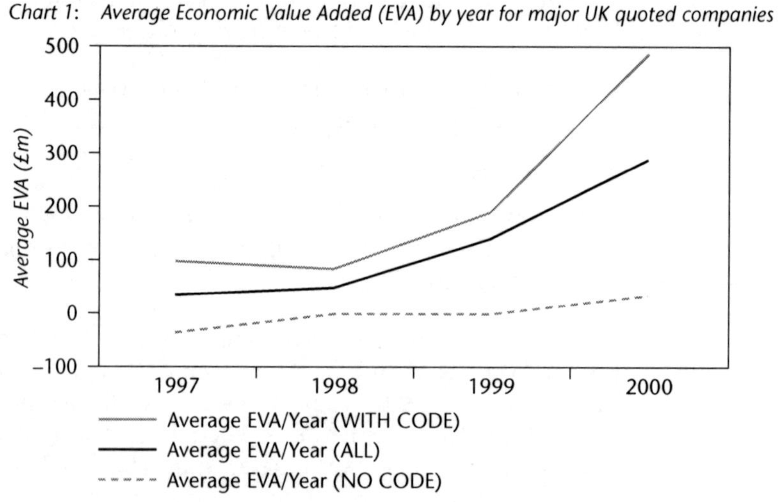

Figure 1.1 Does business ethics pay: does it add value?
Source: Webley and More 2003

2. Is having an ethical code consistent with enhanced market value?

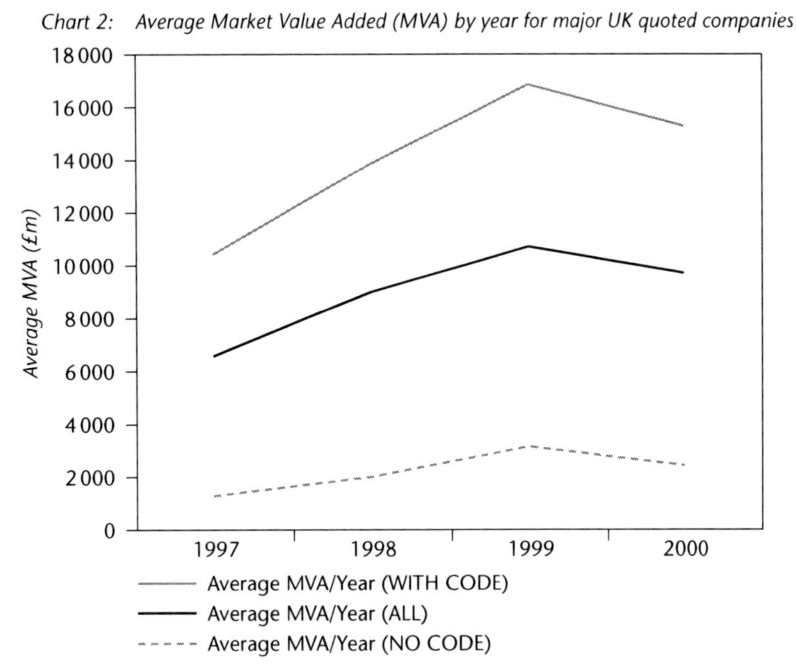

Figure 1.2 Does business ethics pay: does it enhance market value?

Source: Webley and More 2003

3. Is having an ethical code consistent with an improved return on capital?

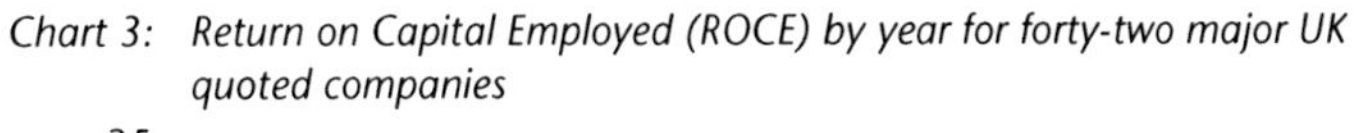

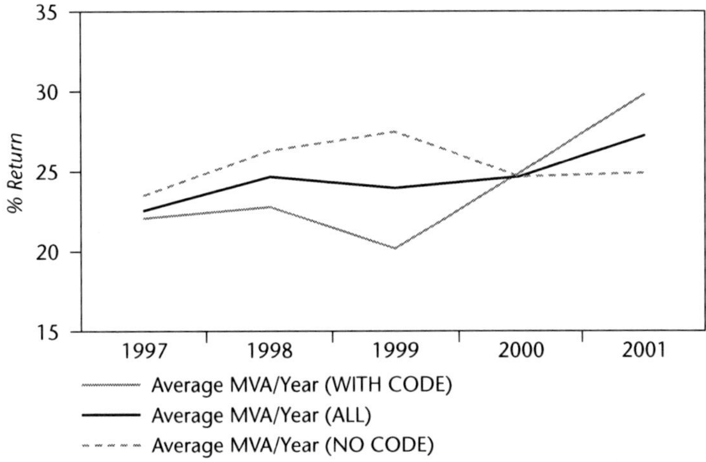

Figure 1.3 Does business ethics pay? Does it improve return on capital?

Source: Webley and More 2003

4. Is having an ethical code consistent with a more stable Price/ Earnings Ratio?

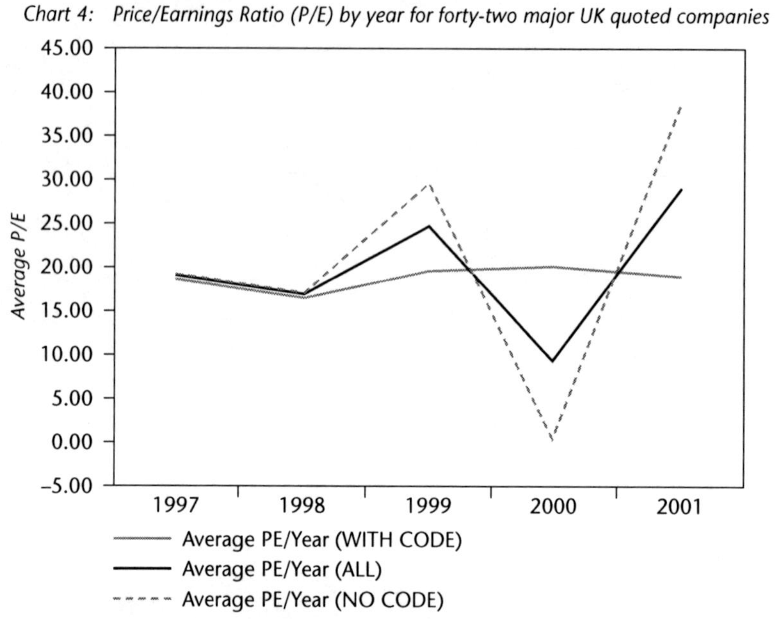

Figure 1.4 Does business ethics pay: does it improve the P/E ratio?
Source: Webley and More 2003

However, this is not necessarily proof of the business case for business ethics. A statistical association does not mean that the adoption of ethical business practices is the cause of financial improvement. It could be the result of some different, and as yet unconsidered, factor.

Moore (2001) conducted a study of the financial and social performance of eight retail supermarket companies in the UK over a three-year period. He found a number of statistical correlations but, because of the small sample size, only one was statistically significant. The social performance of companies was measured by a sixteen-factor index prepared by EIRIS (see p. 11). The correlations were:

- That social performance got worse as financial performance improved.
- But if social performance was compared with financial performance three years earlier the association was positive.
- That older companies did better on social performance than younger ones.
- And larger companies had a better performance than smaller ones; this was the one statistically significant finding.

These findings suggested that far from good social performance leading to improved financial effects the cause and effect relationship worked the other way around. That is to say, companies that do well financially find themselves with some money that they can spend on good works and improving their social and environmental performance. It takes time to implement these policies, hence the three-year time lag. The Institute of Business Ethics research could not be expected to identify this time lag because their key indicator, the presence or absence of a code of ethics, is not one that would fluctuate year on year, but the index that Moore used would. This direction of causation, from financial to social, is known as the Available Funding Hypothesis (Preston and O'Bannon, 1997). However, giving attention to these new social projects causes companies to take their eye off their main objective, making money. This distraction of attention, plus the fact that these projects can cost a lot of money, causes the financial performance to worsen. In response the companies would return their efforts to financial performance. Commentators within the supermarket industry anticipated that as Sainsbury and Marks and Spencer were performing less well financially their social and environmental efforts would decrease.

These same commentators also speculated whether social and environmental performance might be related to the social class of its customers (Moore and Robson, 2002: 27). Tesco and Morrisons served lower socio-economic groups (on average) who were less likely to be conscious of social and environmental concerns and so there would be no advantage to the company in taking a lead on such matters. The higher status groups who shopped in Sainsbury and Marks and Spencer were more likely to be careful conservers of the natural and social world and might begin to boycott the stores if they were not seen to be sufficiently interested in sustainability.

In a later study (Moore and Robson, 2002: 28–9) a more detailed statistical analysis was carried out between the 16 social performance indicators (instead of the aggregate result as in the first study) and an extended range of financial performance indicators. Negative, and statistically significant, correlations were found between growth in turnover and the league table rank of:

- the mission statements compared with those of others;
- the proportion of women managers compared with other companies;
- the environmental policy;
- the environmental management systems;
- the social performance total.

In summary, this suggests that as companies increase their turnover their social performance worsens, or the obverse, that as their social performance improves their turnover declines. This adds support to the second part of the cycle suggested above, that social performance endangers financial performance, but does not of itself support the first part of the cycle, that companies flush with profits are inclined to spend some of the profits on social performance, even though as we saw above this is precisely what Sir Richard Branson says they should do. These results of course only apply to one industry – retailing and supermarkets.

There is an association between good social performance or ethical business practices and good financial returns. It is not clear, however, that it is the good social performance that increases profits. It may be the other way around. This conclusion is not necessarily dismissive of all concerns with business ethics from an organisational point of view. There may not be a financial case for actively and purposefully seeking to make a better social and environmental world. This does not mean that companies should not seek to minimise the potential costs of being found to have acted unethically or improperly. If a company or government department is sued for damages arising from its negligence or its bad behaviour, the costs of the case and the costs of the award can be very high. It may be wise to seek to avoid those actions and practices that could cost dearly; this management function is known as risk management. If a company can be shown though its risk management procedures to have taken every reasonable precaution to identify a potential malpractice or problem and to do what is reasonable to prevent it, then, even if the problem or malpractice happens and damages others, the company will have a legal defence.

So, unfortunately (fortunately for text book writers for if otherwise we would have to close the book at this point), it is not clear that there is a business case for business ethics, although on the defensive principle there is one for managing the financial risk of unethical or improper organisational behaviour. It is necessary to turn to other ways of deciding whether companies and organisations should act ethically and responsibly. This comes down to the question of whose interests companies and organisations should exist to serve. Should they serve the interests of society generally? Or should they serve the interest of particular groups within society? If so, which groups should they serve? It is the answer to these questions we now turn to.

Stakeholder theory

Connexion point

Stakeholder theory is a key and recurring theme in this book because ethics is concerned with the harm or good done to people. As different people may be affected differently by the same action then it is important to take these various impacts, some good and some bad, into account. The simplest way of doing this is to use stakeholder theory. The theory will be used and discussed in Chapters 2, 8 and 12.

If we continue with the storytelling metaphor it is important to know who the characters in the story are. In terms of business ethics stakeholder theory provides an answer. It might be more accurate to say stakeholder theories since there are various interpretations of what the term means. They share one attribute, however, which is that for any organisation there are a number of definable groups who have an interest, or a stake, in the actions of that organisation. There is more disagreement about what constitutes a stake. It is clear that the shareholders, the owners if it has any, have a legitimate stake in an organisation. So do its employees. At the other extreme the 'phishers', who try to gain fraudulently customers' bank account details through fake, spammed emails, obviously have an interest in the banks they attack; but it is hardly a legitimate one. So the issue is three-fold:

- What responsibilities or duties, if any, does an organisation owe to its stakeholders? The fact that a stakeholder group may have a legitimate interest does not, of itself, mean that the organisation owes anything to it. At one extreme of the spectrum of possibilities an organisation may be obliged to do what its stakeholder group requires. If that group is society at large, as it expresses its will through legislation, then the organisation should submit to it. At a level below this stakeholders could have the right to participate in the organisation's decision making. This might be accepted in the case of employees who are expected to commit to the organisation's objectives and decisions. It might not be right in the case of a judicial system's obligations to those being tried in a court. A lesser obligation might be a stakeholder group's right to be consulted before major decisions are taken. If not this, then at least the group might expect the organisation to give them an account of why they did what they did. At the other extreme the organisation might owe the stakeholder group nothing.
- How should an organisation decide between its obligations to two or more stakeholders if they demand incompatible things from an organisation? What criteria should the organisation use when deciding which stakeholder group's wishes it should prioritise? Often in public service organisations the criterion used is a crude one that the group that shouts loudest is the one listened to. There is an interesting issue involved here. What if a constituency is not a person or persons but a thing or collection of things or ideas (these are known in sociological jargon as actants) such as rivers, nature reserves, spirituality? How can these things be given a voice? An easy answer might be that their voices are those of the lobby groups that support each particular cause. There is a problem here though. Some research indicates that, when lobby groups cause too much irritation to the organisation they are trying to influence, their reward is not to be listened to but to be shut out. If the cause of environmentalism is voiced by overaggressive agitation then an organisation might close its ears to the problem when the cause itself is more deserving than its supporters' actions.
- What legitimate interests justify a group of people being regarded as a stakeholder in an organisation? A criterion often proposed is that stakeholders are any group that is affected by an organisation's actions. But this would give a commercial company's competitors a voice in its activities because their performance would be affected by the organisation's performance, which would not seem fair.

The subject matter of business ethics is an attempt to answer these three questions. In the next section we consider four different answers, or perspectives, that are given in modern western, capitalist societies.

Business and organisational ethics

In this section four broad theories of the firm, and the assumptions and implications of these perspectives for prioritising the various stakeholders' needs and for the exercise of moral agency, are considered.

> **DEFINITION**
>
> **Moral agency** within organisations is the ability of individuals to exercise moral judgement *and behaviour* in an autonomous fashion, unfettered by fear for their employment and/or promotional prospects.

Organisation, in the sense we are using the term here, refers to any configuration of people and other resources that has been created to coordinate a series of work activities, with a view to achieving stated outcomes, or objectives. At this stage we make no distinction as to whether an organisation is profit seeking, located within the public sector, or is a charitable/voluntary organisation. The issues we discuss are largely, but not exclusively, sector-blind, although the intensity with which the issues are experienced may vary significantly between organisational types.

As will become evident as we progress through the chapters, the location of an organisation within the public sector does not make it immune from economic constraints, even economic objectives. Likewise, there is a growing body of opinion that argues forcibly that profit seeking organisations should be more accountable to a body of citizens that extends considerably beyond shareholder-defined boundaries. While the distinctions between private sector and public sector, profit seeking and non-profit seeking, have become less clear-cut in recent years, we do not argue that all organisations are equivalent, and that the sector of the economy in which an organisation is located is irrelevant to understanding the ethical, political, economic and social constraints within which it operates. Penalties or sanctions for poor performance are possibly more obvious and severe in the profit seeking sectors, but it can be argued that the multiplicity and complexity of the objectives managers are required to achieve in certain parts of the public sector make managing in such a context a far more demanding and ethically fraught role. Although each perspective assumes that organisational relationships are largely, if not exclusively, mediated by market dynamics, the extent to which 'the market' is relied upon as an exclusive mediating mechanism does vary.

Table 1.1 presents the schema of four perspectives to highlight the point that different imperatives and assumptions may underpin market-based, capitalist economies.

Within the four categories in Table 1.1 different assumptions are made about the relationships between:

- organisations and the state;
- organisations and their employees;
- organisations and their various stakeholder groups (i.e. beyond the employee group).

Table 1.1 Theories of the firm and their ethical implications

Issue	Classical liberal economic	Pluralist (A and B)	Corporatist	Critical
Status of the category	1. For its advocates it is the only game in town, not merely the most efficient, but the most ethically justifiable. 2. For others the 'pure' model must be tempered by interventions to (a) minimise problems of short-termism, or (b) correct power imbalances. 3. Whilst for others the neo-classical model is a corrupting chimera that acts as a cover to camouflage the interests of the powerful.	1. Type A. A stakeholder perspective is advocated in corporate decision making, with key interest groups physically represented on decision-making boards. 2. Type B. Individual managers weigh the full ethical and social considerations of their actions and decisions. Stakeholder groups would not necessarily be present at decisions.	Refers to the business relationships in countries such as Germany, Sweden and Japan (although the approaches adopted are not identical). The interests of employee groups, non-equity finance, and sometimes the state, are represented alongside the interests of equity shareholders, on senior decision-making boards.	Ranging from descriptive theories of the firm that portray how organisations appear to be (or are), rather than how they should be, to critical theorists who portray an organisational world beholden to the demands of capitalism or managerialism (these terms are not the same). Both approaches reflect messier and more ethically fraught worlds than tend to be suggested in the other three categories.
Number of objectives recognised	One – meeting the demands of equity shareholders.	Multiple, reflecting an array of stakeholder perspectives, although the actual mechanics remain problematic.	A mix of equity shareholder, employee and non-equity finance perspectives, although long-term economic interests of the firm are dominant.	Multiple, reflected by the various coalitions and power groups within an organisation, particularly economic interests.
Status of financial targets	Regarded as the organisation's primary or sole objective, because they will reflect the efficiency with which resources are being employed.	Important, but not to the domination of all other considerations. Ethical as well as multiple stakeholder perspectives are weighed in decision making.	Important, but greater attention paid to the medium to longer-term financial implications of decisions than appears to be the general case in Anglo-American corporations.	In highly competitive markets, or during periods of crisis, likely to be the dominant, although not the exclusive, organisational consideration. During periods of relative stability, other considerations will gain in significance and could dominate.
Significance of ethical behaviour (both individual and corporate)	Defined by national and international laws, which are seen as both the minimum and maximum of required ethicality. The neo-classical model is argued to be the only approach that allows the primacy of individual interests to be reflected in economic and social coordination.	At the heart of the debate for those who bemoan what is seen as the exclusive, or overly dominant, economic orientation of organisations.	No clear evidence that ethical considerations feature more strongly in corporate decision making, although the lack of an exclusive shareholder perspective might offer greater potential for a broader societal perspective.	An important, but variable, element in defining the reputation of the organisation. Will be shaped by the power of influential individuals and groups within and external to the organisation.

Table 1.1 Continued

Issue	Classical liberal economic	Pluralist (A and B)	Corporatist	Critical
Role of managers	Portrayed as functionalist, technicist and value neutral.	Type A. Managers come into direct contact with specific sectional interest groups, which should affect decision making. Type B. Individual managers are required to have internalised a societal ethic into their decision making.	The structures of organisations reflect a formal involvement of employee representatives, non-equity financiers, and sometimes state representatives, alongside shareholder interests, on corporate decision-making boards.	Complex, with competing and sometimes/often mutually exclusive interests and demands being required to be satisfied, including the managers' own agendas.
Status of employees	Resources to be used by the organisation in its quest to satisfy shareholder interests.	Employees represent an important interest/stakeholder group within the organisation, although economic considerations are not ignored.	Employee representation is guaranteed on some of the organisation's senior decision-making boards, e.g. supervisory boards in Germany.	Operating within a capitalist mode of production, employee interests will vary between organisations, depending upon the power of individuals and groups of individuals.
Values	Competition seen as the bulwark against power imbalances. Efficient resource allocation facilitated by profit-maximising behaviour.	Inherently societal in orientation, but the views of those actually making decisions will be important.	Those of the shareholders, employees, non-equity financiers (possibly the state) are likely to dominate.	A complex interaction of multiple individual and corporate values. Critical theorists would single out the values that underpin capitalism.
The possibilities for moral agency in organisations	The individual as consumer, as chooser, is the personification of moral agency, but the individual as moral agent when selling his or her labour is troublesome. The atomisation of society, which appears to be an inevitability of this form of individualism, is seen by many as leading to feelings of alienation and anomie.	Type A. Multiple perspectives offer heightened possibilities, but medium to long-term organisational survival will dominate concerns. Type B. Very similar to Type A, but the confidence and integrity of individual managers becomes a critical issue.	With employee representatives on the supervisory boards of organisations (as in Germany), the possibilities again appear stronger than with the liberal-economic perspective. However, economic considerations will remain dominant.	Empirical evidence indicates that the suppression of moral agency might be more than minor and isolated aberrations in an otherwise satisfactory state of organisational affairs. Critical theorists would see these problems as an inevitable consequence of the demands of capitalism.

We need to understand these perspectives because they are helpful in appreciating the potential for, and the constraints we each face in exercising, moral agency within business contexts.

With the exception of the 'classical-liberal' category, each of the categories is an amalgam of a variety of theories, ideas and practices. The corporatist approach is referred to by Crouch and Marquand (1993) as 'Rhenish'. This latter term refers to a particular (German) approach to a market-based, capitalist-oriented economy, although the writers broaden their consideration beyond Germany to take in a wider group of non-Anglo-American market-based economies. Whilst the German approach displays important differences from the Japanese and the Swedish approaches, they have, for our purposes, been grouped together as representing a more corporatist approach, where the overt involvement of the state and employees in the running of individual organisations is an accepted practice.

This is not to say that the Anglo-American approach to economic development can be simply categorised within the 'classical-liberal-economic' group. Notwithstanding the rhetoric of various UK and US governments, state involvement has been required and forthcoming on many occasions in these two countries, often to overcome what is known as market failure. However, the common belief in the UK and America leans towards the need for less, or minimal, government interference in business, and a drive towards market dynamics to facilitate organisational coordination.

The following is a closer examination of the four theories of the firm and their implications for moral behaviour within, and of, organisations.

The classical-liberal-economic approach

A classical-liberal theory of the firm places the organisation within an economic system that is made up of a myriad of interconnecting but legally separate parts, and where relationships between these many parts are defined in terms of free exchange. Money acts as the facilitator of exchange, thus performing the role of the oil that greases the economic system's wheels. The 'invisible hand' that Adam Smith spoke of is the force that drives the mass of individual transactions. The argument is that, with no individual person or company able to affect price, the resulting transactions, and the prices that draw both suppliers and customers into the marketplace, reflect people's wishes. This is the strength of the claims for the ethicality of 'free' markets as espoused by writers such as Milton Friedman, Friedrick von Hayek and Ayn Rand. Individual choice, free of government coercion, is seen as the only ethical influence in shaping economic and social development.

Rand is probably the least well known of the three advocates of free markets mentioned above, although her advocacy appears to have been influential. She is reputed to be a favourite writer of Alan Greenspan, the Chairman of the American Federal Reserve at the time of writing. Friedman's arguments in defence of a business world free of government or social obligations beyond those defined in law are considered in more depth in Chapter 8, so a little more time will be given here to consider some of the key thoughts of Rand on the subject of markets as the basis of economic and social coordination.

Ayn Rand was born in Russia in 1905, but she emigrated to America when she was twenty-one, nine years after the 1917 Bolshevik uprising in Russia and four years after the civil war that followed the uprising. On arriving in America, Rand took a variety of low-paid, menial jobs. She is quoted as saying: 'I had a difficult struggle, earning my living at odd jobs, until I could make a financial success of my writing. No one helped me, nor did I think at any time that it was anyone's duty to help me.' Rand depicted man as 'a heroic being, with his own happiness as the moral purpose of his life, with productive achievement as his noblest activity, and reason as his only attribute'.

Such snippets of historical context are helpful in understanding some of the factors that might explain an individual's philosophical position on key issues. Randianism (the term used by followers of Rand) rejects government in anything other than its minimalist form, i.e. that which can be justified to protect individual rights, such as the police, the law courts and national defence forces. All other functions can and should be operated by 'the people', preferably via market mediation, and paid for (or not) by choice.

Case study 1.2

Biography and philosophy

Bauman (1994) contrasts two philosophers, Knud Logstrup and Leon Shestov. Logstrup lived a tranquil and civilised life in Copenhagen. He wrote of human nature, 'It is characteristic of human life that we mutually trust each other ... Only because of some special circumstance do we ever distrust a stranger in advance ... initially we believe one another's word; initially we trust one another' (Bauman, 1994: 1). Shestov, on the other hand, experienced great persecution during his life, under both the tsarist and anti-tsarist regimes and as a consequence had a far more pessimistic view of human nature, portraying the individual as one who is vulnerable and must at all times be ready to be betrayed. 'In each of our neighbours we fear a wolf ... we are so poor, so weak, so easily ruined and destroyed! How can we help being afraid?' (Bauman, 1994: 2).

Rand is credited with developing the philosophical position that is known as objectivism. Objectivism has three key elements:

1. '*Reason* is man's [*sic*] only means of knowledge', i.e. the facts of reality are only knowable through a process of objective reason that begins with sensory perception and follows the laws of logic. Objectivism rejects the existence of a God, because it lacks (to date) empirical support. However, in America, some of the most strident advocates of free markets come from politically powerful religious groups.
2. *Rational self-interest* is the objective moral code. Objectivism rejects altruism (i.e. the greatest good is service to others) as an unhelpful and illogical human attribute. Individuals are required to pursue their own happiness, so long as it does not negatively affect anyone else's. This is compatible with negative

freedom, one of Isaiah Berlin's two forms of freedom. It relates to a 'freedom from' approach that grants people a right to be free from interference by others, including, and in particular, government.

3. *Laissez-faire capitalism* is the objective social system. It is important to recognise that laissez-faire capitalism is referred to by its advocates as a social system, and not just an economic system. This is an important issue and one towards which critics of the approach feel unified in their opposition, although such opponents have differing views on how to respond. Some would argue for an overthrow of the capitalist ethic and practice, whilst others would retain a market-based framework, but define boundaries of relevance and ethical justification for markets. The latter is exemplified by writers such as Walzer (1983) and is discussed below.

DEFINITION

Laissez-faire means unrestricted. So laissez-faire capitalism refers to a preparedness to let markets 'sort themselves out', even during periods of disequilibrium and apparent malfunctioning. The belief is that a 'market' will self-correct in time (a natural law, or Darwinist view within economics). Self-correction rather than external intervention is deemed infinitely preferable in the long run for all concerned.

The attachment of modern-day libertarian-economists to a myopic focus upon competition can be criticised for ignoring two other significant elements of economic systems, which are:

- *Command* (the extent to which power, coercion and hierarchy affect economic relationships), and
- *Change* (the way that capitalism effects change and is itself affected by change).

These three central elements of capitalism, competition, command and change have ethical and moral implications and it is argued here that they are interconnected, not subject to easy and simplistic separation. However, the classical-liberal perspective eschews these arguments and presents a schema in which the operations of the firm, both those within the firm and how it interacts with its external environment, are treated as if they are value neutral.

Within the simple competitive model of economic behaviour managers are expected to behave in ways that reflect what is known as economic rationality. This normative theory is open to challenge in terms of its descriptive rigour, hence the existence of alternative theories of the firm. Supporters of the neo-classical-economic perspective would accept that actual practice is likely to be variable around the preferred norm, but it is argued that economic rationality is the goal towards which organisations should strive. They argue that those organisations that get closest to the normative position will prosper, with competitors having to respond in a similar fashion, or wither on the economic vine.

The corporatist approach

The corporatist approach does not deny the primacy of competitive market forces, but an exclusive equity shareholder perspective is eschewed in favour of a broader-based set of perspectives in some of the organisation's decision making. These additional perspectives are those of employee representatives, debt financiers, and in some cases state interests. This broadening of the decision-making base is claimed, and appears to offer, a longer-term view to certain aspects of corporate decision making. For Crouch and Marquand (1993: 3).

> The system as a whole trades-off losses in the short-term efficiency on which the Anglo-American tradition focuses against gains in consensual adaptation and social peace. It owes its extraordinary success to its capacity to make that trade-off ... In a high skilled – or would be high skilled – economy, consensual adaptation and social peace are public goods, for which it is worth paying a price in strict allocative efficiency.

The sphere of inclusion reflected in this approach goes beyond the exclusivity of the shareholder orientation of the classical-liberal perspective espoused by most Anglo-American corporations. Evidence suggests that the corporatist-type approach has avoided, or minimised, many of the worst effects of short-term economic 'adjustments' in world trade that have been experienced since about 1960. This is not to say that countries such as Germany, Sweden and Japan (examples of the corporatist perspective) can be immune from significant movements in world economic activity, but it is argued that significant economic lurches have been avoided in these countries, thus minimising significant rises in unemployment levels, with the attendant impacts upon social cohesion. The significant economic downturns experienced by a number of Asian economies in the late 1990s, including Japan, were associated more with structural factors within these economies than with inherent weaknesses in Japan's more corporatist approach to market coordination.

Whether the corporatist approach is preferred by some because it offers a greater likelihood of economic, and thus political, stability, with the greater apparent value placed upon the interests of individual citizens/employees merely an ancillary benefit, or whether the rationale for employing this approach is reversed (i.e. the ethics of the corporatist approach are argued to be the main reasons for its adoption), is not critical for our discussion. What is relevant is that both the 'classical-liberal-economic' and the 'corporatist' approaches can cite ethical justifications for their superiority as economic and social systems. The former can do so because of the primacy attaching to the notion of individual choice, the latter because of its attachment to social cohesion and the desire to avoid, or minimise, what might be deemed unnecessary social disruption and distress to individual lives during periods of economic correction or recession.

The pluralist perspectives

There are two main pluralist perspectives. The first (referred to as Type A pluralism) sees broad stakeholder interests being represented (as far as this is possible) by elected or appointed members of corporate boards. This is a development of the corporatist perspective, but with the stakeholder groups being drawn more widely. The corporatist approach is evident in the countries cited above on a reasonable scale, whereas the two pluralist perspectives currently exist as arguments and debates, rather than as practice. Companies such as The Body Shop are very much the exceptions that prove the rule.

In Type A pluralism stakeholder groups are required to do more than argue their particular, vested-interest, case. They are expected to be representative of societal interests. Clearly the extent to which the latter are adequately represented will depend upon the composition of the stakeholder groups. Thus, as compared with the classical-libertarian-economic perspective, where the unconscious forces of individual decisions are deemed to give expression to society's preferences, within Type A pluralism societal preferences are given voice by the presence (or not) of stakeholder groups on company boards or committees.

The second pluralist perspective (referred to as Type B pluralism) does not dispute the possibility of stakeholder groups being physically represented within corporate decision-making processes, but this is neither a prerequisite, nor part of the basic arguments. This second variant of pluralism sees economic rationality being moderated by concerns for, and recognition of, wider social implications of corporate decisions, with these factors being weighed by individual decision makers. Type B perspectives can be presented as a continuum, with writers such as Casson (1991) at one pole, and Maclagan (1998), Maclagan and Snell (1992) and Snell (1993) at the other.

The perspective argued by writers such as Casson is that competition via market-based economies is the preferred economic system, but that reliance upon unadulterated economic rationality as the sole explanation of individual behaviour is both naïve and unhelpful. For the discipline of economics to retain relevance Casson argued that it must recognise behaviours that are explained by drives other than, or in addition to, economic rationality.

> These professional prejudices must be overcome if economics is to handle cultural factors successfully. They are the main reasons why, in spite of its technical advantages ... economics has not contributed more to the analysis of social issues.
>
> (Casson, 1991: 21–2)

Classical-libertarian economics retains a view of human behaviour that sociologists would describe as 'under-socialised' (i.e. unrepresentative of the complexity and variability of actual human behaviour). Type B pluralism argues for a recognition of the realities of everyday market conditions, but also a more socialised set of assumptions of human behaviour. Whilst a market-based economy is seen as the foundation upon which organisational coordination takes place, structural issues and problems within markets are recognised, e.g. power imbalances between competitors; information asymmetry between producers and customers; and the capricious nature of (the owners of) capital. Greater responsibility, ethicality and humanity are required of corporate decision makers.

In a similar vein, but with less of Casson's implicit instrumentalism, Etzioni (1988) employed a moral justification for an overt recognition of broader perspectives beyond short-term profit motives. In the following quotation Etzioni used the term 'deontological'. This is an important word in any consideration of business ethics and it is considered in more depth in Chapter 3. However, we offer a brief definition of the term here to allow you to understand the argument that Etzioni was making.

DEFINITION

A **deontological** approach to moral behaviour is one that believes that moral reasoning and action should be guided by universal principles that hold irrespective of the context in which an ethical dilemma might exist.

> Instead of assuming that the economy is basically competitive, and hence that economic actors (mainly firms) are basically subject to 'the market' possessing no power over it (monopolies are regarded as exceptions and aberrations), the deontological 'I & We' paradigm evolved here assumes that power differences among the actors are congenital, are built into the structure, and deeply affect their relationships. We shall see that power differentials are gained both by applying economic power (the power that some actors have over others, directly, within the economy) and by exercising political power (the power that some actors have over others, indirectly, by guiding the government to intervene on their behalf within the economy). These fundamentally different assumptions make up what is referred to here as the I & We paradigm (one of the larger possible set of deontological paradigms). The term [I & We] highlights the assumption that individuals act within a social context, that this context is not reducible to individual acts, and most significantly, that the social context is not necessarily wholly imposed. Instead the social context is, to a significant extent, perceived as a legitimate and integral part of one's existence, a whole of which the individuals are constituent elements ... The deontological paradigm evolved here assumes that people have at least some significant involvement in the community (neo-classicists would say 'surrender of sovereignty'), a sense of shared identity, and commitment to values, a sense that 'We are members of one another'.
>
> (Etzioni, 1988: 5)

Etzioni continued:

> The issues explored here range way beyond the technical, conceptual matters of what constitutes a workable theory of decision-making in economic and other matters. At issue is human nature: How wise are we, and what is the role of morality, emotions and social bonds in our personal and collective behaviour.
>
> (Etzioni, 1988: xii)

Progressing along the continuum, past Etzioni's position, one moves towards those who argue for Type B pluralism on the grounds that a broader ethic than that required by classical-liberal economics is desirable, even essential, on the grounds that society as a whole needs organisational decision-makers who understand and can exercise moral judgement in complex situations (Maclagan, 1996,

1998; and Snell, 1993). These writers see management practice as essentially a moral practice, set in a complex and challenging arena (business organisations), for individual moral development.

Thus, our pluralist continuum moves from writers, such as Casson, who argued for theories of decision making to recognise actual human behaviour and instincts in order to make economic theorising more relevant and realistic, to the arguments of writers such Maclagan and Snell, who justify the inclusion of the moral dimensions within business decision making on the grounds of the ethical demands of society as a whole.

The critical perspective

The critical perspective is composed of many different theories about human and collective behaviour, including the politics of organisations (Simon, 1952, 1953 and 1955); expectation theory (Vroom, 1964); the use of ambiguity and hypocrisy as managerial tools (Brunsson, 1986 and 1989); the theory of coalitions (Cyert and March, 1992); the exploitation of people (Marcuse, 1991); the benefits that people seek at work and the importance of these benefits (Maslow, 1987); power and identity in organisations (Knights and Willmott, 1999); and the range of strategic resources that individual managers draw upon to allow them to cope with managerial life (Watson, 1994). This is far from an exhaustive list, but it gives a flavour of the range of research and theories that have been developed to explain actual behaviour within organisations. What these works share is a picture of organisational life that is far more complex and messy than classical-liberal economics would prefer to work with. The behavioural and critical theories are not normative theories (i.e. theories of how things should be, such as the classical-libertarian-economics perspective), but what are referred to as descriptive theories, i.e. theories of how things actually appear to be. However, behavioural theorists and critical theorists do vary in terms of the intentions of their respective arguments.

Behavioural theories are amoral in their stance in that, unlike the liberal-economic, corporatist and pluralist perspectives, they do not put forward a preferred ethical foundation for their theorising. They might however highlight examples of laudable, contentious or downright immoral behaviour. They do so by acting as organisational windows through which we can observe the ways in which employees at all levels in organisations appear to react, and behave, when faced with ethically complex situations. For example, you become aware that a friend and work colleague, who you know has a very difficult financial situation at home, unlawfully takes a small toy (a company product) home to one of their children. Such situations could involve divided loyalties between either colleagues or concepts, where the ethics of a situation are not clear-cut or neat; or where moral agency is compromised by power imbalances that jeopardise future employment and promotional prospects.

Critical theorists, however, have an avowed commitment to societal change, for the emancipation of employees from the shackles of capitalism. However, critical theorists make different analyses (for example, Foucaudian perspectives, e.g. McKinley and Starkey, 1998, and neo-Marxist perspectives, e.g. Alvesson and

Willmott, 1996) and there is no consensus on the preferred replacement for market-based societies. Habermas (whose ideas are discussed in Chapter 3) does, however, outline the necessary conditions for a societally acceptable economic set of relationships to develop.

Boundaries of jurisdiction or spheres of justice

The fear of market-based relationships as the bedrock upon which all societal and interpersonal relationships are based is articulated by a number of writers. Walzer (1983), for example, wrote:

> One can conceive of the market as a sphere without boundaries, an unzoned city – for money is insidious, and market relations are expansive. A radically laissez-faire economy would be like a totalitarian state, invading every other sphere, dominating every other distributive process. It would transform every social good into a commodity. This is market imperialism.
>
> (Walzer, 1983: 119–20)

Taking his cue from Walzer, Keats (1993) argued that:

> It is as if their [liberal economists'] theoretical energy has been so fully utilised in demonstrating the virtues of the market that little has been left to deal with the arguably prior question of what it is that defines the nature – and hence limits – of that 'economic' domain with respect to which market and state are seen as the chief rival contenders.
>
> (Keats, 1993: 7)

As a way of handling this problem Walzer argued that societal life should be seen as a series of spheres, which contain and constrain differing elements of societal existence. One of these spheres is the economic, in which markets are recognised as the most effective mediating mechanism, and competition the most defensible form of organisational coordination. Whilst markets, contract and competition are seen as appropriate mediating elements, their relevance is largely constrained within this sphere. Within the spheres representing non-economic interpersonal relationships we find notions of trust, care, welfare, sharing, friendship, leisure and possibly even altruism (although this is not highlighted by Walzer). There is some similarity between Walzer and the earlier work of the German philosopher Hegel (1770–1831) who also used the notion of spheres to conceptualise the social world (Singer, 1983). Hegel spoke of the spheres of state, family and civil society, and to these Walzer adds the economic as worthy of consideration.

McMylor comments upon the development of market-based capitalism from feudal societies. He presented the development from non-market societies as a process whereby the economic moved from being enmeshed 'within other dominating frameworks' to a situation in market societies when:

> the economy, with a capital 'E' is no longer so embedded. The market means that there is in some sense, a differentiation of economic activity into a separate institutional sphere, no longer regulated by norms that have their origin elsewhere. The individual economic agent is free then to pursue economic self-interest, without 'non-economic' hindrance.
>
> (McMylor, 1994: 100)

From a moral perspective one of the problems with dividing the human world into separate spheres is that it might suggest the spheres are independent to the point of allowing differing forms of behaviour to prevail within each. Behaviour might be accepted, or at least tolerated, in one sphere that would not be acceptable in another. It has been argued that this is a recognition that people sometimes act (or feel they need to act), when in 'business mode', in ways that they would not employ within their private, domestic lives. Walzer recognised this and argued that the spheres should not be seen as totally autonomous and independent. Rather, he portrayed a dynamic set of relationships between the spheres in which shifts between spheres of particular facets of societal life do happen, and that a sphere's scope and importance may wax and wane. Boundary conflict thus becomes endemic:

> The principles appropriate to the different spheres are not harmonious with one another, nor are the patterns of conduct and feeling they generate. Welfare systems and markets, offices and families, schools and states are run on different principles: so they should be.
>
> (Walzer, 1983: 318)

However, Walzer went on to say that 'the principles must fit within a single culture' (1983: 318). This is highly problematic, unless the single culture is one that recognises difference, a multiplicity of cultures. Within such a complexity of perspectives, the notion of wisdom becomes an important mediating factor, but this has to be an active wisdom, i.e. it is always in a state of emerging through dialogue and debate. Within this perspective the dynamic of change is recognised, is debated and matures through processes that are demanding but which, it must be stressed, are subject to 'social capture' by active groups and voices if participation is shirked by the general polity.

DEFINITION

Social capture is a term used to describe a mechanism, e.g. a committee, a regulatory body or a political process, which is established to oversee a particular facet of social life, but which becomes dominated by, or heavily influenced by, the very sectional interests the mechanism was intended to monitor or control. The original intentions behind the creation of the mechanism thus become at best neutralised, and at worst subverted.

To minimise the risk of social capture and other such distorting influences within political, economic and social systems requires an active citizenry, prepared to be interested in, even involved in, micro- and macro-level debates about equity and justice – the very morality of life's various spheres. Hegel spoke of the dialectic, the processes of debate and argument that are required to surface and (possibly) resolve differences of view and contradictions. The dialectical approach is to be found in the teachings of Socrates, certainly in the way that Plato presents the work of his master. Billig (1996) makes a plea for a resurgence of the practice of rhetoric, not in the pejorative sense in which the term tends to be viewed in contemporary society, but as a return to an engagement in debate and argument, for these are the mechanisms and processes by which civilised societies develop and progress.

Defining the boundaries of the economic sphere

One of the principal virtues of competitive markets, as the mechanisms by which business and social interaction is mediated, is that the 'invisible hand' of the market is amoral, i.e. value neutral. Although some may suffer as a result of market-based outcomes, through unemployment or loss of capital, the outcomes are not intended from the start. They are simply the unintended consequences of the multitude of transactions that comprise a free market. Sir Keith Joseph, a notable politician of the 1970s and 1980s and an architect of the political period and philosophy referred to as Thatcherism, was a devotee of Hayek and Friedman. As Heelas and Morris (1992: 19) observed:

> Policies designed to effect more equal distribution of resources, Joseph claims, are not only coercive and threaten individual liberty but are counterproductive and give rise to a series of negative consequences (economic, psychological, moral and political) ... Liberty is primarily to be exercised by the self-interested consumer in the market place, including the political, educational and medical 'markets'.

Plant (1992), taking up the theme of markets being the most appropriate mediating mechanism for medical services, explored the possibilities for a free market in body parts (human organs), as well as the justification for a market-based ethos replacing a service ethic in non-voluntary, public service organisations. With regard to a market for human body parts Plant (1992: 91) observed:

> On a strictly capitalist view of market principles, it is very difficult to see why there should not be such a market. The scope for a market is clearly quite wide. There could be a market in blood and blood products; in kidneys; in sperm; in renting out a uterus for surrogate pregnancy; and so forth.

Plant argued that, from a market perspective, at least three principles would favour a market in these areas:

1. There is a clear demand.
2. The current donor system is failing to meet demand.
3. Ownership of the human organs is clear and would not be undertaken by the donor if it were not in their personal interest.

Despite strong advocacy for such markets, broad public support was (and appears to continue to be) lacking. Plant argued that this reluctance reflected a boundary being drawn by society, with human organs currently residing outside the boundary that defines the limits of market application.

Titmuss (1970), in a seminal work on the marketisation/commercialisation of blood donor services, observed, when responding to arguments that blood should be seen as a commodity and thus private blood banks should be introduced to improve the productivity of the blood giving process:

> In essence, these writers,[ ] are making an economic case against a monopoly of altruism in blood and other human tissues. They wish to set people free from the conscience of obligation. Although their arguments are couched in the language of price elasticity and profit maximisation they have far-reaching implications for human values and all 'social service' institutions ... The moral issues that are raised extend beyond theories of pricing and the operations of the marketplace.
>
> (Titmuss, 1970: 159)

Titmuss worried about the wider implications of commercialising the blood donor service in the UK. If the altruism that, it is argued, is reflected in the voluntary and unpaid giving of blood is replaced by a commercial relationship, what, asked Titmuss, fills the space that used to be occupied by the sense of community inherent within the existing system?

> There is nothing permanent about the expression of reciprocity. If the bonds of community giving are broken the result is not a state of value neutralism. The vacuum is likely to be filled by hostility and social conflict, a consequence discussed in another context ... the myth of maximising growth can supplant the growth of social relations.
>
> (Titmuss, 1970: 199)

Titmuss discussed four economic and financial criteria, excluding the much wider and unquantifiable social, ethical and philosophical aspects to concentrate upon those aspects that economists (the focus of his criticism) would recognise. These were:

1. Economic efficiency.
2. Administrative efficiency.
3. Price – the cost per unit to the patient.
4. Purity, potency and safety – or quality per unit.

> On all four criteria the commercialised blood market fails. However, paradoxically ... the more commercialised a blood distribution system becomes (and hence more wasteful, inefficient and dangerous) the more will the GNP be inflated. In part, ... this is the consequence of statistically 'transferring' an unpaid service (voluntary blood donors, voluntary workers in the service, unpaid time) with much lower external costs to a monetary and measurable paid activity involving costlier externalities.
>
> (Titmuss, 1970: 205)

The discussion so far in this chapter has laid out the arguments for claiming that the market system is:

- The only defensible economic and social system for protecting the freedom of the individual to exercise personal choice, which allows the development of economic and societal relationships that are free from government coercion and intervention. This is the liberal-economic perspective.
- Something that is preferable to alternative economic systems, but which needs to be carefully watched and, if necessary, modified from time to time to ensure that the economic system is compatible with broader societal aims. This incorporates the corporatist and pluralist perspectives.
- An intrinsically corrupting system that pits human beings against each other, with only an elite few dictating the life chances of the many. This is the critical perspective.

The argument has been about the place of ethics in business life, and the place of business in the ethics of life.

Descriptive, normative and reflective approaches

Two ways of discussing ethical matters, normatively and descriptively, are often proposed. Normative discussion is concerned with rules and principles that ought to govern our thoughts and actions. Normative arguments are focused in particular on how such prescriptive claims can be shown to be legitimate or valid. Descriptive discussion focuses on how things *are* rather than how they should be. A descriptive approach to ethics would give an account of the values and ethics of particular groups and try to explain how they have emerged. It would analyse value systems to look for norms and the tensions between them. The word normative is troublesome in a subject, such as business ethics, that spans both philosophy and sociology. In sociology, normative refers to that which is the norm within a group or society. The term is both descriptive – the norms are those of a particular group, and also normative – they define right and wrong within that group. In philosophy normative and descriptive are seen as opposing terms. In this book normative will be used in its philosophical sense.

Many business ethics textbooks take a normative approach. They identify ethical difficulties in business, rehearse the arguments about what should be done about them and then present a resolution or a set of principles. Rather than taking a normative and prescriptive approach this textbook takes a descriptive and analytical approach. It attempts to describe how people in organisations interpret and respond to ethical issues at work. It does not propose solutions to the many ethical dilemmas and problems that face managers and organisations. However, by explaining how others think about and respond to ethical matters, and by providing you with the appropriate tools for thinking, we hope the book will enable you to analyse the issues and to come to your own conclusions.

The intention of the book brings us to a third way of talking about business ethics, the reflective and reflexive approach. Reflection implies careful consideration of ethical issues. Reflexive means to turn back on one's own mind and to consider one's own values and personality. This textbook therefore tries to help you examine your own positions and thoughts. This can be done in part by reflecting on the material in this book and other publications. But this is vicarious learning, piggy-backing on the experiences of others. Reflexive learning occurs when you use your values to challenge your actions and your experiences to challenge your values.

Reflections

One of our concerns in this book is the possibility of the existence of moral agency and ethical practice within organisations. Integrity is one of the concepts that would form part of any definition of business ethics. The importance of integrity within organisational life in general, and executive decision making in particular, is discussed by Srivastva and Cooperrider (1988), although they stress that the way forward is not easily mapped. It can only be navigated and negotiated through dialogue, reflection, learning, tolerance and wisdom.

> Executive integrity is dialogical. Executive integrity is more than the presence of morality or the appropriation of values; integrity involves the process of seeing or creating values. Whereas ethical moralism is blindly obedient, integrity represents the 'insightful assent' to the construction of human values. In this sense, organisation is not viewed as a closed, determined structure but is seen as in a perpetual state of becoming. Dialogue is the transformation of mere interaction into participation, communication, and mutual empathy. Executive integrity is, therefore, a breaking out of a narrow individualism and is based on a fearless trust in what true dialogue and understanding might bring, both new responsibilities and new forms of responsiveness to the other.
>
> (Srivastva and Cooperrider, 1988: 7)

The big weakness of a heavy reliance upon the notion of a dialectic transformation of society is that the associated processes are subject to the risk of social capture. The best chance of minimising this possibility is for all of us to take ourselves seriously and to believe that our individual voices count in shaping the societies in which we live.

We end this opening chapter on a qualified, optimistic note. Spaemann (1989) refused to accept that conscience is either purely instinct or exclusively a function of upbringing:

> In every human being there is the predisposition to develop a conscience, a kind of faculty by means of which good and bad are known.
>
> (Spaemann, 1989: 62–3)

However, Spaemann went on to say that conscience has to be nurtured and supported – shown good practice in order for it to flourish and mature. Fail to do this and the development of a strong conscience becomes 'dwarfed'. The term 'dwarfing' is used by Seedhouse (1988) when discussing the growing attention to a 'business mentality' within UK health care, at the expense of a prioritising of the individual. Both Spaemann and Seedhouse saw the individual as central to any challenge to the primacy of business interests, although, as you will see in Chapter 7, conscience is often the victim of the need to maintain organisational and personal relationships.

Hannah Arendt (cited in Bauman, 1994) also placed the individual at the centre of any developments towards making ethics a live and legitimate subject for debate within organisations. Arendt wrote, 'there are no rules to abide by ... as there are no rules for the unprecedented'. Bauman continued

> in other words, no one else but the moral person themselves must take responsibility for their own moral responsibility.
>
> (Bauman, 1994: 14)

With this in mind, this book is intended to inform your understanding of some of the key issues that bear upon this critical element of modern society – the possibilities for business ethics.

Summary

In this chapter the following key points have been made:

- Business ethics issues can be illustrated through stories; sometimes these are expressed as romances, as tragedies, as satire, as comedies and sometimes as farces.
- Many writers, and indeed organisations, argue that there is a business case for companies to behave ethically and responsibly. There is an association between the two, but whether good companies are profitable because they are good, or good because their profitability means they can afford to be, is not easily proven one way or the other.
- Many business ethics issues are best understood by using a stakeholder approach.

- Four different perspectives: the classical-liberal, the corporatist, the pluralist and the critical, on the question of whether organisations, and their role within market systems, are ethically proper.
- The doubts about the classical-liberal model place a premium on the role of the moral agency of individuals within organisations. Moral agency involves reflection on what is right and wrong and working for the good within organisations.

Quick revision test

1. What is meant by the term 'moral agency'?
2. Ayn Rand is credited with being the founder of the philosophical position known as 'objectivism'. What are objectivism's three core elements?
3. What does the criticism of neo-liberal economics being 'under-socialised' mean?
4. What is the difference between 'normative' theories and 'descriptive' theories of ethical behaviour within organisations?

Typical assignments and briefs

1. Is there an effective 'business case' for corporations acting in a socially, ethically and environmentally responsible way?
2. Compare and contrast the four approaches to the involvement of stakeholders' business decision making (classical liberal, pluralistic, corporatist and critical) outlined in this chapter.
3. How should a company decide which interest groups should be treated as stakeholders and which should not?
4. What can we learn about business ethics issues at work by studying the stories in which they are reported?

Group activity 1

A delphi exercise on reasons to be an ethical organisation

Delphi is a technique for creating a consensus on difficult matters of prioritising or forecasting. In this instance it will be used to answer the question:

Why should organisations choose to behave ethically and socially responsibly?

The exercise needs the group to divide into groups of between five and eight people. Each group should then follow the following steps.

1. Each person, working on their own, should think of as many reasons as they can why an organisation should behave ethically and socially responsibly. Write each reason down on a Post-it note and make a pile of them.
2. Everyone then posts their Post-its in random order on a convenient board.
3. The group should gather around the Post-its and sort and cluster them, putting similar points together, until the mass of Post-its has been reduced to about five or six reasons.
4. The group should then write a simple, one-page, questionnaire that lists the five or six reasons and asks respondents to score each reason according to its importance. The scoring should be done using percentages, the larger the percentage the more important the reason. Photocopy a batch of the questionnaires (or, if you are inclined, create a small spreadsheet).
5. Each member of the group then completes the questionnaire on their own.
6. The scores are then totalled and averaged and presented to the whole group.
7. Each group member then completes a new questionnaire taking into account the average scores of the whole group.
8. The process continues through cycles of individual scoring and group feedback until the group reaches a consensus, or nearly does, on the scoring and importance of the five or six reasons.
9. You will then have decided why organisations should behave ethically and socially responsibly.
10. Discuss in the group how the arguments you have identified are similar to or differ from those presented in this chapter.

Useful websites

Topic	Website provider	URL
Business Ethics A general website including articles, corporate codes of ethics, resources and so on.	Sharon Soerger	http://www.web-miner.com/busethics.htm#additional%20
Business case for ethics	World Economic Forum	http://www.weforum.org/site/knowledgenavigator.nsf/Content/_S3576
A news digest service that provides useful updates on stories about business ethics.	Institute of Business Ethics	http://www.ibe.org.uk/ethicsnews.html
A website on a research project into stakeholder theory. It includes a bibliography of articles on stakeholder theory.		http://www.mgmt.utoronto.ca/~stake/Articles.htm http://www.mgmt.utoronto.ca/~stake/index.htm
Business case for ethics	World Economic Forum	http://www.weforum.org/site/knowledgenavigator.nsf/Content/_S3576
FTSE4Good Home page	FTSE	http://www.ftse.com/ftse4good/index.jsp
Dow Jones Sustainability Index Home page	Dow Jones STOXX Ltd	http://www.sustainability-index.com/
EIRIS home page	Ethical Investment Research service (EIRIS)	http://www.eiris.org/index.htm

Whistleblower or witness?

Learning outcomes

Having read this chapter and completed its associated activities, you should be able to:

- Examine the various issues that relate to the act of whistleblowing.
- Debate the role that whistleblowing potentially has to play within corporate governance processes.
- Discuss possible explanations of the whistleblower's plight.
- Evaluate the legislation which seeks to protect whistleblowers in the UK.

Introduction

Chapter 6 considered possible stances or ethical positions that people facing ethical challenges may move through. The stances are ways of labelling the different forms of responses people might display in ethically complex situations. In this chapter we discuss the issue of those employees, who, for a variety of reasons, come to a position where they are so uncomfortable with a particular practice or activity within their employing organisation that they feel no alternative but to raise the matter with another person. This other person might be a work colleague, a senior member of the organisation, a family member, or a non-related third party who is external to the employing organisation. The person to whom the revelation is made can be important because in the UK, for example, it can affect the degree of legal protection that is available to the concerned employee. However, to whomever the concerned employee confides, the act is the same. It is often referred to as whistleblowing and the people who whistleblow are usually referred to as whistleblowers. However, this can be a pejorative term and some writers prefer other descriptions, e.g. Beardshaw (1981) described such employees as 'conscientious objectors at work', while Winfield (1990) preferred 'principled dissenters'. Borrie and Dehn (2002: 5) offered some thoughts on how whistleblowers might be viewed in the future and in order to help change people's perceptions they suggested the alternative nomenclature of 'witness', not 'complainant'. This is an interesting suggestion because changing people's perception of those who whistleblow is an important stepping stone in altering the likely outcomes experienced by those who reveal organisational malpractices.

Connexion point

The issues and arguments discussed in this chapter build upon Chapters 5 and 6 by focusing attention upon those individuals who encounter an issue within their organisation that challenges their personal values and ethics in a profound way, but for which they can find no satisfactory resolution.

The words we use to describe people or things are important because they create an initial context and orientate our emotions towards the discussion that might follow. Thus, if the term whistleblower brings to mind the notion of a snitch, or a grass, then you are more likely to be inclined, initially at least, towards a negative view of a whistleblower with regard to any discussion of a particular whistleblowing case. If, however, you prefer the descriptions proffered by writers such as Winfield, Beardshaw or Borrie and Dehn, because that is how you see most whistleblowers, then your interpretation of the 'rights' and 'wrongs' of a particular case is likely to lean towards the position of the whistleblower. Our quest in this chapter is to consider the issue of whistleblowing and whistleblowers, using the terms neither pejoratively nor exaltingly, but merely descriptively.

In this chapter we will present you with the arguments surrounding whistleblowing, but also with evidence of the pressures within organisations that can constrain potential whistleblowers and the implications of such 'muteness'. We will use actual cases to illustrate the arguments, reflecting the messiness that is often to be found in organisational life, and the organisational impotency that many employees feel, irrespective of their position within the organisation. This is not to justify or to recommend an uncritical acceptance of the messiness and personal impotency that can be experienced in ethical dilemmas. The tools of analysis and the implications of the differing philosophical positions discussed in Chapters 3 and 4 will allow you to form reasoned judgements on the questions, issues and cases relating to whistleblowing that you will now consider.

However, before we progress, we would like you to work through Activity 7.1.

Activity 7.1

On the scales shown, identify your feelings towards the person raising the alarm.

Case A

You are playing in a team and a player on your side fouls a player on the opposing side, but the referee misses the incident. However, one of your team mates suddenly stops the game and brings the foul to the attention of the referee.

Extremely supportive Extremely angry

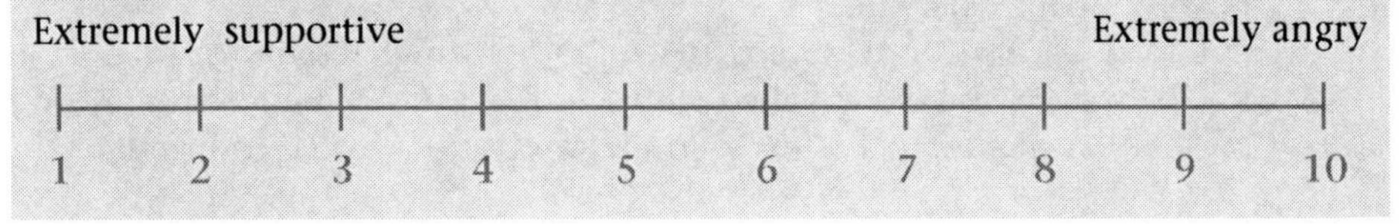

Case B

You read in the newspaper that an employee of a building company has provided evidence to a national newspaper of practices on building sites that contravene health and safety legislation and which have resulted in fatalities and serious injuries during the past two years.

Extremely supportive Extremely angry

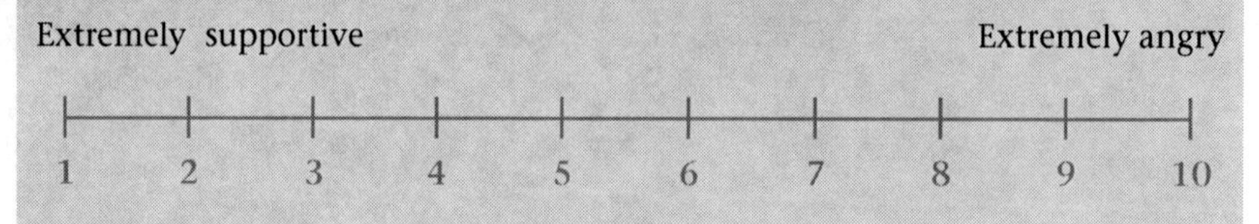

Case C

You work for a car manufacturer and a fellow employee, whom you do not know personally, releases information to the press of a design fault in one of the company's best-selling models that is potentially life threatening. Sales of the car plummet and significant layoffs are announced.

Extremely supportive Extremely angry

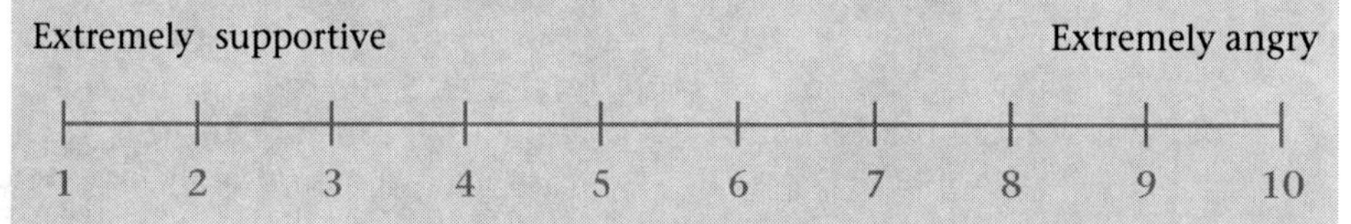

When is a whistleblowing act performed?

A commonly held understanding of a whistleblowing act is the release of confidential organisational information to an external third party, often, but not exclusively, the media. However, as suggested above, a whistleblowing act can be a conversation, a remark even, to a work colleague or a family member in which organisational information, unknown to others participating in the conversation, is revealed. If these concerns are relayed back to 'management' before the employee concerned has raised the issue through the company's formal procedures (assuming they exist), and they are dismissed as a result of the revelation, then, in the UK, they are likely to lose the protection of the law that was introduced to protect whistleblowers. This is the Public Interest Disclosure Act 1998 (PIDA), which is discussed in more detail later in the chapter.

The PIDA was designed to provide protection to those who raise awareness of an act or practice that poses problems for public safety, or threatens other, specific areas of public interest. From the above it is clear that, whilst whistleblowing is normally a purposeful and intentional act, it might also be unintended and innocent. The law makes little, if any, distinction between intended and unintended whistleblowing.

Reacting to a particular organisational activity or practice in a way that does not comply with the requirements of the PIDA does not mean that legal recourse is denied to a whistleblower, should they wish to bring a case for wrongful dismissal. A civil action will still be possible. It is simply that the protection afforded by the PIDA will not be available.

Why whistleblow?

The personal outcomes experienced by many whistleblowers have been damaging, whether the outcomes are considered at a psychological, financial or social level (*see*, for example, Soeken and Soeken, 1987; Winfield, 1990; Miceli and Near, 1992; Hunt, 1995, 1998). Loss of employment is common for the whistleblower, with opportunities to gain alternative employment often limited. Some whistleblowers have become unemployable as their names have been circulated among employing organisations as 'troublemakers'. Borrie and Dehn (2002) refer to such an example.

Case study 7.1

Paying a heavy price

Robert Maxwell, who was chief executive of Maxwell Communications, stole $1M from the pension funds of the company, which included the pension funds of the *Daily Mirror* group of newspapers. He sacked a union official who had challenged what he was doing with the pension money at a Scottish Newspaper. Maxwell, a powerful businessman, was able to ensure that the man could not get another job in the industry. Subsequently the claims of the union official were found to have been accurate, but that was little consolation for the union official whose career in the print industry had been ruined.

The whistleblower and his or her family often experience great financial and emotional hardship, with break-ups in marriages or partnerships frequently reported. Suicides of whistleblowers have also been attributed to the financial and psychological fallout from their whistleblowing experiences (Soeken and Soeken, 1987). However, not all whistleblowing cases end in such unhappiness, although it is difficult to overplay the trauma that is likely to be experienced while the scenario is unfolding, even if the final outcome shows the whistleblower both vindicated and adequately compensated. Sherron Watkins was an accountant and a former vice-president at Enron before she 'blew the whistle' on the corrupt practices at Enron. Watkins has enjoyed something of a celebrity status since her whistleblowing act, but this might have something to do with the scale of the fraud at Enron and the ease with which it was possible to identify key individuals at the top who were directly implicated in the fraud. A less clear-cut scenario, with slightly less media scrutiny, can find the potential whistleblower in a more vulnerable and exposed position. As it was, Watkins was faced with some hostility from her work colleagues. It must be recognised that the revelation of an organisational malpractice, however corrupt and indefensible it might be, risks damaging the employing organisation's share price and standing in its various product or service markets. This could place jobs at risk, the jobs of one's work colleagues and perhaps their pension funds.

The situation at Enron was complicated by the fact that many of the employees had invested heavily in the stocks and shares of Enron, believing that the phenomenal growth in the share price that had been experienced over the previous seven or so years would continue, allowing their portfolio to be converted upon retirement into a sizeable pension fund. Thus, anyone blowing the whistle at Enron would be putting at risk both jobs and personal retirement/pension funds. Without minimising the courage displayed by Sherron Watkins, her position was possibly eased slightly because she first formally raised her concerns in an internal letter to Kenneth Lay (CEO and Chairman) on 15 August 2001. This was only two months before Enron made a public announcement that it was making significant write-offs and only three and half months before Enron filed for bankruptcy. The scale of the fraud and the perpetrators became evident quite quickly, a state of affairs not often experienced by whistleblowers.

The PIDA does appear to have made a difference in some cases, and with compensation claims now having no ceiling (which was not the case when the Act was first introduced), the compensation awards to some wronged whistleblowers have been significant. The organisation Public Concern at Work has undertaken a review of the first three years' working of the Act. During this period employees lodged over 1,200 claims alleging victimisation for whistleblowing. Of these two-thirds were either settled out of court or withdrawn without a public hearing. Of the remaining one-third, 54 per cent of claimants lost, 23 per cent won their case, but under a different employment or discrimination law, and the final 23 per cent won their case under the PIDA. The highest award made was for £805,000 and the lowest £1,000. The average value of award made during this first three-year period was £107,117.

Although the protection afforded by the PIDA may encourage some potential whistleblowers to become actual whistleblowers, whistleblowers have followed their respective consciences for millennia without the protection of the PIDA, so what might explain such acts? The answer may be found in a number of tragedies, but we will focus upon only those of recent times. In these instances we often find evidence of employees who have raised concerns prior to the final incident occurring. Had these concerns been acted upon the tragedy in question might not have happened. Whether we look at examples such as the Piper-Alpha disaster or the Zeebrugge (*Herald of Free Enterprise*) tragedy, BCCI, Maxwell Communications, Barlow Clowes, the Lyme Bay canoeing tragedy, the Southall rail crash, the Clapham rail crash, or the incidence of high fatality rates among operations on young children at Bristol Royal Infirmary, we find evidence of the ignored concerns of employees.

These were tragedies in the Greek sense. They could have been predicted from their specific circumstances yet the final dénouement appeared inexorable. The circumstances in question often related to lax controls and practices and/or a failure to listen to the concerns of employees. The concerns had either been reported to management, but not acted upon, or unreported due to oppressive and authoritarian management practices or misguided feelings of loyalty. An example of the former is the case of the *Herald of Free Enterprise*, which capsized as it left Zeebrugge harbour because its bow doors had been left open, resulting in the deaths of 192 passengers and crew. A more detailed account of the case is provided in Chapter 8 in Case study 8.6 (*see* p. 328), but some relevant details are provided here. The inquiry report into the disaster, concluded,

> If this sensible suggestion ... had received the serious consideration it deserved this disaster might well have been prevented.
>
> (Lewis, 2000:3)

The suggestion in question was the fitting of lights to the bridge that would have indicated whether or not the bow doors were closed. On five occasions prior to the *Herald of Free Enterprise* capsizing, P&O staff had experienced ferries leaving port without the bow doors being fully closed and had expressed their concerns, but these were not acted upon. The concerns, although communicated to the ferries' management, had not been conveyed to the top management of the company. The concerns appear to have become lost in the middle management tiers of the organisation. Tragedies, such as those mentioned above, created a sufficiently supportive socio-political climate that allowed the PIDA to be passed as an Act of Parliament in 1998 and to become operative in 1999.

Case study 7.2

The Lyme Bay canoeing tragedy

Once again the term 'tragedy' is appropriate, because this appears to have been an accident waiting to happen. The company OLL Ltd offered outdoor adventure holidays, breaks and vacations for younger people. However, two of the instructors were concerned at the lack of attention to safety issues within the company. They became exasperated at the refusal of the owner of the company to take their concerns seriously, so that they felt compelled to resign, although not before they wrote to the owner, detailing their concerns. Not long after their resignations a group of school children were taken canoeing in Lyme Bay, England, by the company, but the weather and sea conditions changed and four of the school children lost their lives. Because there was evidence that the safety failings in the company had been brought to the attention of the owner, 'the guiding mind' (which is discussed in more detail in Chapter 8), a case of corporate manslaughter could be brought. The company was fined £60,000 and the owner was jailed for three years.

The penalties imposed upon the corporations and individuals found complicit in the injuries or deaths of others are not necessarily adequate to influence adherence to health and safety regulations. Slapper and Tombs (1999) cite a couple of cases that illustrate this point. The first relates to Mr Roy Edwin Hill, who was a director of a demolition company. In 1994, the company won the contract to demolish the former Lucas Building in Brislington, which is near Bristol. The factory was demolished with an excavator, but, in violation of Health and Safety legislation, no precautions were taken to prevent the spreading of asbestos and asbestos dust contained in the roofing and pipework lagging. In 1995 Mr Hill received a jail sentence of thee months and a fine of £4000. While these penalties might be surprising, what is possibly more surprising is that Mr Hill's sentence was the first custodial sentence under Health and Safety legislation in 193 years!

The next case has some gruesome details, but it reveals the types of practices that are still prevalent.

Case study 7.3

Dickensian practices, but in modern times

A 19-year old man, Michael Pollard, was employed as a heavy goods vehicle mechanic by a company that manufactured fibres that were used in carpet felt. Mr Pollard was not employed to maintain the equipment in the factory, but on the day in question he was instructed to correct a problem on one of the factory machines. A safety gate was not working and this allowed Mr Pollard to enter the machine while it was still operative. His arm became trapped between spiked rollers and was torn off at the shoulder and shredded in the machine. The Health and Safety Executive immediately maintained that a Prohibition Notice that was served on the company to prevent the use of the dangerous equipment was ignored by the directors. Two of the company's directors were sent to jail for ignoring the Prohibition Notice, but the maximum sentence under the legislation is six months.

The next case provides further evidence of the calculative approach companies can adopt in weighing up whether it is cost-effective to comply with legislation.

Case study 7.4

What is a life worth?

James Hodgson was 21 years old. In 1996, while cleaning the chemical residues from a road tanker, Hodgson was sprayed in the face with a toxic chemical and died. The company was found guilty of gross negligence in the supervision, training and the equipment it supplied to handle dangerous chemicals. The company was found guilty of corporate manslaughter and fined £22,000 (£15,000 of which related to the corporate manslaughter) and the owner of the company was sent to prison for 12 months (subject to early release for good behaviour).

So, in response to the question 'why whistleblow?', examples, such as those above, can be cited of situations in which (many) lives might have been saved, had the concerns of employees been listened to and acted upon. Alternatively the concerned, but ignored employees might have taken their worries on to a broader public platform and made the general public aware of their concerns. So does this type of evidence make the general argument in favour of whistleblowing correct, justifiable, and to be encouraged? If so, why is the act of whistleblowing and of a whistleblower so often portrayed and perceived as a negative force within society?

A contributory factor in explaining why one person might choose to whistleblow in a given situation, while another, when faced with the same circumstances, would opt for a different strategy, is associated with the issues we discussed in Chapter 3.

Connexion point

Although no substantial evidence exists concerning the ethical orientation of whistleblowers (and more significantly suppressed whistleblowers), we can employ our understanding of ethical theories to hypothesise about their likely ethical orientation. In terms of the ethical theories represented in the quadrants of Figure 3.1, people who display a predominantly deontological orientation towards ethical issues, whose ethical thinking, and possibly action, reflects principle-based responses, are more likely to feel compelled to whistleblow if resolution of an ethical dilemma proves impossible.

With concepts such as justice, honesty and integrity normally included in any set of virtues, a virtue ethics orientation (the top left-hand section of Figure 3.1) would also suggest that someone possessing such an orientation would be more likely to resist pressure to compromise themselves should an ethical issue prove insoluble. Likewise, for a Kantian oriented person, whistleblowing would be a likely outcome to an intractable ethical issue.

This contrasts with someone whose ethical orientation reflects consequentialist thinking, i.e. whose decision making will be determined by a thinking through of the consequences of the available options before choosing a course of action. With this orientation, the course of action chosen will depend upon the circumstances of each situation. Given the history of whistleblowing cases (and not just the negative outcomes for the whistleblowers, but also for other employees and the organisation concerned), whistleblowing becomes a far less likely outcome if the concerned employee displays a consequentialist orientation.

The above discussion assumes, of course, that the individual is free to adopt the ethical reasoning which reflects their personal orientation. This, however, is often not possible, due to powerful pressures upon individuals to suppress personal values and to compromise their principles. We discuss the implications of these pressures in the case examples that follow.

Activity 7.2 What would you do?

If your knowledge of an organisational malpractice could, if revealed, cause job losses among your colleagues and possibly harm their pension funds, do you believe that you could undertake a whistleblowing act?

What, if any, organisational issue would be likely to force you ultimately to whistleblow?

Connexion point

In terms of the theoretical framework presented in Chapter 3, the organisation that develops and employs a bona fide whistleblowing process can be located in the top right-hand section of Figure 3.1, the 'ethical learning and growth' section. Such an approach would suggest a reflective, thoughtful orientation towards organisational development, with employees seen as important stakeholders and contributors to that development. Such processes would reflect the best of practices.

When might whistleblowing be justified?

Some writers have set out what, for them, are the essential conditions that make whistleblowing acts justifiable. De George (1999) argued that there are six such conditions. De George's position on whistleblowing is a consequentialist one. Because any whistleblowing act is likely to do harm to the employing organisation, the act can only be justified if the overall effects of the act are likely to be positive. There is no reference to principles or virtues. For De George, it is the overall consequences of a whistleblowing act that determine its justification. The first three conditions (shown below) are argued to make whistleblowing permissible, but not obligatory. If conditions 4 and 5 can be satisfied then whistleblowing becomes a far more persuasive option, in De George's terms, morally obligatory. Another way of interpreting these conditions is to say that, without them, an act of whistleblowing cannot be morally justified as the likely outcome will be painful and probably fruitless for the whistleblower, and detrimental to the organisation. The conditions are as follows:

1. A product or policy of an organisation needs to possess the potential to do harm to some members of society.
2. The concerned employee should first of all report the facts, as far as they are known, to their immediate superior.
3. If the immediate superior fails to act effectively, the concerned employee should take the matter to more senior managers, exhausting all available internal channels in the process.
4. The prospective whistleblower should hold documentary evidence that can be presented to external audiences. In this condition De George argues that the evidence should show that the product or policy 'poses a serious and likely danger to the public or to the user of the product' (De George, 1999: 255).
5. The prospective whistleblower must believe that the necessary changes will be implemented as a result of their whistleblowing act.
6. The sixth condition is a general one and it is that the whistleblower must be acting in good faith, without malice or vindictiveness.

These conditions will now be considered to assess their defensibility, but first we would like you to ponder their appropriateness and helpfulness.

Activity 7.3 Challenging the conditions for justifiable whistleblowing

The six 'conditions of whistleblowing' mentioned above suggest that, if they cannot be fulfilled, then a whistleblowing act cannot be justified. Develop arguments against as many of the six conditions as possible to justify acts of whistleblowing.

A consideration of the conditions

1. *A product or policy of an organisation needs to possess the potential to do harm to some members of society.*

At first sight it might seem difficult to find fault with this requirement, because if no public safety or public concern issue exists, where is the public interest in 'the problem'? What can be the justification for any revelation? An important caveat would be that harm must be interpreted widely and not confined to physical harm. Economic harm, as in the cases of Enron and WorldCom, or psychological harm in the form of race or gender discrimination can be just as damaging as physical harm.

2. *The concerned employee should first of all report the facts, as far as they are known, to their immediate superior, and*
3. *If the immediate superior fails to act effectively, the concerned employee should take the matter to more senior managers, exhausting all available internal channels in the process.*

These two conditions are considered together because of their obvious linkage. Some would argue that organisations should view internal whistleblowing procedures as important mechanisms within their corporate governance processes. It might seem common sense that organisations would wish to be informed about practices that threaten the well-being of their customers, or the public at large. After all, reputations and brands can take years and considerable expenditures to build, but be destroyed in a very short time by adverse publicity. Thus, enlightened self-interest would seem to dictate an interest in encouraging internal whistleblowing. So why are many organisations not more receptive to the concerns and criticisms of their employees?

The roots of the explanation are complex, but they have to include personal reputations and relationships. By suggesting that 'organisations' would wish to be informed about unsafe practices or products gives a physical status to the term 'organisation' which is, in this context, inappropriate and unhelpful. Criticisms made of products and practices will invariably be criticisms of people, usually more senior than oneself. Condition 2 implies that one's immediate superior within the organisation should be consulted, even if they are part of the problem, hence condition 3. The PIDA also recognises this potential problem and allows the whistleblower to bypass their immediate supervisor if this can be shown to be warranted.

Condition 3 assumes that some form of internal whistleblowing process exists and is operated with integrity. A good example is Nottinghamshire County Council's website, from which you can access a report prepared for the Council on its whistleblowing procedures. The County Council employs an external organisation to operate its anonymous whistleblowing procedure. This is a laudable approach and the County Council operates a refreshingly open policy to its procedures.

However, it is quite possible that the cause of one's concerns lies with the policies or practices of the senior management. For example, budgetary pressures to achieve improved output targets within existing or reduced resources might compromise quality, including safety checks. Alternatively, managers at differing levels within their organisation might each, unknown to the others, impose planned efficiency savings on budgetary forecasts in order to impress senior management (De George, 1999: 244, cites such a scenario). In the process a final budget is created that might involve production outputs and cost levels that are wholly unrealistic. As a consequence corners are subsequently cut to try to approach the agreed output or cost budgets. Any expression of concern by an employee may become 'lost' within the management hierarchy. Finding out where the blockage exists might be a far from simple task. Expecting employees who are employed 'at the coal face' to have the awareness or confidence to express their concerns higher up the management tree (assuming one can identify how far one needs to go to escape the vicious circle of partially implicated managers) could be an unrealistic assumption. In real life, raising one's concerns internally can simply mean that management can identify which employees are likely to reveal problems that are of the managers' making.

A number of cases reported on the *Public Concern at Work* website (www.pcaw.co.uk) illustrate how the PIDA has been used and several cases relate to whistleblowers being victimised following internal disclosure of concerns.

Case study 7.5

Victimisation and its consequences

In the case Fernandes v. Netcom (2000), Fernandes (F) was the finance officer of a subsidiary of a large US telecoms company. F became concerned at the level of expenses claimed by the CEO of the subsidiary company. F was initially told by his contact in America to 'turn a blind eye', which initially F appears to have done. However, when the CEO's expenses went above £300,000, F took his concerns to the US Board. F was immediately put under pressure to resign (not the CEO), but F refused. F was disciplined and then sacked for authorising the CEO's expenses. F brought a claim using the PIDA. Contrary to the claims of the American parent company, the UK Employment Tribunal found that F had been dismissed for his whistleblowing, not for authorising the expenses, and because he was 58 and unable to secure similar work, he was awarded £293,000.

Returning to De George's conditions, it might be argued that conditions 2 and 3, while initially suggesting a way for concerned employees and enlightened organisations to operate open channels of communication, might in fact be more reflective of a desire to keep the problem within the organisation, as experienced by Fernandes. This implies an emphasis upon loyalty to the organisation, loyalty which history would question in terms of reciprocated loyalty and commitment.

So far we have shown that a number of circumstances can exist that make conditions 1, 2 and 3 problematic. Yet these are only considered to be conditions that would make a whistleblowing act permissible. They are argued to be insufficient on their own to constitute the necessary conditions for an act of whistleblowing to be morally obligatory. To achieve this, De George argued that conditions 4 and 5 need to be satisfied.

4. Documentary evidence should be in the possession of the prospective whistleblower that can be presented to external audiences.

Here it is being argued that, without hard evidence of your concerns, you are not obliged to reveal them to an external (or internal) audience. The rationale is that without strong evidence you may risk the negative outcomes experienced by many whistleblowers, without being able to expose the bad practices that concern you. This has to be a sensible, cautionary note for any potential whistleblower to weigh in their deliberations about expressing their concerns, but it does not address the moral dilemma that the concerned employee faces.

Obtaining the evidence one requires to substantiate one's concerns can be extremely difficult. First there is the problem that ownership of the information is likely to rest with the organisation. The law of property rights would make the photocopying of such evidence a criminal offence. However, to blow the whistle without such evidence would be naïve in the extreme. Most whistleblowers obtain as much evidence as they can and let the courts decide whether accusations of stealing company property are an adequate defence by the employing organisation.

The other major problem is that sometimes incriminating evidence is either too difficult to obtain or simply not available. In the example of the misappropriation of pension fund monies by Robert Maxwell, the case was so complex, due to the interlocking nature of so many of the subsidiary companies within the *Maxwell Communications* empire, that the task for one, or a few, employees of obtaining sufficient corroborating evidence to support their concerns was simply impossible. It took a team of accountants nearly two calendar years, and many more person years, to unravel the web that Maxwell had woven.

So if one has deep concerns about a particular issue (say the use of pension funds as in the Maxwell case), but a lack of hard evidence, is one absolved from one's civic responsibilities? The financial loss suffered by the pensioners of the Maxwell companies, as was experienced by the employees of Enron and WorldCom, were significant. These were not minor financial scams. A lot of people were financially hurt; in a significant number of cases their lives were damaged irrevocably.

While it is wise to counsel caution to prospective whistleblowers if their corroborating information is not strong, society as a whole might be the lesser if this condition was used as an ethical loophole, through which individuals could escape their personal dilemma, i.e. to divulge or not to divulge. It is unlikely that sufficient corroborating evidence will be gathered in many cases to prove irrevocably that a particular revelation is watertight. This is why the PIDA uses phrases such as the whistleblower should 'reasonably believe' and should believe the accusation to be 'substantially true'. UK law does not require that the accusation be 'true', only that it was reasonable to believe that it was true.

5. The prospective whistleblower must believe that the necessary changes will be implemented as a result of their whistleblowing act.

The emphasis here is again on the protection of the whistleblower. Given the negative personal outcomes that the majority of whistleblowers have experienced, this condition is merely saying, 'If the probabilities are that nothing will change as a result of your action, you are not duty bound to make your revelation'. Although the condition is expressed in a positive sense, i.e. 'if conditions 1–5 exist and you are of the view that your revelation will cause the offending or dangerous practice to cease, then you are morally obliged to make your revelation', the condition can be reinterpreted as possessing a negative slant. In its negative form the condition is effectively offering an escape route to the uncertain whistleblower.

6. The whistleblower must be acting in good faith, without malice or vindictiveness.

This is a contentious condition. It begs the question, 'Why are the motives of the whistleblower important or relevant?' If, say, the whistleblower can be shown to have grounds for harbouring resentment at being passed over for promotion at some time in the past, or for being disciplined for an organisational infraction, why should this invalidate or undermine any revelation that they might make about an organisational malpractice? If, as some managers claimed in our research interviews, the disgruntled employee was lying, out of spite, about an alleged wrongdoing, then clearly the claimed whistleblowing act would not in fact be one, because no wrongdoing took place. Such acts are simply lies, not whistleblowing.

We might prefer that those revealing organisational malpractices do so for honourable reasons, and the purity of the whistleblower's position is an oft-cited requirement for acceptable whistleblowing, but it is a doubtful argument. As you will see when we discuss the PIDA, one of the requirements of the Act is that, for a whistleblower to gain the protection of the Act, they must not profit from the whistleblowing, e.g. being paid as a result of publishing their revelations in a newspaper or book. While it might not be wholly desirable for whistleblowing to be stimulated by thoughts of personal gain, it has to be asked whether the public interest is served by denying such whistleblowers legal protection. Practices for encouraging whistleblowing are followed when rewards are offered for information leading to the successful prosecution of criminals in cases of robbery, murder, hijacking and so on, and nothing is judged to be untoward in these circumstances. One must ask what the distinctions are that make whistleblowers of organisational malpractices less valued by society than whistleblowers of other crimes?

The 'crime' of revealing corporate malpractices is sometimes seen as greater than the corporate malpractices themselves. Whilst offering rewards for the capture of, say, criminals who have robbed a bank is acceptable, the offering of rewards for evidence against companies who have 'robbed' shareholders and employees is somehow seen in a different light.

Whistleblowing: a positive or negative force within society?

The tragedies referred to earlier in the chapter might suggest that organisations would be wise to institute internal whistleblowing procedures to allow employees to raise their concerns and thus create early warning systems upon which the employing organisations could act. Indeed, internal whistleblowing structures can be seen as essential to good corporate governance. So is whistleblowing a characteristic of a healthy, self-aware and self-critical society, with those who reveal organisational malpractices regarded as performing positive civic acts? The evidence would suggest that as a society we are some way away from such a position, although Borrie (1996) observed that the development of organisations such as *Childline* might be heralding a changing view in relation to those who reveal evidence of abuse, recklessness, and disregard for the integrity and sanctity of fellow human beings.

Sternberg (1996) argued that companies should look upon whistleblowing processes as critical elements within good corporate governance practice, and Borrie and Dehn (2002: 5) have also discussed the development of a whistleblowing culture in which, the whistleblower would be seen 'as a witness, not as a complainant'. They argued that, thirty years ago, it was rare to find a company seeking the views of its customers about the quality of the company's products or services. Now it is regarded as central to staying competitive. Borrie and Dehn suggested that perhaps by, say, 2030 whistleblowing processes will not merely be the norm, but seen as essential elements of a corporation's information gathering processes.

Connexion point

Whilst a Kantian perspective (discussed in Chapter 3) would see the instrumental rationale implicit in such a development as reducing its ethical integrity, prospective whistleblowers might just be grateful for the development.

A more serious concern for the development of supportive whistleblowing cultures is that, if their justification is based upon economic rather than ethical grounds, then if the economic justification ceases to exist (i.e. the costs of operating a whistleblowing process are judged to outweigh the benefits being derived), then whistleblowers will once again be seen as impediments to organisational competitiveness.

As mentioned earlier, incidents such as the Lyme Bay canoeing disaster and the *Herald of Free Enterprise* disaster created the social and political conditions that allowed the Public Interest Disclosure Act to become law, but history is replete with examples of individuals who have revealed organisational malpractices, invariably to their own personal cost. Peter Drucker (cited in Borrie, 1996) referred to whistleblowers as informers and likened societies that encouraged whistleblowing as bearing some of the characteristics of tyrannies such as those of Tiberius and Nero in Rome, the Spanish Inquisition, and the French Terror, a view that not all would share. Others see the acts of whistleblowers as equivalent to referees who maintain 'the rules of the game'. However, the analogy of the whistleblower as a referee in a sporting contest is flawed and a closer examination of the acts of whistleblowing within the context of a sporting event goes some way to explaining the antipathy that some feel towards whistleblowing and whistleblowers.

A whistleblower in a sporting event would not be the referee, but a member of one of the opposing sides who, upon seeing an infringement by one of his own side, stops the game and calls the referee's and the crowd's attention to the incident. This would be referred to as displaying a Corinthian spirit, i.e. placing the ideals and integrity of the sport above the mere winning of the immediate contest. Whether the supporters and fellow team members would see the incident in exactly the same light is debatable.

The sporting analogy should not be taken too far, because whistleblowing cases involve far greater consequences than the result of a game. The point of the analogy is that whistleblowers are not the appointed referees of organisational affairs. Neither do they claim to be so. They are usually unfortunate individuals who become ensnared in the maelstrom of a situation, which for a variety of reasons becomes irresolvable, at least to their satisfaction. They are then faced with the predicament of either allowing their concerns to subside and to 'keep their heads below the parapet', or to seek to get the issue resolved by revealing their concerns to either an internal or external audience. Some have described whistleblowing acts as heroic acts, because the outcomes for many whistleblowers tend to be so negative. But why are whistleblowers so often maligned and cast as the wrongdoers, in situations where others have created great potential harm?

Besides the unpleasantness of being seen as a 'snitch' or an informer, the prospective whistleblower has to weigh the implications for an organisation of news reaching its critical markets about the practices in question. These markets include both product markets and securities' markets. In competitive markets, ground lost to rival organisations can be difficult to make up, and confidence lost by investors in the organisation difficult to restore. The threat of lost jobs can mean that even long-term colleagues may not support the whistleblower. Whilst the architect of such a situation is the person/s who have committed the malpractice, the innocent employee who becomes knowledgeable of the malpractice is placed in a complex, vexed situation. In some respects they could be damned if they do (i.e. whistleblow) by their colleagues, but damned if they don't (i.e. stay silent) by members of the public who might subsequently be harmed as a result of the malpractice.

The following example, which is taken from a study conducted by the authors (Fisher and Lovell, 2000), indicates that such bad practices are not confined to small, back-street operators who exploit the vulnerability of a low-skilled workforce. The company concerned was a large, internationally known engineering organisation.

Case study 7.6

The Engineering Company and its overseas markets

This company operated in a range of domestic (UK) and overseas markets. In at least one of the overseas markets 'arrangements' were sometimes negotiated with overseas agents that involved exported goods being artificially reclassified to reduce the level of import duties in the overseas country. For example, a £1M order for engineered products would be reclassified for invoice purposes as £700K engineered products and £300K consultancy services. In this particular overseas country consultancy services were not subject to import duty.

The engineering company did not suffer as a result of the reclassification, and the importing agents acquired the goods at a lower cost (taking import taxes into account) than they would otherwise have had to pay. The only losers were the governments of the countries concerned. When these situations arose, the unofficial, but well understood, procedure within the engineering company was for the requested 'arrangement' to be passed directly to the sales director and managing director of the engineering company. This ultimate decision-making unit would weigh the risks, the returns and the implications of the decision and then decree whether the proposed deal with the agent would be sanctioned. Clearly this act was illegal, yet it was argued that such behaviour was necessary in order to stay in the markets concerned and to protect jobs in the UK. Other operators in these markets were claimed to offer similar 'arrangements'. Here the consequentialist argument that all the implications of a decision should be weighed in order to identify the decision that offers the greatest good to the greatest number might be tabled. The waters become further muddied when the management of the engineering company argued that the government of the overseas country operated a repressive regime, employing punitive import taxes in order to shore up excessive government expenditure on military equipment and government largesse.

None of the claims about the foreign government could be validated, but, assuming they were accurate, what did the actions of the senior management of the company say to the employees of the engineering company? Whatever the rights and wrongs of the situation, the engineering company was employing criteria and a decision process that sanctioned law-breaking activity.

Interestingly, Tony Blair, the British Prime Minister, made the problems of Africa one of the major challenges of his 2005 G8 presidency. Having previously established the Commission for Africa, one of the principal areas of focus of the Commission was the issue of fraud within African governments and between those governments and multinational corporations. If progress ensues from the work of the Commission then the type of incident portrayed in Case study 7.6 might become a thing of the past, but history would suggest that progress may be slow and uneven. This is particularly so if the account provided by Evans (2004) is indicative of the UK Government's commitment to the principles of the Commission for Africa. Evans reported that secret documents, which were revealed in the high court on 22 December 2004, showed that the Trade Secretary, Patricia Hewitt

> overruled her civil servants to water down rules to curb corruption by companies after lobbying by the Confederation of British Industry (CBI) and Rolls Royce, BAE Systems and the Airbus aircraft maker,. ... previously confidential documents showed that the CBI had appreciated the 'full engagement and (continuing friendliness) on this very important issue' shown by Mrs Hewitt and 'our friends at the Department of Trade and Industry'... the government and business were 'really playing together now on this'!

If the argument is raised that business is not a precise and neat ethical practice and that one has to accept that in certain cases the ends justify the means, one is accepting a situation where different rules are known to apply in different contexts. No part of a code of behaviour can be seen to be inviolate and every organisational value has its price. This is not to suggest that all laws have to be respected, however repressive and immoral, but the behaviour of the engineering executives was not lawbreaking born from high ideals, but rather lawbreaking born of organisational or personal gain and/or prejudice.

Case study 7.7

A postscript to Case study 7.6

An interesting development to the previous case was that the practice involving the reclassification of exported products had come to the attention of an overseas government and the major operators in this market (including the UK engineering company) were making provisions for substantial repayments of undeclared import taxes. There was also the possibility that a number of the operators could be barred from selling in the overseas market in the future. This development does not suddenly make the decision-making procedures employed invalid, when previously they could be justified on an ends–means basis. An action does not acquire the status of being ethical or unethical merely on the grounds that its existence is either publicly known or unknown.

An obvious question regarding the engineering company is why the employees we interviewed tolerated their organisational environment. The answer to this question is not explained by one single factor, but it did appear that the most senior managers of the organisation were implicated in the practices. Fear that any form of dissent would be quickly suppressed and impair future promotional prospects was the overriding reason offered by the interviewees for their muteness. There were no whistleblowers within this organisation. Was this a state of affairs to be applauded or encouraged, and how and why can middle and senior managers possess such feelings of organisational impotence?

Within the engineering company many understood the practices, but no one possessed the courage, the will or the independence (as a result of the need to retain their employment) to raise their concerns, either within the organisations or to external agencies. The extent of the malpractices acted like a cancer, corrupting others who might otherwise have exercised moral judgement. There appeared to be a view among certain middle and junior management levels of 'what is sauce for the goose (senior management) is sauce for the gander (themselves)'.

The engineering company might seem an extreme example of modern organisational life. However, the continuing evidence of unacceptable organisational practices and whistleblowing cases (*see* for example Hartley, 1993; Hunt, 1995, 1998), and the work of organisations such as Public Concern at Work and Freedom to Care, do not provide much support for benign assumptions about respect for the moral agency of individual employees.

Suppressed whistleblowing

For the concerned employee, there are not only potential costs associated with revealing organisational malpractices; there are also costs associated with suppressing whistleblowing. The latter costs tend to be emotional and psychological and are associated with a loss of self-esteem. This is illustrated in Figure 7.1. A fuller account of the issues relating to this framework is given in Lovell (2002).

The framework possesses two layers. The first of these is concerned with two non-organisational factors that are significant in shaping the third element, that of the individual's personal autonomy. The three elements of layer 1 are:

- The individual's personal value system, born of past experiences, including family values and perspectives (both nature and nurture are included).
- Broader societal values, which are unlikely to be homogenous or consistent.
- The feeling of personal autonomy held by the individual.

Layer 2 also possesses three elements, which are context specific. These are:

- Values derived from within the organisation.
- The ethical intensity of a situation or problem felt by the concerned employee.
- The support from others, normally organisational colleagues, both peers and hierarchical superiors, and family, but also support groups, professional associations, etc.

In Figure 7.1 the six cells are shown as the same size. However, the figure can be used to describe the relative importance of the six elements in different potential whistleblowing situations. The relative size of the cells is contingent on the specifics of each case.

The emboldened part of Figure 7.1 represents an inflexible organisational boundary. If an ethically charged situation develops in which the position of the troubled employee is at loggerheads with the senior management, it is likely that the organisational mores/strength of practices will flex and grow in scale. With the boundaries of Figure 7.1 fixed, either one or more of the other elements has to shrink, or a fracture in the boundary will occur. If this happens, then confinement of the problem within the organisation will have ceased and an external whistleblowing situation could follow.

If the troubled employee wishes to retain employment within the organisation, but retains a belief that the organisational practice is wrong, their personal autonomy will need to shrink to accommodate organisational/managerial interests. As a consequence of this diminution of personal autonomy, the ability to exercise moral agency is driven out.

LAYER 2	Intensity of problem	Organisational values/ strength of practices	Support of others
LAYER 1	Personal values	Personal autonomy	Societal values

Figure 7.1 Elements of ethical complexity

Effectively an individual's personal autonomy acts as a type of shock absorber, allowing confinement of the issue within the organisational boundary. As a consequence, however, the confidence of the suppressed whistleblower can be severely affected. This was particularly so with respect to the individual featured in Case study 7.6. The shrinking of personal autonomy is also significant in Case study 7.8.

Case study 7.8

The charity

G possessed a strong religious faith, which reflected his family upbringing. He worked for an internationally known charitable organisation, whose *raison d'être* was love, understanding, tolerance and forgiveness. During the initial interview G revealed that he had an interesting example of principle that was live at the time of the interview. Having recently attended a seminar on value-added-tax (VAT), G had realised that a practice operated by the charity was liable to VAT, but the practice had never been declared for VAT purposes. On returning from the seminar G brought the matter to the attention of the directors, believing that the correct approach would be to notify Customs and Excise and to discuss the issue with them. G was very aware that the charity could not afford to repay the sums that were now clearly owing to Customs and Excise, but G believed that Customs and Excise would agree that the VAT rules were never intended to apply to charities like his own, and at worst the charity would need to lobby Parliament and the Treasury to get the rules changed retrospectively. Being an internationally known charity that attracted widespread public support, G believed this would be possible.

At a subsequent meeting with G, he was clearly less buoyant than at the first meeting. He described how the charity's solicitors had been contacted to obtain a legal ruling on the practice in question and they had confirmed G's assessment. However, the attitude of the senior management towards G was not one of gratitude, but rather coolness, even a degree of wariness. At the third meeting with G, he revealed that the affair had been a sickening experience for him. The legal advice had been that the practice should be terminated immediately, but that no mention should be made to Customs and Excise. The belief was that Customs and Excise would demand a refund of the unpaid taxes and that the probability of the Treasury seeking a change to taxation legislation to exclude the charity from future liability was low, with no chance of retrospective legislation. G's wishes to be honest and 'come clean' with Customs and Excise' were dismissed as naïve. What particularly vexed and troubled him was that he was now, in his own words, 'perceived as a potential whistleblower'. His relationship with members of the charity's Board of Directors had changed from a close and friendly one to one characterised by considerable wariness and mistrust. He had no intention of whistleblowing (out of loyalty to the organisation, not to the senior management), but it hurt greatly to come face to face with his organisational impotency, when he had thought that he and his work were highly valued.

At the start of his ethical dilemma, G carried with him a set of values that he argued reflected a strong commitment to notions of fairness, equity and justice. These underpinned his initial reasoning of the problem. These were values that he believed corresponded with those of the broader society and the charity in question.

Connexion point

The Golden Rule

G enjoyed a quite senior position within the charity. A quiet and softly spoken man, G initially considered his individual autonomy to be high. He was confident of his (moral) position and his arguments. During the interviews, he even cited the 'Golden Rule', in his words, 'treat others as you would want to be treated yourself'.

For G, the intensity of the problem was initially high, but he quickly realised that the support of others did not exist, particularly at a very senior level. This mix of level 2 elements (high problem intensity; total resistance from senior management; and low support from others) transformed the issue from one, in G's eyes, capable of resolution within notions of justice and equity, to an ethical dilemma. G's preference to discuss the issue with Customs and Excise put him at variance with the charity's board of directors. G became isolated and was seen as a deviant. He had a loyalty to both the organisation, whose values and mission he wholeheartedly believed in, and to his fellow employees, whose livelihoods would certainly be affected if the tax authorities did demand a repayment of back taxes.

G expressed the view that, if he really believed that Customs and Excise would be successful in demanding repayment of back taxes, he too would support concealment, as the work of the charity would be affected to the point of ruin. However, he simply could not accept that this would be the ultimate outcome. He believed that the Board of Directors did not wish to be seen as having made a serious error in the decisions they had taken over the configuration of the organisation that had led to the practice in question attracting VAT liability, a ramification they had overlooked.

Connexion point

Kohlberg's hierarchy of moral reasoning

G's apparent willingness to 'break the law' is not necessarily a reprehensible position to hold. In G's view the particular VAT law in question represented a failing in the legislation's drafting. It was 'bad law', and could be corrected once its failings were brought to the attention of the relevant authorities. This form of reasoning would normally be considered to reflect high levels of moral reasoning, that is, 5, possibly even 6, within Kohlberg's hierarchy (*see* p.252–4), depending upon how hard G was prepared to fight for his convictions.

G considered the concealment decided upon by the directors reflected an avoidance of pain motive on their part, the very lowest stage of reasoning within Kohlberg's hierarchy. The values imposed upon the situation by the Board of

Directors effectively challenged G. He either stayed and kept quiet or he left. Due to family commitments and a strong belief in the work of the charity G stayed, but his personal autonomy was severely diminished and he viewed the future with sadness and apprehension. Figure 7.2 reflects an application of the elements of ethical complexity to the case.

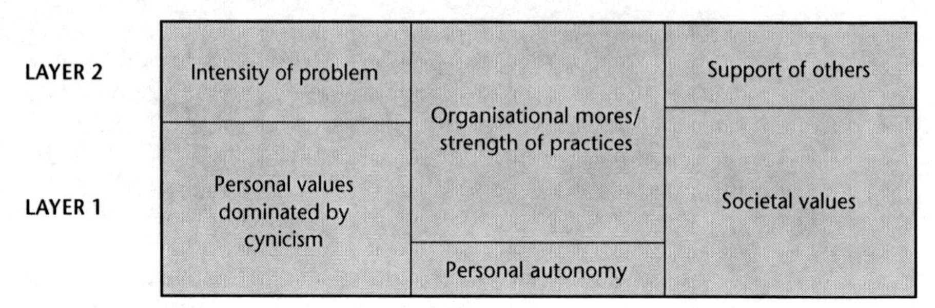

Figure 7.2 Elements of ethical complexity (Case study 7.8)

If a whistleblower reveals an organisational practice that they consider to be against the public interest, such a whistleblowing act could be considered a civic act. In the sense used here, civic describes an act that an individual citizen carries out as a member of a community or state. The term citizen is an inclusive term. It locates the individual within a community of others. It stresses relatedness, without the integrity and specialness of the individual being lost in the blandness of a crowd. The citizen is both part of a community, but identifiable and separable within it.

There is no suggestion that in such a society every individual is perpetually and desperately seeking to achieve a utopian form of communitarian existence, a form of societal nirvana. What the term civic describes is a context in which justice and understanding are at the bedrock of social relationships. Thus, when a (potentially) significant injustice is observed, the civic-minded individual does not walk away from their civic responsibilities by ignoring the injustice or public hazard. They seek to change the practice, and if this is unsuccessful they seek to bring the problem to public attention. They act in an autonomous way, i.e. they act as free people. They act with moral agency. This is what many whistleblowers would claim for their acts. This is not an argument for a form of societal or organisational chaos that would encourage everyone to challenge everything. As with all aspects of human relations, rights should normally carry with them responsibilities. As a consequence the right to exercise moral agency requires that individuals also respect the beliefs of others insofar as they represent commonly held views.

The whistleblower can be portrayed as a somewhat heroic figure, and some writers do argue this position. While no attempt will be made to suggest that whistleblowing is a saintly act, there is no doubt that particular whistleblowing cases portray individuals who have displayed personal courage and determination to overcome legal, financial, psychological and physical obstacles in their attempts to stop a particular organisational practice, or to bring it to public attention (see Hoffman and Moore, 1990; Hunt 1995, 1998; Lovell and Robertson, 1994; Matthews, Goodpaster and Nash, 1991; Miceli and Near, 1992 for examples). But, for some, there can be an exhilaration associated with whistleblowing. Paul van Buitenen (2000) was the EU employee whose revelations about the misuse of EU funds contributed to the resignation of the entire European Union Commission in 1999. His autobiography reveals that, although his whistleblowing damaged him, he also relished the excitement of the clandestine meetings and the media attention that arose from it.

Returning to our consideration of the societal role and defensibility of whistleblowing, we consider Case study 7.9. This case provides further evidence of the psychological damage that can be inflicted upon an employee who rails against an organisational practice. The person in question occupied a senior position within the organisation concerned, but was judged to pose a threat to certain key individuals within the organisation.

Case study 7.9

The costs of whistleblowing

W had worked for the organisation concerned for seven years and had risen to a senior position, effectively being the joint deputy head of finance. However, his unease about certain accounting 'adjustments' he was being asked to make and the obstacle that he represented to the advancement of a junior colleague whom the chief executive appeared to favour, meant that W suddenly appeared to be a 'persona non grata'. This was surprising to all those who were interviewed to corroborate this case, because, without exception, they all held W in very high esteem. A decision appeared to have been made by the chief executive that W had to go, and considerable psychological pressure was exerted on W to encourage him to resign. W's last annual appraisal spoke about his failing performance, despite glowing previous appraisals. W finally resigned, although he appeared to have been 'constructively dismissed', and an out-of-court settlement was made to remove the threat of an industrial tribunal hearing for wrongful dismissal. The words of W are illuminating:

> ... they drag you down to such an extent that your confidence is absolutely rock bottom. You have no confidence in your own ability and it takes you a long time to realise that you didn't deserve this. You hadn't done anything wrong... in the back of your mind you're thinking, did I do something wrong to deserve this? Until now, I have not said anything about my case ... You want a career and you're not quite sure what influence they have in the rest of the public sector – I still haven't got a permanent position.

The governance structures of W's organisation were clearly deficient.

Whistleblowing was not on the agenda of any of the central characters within the cases considered in this chapter because of their fear for their respective employment prospects. Many of those who, in a study of accountants and HR managers (Fisher and Lovell, 2000), expressed disgust over certain organisational practices felt impotent and unable to do anything to put things right.

The words of a hospital's deputy director of finance reveal behaviour that might surprise some.

Case study 7.10

The hospital case

This case was recounted to the researchers by a range of middle ranking HR managers and accountants within a hospital, as well as by H, the Deputy Director of Finance. It was a situation that troubled many in the hospital (see Case study 2.21 for another interviewee's perspective).

The case relates to the waiting lists initiative instigated by the Department of Health in 1998. The intention of the initiative was to provide additional funds to hospitals to allow them to reduce hospital waiting lists in key areas. The following are the words of the Deputy Director of Finance.

> The government has just put all this money into the waiting list initiative, to treat patients and get them off the waiting list. It's taxpayers' money – the spirit of that money was not to line consultants' pockets. In theory, it's NHS money, health sector money. A number of the specialties reacted as one would hope. However, the ophthalmologists said, 'Yes, we will do this, if you pay me something like £750 per case. We will pay the nurses time and a half. ... And if you don't pay us that rate we won't do the list'. So ophthalmologists got their way – a very dirty deal – nurses get a bit and porters and cleaners get nothing. The ophthalmologists are getting about £15,000 extra per list.

In addition to the ophthalmologists, ENT specialists and anaesthetists at this hospital also negotiated their own special deals with regard to the waiting lists' initiatives. When asked how particular specialties could drive through such arrangements, the response was, 'They confronted the organisation. The chief executive is frightened of the power of these groups, so he is prepared to do deals, rather than risk not getting patients done.'

When asked to describe his own feelings towards this situation, H replied, 'Perhaps I am naïve, but I wouldn't have let it happen. I think all staff should be treated equally and I would have waged war with the consultants and said, I am sorry – we are not playing.'

Had H ever been tempted to blow the whistle at any time? The answer was yes and the above situation was such a time. He had not because, 'I have to respect the chief executive's decision. My loyalty to him, my accountability – I haven't done anything wrong.'

'I haven't done anything wrong.' These are words to ponder.

Connexion point

Using De George's six criteria for justifiable whistleblowing (see p. 268) it is possible to argue that H could have responded positively to conditions 1, 2, 4 and 6.

- H would have been acting honourably, assuming he did not sell his story to the press, if he had chosen to go public with his knowledge (condition 6).
- It was disgust with the way senior consultants were using their organisational power to 'line their pockets' with public money that was at the heart of H's angst (condition 1).

- H had also discussed the issue with the finance director (condition 2), although the latter seemed resigned to the realities of organisational power within the hospital.
- H also had the documentary evidence to substantiate his case, had he chosen to use it (condition 4).
- However, H had not taken the matter to the chief executive because the chief executive was a central figure in the affair (condition 3), and
- He doubted whether a whistleblowing act would change much, after the initial furore had died down (condition 5).

Thus, against the six criteria H would have found a degree of support for an act of whistleblowing, although the belief that little if anything would change as a result of a whistleblowing act (condition 5) does provide a justification (within De George's framework) for 'keeping quiet'.

A further consideration was that H feared that the adverse publicity that such a revelation would attract would do the hospital great harm, at a time when hospitals across the UK were under considerable media scrutiny due to revelations about the concealment of negligent practices by clinicians (*see* Case study 2.19). It is not just organisations operating in the profit seeking sectors that can suffer from adverse publicity and falling 'client' confidence. H's concerns over the ramifications for 'his' hospital of any disclosure about the greed of a significant number of consultants were real.

Within this account of H's case, there are a number of issues that need to be explored further. The first is the harm that can be caused by an act of whistleblowing. Notwithstanding the existence of unacceptable organisational practices, or shortcomings in quality and/or safety, the whistleblowing act itself may inflict harm upon individuals and organisations including individuals known personally to the whistleblower. To present whistleblowing situations as always clear-cut, with 'good guys' and 'bad guys' clearly demarcated, and issues neatly packaged with 'right' and 'wrong' labels attached, would be misleading. Life is messy, and organisational life is particularly messy on occasions. However, this is not an excuse to do nothing. Judgement has to be a major factor in shaping personal decision making, but when that judgement is constrained by employment fears, moral agency is undermined and impoverished. This takes us to the second point, that of floating responsibility (Bauman, 1994).

Floating responsibility

DEFINITION

Floating responsibility refers to the situation where all the individuals that were potentially involved or implicated in a particular incident or problem are all able to explain that responsibility for the problem was not theirs. Responsibility becomes impossible to pinpoint. It appears to fall between the cracks of job descriptions and roles.

H's closing words 'I haven't done anything wrong' could be seen as an example of floating responsibility. It becomes an organisational defence against individual conscience. In this way the following of rules and adherence to the commands of superiors make identification of responsibility difficult to isolate. 'I was only following orders' is a plea heard from junior clerks to senior military officers.

The third point to consider is H's expressed loyalty to the chief executive. 'I have to respect the chief executive's decision. My loyalty to him, my accountability.' Besides loyalty to the chief executive, H was also thinking of his other work colleagues. As the case indicates, H was not alone in his knowledge of the affair, yet H indicated that no one else would 'rock the boat'. These others preferred to 'keep their heads down' for fear of the personal consequences. Colleagues (and their families) who choose to ignore the implications of a malpractice could be significantly affected by any revelations. These are heavy considerations to weigh in the decision of whether or not to whistleblow. The vulnerability and aloneness of the potential whistleblower, but also those who adopt a 'not my business' stance, need reflecting upon. Jos (1988: 323) argued that,

> Modern organisations require workers to do things they might not otherwise do.... [they] undermine the capacity of workers to make their own judgement about what they should do. By uncritically deferring to others, workers may become party to immoral or illegal activities and policies. In short, it is the worker's autonomy, his status as a chooser that is at stake.

Jos's lament over the demise of moral autonomy needs to be juxtaposed with the celebration of 'the individual' as evidenced in much political and corporate rhetoric. The wishes of the individual consumer are claimed to be sovereign. Citizen charters abound, and organisations, both public and private sector, claim to dance to the tune of consumer preferences. Nisbet (1953), while addressing issues of political economy, offered some thoughts that are relevant to this debate.

> The political **enslavement** of man requires the **emancipation** of man from all the authorities and memberships ... that serve, one degree or another, to insulate the individual from the external political power ... totalitarian domination of the individual will is not a mysterious process, not a form of sorcery based upon some vast and unknowable irrationalism. It arises and proceeds rationally and relentlessly through the creation of new functions, statuses and allegiances which, by conferring community, makes the manipulation of the human will scarcely more than an exercise in scientific social psychology ... there may be left the appearance of individual freedom, provided it is only individual freedom. All of this is unimportant, always subject to guidance and control, if the primary social contexts of belief and opinion are properly organised and managed. What is central is the creation of a network of functions and loyalties reaching down into the most intimate recesses of human life where ideas and beliefs will germinate and develop.
>
> (Nisbet, 1953: 202, 208, emphasis in the original)

Thus, Nisbet argued that the freedom inherent within current conceptions of individualism is a particular and partial form of individualism, located precisely in the economic sphere. This ideology has, however, facilitated the neutering of people as political actors. Yet in the economic sphere individualism is again prescribed, with certain forms of action almost proscribed. Sarason (1986) commented on a society in which individuals affected by social dilemmas perceive their dilemmas as their, and only their, responsibility. Paraphrasing Sarason,

> If **your** ethical dilemma is **your** responsibility according to **my** morality, this is quite consistent with the increasingly dominant ideology of individual rights, responsibility, choice and freedom. If I experience the issue as **yours**, it is because there is nothing in my existence to make it **ours**. And by **ours** I mean a socio-cultural network and traditions which engender an obligation to be part of the problem and possible solution.
>
> (Sarason, 1986, emphasis in the original)

What we hope is becoming evident is that whistleblowing is a complex, many-sided debate that cannot be removed from the social, cultural and economic contexts to which it relates.

Whilst individual attitudes might be difficult to change, certainly in the short term, maybe the least that might be expected of a civilised society is that those of its members who do act in ways that reflect a civic orientation in their whistleblowing should enjoy the protection of the law. Thus, it is appropriate that we now progress to a consideration of the law relating to whistleblowing in the UK, The Public Interest Disclosure Act, 1998.

The Public Interest Disclosure Act (1998) (PIDA)

There are two central elements to the PIDA to recognise from the outset. The first is that it does not give a right to an employee to whistleblow. The Act has been constructed upon the premise that confidentiality of corporate information is the primary principle, from which there a few exceptions. It is to these exceptions that the Act speaks. It offers protection to those who speak out (in the parlance of the Act, make a 'disclosure') against specific types of organisational malpractices, as long as certain conditions are met. The construction of the Act encourages disclosure to be kept within the employing organisation's boundaries by increasing the conditions that have to be satisfied if one makes a disclosure outside the confines of the employing organisation.

The second element that lessens the Act's potential from the perspective of the concerned employee is that the burden of proof is upon the employee to show that a malpractice has occurred, although the burden of proof does vary depending upon to whom a disclosure is made. In circumstances where the work environment is intimidatory and oppressive, obtaining supporting evidence, such as corroboration from current employees, could prove extremely difficult.

The term 'protected disclosure' relates to the type of whistleblowing act that falls within the protection of the Act. The malpractice must normally relate to the employing organisation. However, in certain, restricted situations a protected disclosure can be made against third-party organisations. Interestingly, auditors, with the exception of matters relating to terrorism and money laundering, do not have a duty to report wrongdoing, and neither are they protected by the PIDA if they do make such a revelation. It could be argued that this exclusion from protection by the Act and the omission of a duty to report wrongdoing, other than in the two areas mentioned, suits the practising members of the accountancy profession, as it avoids their coming into conflict with their clients. Audit income is but a part of the income that most practising accountancy firms earn from their audit clients. It is not in the interest of practising accountancy firms to be required to play the role of society's watchdog on the activities of their clients.

For a disclosure to fall within the protection of the Act, the disclosure itself must relate to a specified set of malpractices. These are:

- A criminal offence.
- A failure to comply with any legal obligation.
- A miscarriage of justice.
- Danger to the health and safety of any individual.
- Damage to the environment.
- Deliberate concealment of any of the above.

To comply with the PIDA (and thus to stay within its protection), an ethically concerned employee must use to the full the organisation's internal procedures for handling such concerns. Such procedures can be avoided only if:

- at the time the disclosure was made the employee reasonably believed that they would be 'subject to a detriment' by the employer if a disclosure was made to the employer;
- the employee is concerned that evidence relating to the malpractice would be concealed or destroyed by the employer;
- the employee has previously made a disclosure to the employer of substantially the same information.

DEFINITION

Detriment is defined in the Act as being penalised by the employer, e.g. being fined, demoted, sacked or denied promotion.

Internal procedures can be sidestepped if they are shown to be seriously flawed, because of legitimate fears of information being confiscated or destroyed. Other fears, such as the existence of an oppressive and threatening employment environment, can be more difficult to substantiate. This is because obtaining corroborating evidence from fellow employees (who might be fearful for their own jobs) can be extremely difficult to obtain.

One concern about the Act is that it addresses the circumstances of the employee once that employee has made a disclosure. It is possible that, if only the *threat* of disclosure is made by the concerned employee, the Act would not protect the employee in the event of the employee being sacked before a full disclosure was made. In addition, whilst expressions of concern by one employee to another employee about a particular organisational (mal)practice might constitute a breach of confidentiality (and thus create the possibility of dismissal), the PIDA would not be available to the sacked employee if he had not raised the issue with the organisation's management.

While the establishment of an internal whistleblowing procedure may, at first sight, be a laudable development by any organisation, in the hands of unscrupulous employers it might be a mere device for complying with the letter of the law but not the spirit. Warren (1993) questioned the rationale for American firms introducing corporate codes of conduct. The same might be said of internal whistleblowing procedures.

There is also the issue of gaining sufficient evidence to feel able to lodge a concern. Raising a concern within the employing organisation requires that the concerned employee must satisfy two tests. The first is that he must 'reasonably believe' that one of the above mentioned malpractices has occurred. Secondly, the disclosure must be made in 'good faith'. However, the process of gaining evidence, as mentioned in relation to the Maxwell affair, can be a big problem. In such situations, being able to prove that sufficient evidence existed to allow individuals to 'reasonably believe' there were malpractices afoot could be extremely difficult. In addition, the use of internal procedures could prove unattractive to an employee (as in the Maxwell case). This would leave the concerned employee with only external whistleblowing to contemplate. However, the burden of proof required to stay within PIDA protection increases as soon as one raises one's concerns with external third parties. If information is revealed within the firm then the 'reasonably believe' test applies. However, if concerns are expressed to an external third party then the test becomes, 'the employee ... reasonably believes that the information and any allegation contained in it are *substantially true'* [emphasis added]. Thus the concerned employee must be able to show that there were reasonable grounds for them to believe that the allegation being made was 'substantially true' – a far more rigorous criterion than 'reasonably believe'.

Even if this condition is met, the concerned employee loses protection of the PIDA if the employee is rewarded for disclosing the wrongdoing, e.g. receiving payment from a newspaper. Thus, motive for the disclosure affects the protection provided by the PIDA. As mentioned earlier, rewards for information (including that provided anonymously) that leads to the successful prosecution of a criminal are quite acceptable. So why the different treatment of those who report the criminal activity of organisations?

If the internal whistleblowing procedures of an employing organisation are judged to be unsafe by a concerned employee, they will normally be expected to use the offices of a 'prescribed body'. Such a prescribed body is likely to be a regulatory body of an industry (e.g. OFWAT for water companies, or the Financial Services Authority for financial service companies). Within the public sector, such prescribed bodies are less likely to exist. It will be important for the concerned employee to establish whether a 'prescribed body' exists to handle their concerns.

Failure to follow the required procedures might take the complaint outside the protection of the PIDA. Notwithstanding this, there exists no requirement on the part of a regulator to act in response to the information supplied by a concerned employee, other than the rules under which the regulator normally acts.

The above uncertainty over the 'actual' protection afforded by the PIDA is at the heart of concerns expressed about the Act. The evidence provided by *Freedom To Care* on those cases it has investigated is that the PIDA would not have provided the protection the whistleblowers needed to withstand losing their jobs.

Employees working in areas covered by the Official Secrets' Act are also not protected by the PIDA. There are many examples of classified information within central government and (to a lesser extent) local government that are of dubious sensitivity, yet the information is covered by the Official Secrets' Act. There is a need for a concerned employee to check whether any information that relates to the cause of their concern is of a classified nature.

If all the requirements of the PIDA are satisfied (including the requirement that the alleged malpractice be deemed to be a sufficiently serious offence, plus all the other requirements mentioned above), the Act does provide protection that previously did not exist. Additional features of the PIDA are:

1 Gagging clauses. Gagging clauses are restrictive clauses in employment contracts that prevent the mentioning of anything of an organisational nature to anyone outside the employing organisation. These were a very real problem for many employees prior to the PIDA, but they appear to be void under the Act – other than those covered by the Official Secrets Act.

Whilst gagging clauses appear to be outlawed by PIDA, it must still be remembered that an implied term of employment contracts is the duty of confidentiality to the employing organisation on the part of the employee. It is this 'duty of confidentiality' that explains the considerable restrictions that have been placed upon the definition of a 'protected disclosure'. Only when the conditions of the PIDA have been judged to have been complied with, can the 'duty of confidentiality' be usurped by the PIDA in the specified situations identified above.

2. Interim Relief (keeping one's salary if dismissed for whistleblowing). Under section 9, the PIDA extends one of the provisions of the Employment Rights Act (ERA). If an employee suffers dismissal as a result of making a 'protected disclosure', they should make representation to an Employment Tribunal within seven days of dismissal. This aspect is known as interim relief. If the Employment Tribunal considers that the disclosure is likely to fall within the definition of a protected disclosure, the Employment Tribunal *may* order the employer to reinstate the employee. If the employer fails to comply with such an order, 'the employee is deemed to remain in employment until the hearing and entitled to continue to be paid as such'. However, before these conditions are activated on behalf of the employee, three further conditions must be met.

1. The claim for an interim relief must be lodged within seven days of dismissal.
2. The Employment Tribunal must first decide that the employee is likely to be found to have made a protected disclosure (not an obvious decision without studying all the relevant information); **and**

3. An order is likely to be made to the employing organisation to reinstate the employee (and this ruling happens relatively infrequently).

Thus, an interim order, while appearing to be a positive aspect of the PIDA, is likely in practice to be much less frequently activated than it might first appear. For example, in the case, *Bladon v. ALM Medical Services ET*, reported by Myers and Dehn (2000), an application for interim relief was rejected by the Chairman of the Employment Tribunal without hearing evidence. The basis for this judgement was that the Tribunal Chairman considered the claimant's (the whistleblower) case to be 'implausible'. Yet, when the case was finally heard, the whistleblower's actions were upheld and he was awarded damages. However, in the many months between the application for an interim relief and the actual Tribunal hearing, the whistleblower was denied any salary from his former employer.

If an employee's case falls within the protection of the PIDA then:

- The employee will be entitled to a compensation payment if victimisation is experienced as a result of the whistleblowing act (e.g. the employee stays within the employing organisation but suffers demotion). The level of compensation will depend upon the specifics of each case.
- If dismissed, the employee will be entitled to a compensation payment in line with the awards available through Employment Tribunals. These rates change over time, but, as mentioned earlier, the ceiling has now been removed.

Reflections

This chapter has considered various aspects of whistleblowing. Although examples can be cited of revelations of organisational malpractices that have been shown to be both accurate and serious, as well as examples of where the concerns of employees have been ignored or 'lost' in managerial structures and disasters involving loss of life have followed, the prospects for those contemplating whistleblowing remain uncertain. Employment law and the PIDA are written with the primary intention of protecting the commercial confidentiality of organisations that operate in legally compliant ways. There is thus a fundamental tension between, on the one hand, the need for employees to feel able to exercise moral agency and raise awareness of issues that have a genuine public interest and, on the other hand, the need for organisations to retain commercially sensitive information, and be protected from malicious and ill-founded accusations by disgruntled employees. The extent to which the balance between these competing requirements is acceptable and appropriate needs to be revisited regularly.

In modern times strong economies and vibrant business sectors are essential if political and social goals are to be achieved. It is difficult to refute the centrality of a strong economy to many societal aspirations, whether the economy is located in the so-called developing or developed worlds. As a result, businesses, and pressure groups representing business interests, act as powerful influences in the creation and maintenance of the legal frameworks that govern business activities. In this context it is perhaps not surprising that the PIDA was framed in the way that it was, if it was to receive sufficient support in the UK Parliament and thereby become law. Yet the very necessity to support and protect business interests creates loopholes for unscrupulous organisations to use. In addition there are those situations in which organisations flout the laws that society has passed, and the question then arises as to how and when society should be made aware of these infractions.

There are also questions about the relationships between business, environmental and societal interests, with the latter relating as much to future societies as to present ones. It is important that assumptions regarding the roles and power of organisations are challenged – not taken for granted. Related to, but separate from, these assumptions are the issues relating to notions of individualism and civic perspectives that have been alluded to in this chapter. These need revisiting on a regular basis to ensure that the issues and debates are themselves comprehended, and not overpowered by the pre-eminence of business interests.

Summary

In this chapter the following key points have been made:

- Whistleblowing includes, but is not limited to, the revelation of an organisational issue to an external party.
- Whistleblowing help-lines can be both important organisational mechanisms for the raising of ethical concerns, and early warning systems of unacceptable practices.
- Protection offered to whistleblowers by the PIDA is constrained and cannot limit the trauma that tends to accompany whistleblowing acts.
- The pejorative connotation of whistleblowing needs to be reflected upon and understood. Whilst perpetual whistleblowing is an unattractive proposition, the organisational impotence reflected in the case studies cited is equally unpalatable.
- Viewing whistleblowers as witnesses rather than snitches would be a positive development.
- If it is right to reveal the identity of those who break the law outside organisational life, why is it less right to reveal those who break the law or who endanger human life in their capacities as organisational employees?

Quick revision test

1. Is an act of whistleblowing confined to the release of organisational information to an external third party?
2. Is it appropriate or helpful to view whistleblowers as equivalent to referees?

3. What is the name of the Act that can offer protection to those who reveal an organisational malpractice in the public interest?
4. Rewards are often offered by the police to those who reveal the identity of those who commit a crime, such as robbery or theft. Does the PIDA take a similar view to those who make a financial gain as a result of their whistleblowing?

Typical assignments and briefs

1. Debate the strength of the arguments that seek to change the terminology for describing those who reveal organisational malpractices as whistleblowers.
2. To gain the protection of the Public Interest Disclosure Act, those who reveal organisational malpractices have to satisfy a number of conditions that witnesses in other criminal investigations do not have to satisfy, e.g. deriving no financial gain from the case and not having been involved in the crime at any stage. Critically evaluate the merits of these conditions.
3. Evaluate the argument that internal whistleblowing procedures are an essential part of any learning organisation.
4. Assume that a person has responded to Activity 7.1 in the following way. He has indicated:
   - an extreme level of anger (point 10 on the scale) in response to Case A;
   - a high level of support (point 2 on the scale) in Case B; and
   - a fair degree of anger (point 6 on the scale) in Case C.

   Discuss the factors that could explain these variations in the responses to the questions posed and what this might say about ethical principles.

Group activity 7

Consider the PIDA and make recommendations to reduce or add to the scope of the Act. Your proposals should be able to withstand critical appraisal at both a practical and theoretical level. Divide a sheet of paper into four columns. In the first column list your proposals. In the second column state against each proposal why you believe the amendment is justified. In the third column you should identify the principal objections or problems associated with your proposal. The final column should reflect your thoughts on the strengths of the objections/problems identified in column three, and whether you believe they are surmountable.

Recommended further reading

The two main authors writing on the topic of this chapter are Borrie and Hunt. We recommend that you read Borrie (1996), 'Business Ethics and Accountability', in Brindle, M. and Dehn, G. (1996), *Four Windows on Whistleblowing*, pp. 1–23, Public Concern at Work. Also Borrie, G. and Dehn, G. (2002), *Whistleblowing: The New Perspective*, Public Concern website, http://www.pcaw.co.uk/policy_pub/newperspective.html. Hunt's books (1995), *Whistleblowing in the Health Service: Accountability, Law & Professional Practice*, Edward Arnold and (1998), *Whistleblowing in the Social Services: Public Accountability and Professional Practice*, Edward Arnold are also useful. A more recent work is by Lewis, D.B. (2000), *Whistleblowing at Work*, Athlone Press.

Useful websites

Topic	Website provider	URL
The website of the leading charitable organisation providing advice to both individuals and organisations on whistleblowing issues/organisational hotlines	Public Concern at Work	http://www.pcaw.co.uk
An impressive organisation that acts as an advocate for those who stand up for freedom of speech in the workplace. Publishes an extremely thought provoking and important newsletter	Freedom to Care	http://www.freedomtocare.org

Corporate responsibility, corporate governance and corporate citizenship

Learning outcomes

Having read this chapter and completed its associated activities, you should be able to:

- Discuss the development of corporate social responsibility (CSR), and the more recent attachment to the notion of corporate responsibility.
- Critically evaluate the counter-arguments to CSR.
- Debate the scope and appropriateness of developments in Anglo-American corporate governance since the early 1990s.
- Discuss the challenges posed to Anglo-American development in corporate governance by the King Report.
- Review the UN Global Compact and the development in orientation reflected in the 2004 *Gearing Up* report.
- Understand the notion of the social contract as reflected in *Integrated Social Contract Theory*.
- Discuss the position of corporate manslaughter as an indictable offence in the UK and America.

Introduction

Corporate responsibility is a term that is supplanting the term corporate social responsibility. The 'social' is increasingly being omitted in order to emphasise the (claimed) broader responsibilities of business corporations, particularly their responsibilities with regard to the environment, as discussed in the next chapter.

Corporate governance is a phrase with some longevity, but which has gained greater prominence since the early 1990s. The issues of whether corporations can assume the status of citizens and, if so, whether such a development is desirable, will also be discussed. The three terms have been purposely linked in this chapter because, whilst they possess different associations, within corporate governance reforms in the UK and America, there have been strenuous and largely successful attempts to deny their relationship, or at least to contest the notion of corporate responsibility, let alone debate the notion of corporate citizenship.

The early calls for corporate social responsibility (CSR)

The desire to encourage, nay require, corporations to assume greater responsibility for their actions can be traced back over many decades, and reflects growing concerns regarding the power and influence of corporations over people's lives and even the independence and integrity of governments. For example, Oberman (2000) refers to academic debates over corporate social responsibilities taking place in the 1920s.

As the power and influence of business corporations have assumed ever greater proportions, so too have the calls increased for mechanisms to be put in place that would make corporations more accountable as well as responsible to a wider constituency than merely their shareholders. Within this latter aspect of the debate the use of the term *stakeholder* has gained currency in recent years and is a subject to which we will return later in this chapter.

The development of the argument from one of requiring corporations to act in socially responsible ways, to more recent calls for corporations to be seen as corporate citizens, reflects a desire to lock corporations, both formally and possibly legally, into the responsibilities that this status would confer. As indicated in the definition below, the citizenry is, in theory, sovereign to the state, yet the citizenry has little or no access, and certainly few, if any, rights with respect to corporations. With corporations playing an increasingly influential role over very many aspects of social and political life, the demand for more accountability and responsibility on the part of corporations is unlikely to diminish.

DEFINITION

The term **citizen** normally relates to the relationship between an individual and the political state in which the individual lives. It carries with it notions of rights and responsibilities on the part of the individual and the state. However, this reciprocity (i.e. two-way relationship) is unlikely to be an equal one. Within democratic theories of the state, citizens have ultimate sovereignty over the state, or at least sovereignty over those who represent the citizenry within government. Practice, however, usually reflects a quite different balance of power.

Being described as a citizen does not of itself imply much about morality. It is a noun in need of an adjective such as 'good' or 'moral' before it can confer a positive societal influence. Wood and Logsdon (2001) referred to this issue when they observed, in the context of the corporate citizen debate,

> One important debate distinguishes the concept of citizenship-as-legal-status from the concept of citizen-as-desirable-activity. The minimum requirements to be called a citizen are very different from the requirement to be called a 'good citizen.'
>
> (Wood and Logsdon, 2001: 88)

The role of the citizen can vary from the active notion of citizenship evident in ancient Greece (for those conferred as free men) to a passive acceptance of governance from a sovereign body (à la Hobbes) or from the bureaucratic state (à la Weber). Within the corporate citizen debate, the demands made of corporations vary from a minimalist societally neutral influence, to a proactive role. The societally neutral arguments do not, however, reflect a status-quo situation, or even a single understanding of what might be meant by societally neutral. For example, would being societally neutral mean that:

- Negative and positive effects of corporate activities could be balanced out (possibly involving an international perspective), or would a corporation's impacts need to harm no one or nothing at any time?
- Acting within legal constraints would be acceptable, even if the law was judged by many to be inadequate (as a result of the political lobbying by corporations)?
- There is a general acceptance that corporations do have social responsibilities?

These debates are still developing and represent just some of the issues that make the general area of business and values both dynamic and vital.

Hobbes (*see* Pojman, 1998) held a pessimistic view of human nature, seeing people as essentially selfish and untrustworthy. Thus, Hobbes deemed that a sovereign power was necessary to which the people would owe allegiance. The relationship between the sovereign power and the citizen is, in a Hobbesian world, a subjugated one. In this context, being a citizen within a Hobbesian state is a quite different one from that which would be acceptable in the twenty-first century. However, if the idea of conferring citizenship status upon corporations is one that concerns people, due to their distrust in corporations to act in socially beneficial ways, then a Hobbesian notion of citizenship has some appeal. But much depends upon the constitution and constituent parts of the sovereign power.

As societies have developed and the scope of governments has increased, the lack of possibilities for active participation of citizens has come to be viewed as a weakness of modern conceptions of democratic states. In contemporary societies political citizenship is increasingly limited to periodic elections of political representatives, and even the relevance of these is being questioned. For example, in the 2001 general election in the UK, only 58 per cent of those eligible to vote did so, the lowest turnout for many years. In the UK, local elections and those for the European Union achieve even lower levels of elector participation. In these elections approximately two out of three people do not vote. Thus, when we, or others, use the term citizen, we need to be clear about the form of citizenship we are discussing.

Activity 8.1

The next time you are in a group – in a seminar room, pub or other social gathering, try to establish how many people voted at the last general election, and if you think the conversation will stand the enquiry, how many people voted at the last local election when it was held independently of a general election. Do you think the percentages you establish sit comfortably in a democratic state?

One of the most widely expressed concerns about modern corporations is that they have relatively unfettered authority, with only limited responsibilities (basically to keep within the laws of the land), but there is a need to be more specific about the form and level of participation in the operations of the state that are being suggested when the phrase corporate citizenship is employed. Given the significance of business organisations within democratic (as well as undemocratic) states, the presumption must be that the notion of corporate citizenship assumed by its advocates would reflect the acceptance of certain societal responsibilities, although whether there is envisaged to be an equal bestowing of citizens' rights on corporations is far from clear.

Before progressing any further, it is worth reflecting upon the observations of Charles Lindblom, a former Professor of Economics and Political Science at Yale University. In his book *Politics and Markets* (1977), Lindblom concluded his analysis of the relationships between large corporations and political systems (and the book itself) with the following paragraph.

> It has been a curious feature of democratic thought that it has not faced up to the private corporation in an ostensible democracy. Enormously large, rich in resources ... they can insist that government meet their demands, even if these demands run counter to ... citizens .... Moreover they do not disqualify themselves from playing the role of citizen ..... they exercise unusual veto powers .... The large private corporation fits oddly into democratic theory and vision. Indeed it does not fit.
>
> (Lindblom, 1977: 356)

The final five-word sentence is the last in the book and is particularly piercing. Lindblom was bringing into sharp focus the lack of compatibility between democratic aspirations for political systems and the autocratic, sometimes feudal, systems that operate in many, if not the majority of, corporations, and it is the latter in which most people spend most of their waking lives. Large corporations have influence in and upon even the most significant of political powers. Table 8.1 illustrates the sort of evidence that gives rise to such concerns. The table reflects some of the donations made to the Republican Party during the 2000 American presidential campaign and the actions taken immediately following the inauguration of George W. Bush as President of the United States of America in 2001. All the actions were taken by the President during the first three months of his presidency.

Table 8.1 Actions taken by President G.W. Bush within three months of his inauguration in 2001

Industry	$M donated	Actions taken
Tobacco	7.0	Removal of federal lawsuits against cigarette manufacturers
Timber	3.2	Restrictions on logging roads scrapped
Oil and Gas	25.4	Restrictions on CO2 emissions abandoned; Kyoto agreement scrapped; moves to open Arctic refuge to drilling
Mining	2.6	Scrapping of environmental clean-up rules, e.g. arsenic limits in water supply
Banks and credit card companies	25.6	Bankruptcy bill making it easier for credit card companies to collect debts from bankrupt customers
Pharmaceuticals	17.8	Medicare (government-supported health insurance) reform removing price controls
Airlines	4.2	Federal barriers to strikes introduced; back-pedalling on antitrust (mergers and monopolies) legislation

Source: *Guardian* G2, 27 April 2001, p. 2

It would be wrong to imply that concerns are only ever expressed with regard to American corporate–political relationships. The following are just two examples taken from the UK that have raised similar concerns.

1. In 1997, the incoming Labour government had a manifesto commitment to a total ban on tobacco advertising, yet no such proposed legislation was ever formally debated in Parliament during the 1997–2001 administration. By the time the Labour Party's 2001 manifesto was published, the commitment to a complete ban on tobacco advertising was noticeable by its absence, although in March 2002 the Minister for Health announced legislative plans for an almost complete ban on tobacco advertising and sponsorship, the one exception being motor racing sponsorship. It might be just a coincidence that Bernie Ecclestone, who effectively controls world-wide Grand Prix motor racing, donated £1M to the Labour Party, which was subsequently repaid when the donation became public knowledge.
2. The Labour Party's 1997 manifesto also included a commitment to a reform of company law by recognising a stakeholder perspective (as opposed to an exclusively shareholder responsibility). Upon election the Labour government established a committee to consider how the stakeholder commitment could be operationalised. The committee deliberated for nearly two years. An interim report was published after the first year, which retained an attachment to the notion of pluralism in corporate decision making, although the wording can be seen to be becoming a little ambiguous.

> The principle arguments are that the present scheme of law fails adequately to recognise that businesses best generate wealth where participants operate harmoniously as teams and that managers should recognise the wider interests of the community.
>
> One year later the committee published its final report, but by now the term pluralism had been lost and in its place appeared the term 'enlightened shareholder value'. The removal of the commitment to pluralism led to the resignation from the committee of the finance director of *The Body Shop*. He described himself as an advocate of social and environmental responsibility and was not prepared to remain a member of the committee once the commitment to enlightened shareholder value had replaced pluralism. Newspaper reports on the outcome of the committee's work talked of frantic lobbying by business interests that ultimately led to not only the retention of the shareholders' interests being the only one formally recognised in UK law, but also the conversion of the committee's proposals for compulsory statements on corporate issues into proposals that would only be voluntary, i.e. at the discretion of directors.

The above examples are not cited to claim that all businesses are corrupt or corrupting. However, just as a few examples of negative or unethical business practices should not tar all businesses with these behaviours, neither should a few examples of positive business behaviour suggest that all is right in the corporate and political worlds. For our purposes the point the cases illustrate is the way the business lobby groups successfully influenced legislative matters. The cases illustrate the significant ramifications for social and democratic processes of the lobbying phenomenon which, by its very nature, is opaque. An image thus emerges of business interests playing an active, although not always transparent, role in political and social, as well as economic, matters.

The question is thus raised, 'To what extent is ethical egoism, with its appeal to emotive and fundamental concepts such as freedom and individuality, merely a convenient façade behind which privileged and powerful self-interests hide?'

Connexion point

Ethical egoism was discussed in Chapter 3 and relates to the ethical stance that sees the protection of individual freedom as the touchstone of ethics. It draws upon notions of choice, meritocracy and a form of justice, but it can conceal extreme selfishness, protectionism and callousness.

With many large corporations now (and for some time) more powerful than the majority of governments, the feudal nature of corporate realpolitik is masked by the veil of democratic political paraphernalia for the majority of people living on the planet. Thus, if large corporations are to exist within democratic states there have to be certain developments that democratise the corporations and other developments that make them less of a threat to political and social democracy.

When put in this context the subject of corporate governance ceases to be (if it ever was) an arcane and dry technical subject. As we will see, different notions of corporate governance exist in different parts of the world, with some of the most enlightened thinking emanating from South Africa.

The recurring issue of corporate governance

As with notions of CSR, issues relating to corporate governance have featured regularly through time. For example, the 'Bubble Act' of 1719 came into being as the result of a corporate scandal which, in relative terms, involved sums of money greater than the combined value of Enron and WorldCom.

Lee (1984) and Edey (1984) referred to the manipulation of company accounting information by managers at the expense of the owners' interests during the early nineteenth century, while Carey (1984) referred to the contribution of William Z. Ripley, a Harvard professor, who, in the early 1920s wrote about the 'docility of corporate shareholders permitting themselves to be honeyfuggled'. In relation to the public utilities industries, Ridley referred to 'the hoodwinking of the shareholders', and of accountants Ripley observed, 'accountants are enabled to play ball with figures to an astounding degree' (Carey, 1984: 243).

The concerns over corporate governance continued through the latter part of the nineteenth century and into the early part of the twentieth century, culminating in Berle and Means' seminal publication in 1932. In this publication Berle and Means charted the history and implications of the decoupling of ownership (shareholders) from control (senior management) within the modern corporation. Niebuhr (1932) also wrote powerful critiques of corporate power and the exploitative and alienating tendencies of the capitalist system. Since the early 1990s there has been increasing attention to corporate governance as a result of major corporate scandals such as Maxwell Communications, BCCI and Polly Peck in the late 1980s and in the early 2000s Enron, WorldCom, Global Crossing and Parmalat. We will return to the issues raised by these corporate collapses and scandals shortly, but first we address the issue of whether we should just accept such corporate débacles as a fact of economic life and not be too concerned about them.

Are not corporate failures just a fact of economic life?

It is clear from the very brief overview above that concerns over corporate governance are not new, but reactions to corporate scandals of the 1990s and early twenty-first century by organisations such as the major stock exchanges, professional accountancy bodies and governments appear to have been more obvious and public than before. Could this reflect a degree of vulnerability and sensitivity that was not felt in the past? It is difficult to say, although débacles such as Enron and WorldCom, Global Crossing and Parmalat pose fundamental problems for securities' markets. Investing in companies is a risky business and any investor must recognise and accept this fact. Thus, it is not the losing of money that is the problem. The problem is the failure of market mechanisms to provide the information and warning signals that the investing public has a right to expect. In all the corporate failures referred to in this chapter the most recent accounts of the corporations concerned gave little if any hint of the financial turmoil the corporations were experiencing.

In the cases of Enron and WorldCom the auditors appear to have been complicit in the deceit, whilst in the cases of Maxwell Communications and BCCI (financial scandals of the late 1980s and early 1990s) the causes of the auditors' performance are more opaque. Whatever the reasons, the important market mechanism that the role of audit is supposed to play (verifying the reliability of the financial information supplied to shareholders) failed. The accounting profession was seen to be, at best, an unreliable scrutineer of financial information. More significantly the independence and integrity of accountants and accounting firms were increasingly being called into question.

In addition to the failings of the audit function, market analysts were still recommending Enron and WorldCom stocks as 'buys' to the investing world until days before the companies crashed, although again the integrity of the market analysts concerned has subsequently been shown to have been heavily compromised. As a result of these failings of the securities' markets, confidence in their fairness, transparency and integrity was undermined, with the risk that investors might turn to other investment options, such as property, currencies, works of art, etc. Thus, while it might only be out of enlightened self-interest, the securities' markets cannot afford to tolerate unethical corporate behaviour. However, at the same time, the intensity of the demands of the securities' markets is unrelenting in terms of the enormous pressures placed upon company executives to deliver improved 'financials' (profits) year upon year, half-year upon half-year, quarter upon quarter.

Developments in corporate governance

There has been a lot of activity with regard to corporate governance in the UK since the early 1990s and Figure 8.1 presents a schema of the various reports, with the addition of one notable reform in the USA, that of the Sarbanes–Oxley Act in 2002. A brief overview of these reports is provided so that the contestability of corporate responsibility and corporate governance can be discussed.

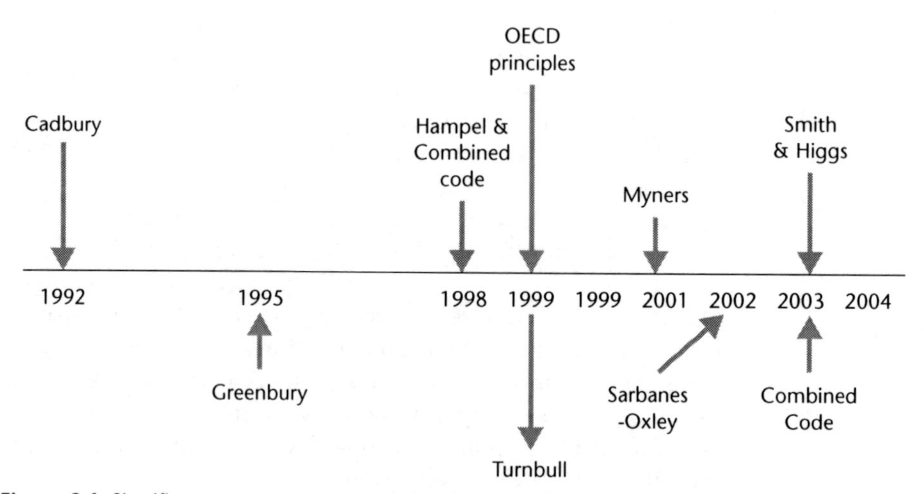

Figure 8.1 Significant recent reports and developments in corporate governance

The **Cadbury Committee** was established as a response to some significant corporate collapses/scandals in the late 1980s and early 1990s, including BCCI, Polly Peck and Maxwell Communications. Given the comments made above regarding the questioning of the audit function performed by the large accounting firms and the resulting undermining of confidence in the London Stock Exchange, it will come as no surprise to learn that these were the two major sponsoring organisations of the Cadbury Committee. The major recommendations of the committee included the increased use of non-executive directors to counter what is referred to as the agency effect, and the splitting of the roles of chief executive and chairperson.

DEFINITION

The **agency effect** is derived from agency theory, which assumes that people are, at heart, untrustworthy. As a result of the privileged position that executive directors enjoy over shareholders with regard to the control of information, executive directors are deemed likely to exploit this power situation to their own advantage. This might manifest itself in 'managing' information (hence the importance of the audit function) and large remuneration packages.

The **Greenbury Committee** was set up to look into the issue of executive pay (Sir Richard Greenbury was at the time Chief Executive of Marks & Spencer and one of the highest paid directors in the UK). Even at this time the issue of executive pay, sometimes referred to as 'fat-cats pay', was a vexed issue but the work of the Greenbury Committee seems to have had little constraining effect, as indicated by Table 8.2. This table contrasts the movement in the FTSE 100 index with the average increase in the remuneration of the executive directors of the same top 100 UK corporations. If the movement in a company's market worth is a fair reflection of the performance of the company's senior management, then is it not reasonable to expect that there would be a close correlation between the change in corporate executives' remuneration and the change in market worth of the companies they manage, certainly over a reasonable period of time like three years?

Table 8.2 Average increases in the remuneration of the directors of the FTSE 100 companies for 2000–2002 compared with movements in the FTSE 100 share index over the same period

Year	Movement in directors' remuneration	Movements in FTSE 100 index
2000	+ 28%	– 8%
2001	+ 17%	– 15%
2002	+ 23%	– 23%
Overall movements from Jan. 2000 to 31 Dec. 2002	+ 84%	– 40%

A similar picture is evident in the USA. With the boundaries of self-control removed during the 1990s, but with the retention of the rhetoric of free markets, rapacious has been a frequently used adjective in discussions of corporate and executive behaviour. In both America and the UK stock options became a central part of executive remuneration packages during the 1990s, as attempts were made to tie the pay of senior executives to the performance of their companies, thereby trying to minimise the agency effect. The result was startling, although not necessarily in the way intended. Robert Monks (2003) commented upon the transfer of wealth reflected in the value of stock options held by a very small minority of senior executives in America.

> The most important component of compensation was the grant of options that, according to the accounting rules after 1994, did not have to be accounted for as an expense by the issuing company. Typically, the top five executives in a company held 75% of the total options granted; the ratio of options to the total outstanding rose in the 1990s from 2% to 12%. This must be the greatest 'peaceful' transfer of wealth in recorded history.
>
> (Monks, 2003: 165)

Two per cent or one-fiftieth, of the value of the equity capital of corporate America is a huge figure. Twelve per cent, or nearly one-eighth, is a gargantuan number and this proportion of American equity capital is held by a relatively small number of senior of executives.

Returning to reports on UK corporate governance, the **Hampel Committee** (1998) was formed to take stock of both the Cadbury and Greenbury reports and to suggest how best to implement their recommendations. Interestingly, the Hampel report, while recognising that boards of directors have a responsibility for *relations* with stakeholders, felt the need to emphasise that the *responsibility* of directors is to shareholders. Stakeholders are of concern to directors, but only in as far as they can contribute to the maximisation of shareholder wealth.

The Hampel Report led to the first **'Combined Code'**, which was issued by the London Stock Exchange in 1998. The Code specifies the corporate governance practices that quoted companies should follow if they wish to have a listing on the London Stock Exchange. The Code is not backed by law and if a quoted company chooses not to follow the Code the company must explain the rationale for its different practice. For example, the supermarket chain, Morrisons, had, until it bought the Safeway group in 2004, combined the roles of chief executive and chairman, which was contrary to the 1998 Combined Code. Morrisons claimed that combining the two roles made sense for them and this was accepted by the London Stock Exchange.

The 'comply or explain' approach towards corporate governance developments in the UK is different from the approach of the United States, where changes are passed through the legislative processes and are thus legally binding. Such an example is the Sarbanes–Oxley Act of 2002. The latter was the result of two Congressmen formulating their response to a number of financial scandals, notably those of Enron, WorldCom and Global Crossing. The Act places specific responsibilities upon chief executives and the chief financial officers (in UK terms, the finance directors) to personally sign off the accounts. In addition certain accounting services that audit firms might wish to provide to their audit clients have been proscribed by the Act. This reflects the concerns that have been expressed for many years that the level of non-audit fee income earned by accounting firms from their audit clients might compromise their independence and objectivity. The fact that Andersen's (Enron's auditors) generated around $25M of non-audit fee income from Enron, on top of the $25M audit income, was felt by many to have been an unhealthy situation, and it was not unique. Interestingly, Andersen's were also WorldCom's auditors.

The **Turnbull Report** of 1999 concerned itself with internal controls and internal audit, while the **Myners' Committee** was sponsored by the UK Treasury to look into the role of institutional investors in company affairs. With institutional investors (banks, pension funds, unit and investment trusts) such influential players on securities' markets, any hope of improved shareholder activism to challenge the power of directors would need to come from the institutional investors. In a nutshell, Myners recommended that institutional investors *should* be more active, but not a lot more.

The statements of corporate governance principles by the **OECD** (Organisation for Economic Cooperation and Development) in 1999 and 2005 represent a very Anglo-American view of the subject and bear a close resemblance to the 1998 and 2003 UK Combined Codes.

The reports of the **Higgs** and **Smith** Committees were published in 2003, the former being concerned with the roles of non-executive directors (NEDs) and the latter concerned with the work and roles of Audit Committees. Higgs recommended a scaling up of the importance of NEDs, such that the majority of main board directors should be NEDs, presumably to further minimise the agency effect. The Report makes further recommendations with respect to how many NED appointments executive directors can hold etc., but these need not concern us. However, three questions remain unanswered by the Higgs Report and corporate governance developments in general.

1. The majority of directors on Enron's main board were NEDs, but this did not prevent the corruption that appears to have taken place at Enron. So why was the main recommendation of the Higgs Report that the majority of main board directors should be NEDs?
2. NEDs only attend the companies of which they are NEDs on one, possibly two, days each month. Does this not place even more power in the hands of the few remaining executive directors, who agency theory claims should not be trusted?
3. If minimising the agency effect is a key role of NEDs, why is it that the vast majority of NEDs are also executive directors in their primary employment? Why should person 'A', who is an executive director of company 'X' be subject to the agency effect and be untrustworthy in this role, but upon taking on the mantle of NED of company 'B' become a trustworthy individual whose role it is to ensure the integrity of company B's practices? What is the transformation process that turns A from untrustworthy to trustworthy?

As for the Smith Report on Audit Committees, it makes various recommendations, but it stops short of requiring accounting firms to stop providing any of their non-audit services to their audit clients. This is a far less prescriptive or punitive approach than that reflected in the Sarbanes–Oxley Act.

What have the developments in corporate governance achieved?

What do all these reports and recommendations say about corporate governance and ethics in business? For many they say very little and what they say is inadequate, given the scale of corporate governance issues. A more inclusive view of corporate governance sees the disregard for shareholder interests displayed by executives as but one of the corporate governance issues to be addressed. All the developments in corporate governance since 1992 amount to very little. An increase in NEDs here, some concerns expressed about accounting firms there, but really it is a 'steady-as-she-goes' approach, with only minor adjustments to the tiller.

Frustration with the myopia and impotence displayed by governments to correct what are seen as the inadequate responses to profound corporate governance issues such as child labour, forced labour, inhuman working conditions, despoliation of the environment, and the connivance and corrupt practices of governments (*see* the *Transparency International* website for an examination of the latter) with corporations has led to a series of other initiatives, which are highlighted in Figure 8.2.

The King Report on corporate governance

Before progressing to the issues reflected in the UN Global Compact, reference will be made to the second King Report, which was published in 2002 (the first having been published in 1994) and which relates to corporate governance in South Africa. The opening of the report is interesting in that it refers to a state-

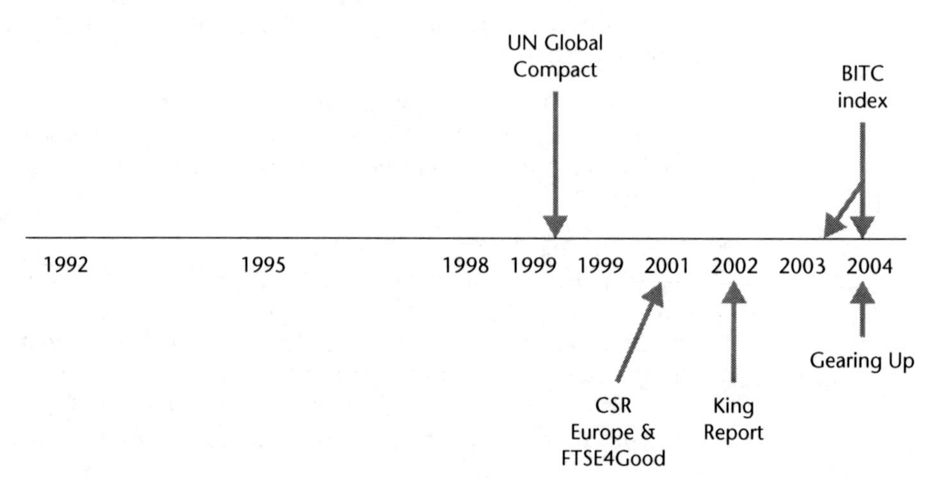

Figure 8.2 Other interesting developments in corporate governance that have not impacted upon UK and American stock exchange listing requirements

ment made by Sir Adrian Cadbury (the same Cadbury who gave his name to the 1992 UK Cadbury report on corporate governance), but this time the statement was made by Cadbury in the World Bank's 1999 report on corporate governance.

> Corporate governance is concerned with holding the balance between economic and social goals and between individual and community goals. ... The aim is to align as nearly as possible the interests of individuals, corporations and society.
>
> (King, 2002: 6)

This is a much more expansive and inclusive view of corporate governance than that articulated in the 1992 UK Cadbury Report, or in any UK or US financial corporate governance reports since. There are further important features of the King Report that are highly relevant to the considerations of this chapter. The first is the continuation in the second (2002) King Report of the inclusive orientation of the first (1994) King Report. This orientation is reflected in the following extract.

> Unlike its counterparts in other countries at the time, the King Report 1994 went beyond the financial and regulatory aspects of corporate governance in advocating an integrated approach to good governance in the interests of a wide range of stakeholders having regard to the fundamental principles of good financial, social, ethical and environmental practice. In adopting a participative corporate governance system of enterprise with integrity, the King Committee in 1994 successfully formalised the need for companies to recognise that they no longer act independently from the societies and the environment in which they operate.
>
> (King, 2002: 6)

In contrast, Anglo-American reforms to corporate governance have been allowed to concentrate exclusively upon corporations' responsibilities to shareholders. The King Committee took an explicitly inclusive view of a corporation's stakeholders, although it was not a naïve report that ignored or undervalued the economic imperatives faced by companies. It is a thoughtful, scholarly report that distinguishes between accountability and responsibility, which UK reports on corporate governance have failed to articulate. The King Report was not a maverick study located at the margins of South Africa's economic interests. It was a study sponsored by the South Africa Institute of Directors, and whilst operating in the context of a market-based capitalist economy the King Report reflects a very different conception of the business–society debate. This is most intriguingly reflected in paragraph 38 and its subsections where the report focuses upon the values that underpin South African society. This is a dimension to corporate governance that has not only been missed by UK and US corporate governance reports; it would currently not be countenanced as it reflects a profoundly different world view of the business–society relationship.

The very first of the values considered in the King Report is 'spiritual collectiveness'. Paragraph 38.1 reads as follows:

> Spiritual Collectiveness is prized over individualism. This determines the communal nature of life, where households live as an interdependent neighbourhood.

Other values considered include:

> Humility and helpfulness to others is more important than criticism of them. (paragraph 38.3)
>
> There is an inherent trust and belief in fairness of all human beings. This manifests itself in the predisposition towards universal brotherhood, even shared by African-Americans. (paragraph 38.6)
>
> High standards of morality are based on historical precedent. These are bolstered by the close kinship observed through totem or clan names and the extended family systems. (paragraph 38.7)

The above claims to community values and beliefs do not deny the historic tribalism that has seen African peoples at war with one another over centuries. However, it draws out the common values that unite rather than separate the tribes (which are effectively mini-nation states in western terms) and seeks to build notions of corporate governance that reflect cultural mores and values, rather than allow more recognisable business values and beliefs to migrate from the economic sphere, driving out the more inclusive, community-oriented values in the process.

Interestingly, paragraph 39 opens with the statement, 'Corporate governance is essentially about leadership', followed by the essential values that a leader should possess and display. The African 'great-soul-man' appears to being alluded to here, who is noticeable by his absence from Anglo-American debates.

The twentieth century was traumatic for South African society. The release of Nelson Mandela in 1990 heralded the ending of the brutal apartheid policies, and the King Report must be seen in this social and cultural context, but it should not be side-stepped or minimised as a result. It is a report that should demand our attention. It offers a very different perspective on corporate governance, arguing that business is a part of society rather than apart from society. This challenge to the assumptions implicit within Anglo-American corporate governance reforms leads us to a consideration of the UN Global Compact.

The UN Global Compact

In 1999, frustrated by the lack of progress of governments to respond adequately to addressing issues such as child labour and inhuman working conditions in companies located in the developing economies, but which are part of the supply chains of large international organisations, the United Nations set up the UN Global Compact. In the words of Global Compact's Chief Executive, the Global Compact was established to fill a void, to 'respond to demands and needs that governments were either unwilling or unable to meet' (Kell, 2004).

The Compact was, and remains, a voluntary code that is intended to influence corporate practices by:

(i) gaining the support and membership of leading organisations, and then
(ii) increasing the acceptance and take-up of corporate responsibility by disseminating examples of good practice that hopefully other organisations will adopt.

The Compact focuses upon nine key principles of corporate activity, which are grouped into three categories.

Human rights
Principle 1 – Businesses are asked to support the protection of international human rights within their sphere of influence; and
Principle 2 – To ensure their own corporations are not complicit in human rights abuses.

Labour
Principle 3 – Businesses are asked to uphold the freedom of association and the effective recognition of the rights to collective bargaining;
Principle 4 – To eliminate all forms of forced and compulsory labour;
Principle 5 – To abolish child labour; and
Principle 6 – To help eliminate discrimination in respect of employment and occupation.

Environment
Principle 7 – Businesses are asked to support a precautionary approach to environmental challenges;
Principle 8 – To undertake initiatives to promote greater environmental responsibility;
Principle 9 – To encourage the development and diffusion of environmentally friendly technologies

In 1999 those responsible for the Compact saw the future for social change to be through international corporations, hence the focus on working with significant organisations to both gain their support (patronage) and stimulate corporate responsibility (CR) by highlighting examples of good practice that 'work' and that could be seen to be compatible with being a successful company.

The Foreword to the 2004 report *Gearing Up*, which was commissioned by the executive of Global Compact, reflected a development in this thinking and strategy. There now appears to be a recognition that it was unrealistic to expect corporations to respond to initiatives such as the Global Compact independent of governments. While the original Global Compact may have been a response to political failings, a voluntary initiative that appears to ask businesses to make good the failings of governments, ironically, needs the commitment and positive engagement of governments to help it develop. For this reason *Gearing Up* argues for a greater level of dialogue, collaboration and partnership between businesses and governments for the future development of corporate responsibility.

A more critical voice is that of Christian Aid. In its 2004 report, *Behind the Mask*, Christian Aid dismissed the UN Global Compact as having had 'almost no impact' (p. 16). The lack of transparency associated with the Global Compact and its lack of monitoring and verification are other failings in the initiative's credibility. For Christian Aid it would seem that the Global Compact is an example of the worst sort of CSR initiative, that is one that enjoys a lot of publicity and hype, but is in fact a toothless tiger, with few if any monitoring and/or verification powers or resources. For some it is a sham and governments are complicit, instrumental even, in this charade.

The Global Compact contains the sorts of commitments and aspirations that many supporters and advocates of CSR or CR (corporate responsibility) would welcome, as well as displaying many of the limitations of a number of CR initiatives. Thus, with the important caveat from Christian Aid expressed in the above paragraph, we return to a key aim of the *Gearing Up* report, which is stated as making 'the link between corporate responsibility ... initiatives and wider sustainable development challenges', with the report linked to the Millennium Development Goals (MDGs) (*see* Table 8.3).

The *Gearing Up* report moves on, via a discussion of its findings and case studies, to identify six possible ways (or, probably more accurately, rates of change) that CR could reflect. The six possibilities reflect different levels of engagement by 'business' in economic and non-economic development, including one option (termed 'reverse') which reflects the possibility that businesses might publicly articulate a commitment to being catalysts for change, while, behind the scenes, doing all they can to frustrate and hinder developments.

Table 8.3 The Millennium Development Goals

1	Eradicate extreme poverty and hunger
2	Achieve universal primary education
3	Promote gender equality and empower women
4	Reduce child mortality
5	Improve maternal health
6	Combat HIV/AIDS, malaria and other diseases
7	Ensure environmental sustainability, and
8	Develop a global partnership for development (this relates to trade issues, but also debt relief and access to affordable, essential drugs in developing countries).

Connexion point

One can construct both consequentialist and deontological arguments to support the development of CSR. Produce two brief justifications for adopting CSR based upon (i) consequentialist arguments, and (ii) deontological arguments. Refer back to Chapter 3 if you need to refresh your memory on these respective ethical stances.

Activity 8.2 An important question

Notwithstanding the ethical arguments you have raised in response to the above connexion point, is it fair, sensible and/or ethical to ask, let alone expect, business organisations to take on the role of correcting the world's ills? How can organisations, established to fulfil a very specific economic role, take on the responsibility for enacting or at least contributing to roles that might be expected to be the responsibility of governments?

Activity 8.2 raises a fundamental question. To explore both the implications of the question and how one might respond to the question we turn to the arguments of Milton Friedman (1970).

Milton Friedman's arguments against corporations being charged with social responsibilities

Milton Friedman was a Nobel prize-winning economist, whose ideas were very influential in America and the UK during the 1980s and 1990s. It is worth reading Friedman's oft-cited 1970 article on why the only social responsibility of business is to increase its profits, and not to indulge in social interventions such as sponsorship of community activities, the funding of charities, community activities, or other 'good deeds'.

Friedman's article was a response to what were becoming increasingly frequent calls for corporations to act in socially responsible ways in the late 1960s and early 1970s. Precisely what was meant by 'socially responsible ways' was often left vague and poorly explained, save for concerns being expressed that corporate power was authority without responsibility. Friedman's criticisms were rehearsed by Wolf (2000) thirty years later when the latter accused those (still) calling for greater corporate social responsibility as not only distorting business activity, but confusing and misunderstanding the rationale of business. 'The role of well run companies is to make profits, not save the planet', Wolf argued.

Friedman criticised the arguments for corporate social responsibility on three fronts. The first criticism was an economic one, with ethical undertones. If corporations are required to engage in corporate philanthropy, e.g. making a donation to a charity, school or hospital, these acts will distort allocative efficiency, i.e. the profitability with which capital is employed. Friedman argued that corporations are responsible for using shareholders' funds in profitable ways, in legally acceptable ways – nothing more. Worrying about which charity to support, or which good deed/s to perform, merely 'takes management's eye off the ball', the ball being how to increase profits. Thus, the only form of corporate philanthropy that Friedman's argument would accept is where it could be shown that a donation, or good deed, would improve a company's profitability in ways superior to alternative investment opportunities. We can view this as 'prudential altruism'. In such a case the charitable donation would in fact be described more accurately as a commercial investment. Porter and Kramer (2002) makes a similar point but refers to such acts as 'strategic philanthropy', which, given the points he makes in the article, stretches the notion of philanthropy a little. Windsor (2001) reinforced the philanthropy argument with the demand that all business activities, including 'good deeds', should 'add-value', or more precisely 'add-shareholder-value'. This is most emphatically a Friedmanite position.

The second of Friedman's criticisms draws upon both ethics and political philosophy. It is that it is undemocratic for corporations to use shareholders' funds to support charities or other 'good causes'. Any such donation can only come at the expense of lower dividends, higher prices or lower wages (or a combination of all three). Friedman asked, 'How can it be ethical that a corporation should act first as unpaid tax collector (i.e. levying a tax on the shareholders, customers and/or employees) and then as unaccountable benefactor?' It is either for publicly elected representatives of the people (i.e. national or local politicians) to provide financial support to public services or charities, etc. from public funds, or for individuals to decide to which charities they wish to make private donations.

The third criticism was a philosophical one. It was that corporations cannot possess responsibilities. Corporations are social constructs, i.e. they have been brought into existence by societies passing laws that give legal protection to certain forms of business associations and structures. Without these legal and social devices, corporations could not and would not exist. In Friedman's terms only individuals can have responsibilities, not corporations.

Activity 8.3 Challenging Friedman

Taking the three criticisms that are raised by Friedman, try to develop arguments that challenge Friedman's claims. It is important that you think through the arguments that Friedman is making, so take your time.

Responding to Friedman's arguments

From the perspective of advocates of unfettered (or as unfettered as possible) market-based economies, which we referred to in Chapter 1 as the *neo-liberal economic position*, or simply neo-liberalism, the best hope for the protection of individual freedoms is the maintenance of open markets (i.e. no barriers to trade) and minimum interference in the workings of business by governments.

Connexion point

Adopting the stance that governments should play as small a part as humanly possible in economic and social affairs is the concept known as 'negative freedom', i.e. freedom 'from', as discussed in Chapter 3.

Not only is interference by government seen as economically counter-productive in the medium to long run, but such interventions are themselves argued to be unethical, i.e. they impose a big-brother-knows-best mentality over individual preferences and thus undermine the sovereignty of individual choice. From the perspective of the neo-liberalist position the first and second objections raised by Friedman are both strong objections. Non-accountable tax-raising, whether by government or corporate leaders, is a distortion to allocative efficiency, injurious to the sovereignty of the individual and undemocratic, and thus to be opposed.

Friedman did not argue that corporations should be above the law, but he did argue that corporations should not be expected to exceed what the law defines as minimum levels of behaviour. Laws are assumed to represent what societies deem to be acceptable behaviour (of both individuals and corporations) and only if a society increases the burden upon business in terms of legally defined levels of performance (e.g. increased levels of pollution control) should corporations have to raise their performance. This obviously ignores the pressures for increased performance resulting from normal competitive forces, although such pressures will often present countervailing forces to those emanating from environmental concerns.

Neo-liberal supporters would accept that there are sometimes considerable negative human consequences resulting from economic fluctuations. For example, large-scale redundancies and/or high levels of unemployment can result from significant economic downturns, with resulting impacts upon local infrastructure in the form of, say, lower than desired levels of expenditure on education, health care, transport, etc. The latter would be the economic consequences of lower levels of taxes being collected, coupled with increased social security benefits. These are seen as unfortunate, but unavoidable, consequences that societies must accept in order to protect the overall integrity of the market system. Yet the increasing impact of what is known as globalisation and the powerful moves towards full deregulation of markets across the world by the World Trade Organisation (WTO) have raised the political and social stakes in this debate.

Within the arguments presented by Friedman, either the role and impact of business in general must be benign, or, the more traditional argument, the acknowledged inequities and imperfections in market-based systems are more than counterbalanced by the claimed advancements and advantages that everyone ultimately enjoys, as a result of the market dynamics levering change and economic progress. That everyone does not benefit to the same extent as a result of these claimed economic advances is not disputed, but everyone is argued to be better off, to some extent, in the long run. You may recognise something of the Rawlsian position (which was discussed in Chapter 3) in this argument, that whilst the poorest of society are indeed relatively poor they are better off than they would be, or could be, under any other economic system. This claim can be considered at two levels.

(i) The first is the empirical question. Does the evidence we have of the globalising and deregulating effects on world markets display an overall elevation of people's well-being and is this elevation superior to all other options?
(ii) The second is the ethical question. Does this approach stand up to scrutiny when judged against notions of justice, fairness, wisdom and care?

The evidence that is available with regard to question (i) is incomplete, but at best it is mixed. At worst we are experiencing even greater concentrations of power over resources that lie outside the political arena, with fundamental questions regarding authority, responsibility and accountability remaining unanswered.

Connexion point

The observations of Anita Roddick, founder of The Body Shop organisation, are interesting in this context. She was responding to an article by Philippe Legrain that had appeared in the *Guardian* newspaper (on the day before the publication of her letter). Legrain had made the case that the deregulation of world markets, in line with the actions of the WTO, should be welcomed by all, as ultimately all would benefit (the argument outlined above). The words of Ms Roddick are shown on p. 464.

It is always possible to highlight acts by individual people or specific corporations that present a poor image of the groups they are said to represent. Proverbially speaking, bad apples do not necessarily tell us much about the rest of the apples in a barrel. However, if one can point to trends, allegiances, purposeful manipulation of power by large corporations, or groups of corporations, then we might have something more than the odd bad apple. The following are just a selection of possible examples that could be used.

Case study 8.1

The tobacco industry

For many years, medical research had indicated a clear link between the use of tobacco products and various forms of cancer, although these findings had always been contested vigorously by the tobacco industry. Yet, in 2000, the tobacco company Reynolds broke ranks and announced in court that it was accepting liability for certain smokers' ill-health. There is evidence to suggest that the tobacco companies had confirmed the link between their products and cancer-based illnesses many years previously but concealed the evidence. Since sales of tobacco products in most western countries have been either stagnant or in decline since the early 1990s, the tobacco companies had targeted developing countries (and particularly young people) as growth markets for their products.

Notwithstanding the many previous denials of the tobacco companies of the link between cigarettes and cancer, it is now clear that such a link is accepted. This is exemplified by the use made of a study commissioned by the multinational tobacco company, Philip Morris. In 2001 the tobacco firm, one of the world's leading producers of tobacco products, and responsible for 80 per cent of the cigarettes sold in the Czech Republic, felt the need to respond to claims that cigarette smoking was costing the Czech economy significant sums by virtue of high levels of hospitalisation, absenteeism from work and thus lower tax collection levels caused by smoking-related illnesses. The study commissioned by the tobacco company concluded that, rather than impose costs on the Czech economy, cigarettes saved the Czech government over £100M each year. The basis for this assessment was that, because cigarette smokers would be dying earlier than non-smokers, due to smoking-related illnesses, this would save the government hospitalisation costs associated with old age, as well as lower pension costs and lower housing costs.

Case study 8.2

When can genetically modified crops be grown?

In many western countries, including the UK, the planting of genetically modified (GM) crops is limited and tightly controlled by governments. Following a series of trials the UK government announced that only one genetically modified crop had passed its tests. The principal companies concerned had accepted the need to monitor the trials and to develop a thorough body of evidence before large-scale commercial planting could be considered. Yet, at the very time the UK government was proclaiming a moratorium in the UK, in the

Indian state of Andhra Pradesh, a 384 square mile area known as Genome Valley, was being developed for GM crop production, funded by overseas aid from the UK government. In excess of £50M was allocated to this project by the UK government in 2001. Monsanto, the principal company involved in the controlled trials in the UK, was among the companies invited to participate in the development in Andhra Pradesh. Farmers in Andhra Pradesh expressed concerns that development of prairie-style fields would result in the mass migration of millions of small farmers and labourers to the cities in search of work. The Andhra Pradesh project (known as *Vision 2020*) was the result of a study undertaken by a large American consulting firm, which, critics argue, gave little, if any, consideration to alternative forms of raising agricultural efficiency that utilised local resources more effectively and sensitively. Local farmers in Andhra Pradesh wished to control their own destinies, but the fear was that this scheme, with such influential corporate involvement, involvement that will have secured governmental support before it was officially announced, would lead to a social disaster in the region.

The case of the carving up of Indonesia, following the overthrow of President Sukarno in 1966 (reported in Chapter 12), is a further example of what appear to be structural, rather than aberrational, problems in the workings of business-society-political relationships.

Case study 8.3

Markets, prices and need

The pharmaceutical industry tends to be the target of a lot of angst when it comes to illustrating the problems/issues raised by global markets and global corporations. Among other things, the pharmaceutical corporations are often criticised for concentrating the overwhelming proportion of their research and development budgets on diseases of the rich. For example, there are new products continually coming to the market which claim to address issues of impotence, hair loss, wrinkles, obesity, etc., whereas diseases such as malaria, Ebola and HIV AIDS either remain under-investigated or the drugs available are too expensive for millions of people experiencing the diseases. However, the drugs companies point out that they are commercial corporations, subject to the disciplines of financial markets. If governments wish them to channel/divert research and development budgets into specific areas of medical treatment, then the pharmaceutical companies need to be compensated for the opportunity cost of this activity. One of the responses to these claims is that generic producers can manufacture HIV-AIDS drugs, for example, for a fraction of the price charged by the global pharmaceutical companies (around one-eighth of the price). The pharmaceutical companies respond by arguing that they need to recover the research and developments costs of those drugs that never reach their intended markets, costs that the generic producers do not incur.

Whilst the ethical weight of the above arguments are not suggested to be equal, we will sidestep offering a view on where the balance lies, but consider one of the ways the pharmaceutical companies (Big Pharma) responded to criticisms of their policies with regard to HIV-AIDS.

In 2001 the South African Government took Big Pharma to court in South Africa over the pricing of retro-viral drugs (the drugs used to treat HIV AIDS). The day before the judicial decision was to be given, the pharmaceutical companies, realising that they were going to 'lose' the decision, effectively began to discuss an 'out-of-court settlement'. This took the form of initially a fifty-word statement, which, after many months of 'debate', became a massive obfuscating document. Many felt the pharmaceutical companies had pulled victory from the jaws of defeat. This feeling was reinforced when in October 2003 the US Senate announced the name of the person who was to head the American AIDS Initiative. It was Randall Tobias, a former head of Eli Lilly, one of the world's big pharmaceutical companies. He was not required to sell his share holding in pharmaceutical companies, meaning that, if Mr Tobias took any decisions that harmed the interests of Big Pharma, he would also be negatively affecting his own wealth position. The question of a conflict of interest was raised by many but never adequately responded to.

The relationship between government and business is complex and in continuous need of scrutiny. It is far more complex than the simplistic call for minimal government that is heard from free-market fundamentalists would suggest. In a market system businesses require the autonomy to respond to market signals and claim the right of freedom from government interference in business decisions. Yet, that claim is disingenuous. It ignores the role of governments in setting fiscal policies; the management of government borrowing and macro-economic affairs; the support given to businesses during times of local or national recessions; the funding provided by governments to support both pure and generic research; and the funding of major projects that might be too large for private capital formation.

In addition, business in general has a vested interest in the maintenance of particular economic and legal conditions. As part of the pluralist political system, business organisations lobby governments and parliaments to achieve the conditions and laws that suit them. In the modern era it is argued that pressure groups, particularly business pressure groups, have a far more significant influence upon the construction of legislation than the polity in general.

The ethical question is immensely complex and not just in terms of disentangling competing notions of justice, fairness and care from one another. However, it is not clear whether this question is being asked at all. The power and influence of large corporations appear to dominate political agendas, stunting debate and maybe thinking.

So, to summarise the argument so far, corporations, via their economic power, have the potential to do significant good and significant harm. The UN Global Compact was initially a reaction to multi-government failure in adequately addressing critical global issues. It was an attempt to by-pass governments and to seek social intervention by large corporations. More recently, in 2004, the *Gearing Up* report has recognised this approach as unrealistic and set itself the task of trying to facilitate greater corporate and government bi-partisanship in tackling the world's great challenges. Are we entering a period when corporate executives become engaged with addressing the world's great social and environmental challenges without jeopardising their economic well-being? It is much too early to say, but what is clear is that the issue of ethics in business has never been more relevant and high profile.

Profit as the lever and the lure

The types of examples highlighted above regarding globalisation and deregulation issues challenge the claim that the overall effects of liberalism will necessarily be a benefit for all. An application of the Rawlsian original position test might cast doubt upon the efficacy, let alone the ethicality, of the poor being better-off as a result of MNC-influenced globalisation and WTO strictures, rather than the employment of other, more culturally and socially sensitive, approaches to economic development. For example, Chang (2002) makes the case that the principal countries that now fund and direct WTO free-trade policies did not follow WTO-type strictures when they were developing economies. The UK and the USA both employed protectionist policies to allow their economies to grow.

In a similar attack on free-trade ideology, but this time aimed at the IMF and World Bank, Burgo and Stewart (2002) used Malawi as an illustration of enforced privatisation policies that had created a food crisis. The case is explained in more detail in Chapter 13 (*see* Case study 13.3 on p. 513). In summary, in the mid-1990s the IMF insisted on the deregulation of the grain and foodstuffs agency before any further loans and aid finance were to be granted. The result, which Burgo and Stewart attribute principally to the deregulation policy, was a collapse in grain supplies and widespread famine in 2002. Interestingly, the Commerce and Industry Minister of Malawi, Mr Mpasu, was asked by the UK Government to speak to a meeting of G7 ministers in Cancun of the benefits of liberalising the Malawi economy. He stood up and said, 'We have opened our economy. That's why we are flat on our backs' (Elliott, 2003).

An issue emerging from this discussion is the complex question of how can the demands of economic imperatives be tempered within socially acceptable parameters? Nearly 200 years ago, David Ricardo (a significant figure in British economic thinking) described profit as 'the lever and the lure'. The lure because it is the indicator of how successfully capital has been invested, thereby acting as a lure to new capital investment. The notion of the lever, however, speaks to the social, as well as the economic, impact that capital migration can have on whole communities. The migration of capital from one region to another, from one country to another, as it seeks out the most advantageous investment opportunities, can have destabilising impacts upon those areas affected by the capital flows. While Friedman points to the undemocratic nature of corporate social responsibility, the argument to leave business alone ignores the profound influence of corporate decisions and their impact upon, potentially, millions of lives. Corporate decisions are made by unseen and largely unaccountable decision-makers. Critics of Friedman's 'undemocratic' argument see these issues as far more significant and serious threats to democratic processes than those raised by Friedman.

Friedman's third argument

Moving to the third of Friedman's criticisms, we find that it is open to challenge at the levels of principle, of legal argument and empirical evidence. To remind you, the third of Friedman's arguments was that businesses cannot have responsibilities because they are not real people; they are social constructs, i.e. they are artificial entities. While accepting Friedman's argument that a corporation is a social construct, this does not deny the possibility that the passage of time may confer upon business organisations new constraints, attributes, rights and/or responsibilities. In essence, social constructs can be reconstructed. Therefore, the simple fact that corporations are social constructs does not deny the possibility that the significance of such entities can develop to such an extent that society deems it necessary to place constraints, or responsibilities, upon corporations. There would be nothing philosophically objectionable, or flawed, in such developments. Whether such moves would achieve their desired ends is, however, a quite different question and set of issues.

In addition to challenging the validity of Friedman's third criticism at the level of principle, corporations have themselves undermined the strength of the criticism by their own actions. Corporations in America have claimed the same rights as individuals under the American Constitution. For example, in 1996 the US Supreme Court unanimously overturned a Rhode Island law which had stood for forty years. This law had prohibited businesses advertising the price of beers and spirits. Referring to the First Amendment the Supreme Court ruled that corporations could claim the same rights of protection as individuals. In 1998 in *First National Bank of Boston v. Bellotti* the American Supreme Court ruled again that corporations are protected by the First Amendment in the same way that individuals are in terms of freedom of speech. Thus, notwithstanding that they are social constructs, the corporations involved in these cases were granted the same rights under the American Constitution as those available to individual American citizens.

In the King Report, a further and critical legal point is highlighted. The conventional rhetoric is that corporate executives are required to run corporations in the interests of shareholders. However, the King Report challenges this claim by referring to some jurisdictions in which, upon incorporation,

> the company becomes a separate persona in law and no person whether natural or juristic can be owned. Courts have also held that shareowners have no direct interests in the property, business or assets owned by the company, their only rights being a right to vote and a right to dividends. Shareowners also change from time to time while, as the owner, the company remains constant. Consequently, directors, in exercising their fiduciary duties, must act in the interest of the company as a separate person.
>
> (King Report, 2002: 10)

Following the logic of this separation, the corporate executives are committed to act in the interests of the company, which would suggest that, if they deem it appropriate, this could include acting in ways that could be labelled corporately socially responsible. This approach places the company's long-term economic survival above all others. The interests of shareholders and those of the company would coincide via the process known as 'the correspondence principle', in which investors select companies to invest in on the basis of each company's known objectives and performance. Thus corporate executives do not have to worry about acting in the ways shareholders would prefer. If the actions of corporate executives are consistent with past decisions and rationale, then this will correspond with the interests of the shareowners, because the shareowners would have decided to invest in the company on this very basis.

As a recognisable legal entity, it might also be argued that, if corporations can be assigned the rights of citizenship, why should they not be assigned equivalent levels of responsibilities? If this argument is accepted then it raises questions about how one operationalises a broader view of a corporation's responsibilities and this in turn heralds the notion of stakeholders.

Stakeholding and stakeholders

The term stakeholding refers to an idea, a principle or argument, whereas the term stakeholder refers to a specifiable person or groups of people (sometimes in an organised form), with clear implications for how the interests of such groups might be incorporated or represented within organisational decisions. This distinction is important because, for some writers who support and argue for the concept of stakeholding, the operationalising of the concept presents enormous problems that possibly cast doubt upon the usefulness of the concept. Writers such as Bucholz (1998) and Rosenthal (1990) are examples of commentators who have expressed support for the stakeholding concept, but also expressed concerns about its real-world potential.

Notwithstanding these concerns, there is growing empirical evidence to suggest that an increasing number of organisations can be said to be adopting more inclusive perspectives into their ways of working that deny an exclusive shareholder focus to their decisions. This does not imply that shareholders are no longer an important consideration of managerial thought and action. Indeed, economic imperatives will often/invariably have to take precedence when stakeholder interests clash, but maybe, just maybe, the interests of shareholders are becoming more of a minimum constraint than a maximising objective.

In many ways a constraint is more demanding than an objective in that a constraint is invariably expressed as a specific number, e.g. the minimum dividend return next year must be 6 per cent, or the minimum earnings yield must be 11 per cent, whereas to state that 'we aim to maximise shareholder wealth' is a very loose statement, with no identifiable performance target. The minimum returns specified in the 'constraints' would need to take account of competing investment opportunities, so what is being suggested here is not 'pie-in-the-sky' wishful thinking, but rather a possible explanation of what might already be happening in some corporate board rooms in an osmotic sort of way. Thus the change process, if it reflects a genuine long-term change rather than something of faddish duration, is not an abrupt sea-change in perspective, which is heralded by a fanfare of trumpets, but rather a more incremental, less obvious change. Clearly more empirical evidence is required to allow more confident statements to be made on this point.

By turning shareholder considerations into a constraint, maybe seeing ordinary shareholders as becoming akin to first-order preference shareholders, managerial attention can then turn to considering how an organisation can become more a part of the societies with which it interacts, rather than apart from them. How might this work in practice?

There are various ways of approaching this issue, but one way that would *not* work is for an organisation to wait until it is confident that it will definitely achieve its shareholder 'constraint' target (i.e. the minimum dividend or earnings return) before debating how it should position itself as a social-economic entity. It might not be until, say, month eleven or later that attainment of the minimum shareholder return can be confirmed, leaving no time to begin thinking about other stakeholder issues.

If stakeholder engagement is to be a realistic and meaningful idea, then a longer-term stakeholder strategy becomes essential, just as a market strategy is essential for product or service development. Organisational development then becomes the sum of the two. To counter the concerns articulated by Friedman (and acolytes such as Elaine Sternberg, 2000), a number of organisations are firmly of the view that employee participation in social projects, which are outside the organisation's normal line of business, has a positive effect upon staff morale and aid organisational performance. The application of staff time in 'social projects' can be shown to be an effective 'value-adding' activity. Case study 8.4 is a specific example.

Case study 8.4

An economically successful corporation with a view of its social position

Capital *One* is a credit card company that chooses not to publicise its social projects because it is uneasy that it might be accused of only undertaking its social activities in order to gain publicity. Most of its social engagements go unreported and thus unrecognised, but the following example did attract media attention and the company acknowledged its role in the programme.

The projects in question related to the development of sophisticated software to facilitate the interrogation of differing national databases by a local police force in the pursuit of suspected paedophiles. The company supported a number of its programmers in working with the local police force over many months in developing the software, which has subsequently proved to be an important advance in police work and adopted by other police forces. The programmers also committed a lot of their own free time to the project. When talking with people at the company, one of the authors was left in no doubt that everyone was extremely supportive of the project and that its effect upon staff morale had been both positive and significant, manifesting itself in enhanced levels of efficiency and innovation in all areas of the programming division's work.

The Friedmanite response might be that such an example is fine, as long as it is undertaken in the belief that it will positively affect shareholder interests. If this is thought unlikely then such activities should not be undertaken. Interestingly the senior management argued strenuously that the decision to support the project was not taken for Friedmanite reasons. The senior executives argued that decisions relating to their 'social projects' were taken on non-consequentialist grounds. The senior management review projects that have been identified by the 'Social Resonsibility Team' (which comprises four full-time staff). There also appeared to be some consultation with all the employees to help shape the 'social projects' agenda' for the coming year.

The senior management argued that they saw their company as part of the local community and wanted to be regarded as a part of that community. They wanted to be regarded as a good employer, thereby attracting not just 'good' employees, but employees coming with the right approach and commitment. Such a policy did enhance organisational efficiency, but the senior management regarded the policy decision as reflecting more of a principled than an instrumental stance. At its root, the senior management philosophy was an inclusive approach to organisational 'Being'.

The 'everybody wins' feel of the closing sentence of Case study 8.4 does not have to be seen in a cynical light. The basic argument harks back to the original conceptualisation of the word 'company'. The etymology of the word 'company' relates to a community of interest, a mutually beneficial partnership of employers, employees and investors. Such an approach does not deny the significance of competition in an organisation's financial market as well as its product and service markets, but the 'shareholder-as-constraint-perspective' offers a possible way of negotiating the conundrum that the notion of stakeholding appears to present when set in the context of market-based, capitalist systems.

Corporate governance and trust

We discuss codes of ethics and conduct in Chapter 10, where we make the point that codes of ethics tend to be concerned with values and virtuous qualities. Certainly the most efficient and economic form of corporate governance is a relationship built upon trust, buttressed by the requisite levels of accountability and transparency. As soon as one begins to doubt a person's integrity and trustworthiness then monitoring and control processes come into play, but these are expensive and can themselves exacerbate a situation and breed an air of mistrust.

If an organisation wishes to develop a culture based upon virtues such as integrity, honesty, objectivity, justice and fairness, partly to reduce the costs of monitoring and control processes, then consistency in practices and the avoidance of double standards are essential. Unfortunately this is too often not the case, as indicated by Table 8.4.

Table 8.4 Organisational principles and human behaviour

Issue	General employees	Senior executives
Working for other organisations	Taking time off to do 'other' work would be described as moonlighting and subject to instant dismissal. Working for other organisations considered to be a vice.	Taking consulting or NED-type role with another organisation invariably seen as broadening for all concerned and a virtue.
Pay–motivation relationship	Paying people low wages incentivises employees to work hard. High wages merely breed sloth and inefficiency.	Senior executives need increasing levels of pay to incentivise them. The higher the pay, the higher the motivation.
Pensions	It is unreasonable to expect the state or organisations to provide for income after employment.	Generous pension packages are essential to entice the appropriate level of executive talent.
Working conditions	General working conditions should reflect basic functional requirements. To do more would reflect an unnecessary diversion of shareholder funds.	Require high-quality accommodation and to provide less will act as a disincentive to prospective appointees.
Perks	Very few and where they exist will need to reflect a close relationship between performance and perk. No such thing as a 'free lunch'.	Come in many forms from first-class travel to company cars (when little corporate travel is undertaken by road), to executive boxes at arts or sporting arenas, to company accommodation and company loans. Lunches may still not be free but are paid for by 'others'.

Moving the debate forward

So where have we arrived in terms of our consideration of Anglo-American developments in corporate governance and corporate responsibility? It brings us to the point where it is fair to ask, if the Friedmanite position on corporate responsibility can be successfully challenged, how can one operationalise notions of ethics in business which recognise the dynamics of market conditions, but which also recognise the differences in ethical perceptions and stances? Any such framework needs to have at its core some universally held principles relating to human dignity and rights, but also a flexibility to allow certain, 'acceptable' local variations to apply. This might be regarded as the Holy Grail, yet an attempt has been made to develop such a framework. What we are about to discuss is not a prescriptive approach to developing specific ethical principles in complex, multicultural contexts, but rather an over-arching framework that at least provides a general structure upon which organisations can begin to shape their respective approaches to managing in ethically complex contexts.

The social contract and the business case

The social contract is an interesting concept that can be traced back to Plato (Bosanquet, 1906) and Aristotle (Aristotle, 1976), but more recently to Hobbes (1968), Locke (1952) and Rousseau (1913). Lessnoff (1986) provides a good introduction to the history of social contract as an idea and as an argument.

A more recent articulation of the social contract is found in the argument that corporations have to earn and maintain a 'license to operate'. The license to operate reflects a commitment to more than economic imperatives, although the approach does not ignore economic issues. Two interesting writers working in this area are Thomas Donaldson and Thomas Dunfee. They have published in various forms over the past twenty years, for example, Donaldson (1982, 1989, 1990, 1996); Donaldson and Dunfee (1994, 1995 and 1999); Dunfee (1991, 1996); and Dunfee and Donaldson (1995). Donaldson and Dunfee have taken the social contract idea and developed a distinctive approach that they call *Integrative Social Contract Theory* (ISCT). At the core of the theory are four norms, or categories of values. One way to visualise ISCT is in the form of concentric circles, with the core foundational values at the centre (Figure 8.3).

The norms are described as follows.

Hypernorms These are argued to be fundamental human rights or basic prescriptions common to most religions. The values they represent are by definition acceptable to all cultures and all organisations. These have the characteristics of universal norms and in order to be workable will be few in number. What is and what is not a hypernorm would be agreed by rational debate and any contender for 'hypernorm' status would fail if it could be shown not to be universalisable. The issue of universal norms raises all the problems that Kantian ethics encounter, but rather than turning to something akin to Ross's (1930) *prima facie obligations*, Donaldson and Dunfee introduce two 'lower level' norms that allow for 'local' variations to be possible. The first of these is *consistent norms*.

Consistent norms These values are more culturally specific than hypernorms, but they will be consistent with hypernorms and other legitimate norms, the latter being defined as a norm that does not contradict the hypernorm test (Donaldson and Dunfee, 1999: 46). Donaldson and Dunfee cite corporate mission statements as examples of 'consistent norms'.

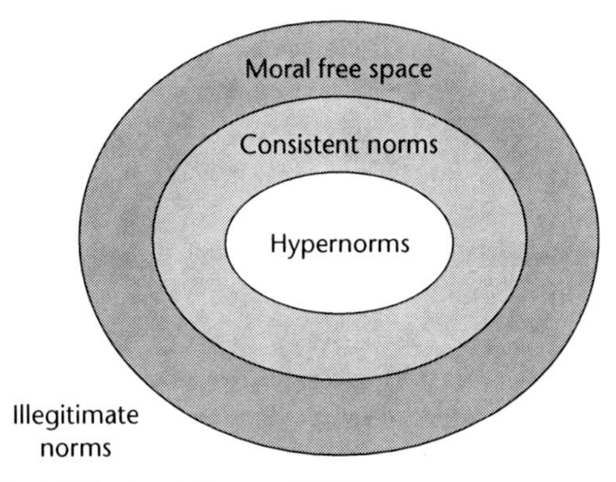

Figure 8.3 Integrated Social Contract Theory (ISCT)

Moral free space This is an interesting concept and allows Donaldson and Dunfee to contain norms that might be in tension (or limited contradiction) with any of the hypernorms within ISCT. An example of such a tension could be the use of child labour. Donaldson and Dunfee cite two examples involving the company Levi-Strauss.

Case study 8.5

Levi-Strauss

In the first example Levi-Strauss severed its links with the Tan family (and their businesses) because they (the Tan family) reportedly 'held twelve hundred Chinese and Philippine women in guarded compounds working them seventy four hours a week' (*The Clean Clothes Campaign*, 1992). These practices contravened Levi-Strauss's Business Partners Terms of Engagement'. The actions of the Tan family could be said to have contravened the hypernorms of respect for human dignity and justice.

The second example relates to the reaction of Levi-Strauss when it became aware that two of its suppliers in Bangladesh were employing children under the age of fourteen (a generally internationally accepted minimum age of employment). The company did not sever its relationship with the suppliers but chose an alternative course of action. The company required that the children be sent to school, with Levi-Strauss paying the children's tuition and associated fees, but also paying the children's wages to their families, so the latter did not suffer, but only while the children were at school. The company also agreed to re-employ the children when they reached fourteen. Whilst the exploitation of children has to addressed by the hypernorms, ISCT can cope with the actions of Levi-Strauss in this case because, whilst the use of the child labour must have been in contravention of at least one hypernorm, the practice was also recognition of a locally 'accepted' practice, something that might, for the time being, be seen to reside within the 'moral free space'. This is not to say that for all companies the 'right' action would be to react as Levi-Strauss had. For some the use of children under the age of fourteen may have meant a severing of links with the suppliers concerned, irrespective of the ripple effects of this action. In this case the moral free space would not allow the inclusion of the use of children less than fourteen years of age, notwithstanding that it is an 'accepted' local norm. ISCT allows both of these (re)actions because of the relationship of 'moral free space' to 'hypernorms' and 'consistent norms'. The example does illustrate that it is for individual groups and organisations to define what constitutes their 'moral free space'.

Illegitimate norms These norms are irreconcilable with *hypernorms*. For some this might be the case with regard to the treatment of women and children in some societies, but for others some of these 'problems' might fit within a 'moral free space' that would allow some development of understanding on all sides to see if a longer-term relationship might be possible with some modification to the 'problems' in question.

Connexion point

In this form of application, *moral free space* becomes something of a utilitarian concept (which, you will recall from Chapter 3, weighs ethical decisions in the context of a decision's consequences), but only on the understanding that the intention is to achieve longer-term correction of the offending practice and, to do this most effectively, it is better to work at the offending practice and to achieve change.

It would seem possible for principle-based *hypernorms* to be 'suspended', for some short passage of time, to allow utilitarian considerations to be located within the *moral free space*. This is contentious, and this interpretation might not meet with universal agreement, but it does show the flexibility that would be essential for such a framework to be useful for a multi-national corporation endeavouring to make sense of developing an ethical framework where certain practices, for example nepotism, might be unacceptable in most western cultures, but acceptable and important in others, e.g. Indian society. For an international corporation with operations in many parts of Asia and Europe, how should they handle this tension? They will require a short-term strategy guided by a longer-term principle.

As a result of the above type of example, ISCT has been criticised for being relativist. Donaldson and Dunfee refute this, arguing that ISCT is pluralist, combining the notion of universal norms of behaviour (hypernorms) with the recognition of important cultural differences (consistent norms and moral free space). The authors also recognise that, within the theory, individuals, corporations and communities have to work out for themselves what are their respective 'norms', at all levels.

> Business ethics should be viewed more as a story in the process of being written than as a moral code like the Ten Commandments. It can, and should ... adjust over time – to evolving technology, and to the cultural or religious attitudes of particular economic conditions.
>
> (Donaldson and Dunfee, 1999: viii)

Donaldson and Dunfee go on to say,

> At the heart of social contract effort is a simple assumption, namely that we can understand better the obligations of key social institutions, such as business or government, by attempting to understand what is entailed in a fair agreement or 'contract' between those institutions and society and also in the implicit contracts that exist among the different communities and institutions within society. The normative authority of any social contract derives from the assumption that humans, acting rationally, consent – or at least would consent hypothetically – to the terms of a particular agreement affecting the society or community of which they are a member. In this manner contractarian theories utilise the device of consent, albeit it is often *hypothetical* consent, to justify principles, policies and structures.
>
> (Donaldson and Dunfee, 1999: 16–7)

In order to provide a mechanism that might help operationalise ISCT, Donaldson and Dunfee employ a modified form of Rawls' veil of ignorance. Unlike Rawls' conception of the veil of ignorance, in which those (metaphorically) placed behind the veil have no knowledge of any aspect of their status, ethnic origin, physical abilities, gender, geographic location, political and economic system, etc., in Donaldson and Dunfee's conception only those aspects of a person's identity that are economic in nature, e.g. level of personal skill, nature of economic system, type of employing organisation, employment position held, etc., are concealed. This modified Rawlsian artifice is hoped to facilitate reflection and debate about an 'objective' fairness that should be inherent within an economic system and the ethical and moral base of that system.

ISCT attempts to hold on to both the integrity of universalisable norms (minimum accepted standards of behaviour irrespective of where in the world the norms are being considered), but avoiding the inflexibility of non-consequentialist stances. This is addressed by the introduction of the consistent norms and the moral free space. It is an interesting development, providing as it does a schema or framework that business people can employ to interrogate the ethical and moral issues that might be at stake in a particular situation. Donaldson and Dunfee are emphatic that ISCT is not a framework, let alone an approach, that can be employed unthinkingly. By its very nature it is a framework for facilitating discussion, debate and argument. It is not a decision-making tool, for the type of ethically charged situations that corporations are often faced with are invariably too complex and multi-faceted to lend themselves to easy formulation and calculation. However, the ideas and categories within ISCT do provide a language and a set of concepts that may help parties to a decision think constructively about the different issues and dimensions inherent within a complex business scenario.

Corporate manslaughter

The concluding major topic in this chapter continues the theme of attempts to hold corporations to account for their roles in, or impacts upon, society. To do this, there is a need to consider both the legal position and the philosophical position of corporations with regard to this issue.

Within the UK the prosecution of corporations, as distinct from individual employees, for claimed acts of wilful neglect of a duty of care has been difficult, at least via criminal law. Actions through the civil courts against corporations have been possible for many years, but the expense and the many years involved in prosecuting such cases make the civil law option one that is rarely taken up by members of the public.

Recent developments

Recent developments, reflected in proposals to change UK criminal law with respect to corporate manslaughter, by possibly bringing it in line with US criminal law, suggest that corporations might, in future, face the prospect of being held to account for criminal neglect of their duty of care. However, the UK administrations of Prime Minister Tony Blair have been reticent to bring the proposed law to Parliament for debate, despite a manifesto pledge since 1997. The inclusion of a corporate manslaughter bill in the 2004 Queen's Speech (the mechanism that announces the proposed bills to be discussed in the forthcoming parliamentary session) was seen by many as a deceit, because it was generally believed that the Prime Minister would call a general election in May 2005, which proved to be correct, thereby relegating all the proposed bills to the 'bills lost' bin.

Why this reticence to instigate a corporate manslaughter bill? It is difficult to see beyond the power of the corporate lobby persuading government that 'it would not be a good thing'. Yet in the United States it is possible for corporations to be forced to stop trading because of corporate wrongdoings. Such acts, known as charter revocation acts, are very rarely used, but at least they exist. In the UK no such possibilities exist, other than for the Department of Trade and Industry in special situations and for creditors. In America, however, a private citizen can instigate a winding-up procedure as a result of a corporate wrongdoing. There the death penalty exists for corporate acts of murder as it does for individuals. Notwithstanding that the death penalty for citizens has long been abolished in the UK, the possibility of such a punishment in the corporate field raises very different issues and arguments. The possibilities for a charter revocation law in the UK are discussed in a little more detail in Chapter 13 where we introduce our 'modest proposal' for affecting change in the ethics of business.

The 'identification principle' and the 'guiding mind'

As it currently stands, the first impediment to criminal prosecution for corporate manslaughter in the UK has been the argument, with which you will by now be familiar, that corporations do not commit acts; only individuals do. Thus, individual employees can be charged with manslaughter, e.g. a train driver involved in a rail crash, but charging the relevant rail company is a more difficult task. To do so, one has to be able to prove that an individual, who sits at the nerve centre of corporate decision making, and who should have acted in ways that could have prevented the accident occurring, was negligent in their duties. This is known in law as the *identification doctrine*, i.e. one has to be able to identify the negligent individual who could be said to represent the failure of the corporation as a whole.

In law, as in many other walks of life, one has to be clear about the precise meaning of words. So, when we use the phrase 'who sits at the nerve centre of corporate decision making', what do we mean? For the corporation to be charged, the identified individual has to be shown to be the person with overall responsibility for this particular aspect of corporate activity, for example health and safety matters, or rail track inspection. The need for this requirement is that because the law has, to date, only viewed corporations as being answerable via their employees, the employee concerned must be recognised as the person who was 'guiding' this aspect of corporate activity. This is the second legal principle to recognise, i.e. to be able to prosecute a corporation for corporate manslaughter, the *guiding mind* of the organisation has to be identified, and be shown to be implicated in the negligent act/s. Some real-life examples of this principle will help to illustrate the issues involved.

Case study 8.6

The *Herald of Free Enterprise*

The case has already been mentioned in Chapter 7. It relates to the capsizing of the P&O ferry *Herald of Free Enterprise* outside Zeebrugge harbour in which 192 people lost their lives. It is possible that the captain of the ferry might have been able to be prosecuted for not fully checking that the bow doors were securely closed before the ferry set sail. However, the fact that crew members had, on five previous occasions, expressed concerns to their seniors about the lack of any warning lights on the bridge relating to the position of the bow doors was insufficient to bring a prosecution against the P&O Corporation. It was not possible to prove that these expressions of concern had reached the top echelons of the P&O corporation, the 'guiding mind'. Although comparative evidence was available concerning the (lack of) commitment that P&O was claimed to have towards safety issues, the prosecution lawyers were refused permission by the trial judge to call captains of the Sealink corporation (at the time of the trial Sealink was a rival ferry company), to contrast the safety practices of P&O ferries with those of other ferry operators. Four years after the capsizing of the *Herald of Free Enterprise*, safety issues at P&O were again raised when it was revealed that P&O crew members had to pay for their own basic safety training. One recruit recounted, ' I was sent to a college and given pages of information on things like where lifeboats are kept on a ferry, and how to evacuate in an emergency. But you don't get a chance to practise any of this on a ship. When I worked on a ferry for the first time it was up to me to find out where the evacuation points and passengers' lifejackets were' (Crainer, 1993: 67).

Even actions that might have appeared doubtful did not attract the judge's concerns. For example, while the inquests into the deaths of the 192 passengers and crew were still in progress, the *Herald of Free Enterprise*, which, unaccountably, had been renamed *Flushing Range* and with its bow doors welded together, was being towed to a scrap yard in Taiwan. Members of the Kent police had to fly to South Africa to intercept and inspect the renamed ship. As Crainer (1993) observes, for many concerned in the case, the vessel was 'regarded as an important piece of evidence in a criminal investigation'.

In terms of the 'guiding mind' P&O's marine superintendent admitted that he had misled the original inquiry into the disaster about when he had first heard of a proposal to fit warning lights on ferry bridges. It was also revealed that he discounted warnings from one of the company's senior masters about potential dangers because he thought the captains were exaggerating. Sheen (who chaired the initial enquiry) described Develin's [P&O's marine superintendent] responses to the legitimate concerns of the masters as 'flippant, facetious and fatuous' (Crainer, 1993). Yet Develin was not deemed sufficiently senior to equate with being (or being part of) P&O's 'guiding mind'.

Similar scenarios regarding the chasm that can appear to exist between a corporation's executive and operational management can be seen in other examples. A report in a safety journal during the inquiry into the disaster at *Piper Alpha* oil rig noted,

> The whole management evidence from Occidental [the owners of the oil rig] paints a picture of complete ignorance of the problems which existed. The senior management provided no support to the platform staff. They provided no training. They provided no guidance. The laid down no procedures. They did not participate in discussions with the operators. They did not seek the views of their employees.
>
> (*Safety Management*, December, 1989, reported in Crainer, 1993: 116)

Similarly, King (2001) remarked upon the actions of senior management at British Rail following the 1999 Paddington rail crash.

> It should come as no surprise that soon after the UK suffered its second worse rail disaster of recent times – the 1999 Paddington crash – it was revealed that the rail companies had resisted calls to introduce a confidential reporting procedure, i.e. 'whistleblowing' procedure through which staff could report safety concerns without fear of recrimination.
>
> (King, 2001: 152)

Of course, if a company has an internal grievance/concerns procedure, and issues are raised by employees within this process, senior management cannot later feign ignorance of any problems that subsequently result in injuries or death to consumers or general members of the public.

A little over 12 months after the Paddington rail crash, in October 2000, another serious incident occurred involving rail transport when a train left the track at Hatfield due to faults in the track. This time four people lost their lives and many more were injured. Again management failures regarding reluctance to heed concerns about the quality of the track and its maintenance were suggested to be a significant feature of the case, but on 23 September 2004 a high court judge announced that no charges would be brought against either the company *Railtrack* (which was later renamed *Network Rail*) and three of its directors, including the former chief executive. The reason – lack of evidence.

The issue of aggregation

Unlike the situation in the United States, UK courts will not accept the principle of *aggregation*. This relates back to the 'guiding mind' principle. In essence the refusal of UK courts to accept aggregation means that the guiding mind of an organisation needs to be held within a tight area of the corporate structure. However, the US Court of Appeal ruled in 1987 that,

> corporations compartmentalise knowledge, subdividing the elements of specific duties and operations into small components. The aggregate of those components constitute the corporation's knowledge of a particular operation.
>
> (Crainer, 1993: 122)

The US Court of Appeal thus recognised the complexity of corporate structures, and allowed that, if responsibility for a particular facet of corporate activity, such as health and safety, was located in many different parts of a corporation, this was not a defence a corporation (as a totality) could employ to deny responsibility for a failure to adhere to acceptable safety practices. As a result of this approach, all the various parts of a corporation that are responsible for safety can be added together (aggregated) to produce the sum of the corporation's health and safety practices (or lack of).

As mentioned above, the past decade has seen calls for a crime of corporate manslaughter grow louder and more frequent in the UK, so much so that in 2000 the UK Government, via the Home Office, published its own proposals, *Reforming the Law on Involuntary Manslaughter*. However, no time in parliamentary sessions could be found. We have already mentioned what happened to the Queen's Speech in the Autumn of 2004. The situation in the UK with regard to corporate manslaughter remains a contentious issue. The influence of industry lobby groups in the stunted progress of a corporate manslaughter bill is a worrying issue for many.

The UK government's and EU proposals on corporate manslaughter

Notwithstanding the fact that a general election in 2005 frustrated parliamentary time on a bill, the government's proposals do acknowledge the inadequacies of the current law. Four significant disasters were cited in the report *Reforming the Law on Involuntary Manslaughter*. These were: the capsizing of the *Herald of Free Enterprise*; the Kings Cross fire; the Clapham rail crash; and the Southall rail crash, with the implicit view that the law inhibited the successful prosecution of what appeared to be culpability within and of the organisations concerned. The identification doctrine was seen as the principal stumbling block to successful prosecution of companies.

The Government's proposals were based upon the Law Commission Report No. 237, *Legislating the Criminal Code: Involuntary Manslaughters*. The principal proposals were:

- There should be a special offence of corporate killing, broadly corresponding to the proposed offence of killing by gross carelessness.
- The corporate offence should (like the individual offence) be prosecuted only where the corporation's conduct fell far below what could be reasonably expected.
- The corporate offence should not (unlike the individual offence) require that the risk be obvious or that the defendant be capable of appreciating the risk.
- A death should be regarded as having been caused by the conduct of the corporation if it is caused by a 'management failure', so that the way in which its activities are managed or organised fails to ensure the health and safety of persons employed in or affected by its activities.
- Such a failure will be regarded as a cause of a person's death even if the immediate cause is the act or omission of an individual.

- That individuals within a company could still be liable for the offences of reckless killing and killing by gross carelessness, as well as the company being liable for the offence of corporate killing.

Switching the burden of proof to the corporation

A different approach has been proposed by the Council of Europe (European Union). This proposal would make companies responsible for all offences committed by their employees, but corporations would be allowed a due diligence defence, i.e. corporations would be exempted from liability if they could show that every precaution to avoid or minimise such an act occurring had been implemented. In this proposal the conventional approach to law is turned on its head, i.e. the initial presumption is that of guilt on the part of the accused, and it is then the responsibility of the accused (the corporation) to present evidence of its existing practices that would exempt it from liability. Clarkson (1998) has expressed concern at the implications of this proposal in that (from a legal perspective) it would change the offence committed to one of a lesser order than criminal manslaughter. The new offence would be offset by a possible due diligence defence. The result would be the attribution of lesser sanctions than under a criminal prosecution for manslaughter.

The possibilities for the senior management of corporations to deny personal or corporate responsibility for criminal neglect appear to be entering a new era. In 1993, Crainer observed,

> Sadly the failure of the Zeebrugge corporate manslaughter trial seemed to condone an all-too-prevalent attitude among senior managers: 'Don't tell me what is going on because if I know, I might be held accountable'.
>
> (Crainer, 1993: 142)

Clarkson made a similar point when he observed,

> If the company's structures are impenetrable or if its policies are so 'sloppy' that no person has been made responsible for the relevant area of activity, a company can still shield itself from corporate criminal liability. In the *P&O* case, where there was no safety manager or director, there would be no person whose acts and knowledge could be attributed to the company.
>
> (Clarkson, 1998: 6)

Drawing upon the findings of the Sheen Report into the *Herald of Free Enterprise* disaster, in which the corporation was accused by Sheen of 'being infected with the disease of sloppiness' (Department of Transport, 1987), Clarkson observes, 'the worse the disease of sloppiness, the greater is the immunization against criminal liability'. The inference of Clarkson's comments regarding the 'P&O case' (*Herald of Free Enterprise*) is that the interpretation of the identification principle during the trial was too tight. It is not just the weight of the evidence that determines the outcome of legal prosecutions. The interpretations of law and decisions concerning the admissibility of evidence make the judiciary crucial elements within legal processes.

An example of the power of judges to create legal precedent is exemplified in the ruling relating to *Meridian Global Funds Management Asia Ltd v. Securities Commission* (reported in Clarkson, 1998: 3). The presiding judge ruled that the 'directing mind and will' of a company did not have to be a very senior person, if the person committing the act was authorised to undertake the act on the company's behalf. This ruling still leaves identification necessary, at the present time at least, but the clear implication is that the responsible person does not have to be a very senior person in order for a corporation to be held responsible for an act of negligence (Clarkson, 1998: 3).

Twelve years after the *Herald of Free Enterprise* disaster, and following the high-profile rail crashes involving loss of life at Clapham and Southall, two trains collided just outside Paddington Station in 1999, killing 31 people and injuring over 400. In the report published in June 2001 into the causes of the crash, Lord Cullen, the enquiry Chairman, condemned the entire rail industry for 'institutional paralysis'. He described the failure of the track operator, Railtrack, to act on previous reported incidents of train drivers passing through red signals as 'lamentable'. He was extremely critical of one of the train companies involved, Thames Trains (whose driver passed the red signal), and the company's safety culture which he described as 'slack and less than adequate'. Lord Cullen also spoke of the 'significant failures of communication within the organisation'.

The driver of the train operated by Thames Trains was inexperienced and had not been notified by the company of information that was in its possession that the signal just outside Paddington Station had been passed at danger (i.e. on red) eight times before. The problem appears to have been related to the signal being obscured at certain times of day due to the glare of the sun and/or overhanging foliage.

Lord Cullen was also critical of the quality of training given by Railtrack to its signallers, the 'slack and complacent regime at Slough' (the control centre for the signals in question). He was also extremely critical of the Railway Inspectorate which he deemed 'lacked resources, acted without vigour and placed too much faith in Railtrack'. These words carry echoes of those used by Sheen, the chairman of the Department of Trade inquiry into the *Herald of Free Enterprise* disaster. Sheen spread the blame far more widely than those directly involved on the night of the disaster. Guilt lay with 'all concerned in management. From top to bottom, the body corporate was infected with the disease of sloppiness.' No actions were ever brought against the corporations concerned!

The UK Government's earlier proposals allow for criminal prosecutions of corporations, as well as individuals, if practices that a reasonable and careful corporation would employ are absent. The speed with which the Government's proposals move from discussion paper to actual law will be interesting to observe following the 2005 election. American law would be a good precedent to follow in this case.

Clarkson offered a further variation on the quest to hold corporations to account, by the application of what he describes as 'corporate *mens rea*'. Clarkson offers his proposal because he fears that the doctrines of 'identification' and 'guiding mind' remain problematic within the government's proposals.

DEFINITION

Mens rea is a legal term that means criminal intention, or knowledge that an act is wrong. Thus, corporate *mens rea* refers to an act or set of practices (or lack of) perpetrated in the name of a corporation that possess the essence of wrongdoing.

Clarkson argued,

> Doctrines – identification, aggregation, etc. – involve fictitious imputations of responsibility. The real question is not whether the question of corporate mens rea involves a fiction, but whether, of all the fictions, it is the one that most closely approximates modern-day corporate reality and perceptions. ... the important point about this approach is that it is not whether any individual within the company would have realised or foreseen the harm occurring but whether in a properly structured and organised, careful company, the risks would have been obvious.
>
> (Clarkson, 1998: 10)

What this argument is saying is, 'Yes, corporate culpability is a fiction, or a problematic concept, but then so are many of the concepts that are involved in this debate'. Clarkson referred to legal concepts such as identification and aggregation as equivalent fictions/problematic concepts, but we could just as easily refer to concepts such as citizenship, democracy, property rights, free trade, a living wage. Property rights are an entirely socially constructed phenomenon, yet this has not prevented millions of lives being lost in its defence over the centuries. It is for societies to decide the laws that are appropriate for their own well-being and development. In many respects the fact that some of the laws relate to human beings, whilst others relate to socially constructed beings, is irrelevant.

Connexion point

Earlier in this chapter we discussed one of Milton Friedman's main criticisms of corporations being required to be 'responsible' for their actions beyond economic responsibility. The criticism in question was that as social constructs corporations could not have responsibilities; only people can. The reference, immediately above, to 'It is for societies to decide the laws that are appropriate for their own well-being and development. In many respects the fact that some of the laws relate to human beings, whilst others relate to socially constructed beings, is irrelevant', is extremely apposite in the context of Friedman's objections to calls for CSR.

This still leaves us with the issue of whether corporations can be construed or treated as corporate citizens. From the Heideggerian position (which we discuss in more detail in Chapter 9), corporations cannot be citizens, because the best that can be expected of corporations is that they view nature in exclusively instrumental ways. From a Heideggerian perspective, corporations have to be controlled in ways other than 'wishing' them to act in socially responsible ways. Windsor (2001) supported this view.

> The corporate citizenship notion conflates citizen (which a firm cannot be) and person (which a firm can be, but only as a legal fiction). The portrayal is fictional .... Fictional personhood is not a sound basis for artificial citizenship.
>
> (Windsor, 2001: 41)

The key proposal of the Law Commission report on involuntary manslaughter, which the UK government appears to have accepted, is that management failure to introduce and ensure the application of reasonable safety practices is sufficient to justify the prosecution of corporate manslaughter. This is a fundamental change. Whether it could be cited, retrospectively, against Railtrack and/or Thames Trains is a moot point, but the position of corporations vis à vis the death of their employees and/or members of the public due to actions or inactions of the corporation is undergoing fundamental scrutiny. As mentioned above, whether any alterations to the law will reflect such a fundamental change remains to be seen.

Summary

In this chapter the following key points have been made:

- The changes in terminology, as reflected in the initial use of corporate social responsibility, which is beginning to mutate into corporate responsibility, while along the way the notion of corporate citizenship has also been employed, reflect an ongoing search for a concept that can encapsulate a business–society set of relationships that satisfies all aspects of the debate, but, particularly, that extends corporate executives' responsibilities beyond those to the providers of equity capital.
- Corporate governance reforms in the UK and America have retained an exclusive focus upon the interests of shareholders, unlike the King Report on corporate governance in South Africa.
- The King Report also raised the issue of values and beliefs as an explicit consideration of corporate governance, which in a South African context emphasised kinship, community and 'an inherent trust and belief in fairness of all human beings'. The issue of values within Anglo-American approaches towards corporate governance is not explicit, but implied. They are underpinned by ethical individualism and (from agency theory) a belief that individuals are self-serving and inherently untrustworthy.
- The 1999 UN Global Compact reflected a frustration with governments to address corporate governance reforms which focused upon basic human rights, such as humane living conditions; freedom of association at work; respectful working conditions, including hours of work; child labour; forced labour; and extreme poverty.

- However, the 2004 *Gearing Up* report reflects a recognition that the initial Global Compact placed too much of the responsibility for making a difference on these issues on to business corporations. The *Gearing Up* report acknowledges that there has to be a genuine bipartisan approach between governments and business if any significant outcome is to be achieved on profound global and national structural problems.
- Integrated Social Contract Theory (ISCT) offers a framework to allow us to begin to identify core organisational values that can stand the test of universalisation, but that retain the flexibility for local variations in customs and values.
- Corporate manslaughter, as a criminal offence, remains profoundly difficult to prosecute under UK law. Proposals to remedy this situation continue to be frustrated and the reasons for this stifling of progress are worrying in terms of democratic principles. The Law Commission and the Council of Europe have both pronounced on the issues and their recommendations await parliamentary time. It is now for government to choose whether or not to act.
- We may be entering, or have already entered, a period when the business–society relationship becomes far more openly debated. As a result we might find that in, say, 10 or 15 years' time the evolution of the limited liability company may have moved on apace from where it was at the turn of the century.
- Within the next 10–15 years, perhaps the notion of shareholder-as-constraint, rather than shareholder-as-maximising-objective, might have become more recognised and part of practice. As a result the notion of stakeholding may have become less of a practical conundrum. Business ethics and values have never been more relevant and centre-stage.

Quick revision test

1. Have calls for corporations to display greater levels of social responsibility only arisen during the past fifteen years?
2. What was the view of Charles Lindblom regarding the fit of large corporations in democratic states?
3. What is agency theory?
4. What is the paradox concerning non-executive directors that relates to agency theory?
5. What admission was made in the 2004 *Gearing Up* Report concerning the 1999 UN Global Compact?
6. What were Christian Aid's principal criticisms of the UN Global Compact?

Typical assignments and briefs

1. The ethical principles that underpin official approaches towards corporate governance in South Africa (the King Report) and the UK (2003 Combined Code) both defend issues of rights, but the extent of those rights and to whom they relate varies significantly. Debate, using contrast and comparison, where you believe the weight of ethicality and pragmatics lies.
2. International codes of conduct reflect attempts to move a more socially oriented agenda into the board rooms of corporations. Employing three different international codes,
   (i) compare and contrast the ethical principles upon which each is based; and
   (ii) given the explicit or implicit objectives of the codes you have chosen, provide a reasoned analysis of their respective likely efficacy.
3. You are an advisor to the cabinet minister who has been charged with the responsibility of responding to a parliamentary question as to why the government has chosen not to introduce the crime of corporate manslaughter. You are required to present a paper to the minister that evaluates the ethically based arguments that could be used to defend the government's position during the debate.
4. Critically evaluate Integrated Social Contract Theory as a possible way forward for reconciling a universal code of behaviour in multi-ethnic, multi-national corporations.
5. Critically contrast the 'shareholder as constraint, not objective' proposal, from both the ethical egoist and Rawlsian 'justice as fairness' perspectives.

Group activity 8

You are asked to work in groups of between three and six members and to assume the role of being the senior decision-making team of a leading institutional investor. Your tasks are as follows, with tasks A and B ideally completed before the commencement of the group session.

A Define the principles that will guide your investment strategy. To do this you will need to consider, among other issues, the following:
   (i) On whose behalf are you making decisions?
   (ii) Are there any types of organisation in which you would not invest?
   (iii) Are there any sectors in which you emphatically wish to invest?
   (iv) What do you expect of the companies in which you invest in terms of communications and information updates?
   (v) Are there any aspects of corporate governance that you would prioritise?
   (vi) What will be your attitudes towards growth and risk?
   (vii) What will be your expectations and attitude towards rates of return?

An example of a leading institutional investor that has published its investment principles is the Hermes organisation. The following website will allow you to access the Hermes Principles, as well as a number of other important corporate governance publications.

http://www.ecgi.org/codes/country_pages/codes_uk.htm

B Having established your investment principles, you must now select ten quoted companies that will form your investment portfolio. You are not required to worry about how well these organisations have performed in the past year. For now, simply select ten companies that you believe satisfy your investment principles.

C You should prepare to discuss in open session the basis upon which you established your investment principles and the rationale for selecting the ten companies in your investment portfolio.

Recommended further reading

You might find the following publications helpful.

Donaldson, T. (1989) *The ethics of international business*, New York: Oxford University Press.

Donaldson, T. and Dunfee, T.W. (1999) *Ties That Bind: A Social Contracts Approach to Business Ethics*, Harvard Business School Press.

Lindblom, C.E. (1977) *Politics and Markets: The World's Political-Economic Systems*, New York: Basic Books Inc.

SustainAbility (2004), *Gearing Up: From corporate responsibility to good governance and scalable solutions*, New York: UN Global Compact.

Useful websites

Topic	Website provider	URL
Corporate governance	European Corporate Governance Institute	http://www.ecgi.org/
International corporate governance	International Corporate Governance Network	http://www.icgn.org/
Corporate governance – The King Report		http://www.ecseonline.com
Gearing Up Report	SustainAbility	http://www.sustainability.com
Global Compact	United Nations	http://www.unglobalcompact.org

Sustainability and the responsible corporation

Learning outcomes

Having read this chapter and completed its associated activities, you should be able to:

- Discuss the importance of sustainability as a concept that applies to social and economic, as well as environmental, aspects of human activity.
- Debate both the principled and consequentialist positions that underpin sustainability arguments.
- Participate in debates concerning various global initiatives on sustainability.
- Evaluate the strength of the ethical egoist arguments for market-based, price-led sustainability solutions.
- Debate the 'enframing of technology' mind-set that represents one of the major obstacles to moving to more sustainable activities, practices and processes.
- Discuss reconceptualising the relationship between shareholder and corporate executives that could allow the stakeholder perspective to become a less problematic issue.

Introduction

The immediate question we have to address is, 'What do we mean by sustainability?' Sustainability of what, for whom, and over what timescale?

When the term sustainability was first used in the context of social and economic activities it was used exclusively in the context of the use and depletion of environmental resources. There are a number of statements that capture the essence of this notion of sustainability and one of the earliest came from the United Nations Brundtland Commission (1987), which referred to sustainability as

> development that meets the needs of the present without compromising the ability of future generations to meet their own needs.

A variation on this theme is to see members of the human race as always in the role of lessees or guardians of the planet. From this perspective, statements such as the following flow, 'We lease nature from our children, and they from their children. We must all act wisely'.

Significant political initiatives

There have been a number of political initiatives that have attempted to address pressing (environmental) sustainable development issues, culminating in agreements such as the Rio Declaration (1992); the Kyoto Protocol (1997); and the Johannesburg World Summit (2002). Implementation of the Kyoto Protocol was intended to be a major advance in the global approach to climate change issues, with commitments to reduce by 5.2 per cent the 1990 level of global greenhouse gas (GHG) emissions by 2012 and by 50 per cent by 2050.

As indicated above the protocol was drawn up in 1997, but the base line year for calculations was agreed as 1990. However, the subsequent withdrawal of America and Australia from the protocol undermined its status, and the tenth annual UN Conference on Climate Change, held in Buenos Aires in December 2004, witnessed further erosion of its credibility. The purpose of the conference in Buenos Aires was to gain agreement on Kyoto 2, i.e. post-2012. However, the dominant developing economies of India and China joined forces with the USA and Australia to scupper any talks concerning post-2012 GHG emission levels. India and China considered that such levels of GHG emission controls threatened their economic growth and might just be a ploy by the developed economies to slow the economic growth of India and China.

At the present time it is impossible to see the adjustments required to move to a globally sustainable position on natural resource usage without major adjustments being made to people's perceptions of acceptable ways of living. This statement denies neither the claim that present ways of living for many western societies are unsustainable, nor that the adjusted standard of living required is in any way unacceptable to rational human beings. However, it has to be recognised that, at the present time, with ethical egoism such an apparently powerful descriptive theory of human behaviour, for a political leader to claim that their policies will lead to fundamental adjustments and, some might argue, reduced standards of living would be political suicide.

You might ask what types of 'adjustments' are being referred to here. One of the major areas of potential impact would be in terms of modes of transportation. An interesting example is described in Activity 9.1.

Activity 9.1

For example, an inter-city train can carry many more passengers than a plane on an internal flight, yet, in early 2005, it costs under £27 (including airport taxes) for a scheduled return flight from Nottingham (in England) to Edinburgh (in Scotland), a distance of 260 miles each way. With the round trip amounting to 520 miles, this works out at 5p per mile! The cheapest return ticket for a train journey from Nottingham to Edinburgh is an Apex ticket that costs £50, but there are always relatively few of these tickets available. The next cheapest ticket costs £85, while the standard return (not first class) is £135. In addition, the train travel time is three hours longer, even allowing for a one-hour early arrival time at the airport. In this context you might like to make enquiries as to the cost of rail travel versus internal air flights in your own part of the UK or your own country.

With the cost of running an average family motor car estimated to be around 30p per mile and rising, and the accepted mileage rate for car travel approved by the Inland Revenue to be 40p per mile, it is puzzling in the extreme to understand how an airline can charge the equivalent of 5p per mile and still find it economically worthwhile. One of the reasons for the difference in price in the UK is that aviation fuel is not taxed. Even though this concession to the airlines is estimated to cost the UK taxpayer £6bn each year (The *Guardian*, 2005), it is not the only concession. In addition, the cost of an airline ticket is 'subsidised' in the sense that no value added tax (VAT) is levied by the government, despite the fact that air travel is the most polluting form of transportation one can choose. Excluding food products, it is difficult to identify any product or service provided by a private sector organisation that is free of VAT. This situation has to say something about the influence the airline industry has in the corridors of power.

While an element of the price differences may have something to do with the respective efficiency levels of the organisations concerned, any government espousing its commitment to a sustainability agenda has to address the cost of air travel. Interestingly, the owners of airports (often local authorities) sometimes offer incentives to airlines to fly to their destination to facilitate local economic development, which once again illustrates the complex intertwining of governments and business and the vulnerability of sustainability issues to economic, social and political interests.

Likewise, the motor car and its place in modern society cannot be exempt from political attention. The taxation of all the different facets of road travel (e.g. fuel costs, road tolls, recycled materials, fuel types, etc.) is a further issue upon which politicians can be said to be dragging their feet. In many societies the motor car has become a fundamental part of modern living, with public transport sometimes barely a viable option. Changing attitudes to reduce dependency upon the motor car is a monumental task and at the present time, potentially, a political suicide note.

Activity 9.2

Employing the following scale, think about where your position lies on the scale with regard to each of the questions shown below.

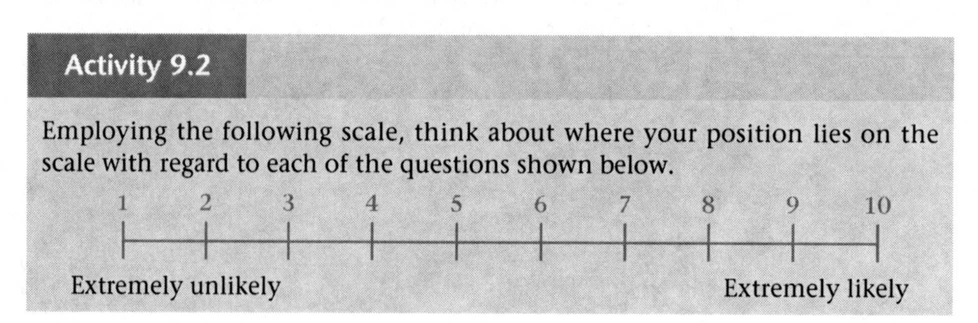

Questions

1. Can you envisage *not* owning a car – ever?
2. Would you support an increase in motor fuel tax that would double the price of a litre of fuel?
3. Would you support an increase in motor fuel tax that would quadruple the price of a litre of fuel?
4. Assuming the price adjustment relates to an airline flight that you might take, would you support a levy on aviation fuel that would raise the price of an economy airline ticket from its current price of £300 to £1800?
5. Assuming the price adjustment relates to an airline flight that you might take, would you support a levy on aviation fuel that would raise the price of an internal air flight from, say, £27 to £270?
6. How likely do you think it is that the fuel tax rises suggested in the questions above would address the worldwide issue of GHG emissions?

Activity 9.3 A moral choice

In a radio interview of January 2005, Jonathon Porritt, the UK government's advisor on environmental issues, gave an example of the tension between social ethics and environmental ethics. He argued that, whilst it might be a socially moral act to attend one's sister's wedding in New York, the environmentally moral case is not to attend (but with profuse apologies). What is your reaction to this statement?

The changes required to address the environmental problems facing the world in the early stages of the twenty-first century are not all as startling or lifestyle-changing as these examples and questions imply, but it is probable that many required changes do represent changes of a stepped and profound nature.

Returning to the UN Climate Change Conference in Buenos Aires in December 2004, the problems of achieving an outline agreement on a Kyoto 2 accord were further exacerbated when Italy joined the dissenting countries (Australia, China, India and America) and thereby undermined a previously united EU position. This was clearly a significant setback for the coordinated European position, but the UK's position is itself not wholly consistent. For example, the UK government had previously announced that it had set itself the task of achieving the Kyoto target of GHG emissions by 2010 and by a greater amount than the EU as a whole had agreed. The commitment to achieve higher levels of reduction of carbon dioxide emissions, and two years ahead of the time the EU was requiring its member states to achieve the Kyoto targets, was a demanding commitment by the UK government. However, by doing so the UK government was announcing its commitment to environmental issues.

In April 2004 the UK Secretary of State for the Department of Environment, Food and Rural Affairs (DEFRA) announced that for the period 2004–2007 the UK's reduction in carbon dioxide emissions would be 756m tonnes. However, on 27 October 2004, and after significant lobbying by industry groups, the Secretary of State announced that the UK government had made adjustments to the base line number to allow British industry to remain 'competitive' (i.e. to allow it to spend less on GHG-reducing measures). The reduction in carbon dioxide emissions had been recalculated as 736m tonnes. The overall target reduction for 2010 remained unchanged, which meant that the reductions between 2007 and 2010 would have to be even more significant than before, although maybe that was seen as the next government's problem!

Emissions Trading Scheme

The commitment to the GHG targets may have been initially well intentioned, but the political will appears to have been found lacking when confronted by powerful industrial pressure groups. However, the story does not end there. The EU Commission refused to accept the UK's revised figures and insisted that the original target be reinstated. After much 'discussion' the UK Government acceded to the EU ruling, but announced that it would challenge the ruling in the courts. This decision allowed the UK to enter the Emissions Trading Scheme (ETS) but left unresolved, for the time being, the reduction in GHG emissions that UK companies would need to achieve. As we write this chapter the situation remains unresolved. The ETS officially began operating on 1 January 2005, although the dispute between the UK government and the EU Commission delayed its start.

The ETS is a market-based response to the need to reduce GHG emissions. As part of the Kyoto Protocol, the EU committed its member states to reduce GHG emissions by 8 per cent by 2012, but as mentioned above the UK government committed itself to achieve a 12 per cent reduction by 2010, so relatively speaking this was a far more ambitious, environmentally sensitive and bold stance than the EU had committed its member states to.

Each EU country has had to develop a National Allocation Plan (NAP). Within the respective NAPs organisations generating more than a certain level of carbon dioxide emissions have to apply for a permit, which may or may not represent the organisation's current carbon dioxide emissions level. If during the year an organisation believes it will exceed its permitted allowance then it will need to enter the ETS and buy additional 'credits'. Alternatively, if an organisation believes that it will not require all its allocated credits (maybe as a result of installing equipment and plant that are very energy efficient) then the organisation can consider selling its surplus 'credits' on the ETS.

Environmental pressure groups and other agencies (including governments) may wish to increase the pressure on companies to replace existing plant with more energy-efficient plant by entering the market and buying credits, thereby reducing the available pool of credits and increasing the price of those credits still available. The intention would be that by driving up the price of credits the cost of purchasing energy-efficient plant and equipment becomes more attractive than buying the GHG credits. In addition, by investing in energy-efficient plant and equipment a company may not need all its credits and thus be able to sell them in, ideally, a rising market for credits. It will be interesting to see the extent to which agencies such as pressure groups and governments act as buyers to push up the price of credits. Without such intervention it is difficult to see how the market will stimulate the desired transfer to energy-efficient plant.

Whether this 'solution' to global warming is the ideal solution, or even a suitable one, is a moot point. It is a business solution to a problem that has profound social, political and, ultimately, survival consequences. As discussed above, unless a market price fully reflects all opportunity and externality costs, including those of future societies, it remains incomplete as an expression of societies' preferences. For example, the approach encourages a highly calculative stance with regard to investment in new energy-efficient plant. As an alternative to possessing sufficient credits that equate with one's GHG emissions, a corporation may simply decide to pay whatever fine is levied upon corporations that fail to comply with the ETS and the Kyoto defined emission levels. Thus, to make engagement with the ETS economically logical, non-compliance fines will need to be high, even punitive. Will governments be strong enough to levy fines of this scale? History does not offer encouragement for this prospect.

Thus, ETS credits could remain only a partial solution to the problem, but be presented as if they were the complete answer. Societies and their governments are likely to have important roles still to play on the issue of global warming.

When is the environment precious?

The perception that nature is simply a resource at our disposal and that the only factor that will shape our usage of, and attitudes towards, it is the exhaustion of these resources is a very specific view. We will explore a counterview to this stance later in the chapter when we consider the ideas and arguments of Martin Heidegger, but for now it is worth reflecting upon a study by Sterman and Sweeney (2002).

The authors conducted a study of American interviewees' understanding of climate change and global warming issues. Their findings were that, while most who took part in the study accepted that the available facts bear out the claims that climate change and global warming are real phenomena, their understanding of the trajectory of the different issues was usually illogical and/or irrational (the researchers' judgement). Coupled with this was a widespread preference on the part of the study's participants for a wait-and-see policy towards implementing environmental protection policies and practices. The arguments of the researchers were that a 'wait-and-see' approach is inadequate and that merely reducing environmental usage, other than a radical step-change, is unacceptable, but that the interviewees would not consider this as an acceptable position. In terms of the questions posed in Activity 9.2 above, the researchers would argue that, with ozone depletion and global warming occurring at such a pace, nothing short of stopping certain actions and practices is required.

Connexion point

The claims of ethical egoism, as discussed in Chapters 3 and 8, are that neo-liberal economics (including free trade, free markets and no government interventions) offers the best prospect for the protection of individual liberties and freedoms and democratic ideals.

Yet, in terms of Activity 9.2, there are, paradoxically, important aspects of a 'business/market-based' solution to GHG emissions and transportation choices that are profoundly undemocratic. Even the intervention of governments by raising fuel taxes by factors of 2, 3, 10, 20, or whatever, but in doing so employing the price mechanism to shape behaviour and achieve a critical environmental policy, suffers the same undemocratic potential.

At one level, by using the price mechanism as a moderator of behaviour, the notion of individual choice is maintained. This, as we have discussed, is the neo-liberal argument regarding the morality of the price mechanism to reflect freedom of choice. However, how democratic is it that only the very wealthy might be able to afford such amenities, and how democratic is it that many, many millions of people may never be able to afford these facilities?

Possibly a more profound question in terms of democratic ideals is, if certain practices and activities are major contributors to ozone depletion and GHG emissions and are thereby harmful to the vast majority of people, possibly even threatening the survival of many species, including *homo sapiens*, why should a few people be allowed to inflict harm upon the vast majority, simply because they are able to use their wealth to exercise their freedom to fly? Is the price mechanism as democratic a tool of resource allocation as it is invariably portrayed?

Redclift (1984, 1987) presented a thoughtful analysis of the tensions and contradictions within the sustainability debates. One of the early statements in his 1987 book asserts, '... the environment, whatever its geographic location, is socially constructed' (1987: 3). What might he have meant by this?

One way to understand this statement is to think of a woodland comprised of ancient trees, glades, brooks, and with special flora and fauna. Today the woodland might be a prized place, maybe designated an SSI (a place of Special Scientific Interest) and consequently protected from exploitation. This is how we see it (socially construct it) today, but that is unlikely to be how it has always been seen by those who have lived by the woodland and in the woodland. At times it might have been seen as a source of social and possibly economic survival. At the social, human existence level, the woodland would have presented wood for building homes and fires, while the animals and bushes would have been the sources of food and sustenance. The notion of a prized place would have been meaningless beyond its relative fruitfulness in terms of hunting, shelter and sustenance. The woodland, and its immediate environs, represented the world as the inhabitants knew it, assuming they had forsaken a nomadic existence. They had neither the time nor the reason to consider the woodland beyond its functionality. If the woodland lacked wildlife it is extremely likely the local people would have held the woodland in low esteem and moved on to more plentiful pastures. A woodland's value would have been determined by its ability to sustain human existence.

At other times the woodland may have been a place of foreboding, a place to be avoided as it could have harboured dangerous and predatory animals and/or people. Highwaymen may have roamed the woodland and trees would have been considered negative elements, providing cover for robbers and brigands. The notion of the woodland as a special place would have been scoffed at and derided. Yet it is the same woodland that we prize today. This is what is meant by the phrase, 'the environment is socially constructed'. In one era the felling of trees (to remove the camouflage that robbers seek) would have been considered desirable and sensible. In another era (today) the felling of many species of trees without special permission is considered a crime and subject to criminal prosecution. With regard to our perceptions of the environment, it is clear that we are once again discussing values, ethics and arguments and not irrefutable and indisputable facts. With regard to issues such as global warming and GHG emissions, while we are discussing (disputed) 'facts', our behaviours and responses to these 'facts' will be reflective of our ethics and our values.

Broadening the concept of sustainability

For many people the concept of sustainability still refers to the effects of human, particularly corporate, activity on the environment. However, for others the concept needs broadening. With social and political systems so intertwined with economic activity, any hope of addressing the exploitation of people and natural resources has to involve corporate and political forces. In addition, whilst national initiatives on environmental and social issues are important, coordinated international initiatives are equally important, even though the refusal of America and Australia to comply with the Kyoto Protocol (and now India, China and Italy refusing to agree on a Kyoto 2) bears testimony to the problems of achieving meaningful progress on environmental issues. However, the important point is that recognition needs to be given to the engagement of large corporations. It is not enough to highlight that corporate activity (often with governmental support or acquiescence) is the principal cause of many environmental and social problems. The active collaboration of the corporate world has to be an important element in any successful set of initiatives that are implemented to address the world's environmental and social problems.

Part of this argument is that for corporations to remain sustainable (the notion of business sustainability is the interesting twist to current debates) they have to operate within socially acceptable parameters, which include how corporations use and treat the environment and people. This is part of what can be called the 'social contract', as discussed in Chapter 8. The UN Global Compact (1999) and the *Gearing Up* (2004) report are also important documents in attempts to shape thinking, debate and action.

To illustrate some of the tensions that can exist between competitive forces delivering lower prices, but only as the result of what some argue are unsustainable practices, we reflect on the challenges being made against the alleged practices of the supermarkets.

Case study 9.1

Low, low prices – but at whose cost?

Tesco has risen from the third most significant food retailer in the UK to the UK's largest retailer (not just food) within a 15-year period. In 2005, for every £8 spent in retail outlets in the UK – on all goods – £1 was spent at Tesco. This is a phenomenal growth record and achievement. Tesco has branched out into clothes and white goods (e.g. fridges and freezers) and other electrical and electronic goods, with good quality goods being sold at prices that customers judge to be excellent value for money. For example, both Tesco and Asda sell good quality jeans for just £3, and a pint of milk cannot be purchased more cheaply than at these stores. However, the low prices of certain goods (not all goods are so 'competitively' priced) come at costs. There are accusations of unethical practices and in some cases illegal practices.

Farmers' unions and allied pressure groups accuse Tesco (and the other large food retailers) of making the farmer carry the burden of the falling price of milk. Tesco is accused of being able to sell milk at the price that it does only because it pressurises the farmer to sell, in some cases, at less than the costs of production.

Tesco has also accepted that quality garden furniture was sold at 'extremely competitive prices', but was made from illegally logged wood from the Indonesian rain forests. In 2003, Friends of the Earth identified that 70 per cent of Tesco's garden furniture was made from illegally logged timber. The Malaysian timber industry has greatly outstripped the supply of suitable Malaysian timber, and highly profitable, but illegal, trafficking in protected Indonesian timber has flourished through Malaysia. However, this was a known phenomenon and having been a signatory to the 95+ Group, which was set up by the World Wildlife Fund (WWF) to protect endangered rain forests, it might have been expected that great care would have been taken by Tesco to ensure that it did not undermine the WWF campaign. A spokesperson for Tesco stated, 'We didn't knowingly buy timber from illegal sources ... We haven't done such a good job of checking where the material is coming from, and the ability to track it isn't up to our usual standards' (*Independent on Sunday*, 13 July 2003). Just how rigorous 'usual standards' are was not explained.

The issue is, that while the consumer is able to enjoy low prices, it is the food producer, or the inhabitants of the rain forests, or the garment maker in a sweatshop somewhere, or the assembly worker on an electrical goods production line where health and safety standards bear little resemblance to western conditions, who is shouldering the price cuts, not the superstores. 'Low' and declining prices can rarely be explained exclusively by economies of scales, or the learning curve effect. Someone, somewhere, along the supply chain is being squeezed hard and invariably it will be the least powerful links in the chain.

Tesco, and the other supermarkets, refute these claims and a continuing 'debate' moves back and forth between the companies and their critics.

Interestingly, Bennett (2005) questions why consumers show considerable concern for dolphin-friendly tuna, inappropriately reared prawns or battery-farmed chickens, but express few such qualms regarding jeans that retail at £3 per pair and are sold at the rate of 50,000 pairs per week from Tesco stores alone. National newspapers, so quick to focus upon unsatisfactory farming and harvesting practices when it comes to fish or poultry, laud the cheap, but high-quality garments now on sale, not just at Tesco or Asda, but at designer outlets such as Hennes and Top Shop (Bennett, 2005: 5). The big clothing retailers argue that they meet local employment and payment conditions and often exceed them, but a quick study of local laws and conditions should raise important questions regarding the acceptability of these rules. For example, the internationally agreed Sweatshop Code requires the following conditions in terms of hours of work to be respected if companies are to claim compliance with the Code.

> Except in extraordinary business circumstances, employees shall (i) not be required to work more than the lesser of (a) 48 hours per week and 12 hours overtime or (b) the limits on regular and overtime hours allowed by the law of the country of manufacture or, where the laws of such country do not limit the hours of work, the regular work week in such country plus 12 hours overtime and (ii) be entitled to at least one day off in every seven-day period.

Thus, depending upon how vigorously the Code is policed and monitored, company owners can require 60 hours per week as long as they claim that the circumstances are 'extraordinary', or local employment law stipulates a lower ceiling. With regard to the latter, it would be interesting to learn how vigorously the large international corporations lobby for greater employee protection legislation in countries such as Guatemala, Indonesia, China, India, El Salvador and Cambodia, compared with, say, corporate-friendly taxation policies or inward investment incentives.

However, it is not just corporations that should be the focus of attention. As indicated above, while the living conditions of poultry and prawns have grabbed the attention of the media and consumers, the living and working conditions of fellow human beings appear to be less/not important. If we wish markets to reflect different values from those that currently prevail, then it is for individual consumers to exercise their voice. This can be expressed via purchasing decisions or political voting and/or through other media, such as radio and television phone-in programmes etc. These issues are not just issues for businesses to address. Individuals have a part, some would say a responsibility, to express their views. It is too easy to pass all the responsibility for curing the ills of the world on to corporate executives, with consumers accepting no responsibility. If the 'C' in CSR relates only to 'corporate' and not 'consumer' then, should corporations who take their broader social and environmental responsibilities seriously suffer consequential cost increases, but consumers retain price as their primary decision criterion, executives have every right to feel double standards at play in the CSR debate. In such situations the 'market' may need help from governments in the form of differential taxation policies with regard to CSR products or organisations. Contrary to market-fundamentalist belief, maybe this is an example where governments could intervene to reward those companies that operate socially and environmentally sensitive practices and policies, or conversely penalise those organisations that do not. On its own the 'market' cannot equalise the product costs of the different corporate approaches. As the Secretary-General of the United Nations stated at the launch of the UN Global Compact in 1999, 'Markets are not embedded in universal human rights'.

Activity 9.4 **£3 jeans – a good buy?**

Having read the above discussion, would you:	*Yes*	*No*	*Maybe*
1. Now think twice before purchasing jeans at very low prices?	☐	☐	☐
2. Wait until you are earning a reasonable wage before being able to be a discriminating consumer? or	☐	☐	☐
3. Not worry about the possible implications of the low prices on the basis that the 'workers' would be worse off without the work?	☐	☐	☐

The issue of consumer responsibility, as distinct from corporate responsibility, is an interesting issue to which we will return. However, for the moment, we will concentrate upon environmental sustainability and its various dimensions.

Environmental sustainability

It might be assumed that concerns at the rate of environmental depletion and contamination are relatively recent, with the levels of social and economic activity of earlier times too limited to have raised concerns over the environmental impacts of human activity. How long ago do you think the following words were written?

> Human beings have been endowed with reason and a creative power so that they can add to what they have been given. But until now they have not been creative, but destructive. Forests are disappearing, rivers are drying up, wildlife is becoming extinct, the climate's being ruined and with every passing day the earth is becoming poorer and uglier.

These are familiar and contemporary concerns, expressed in modern language, but the words were written not five or ten years ago but in 1897 by the Russian dramatist and short-story writer, Anton Chekhov. Does this mean that current concerns over, for example, global warming, deforestation, changes in sea levels and pollution levels are merely a continuation of long-standing worries, and that these concerns underestimate the ability of the environment to absorb and cope with the worst excesses of man?

Even if the answer to the above questions is agreed to be 'No', that is, the depletion of natural resources and evidence of climate change and global warming do pose a threat to political, social and economic structures, the question remains, 'Are these issues really about ethics and morals?' Can we not simply categorise the arguments about pollution levels, climate change and the depletion of natural resources as commonsense? Will not the logic of adverse developments in any or all of these areas force people to behave sensibly, even if only out of enlightened self-interest?

We will take these questions separately, with our responses shown in italics, before returning to the standard font for the general discussion.

Question 1 – Are we over-reacting and over-estimating the extent of environmental degradation and despoliation and their effects?

There are a few voices that argue that most, if not all, of the claims over the effects of environmental degradation and despoliation are misguided and/or exaggerated. An interesting contribution to the debates has been that of the thriller crime writer Michael Crichton, whose book 'State of Fear' (2004) tells a fictional but, it is argued, rigorously researched story of environmental news distortion, exaggeration and manipulation. It reflects most of the arguments, plus new claims, used by the Kyoto dissenting countries. However, the counter-view is supported by a considerable weight of evidence. The latter evidence highlights climate change and global warming and the factors that appear to be triggering these changes, plus the rate of natural resource depletion. All this evidence appears to reflect fundamental and potentially destabilising changes. In view of this, the evidence would argue forcibly for profound changes to our collective and individual behaviours and practices, particularly on behalf of future generations.

From an ethical perspective, a response to the above statement can be justified using both principled (deontological) and consequentialist (utilitarian) arguments.

The principled argument

Natural justice would be the basis for opposition to what many would argue to be unsustainable environmental depletion and pollution linked to the double standards of critical decision-makers. An important factor in this debate is the issue of property rights. We (societies) have created the construct of property rights as a way of managing important parts of our lives. This development has been a significant force in economic development, but it has not been a universal approach. Various groups and societies through time, often but not always nomadic, have seen man and nature's relationship as far more respectful and symbiotic than tends to be the case in many contemporary societies. Nature, in its various forms, has often been represented by gods to be revered and worshipped. Taking from the gods was only possible through compensatory offerings and devotion to rituals.

Irrespective of contemporary religious (and secular) perspectives on nature, the social construct of property rights has located control over natural resources (*see* definition below) in the hands of relatively few people, those with great personal wealth, or those in critical decision-making roles in business or political organisations. A natural justice argument would see this 'arrangement', at least as it involves non-politicians, as undemocratic, not just for those members of contemporary societies that are excluded from important decisions by virtue of the existence of property rights legislation (e.g. because they do not own equity shares in companies), but also members of societies that are denied involvement owing possibly to their age, gender or ethnicity, or maybe because they have yet to be born.

DEFINITION

The term **resource** is a value-laden concept, carrying with it connotations of something to be used. Even the notion of usage is usually considered in terms of economic usage. This is a particular way of 'seeing' nature – as a resource, as something to be exploited. The notion of nature as a resource will be explored in more depth when we consider the work of Martin Heidegger.

Planning laws have been instituted to address some of these concerns, but the power of 'economic logic' in planning decisions is such that governments, both national and local, are often incapable of resisting proposals to exploit natural resources or to build constructions (including large-scale quarrying) that despoil landscapes or localities. The promise of jobs and the associated economic benefits, or the consequences of losing the proposal to other areas, can be powerful reasons for overriding environmental and other planning considerations. Even Deputy Prime Ministers seem to feel the need to instruct planners to 'take developers' business arguments into account' when considering planning applications (Russell, 2005).

The double standards argument

This argues that the people who make these decisions rarely live close to, or are affected by, these decisions. Indeed they invariably live in beautiful areas and fight aggressively and generally effectively to defend 'their' environmental habitats. Their access to political networks and their ability to engage influential legal and other resources make their prospects for defending their environments from exploitation by others far greater than is the norm. A defence of this state of affairs might be that it is a system that is open to all, but this would be a very particular form of democratic logic, because many do not possess the networks or financial resources to employ 'the system' so effectively.

The reason that the above is referred to as a principled argument is that it is an argument that is independent of consequentialist issues. No reference has been made to particular decisions being 'wrong' or 'right' because of the specific ramifications of those decisions. To be a principle-based argument, the case has to be that the decisions and/or the processes by which such decisions are made are inadequate and unjust at the general, societal level.

The consequentialist argument

Opposition to and criticism of current decision-making processes that impact upon sustainability issues that stem from a consequentialist perspective will be as a result of weighing all the ramifications of the decisions in terms of their effects upon various groups. As a result of this calculative approach, the consequentialist perspective is a stance that can be employed to both support and condemn environmental exploitation. Much depends upon how far one draws the boundaries of affected or relevant individuals and groups. Just how far should one allow one's considerations to be stretched before it is agreed that all the relevant parties' interests have been adequately weighed to allow the hypothetical scales of utilitarian justice to show where the balance of the argument lies?

These are often far from easy decisions and decision processes, although utilitarian considerations will often lie at the heart of political and planning decisions. The following case illustrates some of the complexities of such decisions.

Case study 9.2

Removing a mountain on the Isle of Harris

The Isle of Harris lies to the north-west of the Scottish mainland and is part of the Outer Hebrides. It is an island, along with the attached Isle of Lewis, of significant natural and archaeological interest and beauty. It is also of considerable geological interest because, unlike the other islands that form the Inner and Outer Hebrides, it was not once part of the Scottish mainland. It 'drifted' to its current position over millennia, as a result of the movement of tectonic plates. The only other areas of the world displaying similar rock formation and composition are to be found in New Zealand and South Africa.

Shortly before this case study was written, the Scottish Parliament announced that it had turned down an application to allow mining of a mountain area on the Isle of Harris. The economic, social and political dimensions to the case were considerable and it is unlikely that the recent decision by the Scottish Parliament is the last act in this unfolding drama.

The mountain in question lies in the south-east corner of the island and is composed of rock that is both extremely hard (wearing) and has luminous qualities, ideal qualities of aggregates to be used in the construction of roads and motorways. With the mining completed the mountain would have effectively been removed, leaving an enormous cavity in the ground. The hole would cover a very wide area and the belief/fear was/is that it would then be a convenient site for the dumping of much of Scotland's 'undesirable' waste, which could include toxic waste.

One of the authors visited the island in 2004 for a holiday and was impressed with the level of opposition to the proposal by islanders in the north of the island, particularly those who were relatively recent inhabitants of the island. Their opposition was based upon environmental and, to a lesser extent, economic considerations. The latter reflected concerns over the impact upon tourism of the massive quarrying and then dumping operations. However, when he visited the south of the island the reaction of the locals was far more mixed, with possibly a majority of those he met (in a very unscientific study!) in favour of the proposal. Their reasoning? It reflected the locals' concern over the significant haemorrhaging of young islanders to the mainland in search of work (although there was a strong argument that the jobs issue could be handled by other approaches). The islands were becoming the repositories of elderly (usually English) people, seeking peaceful retirements and those seeking an alternative lifestyle to the pressures and demands of modern life. In the words of those who supported the proposal, the island was dying as its young people continued to migrate to the mainland.

The following are some of the difficult questions that demand attention if adopting a utilitarian approach to the ethically appropriate decision for the Isle of Harris.

1. Where does the balance of the consequentialist argument lie?
2. Is a simple calculative approach adequate?
3. Is it simply a case of counting the number of people likely to be affected, both negatively and positively, by the decision, and opting for the decision that affects the larger number of people positively?
4. Or should the decision be based upon the option that affects the smaller number of people negatively?
5. If a higher value is placed upon avoiding harm, then avoiding negatively affecting people will carry a higher (political) weighting, which might result in a different decision from that suggested by 3 above.
6. How much attention and weight should be given to the financial implications of the decision?
7. How does one take into account those people who live elsewhere in Scotland or other parts of the UK, who might be affected by a landfill site being located near their homes if the planning application for the Isle of Harris site is refused?
8. Within a utilitarian stance should the views of the indigenous islanders be weighed more significantly than those of the 'newcomers'?

This is a real case with which the Scottish Parliament has had to wrestle and which it might have to revisit, should an appeal be lodged against the planning rejection.

To conclude this section we highlight the murkiness and business–political intrigue at play on the critical subject of environmental sustainability with reference to an article written by Lord May, who in 2005 was President of the Royal Society and between 1995 and 2000 was the UK government's chief scientific advisor. The following case summarises the article.

Case study 9.3

An insider's view

During the 1990s, parts of the US oil industry funded – through the so-called Global Climate Coalition (GCC) – a lobby of professional sceptics who opposed action to tackle climate change by cutting greenhouse gas emissions. The GCC was 'deactivated' in 2001, once President Bush made it clear he intended to reject the Kyoto Protocol. But the denial lobby is still active , and today it arrives in London.

The UK has become a target because the government has made climate change a focus of its G8 presidency this year [2005]. A key player in this decision is chief scientific advisor Sir David King, who became public enemy number one for the denial lobby when he described climate change as a bigger threat than terrorism.

> In December [2004], a UK-based group, the Scientific Alliance, teamed up with the George C. Marshall Institute, a body headed by the chairman emeritus of the GCC, William O'Keefe, to publish a document with the innocuous title 'Climate Issues & Questions'. It plays up the uncertainties surrounding climate change science, playing down the likely impact that it will have.
>
> It contrasts starkly with the findings of the Intergovernmental Panel on Climate Change (IPCC) ... the world's most reliable source of information on the effects of greenhouse gas emissions.
>
> (*Source*: Lord May, 2005)

Lord May was pointing out that powerful interest groups in the shape of the major US oil corporations were funding organisations that were seeking to undermine the evidence-based arguments of respected scientific bodies such as the IPCC. You might feel that if the claims being made by organisations such as the George C. Marshall Institute are unfounded and spurious then they will be derided. However, one should not trust reason and logic to prevail when such powerful economic interests are at risk.

Later in his article, Lord May expressed concern that major UK daily newspapers were running articles and leaders in 2005 that undermined the evidence-based arguments of the IPCC. Public opinion becomes influenced by such sources. The American tobacco industry denied for decades the causal link between smoking and different forms of cancer. In the mid-1990s all the CEOs of the seven largest tobacco companies testified before a congressional hearing that in their view there was no causal link, despite the fact the tobacco industries' own (private) research revealed the connections. It was only when one of the tobacco industries' own scientists 'blew the whistle' on the suppressed evidence that the tobacco companies accepted the causal relationship. The oil industry cannot suppress the scientific evidence that is published on climate change, so an alternative strategy is to challenge and undermine the evidence and arguments.

In all discussions on environmental sustainability the American perspective is critical. With America accounting for only 4 per cent of the world's population, but with 22.5 per cent of the world's GHG emissions emanating from the United States, gaining the support of the American political establishment is critical. A different way of looking at this situation is that any American president has an incredibly difficult and high-risk task in making environmental issues a major political issue for the American electorate. Some argue that it would be a political suicide note.

Interestingly, the UK Prime Minister, Tony Blair, when he gave the keynote speech at the opening of the World Economic Forum at Davos, Switzerland, on 26 January 2005, softened his own commitment to making climate change issues his primary challenge, when he asserted that climate change was 'not universally accepted'. Elliot (2005) observed, 'with chief executives of many US firms in the audience, [Blair] said, "the evidence is still disputed"'. Mr Blair went on to state that no significant adjustments to business behaviour towards the environment can be expected if such adjustments threaten economic growth. This may or may not be a realistic assessment of the economic and political power positions (the so-called *realpolitik*), but the assertion is as much puzzling as it is concerning, because it ignores both the morality and the physical consequences of a 'do-nothing' attitude to environmental despoliation and degradation, whether from a principled or consequentialist perspective.

Question 2 – What are the implications of relying exclusively upon enlightened/rational self-interest to drive sustainable corporate behaviour and practices?

There has been a variety of evidence available over many years that has highlighted the unsustainability of the rate of environmental depletion and waste across the globe. However, to date, this evidence and official responses have had limited impact upon our practices. For example, in the early 1990s and in response to concerns over carbon dioxide emissions, the Intergovernmental Panel on Climate Change called for carbon dioxide emissions to be 50 per cent lower by 2050 than their 1990 levels. Given the likely increase in global economic activity between 1990 and 2050, such a reduction represents a significant change in consumption and will not be achieved without new technologies and practices, as well as possible revisions to economic growth assumptions. Yet between 1990 and 2004 carbon dioxide emissions actually rose by 8.9 per cent! The implications of these (in)actions and behaviours are likely to affect all members of the human race to some extent, but possibly most significantly, those yet to be born. Thus, a decision based exclusively upon rational self-interest fails to address the wider significance of individual choices and decisions. Whilst our actions and behaviours affect others, they have ethical import.

The assumptions regarding economic growth rates contained within the calculations regarding carbon dioxide emissions do reflect an economic mind-set that now goes almost unchallenged. Whilst writers such as Dickson (1974), Sawyer (1978) and Schell (1982) presented arguments that challenged the wisdom and sustainability of economic growth assumptions in the 1970s and 1980s, these arguments are far less frequently discussed today, even though the economic growth assumptions have been outstripped – such is the dominance of economic imperatives and their relationships with political objectives. The notion of short-termism in decision making, whether it be related to political or economic decisions (and often they are linked), is a central issue within these debates and can be said to reflect an ethical egoist perspective, as discussed below.

Activity 9.5 **Putting yourself in the shoes of 'others'**

The refusal to recognise the evidence that exists regarding environmental degradation and depletion represents an act with ethical significance. A decision to do nothing is still a decision. What will be the consequences of maintaining existing rates of resource consumption and thus depletion by 2105? If you were to be living in 2105, what do you think would be your attitude towards those living in 2005 who refused/failed to curb their consumption of finite natural resources and/or did little to address global warming and climate change issues?

Ethical egoism (sometimes referred to as possessive egoism), with its reliance upon market signals to reflect social preferences would, at best, appear to require an ambivalent stance towards environmental issues.

Ethical egoism and sustainability

From an ethical egoist perspective, market-based forms of coordination of economic and social activity are argued to be at the bedrock of basic freedoms. The more all facets of human interaction can be coordinated by market dynamics, the more the resulting outcomes will reflect the independent, 'free' choices of all participants. As we discussed in Chapter 3, this argument has certain strengths, but it also ignores important structural issues which challenge its integrity (principled-based objection) and efficacy (utilitarian-based objection).

Allowing markets to be the dominant forms for allowing societal preferences and choices to become known assumes that prices contain all relevant information and markets are not unduly skewed owing to power imbalances. Yet, as suggested in the Isle of Harris case, there might be certain situations where the opinions and arguments of particular groups might justify higher weightings than other groups in a decision-making process. If it was left to simple market dynamics to reflect these different weightings, then it is likely that the economically powerful would secure the largest weightings, possibly usurping those with higher, principle-based claims to justice, or deservingness.

As mentioned already in this chapter, the voice of the yet to be born is a complex one to include in such debates, but it is almost impossible to envisage how the price mechanism would incorporate the views of future generations, other than perhaps taxes levied by governments on behalf of future generations, to pay for 'clean-ups' or detoxifying processes, reclamation, compensation payments, etc. However, if the voice of future generations was truly able to be heard, it could be that they would be at one in rejecting the decision in its entirety, thus obviating the need for compensation payments or other such contingency plans. Designating areas of special scientific interest is one way of protecting certain parts of the environment for current and future generations, but these designations are vulnerable to powerful interests and can be overridden. One such example is the opening up of a previously protected region of the Arctic Circle in Alaska for oil drilling, as evidenced in Table 8.1 in the previous chapter.

In the context of environmental protection it would seem that market signals have limited application, an example of what can be called 'market failure', making the intervention of governments essential as the representatives of the people and their adjudicators. However, governments' interventions in economic and social affairs are anathema to market fundamentalists, with any exceptions to this principle seen as the start of a very slippery slope. For those with more acceptance of political intervention in such situations, their concerns are with the corruptibility of political processes. The latter are seen as too susceptible to the influence of powerful individuals and corporations.

Connexion point

Refer back to Table 8.1 to refresh your memory on the political donations made to the Republican Party during the US Presidential elections of 2000 and the resulting changes to the law that immediately followed President Bush's inauguration.

A different perspective on environmental issues

If you refer back to Chapter 1, three of the theories of the firm, *Classical liberal economic, Pluralist (A and B)* and *Corporatist*, each locate the business corporation within a capitalist-driven, market-based economy. Each perspective accepts the need for corporations to legitimately seek out new ways to generate profits on behalf of shareholders, but with other interest groups (employees, customers and suppliers) benefiting in differing ways as a result of these corporate activities. Within these perspectives, nature, in all its various forms, is seen as a resource, at the behest of society in general, and corporations in particular, to be employed in whatever ways are deemed socially and legally permissible to facilitate economic activity.

Before these issues are discussed in more detail, we would like you to take a few minutes to undertake the following task.

Activity 9.6 Subjects and objects

Try to identify a place or an object that has a special significance for you. The place or object might be very commonplace (e.g. a ring, an ornament, a book, a photograph) or it might be a little unusual, a location for example. Whatever it is, for you it is special. If you cannot identify such a place or object, try to identify a place or object that you know to be special to someone else, your mother or father perhaps, or your brother or sister. If you were then asked to place a value on that place or object, how might you express that value as a number, a monetary value?

Prior to Activity 9.6, the perspective that has so far underpinned our discussions in this chapter has been that of a clear distinction between ourselves (subjects) and the world of objects that surround us. We have assumed that we are separate from nature and nature is separate from us. We possess the technologies to control, manipulate and direct nature, and we possess the capabilities, and some would argue the right, to do with nature as we see fit. The law of property rights underpins this belief. Landowners can prohibit access to their lands because laws have been passed that allow such prohibitions. Countries fight over, or at least contest, ownership of areas of land and sea (the Arctic and Antarctic regions for example) because of their mineral deposits and other valued resources. Even the moon is subject to property rights' claims for its mineral deposits. Currently companies are seeking to decode human DNA so that they can patent and thus 'own' the codes. The ability of humanity to benefit from such 'code-breaking' research will then be subject to commercial exploitation of these medical understandings. At one level this is no different from the patent rights and copyright constraints existing in many areas of organisational activity, but deeper philosophical issues can be argued to be at play when one considers knowledge breakthroughs that can possibly alleviate great human suffering, e.g. in the areas of genetically inherited diseases and disabilities.

Practically everything you see around you, can touch, or what you are wearing, represents some form of intervention of human activity on nature. This is not to say that these interventions have been/are bad or wrong. The question is, how do we view nature and, equally importantly, how do we view ourselves with respect to nature?

Martin Heidegger (1959, translation 2000) is the person who is most identified with the perspective we are about to discuss. It is known as Phenomenology.

DEFINITION

Phenomenology is the belief that the world around us can only be understood through our lived experiences. The world does not exist beyond those experiences. We impose understandings and interpretations on that world, or worlds, based upon the values, perspectives and beliefs we hold. The relationship between ourselves and nature is a symbiotic one (i.e. mutually dependent) and not one of independence. This perspective has a strong resonance with the discussion earlier in the chapter concerning the way a woodland might be perceived through time.

Whilst Heidegger was not the first to challenge the notion that subjects and objects are distinct and separate entities, his analysis was more radical than those who had come before him, for example, Edmund Husserl (1931, 1965), who was Heidegger's teacher. Heidegger died in 1976, so by the standards of notable philosophers his arguments are quite new.

As the definition above indicates, Heidegger's principal argument was that we cannot understand nature other than how we experience it. Nature does not exist beyond our experiences of it. Those experiences might have come to us via first-hand knowledge, or stories, accounts, films, newspapers, books, the Internet, conversations, whatever. When we look at something or hear something, what we see and hear is filtered through our mental faculties, which in turn process information and understanding through many subtle processes including emotions, memories, existing values, beliefs and understandings – essentially our experiences. For example, when we look at something, say an NHS hospital, what do we see? Some would simply say that they see a place where those who are unwell or injured are taken in order to receive treatment. Others might see the building as representing a symbol of a civilised society that has created facilities to tend to the sick or the injured, irrespective of their ability to pay for their treatment. Others might see the building as representing a bundle of resources, which are outstripped by demand for its services. From the latter perspective, the hospital is a cauldron of ethical dilemmas in terms of the choices over which treatments to prioritise and which to de-prioritise.

The same object can represent different visions to different people. Think back to Acitivity 9.6. Why was the place or object you selected special? The answer will be related to the place or object's history. It is likely to hold memories that are important to you. The place or object keeps you in touch with something or someone you want to hold on to. History and context are central to this debate. Were you able to place a monetary value upon your object or place? For some, the importance of the object or the place will be incalculable because of the memories it reveals, what it represents.

Whilst the argument that different people will have different views about the importance of places and objects is reasonably uncontentious, you might ask, 'Are we moving towards a position that simply admits that all we are likely to agree upon is that we are likely to disagree upon the values we are prepared to place upon various objects?' If so, how is this going to help individuals and corporations make choices over the use of natural resources, whether they be tropical rain forests, a local park, playing field, a set of allotments or the survival of a threatened species of animal? Heidegger does not offer a magic formula, but he does offer a way of thinking, a way of seeing, that could prove helpful.

Heidegger's concern was with what he described as the 'enframing of technology', or what we might call a technology mentality, i.e. the seeing of nature as purely instrumental, as simply a means to an end. If nature represents merely the opportunity to make money, if that is all nature means to us, then, from a Heideggerian perspective, society has become emotionally and spiritually bankrupt.

DEFINITION

If an object is viewed in purely **instrumental** terms then it possesses no worth beyond its functional use, that is, what might be obtained for it by either selling it as it is or converting it into another form of tradable object. It is purely a means to an end. The end in this case is to make money, although this is not the only 'end' that can be considered.

Heidegger was not anti-technology. He recognised the contributions that technological advancements had made, and continue to make, to people's lives. Improvements in sanitation, health care, education, etc. can be seen as benefiting either directly or indirectly from technology. In Heidegger's view, we have a symbiotic relationship with nature, i.e. the relationship between humans and nature is one of mutual dependency. As we exploit nature, we cannot avoid, to a greater or lesser extent, having an impact upon ourselves. In this context 'ourselves' is used in a very broad sense, reflecting impacts not necessarily upon our own generation, but those that are yet to come.

The treatment of nature in purely instrumental ways is not limited to profit seeking organisations. Neither is the 'enframing of technology' limited to capitalist systems. Examples of the destruction of the environment in the name of 'progress' can be seen in many different political and economic contexts. However, in an economic system in which:

(a) the *raison d'être* (the reason for being) of business enterprises is to maximise profits on behalf of shareholders, and

(b) the nature of competitive capitalism is that a company incurring additional costs by way of laudable, but not legally required, pollution controls that result in its being put at a cost and price disadvantage to its competitors is likely to fail,

the question has to be asked, 'How is it possible for corporations to view nature in anything other than an instrumental fashion'? In addition, if we cannot expect everyone to value the same objects that we regard as important as highly as ourselves, and vice versa:

- How can a corporation place a value upon any object, other than in terms of its instrumental worth to the corporation?
- How can objects have meaning to a corporation beyond their functional or instrumental worth?
- Where is a corporation's memory that might allow it to attach feelings to objects that transcend their instrumental worth?
- What is the market value of the site of the Parthenon of ancient Greece to a property developer or, for a mining company, a spectacular ravine in a site of special scientific interest that contains valuable mineral deposits?

A moment of reflection

We are approaching a possibly critical point in our consideration of sustainability, corporate social responsibility and corporate citizenship, certainly in terms of Heidegger's view of a 'technology mentality'. Asking where a corporation's memory might lie, or whether a corporation can possess feelings towards objects, is attributing human characteristics to business enterprises that many would regard as simply unrealistic, as silly. The technical term is reification, that is, giving concrete (human) form to an abstract idea (a corporation). When we use the term 'corporation' in the sense being discussed here, we are referring to the senior decision-makers. A corporation's 'memory' will reside with individuals, or possibly in the form of company stories and myths. The use of 'corporation' is in fact a form of shorthand.

If corporations can only ever view objects in instrumental ways, then society cannot expect corporations to value and to treat nature in ways that it (society) might wish or demand. To repeat, this is not to suggest that all members of society will hold the same views on particular aspects of nature, but at least a debate can ensue between interested parties about the various merits of different choices under debate. And the debate will embrace many value systems that go beyond instrumentality.

Following Heidegger, the fundamental objection is that corporations *cannot* fully act in socially responsible ways because they possess a perspective on nature that is extremely limited. A societal perspective on nature that is compatible with a Heideggerian perspective is denied to a corporation, as long as corporations are constituted in their current form. Corporations cannot be citizens because their value systems are highly constrained and unable to handle concepts of value beyond instrumentality. A corporation's perspective is 'enframed by technology'. However, this does not dismiss corporations as irrelevancies to modern life. Clearly, business, in its many forms, is fundamental to the way we live. In many respects it is the dominant force in modern societies. The central issue concerns the relationship between corporations and society, but is citizenship a realistic or appropriate concept in this debate? Welford (1995), when discussing issues of sustainable development, referred to this issue when, in the six areas that are argued to require shifts of thinking, he stated that a key transformation is the move from 'objects to relationships'.

Thinking about the Self and Others

Central to any debate concerning objects and subjects is the notion of the Self. We have referred to ethical egoism on a number of occasions in this chapter, with an example of its manifestation reflected in the previous chapter in Table 8.2 on page 303. This table contrasted the remuneration of executive directors of FTSE 100 between January 2000 and December 2002 (up 84 per cent), with the movement in the FTSE 100 index (down 40 per cent). It is intriguing how the behaviour of corporate executives, in relation to their own remuneration, or the ownership of many, many gas-guzzling motor cars by certain wealthy individuals, is sometimes accepted on the basis that, 'Well, I would do the same in their shoes'! Why is there this apparent acceptance of such behaviour and the belittling of one's own ethics? It might have something to do with the promulgation of the Self as a self-serving, myopic, selfish individual as exemplified in agency theory and ethical egoism.

DEFINITION

Agency theory, as used here, refers to the division of ownership and control of corporations, with shareholders the principals and management their agents. With human behaviour assumed to be essentially self-seeking and self-focused and management 'enjoying' a privileged control of information over shareholders, this control is assumed to manifest itself in sub-optimum decision making (from the shareholders' perspective), as reflected in Table 8.2.

This view of human nature was argued for by Thomas Hobbes and David Hume among others. Both were eminent philosophers, but their position on this issue is an argument, not a fact, and it is up to us, individually and collectively, to decide where we stand on this issue. If we are to see as 'natural' a regard for the Self as the primary, maybe sole, driver for determining our collective attitudes towards sustainability, who speaks for those who cannot speak, the dispossessed, the unborn? These tensions are explicitly addressed in the following statement taken from the Sustainability Strategy and Action Plan 2000–2005 of the UK's second largest city, Birmingham. A local authority, like Birmingham City Council, has an immensely difficult task to develop a sustainability strategy or, more accurately, a series of sustainability strategies that cohere and are mutually supportive and sustaining. The statement from which the following extract is taken is headed 'The Challenge'.

> A Sustainability Strategy for the City Council could be huge, involving almost every policy and strategy of every department. Clearly this would be undesirably unwieldy. Suffice it to say that Community Safety and Nature Conservation Strategies, policies on Disability, Employment, Equalities and the City's commitment to lifelong learning are a fraction of the existing policies, strategies and actions which are relevant to our drive towards sustainability (p. 3).

Having hinted at the complexity of the task facing the City Council, the 'challenge' is then articulated.

> **The Challenge**
> Delivering sustainability for a large Metropolitan city in the developed world is not an easy or comfortable matter. It is about making choices about the distribution of benefits between generations, and denying people benefits now, for the yet unborn. Such decisions will never be universally popular. There will always be special reasons for not taking the sustainability route. Indeed tensions will sometimes even exist between alternative sustainability options. Facing up to this dilemma is one of the biggest challenges the Council needs to address.
>
> (Sustainability Strategy and Action Plan 2000–2005, Birmingham City Council, p. 4)

Birmingham City Council cite the Brundtland Commission's definition of sustainability (which was shown at the start of this chapter) to define what they mean by sustainability. An interesting definition of sustainable communities and one that offers an insight into the complexity of the notion of sustainable communities is reflected in the UK Government's Sustainable Communities' initiative.

Sustainable communities DEFINITION

Places where people want to live and work, now and in the future. They meet the diverse needs of existing and future residents, are sensitive to their environment, and contribute to a high quality of life. They are safe and inclusive, well planned, built and run, and offer equality of opportunity and good services for all.

The above reflects the challenges that a sustainability commitment involves, but the philosophical position of the ethical egoist position is a powerful one in modern western societies and it is important that we study the issues in more depth. The discussion which follows explores the issues through the lens provided by Adam Smith, who is sometimes referred to as the father of market-based capitalism.

Smith lived during the eighteenth century and was an acquaintance of David Hume. Smith was a prominent Scottish academic who applied his intellect to a number of fields, but he is most notably remembered for his seminal work, the title of which is usually shortened to *The Wealth of Nations*. This treatise argues for the primacy of market-based capitalism to be the basis for social and economic coordination. However, while markets were his principal means of releasing the individual from the demands of kings, governments and religious interference, Smith's advocacy was conditional and dependent on two central elements, that of *competitive* market-based capitalism and *constrained self-love*.

Smith is referred to as a 'classical economist', which means that he considered economic issues from a broader, more socially inclusive perspective than is allowed or recognised in neo-classical economics. In 1751 and at the age of 28, Smith was appointed to the Chair of Logic at Glasgow University. One year later he was appointed to the Chair of Moral Philosophy. It was from the perspective of a Professor of Moral Philosophy that Smith wrote his two seminal treatises. *The Wealth of Nations* has already been referred to, but the second major treatise to flow from Smith's pen was *The Theory of Moral Sentiments*. The importance of this is that, within *The Wealth of Nations*, Smith did not elaborate on his notion of self-love. However, the concept is explored by Smith in *The Theory of Moral Sentiments*, which was first published in 1759, sixteen years before *The Wealth of Nations* was first published, while the final edition of *The Theory of Moral Sentiments* was published in 1790, the year of Smith's death. Thus, it can be seen that the notion of self-love would have developed as a result of Smith's work on his two famous treatises over a period of some forty years. *The Theory of Moral Sentiments* allows us to understand that Smith's conception of self-love was not the distorted version that travels today under the banner of selfishness, nor as it appears to have become corrupted by certain writers, e.g. Levitt (1956), who argued,

> What is important is that the pursuit of Self-interest has become institutionalized ... this is of the greatest importance for the future of capitalism.
>
> (Levitt, 1956: 109)

As indicated above, although Smith placed competition at the centre of his economic thought, he did not leave his economic ideal to the mercy of rapacious individuals or groups, or imperfections in market conditions. Smith sympathised with Platonic and Aristotelian notions of self-control as a core human virtue in its own right, but his commitment to the importance of self-control within his economic theorising might be argued to be as much prosaic as principled. Self-control was attributed a key position within his economic schema to buttress situations where economic equilibrium would be less than perfect. Self-control was not argued to be regretted, but rather a necessary constraint on human action. Self-control was recognised in respect of freedoms, but not just those of the Self. In sympathy with Aristotelian arguments, the perception of Others was also important.

Smith's recognition of Others was more than a recognition of the plight of others out of a sense of pity. Smith used the term 'sympathy', with this describing a notion of empathy, a 'fellow-feeling'. The opening sentence of *The Theory of Moral Sentiments* reads as follows:

> How selfish soever man may be supposed, there are evidently some principles in his nature, which interest him in the fortunes of others, and render their happiness necessary to him, though he derives nothing from it, except the pleasure of seeing it.
>
> (Smith, 2000: I, 3)

The recognition of Others and their interests, whilst not equating to altruism, leads to Smith's important mechanism for operationalising his conception of self-control. The notion of fellow-feeling has been termed 'imaginative sympathy' (Wilson and Skinner, 1976), allowing an understanding to be developed of the position of other people by trying to view our own conduct through their eyes. As Wilson observed,

> To use Smith's own imagery, we learn to observe our own behaviour as it might be seen by an imaginary spectator who is at once impartial and well-informed with regard to our motives.
>
> (Wilson, 1976: 74)

Smith used the idea of a 'stranger' or 'spectator' to convey the imagery of an independent arbiter, unfettered by bias and preconceptions.

> The constancy or equality of temper which is more valuable for Smith than virtues like humanity, generosity etc., is obtained through a society where everyone has continuously tried to moderate his emotions ... everyone is accustomed to think how Others will judge his action and passion and to act accordingly ... and ... it must be repeated that Self-control in Smith cannot be established without the judgement of strangers.
>
> (Skinner and Wilson, 1975: 122)

In a footnote Skinner and Wilson add,

> The stranger is not a friend from whom we can expect any special favour and sympathy. But at the same time he is not an enemy from whom we cannot expect any sympathy at all. Everyone in society is as independent of every other stranger, and is equal with every other as they can exchange the situations. The famous impartial stranger is no one else but the spectator who is indifferent to, and does not take the part of either side.
>
> (Skinner and Wilson, 1975: 122)

Smith argued that man is keen to obtain the respect of Others, but, because this is insufficient to ensure appropriate behaviour, he also argued that man is subject to two forms of jurisdiction, that of conscience (the man within) and that of the 'spectator' (the man without) (Smith, 1776/1982: 20/1).

The above represents a portrayal of Smith's notions of the Self that runs counter to the *a priori* assumptions of man as self-serving, atomised egoist for whom self-love equates with selfishness, traits that are to be found at the root of ethical egoism and agency theory. However, the atomisation of the individual, so dominant in neo-classical economics, is also observable in other disciplines. In political science the elevation of the Self as consumer, but with little other political relevance, was commented upon by Nisbet over fifty years ago.

> The politics of enslavement of man requires the emancipation of man from all the authorities and memberships ... that serve, one degree or another, to insulate the individual from the external political power ... totalitarian domination of the individual will is not a mysterious process, not a form of sorcery based upon some vast and unknowable irrationalism. It arises and proceeds rationally and relentlessly through the creation of new functions, statuses and allegiances which, by conferring community, makes the manipulation of the human will scarcely more than an exercise in scientific, social psychology ... there may be left the appearance of individual freedom, provided it is only individual freedom. All of this is unimportant, always subject to guidance and control, if the primary social contexts of belief and opinion are properly organized and managed. What is central is the creation of a network of functions and loyalties reaching down into the most intimate recesses of human life where ideas and beliefs will germinate and develop.
>
> (Nisbet, 1953: 202, 208)

Sarason (1986) echoed Nisbet's concerns. The following paraphrases Sarason, setting his argument at the general level of concern about modern conceptions of individualism.

> If *your* ethical dilemma is *your* responsibility according to *my* morality, this is quite consistent with the increasingly dominant ideology of individual rights, responsibility, choice and freedom. If *I* experience the issues as *yours*, it is because there is nothing in my existence to make it *ours*. And by *ours I* mean a social-cultural network and traditions which engender in members an obligation to be part of the problem and possible solution.

One line of thinking has been that the primacy of the Self has been reinforced by the attention given in psychology, and more particularly psychoanalysis, to patients being directed to 'look within' and to see solutions to their personal problems taking the form of much greater attention to the Self – to be far more self-aware and self-actualising. Goodwin (1974: 75), cited in Wallach and Wallach (1983), observed,

> The ideology of individualism is so powerful that we ... look on bonds as restraints; values as opinions and prejudices; customs as impositions.
>
> (Goodwin, 1974: 75)

Within this conception the Self is seen as a fully autonomous unit that should be responsible to no authority in the forming of its relationships beyond the exercise of its own volition – what it voluntarily wills and wishes to do. The social arrangements remaining that permit a sense of community or shared social purpose 'are assaulted as unjust restraints on liberty, impediments to the free assertion of the self' (Goodwin, 1974: 75). The proper mode of living is to be oneself – to find out who one is and to let no one and nothing interfere with one's self-realisation. This is ethical egoism in its raw form.

Challenging psychoanalysis's focus upon the Self, to the exclusion of broader social relationships and behaviours, Wallach and Wallach (1983) asserted,

> If, ... human beings can be motivated towards ends quite other than themselves, and it is in fact better for them when this is the case, then perhaps the usual lines of therapeutic advice might well be redirected. The problems and troubles that lead people to seek psychotherapy may derive less than is commonly supposed from not expressing themselves, fulfilling themselves, or satisfying needs directed toward themselves and more from not having a workable way of living in which they participate in and contribute to matters they care about beyond themselves.
>
> (Wallach and Wallach, 1983: 274)

Maybe we need to think more carefully before accepting the arguments of agency theory and ethical egoism that human beings are by nature self-serving, possessively egoistic, with little other consideration than their own well-being. As in psychoanalysis, we need to think afresh about both the empirical and philosophical justification of this position. The assumptions concerning human behaviour explicit within agency theory and ethical egoism to explain the behaviour of senior corporate executives might simply be philosophical camouflage to mask the greed of those in privileged and powerful positions.

Smith was not blind to the risks of competitive capitalism, hence his advocacy of self-control, a virtue that appears to be in very short supply in many corporate board rooms (as evidenced by Table 8.2). What might be the issue is that too many corporate executives lack a fundamental quality of Smith's advocacy of competitive market-based capitalism. Do contemporary corporate executives (as well as politicians) possess the requisite qualities and values that issues, developments and challenges such as the GHG emissions, the power of large corporations, global poverty, and the exploitation of weak and corrupt governments, require?

Is it all doom and gloom?

There is much within modern experiences to make the heart heavy with concern, but it would clearly be a fundamental mistake to imply that all corporate executives are greedy individuals with no care for the environment, or that corporate activity is exclusively negative, both socially and environmentally. Although one or two examples of impressive individual and/or corporate activity 'do not a summer make', it is important to be aware of the excellent initiatives that are under way at the local and individual (including corporate) level to address sustainability issues, and which in some cases have been established for some time. The following are some examples of organisations that are working with corporations to develop more sustainable processes, practices, attitudes and beliefs. The last two elements are possibly the most important because without them changes to processes and practices are likely to be short-lived and/or poorly implemented and operationalised.

Case study 9.4

Capital *One*

In the corporate sector the company Capital *One* is a large credit card organisation. It has a 'corporate responsibility' team of four full-time employees, headed by a 'Corporate Social Responsibility Manager'. The initiative to establish the team came from the main board and replicates its American parent company's belief in corporate responsibility. A 'corporate responsibility' commitment was not the result of the company receiving bad publicity and feeling the need to be 'seen to be doing something'. At one level it might be argued that all the company is displaying is a form of enlightened self-interest, in that by performing good deeds it wishes to attract employment applications from high-quality people who wish to work for such an organisation. The company does not dispute that it hopes to attract 'better' applicants for posts at the company, but the primary stimulus is the belief of the senior management that 'this is the way companies should behave'. The company does not publicise many of the projects in which it becomes involved, the reason being that it does not wish to be accused of merely undertaking the projects to obtain the favourable publicity. It is something of a Catch 22 situation, with the company potentially damned if it does and damned if it doesn't.

An example of one of the projects with which it has been involved relates to the collaboration between the company's programming team and Nottinghamshire Police Force. Following the murder of two young girls in Soham, UK, the Nottinghamshire Police Force wished to create a database of all known paedophiles; however, they lacked the expertise to do this. The programming team of Capital *One*, over a period of some months, developed the database, which has now been adopted by other police forces in the UK. Initially the company kept its involvement in the project low-key. It was only when the system was rolled out to a number of other police forces that it publicly acknowledged its collaboration.

Case study 9.5

The Citizen Group

The Citizen Group is an interesting organisation, noted for its watches and other timepieces. The reason for featuring the corporation is not so much for any specific 'good deeds', but rather the company's broader commitment to notions of corporate citizenship. The President of the company heads the 'Citizen CSR Committee', which was instituted in October 2003. The company has developed a 'Citizen Code of Conduct' that speaks to the corporation's values and ethics. The code has eight commitments, with commitments 1–4 concerned with, respectively, products and services; open competition; corporate information; and a respectful environmental policy. These are laudable and hopefully reasonably standard commitments. For our purposes, in terms of corporations that appear to be moving beyond specific but localised CSR initiatives, the Citizen Group displays in commitments 5–8 an articulation of a corporation that does appear to be 'walking the talk' of corporate citizenship (the name of the corporation being highly apposite).

No.	Commitment
5	Value symbiosis with the regional society as a good corporate citizen, and strive to make a social contribution.
6	Ensure a safe and good work environment, encourage the development of our employees' abilities and energies while respecting their character and individuality.
7	Respond to anti-social and corruptive behaviour in a decisive manner.
8	Value and respect different cultures and customs in foreign countries and contribute to the development of the locale.

In an extract from the company's 2004 'Environmental and Social Report' (p. 26), the following statements appear.

> In my view [Chair of the CSR Committee] CSR initiatives are an integral part of our business activities. It's not something new that we have to begin. Rather, the way I see it, what we need to do is have a fresh look at our business activities in the context of our relationships with the various stakeholders who support Citizen, and ask anew how we can put this new CSR approach into our business activities ... last year when other companies in Japan suffered from various corporate scandals, I felt that Citizen's culture served us well as a precious asset to help us avoid such problems. Now that Citizen has announced CSR as an important pillar of management, I would like to do my best to help preserve our corporate culture, robustness, honesty and openness.

Case study 9.6

The 'DEEP' fish restaurant chain

A fish restaurant chain was established in 2005, trading under the name 'DEEP'. The menu in the restaurants is limited to only those fish that are *not* 'at risk'. So you will not find Atlantic cod, haddock, blue fin tuna, monkfish or halibut on the menu. Instead there are herring, mackerel and pollack, and others whose stocks are not endangered. The restaurant chain is committed to serving only fish that are taken from the sea within a sustainable fishing policy. Interestingly, fish farms, because of health and safety concerns, as well as the practice of feeding fish sprats to the salmon in the form of food pellets, are not regarded as an appropriate source. In addition, the restaurant chain makes an explicit statement that £1 is added to every bill, which will be used as a donation to a named pressure group that is lobbying for sustainable fishing policies throughout the world.

These are encouraging developments from the corporate world. Moving to the non-profit seeking organisation, a number of interesting developments can be cited, of which the following are but illustrative.

Case study 9.7

The Natural Step Organisation

The Natural Step Organisation was founded in 1989 by Dr Karl-Henrik Robèrt, who at the time was a leading Swedish oncologist (cancer specialist). Dr Robèrt had become concerned about a significant increase in childhood leukaemia cases in particular parts of Sweden, and traced the cause to increasing toxins in the environment. These appeared to have been the result of particular production processes. Dr Robèrt's concern at the production methods used to manufacture so many goods led him to found The Natural Step Organisation to address the systemic causes of environmental problems. Society's apparent preferencing of commercial activity has echoes of Heidegger's 'enframing of technology' or 'technology mindset'.

With the help of fifty Swedish scientists, Dr Robèrt developed a consensus document that described the basic knowledge of the earth's functions and how humans interact with it. The organisation's website tells how the document went through 21 iterations and upon completion was sent to every household and school in Sweden.

In the early 1990s, Dr Robèrt worked with physicist, John Holmberg, to define a set of guiding principles for a sustainable society that are based on the laws of thermodynamics and natural cycles. These principles of sustainability are the foundation of The Natural Step's content and approach. The organisation now has centres in many countries, with its American operations having been established in 1995. The Natural Step Organisation works with corporations and governments in developing sustainable programmes of industrial and commercial activity, but that is not to say that its four guiding principles are easily absorbed within many corporate practices. Changes are required.

Case study 9.8

The Sustainability Institute

The Sustainability Institute was founded in 1996 and possesses an interesting statement of its philosophy.

> Unsustainability does not arise out of ignorance, irrationality or greed. It is largely the collective consequence of rational, well-intended decisions made by people caught-up in systems – ranging from families and communities to corporations, governments and economies – that make it difficult or impossible to act in ways that are fully responsible to all those affected in the present and future generations.
>
> (http://www.sustainabilityinstitute.org)

Once again the issue of an 'enframing technology' mind-set underpins the perspective. We are dealing with, in many respects, a need to change people's assumptions about what is possible and acceptable in terms of sustainable systems, communities, economies and societies. However, it must be stressed that what sustainable futures will look like is up to people, individually and collectively, to negotiate, debate and work towards. The mission statement of The Sustainability Institute adopts just this line of reasoning. It possesses three elements, namely:

- to shift mind-sets – values, attitudes and beliefs – when they are out of step with the realities of a finite planet and a globally dominant human race;
- to restructure systems when the rewards and incentives of the system are inconsistent with long-term social, environmental and economic goals; and
- to build the capability to manage and learn in complex, environmental, social and economic systems.

Case study 9.9

The Sustainable Business Institute

The Sustainable Business Institute (SBI) is another organisation that seeks to work with corporations to address the challenges of sustainable economic, social and environmental systems.

The SBI was founded in 1994 and aims to educate senior executives about 'what is sustainability' and how sustainable practices are working effectively across industries. In sympathy with the Global Compact's approach of disseminating good practice, the SBI places considerable emphasis upon using workshops, forums and the media, particularly television programmes, to spread its ideas and approaches among senior executives.

Case study 9.10

The International Institute for Sustainable Development

The International Institute for Sustainable Development (IISD) was established in 1990 and aims to contribute to sustainable development by advancing policy recommendations in a number of areas, *viz.*

- international trade and investment,
- economic policy,
- climate change,
- measurement and indicators, and
- natural resource management.

By using Internet communications the IISD aims to report on international negotiations and broker knowledge gained through collaborative projects with global partners, resulting in more rigorous research, capacity building in developing countries and better dialogue between North and South.

Case study 9.11

The Institute for Market Transformation to Sustainability

The Institute for Market Transformation to Sustainability (MTS) is another organisation with a commitment to exploring, identifying and supporting sustainable economic activity. However, this organisation is much more upbeat and bullish about the power of markets to be the force in activating change, albeit with an initial helping hand. Its website includes the following statement.

> MTS brings together a powerful coalition of sustainable products manufacturers, environmental groups, and key state and local government leaders using market mechanisms [to] increase sales and market share of sustainable products. We have identified consensus protocols for sustainable products such as FSC Certified Wood, Certified Organic Products, and the Clean Car Standard. When such a consensus is reached, the next steps are to increase awareness and sales of these products until profit motives and other marketplace incentives kick in and drive the transformation. Awareness and sales are manageable steps. ... Because the 100 largest companies account for more than 90% of the world's products, our mission is attainable. All companies want to increase their profits while contributing to an unpolluted, safer environment, and improved public welfare. ... Sustainable products increase corporate profits while enhancing society as a whole, because they are cheaper to make, have fewer regulatory constraints, less liability, can be introduced to the market quicker, and are preferred by the public.
>
> (http://mts.sustainableproducts.com)

The commitment to the notion of markets being the primary, if not exclusive, driver of sustainable development is contestable, for such an approach requires that:

(a) all the salient facts can be expressed in numerical form;

(b) all the salient information (including that relating to the preferences of future generations) can be articulated in the final 'market' price; and

(c) all decisions are simply the art, or science, of obtaining the 'right balance' of resource usage and that placing the resource in the hands of those who are able to pay the highest price is the most appropriate 'solution'.

The first two points are concerned with the feasibility of developing inclusive and articulate prices. The third and final point is one that raises profound philosophical issues, both political and ethical.

Moving to the academic community, we find that a number of universities have established sustainability research centres such as:

- the **Sustainable Futures Institute** at Michigan Technological University, USA;
- the **Sustainable Development Research Initiative** at the University of British Columbia, Canada;
- the **World Business Council for Sustainable Development**, which has close links with the Royal Melbourne Institute of Technology, Australia;

- the **Institute of Sustainable Development in Business** at Nottingham Trent University, England; and
- the **Sustainable Development Research Centre**, at Forres, Scotland, which has strong links with St Andrews University, Scotland, and the University of the Highlands and Islands, Scotland.

All of these institutes, and the many more that exist, are important developments. Local, grassroots initiatives are necessary developments for sustainable communities and societies. However, for the national and global sustainability agendas to be adequately addressed, there is an unavoidable need for the active and sincere engagement of large corporations and governments. As the MTS website announces, the largest 100 corporations account for 90 per cent of the world's production output. Without these corporations 'on board' and the active support of governments in encouraging and enforcing sustainable economic, social and environmental policies, all the individual initiatives, as important as they are, will not be anywhere near sufficient to address the pressing sustainability problems.

The triple bottom line

A phrase that was in vogue in the early 2000s was to talk of organisations having a 'triple bottom line', as distinct from the traditional use of the term 'bottom line' meaning simply profit. The triple bottom line encompasses economic, social and environmental concerns, but its articulation and operationalisation has remained problematic. Explanations of what is meant by 'triple bottom line' do not suggest an equal weighting being given to the three elements. Birch (2001), in reviewing a draft charter of corporate citizenship developed by BP Australia, referred to a statement contained within the draft charter. Under the heading 'sustainable development' the following statement appeared.

> BP is committed to a socially, environmentally and economically responsible business. This means maximising profit in order to create wealth and sustainable jobs, always intending to have a positive social and environmental impact.
> (Birch, 2001: 62)

The reference to maximising profit is interesting. Within the draft charter no attempt is made to discuss the tension between this commitment and the commitments made to the social and environmental issues mentioned elsewhere in the draft charter. However, Birch does refer to earlier discussions with BP Australia during which these issues appeared to have been raised.

> The tensions between capitalism and democracy as currently defined are irreconcilable without serious change. We agreed that we could not achieve long-term sustainability without change. Business needs, therefore, significant policy directions to enable this change to occur, not just within business practices but also within society overall.
> (Birch, 2001: 59)

The phrase 'business needs ... significant policy directions' refers directly to the need for a 'sovereign power', à la Hobbes. There is no suggestion that business can be assumed to resolve these tensions itself. The 'hidden hand' of the market is viewed as too unreliable to be left to its own devices in this context.

The triple bottom line is part of the Global Reporting Initiative (GRI) which in turn is a voluntary initiative that has so far been through two iterations. As we write the second edition of this book, the GRI team is receiving comments and advice from users and preparers as to how the GRI reporting requirements should be developed for the future. The process is open, mirroring the GRI's commitment to a stakeholder approach to corporate reporting. The third version of the GRI is due in 2006.

The current requirements of the GRI require organisations to report on corporate environmental, social and economic performance information, in essence a corporation's sustainability performance. There are five framework documents to the GRI, which are:

- Sustainability reporting guidelines (these are core requirements for all organisations).
- Sector supplements (which indicate additional information for different sectors, if such information is available).
- Technical protocols (these provide details of individual indicators, their definition, formulae and cross-referencing to minimise problems in comparability).
- Issue guidance documents (which are non-sector specific issues affecting a range of organisations, such as 'diversity' and 'productivity'), which all lead to:
- The Sustainability Report.

A two-way social contract?

What every sustainability and corporate responsibility initiative has to recognise and accept is that with the best will in the world, business corporations, in the form of their chief executives, have to be competitive in their respective marketplaces. Until consumers not only express a wish for corporations to move beyond legal minima, but are prepared, in certain cases, to pay slightly higher prices for products or services produced and delivered in ways that are more socially or environmentally sensitive than rival products, then corporate executives will feel there is too much hypocrisy and double standards in many of the corporate responsibility debates. The social contract, which was discussed in Chapter 8, tends to be presented as a one-way contract, that is, the conditions within the contract are placed exclusively upon corporations for them to maintain their (theoretical) 'licence to operate'. This poses a significant and fundamental question.

A fundamental question

Do the demands of global environmental and social issues, as articulated in the Global Compact, suggest that we must think more carefully about the notion of a two-way social contract?

What do we mean by this?

The transfer of production capacity to less-developed economies is not only a reflection of capital seeking out the most profitable investment opportunities, but is also evidence of the perpetual downward pressure on prices. The 'real' (inflation adjusted) cost of many products has been and continues downwards. For most customers, assuming the quality differential is not too marked, then price is a/the critical purchase criterion. Corporate executives need to feel reassured that, assuming any price differential between their own products and those of their competitors can be explained by the more environmentally and/or socially sensitive policies of their organisation, then consumers will respect this and not prejudice the more sustainable policies of the company by switching their purchasing allegiance to companies with lower prices but less sustainable policies. In this respect governments have a potentially important part to play in either rewarding companies that operate with leading-edge environmental and social policies or penalising those that do not. Such interventions could be via grants, tax concessions or tax penalties. Such an approach might be anathema to market fundamentalists, but 'the market' (or more particularly 'the consumer') might be too capricious and fickle a coordinating mechanism in these circumstances to be seen as the principal tool for resource allocation. Is there a need for a term such as 'consumer social responsibility'?

These issues reflect the profoundly important debates that need to be increasingly part of political and social agendas.

Summary

In this chapter the following key points have been made:

- The notion of sustainability should be seen as the symbiotic relationship between social, economic and environmental issues.
- Different ethical stances can be drawn upon to support particular sustainability positions.
- However, weighting the different claims in a utilitarian analysis can be extremely problematic. Not all those involved in or affected by a decision should necessarily attract the same level of importance.
- The leadership required of all political leaders concerning sustainability issues and the global crises of extreme poverty, child labour, inhuman working conditions, global warming, greenhouse gas emissions and political corruption has been found wanting.

- However, the decision by Global Compact to by-pass the political processes in 1999 and to go directly to the largest corporations to gain their active support in addressing the great global challenges of our time has, with hindsight, been recognised as flawed. Notwithstanding their poor track records, governments have to be a critical part of the strategies to address the many sustainability issues.
- Exclusive reliance upon the price mechanism to adjudicate and reflect societal preferences over sustainability issues has a number of profound weaknesses.
- The 'enframing of technology' mindset has to be successfully challenged.
- Current debates and demands concerning sustainable corporate practices tend to exclude the role consumers and governments can/must play in supporting those corporations employing sustainable and responsible practices and processes.
- The choices before us involve many issues, but above all they are choices that speak to the ethics and morals that we wish to underpin our communities and societies.

Quick revision test

1. Is the price mechanism without blemish as the key mechanism for resolving societies' preferences for addressing global warming issues?
2. What is meant by the phrase 'the enframing of technology'?
3. What is meant by the environment being socially constructed?
4. Who is the philosopher normally associated with the phrase 'the enframing of technology'?
5. What is the difference between Adam Smith's notion of self-love and selfishness?
6. What might be meant by 'consumer social responsibility'?
7. What is the triple bottom line?

Typical assignments and briefs

1. In the context of global warming, debate the appropriateness of the price mechanism as the primary democratic tool of resource allocation.
2. Critically evaluate Heidegger's notion of the 'enframing of technology' in terms of its contribution to debates concerning global economic growth rate forecasts.
3. Discuss the notion that 'consumer social responsibility is as important as corporate social responsibility'.
4. Evaluate the usefulness of Adam Smith's 'stranger' to debates concerning corporate executive behaviour and sustainable business practices.

Group activity 9

For Group Activity 8, you established an investment portfolio of ten companies. Having considered the issues covered in Chapter 9, you are now required to carry out the following tasks.

1. Revisit your investment principles to consider whether you wish to amend, add to or subtract from your previously agreed principles.
2. Decide whether you are comfortable with the ten corporations you have in your portfolio. You are allowed to make any changes you wish, but the final number of corporations in your portfolio must remain ten.
3. During the group session you will be provided with two sets of information of the share prices of quoted companies, taken from the financial pages of daily newspapers. One set will be dated within seven days of the group session, while the other will be twelve months old. From these two sets of information you will identify how the share prices of the companies in your portfolio have moved during the past twelve months, both absolutely and in terms of the sector index. You can include the dividend return in your calculations if this information is available, but for the purposes of the exercise it is not crucial.
4. Within your teams, you can briefly discuss your level of satisfaction with your portfolio's performance and whether you would wish to make any further changes to your portfolio.
5. You should prepare to discuss your team's judgement on your portfolio's performance, whether you have intentions to make adjustments and the basis for your decisions.
6. You should consider (with complete honesty and openness) how the issues of sustainability and social practices weighed
   - in your initial portfolio selection; and
   - in your considerations about possible changes your team might make in the light of the first year's financial performance.
7. You should also consider the knowledge that, in your employment as a portfolio manager, 40 per cent of your personal remuneration package is represented by a performance-related payment, based upon the financial performance of your team's portfolio's performance, and this payment is calculated every three months, i.e. it is not based upon the overall performance of your portfolio for the full twelve months, but is calculated for each quarter.

Recommended further reading

The most useful book on the issues covered in this chapter is Redclift, M. (1987) *Sustainable Development: Exploring the contradictions*, London: Routledge.

Useful websites

Topic	Website provider	URL
Sustainability	The Sustainability Institute	http://www.sustainabilityinstitute.org
	The Sustainable Business Institute	http://www.sustainablebusiness.org
	The International Institute for Sustainable Development	http://www.iisd.org
	The Sustainable Futures Institute	http://www.sustainablefutures.mtu.edu
	The Sustainable Development Research Centre	http://www.sustainableresearch.com/about-sustainable-research/news.asp
	The Institute for Sustainable Development in Business	http://www2.ntu.ac.uk/susdev/about_us.htm

Ethical conformance: codes, standards, culture, leadership and citizen power

Learning outcomes

Having read this chapter and completed its associated activities, readers should be able to:

- Discuss the pressures upon organisations to employ codes of practice.
- Differentiate between various types of codes.
- Describe the practical problems faced when drafting codes.
- Understand the arguments for and against the employment of codes of practice within organisations.
- Show an awareness that codes of practice can sometimes conflict with one another, creating organisational tensions.
- Understand the significance and power of organisational culture and unwritten codes of conduct.
- Evaluate the role of ethical leadership.
- Evaluate the role of public pressure on maintaining organisational good behaviour.

Introduction

This chapter considers the developments that have become evident as the attention paid to ethical issues in business has intensified. Broadly speaking, these developments have reflected reactions to one or more problems affecting either a specific firm or an industrial/commercial sector. Sometimes developments can be seen in the form of organisations and/or groups of companies working in tandem, sometimes with governments and/or pressure groups, to draw up codes of practice and conduct.

The International Labour Organisation (ILO) argued that worldwide interest in corporate codes of conduct was initially awakened in the 1980s by scandals in the US defence industry and the overt greed that was displayed on Wall Street. The ILO sees business ethics as a way for companies to promote self-regulation, thereby deterring government intervention and possible regulatory action.

Corporate interest quickly led to the institutionalisation of business ethics programmes, consisting largely of codes of conduct, ethics officers and ethics training. However, Brytting (1997) cited the Zeiss organisation as having a recognisable code of conduct for its employees in 1896, and Mill, writing in 1861 but cited by Warren (1993: 187), observed that 'it is the business of ethics to tell us what our duties are or by what test we may know them'. It has been argued that the more recent increase in the growth of corporate codes of conduct relates to the potential for such codes to reduce corporate exposure to punitive damages in claims of negligence. As Warren (1993: 109) observed in terms of the situation in the United States,

> The 1984 Sentencing Reform Act and the US Sentencing Commission's 1991 Federal Guidelines for Sentencing Organisations, allow for a fine on a corporation to be reduced by up to 95% if it can show that it has an effective program to prevent and detect violations of law.

Attempts to reduce negligence claims are not the only reason for organisations to be seen to be addressing the ethicality of their practices. Multi-national corporations (MNCs) are not only increasingly powerful, but also open to critical scrutiny of any of their practices in all parts of the world. MNCs thus have a vested interest in harmonising and standardising practices throughout their respective organisations in order to minimise the risk of aberrant behaviour. We consider later in this chapter the initiatives being employed by MNCs to address concerns about their practices and those of their supplier networks.

An overview of the pressures upon organisations for ethical development

Figure 10.1 reflects the differing pressures on organisations to institute and formalise their ethical practices.

Of all the connections depicted in Figure 10.1, the only unbroken line is that between 'Governments' and 'The organisation'. This reflects the mandatory nature of laws, as opposed to the other relationships that are characterised by frameworks, agreements, codes, understandings or memoranda, none of which is legally binding. The agreements, or framework documents, between governments and MNCs reflect the dilemma faced by many governments, particularly those of developing countries. The presence of MNCs within the host country can bring the prospect of accelerated economic development, but the support, incentives and conditions that must be agreed to by the host government, in the face of alternative offers by other countries to the MNCs, can weaken the host government's bargaining powers. In such circumstances, legislation is unlikely to be deemed 'appropriate' to control the operations of the MNCs, and more adaptive, negotiable instruments such as framework agreements, or codes,

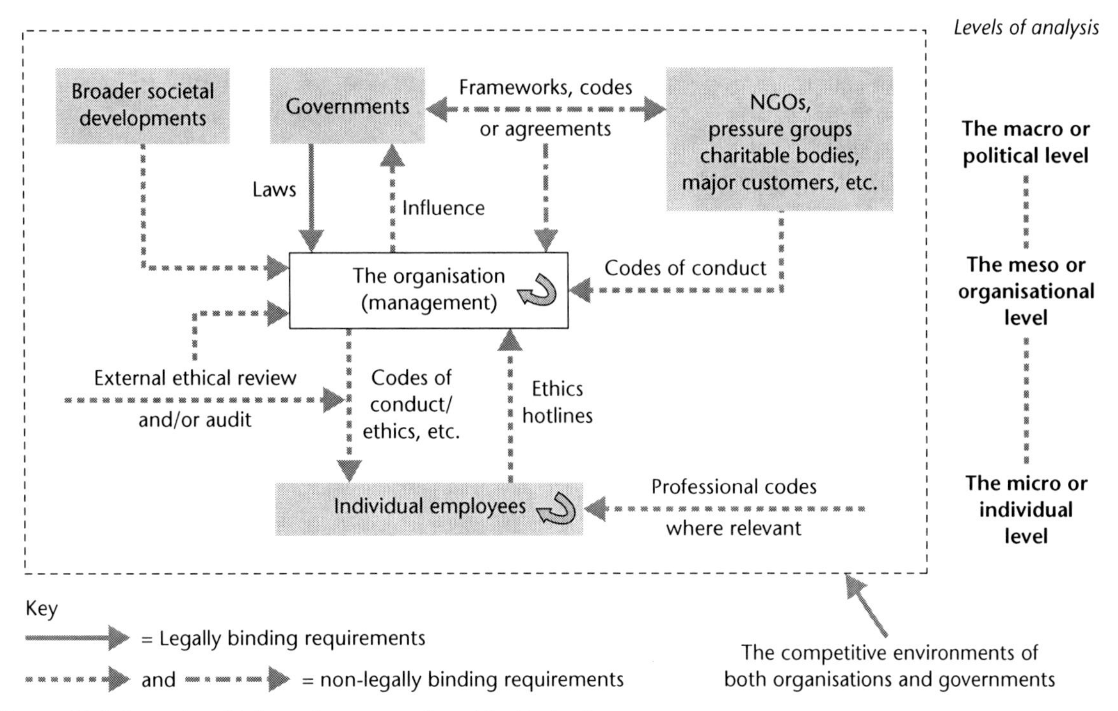

Figure 10.1 Formal and informal pressures for ethical behaviour

become the norm. The non-legally binding agreements or codes of practice may be developed with or without the involvement of pressure groups and interested charitable bodies.

In turn, non-governmental bodies (NGOs), pressure groups and charitable bodies can exert pressure upon organisations independently of governments by developing their preferred codes of practice for business organisations and then contrasting these codes with the behaviour of specific organisations. These comparisons can reveal considerable discrepancies between espoused and actual behaviour and, given the glare of national and international publicity, can involve discussions about change. These relationships are reflected in the additional lines emanating from the 'NGOs, pressure groups' box and going towards the 'The organisation' box. Organisations such as Greenpeace, Friends of the Earth and the International Baby Food Action Network (IBFAN) are notable in this field.

Business organisations do not have to wait for external pressure before they act to enhance their own practices and behaviour. We illustrate below examples of ethical initiatives that appear to have come from within organisations, although the initiatives may have been in anticipation of government or pressure group involvement if the organisation did not respond in some way to an ethical issue.

There are examples of cooperation and collaboration between governments and pressure groups, between pressure groups and organisations/industries and between governments, pressure groups and business organisations, that appear to be addressing matters of ethical concern in effective ways. We also highlight, however, examples of apparent 'good' practice, which, when carefully scrutinised, are possibly less effective than they might at first appear.

Within Figure 10.1 the introduction of a corporate code of conduct by an employing organisation is shown by the downward-pointing arrow, aimed at 'Individual employees'. This is because such codes are invariably the result of a 'top-down initiative', with relatively little, or no, involvement from non-senior managerial staff. These codes tend to be statements of how employees are required to behave by the company/senior management.

Connexion point

However, companies can also incorporate 'ethics hotlines' to allow those employees with concerns about the ethicality of particular business practices to express their concerns, as we discussed in Chapter 7. These organisational vents can be both important mechanisms for concerned employees to express their worries, and effective early warning systems for organisations about potentially damaging practices and behaviour.

Both the ethics hotlines and the codes of conduct can be supported by external ethical review, e.g. an annual or periodic ethics audit, but because all of these mechanisms are optional they are shown as broken lines.

An important point to emphasise is that the 'Codes of conduct, etc.' link between 'The organisation' and 'Individual employees' is not just about codes of conduct. The 'etc.' encompasses a range of other ways of communicating, inculcating and nurturing corporate values. McDonald and Nijhof (1999) cited:

- training
- story telling
- reward systems
- monitoring systems
- communication channels
- job design
- ethics officers
- information systems
- recruitment and selection policies and processes, and
- organisational strategies

as further examples of ways in which organisations can influence the values and practices that become accepted as 'the ways things are done around here'. Many of these elements come within what is known as organisational culture. This is a very significant area, upon which many books have been written. A consideration of some of the important issues of organisational culture for values and ethics, and vice versa, is undertaken towards the end of this chapter.

The arrows within 'The organisation' and 'Individual employees' boxes that appear to turn on themselves indicate that neither organisations, nor individuals, should expect or passively wait for developments on ethical behaviour to be externally imposed or influenced. If terms such as 'learning organisation' and 'reflective practitioner' are to mean anything, they will need to be evident in the critical reflection of both organisations and individuals on their respective practices. In many respects the integrity with which organisations and individuals reflect upon notions of ethicality are fundamental elements of Figure 10.1. If change is only ever externally stimulated, rather than the result of internal reflection and action, then such change is subject to whims and pressures that will not necessarily be rooted in well-argued principles and values.

The arrow moving from the 'The organisation' to 'Governments' acknowledges that business organisations are not passive or disinterested bystanders in the development of laws affecting corporate practice. This arrow acknowledges the quite significant influence that specific organisations and industrial/commercial sectors can have on governments and the laws that are passed. Equally, it must be emphasised that the whole of Figure 10.1 sits within a commercial and competitive environment that bears upon the practices of individuals, organisations and governments.

The levels of analysis

Researchers and organisations that study and work with the many issues that comprise business ethics and values tend to do so from one of three perspectives, as reflected in the column on the right-hand side of Figure 10.1. These levels are the macro or political level, the meso or organisational level and the micro or individual level. Those working at the macro-political level are seeking to understand, and possibly influence, the way that political and particularly economic systems impact upon broad national and societal issues. Examples of interesting monitoring organisations that operate at national and international government levels include Transparency International and One World Trust. Their respective websites are provided in the list of business ethics resources on the World Wide Web at the end of the chapter.

At the meso, or organisational, level we find pressure groups, professional associations, trade bodies and labour organisations which are working to monitor, analyse, understand, support, defend and develop the ethicality of business practice within organisations. Researchers working at this level study issues such as ethical awareness and training programmes; the development of corporate codes of conduct and/or ethics; and controversies such as those relating to the production, distribution and selling of bananas; the retailing of breastmilk substitutes in developing countries; and sweatshop and child labour issues. In addition to the material on the websites given at the end of the chapter, there are some interesting ideas and arguments concerning ethical development at the organisational level in Schein (1992); Watson (1994); Fineman and Gabriel (1996); McDonald and Nijhof (1999); Gabriel, Fineman and Sims (2000); and Sternberg (2000).

At the individual level we find debates and research that consider the possibilities for moral agency in organisations. This level is discussed in a number of places in this book, but particularly Chapter 7.

Codes of conduct and codes of ethics

In market contexts where competitive forces are significant, consistency in all aspects of an organisation's operations is imperative. In order to stimulate, foster and maintain consistency in the behaviour of employees, consistency that also reflects the standards of behaviour that an organisation wishes its employees to adopt, organisations often develop codes of conduct and ethics. A distinction can be made between codes of ethics and codes of conduct that is helpful in examining the roles these types of statements perform. Although this distinction is not universally employed, indeed you may find some organisations employing codes of ethics that by our definition would be classed as codes of conduct, it offers some insight into the purpose of such codes. A study by Farrell and Cobbin (1996) discusses variations between codes of conduct and codes of ethics and the findings of this study add support to the distinction. A much higher level of prescription was found in the codes of conduct studied (average number of rules equalled 30.6), compared with the average number of rules contained in the codes of ethics (16.5).

DEFINITIONS

Codes of conduct tend to be instructions, or sets of rules, concerning behaviour. As a result they are likely to be reasonably prescriptive and proscriptive concerning particular aspects of employee behaviour. They identify specific acts that must be either adhered to (prescription), or avoided (proscription). However, the extent to which all possible situations can be addressed within a code of conduct is problematic.

Codes of ethics tend to be reasonably general in their tenor, encouraging employees to display particular characteristics such as loyalty, honesty, objectivity, probity and integrity. They do not normally address specific types of decisions; rather they encourage the application of what might be called 'virtues', although, as noted in Chapter 3, what are regarded as virtues can vary over time. While notions of honesty and integrity remain fairly constant over time, concepts such as justice and loyalty are more contentious.

From these definitions it is evident that, where all possible scenarios that an employee might face can be predicted with a high degree of confidence, as well all the circumstances relating to those scenarios, then a specific code of conduct might be possible, because ethical judgement becomes redundant. However, where the likely scenarios that an employee might face cannot be predicted in the requisite detail, then reference to general qualities and principles will be preferred, i.e. codes of ethics become more appropriate.

The risk of confusing these two general positions is that, if a code of conduct fails to address a particular scenario that an employee actually faces, then the silence of the code on the matter in question might be interpreted by the employee as an indication that the employing organisation is at best indifferent to the ethics of the decision in hand.

In this discussion the employee might be said to be (or be treated as) morally immature, requiring a code of conduct or ethics to act as a reference point in times of need, but that is just what codes imply. By issuing such codes, a company is stating that it does not have sufficient confidence in all of its employees to be able to view a code of conduct or ethics as unnecessary. This is an implication that some, perhaps many, employees might find objectionable, but for an organisation that straddles many countries and cultures in its operations the need for an articulation of expected behaviour and practices throughout its operations can be overwhelming.

The purposes of codes of conduct and ethics

At one level, codes of conduct and ethics can be seen as legitimate and necessary devices for senior management to develop in order to specify expected codes of behaviour of all employees. Each employee of an organisation will be seen as a representative of that organisation by others external to the organisation. Thus, it is important that employees reflect behaviour that is commensurate with the persona and reputation that the organisation wishes to project. In this context some writers see codes of conduct as principally manipulative control devices to achieve managerial ends. Stevens (1994: 65) argued that 'some ethical codes are little more than legal barriers and self-defence mechanisms; others are intended to influence and shape employee behaviour'. These were observations that had been made earlier by, among others, Mathews (1988) and Warren (1993).

Developing and adding to the work of Bowie and Duska (1990), we have listed below eight roles for corporate codes. These are:

- *Damage limitation* – to reduce damages awarded by courts in the event of the company being sued for negligence by one its employees.
- *Guidance* – the 'reference point' role, similar to what Passmore (1984) referred to as 'the reminding role'. An aide-memoire for employees when faced with an ethically complex situation.
- *Regulation* – this is the prescribing and proscribing roles that will stipulate specific qualities that are essential, e.g. independence, objectivity, etc., or acts that are prohibited.
- *Discipline and appeal* – this is the role of a code as a benchmark for an organisation or professional body to decide whether an employee/member has contravened required conduct and what form of punishment might ensue. In addition the code can form the basis of an appeal by the accused.
- *Information* – a code expresses to external audiences standards of behaviour that can be expected of employees/members.
- *Proclamation* – this has echoes of 'information', but it relates more to the role of codes of conduct developed by professional bodies. To achieve 'professional' status trade associations are normally required to assuage public concerns over the granting of monopoly rights to specific areas of commercial/social activity (e.g. auditing, doctoring, etc.). Ethical codes will attempt to reassure that these monopoly powers will not be abused.

- *Negotiation* – this is not dissimilar to *guidance* in that codes can be used as a tool in negotiations and disputes with and between professionals, colleagues, employers, governments, etc.
- *Stifling* – this is the creation of internal procedures for handling the ethical concerns of employees that are more concerned with management keeping a lid on internal dissent than acting as a conduit for internal debate and examination. Hunt's (1995 and 1998) work on whistleblowing in the health and social services reflects a number of examples of this use of codes of conduct and internal whistleblowing processes.

The attention paid to codes of conduct by both organisations and researchers does presume both that codes are a 'good' thing and that they do have a positive impact upon individual and corporate behaviour. With regard to the latter, Mathews (1988) was able to identify only a weak link between the existence of ethical codes and corporate behaviour. This latter point was taken up by Cassell, Johnson and Smith (1997: 1078) who argued that:

> An important, if implicit, assumption of many writings on corporate codes ... is that such codes do have a 'real' effect upon behaviour. This tends to be something that is taken for granted, but it is not empirically validated by subsequent investigation ... recipients of the code: those who are required to make sense of it, and respond to it, often as one more instance of managerially-inspired change, amidst a plethora of pre-existing formal and informal control processes within which the impact of the code must be located. As with any example of formal organisational control, the actual, as opposed to the intended, effect may be subject to processes that entail negotiation and bargaining.

Stevens' (1994) observations were that codes were:

- primarily concerned with employee conduct that might damage the firm, that is, they were thus skewed towards self-protection, and
- preoccupied with the law.

The legalistic orientation of many codes has been noted by a number of writers, including Farrell and Cobbin (1996). The latter identified differences between American, Australian and UK corporate codes of conduct. They concluded that, of the codes they studied, the Australian codes tended to concentrate upon a reiteration of the legal environment within which individuals and organisations operate, emphasising the importance of not doing anything to harm the employing organisation's reputation. American codes included, but went beyond, this orientation, emphasising customers, equal opportunities and insider dealing, while the UK codes made more frequent reference to the community, customer welfare and the environment than the Australian or American codes. However, all of these are relative terms, 'the level of specific guidance on ethical content in each country's codes was very low' (1996: 54). As lawyers were identified as the most frequent developers of such codes (30 per cent), a legalistic orientation to the codes was not surprising.

Factors that will affect the impact of a code

Cassell *et al.* (1997), combining the work of Hopwood (1974) and Kelman (1961), identified three possible explanations why individuals might display behaviours that conform with desired organisational behaviours. These are:

1. *Internalisation*, in which the behaviours are accepted by the individual as their own, even though they are set externally. This does suggest, however, that the ethical values displayed will be subject to, and influenced by, further external forces, unless the organisational values are held by the individual at a profound and deep level.
2. *Compliance*, in which the displayed behaviour is associated with the desire to achieve some form of reward, or avoid an identifiable punishment. This form of behaviour will last as long as the punishment or reward is regarded as both significant and realisable by the individual/s concerned, but not beyond. This form of behaviour is thus not ethically based, but instrumental, calculating and unreliable.
3. *Identification*, in which behaviour is shaped by, and mirrors, the behaviours of significant others with whom the individual wishes to identify. Again because of the instrumental and externally located locus of a behaviour's rationale, the reliability of the behaviour in question is problematic.

Of these three possible explanations, only the first holds out the prospect of consistency for the organisations, the other two being unreliable due to external corruption. If this is so then the individual must absorb the organisation's values in a conscious and knowing way because either:

- The individual's existing values correspond closely with those espoused by the organisation and, thus, little change is required to the individual's own ethics, or
- The individual recognises in the organisation's values a set of principles that transcend their own and to which they wish to aspire.

Alternatively the internalisation is not conscious, but unconscious, achieved by the constant drip-drip of organisational images and rhetoric. This might seem a very distant possibility in the current day and age, but one of the authors is reminded of an ethics workshop he held for a group of managers on a Master's programme. One of the managers worked for a well-known and respected retail organisation, respected among other things for the apparently strong employee benefits and care provided by the company. However, during the course of the workshop all the participants reviewed different aspects of their organisation's practices, and this particular manager gradually shifted from a view of his employing organisation's paternalistic care as benign, to one which was more oppressive and manipulative. This change in interpretation came not from questioning by the tutors, but from a series of interactive exercises with other members of the course. The manager in question had worked for the retail organisation for over 15 years and during that time had accepted the organisation's house journal, the management conferences he attended and other practices as evidence of his employer's good intent. His now more critical interpretation did not suddenly make his employers 'bad' employers, when for the previous 15 years they had been 'good' employers. What unsettled him was how uncritical he had been in accepting a particular interpretation of some of the organisation's actions and decisions over the years, some of which did not square with his original uncritical, 'rose-tinted' description of his organisation.

Using Goffman's (1959) dramaturgical metaphor, individuals can be said to 'act out' their preferred view of themselves on the stage of life. Information likely to enhance others' opinions of oneself is kept 'centre stage' rather than 'in the wings'. The concept of impression management pervades the literature on business ethics, and is particularly apparent in ethnographic accounts of how managers deal with ethical problems (e.g. Jackall, 1988; Schein, 1992; Toffler, 1991; Watson, 1994). Interestingly, the 'management' and 'organisational behaviour' literature is a much richer and a more academically robust source of material on this point than much of the business ethics literature.

Jackall (1988) argued that the unethical actions of managers do not result from the individual's moral deficiencies, but rather from the bureaucratic structures of modern organisations that encourage managers to behave unethically. This view has been echoed by others within the literature. For example, Liedtka (1991) concluded that many of the managers in her study found themselves forced to choose between preserving their relationships within the firm (operating within the organisational political model) and following their own values (using a value-driven model). We will conclude our consideration of this issue with a quote from Cassell *et al.* (1997: 1088):

> It is our contention that although individual psychological and demographic factors play a role in influencing behaviour in relation to codes, that role is relatively minor given the significance of the organisational context and culture within which behaviour takes place.

Cassell *et al.* (1997) identified three factors they argued would determine the influence a code would have upon the behaviour of organisational members, namely:

1. The nature of the code, its content and the processes by which it has been designed, developed and implemented.
2. The organisational control mechanisms (both formal and informal). For example, will the employees see the introduction of a (new) code as just another mechanism by which the employing organisation wishes to determine individual behaviour, or a genuine attempt to help employees cope with complex ethical issues that they will face during their day-to-day practice?
3. Individual influences which focus upon perceptual and self-control processes.

Thus, if the individual employee acts in keeping with required organisational behaviour out of either compliance or identification motives, and is sceptical about factors (1) and (2) above, the prospects for a newly introduced code of conduct or practice are likely to be unpredictable and variable throughout an organisation, two outcomes the code was presumably intended to obviate.

Writing a code of ethics

The difficulty of writing a code of ethics is that, when they are completed, they look banal, and people comment, 'Well, that is all just common sense'. Their commonplaceness is intensified when they are reduced to the basics and provided to all employees as laminated cards that can be stored in wallets and purses with the credit cards. Commonplaces of course are mostly true and important statements about trust, integrity, honesty and fairness. The intention is clearly that employees should carry these cards around with them as reminders, thus implying that the staff need constant admonition to be honest and so on. In our research interviews one respondent reported a debate in a focus group set up to discuss what should be included in the new code of ethics. One side of the argument was that 'Employees should act honestly' should be included. The contrary view was that this was such an obvious requirement that it did not need stating, and that if it was it implied that the management thought their employees potentially dishonest. It was decided not to include it.

Most organisations go to great trouble to ensure that their code of ethics is particular to them and their business and circumstances. Yet most codes of ethics look alike. It is unusual for codes to go against convention or the norms and institutions of the surrounding society. Table 10.1 attempts to illustrate this phenomenon by comparing the ethical code for the conduct of pharmaceutical medicine of Johnson and Johnson (n.d.) with that of the Covenant of the Goddess (Center for the Study of Ethics in the Professions, 2003), which is an association of white witches.

As there is much common ground between different organisations' codes of ethics it is possible to identify the topics and themes most commonly mentioned. In the analysis in Table 10.2 the examples are taken from Johnson and Johnson's Credo, the UK Civil Service Code of Conduct (The Cabinet Office, 2004), BP's business policies and the statement of core values of Carbo Ceramics (2002) (which was more or less chosen at random from the many company statements available); note that none of these uses the term code of ethics, but nevertheless that is what they are.

Table 10.1 A comparison of the code of ethics for the conduct of pharmaceutical medicine of Johnson and Johnson and the Covenant of the Goddess Code of Ethics

Common theme	Ethical code for the conduct of pharmaceutical medicine of Johnson and Johnson	Covenant of the Goddess ethical code
Credo based	'It is our responsibility to apply Credo-based values and judgment regarding the design, conduct, analysis and interpretation of clinical studies and results.'	'Members of the covenant should ever keep in mind the underlying unity of our religion as well as the diversity of its manifestations.' 'These ethics shall be understood and interpreted in the light of one another, and especially in the light of the traditional laws of our religion.'
The credos are of similar antiquity	The Johnson and Johnson credo was first published in 1943	Modern witchcraft was probably invented as a religion in the 1920s and 1930s when there was a fashion for magic and druidism. It is only slightly older than the Johnson and Johnson credo.
Do no harm	'It is our fundamental responsibility to place the well-being of the patient first by appropriately balancing risks and benefits and to ensure that the best interests of patients and physicians who use our products receive utmost consideration. '	'An ye harm none, do as ye will'
Respect the differences and autonomy of others	'It is our responsibility to understand differences in values across cultures and to appropriately adapt our behaviors without relaxing our ethical principles.'	'Every person associated with the covenant shall respect the autonomy and sovereignty of each coven, as well as the right of each coven to oversee the spiritual, mental, emotional and physical development of its members and students in its own way, and shall exercise reasonable caution against infringing upon that right in any way.'
A position on openness and secrecy	'It is our responsibility to ensure all Company-based, medically relevant product information is fair and balanced, accurate and comprehensive, to enable well-informed risk-benefit assessments about our products.'	'All persons associated with this covenant shall respect the traditional secrecy of our religion.'
Right to a fair return	Not included in the code but the credo states, 'When we operate according to these principles, the stockholders should realize a fair return.'	'All persons have the right to charge reasonable fees for the services by which they earn their living, so long as our religion is not thereby exploited.'
Professional standards of those who practice the activity	'It is our responsibility to adhere to the principles of good clinical practice.'	'Since our religion and the arts and practices peculiar to it are the gift of the Goddess, membership and training in a local coven or tradition are bestowed free, as gifts, and only on those persons who are deemed worthy to receive them.'

Table 10.2 Common themes in codes of ethics

Theme	Example	Source of example
Integrity	The constitutional and practical role of the Civil Service is, with integrity, honesty, impartiality and objectivity, to assist the duly constituted Government [ ] whatever their political complexion, in formulating their policies, carrying out decisions and in administering public services for which they are responsible.	UK Civil Service Code
	We conduct our business with the highest ethical standards. We are truthful and honor our commitments and responsibilities.	Carbo Ceramics
Loyalty	Civil servants are servants of the Crown. Constitutionally, all the Administrations form part of the Crown and, subject to the provisions of this Code, civil servants owe their loyalty to the Administrations in which they serve.	UK Civil Service Code
No harm and risk management	We believe our first responsibility is to the doctors, nurses and patients, to mothers and fathers and all others who use our products and services. In meeting their needs everything we do must be of high quality.	Johnson and Johnson
	We will regularly identify the hazards and assess the risks associated with our activities. We will take appropriate action to manage risks and hence prevent or reduce the impact of potential accidents or incidents.	BP
Respect for individual employees	We are responsible to our employees, the men and women who work with us throughout the world. Everyone must be considered as an individual. We must respect their dignity and recognize their merit. They must have a sense security in their jobs. Compensation must be fair and adequate, and working conditions clean, orderly and safe. We must be mindful of ways to help our employees fulfil their family responsibilities. Employees must feel free to make suggestions and complaints. There must be equal opportunity for employment, development and advancement for those qualified. We must provide competent management, and their actions must be just and ethical.	Johnson and Johnson
Respect for the law	We will respect the law in the countries and communities in which we operate.	BP
Trust	Our commitment is to create mutual advantage in all our relationships so that people will trust us and want to do business with BP.	BP
Relationship with stakeholders	We will enable customers, governments, communities and our own people to participate in a new constructive dialogue. We aim for a radical openness – a new approach from a new company, transparent, questioning, flexible, restless and inclusive.	BP
	Our suppliers and distributors must have an opportunity to make a fair profit.	Johnson and Johnson
Developing communities	We are responsible to the communities in which we live and work and to the world community as well.	
	We must be good citizens – support good works and charities and bear our fair share of taxes.	
	We must encourage civic improvements and better health and education. We must maintain in good order the property we are privileged to use, protecting the environment and natural resources.	Johnson and Johnson

Table 10.2 Continued

Theme	Example	Source of example
Goals and achievement	We set aggressive goals and strive to exceed them. We value and celebrate a high level of individual achievement and team performance.	Carbo Ceramics
Return to shareholders	Our final responsibility is to our stockholders. Business must make a sound profit.	Johnson and Johnson
Environmental sustainability	We are committed to [ ] demonstrating respect for the natural environment and work towards our goals of no accidents, no harm to people and no damage to the environment.	BP
Political activity and contributions	BP will never make political contributions whether in cash or in kind anywhere in the world.	BP
Personal advantage	Civil servants should not misuse their official position or information acquired in the course of their official duties to further their private interests or those of others. They should not receive benefits of any kind from a third party which might reasonably be seen to compromise their personal integrity or judgement.	Civil Service Code
Commitment to external standards or assurance	BP supports the principles set forth in the UN Universal Declaration of Human Rights and will respect the 2000 International Labour Organisation, the 'Tripartite Declaration of Principles Concerning Multinational Enterprises and Social Policy' and the 2000 OECD 'Guidelines for Multi-national Enterprises'.	BP

Arguments against the employment of codes of conduct and ethics

Activity 10.1

Although our consideration of codes of conduct and ethics has identified limitations in practice and referred to evidence that casts doubt upon the actual impact of codes 'on the ground', we have not suggested that the development and introduction of a code would be a negative development. There are, however, such arguments, and before discussing these we would like you to think through what these might be.

Identify as many negative aspects as possible associated with the development of a code of conduct or ethics.

While the employment of codes has an intuitive appeal, we can identify five possible objections to their development and employment.

1 Justification

This relates to the lack of any universally accepted set of common principles and ethics. If 'everything is relative' is taken to its logical conclusion and codes can only ever be culturally and socially specific, the notion of universal laws is rejected and with it the argument that a corporation can have a single code of conduct. If a multi-national organisation produces a code of conduct that reflects a basic set of values, by definition this implies there are certain basic concepts that it wishes to universalise, at least within its own worldwide operations, but is this possible? The question might become one of distinguishing between negotiable and non-negotiable values – how and when does one balance local customs and traditions with one's own sense of values when the two are in conflict? For example, when is a gift a bribe? We discuss this particular issue in the next chapter.

2 The inability of rules to govern actions

If codes cannot guarantee changes in behaviour, and empirical evidence is very limited with respect to examples of codes shaping behaviour in desired ways, will the negative signals being sent out to employees, that the organisation does not trust them, be the abiding impact of the introduction of a code? If so, then the overall impact of a code is likely to be negative.

Connexion point

Re-read our discussion of *Integrative Social Contract Theory* in Chapter 8 (pp. 323–6) and consider how it argues the issues relating to universal versus relativist ethics can be handled.

3 Support structures

There is a need for, but paucity of, support structures within organisations for employees to feel able to act in accordance with specified codes of behaviour. Where codes of conduct do exist, Warren (1993: 189) argued that:

> All too often ethical codes are handed down to employees from the executive above and the importance of trying to create a community or purpose within the company is ignored.

Warren (1993) referred to the field of industrial relations where evidence indicates that rules governing industrial relations need collective agreement if they are to be honoured in the observance as well as in the breach (e.g. Terry, 1975). This perspective is supported by Bird and Waters (1989: 83). They argued that just talking about ethical issues is unlikely to enhance the significance of the issues unless mechanisms are found for 'connecting this language with the experiences and expectations of people involved in business'. Taking this argument forward, Bird and Waters (1989: 84) argued that

> Business people will continue to shun open discussions of actual moral issues unless means are provided to allow for legitimate dissent by managers who will not be personally blamed, criticised, ostracised, or punished for their views.

They found that talking to managers individually revealed that the managers had many concerns of an ethical nature. However, when asked if these issues were ever raised among managerial colleagues, either formally or informally, the managers replied that they were not. The managers identified a range of explanations for the collective managerial muteness on ethical issues. Such talk was perceived to be a threat to:

- efficiency (i.e. the imposition of rigid rules and regulations);
- the image of power and effectiveness (i.e. previous attempts had resulted in the dissenting manager being shown to be organisationally impotent); and
- organisational harmony (i.e. discussion of moral issues at work was perceived to be dysfunctional).

Thus, the introduction of a code of conduct requires an environment in which expressions of concern over particular practices are not perceived as simplistically 'anti-company' or 'wimpish'. Without such an environment, cynicism is likely to be fuelled, and the overall impact of the code will be negative.

4 The marginality of codes

Codes tend to be treated as 'add-ons', as constraints upon action, and thus act at the margins of corporate activity. To be effective, codes need to be at the centre of corporate beliefs or, more particularly, a code becomes redundant if the corporate culture encapsulates those values and beliefs that would be reflected in a corporate code of conduct or ethics. If left at the margins, a code might be interpreted as a necessary accoutrement (garnish) to corporate activities, but one that can be circumvented, or 'negotiated' in certain circumstances. If so, then cynicism about corporate motives would be heightened and the overall effect of the code would be negative.

5 The diminution and ultimate invisibility of individual responsibility

Codes that specify behaviour in particular situations seek to take judgement out of ethically charged situations. Whilst this has the advantage of standardising behaviour throughout an organisation and potentially minimising the risk of behaviour that is unacceptable, there is also the risk of the individual using the 'I was only following orders' defence in the event of an enquiry into a dispute over a particular incident. This shifting of responsibility has been termed by Bauman (1994) as 'floating responsibility' and was discussed in Chapter 7. It becomes an organisational defence against individual conscience. The following of rules and adherence to the commands of superiors makes identification of responsibility difficult to isolate. Identification of responsibility for a particular action or inaction falls between the cracks of job descriptions and responsibilities, and codes of conduct. Morality (or the defining of it) thus becomes someone else's responsibility. The actions of individuals become automatic, with little thought or judgement on the part of the individual required. Whilst actual situations will often present complexities and nuances that take the individual into contexts not addressed adequately by a code, the existence and 'failings' of the code present the individual with an escape route from responsibility. To obey instructions is less demanding and far less risky than exercising moral judgement.

Bauman (1994) identified a second tendency, that of organisational actions being deemed amoral, that is neither good nor bad, only correct or incorrect. In this context codes of conduct can be used to make what could be transparent opaque. Codes might be expressed, not so much in moral terms, but in technical terms, implying a moral neutrality to the issues being addressed in the code.

The difficulties of writing codes of conduct – the ethics of e-communication

With the coming of new forms of electronic communication and diffusion of information, in particular email and the Internet, new forms of ethical problems have appeared in organisations. As this has happened organisations have tried to develop new codes of conduct governing e-communications, to minimise abuse. Their attempts to respond to new problems illustrate many of the problems and difficulties with codes of conduct discussed in the previous section. The matter is not an inconsequential one. In 1998 an IT manager was sacked from her job because she had booked her holiday on the Internet, using the company's computers, during work time (Wakefield, 1999). In 2003 four lawyers lost their jobs at a top London law firm after circulating an email about oral sex among their colleagues; at some point it was emailed to a further 20 million people worldwide. A year later ten clerical workers at the Royal Sun Alliance in Liverpool were dismissed after emailing a risqué cartoon involving Bart Simpson and a donkey (*The Observer*, 2004). People have no control over what they are sent by email, and they may inadvertently, or so they will claim, download a pornographic image for example. Even if they delete it immediately a record will remain, in this networked age, that they received the image. It might be difficult for them subsequently to disprove that they were simply an innocent dupe.

It is estimated that 36 per cent of employees have an email address provided by their employers. As access to email and the Internet grows so the ethical issues become more important. The main problems are listed below.

1 Misuse by employers

- Employers have the capacity, but not always the inclination, to monitor every action that employees take while using networked computers at work. Employees' net surfing and email correspondences are all logged. The question is the extent to which such surveillance is ethical and legitimate and when it could be claimed to break an employee's right to privacy. In 2003 the UK government passed the Regulation and Investigatory Powers Act that made it illegal to monitor employees' emails without their consent. Guidelines issued by the Department of Trade and Industry, however, construed the Act as allowing surveillance if contracts of employment included a clause that allowed employers to monitor email and Internet usage. The employers argued that they needed this right as all emails sent from their systems were their legal responsibility, which is why most emails now sent from organisational systems have a disclaimer (often longer than the message) denying any such responsibility.

- Assuming that by emailing all staff they have exhausted their responsibility to communicate effectively with their staff.

2 Misuse by employees

- Stealing employers' time by surfing the net when they should be working.
- Using the email and Internet facilities for improper purposes, such as distributing racist messages or obscene materials.
- Conducting a personal business using their employer's systems.
- Harassing or stalking other employees by email, a practice that has been recognised by Industrial Tribunals as illegal behaviour (Taylor, 2001).
- Sending an internal email communication to an external body. For example, an aggrieved employee who had taken Prince Charles to an Industrial Tribunal complaining of sex discrimination used an internal email from the Prince's household as evidence in support of her case.
- Misusing online selection and recruitment testing to misrepresent oneself to a potential employer. In 2003 6 per cent of organisations were using some form of online testing for recruitment and selection purposes (Czerny, 2004).

3 Abuses of good communication

- Email communication is anomalous; on the one hand it is seen as quick and informal yet on the other it is a recorded form of communication that can be used in a court of law. This leads people to show a lack of courtesy in their communications with others that they would not think of exhibiting on the telephone or in face-to-face communication (Taylor, 2001).
- People often use emails to avoid giving news, often bad, that ought to be given personally. There was in 2004 a case of a large number of employees being informed by email that they were redundant.
- The informality and distance of emails encourage people to be ruder, especially when they are angry, than they would be if addressing the subjects of their disgust directly. Reliance Industries (RIL) is a very large family firm in India. When the founder died there was a power struggle between his two sons that was conducted almost entirely in emails leaked to the media. The directors of the company thought the dispute would never be resolved by emails and said,

> [we do] not find the mode of e-mail suitable. Instead of e-mail it should be love mail. It is better to sit and talk.
>
> (*Hindustan Times*, 2004: 1)

The extreme email discourtesy is when someone writes an email complaining about some hurt from another and then copies it to the entire company. This may have a beneficial aspect, such as when an email that affects all staff, but which was intended to be confidential to a select group, is forwarded by one of that group to all employees. This can lead to a vigorous and democratic debate about the issue between all staff. Emails can be an effective forum for rapid debate.

- Overusing mailing lists and the 'cc' function to flood people with emails that are of little interest to them.

One of the difficulties of writing a code of conduct to cover these issues is that most employers wish to draw a sensible balance between the employees' rights and those of the companies. Most organisations are happy to allow their employees to use email and Internet access for personal use, but, as one code expresses it,

> this should not interfere with or conflict with business use. Employees should exercise good judgement regarding the reasonableness of personal use.

This particular employer provided a junk mail group so that employees could post messages such as 'looking to rent' or 'something to sell'. Only a few organisations go to the extreme of prohibiting all personal use of the Internet and email. One American University did, and incurred the wrath of its academic staff. (Woodbury, 1998). One of the reasons for employers to exercise some discretion is that the custom and practice, the work culture, of many occupational groups does not see personal use of ICT as an ethical wrong. Stylianou *et al.* (2004) conducted research that shows that R&D staff think it is right to violate both intellectual property (IPR) and privacy rights (when using ICT) to favour open access to data and knowledge. Programmers, more restrictively, think it acceptable to plagiarise (ignore IPR) but not to breach an employee's right to privacy. Some of the standard clauses in a code of conduct on the use of email and the network might be as follows.

- No email or communication should violate the law or company policy.
- Employees should take care to maintain the security of their passwords.
- Accessing and using copyright information in ways that break the law is a disciplinary offence.
- Confidential internal messages should not be posted outside the organisation.
- Chain messages should not be originated or passed on.
- Emails should be brief, courteous and only sent to individuals with an interest in them, and not en bloc to groups.
- Employees should be informed of the level of monitoring of their email and Internet usage that will be carried out.
- The monitoring of an individual's private emails will not be routinely conducted unless it has been specifically authorised by a senior manager in support of a specific allegation of wrongdoing. (This is a particularly contentious clause.)

- Employers should give warnings to staff about misuse and make the penalties clear. Cronin (2004) has carried out some intriguing research on the efficacy of such warnings.

Of course once someone starts to draft such regulations the creation of a rule to prevent one problem, not using email to distribute political messages to staff for example, quickly creates another. Does this mean that Trade Union officials cannot use organisational email to send messages to its members? The other problem is the rate of innovation in e-communication. Each new development probably creates a new opportunity for misuse that had not been anticipated by the writers of codes (*see* the story of the Delhi schoolboy, p. 6).

Activity 10.2

In what ways, if any, might a code of conduct designed to govern email and Internet use at work in a:

- research and consultancy company with a small staff of professional IT employees, and a
- large call centre dealing with service and other enquiries differ? If they do differ, why?

When codes of conduct collide

A fundamental problem within many types of organisation, but particularly those in the public and non-profit seeking sectors, is the issue of the codes of conduct of differing professional groupings and the potential conflicts that the respective codes can create. For example, the role of internal accounting information as a management information support system places the role of accountants within the managerial structures. This does not of itself set accountants and those professionals located within an organisation's managerial structures against those professionals who are outside those structures, but it creates the possibilities of conflict. One of the six principles upon which the International Federation of Accountants' Code of Ethics is based, and which is reflected in the codes of conduct of all the UK professional accountancy bodies, is that of confidentiality. The duty to protect the confidential nature of corporate information is underscored, even after a contract of employment is terminated.

A consideration of the codes of conduct or ethics within which other professionals must operate indicates the potential for conflict. For example, the United Kingdom Central Council for Nursing, Midwifery and Health Visiting (1996) states that 'each registered nurse, midwife and health visitor shall act, at all times, in such a manner as to safeguard and promote the interests of individual patients and clients'. In an environment that has seen health care subjected to considerable financial strictures over the past twenty years, a number of cases have highlighted the extremely difficult situations health care workers face in delivering effective and appropriate medical care 'that is in the interests of individual patients and clients'. The creation of managerial posts for medical staff such as nurses has only served to emphasise these tensions. Hunt (1995 and 1998) recounted cases in health care and social services where individuals have tried to speak out about their concerns, but found their actions thwarted and future career progression blighted.

The very nature of the codes of conduct of nurses and accountants maps out the territory of potential conflict. While the nursing code requires patient advocacy, the accountants' code reflects an orientation of organisational loyalty. Indeed, in the cases of the codes of conduct developed by the American Institute of Internal Auditors and the (American) Government Finance Officers Association (Harris and Reynolds, 1993), explicit reference is made to loyalty to the employer. Even the human resource managers interviewed in the Fisher and Lovell (2000) study displayed a greater organisational orientation than the stereotypical portrayal of human resource managers might suggest.

The respective codes of conduct under which professional accountants and health care workers must operate are both understandable and defensible when viewed separately. However, when placed within a single organisational context, the potential for conflict is evident.

Even within a code of conduct, tensions often exist. Proctor *et al.* (1993: 166) highlight the contradictory situation that confronts social workers:

> The preamble to the Code itself acknowledges that multiple principles could bear on any practice situation ... thus, the potential for conflict is inherent in the profession's values and is reflected in its Code of Ethics.

At least the code of the social workers' professional body recognises these tensions. For accountants, the needs both to respect the confidentiality of corporate information and to respect the public interest are not usually formally recognised as posing any particular dilemma for accountants.

Interestingly, Article IV of the code of conduct of the Project Management Profession (1996: 2) contains the following clause:

> Project management professionals shall protect the safety, health and welfare of the public and **speak out** against abuses in the areas affecting the public interest [emphasis added].

Some would argue that more than a pinch of salt needs to be on hand when considering the pronouncements of aspiring professional associations, but it is quite clear that this aspiring professional body expects its members to take public stands when appropriate. This is an unusually explicit statement from a trade association.

The above discussion has introduced an additional dimension, that of the ethics codes of professional associations. Much has been written on the rise of the professions (*see* Durkheim, 1992; Koehn, 1994; and Larson, 1977, for a discussion of these issues) and the roles of codes of ethics have been influential in this rise. Any trade association that gains the statutory right to control the membership of a particular aspect of human activity (e.g. the British Medical Association and doctoring; the Law Society and particular legal work; and certain professional accountancy bodies and auditing) will possess a code of ethics for its members to follow. The existence of a code of ethics will have been an essential element of the trade association's submission to control the membership of those who wish to practise as specific 'professionals', such as doctors, lawyers and auditors, etc. This is because the trade associations will need to assuage public concern that their state-granted monopolies will not be abused. The 'professional' bodies concerned will commit their members, above all else, to act 'in the public interest' whenever there is a clash of interest.

The 'public interest' is a very slippery concept. It refers to the interests of the public at large, not in a simplistic majority-type way, but rather in terms of what should be in the general interest of civic society if a rational, objective, long-term assessment of a situation is taken. Major scandals involving professional people cast very long shadows over the veracity and intentions of codes of conduct when employed by so-called professional bodies. Examples include the involvement of the international firm of accountants, Arthur Andersen, in the Enron affair. Shortly after Enron's collapse and the complicity of the auditing arm of Andersen's was revealed this part of the company collapsed. Other examples are the failure of the accountancy profession to respond in any meaningful way to the travails of its senior members, or the way that doctors appear to have placed the interests of their profession and fellow colleagues' status above that of the public interest in cases such as the Bristol Heart Surgery Unit, or the body-parts shambles (*see* Case study 2.19). Yet to stay within the membership of a 'profession' the individual member must attempt not to bring the profession into disrepute. As mentioned above, individual professional codes of ethics, while defensible when considered on their own, can present a conflict situation when juxtaposed in particular organisational contexts.

In the Fisher–Lovell (2000) study, few of the accountants and HR professionals had studied their respective professional bodies' code of ethics and little weight seemed to be placed on them. In some senses the issue of the codes of ethics of professional associations has diminished in its relevance as an area of interest and study, as the mantle of professional bodies has slipped, and their claims to be acting in the public interest are seen as little more than façades behind which opaqueness is maintained and vested interests are concealed.

Given the arguments posed in this section against the use of codes, the question might be asked, 'So do codes have a future?' Judging by the increase in the number of organisational codes in evidence, codes certainly have a present. A survey conducted by Arthur Andersen and London Business School (1999) contrasted the prevalence of codes of conduct in 1996 and 1999. Whereas 59 per cent of companies surveyed in 1996 acknowledged the use of a code of conduct, the figure had grown to 78 per cent by 1999, and 81 per cent of companies surveyed in 1999 had values or mission statements. The question is whether this recent upsurge in interest is anything more than a defensive reaction against potential legal claims, or, as in the case of public sector bodies, merely a necessary response to the outcome of the Nolan Committee reports. Does managerial attention to codes of conduct represent anything more than the latest management fad – after quality circles, business process re-engineering, the balanced scorecard, the learning organisation, etc.?

Connexion point
The Nolan principles, which were published in the First Nolan Committee Report on Standards in Public Life, can be read in Chapter 2, p. 71.

So far we have focused upon organisational responses to ethical issues by way of the development and employment of a range of different forms of codes of practice. We now move to a consideration of less overt, more subtle, but possibly more effective ways of shaping behaviour within organisations. This is the notion of corporate cultures, either singular or multiple. The development of a particular culture does not preclude the employment of a code of conduct; indeed the unwritten understandings that invariably comprise a particular culture often act as inviolate rules of conduct. All organisations will have 'ways of working', although those ways may be many and varied, with espoused behaviour sometimes deviating from actual behaviour.

Ethical culture and ethos

There are ethical issues about the propriety of using culture as a device for encouraging people to behave in one way rather than another. However, if we assume for the moment that it is acceptable for managers to foster a culture that encourages ethical behaviour, what would such a culture look like? Snell (1993 and 2000) used the term moral ethos, rather than ethical culture, when he discussed this issue. He defined moral ethos as comprising a set of 'force-fields',

> all of which impinge on members' understandings, judgements and decisions concerning good and bad, right and wrong.
>
> (Snell, 2000: 267)

Snell argued that the moral ethos emerges from the interactions of such forces. For example, if the demand for loyalty is low this may encourage openness within an organisation that supports criticism and acting with integrity. Contrarily an organisation's demand for loyalty may inhibit the exercise of integrity. From an organisational perspective, loyalty is possibly the most important behaviour to cultivate among employees. Willmott (1998: 83) highlighted the contentious nature of codes of conduct and the implicit role of loyalty within them when he observed:

> the value ascribed to the adoption of codes is made conditional upon their contribution to business objectives. This implies that, in principle, the codes will be refined or discarded according to calculations about their continuing contribution to these objectives.

Integrity is less amenable to codes of conduct. For example, a code or rule to respect the confidentiality of corporate affairs in all circumstances might conflict with a broader social perspective of integrity.

Paralleling Kohlberg's stages of moral reasoning, Snell (1993: Chapter 6) identified six types of moral ethos that could arise within organisations. They are:

1. *Fear-ridden ethos*. Behaviour that is characterised by coercion, blind obedience and a myopic focus on organisational survival at any cost.
2. *Advantage-driven ethos*. Employees are rewarded for getting the best for the organisation even if this might involve deception, gamesmanship and exploitation of others if necessary. The ethos encourages private alliances, secrecy and personal advantage.
3. *Members-only ethos*. This ethos demands loyalty and a shared concern to present a good image to those outside the organisation. Clever upstarts are to be tamed and brought into the fold. Internally the focus on group membership can encourage paternalism, sexism and racism.
4. *Regulated ethos*. Regulation and accountability are typical of this ethos. Codes of conduct are written and employees are often expected to self-certify that they have obeyed the rules.
5. *Quality-seeking ethos*. This ethos seeks to encourage everyone to work to the highest ethical standards. Training and development encourages debate and argument about what those standards should be. The ethos can create a sense of arrogance and over-commitment.
6. *Soul-searching ethos*. The organisational ethos supports a spiritual learning community that emphasises integrity and an ongoing ethical dialogue.

Given that corporate cultures can be employed in manipulative ways, the issues of ethicality that pervade this area ultimately resolve themselves around

> the process of moral thought and self-scrutiny that precedes it. This understanding of ethics puts weight on the process of thought that precedes action, to qualify behaviour as ethical.
>
> (Sinclair, 1993: 69)

Thus, the ethicality of a decision lies not in the behaviour displayed, or the decision taken, but in the forethought that preceded the behaviour or decision. This suggests that we need to think more critically about notions of culture. The 'forces' that Snell referred to can be seen at the visible level (e.g. the behaviour of individuals) or at more subtle, less visible levels (e.g. assumptions and beliefs that inform behaviour). Thus it is argued that culture operates at different levels, with important implications for business ethics.

Connexion point

Kohlberg's staged theory of moral development is discussed in detail in Chapter 6, pp. 252–4 ,if you wish to confirm the parallels between the theory and Snell's stages of development of ethical ethos.

Levels of culture

Schein (1992) offered an analysis that reflects three levels of culture, each with a different level of visibility. The top or first level is the most visible level of culture. Within this category would be included evidence such as signs, symbols, written codes, forms of address (i.e. how seniors, peers and juniors are expected to be addressed), clothing (formal, informal), stories and myths (usually about past leaders), rituals, architecture and décor of the company's premises. These visible signs, practices and images are described as artefacts of culture. Schein argues that while these are the most visible evidence of culture they are not always easy to decipher by the external observer. Forms of initiation and 'apprenticeship' are often required before the full significance of these artefacts is revealed.

The second level of culture is represented by the espoused values of a group. These are the beliefs that are articulated, that are audibly expressed. Sometimes these beliefs can be represented by a 'go-get-'em' philosophy, with staff encouraged to 'take the moment' or to 'go for it'. Whether these values are wholeheartedly believed is a matter of question, but if the stated values or beliefs tend to deliver the outcomes sought, then the credibility of the beliefs will grow and become accepted as 'the way things are done around here'. An interesting example of how language is used to create particular attitudes and cultures is reflected in the refusal of one leading security firm to allow its employees to use the term 'failure'. This reflects a refusal by the senior management to accept any level of underachievement by employees, or for the employees to see any demand as unattainable.

Schein referred to the third level as basic assumptions. These are the unspoken beliefs that exist within an organisation. They are the least visible, yet the most pervasive, form of culture because they represent deeply embedded ways of thinking about such questions as the nature of human nature, humanity's relationship with the environment, the nature of truth and of human activity. Basic assumptions are difficult to bring to the surface and challenge. Consequently they operate below the level of consciousness and can undermine the idea of moral agency, which requires conscious deliberation. If corporations are capable of subliminal influence on their employees' basic assumptions then this would be a potent threat to moral agency. There is much debate (Smircich, 1983), however, about whether top managers do have this power or whether any attempts they make to guide cultures lead only to unanticipated changes. That corporations can shape employees' beliefs is not questioned; whether those influences can be controlled to the organisation's benefit is doubtful, at least in the short term.

How to develop the ethical ethos of organisations leads us to a consideration of ethical leadership.

Ethical leadership

The direction and example presented by senior management in terms of what is considered to be acceptable practice within an organisation must inform and shape the behaviour of others. Most textbooks argue that it is a leader's role to define the vision and core values of an organisation. The UK government, through an agency called the CSR Academy, has published a set of CSR competencies. These can be seen as a tool for establishing a set of behaviours and core values within organisations that would support the development of a CSR culture within an organisation. In Schein's terms they would be cultural artefacts. The competencies are intended to make CSR an integral part of business practice not only in large companies but also in small ones. The competencies (CSR Academy, 2004)

- focus on the personal qualities, attitudes and mind-sets which managers need to learn and which will in turn drive improvements in business performance.
- should become embedded into the education, training and development of managers and staff,
- are a tool for assessing performance in all business functions.

The competencies are:

1. Understanding society and business's roles and obligations within it
2. Building capacity within an organisation to work effectively in a responsible manner
3. Questioning business as usual
4. Stakeholder relations
5. Strategic view and ensuring that social and environmental concerns are considered in broad decision making
6. Harnessing diversity.

Alongside these competencies are a set of benchmark indicators that can be used to assess whether people in the company

- are aware of CSR
- understand the issues around CSR
- apply the competencies at work
- integrate the competencies into the culture of the company
- provide leadership on CSR across the organisation.

Competencies have normally been defined as an ability to do something. Distinctively, these CSR competencies are about understanding at the lower levels of attainment and only about action at the higher levels. As a cultural artefact the extent to which the competencies will affect the levels of values and basic assumptions in organisations is limited. They are probably best seen as a way of raising the priority given to CSR in businesses, especially smaller ones, and of creating a market for training courses in CSR.

Kanungo and Mendonca (1996) pointed out that employees will not believe leaders who lack ethical integrity and the leaders' values will not be accepted. They suggested that ethical leadership has to be altruistic, putting the well-being of others in the organisation before self-interest. However, they noted that western culture was better known for its emphasis on egoism than on altruism. The human resource management function has been identified (Connock and Johns, 1995: 159) as the natural repository of organisations' consciences, although a survey found that, in those companies that allocated business ethics to a particular department, responsibility was given to a range of departments (Arthur Andersen and London Business School, 1999: 19).

To suggest that where there is a virtuous set of senior managers all employees will automatically follow their examples of desired practice would be naïve. However, negative examples of immoral behaviour by senior executives can act like a cancer on ethical behaviour throughout an organisation, as the example provided in Case study 7.1 illustrated. The organisation in question appeared to harbour unpalatable practices and beliefs at a senior level, which created moral indifference within the headquarters.

A significant problem for any organisation that publicises its commitment to high ethical standards in all its business dealings is that any one single departure from such standards is likely to attract considerable media attention and cast doubt upon the full range of the organisation's activities. If this does happen, the reaction could be both unreasonably harsh (depending of course upon the nature and scale of the alleged infraction), and also a somewhat disingenuous approach to the analysis and reporting of the incident. Even if the infraction in question is finally judged to be an intentional and knowingly unethical act on the part of the individual employee concerned (however senior), the individual transgression might be just that, an individual's error of judgement. It might not be a revelation of institutionally entrenched unethical practices. In such a situation the more telling test of organisational commitment to a broadly accepted notion of corporate ethical behaviour would be how the organisation's senior management respond to the transgression and the steps they take to remedy the problem. In short, no one is perfect, but when errors are made, or misjudgements are revealed, how do we as individuals and corporations react and respond? The openness of individuals and organisations to acknowledge an error or problem, and the learning that ensues from the incident in question, are more likely to reflect the depth of commitment to ethical practice than are pious claims to high ethical standards made in mission statements or corporate reports. It is at times of tension or challenge that ethical credentials are more likely to be revealed. Organisational learning is a much vaunted but also a most demanding and challenging notion. The processual model of managing is commensurate with such an approach, and Buchholz and Rosenthal (1998) adopt it to explain their view of moral development within organisations.

> The adjustment between the self and the other is neither assimilation of perspectives, one to the other, nor the fusion of perspectives into an indistinguishable oneness, but can best be understood as an 'accommodating participation' in which each creatively affects and is affected by the other through accepted means of adjudication ... because of these dynamics, the leader does not 'stand apart' from a following group, nor is the leader an organizer of group ideas, but rather leadership is by its very nature in dynamic interaction with the group, and both are in a process of ongoing transformation because of this interaction.
>
> (Buchholz and Rosenthal, 1998: 418–19)

Connexion point

The idea of 'accommodating participation' is closely associated with those of the learning organisation and ethical learning discussed in Chapter 3, pp. 119–21.

Such a processual and 'accommodating participatory' approach would represent a fundamental change of perspective for the type of managers represented in the studies reported by Bird and Waters, 1989; and Lovell, 2002. The processual perspective offers, on the one hand, the prospects for moral chaos, but, on the other, possibly the best hope for moral agency. The former because the type of leadership implied in the processual model requires a degree of maturity and humility, but also a strength of belief and conviction that might be beyond many managers and leaders. However, if some form of accommodation is achievable in ways that eschew indoctrination, the debates that would be evident might do much to address many of the concerns raised throughout this book.

An important caveat with respect to greater openness and transparency in corporate dealings is the issue of litigation. The greater demands made of public corporations in terms of their various impacts are in many respects a sign of a maturing society. However, there has been an attendant increase in the propensity of members of the public to take legal action against corporations when infractions occur. In such a context it should not be surprising that corporations become very wary of revealing their 'failings' in public for fear of how such information might be employed. These complex issues can only be moved forward by debate and a developing sense of balance between:

- on the one hand, reparation for any 'injuries' experienced as a result of substandard performance by an individual or organisation, where culpability is evident; and
- on the other, a recognition that 'things' will and do go less than satisfactorily on occasions and that if the 'failing' was innocent, and all reasonable measures had been taken to avoid its occurrence in the first place, then retribution should be avoided, to encourage and foster learning from the experience.

These words are easy to say and write, but much more difficult to put into practice. Yet this is the challenge facing organisations. No easy compromise or solution is on offer, only the prospect of continued action and attention to the levels of behaviour deemed acceptable within our societies.

Best practice standards

In the past ten years a number of standards for business ethics have been developed. These differ from codes of conduct and ethics in that they are meant to have a wide application, and are not written for particular organisations or professional groups. More importantly, whereas a code determines rules or principles for behaviour, standards set a minimum benchmark of behaviour against which organisations can be compared and judged. A standard often accredits, or gives a badge to, any organisation that meets the minimum standard. Membership-based organisations, often referred to as compacts, and international agreements concerned with improving the ethical standards of international business are discussed in Chapter 12.

Accountability 1000 (AA1000)

AA1000 is a quality assurance standard. That is to say it focuses, not on whether an organisation is acting ethically, but on whether it has good systems that will identify whether it is acting unethically and so enable it to put things right. It is like ISO 9000 which is also a process standard, but one concerned with quality assurance systems generally and not just those that focus on ethical matters. It was announced in 1999 by the Institute of Social and Ethical Accountability, which works under the name AccountAbility. It contains both principles and a set of standards against which an organisation can be assessed. The issue of accountability always raises the question of accountability to whom, and in this standard the answer is to stakeholders. The components required in a system that makes an organisation accountable to its stakeholders include:

- planning
- accounting
- auditing and reporting
- embedding and
- stakeholder engagement.

Embedding means ensuring that everyone in the organisation takes the meeting of ethical and social standards seriously and takes it into account in their daily work. This is contrary to the suspicion, about all standards, that organisations only pay attention to them when they are to be accredited or re-accredited and only then to the extent of making sure that the right boxes on the correct forms have been ticked. The standard is also concerned with materiality, that is to say whether the accountability systems include the entire range of topics, such as:

- environmental issues
- work place and employment issues
- health and safety
- behaviour of supply chain partners
- employee involvement
- training and people development
- community involvement
- sustainable development.

In 2004 there were 22 companies using the standard, of which 16 were companies providing assurance services. This was a decrease from the 55 companies who were using the service in 2003 (AccountAbility, 2004). The International Standards Organisation (ISO) reported in 2004 that it was to prepare a set of standards for corporate social responsibility.

Global Reporting Initiative (GRI)

The GRI was initiated in New York and although originally directed at US businesses it is now based in Amsterdam. The original sponsor was CERES but the initiative was subsequently funded and supported by the UN. Its purpose is to propose guidelines for organisations to report on the economic, environmental and social implications of their business practices. The GRI provides a series of performance indicators that it recommends organisations should publish. Some of these are regarded as core and others as optional. But in either case they are divided between:

- *Economic*: monetary flows to stakeholders, e.g. donations to community, civil society or other groups
- *Environmental*: for example, in the area of bio-diversity the impact of a company's activities on sensitive or protected land
- *Social*: for example, the composition of the senior management team, the number of men and women on it.

The performance indicators are either

- descriptions of policy and procedures or
- numerical measures of impacts and outcomes.

The full list can be seen in the Sustainability Reporting Guidelines. In brief, the Guidelines can be seen as a crib for those who need to write triple-line (*see* p. 371) reporting documents.

Social Accountability 8000 (SA8000)

SA8000 is an international standard for corporate behaviour that identifies a range of criteria against which the activities and performance of organisations can be mapped and compared. The intention is that the standard (and the beliefs, values and ethics assumed within it) should be applicable throughout the world, with no exceptions. It is thus an attempt to specify a standard of employment conditions and practices with universal application.

The standard was developed by the Council on Economic Priorities Accreditation Agency (CEPAA). In 2000 it changed its name to Social Accountability International (SAI) and it keeps the standard under review, updates it from time to time and invites comments and advice. Indeed, once you have visited the website you may wish to pass on your own thoughts about the standard's comprehensiveness or robustness.

The standard has nine categories. These are:

- Child Labour
- Forced Labour
- Health and Safety
- Freedom of Association and Right to Collective Bargaining
- Discrimination
- Disciplinary Practices
- Working Hours
- Remuneration
- Management Systems.

Each of the categories has sub-headings. For example, 'Forced Labour' has only one, which effectively states, 'Thou shalt not be engaged in, or associated with, forced labour'. 'Management Systems', on the other hand, has 14 sub-headings. The standard is not enforced by any national law, but it is hoped that, as its use grows as a standard against which corporate practices and behaviours are judged, compliance will become the norm.

As the SA8000 standard is a recent development only a small number of companies have been accredited. Although a wide range of companies, governments and NGOs were consulted during the development of the standard some NGOs concerned with international labour standards criticise CEPAA for being too close to the views of industry. Nevertheless the standard is an attempt to formalise universal ethical standards for businesses and organisations.

The Ethics Compliance Management System Standard (ECS2000)

This standard was developed by the business ethics research project at the Rietaku Centre for Economic Research in Japan. This standard is fully committed to the business case for ethical behaviour in business and assumes that through a continuous improvement process unethical behaviour can be reduced, to the economic and financial benefit of the company. Not surprisingly, since Japan was the home of the Total Quality Management (TQM) movement and the commitment to *Kaizen*, it is not unexpected that they would apply a similar approach to business ethics reporting. The standard proposes four stages in the creation of an ethical compliance system:

- Preparing a legal compliance manual and clarifying the organisation's ethical policy and values.
- Appointing an individual or group to oversee the implementation of the compliance manual.
- An independent audit to check that the manual has been implemented.
- Identifying areas for development and improvement using the audit results.

This standard is a process-centred one. It cannot report on whether a company is acting ethically because each company will produce:

- a set of ethical standards which the organisation will implement according to its own traditions and management beliefs [a code of ethics] and
- a body of rules and regulations [a code of conduct] of specific relevance and importance to the organisation considering its work content, scale and the materials and services in which it deals.

(Reitaku Centre for Economic Studies, 1999: 8)

The standard can only report on whether the company is doing what it says it would do.

Q-RES

This is an Italian initiative; the documents are available in English. The standard was published in draft form in 2001 and was piloted by seven companies. It aims to provide guidance on how to:

- draw up codes of ethics and conduct;
- improve training and communication on social responsibility matters;
- produce externally verified reports.

The project has identified a number of indicators that can be used to indicate social and ethical performance as far as the following stakeholder groups are concerned (Tencati *et al.*, 2003: 19–21):

- Human resources
- Members/shareholder/financial community
- Clients/customers
- Suppliers
- Financial partners
- Government and local authorities
- Community
- Environment.

The indicators that were identified during the pilot projects were a mixture of qualitative, quantitative, and in particular economic measures.

Activity 10.3

Compare and contrast the best practice standards just discussed. Identify the relevant strengths and weaknesses of each. Which would you recommend to a multi-national company?

The challenge of the citizen

In Chapter 8 we considered the possible implications of the notion of corporate citizenship developing along the lines of (theoretical) individual citizenship. We also considered, in Chapter 9, a simultaneous process identified by many commentators as the diminishing and stunted notion of the individual, as reflected solely in the self-seeking consumer. Yet, paradoxically, groups opposed to particular corporate practices have focused their attention upon consumer groups in order to try to change the practices in question. The oil corporations Esso (Exxon in America) and Shell have both been the subject of boycott campaigns. In the case of Esso, the issue was the corporation's oil-drilling activities in the Arctic Circle, whereas for Shell it has been the continuing problems of oil extraction in the Niger delta.

Other specific examples include:

- The picketing of Cartier, one of the premier jewellers on New York's Fifth Avenue, by members of the Campaign to Eliminate Conflict Diamonds, in September 2000.

  As thousands of potential shoppers filed past, the demonstrators brandished signs depicting children whose hands and feet had been amputated by rebels fighting a brutal war in Sierra Leone. 'Did your diamond do this?' the placards screamed. The protest, which was reinforced later by prime-time television advertising, was aimed at forcing the US diamond industry to support legislation to stem the flow of illegal diamonds, thereby robbing rebels in Sierra Leone and Angola of their main funding source. By linking the diamond industry with such extreme violence, the campaign tried to tarnish the image of diamonds as a sign of love and fidelity... NGOs have realised that the quickest way to get the results is to go directly after companies by targeting their customers, their investors, or both.

  (Alden, 2001: 11)

- The picketing of Huntingdon Life Sciences (HLS) is discussed in Chapter 2 (Case study 2.26). In 2002 a number of major clients removed their custom from HLS because of the damage the association was causing the client companies.
- The criticisms levelled at corporations such as Nike for their involvement in Indonesia and other third world countries. In response to adverse publicity and campaigns against their products, some companies, including Nike, have agreed to pay certain non-government organisations (NGOs) to monitor the operations of suppliers to ensure compliance with agreed codes of conduct.
- Conversely the rise of retailing initiatives such as 'Trade Fair' reflects the ability and opportunities that are beginning to occur that allow consumers to display their preferences for ethical practices in business.
- In a similar vein, it can be argued that the significance of US and UK pension funds, unit trusts and investment trusts has increased the importance of the capital and securities markets as potential points of leverage for NGOs. One

of the most active, and famous, pension funds in the field of ethical investing is CalPERS (The California Public Employees Pension system). In July 2001 the *Financial Times* announced the launch of four sets of indices that were designed to reflect the ethicality of corporate practices and activities. An ethical share index was launched. One of the indices relates to companies operating in the UK, one relates to Europe, the third to the USA and the fourth to the whole world. The UK-based index was the first to go 'live' in July 2001.

To be included in the index a company must satisfy a range of criteria including employment issues; types of products produced and/or sold; the human rights records of the countries in which the companies operate; health and safety issues; and community involvement. Of the top 100 UK companies, as measured by the traditional *Financial Times* index, 36 were not included in the first publication of the ethical share index. In some way each of these companies had failed against one or more of the index's criteria.

The Confederation of British Industry (CBI) expressed reservations about the index, fearing that those companies omitted from the index would be perceived as 'bad' companies, whereas any exclusion might reflect merely a difference in terminology or definition. However, pressure groups expressed concern at the inclusion of certain companies in the index. The Free Tibet Campaign, for example, objected to BP's inclusion.

A further development comes from the EU. In 2001 the EU part-financed a business organisation called CSR Europe, which was intended to add impetus to the developments in corporate social responsibility. CSR Europe was charged with promoting corporate social responsibility throughout Europe, culminating with 'European Year on corporate social responsibility' in 2005. Whilst free-market critics accused CSR Europe of being anti-capitalist and anti-market, those on the left have been critical of CSR Europe, seeing it as a 'camouflage', 'allowing big business to claim responsibility without doing anything more than paying its subscriptions. Trade unionists worry that voluntarism cannot provide sufficient protection for workers' (Cowe, 2001).

Those companies initially supporting CSR Europe included Nike, Shell and BP, companies with much adverse publicity to overcome. The reasons for joining CSR Europe are varied but Cowe (2001) observed that, 'while social responsibility is much more than philanthropy, it is about money, not morals'. BT's group personnel director made the following observation, 'It is about doing business in a way that persuades our customers to buy from us, our employees to work hard for us and our communities to accept us'.

The phenomenon of the rise of citizen pressure groups, whether they are human or animal rights based, or associated with environmental issues, is a development that contains the seeds of positive and negative potentialities. The positive aspects relate to the challenging (and sometimes overturning) of unethical corporate practices. Campaigns and protests can reflect active citizen participation in the social, political and economic evolution of nation states and super-nation states. However, there is also the downside potential, the risks associated with these developments. These risks are three-fold.

1. The first relates to the ability of the under-represented, the already socially and economically excluded, to be able to articulate their concerns – and be listened to. At least with universal suffrage, each person has only one vote. In pressure group politics, the super-organised, media-wise, politically adept pressure group is likely to have a considerable advantage over less well-organised groups. In the latter scenario, 'might is right' might well prevail, which is hardly an ethically sound approach.
2. The second concern is that, if scarce resources are to be effectively harnessed and utilised (a justifiable ethical concern), decision making in corporations cannot become paralysed by rules, by interminable meetings, or by an inability to achieve consensus on every decision.
3. The third concern is associated with the way opposition to corporate or government practices is expressed. The violence witnessed at the G8 summits at Genoa, Seattle and London shocked many people. Unintentional violence can be seen as one of the possibilities of democratic expression, but a number of the pressure groups present at these summits were also concerned by the violence, not just because it was never their intention that the demonstrations would develop in the ways they did, but also because the violence detracted from their important messages.

The ways societies evolve to handle these aspects of the corporate citizen relationship is of fundamental importance to societal development.

Reflections

From the Hobbesian view of human behaviour, that people will not behave morally without the fear of retribution, flows the necessity for rules, of which codes of conduct are an obvious example. Bauman saw rules and codes, based upon reason, as leading to a morality associated with law – the laws of business and bureaucracy. This adherence to procedural rationality requires that

> all other emotions must be toned down or chased out of court . . . the most prominent of the exiled emotions are moral sentiments; that resilient and unruly 'voice of conscience'.
>
> (Bauman, 1994: 8)

Interestingly, Bauman argued that when the term ethics appears in the vocabulary of bureaucracy it is invariably in connection with 'professional ethics'. The latter term is considered to be breached when a member shows disloyalty either to the organisation or to (organisational) colleagues. A qualified notion of honesty thus becomes of critical importance, i.e. the keeping of promises and contractual obligations. This leads to predictability and consistency in organisations, an extremely important managerial need. When this is coupled with the notion of 'floating responsibility', an escape route is provided for those seeking a quiet life in the face of an awkward organisational issue.

People's instrumentalism is seen as something to be encouraged by Clutterbuck (1992: 100–1) as he exhorted organisations to reward exemplary behaviour, possibly with cash payments, and to 'punish breaches of the code publicly; use the key motivators of influence, promotion and access to resources'. This simplistic view of human nature and notions of managing assumes that instrumentalism is the only determinant, or at least the dominant explanation, of human behaviour. From a purely instrumental perspective, it is also an expensive option. In the governing of human relationships, trust is a far less expensive option than contractualism or financial incentives. But the problem remains of whether trust can be relied upon. When associated with notions of loyalty, it becomes increasingly problematic. For example, in a situation where it has become known to you that a product of your employing organisation poses health risks to consumers, which is paramount, your loyalty to:

- your work colleagues,
- your employing organisation,
- your family (who depend on your income),
- the consumer, or
- the general public?

The converse of the loyalty question is which of these groups has the right to trust you and your actions in such a situation?

Maybe the least that can be said for codes of ethics is that they give the principled employee a reference point should times become ethically challenged and certain organisational practices give rise to serious cause for concern. At its best a code can reflect an honestly expressed expectation about moral conduct within an organisation, with the code probably written in terms of principles rather than in a prescriptive or proscriptive fashion. Employees would be encouraged to act with moral agency and the codes would be supported by mechanisms that would allow concerned employees to raise concerns in a neutral and anonymous forum, preferably using external counsellors.

The roles of codes and agreements relating to the relationships between MNCs, national governments and supplier networks are important and interesting elements in the debates on codes of conduct. At the same time debates relating to codes of ethics and professions, an area of much academic activity at one time, have become less relevant as the compromised positions of many business professions have come to general attention.

Within the complex arenas that are modern business corporations, codes of conduct, codes of ethics and the prevailing culture/s will be important reference points for many of the players involved with, or affected by, the activities of the corporation. At different times the eight roles of codes discussed in this chapter will be seen in operation. Yet if ethics is at the heart of an organisation's practices and its *raison d'être*, embedded within its culture/s, written codes become less important. They become less defensive in terms of their tenor, being essentially codes of ethics.

Summary

In this chapter the following key points have been made:

- While not universally or uniformly recognised, distinctions between codes of conduct and codes of ethics help crystallise the intended purpose of a code.
- Codes of practice can be important mechanisms that allow business corporations to negotiate their position in a society.
- Codes of practice have multiple roles within organisations, which will not necessarily be mutually exclusive.
- The development of a code of practice is, at one and the same time, an understandable development by a corporation, but also a reflection of a lack of trust in the integrity and reliability of its employees.
- There are arguments against developing codes of practice that require ethical practice to be at the heart of an organisation's activities and 'ways of working'.
- The various international and public ethical best practice standards that companies can commit to each have separate priorities and emphases.
- Organisational cultures and leadership are critical to understanding an organisation's actual (as distinct from espoused) values.
- The challenges to corporations by organised lobby groups of citizens are also an important means of monitoring the ethical performance of companies and their degrees of adherence to codes.

Quick revision test

1. Identify the possible roles of codes of ethics.
2. What are the arguments against the employment of codes of practice within organisations?
3. What other means can organisations employ to communicate and inculcate organisational values, in addition to codes of conduct and ethics?
4. How many levels of culture does Edgar Schein identify; which are the most changeable?

Typical assignments and briefs

1. Why have codes of ethics become so commonplace in corporations and how useful are they?

2. Draft a code of conduct to cover e-communications (email, Web use and so on). Explain and justify your proposed code.
3. What are the drawbacks and problems associated with codes of ethics?
4. Discuss the role of leadership and organisational culture in developing a socially responsible company.

Group activity 10

Search the World Wide Web to find a code of ethics that you can download. The easiest way might be to think of a company you have heard of and track down its code. Analyse it by answering the following questions.

- Is it a code of ethics, a code of conduct or both?
- Does it look like a standard code, the same as everyone else's, or does it look as if it has been tailored to that organisation?
- Is it a code that recognises that some things within it are likely to be aspirations?
- Is it clear and unambiguous or does it leave lots of 'wriggle room'? If it does is such a 'fudge factor' necessary?
- Does it look like a PR document or one that will be helpful to employees?
- If you were an employee of the organisation what would you think the code implied about the organisation's view of its staff?

Recommended further reading

A useful text is R.A. Buchholz and S.B. Rosenthal (1998) *Business Ethics: The Pragmatic Path Beyond Principles to Process*, London: Prentice Hall. Deborah Smith's pamphlet, *Demonstrating Corporate Values – which standard for your company?*, published by the Institute of Business Ethics in 2002 is an excellent comparative guide to the various codes and standards of ethical business available to organisations.The following articles will be of interest to those who wish to study the topic further: C. Cassell, P. Johnson and K. Smith (1997), 'Opening the Black Box: Corporate codes of ethics in their organisational context', *Journal of Business Ethics*, 16, 1077–93; G. McDonald and A. Nijhof (1999) 'Beyond codes of ethics: an integrated framework for stimulating morally responsible behaviour in organisations', *Leadership & Organisation Development Journal*, 20(3), 133–46; R.C. Warren (1993) 'Codes of ethics: Bricks without straw', *Business Ethics: A European Review*, 2(4), 185–91. *See also* S. Srivastva and D.L. Cooperrider (1988) *Executive Integrity: The Search for High Human Values in Organisational Life*, San Francisco: Jossey-Bass Inc., 1–28.

Useful websites

Topic	Website provider	URL
The CSR Competency framework	The CSR Academy	http://www.csracademy.org.uk/competency.htm
The AA1000 quality standard for corporate social responsibility	AccountAbility	http://www.accountability.org.uk/aa1000/default.asp
The One World Trust website	One World Trust	http://www.oneworldtrust.org/
Transparency International website	Transparency International	http://www.transparency.org/
The Global Reporting Initiative Web page	CERES/UN	http://www.globalreporting.org/
Social Accountability SA8000 Web page	Social Accountability International	http://www.cepaa.org/SA8000/SA8000.htm
The Ethics Compliance Management System Standard (ECS2000)	Reitaku Centre for Economic Studies	http://www.ie.reitaku-u.ac.jp/~davis/assets/applets/ecs2k-e.pdf
Q-RES Report		http://www.biblio.liuc.it:8080/biblio/liucpap/pdf/95e.pdf
This is a good place to find copies of professional, governmental and organisational codes of ethics. Particularly fun is the code of ethics for witches (the Covenant of the Goddess). Most of the codes on this site are utterly serious.	Centre for the Study of Ethics in Professions	http://www.iit.edu/departments/csep/PublicWWW/codes/
An interesting corporate ethics website	Texas Instruments	http://www.ti.com/corp/docs/company/citizen/ethics/benchmark.shtml
Issue brief on codes of ethics/values	Business for Social Responsibility	http://www.bsr.org/CSRResources/IssueBriefDetail.cfm?DocumentID=395
Shell Canada: Statement of general business principles	Shell Canada	http://www.shell.ca/code/values/commitments/principles.html

Globalisation and international business

Learning outcomes

Having read the chapter and completed its associated activities, readers should be able to:

- Define globalisation and the ethical issues that it raises.
- Evaluate the evidence and arguments concerning the fairness of the economic impact of world trade liberalisation.
- Evaluate the roles of multinational enterprises in relation to developing the institutions of ethical business practice.
- Identify the potential for close relationships between multinational enterprises and governments to damage ethically responsible business practices.
- Identify the risks to peace and stability that multinational enterprises may cause by their operations in politically and militarily unstable regions.
- Judge the arguments for multinational enterprises remaining within ethically dubious countries, and trying to change things from the inside, or for withdrawing.
- Rehearse the argument about the social and cultural impact of globalisation.
- Identify the strengths and weaknesses of various approaches to developing codes and compacts for the conduct of international business.

Introduction

The ethics of globalisation, for most, rests on a fine point of utilitarianism. Does globalisation result in more harm than good? If it creates both harm and good in large measures, but the harm and the good are felt by different groups of people, how should the benefits experienced by some be weighed against the disadvantages heaped on others? It would probably not be sufficient to quieten the disadvantaged to simply point out that in aggregate the good outweighs the bad.

Connexion point

Utilitarianism is one of the major ethical theories. It is discussed in detail in Chapter 3, pp. 127–36. Those who take a human rights perspective, which is also discussed in Chapter 3, do not approach the ethical issues of globalisation from a utilitarian perspective but simply argue that companies operating in the global marketplace should take care to respect human rights.

A consideration of the ethics of globalisation, and of the role of multi-national enterprises (MNEs) within it, must therefore include an analysis of its impact. The likely areas of impact can be deduced from the definition of globalisation.

DEFINITIONS

Globalisation is a process which is bringing societies that were previously economically, politically and culturally diverse into convergence. This is being achieved by a combination of the success of capitalism, the growth of a common mass culture (McLuhan and Powers' (1989) 'global village') and the wish of people in all societies, through their rational choices, to choose the same goals. It is a process that affects three domains, the political, the economic and the cultural and social.

The World Commission on the Social Dimension of Globalization (WCSDG, 2004: §132–5) identified the following characteristics of globalisation.

- Liberalisation of international trade.
- Growth of foreign direct investment (FDI) and massive cross-border financial flows.
- Growth of the new technology of IT and communications that makes communication between countries easier.
- The greater ease of transporting goods and people around the world that now makes it possible for markets to be global in scope.

This last characteristic gives rise to a different definition of globalisation that sees it not as a description of a process but as a strategy that a company can choose to adopt. Companies may decide to produce and market their goods and services for a global market (Holden, 2002: 44).

In this chapter the impacts and ethical considerations of globalisation will be reviewed under the following headings.

- Trickle down or just trickery? Does the opening of national markets to world trade and an increase in international trade benefit all countries?
- Developing institutions or taking advantage? Do multi-national companies seek to improve the institutional arrangements (by advocating and practising good employment practices and operating to high standards of business) in host companies or do they seek to benefit from the weak institutional and legal frameworks governing business in many developing countries?

- Creating political tensions between and within states. Does the involvement of multi-national companies, many of which have a higher turnover than developing countries have gross domestic product (GDP), exacerbate regional political instabilities and create political disturbances and unrest?
- Staying put or withdrawing? Multi-national enterprises may find themselves operating in countries where they become complicit with intolerable unfairness and abuses of human rights, and they have to decide whether to remain or withdraw.
- Cultural diversity or cultural homogenisation? Does the global reach of multinational companies threaten indigenous cultures and values and lead all societies to a standardised culture that diminishes the variety of human cultures?

The remainder of the chapter will consider the various attempts to create a worldwide framework of global governance to guide and police the propriety and fairness of international trade and its globalising consequences.

However, the ethical issues of globalisation are not new. They could be found in the actions of colonial companies, such as the Dutch and English East India Companies, which were as powerful and globally dominating in the eighteenth and nineteenth centuries as multi-nationals are today. The modern themes listed above for this chapter had their equivalents in the eighteenth- and early nineteenth-century history of the British East India Company in particular.

- **The charge that the East India Company impoverished India.** In the eighteenth century it was a common charge that the Company was draining India of its wealth and transferring it to Britain. It was accused of enriching new elites, both Indian and British (called nabobs), while the mass of the Indian population suffered intermittent famines. The charges were crystallised when Warren Hastings, the Governor-general, was impeached by Parliament in 1786 over issues that would today be termed corporate governance. He was found not guilty in 1795.
- **Exploiting weak institutions in host countries.** When the East India Company was establishing itself in India in the eighteenth century the nominal sovereign power was the Moghul Empire, which by that time was in decline. The company was able to exploit the empire's institutional weaknesses to its own commercial advantage by acquiring formal government roles, such as the tax collecting function of the *diwani* of Bengal.
- **Increasing political tensions in a region.** The decline of the Moghul Empire created military and political tensions as different groups sought to fill the political vacuum. The East India Company was one of these and it developed its own armies and spent much of the eighteenth century fighting wars in India.
- **Staying in or withdrawing decision.** The company's business stretched as far as China, from where it imported tea to Britain. The tea had to be paid for and conveniently the Company had a monopoly of opium production in India. It was convenient to ship the opium to China, where there was a good market, and use the proceeds to buy the tea. Unfortunately the Chinese government banned the sale of opium in 1729 because of its damaging effects on the users.

The Company formally withdrew from the illegal trade, but it would sell the opium to private traders in Calcutta and then turn a blind eye when they exported it at their own risk to China. However, by the 1830s the revenues from the opium trade which in the eighteenth century had been only about 5 per cent of the Company's turnover had become much more important and Britain engaged in gunboat diplomacy in China, not just to protect the opium trade but to protect its much more important general monopoly of trade with China.

- **Cultural diversity or cultural globalisation?** William Dalrymple's (2002) book on the interaction between the Company's officials and the Mughal elite in India in the eighteenth century tells an intriguing history of how originally many of the British in India were fascinated by the culture of the Mughal courts, adopted its customs, married Mughal women and became 'white Mughals'. But in the late eighteenth century, and certainly during the Victorian era, the British came to despise Indian culture and kept aloof from it so that those Indians who wished to benefit from the opportunities that the Company offered had to adapt to British ideas, values and customs.

The World Commission (WCSDG, 2004: §134) has pointed out that one difference between eighteenth- and nineteenth-century globalisation and that of today is that the earlier period involved large migrations of people – Africans to the Americas, Indians to East and South Africa, the Welsh to Patagonia and so on. Many of these movements themselves raised moral questions because the migrations were enforced by the slave trade. In the current phase of globalisation money and goods are free to cross borders but in general people are not. However, this is not to say that globalisation does not still create some problems associated with migration. The ethical charge is still that people are moved to the advantage of the first world and the disadvantage of the third world. One particular instance concerns the National Health Service (NHS) in the United Kingdom. The NHS is short of doctors and it will be several years before the expansion of medical education delivers the needed fully qualified doctors. To fill the immediate gap the NHS has recruited doctors from other countries, from Africa in particular. In 2004 two-thirds of newly registered doctors in the UK came from abroad. Many African countries desperately need the doctors they train to remain, not least to help deal with the AIDS epidemic they face. Yet in Zambia, to take one example, only 50 of the 600 doctors trained there since independence are still practising in the country. This migration also has the advantage for the UK that it does not have to bear the cost of training many of the doctors it employs. This movement of doctors is seen by both the British government and the British Medical Association as an ethical problem. In this case, however, the migration is not an enforced one. Doctors trained in Africa are inevitably attracted by the better salaries and working conditions that they would experience in the UK (BBC, 2005).

Although the claims that globalisation has brought new ethical problems need to be seen in historical context, globalisation has increased the velocity and awareness of the ethical problems of worldwide economic integration. As Petrick (2000: 1) expressed it, the 'high velocity global market place is complex and challenging'. The international marketplace can now operate in real time – as do the world's stock exchanges as trading moves through time zones from one exchange to another – and not have to deal with the time lags in communication that characterised earlier times. This is the other main difference between the current and the historical periods of globalisation.

The networks of global, multi-national and transnational companies and organisations and NGOs form the arenas in which such problems may arise and the business cultures of different societies and countries may come into contact with each other. It will be useful to define the differences between them.

DEFINITIONS

Multi-national enterprises (MNEs) have been divided into three types (Harzing, 2000):

- **Multi-domestic companies** are federations of autonomous subsidiaries that operate in different countries.
- **Global companies,** by comparison, view themselves as operating in a world market and their products and services make relatively little concession to the particularities of different national markets.
- **Transnational companies** are networks and tend to have little specific national identification or base, although they do have a legal base in a particular country. Worldwide consultancy and accountancy firms are a good example of this type of organisation. They are run by international managements and are willing to move their capital and operations to any favourable location (Hirst and Thompson, 1996: 11).

Now that the key terms have been defined we can consider the ethical issues of globalisation in turn.

Trickle down or just trickery?

Does the evidence we have of the effects of globalisation and trade deregulation on world markets display an improvement of people's well-being? The available evidence is at best mixed. At worst we are experiencing even greater concentrations of power within corporations over resources that lie outside the political arena, with fundamental questions regarding authority, responsibility and accountability remaining unanswered. The observations of Anita Roddick, founder of the Body Shop organisation, are interesting in this context. She was responding to an article by Philippe Legrain that had appeared in the *Guardian* (on the day before the publication of her letter). The latter had made the case that the deregulation of world markets, in line with the actions of the WTO, should be welcomed by all, as ultimately all would benefit. Case study 12.1 presents the words of Ms Roddick.

Case study 12.1

Anita Roddick's views on globalisation

I went to Seattle in November 1999 to speak at a teach-in on globalisation and to peacefully protest against the WTO. Probably the only international retailer on the 'wrong' side of the police lines. I was baton-charged and tear-gassed by riot police. It was a frightening experience of what corporate controlled reality might look like. Perhaps it prejudiced me against the WTO, it certainly re-radicalised me. Mr Legrain trots out the free traders' familiar falsehood that globalisation is all about making the poor richer. No, Mr Legrain, it's about making the rich even richer ... I can only presume his travels haven't taken him out of the international conference centres into the slums and shanty towns where the poorest and most exploited people live. How else could he glibly state that seamstresses in Bangladesh are not exploited because 'they earn more than they would as farmers'? I recently visited Nicaragua, a country restructured to comply with the WTO and IMF vision of economic progress. There I met workers from the free trade zone, who are paid less than $5 a day to make jeans and shirts exported to the US and sold at obscene mark-ups. Does their pay afford them [the means] to live decently? Depends if a 10 ft square, dirt floored, shack with no plumbed in water or sanitation is decent.

I also visited a cooperative of peasant farmers who grow sesame seed in a remote part of Nicaragua. The price of sesame crashed in 1993. Working with Christian Aid, Body Shop now community trades with the cooperative, sustaining the farmers' livelihoods and culture. They may not be rich, but they do lead dignified lives off the rollercoaster of the commodity market. When the WTO promotes such fair trade, I may 'dump my prejudices'.

(*Source*: Anita Roddick, Letter to the *Guardian*, 13 July 2001)

Discussion activity 12.1

What were the positions taken on international free trade and its impact on developing countries at the Gleneagles G8 meeting in 2005? Had postions changed since Seattle in 1999?

The two sides of this debate are:

1. The trickle down case – that freeing international trade from restrictions increases the total wealth of the world and that, while this will inevitably reward the elites, the benefits will also trickle down to everyone. This argument is based on standard economic theory which proposes that free international trade encourages countries to specialise in exporting those services and products in which they have a competitive advantage and not to produce those that other countries can produce more efficiently. This leads to a situation in which all countries are producing the most added value they can and are not wasting resources on producing things inefficiently that could better be imported from elsewhere. This maximises the world's wealth, and all benefit.

2. The contrary case argues that, whilst the trickle down case may be logical, the international trade market has a number of imperfections that can prevent the anticipated benefits for all emerging. The first is that large companies from the industrialised countries have greater bargaining power than the small-scale companies and traders in the developing world from whom they buy goods. The former therefore gain the most advantage from international trade. The second imperfection is that the industrialised countries demand that the developing countries place no barriers on international trade but do not return the favour. The most obvious example is that the European Union's Common Agricultural Policy subsidises food production in Europe and so makes it difficult for food producers in the developing world to export their produce to Europe. The third imperfection is that the global institutions set up to regulate international trade, notably the World Trade Organisation (WTO), do not fairly represent the interests of the many parties to them. The institutions respond more to the needs of the industrialised countries, which have their own global institutions such as the G8, and less to the voices of the countries of the developing world. The consequence of these imperfections is that international trade does not necessarily deliver what it promises, and that its promises are sleight of hand and trickery to disguise the fact that the poor in the poorest countries do not benefit from the liberalisation of foreign trade. Even if international trade does make some poor countries better off there is no guarantee that those benefits will be fairly enjoyed by the whole population. Most of the oil exported from Nigeria comes from the Niger delta region. The major oil companies are inevitably active in the region and the Government of Nigeria receives most of its revenues from the oil industry, but the population of the delta has not benefited economically. Indeed the environmental damage to agricultural land caused by the oil operations has worsened even that poor standard of living it used to have.

It is necessary to consider the evidence relating to this debate. Some researchers have focused on identifying whether there is a statistical correlation between growth in world trade and changes in the level of income inequality between countries. As is often the case, research studies do not agree. Lundberg and Squire (2003) found that increasing the openness of international trade makes for greater income inequality between countries. Dollar and Kraay (2002 and 2004), however, found that increasing international trade had little or no impact on income inequality. The figures for countries' poverty levels (percentage of people living on less than $1.08 a day at 1993 purchasing levels) and countries' growth in international trade (measured by exports as a percentage of GDP) was studied by Ravallion (2004). He found a negative correlation between the two, namely as a country's trade increases the amount of poverty decreases, but the correlation was too weak to carry conviction.

China has often been cited as a case where the expansion of its international trade following the start of its 'Open Door 'policy in the early 1980s was a major factor in its success against poverty (World Bank, 2002). An analysis of the statistics by Ravallion and Chen (2004) gives a negative correlation of –0.75 between trade increases and decreases in poverty. As always with correlations, however, it may be dangerous to assume that statistical association implies a cause and effect relationship. The greatest decrease in poverty in China occurred in the early

1980s when trade was liberalised. The poverty rate fell from 76 per cent in 1980 to 23 per cent in 1985 (Ravallion, 2004: 9). However, this was also a period of great increases in agricultural production following the de-collectivisation of agriculture. Conversely the greatest changes in China's openness to international trade occurred after 1985 when poverty had already fallen. It is at least arguable that the reduction in poverty was more to do with agrarian reform than with trade liberalisation. Ravallion also studied the differential impact of China's accession to the WTO in 2001 which involved massive reductions in China's tariff barriers to trade. His analysis suggests that between 2001 and 2007

- 75 per cent of rural households are predicted to lose income but only 10 per cent of urban households would suffer similarly.
- Some areas of China will lose income while other areas will gain.
- In rural areas larger households will benefit more from trade liberalisation than small ones.
- In urban areas smaller households will benefit more than larger ones.

Similar patterns can be found in other countries. In India some states have benefited massively from trade liberalisation and the growth of the IT industry. Other states, notably Bihar on the Gangetic plain, continue with a subsistence economy with increasing levels of poverty. Equally it is the urban areas that benefit from increasing international trade and the rural populations that mostly suffer. The World Bank completed a study of the likely impact of a decrease in the tariffs protecting cereal production in Morocco. The impact of a 30 per cent reduction in tariffs would have been to increase rural poverty while improving the lot of urban households.

The general conclusion concerning the relationship between the opening up of countries to international trade and the level of poverty is that trade openness may not be the key issue in decreasing poverty but that its impact within a particular country is likely to be variable between regions and groups within the country.

It seems unlikely therefore that world trade liberalisation can be morally justified by its impact on reducing poverty. Rather, the consequence of world trade liberalisation for developing countries may be to create a two-track economic and social system, sometimes known as dualism and sometimes as the informal economy.

Dualism or the informal economy

Dualism was first observed in the British and Dutch empires in South Asia, the British in India and the Dutch in what is now Indonesia. The term means that two economic systems exist in one place in parallel with one another but with little connection or interaction between them. In the nineteenth-century Asian empires there would typically be a capitalist plantation economy that was integrated into international trade by exporting raw material to the west and which used hired labour. Alongside it would be a subsistence agricultural sector that ate what it produced and participated very little in markets. An argument was often made that the plantation managers acted in an economically rational way while the peasant producers exhibited a backward sloping supply curve for labour; in other words the more they earned the less inclined they were to work. However, subsequently it was recognised that this phenomenon was explained by structural barriers that made it too difficult for subsistence producers to put effort into the production of risky cash crops that they would not be able to eat if the market failed to offer them a worthwhile price, quite a likely consequence as they were forced to sell to monopsonistic middlemen. The modern equivalent of this situation is known as the informal economy, which exists in many countries. It consists of small-scale manufacturing, service provision and agricultural work. It is characterised by:

- A lack of recognition and formality: these enterprises do not submit accounts or have legal recognition, they do not recognise laws and regulations and, in many countries, will obtain their electricity by tapping into the grid illegally. The informal market will often specialise in pirated goods such as tapes and CDs. They are a tolerated, but therefore fragile, form of enterprise.
- No access to the formal sources of credit.
- They do not have access to wider regional, national and international markets.
- A lack of rights and legal protections for the people within it.
- Women forming a large proportion of the informal workforce.
- Wages and income being at or close to poverty levels.
- An entrepreneurial creativity and energy that helps respond very quickly to market demand.

The World Commission on the Social Dimension of Globalisation (WCSDG, 2004) reported that globalisation had a great potential for good but that this potential was not yet being fulfilled. Their vision was a moral one.

> We have come to an agreement on a common goal: a fair globalisation which creates opportunities for all. We wish to make globalisation a means to expand human well-being and freedom, and to bring democracy and development to local communities where people live. [ ] Our primary concerns are that globalisation should benefit all countries and should raise the welfare of all people throughout the world.
>
> (WCSDG, 2004: §3 and 171)

It is clear that the liberalisation of international trade will not automatically meet that vision through a trickle down process.

- Between 1985 and 2000 16 developing countries had a per capita income growth of more than 3 per cent, 32 developing countries grew at less than 2 per cent, 23 countries showed negative growth. China and India were transitional countries with high growth rates.
- The gap between GDP per capita in the poorest and richest countries has increased. In the early 1960s per capita income was 50 times higher in the 20

richest countries than in the 20 poorest. By the new millennium this figure had increased to 110.

- In the developed countries, particularly in the UK and the USA, the ratio between the top 10 per cent highest earners and the lowest 10 per cent earners has increased between the mid-1980s and the mid-1990s by 35.1 per cent in the UK and 36.8 per cent in the USA.
- In the developing countries the volatility of flows of foreign direct investment has brought new jobs to countries, most obviously in the movement of call centres from the West to South Asia, but has also decreased the security of jobs in these mobile industries. (WCSDG, 2004: §210)

If there is no global action to help spread the undoubted benefits of increasing trade then unfairness will result.

Developing institutions or taking advantage?

Many of the ethical criticisms of multinationals and transnationals arise from their tendency to exploit local conditions for commercial advantage. In practice, developing countries may have lower expectations, and weaker laws, concerning acceptable conditions of employment, minimum wage rates, pollution control, health and safety, and many other factors concerning management and business. The problem is to determine to what extent it is right and proper to exploit these circumstances to gain a commercial advantage. There will be extreme cases when it would be uncontroversial to say that such exploitation is bad. A company dumping in third world markets a product that has been declared unfit for use or consumption in the country of origin is such as case. It is perhaps a little more difficult when we consider companies that move their manufacturing operations to new countries where the cost of labour is much lower. It would be clear that they are taking advantage of the lower wages; the question is whether this is simply the market working effectively or an unethical taking of advantage. The typical corporate response to this charge is that inward investment gives jobs to those who would not otherwise have them. The company is thus doing good by giving people jobs and ought not to be expected to pay them wages above the going rates. Local employers would also object and claim they were being harmed if a multi-national started to pay its staff above the labour market rate. Often, however, a form of dual economy emerges in which the multinational companies in a developing country exist in parallel with the local companies but occupy a separate economic 'world', paying higher wages and granting better employment conditions than companies in the local economy. Such a development seems to have happened with the development of the IT industry in India. As the *Economist* (2001) reported, most of India's new economy holds aloof from the old Indian economy. Software engineers in Bangalore, the capital of India's IT industry, work in good conditions in state-of-the-art corporate campuses whereas the rest of the economy operates in poor to bad conditions. Such dual economies produce their own ethical problems and critics demand to know why the benefits of inward investment are not being spread more widely in society.

Chakraborty (1999: 20) laments the impact of western companies employing Indian MBAs at a salary three times that which an Indian company would pay, but still lower than an equivalent person would be paid in the USA, because of the disaffection produced among those not lucky enough to be employed by a multi-national.

Case study 12.2

The Bhopal disaster

This episode is a tragic and classic case study in business ethics. Union Carbide, an American-owned company, owned 50.9 per cent of a pesticide plant in Bhopal, central India. The government of India had apparently been so keen to receive this inward investment that it had found a way around its own legislation, which at that time allowed overseas companies to own no more than 40 per cent of any Indian company in which they invested. On the night of the 2–3 December 1984, 40 tonnes of poisonous gases were thrown into the air over Bhopal from the plant. The gases burned the eyes and lungs of people on whom it settled and, when it crossed into their blood stream, it damaged many physiological systems. Over 3,000 people died and 20,000 were injured. At least that was one estimate; the death and morbidity rates of the accident are still the subject of controversy. Campaigners claim that the accident has caused 20,000 deaths in the twenty years since the accident and that half a million have become chronically ill (Ramesh, 2004).

There appear to have been a number of contributory factors that led to the leakage. They mostly related to a cost-cutting culture in a factory that at that time was making a loss and only working at a third of its capacity. On the night of the disaster six safety measures designed to prevent a leak were inadequate, malfunctioning or switched off. Safety audits had been done that had revealed major safety concerns but no action had been taken. These all raise the question of the extent to which Union Carbide had taken advantage of low levels of safety monitoring and expectations to save costs.

It can be argued that a concern to save costs characterised the company's behaviour during the aftermath of the disaster. On one account the company's legal team arrived in Bhopal days before their medical team (Bhopal.net, 2001). One of the issues after the accident was whether the case should be settled in an American court, as the government of India wanted, or in an Indian court, as the company wished, and as was in fact the case. The company fought liability for the accident and agreed an out-of-court settlement five years later with the government of India for $470m. The families of those who died received an interim payment of $550 per fatality. Had the deaths occurred in the USA the families might have received a hundred times that amount (De George, 1999: 511). Associations of the injured are still fighting for further compensation (Corpwatch, 2001). The Bhopal.com website (2001), owned by the Union Carbide Corporation, argues that the 1989 settlement has provided sufficient money from its investment to provide the compensation, and that the compensation was much higher than any settlement that would have been payable under Indian law. The company saw this settlement as complete and final.

It was the twentieth anniversary of the incident in 2004 and this became a time for taking stock. The site of the plant in 2004 belonged to the government of India. The site had not been cleared and there were reports that it still contained potentially damaging chemicals. Dow Chemicals, which had taken over Union Carbide, claimed that it had no further responsibilities in India while the government of India was still pursuing its demand, that Dow Chemicals should clean up the site, through the Indian Courts.

There is an outstanding criminal case against Warren Anderson, the former Chief Executive of Union Carbide. The Indian CBI (Criminal Branch Investigations) had sought Anderson's extradition from his retirement in the United States to stand trial in India. However, the American Government had not responded, pointing to technical difficulties in the claim. The CBI was still pursuing the case, however (*Times of India*, 2004).

The poor of Bhopal, who had borne the brunt of the toxic effects of the discharge, were often still living close to the plant. Only part of Union Carbide's payment had been distributed to the victims. By 2004 there was a balance of £174m (the compensation fund had been swelled by interest over fifteen years). The problems of identifying the victims and deciding what proportion of the compensation sum each should receive had brought the payments to a standstill. In 2004, however, the Supreme Court of India demanded that the government should pay the money out on a per-capita basis (Brown, 2004); which would mean that each victim would receive about $300. There was some scepticism among the activists in Bhopal as to whether the money would appear in the victims' hands.

A group of activists, the 'Yes Men Group', arranged an elaborate hoax so that when BBC producers arranged an interview with a representative of Dow Chemicals (the successor company to Union Carbide) they were actually talking to one of the hoaxers who stated, when interviewed on radio, that Dow Chemicals was accepting full responsibility for the Bhopal disaster. He later said that he was 'speaking on behalf of Dow in a certain way. I was expressing what they should express' (Wells and Ramesh, 2004). Residents of Bhopal had broken down in tears when they heard that Dow had finally accepted their responsibilities, a collapse that was no doubt repeated when they learnt it was not true.

Discussion activity 12.2

The harm caused by an event such as the Bhopal gas leak can have consequences for many years; yet the corporations, who may be liable for the harm through their negligence, cannot, as commercial organisations, tolerate having long-term, open-ended liabilities on their balance sheets. Discuss whether the belief that responsibility can be ended by a one-off payment in final settlement can be sustained when the harm may be so extensive and widespread?

The Bhopal case illustrates the ability of MNEs to exercise some choice over which legal jurisdiction they choose to submit to, as a way of taking advantage of the different institutional contexts of different countries. Sometimes organisations attempt to do this but fail to achieve the hoped for advantage. An example is the giant Russian oil company Yukos. Yukos was accused by the Russian government of having evaded the payment of taxes. The Government enforced the sale of Yukos's largest asset, a company called Yuganskneftegaz that produced two-thirds of Yukos's oil production. It was likely that Gazprom, the Russian state-owned oil company, would become the purchaser and it had arranged financial backing for the deal from Deutsche Bank. It so happens that the United States courts claim worldwide bankruptcy jurisdiction for companies that operate in the United States. Consequently Yukos opened an office in Dallas and put $2m into its American bank account. It then applied to the courts in Dallas for temporary bankruptcy protection. This was granted and a restraining order was issued to stop the sale of Yugansk. The sale went ahead but the displeasure of the US legal system was enough to frighten away Gazprom's western financial backers, and Deutsche Bank withdrew its financial support. The restraining order made it illegal for any company to work with Gazprom, and Deutsche Bank has a large American operation. The bank has applied to the American courts to have the restraining order removed (Mortished, 2004).

There have been cases where MNEs have avoided the institutional arrangements of industrialised countries. One such case is McDonald's operations in Europe. Most European countries have legislation on worker participation that is designed to give employees some influence on company decision making. This is known as co-determination and in Germany the legislation allows for both supervisory boards and works councils. Supervisory boards are strategic bodies within a company, and companies with more than 2,000 employees should have employee representatives on the supervisory board. If McDonald's operations in Germany were registered in Germany it would have to have a supervisory board; however, it is a fully owned subsidiary of the American parent company and so has avoided the necessity (Royle, 2000: 124). McDonald's are however obliged to allow, and meet with, a plant level Works Council if the employees request it. The company had 350 fully owned restaurants in Germany and 650 franchises and each one was entitled to have a Works Council as well as a company level and a group level Works Council. In practice, in 1999, there was no group or company Council and there were only between 40 and 50 plant level Councils in the 1,000 restaurants. McDonald's management had used a number of tactics to discourage its employees setting up Works Councils. The simplest was sending flying squads of managers to restaurants to dissuade staff from setting up a Works Councils and to use McDonald's own systems of communication and feedback. On occasion the company would transfer the ownership of a company between holding companies, an action that had the effect of delaying the election of a Works Committee. Most commonly they would 'buy out' Works Council representatives with cash and then nominate their own candidates to capture the Council and keep it compliant with management's wishes (Royle, 2000: 126–127). It was reported in 1995 that McDonald's spent £250,000 buying out 46 works councillors and their supporters. US companies, used to unregulated labour markets, would inevitably find continental European labour markets uncongenial, sufficiently so for them on occasion to seek to avoid the legal and institutional requirements.

However, most examples of MNEs taking advantage of easier institutional conditions refer to developing countries that have a strong desire for foreign direct investment (FDI). It is arguable that the exploitation of institutional weaknesses is an unsatisfactory form of advantage. The problems of investing and operating in a country that has weak institutions and poor governance outweigh, in the long term, the advantages. As the Report of the Commission for Africa (2005: 24–5) points out, both MNEs and developing countries would benefit if those countries could develop an effective form of governance that encourages investment. By effective governance is meant

- security and peace
- sound economic policies under the law
- collecting taxes and providing adequate public services
- adequate physical infrastructure such as transport and telecommunications
- effective legal systems and respect for contracts and property rights
- maintenance of human rights
- appropriate constitutional checks on the actions of government.

Multi-national and transnational countries should act as good corporate citizens in the host countries in which they operate. They should play a part in developing the ethical codes, norms and practices of business. This may be particularly important in developing countries which, through lack of resources or of opportunity, have poorly developed legal and voluntary frameworks intended to encourage ethical business behaviour.

Collusion between governments and corporations

Since Eisenhower invented the term 'military–industrial complex' in 1961 there have been concerns that the American government and large American companies, especially those involved in strategic industries, have become mutually dependent in a way that damages government's ability to ensure that the market-place operates fairly and ethically. Governments anywhere may use their discretion to take decisions that unfairly advantage companies based in their countries. Very often the criticisms concern the actions of government to support domestic companies' export sales.

An example occurred in the UK in 2005 when the Government was found to have been publicly supporting moves to prevent UK companies paying facilitation payments overseas while, at the same time, supporting the business lobby's opposition to the controls (Eaglesham and Tait, 2005). In May 2004 the government's Export Credits Guarantee Department (which underwrites British companies' export deals) introduced tough anti-corruption rules. Among other provisions these would have forced companies to guarantee that their joint venture partners would not act corruptly and to disclose commissions paid to agents. A number of British companies, including Airbus, Rolls Royce and BAE Systems, lobbied against the rules. They argued that if these rules stood major contracts would be lost. The Secretary of State for Trade and Industry relented and agreed a new set of rules in which these requirements were dropped, even though her civil servants had advised that any changes should have been put out for public consultation. However, Corner House, an anti-corruption group, threatened to go to Court to have the old rules reinstated because the anti-corruption groups had not been consulted. On this occasion the Secretary of State relented to the demands of the anti-corruption lobby and a process of public consultation was agreed. If it had not been for some leaked documents however the regulations would have been quietly changed in order to protect the interests of some major companies, and consequently, as some would argue, the interests of the UK. The price would have been tacit collusion with bribery in the world marketplace.

Connexion point

The nature of bribery and of grease payments in particular is discussed in Chapter 11, pp. 424–7. This particular case is also raised in Chapter 13, p. 00.

Case study 12.3

Indonesia

The situation regarding the fate of Indonesia since 1965/6, as documented by Pilger (2001), is one of the most troublesome examples of corporate capital and western governments working in tandem, first to engineer a change in political leadership, and then to dictate both economic policy and the way ownership and control of a nation state's natural resources would be allowed to develop. It involves the overthrow of the then leader President Sukarno in 1965/6 by General Suharto, with significant western support. The prize in ousting Sukarno was great. Of Indonesia, Richard Nixon, a former President of the United States, said, 'With its 100 million people, and its 300-mile arc of islands containing the region's richest hoard of natural resources, Indonesia is the greatest prize in southeast Asia.'

The UK also had a vested interest in seeing a regime in power that was friendlier to the West than Sukarno and his ruling Communist party. In 1964 the UK Foreign Office produced an analysis of the region and 'called for the "defence" of western interests in south-east Asia, a major producer of essential commodities. The region produces nearly 85% of the world's natural rubber, over 45% of the tin, 65% of the copra and 23% of the chromium ore' (Pilger, 2001: 26).

The complicity of America and the UK in the bloody aftermath of the Suharto take-over (it is claimed that as many as one million have been murdered) appears to have been considerable and is documented by Pilger (2001). The American Central Intelligence Agency (CIA) reported that, 'in terms of the numbers killed the massacres rank as one of the worst mass murders of the 20th century' (Pilger, 2001: 24).

With Suharto in power, a conference took place between corporations, predominantly American, but also including some UK and other European corporations, and the Indonesian government. In Pilger's words, 'the Indonesian economy was carved up, sector by sector. In one room, forests; in another minerals. The Freeport Company got a mountain of copper in West Papua. A US/European consortium got West Papua's nickel. The giant Alcoa company got the biggest slice of Indonesia's bauxite. A group of US, Japanese and French got the tropical forests of Sumatra, West Papua and Kalimantan. In addition a foreign investment law was hurried on to the statute books by Suharto, allowing all profits made by foreign companies to be tax-free for at least the first five years of operations.'

Over the next thirty years the World Bank provided loan finance amounting to £30bn to Indonesia. Of this, it is estimated by the World Bank itself that up to £10bn went into Suharto's own pockets, or those of his family and associates.

'In 1997 an internal World Bank report confirmed that at least 20–30% of the bank's loans [to Indonesia] are diverted through informal payments to GOI [Government of Indonesia] staff and politicians' (Pilger, 2001: 22).

In recent years attention has been drawn to the working conditions (e.g. up to 36-hour shifts) and pay (equivalent to 72p per hour) of factory workers in Indonesia making products for major companies such as Nike, Adidas, Reebok and GAP, and the squalor of the living conditions they endure in the camps located next to the 'economic processing zones' (i.e. the factories). In 1998, following mounting demonstrations in the Indonesian capital of Jakarta by large crowds protesting at their poverty and their desperate living conditions, Suharto left office, taking with him many billions of pounds sterling provided for his country over the years by the World Bank. These are monies that the country is obliged to keep paying the interest on, before it can even start repaying the capital.

The fall of Suharto might have marked the end of Indonesia's plight, but it may not have done. In 2000 the IMF offered the post-Suharto government a 'rescue package' of multi-million-dollar loans. However, there were conditions. These included the elimination of tariffs on staple foods. 'Trade in all qualities of rice has been opened to general importers and exporters' (Pilger, 2001: 24), decreed the IMF's letter of intent. Fertilisers and pesticides lost their 70 per cent subsidy, thereby ending for many farmers the prospect of staying on their land. They too will be forced to try to find work in the cities, which are already overburdened with unemployed 'citizens' looking for work. However, 'it gives the green light to the giant food grains corporations to move into Indonesia' (Pilger, 2001: 24).

Discussion activity 12.3

Use a World Wide Web search engine to find material on the relationships between the American oil company Halliburton and the American administration of President Bush concerning the re-building of Iraq after the defeat of Saddam Hussein. Discuss the issues the case raises about close connections between governments and global businesses.

Creating political tensions between and within states

As MNEs are often bigger than many states they frequently begin to act as sovereign bodies and players in international power politics or realpolitik.

DEFINITION

The term **Realpolitik** originated in Germany in 1853 to describe an approach to relations with other countries. It does not mean a naked self-interest or use of power but it does imply that ethical considerations have to be balanced against what is possible, where the balance of power lies, and self-interest. The idea of course is an ancient one. It can be found in the Arthrashastra of Kautilya.

> A King whose territory has a common boundary with that of an antagonist is an ally.
>
> (Rangarajan, 1992: 555)

In other words, my enemy's enemy is my friend. This is the principle that MNEs may have to follow. It would explain why the oil companies in the following case study found themselves in alliance with the federal Nigerian government, which was then a military dictatorship.

The natural aim of trading companies is to achieve political stability so that their trading plans are not inconvenienced. However, since the days of the European colonial trading companies – the Dutch East India Company, The English East India Company, the Hudson Bay Company and many others – international trading companies have been drawn into regional power struggles between and within states. Their ambition may be profit but the pursuit of that goal often requires them to act as political entities and, in some cases, to take on aspects of sovereignty. Inasmuch as they become additional factors in regional conflicts they have the opportunity to act to diminish or inflame these disputes. When companies intervene in local and regional politics and conflict in support of their commercial objectives they cannot be certain that the outcomes will be the ones they wished for. Companies may have good intentions but their actions may make matters worse. Consequently, serious ethical implications attach to companies' decisions to act politically; they may seriously disturb the peace and prosperity of communities and societies.

Case study 12.4

The oil industry and the Niger Delta

The Nigerian oil fields are in the Niger Delta in the south-eastern part of the country, and this has been a politically troubled area for many years. Since 2001 there has been ethnic violence in the area between Muslims and Christians with 5,000 people killed in four years. There is conflict between tribes indigenous to the area and the Nigerian government and consequently a large military presence in the region. Much of the political instability however is a consequence of the presence of the international oil industry in the region. The peoples of the delta feel that they have not benefited from, and in fact have been damaged by, the presence of the oil industry. A sense of deprivation is often expressed as resentment against other groups who, it is felt, have fared better. Link this relative sense of deprivation to the tribal diversity of the delta and the probability of civil unrest is much increased. This of course is the opposite of what the oil companies wanted and they allied themselves with the Nigerian government, then a military dictatorship, by supporting a military crack-down against what they saw as greed by the communities in the delta who were prepared to foment unrest to extract the maximum benefits from and damage an oil industry that was necessary to the economic well-being of the whole of Nigeria.

Two of the major ethnic groups in the delta are the Ogoni and the Ijaw. The Ogoni started a campaign against the environmental damage, social exclusion and poverty caused by the oil industry. These troubles came to the world's notice in 1995 when activists linked Shell to the military government's trial and execution of the Ogoni activist Ken Saro-Wiwa (Planet Ark, 2004). It was also argued that the government encouraged violent conflicts between the Ogoni and neighbouring communities – the Andoni, the Okrika and the Ndoki. This violence then gave the government an excuse to use the security forces against the Ogoni whose uprising ended when the Ogoni leadership split amidst mutual accusations that competing leaders were only interested in furthering their own financial and political ambitions. By the late 1990s the struggle against the petro-business had been taken up by a youth movement among the Ijaw. This developed into what became known as the first and second Egbusu wars.

The presence of the international oil industry was the focus of violent conflicts between sections of the Nigerian population and its government and between Nigerian communities. It is not claimed that there would have been only peace if there had been no oil industry. But it can be claimed that by allying themselves to the government, rather than responding to the concerns of the communities, the presence of the oil industry made the problems worse. A class action being prepared against Shell will accuse the company directors of supporting military operations by Nigeria's former government against Ogoniland separatists in the Niger Delta in the 1990s.

In 2003 Shell commissioned a conflict resolution consultancy based in Lagos to prepare a report on its troubles in the Niger River Delta. The 93-page report was published in 2004. In that year's annual sustainability report the Community Development manager, Emmanuel Etomi, wrote that he accepted that the oil industry was 'inadvertently contributing' to conflict in the country; and

> How we sometimes feed conflict by the way we award contracts, gain access to land and deal with community representatives; how ill-equipped our security is to reduce conflict; and how drastically conflict reduces the effect of our community development programmes.

The consultants' report argued that ethnic violence would cause Shell to withdraw from the area by 2009 (Hope, 2004).

(*Sources*: Ibeanu (2000); Ojefia (n.d.))

Discussion activity 12.4

Corporations working in politically troubled areas will often need the support of the local government. This might lead such corporations to assume that their ally's enemy is also their enemy, and cause them to come into conflict with local communities, who are antagonistic towards the government, but whose support they also need to conduct their business. Discuss how corporations might avoid this dilemma.

The oil industry is the natural one to consider in this section because it deals with the most strategically important product in the world. Oil has become the driving force of much international politics as the USA seeks to protect its sources of oil from the inconvenient fact that much of the oil comes from countries with which it is out of sympathy, Russia seeks to maintain its control over central Asian oil fields, and China desperately seeks the oil it needs to finance its rapid industrialisation. Whereas the previous case study dealt with the impact of the oil industry on the internal politics of a country, Case study 12.5 deals with its impact on the relationships between states.

Case study 12.5

The Baku – Tblisi – Ceyhan (BTC) oil pipeline

The Caucasus region, like the Balkans, has long been an area of nationalist, ethnic and religious rivalries. When the region was part of the Soviet Union these tensions were held in check. Now that each of the groups within the region has its own sovereign territory, and the few who do not, the South Ossetians and the Chechens for example, are seeking it, the conflicts between them have again become palpable. If to this mixture is added the internationally strategic significance of the new oil fields discovered under the Caspian Sea then the industrialised countries, who need the oil and the multinational oil companies, who need the business, also become involved in what has become called the New Great Game, in homage to the strategic conflict between Britain and Russia in the nineteenth century over who was to control the region (Kleveman, 2003).

Azerbaijan is a central player in this game. The modern oil industry had its origin in the Azerbaijani capital Baku in the 1880s and the city experienced an oil boom that lasted until 1905. The industry revived after the Second World War when Azerbaijan was an important component of the Soviet Union's oil industry. When Azerbaijan gained independence in 1991 it wished to assert its actual as well as legal independence from Russia. Its only asset for achieving this was the state-owned oil company SOCAR. The new state went into partnership with BP and Amoco by forming the Azerbaijan International Operating Company (AIOC). BP later took over Amoco and so became the major western oil company operating in Azerbaijan.

If Azerbaijan were more conveniently located, so that oil could be easily taken to the west, there would be few problems. However, the country is landlocked and a long pipeline is needed. There were several possible routes.

- To a port on Turkey's Black Sea coast; but Turkey rejected this option because it would have involved oil tankers going through the narrow Bosporus that links the Black Sea to the Mediterranean and the danger of pollution was unacceptable.
- Through Armenia to either the Black Sea or Mediterranean coast; but Azerbaijan and Armenia had fought a war over, and Armenia still occupies, the Azerbaijani province of Nagorno-Karabakh. Although hostilities have ceased peace talks between the two countries make little progress.
- Through Russia; but Azerbaijan is trying to assert its independence from its former masters.
- Through Iran; but the United States would not wish to entrust the security of a pipeline from which it drew oil to a fundamentalist Shiite state with which it is already in diplomatic dispute.
- Through Georgia; but Georgia is politically unstable with intrusions from Chechen rebels in the north and its own internal separatist movements among the Abkhazians and the South Ossetians.

The route finally chosen was from Baku, through Georgia and then through Turkey to the Mediterranean coast. BP and the other oil companies grumbled about the cost of the pipeline which was inevitably taking a circuitous route. The additional costs also made the oil companies feel more anxious about the potential political problems of building and operating the pipeline.

This insecurity was perhaps what led the oil companies to insist on international treaties, rather than commercial contracts, to govern the pipeline. Consequently an inter-governmental agreement and three host government agreements (HGAs) were drafted, largely by BP's lawyers, and signed by the governments. Pressure groups such as Corner House (*et al.*, 2003) have argued that these agreements give the oil companies virtual sovereign powers over the territory that the pipeline will traverse in its long journey through Turkey, Georgia and Azerbaijan. They effectively exempt BP and its partners from any laws in the three countries, present or future, that would conflict with the pipeline project. The governments have to compensate BP if any law or tax damages the financial viability of the pipeline. The consortium is also given the right to prevent building development in the pipeline zone and to restrict the movement of livestock. Amnesty International (2003) argued that the HGA signed by Turkey creates a disincentive for Turkey to improve its human rights record. Turkey has to pay the consortium compensation if there is any economic disruption to the project. Such disruption might take the form of local protests against the pipeline, especially as 30,000 people will have to give up their property rights to make way for the pipeline. The government of Turkey might be prepared to sacrifice the human rights of any protestors to avoid paying compensation. The agreements were a revival of the OECD proposals for a Multilateral Agreement on Investment that was dropped in 1998 because of the public outcry it caused (Friends of the Earth, 1997).

Despite these treaty provisions some of the Caucasian states are flexing their muscles against the oil companies. In 2003 Edward Shevardnadze was forced out of government by popular pressure. In 2004 the new government ordered BP to stop work on the pipeline in Borjormi, an area of Georgia that is classified as an area of natural beauty and in which are located mineral water springs that provide a good proportion of Georgia's exports. The government argued that BP had not provided a full environmental assessment (Malhiason, 2004).

There is a danger that the presence of the pipeline will exacerbate the political and military tensions in the areas it traverses. The pipeline passes near to Nagorno-Karabakh, near to South Ossetia and near to the Kurdish area of Turkey where there is a conflict between the PKP and the Turkish military. All the countries in the region are also the seats of conflict between Russia and western nations as to who can include the region in its sphere of influence. The pipeline could become a focal point for military or terrorist attack, and to protect from this possibility it is likely that western troops will be posted to protect it and create a militarised strip running through the region. The oil companies could only be grateful for the support even if they knew that the military presence might increase the probability of an attack on the pipeline.

There is a dilemma for companies pursuing projects in politically unstable areas. Their presence makes them an object of contention between competing political factions and interests. This causes them to seek means of protecting their investment. But the means they use, presence of foreign troops, HGAs, creates local objections and protests making them even more the focus of political and, possibly military, conflict.

(*Additional sources*: baku-ceyhan campaign, 2003a, 2003b and n.d.)

Discussion activity 12.5

In the past western governments have sometimes assumed sovereign powers in other countries to secure vital trade links. Two examples are the US government and the Panama Canal and the British and French governments who had control over the Suez Canal. Use a World Wide Web search engine to discover what the historical outcomes were in these two cases. Then discuss what lessons, if any, can be drawn from these examples for projects such as the BTC pipeline.

Staying put or getting out?

The issue facing multi-national companies, however, may not just be that the norms of business behaviour in the countries they operate in are undeveloped. Companies may find themselves in countries where the regimes are commonly regarded as oppressive and human rights are being denied. This situation raises the question of what obligations private companies might have to challenge unethical behaviour by states. Murphy (2001) proposed a theory of benevolence in which people (he was not discussing companies) are not morally obliged to do more to solve the world's problems than would be their portion if everyone else were doing their share. In other words people (and companies?) should only do their portion even if others are not doing theirs and so there remains much that the individual or company could do.

Unethical states may, however, seek to influence how international companies conduct their business. If such regimes demand that companies use unacceptable employment practices, for example, or direct their investments in ways that reward their political supporters, then companies may be forced to consider whether it is ethical to remain in that country

Lord Browne (Browne of Madingley, 2004), Group Chief executive of BP, put forward an unambiguous principle.

> Companies must obey the law in every jurisdiction in which we operate and if we find the law unacceptable and at odds with our own values we shouldn't be operating in that jurisdiction.

Withdrawing from a failed or oppressive state may meet ethical requirements because the organisation would cease to be complicit in wrongdoing, but such a move may make the situation of the population in the state worse. Talisman is a Canadian oil company that was active in Sudan, a country that has been suffering a civil war between its Muslim north and its Christian and Animist south for two decades. Talisman was charged by human rights groups that its presence exacerbated the civil war, that the money it paid for the oil was used to buy arms and that its oil development had displaced thousands of people. In 2003 Talisman withdrew from the Nile Petroleum Operation Company (NPOC), which it owned in partnership with the China National Petroleum Corporation, Petronas the Malaysian oil company and the Sudanese state-owned oil company. Talisman sold its share of NPOC to an arm of India's Oil and Natural Gas Corporation. The organisations that now own NPOC are all state owned. They do not raise their capital on the international markets nor are they accountable to shareholders. Seymour (2003) argued that these organisations benefited from the political turmoil in Sudan, which acted to keep their western competitors out. (Since a peace deal brought the civil war to an end in 2005 western oil companies have shown a renewed interest in Sudan.) He also argued that because they are companies owned by governments, which were often intolerant of critical voices within their own countries, these corporations are immune from the demands of human rights groups such as had encouraged Talisman to quit Sudan.

> [ ] with the sale of Talisman's share, a company that its critics had ensured had an interest in attempting to moderate the government of Sudan's policies has left. What remains are companies that actively support the government of Sudan and its war against southerners, with all its attendant human rights abuses. The moral calculus is thus vastly more complex, and our celebration of Talisman's departure utterly displaced.
>
> (Seymour, 2003: 5)

Case study 12.6

Businesses and South Africa in the apartheid era

In the 1950s the apartheid regime in South Africa was created by a series of laws that enforced racial segregation by restricting the areas in which blacks and coloureds could live and by limiting the jobs they could apply for. There were many foreign-owned companies that had long been present in South Africa. These companies had to obey the apartheid laws. As, by common consensus in the world beyond South Africa, apartheid was evil, and the foreign-owned companies were not in a position to change it, the question arose as to whether in conscience they should disinvest from South Africa. In 1977 Leon Sullivan, a director of General Motors, a company that had a subsidiary in South Africa, proposed a set of principles to govern its business in South Africa (Minnesota Center for Corporate Responsibility, 2001). They amounted to a refusal to obey the apartheid laws. Segregation was not to be practised in its plants and staff were to be paid and promoted according to merit not race. They also imposed an obligation to improve the quality of life in those communities in which companies did business. Many American companies trading in South Africa signed up to the principles. It was hoped that such large numbers would discourage the South African government from prosecuting the companies for breaking the apartheid laws and that their efforts might lead to the collapse of apartheid.

However, in 1987 Sullivan declared that the experiment was showing no sign of undermining apartheid. He claimed that American companies should withdraw from their South African operations. In that year General Motors sold its holdings in South Africa. In 1991 the South African government began to repeal the apartheid regime. Nelson Mandela was elected President of South Africa in 1994.

The issue of the moral, and perhaps legal, responsibility of MNEs for the apartheid era has remained. The issue came into prominence in 2004, as in the Yukos case (*see* p. 471), because the United States judiciary was claiming a worldwide jurisdiction in certain circumstance. The American Alien Tort Claims Act of 1789 allows American companies to be sued in the American courts for certain classes of wrong that were committed in other countries. The validity of this law was confirmed by a Supreme Court ruling in 2004. An American law firm proposed to start a case on behalf of the Khulumani Support Group of South Africa against IBM. The allegation is that IBM supplied the then South African government with the computers that enabled them to put the pass laws, which allocated individuals to a racial category that determined where they might go and what they might do, into effect. The pass laws were at the heart of the apartheid system. In case it be argued that in supplying the hardware IBM cannot be liable because they could not determine the use to which the computers might be put, the allegation also argues that IBM supplied the software (Robins, 2004).

The South African government is opposed to the case although many human rights groups are supporting it. They point out that the MNEs are fully cooperating in rehabilitating the lives of those damaged by apartheid. It is also no doubt seen to be in the country's national interest to keep the MNEs engaged with South Africa's economic growth.

Discussion activity 12.6

Draw up and discuss guidelines that could be used to help a company decide whether a country it was working in had such a corrupt government and institutions that they should withdraw from it.

Cultural diversity or cultural homogenisation?

The World Commission on the Social Dimension of Globalisation (WCSDG, 2004) identified a number of broadly cultural aspects of globalisation. The major impact concerns what they term interconnectivity (WCSDG, 2004: §218). The rapid spread of telecommunications and the Internet, and in particular of television and the global entertainment industry, has made people everywhere more conscious of each other's ambitions, expectations and circumstances. For the relatively poor this process creates a sense of missing out that they would not have if their horizons were more local and circumscribed. For the relatively rich it increases their sense of privilege, which may create a feeling of obligation to those less fortunate. This may well explain the growth of NGOs and international charities and indeed the increase in anti-globalisation activisms. Travel is an aspect of this increasing interconnectivity and the fact that many Europeans had travelled to Thailand, in particular, explains both the high loss of life of European tourists in the 2004 Asian tsunami and the huge and sympathetic response from the western world.

A common cliché is that travel broadens the mind. However, ironically, as we travel more, taking advantage of the spread of budget airlines, our ethical horizons can become narrower. If we visit the places much frequented we may only see a Disney-fied version of the local culture – folkloric evenings in Greece, having lunch with the inhabitants of the floating islands on Lake Titicaca – and mistakenly think it true. Julian Barnes' (1998) comic novel *England, England* explores the idea of a replica England built on the Isle of Wight to attract the tourists. Merely flying to broaden our minds may show a lack of awareness of sustainability issues. Aviation fuel is untaxed, which makes flying cheaper than if it were taxed as are other forms of transport. Therefore as the demand for air travel, especially for holidays, increases aeroplanes become a major source of the greenhouse gases that may contribute to global warming. Therefore our desire to travel may be harming us all.

A particular criticism of globalisation is the tendency of powerful countries and companies to impose their values on weaker societies. This is sometimes called McDonaldisation, a process by which western brands and organisational methods and structures replace local products and thereby reduce choice and variety.

The charges of McDonaldisation and Logo-isation define the ethical questions surrounding the cultural and social aspects of globalisation. Do these processes destroy local cultures and replace them with North American values, and if they do is this a bad thing?

DEFINITION

Ritzer (1993) in his book *The McDonaldization of Society* took the global success of McDonald's as an example of the growth of a common, worldwide, mass culture. Ritzer argued that the process of **McDonaldisation** represents the expansion of instrumental rationality – a drive for efficiency, predictability, calculability and control – with no questioning of the ends being sought. The criticism of mass culture, of which McDonaldisation is a modern example, is that it causes people to be satisfied with a 'vulgar simplicity' (Harrington, 1965: 188). Advertising and sound-bite communications, it is alleged, diminish the masses' ability to exercise moral agency. They lose the ability to distinguish the good from the bad, gourmet cooking from burgers, the noble life from consumerism.

This criticism was taken up and popularised by Naomi Klein (2000) in her book *No Logo*. She argues that globalisation, and in particular the branding of consumer goods, has limited people's choices throughout the world. This has been done by:

- Replacing culture and education by marketing. Brands divert people from the product or service they are buying and focus them on purchasing the perceived status and values that are associated with the brand. People buy coffee from Starbucks, she argues (Klein, 2000: 21), for the sense of being a member of a warm, bookish, jazz listening, armchair lounging community; and not for the coffee. The purchase of coffee therefore ceases to be a rational expression of personal values but an entrapment by emotional lures. It may of course have always been so. If one replaces jazz and armchairs with tobacco fug, cosy booths and clubbable warmth one has a description of the original coffee shops in eighteenth-century London.
- Creating less secure, less fulfilling and poorly paid jobs for people, not just in the developing world but in the industrialised worlds as well. This has been achieved by the casualisation of labour through outsourcing, flexible work and part-time employment. Interestingly, again, a return to the nature of the work force in eighteenth-century England.

Klein however is not simply an observer; her intention is to report on and encourage the forces of anti-globalisation and the activities of anti-brand warriors.

Connexion point

The discussion of McDonaldisation and Logo-isation is a particular aspect of a more general issue that is discussed in Chapter 11, namely the extent to which different countries or cultural groups wish to develop or maintain their own values and priorities in relation to business and management.

Does globalisation damage indigenous and local cultures?

The first of these questions is slightly easier to address because it is a practical matter. MNEs may take a range of actions concerning the introduction of their international brands into new countries.

- Introduce the brand and product in its traditional form. Such is the case with Coca Cola that is marketed as a global product.
- Introduce the brand but adapt the product to local tastes and preferences. In Greece, for example, McDonald's burgers are mostly lamb, in recognition of local tastes; in India they sell no beef or pork patties at all in response to religious prohibitions.
- Decide not to enter the market but wait to see if local demand develops. No major western coffee chain has yet opened in India to sell espressos and lattes. However, in Delhi and other metropolitan areas local chains such as Barista are expanding.
- In some cases an MNE may prevent the importation of a western product or service into a country. China has opened its market but its government is concerned that this should not present any threat to its ideology and policies. MNEs therefore will take care not to offend the Chinese government lest they experience some problems with their licences to operate in China. The country is a vast potential market for satellite television and other services and News Corporation International is a major provider through its Star TV service. News Corporation International dropped the BBC World Service from the range of channels it provided to China because the government objected to a documentary that the BBC had broadcast on Mao Tse-tung (Klein, 2000: 171).
- The case of what the WCSDG calls indigenous and tribal peoples (WCSDG, 2004: §311) is a particularly difficult one. There are a few communities in the world that are totally separated from life in the rest of the world. The question is whether these societies should be protected not only from intrusion by companies but also from all other forms of contact including tourism.

Case study 12.7

McDonald's fries

The original McDonald's fries were cooked in beef fat. This of course made them objectionable to vegetarians and to Hindus for whom the cow is sacred. In 1990 McDonald's announced that in future all its fries would be cooked in vegetable oil. It emerged in 2001, however, that this was only part of the story. In North America the fries were first cooked in centralised plants using beef fat. They were then frozen and transported to the restaurants for further frying in vegetable oil. McDonald's announced that it was 'not too big to apologise' and that it had given incomplete information to its customers. American Hindus have started seeking damages. Other customers have no problem with the use of beef fat and may even think that it improves the taste of the fries. McDonald's has nearly thirty restaurants in India, where its burgers are made from lamb rather than beef. It assured its Indian customers that its cooking methods were strictly vegetarian.

(*Source*: Evans, 2001)

The situation is not a simple one therefore of the imposition of western brands and products, and by implication western consumer values, on local cultures. Such an argument in any case implies a naïve and orientalist distinction between the spiritual east and the materialist west, and presumes a story in which the simple and non-materialist lives of the east are destroyed by crass western commercial values. Social and economic histories point out that people and communities in the east are as concerned with material things and profits as those in the west. For a detailed and very local account of the importance of the market – the bazaar – in the lives of local people in the Gangetic plain of India in the nineteenth and twentieth centuries, read Yang (1998).

Orientalism **DEFINITION**

This term was coined by Edward Said (1978) to explain the stereotyped view that the western imperial powers had of the eastern societies they were colonising.

> This is the apogee of Orientalist confidence. No merely asserted generality is denied the dignity of truth; no theoretical list of oriental attributes is without application to the behaviour of orientals in the real world. On the one hand there are Westerners, and on the other there are Arab-orientals; the former are (in no particular order) rational, peaceful, liberal, logical, capable of holding real values, without natural suspicion; the latter are none of these things.
>
> (Said, 1978: 49)

Said argued that such stereotyping was an ideological device to support colonialist exploitation of the east.

Connexion point
The concept of orientalism is closely associated with that of essentialism, which is discussed in Chapter 11, p. 420.

Globalisation and consumer choice

Let us assume, and it is a big assumption, that western brands and products are changing the local and family values of developing countries. Is this a bad thing? We will not answer the question but we will try to lay out the form that an argument about the matter might take. The process would be bad

- if it were accepted unwittingly by those affected, who were unaware of the changes and their significance.
- or if it broke some generally accepted ethical principle.

The main commentators on these questions take different positions.

- Klein argues that branding and marketing are devices to circumvent people's tendency to make rational choice by appealing to them through symbolism and emotion. She would also argue that this effect is just as strong, and perhaps stronger, in the industrialised west than it might be in developing countries. Branding is therefore to be regarded as a bad thing because people are unconscious of the changes they were experiencing. This argument is a version of the Marxist concept of false consciousness (Sklair, 1995). This states that in capitalist societies the masses are exploited but are lured into believing that they are living in the best of all possible worlds. They are not able to recognise their own oppression.
- The Ritzer argument in McDonaldisation (*see* p. 483) is not that people do not make rational choices in a consumer society, simply that they use the wrong sort of rationality. Instrumental rationality, which is what it is argued consumers use, is conscious and calculated but it is focused on achieving the wrong ends. Instead of seeking the good life, as Aristotle demanded in the west and as is required by many other philosophies and religions, modern consumers satisfy themselves with designer labels and the newest gadgets. This is essentially a Weberian analysis in which the day-to-day operations of modern organisations constrain people's actions to implementing means, and mistakenly assuming them to be ends. On this basis consumerism can be seen as breaking an important ethical principle and thus is to be seen as a bad thing.
- The third position believes that in the new global village people in different societies choose freely to enjoy the benefits and comforts provided by iPods, computer games, Internet access and coffee lattes. This view was taken by Kerr *et al.* (1960). On this argument globalisation, and the standardisation of tastes it brings, are to be thought a good thing.

DEFINITION

Weberian is the adjectival form of the name of the sociologist Max Weber. He defined bureaucracy (the following definition is heavily dependent on Watson (2002: 240–2)) as a distinctive form of organisation and decision making that had replaced traditional methods. In bureaucracies decisions are made using instrumental or formal rationality that involves a calculation as to which option would best meet the desired objectives. This approach has many benefits; it enables, for example, doctors to develop ever more complex means of assisting human conception. However, Weber also noted that a fixation on techniques would lead to a neglect of discussion of the value of the ends being sought. This was his idea of the *stalhartes Gehäuse* (meaning steel-hard house but often translated as iron cage). In the example given instrumental rationality could mean that if the technology to clone human beings is developed it would be used without considering whether it was right to do so.

The net effect of globalisation would seem to be one in which the populations of the developing and the transitional countries are increasingly sharing common expectations and demands for services and products. The expansion of international trade and foreign direct investment (FDI) that fuels globalisation has increased the wealth of the world. However, the distribution of these beneficial impacts has been skewed. Some areas, notably Asia and Latin America and the Caribbean, have received much larger inflows of FDI than other areas such as Africa and Eastern Europe (International Labour Organisation, ILO 2004: 28). Within the developing countries the elite have benefited more than the bulk of the populations, who in some cases have become worse off. At an ethical level these outcomes offend against Rawls' fairness principle (*see* p. 115); in practice it creates a destabilising situation in which many people's expectations are increasing while their conditions are worsening. There is recognition among international institutions, such as the United Nations, The Group of Eight (G8) and many others, that this situation is unfair and potentially a source of conflict within the world. There is consequently much discussion about the governance of international businesses, and it is to this topic that we now turn.

Global governance

At the close of the second world war a series of international conferences set up the basic institutions of global governance, namely the United Nations, the World Bank, the International Monetary Fund and the General Agreement on Tariffs and Trade (GATT). There have been changes since; GATT was replaced in 1995 by the World Trade Organisation (WTO) for example. Although the number of sovereign states has increased, from about 50 after 1945 to 190 now, the system of global governance has remained much the same. A number of deficiencies in this system of governance have been recognised by the WCSDG (ILO: §340–52).

- The western industrialised companies have an excessive influence in the formal bodies of global governance. The emergent industrialised countries such as China, India and Brazil can exert influence in such bodies when they act in concert, but the western countries still have the greatest influence and the developing countries have little. This is so even in organisations like the WTO where the developing countries have a formal equality with the industrialised ones.
- The developing countries often cannot afford to attend the many international conferences that influence global governance and do not have the technical expertise necessary to make their cases as strong as they might be.
- An international civil society has emerged since the end of the second world war formed of non-governmental organisations (NGOs) such as international charities and lobby organisations such as Greenpeace. These organisations have no formal role in the institutions of governance.

- The MNEs have become much more significant in the world. They have become bigger and more globally extensive. They have great influence on global governance through private lobbying and public relations activities. They are not however formally involved in the institutions and do not carry the accountability that formal membership would imply.
- Many decisions that affect global governance are made by exclusive bodies, such as the G8 and the Organisation for Economic Cooperation and Development (OECD).
- The system of global governance is disjointed and unconnected. There are many bodies operating separately – and often doing much good, such as the development of international accountancy standards. However, these initiatives are often unconnected and carry differing levels of authority. Some aspects of global governance have the status of international law and treaty obligations: there are voluntary agreements backed by public bodies such as the United Nations and voluntary agreements between any permutation of private companies, NGOs and governments.

Global governance is the set of rules set up by the international community of governments, companies and NGOs and formal bodies to govern political, economic and social affairs. Some of these are discussed in the next section of the chapter.

Connexion point

There is a general discussion of ethical codes in Chapter 10. In this chapter we concentrate on those standards and codes that are concerned with the consequences of international trade.

Voluntary codes

Mention was made earlier in the chapter of the dilemma that national governments, particularly those of developing countries, sometimes face when wishing to encourage inward investment by MNEs, but also wishing to maintain some form of influence, if not control, over the activities of the MNEs in the host country. Some form of middle ground is often required between the polar extremes of legislation governing particular aspects of economic or corporate activity on the one hand, and a totally laissez-faire approach on the other. Codes of conduct, agreements and framework documents are examples of such 'middle ground'.

If a code of conduct for MNEs has the support of sovereign states, this does not mean the issues encompassed by the code have become international law. Until they do the codes are not legally binding on MNEs. Thus, the obligations cited by a code will be moral, but not legal.

An example of such a code of practice that has received much publicity concerns the selling of breastmilk substitutes in developing countries.

Case study 12.8

The International Code of Marketing of Breastmilk Substitutes

The International Code of Marketing of Breastmilk Substitutes, the first international code of its kind, was adopted by the World Health Organisation (WHO) in 1981 and by the World Health Assembly (WHA) in 1984. The code was intended to control the practices of those producing and selling breastmilk substitutes and related products (e.g. feeding bottles), particularly in developing countries. These countries tend to have relatively high birth rates but weak economies. It can be argued that expenditure on breastmilk substitutes is a misuse of a nation's resources, when the natural alternative is cost free and more nutritious for the child. However, to the large corporations producing these products the markets of the developing world represent significant profit opportunities. The problem had become so acute in certain African countries that breastfeeding had become almost eradicated. The international code bans free supplies of breastmilk substitutes in hospitals, because once mothers leave hospital the breastmilk substitutes are no longer free. Yet in 1996 Nestlé, a significant producer of breastmilk substitutes, was reported to be providing free and low-cost supplies of infant formula to hospitals in Kunming Province in China. Save the Children reported:

> Nestlé has made Lactogen widely available in six hospitals in Kunming, where it has targeted health professionals with both free and discounted supplies of the formula. This helps to create an incentive for the health workers, not only to use the formula within the hospitals, but also actively to encourage its use among mothers of newborn children. Lactogen has been displayed in some of the hospitals for sale. The report prepared by our China staff and local health workers alleged that there had been an increase in the consumption of Lactogen and that breastfeeding rates had fallen.

Despite getting companies to sign up to the International Association of Infant Food Manufacturers (IFM) and in 1991 pledging to eradicate the supply of free and discounted supplies, a monitoring report entitled 'Breaking the Rules, Stretching the Rules' found that in 19 of 31 countries surveyed contraventions of the pledge were evident. In addition, a study in Pakistan in 1998 found widespread use and distribution of free supplies, with doctors being 'purchased by the companies'.

(*Source*: IBFAN, n.d.)

Even when codes of practice are established, compliance by MNEs is not necessarily automatic, and enforcement can be difficult, as evidenced by the selling of breastmilk substitutes in Malawi.

Case study 12.9

Breastmilk substitutes in Malawi

In 1994 the Health Ministry of Malawi had discussed with Nestlé the need to have the instructions on their products written in Chichewa, the national language of Malawi, a requirement that was in compliance with Article 9.2 of the International Code of Marketing of Breastmilk Substitutes. Despite these discussions, Nestlé did not respond positively and the instructions remained in English. The level of literacy is not high in Malawi and, of those women who could read at the time, it was estimated that only a little over one-half could read English.

Under Article 9.1 of the Code, labels on breastmilk substitutes should not discourage breastfeeding. However, on its Bona infant formula, Nestlé continued to assert in a section headed 'Important Notice', 'Infant formula can be used from birth onwards when breastfeeding is not possible, or as a supplement to breastfeeding'. This statement was retained on the packaging despite there being general recognition that supplementing breastfeeding with breastmilk substitutes brings forward the time when a mother's natural milk dries up, thereby bringing forward the time when breastmilk substitutes will be required as the sole source of infant nutrition.

Discussion activity 12.9

Should the response to the difficulties in implementing voluntry codes illustrated in Case studies 12.8 and 12.9 be:

- Work harder at convincing companies to adhere to the codes

or

- pass legislation in the companies' base countries that make it illegal not to adhere to the codes?

Humanitarian aid provides another opportunity for breastmilk substitute products to be introduced into vulnerable, but lucrative, markets. The International Baby Food Action Network (IBFAN) claims that:

> The baby food industry has used emergencies generally to promote its products and used 'humanitarian aid' as a way of entering into the emerging markets of Europe and the former Soviet Union.
>
> (IBFAN, n.d.)

These cases illustrate some of the problems inherent within a 'pledge', 'code' or 'framework agreement' that is not supported by legal or meaningful sanctions.

Another area of contention relates to the use of child labour. Corporate policy statements of MNEs on the use of child labour within its supplier networks tend to reflect one of four options:

1. Stipulate a minimum age for employment by their suppliers.
2. Refer to national laws of the host country regarding minimum age of working.
3. Refer to international standards, or
4. A combination of some or all of the above.

However, some company policy statements that prohibit the use of child labour in the production of their products do not define what they mean by child labour, thus leaving discretion and judgement to local suppliers. This takes us to the issue of the rigour with which codes of practice are implemented and monitored, particularly those relating to overseas suppliers.

Putting MNE codes of practice into effect

Codes of conduct for MNEs can take various forms and the ILO cites three factors that tend to determine the credibility with which codes for MNEs are regarded.

1. The specific governments that have adopted and support the codes, and the particular MNEs that have 'signed up' to the codes.
2. Whether a code actually addresses the critical issues of the business activity being considered.
3. The effectiveness of the monitoring mechanisms employed and the sanctions available.

The International Chamber of Commerce (ICC) is active in pursuing a self-regulatory framework for business operations on the world stage. It sets standards that recognise the tensions inherent within any competitive market setting. The following statement is drawn from one of its publications.

> The globalisation of the world's economies, and the intense competition which ensues therefrom, require the international business community to adopt standard rules. The adoption of these self-disciplinary rules is the best way that business leaders have of demonstrating that they are motivated by a sense of social responsibility, particularly in light of the increased liberalization of markets.
>
> (International Chamber of Commerce, 1997)

A number of initiatives and codes have been developed to address specific global business issues. Examples include the following:

- The 1990s saw the scope of some agreements expand to take in broader social issues. An example is the Japan Federation of Economic Organisations. Established in 1996, it covered a number of issues including philanthropic activities, resistance against organisations that undermine social cohesion, policies to enrich the lives of employees, safe and comfortable work environments, a respect for individual dignity and 'specialness' and corporate transparency.
- In 1996 the British Toy and Hobby Association developed a code of practice that forbids the use of forced, indentured or under-age labour in the production of toys. The agreement also speaks to the working and living conditions of employees. An amended form of this code was adopted by the International Council of Toy Industries later in 1996.

- In February 1997, the ILO, the Sialkot Chamber of Commerce (SCCI) in Pakistan and UNICEF formed an agreement to eliminate child labour in the production of footballs by 1999. This specific initiative was the result of worldwide publicity of the use of child labour in the production of footballs, although no other products or industries were specifically targeted. It appears that this initiative has been largely, if not completely, successful. It does appear that high-profile media coverage is conducive to, and possibly necessary for, change to be levered and achieved.
- In the USA similar codes have been developed in relation to other industries, e.g. the Apparel Partnership on Sweatshops and Child Labour which was adopted in 1997.
- The Organisation for Economic Cooperation and Development (OECD) has also produced guidelines for MNEs covering labour relations.
- A variety of organisations have sponsored the Sweatshop and Clean Clothes Codes, which cover labour relations, health and safety issues, freedom of association, wages and benefits and hours of work.
- The Declaration of Principles concerning Multinational Enterprises, developed in 1997 and involving the ILO, is a code that addresses issues such as freedom of association, terms and conditions of work.

At first sight the existence of such codes presents a preferable state of affairs to that of no codes at all. However, a closer inspection of such codes poses some uncomfortable challenges to this assumption. For example, within the Sweatshop Code, the wording relating to 'wages and benefits' specifies:

> Employers shall pay employees, as a floor, at least the minimum wage required by local law or the prevailing industry wage, whichever is the higher, and shall provide legally mandated benefits.

This leaves much responsibility with governments to institute laws that enhance working and employment conditions. The lobbying of governments by business organisations, including MNEs, will clearly be listened to in government circles. Those employed in sweatshop conditions are not often well represented at the political negotiating table. In the meantime global organisations and western customers of the manufacturing output of developing countries remain free to exploit the cost differentials of sourcing their production capacity overseas. Indeed, the very reason why many western apparel companies have closed their western production capability and transferred production to locations in the Philippines, India, Honduras, etc. has been to exploit the cost advantages of the developing world, cost advantages that have often involved sweatshop conditions and child labour.

With regard to 'hours of work' the Sweatshop Code states:

> Except in extraordinary business circumstances, employees shall (i) not be required to work more than the lesser of (a) 48 hours per week and 12 hours overtime or (b) the limits on regular and overtime hours allowed by the law of the country of manufacture or, where the laws of such country do not limit

> the hours of work, the regular work week in such country plus 12 hours overtime and (ii) be entitled to at least one day off in every seven day period.

Thus, unless local laws state otherwise, an employer can require their workers to work 60 hours per week, and stay within the obligations of the code. Employees might be entitled to one day off per week, but whether they will get this is another matter. In addition, when demand is high, the working week can extend beyond the 60 hours. This should be constrained to 'extraordinary business circumstances', but the latter is not defined and less than scrupulous employers will use this as a loophole to work employees for all seven days of the week and exceed the 60 hours per employee. The code could be far more stringent in its demands on behalf of the employees (the majority of whom tend to be women), but of course, the closer wage rates and working conditions are pushed towards western levels, the less the original decision to source production to the developing country makes economic sense.

There are examples of organisations appearing to make serious efforts to put their codes into practice. The ILO reported that Levi-Strauss, for example, conducts annual global training programmes to ensure its audit managers are familiar with their internal code, and has conducted five-day training programmes in the Dominican Republic for 'terms of engagement' auditors. Liz Claiborne (an American retail organisation of women's fashion clothes) has also reported that it had intensified its efforts to identify and remove labour abuses.

An example is provided by McDonald and Nijhof (1999: 140) of an organisation that employed 6,000 people, and whose CEO sought to roll out an ethics awareness-raising programme across the whole organisation. This involved writing the associated code of conduct in both English and Chinese and then training a series of trainers to deliver the associated workshops. The latter included a video message from the CEO, in which he stated that he would rather the organisation lose a contract than undermine the code. The programme was delivered throughout the company. For the CEO, 'the code needs to come off the pages and into people's lives'. As McDonald and Nijhof report, elements that were not included in the initiative were an annual ethics audit and an ethics hotline. Whether these have since been instituted is unknown.

The rigour with which MNEs police their own codes of conduct (particularly those they apply to their suppliers) does appear to vary. Of the organisation Liz Claiborne, the plant manager of Primo Industries, an apparel contractor based in El Salvador, stated, 'they are the toughest on child labour'. The plant manager told US Department of Labor officials that inspectors from Liz Claiborne visited the plant 'approximately twice a month to check on quality control and see whether rules and regulations are being implemented'. Such vigilance by the Claiborne organisation must involve costs that some other organisations (maybe its competitors) do not appear to incur, at least not to the same extent. A manager with the Indian company, Zoro Garments, 75 per cent of whose output goes to US markets, is quoted as saying that:

> Representatives of US customers have visited Zoro's factory occasionally for quality control inspections, [but] most of the visits were walk-throughs with some general questions raised about the use of child labour, but no check-list of requirements was administered.
>
> (ILO, n.d.)

A complicating issue occurs where the MNE sources products from a variety of overseas suppliers, with some of these suppliers being in monopsony relationships with the MNE, while for other suppliers the MNE in question might be only one among a range of customers. Thus, can an MNE be held responsible for the work conditions and labour practices of a supplier from which it sources relatively few orders? Whatever one's position on this question, it has to be taken for granted that, for production costs of suppliers in developing countries to be so much lower than those of their western competitors, wage rates and employment conditions cannot be equal. Thus, for MNEs, or any other form of organisation, to feign ignorance of the working conditions of some of its suppliers ignores the logic of the situations. Rather than assuming that all is satisfactory, they must know that the cost differentials between suppliers in developing and developed countries would suggest a default position that all is not satisfactory, and that evidence is required to disprove this assumption.

Establishing a corporate code of conduct is one thing; making it a part of everyday practice is another. Of the 42 apparel companies surveyed by the US Department of Labor in 1996, to establish how many of them had endeavoured to ensure that workers in their overseas suppliers were aware of their code of conduct, 'very few respondents indicated that they had tried'. Only three companies insisted on their codes being posted on their suppliers' notice boards. In a further study reported by the ILO, of 70 supplier companies, 23 (33 per cent) indicated that they were not aware of corporate codes of conduct issued by their US customers.

The US Department of Labor also undertakes company visits and the ILO website gives information on ILO visits to a variety of countries including El Salvador, the Dominican Republic, Honduras, India and the Philippines. In a study of 70 companies, managers at only 47 of these stated an awareness of such codes, and of these only 34 could produce a copy of a code. Thus, less than half of the sites visited could produce a principal customer's code, yet the US retailers refer to their supplier codes as evidence of their (the apparel retailers') commitment to ethical practices at their overseas suppliers.

Awareness of such codes was highest in El Salvador, where managers at six out of the nine companies visited were aware of such codes, whereas in India managers at only two of the seven producer sites visited were aware. Even where awareness was acknowledged, awareness was not the same as accepting the codes and adhering to them. As the ILO observed,

> Although a significant number of suppliers knew about the US corporate codes of conduct, meetings with workers and their representatives in the countries visited suggested that relatively few workers were aware of the existence of codes of conduct, and even fewer understood their implications.

The UN Global Compact

This international standard is worth separate consideration because it was initiated by the UN Secretary-General at the Davos World Economic Forum in 1999. This is an informal conference at which politicians, MNE chief executives, NGO representatives and high-profile lobbyists meet. The Compact is supported by the International Labour Office (ILO), The Office of the UN Commissioner for

Human Rights (OHCHR), the United Nations Environment Programme (UNEP), the UN Industrial Development Organisation (UNIDO) and others. It therefore carries the support of many of the world's institutions of global governance. It is however also a voluntary code.

Connexion point

The principles that companies have to sign up to when they join the Global Compact are discussed in Chapter 8, pp. 308–10. The chapter also provides an evaluation of the Compact's impact.

A major criticism of the Global Compact from a globalisation perspective is that it covers only a narrow range of issues. For example, several of the matters raised in this chapter, such as the justice and fairness of the governance of international trade, and the effect the operations of MNEs might have on exacerbating political and military tensions in regions in which they operate are not covered.

The Global Compact, however, is developing in a different form from that of other ethical and CSR standards which take an assurance based ('ticking the box') approach. The Compact is more like a learning network in which understanding and learning about the problems of behaving in a socially and environmentally responsible way are discussed and explored. Those who have signed up to the Compact are encouraged to take part in seminars, act as mentors, join networks and enter into partnerships to carry out projects. Many of the world's well-known companies have signed up including BT, BMW, Standard Chartered Bank, Nike, Novartis, Shell, Warburg and Unilever.

In 2001 the theme of the Global Compact policy dialogue was 'the role of the public sector in zones of conflict'. So, despite the criticism often made of it, it does address the issues of globalisation and conflict. The participants were from businesses, NGOs, trade unions and the UN. Tools and techniques for ameliorating conflict, such as risk assessment and multi-stakeholder processes of community development (*see* the Shell case study on p. 475). It was also agreed that partnership projects would be set up to try to make practical changes in selected regions (McIntosh *et al.*, 2003: 182). The Global Compact also undertakes outreach activities and tries to involve small and medium-sized companies as well as city governments.

Reflections

Individual MNEs have, in many cases, become so large that as individual corporations they can have a major impact on the prosperity and the peacefulness of the communities, countries and regions they work within. This gives them a power equivalent to that of governments. If they have the influence of governments then they ought also to have the accountability that goes with it.

Historically large corporations have become governments. The British East India Company, for example, formed in the seventeenth century as a company of merchants, became by degrees the government of India in the nineteenth century. The task for the development of global governance is to find the institutions and mechanisms by which large corporations can be brought to account for their global impacts.

Corporations may have an ethical responsibility to behave well in their international dealings but it is the individual managers in multinationals, transnationals and international NGOs who exercise that responsibility. In Case study 12.6 it was an individual, Leon Sullivan, who drove forward the response to apartheid.

Summary

In this chapter the following key points have been made:

- Globalisation concerns the economic, political and cultural impact of the expansion of international trade and international interconnectivity.
- The ethical issues surrounding globalisation include whether MNEs do or do not offend against human rights and/or benefit themselves and certain others but only at the cost of making others worse off in their pursuit of global business.
- The standard argument in favour of the liberalisation of world trade is that it increases the total sum of wealth in the world, which through a 'trickle down' effect benefits all. The evidence suggests that the benefits of increasing world trade are patchily distributed. Some countries, notably China, Brazil and India, have benefited but others have experienced a worsening of their relative economic performance. Within developing and transitional countries some sections of the population have paid a price for trade liberalisation while other groups have benefited.
- MNEs are tempted to choose the location of their operations to gain the benefits of institutions and legal jurisdictions that will give them better financial returns.
- The foreign and domestic policies of the governments of countries can be distorted by the needs and demands of MNEs that are based in those countries in ways that diminish the public good.
- The operations of MNEs in developing countries can make internal political and ethnic tensions worse. When their operations stretch over several mutually antagonistic countries in a region the presence of the MNEs can either make the tensions worse or, at the least, act as a focus of discontent for the disaffected.
- MNEs may find themselves operating in countries whose governments are thought to be tyrannical and dismissive of human rights. This raises the ethical question of when the situation is so bad that the company should withdraw from that country.

- Globalisation is in part a diminution of cultural diversity across the world and the growth of a worldwide consumerist and brand led culture. The ethical issue is whether this change is one that people have entered into freely and in full knowledge or whether they have been manipulated into acceptance because it suits the purposes of the MNEs.
- Cultural change is an unpredictable process, however, and it is likely that different cultures will absorb western consumerist values and adapt and change them in unexpected ways.
- There has been much development of voluntary codes that are intended to provide a framework for the global governance of MNEs and world trade. Although this is a good development the implementation of such standards and codes is a difficult one when the demands conflict with commercial imperatives.
- The Global Compact is a development that promises a new type of approach to global governance, one based on networks of learning rather than the assurance of adherence to bureaucratic standards.

Quick revision test

1. What is a trans-national company?
   (a) A company that trades globally
   (b) A company that trades internationally but makes little concession to the particularities of national markets.
   (c) A network-based international organisation that has little or no identification with a particular country.
2. What are the Sullivan principles?
   (a) Companies should not continue to operate in countries whose systems of government and governance are below minimum, acceptable ethical standards.
   (b) Companies should work to meet the human rights of their employees even when they are operating in countries where those rights are ignored or undermined.
   (c) Companies should strive to change the system of government and governance in countries where those systems are below minimum, acceptable ethical standards.
3. What does dualism mean when applied to developing countries?
   (a) Where an advanced and international economic system coexists, but does not connect, with an informal local economy.
   (b) An economic system that meets the objective of both national economies and international companies.
   (c) A business strategy that adapts international brands to local market conditions.

4. The host government agreement (HGA) that governs the Baku-Tblisi-Ceyhan oil pipeline...
   (a) requires the governments to compensate the oil companies if there is any disruption to the pipeline project
   (b) requires the oil companies to invest in the social and cultural development of the host countries
   (c) gives local communities a veto over the specific location of the pipeline.

Typical assignments and briefs

1. In what circumstances should an MNE withdraw from a country for ethical reasons? Illustrate your argument with examples.
2. To what extent does the UN Global Compact represent an innovative and effective approach to the governance of MNEs?
3. What responsibilities, if any, do MNEs have in helping countries develop fair and effective systems of governance?
4. Does the expansion of international trade benefit everybody? Does it matter if it does not?

Group activity 12

For the purposes of this activity, you should assume that most desktop computers are made in a variety of Asian countries. Three parties are in discussions over the development of a code of practice that might cover the activities of the local suppliers to the multinational corporate purchasers of the computers.

The code of practice would cover the operations of the MNEs in **one** of the countries concerned. The three parties are a spokesperson for the Society of Computer Manufacturers and Assemblers, a representative from the host country's Ministry for trade and industry and a representative from the pressure group Workers in the Manufacture and Assembly of Computers (WMAC), who is also a local trade union representative.

Divide the seminar group into three sub-groups (one for each of the parties involved). Each sub-group should decide its position, in terms of what is:

(a) morally justifiable, and

(b) likely to be achieved,

on the following issues:

- standard hours of work;
- acceptable overtime working;
- pension rights;
- accident and injury protection and benefits for dependants;
- number of continuous working days in normal and abnormal circumstances;
- health and safety standards (equivalent to western standards?);
- employment rights (e.g. period of notice required by both employer and employee);
- minimum employment age;
- social infrastructure support (e.g. support for local schools, sports clubs, youth clubs, medical facilities);
- grievance procedures.

Then, as a complete group, debate the contrasts between the three perspectives.

Recommended further reading

Jan Aart Scholte's book *Globalisation: a critical introduction* (2000) provides a good introduction to the topic, as does Held and McGrew (2000) *The Global Transformations Reader*. Another very popular book is *Globalisation and its Discontents* by Joseph Stiglitz (2004). *Living Corporate Citizenship* by McIntosh, Thomas, Leipziger and Coleman (2003) is a good read and describes most of the main standards for international business but it also has a particularly extensive discussion of the Global Compact and lots of case studies of projects undertaken by companies. Unusually, two semi-official publications make good introductions to the topic of globalisation. The first is the World Commission on the Social Dimension of Globalisation (2004) *A Fair Globalisation: Creating Opportunities for All* and the second is the Report of the Commission for Africa (2005) that was instigated by the British government.

Useful websites

Topic	Website provider	URL
A very useful site providing links to materials on businesses and human rights. The materials are classified by topicality, regions, sectors, individual companies, laws and principles	Business & Human Rights Resource Centre	http://www.business-humanrights.org/Home
International poverty measures	Povcal website	http://iresearch.worldbank.org/povcalnet
The Corner House anti-corruption organisation	The Corner House	http://www.thecornerhouse.org.uk/
Global Compact	The Global Compact Secretariat	www.unglobalcompact.org
Businesses and human rights	Amnesty International Business group	www.amnesty.org.uk/business
Private sector initiatives on labour and social conditions	The Business and Social Initatives Database (BASI)	www.oracle02.ilo.org/dyn/basi/vpisearch.first
The Sullivan principles website	The Sullivan principles organisation	www.globalsullivanprinciples.org
World Trade Organisation	World Trade Organisation	www.wto.org/
International Forum on Globalisation web page	International Forum on Globalisation	http://www.ifg.org/
A vast list of resources on globalisation	The Róbinson Rojas Archive	http://www.rrojasdatabank.org/dev3000.htm

Organisation Management

ORGANISATION DEVELOPMENT, CULTURE AND CHANGE

> **Behaviour change is a personal issue. Groups don't change, teams don't change, companies don't change: *individuals change.* Teams change the way they operate when every member of the team changes the way he or she operates. Companies change the way they operate when the people in them change the way they behave.**
>
> **Robin Stuart-Kotze** – Chair of Behavioural Science Systems Limited, Oxford
>
> *Performance: The Secrets of Successful Behaviour*, Financial Times Prentice Hall (2006), pp. 17–28

Organisation development (OD) is concerned with the diagnosis of organisational health and performance, and the ability of the organisation to adapt to change. It involves the applications of organisational behaviour and recognition of the social processes of the organisation. The manager needs to understand the nature and importance of organisational culture and climate, employee commitment, and the successful implementation and management of organisational change.

Learning outcomes

After completing this chapter you should be able to:

- explain the meaning and nature of organisation development;
- examine the nature, types and main features of organisational culture;
- evaluate influences on the development of culture and the importance of culture;
- detail the characteristics of organisational climate and employee commitment;
- explore the nature of organisational change and reasons for resistance to change;
- examine the management of organisational change, and human and social factors of change;
- review the importance of organisational culture and the ability of the organisation to adapt to change.

Critical reflection ????

'Surely an organisation can't develop or change.'

'Perhaps not, but it is people who make up the organisation, and as people change and develop, so does the performance of the organisation.'

What do you think? Do you agree that the study of organisation development is ultimately all about the actions, behaviour and effectiveness of individuals?

THE MEANING OF ORGANISATION DEVELOPMENT

Organisation development is a generic term embracing a wide range of intervention strategies into the social processes of an organisation. These intervention strategies are aimed at the development of individuals, groups and the organisation as a total system. In a very general sense, OD is concerned with attempts to improve the overall performance and effectiveness of an organisation. Essentially, it is an applied behavioural science approach to planned change and development of an organisation.

The broad nature of OD means that many interrelated topics could be included under this heading or 'label'. Given the importance of people, topics that are normally included under the heading of organisational behaviour can also be seen as relevant to the study of OD. However, the emphasis of OD is more on the development of the organisation than the actual processes of organisation and management. **Two major topics that are central and critical features of OD are organisational culture and organisation change.**

Organisation culture

An example of a comprehensive definition of OD in the behavioural science sense of the term is given by French and Bell:

> *Organisation development is a long-term effort, led and supported by top management, to improve an organisation's visioning, empowerment, learning, and problem-solving processes, through an ongoing, collaborative management of organisation culture – with special emphasis on the culture of intact work teams and other team configurations – utilizing the consultant-facilitator role and the theory and technology of applied behavioural science, including action research.*[1]

French and Bell include culture prominently in their definition as they believe that culture is the bedrock of behaviour in organisations. They summarise the primary distinguishing characteristics of organisation development in terms of the following:

- a focus on culture and processes with specific encouragement of collaboration between leaders and members;
- a focus on the human and social side of the organisation, the importance of teams of all kinds, and participation and involvement in problem-solving and decision-making;
- a focus on total system change with organisations viewed as complex social systems;
- OD practitioners as facilitators, collaborators and co-learners with the overarching goal to make the client able to solve problems on their own;
- a reliance on an action research model and the adoption of a developmental view that seeks betterment of both individuals and the organisation.[2]

Organisation change

The relationship between OD and change is emphasised by *Hamlin, Keep and Ash,* who maintain that: 'For organisations that do manage change effectively, change itself becomes the driving force that perpetuates future success and growth. In these organisations, every change becomes welcomed as an opportunity for increasing efficiency and building new organisational success.'[3]

According to Church, OD ought to be about large-scale organisational change that is based on people's perceptions and behaviours–human data.

I would draw the line at that kind of work. I would say that downsizing is not OD. I would say that a lot of training and development is not OD. Process consultation is, in my way of thinking, not OD. It's a skill that OD practitioners have, but it's not doing OD. I really think of OD as being systematic organisational change.[4]

Management development

Patching refers to the importance of the relationship between the three levels of business strategy, management strategy and organisation and management development strategy. Patching maintains that 'management development is organisation development'.

Management development is discussed in Chapter 20.

> *Management and organisation development interventions make no direct physical impact on organisations as such; they create no product; yet they change things. What they change is managers' minds ... And in changing managers' minds, such interventions thereby change those constructs which comprise organisations, markets, careers, and so on. In other words, as managers' minds change, so do their organisations.*[5]

The implementation of OD

In order to bring about effective change, OD makes use of a number of approaches – often referred to as **intervention strategies** – including survey research and feedback, T-groups, teambuilding and grid training.

- **Survey research and feedback** involves the use of questionnaire surveys to help determine the attitudes of members to the functioning of the organisation. Results of the surveys are fed back to top management and then to work groups for interpretation and analysis. Group members participate in discussions on the implications of the information, the diagnosis of problems and the development of action plans to help overcome the problems identified.
- **T-groups (or sensitivity training)** involve small, unstructured, face-to-face groupings who meet without a planned agenda or set activities. Training is intended to concentrate on process rather than content: that is, on the feeling level of communication rather than the informational value of communication. With the guidance of the trainers, participants' patterns of behaviour become the focus of attention for the group. The objectives are usually to increase participants' sensitivity to the emotional reactions in themselves and others, their diagnostic ability, and their behavioural flexibility and effectiveness. (T-groups were discussed in Chapter 9.)
- **Teambuilding** is the process of diagnosing task procedures and patterns of human interaction within a work group. The basic objective is to improve the overall performance of the organisation through improvements in the effectiveness of teams. Attention is focused on work procedures and interpersonal relationships, and especially the role of the leader in relation to other members of the group.
- **Grid training** is a development from the *Blake and Mouton* Managerial Grid approach (discussed in Chapter 12). An implied goal of grid training is that changes are aimed at attaining a 9,9 orientation (maximum concern for both production and people) on the Grid.[6]

There are, however, a number of other possible intervention strategies. *Naylor* refers also to the following 'OD techniques':

- **role analysis** – the systematic clarification of roles and allocation of them among group members;
- **life and career planning** – people are encouraged to develop and express personal goals with strategies for integrating these goals with those of the organisation;

- **quality of work life** – links between quality of work life and career planning, and a philosophy of improving the climate in which work occurs; and
- **counselling** – to help individuals better understand what it is like to work with them and, through this, assist them to attain their goals.[7]

OD action-oriented

No two organisations are the same. Each organisation has its own types of problems and most appropriate remedies. OD is action-oriented and tailored to suit specific needs. It takes a number of forms with varying levels of intervention. OD concerns itself with the examination of organisational health and the implementation of planned change. This may include training in interpersonal skills, sensitivity training, and methods and techniques relating to motivational processes, patterns of communication, styles of leadership and managerial behaviour.

Although an OD programme is legitimised by the formal system, it focuses on both the formal and the informal system. The initial intervention strategy is usually through the informal system, which includes feelings, informal actions and interactions, group norms and values, and forms part of the culture of an organisation. In Chapter 1, it was suggested that the term 'organisational behaviour' is a misnomer. The same caveat also applies to the term 'organisation development'. An organisation is made up of people. When we talk about organisation development it is important to emphasise a pluralistic approach and remember that, in practice, we are referring to the development and performance of those individuals and groups of people who comprise the organisations.

ORGANISATIONAL CULTURE

Although most of us will understand in our own minds what is meant by **organisational culture**, it is a general concept that is difficult to define or explain precisely. The concept of culture has developed from anthropology. Although people may not be aware consciously of culture, it still has a pervasive influence over their behaviour and actions. There is, however, no consensus on its meaning or its applications to the analysis of work organisations.[8] The wide diversity of interpretations relating to OD gives rise to a large number of different, and sometimes conflicting definitions.[9] Furthermore, there is sometimes confusion over the difference between the interpretation of organisational culture and organisational climate (discussed later in this chapter).

A popular and simple way of defining culture is 'how things are done around here'. For example, *Atkinson* explains organisational culture as reflecting the underlying assumptions about the way work is performed; what is 'acceptable and not acceptable'; and what behaviour and actions are encouraged and discouraged.[10]

A more detailed definition is:

> *The collection of traditions, values, policies, beliefs, and attitudes that constitute a pervasive context for everything we do and think in an organisation.*[11]

The culture of an organisation is also often likened to the personality of an individual.[12]

Cartwright sees culture as a system of management authority. When accepted by employees, cultural values increase the power and authority of management in three ways. Employees:

- identify themselves with their organisation and accept its rules when 'it is the right thing to do';
- internalise the organisation's values when they believe they are right; and
- are motivated to achieve the organisations objectives.[13]

Levels of culture *Schein* suggests a view of organisational culture based on distinguishing three levels of culture, from the shallowest to the deepest: artefacts and creations; values and basic assumptions.[14]

- **Level 1: Artefacts.** The most visible level of the culture is artefacts and creations – the constructed physical and social environment. This includes physical space and layout, the technological output, written and spoken language and the overt behaviour of group members.
- **Level 2: Espoused values.** Cultural learning reflects someone's original values. Solutions about how to deal with a new task, issue or problem are based on convictions of reality. If the solution works, the value can transform into a belief. Values and beliefs become part of the conceptual process by which group members justify actions and behaviour.
- **Level 3: Basic underlying assumptions.** When a solution to a problem works repeatedly it comes to be taken for granted. Basic assumptions are unconsciously held learned responses. They are implicit assumptions that actually guide behaviour and determine how group members perceive, think and feel about things.

Schein suggests that the basic assumptions are treated as the essence – what culture really is – and values and behaviours are treated as observed manifestations of the culture essence.

TYPES OF ORGANISATIONAL CULTURE

There are a number of ways in which to classify different types of organisational culture. Developing the ideas of *Harrison*,[15] *Handy* describes four main types of organisational cultures: power culture; role culture; task culture; and person culture.[16]

- **Power culture** depends on a central power source with rays of influence from the central figure throughout the organisation. A power culture is frequently found in small entrepreneurial organisations and relies on trust, empathy and personal communications for its effectiveness. Control is exercised from the centre by the selection of key individuals. There are few rules and procedures, and little bureaucracy. It is a political organisation with decisions taken largely on the balance of influence.
- **Role culture** is often stereotyped as a bureaucracy and works by logic and rationality. Role culture rests on the strength of strong organisational 'pillars' – the functions of specialists in, for example, finance, purchasing and production. The work of, and interaction between, the pillars is controlled by procedures and rules, and co-ordinated by the pediment of a small band of senior managers. Role or job description is often more important than the individual and position is the main source of power.
- **Task culture** is job-oriented or project-oriented. In terms of structure the task culture can be likened to a net, some strands of which are stronger than others, and with much of the power and influence at the interstices. An example is the matrix organisation. Task culture seeks to bring together the right resources and people, and utilises the unifying power of the group. Influence is widely spread and based more on expert power than on position or personal power.
- **Person culture** is where the individual is the central focus and any structure exists to serve the individuals within it. When a group of people decide that it is in their own interests to band together to do their own thing and share office space, equipment or clerical assistance then the resulting organisation would have a person culture. Examples are groups of barristers, architects, doctors or consultants. Although it is found in only a few organisations, many individuals have a preference for person culture, for example university professors and specialists. Management hierarchies and control mechanisms are possible only by mutual consent. Individuals have almost complete autonomy and any influence over them is likely to be on the basis of personal power.

Every organisation will have its own unique culture and most large businesses are likely to be something of a mix of cultures with examples for each of the four types in varying areas of the organisation. Different people enjoy working in different types of organisation culture and they are more likely to be happy and satisfied at work if their attributes and personalities are consistent with the culture of that part of the organisation in which they are employed.

Four generic types of culture

From an examination of hundreds of business organisations and their environments, *Deal and Kennedy* categorise corporate cultures according to two determining factors in the marketplace:

- the degree of risk associated with the organisation's activities; and
- the speed at which organisations and their employees receive feedback on the success of decisions or strategies.

These factors give rise to four generic types of culture: the tough-guy, macho culture; the work-hard/play-hard culture; the bet-your-company culture; and the process culture.[17]

- **Tough-guy, macho culture** – an organisation of individualists who frequently take high risks and receive quick feedback on the right or wrong of their actions. Examples cited include police departments, surgeons, construction, cosmetics, management consulting and the entertainment industry. Financial stakes are high and there is a focus on speed. The intense pressure and frenetic pace often results in early 'burn-out'. Internal competition and conflict are normal, stars are temperamental but tolerated. A high staff turnover can create difficulties in building a strong cohesive culture.
- **Work-hard/play-hard culture** – characterised by fun and action where employees take few risks, all with quick feedback. There is a high level of relatively low-risk activity. Examples include sales organisations such as estate agents and computer companies, mass consumer companies such as McDonald's, office equipment manufacturers and retail stores. Organisations tend to be highly dynamic and the primary value centres on customers and their needs. It is the team who produce the volume, and the culture encourages games, meetings, promotions and conventions to help maintain motivation. However, although a lot gets done, volume can be at the expense of quality.
- **Bet-your-company culture** – where there are large-stake decisions with a high risk but slow feedback so that it may be years before employees know if decisions were successful. Examples include oil companies, investment banks, architectural firms and the military. The focus is on the future and the importance of investing in it. There is a sense of deliberateness throughout the organisation typified by the ritual of the business meeting. There is a hierarchical system of authority with decision-making from the top down. The culture leads to high-quality inventions and scientific breakthroughs, but moves only very slowly and is vulnerable to short-term fluctuations.
- **Process culture** – a low-risk, slow-feedback culture where employees find difficulty in measuring what they do. Typical examples include banks, insurance companies, financial services and the civil service. The individual financial stakes are low and employees get very little feedback on their effectiveness. Their memos and reports seem to disappear into a void. Lack of feedback forces employees to focus on how they do something, not what they do. People tend to develop a 'cover your back' mentality. Bureaucracy results with attention to trivial events, minor detail, formality and technical perfection. Process cultures can be effective when there is a need for order and predictability.

Note, however that in a subsequent publication, *Deal and Kennedy* suggest revisions to the original typology. For example, under process cultures, banks might not yet fit into the work-hard/play-hard culture but have evolved more into sales-type organisations.[18]

INFLUENCES ON THE DEVELOPMENT OF CULTURE

The culture and structure of an organisation develop over time and in response to a complex set of factors. We can, however, identify a number of key influences that are likely to play an important role in the development of any corporate culture. These include history, primary function and technology, goals and objectives, size, location, management and staffing, and the environment.[19]

- **History**. The reason, and manner in which, the organisation was originally formed, its age, and the philosophy and values of its owners and first senior managers will affect culture. A key event in the organisation's history such as a merger or major reorganisation, or a new generation of top management, may bring about a change in culture. Corporate history can be an effective induction tool to assist a growth programme, and to help integrate acquisitions and new employees by infusion with the organisation's culture and identity.[20] Failure in merger and acquisitions can arise from cultural clashes and failure to integrate different cultures.[21]
- **Primary function and technology**. The nature of the organisation's 'business' and its primary function have an important influence on its culture. This includes the range and quality of products and services provided, the importance of reputation and the type of customers. The primary function of the organisation will determine the nature of the technological processes and methods of undertaking work, which in turn also affect structure and culture.
- **Goals and objectives**. Although a business organisation may pursue profitability, this is not by itself very clear or a sufficient criterion for its effective management. For example, to what extent is emphasis placed on long-term survival or growth and development? How much attention is given to avoiding risks and uncertainties? Or how much concern is shown for broader social responsibilities? The organisation must give attention to objectives in all key areas of its operations. The combination of objectives and resultant strategies will influence culture, and may itself be influenced by changes in culture.
- **Size**. Usually larger organisations have more formalised structures and cultures. Increased size is likely to result in separate departments and possibly split-site operations. This may cause difficulties in communication and inter-departmental rivalries with the need for effective co-ordination. A rapid expansion, or decline, in size and rate of growth, and resultant changes in staffing will influence structure and culture.
- **Location**. Geographical location and the physical characteristics can have a major influence on culture – for example, whether an organisation is located in a quiet rural location or a busy city centre can influence the types of customers and the staff employed. It can also affect the nature of services provided, the sense of 'boundary' and distinctive identity, and opportunities for development.
- **Management and staffing**. Top executives can have considerable influence on the nature of corporate culture. Examples are the key role played by Anita Roddick, founder of The Body Shop,[22] and Marjorie Scardino and her change of style when she took over as the new chief executive of Pearson.

Her candour works ... As an example of straight talking winning over a sceptical City and press, it is brilliant. As an example of just how much a company's culture can change under a new chief executive, it is breathtaking.[23]

Another example is Louis Gerstner, who defined a strategy for the computing giant IBM and remade the ossified culture bred by the company's success, rebuilt the leadership team and gave the workforce a renewed sense of purpose.[24]

However, all members of staff help to shape the dominant culture of an organisation, irrespective of what senior management feel it should be. Culture is also determined by the nature of staff employed and the extent to which they accept management philoso-

phy and policies or pay only 'lip service'. Another important influence is the match between corporate culture and employees' perception of the psychological contract.
- **The environment.** In order to be effective, the organisation must be responsive to external environmental influences. For example, if the organisation operates within a dynamic environment it requires a structure and culture that are sensitive and readily adaptable to change. An organic structure is more likely to respond effectively to new opportunities and challenges, and risks and limitations presented by the external environment.

Critical reflection

'The proliferation of definitions and explanations of culture, its anthropological origins and lack of clarity arguably undermine its value to our understanding of organisational behaviour.' Do you agree? What role does culture play in the management of modern work organisations?

THE CULTURAL WEB

In order to help describe and understand the culture of an organisation, *Johnson, Scholes and Whittington* present a cultural web, which brings together different aspects for the analysis of organisational culture (*see* Figure 19.1).

- **Routine behaviours** – the ways in which members of the organisation behave towards each other and towards those outside the organisation and which make up how things are done or how things should happen.
- **Rituals** – the particular activities or special events through which the organisation emphasises what is particularly important and can include formal organisational processes and informal processes.
- **Stories** – told by members of the organisation that embed the present and flag up important events and personalities, and typically have to do with successes, failures, heroes, villains and mavericks.
- **Symbols** – such as logos, offices, cars, titles, type of language or terminology commonly used which become a shorthand representation of the nature of the organisation.
- **Power structures** – the most powerful individuals or groups in the organisation that may be based on management position and seniority but in some organisations power can be lodged with other levels or functions.
- **Control systems** – the measurement and reward systems that emphasise what it is important to monitor, and to focus attention and activity upon – for example, stewardship of funds or quality of service.
- **Organisation structure** – which reflects power structures and delineates important relationships and activities within the organisation, and involves both formal structure and control and less formal systems.
- **Paradigm** – of the organisation that encapsulates and reinforces the behaviours observed in other elements of the cultural web.[25]

Other focuses of analysis

There are, however, many other ways in which people attempt to describe and understand what constitutes organisational culture, and different areas of attention for analysing the elements of culture. *Wilson* suggests that culture is a characteristic of the organisation, not of individuals.

Figure 19.1 The cultural web of an organisation

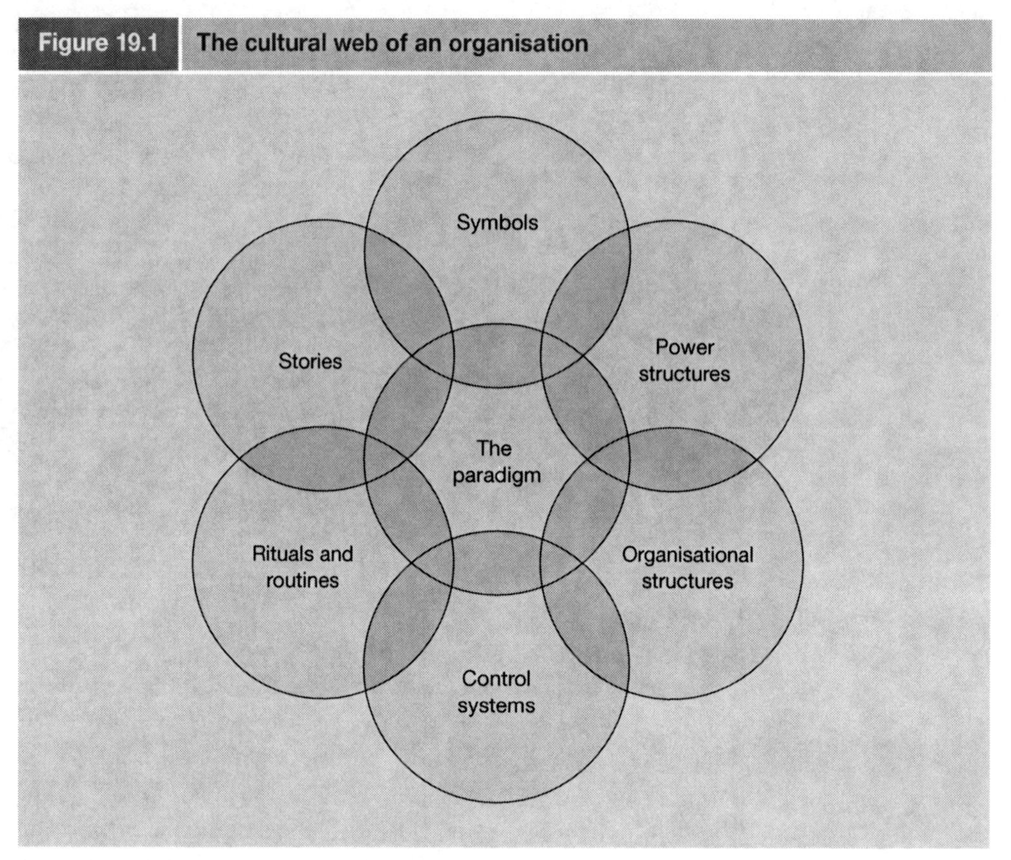

Source: Johnson, G., Scholes, K. and Whittington, R., *Exploring Corporate Strategy*, Seventh Edition, Financial Times Prentice Hall (2005), p. 202. Reproduced with permission from Pearson Eduction Ltd.

One way of examining the culture of an organization is to look at its corporate image to see what and who is valued in the organization. A corporate image is the mental picture the clients, customers, employees, and others have of an organization. The impression is the combination of unconscious, unintended, conscious, and intended factors that arise.[26]

ACAS distinguishes two different organisation cultures and different ways of doing things:

- **Control culture** with the emphasis on rules and procedures, control and compliance with precedent providing guidelines; and
- **Quality of working life culture** with the emphasis on core values, with mission statements providing guidance and commitment via shared goals, values and traditions.[27]

Naylor suggests that quite what forms organisational culture is a difficulty and to make a start we need to recognise both the visible and invisible layers. On the surface is the visible layer made up of elements such as artefacts, symbols, languages, stories and activities which can be collected, compared and assembled into a description of the organisation. Underpinning this 'visible culture' is the invisible layer of beliefs, values, norms, basic assumptions and understanding.[28]

Charters questions the extent to which the concept of 'folklore' offers the potential to explore the existence of company myths and legends. Dictionary definitions and discussions of the term in research papers, point to its close connection with culture.

Elements of folklore include myths and legends, and hence the concept of folklore appears to validate the exploration of organisational stories as part of cultural research ... If folklore really is an expression of culture, then it could be argued that it should be possible to discern aspects of the culture of an organisation through the legends and myths of that organisation, the stories told which may or may not have a foundation in history.[29]

THE IMPORTANCE OF CULTURE

Applications of organisational behaviour and the effective management of human resources are dependent not only upon the nature of the industry or business, but also upon the characteristic features of the individual organisation – and its culture. The pervasive nature of culture in terms of 'how things are done around here' and common values, beliefs and attitudes will therefore have a significant effect on organisational processes such as decision-making, design of structure, group behaviour, work organisation, motivation and job satisfaction, and management control. For example, many managers claim that their organisation's culture contributes considerably to their stress.[30]

Harrison and Stokes maintain that organisational culture influences the behaviour of all individuals and groups within the organisation.

Culture impacts most aspects of organizational life, such as how decisions are made, who makes them, how rewards are distributed, who is promoted, how people are treated, how the organization responds to its environment, and so on.[31]

A similar point is made by *Reigle*, who refers to culture as an important factor in successful technology implementation, innovation, mergers, acquisitions, job satisfaction, organisational success and team effectiveness, and to the importance of determining whether organisations exhibit organic or mechanistic cultures.[32]

Culture and organisation control

Egan refers to culture as the largest organisational control system that dictates how crazy or idiosyncratic people can be. Companies and institutions have both an overt and covert culture that influences both business and organisational behaviour.

The covert set can be quite dysfunctional and costly. Culture – the assumptions, beliefs, values and norms that drive 'the way we do things here' – is the largest and most controlling of the systems because it affects not only overt organisational behaviour but also the shadow-side behaviour ... Culture lays down norms for the social system. In one institution you had to be an engineer to rise to the top. There was no published rule, of course, it was just the way things were. In one bank you could never be made an officer of the company if you wore polyester clothes. Culture tells us what kind of politics are allowed and just how members of an organisation are allowed to play the political game.[33]

Egan also distinguishes between the 'preferred culture' which serves the business and the 'culture-in-use'. This culture-behind-the-culture carries the real beliefs, values and norms that drive patterns of behaviour within the company. These remain unnamed, undiscussed and unmentionable and these covert cultures lie outside ordinary managerial control. The first step in changing such limiting behaviour features is to identify the preferred culture and to ensure that the company's way of operating effectively serves the business right now.[34]

Culture in short-life organisations

The importance of culture raises interesting questions relating to its nature and influence in 'short-life' organisations – that is, organisations created to run for only a short period of time such as arts festivals or national garden festivals. For example, how does culture develop when the organisation has little or no prior history, has short-term goals and objectives and has only limited time for top management to exercise influence? How do managers in such organisations attempt to inculcate culture? From a study of the Garden Festival Wales, *Meudell and Gadd* found that success in creating a culture occurred as a direct result of their recruitment and training initiatives. However, it is not only culture but climate that is important for organisational effectiveness.

> *Rigorous training in customer care/corporate culture might produce an automatic 'Have a nice day' but only the engendering of a suitable climate will encourage people to say it and mean it.*[35]

Culture and organisational performance

Culture is clearly an important ingredient of effective organisational performance. In their study of 62 American companies with outstandingly successful performance, *Peters and Waterman* draw attention to the importance of corporate culture.

> *Without exception, the dominance and coherence of culture proved to be an essential quality of the excellent companies. Moreover, the stronger the culture and the more it was directed to the market-place, the less need was there for policy manuals, organization charts, or detailed procedures and rules. In these companies, people way down the line know what they are supposed to do in most situations because the handful of guiding values is crystal clear.*[36]

Although a number of the original 'excellent' organisations have since fallen from grace, the importance of culture to effective organisational performance still stands and has been reinforced by a study by Heller of Europe's top companies. For example, in commenting on Heineken's superiority in world markets, *Heller* makes the point that it rests in part on its remarkable corporate culture:

> *There is nothing accidental about cultural strengths ... There is a relationship between an organisation's culture and its performance.*[37]

In their original study of highly successful companies, *Goldsmith and Clutterbuck* identified eight characteristics built into the day-to-day culture of the organisation. From their subsequent study of the world's top companies, a key characteristic of high-performing companies is a challenge culture. All the companies are very demanding of the people who work for them but this is balanced by a nurturing culture that shows that they also care for their employees in numerous ways.[38]

And according to *Cummings and Worley*:

> *An organization's culture is the pattern of assumptions, values and norms that are more or less shared by an organization's members. A growing body of research has shown that culture can affect strategy formulation and implementation as well as a firm's ability to achieve high levels of excellence.*[39]

Use of managerial tools

Chatman and Cha suggest that every company has a culture – good or bad. However, there is more to a good culture than happy staff. In order to aid long-term performance, there are three main criteria needed to develop a suitable culture:

- it must be strategically relevant;
- it needs to be strong in order that people care about what is important; and
- the culture must have an intrinsic ability to adapt to changing circumstances.

In order that leaders can develop, manage and change their culture for better performance, Chatman and Cha refer to the use of three managerial tools.

- **Recruitment and selection** – hire people who fit the company's culture even if this may involve overlooking some technical skills for a better cultural fit. Look carefully at the characteristics of your recruiters and consider your selection decision in the light of culture.
- **Social tools and training** – develop practices that enable new people to understand the values, abilities, expected behaviour and social knowledge in order to participate fully as an employee, and to create strong bonds among members.
- **Reward system** – culture is an organisation's informal reward system but it needs to be intricately connected to formal rewards. Examples include staff meetings where the seat-

ing arrangement is in accordance with level of sales, name badges that include inventory losses, and payments of large commissions in front of customers and other staff.[40]

Culture change

The pervasive nature of organisational culture means that if change is to be brought about successfully, this is likely to involve changes to culture. For example, *Stewart* makes the following comment on the relationship between culture and change.

> *In recent years attention has shifted from the effects of the organization of work on people's behaviour to how behaviour is influenced by the organizational culture. What is much more common today is the widespread recognition that organizational change is not just, or even necessarily mainly, about changing the structure but often requires changing the culture too.*[41]

A similar view is held by *Naylor*, who points out that: 'In the holistic system, any change will affect the culture and the culture will affect or constrain the change ... Cultural change is intimately bound up with the process of organisational change.'[42]

However, although attention is often given to shifting the prevailing activities and atmosphere of an organisation to a brighter future, changing the ethos and culture of an organisation is not easy. In practice, organisations usually appear to alter their underlying ethos only on a gradual basis and the complexity of environmental pressures may itself hinder rapid change. Culture is often deep-rooted and commitment to the objectives and policies of the organisation, people's cognitive limitations and their uncertainties and fears, may mean a reluctance to accept a change in behaviour. Culture is reinforced through the system of rites and rituals, patterns of communication, the informal organisation, expected patterns of behaviour and perceptions of the psychological contract.

> *Clearly most organisations are not the stable, predictable structures of the past. Keeping followers motivated and committed in an era of unrelenting change, means that leaders must be able to create organisational cultures that foster not only performance, but also a sense of pride and fun. Because cultures evolve over many years and are usually deep-rooted, they can be difficult to change. Some commentators have observed that it is easier to change behaviour by changing processes and systems in an organisation than it is to change people's attitudes. While goals change in the course of a person's life, values tend to remain constant and help determine an employee's attitudes to their employer.*
>
> DTI (2004)[43]

The nature of organisational change is discussed later in this chapter.

National and international culture

Culture helps to account for variations among organisations and managers, both nationally and internationally. It helps to explain why different groups of people perceive things in their own way and perform things differently from other groups.[44] With greater international competition, an understanding of national culture has become of increasing importance for managers. According to *Siddall*, for example: 'International business, the issue of culture and the need for better understanding have become major parts of organisational behaviour.'[45] Cultural practices vary widely among different countries and because of our own values may be difficult to understand.

Schneider and Barsoux suggest that cultural beliefs and values influence the meaning of management and also show up differences in conceptions of organisations. National differences and cultural reasons raise concerns about the transferability of organisational structures, systems and processes and question the logic of universal 'best practice'.[46] *Cheng*,

Sculli and Chan also question the universality of theories of management and organisational behaviour on the ground that they have not adequately addressed the factor of culture.[47] Those fortunate enough to have shared the experience of the author in visiting both Disneyland in Florida and Disneyland Paris would probably have witnessed the cultural differences in the attitudes to, and acceptance of, the Disney approach and procedures between American and French employees.

According to *Francesco and Gold*, culture has recently been accepted as an explanation of organisational behaviour. One reason is the increase in competitiveness of nations and a second reason is that managers encounter different cultures in their contacts with people from other nations. However, there are limits to the use of culture to explain organisational behaviour, and the relationship between national cultural values and actual behaviour in organisations is complex.[48]

Refresh your understanding
Activity 19A
www.pearsoned.co.uk/mullins

Recall also the discussion on the international context of management and organisational behaviour in Chapter 1.

ORGANISATIONAL CLIMATE

In addition to arrangements for the carrying out of organisational processes, management has a responsibility for creating a climate in which people are motivated to work willingly and effectively. **Organisational climate** is a general concept and difficult to define precisely. It is more something that is felt. It can be likened to our description of the weather and the way in which the climate of a geographical region results from the combination of environmental forces. Some of these forces are better understood than others.

Applied to organisations, **climate** can be said to relate to the prevailing atmosphere surrounding the organisation, to the level of morale, and to the strength of feelings of belonging, care and goodwill among members. Climate will influence the attitudes that members of the organisation bring to bear on their work performance and personal relationships. The extent to which employees accept the culture of the organisation will have a significant effect on climate.

From a detailed study of approaches to organisational climate, *Moran and Volkwein* conclude that:

> *... since climate operates at a more accessible level than culture, it is more malleable and, hence, the more appropriate level at which to target short-term interventions aimed at producing positive organisational change ...* [however] *interventions to change climate must consider the deeper patterns embedded in an organisation's climate.*[49]

Whereas organisational culture describes what the organisation is about, organisational climate is an indication of the employees' feelings and beliefs of what the organisation is about. Climate is based on the perceptions of members towards the organisation.

> *Organisational climate is a relatively enduring quality of the internal environment of an organisation that (a) is experienced by its members, (b) influences their behavior, and (c) can be described in terms of the values of a particular set of characteristics (or attributes) of the organisation.*[50]

Climate also relates to the recognition of the organisation as a social system and the extent to which membership is perceived as a psychologically rewarding experience. It can be seen as the state of mutual trust and understanding among members of the organisation. For example, *Rentsch* suggests that: 'One assumption of climate theory is that organisational members perceive and make sense of organisational policies, practices, and procedures in psychologically meaningful terms'.[51]

Characteristics of a healthy organisational climate

Organisational climate is characterised, therefore, by the nature of the people–organisation relationship and the superior–subordinate relationship. These relationships are determined by interactions among goals and objectives, formal structure, the process of management, styles of leadership and the behaviour of people.

Although similar types of organisations will share certain common features and norms, each organisation will have its own different and distinctive features. In general terms, however, a healthy organisational climate might be expected to exhibit such characteristic features as:

- the integration of organisational goals and personal goals;
- the most appropriate organisation structure based on the demands of the socio-technical system;
- democratic functioning of the organisation with full opportunities for participation;
- justice in treatment with equitable HRM and employment relations policies and practices;
- mutual trust, consideration and support among different levels of the organisation;
- the open discussion of conflict with an attempt to avoid confrontation;
- managerial behaviour and styles of leadership appropriate to the particular work situations;
- acceptance of the psychological contract between the individual and the organisation;
- recognition of people's needs and expectations at work, and individual differences and attributes;
- concern for job design and the work/life balance;
- opportunities for personal development and career progression;
- a sense of identity with, and loyalty to, the organisation and a feeling of being a valued and important member.

If organisational climate is to be improved, then attention should be given to the above features. A healthy climate will not by itself guarantee improved organisational effectiveness. However, an organisation is most unlikely to attain optimum operational performance unless the climate evokes a spirit of support and co-operation throughout the organisation, and is conducive to motivating members to work willingly and effectively.

Whitmore suggests that two human drives rise above all others; the need for self-belief, and the need for a sense of meaning and purpose in our lives. They exist independent of race, creed and culture. These two needs are the fundamental bedrocks that underlie business performance, and the importance of generating a climate of creativity within an organisation stems from recognition of their significance.[52]

EMPLOYEE COMMITMENT

Among the factors that contribute to a healthy organisational climate is the extent to which members of staff have a sense of commitment to the organisation. The extent of their commitment will have a major influence on the level of work performance. *Walton* suggests that a significant change in approaches to the organisation and management of work is from organisational control to commitment in the workplace. The evidence is well grounded that underlying all the policies of commitment strategy is a management philosophy at the centre of which 'is a belief that eliciting employee commitment will lead to enhanced performance'.[53]

The concept of **employee commitment** itself, and the manner in which it is actually created, is not easy to describe. There does, however, appear to be a growing acceptance of the notion of attachment and loyalty. *O'Reilly* refers to the term 'organisational commitment' as 'typically conceived of as an individual's psychological bond to the organization, including a sense of job involvement, loyalty, and a belief in the values of the organization'.[54]

Securing the commitment of staff

Genuine commitment requires not just a recognition or understanding of what the organisation expects but an emotional and behavioural response from staff. If loyalty, long service or expertise appear to be no longer rewarded, this may well have an adverse effect on those members of the organisation who do survive and they are less likely to have a high level of commitment to the organisation.[55] *Guirdham* suggests that 'commitment of staff to the organisation has long been valued and is coming back into fashion as the costs to loyalty of downsizing and re-engineering come to be felt'.[56]

After the downsizing, de-layering, streamlining and outsourcing of recent years, *Altman, Cooper and Garner* question whether companies can continue to count on commitment from employees when they are no longer seen to be committed to them. The more companies downsize, the more they are seen to be breaking the psychological contract. A new psychological contract needs to consider the organisation of the future.

> *The old 'command and control' interpretation of loyalty in the workplace needs to be replaced with an attitude of commitment by both sides which leads to a more pragmatic relationship within the limited horizons against which businesses are being managed today worldwide. Employers will still commit themselves to their employees but employment can no longer be guaranteed.*[57]

Galunic and Weeks suggest that with the demise of job security, companies need other strategies to encourage commitment. Examples include paying more attention to compensation, flexible working, spending to support telecommuting and lifestyle-friendly perks. However, while such initiatives may encourage employees to work hard, they are no substitute for job security. In order to help restore commitment without again offering job security, Galunic and Weeks propose that in addition to company-specific training, there is a programme of investment in generic training that focuses on general skills and education to raise the professional level of employees. By developing 'employability' and the ability to earn a living through professional or occupational – not job – security, employees are in turn likely to respond with greater commitment to the company.[58]

According to *Gratton*, the obligations of the firm to individual members are expressed continuously and the first obligation is true commitment to people.

> *On the face of it 'true commitment to people' is an overused phrase, appearing as it does on every CEO's annual business report. The obligation or 'true commitment' is tested, not when times are good, but when times are hard.*
>
> Lynda Gratton, *The Democratic Enterprise*[59]

Managerial control and commitment

Watson refers to the basic choice that managers can make in trying to achieve managerial control. The choice between direct and indirect control influences the extent of the psychological commitment that is sought from staff. An organisation leaning towards direct control principles would be highly centralised with a tight bureaucratic structure, and close supervision and monitoring of activities. There would tend to be a culture involving a low level of mutual commitment between the organisation and its members. Because of the implication that management are putting little trust in employees to use their own discretion a 'low-trust' culture emerges. By contrast, an organisation leaning more towards the use of indirect control would be less centralised with a looser bureaucratic structure. Rules would be relatively loose and procedures more flexible as employees have more empowerment and discretion about how to carry out their activities. The high level of trust between members of the organisation would be associated with a culture of mutually high-level commitment.[60]

Underlying influences

In addition to the above, there are a number of underlying influences on the extent of employees' commitment to the organisation.

- People differ in their **work ethic** and the manner of their involvement with, and concern for, work (discussed in Chapter 1) and the extent to which they have an instrumental, bureaucratic or solidaristic orientation. Some people may well have a set attitude to work, whatever the nature of the work environment.
- People's behaviour and the level of their commitment is also influenced by the nature of the **psychological contract** and the degree to which it is perceived as fair by both the individual and the organisation.
- In terms of their relationship with the work organisation, employees may reasonably have the approach of 'what's in it for me'. An important influence on the strength of commitment is the **nature of the reward system** and the satisfaction of needs and expectations at work in terms of economic rewards, intrinsic satisfaction or social relationships (*see* Chapter 7).

Critical reflection

'The socialisation of new members into an organisation's culture is no more or less than the manipulation of the individual, and is therefore unethical and should be condemned.' How would you challenge the validity of this statement?

THE NATURE OF ORGANISATIONAL CHANGE

Change is a pervasive influence. It is an inescapable part of both social and organisational life and we are all subject to continual change of one form or another.

The effects of change can be studied over different time scales, from weeks to hundreds of years, and studied at different levels. Change can be studied in terms of its effects at the individual, group, organisation, society, national or international level. However, because of its pervasive nature, change at any one level is interrelated with changes at other levels, and it is difficult to study one area of change in isolation. But our main focus of attention is on the management of organisational change. Organisational change can be initiated deliberately by managers, it can evolve slowly within a department, it can be imposed by specific changes in policy or procedures or it can arise through external pressures. Change can affect all aspects of the operation and functioning of the organisation.[61]

The forces of change

An organisation can perform effectively only through interactions with the broader external environment of which it is part. The structure and functioning of the organisation must reflect, therefore, the nature of the environment in which it is operating. There are factors which create an increasingly volatile environment, such as:

- uncertain economic conditions;
- globalisation and fierce world competition;
- the level of government intervention;
- political interests;
- scarcity of natural resources;
- rapid developments in new technology and the information age.

In order to help ensure its survival and future success the organisation must be readily adaptable to the external demands placed upon it. The organisation must be responsive to change. Other major forces of change include:

- increased demands for quality and high levels of customer service and satisfaction;
- greater flexibility in the structure of work organisations and patterns of management;
- the changing nature and composition of the workforce; and
- conflict from within the organisation.

According to a survey from Management Consultancies Associations, four interrelated forces are driving change, each of which brings organisations and individuals into conflict:

1 outsourcing and the continual redefinition of what constitutes an organisation's core business;
2 the distribution of work across different people, organisations and locations, and the extent to which this makes work fragmented;
3 changing demographics and expectations that create an employees', rather than employers', market;
4 the doubled-edge sword of technology, which enables people to do more but tempts organisations to do too much.[62]

Change within the organisation

Change also originates within the organisation itself. Much of this change is part of a natural process of ageing – for example, as material resources such as buildings, equipment or machinery deteriorate or lose efficiency; or as human resources get older, or as skills and abilities become outdated. Some of this change can be managed through careful planning – for example, regular repairs and maintenance, choice of introducing new technology or methods of work, effective human resource planning to prevent a large number of staff retiring at the same time, and management succession planning – training and staff development. However, the main pressure of change is from external forces. The organisation must be properly prepared to face the demands of a changing environment. It must give attention to its future development and success and this includes public sector organisations and the armed forces.[63]

Public sector executives face unique obstacles in leading organisational change, in part because of entrenched civil service bureaucracies, procedural constraints such as managing performance and firing employees, and dealing with many different stakeholders with competing priorities.[64]

A concept map of sources of change is presented in Figure 19.2.

Increasing pace of change

The latest 'Quality of Working Life' report published by the Chartered Management Institute draws attention to the intensifying pace, scale and complexity of organisational change.

What has emerged is a picture of managers coming under increasing pressure from the imposition of targets, performance management systems and league tables against a backdrop of global competition, technological change, the drive to maximise shareholder value and, in the public sector, a modernisation agenda.

Not surprisingly, managers in larger organisations in all sectors experienced most change. While a higher proportion of managers working in the public sector had experienced change initiatives compared to managers working in PLCs, those working in the private sector experienced a greater variety of change initiatives.[65]

Figure 19.2 Concept map of sources of change

SOURCES OF CHANGE

CHANGE MAY ORIGINATE FROM
• OUTSIDE THE ORGANISATION
• INSIDE THE ORGANISATION

IN ORDER TO
• promote change
• adapt to change

IT IS ESSENTIAL TO DEFINE
• the origin of the NEED to change
• the NATURE of any PROPOSED change

THE NEED FOR REORGANISATION
within an organisation can arise from several sources:
ORGANISATION IS GROWING
→ requires more staff →
requires tighter control of
– administrative procedures
– employment conditions
– wages structure e.g.
In small company salaries/wages agreed on a personal basis
In large companies – a hierarchal structure of salaries wage level and bargaining conditions
ORGANISATION IN DECLINE
– staff reduction
– frozen or reduced wages
– lack of motivation
ORGANISATION TAKES NEW DIRECTION/ ADDITIONAL DIRECTION
– changes in staff roles
– changes in conditions of employment
– changes in culture/social attitudes

REORGANISATION IS ACCOMPANIED BY CHANGES IN CULTURE
• less social contact between staff at all levels
• less opportunity for co-operation between management and staff
• decrease in motivation by staff

INTERNAL FORCES FOR CHANGE INCLUDE
• profitability
• reorganisation
• conflict between organisational components
– departments
– people
• changes in culture/social environment

CONFLICT CAN BE A SOURCE OF CHANGE
Between
– senior management on strategy
– departments on respective roles/areas of responsibility
– all staff on levels/areas of responsibility
e.g. in a company
• production manager/service manager has tie-up with clients on technical matters
• accounts manager has tie-up with client on payment of bills
• one manager commandeers the dual role

EXAMPLE
A travel company is losing money/making lower profits
Causes may be
– inefficient managers
– more efficient management of competitors
– more attractive holidays from competitors
– less competitive prices
– poor exchange rates
– improved weather conditions in the UK
Having identified causes, solutions can be planned at
• company level
• branch level

EXTERNAL FORCES FOR CHANGE INCLUDE
• Market forces
• Legislation
• Tax structures
• New technologies
• Political

NEW TECHNOLOGIES
– these may be
• New process equipment
• New computer technology
• New information/data processing systems

MARKET FORCES FREQUENTLY DICTATE NEED FOR CHANGE
• Financial pressures
e.g. increased cost of imports, effect of VAT on fuel
• Competition – need to develop new/improved products
– need to continually develop competitive pricing policies e.g. supermarket price war, travel agent price war
– need to provide new and improved services and quality of services

TAX STRUCTURES
– Value Added Tax changes
– National Insurance contributions
– Windfall taxes
– Local taxes, e.g. community charges business rates

PROFITABILITY IS A MAJOR THRUST FOR CHANGE
Source of change to improve profitability
– attitudes and skills of senior management
– products of research
– improved production facilities
– reductions in staff
– take-overs/mergers
• of other organisations
• by other organisations

LEGISLATION
– in particular environmental and employment legislation
• Quota controls
• Equal opportunities
• Discrimination
• Workers' charter
• Data protection

POLITICAL REASONS FOR CHANGE
A source of change which encompasses many of the above –
• world politics/transnational policies
• national politics
• organisational politics

TAKE-OVERS/MERGERS
This source (origin) of change
take-over or combination of firms
– to improve efficiency/efficient use of assets
e.g. economics of sales
reduce duplication
increased market pull
more dynamic pull
more dynamic management
– to improve profitability

Source: Training Learning Consultancy Ltd, Bristol, England. Reproduced with permission.

PLANNED ORGANISATIONAL CHANGE

Most planned organisational change is triggered by the need to respond to new challenges or opportunities presented by the external environment, or in anticipation of the need to cope with potential future problems, for example, intended government legislation, a new product development by a major competitor or further technological advances. Planned change represents an intentional attempt to improve, in some important way, the operational effectiveness of the organisation.

The basic underlying objectives can be seen in general terms as:

- modifying the behavioural patterns of members of the organisation; and
- improving the ability of the organisation to cope with changes in its environment.

ACAS refers to initiating and maintaining a Quality of Working Life (QWL) change programme. Such initiatives could stem from a variety of issues that might provide 'a window for change' to management and/or worker representatives. Examples include:

- a general sense that the organisation could perform better;
- the need to improve organisation flexibility, quality or to develop new customer concern;
- a sense that skills and abilities of people are under-utilised or concerns about a lack of commitment from employees;
- the need to introduce changes in technology or working practices;
- workers feeling over-controlled by supervision or by the process or jobs seen as being boring;
- concerns about ineffective communications or poor performance indicators;
- fractious relationships between managers and the managed.[66]

Behaviour modification

A programme of planned change and improved performance developed by *Lewin* involves the management of a three-phase process of behaviour modification:

- **unfreezing** – reducing those forces which maintain behaviour in its present form, recognition of the need for change and improvement to occur;
- **movement** – development of new attitudes or behaviour and the implementation of the change;
- **refreezing** – stabilising change at the new level and reinforcement through supporting mechanisms, for example policies, structure or norms.[67]

French, Kast and Rosenzweig list eight specific components of a planned-change effort related to the above process (*see* Figure 19.3).[68]

Figure 19.3 Stages in a planned-change effort

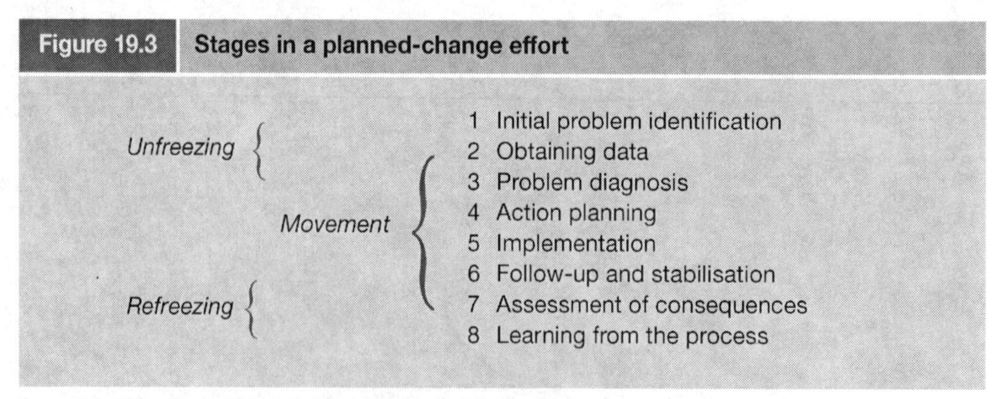

Source: Adapted from French, W. L., Kast, F. E. and Rosenweig, J. E., *Understanding Human Behaviour in Organizations*, Harper and Row (1985), p. 9. Reproduced with permission from Pearson Education, Inc.

Changes in managerial work Change is reciprocal and changing organisations will affect the nature of managerial work. *Stewart*, for example, describes how changes in organisations affect the kinds of jobs that managers have to do and the nature of their lives and careers. Older managers now work for very different kinds of organisations from those in which they first became managers. Although hierarchies of authority will continue to exist in large organisations they will be shorter and there will be wider networking. There will be a smaller number of middle managers but with more responsible roles. Managers' jobs are more complex and demanding, and managers' careers are much less predictable. But managers now have a greater choice in their work and careers.[69]

However, according to *Crainer*, many managers refuse to accept the necessity of change. Instead of being proactive, change is often reactive, the last resort.

> *Research repeatedly shows that it is managers who are the chief stumbling block to making change happen. Changing organizational structures and managerial thinking challenges and undercuts traditional power bases ... For the manager reared on the old functional certainties, the new world organization is very difficult to manage. Indeed, the vast majority of managers are neither trained nor equipped to manage in such an environment.*[70]

And, according to *Gratton*, 'understanding the soul of the organisation and building trust and commitment is crucial to ongoing adaptation and change'.[71]

The challenge of e-business It is impossible to know exactly what the future of e-business will bring but it will continue to bring tremendous change. One of the biggest changes for managers, especially within large organisations, is learning how to get to grips with an increasingly flexible workforce. As a result of the e-business environment many people can work at any time, anywhere and at any place. Many employees work at home but although the virtual office may help organisations to cut costs, it also poses many management challenges including the challenge to put structures in place to ensure regular meetings take place. Flexible working calls for flexible managers. This means that the traditional line managers need to become leaders, coaches and facilitators. Given the accelerating rate of change particularly with the intranet, it is essential that organisations invest in and develop their managers to succeed with this change.

RESISTANCE TO CHANGE

Despite the potential positive outcomes, change is often resisted at both the individual and the organisational level. Resistance to change – or the thought of the implications of the change – appears to be a common phenomenon. As long ago as 1970, *Toffler* wrote about the psychological dimension of 'future shock', and that people are naturally wary of change. 'Among many there is an uneasy mood – a suspicion that change is out of control.'[72]

Resistance to change can take many forms and it is often difficult to pinpoint the exact reasons. The forces against change in work organisations include: ignoring the needs and expectations of members; when members have insufficient information about the nature of the change; or if they do not perceive the need for change. Fears may be expressed over such matters as employment levels and job security, de-skilling of work, loss of job satisfaction, wage rate differentials, changes to social structures and working conditions, loss of individual control over work, and greater management control.

Individual resistance Some common reasons for individual resistance to change within organisations include the following:

- **Selective perception**. People's interpretation of stimuli presents a unique picture or image of the 'real' world and can result in selective perception. This can lead to a biased view of a particular situation, which fits most comfortably into a person's own perception of reality, and can cause resistance to change. For example, trade unionists may have a stereotyped view of management as untrustworthy and therefore oppose any management change, however well founded might have been the intention. Managers exposed to different theories or ideas may tend to categorise these as either those they already practise and have no need to worry about or those that are of no practical value and which can be discarded as of no concern to them.

- **Habit**. People tend to respond to situations in an established and accustomed manner. Habits may serve as a means of comfort and security, and as a guide for easy decision-making. Proposed changes to habits, especially if the habits are well established and require little effort, may well be resisted. However, if there is a clearly perceived advantage, for example a reduction in working hours without loss of pay, there is likely to be less, if any, resistance to the change, although some people may, because of habit, still find it difficult to adjust to the new times.
- **Inconvenience or loss of freedom**. If the change is seen as likely to prove inconvenient, make life more difficult, reduce freedom of action or result in increased control, there will be resistance.
- **Economic implications**. People are likely to resist change that is perceived as reducing either directly or indirectly their pay or other rewards, requiring an increase in work for the same level of pay or acting as a threat to their job security. People tend to have established patterns of working and a vested interest in maintaining the status quo.
- **Security in the past**. There is a tendency for some people to find a sense of security in the past. In times of frustration or difficulty, or when faced with new or unfamiliar ideas or methods, people may reflect on the past. There is a wish to retain old and comfortable ways. For example, in bureaucratic organisations, officials often tend to place faith in well-established ('tried and trusted') procedures and cling to these as giving a feeling of security.
- **Fear of the unknown**. Changes which confront people with the unknown tend to cause anxiety or fear. Many major changes in a work organisation present a degree of uncertainty, for example the introduction of new technology or methods of working. A person may resist promotion because of uncertainty over changes in responsibilities or the increased social demands of the higher position.

Organisational resistance

Although organisations have to adapt to their environment, they tend to feel comfortable operating within the structure, policies and procedures which have been formulated to deal with a range of present situations. To ensure operational effectiveness, organisations often set up defences against change and prefer to concentrate on the routine things they perform well. Some of the main reasons for organisational resistance against change are as follows.

- **Organisation culture**. Recall that the culture of an organisation develops over time and may not be easy to change. The pervasive nature of culture in terms of 'how things are done around here' also has a significant effect on organisational processes and the behaviour of staff. An ineffective culture may result in a lack of flexibility for, or acceptance of, change.
- **Maintaining stability**. Organisations, especially large-scale ones, pay much attention to maintaining stability and predictability. The need for formal organisation structure and the division of work, narrow definitions of assigned duties and responsibilities, established rules, procedures and methods of work, can result in resistance to change. The more mechanistic or bureaucratic the structure, the less likely it is that the organisation will be responsive to change.
- **Investment in resources**. Change often requires large resources that may already be committed to investments in other areas or strategies. Assets such as buildings, technology, equipment and people cannot easily be altered. For example, a car manufacturer may not find it easy to change to a socio-technical approach and the use of autonomous

work groups because it cannot afford the cost of a new purpose-built plant and specialised equipment.

- **Past contracts or agreements**. Organisations enter into contracts or agreements with other parties, such as the government, other organisations, trade unions, suppliers and customers. These contracts and agreements can limit changes in behaviour – for example, organisations operating under a special licence or permit, or a fixed-price contract to supply goods/services to a government agency. Another example might be an agreement with unions that limits the opportunity to introduce compulsory redundancies, or the introduction of certain new technology or working practices.
- **Threats to power or influence**. Change may be seen as a threat to the power or influence of certain groups within the organisation, such as their control over decisions, resources or information. For example, managers may resist the introduction of quality circles or worker-directors because they see this as increasing the role and influence of non-managerial staff, and a threat to the power in their own positions. Where a group of people have, over a period of time, established what they perceive as their 'territorial rights', they are likely to resist change.

Perceptions and change

Although change is often resisted, *Cunningham* maintains that one of the greatest myths in management is the generalisation that people resist change. In fact people love change. The commonest reason for resistance is where people perceive a potential loss. For example because of negative rumour-mongering, people may perceive that they will be worse off from a proposed change even if the opposite is in fact true. In a different context, changes that result, for example in the loss of one's job, can create real, fact-based resistance. While people welcome change that they want, they have to be careful about the pace of change. In a more general context people may be enthusiastic for change, for example in large organisations where some people want to see changes and improvements in communication.

> *What seems to get in the way is the continual chanting of the untrue generalisation that 'people resist change'. People resist some change – if they perceive that they are going to lose out. People welcome change that makes things better.*[73]

Critical reflection

Change is nothing new and a simple fact of life. Some people actively thrive on new challenges and constant change, while others prefer the comfort of the status quo and strongly resist any change. Do you agree that it is all down to the personality of the individual? Do you accept that despite all the attention there is little management can do about resistance to change?

THE MANAGEMENT OF ORGANISATIONAL CHANGE

The successful management of change is clearly essential for continued economic performance and competitiveness. New ideas and innovations should not be perceived as threats by members of the organisation. The efforts made by management to maintain the balance of the socio-technical system will influence people's attitudes, the behaviour of individuals and groups, and thereby the level of organisational performance and effectiveness.

Stewart is among those writers who point out how changes in technology and in domestic government policies have had a radical impact on managers in many companies and in public service organisations.

One of the most difficult problems for managers is rapid change. How British managers react to change will have an important influence on Britain's economic future. This is true for managers in the public service as well as for those in industry and commerce. The tempo of change has speeded up; hence the demands made on managers to plan for, and adjust to, change are greater. All change requires both abilities.[74]

Organisational responses to change

Christensen and Overdorf suggest a framework to help managers understand what types of change the organisation is capable and incapable of handling. They identify three factors that affect organisational responses to different types of change and what an organisation can and cannot do:

- **resources** – access to abundant, high quality resources increases an organisation's chances of coping with change;
- **processes** – the patterns of interaction, co-ordination, communication and decision-making employees use to transform resources into products and services. Processes may be formal and explicitly defined and documented, or informal and routines or ways of working that evolve over time;
- **values** – the standards by which employees set priorities that enable them to judge whether an order is attractive, whether a customer is more or less important, whether an idea for a new product is attractive or marginal.

The factors that define an organisation's capabilities and disabilities evolve over time – they start in resources, then to move to visible, articulated processes and values, and finally migrate to culture. Christensen and Overdorf maintain that when an organisation faces the same sort of problem that its processes and values were designed to address, managing can be straightforward. However, when the problem facing the organisation is fundamentally different these same factors constitute disabilities, especially when the organisation's capabilities have come to reside in processes and values. There are three possible ways in which managers can develop new capabilities to cope with change:

- create organisational structures within corporate boundaries in which new processes can be developed;
- spin out an independent organisation from the existing organisation and develop new processes and values;
- acquire a different organisation whose processes and values match closely the new requirements.[75]

Actions to secure effective change

Many books and articles refer to the steps or actions to be taken to secure successful and sustainable change.[76] For example, *Kotter and Cohen* list the following eight steps for successful large-scale change:

1 **Create a sense of urgency** among relevant people, whatever the nature or size of the organisation.
2 **Build a guiding team** with the credibility, skills, connections, reputations and formal authority to provide change leadership.
3 **Create visions** which are sensible, clear and uplifting, and sets of strategies.
4 **Communicate** the vision and strategy in order to induce understanding and commitment.
5 **Empower action** and remove obstacles that stop people acting on the vision.
6 **Produce short-term wins** that help to provide credibility, resources and momentum to the overall effort.
7 **Don't let up** but maintain the momentum, consolidate early changes and create wave after wave of change.
8 **Make change stick** by nurturing a new culture, and developing group norms of behaviour and shared values.[77]

Minimising the problems of change

Activities managed on the basis of technical efficiency alone are unlikely to lead to optimum improvement in organisational performance. A major source of resistance to change arises from the need of organisations to adapt to new technological developments. The following discussion on how to minimise the problem of change centres on the example of the impact of information technology. The general principles, however, apply equally to the management of change arising from other factors.

- **An important priority is to create an environment of trust and shared commitment, and to involve staff in decisions and actions that affect them.** There is a considerable body of research and experience that demonstrates clearly the positive advantages to be gained from participation. It is important that members of staff understand fully the reasons for change. Organisations should try to avoid change for the sake of change as this can be both disruptive and lead to mistrust. However, considerations of the need to change arising from advances in information technology simply cannot be ignored.
- **There should be full and genuine participation of all staff concerned as early as possible, preferably well before the actual introduction of new equipment or systems.** Information about proposed change, its implications and potential benefits should be communicated clearly to all interested parties. Staff should be actively encouraged to contribute their own ideas, suggestions and experiences, and to voice openly their worries or concerns. Managers should discuss problems directly with staff and handle any foreseen difficulties in working practices or relationships by attempting to find solutions agreed with them. The use of working parties, liaison committees, steering groups and joint consultation may assist discussion and participation, and help to maintain the momentum of the change process.
- **Team management, a co-operative spirit among staff and unions and a genuine feeling of shared involvement will help create a greater willingness to accept change.** A participative style of managerial behaviour that encourages supportive relationships between managers and subordinates, and group methods of organisation, decision-making and supervision, are more likely to lead to a sustained improvement in work performance. There is an assumption that most people will direct and control themselves willingly if they share in the setting of their objectives.
- **As part of the pre-planning for new technology there should be a carefully designed 'human resource management action programme'.** The action programme should be directed to a review of recruitment and selection, natural wastage of staff, potential for training, retraining and the development of new skills, and other strategies to reduce the possible level of redundancies or other harmful effects on staff. Where appropriate, arrangements for a shorter working week, and redeployment of staff with full financial support, should be developed in full consultation with those concerned. If job losses are totally unavoidable, there should be a fair and equitable redundancy scheme and provision for early retirement with protected pension rights. Every possible financial and other support should be given in assisting staff to find suitable alternative employment.
- **The introduction of incentive payment schemes may help in motivating staff by an equitable allocation of savings which result from new technology and more efficient methods of work.** Incentive schemes may be on an individual basis, with bonuses payable to each member of staff according to effort and performance; or on a group basis, where bonus is paid to staff in relation to the performance of the group as a whole. An alternative system is 'measured day work'. Staff receive a regular, guaranteed rate of pay in return for an agreed quantity and quality of work based on the capabilities of new equipment and systems. Management may also be able to negotiate a productivity bargain with unions. By accepting changes in work methods and practices, staff share in the economic benefits gained from the improved efficiency of information technology and automated systems.

- **Changes to the work organisation must maintain the balance of the socio-technical system.** Increased technology and automation may result in jobs becoming more repetitive and boring, and providing only a limited challenge and satisfaction to staff. It is important, therefore, to attempt to improve the quality of work, to remove frustration and stress from jobs, and to make them more responsible and interesting. Actual working arrangements rely heavily on the informal organisation and effective teamwork. Groups and teams are a major feature of organisational life and can have a significant influence on the successful implementation of change. New working practices should take account of how best to satisfy people's needs and expectations at work through the practical application of behavioural science.
- **Careful attention should be given to job design, methods of work organisation, the development of cohesive groups, and relationships between the nature and content of jobs and their task functions.** The introduction of new technology has also highlighted the need to give attention to the wider organisational context including the design of technology itself, broader approaches to improved job design, employee involvement and empowerment, the development of skills and problem-solving capacity, and the effective management of change.

Style of managerial behaviour

One of the most important factors in the successful implementation of organisational change is the style of managerial behaviour. Some members may actually prefer, and respond better, to a directed and controlled style of management. (Recall, for example, the discussion on Theory X and Theory Y styles of managerial behaviour in Chapter 12.)

In most cases, however, the introduction of change is more likely to be effective with a participative style of managerial behaviour. If staff are kept fully informed of proposals, are encouraged to adopt a positive attitude and have personal involvement in the implementation of the change, there is a greater likelihood of their acceptance of the change. However, *Reis and Pena* maintain that too often, management ignores human resistance issues and the need to address them in the implementation plan.

> *The success of any change depends on the willingness of employees to accept it with enthusiasm and implement it with care. Yet, business changes at times are undertaken without understanding how the human element influences the success or failure of a project. Frequently, companies develop impressive technical plans and simply assume the change – technical or organizational – will occur. The difficult and often neglected part of such initiatives is leading and managing behavioural change with those persons who interface with the new technology or the new initiatives.*[78]

McHugh, O'Brien and Ramondt point out that many public sector organisations have embarked upon far-reaching programmes of unsettling strategic change. They argue that such change programmes initiated by senior management without involvement of organisational members are unlikely to be successful. Organisations are more likely to experience the desired metamorphosis where the change is led by relatively junior front line staff with senior management practitioners acting as facilitators of organisational transformation.[79]

OVERCOMING RESISTANCE TO CHANGE

The effective management of change must be based on a clear understanding of human behaviour at work. Most people are not detached from their work but experience a range of emotional involvements through their membership of the organisation, they feel threatened and disoriented by the challenge of change. Emotions such as uncertainty, frustration or fear are common reactions. It is understandable therefore that people often adopt a defensive and negative attitude, and demonstrate resistance to change. It is important to remember that change is a complex and powerful psychological experience, and that individuals react internally to change.

According to *Atkinson*, a major problem in driving change in organisations is dealing with and managing the resistance that will be encountered – but that resistance should be welcomed as a healthy response. Resistance is natural and should not be viewed only as a negative response to change. In the absence of really positive benefits from the proposed change, the 'default' response of resistance is acceptable.

> *It is unusual for any change not to attract some resistance. Even with foresight, pre-planning and all the apparent logic behind the need to change, you should expect some resistance as the norm. Recognise and welcome it as a healthy response and an opportunity to openly debate possibilities and treat resistance as a powerfully ally in facilitating the learning process.*
>
> Philip Atkinson, 'Managing resistance to change'[80]

People are the key factor

The successful implementation of new work methods and practices is dependent upon the willing and effective co-operation of staff, managerial colleagues and unions. People are the key factor in the successful management of change. If change is to work, it must change the perceptions, attitudes and behaviour of people.

However, *Lucas* reminds us that a high proportion of change initiatives fail, derailed by the people factor.

> *Given that change has become such a fact of business life, it is worrying that so many change management programmes fail to fulfil their potential. The consensus among the experts is that it is often the people factor that derails the effort. Put simply, organisations know where they want to go – but they are not taking their people with them.*[81]

Responsibilities of top management

The successful management of change is a key factor of organisational performance and effectiveness and should emanate from the top of the organisation. Top management has a responsibility for the underlying philosophy and attitudes of the organisation, for creating and sustaining a healthy climate; and establishing appropriate and supportive organisational processes. The successful implementation of change demands positive action from top management and a style of transformational leadership in order to gain a commitment to change.[82]

However, *Champy* points out that one of the biggest challenges occurs not with middle management or deep in the organisation but at the level of senior managers.

> *I don't agree with the old song that people resist change. I think that people are fearful of change when they don't know where they're going, but they can get excited about these changes once they have a sense of where the whole operation is heading.*[83]

Change leaders

From a study of 25 chief executives in the UK and abroad, *Hooper and Potter* investigated what were thought to be the crucial attributes for effective change leaders. They point out that effective change leadership is not easy but found the following key factors and behaviours that have been crucial to the success of top people:

- effective communication of the reasons for change and developing an open communications culture;
- releasing the potential of everyone involved in the change, and championing innovation and creativity;
- setting a good personal example; and
- self-pacing to avoid unnecessary stress.[84]

An interesting proposition is put forward by *Drucker*, who contends that 'one cannot manage change. One can only be ahead of it. We do not hear much anymore about "overcoming resistance to change"'. Everyone now accepts that change is unavoidable.

But in a period of upheavals, such as the one we are living in, change is the norm. To be sure, it is painful and risky, and above all it requires a great deal of very hard work. But unless it is seen as the task of the organization to ***lead change****, the organization – whether business, university, hospital and so on – will not survive. In a period of rapid structural change, the only ones who survive are the* ***Change Leaders****. It is therefore a central 21st-century challenge for management that its organization become a change leader. A change leader sees change as opportunity. A change leader looks for change, knows how to find the right changes and knows how to make them effective both outside the organization and inside it. This requires:*

1. *Policies to make the future.*
2. *Systematic methods to look for and to anticipate change.*
3. *The right way to introduce change, both within and outside the organization.*
4. *Policies to balance change and continuity.*[85]

Activity 19C

www.pearsoned.co.uk/mullins

Critical reflection

'The study of organisation development may not help us solve all of the new problems that we face in our organisational lives, but it can help us to solve some of the old ones!' What do you think? What do you see as the value and relevance of organisation development?

MANAGEMENT IN THE NEWS

Being charitable

The business of doing good

Sathnam Sanghera

Almost everyone I know approaching 30 is suddenly making unrealistic threats to quit their lousy well-paid job in the City of London to do something less stressful and more meaningful instead. This always irritates me because my brother works as a manager at a housing charity and over the years I have learned that:

- **Working for charity is more stressful than working in business.** There seems to be a view among City types that switching to the voluntary sector is a form of downshifting. But this is not the case, not least because businesses have simpler aims than charities: making sure pre-tax profits increase by 7 per cent is easier than making poverty history, for instance. Also, although it may not feel like it for the jaded executive, the power structure of the typical company is pretty simple: the chief executive reports to the board and the staff report to the chief executive. At a charity a chief executive has multiple stakeholders to deal with, from the recipients of aid to donors, volunteers and a powerful board of trustees, who will not always do what they are told. It is hard work.

Want to turn your back on the big bucks in the city for a less stressful job with a charity? Think again.

- **Charities do not necessarily offer respite from office politics.** Another common assumption is that because their minds are focused on saving the world, charity workers have no time for stabbing each other in the back. In reality, because they are all so passionate about what they do, they are more likely to do so. Sir Christopher Bland, the chairman of BT Group, put it well in a *Financial Times* interview when he explained that in his experience 'the amount of backbiting, in-fighting and general skullduggery in an organisation is in direct proportion to the nobility of its goals'. He added: 'In seven years as a management consultant, the worst behaviour I found was in a home for handicapped children in north London, closely followed by a large teaching hospital. Compared with that, British American Tobacco was relatively well behaved.'
- **Charities do not necessarily offer an escape from corporate culture.** There is no better illustration of this than *It's Tough at the Top*, a new management guide by Debra Allcock Tyler, chief executive of the Directory of Social Change, a charity providing training for charities. It is aimed at the voluntary sector, but with its Venn diagrams and talk of 'action-centred leadership', it is like most management books aimed at the private sector. There is a sound reason for this: charities in the UK alone have an annual income of £26.3bn ($49.2bn) and, with the ever increasing pressure to get value for money from donations, they are increasingly run like businesses.
- **Just because you work for charity, it does not mean that the charity that employs you will be charitable towards you.** While more than 290 charities in Britain have an annual income in excess of £10m, 56 per cent have an annual income of less than £10,000 and many of these have to sacrifice investment in staff, and often the staff themselves, for the sake of survival. 'The difficulty with being the chief executive of a charity is that staff expect you to be generous towards them,' says Ms Tyler. 'But the brutal reality of funding means that you can't afford to be.'

Of course, I do not mean to suggest that people should not consider working for charity. It is a fantastic thing to do: my brother loves it and in a recent survey, 95 per cent of British charity workers said they regarded their job as rewarding. But the sector has enough to deal with without becoming a rest home for the professionally disillusioned.

Maybe, as unfashionable as it is to say so, you could remind yourself that business also makes a contribution to society and that there is something to be said for creating wealth and opportunity.

Source: Sanghera, S., 'The business of doing good', *Financial Times*, 25 May 2006.

Discussion questions

1. **Analyse and review what this article reveals about the nature of employee commitment.**
2. **What sources of conflict exist in a charitable organisation? Identify and explain what different strategies managers working for charities might have to use when dealing with conflict, compared with those used by managers in a business organisation.**

SYNOPSIS

- Organisation development (OD) is a generic term embracing a wide range of intervention strategies into the social processes of an organisation. In a very general sense, OD is concerned with attempts to improve the overall performance and effectiveness of an organisation. The broad nature of OD means, however, that many interrelated topic areas could be included under this heading. OD makes use of a number of intervention strategies, and is action-oriented and tailored to suit specific organisational needs. Two central and critical features of OD are organisational culture and organisational change.

- Applications of organisational behaviour and the effective management of human resources are dependent upon organisational culture and climate. Organisational culture helps to explain how things are performed in different organisations. Culture is, however, a general concept, and difficult to explain precisely. There are a number of ways to classify different types of organisation culture. It develops over time and in response to a complex set of factors. There are a number of different ways in which to understand what constitutes organisational culture.

- Applications of organisational behaviour and the effective management of human resources are dependent upon the characteristic features of the individual organisation – and its culture. The pervasive nature of culture has an important effect on the behaviour and actions of individuals, the process of management and on organisational performance. It describes what the organisation is all about. Culture helps to account for variations among organisations and managers, both nationally and internationally.

- Organisational climate is based on the perception of members towards the organisation, and can be seen as the state of mutual trust and understanding among members of the organisation. Climate influences the attitudes that staff bring to bear on their work performance and personal relationships. Among the factors which contribute to a healthy climate is the extent to which employees have a sense of commitment to, and psychological bond with, the organisation.

- Organisations operate within an increasingly volatile environment and are in a state of constant change. Change is a pervasive influence and an inescapable part of social and organisational life. There is a wide range of forces acting upon organisations which make the need for change inevitable. Change can affect all aspects of the operation and functioning of the organisation. Planned organisation change involves a process of behaviour modification. Change is reciprocal and changing organisations may affect the nature of managerial work.

- Despite the potential positive outcomes, change is often resisted at both the individual and the organisational level. Resistance to change can take many forms and it is not always easy to pinpoint the exact reasons. It is important that management adopt a clearly defined strategy for the successful initiation of change, including attention to the style of managerial behaviour, and the human and social factors of change. The effective management of change is a key factor of organisational performance and competitiveness, and should emanate from the top of the organisation.

Refresh your understanding, assess your progress and begin your research with online resources at www.pearsoned.co.uk/mullins

REVIEW AND DISCUSSION QUESTIONS

1. Explain fully what you understand by the meaning and nature of organisation development (OD).
2. Suggest how you would attempt to explain the concept of organisational culture. What factors might influence the development of culture?
3. Discuss critically the importance of culture for effective organisational performance. Give practical examples from your own organisation.
4. What do you understand by organisational climate and what do you think are its main characteristic features? From your own organisation, give examples of features that have contributed to and/or detracted from a healthy climate.
5. Explain the concept of employee commitment and suggest how it might actually be created. Give examples of factors that have contributed to your own strength of commitment in any work situation.
6. Give specific examples of major changes confronting management today and their probable implications for an organisation of your choice.
7. Why do individuals and organisations tend to resist change? To what extent do you believe such resistance can be effectively overcome?
8. Explain fully what *you* believe are the most important features in the successful implementation of organisational change.

ASSIGNMENT

Rate your readiness to change

A Quiz

The left-hand column lists 17 key elements of change readiness. Rate your organisation on each item. Give three points for high ranking ('We're good at this; I'm confident of our skills here'), two for medium score ('We're spotty here; we could use improvement or more experience') and one point for a low score ('We've had problems with this; this is new to our organisation'). Be honest. Don't trust only your own perspective; ask others in the organisation, at all levels, to rate the company too. The consultants at Symmetrix believe – no surprise – it helps to have an outsider do the assessment with you.

Readiness scoring

How to score: High = 3 Medium = 2 Low = 1

Category		*Score*
Sponsorship	The sponsor of change is not necessarily its day-to-day leader; her or she is the visionary, chief cheerleader, and bill payer – the person with the power to help the team change when it meets resistance. Give three points – change will be easier – if sponsorship comes at a senior level; for example, CEO, COO, or the head of an autonomous business unit. Weakest sponsors: midlevel executives or staff officers.	☐
Leadership	This means the day-to-day leadership – the people who call the meeting, set the goals, work till midnight. Successful change is more likely if leadership is high level, has 'ownership' (that is, direct responsibility for what's to be changed) and has clear business results in mind. Low-level leadership, or leadership that is not well connected throughout the organization (across departments) or that comes from the staff, is less likely to succeed and should be scored low.	☐
Motivation	High points for a strong sense of urgency from senior management, which is shared by the rest of the company, and for a corporate culture that already emphasizes continuous improvement. Negative: tradition-bound managers and workers, many of whom have been in their jobs for more than 15 years; a conservative culture that discourages risk taking.	☐
Direction	Does senior management strongly believe that the future should look different from the present? How clear is management's picture of the future? Can management mobilize all relevant parties – employees, the board, customers, etc. – for action? High points for positive answers to those questions. If senior management thinks only minor change is needed, the likely outcome is no change at all; score yourself low.	☐
Measurements	Or in consultant-speak, 'metrics'. Three points if you already use performance measures of the sort encouraged by total quality management (defect rates, time to market, etc.) and if these express the economics of the business. Two points if some measures exist but compensation and reward systems do not explicitly reinforce them. If you don't have measures in place or don't know what we're talking about, one point.	☐
Organizational context	How does the change effort connect to other major goings-on in context of the organization? (For example: Does it dovetail with a continuing total quality management process? Does it fit with strategic actions such as acquisitions or new product lines?) Trouble lies ahead for a change effort that is isolated or if there are multiple change efforts whose relationships are not linked strategically.	☐

Assignment – continued

Category		*Score*
Processes/ Functions	Major changes almost invariably require redesigning business processes that cut across functions such as purchasing, accounts payable, or marketing. If functional executives are rigidly turf conscious, change will be difficult. Give yourself more points the more willing they – and the organisation as a whole – are to change critical processes and sacrifice perks or power for the good of the group.	☐
Competitor benchmarking	Whether you are a leader in your industry or a laggard, give benchmarking yourself points for a continuing programme that objectively compares your company's performance with that of competitors and systematically examines changes in your market. Give yourself one point if knowledge of competitors' abilities is primarily anecdotal – what salesmen say at the bar.	☐
Customer focus	The more everyone in the company is imbued with knowledge of customers, the more likely that the organization can agree to change to serve them better. Three points if everyone in the work force knows who his or her customers are, knows their needs, and has had direct contact with them. Take away points if that knowledge is confined to pockets of the organization (sales and marketing, senior executives).	☐
Rewards	Change is easier if managers and employees are rewarded for taking risks, being innovative, and looking for new solutions. Team-based rewards are better than rewards based solely on individual achievement. Reduce points if your company, like most, rewards continuity over change. If managers become heroes for making budget, they won't take risks even if you say you want them to. Also: If employees believe failure will be punished, reduce points.	☐
Organizational structure	The best situation is a flexible organization with little churn – that structure is, reorganizations are rare and well received. Score yourself lower if you have a rigid structure that has been unchanged for more than five years or has undergone frequent reorganization with little success; that may signal a cynical company culture that fights change by waiting it out.	☐
Communication	A company will adapt to change most readily if it has many means of two-way communication that reach all levels of the organization and that all employees use and understand. If communications media are few, often trashed unread, and almost exclusively one-way and top-down, change will be more difficult.	☐
Organizational hierarchy	The fewer levels of hierarchy and the fewer employee grade hierarchy levels, the more likely an effort to change will succeed. A thick impasto of middle management and staff not only slows decision-making but also creates large numbers of people with the power to block change.	☐
Prior experience with change	Score three if the organization has successfully implemented major changes in the recent past. Score one if there is no prior experience with major change or if change efforts failed or left a legacy of anger or resentment. Most companies will score two, acknowledging equivocal success in previous attempts to change.	☐
Morale	Change is easier if employees enjoy working in the organization and the level of individual responsibility is high. Signs of unreadiness to change: low team spirit, little voluntary extra effort, and mistrust. Look for two types of mistrust: between management and employees, and between or among departments.	☐

Category		Score
Innovation	Best situation: The company is always experimenting; new ideas are implemented with seemingly little effort; employees work across internal boundaries without much trouble. Bad signs: lots of red tape, multiple signoffs required before new ideas are tried; employees must go through channels and are discouraged from working with colleagues from other departments or divisions.	☐
Decision-making	Rate yourself high if decisions are made quickly, taking into account a wide variety of suggestions; it is clear where decisions are made. Give yourself a low grade if decisions come slowly and are made by a mysterious 'them'; there is a lot of conflict during the process, and confusion and finger pointing after decisions are announced.	☐
	Total score	☐

After completing your total score, compare and discuss your response with those of your collegues.

Source: Stewart, T. A., 'Rate your readiness to change', *Fortune*, 7 February 1994, pp. 63–4.

PERSONAL AWARENESS AND SKILLS EXERCISE

Objectives

Completing this exercise should help you to enhance the following skills:

- Relate classifications of culture to different types of organisations.
- Assess influences on the development of culture.
- Evaluate the appropriateness of culture for specific organisations.

Exercise

Using the classifications of organisational culture proposed by Handy, and by Deal and Kennedy, you are required to:

1. Compare and contrast the influences on the development of culture in any two different types of organisations. Your two organisations could be, *for example*:

   Private and public sector; For profit and not-for-profit; Service sector and manufacturing sector; Production and academic.

2. Suggest, with supporting reasons, which of **either** the Handy or the Deal and Kennedy typologies you would try to foster if you were appointed as a senior manager in any two of the following organisations:
   - wheel-clamping contractor;
   - research laboratory;
   - battleship;
   - private hospital;
   - second-hand car business;
   - high-fashion clothing store;
   - fast-food chain;
   - advertising agency.

→

Personal awareness and skills exercise – continued

Discussion

- How important is organisational culture? How would you attempt to foster a change in the prevailing culture of an organisation?
- To what extent do textbook classifications aid our practical understanding and analysis of organisational culture?
- Should there be/is there a most 'suitable' culture for specific organisations?

CASE STUDY

The Haier Corporation

Haier is one of the most remarkable success stories associated with the extraordinary growth of the Chinese economy over the last 20 years. Its story shows the importance of a strong culture, deliberate strategy and a successful focus on operational management and quality.

In 1984, Haier was a small, unsuccessful state-owned corporation in Qingdao, a city of about 7 million people in eastern China. It was losing $178,000 on annual revenues of $421,000 and had 600 employees.[86] Twenty years later, it was profitable, with an annual sales revenue of almost $10 billion. Over that period, it had built up export sales to more than 160 countries, together with a range of manufacturing and other alliances and investments around the world. Its product range – originally just refrigerators – had expanded massively to cover dozens of categories in the domestic electrical appliance market, with thousands of individual products. As an article in *Forbes* magazine in 2001 pointed out, Haier had achieved this growth by deploying a genuinely international approach, unlike many other Chinese manufacturers: it traded, for example, under its own brand rather than making products anonymously for other companies.[87] It also ran manufacturing operations in other countries and was always looking for opportunities to adapt its products to local tastes. In the United States, for example, a successful wine fridge was designed by Haier America's President. Unexpectedly for many in the West (given its origins in what is still a one-party communist state), Haier seemed to be growing into a fully fledged multinational corporation, competing successfully with longer-established rivals.

Source: Lou Linwei/Alamy

Zhang's hammer forged a successful organisational culture in China, but can it succeed in global markets?

Zhang's hammer

However, Haier is far from a standard faceless, stateless multinational: its culture, style and operational approach reflect its Chinese traditions and its successes are clearly identified with some of its key leaders. In *Fortune* magazine in 2005, Haier president Yang Mianmian was listed as the fifteenth most powerful businesswoman in the world: her strategy of 'one low (price), three high (value, growth and quality)' was cited as a key foundation of Haier's continuing success.[88] The corporation's superstar, however, must be CEO Zhang Ruimin, who took the company over at its low point in 1984 and whose drive, imagination and personal philosophy largely powered its transformation into a truly global player. One story that crops up again and again in reports about Haier concerns the day in 1985 that CEO Zhang took a sledgehammer to a row of 76 faulty Haier fridges, to the great distress of the workforce who were lined up to watch (a fridge cost about two years' wages in that year).[89] Explaining his dramatic action, Zhang said:

> *If we don't destroy these refrigerators today, what is to be shattered by the market in the future will be this enterprise!*[90]

The hammer is reportedly on display in Haier's exhibition hall, a symbol of Zhang's complete rejection of the previous company attitude that defective products could be tolerated and knocked out at a discount. Perhaps the story has been idealised a little over the years; the point, however, is that Haier is a corporation with a soul – one that creates and retells stories about itself, one with a strong and distinctive culture.

Some of that distinctive identity can be seen in the nature of its external relationships. As mentioned above, its international strategy seeks to make maximum use of local human resources and capital, an approach that also helps Haier to offer fast delivery and very good service to its customers and distribution partners. It is always open to opportunities to adapt its products to local preferences and habits (as with the wine fridge), a practice that could become costly in terms of complexity and logistics. Its international strategy has been to go for the difficult markets first on the basis that success in these markets would require the company to improve faster than seeking to dominate less fiercely contested markets.[91] Haier is, of course, very strong in its enormous and fast-growing home market and has built up an enviable distribution network in China. This has helped it to dominate the Chinese market, but Zhang has also sought to expand the network via multinational alliances, such as the 2002 agreement with Japan's Sanyo, through which Sanyo products are distributed by Haier in China and vice versa in Japan.[92]

Haier's strong culture can be seen most clearly in its internal relationships: for all of its willingness to adapt its output to local preferences and demands, Haier seems to be much less flexible about how things should be done within the corporation. As with so many organisations with strong cultures, there is a well-articulated Haier way of doing things, which new Haier employees must become used to. The company's philosophy and values are set out in some detail on its website and the sentiments include some fairly standard rallying cries about excellence and innovation:[93]

> *Haier spirit: we work diligently to serve the country and to pursue excellence through innovation.*
>
> *Management accountability – the 80/20 principle: management is 80 per cent responsible for any subordinate's wrongdoing.*
>
> *Quality focus: excellent employees produce high quality products.*
>
> *Team spirit – 10/10 principle: The top 10 per cent of performers ought to help the bottom 10 per cent performers to improve the firm's competitive advantage.*
>
> *Haier should be like the sea and make contributions to mankind 'sincerely and forever'. In so doing, it will exist forever for the good of all and Haier will be part of the whole society.*[94]

The philosophy and values section also contains a series of gloriously off-the-wall metaphors and statements that would make a newly formed creative advertising agency proud (check the website for a discussion of the dietary and behavioural differences between 'shockfish' and 'sharks', for example).

These strangely (to Western ears) poetic sentiments do not intrude, however, into the Haier 'OEC' management control system. This is defined by Haier's HRM Director Wang Yingmin as follows:[95]

- O stands for Overall.
- E stands for Everyone, Everything, Everyday.
- C stands for Control and Clear.
- OEC means that every employee has to accomplish the target work every day. The OEC management-control system aims at overall control of everything that every employee finishes on his or her job every day, with a 1 per cent increase over what was done the previous day.

The OEC system is designed to ensure high levels of discipline in the company's operations, through a set of rewards and punishments, including detailed fines; for instance, failing to check or maintain equipment daily (5 yen), not cleaning up their work environment (2 yen), being late to work (2 yen) or 'gathering for fun or chat during work time' (2 yen). Rewards include a bonus for saving raw materials of 5 per cent of the value of the savings. This approach was developed as part of Zhang's turnaround strategy for Haier in the bad days of the 1980s and early 1990s, with the aim of getting the workforce to focus on creating quality products for customers and on the process of innovation, which is actively encouraged at the working level. The OEC approach has now become part of Haier's internationalisation strategy, to be applied in the company's many operations around the world. It is backed by a detailed target-setting and monitoring system, together with a series of incentive bonuses for the best performers.

Exporting the Haier culture

Remarkably, Haier built and opened a factory in South Carolina to serve the US market. Initially, its methods were strange to the new employees from the local labour market. However, according to a report in the *Chinese People's Daily*:

... both sides have harmonious exchanges, the difference of cultural background, instead of causing estrangement between the Chinese and American workers in their work, has increased their interest in mutual understanding.[96]

At first, the US workers were slow to volunteer for overtime to complete the day's target work, but (according to the report) all accept the importance of the Haier system and are even sometimes prepared to call into work on Independence Day to prepare for the next day's work. For all that one would expect an enthusiastic report from this particular source, Haier does seem to have established a reputation as a good employer in the area.

Haier has done spectacularly well during its brief life. It has established a strong international brand based upon high quality and value for money. It has internationalised on the basis of a strong culture, which sets out the company way of doing things but which also contains a commitment to local adaptation and content. Having become so big in such a short time, it must now face new challenges as a global player. Longer-established Western brands are competing vigorously in Haier's rapidly developing home market as well as in the richer markets of Europe and North America. Many of today's superbrands started as local Japanese operations with successful export systems that managed to establish and consolidate their global position. Haier may manage to do the same, but it is not going to be easy. As CEO Zhang put it, with characteristic eloquence:[97]

Another challenge unique to China is we have started our brand development very late. So we have to catch up in a very short period of time. I will give you an analogy: It's like constructing a 10-story building. Our foreign competitors have already finished all the way up to the ninth floor. The Chinese market is their 10th floor. Once they have moved successfully into the China market, they will be finished with building this highrise. But in China, we have only built the first floor. There are still nine floors to be built.

Your tasks

1. What type of organisational culture appears to exist at Haier? To what extent can that be explained by the cultural influences (p. 724) discussed in this chapter? How can the ideas of national culture (discussed in Chapter 1) add to this explanation?
2. Using the components of Johnson *et al.*'s cultural web, Figure 19.1, critically review the cultural aspects of the Haier Corporation over the course of its development.
3. Given Haier's prominent position in global markets, what external influences on Haier's culture are likely to be important over the next few years? What challenges does this pose for Haier's management and what key management skills are likely to be needed in responding to these challenges?

Notes and references

1. French, W. L. and Bell, C. H. *Organization Development: Behavioral Science Interventions for Organization Improvement*, Sixth edition, Prentice-Hall (1999), pp. 25–6.
2. Ibid., p. 29.
3. Hamlin, B., Keep, J and Ash, K. *Organizational Change and Development*, Financial Times Prentice Hall (2001), p. 13.
4. Maier, D., Leban, B. and Orr-Alfeo, D. 'A values statement on OD: An interview with practitioner-scholar Dr Allan Church RODC', *Organization Development Journal*, vol. 19, no. 3, Fall 2001, pp. 69–74.
5. Patching, K. *Management and Organisation Development*, Macmillan Business (1999) p. 27.
6. Blake, R. R. and Mouton, J. S. *The Managerial Grid III*, Gulf Publishing Company (1985).
7. Naylor, J. *Management*, Second edition, Financial Times Prentice Hall 2004, pp. 645–6.
8. See, for example: Smircich, L. 'Concepts of Culture and Organizational Analysis', *Administrative Science Quarterly*, vol. 28, 1983, pp. 339–58.
9. See, for example: Brown, A. D. *Organisational Culture*, Second edition, Financial Times Management (1998).
10. Atkinson, P. E. 'Creating Cultural Change', *Management Services*, vol. 34, no. 7, 1990, pp. 6–10.
11. McLean, A. and Marshall, J. *Intervening in Cultures*, Working Paper, University of Bath, 1993.
12. See, for example: Oswick, C., Lowe, S. and Jones, P. 'Organisational Culture as Personality: Lessons from Psychology?', in Oswick, C. and Grant, D. (eds) *Organisation Development: Metaphorical Explorations*, Pitman Publishing (1996), pp. 106–20.
13. Cartwright, J. *Cultural Transformation*, Financial Times Prentice Hall (1999), p. 34.

14 Schein, E. H. *Organizational Culture and Leadership: A Dynamic View*, Third edition, Jossey-Bass (2004).
15 Harrison, R. 'Understanding Your Organization's Character', *Harvard Business Review*, vol. 50, May/June 1972, pp. 119–28.
16 Handy, C. B. *Understanding Organizations*, Fourth edition, Penguin (1993).
17 Deal, T. E. and Kennedy, A. A. *Corporate Cultures: The Rites and Rituals of Corporate Life*, Penguin (1982).
18 Deal, T. E. and Kennedy, A. A. *The New Corporate Cultures*, Perseus Books (2000).
19 See, for example: Handy, C. B. *Understanding Organizations*, Fourth edition, Penguin (1993); and McLean, A. and Marshall, J. *Cultures at Work*, Local Government Training Board, October 1988.
20 Kransdorff, A. 'History – A Powerful Management Tool', *Administrator*, October 1991, p. 23.
21 See for example: Beckett-Hughes, M. 'How to Integrate Two Cultures' , *People Management*, vol. 11, no. 5, 10 March 2005, pp. 50–1.
22 Roddick, A. *Body and Soul*, Ebury Press (1991) and Roddick, A. *Business As Usual*, Thorsons (2000).
23 Blackhurst, C. 'Up Front at Pearson', *Management Today*, May 1997, pp. 50–7.
24 Gerstner, L. V. Jr. *Who Says Elephants Can't Dance?: Inside IBM's historic turnabout*, HarperBusiness (2002).
25 Johnson, G., Scholes, K. and Whittington, R. *Exploring Corporate Strategy*, Seventh edition, Financial Times Prentice Hall (2005).
26 Wilson, F. *Organizational Behaviour and Work: A Critical Introduction*, Second edition, Oxford University Press (2004), p. 185.
27 'Effective Organisations: the People Factor', Advisory Booklet, ACAS, November 2001.
28 Naylor, J. *Management*, Second edition, Financial Times Prentice Hall (2004).
29 Charters, J. 'Are You a "Woodentop?"', *The British Journal of Administrative Science*, May/June 2000, p. 20.
30 Oliver, J. 'Losing Control', *Management Today*, June 1998, pp. 32–8.
31 Harrison, R. and Stokes, H. *Diagnosing Organizational Culture*, Pfeiffer & Company (1992), p. 1.
32 Reigle, R. F. 'Measuring organic and mechanistic cultures', *Engineering Management Journal*, vol. 13, no. 4, December 2001, pp. 3–8
33 Egan, G. 'The Shadow Side', *Management Today*, September 1993, p. 37.
34 Egan, G. 'Cultivate Your Culture', *Management Today*, April 1994, pp. 38–42.
35 Meudell, K. and Gadd, K. 'Culture and Climate in Short-Life Organizations: Sunny Spells or Thunder-storms?', *International Journal of Contemporary Hospitality Management*, vol. 6, no. 5, 1994, pp. 27–32.
36 Peters, T. J. and Waterman, R. H. *In Search of Excellence*, Harper and Row (1982), pp. 75–6.
37 Heller, R. *In Search of European Excellence*, HarperCollins Business (1997), p. 229.
38 Goldsmith, W. and Clutterbuck, D. *The Winning Streak Mark II*, Orion Business Books (1998).
39 Cummings, T. G. and Worley, C. G. *Organization Development and Change*, Eighth edition, Thompson South-Western (2005), p. 509.
40 Chatman, J. A. and Cha, S. E. 'Culture of Growth', Mastering Leadership, *Financial Times*, 22 November, 2002, pp. 2–3.
41 Stewart, R. *The Reality of Management*, Third edition, Butterworth Heinemann (1999), p. 123.
42 Naylor, J. *Management*, Second edition, Financial Times Prentice Hall (2004), p. 79.
43 'Inspired Leadership: Insights into people who inspire exceptional performance' DTI, August 2004.
44 Potter, C. C. 'What is Culture: And Can It Be Useful For Organisational Change Agents?', *Leadership and Organization Development Journal*, vol. 10, no. 3, 1989, pp. 17–24.
45 Siddall, P. 'Working With Cultural Differences', *Chartered Secretary*, February 1998, p. 30.
46 Schneider, S. C. and Barsoux, J. *Managing Across Cultures*, Second edition, Financial Times Prentice Hall (2003).
47 Cheng, T., Sculli, D. and Chan, F. 'Relationship dominance – Rethinking management theories from the perspective of methodological relationalism, *Journal of Managerial Psychology*, vol. 16, no. 2, 2001, pp. 97–105.
48 Francesco, A. M. and Gold, B. A. *International Organizational Behavior*, Second edition, Pearson Prentice Hall (2005).
49 Moran, E. T. and Volkwein, J. F. 'The Cultural Approach to the Formation of Organizational Climate', *Human Relations*, vol. 45, no. 1, 1992, p. 43.
50 Tagiuri, R. and Litwin, G. H. (eds) *Organizational Climate*, Graduate School of Business Administration, Harvard University (1968), p. 27.
51 Rentsch, J. R. 'Climate and Culture: Interaction and Qualitative Differences in Organizational Meanings', *Journal of Applied Psychology*, vol. 75, no. 6, 1990, p. 668.
52 Whitmore, Sir John 'Breaking Down the Barriers to Management Creativity', *The British Journal of Administrative Management*, September/October 2002, pp. 24–5.
53 Walton, R. E. 'From Control to Commitment in the Workplace', in Steers, R. M. and Porter, L. W. (eds), *Motivation and Work Behavior*, McGraw-Hill (1991), p. 448.
54 O'Reilly, C. 'Corporations, Culture and Commitment: Motivation and Social Control in Organizations', in Steers, R. M., Porter, L. W. and Bigley, G. A., *Motivation and Leadership at Work*, Sixth edition, McGraw-Hill (1996), p. 374.
55 See, for example: Thornhill, A., Saunders, N. K. and Stead, J. 'Downsizing, Delayering – But Where's the Commitment?', *Personnel Review*, vol. 26, no. 1/2, 1997, pp. 81–98.
56 Guirdham, M., *Interactive Behaviour at Work*, Third edition, Financial Times Prentice Hall (2002), p. 341.
57 Altman, W., Cooper, C. and Garner, A. 'New Deal Needed to Secure Commitment', *Professional Manager*, September 1999, p. 40.
58 Galunic, C. and Weeks, J. 'Survey – Mastering People Management', *Financial Times*, 12 November 2001.
59 Gratton, L. 'The Democratic Enterprise', Financial Times Prentice Hall (2004), p. 184.
60 Watson, T. J. *Organising and Managing Work*, Second edition, Financial Times Prentice Hall (2006).
61 For a discussion of change in relation to the complexities of organisational life, see: Senior, B. and Fleming, J. *Organizational Change*, Third edition, Financial Times Prentice Hall (2006).
62 Czerniawska, F. 'From Bottlenecks to Blackberries: How the relationships between organisations and individuals is changing' MCA/FT, September 2005.

63 See, for example: Henderson, H. (Squadron Leader) 'Flying High', *The British Journal of Administrative Management*, January/February 1998, pp. 10–13.
64 Fenlon, M. 'The Public Spirit', Mastering Leadership, *Financial Times*, 22 November 2002, p. 4.
65 Worrall, L. and Cooper, C. 'Managers just soldiering on', *Professional Manager*, vol. 15, no. 3, May 2006, pp. 30–2.
66 'Effective Organisations: the People Factor', Advisory Booklet, ACAS, November 2001.
67 Lewin, K. *Field Theory in Social Science*, Harper and Row (1951).
68 French, W. L., Kast, F. E. and Rosenzweig, J. E. *Understanding Human Behavior in Organizations*, Harper and Row (1985).
69 Stewart, R. *Managing Today and Tomorrow*, Macmillan (1991).
70 Crainer, S. *Key Management Ideas: Thinkers that Changed the Management World*, Third edition, Financial Times Prentice Hall (1998), pp. 144–5.
71 Gratton, L. *Living Strategy: Putting People at the Heart of Corporate Purpose*, Financial Times Prentice Hall (2000), p. 191.
72 Toffler, A. *Future Shock*, Pan Books (1970), p. 27.
73 Cunningham, I. 'Influencing people's attitudes to change', *Professional Manager*, vol. 14, no. 3, May 2005, p. 37.
74 Stewart, R. *The Reality of Management*, Third edition, Butterworth Heinemann (1999), p. 161.
75 Christensen, C. M. and Overdorf, M. 'Meeting the Challenge of Disruptive Change', *Harvard Business Review*, vol. 78, no. 2, March–April 2000, pp. 67–76.
76 See, for example: 'Mapping an Effective Change Programme', *Management Checklist 038*, Institute of Management, November 2001; and Covington, J. and Chase, M. L. 'Eight steps to sustainable change', *Industrial Management*, vol. 14, no. 6, November/December 2002, pp. 8–11.
77 Kotter, J. P. and Cohen, D. S. *The Heart of Change*, Harvard Business School Press (2002).
78 Reis, D. and Pena, L. 'Reengineering the Motivation to Work', *Management Decision*, vol. 39, no. 8, 2001, pp. 666–75.
79 McHugh, M., O'Brien, G. and Ramondt, J. 'Organizational Metamorphosis Led by Front Line Staff', *Employee Relations*, vol. 21, no. 6, 1999, pp. 556–76.
80 Atkinson, P. 'Managing resistance to change' *Management Services*, Spring 2005, p. 15.
81 Lucas, E. 'Riding the Change Roller-coaster', *Professional Manager*, September 2002, pp. 27–9.
82 See, for example: BBC, *Building Tomorrow's Company, Leadership – Supporting Notes*, BBC for Business; and The Centre for Tomorrow's Company and William Tate, 1999.
83 Champy, J. *Reengineering Management: The mandate for new leadership*, HarperBusiness (1996) p. xxi.
84 Hooper, A. and Potter, J. 'Take It from the Top', *People Management*, vol. 5, no. 16, August 1999, pp. 46–9.
85 Drucker, P. F. *Management Challenges for the 21st Century*, Butterworth Heinemann (1999), p. 73.
86 Lin, T.W. (2005) 'OEC Management-Control system helps China Haier group achieve competitive advantage', *Management Accounting Quarterly*, Spring 2005, retrieved from www.allbusiness.com.
87 Flannery, R (2001), China goes global, *Forbes* 6 August 2001.
88 'The 50 most powerful women in business', *Fortune*, 14 November 2005.
89 Other versions of the story suggest that Zhang had some help: those who made the faulty fridges were obliged to smash them in front of their colleagues.
90 *Chinese Peoples' Daily*, Opinion, 8 August 2001.
91 *Business Week*, 31 March 2003.
92 http://www.sanyo.co.jp/koho/hypertext4-eng/0201/0108-e.html.
93 http://www.haier.com/abouthaier/CorporateCulture/index.asp.
94 Lin, T.W. (2005) 'OEC Management-Control system helps China Haier group achieve competitive advantage', *Management Accounting Quarterly*, Spring 2005, retrieved from www.allbusiness.com.
95 Quoted in Lin, T.W. (2005) 'OEC Management-Control system helps China Haier group achieve competitive advantage', *Management Accounting Quarterly*, Spring 2005, retrieved from www.allbusiness.com.
96 *Chinese People's Daily*, 19 February 2002.
97 *Business Week*, 31 March 2003.